» INTRODUCTION TO COMPARATIVE POLITICS: POLITICAL CHALLENGES AND CHANGING AGENDAS

Fifth Edition

WADSWORTH
CENGAGE Learning

Australia • Brazil • Japan • Korea • Mexico • Singapore • Spain • United Kingdom • United States

WADSWORTH
CENGAGE Learning™

**Introduction to Comparative Politics:
Political Challenges and Changing
Agendas, Fifth Edition**
**General Editors: Mark Kesselman,
Joel Krieger, William A. Joseph**

Executive Acquiring Sponsoring Editor:
Carolyn Merrill

Acquiring Sponsoring Editor: Edwin Hill

Development Manager: Jeffrey Greene

Associate Editor: Katherine Hayes

Editorial Assistant: Matt DiGangi

Media Editor: Laura Hildebrand

Senior Marketing Manager: Amy Whitaker

Marketing Coordinator: Josh Hendrick

Marketing Communications Manager:
Heather Baxley

Content Project Manager: Aimee Chevrette
Bear

Art Director: Linda Helcher

Print Buyer: Miranda Klapper

Senior Rights Acquisition Account Manager:
Katie Huha

Senior Photo Editor: Jennifer Meyer Dare

Photo Researcher: Lisa Jelly Smith

Compositor: Pre-PressPMG

For product information and technology assistance, contact us at
Cengage Learning Academic Resource Center, 1-800-423-0563

For permission to use material from this text or product,
submit all requests online at **www.cengage.com/permissions**
Further permissions questions can be e-mailed to
permissionrequest@cengage.com

Library of Congress Control Number: 2009920555

Student Edition:
ISBN-13: 978-0-547-21629-4

ISBN-10: 0-547-21629-7

Wadsworth
20 Channel Center Street
Boston, MA 02210
USA

Cengage Learning is a leading provider of customized learning solutions with
office locations around the globe, including Singapore, the United Kingdom,
Australia, Mexico, Brazil, and Japan. Locate your local office at:
international.cengage.com/region

Cengage Learning products are represented in Canada by
Nelson Education, Ltd.

For your course and learning solutions, visit **www.cengage.com**

Purchase any of our products at your local college store or at our preferred
online store **www.ichapters.com**

Printed in Canada
1 2 3 4 5 6 7 13 14 12 11 10

Contents ⟫⟫

CHAPTER 3 France 99

MARK KESSELMAN

CHAPTER 4   Germany   157

CHRISTOPHER S. ALLEN

CHAPTER 5   Japan   211

SHIGEKO N. FUKAI AND HARUHIRO FUKUI

CHAPTER 6 India 265

ATUL KOHLI AND AMRITA BASU

CHAPTER 9   Brazil   415

ALFRED P. MONTERO

CHAPTER 10   Mexico   471

CHAPTER 11   Russia   517

Part 4 Non-Democracies   577

CHAPTER 12   IRAN   579

CHAPTER 13 China 625

WILLIAM A. JOSEPH

Preface »»

We began the preface to the third edition of *Introduction to Comparative Politics* (ICP), which was published in 2004, with the following observation: "Politics throughout the world seems more troubled today than even a few years ago, when celebrations around the globe ushered in the new millennium." In our preface to the fourth edition in 2004, we noted the wisdom of Francis Fukuyama's famous prediction that the demise of communism heralded the end of the kind of ideological conflict that had animated politics since the Industrial Revolution,[1] but also cautioned that the appearance of the end of history was misleading. The world of politics was as turbulent as at any time in recent memory, with clearcut trends more elusive than ever.

If anything, the years since the publication of the fourth edition of ICP have witnessed as much—or more—turmoil and uncertainty as the preceding years. Like Mark Twain's famous quip, "the report of my death was an exaggeration," any report of the end of history must await additional proof. Although in ICP we don't intend to present such proof or, for that matter, refute Fukuyama, we will do everything we can to provide a clear and comprehensive guide to these unsettled political times. In the Introduction, we set the stage and preview the thematic focus of the book by analyzing three critical junctures: 1989, which symbolizes the end of the cold war, and the eruption of capitalist democracies that transcend East versus West divisions in Europe and much of the world; 9/11, which reframes globalization, shifting attention away from the development gap and on to terrorism, security, and the use of force; and 2008, the year when nothing as dramatic as 1989 or 9/11

occurred, but when a series of spikes in the price of oil, reverberating credit, and home mortgage crises intensified concern about climate change, and mounting worry about a reverberating set of financial crises topped the political charts, bedeviled policy-makers, and mobilized citizen activism around the world. Add to this recipe for political turmoil uncertainty about the global role of the United States under new leadership; worries about nuclear weapons in Iran and continued instability in the Middle East; humanitarian catastrophes in the Sudan, China, Myanmar, and many other locales; and wars without any apparent end in sight in Iraq and Afghanistan. Not much is certain, except that the political world will be endlessly fascinating and analysis will be quite a challenge. Welcome aboard!

Structure and Approach of the Book

Like previous editions of ICP, this edition employs a country-by-country approach built around four core themes that strikes a balance between the richness of each country's distinctive pattern of political development and cross-country comparative analysis.

Our approach to comparative politics emphasizes patterns of state formation, political economy, domestic political institutions and processes, and the politics of collective identities, all within a context shaped by globalization. We use four comparative themes to frame the presentation of each country's politics. We explain the themes in Chapter 1 and present an intriguing "puzzle" for each to stimulate student thinking. These themes—described in the first section of each country study and analyzed throughout the chapter—focus attention on the patterns of similarity and difference among the twelve country studies:

- **A World of States** focuses on the importance of state formation, the internal

---

[1]Francis Fukuyama, "The End of History?" *The National Interest* 16 (Summer 1989): 3–18. The article is reprinted in Mark Kesselman, ed., *Readings in Comparative Politics: Political Challenges and Changing Agendas*, 2nd ed. (Boston: Wadsworth/Cengage, 2010).

organization of the state, and the effects of the interstate system for political development. We emphasize the interactive effects of globalization and state power.

- **Governing the Economy** emphasizes the crucial role of economic performance in determining a state's political legitimacy, analyzes state strategies for promoting economic development and competitiveness, and stresses the effects of economic globalization on domestic politics.
- **The Democratic Idea** explores the challenges posed to the state by citizens' demands for greater control and participation in both democracies and authoritarian regimes and discusses the inevitable gap between the promise of democracy and the imperfect expression of democracy.
- **The Politics of Collective Identities** considers the political consequences of race, ethnicity, gender, religion, and nationality and their complex interplay with class-based politics.

Through our four themes, the methods of comparative analysis come alive as students examine similarities and differences among countries and within and between political systems. The thematic approach facilitates disciplined analysis of political challenges and changing agendas within countries.

Organization of Chapters and Special Features

Chapter 1 explains the comparative method, analyzes the four key themes of the book, and describes core features of political institutions and processes. Each country chapter that follows consists of five sections. **Section 1** treats the historic formation of the modern state, its geographic setting, critical junctures in its political development, its relationship to the international political and economic system, and the country's significance for the study of comparative

politics. **Section 2** describes the political economy of past and current national development. **Section 3** outlines the major institutions of governance and policy-making. **Section 4** explains the widely varying processes of representation, participation, and contestation. Finally, **Section 5** reflects on the major issues that confront the country and are likely to shape its political future.

Several special features assist in the teaching and learning process.

- Throughout the chapters a wide array of maps, tables, charts, photographs, and political cartoons enliven the text and present key information in clear and graphic ways.
- Each country study includes several sidebar boxes that highlight interesting and provocative aspects of politics. These vary somewhat chapter by chapter, but generally include the following:
  - **Leaders:** biographies of important political leaders;
  - **Institutional Intricacies:** important features of a political system that warrant careful discussion;
  - **Citizen Action:** politically potent expressions of citizen participation and protest;
  - **Global Connection:** examples of links between domestic and international politics;
  - **Current Challenges:** issues of today and the future that help shape important dimensions of national politics.
- Key terms are set in boldface when first introduced in each chapter and are defined in the Glossary at the end of the book. Students will find that the Glossary defines many key concepts

that are used broadly in comparative politics.

- Each chapter concludes with a list of suggested readings and websites. The Introduction (Chapter 1) includes a sidebar box that discusses the use of the Internet in the study of comparative politics.

New to This Edition

As our discussion of the critical junctures of 1989, 9/11, and 2008 suggests, history and politics have not ended, and as this text will amply demonstrate, interpretive debates have not ended either. To capture these epochal developments, we have expanded coverage in a number of ways that are new to this edition:

- We deepen and widen our treatment of globalization in each country study and analyze in greater detail the impact of globalization on a country's politics and political economy.
- We take special note of the social policies and their outcomes in each country, in particular their implications for the household and the role of women in society.
- We assess significant changes in the maintenance of internal security since 9/11, and the trade-offs between security and civil liberties or human rights.
- We consider how the war in Iraq and American foreign and security policy and influence have affected politics as well as foreign and security policy in each country.
- We address how concerns about climate change and environmental politics have shaped party competition and electoral behavior, and produced social movements and political protests.

In addition, we have provided a more visually interesting presentation of data in a way that is intended to enhance cross-country comparative analysis.

Teaching and Learning Aids and Database Editions

ComparingGovernments.org This online learning tool engages students through a variety of media, including original videos, short-form documentaries, writing excerpts, and additional resources. Correlated to the table of contents in the text, the site offers instructors four quality homework assignments per chapter that can be recorded in an online "Notebook." In addition, newsfeeds from the BBC World News and top stories from the United Nations News Centre keep students current with world affairs. Ask your Wadsworth/Cengage rep about packaging ComparingGovernments.org with your text.

In addition, instructors have access to an **Instructor's Resource Manual** and PowerPoint slides for classroom presentation. These are available on the instructor website along with practice test questions for students. And finally the **Test Bank** is available electronically and as Word files on the Diploma Testing CD-ROM. It is available from your Wadsworth/Cengage sales representative.

Acknowledgments

We are grateful to colleagues who have reviewed and critiqued ICP5:

Donn Kurtz, *University of Louisiana*
Julie M. Mazzei, *Kent State University*
Derwin S. Munroe, *University of Michigan at Flint*
Lisa Elizabeth Huffstetler, *University of Memphis*
Nicholas Toloudis, *Rutgers University*
Dag Mossige, *Ohio State University*
Thomas Kolasa, *Troy University*

In addition, we are grateful to the talented and professional staff who helped edit and publish ICP5: Edwin Hill, acquiring sponsoring editor; Jeff Greene, development manager; Aimee Bear, content project manager; Matt DiGangi, editorial assistant; and Leslie Kauffman, senior project manager, development at LEAP Publishing Services.

M. K.
J. K.
W. A. J.

Part 1 >> Introduction

Chapter 1   **INTRODUCING COMPARATIVE POLITICS**

Mark Kesselman, Joel Krieger, and William A. Joseph

Chapter 1 »» INTRODUCING COMPARATIVE POLITICS

The Global Challenge
SECTION 1 of Comparative Politics

Three dates are useful markers to define the current era of world politics: 1989, 2001, and 2008. Each one can focus our attention on a different element of the current world order. *Introduction to Comparative Politics* studies how different countries both shape and are shaped by the world order created by watershed events such as those that occurred in 1989, 2001, and 2008. Each of these events describes a particularly important moment—what we call a **critical juncture**—that helps define key transitional moments.

When did our current era begin? A frequently cited date is 1989, when the Berlin Wall, that separated communist-controlled East Berlin from West Berlin, was dismantled. More broadly, the Berlin Wall separated the communist regime of the German Democratic Republic (GDR), allied with the Soviet Union, from the Federal Republic of Germany, a country that belonged to the rival alliance of the United States and other democratic countries. The wall served as a powerful symbol of the division of the world into a communist bloc of countries under the control of the Soviet Union, and the "Western" world, led by the United States. Until 1989, the two alliances stood toe to toe, glaring at each other across the Berlin Wall and a frontier that stretched across Europe and the entire world. The Soviet Union and the United States each possessed an arsenal of many thousands of thermonuclear-tipped missiles that targeted the other.

In 1989, the Soviet Union weakened its grip on the countries in East Central Europe, including the GDR. One result was the collapse of the Berlin Wall, when Germans and others in East Central Europe breached the wall in order to escape the harsh conditions in which they lived and flee to the West to pursue freedoms and economic opportunities that were unavailable in the East. The crumbling of the Berlin Wall was soon followed by a series of peaceful revolutions against the **communist party-states** of East Central Europe and the Soviet Union. The implosion of these **regimes**, and their replacement by governments proclaiming a commitment to democratic rule, marked the end of the grim and sometimes deadly **cold war** that had pitted the Soviet and American alliances against one another not only in Europe but in many parts of the world.

Soon after the Berlin Wall was torn down, an important and controversial analysis of world events was published with an audacious title, "The End of History?"[1] For its author, Francis Fukuyama, the failure of communism was of historic significance not only in itself, but also because it signified the end of any feasible alternative to Western-style regimes, that is, regimes that combine capitalist organization of the economy with a democratic political system. (This combination is known as **liberal democracy**.) He recognized that the political and economic transitions to this new era would not be easy for many countries. Fukuyama predicted that because of deeply entrenched nationalist and ethnic divisions, many parts of the world would "be a terrain of conflict for many years to come." But, according to Fukuyama, henceforth, there would only be one model of political and economic development for the world. The global struggle between competing **ideologies** (a set of beliefs and preferences) that had marked previous eras and that, in the twentieth century alone, had led to two world wars and the cold war, was over.

Fukuyama recognized that, in the short run, several crucial issues presented the post-cold war world with both promise and peril. Every country faces the challenges of adjusting to a global economic system dominated by developed capitalist countries and international organizations committed to promoting free market capitalism. Many are also struggling, often under intense pressure, to build democratic governments in difficult economic and social circumstances and after decades of **authoritarian** rule. And Fukuyama was certainly correct—as **ethnic cleansing** and **genocide** in Rwanda, the former Yugoslavia, and the Sudan painfully remind us—that violent antagonisms can produce a terrible toll in some countries.

1989 ushered in three important changes. First, it marked the end of a bipolar world, in which two superpowers, the Soviet Union and the United States, vied to dominate global affairs. It marked the emergence of a unipolar world dominated by what a French foreign minister dubbed a "hyperpower"—the U.S. Second, as Fukuyama pointed out, 1989 marked the triumph of one model of political and economic development: liberal democracy. Third, 1989 was a gateway to **globalization**.

In the years following 1989, globalization provided a new and distinctive lens for analyzing politics within and among countries. The key new question that promised to dominate the political agenda was whether the global diffusion of investment, trade, production, and electronic communication technologies would promote a worldwide expansion of opportunity and enhance human development—or whether it would reinforce the comparative advantages of the more prosperous and powerful nations, transnational corporations, and peoples; undermine local cultures; and intensify regional conflicts.

These issues are very much with us today and frame the country studies in this book. Yet we have been forced to rethink the meaning of globalization because of what occurred on September 11, 2001, the second date framing the current era. On that day, the Islamic terrorist group, Al Qaeda, led by Osama Bin Laden, launched deadly attacks on the World Trade Center in New York and the Pentagon in Washington, D.C. Before 9/11, the economic aspects of globalization claimed much of the world's attention. The attacks on that fateful day constituted a new challenge, and produced a tragic and somber critical juncture following the brief post-cold war period when the issues of political reform and improved economic performance dominated the global agenda.

Terrorist attacks on the United States and countries throughout the world were not a new phenomenon. Consider the United States. There was a car bomb attack on the World Trade Center by Al Qaeda in 1993, the 1995 bombing by domestic terrorists of a federal office building in Oklahoma City, and an attack by Islamic terrorists on a U.S. Navy destroyer, the *U.S.S. Cole*, in Yemen in 2000. Many other countries in the world were also the target of terrorist attacks before 9/11. But the 9/11 attacks were different because of the scale—more than 3,000 deaths; the targets: the Pentagon, the nerve center of the U.S. military, and

the 112-story twin towers of New York's World Trade Center; and the impact on global politics—comparable to the crumbling of the Berlin Wall in 1989.

The attacks of 9/11 were not an isolated event. They were soon followed by the bombing of a beach resort in Bali, Indonesia; a train station in Madrid, Spain; an elementary school in Beslan, Russia; a subway and bus in London; and a host of other highly politicized attacks on targets throughout the world, which have come to characterize the contemporary era. Since 9/11, security concerns have risen to the top of nearly every government's agenda and transformed domestic politics in countries around the globe. The attacks have also led to a recasting of global alliances and the development of new domestic and foreign policies to counter the threat of Islamic radicalism.

The 9/11 attacks triggered a rapid U.S. response, named by President George W. Bush "the war on terror." With wide international support and near-unanimity at home, the United States launched an attack in October 2001 on the Taliban regime in Afghanistan. The reason, according to President Bush, was that the regime had provided a safe haven for Al Qaeda and its leader, Osama Bin Laden. However, not long after the U.S.-led coalition toppled the Taliban regime in Afghanistan, the United States provoked the strong opposition of most governments and global public opinion when it attacked the Iraqi regime of Saddam Hussein in 2003. President Bush and prominent administration officials—as well as a few key allies, notably Britain's prime minister Tony Blair—defended the decision on the grounds that Saddam Hussein possessed, and could rapidly deploy, weapons of mass destruction, including nuclear, biological, and chemical armaments. It was further alleged that there were close links between Iraq and Al Qaeda and that the invasion and occupation of Iraq were a critical part of the war on terror.

Opposition to the United States and its allies increased after Saddam's regime was quickly toppled when the U.S. failed to produce evidence that Saddam possessed weapons of mass destruction or had links to Al Qaeda and the attacks of 9/11. Moreover, establishing order, reconstructing Iraq, and creating an effective democratic government proved far harder than removing Saddam. Many years after President Bush

Introduction

Two events symbolically mark the major changes in world politics in the late twentieth and early twenty-first centuries: The fall of the Berlin Wall (left), in November 1989, ushered in the post-cold war era, while the terrorist attack on the World Trade Center towers in New York City on September 11, 2001 (right), reflected a particularly violent form of the forces of globalization that now affect politics in all countries.   *Sources:* (Left) Lionel Cironneau/AP Images. (Right) Gulnara Samoilova/AP Images.

prounounced in May 2003, "mission accomplished," military hostilities and civil war continued to claim the lives of Iraqis and American troops.

The events following September 11 have added to rather than replaced concerns about economic globalization. As a result, we are challenged to develop a more complex understanding of globalization and how it frames both political realities on the ground and the study of comparative politics.

Globalization and terrorism make the current era complex and fraught with uncertainties. And those are not the only challenges facing the world. 2008—the third date that serves to define the context in which countries included in *Introduction to Comparative Politics* must navigate—points to yet another key development in the world today. At first glance, no noteworthy event occurred in 2008 that was comparably important to 1989 and 2001. Yet 2008 was a noteworthy year because of a cascade of economic challenges.

For a starter, the price of crude oil on world markets first reached $100 a barrel in 2008. Nor was this price increase a blip: by the summer of that year, the price of oil exceeded $140 a barrel and gasoline at the pump cost over $4 a gallon. When a world-wide recession erupted in late 2008, the demand for oil plummeted. As one might expect, given the law of supply and demand, the price of oil also quickly fell. However, the same law dictates that oil prices will soar when the recession ends.

Why does the price of petroleum matter? Because the world runs on oil. It fuels the global economy, from the industries that churn out the products of a modern society to the electricity that lights our homes. The high price of crude oil reflects four factors, each of which is troublesome. When the four coincide, as they do in the current era, the challenges confronting governments and citizens throughout the world are daunting. First, the world's supply of petroleum

is finite, nonrenewable, and becoming increasingly scarce. Second, competition for access to petroleum has considerably increased in the twenty-first century. This is largely because China and India, the two most populous nations in the world, have achieved extraordinarily rapid industrialization and economic growth that requires huge amounts of oil. Third, many of the major petroleum exporters have somewhat unstable regimes, including Iraq and Nigeria. Disruption of supplies spells higher oil prices. Finally, the cost of petroleum is measured in dollars, and the value of the U.S. dollar has significantly declined recently. Thus, more dollars are needed to purchase a barrel of oil.

The fact that petroleum soared to well over $100 a barrel in 2008 warrants identifying that year as a turning point. Other developments in 2008—some of which are linked to the oil price hike—provide additional reasons. The effect of rising oil prices rippled throughout the global economy. The impact has been

especially harsh for the several billion people at the low end of the income scale. As airline passengers and commuters filling up at the pump well know, the cost of transportation rises when oil costs more. The cost of food also rises: it takes petroleum to produce fertilizers, operate farm machinery, and transport crops to market. Further, the supply of food is reduced when crops are diverted for use as biofuel. In 2008, as the price of basic necessities—rice, corn, soybeans, and wheat—soared, desperate citizens participated in food riots in Egypt, Haiti, Burkina Faso, and elsewhere.

2008 is an important date for another reason, also linked to petroleum. That year, global awareness of climate change and global warming claimed the world's attention. As every schoolchild has learned, burning fossil fuels increases man-made greenhouse gases, a prime cause of global warming. In 2008, scientists warned that CO_2 emissions may produce an irreversible tipping point within several decades, involving the melting of the polar ice caps and a rise in sea levels. The results would be disastrous for people living in coastal areas in Bangladesh, Sri Lanka, the U.S., and elsewhere.

Another series of economic difficulties in 2008 further contributed to making that year a critical juncture. When a financial bubble in the U.S. housing sector burst, it forced a large number of financial giants based in the United States, including Bear Stearns, Lehman Brothers, Merrill Lynch, and American International Group, to declare bankruptcy or accept buyouts at bargain-basement prices. Given the close interconnections among industrial and financial firms and among regions of the world, the entire global economy tottered on the brink of disaster. The crisis was at least temporarily resolved when the U.S. government created a new facility to purchase the bad debt held by banks and other financial institutions. The government provided a whopping $700 billion for this purpose—a larger sum than the Pentagon's annual budget! The financial turmoil in the U.S. whipsawed through the entire global financial system and provoked widespread calls for substantially restructuring the relationship between governments and private markets.

The changes occurring in 1989, 2001, and 2008 have not occurred in a clear linear sequence: they overlap to produce the charged global era in which we live. *Introduction to Comparative Politics* analyzes how important governments throughout the world attempt to govern effectively and produce desirable results for citizens in a context shaped by these challenges (and others that we will identify shortly).

Globalization and Comparative Politics

The three developments that we have just reviewed help define our global era. Given its importance, it is useful to explore the features of this global era more fully. The terms *globalization* and *global era* are applied everywhere as general catch phrases to identify the growing depth, extent, and diversity of cross-border connections that are a key characteristic of the contemporary world. Discussion of globalization begins with accounts of economic activities, including the reorganization of production and the global

redistribution of the work force (the "global factory" and "global supply chains"), as well as the increased extent and intensity of international trade, finance, and foreign direct investment. Globalization also involves the movement of peoples due to migration, employment, business, and educational opportunities.[2]

Globalization includes other profound changes that are less visible but equally significant. For example, new applications of information technology (such as the Internet) and new ways to deliver news and images around the world (such as CNN) blur the traditional distinction between what is around the block and what is around the world—instantly transforming cultures and eroding the boundaries between the local and global. These technologies make instantaneous communication possible and link producers and contractors, headquarters, branch plants, and suppliers in real time anywhere in the world. Employees may be rooted in time and place, but employers can take advantage of the ebb and flow of a global labor market. A secure job today may be gone tomorrow. Globalization both offers opportunities and fosters insecurity in everyday life, and presents extraordinary challenges to governments in all countries, large and small, rich and poor.

Globalization has forged new forms of international governance, from the **European Union (EU)** to the **World Trade Organization (WTO)**, in an attempt to regulate and stabilize the myriad flows of globalization. An alphabet soup of other organizations and agreements—such as UNDP, IMF, IBRD, OECD, NAFTA, and APEC,[3] to name but a few—have also been enlisted in this attempt. Globalization has also provoked challenges from grassroots movements in every region of the world that are concerned with its negative impact on, for example, poor people, the environment, and labor rights. All of these globalization processes complicate politics, just as they erode the ability of even the strongest countries to control their destinies. No state can achieve the economic security and general well-being of its citizens in isolation from the rest of the world. None can preserve pristine national models of economic governance or distinctly national cultures, values, understandings of the world, or narratives that define a people and forge their unity. Many of the most important problems confronting governments are related to globalization, including pandemics like AIDS, global climate change, financial panics, competition for scarce resources, and international terrorism. Although these problems may be global in scope, a government's popularity with its own people depends in considerable measure on how successfully it addresses these problems at home.

It is clear that countries face a host of challenges simultaneously from above and below. The capacities of states to control domestic outcomes and assert **sovereignty** are challenged by regional and global technological and market forces, as well as by growing security concerns. The very stability and viability of many countries are simultaneously assaulted by ethnic, nationalist, and religious divisions that often involve both internal and external components. The bright line separating domestic and international politics has been blurred (some would say rubbed out) by the complex set of cross-border economic, cultural, technological, governance, and security processes, institutions, and relations that constitute the contemporary global order.

Making Sense of Turbulent Times

The flash of newspaper headlines and television sound bites, rush of events, and sheer range and complexity of the cross-border phenomena of globalization tend to make politics look overwhelming and chaotic beyond comprehension. Although the study of comparative politics can help us understand current events in a rapidly changing world, it involves much more than snapshot analysis or Monday-morning quarterbacking, and it requires a longer perspective and a more complex analytic framework than what we have introduced so far by identifying the critical political changes captured by developments in 1989, 2001, and 2008.

Introduction to Comparative Politics describes and analyzes in detail the government and politics of a range of countries and identifies common themes in their development that explain longer-term causes of both changes and continuities. The book provides cross-national comparisons and explanations based on four themes that we believe are central for understanding politics in today's world:

- The World of States: the historical formation, internal organization, and interaction of states within the international order

- Governing the Economy: the role of the state in economic management
- The Democratic Idea: the spread of democracy and the challenges of democratization
- The Politics of Collective Identities: the sources and political impact of diverse **collective identities**, including class, gender, ethnicity, nationality, and religion.

We also expect that these four themes will be useful for charting where the countries discussed in this book may be heading politically (although we hasten to add that we aim to make sense of what exists, not to predict what will exist in the future). The themes are valuable tools that enable us to make political sense of even the most tumultuous times. The contemporary period presents an extraordinary challenge to those who study comparative politics, but the study of comparative politics also provides a unique opportunity for understanding this uncertain era.

In order to appreciate the complexity of politics in countries around the world, we must look beyond any single national perspective. Today, business and trade, information technology, mass communications and culture, immigration and travel, as well as politics, forge deep connections—as well as deep divisions—among people worldwide. It is particularly urgent that we develop a truly global and comparative perspective as we explore the politics of different countries and their growing interdependence on one another.

There is an added benefit of studying comparative politics: by comparing political institutions, values, and processes in countries around the world, the student of comparative politics acquires analytical skills that can be used at home. After you study comparative politics, you begin to think comparatively. As comparison becomes more familiar, we hope that you will look at the politics of your own country differently, with a wider focus and new insights.

The contemporary world provides a fascinating laboratory for the study of comparative politics. We hope that you share our sense of excitement in the challenging effort to understand the complex and ever-shifting terrain of contemporary politics throughout the world. We begin by exploring what comparative politics actually compares and how comparative study enhances our understanding of politics generally.

What—and How—Comparative Politics Compares

To "compare and contrast" is one of the most common human mental exercises, whether in the classroom study of literature or politics or animal behavior—or in selecting dorm rooms or listing your favorite movies. In the observation of politics, the use of comparisons is very old, dating in the Western world to at least from Aristotle, the ancient Greek philosopher. Aristotle categorized Greek city-states in the fourth century B.C. according to their form of political rule: rule by a single individual, rule by a few, or rule by all citizens. He also added a normative dimension (a claim about how societies *should* be ruled) by distinguishing ("contrasting") good from corrupt versions of each type, according to whether those with power ruled in the interest of the common welfare of all citizens or only in their own interest. The modern study of comparative politics refines and systematizes the age-old practice of evaluating some feature of X by comparing it to the same feature of Y.

Comparative politics is a subfield within the academic discipline of political science as well as a method or approach to the study of politics.[4] The subject matter of comparative politics is the domestic politics of countries or peoples. Within the discipline of political science, comparative politics is one of four areas of specialization. In addition to comparative politics, most political science (or government) departments in U.S. colleges and universities include courses and academic specialists in three other fields: political theory, international relations, and American politics.

Because it is widely believed that students living in the United States should study American politics intensively and with special focus, it is usually treated as a separate subfield of political science. The pattern of distinguishing the study of politics at home from the study of politics abroad is also common elsewhere, so students in Canada may be expected to study Canadian politics as a distinct specialty, and Japanese students would be expected to master Japanese politics.

However, there is no logical reason that study of the United States should not be included within the field of comparative politics—and there is good reason to do so. In fact, many important studies in comparative politics

(and an increasing number of courses) have integrated the study of American politics with the study of politics in other countries.[5] Comparative study can place U.S. politics into a much richer perspective and at the same time make it easier to recognize what is distinctive and most interesting about other countries.

Special mention should be made of the distinction between comparative politics and international relations. Comparative politics involves comparing domestic political institutions, processes, policies, conflicts, and attitudes in different countries; international relations involves studying the foreign policies of and interactions among countries, the role of international organizations such as the **United Nations**, and the growing influence of a wide range of global actors from multinational corporations to terrorist networks. In a globalized world, the distinction sometimes becomes questionable, and there is a large gray zone where the two fields overlap. Think of an urgent challenge such as climate change. Most observers would agree that international agreements to limit the use of fossil fuels and the need for concerted action around the world make climate change a proper concern of international relations. It is also true, however, that decisions about energy policy, investments in renewable sources of energy, and government incentives for automobile manufacturers to produce battery-powered cars are made through the prism of country-by-country politics and therefore shaped by the domestic interplay of competing interests. Does the politics of climate change fall within the field of comparative politics or the field of international relations? The answer of course is both.[6]

However, it makes sense to maintain the distinction between comparative politics and international relations. Much of the world's political activity continues to occur within state borders, and comparisons of domestic politics, institutions, and processes enable us to understand critical features that distinguish one country's politics from another's. Furthermore, we believe that, despite increased international economic competition and integration (a key aspect of globalization), national states are the fundamental building blocks in

The Internet and the Study of Comparative Politics

The Internet can be a very rich source of information about the politics of countries around the world. Following are some of the types of information you can find on the web. We haven't included URLs since they change so often. But you should be able to find the websites easily through a key word search on Google or another search engine.

- **Current events.** Most of the world's major news organizations have excellent websites. Among those we recommend for students of comparative politics are the British Broadcasting Corporation (BBC), Cable News Network (CNN), the *New York Times*, and the *Washington Post*.
- **Elections.** Results of recent (and often past) elections, data on voter turnout, and descriptions of different types of electoral systems can be found at the International Election Guide (IFES), Elections by country/Wikipedia, and the International Institute for Democracy and Electoral Assistance.
- **Statistics.** You can find data that is helpful both for understanding the political, economic, and social situation in individual countries and for comparing countries. Excellent sources of statistics are the Central Intelligence Agency (CIA), the Inter-parliamentary Union (IPU), the United Nations Development Program (UNDP), and the World Bank.

    There are some websites that bring together data from other sources. These allow you not only to access the statistics, but also to chart or map them in a variety of ways. See, for example, Nationmaster.com and Globalis.com.

- **Rankings and ratings.** There is a growing number of organizations that provide rankings or ratings of countries along some dimension based on comparative statistical analysis. We provide the following examples of these in the Data Charts that appear at the end of this chapter: the UNDP **Human Development Index**; the **Global Gender Gap**; the **Environmental Performance Index**; the **Corruption Perceptions Index**; and the **Freedom in the World rating.** Others you might look at are UNDP's Gender-Related Development Index (GDI) and Gender Empowerment Measure (GEM); the World Bank's Worldwide Governance Indicators Project; the Global Economic Competitiveness Index; the Globalization Index; the Index of Economic Freedom; the World Audit of Freedom and Democracy; and the Press Freedom Index. *A note of caution: Some of these sites may have a certain political point of view that influences the way they collect and analyze data. As with any web source, be sure to check out who sponsors the site and what type of organization it is.*
- **Official information and documents.** Most countries maintain websites in English. The first place to look is the website of the country's embassy in Washington, D.C., Ottawa, or London. The United Nations delegations of many countries also have websites. Governments often have English language versions of their official home pages, including governments with which the United States may not have official relations, such as Cuba and North Korea.
- **The United States Department of State.** The State Department's website has background notes on most countries. American embassies around the world provide information on selected topics about the country in which they are based.
- **Maps.** The Perry-Castañeda Library Map Collection at the University of Texas is probably the best currently available online source of worldwide maps at an educational institution.
- **General comparative politics.** Several American and British universities host excellent websites that provide links to a multitude of Internet resources on comparative politics (often coupled with international relations), such as Columbia University, Emory University, Keele University, Princeton University, Vanderbilt University, and West Virginia University.

structuring political activity. Therefore *Introduction to Comparative Politics* is built on in-depth case studies of a sample of important countries around the world.

The comparative approach principally analyzes similarities and differences among countries by focusing on selected institutions and processes. As students of comparative politics (we call ourselves **comparativists**), we believe that we cannot make reliable statements about most political situations by looking at only one case. We often hear statements such as: "The United States has the best health care system in the world." Comparativists immediately wonder what kinds of health care systems exist in other countries, what they cost and how they are financed, how it is decided who can receive medical care, and so on. Besides, what does "best" mean when it comes to health care systems? Is it the one that provides the widest access? The one that is the most technologically advanced? The one that is the most cost-effective? The one that produces the healthiest population? None of us would announce the best movie or the best car without considering other alternatives or deciding what specific factors enter into our judgment.

Comparativists often analyze political institutions or processes by looking at two or more cases that are selected to isolate their common and contrasting features. The analysis involves comparing similar aspects of politics in more than one country. Some comparativists focus on government institutions in different countries, such as the legislature, executive, political parties, or court systems.[7] Others compare specific processes or policies, for example, education or environmental policy.[8] Some comparative political studies take a thematic approach and analyze broad issues, such as the causes and consequences of nationalist movements or revolutions in different countries.[9] Comparative studies may also involve comparisons of an institution, policy, or process through time, in one or several countries. For example, some studies have analyzed a shift in the orientation of economic policy that occurred in many advanced capitalist countries in the 1980s from **Keynesianism**, an approach that gives priority to government regulation of certain aspects of the economy, to **neoliberalism**, which emphasizes the importance of market-friendly policies.[10]

Level of Analysis

Comparisons can be useful for political analysis at several different levels of a country, such as cities, regions, provinces, or states. But we believe that the best way to begin the study of comparative politics is with **countries**. Countries comprise distinct, politically defined territories that encompass political institutions, cultures, economies, and ethnic and other social identities. Although countries are often highly divided by internal conflicts, and people within their borders may have close ties to those in other countries, countries have historically been among the most important sources of a people's collective political identity, and they are the major arena for organized political action in the modern world.

Within a given country, the **state** is almost always the most powerful cluster of institutions. But just what is the state? The way the term is used in comparative politics is probably unfamiliar to many students. In the United States, it usually refers to the states in the federal system—Texas, California, and so on. But in comparative politics, the state refers to the key political institutions responsible for making, implementing, and adjudicating important policies in a country.[11] Thus, we use phrases such as the "German state" and the "Mexican state." In many ways, the state is synonymous with what is often called the "government."

The most important state institutions are the national **executive**—usually, the president and/or prime minister and the **cabinet**. In some cases, the executive includes the communist party leadership (such as in China), the head of a military government (as in Nigeria until 1999), or the supreme religious leader (as in the Islamic Republic of Iran). Alongside the executive, the **legislature** and the **judiciary** comprise the institutional apex of state power, although the interrelationships and functions of these institutions vary from country to country. Other key state institutions include the military, police, and the administrative **bureaucracy**.

States claim, usually with considerable success, the right to make rules—notably, laws, administrative, and court decisions—that are binding for people within the country. Even democratic states—in which top officials are chosen by procedures that authorize all citizens to participate—can survive only if they can preserve enforcement (or coercive) powers both internally and with regard to other states and external groups that may threaten them. A number of countries have highly repressive states whose political survival depends largely on military and police powers. But even in such states, long-term stability requires that the ruling regime have some measure of political **legitimacy**; that is, a significant segment of the citizenry (in particular, more influential citizens and groups) must believe that the state is entitled to command compliance from those who live under its rule and acts lawfully in pursuit of desirable aims.

Political legitimacy is greatly affected by the state's ability to deliver the goods to its people through satisfactory economic performance and an acceptable distribution of economic resources. Moreover, in the contemporary period, legitimacy often seems to require that states represent themselves as democratic in some fashion, whether or not they are in fact. Thus, *Introduction to Comparative Politics* looks closely at both the state's role in governing the economy and the pressures exerted on states to develop and extend democratic participation.

Given that the organization of state institutions varies widely, and these differences have a powerful impact on political, economic, and social life, the country studies in this book devote considerable attention to institutional variations—along with their political implications. Each country study begins with an analysis of how the institutional organization of the state has evolved historically. The process of **state formation** fundamentally influences how and why states differ politically.

One critical difference among states that will be explored in our country studies involves the extent to which citizens in a country share a common sense of nationhood, that is, a belief that the state's geographic boundaries coincide with citizens' common identity, anchored in a sense of shared fates and values. When state boundaries and national identity coincide, the resulting formation is called a **nation-state**. A major source of political instability occurs when state boundaries and national identity do not coincide. In many countries around the world, nationalist movements within a state's borders challenge existing boundaries and seek to secede to form their own state, sometimes in alliance with movements from neighboring countries with whom they claim to share a common heritage. Such is the case with the Kurds, who have large populations in Turkey, Syria, and Iraq, and have long fought to establish an independent nation-state of Kurdistan. When a nationalist movement has distinctive ethnic, religious, and/or linguistic ties opposed to those of other groups in the country, conflicts are likely to be especially intense. Nationalist movements may pursue their separatist goal peacefully within established political institutions. Or, as we discuss in several of the country studies, they may challenge established institutions and engage in illegal activity, including violence against political authorities and civilians. India and Nigeria, for example, have experienced particularly violent episodes of ethnonationalist conflict. Tibet is an example of ethnic conflict within a country, China, that otherwise has a very strong sense of national identity.

Causal Theories

Because countries are the basic building blocks in politics and because states are the most significant political organizations within countries, these are two critical units for comparative analysis. The comparativist seeks to measure and hopefully explain similarities and differences among countries or states. One influential approach in comparative politics involves developing causal theories—hypotheses that can be expressed formally in a causal mode: "If X happens, then Y will be the result." Such theories include factors (the independent variables, symbolized by X) that are believed to influence some outcome (the dependent variable, symbolized by Y) that the analyst wants to explain.

For example, it is commonly argued that if a country's economic pie shrinks, conflict among groups will intensify. This hypothesis suggests what is called an inverse correlation between variables: as X varies in one direction, Y varies in the opposite direction. As the total national economic product (X) decreases, then political and social conflict over economic shares (Y) increases. This relationship might be tested by statistical analysis of a large number of cases, a project facilitated in recent years by computers and the creation of data banks that include extensive historical and contemporary data. Another way to study this issue would be to focus on one or several country cases and analyze in depth how the relevant relationships have varied historically. Even when explanation does not involve the explicit testing of hypotheses (and often it does not), comparativists try to identify similarities and differences among countries and to discover significant patterns.

It is important to recognize the limits on just how "scientific" political science—and thus comparative politics—can be. Two important differences exist between the "hard" (or natural) sciences like physics and chemistry and the social sciences. First, social scientists study people who exercise free will. Because people have a margin for free choice, even if one assumes that they choose in a rational manner, their choices, attitudes, and behavior cannot be fully explained. This does not mean that people choose in a totally arbitrary fashion. We choose within the context of material constraint, institutional dictates, and cultural prescriptions. Comparative politics analyzes how such factors shape political preferences and choices in systematic ways. Indeed, one empirical study has concluded that people's political beliefs are, to a certain degree, genetically determined.[12] But there will probably always be a wide gulf between the natural and social sciences because of their different objects of study.

A second difference between the natural and social sciences is that in the natural sciences, experimental techniques can be applied to isolate the contribution of distinct factors to a particular outcome. It is possible to change the value or magnitude of a factor—for example, the force applied to an object—and measure how the outcome has consequently changed. However, like other social scientists, political scientists and comparativists rarely have the opportunity to apply such experimental techniques.

Some political scientists have conducted experiments with volunteers in controlled settings. But laboratories provide crude approximations of natural settings since only one or several variables can be manipulated. The real world of politics, by contrast, consists of an endless number of variables, and they cannot easily be isolated or manipulated. (Further, another reason for the gulf between the laboratory and the world outside is that participants in laboratory experiments are less intensely motivated than they are in natural settings.) Another attempt to deal with this problem is by multivariate statistical techniques that seek to identify the specific causal weight of different variables in explaining variations in political outcomes. But it is difficult to measure precisely how, for example, a person's ethnicity, gender, or income influences her or his choice when casting a ballot. Nor can we ever know for sure what exact mix of factors—conflicts among elites, popular ideological appeals, the weakness of the state, the organizational capacity of rebel leaders, or the discontent of the masses—precipitates a successful revolution. Further,

different instances of a given outcome may result from varying causes. For example, different revolutions may result from different configurations of factors. Thus, one cannot develop a single theory to explain the origins of all revolutions.

There is a lively debate about whether the social sciences should seek scientific explanations comparable to what prevails in the natural sciences, such as physics. Some scholars claim that political scientists should aim to develop what have been called covering or universal laws to explain political outcomes: that is, political phenomena should be explained in a similar way to how physicists develop universally applicable laws to explain specific features of the physical world. Some critics of this view claim that because the social world is essentially different from the natural world, the social sciences should seek to identify particular patterns, mechanisms, and structures that fulfill similar functions that operate in different settings. But they recognize that this is a more modest goal than fully explaining outcomes. Another group of scholars claims that social science should focus on identifying unique configurations of factors that coexist in a particular case. Proponents of this approach do not seek a definitive explanation or the development of covering laws.[13] And yet a fourth approach advocates what the anthropologist Clifford Geertz has designated as "thick description." This approach seeks to convey the rich and subtle texture of any given historical situation, especially the subjective and symbolic meaning of that situation for its participants.[14] Comparativists who favor this approach highlight the importance of understanding each country's distinctive **political culture**, which can be defined as the attitudes, beliefs, values, and symbols that influence political behavior.

An approach largely borrowed from economics, called **rational choice theory**, has become especially influential—and highly controversial—in political science, including comparative politics, in recent years.[15] Rational choice theory focuses on how individuals act strategically (that is, rationally) in an attempt to achieve goals that maximize their interests. Such actions involve such varied activities as voting for a particular candidate or rebelling against the government. Proponents of rational choice generally use deductive and quantitative methods to construct models and general theories of political behavior that they believe can be applied across all types of political systems and cultures. This approach has been criticized for claiming to explain large-scale and complex social phenomena by reference to individual choices. It has also been criticized for dismissing the importance of variations in historical experience, political culture, identities, institutions, and other factors that are key aspects of most explanations of the political world.

Issues involving the appropriate choice of theory, methodology, research approaches, and strategies are a vital aspect of comparative politics. However, students may be relieved to learn that we do not deal with such issues in depth in *Introduction to Comparative Politics*. We believe that students will be in a better position to consider these questions after gaining a solid grasp of political continuities and contrasts in diverse countries around the world. It is this goal that we put front and center in *Introduction to Comparative Politics*.

Returning to our earlier discussion of the level of analysis, most comparativists probably agree on the value of steering a middle course that avoids either focusing exclusively on one country or blending all countries indiscriminately. If we study only individual countries without any comparative framework, comparative politics would become merely the study of a series of isolated cases. It would be impossible to recognize what is most significant in the collage of political characteristics that we find in the world's many countries. As a result, the understanding of patterns of similarity and difference among countries would be lost, along with an important tool for evaluating what is and what is not unique about a country's political life.

If we go to the other extreme and try to make universal claims, we would either have to stretch the truth or ignore significant national differences and patterns of variation. The political world is incredibly complex, shaped by an extraordinary array of factors and an almost endless interplay of variables. Indeed, after a brief period in the 1950s and 1960s when many comparativists tried—and failed—to develop a grand theory that would apply to all countries, most comparativists now agree on the value of **middle-level theory**, that is,

theories focusing on specific features of the political world, such as institutions, policies, or classes of similar events, such as revolutions or elections.

For example, comparativists have analyzed the process in which many countries with authoritarian forms of government, such as military **dictatorships** and one-party regimes, have developed more participatory and democratic regimes. In studying this process, termed **democratic transitions**, comparativists do not either treat each national case as unique or try to construct a universal pattern that ignores all differences. Applying middle-level theory, we identify the influence on the new regime's political stability of specific variables such as institutional legacies, political culture, levels of economic development, the nature of the regime before the transition, and the degree of ethnic conflict or homogeneity. Comparativists have identified common patterns in the emergence and consolidation of democratic regimes in southern Europe in the 1970s (Greece, Portugal, and Spain) and have compared them to developments in Latin America, Asia, and Africa since the 1980s, and in Eastern and Central Europe since the revolutions of 1989. Note that comparing does not require assuming that particular processes are identical in different regions. Indeed, some scholars have highlighted important differences between democratic transitions in Southern Europe and Latin America, on the one hand, and in Eastern and Central Europe on the other.[16]

The study of comparative politics offers many challenges, including the complexity of the subject matter, the fast pace of change in the contemporary world, and the impossibility of manipulating variables or replicating conditions. What can we expect when the whole political world is our laboratory? When we put the method of comparative politics to the test and develop a set of themes derived from middle-level theory, we discover that it is possible to discern patterns that make sense of a vast range of political events and link the experiences of states and citizens throughout the world. Although doubtless we will not achieve definitive explanations, we remain confident that we are able to better understand the daily headlines by reference to middle-range theoretical propositions.

SECTION 3   Themes for Comparative Analysis

We began this introduction by emphasizing the extraordinary importance of the global changes currently taking place. Next, we explained the subject matter of comparative politics and described some of the tools of comparative analysis. This section describes the four themes we use in *Introduction to Comparative Politics* to organize the information on political institutions and processes in the country chapters.

These themes help explain continuities and contrasts among countries. They help us understand what patterns apply to a group of countries and why, and what patterns are specific to a particular country. We also suggest a way that each theme highlights a particular puzzle in comparative politics.

Before we introduce the themes, a couple of warnings are necessary. First, our four themes cannot possibly capture the infinitely varied experience of politics throughout the world. Our framework in *Introduction to Comparative Politics,* built on these core themes, provides a guide to understanding many features of contemporary comparative politics. But we urge students (and rely on instructors!) to challenge and expand on our interpretations. Second, we want to note that a textbook builds from existing theory but does not construct or test new hypotheses. That task is the goal of original scholarly studies. The themes we present are intended to provide a framework to help organize some of the most significant developments in the field of contemporary comparative politics.

Theme 1: A World of States

The theme we call a world of states reflects the fact that for about 500 years, states have been the primary actors on the world stage. International organizations and private actors like transnational corporations—and ordinary citizens, who vote and participate in political parties and social movements—may play a crucial role in politics. But it is the rulers of states who send armies to conquer other states and territories. It is the legal codes of states that make it possible for businesses to operate within their borders and beyond. States provide more or less well for the social protection of citizens through the provision—in one way or another—of health care, old age pensions, aid to dependent children, and assistance to the unemployed. It is states that regulate the movement of people across borders through immigration law. And the policies of even the most influential international organizations reflect to a considerable extent the balance of power among member states.

That said, and as we noted above, states have been significantly affected by globalization. An indication of this development is that, within political science, there is increasing overlap between the study of international relations and the study of comparative politics. Courses in international relations nowadays often integrate a concern with how internal political processes affect states' behavior, while courses in comparative politics highlight the importance of transnational forces for understanding what goes on within a country's borders. The world-of-states theme in *Introduction to Comparative Politics* emphasizes the interaction between domestic politics and international forces.

We distinguish two important components of this theme. One focuses on a state's relationship to the international arena, while the other focuses on the state's internal development. The external element highlights the impact on a state's domestic political institutions and processes of its relative success or failure in competing economically and politically with other states. What sphere of maneuver is left to states by powerful global economic and geopolitical forces? How do CNN, the Internet, McDonald's, television, and films (whether produced in Hollywood or in Bollywood, that is, Bombay, the city that has been renamed Mumbai and that is the site of India's thriving film industry) shape local cultures and values, influence citizen perceptions of government, and affect political outcomes?

States still dwarf other political institutions in the exercise of power that matters, whether with regard to war, peace, and national security, or when it comes to providing educational opportunities, heath care, and pensions (social security). That said, no state, even the most powerful, such as the United States, can shape the world to suit its own designs or achieve its aims autonomously. Nor is any state unaffected by influences originating outside its borders. A wide array of international organizations and treaties, including the United Nations, the European Union, the World Trade Organization, the **World Bank**, the **International Monetary Fund (IMF)**, and the **North American Free Trade Agreement (NAFTA)**, challenge the sovereign control of national governments. Transnational corporations, international banks, and currency traders in New York, London, Frankfurt, Hong Kong, and Tokyo affect countries and people throughout the world. A country's political borders do not protect its citizens from global warming, environmental pollution, or infectious diseases that come from abroad. More broadly, developments linked to technology transfer, the growth of an international information society, immigration, and cultural diffusion challenge state supremacy and have a varying but significant impact on the domestic politics of virtually all countries.[17]

Thanks to the global diffusion of radio, television, and the Internet, people nearly everywhere can become remarkably well informed about international developments. This knowledge may fuel popular demands that governments intervene to stop atrocities in, for example, faraway Kosovo or Rwanda, or rush to aid the victims of natural disasters as happened after a great tsunami struck South and Southeast Asia in late 2004 and a devastating earthquake killed many thousands in China in May 2008. In the case of the cyclone in Myanmar, also in May 2008, that produced catastrophic loss of life, the devastation was made far worse by the resistance of that country's authoritarian regime to outside assistance.

And heightened global awareness may encourage citizens to hold their own government to internationally recognized standards of human rights and democracy. The recent spread of the so-called color or flower revolutions illustrates how what happens in one state can influence popular movements in other states, particularly in this era of globalized media and communications. Such movements have adopted various symbols to show their unity of purpose: the "Rose Revolution" (2003) in Georgia (a country located between Russia and Turkey, not the southern U.S. state), the "Orange Revolution" (2004) in Ukraine, and the "Tulip Revolution" (2005) in Kyrgyzstan all

led to the toppling of dictatorial leaders. The "Cedar Revolution" in Lebanon (2005) didn't force a change of political leadership, but it did cause the withdrawal of unpopular Syrian troops from that country, and the "Blue Revolution" in Kuwait has emerged as an important movement in support of granting women greater political rights.

States may collapse altogether when powerful rivals for power challenge rulers, especially when they are backed by a restive and mobilized citizenry. A similar outcome may occur when leaders of the state violate the rule of law and become predators, preying on the population. Political scientist Robert Rotberg has suggested the term "failed states" to describe this extreme situation, and cited as examples Sierra Leone, Somalia, and Afghanistan before and under the Taliban.[18] The political situation in such countries has approached the anarchical situation described by the seventeenth-century English philosopher Thomas Hobbes. In a state of nature, he warned in the *Leviathan*, the absence of effective state authority produces a war of every man (and woman) against every man, in which life involves "continual fear, and danger of violent death; and the life of man [is] solitary, poor, nasty, brutish, and short."

Although few states decline to the point of complete failure, all states are experiencing intense pressures from an increasingly complex mix of external influences. (Recall our discussion above of global competition for petroleum.) But international political and economic influences do not have the same impact in all countries, and a few privileged states have the capacity partially to shape the institutional structure and policy of international organizations in which they participate. The more advantages a state possesses, as measured by its level of economic development, military power, and resource base, the more global influence it will likely have and the more it will benefit from globalization. Conversely, countries with fewer advantages are more dependent on other states and international organizations, and less likely to derive benefits from globalization.

The second component of the world-of-states theme recognizes the fact that individual states (countries) are still the basic building block in world politics. It analyzes the importance of regime variations among states, in other words, the overall mix of their political institutions that distinguishes, for example, democratic from authoritarian regimes. Country chapters emphasize the importance of understanding similarities and contrasts in state formation and **institutional design** across countries. We identify critical junctures in state formation: that is, key events like colonial conquest, defeat in war, economic crises, or revolutions that had a durable impact on the character of the state. We also study the state's economic management strategies and capacities, diverse patterns of political institutions, such as the contrast between presidential and parliamentary forms in democratic states, the relationship of the state with social groups, and unresolved challenges that the state faces from within and outside its borders.

A puzzle: To what extent can even the most powerful states (especially the United States) preserve their autonomy and impose their will on others in a globalized world? Or are all states losing their ability to control important aspects of policy-making and secure the political outcomes they desire? And in what ways are the poorer and less powerful countries particularly vulnerable to the pressures of globalization and disgruntled citizens?

Increasingly, the politics and policies of states are shaped by diverse international factors often lumped together under the category of globalization. At the same time, many states face increasingly restive constituencies within their country who challenge the power and legitimacy of central governments. In reading the country case studies in this book, try to assess what impact pressures from both above and below—outside and inside—have on the role of the state in carrying out its basic functions and in sustaining the political attachment of its citizens.

Theme 2: Governing the Economy

The success of states in maintaining sovereign authority and control over their people is greatly affected by their ability to ensure that an adequate volume of goods and services is produced to satisfy the needs of their populations. Certainly, inadequate economic performance was an important reason for the rejection of communism and the disintegration of the Soviet Union. In contrast, China's stunning success in promoting economic development has been a major factor in explaining why communist rule has survived in that country.

Effective economic performance is near the top of every state's political agenda, and how a state "governs the economy"[19]—how it organizes production and the extent and nature of its intervention in the economy—is a key element in its overall pattern of governance. It is important to analyze, for example, how countries differ in the balance between agricultural and industrial production in their economies, the strategies that states use to improve economic performance, how successful countries are in competing in international markets, and the relative importance of private market forces versus government direction of the economy.

The term **political economy** refers to how governments affect economic performance and how economic performance in turn affects a country's political processes. We accord great importance to political economy in *Introduction to Comparative Politics* because we believe that politics in all countries is deeply influenced by the relationship between government and the economy in both domestic and international dimensions. However, the term *economic performance* may convey the misleading impressions that there is one right way to promote successful economic performance and one single standard by which to measure performance. In fact, both issues are far more complex.

There are many wrong ways to manage an economy; there are multiple right ways as well. Economic historian Alexander Gerschenkron pointed out long ago that the major European powers developed distinctive ways to promote industrialism because of the different places they occupied in the sequence of industrializing powers.[20] Britain had the good fortune to be the first country in the world to industrialize. Because of its head start in economic competition, it was possible for the state to adopt a relatively hands-off posture and for a market system of production to develop slowly. This arrangement came to be known by the French term **laissez-faire**, which literally means "let do," and more broadly refers to a free enterprise economy. All later developers, both those located in Europe in the nineteenth century and those located elsewhere in the world since then, have had to catch up.

As a result, they did not have the luxury of adopting the British state's style of low-profile management but were forced to develop varieties of crash programs of economic development.

What formula of state economic governance has made for success in this later period? On the one hand, both economic winners and losers display a pattern of extensive state intervention in the economy; thus, it is not the *degree* of state intervention that distinguishes the economic success stories from those that have fared less well. On the other hand, the winners do not share a single formula that enabled them to excel. For example, a study directed by Peter A. Hall and David Soskice of the world's affluent capitalist economies identifies two quite different patterns of political economy, both of which have been associated with strong economic performance.[21] Studies seeking to explain the Asian "economic miracles"—Japan, South Korea, and more recently China—as well as the variable economic performance of other countries highlight the diversity of approaches that have been pursued.[22]

There is agreement on a list of state practices that *hinder* economic development (although it borders on the commonsensical), such as when states tolerate dishonesty and corruption, set tax rates so high as to discourage productive economic activity, and fail to provide public goods like education and transportation facilities that promote a productive economy. However, there is no consensus on the economic policies that states *should* adopt. Moreover, some factors affecting economic performance are beyond a state's control. For example, economist Paul Collier has found that citizens of landlocked countries are especially apt to be among the "bottom billion" poorest people in the world.[23] (However, Collier points out that the examples of Switzerland and Austria suggest that being landlocked does not guarantee failure.)

The matter becomes even more complex when one considers the appropriate yardstick to measure economic success. Should economic performance be measured solely by how rapidly a country's economy grows? By how equitably it distributes the fruits of economic growth? By the quality of life of its citizenry, as measured by such criteria as life expectancy, level of education, and unemployment rate? What about the environmental impact of economic growth?

There is now much greater attention to this question, and more countries are emphasizing **sustainable development**, which promotes ecologically sound ways to modernize the economy and raise the standard of living. (See "How is Development Measured?") We invite you to consider these questions as you study the political economies of the countries analyzed in this book.

A puzzle: What is the relationship between democracy and successful national economic performance? This is a question that students of political economy have long pondered—and to which there are no fully satisfactory answers. Although all economies, even the most powerful, experience ups and downs, all durable democracies have been notable economic success stories. On the other hand, several East Asian countries with authoritarian regimes also achieved remarkable records of development. The Republic of Korea (South Korea), Taiwan, and Singapore surged economically in the 1960s and 1970s, and Malaysia and Thailand followed suit in the 1980s and 1990s. (Korea and Taiwan subsequently adopted durable democratic institutions.) China, a repressive communist party-state that has enjoyed the highest growth rate among major economies in the world since the early 1990s, provides a vivid case of development without democracy.

In light of the contradictory evidence, Nobel Prize–winning economist Amartya Sen has argued, "There is no clear relation between economic growth and democracy in *either* direction."[24] As you read the country studies, try to identify why some states have been more successful than others in "governing the economy," that is, fostering successful economic performance. Are there any consistent patterns that apply across countries?

Theme 3: The Democratic Idea

One of the most important and astounding political developments in recent years has been the rapid spread of democracy throughout much of the world. There is overwhelming evidence of the strong appeal of the democratic idea, by which we mean the claim by citizens that they should, in some way, exercise substantial control over the decisions made by their states and governments.

Global Connection

How Is Development Measured?

As we have already noted, we put particular importance on understanding the relationship between the political system and the economy in the study of the politics of any country and in our overall approach to comparative politics. Each of the country case studies describes and analyzes the role of the government in making economic policy. They also take special note of the impact of the global economy on national politics.

This book makes frequent reference to two commonly used measures of the overall size or power of a country's economy:

- Gross domestic product (GDP): a calculation of the total goods and services produced by the country during a given year.
- Gross national product (GNP): GDP plus income earned abroad by the country's residents.

A country's GDP and GNP are different, but not hugely so. In this book, we use GDP calculated according to an increasingly popular method called **purchasing power parity (PPP)**. PPP takes into account the real cost of living in a particular country by calculating how much it would cost in the local currency to buy the same "basket of goods" in different countries. For example, how many dollars in the United States, pesos in Mexico, or rubles in Russia does it take to buy a certain amount of food or to pay for housing? Many scholars think that PPP provides a relatively reliable (and revealing) tool for comparing the size of an economy among countries. In terms of annual total output according to PPP, the world's ten largest economies are: the United States, China, Japan, India, Germany, Britain, France, Russia, Brazil, and Italy.

But a better way to measure and compare the level of economic development and the standards of living in different countries is to look at annual GDP *per capita* (per person), in other words, to look at total economic output divided by total population. Although China has the world's second-largest economy in terms of total output, from the annual GDP *per capita* perspective China ($5300) falls to 133rd out of 227 countries measured, and India ($2700) falls to 167th place. Qatar and Luxembourg (both over $80,000), with their small populations, rank first and second while the United States is eighth ($45,800). This approach gives us a better idea of which countries in the world are rich (developed) or poor (developing).

The comparative data charts at the end of this chapter provide total GDP and GDP *per capita* as well as other economic, geographic, demographic, and social information for our country case studies. The Comparative Rankings table also provides several ways of evaluating countries in order to compare them along various dimensions of their economic, political, or public policy performance. One of the most important of these is the Human Development Index (HDI), which the United Nations uses to evaluate a country's level of development that considers more than just economic factors. The formula used to calculate a country's HDI takes into account *longevity* (life expectancy at birth), *knowledge* (adult literacy and average years of schooling), as well as *income* (according to PPP).

Based on this formula, countries are annually ranked and divided into three broad categories by the United Nations Development Program (UNDP): "High," "Medium," and "Low" human development. Out of 177 countries ranked according to HDI in 2007–08, the top three were Iceland, Norway, and Australia; the bottom three were Guinea-Bissau, Burkina Faso, and Sierra Leone. Look at the comparative data to see how the countries in this book are ranked, and as you read the case studies try to see what connections there may be between a country's state policies, politics, and its human development ranking.

According to statistical analysis of numerous measures of political freedom and civil liberties, the think tank Freedom House has calculated that in 1973, there were 43 countries that could be considered "free" (or democratic), 38 that were "partly free," and 69 that should be classified as "not free." In 2007, their count was 90 free, 60 partly free, and 43 not free. In terms of population, in 1973, 35 percent of the world's people

Table 1.1

The Spread of Democracy

Year	Free Countries	Partly Free Countries	Not Free Countries
1973	43 (35%)[a]	38 (18%)	69 (47%)
1983	54 (36%)	47 (20%)	64 (44%)
1993[b]	75 (25%)	73 (44%)	38 (31%)
2007	90 (46%)	60 (18%)	43 (36%)[c]

[a]The number of countries in each category is followed by the percentage of the world population.

[b]In 1993, the large increase in the number of free and partly free countries was mostly due to the collapse of communist regimes in the Soviet Union and elsewhere. The main reason that there is a significant drop in the percentage of world population living in free countries since 1993 is that India was classified as partly free from 1991 through 1997. It has been ranked as free since 1998.

[c]The increase in the number of countries and percentage of people rated as not free countries in 2007 compared to 1993 reflects the fact that several countries, most notably Russia, were shifted from partly free to not free.

is no one path to democracy and that democratic transitions can be slow, uncertain, and reversible. Some of the country studies in *Introduction to Comparative Politics* analyze the diverse causes and sources of support for democracy; and some expose the fragility of democratic transitions.

In certain historical settings, democracy may result from a standoff or compromise among political contenders for power, in which no one group can gain sufficient strength to control outcomes by itself.[28] In some (but not all) cases, rival groups may conclude that democracy is preferable to civil war. Or, it may take a bloody civil war that produces stalemate to persuade competing groups to accept democracy as a second-best solution. Democracy may appeal to citizens in authoritarian nations because democratic regimes often rank among the world's most stable, affluent, and cohesive countries. Citizens in authoritarian nations may also crave the political freedoms that are a hallmark of democracy. In some cases, a regional demonstration effect occurs, in which a democratic transition in one country provokes democratic change in neighboring countries. (This occurred in southern Europe in the 1970s, Latin America and parts of East Asia in the 1980s, and Eastern and Central Europe in the 1990s.) Another important pressure for democracy is born of the human desire for dignity and equality. Even when dictatorial regimes appear to benefit their countries—for example, by promoting economic development or nationalist goals—citizens may demand democracy.

Let the reader beware: the authors of *Introduction to Comparative Politics* have a strong normative preference for democracy. We believe, in the words of Britain's World War II Prime Minister Winston Churchill, "Democracy is the worst form of government except for all those others that have been tried." However, we have tried to separate our normative preferences from our analysis.

It should be noted that some theorists have warned of dangers associated with democracy. For example, political commentator Fareed Zakaria asserts, "What we need in politics today is not more democracy but less."[29] He claims that democratic policy-making tends to be dominated by what he terms "short-term political and electoral considerations," whereas wise policy requires a long-range perspective. Zakaria supports

lived in free countries, 18 percent in partly free, and 47 percent were citizens of countries ranked as not free. In 2007, the percentages were 46 percent free, 18 percent partly free, and 36 percent not free.[25] (See Table 1.1.). Amartya Sen has observed, "While democracy is not yet uniformly practiced, nor indeed uniformly accepted, in the general climate of world opinion, democratic governance has now achieved the status of being taken to be generally right."[26] As authoritarian rulers in countries from Albania to Zimbabwe have learned in recent decades, once persistent and widespread pressures for democratic participation develop, they are hard to resist. However, as China demonstrated by its bloody 1989 crackdown on protestors, there is no guarantee that pro-democracy protests will succeed.

What determines the growth, stagnation, or even decline of democracy? Comparativists have devoted enormous energy to studying this question. One scholar notes, "For the past two decades, the main topic of research in comparative politics has been democratization."[27] Yet, for all the attention it has received, there is no scholarly consensus on how and why democratization develops and becomes consolidated or runs out of steam. We have learned that there insulating some key political institutions from partisan swings. He praises agencies within the U.S. government, including the Supreme Court and the Federal Reserve Board, whose members are nominated by the president and who possess ample independent authority. (It may be noted in response that insulating political institutions from the citizenry may be an excellent recipe for corruption.) Consider Zakaria's argument when you read the country studies in this book and consider not only the advantages of democracy, but also the disadvantages.

Is it possible to identify conditions that are necessary or sufficient for democracy to flourish? Comparativists have proposed, among such factors, secure national boundaries, a stable state, at least a minimum level of economic development, the widespread acceptance of democratic values, and agreement on the rules of the democratic game among those who contend for power. Institutional design also matters when it comes to producing stable democracies. Do certain kinds of political institutions facilitate compromise as opposed to polarization and hence greater stability? The balance of scholarly opinion suggests, for example, that parliamentary systems that tie the fates of the legislators to that of the prime minister tend to produce more consensual outcomes than do presidential systems, where the legislature and executive are independent from each other—and often vie for power in setting national political agendas.[30] As you read the country studies, note the patterns of similarity and difference you observe in the degree of conflict or polarization in presidential systems (such as the United States, Mexico, or Brazil) and compare those cases to parliamentary systems (such as Britain, India, or Japan).

We have noted above that certain economic, cultural, and institutional features enhance the prospects of democratic transitions and consolidations. But democracy has flourished in unlikely settings—for example, in India, a country with a vast population whose per capita income is among the lowest in the world—and has failed where it might be expected to flourish—for instance, in Germany in the 1930s. Democracies vary widely in terms of how they came into existence and in their concrete historical, institutional, and cultural dimensions.

Displacing authoritarian regimes and then holding elections does not guarantee the survival or durability of a fledgling democracy. A wide gulf exists between what comparativists have termed a *transition* to democracy and the *consolidation* of democracy. A transition involves toppling an authoritarian regime and adopting the rudiments of democracy; consolidation requires fuller adherence to democratic procedures and making democratic institutions more sturdy and durable. Below, we further explore the important question of how to distinguish what we term *transitional democracies* from *consolidated democracies*. We consider the distinction of such great importance that it forms the basis for our scheme for classifying countries throughout the world.

We want to emphasize that the study of comparative politics does not support a philosophy of history or theory of political development that identifies a single (democratic) end point toward which all countries will eventually converge. One landmark work, published at the beginning of the most recent democratic wave, which began in Latin America in the 1970s, captured the tenuous process of democratization in its title: *Transitions from Authoritarian Rule: Tentative Conclusions about Uncertain Democracies*.[31] A country may adopt some democratic features, for example, elections, while retaining highly undemocratic elements as well. Scholars have suggested that it is far easier for a country to hold its first democratic election than its second or third. Historically, powerful groups have often opposed democratization because they fear that democracy will threaten their privileges. Disadvantaged groups may also oppose the democratic process because they see it as unresponsive to their deeply felt grievances. As a result, reversals of democratic regimes and restorations of authoritarian rule have occurred in the past and will doubtless occur in the future. Recent years have even seen a trend toward "elected dictators," such Hugo Chavez in Venezuela, who are voted into office and then use their power to dismantle important parts of the democratic system. In brief, the fact that the democratic idea is so powerful does not mean that all countries will adopt or preserve democratic institutions.

The theme of the democratic idea requires us to examine the incompleteness of democratic agendas, even in countries with the longest experiences of representative democracy. Citizens may invoke the democratic idea to demand that their government be more responsive and accountable, as in the Civil Rights Movement in the United States. At the same time, **social movements** have targeted the state because of its actions or inactions in such varied spheres as environmental regulation, reproductive rights, and race or ethnic relations. Comparative studies confirm that the democratic idea fuels political conflicts in even the most durable democracies because a large gap usually separates democratic ideals and the actual functioning of democratic political institutions. Moreover, social movements often organize because citizens perceive political parties—presumably an important established vehicle for representing citizen demands in democracies—as ossified and out of touch with the people.

A puzzle: Is there a relationship between democracy and political stability? Comparativists have debated whether democratic institutions contribute to political stability or, on the contrary, to political disorder. On the one hand, democracy by its very nature permits political opposition. One of its defining characteristics is competition among those who aspire to gain political office. Political life in democracies is turbulent and unpredictable. On the other hand, and perhaps paradoxically, the very fact that political opposition and competition are legitimate in democracies can deepen support for the state, even among opponents of a particular government. The democratic rules of the game may promote political stability by encouraging today's losers to remain in the game. They reject the use of violence to press their claim to power, because they may calculate that they have a good chance to win peacefully in future competition. Although there is a disturbing tendency for deep flaws to mar democratic governance in countries that have toppled authoritarian regimes, a careful study finds that, once a country adopts a democratic regime, the odds are that it will endure.[32] As you learn about different countries, look for the stabilizing and destabilizing consequences of recent democratic transitions, the pressures (or lack of pressure) for democratization in authoritarian states, and the persistence of undemocratic elements even in established democracies.

Theme 4: The Politics of Collective Identity

How do individuals understand who they are in political terms? On what basis do groups of people form to advance common political aims? In other words, what are the sources of collective political identities? At one time, social scientists thought they knew. Scholars once argued that the age-old loyalties of ethnicity, religious affiliation, race, gender, and locality were being dissolved and displaced by economic, political, and cultural modernization. Comparativists thought that **social class**—solidarities based on the shared experience of work or, more broadly, economic position—had become the most important source of collective identity. They believed that most of the time, groups would pragmatically pursue their interests in ways that were not politically destabilizing. We now know that the formation of group attachments and the interplay of politically relevant collective identities are far more complex and uncertain.

In many long-established democracies, the importance of identities based on class membership has declined, although class and material sources of collective political identity remain significant in political competition and economic organization. Furthermore, contrary to earlier predictions, in many countries nonclass identities have assumed growing, not diminishing, significance. Such affiliations are based on a sense of belonging to particular groups sharing a common language, region, religion, ethnicity, race, nationality, or gender.

The politics of collective political identity involves struggles to mobilize identity groups as influential participants in the political movement. This struggle involves a constant tug of war among groups over relative power and influence, both symbolic and substantive. Issues of inclusion, political recognition, representation, resource allocation, and the capacity to shape public policies, such as immigration, education, and the status of minority languages, remain pivotal in many countries, and they may never be fully settled.

Questions of representation are especially hard to resolve: Who is included in a racial or ethnic minority community, for example? Who speaks for the community or negotiates with a governmental authority on its behalf? One reason that conflict about these issues can be so intense is that political leaders in the state and in opposition movements often seek to mobilize support by exploiting ethnic, religious, racial, or regional rivalries and by manipulating issues of identity and representation. Another reason is that considerable material and nonmaterial stakes derive from the outcome of these struggles. Race relations in the United States is a powerful reminder of a basic fact of political life: issues about collective identities are never fully settled, although they may rage with greater or lesser intensity in particular countries and at particular times.

Identity-based conflicts appear in every multiethnic society. And given the pace of migration and the tangled web of postcolonial histories that link colonizer to colonized, what country is not multiethnic? As political scientist Alfred Stepan points out, ". . . there are very few states in the entire world that are relatively homogeneous nation-states. . . ."[33] In Britain, France, Germany, and the United States, issues of nationality, citizenship, and immigration—often with ethnic or racial overtones—have been hot-button issues and have often spilled over into electoral politics. Such conflicts have been particularly intense in postcolonial countries, for example, Nigeria, where colonial powers forced ethnic groups together in order to carve out a country and where borders were drawn with little regard to preexisting collective identities. This process of state formation sowed seeds for future conflict and threatens the survival of democracy and perhaps the state itself in many postcolonial nations.

Religion is another source of collective identity— as well as of severe political conflict, both within and among religious communities. Violent conflict among religious groups has recently occurred in many countries, including India, Sri Lanka, Nigeria, and the United Kingdom (again, in Northern Ireland). Such conflicts may spill over national boundaries and involve an especially ugly form of globalization. For example, leaders of Al Qaeda targeted nonMuslim Western military forces stationed in what they regarded as the sacred territory of Saudi Arabia as a principal reason for its attacks. At the same time, the political orientation of a particular religious community is not predetermined. The political posture associated with

what it means to be Christian, Jewish, Muslim, or Hindu cannot simply be read off the sacred texts. Witness the intense conflict *within* most religious communities today that pits more liberal, secular elements against those who defend what they claim is a more orthodox, traditional interpretation.

A puzzle: How does collective identity affect a country's **distributional politics**, that is, the process of deciding who gets what and how resources are distributed? Once identity demands are placed on the national agenda, can governments resolve them by distributing political, economic, and other resources in ways that redress the grievances of the minority or politically weaker identity groups? Collective identities operate at the level of symbols, attitudes, values, and beliefs as well as at the level of material resources. The contrast between material- and non-material-based identities and demands should not be exaggerated. In practice, most groups are animated both by feelings of attachment and solidarity and by the desire to obtain material benefits and political influence for their members. Nonetheless, the analytical distinction between material and nonmaterial demands remains useful. Further, it is worth considering whether the nonmaterial aspects of collective identities make political disputes over ethnicity or religion or language or nationality especially divisive and difficult to resolve.

In a situation of extreme scarcity, it may prove nearly impossible to reach any compromise among groups with conflicting material demands. But if an adequate level of material resources is available, such conflicts may be easier to resolve through distributional politics because groups can negotiate at least a minimally satisfying share of resources.

However, the nonmaterial demands of ethnic, religious, and nationalist movements may be harder to satisfy by a distributional style of politics. The distributional style may be quite ineffective when, for example, a religious group demands that the government require all commercial activity to cease on a religious holiday, or when a dominant linguistic group insists that a single language be used in education and government throughout the country. In such cases, political conflict tends to move from the distributive realm to the cultural realm, where compromises cannot be achieved by simply dividing the pie of material resources. The country studies examine a wide range of conflicts involving collective identities. It is worth pondering whether, and under what conditions, they can be resolved by the normal give and take of political bargaining—and when, instead, they lead to the fury and blood of political violence.

These four themes provide our analytic scaffold. With an understanding of the method of comparative politics and the four themes in mind, we can now discuss how we have grouped the country studies that comprise *Introduction to Comparative Politics* and how the text is organized for comparative analysis.

SECTION 4 Classifying Political Systems

There are more than 200 states in the world today, each with a somewhat distinctive political regime. How can we classify them in a manageable fashion? One possibility would be not to classify them at all, but simply to treat each state as different and unique. However, comparativists are rarely content with this solution—it appears to be a nonsolution. It makes sense to highlight clusters of states that share some important features, to identify what distinguishes one cluster of relatively similar states from other clusters, and to study dynamics, that is, how a state moves from one cluster to another. When comparativists classify a large number of cases into a smaller number of types or clusters, they call the result a **typology**. Typologies facilitate comparison both within the same type as well as between types of states. For example, both Britain and the United States are long-established democracies. What difference does it make that Britain has a parliamentary form of government and the United States a presidential one? Their different mix of democratic institutions provides an interesting laboratory case to study the impact of institutional variation.

We can also compare across clusters or types. In this type of comparison—comparativists call this **most different case analysis**—we analyze what produces the substantial differences we observe. Consider the fact that the world's two most populous countries, China and India, have such different political systems. How do their different political regimes affect such important issues as economic development, human rights, and the role of women?

How do we go about constructing typologies of states? Typologies exist as much in the eye of their beholder as in the nature of the beast. That is, typologies

are artificial constructs, made rather than born. The analyst selects certain features that become the basis for classification. Choosing certain features implicitly downplays the importance of others. It follows that what counts in evaluating a typology is not whether it is "true" or "false," but whether it is useful, and for what purpose. Typologies are helpful to the extent that they permit us to engage in comparisons that yield useful knowledge.

What is the most useful typology for classifying political regimes or states? From the end of World War II until the 1980s, there was a general consensus on the utility of one typology. Political scientists classified states as either Western industrial democracies, dubbed the "First World"; communist states formed the "Second World"; or economically less developed countries in Asia, Africa, and Latin America, many of which had recently gained independence, made up the "**Third World**." As with any typology, it was imperfect. For example, where should one assign Japan, a democratic country not in the West that rapidly developed in the 1960s and 1970s and became the world's second-leading economic power? Nevertheless, the typology was a generally adequate way to distinguish broad groups of countries because it corresponded to what appeared to be durable and important geopolitical and theoretical divisions in the world.

Today, the typology of First, Second, and Third Worlds is less useful. Most important has been the near-disappearance of communist regimes around the world, that is, the "Second World." Beginning in 1989, the implosion of communism in the former Soviet Union and Eastern and Central Europe set off a revolutionary change in world politics. Only a handful of countries—China, Cuba, Vietnam, Laos, and the Democratic People's Republic of (North) Korea—are ruled by communist parties. Even some of these (particularly China and Vietnam) have adopted market-based economic policies and forged close ties with capitalist nations. It follows that the "Second World" is no longer a useful category to classify countries.

Furthermore, scores of countries have become democratic, or at least "partly free," that are neither highly industrialized nor located in the North Atlantic region—the geographic base of the "First World." In Asia, Africa, and Latin America, countries that were formerly colonies or undemocratic states have adopted democratic institutions, which we noted above is one of the most important and promising changes in the modern world.

Finally, the term "Third World" has also become less helpful in understanding the many countries formerly classified in this cluster. Countries in the so-called Third World share few features, other than being less economically developed than industrialized nations (see "Global Connection: How Is Development Measured?"). Moreover, some countries formerly in the Third World have been among the world's economic success stories, including Korea, Taiwan, and Singapore. More recently, India, Brazil, and Mexico have become more economically powerful. At the same time, colonial legacies have receded further and further into the past. The term "Third World" may continue to be a useful shorthand term for the roughly 130 countries that the United Nations classifies as "developing" and that are still separated by a vast economic gulf from the 50 or so industrialized nations. However, one should also take account of the fact that there are about four dozen countries—including Afghanistan, Ethiopia, Chad, and Haiti—that are classified by the UN as "least developed." The majority are located in Africa. They are so poor that the term "Fourth World" is sometimes used to describe them. This group of countries has become absolutely and relatively more poor in recent years, due to the ravages of AIDS, civil war, and failed states.

If the "three (or four) worlds" method of classification is no longer useful, what alternative is preferable? At present, there is a lively debate among comparativists on this question. We suggest a typology based on one of the most important dimensions for understanding similarities and differences among countries in the contemporary world—the extent to which their governments are democratic. However, we preface the discussion by repeating that one might imagine an altogether different typology for classifying regimes. The categories that we have established, the tools we use to measure, and the decisions we have made in classifying particular countries all lend themselves to discussion. We invite students to think critically about how to make sense of the great variety of regimes in the world today and to devise alternative ways to classify countries.

Our typology classifies regimes into three groups: **consolidated democracies**, **transitional democracies**, and **authoritarian regimes**. The typology highlights the bedrock distinction between democratic and undemocratic regimes. Of course, the classification requires rigorously specifying what is meant by democracy and authoritarianism.

What Is the Meaning—or Rather, Meanings—of Democracy?

As with many other important concepts, the meaning of democracy is contentious. The wide popularity of the term conceals some important ambiguities. Should democracy be defined solely on the basis of the procedures used to select top governmental officeholders? That is, for a political system to qualify as democratic, is it sufficient that occupants of the highest offices of the state be selected on the basis of free and fair elections in which opposing parties present candidates and all citizens are entitled to cast a vote for a contending party? Or must there also be respect for civil liberties (including rights of free expression, dissent, and privacy)? What is the relationship between religious practice and the exercise of political power? Must a democratic regime guarantee citizens the right to worship freely—or not worship at all? To what extent must all citizens be guaranteed economic and social rights, such as a minimum income and access to medical care, as distinct from political and civil rights (such as the right to vote and criticize the government)? Put differently, what is the relationship between democracy defined in purely procedural terms and democracy defined as a system that provides an adequate level of resources to its citizens and promotes substantive equalities?

Despite intense debates about the meaning(s) of democracy, a rough consensus has emerged among practitioners and scholars about the minimum political features required for a regime to qualify as democratic. It is generally agreed that the following conditions must be present:

- Selection to the highest public offices is on the basis of free and fair elections. For an election to qualify as fair, there must be procedures in place guaranteeing candidates the right to compete, all citizens must be entitled to vote, and votes must be counted accurately, with the winning candidate(s) selected according to preexisting rules that determine the kind of plurality or majority required to gain electoral victory.

- Political parties are free to organize, present candidates for public office, and compete in elections. The opposition party or parties—those not in power—enjoy adequate rights of contestation, that is, the right to organize and to criticize the incumbent government.

- The elected government develops policy according to specified procedures that provide for due process, transparency in decision-making, and the accountability of elected executives (at the next election, through judicial action, and, in parliamentary systems, to the legislature).

- All citizens possess political rights—the right to participate and vote in periodic elections to select key state officeholders; as well as civil liberties—the rights of free assembly, conscience, privacy, and expression, including the right to criticize the government.

- The political system contains a judiciary with powers independent of the executive and legislature, charged with protecting citizens' political rights and civil liberties from violation by government and other citizens, as well as with ensuring that governmental officials respect constitutionally specified procedures.

- The elected government exercises supreme power within the government and country. In particular, the civilian government controls the military as well as private power-holders (including large landowners, business interests, and so on).

- There is widespread agreement that conflicts—political, social, economic, and identity-based—will be resolved peacefully, according to legally prescribed procedures, and without recourse to violence.

Although these points make a useful checklist of the essential elements of a democracy, several qualifications should be added. First, this definition does not claim that electoral outcomes are always (or possibly even often) rational, equitable, or wise. Democracy specifies a set of procedures for making decisions, but it does not guarantee the wisdom of the outcomes. Indeed, as we discuss below, we believe that political outcomes in all democracies, both elections to office and the decisions of officeholders, are systematically and importantly influenced by economic inequalities that limit the ideal of "one person, one vote."

Second, no government has ever fully lived up to democratic standards. All democratic governments at various points in their histories have violated them to a greater or lesser extent. For example, Britain retained a system of plural votes for certain citizens until after World War II; French women did not gain the right to vote until 1945; and African Americans did not gain full voting rights in the United States until after the passage of the Civil Rights Act of 1964 and Voting Rights Act of 1965.

Third, how the elements on the checklist of democracy are interpreted and implemented can be a contentious political issue. For example, in the 1990s, and again in 2004, there was intense controversy in France about whether Muslim girls should be permitted to wear a headscarf, signifying adherence to Islam, to public school. On the one hand, many public officials and citizens wanted to prohibit girls from wearing the scarf on the grounds that France is a secular state and that displaying the scarf constitutes proselytizing in public schools and symbolizes girls' subordinate status. On the other hand, defenders of the practice argued that Muslim girls were entitled to exercise self-expression.

Fourth, economic inequalities, that exist to a varying extent in all democratic countries, stack the political deck. Wealthy citizens, powerful interest groups, and business firms can use their substantial resources to increase their chances of winning an election and influencing public policy. This creates a tension in all democracies, to a greater or lesser degree, between the formal political procedures (such as voting), in which all are equal, and the actual situation, in which the affluent are, in novelist George Orwell's famous phrase from his satirical novel *Animal Farm*, "more equal than others" because of their greater political influence.

Finally, although all democracies share the seven elements outlined above, the political institutions that implement these democratic principles vary widely. A common distinction among democracies involves differing relationships between the executive and the legislature. In presidential systems, such as in the United States, the chief executive (the president) is elected independently of the national legislature (the House and the Senate) and each branch has powers independent of the other. This means that there is a sharp separation of powers between the executive branch and the legislature. The presidential system is actually an unusual form of democracy. Most of the world's democracies (including Britain, Germany, India, and Japan) have parliamentary governments in which executive and legislative powers are fused rather than separated: the chief executive (whether called prime minister, premier, or chancellor) and the cabinet are chosen from elected members of the legislature and generally are the leaders of the dominant party or party coalition in parliament. In fact, the chief executive in a parliamentary system remains a sitting member of the legislature even while serving as prime minister. As noted above, scholars debate whether the differences between presidential and parliamentary systems influence the stability of a political regime and the capacity of the government to mobilize support for its policies.

The formal and informal rules of the game for reaching and exercising power are very different in presidential and parliamentary systems. In presidential systems, members of the legislature jealously preserve their autonomy. Because the legislature is elected separately from the president, it is constitutionally authorized to set its own agenda, initiate policy proposals, defy presidential directives, and even impeach the president. Presidents have resources that they can deploy in an attempt to persuade the legislature to go along, but even when the same party controls both the presidency and the legislature, the key word is *persuade*. In most parliamentary systems, on the other hand, the legislature may serve as a forum for dramatic policy debate, but it rarely represents an independent source of policy initiatives or poses a decisive obstacle to prevent the government from legislating its own proposals.

The distinction between presidential and parliamentary systems does not exhaust the range of institutional variation within democracies. For example, France's hybrid semipresidential system is quite different from the two "pure" types. France has a dual executive, with both a directly elected president and a prime minister appointed by the president. These differences raise the kinds of questions that are at the heart of comparative politics: Which political institutions and procedures are more likely to represent citizens' demands? Which strike a better balance between participation and leadership? What consequences do these differences have for the effectiveness of government and the distribution of resources?

"So what?" you may ask in response to this discussion of political institutions. Good question![34] Ponder what difference the type of system makes to a country's politics as you study various types of parliamentary and presidential democracies in this book. And note how rare presidential systems are—a point that may surprise those who think that the U.S. presidential system is typical.

A Typology of Political Systems

Our typology of political systems involves a further distinction between long-established, or consolidated democracies, and newly established, or transitional democracies. We claim that there is a difference in kind, and not just of degree, between the two groups. We use two criteria to distinguish these categories. The first criterion divides democratic regimes according to whether their democratic institutions and practices have been solidly and stably established for an ample period of time. (Precisely how long is open to question: more than a few years, possibly at least a decade? In part, the answer depends on the degree to which the next requirement is met.)

The second criterion for distinguishing between consolidated and transitional democracies is the *extent* of their democratic practice. Consolidated democracies are regimes in which there is relatively consistent adherence to the seven democratic principles that we specified above. Examples of consolidated democracies are Britain, France, Germany, India, Japan, and the United States. All have been democracies for more than fifty years and generally practice the democracy they preach.

We do not mean to claim that consolidated democracies never violate democratic norms—they do, and sometimes in shocking ways. For example, police abuse and unequal treatment of citizens who are poor or from a racial or ethnic minority are all too common in countries generally considered high in the democratic rankings, like Britain and the United States. Following 9/11, intelligence agencies in many democratic regimes expanded their surveillance of citizens, for example, by monitoring telephone calls and e-mails. President George Bush declared created a new category—illegal combatants—and authorized interrogation techniques that violated U.S. laws and treaty commitments.

The reason we highlight the importance of adhering to democratic procedures becomes apparent when we turn to the second category of democracy. In many transitional democracies, a façade of democratic institutions conceals informal practices that violate the checklist of bedrock features of democracy.[35] As a general matter, there is greater legal protection of citizen rights and liberties in transitional democracies than in authoritarian regimes—but considerably less than in consolidated democracies. Transitional democracies are to be found on every continent and include Russia, Brazil, Mexico, Nigeria, South Africa, South Korea, and Indonesia.

Transitional democracies are often "hybrid regimes" in which democratic forms of governance coexist with a disturbing persistence of authoritarian elements.[36] In such systems, as compared to consolidated democracies, political authorities are more likely to engage in corruption, control of the media, intimidation, and violence against opponents. Authorities use illegal means to undermine opposition parties and ensure that the ruling party is re-elected. Despite what the constitution may specify, the judiciary is often packed with ruling party faithful, and top military officers often exercise extraordinary political power behind the scenes.

How do we define authoritarian regimes—the third kind of political system in our typology? The simplest way is to change the positive sign to negative in the checklist of democratic characteristics specified above. Thus, authoritarian regimes lack effective procedures for selecting political leaders through competitive elections based on universal suffrage; there are no institutionalized procedures for holding those with political power accountable to the citizens of the country; oppositional politics and dissent are severely restricted; people of different genders, racial groups, religions, and ethnicities do not enjoy equal rights; the judiciary is not an independent branch of government capable of checking the power of the state or protecting the rights of citizens; and coercion and violence are part of the political process.

Clearly, then, authoritarian states are nondemocracies. But it isn't good social science to define something only by what it is not. The term *authoritarianism* refers to political systems in which power (or authority) is highly concentrated in a single individual, a small group of people, a single political party, or institution. Furthermore, those with power claim an exclusive right to govern and use various means, including force, to impose their will and policies on all who live under their authority.

As with states classified as democracies, there is an enormous variety of authoritarian regime types: communist party-states (e.g., China and Cuba); theocracies in which sovereign power is held by religious leaders and law is defined in religious terms (e.g., present-day Iran), military governments (e.g., Myanmar, the country formerly called Burma); absolute monarchies (e.g., Saudi Arabia); and personalistic dictatorships (e.g., Iraq under Sadaam Hussein and Iran under the Shah). Authoritarian regimes frequently claim that they embody a form of democracy, particularly in the contemporary era when the democratic idea seems so persuasive and powerful. For example, according to the Chinese Communist Party, the political system of the People's Republic of China is based on "socialist democracy," which it claims is superior to the "bourgeois democracy" of capitalist countries that, in the end, favors the interests of wealthier citizens. But most political scientists would conclude that there is little substance to these claims and that in such states dictatorship far outweighs democracy.

Nevertheless, even in countries that can be classified as authoritarian, certain features may reflect democratic values and practices. In Iran, a theocratic authoritarian regime, there are vigorously contested multiparty elections, although the extent of contestation is limited by the Islamic clergy who ultimately exercise sovereign power. In China, for more than a decade, a form of grassroots democracy has been implemented in the more than 700,000 rural villages where a majority of the population lives. Even though the communist party still oversees the process, China's rural dwellers now have a real choice when they elect their local leaders. Although such democratic elements in Iranian and Chinese politics are certainly significant, they do not fundamentally alter the authoritarian character of the state.

Like democratic states, authoritarian states are not politically stagnant: they change and evolve over time in response to domestic and international influences. The Soviet Union under Joseph Stalin (1924–1952) and China under Mao Zedong (1949–1976) were extremely brutal dictatorships that closely approximated the model of **totalitarian** regimes that seek to control nearly every aspect of public and private life. Yet the successors to both Stalin and Mao began a process of reform that reduced the extent of repression and control while preserving the ultimate authoritarian power of the communist party. In the Soviet case, this eventually led to the collapse of communism, while in China the outcome actually strengthened communist rule. Why the difference? This is just the kind of interesting and important question that lies at the heart of comparative politics!

Although we believe that there are sharp differences among the three categories of our typology, these categories are not airtight, and some countries may straddle two categories. Which ones? Consider Brazil, which we designate as a transitional democracy. Ever since democracy was restored in 1974, following a period of harsh military rule, Brazil has compiled a solid record of democratic practice. For example, since the return of civilian rule there have been several peaceful electoral alternations between dramatically different political coalitions. One might claim that Brazil should be classified as a consolidated democracy. We believe, however, that because of repeated violations of democratic procedures, political corruption, lack of entrenched democratic values, and extensive inequality (which is heavily coded in racial terms), Brazil remains a transitional democracy.

Another example of the difficulty of classifying states: we consider India a consolidated democracy because it has generally respected most of the democratic procedures on our checklist since it gained independence in 1947. There is intense political competition in India, elections are usually free and fair, and the Indian judiciary is quite independent. However, some might question our decision. For example, India has repeatedly experienced scenes of horrific communal violence, in which large numbers of Muslim, Sikh, and Christian minorities have been brutally massacred, sometimes with the active complicity of state officials.

A further point about our typology is that the boundaries among categories are fluid. Some of the countries classified as transitional democracies are experiencing such political turmoil that they could very well fall out of any category of democracy. Take Russia, for example, where the trajectory in the last few years is in the authoritarian direction. Since Vladimir Putin's reelection as president in 2004 and continuing under his handpicked successor, Dmitry Medvedev (elected in 2008), the Russian government has engaged in numerous undemocratic practices, including arbitrary detention and rigged trials of opponents, repeated violations of the constitution, and extensive political corruption. There are competitive but not fair elections, multiple parties but one dominant establishment party, press diversity in the print media but with significant restrictions, and tightly controlled television news. Therefore a good case could be made that Russia should be classified as authoritarian, even though Putin (now in the position of prime minister) and Medvedev enjoy extensive popular support. In fact, Freedom House classifies Russia as "not free." But a society like Russia may take several decades to transit to democracy and setbacks are to be expected, so we place Russia in the transitional democratic category, but recognize the ominous tendencies that may move Russia into the authoritarian slot in our typology in the next edition of this book.

These observations about Russia underscore an important point about our typology. We do not mean to imply that there is an automatic escalator of political development that transports a country from one category to the next "higher" one. History has demonstrated that one should be wary of subscribing to a theory of inevitable progress—whether political, economic, or social. It is not inevitable that countries will remain anchored in one category or another. Regimes may become more democratic—or a democratic regime can be subverted and replaced by an authoritarian regime. When a new edition of this book appears, several countries classified here as transitional democracies may qualify, according to our criteria, as consolidated democracies—or, on the contrary, they may change in a way that tips the balance toward authoritarianism.

SECTION 5 Organization of the Text

The core of this book consists of a dozen country case studies. We selected them for their significance in terms of our comparative themes and because they provide an interesting sample of types of political regimes, levels of economic development, and geographic regions. Although each of the country studies makes important comparative references, the studies primarily provide detailed descriptions and analyses of the politics of individual countries. At the same time, the country studies have common section and subsection headings to help you make comparisons and explore similar themes across the various cases. The following are brief summaries of the main issues and questions covered in the country studies.

1: The Making of the Modern State

Section 1 in each chapter provides an overview of the forces that have shaped the particular character of the state. We believe that understanding the contemporary politics of any country requires familiarity with the historical process of state formation. "Politics in Action" uses a specific event to illustrate an important political moment in the country's recent history and to highlight some of the critical political issues it faces. "Geographic Setting" locates the country in its regional context and discusses the political implications of this setting. "Critical Junctures" looks at some of the major stages and decisive turning points in the state's development. This discussion should give you an idea of how the country assumed its current political order and a sense of how relations between state and society have developed over time.

"Themes and Implications" shows how the past pattern of state development continues to shape the country's current political agenda. "Historical Junctures and Political Themes" applies the text's core themes to the making of the modern state. How has the country's political development been affected by its place in the world of states? What are the political implications of the state's approach to economic management? What has been the country's experience with the democratic idea? What are the important bases of collective identity in the country, and how do these relate to the people's image of themselves as citizens of the state? "Implications for Comparative Politics" discusses the broader significance of the country for the study of comparative politics.

2: Political Economy and Development

Section 2 looks at the issues raised by our core theme of governing the economy and analyzes how economic development has affected political change. The placement of this section near the beginning of the country study reflects our belief that understanding a country's economic situation is essential for analyzing its politics. "State and Economy" discusses the basic organization of the country's economy, with emphasis on the role of the state in managing economic life and on the relationship between the government and other economic actors. How do the dynamics and historical timing of the country's insertion into the world economy—and its current position within the globalized economy—affect domestic political arrangements and shape contemporary challenges? This section also analyzes the state's social welfare policies, such as health care, housing, and pension programs. "Society and Economy" examines the social and political implications of the country's economic situation. It asks who benefits from economic change and looks at how economic development creates or reinforces class, ethnic, gender, regional, or ideological cleavages in society. "The Global Economy" considers the country's global role. How have patterns of trade and foreign investment changed over time? What is the country's relationship to regional and international organizations? To what degree has the country been able to influence multilateral policies? How have international economic issues affected the domestic political agenda?

3: Governance and Policy-Making

In Section 3, we describe the state's major policy-making institutions and procedures. "Organization of the State" lays out the fundamental principles—as reflected in the country's constitution, its official ideology, and its historical experience—on which the political system and the distribution of political power are based. It also sketches the basic structure of the state, including the relationship among different levels and branches of government. "The Executive" encompasses the key offices (for example, presidents, prime ministers, communist party leaders) at the top of the political system, focusing on how they are selected and how they use their power to make policy. This section also analyzes the national bureaucracy, its relationship to the chief executive, and its role in policy-making. "Other State Institutions" looks at the military, the judiciary and the legal system, semipublic agencies, and subnational government. "The Policy-Making Process" summarizes how public policy gets made and implemented. It describes the roles of formal institutions and procedures, as well as informal aspects of policy-making, such as the influence of lobbyists and interest groups.

4: Representation and Participation

The relationship between a country's state and society is the focus of Section 4. How do different groups in society organize to further their political interests, how do they participate and get represented in the political system, and how do they influence policy-making? Given the importance of the U.S. Congress in policy-making, American readers might expect to find the principal discussion of "The Legislature" in Section 3 ("Governance and Policy-Making") rather than Section 4. But the U.S. Congress is an exceptionally powerful legislature. In most other political systems, the executive dominates the policy process, even when it is ultimately responsible to the legislature, as in a parliamentary system. In most countries other than the United States, the legislature functions primarily to represent and provide a forum for the political expression of various interests; it is only secondarily (and in some cases, such as China, only marginally) a policy-making body. Therefore, although this section does describe and assess the legislature's role in policy-making, its primary focus is on how the legislature represents or fails to represent different interests in society.

"Political Parties and the Party System" describes the overall organization of the party system and reviews the major parties. "Elections" discusses the election process and recent trends in electoral behavior. It also considers the significance of elections (or lack thereof) as a vehicle for citizen participation in politics and in bringing about changes in the government. "Political Culture, Citizenship, and Identity" examines how people perceive themselves as members of the political community: the nature and source of political values and attitudes, who is considered a citizen, and how different groups in society understand their relationship to the state. The topics covered may include political aspects of the educational system, the media, religion, and ethnicity. We also ask how globalization and the events relating to September 11 affect collective identities and collective action. "Interests, Social Movements, and Protests" discusses how various groups pursue their political interests outside the party system. What is the relationship between the state and such organizations and movements? When and how do citizens engage in acts of protest? And how does the state respond when they do?

5: Politics in Transition

In Section 5, each country study returns to the book's four themes and analyzes the major challenges reshaping the world and the study of comparative politics. "Political Challenges and Changing Agendas" lays out the major unresolved issues facing the country and assesses which are most likely to dominate in the near future. Many of the country studies address issues that have generated intense conflicts around the world in the recent period—conflicts involving globalization, collective identities, human rights and civil liberties, the war in Iraq, and the consequences of America's exercise of global hegemony. "Politics in Comparative Perspective" returns to the book's four core themes and highlights the implications of the country case for the study of comparative politics. How does the history—and how will the fate—of the country influence developments in a regional and global context? What does this case study tell us about politics in other countries that have similar political systems or that face similar kinds of political challenges?

Key Terms and Suggested Readings

At the end of each chapter, including this one, is a list of key terms that we think are especially important for students of comparative politics to know. Each term is bolded the first time it appears in each chapter and is briefly defined in the Glossary that appears near the end of the book. Each chapter also has a list of suggested readings: we have provided references to books that reflect important current scholarship in the field and/or that we think would be interesting and accessible to undergraduates. If you find yourself particularly interested in one or more of the countries covered in this text, we urge you take a look at some of the suggested titles. This chapter ends with suggested readings that survey the scope and methods of comparative politics as well as illuminate important issues in the field.

We realize that it is quite a challenge to set out on a journey with the goal of trying to understand contemporary politics around the globe. We hope that the timely information and thematic focus of *Introduction to Comparative Politics* will prepare and inspire you to explore further the often troubling, sometimes inspiring, but endlessly fascinating world of comparative politics.

What's in the Comparative Data Charts?

The following charts and tables present important factual and statistical information about each of the countries included in this book. We hope most of this information is self-explanatory, but a few points of clarification may be helpful.

- The social and economic data largely comes from the CIA *World Factbook*, the World Bank *World Development Indicators*, and the United Nations *Human Development Report*, all of which are issued annually. These reports and other statistics are available from the national statistics or census agencies of individual countries and from the following websites:

- https://www.cia.gov/library/publications/the-world-factbook/
- www.worldbank.org/data/
- hdr.undp.org/
- The data presented are as up-to-date as possible. Unless otherwise indicated, the data are from 2005–2007/8.
- Several important terms used in the data, including gross domestic product (GDP), gross national product (GNP), purchasing power parity (PPP), and Gini Index, are explained in the Glossary and/or the feature called "How Is Development Measured?" on page 20.

Introduction

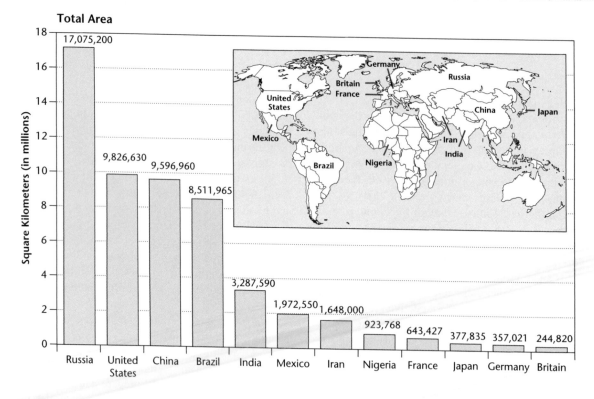

Total Area

Square Kilometers (in millions)

	Russia	United States	China	Brazil	India	Mexico	Iran	Nigeria	France	Japan	Germany	Britain
	17,075,200	9,826,630	9,596,960	8,511,965	3,287,590	1,972,550	1,648,000	923,768	643,427	377,835	357,021	244,820

	Brazil	Britain	China	France	Germany	India
Official Name	Federative Republic of Brazil	United Kingdom of Great Britain and Northern Ireland	People's Republic of China	French Republic	Federal Republic of Germany	Republic of India
Capital	Brasilia	London	Beijing	Paris	Berlin	New Delhi
Comparative Size	Slightly smaller than the U.S.	Slightly smaller than Oregon	Slightly smaller than the U.S.	Slightly smaller than Texas	Slightly smaller than Montana	Slightly more than one-third the size of the U.S.
Population Growth Rate (2008)	0.98%	0.276%	0.629%	0.574%	−0.044%	1.578%

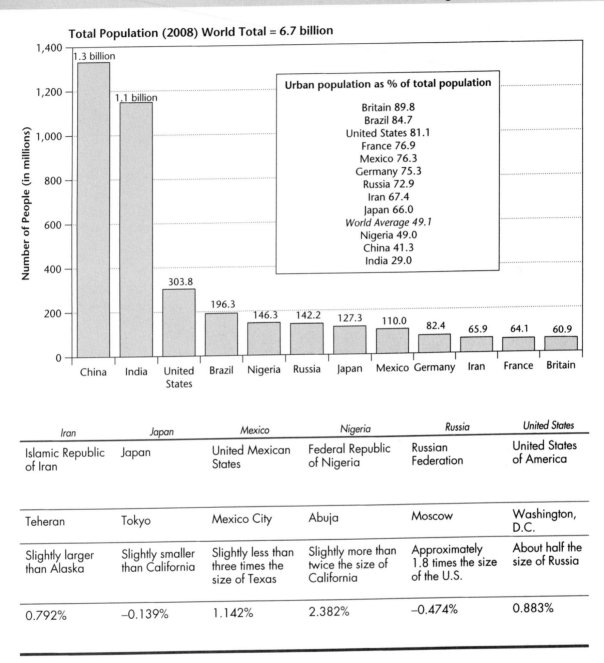

Total Population (2008) World Total = 6.7 billion

Number of People (in millions)

- 1,400
- 1,200
- 1,000
- 800
- 600
- 400
- 200
- 0

China — 1.3 billion
India — 1.1 billion
United States — 303.8
Brazil — 196.3
Nigeria — 146.3
Russia — 142.2
Japan — 127.3
Mexico — 110.0
Germany — 82.4
Iran — 65.9
France — 64.1
Britain — 60.9

Urban population as % of total population

Britain 89.8
Brazil 84.7
United States 81.1
France 76.9
Mexico 76.3
Germany 75.3
Russia 72.9
Iran 67.4
Japan 66.0
World Average 49.1
Nigeria 49.0
China 41.3
India 29.0

Iran	*Japan*	*Mexico*	*Nigeria*	*Russia*	*United States*
Islamic Republic of Iran	Japan	United Mexican States	Federal Republic of Nigeria	Russian Federation	United States of America
Teheran	Tokyo	Mexico City	Abuja	Moscow	Washington, D.C.
Slightly larger than Alaska	Slightly smaller than California	Slightly less than three times the size of Texas	Slightly more than twice the size of California	Approximately 1.8 times the size of the U.S.	About half the size of Russia
0.792%	−0.139%	1.142%	2.382%	−0.474%	0.883%

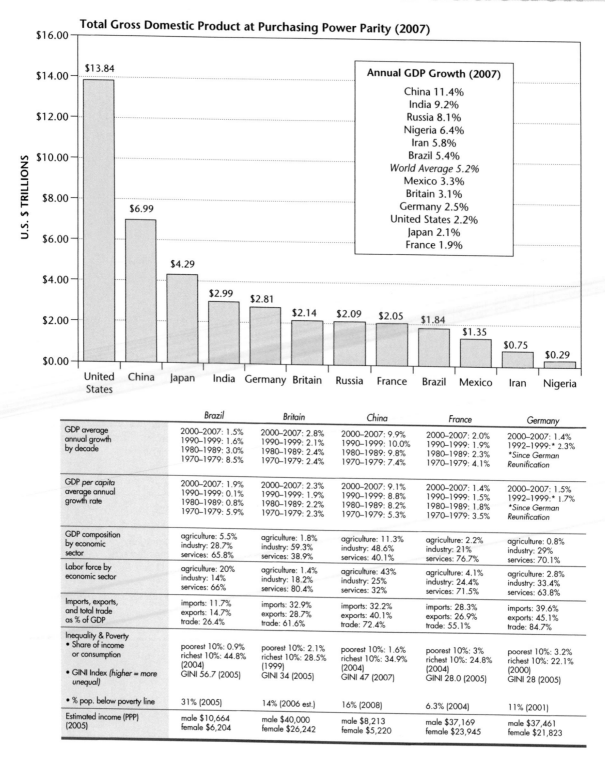

Total Gross Domestic Product at Purchasing Power Parity (2007)

U.S. $ TRILLIONS

- United States: $13.84
- China: $6.99
- Japan: $4.29
- India: $2.99
- Germany: $2.81
- Britain: $2.14
- Russia: $2.09
- France: $2.05
- Brazil: $1.84
- Mexico: $1.35
- Iran: $0.75
- Nigeria: $0.29

Annual GDP Growth (2007)

China 11.4%
India 9.2%
Russia 8.1%
Nigeria 6.4%
Iran 5.8%
Brazil 5.4%
World Average 5.2%
Mexico 3.3%
Britain 3.1%
Germany 2.5%
United States 2.2%
Japan 2.1%
France 1.9%

	Brazil	Britain	China	France	Germany
GDP average annual growth by decade	2000–2007: 1.5% 1990–1999: 1.6% 1980–1989: 3.0% 1970–1979: 8.5%	2000–2007: 2.8% 1990–1999: 2.1% 1980–1989: 2.4% 1970–1979: 2.4%	2000–2007: 9.9% 1990–1999: 10.0% 1980–1989: 9.8% 1970–1979: 7.4%	2000–2007: 2.0% 1990–1999: 1.9% 1980–1989: 2.3% 1970–1979: 4.1%	2000–2007: 1.4% 1992–1999:* 2.3% *Since German Reunification
GDP *per capita* average annual growth rate	2000–2007: 1.9% 1990–1999: 0.1% 1980–1989: 0.8% 1970–1979: 5.9%	2000–2007: 2.3% 1990–1999: 1.9% 1980–1989: 2.2% 1970–1979: 2.3%	2000–2007: 9.1% 1990–1999: 8.8% 1980–1989: 8.2% 1970–1979: 5.3%	2000–2007: 1.4% 1990–1999: 1.5% 1980–1989: 1.8% 1970–1979: 3.5%	2000–2007: 1.5% 1992–1999:* 1.7% *Since German Reunification
GDP composition by economic sector	agriculture: 5.5% industry: 28.7% services: 65.8%	agriculture: 1.8% industry: 59.3% services: 38.9%	agriculture: 11.3% industry: 48.6% services: 40.1%	agriculture: 2.2% industry: 21% services: 76.7%	agriculture: 0.8% industry: 29% services: 70.1%
Labor force by economic sector	agriculture: 20% industry: 14% services: 66%	agriculture: 1.4% industry: 18.2% services: 80.4%	agriculture: 43% industry: 25% services: 32%	agriculture: 4.1% industry: 24.4% services: 71.5%	agriculture: 2.8% industry: 33.4% services: 63.8%
Imports, exports, and total trade as % of GDP	imports: 11.7% exports: 14.7% trade: 26.4%	imports: 32.9% exports: 28.7% trade: 61.6%	imports: 32.2% exports: 40.1% trade: 72.4%	imports: 28.3% exports: 26.9% trade: 55.1%	imports: 39.6% exports: 45.1% trade: 84.7%
Inequality & Poverty • Share of income or consumption • GINI Index *(higher = more unequal)*	poorest 10%: 0.9% richest 10%: 44.8% (2004) GINI 56.7 (2005)	poorest 10%: 2.1% richest 10%: 28.5% (1999) GINI 34 (2005)	poorest 10%: 1.6% richest 10%: 34.9% (2004) GINI 47 (2007)	poorest 10%: 3% richest 10%: 24.8% (2004) GINI 28.0 (2005)	poorest 10%: 3.2% richest 10%: 22.1% (2000) GINI 28 (2005)
• % pop. below poverty line	31% (2005)	14% (2006 est.)	16% (2008)	6.3% (2004)	11% (2001)
Estimated income (PPP) (2005)	male $10,664 female $6,204	male $40,000 female $26,242	male $8,213 female $5,220	male $37,169 female $23,945	male $37,461 female $21,823

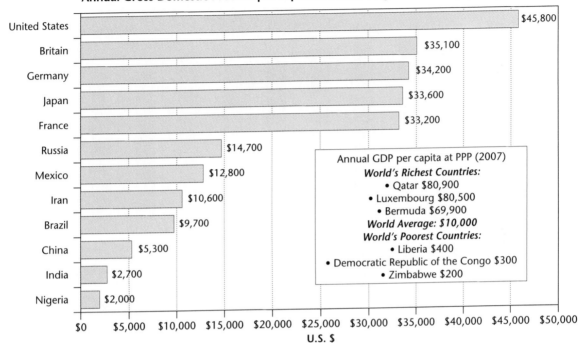

Annual Gross Domestic Product per capita at Purchasing Power Parity (2007)

- United States — $45,800
- Britain — $35,100
- Germany — $34,200
- Japan — $33,600
- France — $33,200
- Russia — $14,700
- Mexico — $12,800
- Iran — $10,600
- Brazil — $9,700
- China — $5,300
- India — $2,700
- Nigeria — $2,000

U.S. $

Annual GDP per capita at PPP (2007)
World's Richest Countries:
- Qatar $80,900
- Luxembourg $80,500
- Bermuda $69,900

World Average: $10,000
World's Poorest Countries:
- Liberia $400
- Democratic Republic of the Congo $300
- Zimbabwe $200

India	Iran	Japan	Mexico	Nigeria	Russia	United States
2000–2007: 7.1% 1990–1999: 5.7% 1980–1989: 5.7% 1970–1979: 2.9%	2000–2007: 3.0% 1990–1999: 4.6% 1980–1989:* 2.3% *Since founding of the Islamic Republic	2000–2007: 1.7% 1990–1999: 1.5% 1980–1989: 3.7% 1970–1979: 5.3%	2000–2007: 3.0% 1990–1999: 3.4% 1980–1989: 2.3% 1970–1979: 4.6%	2000–2007: 5.7% 1990–1999: 3.1% 1980–1989: 0.9% 1970–1979: 7.0%	2000–2007: 6.9% 1992–1999:* –5.1% *Since dissolution of the Soviet Union	2000–2007: 2.6% 1990–1999: 3.1% 1980–1989: 3.0% 1970–1979: 3.3%
2000–2007: 5.5% 1990–1999: 8.8% 1980–1989: 3.5% 1970–1979: 0.6%	2000–2007: 3.7% 1990–1999: 2.9% 1980–1989:* –3.7% *Since founding of the Islamic Republic	2000–2007: 1.5% 1990–1999: 1.2% 1980–1989: 3.1% 1970–1979: 3.5%	2000–2007: 1.8% 1990–1999: 2.0% 1980–1989: 0.1% 1970–1979: 3.3%	2000–2007: 3.1% 1990–1999: 0.4% 1980–1989: –1.9% 1970–1979: 4.1%	2000–2007: 7.2% 1992–1999:* –4.9% *Since dissolution of the Soviet Union	2000–2007: 1.6% 1990–1999: 1.9% 1980–1989: 2.1% 1970–1979: 2.3%
agriculture: 17.6% industry: 29.4% services: 52.9%	agriculture: 10.7% industry: 42.9% services: 46.4%	agriculture: 5.1% industry: 32.7% services: 62.2%	agriculture: 4% industry: 26.6% services: 69.5%	agriculture: 17.6% industry: 52.7% services: 29.7%	agriculture: 4.7% industry: 39.1% services: 56.2%	agriculture: 0.9% industry: 20.5% services: 78.5%
agriculture: 60%, industry: 12% services: 28%	agriculture: 25% industry: 31% services: 45%	agriculture: 4.6% industry: 27.8% services: 67.7%	agriculture: 18% industry: 24% services: 58%	agriculture: 70% industry: 10% services: 20%	agriculture: 10.8% industry: 28.8% services: 60.5%	agriculture: 0.6%, industry: 22.6% services: 76.8%
imports: 25.8% exports: 23.0% trade: 48.8%	imports: 33.6% exports: 41.6% trade: 75.2%	imports: 13.0% exports: 14.3% trade: 27.3%	imports: 33.2% exports: 31.9% trade: 65.1%	imports: 34.7% exports: 56.3% trade: 91.1%	imports: 21.2% exports: 33.9% trade: 55.1%	imports: 16.3% exports: 10.5% trade: 26.8%
poorest 10%: 3.6% richest 10%: 31.1% (2004) GINI 36.8	poorest 10%: 29.6% richest 10%: 2.5% (2004) GINI 38.4 (2004)	poorest 10%: 4.8% richest 10%: 21.7% (1993) GINI 28.6 (1993)	poorest 10%: 1.2% richest 10%: 37% (2006) GINI 50.9 (2005)	poorest 10%: 1.9% richest 10%: 33.2% (2003) GINI 43.7 (2003)	poorest 10%: 1.9% richest 10%: 30.4% (2007) GINI 41.3 (2007)	poorest 10%: 2% richest 10%: 30% (2007) GINI 45 (2007)
25% (2007)	18% (2007)	*Not Available*	17.6% (2004)	70% (2007)	15.8% (2007)	12% (2004)
male $5,194 female $1,620	male $11,363 female $4,475	male $40,000 female $17,802	male $15,680 female $6,039	male $1,592 female $652	male $13,581 female $8,476	male $40,000 female $25,005

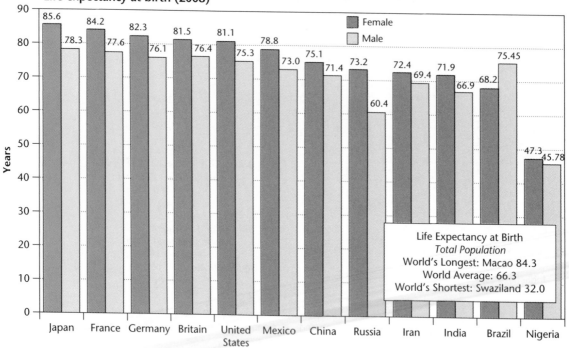

Life expectancy at birth (2008)

Life Expectancy at Birth
Total Population
World's Longest: Macao 84.3
World Average: 66.3
World's Shortest: Swaziland 32.0

	Britain	Brazil	China	France	Germany	India
EDUCATION						
Adult literacy (%)	male & female 99	male 88.4 female 88.8	male 95.1 female 86.5	male & female 99	male & female 99	male 73.4 female 47.8
% of age-eligible population in school	M F primary 98.1 98.8 secondary 90.1 93.5 tertiary 49.6 69.5	M F primary 93.5 95.4 secondary 74.6 82.8 tertiary 22.2 28.8	M F primary 99.0 99.0 secondary 75.2 75.8 tertiary 21.8 21.3	M F primary 98.4 98.8 secondary 97.8 99.7 tertiary 49.5 63.0	M F primary 98.2 98.3 secondary 99.0 99.5 tertiary 50.6 45.1	M F primary 90.4 86.8 secondary 59.0 48.6 tertiary 13.6 9.9
HEALTH						
Physicians/100K	230	115	106	341	344	60
Maternal mortality • per 100K live births • lifetime risk of	8 1/8200	110 1/370	45 1/1300	8 1/6900	4 1/19200	450 1/70
Under 5 mortality rate/1000 live births	male 6 female 5	male 22 female 18	male 21 female 27	male 5 female 4	male 5 female 4	male 72 female 81
Health spending % of GDP % government % private	8.2 87.1 12.9	7.9 44.1 55.9	4.7 38.8 61.2	11.2 79.9 20.1	10.7 76.9 23.1	5.0 19.0 81.0
Adolescent fertility rate (births per 1000 women age 15–19)	26	89	5	9	10	73
OTHER						
Communications & Technology per 100 population	Telephone lines: 55.5 Cell phones: 115.0 PCs: 75.8 Internet users: 55.5 Households with TV: 98	Telephone lines: 20.5 Cell phones: 52.8 PCs: 16.1 Internet users: 22.5 Households with TV: 91	Telephone lines: 28.0 Cell phones: 35.1 PCs: 10.4 Internet users: 4.3 Households with TV: 89	Telephone lines: 55.3 Cell phones: 84.3 PCs: 57.5 Internet users: 49.1 Households with TV: 97	Telephone lines: 65.8 Cell phones: 102.3 PCs: 60.6 Internet users: 46.9 Households with TV: 98	Telephone lines: 3.7 Cell phones: 15.0 PCs: 1.6 Internet users: 5.5 Households with TV: 32
Women as % of national legislatures	Lower House 19.5 Upper House 19.7	Lower House: 9.0 Upper House: 12.3	Single House: 21.3	Lower House: 18.2 Upper House: 18.2	Lower House: 31.6 Upper House: 21.7	Lower House: 9.1 Upper House: 11
Homicides per 100K population	2.1	29.5	2.1	2.6	1.0	3.7
Prison inmates per 100K population	151	219	119	91	88	32

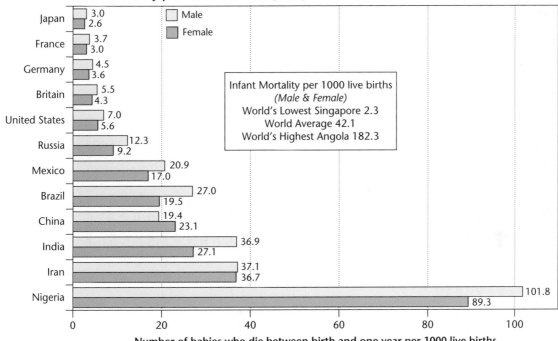

Infant Mortality per 1000 live births (2008)

Legend: ☐ Male   ◼ Female

- Japan: 3.0 / 2.6
- France: 3.7 / 3.0
- Germany: 4.5 / 3.6
- Britain: 5.5 / 4.3
- United States: 7.0 / 5.6
- Russia: 12.3 / 9.2
- Mexico: 20.9 / 17.0
- Brazil: 27.0 / 19.5
- China: 19.4 / 23.1
- India: 36.9 / 27.1
- Iran: 37.1 / 36.7
- Nigeria: 101.8 / 89.3

Infant Mortality per 1000 live births
(Male & Female)
World's Lowest Singapore 2.3
World Average 42.1
World's Highest Angola 182.3

Number of babies who die between birth and one year per 1000 live births

	Iran	Japan	Mexico	Nigeria	Russia	United States
	male 83.5 female 73.4	male & female 99	male 92.4 female 89.6	male 75.7 female 60.6	male 99.7 female 99.2	male & female 99
	M F	M F	M F	M F	M F	M F
primary	90.8 99.9	99.6 100	98.2 97.2	68.1 58.6	90.9 91.0	90.7 92.6
secondary	79.4 75.0	98.5 98.9	70.5 70.1	27.7 23.4	84.8 83.1	94.2 93.5
tertiary	25.4 28.3	60.9 53.5	27.1 25.2	12.0 8.3	61.4 83.4	68.1 96.1
	87	212	150	28	431	260
	140	6	60	1100	28	11
	1/300	1/11600	1/670	1/18	1/2700	1/4800
	male 36	male 4	male 38	male 195	male 15	male 8
	female 33	female 3	female 32	female 187	female 11	female 7
% of GDP	17.8	8.2	6.4	3.9	5.2	15.2
% government	55.8	82.2	45.5	30.9	62.0	45.1
% private	44.2	17.8	54.5	69.1	38.0	54.9
	20	4	67	142	29	
Telephone lines:	31.4	43.2	19.1	1.2	28.0	57.5
Cell phones:	19.5	79.6	54.7	22.3	83.8	77.8
PCs:	10.6	67.6	13.6	0.8	12.2	76.2
Internet users:	25.7	68.5	17.5	5.5	18.0	69.5
Households with TV:	68	99	93	32	98	98
	Single House 2.8	Lower House: 9.4 Upper House: 18.2	Lower House 23.2 Upper House 18.0	Lower House: 7.0 Upper House: 8.3	Lower House: 14.0 Upper House: 4.7	Lower House: 16.8 Upper House: 16.0
	2.9	0.5	13.0	1.5	19.9	5.6
	222	63	198	29	627	751

Comparative Rankings

International organizations and research institutions have developed statistical methods to rate and rank different countries according to various categories of economic, social, political, and environmental performance. Such rankings can be controversial, but we think they provide an interesting approach to comparative analysis. Five examples of this approach are listed below. In addition to the countries included in this book, the top and bottom 5 countries (and in the case of the Freedom House ratings, examples of each level) are also listed.

Human Development Index (HDI)

Human Development Index (HDI) is a measure used by the United Nations to compare the overall level of well-being in countries around the world. It takes into account life expectancy, education, and the standard of living.*

2007–2008 HDI Rankings:
High Human Development
1. Iceland
2. Norway
3. Australia
4. Canada
5. Ireland
8. Japan
10. France
12. United States
16. Britain
22. Germany
52. Mexico
67. Russia
70. Brazil
Medium Human Development
81. China
94. Iran
128. India
Low Human Development
158. Nigeria
173. Mali
174. Niger
175. Guinea-Bissau
176. Burkina Faso
177. Sierra Leone

*http://hdr.undp.org/en/statistics/

Global Gender Gap

Global Gender Gap measures "the extent to which women . . . have achieved equality with men in five critical areas: economic participation, economic opportunity, political empowerment, educational attainment, and health and well-being."*

2007 Gender Gap Rankings:
1. Sweden
2. Norway
3. Finland
4. Iceland
5. New Zealand
7. Germany
11. Britain
31. United States
45. Russia
51. France
73. China
74. Brazil
91. Japan
93. Mexico
107. Nigeria
114. India
118. Iran
124. Saudi Arabia
125. Nepal
126. Pakistan
127. Nepal
128. Yemen

*http://www.weforum.org/en/initiatives/gcp/GenderGap

Environmental Performance Index (EPI)

Environmental Performance Index (EPI) measures how close countries come to meeting specific benchmarks for national pollution control and natural resource management.*

2008 EPI Rankings:
1. Switzerland
2. Sweden
3. Finland
4. Norway
5. Costa Rica
10. France
13. Germany
14. Britain
21. Japan
25. Brazil
28. Russia
39. United States
47. Mexico
67. Iran
105. China
120. India
126. Nigeria
145. Mali
146. Mauritania
147. Sierra Leone
148. Angola
149. Niger

*http://epi.yale.edu/2008EPIOverview

International Corruption Perceptions Index (CPI)

International Corruption Perceptions Index (CPI) defines corruption as the abuse of public office for private gain and measures the degree to which corruption is perceived to exist among a country's public officials and politicians.*

2007 CPI Rankings:
1. Denmark
1. Finland
1. New Zealand
4. Singapore
4. Sweden
12. Britain
16. Germany
17. Japan
19. France
20. United States
72. Brazil
72. China
72. India
72. Mexico
131. Iran
143. Russia
147. Nigeria
175. Uzbekistan
176. Haiti
177. Iraq
179. Myanmar
179. Somalia

*http://www.transparency.org/ Similar numbers indicate a tie in the rankings.

Freedom in the World

Freedom in the World ratings measures how free a country is according to an analysis of its civil and political liberties. 1 = most free; 7 = least free.*

2008 Freedom House Ratings:
"Free" (1.0–2.5)
Britain (1.0)
France (1.0)
German (1.0)
United States (1.0)
Japan (1.5)
Brazil (2.0)
India (2.5)
Mexico (2.5)
"Partly Free" (3.0–5.0)
Turkey (3.0)
Kenya (3.5)
Nigeria (4.0)
Bangladesh (4.5)
Thailand (5.0)
"Not Free" (5.5–7.0)
Russia (5.5)
Iran (6.0)
China (6.5)
Cuba (7.0)

*http://www.freedomhouse.org/

Key Terms ≫≫

critical juncture
communist party-states
regimes
cold war
liberal democracy
ideologies
authoritarian
ethnic cleansing
genocide
globalization
European Union (EU)
World Trade Organization (WTO)
sovereignty
collective identities
comparative politics
Human Development Index
Global Gender Gap
Environmental Performance Index
Corruption Perceptions Index
Freedom in the World rating
United Nations
comparativists
Keynesianism
neoliberalism
countries
state
executive
cabinet
legislature
judiciary

bureaucracy
legitimacy
state formation
nation-state
political culture
rational choice theory
middle-level theory
dictatorship
democratic transitions
World Bank
International Monetary Fund (IMF)
North American Free Trade Agreement (NAFTA)
institutional design
political economy
laissez-faire
sustainable development
gross domestic product (GDP)
gross national product (GNP)
purchasing power parity (PPP)
social movements
social class
distributional politics
typology
most different case analysis
Third World
consolidated democracies
transitional democracies
authoritarian regimes
totalitarian

Suggested Readings ≫≫

Brady, Henry E., and Collier, David, eds. *Rethinking Social Inquiry: Diverse Tools, Shared Standards.* Lanham, MD.: Rowman and Littlefield, 2004.

Chua, Amy. *Day of Empire: How Hyperpowers Rise to Global Dominance—and Why They Fail.* New York: Doubleday, 2007.

Collier, Paul. *The Bottom Billion Why the Poorest Countries are Failing and What Can Be Done About It.* New York: Oxford University Press, 2007.

Diamond, Larry, and Morlino, Leonardo, eds. *Assessing the Quality of Democracy.* Baltimore: Johns Hopkins University Press, 2005.

Diamond, Larry. *The Spirit of Democracy: The Struggle to Build Free Societies Throughout the World.* New York: Times Books, 2008.

Dominguez, Jorge I. and Jones, Anthony. *The Construction of Democracy: Lessons from Practice and Research.* Baltimore: John Hopkins University Press, 2007.

Easterly, Thomas. *The White Man's Burden: Why the West's Efforts to Aid the Rest Have Done So Much Ill and So Little Good.* New York: Penguin Press, 2007.

Friedman, Thomas L. *The World Is Flat: A Brief History of the Twenty-First Century.* New York: Farrar, Straus and Giroux, 2005.

Ghani, Ashraf and Lockhart, Clare. *Fixing Failed States: A Framework for Rebuilding a Fractured World.* New York: Oxford University Press, 2008.

Hall, Peter A., and Soskice, David, eds. *Varieties of Capitalism: The Institutional Foundations of Comparative Advantage.* New York: Oxford University Press, 2001.

Johnston, Michael. *Syndromes of Corruption: Wealth, Power, and Democracy.* New York: Cambridge University Press, 2006.

Katznelson, Ira, and Milner, Helen V., eds. *Political Science: The State of the Discipline.* New York: Norton, 2002.

Kesselman, Mark, ed. *Readings in Comparative Politics: Political Challenges and Changing Agendas.* 2nd ed. Boston: Cengage, 2010.

Kesselman, Mark. *The Politics of Globalization: A Reader.* Boston: Cengage, 2006.

Kohli, Atul. *State-Directed Development: Political Power and Industrialization in the Global Periphery.* Cambridge: Cambridge University Press, 2005.

Krieger, Joel. *Globalization and State Power: Who Wins When America Rules?* New York: Longman, 2004.

Kymlicka, Will. *Multicultural Odysseys: Navigating the New International Politics of Diversity.* New York: Oxford University Press, 2007.

Laitin, David D. *Nations, States, and Violence.* New York: Oxford University Press, 2007.

Lichbach, Mark Irving, and Zuckerman, Alan S., eds. *Comparative Politics: Rationality, Culture, and Structure.* Cambridge: Cambridge University Press, 1997.

Maugeri, Leonardo. *The Age of Oil: The Mythology, History, and Future of the World's Most Controversial Resource.* New York: Praeger, 2007.

Roeder, Philip G. *Where Nation-States Come From: Institutional Change in the Age of Nationalism.* Princeton: Princeton University Press, 2007.

Sen, Amartya. *Development as Freedom.* New York: Knopf, 1999.

Smith, Jackie. *Social Movements for Global Democracy.* Baltimore: Johns Hopkins University Press, 2007.

Stiglitz, Joseph E. *Globalization and Its Discontents.* New York: Norton, 2002.

Tarrow, Sidney. *Power in Movement: Social Movements and Contentious Politics.* 2nd ed. Cambridge: Cambridge University Press, 1998.

Tilly, Charles. *Democracy.* New York: Cambridge University Press, 2007.

Wolf, Martin. *Why Globalization Works.* New Haven, Conn.: Yale University Press, 2004.

Zakaria, Fareed. *The Future of Freedom: Illiberal Democracy at Home and Abroad.* New York: W.W. Norton. 2003.

Suggested Websites ≫

Area Studies and Comparative Politics
www.psr.keele.ac.uk/area.htm
CIA World Factbook
www.cia.gov/cia/publications/factbook
Elections Around the World
www.electionworld.org
Foreign Government Resources on the Web
www.lib.umich.edu/govdocs/foreign.html

Freedom House
www.freedomhouse.org
NationMaster
www.nationmaster.com
Political Resources on the Net
www.politicalresources.net
World Audit
www.worldaudit.org

Endnotes ≫

[1]Francis Fukuyama, "The End of History?" *The National Interest* 16 (Summer 1989): 3–18. The article is reprinted in Mark Kesselman, ed., *Readings in Comparative Politics: Political Challenges and Changing Agendas*, 2nd ed. (Boston: Cengage, 2010). For a counter-argument, see Robert Kagan, *The Return of History and the End of Dreams.* New York: Knopf, 2008.

[2]For collections of articles on globalization, see Mark Kesselman, ed., *Politics of Globalization* (Boston: Cengage, 2006), and Joel Krieger, ed., *Globalization and State Power: A Reader* (New York: Pearson/Longman, 2006). For a lively account of changes involved in the current phase of globalization, see Thomas L. Friedman, *The World Is Flat: A Brief History of the Twenty-First Century* (New York: Farrar, Straus and Giroux, 2005).

[3]United Nations Development Programme (UNDP), International Monetary Fund (IMF), International Bank for Reconstruction and Development (IBRD), Organization for Economic Cooperation and Development (OECD), North American Free Trade Agreement (NAFTA), and Asia Pacific Economic Cooperation (APEC) Forum.

[4]See Philippe Schmitter, "Comparative Politics," in Joel Krieger, ed., *The Oxford Companion to Politics of the World*, 2nd ed. (New York: Oxford University Press, 2001), 160–165. For a more extended discussion and different approach, see David D. Laitin, "Comparative Politics: The State of the Subdiscipline," in Ira Katznelson and Helen V. Milner, eds., *Political Science: The State of the Discipline* (New York: Norton, 2002), 630–659. For a collection of articles in the field of comparative politics, see Kesselman, ed., *Readings in Comparative Politics.*

[5]See Anthony Marx, *Making Race and Nation: A Comparison of the United States, South Africa, and Brazil* (Cambridge: Cambridge University Press, 1998).

[6]For a landmark article that analyzed how political decisions often reflect pressures from both the domestic and international arena, see Robert Putnam, "Diplomacy and Domestic Politics: The Logic of Two-Level Games," *International Organization* 42 (Summer 1988): 427–460.

[7]See, for example, Colin Campbell, *Governments Under Stress: Political Executives and Key Bureaucrats in Washington, London, and Ottawa* (Toronto: University of Toronto Press, 1983).

[8]See for example, Merilee S. Griddle, *Despite the Odds: The Contentious Politics of Education Reform* (Princeton: Princeton University Press, 2004), which compares education policies in several Latin American countries; and Miranda A. Schreurs, *Environmental Politics in Japan, Germany, and the United States* (Cambridge: Cambridge University Press, 2002).

[9]See, for example, Benedict Anderson, *Imagined Communities: Reflections on the Origins and Spread of Nationalism*, rev. ed. (London: Verso, 1991); and Theda Skocpol, *Social Revolutions in the Modern World* (Cambridge: Cambridge University Press, 1994).

[10]Peter A. Hall, *Governing the Economy: The Politics of State Intervention in Britain and France* (New York: Oxford University Press, 1986); and Mark Blyth, *Great Transformations: Economic Ideas and Institutional Change in the Twentieth Century* (Cambridge: Cambridge University Press, 2002).

[11]For reviews of scholarly literature on the state, see Margaret Levi, "The State of the Study of the State," Miles Kahler, "The State of the State in World Politics," and Atul Kohli, "State, Society, and Development," in Katznelson and Milner, eds., *Political Science: State of the Discipline.*

[12]John R. Alford, Carolyn L. Funk, and John R. Hibbin, "Are Political Orientations Genetically Transmitted?", in *American Political Science Review*, vol. 99, no. 2, May 2005: 153–167.

[13]For diverse views, see Gary King, Robert O. Keohane, and Sidney Verba, *Designing Social Inquiry: Scientific Inference in Qualitative Research* (Princeton, N.J.: Princeton University Press, 1994); Mark Irving Lichbach and Alan S. Zuckerman, eds., *Comparative Politics: Rationality, Culture, and Structure,* 2nd ed. (Cambridge: Cambridge University Press, 2009). Katznelson and Milner, eds., *Political Science*; Henry E. Brady and David Collier, eds., *Rethinking Social Inquiry: Diverse Tools, Shared Standards* (Lanham, Md.: Rowman and Littlefield, 2004).

[14]Clifford Geertz, *The Interpretation of Cultures: Selected Essays* (New York, Basic Books, 1973).

[15]For discussion of rational choice theory in the popular press, see "Political Scientists Debate Theory of 'Rational Choice'," in the *New York Times*, February 26, 2000, B11; and Jonathan Cohn, "Irrational Exuberance: When Did Political Science Forget About Politics?," *New Republic*, October 25, 1999, 25–31. For an application of rational choice theory in comparative politics, see Robert H. Bates, Avner Greif, Margaret Levi, Jean-Laurent Rosenthal, and Barry R. Weingast, *Analytic Narratives* (Princeton, N.J.: Princeton University Press, 1998). For a lively exchange about the value of applying this approach to explaining large-scale historical change, see a critical review of *Analytic Narratives* by Jon Elster and a reply by the authors of the book: Jon Elster, "Rational Choice History: A Case of Excessive Ambition," and Robert H. Bates et al., "The Analytic Narrative Project," *American Political Science Review* 94, no. 3 (September 2000): 685–702.

[16]For the most influential example that stresses common patterns across regions, see Juan J. Linz and Alfred Stepan, *Problems of Democratic Transition and Consolidation: Southern Europe, South America, and Post-Communist Europe* (Baltimore: Johns Hopkins University Press, 1996). For a warning that generalizations of this kind may neglect important differences among regimes, for example, between formerly authoritarian and communist regimes, see Valerie Bunce, "Rethinking Democratization: Lessons from the Postcommunist Experience," *World Politics* 55, no. 2 (Jan. 2003): 170–189. Selections of both are included in Kesselman, ed., *Readings in Comparative Politics.*

[17]One statement of the case that globalization has decisively weakened state supremacy is Martin van Creveld, "The Fate of the State," *Parameters* (Spring 1996): 4–17. See also Joel Krieger, *Globalization and State Power.*

[18]Robert I. Rotberg, "Failed States in a World of Terror," *Foreign Affairs* 81, no. 4 (July–August 2002). The article is reprinted in Kesselman, *Readings in Comparative Politics.* Rotberg was referring in his article to Afghanistan when it was taken over by by the Taliban. *Foreign Policy* magazine does an annual "Failed States Index," which is accessible via its website at: http://www.foreignpolicy.com/.

[19]This term is borrowed from Peter A. Hall, *Governing the Economy.*

[20]Alexander Gerschenkron, *Economic Backwardness in Historical Perspective* (Cambridge: Cambridge University Press, 1966).

[21]Peter A. Hall and David Soskice, eds. *Varieties of Capitalism: The Institutional Foundations of Comparative Advantage*

(New York: Oxford University Press, 2001). Also see Herbert Kitschelt, Peter Lange, Gary Marks, and John Stephens, eds., *Continuity and Change in Advanced Capitalist Democracies* (New York: Cambridge University Press, 1998); and David Coates, ed., *Varieties of Capitalism, Varieties of Approaches* (Basingstoke, UK: Palgrave/Macmillan, 2005).

[22]For a sample of an enormous and diverse literature, see Chalmers Johnson, *MITI and the Japanese Miracle: The Growth of Industrial Policy* (Stanford: Stanford University Press, 1982); Stephan Haggard, *Pathways from the Periphery: The Politics of Growth in the Newly Industrializing Countries* (Ithaca, N.Y.: Cornell University Press, 1990); Mancur J. Olson, *The Rise and Decline of Nations: Economic Growth, Stagflation, and Social Rigidities* (New Haven, Conn.: Yale University Press, 1982); Peter Evans, *Embedded Autonomy: States and Industrial Transformation* (Princeton, N.J.: Princeton University Press, 1995); Linda Weiss and John M. Hobson, *States and Economic Development: A Comparative Historical Analysis* (Cambridge: Polity Press, 1995); and Meredith Woo-Cummings, ed., *The Developmental State* (Ithaca, N.Y.: Cornell University Press, 1999). For a review article questioning many commonly offered explanations, see Robert Wade, "East Asia's Economic Success: Conflicting Perspectives, Partial Insights, Shaky Evidence," *World Politics* 44, no. 2 (1992): 270–320. Recent important contributions are Atul Kohli, *State-Directed Development: Political Power and Industrialization in the Global Periphery* (Cambridge: Cambridge University Press, 2005), and Jeffrey D. Sachs, *The End of Poverty: Economic Possibilities for Our Time* (New York: The Penguin Press, 2005).

[23]Paul Collier, *The Bottom Billion: Why the Poorest Countries Are Failing and What Can Be Done About It* (New York: Oxford University Press, 2007), ch. 4.

[24]Amartya Sen, "Democracy as a Universal Value," *Journal of Democracy* 10, no. 3 (July 1999): 3–17. This article is included in Kesselman, *Readings in Comparative Politics*. An influential study of this question, on which Sen draws, reaches a similar conclusion: Adam Przeworski et al., *Democracy and Development: Political Institutions and Well-Being in the World, 1950–1990* (Cambridge: Cambridge University Press, 2000). For a study that finds a positive correlation between democracy and economic growth, see Yi Feng, *Democracy, Governance, and Economic Performance: Theory and Evidence* (Cambridge, Mass.: MIT Press, 2005).

[25]Freedom in World Reports, 2003–2008, available at www.freedomhouse.org.

[26]Sen, 3.

[27]Andrew Roberts, "Review Article: The Quality of Democracy," *Comparative Politics* 37, no. 3 (April 2005): 357.

[28]This view was first developed by Dankwart Rustow. His original article and commentaries are the focus of Lisa Anderson, ed., *Transitions to Democracy* (New York: Columbia University Press, 1999). This approach has been further developed by Adam Przeworski, *Democracy and the Market: Political and Economic Reforms in Eastern Europe and Latin America* (Cambridge: Cambridge University Press, 1991).

[29]Fareed Zakaria, *The Future of Freedom: Illiberal Democracy at Home and Abroad* (New York: W.W. Norton, 2003), 248.

[30]Arend Lijphart, *Patterns of Democracy: Government Forms and Performance in Thirty-Six Countries* (New Haven: Yale University Press, 1999); and Juan J. Linz and Alfred Stepan, *Problems of Democratic Transition and Consolidation,* 139–143.

[31]Guillermo O'Donnell and Philippe Schmitter, *Transitions from Authoritarian Rule: Tentative Conclusions about Uncertain Democracies* (Baltimore: Johns Hopkins University Press, 1986). The concept of waves of democratization is taken from Samuel Huntington, *The Third Wave: Democratization in the Late Twentieth Century* (Norman, Ok.: University of Oklahoma Press, 1991).

[32]Przeworski et al., *Democracy and Development.*

[33]Alfred Stepan, *Arguing Comparative Politics* (New York: Oxford University Press, 2001), 184.

[34]For attempts to answer this question, see Alfred Stepan and Cindy Skach, "Constitutional Frameworks and Democratic Consolidation: Parliamentarism versus Presidentialism," *World Politics* 46, no. 1 (October 1993): 1–22, and Juan J. Linz and Arturo Valenzuela, eds., *The Failure of Presidential Democracy* (Baltimore: Johns Hopkins University Press, 1994).

[35]See, for example, Guillermo O'Donnell, "Illusions About Consolidation," *Journal of Democracy* 7, no. 2 (April 1996): 34–51. Also see Thomas Carothers, "The End of the Transition Paradigm," *Journal of Democracy* 13, no. 1 (January 2002): 5–21; and Steven Levitsky and Lucan A. Way, "The Rise of Competitive Authoritarianism," *Journal of Democracy* 13, no. 2 (April 2002): 51–65; both are reprinted in Kesselman, *Readings in Comparative Politics*.

[36]Larry Diamond, "Thinking about Hybrid Regimes," in *Journal of Democracy*, 13.2 (2002): 21–35.

Part 2 » Established Democracies

Joel Krieger

Chapter 2 ≫**BRITAIN**

Official Name: **United Kingdom of Great Britain and Northern Ireland**

Location: **Western Europe**

Capital City: **London**

Population (2008): **60.9 million**

Size: **244,820 sq. km.; slightly smaller than Oregon**

1688
Glorious
Revolution
establishes power of
Parliament

c. 1750
Industrial
Revolution
begins in Britain

1832
Reform Act expands
voting rights

1837–1901
Reign of Queen Victoria;
height of British Empire

1914–1918
World War I

1929–1939
Great Depression

1939–1945
World War II

1945–1979
Establishment of British welfare
state; dismantling of British
Empire

1973
Britain joins the European
Community

The Making of the Modern British State

Politics in Action

Tony Blair and Gordon Brown met innocently enough as newly elected members of Parliament (MPs) after the 1983 election. They formed a friendship and shared an office: Blair charming, intuitive, telegenic; and Brown more bookish, intense, cautious, and dour. Both were rising stars in the party. Blair pushed the party to modernize and expand its political base well beyond its heritage as a labor party. Brown took on the role of shadow chancellor (the opposition party's spokesman on the economy and potential chancellor should Labour return to office).

But soon they became competitors for leadership of the party. Over dinner at a restaurant in 1994, as the party was selecting a new leader, Brown agreed to withdraw from the leadership contest in favor of Blair—and in return Blair promised one day to resign as prime minister in favor of Brown, who would be given unprecedented power as chancellor under Blair as prime minister. But as time dragged on and both personality and policy differences made for an increasingly testy relationship, Brown chafed at how long it was taking for Blair to make good on his promise. Increasingly, the British government began to look and feel like a dual executive, with Brown in charge of domestic policies and Blair responsible for foreign affairs.

Blair's decision to support the U.S.-led war in Iraq was very unpopular, and questions about the war

Leaders

Gordon Brown

Born in 1951 in Govan, near Glasgow, Scotland, Gordon Brown is the second son of Elizabeth and Reverend John Ebenezer Brown, a Church of Scotland minister. Brown is often termed "a son of the manse"; in other words, someone who grew up in the stately house and the surrounding land assigned to a Presbyterian minister. Like many of his generation, Reverend Brown was appalled by the level of poverty that British people experienced in the interwar years of the 1920s and 1930s.

Although Reverend Brown was not actively involved in politics, he had a strong sense of both duty and social justice. He undoubtedly passed this on to his son, who would later credit his father for teaching him to treat everyone equally. Gordon Brown also learned at an early age to be self-reliant and hard-working: to absorb the values that Margaret Thatcher famously trumpeted as the values of Victorian England, such as self-improvement and industriousness. In repose, Brown often looks stern (he is often called dour or serious).

1979–1990
Prime Minister Margaret
Thatcher promotes
"enterprise culture"

1997
Tony Blair elected prime
minister

2001
Under Blair's leadership,
Britain "stands shoulder to
shoulder" with America in war
against terror

2007
Gordon Brown becomes
prime minister and promises
to renew the party and the
nation

An imposing and rigorous intellectual figure from an early age (a primary school teacher recalls that he was always doing sums), he attended Edinburgh University at the age of 16 and achieved first class honors. He earned a doctorate (he wrote on the Labour Party in Scotland in the early part of the twentieth century) and served as a lecturer at Edinburgh and at Caledonian University. He then worked for Scottish television as a journalist, producer, and current affairs editor before moving on, full-time, to the world of Scottish and British Labour party politics.

As the 1983 election approached, Brown honed his skills as a candidate. He displayed the prudence for which he would become famous, arguing for a significant increase in public spending to save the welfare state from the retrenchment of the Thatcher years, but also promising that the increase on social spending would be measured. He proved himself a skilled political operative, able to pull the levers of machine politics to gain the backing of the powerful Transport and General Workers' Union (TGWU), the British equivalent of the teamsters in the U.S., which he had joined in 1976. The TGWU had the muscle to make him chairman of the Scottish Labour Party and candidate for a safe seat (one that Labour was expected to win) in the 1983 election.

With Tony Blair, this stolid son of the manse modernized and transformed the Labour Party, its organization, its political values and, above all, its electoral fortunes. Brown built his reputation as one of the most powerful, reassuring, and successful chancellors in British history. Given credit for the longest continuous period of growth in Britain since the industrial revolution, he seemed as prepared as anyone could be to take over the reins of government when Blair resigned. How could this unflappable man—known for meticulous planning, formidable intellectual and political skills and, above all, his trademark prudence—turn his lifelong dream into a nightmare in less than six months, making U-turn after U-turn? Of course, Brown could yet become a successful prime minister and confound his current critics but, if he does not, the unraveling of Gordon Brown will become one of the most colossal reversals of fortune in modern British politics.

Sources: William Keegan, *The Prudence of Mr. Gordon Brown* (Chichester, England: John Wiley and Sons, 1994); Francis Becket, *Gordon Brown: Past, Present, Future* (London: Haus Publishing, 2007).

hounded Blair right through the campaign leading to his third electoral victory in May 2005—a feat never before achieved by the leader of Britain's 105-year-old Labour Party. The victory was bittersweet. His parliamentary majority was slashed by nearly 100 seats. And by then, Blair and Brown were barely on speaking terms, and

Brown loyalists in government had the knives sharpened and ready. Soon, a full-scale succession crisis was underway. In June 2007, Blair tendered his resignation to the Queen, who immediately summoned Gordon Brown (he had run unopposed in a leadership election in the Labour Party) to become prime minister.

With the handover to Brown finally consecrated, at the annual Labour Party conference in September 2007, the mood was unusually upbeat. The Blair–Brown feud seemed a distant memory and Labour supporters felt good about the way the new prime minister had handled a set of crises that tested his early leadership: from attempted terror attacks in London and Glasgow, to horrible flooding that displaced thousands in the north of England, to the collapse of Northern Rock, one of the premier banks that provided mortgages to increasingly worried homeowners. Suddenly, with Gordon Brown at the helm, New Labour was on the upswing and the country was buzzing with talk about an early election to give Brown a proper mandate (it is the prerogative of the prime minister to call an election when the time seems right at any point within five years of the previous election). Then, even more suddenly, Brown appeared to get cold feet and dropped plans for a snap election (none is required until spring 2010).

The resurgent Conservatives—with David Cameron, its young and untested but increasingly confident leader leading the charge—made much of Brown's retreat, putting the new prime minister on the defensive not only for retreating on the timing of an election but also for his decision to sign the EU reform treaty in 2007 without committing the UK to a referendum. (Blair had made this promise before the EU constitutional treaty was rejected by French and Dutch voters in 2005). And that was only the beginning of the end of Brown's uncommonly short honeymoon as prime minister. When he ran the economy while Blair was prime minister, Brown was nicknamed the "Iron Chancellor" for his steely determination and unwillingness to back down once a policy was set. But within six months of becoming prime minister, Nick Clegg, the usually mild-mannered head of the Liberal Democrats (Britain's center party) commented to devastating effect that Brown had been transformed "from Stalin to

MORAL COMPASS

At the halfway point between Labour's 2005 victory and the next election to be held by 2010, Brown seemed blown off course, lacking both a political and a moral compass, and uncertain of what direction to take.   *Source:* © Ingram Pinn, Financial Times, April 26/27, 2008.

FIGURE 2.1

The British Nation at a Glance

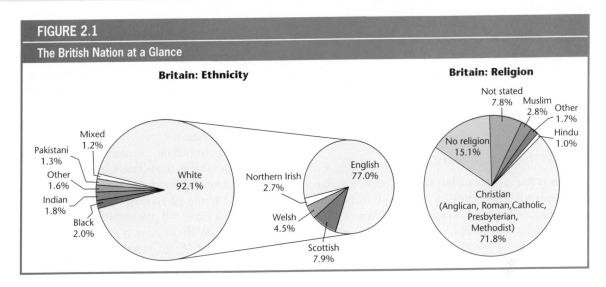

Britain: Ethnicity

Britain: Religion

Mr. Bean" (or from a ruthless dictator to a bumbling and ineffectual slapstick character). By spring 2008, after a much-publicized loss of 25 million records of children receiving benefits, which compromised the bank account details of over 7 million families; a series of policy U-turns on taxes that alienated Labour's traditional working class supporters and increases in corporate taxes that had companies threatening an exodus; a looming mortgage crisis in the UK and concern about declining housing values; Brown seemed beleaguered. Then things went from bad to far worse. Conservative Boris Johnson beat the Labour incumbent

Table 2.1

Political Organization

Political System	Parliamentary democracy, Constitutional monarchy.
Regime History	Long constitutional history, origins subject to interpretation, usually dated from the seventeenth century or earlier.
Administrative Structure	Unitary state with fusion of powers. UK parliament has supreme legislative, executive, and judicial authority. Reform in process to transfer limited powers to representative bodies for Scotland, Wales, and Northern Ireland.
Executive	Prime minister (PM), answerable to House of Commons, subject to collective responsibility of the cabinet; member of Parliament who is leader of party that can control a majority in Commons.
Legislature	Bicameral. House of Commons elected by single-member plurality system with no fixed term but a five-year limit. Main legislative powers: to pass laws, provide for finance, scrutinize public administration and government policy. House of Lords, unelected upper house: limited powers to delay enactment of legislation and to recommend revisions; specified appeals court functions. Reform introduced to eliminate voting rights of hereditary peers and create new second chamber.
Judiciary	Independent but with no power to judge the constitutionality of legislation or governmental conduct. Judges appointed by Crown on recommendation of PM or lord chancellor.
Party System	Two-party dominant, with regional variation. Principal parties: Labour and Conservative; a center party (Liberal Democrats); and national parties in Scotland, Wales, and Northern Ireland.

Ken Livingstone in the race for London's mayor and Labour suffered its worst showing in local elections across the country, slipping to third place behind the centrist Liberal Democrats, and the resurgent Conservatives who beat them by 20 percent. What had become of the Iron Chancellor? What did the government stand for?

Geographic Setting

Britain is the largest of the British Isles, a group of islands off the northwest coast of Europe, and encompasses England, Scotland, and Wales. The second-largest island comprises Northern Ireland and the independent Republic of Ireland. The term *Great Britain* encompasses England, Wales, and Scotland, but not Northern Ireland. We use the term *Britain* as shorthand for the United Kingdom of Great Britain and Northern Ireland.

Covering an area of approximately 94,000 square miles, Britain is roughly two-thirds the size of Japan, or approximately half the size of France. In 2004, the population of the United Kingdom was 60.4 million people.

Although forever altered by the Channel Tunnel, Britain's location as an offshore island adjacent to Europe is significant. Historically, Britain's island destiny made it less subject to invasion and conquest than its continental counterparts, affording the country a sense of security. The geographic separation from mainland Europe has also created for many Britons a feeling that they are both apart from and a part of Europe, a factor that has complicated relations with Britain's EU partners to this day.

Critical Junctures

This study begins with a look at the historical development of the modern British state. History shapes contemporary politics in very important ways. Once in place, institutions leave powerful legacies, and issues that were left unresolved in one period may present challenges for the future.

In many ways, Britain is the model of a united and stable country with an enviable record of continuity and resiliency. The evolutionary nature of British politics contrasts notably with the history of many

countries, ranging from France to Nigeria, which have experienced multiple regimes and repeated transitions between dictatorship and democracy. Some issues that plague other countries, such as religious divisions, were settled long ago in Great Britain proper (although a similar settlement is only now taking shape in Northern Ireland). But others, such as multiple national identities, remain on the agenda.

British state formation involved the unification of kingdoms or crowns (hence the term United *Kingdom*). After Duke William of Normandy defeated the English in the Battle of Hastings in 1066, the Norman monarchy extended its authority throughout the British Isles. With the Acts of Union of 1536 and 1542, England and Wales were legally, politically, and administratively united. The unification of the Scottish and English crowns began in 1603, when James VI of Scotland ascended to the English throne as James I. After that, England, Scotland, and Wales were known as Great Britain. Scotland and England remained divided politically, however, until the Act of Union of 1707. Henceforth, a common Parliament of Great Britain replaced the two separate parliaments of Scotland and of England and Wales.

At the same time, the making of the British state included a historic expression of constraints on monarchical rule. At first, the period of Norman rule after 1066 strengthened royal control, but the conduct of King John (1199–1216) fueled opposition from feudal barons. In 1215, they forced the king to consent to a series of concessions that protected feudal landowners from abuses of royal power. These restrictions on royal prerogatives were embodied in the Magna Carta, a historic statement of the rights of a political community against the monarchical state. Soon after, in 1236, the term *Parliament* was first used officially to refer to the gathering of feudal barons summoned by the king whenever he required their consent for special taxes. By the fifteenth century, Parliament had gained the right to make laws.

The Seventeenth-Century Settlement

The making of the British state in the sixteenth and seventeenth centuries involved a complex interplay of religious conflicts, national rivalries, and struggles between rulers and Parliament. These conflicts

Britain

0 — 100 Miles

0 — 100 Kilometers

Shetland
Islands

Orkney
Islands

Outer Hebrides

Inner Hebrides

SCOTLAND

North Sea

★Edinburgh

•Glasgow

**NORTHERN
IRELAND**

★Belfast

Isle
of Man

Irish Sea

Manchester•
•Liverpool

**REPUBLIC
OF
IRELAND**

Dublin★

Isle of
Anglesey

ENGLAND

•Birmingham

WALES

Thames

Cardiff
★   •Bristol   London⊙   Chunnel

Southampton•

Isle of Wight

ATLANTIC
OCEAN

★Plymouth

English Channel

FRANCE

---

erupted in the civil wars of the 1640s and the forced abdication of James II in 1688. The nearly bloodless political revolution of 1688, subsequently known as the Glorious Revolution, marked the "last successful political coup d'état or revolution in British history."[1] By the end of the seventeenth century, the framework of constitutional (or limited) monarchy, which would

still exercise flashes of power into the nineteenth century, was established. For more than three hundred years, Britain's monarchs have answered to Parliament, which has held the sole authority for taxation and the maintenance of a standing army.

The Glorious Revolution also resolved long-standing religious conflict. The replacement of the

Roman Catholic James II by the Protestant William and Mary ensured the dominance of the Church of England (or Anglican Church). To this day, the Church of England remains the established (official) religion, and approximately two dozen of its bishops and archbishops sit as members of the House of Lords, the upper house of Parliament.

Thus, by the end of the seventeenth century, a basic form of **parliamentary democracy** had emerged. Except in Northern Ireland, the problem of religious divisions, which continue to plague many countries throughout the world, was largely settled (although Catholics and Jews could not vote until the 1820s). As a result of settling most of its religious differences early, Britain has taken a more secular turn than most other countries in Western Europe. The majority of Britons do not consider religion a significant source of identity, and active church membership in Britain, at 15 percent, is very low in comparison with other Western European countries. These seventeenth-century developments became a defining moment for how the British perceive their history to this day. However divisive and disruptive the process of state building may have been originally, its telling and retelling have contributed significantly to a British political culture that celebrates democracy's continuity, gradualism, and tolerance.

In Britain, religious identification has less political significance in voting behavior or party loyalty than in many other countries. By contrast to France, where devout Catholics tend to vote right of center, there is relatively little association between religion and voting behavior in Britain (although Anglicans are a little more likely to vote Conservative). Unlike Germany or Italy, for example, politics in Britain is secular. No parties have religious affiliation, a factor that contributed to the success of the Conservative Party, one of the most successful right-of-center parties in Europe in the twentieth century.

As a consequence, except in Northern Ireland, where religious divisions continue, the party system in the United Kingdom has traditionally reflected class distinctions and remains free of the pattern of multiple parties (particularly right-of-center parties) that occurs in countries where party loyalties are divided by both class and religion.

The Industrial Revolution and the British Empire

Although the British state was consolidated by the seventeenth century, the timing of its industrial development and the way that process transformed Britain's role in the world radically shaped its form. From the mid-eighteenth century onward, the Industrial Revolution involved rapid expansion of manufacturing production and technological innovation. It also led to monumental social and economic transformations and created pressures for democratization. Externally, Britain used its competitive edge to transform and dominate the international order. Internally, the Industrial Revolution helped shape the development of the British state and changed forever the British people's way of life.

The Industrial Revolution. The consequences of the Industrial Revolution for the generations who experienced its upheavals can scarcely be exaggerated. The typical worker was turned "by degrees . . . from small peasant or craftsman into wage-labourer," as historian Eric Hobsbawm observes. Cash and market-based transactions replaced older traditions of barter and production for local need.[2]

Despite a gradual improvement in the standard of living in the English population at large, the effects of industrialization were often profound for agricultural laborers and certain types of artisans. With the commercialization of agriculture, many field laborers lost their security of employment, and cottagers (small landholders) were squeezed off the land in large numbers. The mechanization of manufacturing, which spread furthest in the cotton industry, upset the traditional status of the preindustrial skilled craft workers and permanently marginalized them.

The British Empire. Britain had assumed a significant role as a world power by the end of the seventeenth century, building an overseas empire and engaging actively in international commerce. But it was the Industrial Revolution of the eighteenth century that established global production and exchange on a new and expanded scale, with special consequences for the making of the British state. Cotton manufacture, the driving force behind Britain's growing industrial dominance, not only pioneered the new techniques and changed labor organization during the Industrial Revolution but also represented the perfect imperial industry. It relied on imported raw materials, and, by the turn of the nineteenth century, the industry already depended on overseas markets for the vast majority of its sales of finished goods. Growth depended on foreign markets rather than on domestic consumption. This export orientation fueled an expansion far more rapid than an exclusively domestic orientation would have allowed.

With its leading industrial sector dependent on overseas trade, Britain's leaders worked aggressively to secure markets and expand the empire. Toward these ends, Britain defeated European rivals in a series of military engagements, culminating in the Napoleonic Wars (1803–1815), which confirmed Britain's commercial, military, and geopolitical preeminence. The Napoleonic Wars also secured a balance of power on the European continent, which was favorable for largely unrestricted international commerce (**free trade**). Propelled by the formidable and active presence of the Royal Navy, international trade helped England to take full advantage of its position as the first industrial power. Many scholars suggest that in the middle of the nineteenth century, Britain had the highest per capita income in the world (certainly among the two or three highest), and in 1870, at the height of its glory, its trade represented nearly one-quarter of the world total, and its industrial mastery ensured highly competitive productivity in comparison with trading partners (see Table 2.2).

During the reign of Queen Victoria (1837–1901), the British Empire was immensely powerful and encompassed fully 25 percent of the world's population. Britain presided over a vast formal and informal empire, with extensive direct colonial rule over some four dozen countries, including India and Nigeria. In addition, Britain enjoyed the advantages of an extensive informal empire—a worldwide network of independent states, including China, Iran, and Brazil—whose economic fates were linked to it. Britain ruled as a **hegemonic power**, the state that could control the pattern of alliances and terms of the international economic order, and that often could shape domestic political

Table 2.2		
World Trade and Relative Labor Productivity		
	Proportion of World Trade (%)	Relative Labour Productivity[a] (%)
1870	24.0	1.63
1890	18.5	1.45
1913	14.1	1.15
1938	14.0	0.92

[a]As compared with the average rate of productivity in other members of the world economy.

Source: Robert O. Keohane, *After Hegemony: Cooperation and Discord in the World Economy*, p. 36. Copyright 1984 by Princeton University Press. Reprinted by permission of Princeton University Press.

developments in countries throughout the world. Overall, the making of the British state observed a neat symmetry. Its global power underwrote industrial growth at home. At the same time, the reliance of domestic industry on world markets, beginning with cotton manufacture in the eighteenth century, prompted the government to project British interests overseas as forcefully as possible.

Industrial Change and the Struggle for Voting Rights. The Industrial Revolution shifted economic power from landowners to men of commerce and industry. As a result, the first critical juncture in the long process of democratization began in the late 1820s, when the "respectable opinion" of the propertied classes and increasing popular agitation pressed Parliament to expand the right to vote (franchise) beyond a thin band of men, mainly landowners, with substantial property. With Parliament under considerable pressure, the Reform Act of 1832 extended the franchise to a section of the (male) middle class.

In a very limited way, the Reform Act confirmed the social and political transformations of the Industrial Revolution by granting new urban manufacturing centers, such as Manchester and Birmingham, more substantial representation. However, the massive urban working class created by the Industrial Revolution and populating the cities in the England of Charles

Dickens remained on the outside looking in. In fact, the reform was very narrow and defensive. Before 1832, less than 5 percent of the adult population was entitled to vote—and afterward, only about 7 percent. In extending the franchise so narrowly, the reform underscored the strict property basis for political participation and inflamed class-based tensions in Britain. Following the Reform Act, a massive popular movement erupted in the late 1830s to secure the program of the People's Charter, which included demands for universal male suffrage and other radical reforms intended to make Britain a much more participatory democracy. The Chartist movement, as it was called, held huge, often tumultuous rallies, and organized a vast campaign to petition Parliament, but it failed to achieve any of its aims.

Expansion of the franchise proceeded slowly. The Representation of the People Act of 1867 increased the electorate to just over 16 percent but left cities significantly underrepresented. The Franchise Act of 1884 nearly doubled the size of the electorate, but it was not until the Representation of the People Act of 1918 that suffrage included nearly all adult men and women over age thirty. How slow a process was it? The franchise for men with substantial incomes dated from the fifteenth century, but women between the ages of twenty-one and thirty were not enfranchised until 1928. The voting age for both women and men was lowered to eighteen in 1969. Except for some episodes during the days of the Chartist movement, the struggle for extension of the franchise took place without violence, but its time horizon must be measured in centuries. This is British gradualism—at its best and its worst (see Figure 2.2).

World Wars, Industrial Strife, and the Depression (1914–1945)

With the issue of the franchise finally resolved, in one sense the making of the British state as a democracy was settled. In another important sense, however, the development of the state was just beginning in the twentieth century with the expansion of the state's direct responsibility for management of the economy and the provision of social welfare for citizens. The making of what is sometimes called the *interventionist state* was spurred by two world wars.

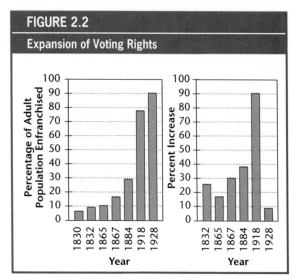

FIGURE 2.2

Expansion of Voting Rights

Expansion of the franchise in Britain was a gradual process. Despite reforms dating from the early nineteenth century, nearly universal adult suffrage was not achieved until 1928.
Source: Jorgen S. Rasmussen, *The British Political Process*, p. 151. Copyright 1993 by Wadsworth Publishing Company. Reprinted with permission of the publisher.

The state's involvement in the economy increased significantly during World War I (1914–1918). It took control of a number of industries, including railways, mining, and shipping. It set prices and restricted the flow of capital abroad and channeled the country's resources into production geared to the war effort. After World War I, it remained active in the management of industry in a rather different way. Amid tremendous industrial disputes, the state wielded its power to fragment the trade union movement and resist demands for workers' control over production and to promote more extensive state ownership of industries. This considerable government manipulation of the economy obviously contradicted the policy of **laissez-faire** (minimal government interference in the operation of economic markets). The tensions between free-market principles and interventionist practices deepened with the Great Depression (which began in 1929 and continued through much of the 1930s) and the experiences of World War II (1939–1945). The fear of depression and the burst of pent-up yearnings for a better life after the war helped transform the role of the state and ushered in a period of unusual political harmony.

Collectivist Consensus (1945–1979)

In the postwar context of shared victory and common misery (almost everyone suffered hardships immediately after the war), reconstruction and dreams of new prosperity and security became more important than ideological conflict. In Britain today, a debate rages among political scientists over whether there was a postwar consensus. Critics of the concept contend that disagreements over specific policies concerning the economy, education, employment, and health, along with an electorate divided on partisan lines largely according to social class, indicated politics as usual.[3] Nevertheless, a broad culture of reconciliation and a determination to rebuild and improve the conditions of life for all Britons helped forge a postwar settlement based broadly on a collectivist consensus that endured until the mid-1970s.

The term *collectivism* was coined to describe the consensus that drove politics in the harmonious postwar period when a significant majority of Britons and all major political parties agreed that the state should take expanded responsibility for economic governance and provide for the social welfare in the broadest terms. They accepted as a matter of faith that governments should work to narrow the gap between rich and poor through public education, national health care, and other policies of the **welfare state**, and they accepted state responsibility for economic growth and full employment. Collectivism brought class-based actors (representatives of labor and management) inside politics and forged a broad consensus about the expanded role of government.

Throughout this period, there was a remarkable unity among electoral combatants. Both the Labour and Conservative mainstream endorsed the principle of state responsibility for the collective good in both economic and social terms. Although modest compared to policies in Europe, the commitment to state management of the economy and provision of social services marked a new era in British politics. In time, however, economic downturn and political stagnation caused the consensus to unravel.

Margaret Thatcher and the Enterprise Culture (1979–1990)

In the 1970s, economic stagnation and the declining competitiveness of key British industries in international markets fueled industrial strife and brought class-based tensions near the surface of politics. No government appeared equal to the tasks of economic management. Each party failed in turn. The Conservative government of Edward Heath (1970–1974) could not resolve the economic problems or the political tensions that resulted from the previously unheard-of combination of increased inflation and reduced growth (stagflation). The Labour government of Harold Wilson and James Callaghan (1974–1979) fared no better. As unions became increasingly disgruntled, the country was beset by a rash of strikes throughout the winter of 1978–1979, the "winter of discontent." Labour's inability to discipline its trade union allies hurt the party in the election, a few months later, in May 1979. The traditional centrist Conservative and Labour alternatives within the collectivist mold seemed exhausted. Many Britons were ready for a new policy agenda.

Margaret Thatcher more than met the challenge. Winning the leadership of the Conservative Party in 1975, she wasted little time in launching a set of bold policy initiatives, which, with characteristic forthrightness, she began to implement after the Conservatives were returned to power in 1979. Reelected in 1983 and 1987, Thatcher served longer without interruption than any other British prime minister in the twentieth century and never lost a general election.

Thatcher transformed British political life by advancing an alternative vision of politics. She was convinced that collectivism had led to Britain's decline by sapping British industry and permitting powerful and self-serving unions to hold the country for ransom. To reverse Britain's relative economic slide, Thatcher sought to jump-start the economy by cutting taxes, reducing social services where possible, and using government policy to stimulate competitiveness and efficiency in the private sector.

The term *Thatcherism* embraces her distinctive leadership style, her economic and political strategies, as well as her traditional cultural values: individual responsibility, commitment to family, frugality, and an affirmation of the entrepreneurial spirit. These values combined nostalgia for the past and rejection of permissiveness and disorder. Taken together, they were referred to as the *enterprise culture*. They stood as a reproach and an alternative to collectivism.

In many ways, Margaret Thatcher's leadership as prime minister (1979–1990) marks a critical dividing line in postwar British politics. She set the tone and redefined the goals of British politics like few others before her. In November 1990, a leadership challenge within Thatcher's own Conservative Party, largely over her anti-EU stance and high-handed leadership style, caused her sudden resignation and replacement by John Major. Major served as prime minister from 1990 to 1997, leading the Conservative Party to a victory in the 1992 general election before succumbing to the New Labour of Tony Blair and Gordon Brown in 1997.

New Labour's Third Way

Under the leadership of Blair and Brown, the Labour party was determined to thoroughly modernize the Labour Party. Although its official name did not change, the party was reinvented as New Labour—a party committed to modernization that promised to fundamentally recast British politics. It offered a "third-way" alternative to Thatcherism and the collectivism of traditional Labour. New Labour rejected the notion of interest-based politics, in which unions and working people naturally look to Labour and businesspeople and the more prosperous look to the Conservatives. Labour won in 1997 by drawing support from across the socioeconomic spectrum. It rejected the historic ties between Labour governments and the trade union movement. It emphasized the virtues of a partnership with business.

It also promised new approaches to economic, welfare, and social policy that emphasized the rights of citizens to assistance only if they took the responsibility to get the needed education and training; and New Labour emphasized British leadership in Europe. Blair undertook far-reaching constitutional changes to revitalize democratic participation. Labour would devolve (transfer) specified powers from the central government to Scotland, Wales, and Northern Ireland.

In the early months of his premiership, Blair displayed effective leadership after Lady Diana's death

and in his aggressive efforts to achieve a potentially historic peace agreement for Northern Ireland. Soon, however, many began to suggest that Blair was better at coming up with innovative-sounding ideas than at implementing effective policy (it was said that New Labour was "more spin than substance"). In addition, Blair's popularity suffered from a set of crises—from a set of fatal train crashes beginning in 1997 to protests over the cost of petrol (gasoline) in September 2000 to an outbreak of mad cow disease in spring 2001. Nevertheless, until the war in Iraq, Blair remained a popular and charismatic leader. A few months before September 11, 2001, New Labour won what it most sought: an electoral mandate in June 2001 for a second successive term. But then its luck began to change.

After September 11. In the aftermath of the September 11, 2001, attacks on the World Trade Center and the Pentagon, Blair showed decisive leadership in assuming the role of a key ally to the United States in the war on terror. Since Britain was willing and able to lend moral, diplomatic, and military support, September 11 lent new credence to the **special relationship**—a bond of language, culture, and national interests, which creates an unusually close alliance—that has governed U.S.–UK relations for fifty years and catapulted Blair to high visibility in world affairs. Before long, however, especially when the central focus of the war on terror moved from Afghanistan to Iraq, many Britons became disenchanted. Blair's willingness to run interference with allies and add intellectual ballast to President George W. Bush's post–9/11 plans was a big help to the United States. However, it also locked Britain into a set of policies over which it had little or no control, it vastly complicated relationships with France and Germany (which opposed the war), and it generated hostility toward the United Kingdom in much of the Arab and Muslim world.

A series of devastating bombings in London on July 7, 2005 (the date of 7/7 is emblazoned in the collective memory like 9/11) was perpetrated by UK citizens who were Muslim and timed to correspond with the G-8 summit in Gleneagle, Scotland. They appeared to confirm that Britain faced heightened security risks because of its participation in the war. Attempted terror attacks in London and Glasgow in

A PLACE IN THE HISTORY BOOKS

In the early years of his premiership, it seemed likely that Blair would leave a glittering legacy behind as modernizer and architect of the Third Way. But Blair's commitment to the "special relationship" led Britain into the war in Iraq, and when no weapons of mass destruction were found, he seemed trapped, his legacy falling down around him.   *Source:* © Ingram Pinn, Financial Times, May 12, 2007.

July 2007 increased the sense of insecurity. Finally, the war in Iraq, which had grown even more unpopular in the UK, eroded Blair's popularity beyond redemption. In addition, the conviction among many Britons that Blair had led them into war under false premises permanently weakened his credibility and tarnished the legacy of New Labour while Blair was at the helm.

As Brown became prime minister, many on both sides of the Atlantic wondered how Brown—who has kept a low profile on the war in Iraq—would reshape the special relationship between the United States and the United Kingdom. What steps would he take to limit the casualties to British forces in Iraq and Afghanistan and to separate his policy in Iraq from that of his predecessor?

Themes and Implications

The processes that came together in these historical junctures continue to influence developments today in powerful and complex ways. The four core themes in this book, introduced in Part I, highlight some of the most important features of British politics.

Historical Junctures and Political Themes

The first theme suggests that a country's relative position in the world of states influences its ability to manage domestic and international challenges. A weaker international standing makes it difficult for a country to control international events or insulate itself from external pressures. Britain's ability to control the terms of trade and master political alliances during the height of its imperial power in the nineteenth century confirms this maxim, but times have changed.

Through the gradual process of decolonization Britain fell to second-tier status. Its formal empire began to shrink in the interwar period (1919–1939) as the "white dominions" of Canada, Australia, and New Zealand gained independence. In Britain's Asian, Middle Eastern, and African colonies, pressure for political reforms leading to independence deepened during World War II and in the immediate postwar period. Beginning with the formal independence of India and Pakistan in 1947, an enormous empire of dependent colonies more or less dissolved in less than twenty years. Finally, in 1997, Britain returned the commercially vibrant crown colony of Hong Kong to China. The process of decolonization ended any realistic claim for Britain to be a dominant player in world politics.

Is Britain a world power or just a middle-of-the-pack country in Europe? It appears to be both. On the one hand, as a legacy of its role in World War II, Britain sits as a permanent member of the United Nations Security Council. On the other hand, Britain invariably plays second fiddle in its special relationship to the United States, a show of relative weakness that has exposed British foreign policy to extraordinary pressures, especially since September 11. In addition, British governments face persistent challenges in their dealings with the EU. Can Britain afford to remain aloof from the fast-paced changes of economic integration symbolized by the adoption of a common currency, the euro, by a majority of the countries in the EU—but not by Britain?

A second theme examines the strategies employed in governing the economy. Since the dawn of Britain's Industrial Revolution, prosperity at home has relied on superior competitiveness abroad. This is even truer in today's environment of intensified international competition and global production. Will Britain's "less-is-more" laissez-faire approach to economic governance, invigorated by business partnerships, survive the daunting challenges of the 2008 global financial crisis? Can Britain achieve a durable economic model without fuller integration into Europe?

A third theme is the potent political influence of the democratic idea, the universal appeal of core values associated with parliamentary democracy as practiced first in the United Kingdom. Even in Britain, issues about democratic governance, citizen participation, and constitutional reform have been renewed with considerable force.

The traditionally respected royal family has been rocked by scandal and improprieties. Few reject the monarchy outright, but questions about the role of the monarchy helped place on the agenda broader issues about citizen control over government and constitutional reform. In addition, long-settled issues about the constitutional form and unity of the state have also reemerged with unexpected force. How can the interests of England, Wales, Scotland, and Northern Ireland be balanced within a single nation-state?

Finally, we come to the fourth theme, collective identities, which considers how individuals define who they are politically in terms of group attachments, come together to pursue political goals, and face their status as political insiders or outsiders. Through the immigration of former colonial subjects to the United Kingdom, decolonization helped create a multiracial and multiethnic society. Issues of race, ethnicity, and cultural identity have challenged the long-standing British values of tolerance and consensus. Indeed, the concept of "Britishness"—what the country stands for and who comprises the political community—has come under intense scrutiny, especially since 9/11, and in the aftermath of the bombings of the London transport system by British Muslims in July 2005.

Implications for Comparative Politics

Britain's privileged position in comparative politics textbooks follows naturally from its historical firsts. Britain was the first nation to industrialize. For much of the nineteenth century, the British Empire was the world's dominant power, with a vast network of colonies throughout the world. Britain was also the first nation to develop an effective parliamentary democracy.

For these reasons, British politics is often studied as a model of representative government. Named after the building that houses the British legislature in London, the **Westminster model** emphasizes that democracy rests on the supreme authority of a legislature—in Britain's case, the Parliament. Finally, Britain has served as a model of gradual and peaceful evolution of democratic government in a world where transitions to democracy are often turbulent, interrupted, and uncertain.

The pressures of global competitiveness and the perceived advantages of a "one size fits all" style of minimalist government have encouraged the movement in many countries toward neoliberal approaches for economic management. A legacy from Thatcher's Britain, **neoliberalism** is a touchstone premise of Gordon Brown's New Labour government. Policies aim to promote free competition among firms, to interfere with entrepreneurs and managers as little as possible, and to create a business-friendly environment to attract foreign investment and spur innovation.

This section analyzes and evaluates the range of strategies that Britain has applied in the post–World War II period for managing the economy, culminating in New Labour's economic and social model. We then consider, in turn, the social consequences of economic developments, and the political repercussions of Britain's position in the international economic order.

State and Economy

Thirty years ago, there was not much to admire in the British economy. Growth was low, and unemployment was high, and in 1976 the country received a Third World–style bailout from the International Monetary Fund to help stabilize the economy. Britain was routinely called the "sick man of Europe." Then times changed for the better. From the mid-1990s until the widening turmoil in financial markets spurred by the mortgage crisis that erupted in the United States in 2007, Britain avoided the high unemployment and recession that has plagued many of the member nations of the European Union (EU). In fact, in 2006 Britain ranked second in income per capita, up from fifth when New Labour took office in 1997.

In general, the British economy reveals a two-track character, with growth in the service sector—the UK is especially competitive in financial services—offsetting a much weaker industrial sector performance. The British economy stands up well in knowledge-intensive high-technology industrial sectors, which account for one-quarter of the country's total exports. International comparisons also reveal superior microeconomic competitiveness, with first- or second-place

rankings in global comparisons of national business environment and company operations and strategy.

On the negative side, however, must be counted a productivity gap in manufacturing between the United Kingdom and key competitors, a persistent deficit in the UK balance of trade, as well as ongoing concern about low rates of domestic investment and spending on research and development. The rising costs of fuel, declining housing values, and the credit crunch are squeezing the economy. By spring 2008, Britain had joined the recessionary club, with growth forecast below 2 percent for 2009. By fall 2008, unemployment, was about 5 and a half percent and creeping upward, still low by European standards, and lower than that in the U.S. However, official Bank of England estimates predicted that growth would be flat for the year, the UK currency was losing value, inflation was expected to hit 5 percent in 2008, and the housing market was collapsing.

The economy New Labour inherited after eighteen years of Conservative stewardship was both prosperous and troubled. It was still in decline relative to the performance of key competitors, but it exhibited a long and significant growth performance relative to British performance. But despite New Labour's best efforts to claim full credit for the longest run of uninterrupted growth since 1701, in fact more than a third of that run came under the Conservatives.[4]

Despite that success, the British economy had been going through, and was continuing to experience, a set of radical shifts that created great political challenges—and headaches. In a few unsettling decades, it had shifted from heavy industry to a predominantly service economy. It was rapidly shedding labor and, from 1983, for the first time since the industrial revolution, it became (as it remains today) a net importer of manufactured goods. So New Labour inherited growth along with economic troubles: relatively weak competitiveness and key industrial sectors that were losing ground to rivals. In short, when Gordon Brown took ultimate responsibility for the economy in 1997, he found a platform for economic stability in the making but, at the same time, not just an economy, but also a society in need of reform—one that was not so easy to govern.[5]

It was an aging society, one with the **gender gap** in voting (in which women favored the Conservatives) and in experiences of work (with women very significantly overrepresented in part-time and nonstandard work). David Coates aptly describes this troubled economic, social, and political context marked by tensions and frustrations, a "patchwork Britain," of vastly disparate experiences of life—with some, especially in London, enjoying a style of life and living standards as elevated as any in the world, while others lived in Second World (the term used for the Soviet Bloc during the cold war) conditions of grim run-down housing estates and the near-certainty of long-term unemployment.

Economic Management

Like all other states, whatever their commitment to free markets, the British state intervenes in economic life, sometimes with considerable force. However, the British have not developed institutions for state-sponsored economic planning or industrial policy. Instead, the British state has generally limited its role to broad policy instruments designed to influence the economy generally (**macroeconomic policy**) by adjusting state revenues and expenditures to achieve short-term goals. The Treasury and the Bank of England dominate economic policy, which has often seemed reactive and relatively ineffectual. Despite other differences, this generally reactive and minimalist orientation of economic management strategies bridges the first two eras of postwar politics in Britain: the consensus era (1945–1979) and the period of Thatcherite policy orientation (1979–1997). How has the orientation of economic policy developed and changed during the postwar period?

The Consensus Era. When it took control of crucial industries during World War I and assumed active management of industry in the interwar years, the state assumed a more interventionist role that belied its laissez-faire traditions. After World War II, the sense of unity inspired by the shared suffering of war and the need to rebuild a war-ravaged country crystallized the collectivist consensus as the British state broadened and deepened its responsibilities for the overall performance of the economy.

The state nationalized some key industries, assuming direct ownership of them. It also accepted the responsibility to secure low levels of unemployment (a policy of full employment), expand social services, maintain a steady rate of growth (increase the output or GDP), keep prices stable, and achieve desirable balance-of-payments and exchange rates. The approach is called Keynesian demand management, or **Keynesianism** (after the British economist John Maynard Keynes, 1883–1946). State budget deficits were used to expand demand in an effort to boost both consumption and investment when the economy was slowing. Cuts in government spending and a tightening of credit and finance, by contrast, were used to cool demand when high rates of growth brought fears of inflation or a deficit in balance of payments. Taken together, this new agenda of expanded economic management and welfare provision, sometimes referred to as the Keynesian welfare state, directed government policy throughout the era of the collectivist consensus.

Before Thatcher became leader of the Conservative Party in 1975, Conservative leaders in Britain generally accepted the terms of the collectivist consensus. By the 1970s, however, public officials no longer saw the world they understood and could master. From 1974 to 1979, the Labour government of Harold Wilson and James Callaghan reinforced the impression that governments could no longer control the swirl of events. The beginning of the end came when trade unions became increasingly restive under the pinch of voluntary wage restraints that had been pressed on them by the Labour government. Frustrated by wage increases that were well below inflation rates, the unions broke with the government in 1978. The number of unofficial work stoppages increased, and official strikes followed—all fueled by a seemingly endless series of leapfrogging pay demands that erupted throughout the winter of 1978–1979 (the "winter of discontent"). There is little doubt that the industrial unrest that dramatized Labour's inability to manage its allies, the trade unions, contributed a great deal to Thatcher's electoral victory a few months later in May 1979. The winter of discontent helped write the conclusion to Britain's collectivist consensus and discredit the Keynesian welfare state.

Thatcherite Policy Orientation. In policy terms, the economic orientations of Thatcher and Major signaled a rejection of Keynesianism. In its place, monetarism emerged as the new economic doctrine. Monetarism assumed that there is a "natural rate of unemployment" determined by the labor market itself. State intervention to steer the economy should be limited to a few steps that would help foster appropriate rates of growth in the money supply and keep inflation low. Monetarism reflected a radical change from the postwar consensus regarding economic management. Not only was active government intervention considered unnecessary; it was seen as undesirable and destabilizing.

New Labour's Economic Policy Approach. From the start of New Labour's time in office, Gordon Brown as chancellor—and later as prime minister—insisted on establishing a "platform of stability." Above all, Brown was determined to reduce public debt. Only as he turned that debt into a surplus did the "Iron Chancellor" reinvent himself as a more conventional Labour chancellor. During his last few years as chancellor, Brown used economic growth to increase spending (rather than cut taxes). The money spent on the National Health Service (NHS) and on education rose dramatically from 2006 to 2008.

In some ways, government policy seems to pursue conventional market-reinforcing and probusiness policies (neoliberalism). In other ways, the New Labour program stands as an alternative to both Thatcherite monetarism and traditional Keynesianism. Does the third way represent a genuine departure in economic policy?

Just as Keynesianism inspired Old Labour, **new growth theory** allowed New Labour to embrace globalization as something positive, to be welcomed, as a rising historical tide—one that the center-left was uniquely well placed to understand and exploit. According to this theory, which Gordon Brown embraced and vigorously applied, a high-skill labor force tilted toward high-tech applications spurs growth and competitiveness.

Brown argues that since capital is international, mobile, and not subject to control, industrial policy and planning that focus on the domestic economy alone are futile. Rather, government should improve the quality of labor through education and training, maintain the labor market flexibility inherited from the Thatcher regime, and attract investment to Britain. Strict controls of inflation and tough limits on public expenditure help promote both employment and investment opportunities. New Labour is very focused on designing and implementing policies that will create new jobs and get people, particularly young people, into the work force in increasingly high-skill and high-tech jobs.

Political Implications of Economic Policy. Differences in economic doctrine are not what matter most in policy terms. In fact, British governments in the past have never consistently followed any economic theory, whether Keynesianism or monetarism or new growth theory. Today, the economic policy of New Labour is pragmatic and eclectic. The political consequences of economic orientations are more significant: each economic doctrine helps to justify a broad moral and cultural vision of society, provide motives for state policy, and advance alternative sets of values. Should the government intervene, work to reduce inequalities through the mildly redistributive provisions of the welfare state, and sustain the ethos of a caring society (collectivism/"Old Labour")? Should it back off and allow the market to function competitively and in that way promote entrepreneurship, competitiveness, and individual autonomy (Thatcherism)? Or should it help secure an inclusive "stakeholder" economy in which business has the flexibility, security, and mobility to compete and workers have the skills and training to participate effectively in the global labor market (New Labour)? As these questions make clear, economic management strategies are closely linked to social or welfare policy.

Social Policy

The social and political role of the welfare state depends as much on policy goals and instruments as on spending levels. Does the state provide services itself or offer cash benefits that can be used to purchase services from private providers? Are benefits universal, or are they limited to those who fall below an income threshold (means-tested)? Are they designed to meet the temporary needs of individuals or to help reduce the gap between rich and poor?

The expanded role of government during World War II and the increased role of the Labour Party during the wartime coalition government led by Winston

Churchill prepared the way for the development of the welfare state in Britain. The 1943 Beveridge Report provided a blueprint for an extensive but, in comparative European terms, fairly moderate set of provisions. In general, welfare state provisions interfere relatively little in the workings of the market, and policymakers do not see the reduction of group inequalities as the proper goal of the welfare state. The NHS provides comprehensive universal medical care and has long been championed as the jewel in the crown of the welfare state in Britain, but it remains an exception to the rule. Compared with other Western European countries, the welfare state in Britain offers relatively few comprehensive services, and its policies are not very generous.

The Welfare State under Thatcher and Major. The record on social expenditure by Conservative governments from 1979 to 1997 was mixed. Given Britons' strong support for public education, pensions, and health care, Conservative governments attempted less reform than many at first anticipated. The Thatcher and Major governments encouraged private, alongside public, provisions in education, health care (insurance), and pensions. They worked to increase efficiency in social services, reduced the value of some benefits by changing the formulas or reducing cost-of-living adjustments, and contracted out some services (purchasing them from private contractors rather than providing them directly). In addition, in policy reforms reminiscent of U.S. "workfare" requirements, they tried to reduce dependency by denying benefits to youths who refused to participate in training programs. Despite these efforts, the commitment to reduced spending could not be sustained, partly because a recession required increases in income support and unemployment benefits.

To some degree, however, this general pattern masks specific and, in some cases, highly charged policy changes in both expenditures and the institutionalized pattern of provision. In housing, the changes in state policy and provision were the most extensive, with repercussions in electoral terms and in changing the way Britons think about the welfare state. By 1990, more than 1.25 million council houses (public housing maintained by local government) were sold, particularly the attractive single-family homes

with gardens (quite unlike public housing in the United States). Two-thirds of the sales went to rental tenants. Thatcher's housing policy was extremely popular. By one calculation, between 1979 and 1983 there was a swing (a change in the percentage of the vote received by the two major parties) to the Conservative Party of 17 percent among those who had bought their council houses.[6]

Despite great Conservative success in the campaign to privatize housing, a strong majority of Britons remain stalwart supporters of the principle of collective provision for their basic needs. And so there were limits on the government's ability to reduce social spending or change institutional behavior. For example, in 1989, the Conservative government tried to introduce market practices into the NHS, with general practitioners managing funds and purchasing hospital care for their patients. Many voiced fears that the reforms would create a two-tier system of medical care for one system for the rich and one for the poor.

More generally, a lack of confidence in the Conservatives on social protection hurt Major substantially in 1992, and it has continued to plague the party. Nothing propelled the Labour landslide in 1997 more than the concern for the "caring" issues. The traditional advantage Labour enjoys on these issues also helped secure victory for Blair in June 2001 and again, in 2005, when he needed a boost from traditional Labour supporters to offset their opposition to the prime minister on the war in Iraq.

New Labour Social Policy. As with economic policy, New Labour sees social policy as an opportunity for government to balance pragmatism and innovation, while borrowing from traditional Labour as well as from Thatcherite options. Thus, Blair and Brown rejected both the attempted retrenchment of Conservative governments that seemed mean-spirited as well as the egalitarian traditions of Britain's collectivist era that emphasized entitlements. Instead, New Labour focuses its policy on training and broader social investment as a more positive third-way alternative. At the same time, New Labour draws political strength from the "Old Labour" legacy of commitment on the "caring" social policy issues.

Under New Labour, the approach to social provision has been refined, with social policy now directed by the Department for Work and Pensions (DWP), focused on ensuring support systems for children and eliminating child poverty, providing benefits and counseling for the unemployed, coordinating disability policy, and more comprehensive retirement planning assistance and benefits for retired people. DWP reflects the modernizing ethos of New Labour, "promoting work as the best form of welfare," and trying to make the bureaucracy more user-friendly—rather than referring to clients or beneficiaries of the welfare state, DWP calls them *customer groups*.

Following Bill Clinton, Blair's New Democratic counterpart in the United States, prime minister Blair promised a modernized, leaner welfare state, in which people are actively encouraged to seek work. The reform of the welfare state emphasizes efficiencies and tries to break welfare dependency. Efforts to spur entry into the labor market combine carrots and sticks. A signature policy initiative of Chancellor Brown, the government offered positive inducements including training programs, especially targeted at youth, combined with incentives to private industry to hire new entrants to the labor market. The threats include eligibility restrictions and reductions in coverage. Referred to as the "New Deal" for the young unemployed, welfare reform in the United Kingdom has emphasized concerted efforts to create pathways out of dependence. Although beginning with a focus on moving youth from welfare to work, New Deal reform efforts expanded in several directions.

The New Deal quickly extended to single parents and the long-term unemployed. In 1999, the government launched a "Bridging the Gap" initiative to provide a more comprehensive approach for assisting sixteen- to eighteen-year-olds not already engaged in education, employment, or training to achieve clear goals by age nineteen through a variety of "pathways" (academic, vocational, or occupational). "Better Government for Older People" was launched in 1998, which was followed quickly by "All Our Futures," a government report issued in the summer of 2000 with twenty-eight recommendations to improve the quality of life and the delivery of public services for senior citizens. A new initiative, the IT New Deal, was launched in 2001 as a government-business partnership to address skill shortages in information technologies.

Although doubts remain about the follow-through and effectiveness of New Labour social and welfare policy initiatives, the intent to create innovative policies and approach social policy in new and more comprehensive ways is clearly there. Late in 1997, the government inaugurated the Social Exclusion Unit. It was charged broadly with addressing "what can happen when people or areas suffer from such problems as unemployment, poor skills, low incomes, poor housing, high crime environments, bad health, and family breakdown." This effort to identify comprehensive solutions to society's ills and reduce the tendency for government to let marginalized individuals fall by the wayside captures the third-way orientation of the New Labour project. In addition, since January 2005, the payment of vouchers to the parents of all British children born since 2002, with a promise to top up the funds periodically, represented an innovative effort to provide a sizeable nest egg of savings available for eighteen-year-olds. This "asset-based" welfare held the promise of reducing poverty and providing a new generation with new economic opportunities.

Nevertheless, New Labour, like all governments in Britain and in many other countries, will be accountable above all for the failure or success of more traditional social policies, especially health care and education. After years of skepticism about New Labour's ability to deliver on promised improvements in providing key public services, by 2005 the tides of opinion—and massive budgetary increases—were beginning to have the desired effect. New Labour had gained considerable credibility on health care as well as education, and increasing success on core policies gave Labour a huge boost heading into the 2005 election. It is also true, however, that Gordon Brown inherited some significant problems with the delivery of key public services, such as health care. Despite the unprecedented increase in resources, health care remains a huge headache for New Labour and Gordon Brown. New Labour's internal market health care reforms have left the system with increasingly untenable deficits. Some hospital trusts are ominously near collapse. Brown needs to find the recipe to provide health care—and other public services such as education—on a sound financial footing and to reassure a restive electorate that the quality of services is high and equitably accessed.

Society and Economy

What were the *distributional effects* of the economic and social policies of Thatcher and Major—the consequences for group patterns of wealth and poverty? To what extent have the policies of the Labour governments headed by Blair and Brown continued—or reversed—these trends? How has government policy influenced the condition of minorities and women? It is impossible to be sure when government policy creates a given distribution of resources and when poverty increases or decreases because of a general downturn or upswing in the economy. The evidence is clear, however, that economic inequality grew in Britain during the 1980s before it stabilized or narrowed slightly in the mid-1990s, and that ethnic minorities and women continue to experience significant disadvantages.

In general, policies initiated by the Conservative Party, particularly during the Thatcher years, deepened inequalities. The economic upturn that began in 1992, combined with Major's moderating effects on the Thatcherite social policy agenda, served to narrow inequality by the mid-1990s. Since 1997, as one observer noted, Labour has "pursued redistribution by stealth, raising various indirect levies on the better-off to finance tax breaks for poorer workers."[7] As a result, Britain has witnessed a modest downward redistribution of income since 1997, although the downward slide of the economy will make that difficult to sustain. Attention to social exclusion in its many forms, a 1999 pledge by the prime minister to eradicate child poverty (even though Britain at the time had one of the highest rates of child poverty in EU Europe), and strong rates of growth seemed to bode well for a further narrowing of the gap between rich and poor in Britain, especially among children. But, despite a strong commitment by both Blair and Brown, the efforts to reduce childhood poverty have not succeeded.

The *Innocenti Report Card* (2007), published by UNICEF, puts a very sobering spotlight on New Labour's high-profile commitment to end childhood poverty in the UK. In this careful assessment of the comparative performance of 21 OECD countries in securing the well-being of children, European countries generally score very well. In fact, in the rankings based on an index that includes measures of relative income poverty, households without jobs, and reported deprivation, to assess the material well-being of children, four European countries—the Netherlands, Sweden, Denmark, and Finland—are at the top of the league tables comparing the twenty-one countries analyzed. However, both the United States and the United Kingdom are in the bottom third for five of the six dimensions under review. Worse still, in the summary table that presents the overall rankings, the UK comes in dead last, just behind the United States (see Figure 2.3).

Inequality and Ethnic Minorities

Poverty and diminished opportunity disproportionately affect ethnic minorities (a term applied to peoples of nonEuropean origin from the former British colonies in the Indian subcontinent, the Caribbean, and Africa). Official estimates place the ethnic minority population in Britain at 4.7 million or 7.9 percent of the total population of the United Kingdom. Indians comprise the largest ethnic minority, at 21.7 percent; Pakistanis represent 16.7 percent, Bangladeshis, 6.1 percent, and Afro-Caribbeans and other blacks, 27.1 percent.[8] Because of past immigration and fertility patterns, the ethnic minority population in the United Kingdom is considerably younger than the white population. More than one-third of the ethnic minority population is younger than sixteen, nearly half is under twenty-five, and more than four-fifths is under age forty-five. Despite the common and often disparaging reference to ethnic minority individuals as "immigrants," the experience of members of ethnic minority groups is increasingly that of a native-born population.[9]

Ethnic minority individuals, particularly young men, have experienced cultural isolation as well as marginalization in the educational system, job training, housing, and labor markets. In general, poor rates of economic success reinforce isolation and distinct collective identities. Variations among ethnic minority communities are quite considerable, however, and there are some noteworthy success stories. For example, among men of African, Asian, Chinese, and Indian descent, the proportional representation in the managerial and professional ranks is actually higher than

FIGURE 2.3

Child Well-Being in Rich Countries

Countries are listed here in order of their average rank for the six dimensions of child well-being that have been assessed.* A light gray background indicates a place in the top third of the table; mid-gray denotes the middle third; and dark gray the bottom third.

Dimensions of Child Well-being	Average Ranking Position (for all 6 dimensions)	Dimension 1 Material Well-being	Dimension 2 Health and Safety	Dimension 3 Educational Well-being	Dimension 4 Family and Peer Relationships	Dimension 5 Behaviors and Risks	Dimension 6 Subjective Well-being
Netherlands	4.2	10	2	6	3	3	1
Sweden	5.0	1	1	5	15	1	7
Denmark	7.2	4	4	8	9	6	12
Finland	7.5	3	3	4	17	7	11
Spain	8.0	12	6	15	8	5	2
Switzerland	8.3	5	9	14	4	12	6
Norway	8.7	2	8	11	10	13	8
Italy	10.0	14	5	20	1	10	10
Ireland	10.2	19	19	7	7	4	5
Belgium	10.7	7	16	1	5	19	16
Germany	11.2	13	11	10	13	11	9
Canada	11.8	6	13	2	18	17	15
Greece	11.8	15	18	16	11	8	3
Poland	12.3	21	15	3	14	2	19
Czech Republic	12.5	11	10	9	19	9	17
France	13.0	9	7	18	12	14	18
Portugal	13.7	16	14	21	2	15	14
Austria	13.8	8	20	19	16	16	4
Hungary	14.5	20	17	13	6	18	13
United States	18.0	17	21	12	20	20	–
United Kingdom	18.2	18	12	17	21	21	20

* OECD countries with insufficient data to be included in the overview: Australia, Iceland, Japan, Luxembourg, Mexico, New Zealand, the Slovak Republic, South Korea, Turkey.

Despite a strong commitment by New Labour to end child poverty, Britain comes in last in a comparison of child well-being among twenty-one wealthy countries.

Source: UNICEF, Child poverty in perspective. An overview of child well-being in rich countries. *Innocenti Report Card No. 7,* 2007. UNICEF Innocenti Research Centre, Florence. © The United Nations Children's Fund, 2007.

that for white men (although they are much less likely to be senior managers in large firms). Also, Britons of South Asian and, especially, Indian descent enjoy a high rate of entrepreneurship. Despite some variations, however, employment opportunities for women from all minority ethnic groups are limited.[10] In addition, a distinct gap remains between the job opportunities available to whites and those open to ethnic minorities. It is clear that people from ethnic minority communities are overrepresented among low-income households in the United Kingdom (see Figure 2.4). Almost 60 percent of Pakistani or Bangladeshi households are in low-income households (defined by income below 60 percent of the median). Just under half of black nonCaribbean households also live on low incomes after housing costs are deducted, as do nearly one-third of black Caribbeans. In contrast, only 16 percent of white people live in such low-income households before housing

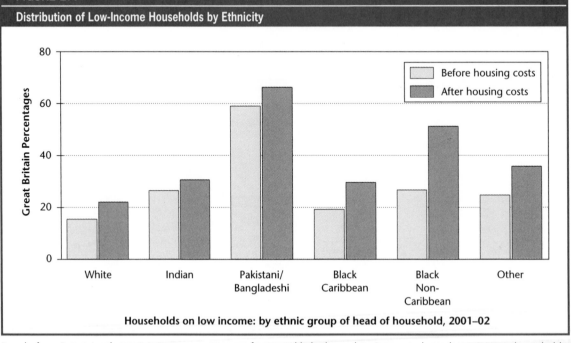

FIGURE 2.4

Distribution of Low-Income Households by Ethnicity

Households on low income: by ethnic group of head of household, 2001–02

People from Britain's ethnic minority communities are far more likely than white Britons to be in lower-income households, although there are important differences among ethnic minority groups. Nearly 60 percent of Pakistani or Bangladeshi households are low-income households, while about one-third of black Caribbean households live on low incomes.

Source: National Statistics Online: www.statistics.gov.uk/CCI/nugget.asp?ID=269&Pos=1&ColRank=2&Rank=384.

costs are deducted, and 21 percent after housing costs are deducted.[11]

The human side behind the statistics reveals how difficult it remains in Britain for ethnic minorities to achieve top posts and how uneven the prospects of success are, despite some pockets of modest success. It seems that the police have been more effective in recent years in recruiting and retaining ethnic minority police officers, and moving them up through the ranks, but the further-education colleges (nondegree-giving institutions providing mainly vocational training for sixteen- to eighteen-year-olds not headed to university) have not done so well. "We don't have one black college principal in London in spite of having one of the most ethnically diverse student populations in the country," observed the mayor of London's senior policy director in 2004. "There are many more young Afro-Caribbean men in prison than there are in university, and more black Met [London police]

officers than there are teachers."[12] Ethnic minority police officers now make up 3 percent of the United Kingdom's 122,000-member police force, but only 2 percent of junior and middle managers in the more than four hundred colleges in Britain, only five of which have ethnic minority principals. It speaks volumes about the level of ethnic minority inequality that a 3 percent representation of ethnic minority police officers is considered evidence that "the police have in recent years been undertaking a much-needed overhaul of equal opportunities."[13]

Inequality and Women

Women's participation in the labor market when compared to that of men also indicates marked patterns of inequality. In fact, most women in Britain work part-time, often in jobs with fewer than sixteen hours of work per week and often with fewer than eight hours (in contrast, fewer than one in every fifteen men is employed part-time). More than three-quarters of women working part-time report that they did not want a full-time job, yet more women than men (in raw numbers, not simply as a percentage) take on second jobs. Although employment conditions for women in Britain trail those of many of their EU counterparts, the gap in the differential between weekly earnings of men and women in the United Kingdom has narrowed. In fact, the gender gap in pay based on median hourly earnings has narrowed from 17.4 percent in 1997 to 12.6 percent in 2006, the lowest value since records have been kept. That's the good news. The bad news is that the part-time gender pay gap (based on a comparison of the hourly wage of men working full-time and women working part-time) for 2006 was 40.2 percent.[14]

New Labour remains committed to gender equality in the workplace and has affirmed its resolve to address women's concerns to balance work and family responsibilities. The government has implemented a set of family-friendly work-related policies, including parental leave and flexible working arrangements and working times. Most of these initiatives only reach the minimum EU standard as required by treaty commitments (under Blair the UK entered into a set of EU treaties governing workers' rights and related social issues from which it had previously opted out). Other measures include a commitment in principle to filling half of all public appointments with women, a review of the pension system to ensure better coverage for women, draft legislation to provide for the sharing of pensions after divorce, tax credits for working families as well as for childcare, and a National Childcare Strategy, to which the Blair government committed extensive financial support and gave high visibility. Nevertheless, the gap between childcare supply and demand is considerable, and the cost for many families remains prohibitive. Moreover, despite its efforts to make it easier for women to balance work and family obligations, "Labour has focused its efforts on persuading employers as to the 'business case' for 'family friendly' working conditions."[15]

This approach limits New Labour's agenda, as witnessed by the government's willingness to let employers opt out of a forty-eight-hour ceiling on the work week (a serious impediment to a healthy family-work balance, especially since UK fathers work the longest hours in Europe).[16] Thus, New Labour's core commitment to management flexibility makes it likely that the general pattern of female labor market participation will change relatively little in the years ahead. A report commissioned by the Cabinet Office's Women's Unit confirms that there is a significant pattern of inequality in lifetime earnings of men and women with an equal complement of skills, defined by both a gender gap and a "mother gap."

Britain in the Global Economy

Britain plays a particular role within the European and international economy, one that has been reinforced by international competitive pressures in this global age. For a start, **foreign direct investment** (FDI) favors national systems, like those of Britain (and the United States), that rely more on private contractual and market-driven arrangements and less on state capacity and political or institutional arrangements. Because of such factors as low costs, political climate, government-sponsored financial incentives, reduced trade union power, and a large pool of potential nonunionized recruits, Britain is a highly regarded location in Europe for FDI. In fact, in 2006 it placed second in the world behind the U.S. in FDI inflows.

The UK scores extremely well in international comparisons of microeconomic competitiveness and growth competitiveness. The competitive strengths of the UK economy are confirmed in some key benchmarks used in the *Global Competitiveness Report, 2005–2006*, published by the World Economic Forum.[17] The UK ranked thirteenth in growth competitiveness and sixth in business competitiveness, with very high rankings for the quality of the national business environment (6), financial market sophistication (1), and, perhaps a mixed blessing, the extent of incentive compensation (1). Britain also displays areas of competitive disadvantage: national savings rate (98), real effective exchange rate (87), and government success in ICT promotion and quality of math and science education (47). This last point was both generalized and reinforced by the results of an executive opinion survey in which respondents rated an inadequately educated workforce as the most troubling factor for doing business in the UK.[18]

On balance, the report indicates success in economic competitiveness, but does not provide heartening news on the new growth theory front, since competitive disadvantages are clustered in the key areas of education and technology acquisition and diffusion, not to mention the availability of scientists and engineers, where the UK ranks 41, below Vietnam and Romania and just above Turkey and Ghana.

Nor does the OECD improve the assessment. The most recent OECD UK survey (conducted in 2005) states, "A wide range of indicators suggests that UK innovation performance has been mediocre in international comparisons," (it ranks sixth among the G7, down from a rank of second, behind Germany, in the early 1980s). The OECD survey also emphasizes the UK's considerable strength in knowledge-intensive services, and points to success in an area that Brown holds dear. The UK achieves a double first—among the G7 and among the thirty OECD countries—in liberal product market regulation. But it is ranked only fifth among the G7 and seventeenth among the OECD countries for the percentage of adults having more than low skills.[19]

Britain preaches a globalization-friendly model of flexible labor markets throughout EU Europe, and its success in boosting Britain's economic performance in comparison with the rest of Europe has won some reluctant admirers, even converts. For example, Chancellor Gerhard Schröder's economic reform package, Project 2010, had much in common with Blair's neoliberal approach to economic governance, and French president Nicolas Sarkozy seems determined to introduce neoliberal economic reforms. Thus, Britain has been shaped by the international political economy in important ways and hopes to take full advantage of the economic prospects of globalization, even as it tries to reshape other European national models in its own image.

As the world-of-states theme suggests, a country's participation in today's global economic order diminishes autonomous national control, raising unsettling questions in even the most established democracies. Amid complicated pressures, both internal and external, can state institutions retain the capacity to administer policy effectively within distinctive national models? How much do the growth of powerful bureaucracies at home and complex dependencies on international organizations such as the EU limit the ability of citizens to control policy ends? We turn to these questions in Section 3.

SECTION 3 Governance and Policy-Making

Understanding of British governance begins with consideration of Britain's constitution, which is notable for two significant features: its form and its antiquity. Britain lacks a formal written constitution in the usual sense; that is, no single unified and authoritative text has special status above ordinary law and can be amended only by special procedures. Rather, the British constitution is a combination of statutory law (mainly acts of Parliament), common law, convention, and authoritative interpretations. Although it is often said that Britain has an unwritten constitution, this is not accurate. Authoritative legal treatises are written, of course, as are the much more significant acts of Parliament that define crucial elements of the British political system. These acts define the powers of Parliament and its relationship with the Crown, the rights governing the relationship between state and citizen, the relationship of constituent nations to the United Kingdom, the relationship of the United Kingdom to the EU, and many other rights and legal arrangements. It is probably best to say, "What distinguishes the British constitution from others is not that it is unwritten, but rather that it is part written and uncodified."[20]

More than its form, however, the British constitution's antiquity raises questions. It is sometimes hard to know where conventions and acts of Parliament with constitutional implications began, but they can certainly be found as far back as the seventeenth century, notably with the Bill of Rights of 1689, which helped define the relationship between the monarchy and Parliament. "Britain's constitution presents a paradox," a British scholar of constitutional history has observed. "We live in a modern world but inhabit a pre-modern, indeed, ancient, constitution."[21] For example, several European democratic countries, including Spain, Belgium, and the Netherlands, are constitutional monarchies, in which policy-making is left to the elected government and the monarch fulfills largely ceremonial duties. In fact, Europe contains the largest concentration of constitutional monarchies in the world. However, Britain alone among western democracies has permitted two unelected hereditary institutions, the Crown and the House of Lords, to participate in governing the country (in the case of the Lords, a process of reform began in 1999, but where the reforms will lead remains unclear).

More generally, constitutional authorities have accepted the structure and principles of many areas of government for so long that appeal to convention has enormous cultural force. Thus, widely agreed-on rules of conduct, rather than law or U.S.-style checks and balances, set the limits of governmental power. This reality underscores an important aspect of British government: absolute principles of government are few. At the same time, those that exist are fundamental to the organization of the state and central to governance, policy-making, and patterns of representation. Yet, the government is permitted considerable latitude.

Organization of the State

The core constitutional principle of the British political system and cornerstone of the Westminster model is **parliamentary sovereignty**: Parliament can make or overturn any law; the executive, the judiciary, and the throne do not have any authority to restrict or rescind parliamentary action. In a classic parliamentary democracy, the prime minister answers to the House of Commons (the elected element of Parliament) and may be dismissed by it. That said, by passing the European Communities Act in 1972 (Britain joined the European Economic Community in 1973), Parliament accepted significant limitations on its power. It acknowledged that European law has force in the United Kingdom without requiring parliamentary assent and acquiesced to the authority of the European Court of Justice (ECJ) to resolve jurisdictional disputes. To complete the circle, the ECJ has confirmed its prerogative to suspend acts of Parliament.[22]

Second, Britain has long been a **unitary state**. By contrast to the United States, where powers not delegated to the national government are reserved for the states, no powers are reserved constitutionally for sub-central units of government in the United Kingdom. However, the Labour government of Tony Blair introduced a far-reaching program of constitutional reform that created, for the first time, a quasifederal system in Britain. Specified powers were devolved (delegated) to legislative bodies in Scotland and Wales and, with the end to decades of conflict, to Northern Ireland as well. (The historic developments in Northern Ireland will be discussed in Section 5). In addition, some powers have been redistributed from the Westminster Parliament to an authority governing London with a directly elected mayor, and additional powers may be devolved to regional assemblies as well.

Third, British government operates within a system of **fusion of powers** at the UK level: Parliament is the supreme legislative, executive, and judicial authority and includes the monarch as well as the House of Commons and the House of Lords. The fusion of legislature and executive is also expressed in the function and personnel of the cabinet. Whereas U.S. presidents can direct or ignore their cabinets, which have no constitutionally mandated function, the British cabinet bears enormous constitutional responsibility. Through its collective decision-making, the cabinet, and not an independent prime minister, shapes, directs, and takes responsibility for government. This core principle, **cabinet government**, however, may at critical junctures be observed more in principle than in practice.

Finally, sovereignty rests with the Queen-in-Parliament (the formal term for Parliament). Britain is a **constitutional monarchy**. The position of head of state passes by hereditary succession, but the government or state officials must exercise nearly all powers of the Crown. Taken together, parliamentary sovereignty, parliamentary democracy, and cabinet government form the core elements of the British or Westminster model of government, which many consider a model democracy and the first effective parliamentary democracy.

Even so, such a venerable constitutional framework is also vulnerable to uncertainty and criticism. Can a willful prime minister overstep the generally agreed-upon limits of the collective responsibility of the cabinet and achieve an undue concentration of power? How well has the British model of government stood the tests of time and radically changed circumstances? These questions underscore the problems that even the most stable democracies face. They also identify important comparative themes, because parliamentary (rather than presidential systems) have been adopted widely by the former Communist states of East-Central Europe, for example, in Hungary, the Czech Republic, and Slovakia.

The Executive

The term *cabinet government* emphasizes the key functions that the cabinet exercises: responsibility for policy-making, supreme control of government, and coordination of all government departments. However, the term does not capture the full range of executive institutions or the scale and complexity of operations. The executive reaches well beyond the cabinet. It extends from ministries (departments) and ministers to the civil service in one direction, and to Parliament (as we shall see in Section 4) in the other direction.

Cabinet Government

After a general election, the queen (or king) invites the leader of the party that emerges from the election with control of a majority of seats in the House of Commons to form a government and serve as prime minister. The prime minister usually selects approximately two-dozen ministers to constitute the cabinet. Among the most significant assignments are the Foreign Office (equivalent to the U.S. Department of State), the Home Office (ministry of justice or the interior, which is responsible for security and order), and the chancellor of the exchequer (a finance minister or a more powerful version of the U.S. treasury secretary).

The responsibilities of a cabinet minister are immense. "The Cabinet, as a collective body, is responsible for formulating the policy to be placed before Parliament and is also the supreme controlling and directing body of the entire executive branch," notes S. E. Finer. "Its decisions bind all Ministers and other officers in the conduct of their departmental business."[23] In contrast to the French Constitution, which prohibits a cabinet minister from serving in the legislature, British constitutional tradition *requires* overlapping membership between Parliament and the cabinet. (In fact, this point was made in dramatic fashion after Blair's 2005 electoral victory when he appointed a former head of his policy unit to the House of Lords so that he could appoint him as a junior education minister. Similarly, Gordon Brown appointed Mark Malloch Brown to the Lords so that he could serve as minister for Africa, Asia, and the United Nations.) Unlike the informal status of the U.S. cabinet, the British counterpart enjoys considerable constitutional privileges and is a powerful institution with enormous responsibility for the political and administrative success of the government.

The cabinet room at 10 Downing Street (the prime minister's official residence) is a place of intrigue as well as deliberation. From the perspective of the prime minister, the cabinet may appear as loyal followers or as ideological combatants, potential challengers for party leadership, and parochial advocates for pet programs that run counter to the overall objectives of the government. Despite this potential for division, the convention of collective responsibility normally ensures the continuity of government by unifying the cabinet. In principle, the prime minister must gain the support of a majority of the cabinet for a range of significant decisions, notably the budget and the legislative program.

The only other constitutionally mandated mechanism for checking the prime minister is a defeat on a vote of no confidence in the House of Commons (discussed in Section 4). Since this action is rare and politically dangerous, the cabinet's role in constraining the chief executive remains the only routine check on his or her power. Collective responsibility is therefore a crucial aspect of the Westminster model of democracy. But does collective responsibility effectively constrain the power of prime ministers, or does it enable the prime minister to paint "presidential" decisions with the veneer of collectivity?

A politician with strong ideological convictions and a leadership style to match, Margaret Thatcher often attempted to galvanize loyalists in the cabinet and either marginalize or expel detractors. In the end,

Thatcher's treatment of the cabinet inspired the movement to unseat her as party leader and stretched British constitutional conventions. John Major returned to a more consultative approach, in keeping with the classic model of cabinet government.

Tony Blair, like Thatcher, narrowed the scope of collective responsibility. Cabinet meetings were often dull and perfunctory, and debate was rare. The prime minister, a few key cabinet members, and a handful of advisers made decisions in smaller gatherings. In a striking example of this process early in the Blair premiership, right after the election when the full cabinet had not yet met, the government announced the decision to free the Bank of England to set interest rates. Blair accentuated the tendency for shorter cabinet meetings (they usually lasted less than an hour) where members couldn't seriously consider (much less resolve) policy differences.

The role of the cabinet in the decision to go to war in Iraq underscores its weakened capacity to exercise constitutional checks and balances. The subject was often discussed in cabinet—and endlessly in bilateral meetings with key ministers and unelected policy advisers—but was never subjected to the full-scale debate and formal cabinet approval that is associated with the model of cabinet government and collective responsibility. The point is not that Blair lacked a majority in cabinet in support of the UK's role in the war in Iraq, but that cabinet meetings had become largely beside the point. In addition, with eyes turned toward bruising debates in Parliament, where, as Blair acknowledged, defeat would compel him to resign, the prime minister took no steps to discipline ministers who spoke out against the war plan. In fact, Blair permitted both Robin Cook (the former foreign secretary and the leader of the House of Commons) and Clare Short (the secretary of state for international development) each to resign in a manner and at a time of their own choosing in protest of the decision to go to war. In March 2003, Blair won the formal support of Parliament that he sought. In so doing, he may have set a precedent: the presumed prerogative power of the prime minister or Crown to declare war had been handed over to Parliament.[24] Alternatively, many contend that the real decision to go to war in Iraq had been made by the prime minister and President Bush long before, probably at President Bush's ranch in April

2002. Either way, the cabinet played a minor, almost incidental role.[25]

As the decision to go to war in Iraq underscores, both Blair and his close aides seemed skeptical about the effectiveness and centrality of the cabinet as well as cabinet committees. As prime minister, Blair preferred to coordinate strategically important policy areas through highly politicized special units in the Cabinet Office such as the Social Exclusion Unit, the Women's Unit, and the UK Anti-Drugs Co-ordination Unit. In June 2001, the Prime Minister's Delivery Unit was introduced to take strategic control of the delivery of public services, a central commitment of Blair's second term of office and one with great significance since it further eroded the principles of collective responsibility and the centrality of the cabinet even further.

On balance, cabinet government represents a durable and effective formula for governance, although the cabinet does not always function in the role of the supreme directing and controlling body that it occupies in constitutional doctrine. It is important to remember that the cabinet operates within a broader cabinet system—or core executive as it is sometimes called (see Figure 2.5)—and that the prime minister holds or controls many of the levers of power in the core executive. Because the prime minister is the head of the cabinet, his or her office helps develop policy, coordinates operations, and functions as a liaison with the media, the party, interest groups, and Parliament. As Martin J. Smith puts it, "The culmination of a long-term process of centralization of power in the hands of the Prime Minister is seen in the declining role of the Cabinet and the increased development of resources inside Number 10."[26]

Before taking office as prime minister, Gordon Brown promised, as a priority, to restore trust in government and indicated that he would make government and ministers more responsible to parliament. But this is easier said than done! Brown likes to rely on a small group of trusted advisers, tends to be secretive, and prefers a very strong top-down management style—none of which make it likely that Prime Minister Brown will operate with the kind of transparency that would restore trust in government or breathe new life into the collective responsibility of the cabinet.

Both cabinet committees (comprising ministers) and official committees (made up of civil servants)

FIGURE 2.5

The Cabinet System

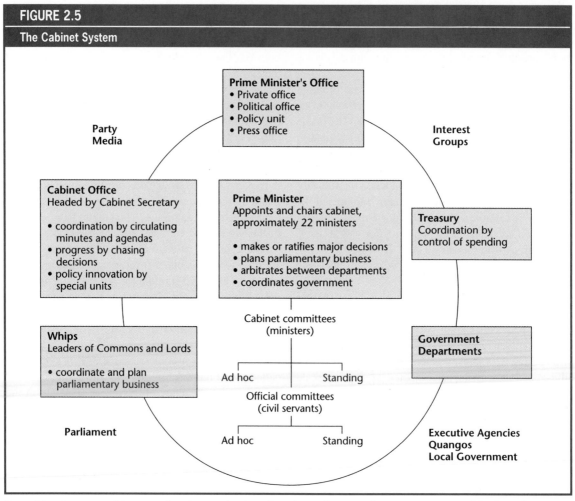

Prime Minister's Office
• Private office
• Political office
• Policy unit
• Press office

Party
Media

Interest
Groups

Cabinet Office
Headed by Cabinet Secretary

• coordination by circulating
  minutes and agendas
• progress by chasing
  decisions
• policy innovation by
  special units

Prime Minister
Appoints and chairs cabinet,
approximately 22 ministers

• makes or ratifies major decisions
• plans parliamentary business
• arbitrates between departments
• coordinates government

Treasury
Coordination by
control of spending

Cabinet committees
(ministers)

**Government
Departments**

Whips
Leaders of Commons and Lords

• coordinate and plan
  parliamentary business

Ad hoc   Standing

Official committees
(civil servants)

Parliament

Ad hoc   Standing

**Executive Agencies
Quangos
Local Government**

The cabinet is supported by a set of institutions that help formulate policy, coordinate operations, and facilitate the support for government policy. Acting within a context set by the fusion of legislature and executive, the prime minister enjoys a great opportunity for decisive leadership that is lacking in a system of checks and balances and separation of powers among the branches of government.

Source: Her Majesty's Treasury Budget Bulletin as found in British Politics: Continuities and Change, Third Edition, by Dennis Kavanagh, p. 251, Oxford University Press, 1996.

supplement the work of the cabinet. In addition, the Treasury plays an important coordinating role through its budgetary control, while the Cabinet Office supports day-to-day operations. The *whips,* leaders in both the Commons and the Lords, smooth the passage of legislation sponsored by the government, which is more or less guaranteed by a working majority.

The cabinet system, and the complex interplay of resources, interdependencies, and power within the core executive that tend to concentrate power at the top, ensure that there is no Washington-style gridlock (the inability of legislature and executive to agree on policy) in London. On the contrary, if there is a problem at the pinnacle of power in the United Kingdom, it is the potential for excessive concentration of power by a prime minister who is prepared to manipulate the cabinet and flout the conventions of collective responsibility.

Comparing the U.S. Presidential System to the British Parliamentary System

Political scientists—especially those engaged in comparative politics—often discuss, and nearly as often argue about, how the design of political institutions affects political outcomes. Near the top of the list of institutional differences that seem to matter the most is the distinction between presidential systems such as the United States and parliamentary systems such as the United Kingdom.

What are the key differences in the two systems of government?

In a presidential system, such as that of the United States, the legislature and executive are *independent*. Both the legislature and the chief executive have their own fixed schedule for election and their own political mandate. Both legislators and presidents have won election, independently of each other. They have different constituencies and often have different political agendas. Each may even gain credibility and support by opposing the other. In presidential systems it is not uncommon to find the agenda and the authority of the president compromised when the president and the majority of the legislators are from different parties—in fact this is the rule, rather than the exception, in the United States and in many other presidential systems. Stalemates on key items of legislation are common. Between presidential elections it is very difficult to remove a president, even one who has very little popular support or who is suspected of acting unconstitutionally. It requires impeachment, which, in turn, requires a finding of extraordinary misconduct and a strong opposition majority in the legislature to push through that finding.

A parliamentary system looks very different. Prime ministers must enjoy the support of the majority of the legislature to achieve office—and they must preserve that support to stay in office, since prime ministers and the governments they head can fall if they lose a vote of no confidence in the legislature. This check on prime ministerial power reveals another fundamental difference between presidential and parliamentary systems—in the parliamentary system the timing of elections is not fixed. When riding high, the prime minister can call for a new election in an effort to win a new mandate and a deeper majority in parliament. When in trouble, a prime minister can be sent packing in an instant through a vote of no confidence.

Parliamentary and presidential systems are very different in institutional design and the differences have consequences. In a parliamentary system like Britain's, because the legislators and prime minister sink or swim together, they tend to cooperate and work through differences. It is a "can do" style of government. In a presidential system like America's, because the legislature and executive are mutually independent—one can swim, while the other sinks—the tendency for finger pointing and stalemate is much greater.

Despite these differences, the distinctions in practice should not be exaggerated. Powerful prime ministers such as Thatcher and Blair were routinely criticized for being too presidential—or even dictatorial. And in Britain, the threat a prime minister faces of losing office as a consequence of a vote of no confidence has all but disappeared—it has happened only once in more than eighty years. In fact, if recent history is a good predictor of the future, an American president is more likely to face a bill of impeachment than a British prime minister is to face a serious vote of no confidence.

This analysis draws heavily from Alfred Stepan, with Cindy Skatch, "Constitutional Frameworks and Democratic Consolidation: Parliamentarism versus Presidentialism," in Mark Kesselman and Joel Krieger, eds., *Readings in Comparative Politics: Political Challenges and Changing Agendas* (Boston: Houghton Mifflin, 2006), pp. 284–293.

Bureaucracy and Civil Service

Policy-making at 10 Downing Street may appear to be increasingly concentrated in the prime minister's hands. At the same time, when viewed from Whitehall (the road that encompasses Parliament Square and many of the government ministries), the executive may seem to be dominated by its vast administrative agencies. The range and complexity of state policy-making mean that in practice, the cabinet's authority must be shared with a vast set of unelected officials.

How is the interaction between the civil service and the cabinet ministers (and their political assistants) coordinated? A very senior career civil servant, called a permanent secretary, has chief administrative responsibility for running a department. Other senior civil servants, including deputy secretaries and under-secretaries, in turn assist the permanent secretaries. In addition, the minister reaches into his or her department to appoint a principal private secretary, an up-and-coming civil servant who assists the minister as gatekeeper and liaison with senior civil servants.

Successful policy must translate policy goals into policy instruments. Since nearly all legislation is introduced on behalf of the government and presented as the policy directive of a ministry, civil servants in Britain do much of the conceptualizing and refining of legislation that is done by committee staffers in the U.S. Congress. Civil servants, more than ministers, assume operational duties. Despite a certain natural level of mutual mistrust and misunderstanding, the two must work closely together.

Since the early 1980s, the pace of change at White-hall has been very fast. Governments have tried to cut the size of the civil service, streamline its operations, replace permanent with casual (temporary) staff, and enhance its accountability to citizens. As a result of the ongoing modernization of Whitehall (known as new public management, NPM), the civil service inherited by New Labour is very different from the civil service of thirty years ago. It has been downsized and given a new corporate structure (divided into more than 120 separate executive agencies). Few at the top of these agencies (agency chief executives) are traditional career civil servants.

In recent years, many observers have expressed concern that New Labour has done—and will continue to do—whatever it can to subject the Whitehall machine to effective political and ministerial direction and control.[27] A related concern is that the centrality and impartiality of civil servants is being eroded by the growing importance of special advisers (who are both political policy advisers and civil servants). This concern came to a head as Blair made the case for war in Iraq. Key special advisers played critical roles in making the case in the famous "dodgy dossier" of September 2002 that the threat of weapons of mass destruction justified regime change in Iraq.

Public and Semipublic Institutions

Like other countries, Britain has institutionalized a set of administrative functions that expand the role of the state well beyond the traditional core executive functions and agencies. We turn now to a brief discussion of semipublic agencies—entities that are sanctioned by the state but without direct democratic oversight.

Nationalized Industries. The nationalization of basic industries—such as coal, iron and steel, gas and electricity supply—was a central objective of the Labour government's program during the postwar collectivist era. By the end of the Thatcher era, the idea of public ownership had clearly run out of steam. For New Labour, a return to the program of public ownership of industry is unthinkable. Instead, when thinking of expanding state functions, we can expect a growing set of semipublic administrative organizations and public/private partnerships.

Nondepartmental Public Bodies and Public/Private Partnerships. Since the 1970s, an increasing number of administrative functions have been transferred to bodies that are typically part of the government in terms of funding, function, and appointment of staff, but operate at arm's length from ministers. They are officially called nondepartmental public bodies (NDPBs) but are better known as quasinongovernmental organizations or quangos. Quangos have increasing policy influence and enjoy considerable administrative and political advantages. They take responsibility for specific functions and can combine governmental and private sector expertise. At the same time, ministers can distance themselves from controversial areas of policy.

Despite Thatcher's attempts to reduce their number and scale back their operations, by the late 1990s, there were some 6,000 quangos, 90 percent operating at the local level. They were responsible for one-third of all public spending and staffed by approximately 50,000 people. Increasingly, the debate about NDPBs is less about the size of the public, semipublic, or private sector, and more about the effective delivery of services.

Alongside quangos, in recent years the government has looked for ways to expand the investment of the private sector in capital projects such as hospitals and schools that provide public sector goods. Thus New Labour continued the private finance initiative (PFI) it inherited from the Conservatives as a key part of its signature modernization program and as a way to revitalize public services. The results are controversial: critics and supporters disagree about the quality of services provided and whether taxpayers win or lose by the financial arrangements. In addition, the tendency of PFI initiatives to blur the line between public and private raises important and controversial issues. Do these initiatives, as Labour modernizers insist, bring welcome resources, expertise, and skills to crucial public sector provisions? Or, as critics contend, do they distort priorities in education and health care, erode vital traditions of universal provision of public goods, and chip away at the working conditions for public sector employees?[28]

Other State Institutions

This section examines the military and the police, the judiciary, and subnational government.

The Military and the Police

From the local bobby (a term for a local police officer derived from Sir Robert Peel, who set up London's metropolitan police force in 1829) to the most senior military officer, those involved in security and law enforcement have enjoyed a rare measure of popular support in Britain. Constitutional tradition and professionalism distance the British police and military officers from politics. Nevertheless, both institutions have been placed in more politically controversial and exposed positions in recent decades.

In the case of the military, British policy in the post–cold war period remains focused on a gradually redefined set of North Atlantic Treaty Organization (NATO) commitments. Still ranked among the top five military powers in the world, Britain retains a global presence, and the Thatcher and Major governments deployed forces in ways that strengthened their political positions and maximized Britain's global influence. In 1982, Britain soundly defeated Argentina in a war over the disputed Falkland/Malvinas Islands in the South Atlantic. In the Gulf War of 1991, Britain deployed a full armored division in the UN-sanctioned

force arrayed against Iraq. Under Blair's leadership, Britain was the sole participant alongside the United States in the aerial bombardment of Iraq in December 1998. In 1999, the United Kingdom strongly backed NATO's Kosovo campaign and pressed for ground troops. Indeed, the Kosovo campaign and Blair's "doctrine of international community," which the prime minister rolled out in a major speech in Chicago on the eve of NATO's fiftieth anniversary in 1999, assumed an important role in Blair's justification for the war in Iraq.[29] According to Blair, global interdependence made isolationism obsolete and inspired a commitment to a new ethical dimension in foreign policy. Throughout the war in Iraq and its bloody aftermath, and to the end of his premiership, Blair persistently characterized Iraq as an extension of Kosovo, an effort to liberate Muslims from brutal dictatorships, whether Serbia's Milosevic or Iraq's Saddam Hussein.

Until Blair's decision to support the American plan to shift the venue of the war on terror from Afghanistan to Iraq, the use of the military in international conflicts generated little opposition. Indeed, even in the case of the war in Iraq, the role of the military (as distinct from the decision to go to war) has generated relatively little controversy. Allegations of mistreatment raised far fewer questions than those directed at the United States for its abuse of prisoners at Abu Ghraib. In addition, UK forces are widely credited with operations in and around Basra that have been as culturally sensitive and effective as could be expected under such difficult circumstances. In September 2007, less than three months after Brown became prime minister, and with little fanfare, British troops completed a pull-out from Basra.

The police have traditionally operated as independent local forces throughout the country. Since the 1980s, however, the police have witnessed growth in government control, centralization, and level of political use. During the coal miners' strike of 1984–1985, the police operated to an unprecedented, perhaps unlawful, degree as a national force coordinated through Scotland Yard (London's police headquarters). Police menaced strikers and hindered miners from participating in strike support activities. This partisan use of the police in an industrial dispute flew in the face of constitutional traditions and offended some police officers and officials. During the 1990s, concerns about police conduct focused on police-community relations. These included race relations, corruption, and the interrogation and treatment of people held in custody. In particular, widespread criticism of the police for mishandling their investigation into the brutal 1993 racist killing of Stephen Lawrence in South London resulted in a scathing report by a commission of inquiry in 1999.

The Judiciary

In Britain, the principle of parliamentary sovereignty limits the role of the judiciary. Courts have no power to judge the constitutionality of legislative acts (judicial review). They can only determine whether policy directives or administrative acts violate common law or an act of Parliament. Hence, the British judiciary is generally less politicized and influential than its U.S. counterpart.

Jurists, however, have participated in the wider political debate outside court, as when they have headed royal commissions on the conduct of industrial relations, the struggle in Northern Ireland, and riots in Britain's inner cities. Some observers of British politics worry that governments have used judges in these ways to secure partisan ends, deflect criticism, and weaken the tradition of parliamentary scrutiny of government policy. Nevertheless, Sir Richard Scott's harsh report on his investigation into Britain's sales of military equipment to Iraq in the 1980s, for example, indicates that inquiries led by judges with a streak of independence can prove highly embarrassing to the government and raise important issues for public debate. The intensely watched inquiry conducted by Lord Hutton, a senior jurist, into the death of David Kelly, a whistle-blower who challenged the government's case for weapons of mass destruction as a justification for going to war in Iraq, confirmed this important public role of judges in the United Kingdom. At the same time, the question of Hutton's independence became very controversial in light of a "verdict" that exonerated the prime minister.

Beyond the politicization of jurists through their role on commissions and public inquiries, potentially dramatic institutional changes in law and the administration of justice are under consideration. In June 2003, Blair announced the government's intention to abolish the office of Lord Chancellor and move the law lords (who hold the ultimate authority of appeal in British law) from the House of Lords to a new

"supreme court." The constitutional reform bill, introduced in 2004, faced strong opposition in the Lords and the prospects for ultimate passage remain clouded.

Subnational Government

Since the United Kingdom is a state made up of distinct nations (England, Scotland, Wales, and Northern Ireland), the distribution of powers involves two levels below the central government: national government and local (municipal) government. Because the British political framework has traditionally been unitary, not federal, no formal powers devolved to either the nation within the United Kingdom or to subnational (really subcentral or sub-UK) units as in the United States or Germany.

Although no powers have been constitutionally reserved to local governments, they have historically had considerable autonomy in financial terms and discretion in implementing a host of social service and related policies. In the context of increased fiscal pressures that followed the 1973 oil crisis, the Labour government introduced the first check on the fiscal autonomy of local councils (elected local authorities). The Thatcher government then tightened the fiscal constraints on local government. Finally, in 1986, the Thatcher government abolished the multicultural-oriented city government (the Greater London Council, GLC) under the leadership of Ken Livingstone, as well as several other metropolitan councils. In 1989, the Thatcher government introduced a poll tax, an equal per capita levy for local finance, to replace the age-old system of local property taxes. This radical break with tradition, which shifted the burden of local taxes from property owners and businesses to individuals, and taxed rich and poor alike, was monumentally unpopular. The poll tax proved a tremendous political liability, made local politics a hot-button national issue, and led to Thatcher's departure.

Although much of New Labour's agenda concerning subcentral government is focused primarily on the political role of nations within Britain, devolution within England is also part of the reform process. Regional Development Agencies (RDAs) were introduced throughout England in April 1999 as part of a decentralizing agenda, but perhaps even more to facilitate economic development at the regional level. Despite the fairly low-key profile of RDAs and their limited scope (they are unelected bodies with no statutory authority), they opened the door to popular mobilization in the long term for elected regional assemblies. Thus far, however, despite opinion polls that indicate some English resentment about devolution in Scotland and Wales, there has been little enthusiasm in England when referenda for regional government in several regions were offered—and a November 2004 referendum in the North-East was soundly defeated.

In addition, the New Labour placed changes in the governance of London on the fast track. The introduction of a directly elected mayor of London in May 2000 proved embarrassing to Blair, since the government's efforts to keep Livingstone out of the contest backfired and he won handily. Livingstone introduced an expansive agenda to spur long-term sustainable growth and advance a policy agenda that emphasizes ethnic diversity and the enhanced representation and leadership of women in London public life. In addition, London's determined effort to reduce traffic congestion by levying per day per vehicle charges within a central London zone have won widespread admiration for one of England's most controversial political leaders. Although Livingstone remained a controversial figure and a spur in the side of Blair and Brown, his May 2008 defeat by an equally colorful and iconoclastic Tory, Boris Johnson, helped create the impression that Brown's Labour party was losing its grip on office.

The Policy-Making Process

Parliamentary sovereignty is the core constitutional principle of the British political system. However, when it comes to policy-making and policy implementation, the focus is not on Westminster but rather on Whitehall. In many countries, such as Japan, India, and Nigeria, personal connections and informal networks play a large role in policy-making and implementation. How different is the British system?

Unlike the U.S. system, in which policy-making is concentrated in congressional committees and subcommittees, Parliament has little direct participation in policy-making; instead, it emerges primarily from within the executive. There, decision-making is strongly influenced by policy communities. These are informal networks with extensive knowledge, access, and personal connections to those responsible for policy. In this private hothouse environment, civil servants, ministers, and members of the policy communities work through informal ties. A cooperative style develops as the ministry becomes an advocate for key players and as civil servants come perhaps to overidentify the public good with the advancement of policy within their area of responsibility.

This cozy insider-only policy process has been challenged by the delegation of more and more authority to the EU. The consequences of the European dimension are profound. Both ministers and senior civil servants spend a great deal of time in EU policy deliberations and are constrained both directly and indirectly by the EU agenda and directives. Although the UK government is still effectively in charge of many areas of domestic policy, more than 80 percent of the rules governing economic life in Britain are determined by the EU. Even when the United Kingdom has opted out, as in the case of the common currency, European influences are significant. Decisions by the Council of Finance Ministers and the European Central Bank shape British macroeconomic, monetary, and fiscal policies in significant ways. Foreign and security policy are not immune from EU influences. The EU's Common Foreign and Security Policy have extended multilevel governance to these spheres, although foreign policy decisions remain the prerogative of national governments. The increasing Europeanization of policy-making will be one of the most interesting and potentially transformative developments in British politics in the next decade.

As discussed in Section 3, parliamentary sovereignty is the core constitutional principle defining the role of the legislature and, in a sense, the whole system of British government. The executive or judiciary can set no act of Parliament aside, nor is any Parliament bound by the actions of any previous Parliament. Nevertheless, in practice, the control exerted by the House of Commons (or Commons) is not unlimited. This section investigates the powers and role of Parliament, both Commons and Lords. It also looks at the party system, elections, and contemporary currents in British political culture, citizenship, and identity. We close by offering an analysis of surprising new directions in political participation and social protest.

The Legislature

Is Parliament still as sovereign in practice as it remains in constitutional tradition? Clearly, it is not as powerful as it once was. From roughly the 1830s to the 1880s, it collaborated in the formulation of policy, and members amended or rejected legislation on the floor of the House of Commons. Today, the Commons does not so much legislate as assent to government legislation, since (with rare exceptions) the governing party has a majority of the seats and requires no cross-party voting to pass bills. In addition, the balance of effective oversight of policy has shifted from the legislature to executive agencies. This section discusses, in turn, the legislative process, the House of Commons, the House of Lords, and reforms and pressures for change.

The Legislative Process

To become law, bills must be introduced in the House of Commons and the House of Lords, although approval by the latter is not required. The procedure for developing and adopting a public bill is quite complex. The ideas for prospective legislation may come from political parties, pressure groups, think tanks, the prime minister's policy unit, or government departments. Prospective legislation is then normally drafted by civil servants, circulated within Whitehall, approved by the cabinet, and then refined by one of some thirty lawyers in the office of Parliamentary Counsel.[30]

According to tradition, in the House of Commons the bill usually comes to the floor three times (referred to as *readings*). The bill is formally read upon introduction (the *first reading*), printed, distributed, debated in general terms, and after an interval (from a single day to several weeks), given a *second reading*, followed by a vote. Usually the bill then goes for detailed review to a standing committee of between sixteen and fifty members chosen to reflect the overall party balance in the House. It is then subject to a report stage during which new amendments may be introduced. The *third reading* follows; normally, the bill is considered in final form (and voted on) without debate.

After the third reading, a bill that is passed in the House of Commons follows a parallel path in the House of Lords. There the bill is either accepted without change, amended, or rejected. According to custom, the House of Lords passes bills concerning taxation or budgetary matters without alteration, and can add technical and editorial amendments to other bills (which must be approved by the House of Commons) to add clarity in wording and precision in administration. After a bill has passed through all these stages, it goes to the Crown for royal assent (approval by the queen or king, which is only a formality), after which it becomes law and is referred to as an Act of Parliament.

The House of Commons

In constitutional terms, the House of Commons, the lower house of Parliament (with 646 seats at the time of the 2005 election), exercises the main legislative power in Britain. Along with the two unelected elements of Parliament, the Crown and the House of Lords, the Commons has three main functions: (1) to pass laws, (2) to provide finances for the state by authorizing taxation, and (3) to review and scrutinize public administration and government policy.

In practical terms, the Commons has a limited legislative function. Nevertheless, it serves a very important democratic function. It provides a highly visible arena for policy debate and the partisan collision of political worldviews. The high stakes and the flash of rhetorical skills bring drama to the historic chambers, but one crucial element of drama is nearly always missing: the outcome is seldom in doubt. The likelihood that the Commons will invoke its ultimate authority, to defeat a government, is very small. MPs from the governing party who consider rebelling against their leader (the prime minister) are understandably reluctant in a close and critical vote to force a general election, which would place their jobs in jeopardy. Only once since the defeat of Ramsay MacDonald's government in 1924 has a government been brought down by a defeat in the Commons (in 1979). Today, the balance of institutional power has shifted from Parliament to the governing party and the executive.

The House of Lords

The upper chamber of Parliament, the House of Lords (or Lords), is an unelected body that is comprised of hereditary peers (nobility of the rank of duke, marquis, earl, viscount, or baron), life peers (appointed by the Crown on the recommendation of the prime minister), and law lords (life peers appointed to assist the Lords in its judicial duties). The Lords also include the archbishops of Canterbury and York and some twodozen senior bishops of the Church of England. There are roughly 700 members of the House of Lords, but there is no fixed number, and membership changes with the appointment of peers. At present, there are approximately 200 Labour and 200 Conservative members, and a roughly equivalent number of members (called Crossbenchers) who are not affiliated with any political party. There are approximately 75 Liberal Democrat members. The House of Lords has served as the final court of appeal for civil cases throughout Britain and for criminal cases in England, Wales, and Northern Ireland. This judicial role, which is performed by the law lords, drew international attention in 1998 and 1999 when a Spanish court attempted to extradite General Augusto Pinochet of Chile on charges of genocide, torture, and terrorism. In modern times, however, the House of Lords, which has the power to amend and delay legislation, has served mainly as a chamber of revision, providing expertise in redrafting legislation. Recently, for example, the Lords considered the Nationality, Immigration and Asylum bill to be too harsh. It battled the government for weeks and forced revisions before approving the legislation.

In 1999, the Blair government appointed a Royal Commission on the Reform of the House of Lords (the Wakeham commission) and in the same year introduced legislation to remove the right of hereditary lords to speak and vote. With the passage of the House of Lords Act 1999, the number of hereditary peers was reduced to ninety-two. In January 2000, the commission recommended a partly elected second chamber, enumerating alternative models. In February 2003, the Commons rejected seven options, ranging

from a fully appointed chamber (Blair's preference) to an entirely elected one. If made into law, the constitutional reform bill, which was introduced in 2004, would transfer that function from the Lords to a new "supreme court." The failure of a joint committee of MPs and peers to achieve consensus has left reform plans in tatters. For now, the future of House of Lords reform has been consigned to a "What is Brown likely to do?" guessing game and given the prime minister's travails there is unlikely to be any breakthrough soon. Most reform options foresee a body that is more or perhaps entirely elected and there seems to be a growing consensus that it should represent regional constituencies.

Reforms in Behavior and Structure

How significant are contemporary changes in the House? How far will they go to stem the tide in Parliament's much-heralded decline?

Behavioral Changes: Backbench Dissent. Ever since the 1970s, backbenchers (MPs of the governing party who have no governmental office and rank-and-file opposition members) have been markedly less deferential than in the past. A backbench rebellion against the Major government's EU policy damaged the prestige of the prime minister and weakened him considerably. Until the war in Iraq was on the horizon, Blair seemed less likely to face significant rebellion from Labour MPs, although divisions did occur—relatively early in his premiership, for example, over social welfare policy and the treatment of trade unions. As Blair's political capital was depleted with the war in Iraq, he faced some bruising rebellions. In January 2004, an education bill, which called for increased tuition fees, produced massive opposition from Labour MPs. It scraped through parliament by only 5 votes on the second reading and 28 on the final reading in March—despite a 161 Labour majority in the Commons and prime minister Blair's statement that defeat on the education bill would be treated as a vote of no confidence and likely result in Blair's resignation. One-third of Labour MPs defected on key votes in February and March 2003 authorizing the use of force in Iraq. This represents a far more historic rebellion. In June 2008, a beleaguered Gordon Brown, intent on expanding the length of time for which suspected terrorists can be held without charge from twenty-eight to forty-two days, narrowly won the vote, but suffered the defection of 36 Labour MPs, and had to rely on the support of MPs from a small party in Northern Ireland (the Democratic Unionist party) to prevail. The vote inspired the most significant rebellion by Labour MPs against prime minister Brown, raised unresolved issues about the loss of civil liberties in the UK, and accentuated Brown's declining authority. In an unprecedented move, David Davis, the shadow Home Secretary (the Conservative Party's spokesman on legal and security affairs who "shadows" and challenges the Home Secretary and would hope to succeed him in a Conservative government) resigned his seat in Parliament to dramatize his strong opposition to what he termed the "insidious, surreptitious and relentless erosion of fundamental British freedoms." Parliament may not be as powerful as it was in the nineteenth century, but can still focus the attention of the country, retain its historic role in critical policy debates, and provoke unexpected—and quite dramatiic—behavior.

Structural Changes: Parliamentary Committees. In addition to the standing committees that routinely review bills during legislative proceedings, in 1979 the Commons revived and extended the number and "remit" (that is, responsibilities) of select committees. Select committees help Parliament exert control over the executive by examining specific policies or aspects of administration.

The most controversial select committees are watchdog committees that monitor the conduct of major departments and ministries. Select committees hold hearings, take written and oral testimony, and question senior civil servants and ministers. They then issue reports that often include strong policy recommendations that may be at odds with government policy. As one side effect of the reform, the role of the civil service has been complicated. For the first time, civil servants have been required to testify in a manner that might damage their ministers, revealing culpability or flawed judgments. As discussed in Section 3, the powerful norms of civil service secrecy have been compromised and the relationship with ministers disturbed. On balance, the committees have been extremely energetic, but not very powerful.

Political Parties and the Party System

Like the term *parliamentary sovereignty,* which conceals the reduced role of Parliament in legislation and the unmaking of governments, the term *two-party system,* which is commonly used to describe the British party system, is somewhat deceiving. It is true that since David Lloyd George, leader of the Liberal party, served as prime minister in a coalition government from 1916–1922, only leaders of the Labour or Conservative parties have served as prime ministers. It is also true that these two parties have had a relatively equal hold on the office of the prime minister. In fact, during the post–World War II period, from 1945 through 2001, the Conservative and Labour parties each won eight general elections, with 2005 giving the lead to Labour. And it is also true that throughout the postwar period, these two parties have routinely divided at least 85 percent of the seats in the House of Commons. But since the 1980s, center parties have assumed a high profile in British electoral politics, with the Liberal Democrats (Lib Dems) sometimes emerging as an important alternative to Conservative and Labour—or perhaps a coalition partner with Labour in the event of a general election that produces no single party with a parliamentary majority (what the British call a "hung parliament"). In addition, Britain has several national parties, such as the Scottish National Party (SNP) in Scotland or the Plaid Cymru in Wales as well as a roster of parties competing in Northern Ireland. (These parties are described below under "Trends in Electoral Behavior.") So it is probably more accurate to classify Britain a two-party dominant system, rather than a two-party system.

The Labour Party

As one of the few European parties with origins outside electoral politics, the Labour Party was launched by trade union representatives and socialist societies in the last decade of the nineteenth century and formally took its name in 1906. But it would be decades before the Labour Party became a contender for government leadership. Its landslide 1945 victory made the party a major player. At the same time, Labour began moderating its ideological appeal and broadening its electoral base by adopting the collectivist consensus described in Section 1. In the 1950s and early 1960s, people who were not engaged in manual labor voted Conservative three times more commonly than they did Labour; more than two out of three manual workers, by contrast, voted Labour. During this period, Britain conformed to one classic pattern of a Western European party system: a two-class/two-party system.

The period since the mid-1970s has been marked by significant changes in the party system and a growing disaffection with even the moderate social democracy associated with the Keynesian welfare state and Labourism. The party suffered from divisions between its trade unionist and parliamentary elements, constitutional wrangling over the power of trade unions to determine party policy at annual conferences, and disputes over how the leader would be selected. Divisions also spilled over into foreign policy issues as well. On defense issues, there was a strong pacifist and an even stronger antinuclear sentiment within the party. Support for unilateral nuclear disarmament (the reduction and elimination of nuclear weapons systems with or without comparable developments on the Soviet side) was a decisive break with the national consensus on security policy and contributed to the party's losses in 1983 and 1987. Unilateralism was then scrapped.

The 1980s and 1990s witnessed relative harmony within the party, since moderate trade union and parliamentary leadership agreed on major policy issues. Labour has become a moderate left-of-center party in which ideology takes a backseat to performance and electoral mobilization, although divisions over the war in Iraq have inspired some soul-searching about what values the party represents.

The Conservative Party

The pragmatism, flexibility, and organizational capabilities of the Conservative Party, which dates back to the eighteenth century, have made it one of the most successful and, at times, innovative center-right parties in Europe. Although it has fallen on hard times in recent years, it would be unwise to underestimate its potential as both an opposition and a governing party.

The association of the Conservative Party with the economic and social elite is unmistakable, but it was the Conservative government of Prime Minister Benjamin Disraeli (1874–1880) that served as midwife to the birth of the modern welfare state in Britain. The creation of a "long-lasting alliance between an upper-class leadership and a lower-class following" made the Conservative Party a formidable player in British politics.[31] Throughout the postwar period, it has also routinely (with some exceptions) provided the Tories, as Conservatives are colloquially called, with electoral support from about one-third or more of the manual working class.

Contemporary analysis of the Conservative Party must emphasize the cost to the party of its internal divisions over Britain's role in the EU. Wrangling among the Conservatives over Europe led to Thatcher's fall from leadership and weakened Major throughout his years as prime minister. The bitter leadership contest that followed Major's resignation after the 1997 defeat reinforced the impression of a party in turmoil; subsequent rapid departures of party leaders after electoral defeat in 2001 as well as the forced resignation of the leader in 2003 lent an aura of failure and self-doubt to the Conservatives.

Once the combative, experienced, and highly regarded Michael Howard—who had served in the cabinets of both Margaret Thatcher and John Major—assumed the party leadership in 2003, the Conservatives seemed revitalized. But Howard could not translate his assured performances from the front bench in Parliament into popular support. Although Howard pounded Blair on the failures of intelligence in the run-up to the war in Iraq, Conservatives gave the prime minister far less trouble on Iraq than did members of the Labour Party itself. Nor could Howard make much headway against New Labour on central social and economic policy concerns—and thus, despite an energetic campaign, and one that will likely be remembered for its xenophobic edge, immediately after the 2005 election Howard succumbed to the same fate as his recent predecessors: electoral defeat followed by a quick resignation as party leader. In December 2005, the Conservatives in a landslide elected David Cameron as party leader.

Cameron wasted little time in reorienting the party, modernizing its appeal, and reaching out beyond its traditional core values. Young (he was born in 1966), smart, and telegenic, Cameron acknowledged that

New Labour had been right in understanding the mood of Britain and right, also, to insist on achieving both social justice and economic success. Cameron promised to reduce poverty both in Britain and globally, take on climate change as a priority, and ensure security from terrorism. He looked for ways to retain a special relationship with America, but he also promised to recalibrate British foreign policy by forging comparable special relationships with countries such as India. As a testament to Blair's success, as well as the uncertainty about Gordon Brown, Cameron worked hard to reposition the Conservatives as a reforming, more centrist party that could compete effectively with post–Blair New Labour across the economic and social spectrum. Cameron also encouraged the view that Brown would drift toward the discredited Old Labour left and, quite remarkably, Cameron claimed that he was the true heir to Tony Blair.[32]

Liberal Democrats

Through the 1970s, the Liberal Party, one of the two governing parties until Labour's rise in the 1920s and thereafter the traditional third party in Britain, was the only centrist challenger to the Labour and Conservative parties. Since the 1980s, a changing roster of centrist parties has posed a potentially significant threat to the two-party dominance of Conservative and Labour. In 1981, the Social Democratic Party (SDP) formed out of a split within the Labour Party. After the Conservative victory in 1987, the Liberal Party and most of the SDP merged to form the Social and Liberal Democratic Party (now called the Liberal Democrats or Lib Dems). In recent years, the Lib Dems have become a major political player.

In the 2001 general election the party increased its vote tally by nearly one-fifth and won fifty-two seats, the most since 1929. This success positioned the party as a potentially powerful center-left critic of New Labour. That said, Labour has not made it easy for them. As the Blair government began to spend massively to improve education and health care, it narrowed the range of policy issues on which the Liberal Democrats could take on New Labour. Party leader Charles Kennedy won the political gamble in spring 2003 by opposing the war in Iraq. But it has not been easy to take electoral advantage of Blair's political weakness.

Thereafter, things went downhill: Kennedy resigned due to problems with alcohol, and his successor Menzies (Ming) Campbell, who took over in March 2006, suddenly resigned. In December 2007, Campbell was replaced by Nick Clegg, a 40-year-old ex-journalist and former member of the European Parliament. Clegg and his party face an uphill battle to make the Lib Dems a serious contender in the next election, but the country's New Labour fatigue, the growing concern about civil liberties that plays to the party's strength, and Clegg's energetic leadership—in fall 2008 Clegg announced a campaign to knock on one million doors to connect with ordinary citizens—seems likely to raise the profile and the prospects of the party.

Elections

British elections are exclusively for legislative posts. The prime minister is not elected as prime minister but as an MP from a single constituency (electoral district), averaging about 65,000 registered voters. Parliament has a maximum life of five years, with no fixed term. General elections are held after the Crown, at the request of the prime minister, has dissolved Parliament. Although Blair has in effect set a precedent of elections with four-year intervals, the ability to control the timing of elections is a tremendous political asset for the prime minister. This contrasts sharply with a presidential system, which is characteristic of the United States, with direct election of the chief executive and a fixed term of office.

The Electoral System

Election for representatives in the Commons (who are called members of Parliament, or MPs) is by a "first-past-the-post" (or winner-take-all) principle in each constituency. In this single-member plurality system, the candidate who receives the most votes is elected. There is no requirement of a majority and no element of proportional representation (a system in which each party receives a percentage of seats in a representative assembly that is roughly comparable to its percentage of the popular vote). Table 2.3 shows the results of the general elections from 1945 to 2005.

This winner-take-all electoral system tends to exaggerate the size of victory by the winning party and

Table 2.3

British General Elections, 1945–2005

		Percentage of Popular Vote						Seats in House of Commons					
	Turnout	Conser-vative	Labour	Liberal[a]	National Parties[b]	Other	Swing[c]	Conser-vative	Labour	Liberal[a]	National Parties[b]	Other	Government Majority
1945	72.7	39.8	48.3	9.1	0.2	2.5	−12.2	213	393	12	0	22	146
1950	84.0	43.5	46.1	9.1	0.1	1.2	+3.0	299	315	9	0	2	0.5
1951	82.5	48.0	48.8	2.5	0.1	0.6	+0.9	321	295	6	0	3	17
1955	76.7	49.7	46.4	2.7	0.2	0.9	+2.1	345	277	6	0	2	60
1959	78.8	49.4	43.8	5.9	0.4	0.6	+1.2	365	258	6	0	1	100
1964	77.1	43.4	44.1	11.2	0.5	0.8	−3.2	304	317	9	0	0	4
1966	75.8	41.9	47.9	8.5	0.7	0.9	−2.7	253	363	12	0	2	95
1970	72.0	46.4	43.0	7.5	1.3	1.8	+4.7	330	288	6	1	5	30
Feb. 1974	78.7	37.8	37.1	19.3	2.6	3.2	−1.4	297	301	14	9	14	−34[d]
Oct. 1974	72.8	35.8	39.2	18.3	3.5	3.2	−2.1	277	319	13	14	12	3
1979	76.0	43.9	37.0	13.8	2.0	3.3	+5.2	339	269	11	4	12	43
1983	72.7	42.4	27.6	25.4	1.5	3.1	+4.0	397	209	23	4	17	144
1987	75.3	42.3	30.8	22.6	1.7	2.6	−1.7	376	229	22	6	17	102
1992	77.7	41.9	34.4	17.8	2.3	3.5	−2.0	336	271	20	7	17	21
1997	71.4	30.7	43.2	16.8	2.6	6.7	−10.0	165	419	46	10	19	179
2001	59.4	31.7	40.7	18.3	2.5	6.8	+1.8	166	413	52	9	19	167
2005	61.5	32.3	35.2	22.1	2.1	8.4	+3.0	197	355	62	9	22	65[e]

[a]Liberal Party, 1945–1979; Liberal/Social Democrat Alliance, 1983–1987; Liberal Democratic Party, 1992–2005.

[b]Combined vote of Scottish National Party (SNP) and Welsh National Party (Plaid Cymru).

[c]"Swing" compares the results of each election with the results of the previous election. It is calculated as the average of the winning major party's percentage point increase in its share of the vote and the losing major party's decrease in its percentage point share of the vote. In the table, a positive sign denotes a swing to the Conservatives, a negative sign a swing to Labour.

[d]Following the February 1974 election, the Labour Party was thirty-four seats short of having an overall majority. It formed a minority government until it obtained a majority in the October 1974 election.

[e]Due to the death of a candidate in one constituency, only 645 parliamentary seats were contested in the May 2005 general election, with one additional seat to be filled through a by-election.

Source: Anthony King, ed., *New Labour Triumphs: Britain at the Polls* (Chatham, N.J.: Chatham House, 1998), p. 249. Copyright 1998 by Chatham House. Reprinted by permission. For 2001 results, http://news.bbc.co.uk/hi/english/static/vote2001/results_constituencies/uk_breakdown/uk_full.stm. For 2005 results, http://news.bbc.co.uk/1/hi/uk_politics/vote_2005/constituencies/default.stm.

minimize the showing of any third party (such as the Lib Dems) that competes broadly across the electoral map. Thus, in 2005, with 35.2 percent of the popular vote, Labour won 355 seats. With 22.1 percent of the vote, the Liberal Democrats won only 62 seats. Thus, the Liberal Democrats achieved a share of the vote that was approximately two-thirds of that achieved by Labour, but won less than one-fifth of the seats won

by Labour. Such are the benefits of the electoral system to the victor (as well as the second major party).

With a fairly stable two-and-a-half party system (Conservative, Labour, and Liberal Democrat), the British electoral system tends toward a stable single-party government. However, the electoral system raises questions about representation and fairness. The system reduces the competitiveness of smaller parties with diffuse pockets of support (regional parties can compete effectively in their traditional strongholds). In addition, the party and electoral systems have contributed to the creation of a Parliament that has been a bastion of white men. The 1997 election represented a breakthrough for women: the number of women MPs nearly doubled to 120 (18.2 percent). The 2001 election saw the number of women MPs decline to 118 (17.9 percent). But a record 128 women were elected in 2005 (19.8 percent). As a result of using women-only shortlists for the selection of candidates in many winnable seats, Labour sent far more women (94) to Parliament than any other party.

In 1992, six ethnic minority candidates were elected, up from four in 1987, the first time since before World War II that Parliament included minority members. The number of ethnic minority (black and Asian) MPs rose in 1997 to nine (1.4 percent), to twelve in 2001 (1.8 percent), and to fifteen in 2005 (2.3 percent). Despite the general trend of increased representation of women and minorities, they remain substantially underrepresented in Parliament.

Trends in Electoral Behavior

Recent general elections have deepened geographic and regional fragmentation. The British political scientist Ivor Crewe has referred to the emergence of *two* two-party systems: (1) competition between the Conservative and Labour parties dominates contests in English urban and northern seats, and (2) Conservative-center party competition dominates England's rural and southern seats.[33] In addition, a third two-party competition has appeared in Scotland, where competition between Labour and the Scottish National Party dominates.

The national parties have challenged two-party dominance since the 1970s. The Scottish National Party (SNP) was founded in 1934 and its Welsh counterpart, the Plaid Cymru, in 1925. Coming in a distant second to Labour in Scotland in 1997, the SNP won 21.6 percent of the vote and six seats. In 2001, support for the SNP declined by 2 percent, and the party lost one of its seats. The 2005 election showed some interesting results in Scotland. Labour lost five seats and the SNP gained two seats (for a total of six). But the Lib Dems overtook the SNP's share of the vote.

Both electoral and polling data indicate that Scottish voters are more inclined to support the SNP for elections to the Scottish parliament than to Westminster and that devolution may have stemmed the rising tide of nationalism.[34] In both 1997 and 2001, the Plaid Cymru won four seats where Welsh is still spoken widely. In 2005, after an absence of eight years, three Conservative MPs were elected in Wales, as the Plaid Cymru lost one seat.

The May 2005 election was not easy to sum up. All three major parties could claim some kind of victory, but also had to come to terms with elements of failure. Blair secured a historic third term with a cautious campaign, riding a strong economy and improvements in education and health care to victory—with recurrent images of Gordon Brown, then a very successful chancellor and heir-apparent, by his side. But the election nevertheless left Blair humbled, his majority slashed, his support often grudging. New Labour won by putting off tough decisions—on pension reform, public spending, climate change, Europe, and a timetable for the withdrawal of British troops from Iraq. They won, too, by locking in the middle of the electoral sentiment. They were perfectly positioned: slightly center-right on security and immigration; slightly center-left on the economy and social policy.

Hence, the other parties couldn't lay a glove on New Labour on the core issues that drive domestic politics. With little to say about the government's solid economic record or about the war in Iraq (which they supported, whatever criticisms they might muster about Blair's credibility), the Conservatives played the race card. As *The Economist* put it, their campaign was an "unseemly scramble for the anti-immigrant vote." The Tories could take solace in the fact that they had a net gain of thirty-one seats, but Michael Howard's hasty departure made it obvious that the campaign was a failure.

One of the most significant features of the 2005 election, an element of continuity with 2001, was the growing importance of the Liberal Democrats. They enjoyed a net gain of ten seats and, perhaps more importantly, their share of the popular vote rose to an impressive 22 percent, but they could not chip away at Labour's dominant position on the core economic and social policies.

Both recent trends in electoral behavior in Scotland and truly historic developments in Northern Ireland will be discussed in Section 5.

Political Culture, Citizenship, and Identity

In their classic study of the ideals and values that shape political behavior, political scientists Gabriel Almond and Sidney Verba wrote that the civic (or political) culture in Britain was characterized by trust, deference to authority, and pragmatism.[35] Looking back, the 1970s appear as a crucial turning point in British political culture and group identities.

During the 1970s, the long years of economic decline culminated in economic reversals in the standard of living for many Britons. Also for many, the historic bonds of occupational and social class grew weaker. Both union membership and popularity declined. At the same time, a growing number of conservative think tanks and mass-circulation newspapers worked hard to erode support for the welfare state. New social movements such as feminism, antinuclear activism, and environmentalism, challenged basic tenets of British political culture. Identities based on race and ethnicity, gender, and sexual orientation gained significance. Thus, a combination of economic strains, ideological assaults, and changes in the social fabric of the country fragmented the political map and inspired a shift to the right.

One of the key changes in political culture in Britain in the last quarter-century has been the weakening of bonds grounded in the experience of labor or, more broadly, the sense of shared fates among people having common socio-economic status. Class still matters in the United Kingdom, but not in the dominating way that it did in the nineteenth century or in the collectivist era. Importantly, as noted in Section 2, the political meaning has changed as the values of working-class families have become largely middle-class aspirations and concerns: a nice home to bring up kids, a secure job, a good education, and health care—whether public or private. As a result, class says far less than it used to about political party preferences in elections: an individual's social class no longer explains more than about 2 percent of voting behavior. Class still matters, but fewer workers are in unions (in December 2006

the rate of union membership for all workers in the UK was down to 25.8 percent), and unions are focused narrowly on the enforcement of individual legal rights in the workplace and bread and butter issues, their concerns magnified by a sense of growing desperation about the cost of fuel and food, fear of unemployment, and worry about the plummeting value of their homes. Collective bargaining has been largely relegated to declining private sector industries and the public sector.[36]

In recent decades the sources and relative strength of diverse group attachments have evolved in Britain under the combined pressures of decolonization, which created a multiethnic Britain, and a fragmentation of the experiences of work, which challenges a simple unitary model of class interest. National identity has become especially complicated. Questions about fragmented sovereignty within the context of the EU, the commingled histories of four nations (England, Scotland, Wales, and Ireland/Northern Ireland), and the interplay of race and nationality in postcolonial Britain have created doubts about British identity that run deep. As ethnicity, intra-UK territorial attachments, and the processes of Europeanization and globalization complicate national identity, it becomes increasingly difficult for UK residents automatically to imagine themselves Britons, constituting a resonant national community.

Thus, the British political community has fragmented into smaller communities of class, nation, region, and ethnicity that exist side by side but not necessarily in amiable proximity. Can any government help recreate a more cohesive political culture and foster a more inclusive sense of British identity? Unlike Thatcher, Blair worked hard to revitalize a sense of community in Britain and to extend his agenda to the socially excluded. But the results were mixed, with every effort to eradicate an emerging underclass, it seems, offset by the divisive aftereffects of 9/11 and fingers pointed at ethnic minorities, immigrants, and asylum seekers.

What about gender politics and identity in the UK? Historically, the issues women care about most—childcare, the treatment of part-time workers, domestic violence, equal pay, and support for family caregivers—have not topped the list of policy agendas of any political party in Britain. Has New Labour significantly changed the equation?

It is fair to say that Labour does well among women voters less because of any specific policies and more because it has made the effort to listen to concerns that women voice. Labour stalwarts insist that they have addressed key concerns that women (and men) share concerning health care, crime, and education. They point with pride to the policy directions spurred by the Social Exclusion and Women's units; to the implementation of a national childcare strategy; to policies intended to help women to balance work and

Current Challenges

Gender and Generation Gaps and Trends

The issue of a gender gap in voting behavior has long been a mainstay of British electoral studies. From 1945 to 1992, women were more likely than men to vote Conservative. In addition, since 1964 a gender-generation gap has become well established and was very clear in the 1992 election. Among younger voters (under thirty years old), women preferred Labour, while men voted strongly for the Conservatives, producing a fourteen-point gender gap favoring Labour; among older voters (over sixty-five years old), women were far more inclined to vote Conservative than were their male counterparts, creating a gender gap of eighteen points favoring the Conservatives.

The modest all-generation gender gap that favored the Tories in 1992 (6 percent) was closed in 1997 as a greater percentage of women shifted away from the Conservatives (11 percent) than did men (8 percent). As a result, women and men recorded an identical[37] percent tally for Labour. The gender-generation gap continued, however, with younger women more pro-Labour than younger men and the pattern reversing in the older generation. Moreover, one of the most striking features of the 1997 election was the generational dimension: the largest swing to Labour was among those in the age group eighteen to twenty-nine years (more than 18 percent), and among first-time voters; there was no swing to Labour among those over age sixty-five.[*]

After the 2001 election, analysis pointed to a generation gap in turnout. BBC exit polls revealed that young voters had the lowest turnout, most often saying the election "didn't matter." The home secretary worried aloud that youth had "switched off politics." Polling data tend to confirm the impression that there is a gender gap in the connection between citizens and mainstream politics, and that younger Britons are

more divorced from politics than older ones. Three-quarters of young people aged fifteen to twenty-four have never met their local councilor, compared with just over half of those aged fifty-five or older. Also, older citizens are more than twice as likely to say that they know the name of their local councilor (46 percent compared with 20 percent of fifteen- to twenty-four-year-olds).[†]

That said, the unprecedented participation of British youth in the massive antiwar protests in February and March 2003 tells a different story—one of young people with strong political views and an unexpected taste for political engagement. A BBC poll of schoolchildren in February 2003 reported that 80 percent opposed the war, while Britain as a whole was more evenly divided. As part of a coordinated day of antiwar protests, thousands of teenagers across the country walked out of school and congregated in city centers, while some five hundred protested at the Houses of Parliament. "What's shocking isn't their opposition but the fact they're doing something about it," noted one electronic journalist on a youth-oriented website. "Considering that most 18–25 year olds couldn't even be bothered to put a cross in a box at the last general election this is a pretty big thing."[‡] It was a big enough thing that New Labour strategists were left to ponder the consequences, knowing that the mobilization of support among young people, which was already a cause for concern, was likely to become more difficult in the aftermath of the war in Iraq.

What are the gender and generational storylines in Blair's historic third electoral victory in May 2005? The most talked about theme regarding youth was their continued disaffection from electoral politics. According to MORI, Britain's highly regarded political polling organization, only 37 percent of the possible eighteen- to twenty-four-year-old voters turned out to vote in 2005 (down from 39 percent in 2001). But this is only one side of the generational story. The other side is that the "gray vote" rose. Voters fifty-five and older made up 35 percent of the electorate in 2005 (up 2 percent from 2001) and since 75 percent voted, they represented 42 percent of those casting ballots. As for women—they delivered a very big chunk of Blair's majority.

While men split evenly between Conservatives and Labour an identical 34 percent (and 23 percent for the Lib Dems), women swung decisively to Labour, giving them a 10 percent advantage over the Conservatives (32 percent to 22 percent).§

* Pippa Norris, *Electoral Change in Britain Since 1945* (Oxford: Blackwell, 1997), pp. 133–135; Pippa Norris,

"A Gender-Generation Gap?" in Pippa Norris and Geoffrey Norris, eds., *Critical Elections: British Parties and Voters in Long-Term Perspective* (London: Sage, 1999).

† Market & Opinion Research International, "Many Councillors 'Divorced' from the Electorate," April 30, 2002, www.mori.com/polls/2002/greenissues.shtml.

‡ David Floyd, "British Youth Oppose 'Bomber Blair,'" *WireTap*, March 28, 2003; www.wiretapmag.org/story.html?StoryID=15505.

§ Robert Worcester, "Women's Support Gives Blair the Edge," *Guardian Unlimited*, May 8, 2005, http://politics.guardian.co.uk/election/story/0,15803,1479 238,00.html#article_continue.

family commitments; and to the creation of women-only shortlists in 2005 for candidates to compete in safe Labour constituencies.

As a result, New Labour has obliterated the old gender gap in which women favored the Conservatives and has begun to establish a new pro-Labour women's vote, which may be particularly significant for its ability to mobilize young women.

Interests, Social Movements, and Protest

In recent years, partly in response to globalization, political protest has increased in Britain. As protesters demanded more accountability and transparency from powerful international trade and development agencies, London became the site of protests timed to correspond with the Seattle meeting of the World Trade Organization (WTO), which generated some 100,000 protesters in November 1999.

In addition, since the mid-1990s, the level and intensity of environmental activism took off with the growing attention to genetically modified (GM) crops in the late 1990s. A newly radicalized movement captured the popular imagination with worries that long-term consumption of GM food might be harmful and that once let loose, GM crops—referred to as "Frankenstein food"—might cross-pollinate with "normal" plants. Opinion polls indicated that nearly 75 percent of the population did not want GM crops

in the United Kingdom, and in November 1999, the government announced a ban on commercially grown GM crops in Britain.

In a movement that galvanized the country and raised critical questions about Blair's early leadership, massive demonstrations in September 2000 to protest high fuel prices cut across constituencies and enjoyed huge popular support. A very successful and well-coordinated week-long protest stalled fuel delivery throughout the country, forced 90 percent of the petrol stations to run out of unleaded gasoline, and required the Queen, on the advice of the prime minister, to declare a state of emergency. By the time the blockades came down, opinion polls for the first time in eight years showed the Conservatives for the moment surging past Labour. In fact, polling data indicates that Blair's popularity never recovered from the bump it took over fuel prices.[38]

A quite different kind of activism spread to the countryside among a population not usually known for political protest. Farmers who had been badly hurt by the BSE crisis (bovine spongiform encephalopathy, more popularly known as "mad cow disease") and other rural populations concerned about the perceived urban bias of the Labour government launched massive protests.[39] As the banning and licensing of fox hunting roiled Parliament, the Countryside Alliance, which represents country dwellers who see restrictions on fox hunting as emblematic of domineering urban interests, held mass demonstrations in an effort to block restrictive legislation. Even after a law banning the hunt went into effect in 2005, they kept up the heat with legal challenges.

On the far more significant matter of war in Iraq, a series of antiwar rallies was held throughout the UK. In September 2002, a huge protest rally was organized in London, led by the Stop the War Coalition and the Muslim Association of Britain. It was one of Europe's biggest antiwar rallies. Another antiwar rally in mid-February 2003 challenged Blair's stand on Iraq with at least 750,000 demonstrators.

Finally, recent developments suggest that rumors about the end of class politics in Britain may have been premature. It is true that strike rates in the UK have generally been below the average of both the OECD and the EU in the last decade, but there have been some notable exceptions. For example, a lengthy dispute between local governments and their employees

In April 2008, opposition to the Brown government by traditional Labour supporters grew alongside growing economic worries. Here, members of the National Union of Teachers [NUT] are joined by striking City Council workers in Birmingham, demanding fair pay for teachers. The first national teachers' strike in twenty-one years closed thousands of schools, forcing parents to stay at home or make emergency childcare arrangements. *Source:* John Giles/AP Images

over pension rights produced a massive one-day strike in March 2006, involving between 400,000 (the estimate by employers) and one million (the estimate by union officials) workers. As Brown's government seemed to lose its way in spring 2008, and the sense grew that the economy was in a downward spiral, strike actions increased. Britain experienced its first national teacher's strike in over twenty years, and strikes by oil refinery workers forced a pipeline that handles almost half of the UK's North Sea oil to close. By September at the annual Trades Union Congress (TUC), the unions in attendance spoke of increasingly angry and underpaid members, threatened job actions on several fronts, especially among public-sector workers, insisted on a windfall tax for energy companies—and voted overwhelmingly to reject the government's pay policy for public-sector employees which would cap raises at 2 percent.

Both within the United Kingdom and among observers of British politics and society, many still endorse the view that British culture is characterized by pragmatism, trust, and deference to authority. This may be true, but the persistence and mobilizing potential of a wide range of social movements suggest that quite powerful political subcurrents persist in Britain, posing significant challenges for British government.

SECTION 5   British Politics in Transition

The 1920 partition of the island of Ireland (which separated the six counties that comprise Northern Ireland, which is part of the UK, from the Republic of Ireland, a separate country, with its capital in Dublin, which occupies the remaining five-sixths of the island) left a legacy of mistrust and violence. The unionists, who were mainly Protestants, insisted on union with the UK (hence the name unionists). The Catholic republicans demanded an independent and unified Irish republic, hence the name republicans. One of the longest festering religious, ethnic, and nationalist struggles in the world, the sectarian strife in Northern Ireland killed more than 3,500 people between 1966 and 1999, bedeviled the governments of Britain and Ireland, and shocked the conscience of the world.

At last, in the fall of 1994, cease-fire declarations made by the Irish Republican Army (IRA) and the Protestant paramilitary organizations renewed hope for a peace settlement in Northern Ireland. Then, in a dramatic new development in early spring 1995, British prime minister John Major and Irish prime minister John Bruton jointly issued a framework agreement, inspiring mounting optimism about a political settlement.

With his 1997 landslide victory, Tony Blair had political capital to spend. He invested a chunk of it on peace in Northern Ireland. Blair arranged to meet Gerry Adams, president of Sinn Fein, the party in Northern Ireland with close ties to the IRA—and shook his hand. He was the first prime minister to meet with a head of Sinn Fein since 1921.

Handshake or not, violent turf battles within and between each camp created fear and repeated crises in the peace process. In 2001, the IRA began disarming under the sponsorship of third-party diplomats, and yet violence rose despite cease-fires by paramilitary groups. In 2002, home rule government was suspended, and British direct rule was reimposed. On numerous occasions, Tony Blair and his Irish Republic counterpart, Bertie Ahern, pledged to redouble efforts to get Northern Ireland's faltering peace process back on track, but progress was not easy.

In January 2005, hopes for a settlement were dashed by the blockbuster announcement that linked the IRA to a $40 million bank robbery. In February, Robert McCartney, a Sinn Fein supporter, was brutally murdered by IRA members in a Belfast bar. McCartney's murder, the wall of silence the IRA imposed on some 70 witnesses, and the IRA's offer to kill the men who were responsible, had significant political repercussions. Despite the May 2005 election, which ousted Unionist moderate David Trimble and strengthened the hands of the more radical parties (Sinn Fein and Democratic Unionist Party), the increasingly vocal popular demands for an end to sectarian violence finally broke the deadlock. By mid-2005, the IRA had exhausted its leverage. Gerry Adams seemed ready to press for their dissolution, and—despite denials—insiders spoke of a pending settlement or even a secret deal all but agreed.

At long last—although as always in Northern Ireland, there would be detours and complications—the optimism was well founded. In March 2007, Gerry Adams and Ian Paisley sat at the same table for the first time, declaring that they would work together in a power-sharing government in Northern Ireland. This was a hard-earned crowning achievement for Prime Minister Blair, supported by Chancellor Brown's commitment to a handsome "peace dividend" (a financial package of some $100 billion over a ten-year period to support development and public services, reduce poverty and social exclusion, and spur business initiatives). In May 2007, the unimaginable came to pass. Devolution was restored to Northern Ireland. Ian Paisley became first minister of Northern Ireland and Martin McGuinness the deputy first minister. The Northern Ireland executive, although highly dependent on budgetary transfers from the UK central government, took over responsibility for regional development, health, and education.

As Ian Paisley put it—in almost biblical terms—on the day the power-sharing arrangement was launched, "Northern Ireland has come to a time of peace, when hate will no longer rule." Let us hope that the decades of sectarian strife ("the Troubles") in Northern Ireland are well and truly over—and nearly everyone thinks they are.

Indeed, the success in Northern Ireland was quickly heralded as the crowning achievement in Blair's legacy. Within hours of Blair's departure as prime minister, he was appointed as a Middle East envoy working on behalf of the United States, Russia, the EU, and the UN. As Blair turned his attention to the Middle East, Gordon Brown found his inbox at 10 Downing Street overflowing.

Political Challenges and Changing Agendas

As our democratic idea theme suggests, no democracy, however secure it may be, is a finished project. Even in Britain, with its centuries-old constitutional settlement and secure institutional framework, issues about democratic governance and citizens' participation remain unresolved.

Constitutional Reform

Questions about the role of the monarchy and the House of Lords have long been simmering on Britain's political agenda. "Why is the House of Commons not sovereign?" wondered one observer somewhat caustically. "Why does it have to share sovereignty with other, unelected institutions?"[40] In addition, the balance of power among constitutionally critical institutions raises important questions about a democratic deficit at the heart of the Westminster model. Britain's executive easily overpowers parliament. Its strength in relation to the legislature may be greater than in any other Western democracy. Add to these concerns the prime minister's tendency to bypass the cabinet on crucial decisions and the bias in the electoral system that privileges the two dominant parties.

Many Britons have raised questions about the accountability of the British government to its citizens and have pressed for constitutional reforms. But the reform agenda has been sidetracked in several areas or slowed to a crawl. For example, the Freedom of Information Act was passed in 2002, but a second stage of implementation only began in January 2005. It was also weakened by the extensive range of information it permitted ministers to withhold and by its limited provision for independent review of such ministerial decisions.[41] The Blair government has begun to implement far-reaching reforms of Parliament, including the removal of the right of most hereditary peers to speak and vote in the House of Lords and the redesign of the historic upper chamber. But the form of the new upper chamber has yet to take shape. In addition, the European Convention on Human Rights has been incorporated into UK law. More controversially, plans have been announced for the creation of a "supreme court," but strenuous opposition in both chambers has clouded the prospects for passage.

Despite these uncertainties, the significance of constitutional reform should not be overlooked. The power-sharing initiatives in Northern Ireland and arrangements between Westminster, the Welsh Assembly, and the Scottish Parliament represent basic modifications of UK constitutional principles. Devolution implies both an element of federalism and some compromise in the historic parliamentary sovereignty at the heart of the Westminster model. The potentially unsettling consequences feared by some have not yet come to pass, but neither is stability certain. In August 2007, Alex Salmond, leader of the Scottish National Party (SNP) and first minister in Scotland, promised to introduce legislation that, if passed, would lead to a referendum on Scottish independence by 2010. In May 2008, Wendy Alexander, Labour's leader in the Scottish Parliament, increased the odds for a referendum—and opened a schism with her fellow Scot Gordon Brown—when she responded to talk of a referendum for Scottish independence by declaring, "Bring it on," a view that caught almost everyone (including Gordon Brown) by surprise.

New Labour's constitutional reform agenda confirms that even long-standing democracies face pressures to narrow the gap between government and citizens. The relatively limited results and slowed pace of reforms are important reminders that democratic changes are not easy, just as the uncertainty about potential Scottish independence is an apt reminder that democracy can be a very messy business.

Identities in Flux

The relatively small scale of the ethnic minority community limits the political impact of the most divisive issues concerning collective identities. It is probably in this area that rigidities in the British political system most severely challenge tenets of democracy and tolerance. Given Britain's single-member, simple-plurality electoral system and no proportional representation, minority representation in Parliament is very low. There are deep-seated social attitudes that no government can easily transform.

The issues of immigration, refugees, and asylum still inspire a fear of multiculturalism among white Britons. Finger-pointing at the Muslim community has intensified since September 11. Government policy has hardened its stance on asylum, refugees, and immigration. Since the London bombings by British Muslims on 7/7 that killed 56 people, intense scrutiny has been focused on the Muslim community, which faces ostracism and harassment. According to police, the number of hate crimes primarily affecting Muslims soared 600 percent in the weeks after the bombings. In October 2006, Jack Straw, a highly visible MP and former foreign minister, sparked a controversy and

angered Muslim groups when he said that the full facial veil worn by some Muslim women had become a "visible statement of separation and difference"—and urged them to remove the veil when they came to see him in his constituency office in Blackburn. Then, in 2007, Salman Rushdie, whose 1998 book, *The Satanic Verses,* offended many Muslims around the world and forced him into hiding in the face of a formal death threat from Iranian religious leaders, was knighted by the Queen. The honor accorded Rushdie was widely held to be an affront to the Muslim community in Britain. In October 2007, the UK announced a sweeping change in immigration policy with the planned introduction of a new points-based system that would limit all non-EU immigration to highly skilled people who could contribute to UK productivity and growth. There is increasing concern across the political spectrum that Britain needs to find a way to deepen the ties of shared political culture and values that hold society together as well as to ensure security. Achieving this result is undoubtedly one of Gordon Brown's (and Britain's) greatest challenges.

British Politics, Terrorism, and Britain's Relationship with the United States

In the immediate aftermath of the terror attacks on the United States, Blair's decisive support for President Bush struck a resonant cord in both countries and (despite some grumbling) boosted Britain's influence in Europe. But by the spring and summer of 2002, Blair's stalwart alliance with Bush was looking more and more like a liability.

As Britons' instinctive support for America after September 11 faded, many wondered whether Tony Blair had boxed himself into a corner by aligning himself too closely with George W. Bush—without knowing where the president's foreign policy initiatives might lead in the Middle East and Asia—and in a host of policy areas from trade policy to the conduct of the continuing campaign in Afghanistan, to global warming, to the International Criminal Court. Yet, throughout the diplomatic disputes in the run-up to war in early 2003, Blair persevered in his staunch support for Bush's decision to go to war—this despite Blair's strong preference for explicit Security Council authorization for the use of force and his strong preference that significant progress in resolving the Israeli-Palestinian dispute be made before any military intervention to topple the Saddam Hussein regime.

Nonetheless, despite his inability to achieve either of these preferences, Blair refused all advice (including counsel from members of his cabinet and his chief of defense staff) to make support of the war conditional on achievement of these ends. Blair was convinced that the threats of weapons of mass destruction (WMDs), Al Qaeda terrorism, and rogue states justified the invasion of Iraq and that Britain should and must support the United States in its leadership of a global war against terrorism. Despite initial denials by the prime minister, most Britons instinctively drew a connection between the war in Iraq and the bombs that exploded in London on 7/7. Britons who displayed enormous resolve in the face of terrorism were shaken by a set of troubling revelations—first, that the July 7 bombers were all British and, second, after a botched bombing attempt two weeks later, that London police had shot and killed an innocent man on a subway. Thus, the repercussions of Iraq continued.

There can be no doubt that when Tony Blair came to office as a modernizer offering a "third way" alternative to the tired Tory and Old Labour recipes for governing the economy, no one anticipated that he would leave office likely to be remembered most (especially in America) for his foreign policy, once the die was cast and the special relationship with the United States became the defining feature of Blair's government after 9/11. It is in Gordon Brown's interest to distinguish his premiership from Blair's in this regard and in his early days as prime minister, he began to do just that—not by any criticism of American policy, but through his key foreign policy appointments. As noted above, Brown appointed Mark Malloch Brown, a vociferous critic of the UK's role in the war in Iraq, as a high-profile minister with broad international affairs responsibilities. More importantly, Brown appointed David Miliband as foreign minister, a young rising star in the party who is known to have reservations about aspects of Blair's policy in the Middle East. Miliband was quick to pledge his commitment to "patient as well as purposeful diplomacy," a signal that issues of development and climate change would be very high on the agenda and a recourse to the use of force more distant. At the same time, Brown quickly made it clear that useful lessons could be learned from the experience of the war in Iraq, leaving few in doubt that he would be reluctant to repeat such an exercise anytime soon. That said, when the military dispute between Georgia and Russia erupted in August 2008, the UK took a hard line against Putin and Medvedev, and expended considerable diplomatic energy in the effort to develop a unified and hard-headed European response to Russia. Clearly, foreign policy priorities are shaped by urgent and sometimes unexpected challenges.

British Politics in Comparative Perspective

Until the Asian financial crisis that began in 1997, it was an axiom of comparative politics that economic success required a style of economic governance that Britain lacks. Many argued that innovation and competitiveness in the new global economy required the strategic coordination of the economy by an interventionist state. Interestingly, however, the United Kingdom escaped the recession that plagued the rest of Europe for much of the 1990s. As Britain approaches the end of the new century's first decade, however, like many countries in the world, it is facing very serious challenges as a result of the crisis in the world financial system. In terms of governing the economy, sluggish growth forecasts, rising inflation, and a severe mortgage and credit squeeze, accompanied by deteriorating home values, suggest very hard times ahead. In November 2008 the International Monetary Fund predicted that as the financial crisis spreads to other sectors, such as manufacturing, the UK will suffer more than any other of the world's rich countries.

In many countries throughout the world, politicians are looking for an economic model that can sustain economic competitiveness while improving the plight of the socially excluded. New Labour's third way—a political orientation designed to transcend left and right in favor of practical and effective policies—has been carefully watched for more than ten years. Observers have seen in New Labour a historic intellectual and political realignment, not only in Britain, but in Clinton's America and Cardoso's (and later Lula's) Brazil, even as it was refashioning Schroeder's Germany in its own image and, in time, drawing others, such as Nigeria's Obasanjo, into its orbit.

If the third way can be sustained, despite the current uncertainty in both its economic and political fortunes, and Brown can rebound in time to reassure his critics in the Labour party and recoup his reputation in the country, New Labour seems destined to be even more widely emulated and assume considerable historic significance in comparative perspective. With growing disaffection with Brown in the country, declining economic fortunes, and increasing signs of political infighting as potential successors considered a challenge to Brown's leadership in September 2008, but the challenge was short-lived. By October, Brown's clarity and quick thinking in the face of the global financial meltdown sent his political stock soaring. While the US dithered, the UK quickly announced and implemented a plan to inject huge doses of equity into wobbly financial institutions and guarantee their debts—a plan that many countries in the world adopted, crediting Brown for global leadership. Suddenly Mr. Bean was gone, and the iron chancellor (now prime minister) was back. Brown was still facing long odds, but it now seemed possible that he might recapture the initiative. Of course, an electorate pounded by years of recession, rising unemployment, and home foreclosures might no longer feel grateful in 2010 to a prime minister or party which, despite decisive action, could not find solutions.

Key Terms »

parliamentary democracy
free trade
hegemonic power
laissez-faire
welfare state
special relationship
Westminster model
neoliberalism
gender gap
macroeconomic policy

Keynesianism
monetarism
new growth theory
foreign direct investment
parliamentary sovereignty
unitary state
fusion of powers
cabinet government
constitutional monarchy
quangos

Suggested Readings »

Beer, Samuel H. *Britain Against Itself: The Political Contradictions of Collectivism.* New York: Norton, 1982.

Coates, David. *Prolonged Labour.* London: Palgrave/Macmillan, 2005.

Coates, David, and Krieger, Joel. *Blair's War.* Cambridge, UK, and Malden, Mass.: Polity Press, 2004.

Coates, David, and Lawler, Peter, eds. *New Labour in Power.* Manchester: Manchester University Press, 2000.

Cook, Robin. *The Point of Departure.* London: Simon & Schuster, 2003.

Cronin, James E. *New Labour's Pasts.* Harrow, UK: Pearson/Longman, 2004.

Dunleavy, Patrick, et al. *Developments in British Politics 7.* New York: Palgrave/Macmillan, 2003.

Gamble, Andrew. *Between Europe and America: The Future of British Politics.* London: Palgrave/Macmillan, 2003.

George, Bruce. *The British Labour Party and Defense.* New York: Praeger, 1991.

Giddens, Anthony. *The Third Way: The Renewal of Social Democracy.* Cambridge: Polity Press, 1998.

Gilroy, Paul. *"There Ain't No Black in the Union Jack": The Cultural Politics of Race and Nation.* Chicago: University of Chicago Press, 1991.

Hall, Stuart, and Jacques, Martin, eds. *The Politics of Thatcherism.* London: Lawrence and Wishart, 1983.

Hobsbawm, E. J. *Industry and Empire.* Harmondsworth, UK: Penguin/Pelican, 1983.

Howell, Chris. *Trade Unions and the State: The Construction of Industrial Relations Institutions in Britain, 1890–2000.* Princeton: Princeton University Press, 2005.

Kampfner, John. *Blair's Wars.* London: Free Press, 2003.

Kavanagh, Dennis, and Seldon, Anthony. *The Powers Behind the Prime Minister: The Hidden Influence of Number Ten.* London: Harper-Collins, 1999.

King, Anthony, ed. *Britain at the Polls, 2001.* New York and London: Chatham House, 2002.

Krieger, Joel. *Globalization and State Power.* New York: Pearson/Longman, 2005.

Krieger, Joel. *British Politics in the Global Age. Can Social Democracy Survive?* New York: Oxford University Press, 1999.

Landes, David S. *The Unbound Prometheus: Technological Change and Industrial Development in Western Europe from 1750 to the Present.* Cambridge: Cambridge University Press, 1969.

Lewis, Philip. *Islamic Britain: Religion, Politics and Identity among British Muslims.* London and New York: I. B. Taurus, 2002.

Marsh, David, et al. *Postwar British Politics in Perspective.* Cambridge: Polity Press, 1999.

Marshall, Geoffrey. *Ministerial Responsibility.* Oxford: Oxford University Press, 1989.

Middlemas, Keith. *Politics in Industrial Society: The Experience of the British System Since 1911.* London: André Deutsch, 1979.

Modood, Tariq. *Multicultural Politics: Racism, Ethnicity, and Muslims in Britain.* Minneapolis: University of Minnesota Press, 2005.

Norris, Pippa. *Electoral Change in Britain Since 1945.* Oxford: Blackwell Publishers, 1997.

Parekh, Bhiku, et al. *The Future of Multi-Ethnic Britain: The Parekh Report.* London: Profile Books, 2000.

Riddell, Peter. *The Thatcher Decade.* Oxford: Basil Blackwell, 1989.

Särlvik, Bo, and Crewe, Ivor. *Decade of Dealignment: The Conservative Victory of 1979 and Electoral Trends in the 1970s.* Cambridge: Cambridge University Press, 1983.

Shaw, Eric. *The Labour Party Since 1945.* Oxford: Blackwell Publishers, 1996.

Thompson, E. P. *The Making of the English Working Class.* New York: Vintage, 1966.

Wright, Tony, ed. *The British Political Process.* London: Routledge, 2000.

Suggested Websites »

Directgov–Portal to public service information from the UK government
www.direct.gov.uk
UK Statistics Authority
www.statistics.gov.uk
The UK Parliament
www.parliament.uk
The Cabinet Office
www.cabinet-office.gov.uk

The Scottish Parliament
www.scottish.parliament.uk
British Broadcasting Corporation (BBC)
www.bbc.co.uk
Market & Opinion Research International (MORI), Britain's leading political polling organization
www.mori.com

Endnotes »

[1]Jeremy Black, *The Politics of Britain, 1688–1800* (Manchester: Manchester University Press, 1993), p. 6.

[2]E. J. Hobsbawm, *Industry and Empire* (Harmondsworth, UK: Penguin/Pelican, 1983), pp. 29–31.

[3]See Duncan Fraser, "The Postwar Consensus: A Debate Not Long Enough?" *Parliamentary Affairs* 53, no. 2 (April 2000): 347–362.

[4]See David Smith, "The Treasury and Economic Policy," in Seldon & Kavanagh, eds., *The Blair Effect 2001–5* (Cambridge University Press, 2005), p. 177.

[5]See David Coates, *Prolonged Labour* (London: Palgrave, 2005), ch.1.

[6]Ivor Crewe, "Labor Force Changes, Working Class Decline, and the Labour Vote: Social and Electoral Trends in Postwar Britain," in Frances Fox Piven, ed., *Labor Parties in Postindustrial Societies* (New York: Oxford University Press, 1992), p. 34. See also David Marsh and R. A. W. Rhodes, "Implementing Thatcherism: Policy Change in the 1980s," *Parliamentary Affairs* 45, no. 1 (January 1992): 34–37.

[7]Steven Fielding, "A New Politics?" in Patrick Dunleavy et al., eds., *Developments in British Politics 6* (New York: St. Martin's Press, 2000), p. 2.

[8]National Statistics Online, "Population Size: 7.9% from a Minority Ethnic Group," February 13, 2003; www.statistics.gov.uk/cci/nugget.asp?id=273.

[9]Office of National Statistics Social Survey, *Living in Britain: Results from the 1995 General Household Survey* (London: The Stationery Office, 1997).

[10]Gail Lewis, "Black Women's Employment and the British Economy," in Winston James and Clive Harris, eds., *Inside Babylon: The Caribbean Diaspora in Britain* (London: Verso, 1993), pp. 73–96.

[11]National Statistics Online, "Low Income for 60% of Pakistanis/Bangladeshis," December 12, 2002; www.statistics.gov.uk/CCI/nugget.asp?ID=269&Pos=1&ColRank=2&Rank=384.

[12]"All White at the Top," *Guardian*, May 25, 2004; education.guardian.co.uk/egweekly/story/0,5500,1223478,00.html.

[13]Ibid.

[14]Women & Equality Unit, "What is the Pay Gap and Why Does It Exist?"; www.womenandequalityunit.gov.uk/pay/pay_facts.htm.

[15]Jane Lewis, "The Pursuit of Welfare Ends and Market Means and the Case of Work/Family Reconciliation Policies," p. 10, paper presented at the Conference on *Cool Britannia: Britain After Eight Years of Labour Government*, Montreal, Cerium, May 4–6, 2005.

[16]Ibid.

[17]Klaus Schwab and Michael Porter, eds., *The Global Competitiveness Report*, 2004–2005 (World Economic Forum/Palgrave Macmillan, 2005).

[18]Ibid., pp. 454–5.

[19]OECD Economic Surveys: United Kingdom (2005), ch. 7.

[20]See Philip Norton, *The British Polity*, 3rd ed. (New York: Longman, 1994), p. 59, for a useful discussion of the sources of the British constitution.

[21]Stephen Haseler, "Britain's Ancien Régime," *Parliamentary Affairs 40*, no. 4 (October 1990): 415.

[22]See Philip Norton, "Parliament in Transition," in Robert Pyper and Lynton Robins, eds., *United Kingdom Governance* (New York: St. Martin's Press, 2000), pp. 82–106.

[23]S. E. Finer, *Five Constitutions* (Atlantic Highlands, N.J.: Humanities Press, 1979), p. 52.

[24]Iain Byrne and Stuart Weir, "Democratic Audit: Executive Democracy in War and Peace," *Parliamentary Affairs 57*, no. 2 (April 2004): 455.

[25]John Kampfner, *Blair's Wars* (London: The Free Press, 2005), p. 294.

[26]Martin J. Smith, "The Core Executive and the Modernization of Central Government," in Patrick Dunleavy et al., eds., *Developments in British Politics 7* (New York: Palgrave/Macmillan, 2003), p. 60.

[27]See Kevin Theakston, "Ministers and Civil Servants," in Pyper and Robins, eds., *United Kingdom Governance* (New York: Palgrave/Macmillan, 2000), pp. 39–60.

[28]See Stephen Driver and Luke Martell, *New Labour, 2nd ed.* (Cambridge, England: Polity, 2006), pp.125–129.

[29]Tony Blair, "Doctrine of the International Community," speech to the Economic Club of Chicago, Hilton Hotel, Chicago, April 22, 1999. For a detailed discussion of the speech and its implications for the war in Iraq, see David Coates and Joel Krieger, *Blair's War* (Malden, Mass.: Polity Press, 2004), ch. 6.

[30]See Dennis Kavanagh, *British Politics: Continuities and Change, 3rd ed.* (Oxford: Oxford University Press, 1996), 282–288.

[31]Samuel H. Beer, *The British Political System* (New York: Random House, 1973), p. 157.

[32]See Stephen Driver and Luke Martell, *New Labour, 2nd ed.* (Cambridge, England: Polity Press, 2006), pp. 8–9

[33]Ivor Crewe, "Great Britain," in I. Crewe and D. Denver, eds., *Electoral Change in Western Democracies* (London: Croom Helm, 1985), p. 107.

[34]John Bartle, "Why Labour Won—Again," in Anthony King et al., eds., *Britain at the Polls, 2001* (New York: Chatham House, 2002), p. 171.

[35]See Gabriel A. Almond and Sidney Verba, *The Civic Culture: Political Attitudes and Democracy in Five Nations* (Princeton, N.J.: Princeton University Press, 1963); Almond and Verba, eds., *The Civic Culture Revisited* (Boston: Little, Brown, 1980); and Samuel H. Beer, *Britain Against Itself: The Political Contradictions of Collectivism* (New York: Norton, 1982), pp. 110–114.

[36]See Chris Howell, *Trade Unions and the State* (Princeton University Press, 2005), ch 6.

[37]David Sanders, "The Political Economy of Labour Support, 1997–2005," paper presented at the Conference on *Cool Britannia: Britain After Eight Years of Labour Government*, Montreal, Cerium, May 4–6, 2005.

[38]David Sanders, "The New Labour and the Electoral Dynamics," paper presented to the *Cool Britannia: Britain After Eight Years of Labour Government*, Montreal, Cerium, May 4–6, 2005.

[39]See Helen Margetts, "Political Participation and Protest," in Patrick Dunleavy et al., eds., *Developments in British Politics 6* (New York: St. Martin's Press, 2000), pp. 185–202.

[40]Stephen Haseler, "Britain's Ancien Régime," *Parliamentary Affairs* 40, no. 4 (October 1990): 418.

[41]Iain Byrne and Stuart Weir, "Democratic Audit: Executive Democracy in War and Peace," *Parliamentary Affairs* 57, no. 2 (2004): 453–468.

Mark Kesselman

Chapter 3 ≫ FRANCE

Official Name: **French Republic
(République Française)**

Location: **Western Europe**

Capital City: **Paris**

Population (2008): **64 million**

Size: **634,427 sq. km.; slightly
smaller than Texas**

Until 1789
Ancien régime (Bourbon monarchy)

1789–1799
Revolutionary regimes
Constituent Assembly, 1789–1791
(Declaration of Rights of Man, Aug. 26, 1789)
Legislative Assembly, 1791–1792
National Convention, 1792–1795:
Monarchy abolished and First Republic established, 1792 Directory, 1795–1799

1800–1814
Consulate and First Empire (Napoleon Bonaparte)

1814–1830
Restoration

SECTION 1 **The Making of the Modern French State**

Politics in Action

In most ways, the evening of May 2, 2007, was like any other in France. Yet it didn't seem like business as usual. Normally lively cities and towns throughout the country were eerily quiet. Streets were deserted. So too were cafés, movie theaters, and restaurants. Why did France come to a halt? The answer: most French were glued to their television sets watching presidential candidates Nicolas Sarkozy and Ségolène Royal face off in the only televised debate of the campaign.

The stakes in the debate were high. Polls suggested that only a few percentage points separated **conservative** frontrunning candidate Sarkozy from **socialist** Ségolène Royal. If "Ségo" could outperform "Sarko"—or if she could provoke him into losing his proverbially bad temper—the debate could decide the election.

For hours, the candidates analyzed the state of France, identified what they regarded as its most pressing problems, presented their reform proposals and—above all—probed for weaknesses in their opponent. As the underdog and a woman, Royal had the harder job: she needed to demonstrate that she possessed the authority and technical competence to become the first female president of France. But Sarkozy also had challenges to overcome: for a starter, he needed to remain cool under fire. Further, because he was the candidate of the major conservative party—the party of Jacques Chirac, France's tired and quite unpopular

president for the past twelve years—Sarkozy had to demonstrate solidarity with less-fortunate citizens and persuade voters that he would break with the past and make a fresh start.

When the debate finally ended—it ran well over the allotted two hours—a majority of French judged that Sarkozy was the winner. And several days later, this opinion translated into a 57 to 43 percent victory for Sarkozy. The intense interest in the debate was evident at the polls as well: 85 percent of registered voters turned out to vote. (Turnout in American presidential elections hovers around 50 percent.)

Three factors probably explain the outcome of the debate and the election. First, Sarkozy appeared more knowledgeable and authoritative. Royal often improvised or evaded answers to tough questions, for example, how to finance and implement her reform proposals. Second, Sarkozy was supported by France's best-organized and unified party, the *Union for a Popular Majority* (UMP). Sarkozy had been president of the UMP since 2004, and the party was solidly behind him. By contrast, Royal won the Socialist Party nomination after a bitter struggle; many party leaders and members gave her candidacy only lukewarm support. Finally, Sarkozy's vision of where he wanted to lead France appealed to more voters than did Royal's. Sarkozy proclaimed the need to unleash private market forces and reward individual initiative and hard work, deregulate the economy, slim down government, and crack down on crime. Royal highlighted the need to

1830–1848
July Monarchy

1848–1851
Second
Republic

1852–1870
Second Empire (Louis
Napoleon)

1871
Paris Commune

1871–1940
Third Republic

1940–1944
Vichy regime

1946–1958
Fourth Republic

1958–Present
Fifth Republic

protect welfare state programs and help the needy. But these were familiar appeals and they fell flat when she failed to explain how she planned to revive France's ailing economy to finance her proposals.

At the same time, Sarkozy and Royal were alike in some ways. Both were in their early fifties and represented a new generation of politicians, a refreshing contrast to most French political leaders, who were well over sixty years old and long-established fixtures of the political scene. Both were mavericks rather than conventional leaders of their respective parties.

How successful has Sarkozy been in implementing his bold vision? Are French political institutions, policies, and culture a help or a hindrance? When other conservative politicians proposed cutbacks in social benefits, the result was nationwide protests and stalemate. To understand why, we need to study how the four major themes of *Introduction to Comparative Politics* have combined to form the exceptional pattern of French politics.

Geographic Setting

France is among the world's favored countries, thanks to its temperate climate, large and fertile land area, and high standard of living. Its natural beauty and superb architecture, culture, and cuisine make France the most popular tourist destination in the world. With that said, the site drawing the most visitors is not Notre Dame Cathedral, the Louvre museum, or

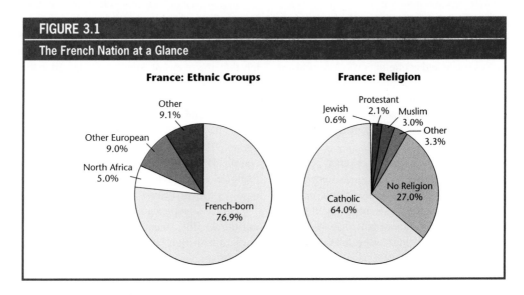

FIGURE 3.1

The French Nation at a Glance

France: Ethnic Groups

- Other 9.1%
- Other European 9.0%
- North Africa 5.0%
- French-born 76.9%

France: Religion

- Jewish 0.6%
- Protestant 2.1%
- Muslim 3.0%
- Other 3.3%
- No Religion 27.0%
- Catholic 64.0%

France

Table 3.1	
Political Organization	
Political System	Unitary republic. Semipresidential system; popularly elected president, popularly elected parliament, and prime minister and government appointed by president and responsible to National Assembly (as well as informally responsible to president).
Regime History	Frequent regime changes since the French Revolution of 1789. Most recently, a dictatorial regime based on Vichy collaborated with the Nazis during World War II; the Fourth Republic existed from 1946–1958; and the Fifth Republic, originating in 1958, has become universally accepted.
Administrative Structure	Unitary, with 22 regions and 100 departments.
Executive	Dual executive: president (five-year term); PM appointed by president, generally leader of majority coalition in National Assembly, and responsible to National Assembly (as well as informally responsible to president).
Legislature	Bicameral. Senate (upper house) has power to delay legislation passed by lower house and to veto proposed constitutional amendments. National Assembly (lower house) can pass legislation and force government to resign by passing a censure motion.
Judiciary	A system of administrative, criminal, and civil courts. At the top, a nine-member independent Constitutional Council named for nonrenewable nine-year terms; president of republic names three members, president of each house of parliament names three. The Constitutional Council exercises right of judicial review.
Party System	Multiparty. Principal parties: Socialist Party (PS); Union for a Popular Movement (UMP); minor parties: National Front (FN); Communist Party (PCF); Green Party; Mouvement Démocratique; and many others throughout the political spectrum.

the Eiffel Tower—but Disneyland-Paris, the most visited tourist site in all Europe.

The French have a reputation for living well (*joie de vivre* is the French term), ranging from a love of art, culture, and romance to appreciation of fine food and wine. On a more mundane level, however, France has its share of social and economic problems. Indeed, France ranked only 64th out of 178 countries in the world in a study of citizen happiness, on a par with Indonesia and El Salvador and far behind Britain—41st, Germany—35th, and the United States—23rd. (Denmark and Switzerland top the list.)[1]

With a population of 60 million, France is among the most populous countries in Western Europe, but its large size—211,000 square miles, which makes it the third-largest country in Europe—means that population density is low (about half that of Britain, Germany, and Italy). An unusual feature of French national boundaries is that five overseas territories—the Mediterranean island of Corsica, the Caribbean

islands of Guadeloupe and Martinique, French Guyana in South America, and the island of Réunion in the Indian Ocean—are considered an integral part of France. Their inhabitants are French citizens with full citizenship rights. For example, they elect representatives to the French legislature. (Their situation parallels that of citizens of Alaska and Hawaii in the United States political system.)

France's gross domestic product (GDP) of over $2 trillion and per capita income of $33,200 make it among the most affluent countries in the world. France ranked 10th out of 177 countries in the 2008 United Nations Development Programme's Human Development Index, a widely respected measure of the overall quality of life.

France occupies a key position in Europe, bordering the Mediterranean Sea in the south and sharing borders with Belgium, Switzerland, and Germany on the north and east, Spain in the southwest, and Italy in the southeast. France is Britain's closest continental neighbor. The two are separated by the English Channel, only twenty-five miles at its most narrow stretch. With the 1994 opening of the "Chunnel," a railroad tunnel under the English Channel, the two countries are even closer. France has quite secure natural borders of mountains and seas everywhere except on the open plains of the northeast bordering Belgium and Germany. The flat, unprotected terrain enabled German forces to invade France three times in the nineteenth and twentieth centuries.

France has a modern economy, and most people work in the industrial and service sectors. But agriculture continues to occupy a significant place in the economy; France is among the world's largest exporters of agricultural products. No other French city rivals Paris, the capital, in size and influence; Lille, Lyon, and Marseille are the next largest cities.

Critical Junctures

A central feature of French history—from premodern times to the present—has been the prominent role played by the state. France was created by monarchs who laboriously united the diverse regions and provinces of what is present-day France—actions that provoked periodic violent resistance. The French have often

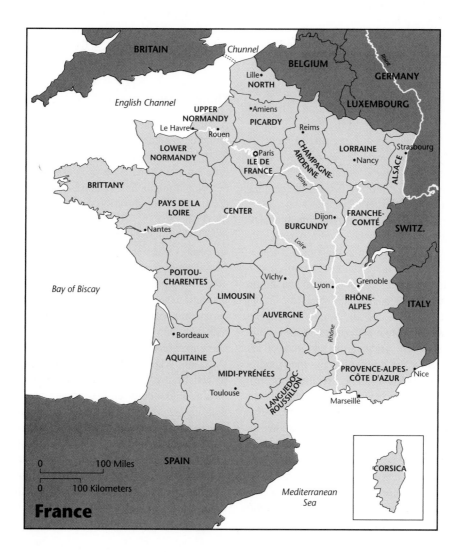

France

France

displayed great respect for the state's achievements—and intense resentment at its high-handed behavior. However, the state's preeminence has recently been jostled by France's participation in the globalized economy and the EU, along with economic reforms and **decentralization** measures. Nowadays, Paris—the national capital and seat of the ministries that govern French life—must vie with regional and local governments throughout France, as well as with Brussels, headquarters of the EU; Frankfurt, where the European Central Bank is located; and Strasbourg, home of the European Parliament.

Creating Modern France

For five centuries at the beginning of the modern era, the area that is now France was part of the Roman Empire. The Romans called the area Gaul (the source of the term *Gallic,* sometimes used to describe the French). France took its current name from the Franks, a Germanic tribe who conquered the area in the fifth century A.D., after the breakup of the Roman Empire. The Frankish Merovingian dynasty ruled France for several centuries. It was succeeded by the Carolingian dynasty, whose most noteworthy ruler, Charlemagne, founded the Holy Roman Empire in the ninth century; it extended throughout Western Europe.

Several decades after Charlemagne's death in 814, his three grandsons divided the empire. Charles the Bald, as he was known, obtained most of the area of present-day France. Hugues Capet was chosen king in 987 by nobles who judged that he would be a more effective ruler than Charlemagne's successors. During the next three centuries, Capetian monarchs struggled to subdue powerful provincial rulers in Burgundy, Brittany, and elsewhere. The country was invaded and nearly conquered by the English during the Hundred Years' War (1337–1453). Joan of Arc, a peasant who believed she had a divine mission, led French forces to victory against the English army. Although Joan herself was captured and burned at the stake, her defeat of the English at Orléans has made her a symbol of intense national pride ever since.

France flourished during the next several centuries, especially after Henri IV (who ruled from 1589 to 1610) eased religious conflict between Catholics and Huguenots (Protestants) by issuing the Edict of Nantes in 1598 granting Protestants limited religious toleration. Protestants lost many of these rights when Louis XIV revoked the edict in 1685.

For a century and a half, France and England competed for control of North America. The rivalry ended with France's defeat in the French and Indian Wars, also known as the Seven Years' War (1754–1763). At a later period, France engaged in further colonial conquests in Africa, Asia, and the Caribbean.

The seventeenth and eighteenth centuries were the high point of French economic, military, and cultural influence. France was the most affluent and powerful country in continental Europe. It was also the artistic and scientific capital of Europe, home of the Enlightenment in the eighteenth century, the philosophical movement that emphasized the importance of scientific reason rather than religious belief or folk wisdom.

The Ancien Régime

A turning point in the struggle between French monarchs and provincial rulers came when Louis XIV (r. 1643–1715) sponsored the creation of a relatively efficient state bureaucracy, separate from the Crown's personal domain. France began to be administered according to a legal–rational code applied throughout the country.

The absolutist state created by Louis XIV and his successors coexisted with a patchwork of taxes and feudal privileges that weighed heavily upon peasants, urban workers, and a rising middle class. Another key institution was the Catholic Church—a large landowner, tax collector, and ally of the feudal authorities. This complex system was later described as the *ancien régime,* or old regime.

Louis XIV and his successor, Louis XV, overplayed France's hand. From the mid-seventeenth to the mid-eighteenth century, France was usually at war with its neighbors and engaged in colonial conquests overseas. As the historian Simon Schama notes, "No other European power attempted to support both a major continental army and a transcontinental navy at the same time."[2] When Britain began to reap the benefits of the Agricultural and Industrial Revolutions while France's economy remained stagnant, the French monarchy was forced to borrow heavily to compete with Britain. By 1788, interest on past French loans consumed over one-half of current state expenditures.[3] When Louis XVI tried to raise taxes in 1789, he provoked a violent reaction that sealed the fate of the French monarchy.

The Two Faces of the French Revolution, 1789–1815

The crowd that stormed Paris's Bastille prison on July 14, 1789, to free the prisoners helped launch the French **Revolution**. In short order, the French monarchy and the entire *ancien régime* of nobility and feudal privileges were abolished. A succession of revolutionary regimes quickly followed, including the Constituent Assembly (which in 1789 issued the world-famous Declaration of the Rights of Man and the Citizen), the Legislative Assembly, the Convention, and the Directory.

It is difficult to overestimate the impact of the Revolution on French and world history. Historian Lynn Hunt observes, "The chief accomplishment of the French Revolution was the institution of a dramatically new political culture. . . . The French Revolution may be said to represent the transition to political and social modernity, the first occasion when the people entered upon the historical stage to remake the political community."[4] The First **Republic**, created in 1792, was the first modern European regime based on the principle that all citizens, regardless of social background, were equal before the law.

The Revolution of 1789 was at the same time a *national* revolution, which affirmed the people's right to choose their own political regime; an *international* revolution, which inspired national uprisings elsewhere in Europe, often promoted by French armed intervention; a *liberal* revolution, which championed individual liberty in the political and economic spheres, as well as **secularism** and religious freedom, instead of state-mandated dominance by the Catholic Church in religious affairs; and a *democratic* revolution, which proclaimed that all citizens have equal rights. The Revolution's provocative ideas have spread far beyond France's borders and have become part of our universal heritage.

The Revolution was seriously flawed. The revolutionary regime betrayed its inspiring message of liberty, equality, and fraternity by acting with brutality and intolerance. During the Reign of Terror, the Jacobin state—the radical faction that gained control after an internal power struggle—guillotined political opponents and many revolutionaries. Despite some reforms that were in women's interests (for example, short-lived divorce legislation), the Revolution was quite hostile to women. As historian Joan Scott notes, "The [First] Republic was constructed against women, not just without them, and nineteenth-century Republicans did not actively counteract this masculinist heritage of republicanism."[5]

In other ways, too, the Revolution left a complex legacy. Alexis de Tocqueville, a brilliant French aristocrat and writer who lived in the early nineteenth century, identified two quite opposite impacts of the Revolution. It produced a rupture with the *ancien régime* by abolishing the monarchy and inherited privileges of all kinds. Yet, like French monarchs for centuries past, it sought to strengthen state institutions and discourage private citizens from forming autonomous associations.[6] (Social theorists describe a country's network of private civic associations as **civil society**.)

Many of the institutions promoting centralization were created by the revolutionary leader—and then emperor—Napoleon Bonaparte, among the most notable political leaders of the modern era. Born on the French island of Corsica in 1769, Napoleon rose through the ranks of the army and became a wildly popular general after leading France's revolutionary forces to brilliant victories in Italy and Egypt. In 1799, he carried out a coup d'état (an illegal seizure of power) and proclaimed himself emperor in 1802. Several of Napoleon's reforms remain to this day. For example, the Napoleonic Code of Law is a detailed legal framework copied in many European countries. He also strengthened the system of central administration. Since Napoleon's defeat in 1815 by a coalition of forces led by Britain, French politics has often involved the question of how to reconcile the state's independence from pressure coming from groups within society with democratic participation and decision-making.

Along with its democratic legacy, the Revolution produced enduring scars. Its hostility toward organized religion, in particular the Catholic Church, deeply polarized French society. Further, the Revolution's disdain for pragmatism and compromise has intensified political conflict and instability. Scholars often compare the French style of historical development with the British. Although Britain saw its share of instability in an early period (notably, the Revolution of the 1640s and 1650s), since then it has exhibited a pattern of relatively peaceful, incremental change that contrasts dramatically with France's political style.

Many Regimes, Slow Industrialization: 1815–1940

During the nineteenth and twentieth centuries, France confronted the powerful and complex legacy of the Revolution of 1789. Following Napoleon's defeat, the monarchy was restored (hence the name, the Restoration). It was overthrown in a popular uprising in July 1830, and the king's distant cousin, Louis Philippe, assumed the throne. (This regime is known as the July Monarchy.) In 1848, another revolution produced the short-lived Second Republic. Louis Napoleon, the nephew of Napoleon Bonaparte, overthrew the republic after three years and proclaimed himself emperor. When France lost the Franco-Prussian War of 1870–1871, a revolutionary upheaval produced the Paris Commune, a brief experiment in worker-governed democracy. The Commune was violently crushed after a few months, to be succeeded by the Third Republic, which was created after France's military defeat and civil war in 1871. Thus, in the century following the Revolution of 1789, France oscillated between monarchy and radical democracy. Since the creation of the Third Republic, France has been ruled by democratic republics, save for a brief period during World War II.

The Third Republic was a parliamentary regime with a feeble executive. Given the legacy of Louis Napoleon's illegal seizure of power and the ideologically fragmented state of French society, the republic was designed to prevent decisive leadership. The Third Republic never commanded much support. (It was described, in a famous phrase by conservative politician Adolphe Thiers, as the regime "that divides us [French] least.") Yet it proved France's most durable modern regime. It survived the terrible ordeal of World War I—when over one million French soldiers were killed—and held firm against extremist forces on the right during the 1920s and 1930s, when republics were crumbling in Germany, Italy, and Spain. However, the Third Republic collapsed when the Nazis invaded France in 1940.

The regime changes in the nineteenth and twentieth centuries were a product of the sharp ideological cleavages and inability of political institutions to regulate conflict. However, in sharp contrast with the dizzying pace at which regimes came and went, the rate of economic change in France during this period was quite gradual. Compared with Germany, its dynamic neighbor to the northeast, France chose economic stability over modernization.

Although France began the nineteenth century as the world's second economic power, close behind Britain, by 1900 it had fallen to fourth, after Britain, the United States, and Germany. A large peasantry acted as a brake on industrialization, as did the fact that France was poorly endowed with coal, iron, and petroleum. Historians also point to the relatively underdeveloped entrepreneurial spirit in France. France excelled in producing custom-made luxury goods, such as silk fabrics and fine porcelain, which could not be produced by mechanized techniques and for which mass markets did not exist.

Another factor inhibiting industrial development was slow population growth. In the mid-nineteenth century, France was the most populous nation in Europe after Russia. However, although Britain's population tripled in the nineteenth century and Germany's doubled, France's population increased by less than one-half.[7] As a result, there was less incentive for businesses to invest.

State policies also contributed to a lag in economic modernization. In Britain, the government removed restrictions on entrepreneurs; in Prussia (later Germany), the powerful chancellor, Otto von Bismarck, imposed industrialization from above. Economic historian Richard Kuisel observes that the French state failed "to promote economic expansion, plan development, or advance economic democracy." Instead, it aimed to "maintain an equilibrium among industry, commerce, and agriculture and attempt[ed] to insulate France from the distress and upheaval that had struck other nations bent upon rapid economic advance."[8] In order to shield domestic producers from foreign competition, France retained high tariff barriers.

Yet the state did not simply prevent economic modernization. In a tradition dating back to Colbert, the finance minister of Louis XIV who created the French merchant marine, the state did organize important economic projects. For example, in the 1860s Louis Napoleon sponsored an extensive rail network throughout France.

In the eighteenth and nineteenth centuries, France conquered vast areas in North America, North Africa, sub-Saharan Africa, Southeast Asia, the Caribbean (including the islands of Haiti, Guadeloupe, Martinique), Pacific islands (Réunion), and South America (French Guiana, known in French as Guyane). France lost a large portion of its colonial holdings in North America when Britain won the Seven Years' War (1754–1763). In 1803, Napoleon Bonaparte sold a vast area that comprises fifteen present-day states of the U.S. and two Canadian provinces, known in the U.S. as the Louisiana Purchase, to President Thomas Jefferson. France's only remaining colonies in North America were two small islands in the North Atlantic. Yet despite its losses in North America, France's vast colonial empire in the nineteenth century was second only to that of Britain.

Under the pretext of bringing civilization to "backward" areas—the French term was "*la mission civilisatrice*"—France extracted natural resources and used the colonies as protected markets for French exports. Most colonies eventually gained their independence in the 1960s, sometimes after violent struggles. However, France continues to maintain informal influence in some former colonies, especially in sub-Saharan Africa. As described above, several others have become an integral part of the French republic, with the same legal status as regions comprising metropolitan France.

Years of trench warfare on French soil took a deadly toll during World War I (1914–18), when over 1 million French troops were killed—more than double the number of American armed forces killed in every foreign war since 1776. France emerged from the war devastated, but with the Third Republic intact. However, France continued to maintain its defensive, conservative posture in the following years, including during the period in the 1930s when Hitler's Nazi regime was modernizing and arming Germany.

To sum up, until World War II, the state sought to preserve political stability rather than promote economic modernization. However, while slow economic growth did not prevent political conflict, it did contribute to France's crushing defeat by Germany in 1940.

Vichy France (1940–1944) and the Fourth Republic (1946–1958)

World War II was one of the bleakest periods in French history. When France was overrun by the Nazi army in 1940, Marshall Henri Philippe Pétain, an aged World War I military hero who was president of France, destroyed the Third Republic by signing an armistice with Hitler. The agreement divided France in two zones. The north was under direct German control. Although the south was considered an independent country whose capital was at Vichy (it is informally known as the Vichy Regime), it was a puppet of Nazi Germany. For example, it sent 1 million French citizens to work in German factories and shipped large amounts of manufactured goods and food to Germany. It was the only regime in Western Europe not directly under German occupation that actively supported the Nazis' anti-Jewish campaign. It rounded up 76,000 French and foreign Jews, including 12,000 children, and shipped them to German death camps.

While most French citizens accepted the Vichy government's authority, a small number of Communists, Socialists, and progressive Catholic forces violently opposed the Vichy regime and German occupation. At immense personal risk, its members provided intelligence to the Allied war effort, blew up bridges, and assassinated Vichy and Nazi officials. Charles de Gaulle, an army general and junior cabinet minister, who opposed the armistice, gained control over the resistance movement. At war's end, he persuaded allied governments to recognize him as France's legitimate leader, and he was able to negotiate a position for France as one of the five permanent members of the United Nations Security Council.

In 1945, following the German defeat, de Gaulle proposed the creation of a new constitution. In his view, the Third Republic's parliamentary system, with its many parties, shifting alliances, and frequent changes of government, had prevented forceful leadership and contributed to France's moral and political decline. When French citizens, with the memory of the **authoritarian** Vichy regime still fresh, rejected de Gaulle's plan for a republic based on strong executive leadership, he abruptly retired from politics.

The Fourth Republic, which was created in 1946 and survived for a dozen years, embodied an extreme form of parliamentary rule with a weak executive. Parliament enjoyed a near-monopoly of power, which it exercised in quite destructive fashion: governments were voted out of office about once every six months! An important reason for the absence of stable governing coalitions in the National Assembly, the powerful lower house of parliament, was that elections were held by **proportional representation (PR)**. This procedure distributes seats in parliament in proportion to the number of popular votes that parties receive. The result is that many parties were represented in parliament. Just as in the Third Republic, rapid shifts in party alliances meant that governments lacked the cohesion and authority to make tough decisions and develop long-range policies. Despite these handicaps, the Fourth Republic promoted economic expansion and modernization. What destroyed the regime was its failure to crush a rebellion by an anticolonial movement seeking independence in Algeria, a territory in North Africa that the French considered part of France.

De Gaulle cleverly exploited the military stalemate in Algeria to regain power in 1958. When the French army stationed in Algeria threatened to invade mainland France and topple the republic to protest what it claimed was indecisive leadership, de Gaulle persuaded parliament to name him prime minister and authorize a new regime that embodied the strong executive leadership that he considered essential. (Several years later, he betrayed the *ultras* who brought him to power by negotiating an agreement to grant Algeria independence.)

The Fifth Republic (1958 to the Present)

The contrast between the Fourth and Fifth republics provides a textbook case of how institutions shape political life. The Constitution of the Fourth Republic granted parliament a monopoly of power. On the other hand, electoral procedures and social cleavages combined to produce a multiparty system whose result was rapidly shifting coalitions, frequent changes of government, and little effective leadership. On the other hand, de Gaulle designed Fifth Republic political institutions to limit parliament's power and enable political leaders to act decisively. At the same time, the regime lacks adequate mechanisms to hold leaders accountable to parliament and public opinion.

Despite the fact that de Gaulle seized power under unsavory circumstances, he commanded wide popular support. Resistance hero and commanding presence, de Gaulle persuaded the French to accept a regime that endowed the executive with extensive power. However, his high-handed governing style as president provoked increasing opposition.

The most dramatic example came in May 1968, when students and workers engaged in the largest general strike in Western European history. For weeks, workers and students occupied factories, offices, and universities, and the regime's survival hung in the balance. Although de Gaulle regained control of the situation, he was discredited and resigned from office the following year.

The Fifth Republic was again tested in 1981. For twenty-three years, the same conservative political coalition that took power in 1958 won every single national election. In 1981, economic stagnation and divisions among conservative forces enabled Socialist Party candidate François Mitterrand to be elected president, along with a Socialist parliamentary majority. The transition was completely peaceful and demonstrated that the institutions of the Fifth Republic could accommodate political alternation.

President Mitterrand's Socialist government sponsored an ambitious reform program: greater autonomy for the judiciary, the media, and local governments; increased social spending; and greater government control of the economy. However, at the very moment that Mitterrand was pursuing a leftward course, conservative leaders Margaret Thatcher in Britain and Ronald Reagan in the United States were elected to leadership positions and initiated a conservative revolution. After the Socialist experiment began to provoke a crisis in 1983–1984, because of political opposition and the high cost of reform programs, Mitterrand

"What!?? The president's a Socialist and the Eiffel Tower is still standing!??" "Incredible!"   *Source:* Courtesy Plantu, Cartoonists and Writers Syndicate/ Cartoon Arts International, Inc., from Le Monde, May 1981.

reluctantly changed course. Since the right turn of that time, French governments of left and right alike have pursued market-friendly policies.

Does the convergence between center-left and center-right parties mean the end of major political conflict in France? Not at all, as events of the past several decades demonstrate.

The Le Pen Bombshell of 2002

Dramatic evidence of political malaise occurred in the 2002 presidential elections, whose results sent shock waves around the world. The procedure for electing a French president specifies that, if no candidate gains an absolute majority at the first round of the election—the typical case, since many candidates compete at this stage—a runoff ballot is held between the two front-runners to decide the election. When the 2002 election campaign opened, it was universally assumed that the two candidates who would face off in the decisive runoff ballot would be center-left Socialist Party Prime Minister Lionel Jospin and center-right President Jacques Chirac. They were candidates of the two mainstream parties that had alternated in office for decades. Everyone believed the first ballot in 2002 would weed out third-party candidates and prepare the groundwork for the runoff between Chirac and Jospin. On the eve of the election, a *New York Times* reporter explained that the campaign was so lackluster because "experts say . . . there is little suspense."[9]

However, when the polls closed, apathy turned to stupefaction. Although Chirac came in first, according to script, Jospin was nudged out of second place by Jean-Marie Le Pen, the candidate of the Front National (FN), a far-right demagogue whose targets include Muslim immigrants, Jews, gays, and mainstream politicians. Commentators routinely described the first round outcome as a bombshell and earthquake. *Le Monde,* France's most influential newspaper, spoke for most French when its front-page editorial declared, "France is wounded."[10]

Immediately after the first ballot, most supporters of Jospin and other leftist candidates swallowed their distaste and voted for Chirac at the runoff ballot. Chirac trounced Le Pen 82 to 18 percent, the most lopsided vote in the history of the Fifth Republic. Yet Le Pen's exploit remains a vivid memory, and the FN remains a significant presence in contemporary French politics.

Five years later, in 2007, another presidential election occurred. The memory of Le Pen's success in 2002 was still fresh. This time, however, Le Pen received only 10.5 percent of the first ballot vote and came in fourth. Did he fare less well because voters rejected his ultraconservative positions? That is not certain. An important reason for his poor showing was that Nicolas Sarkozy, the candidate from the major mainstream center-right party, appropriated some themes from Le Pen's playbook, including the value of patriotism, the need to safeguard national identity, and tough measures to reduce crime and illegal immigration. Many former Le Pen supporters calculated that voting for Sarkozy would be the most effective way to promote a far-right agenda.

Le Monde's cartoonist compares Le Pen's attack on Chirac and Jospin to the bombing of the twin towers of the World Trade Center. *Sources:* Courtesy Plantu, Cartoonists and Writers Syndicate, Cartoon Arts International, Inc., from Le Monde, April 23, 2002.

France after September 11

Following the terrorist attacks on the United States of September 11, 2001, France has been deeply involved in conflicts involving terrorism. A high-profile series of police actions have linked French citizens to Al Qaeda and other terrorist groups. Seven French citizens have been imprisoned at the U.S. detention center in Guantanamo after 9/11, the largest number of Europeans held there. In 2006, Zacarias Moussaoui, a French citizen, was convicted and sentenced to life imprisonment in the United States on charges that he helped plan the September 11 attack. In 2007, French antiterrorism police charged eleven people with participating in an Iraqi insurgency network linked to Al Qaeda. However, in part because of the effectiveness of France's antiterrorism forces, no deadly attacks have occurred in France in recent years comparable to those that occurred in Madrid in 2005 and London in 2006. (Section 5 will describe, however, that for decades before 9/11, France was a target of terrorist attacks.)

Although France is often portrayed as opposing the U.S. war on terror, the reality is more complex.

President Chirac was the first foreign leader to visit the United States after 9/11, and French and U.S. intelligence agencies cooperate closely in antiterrorism activities. France strongly supported the U.S. military action against Al Qaeda and the Taliban regime in Afghanistan in 2001, and French troops have served in Afghanistan ever since. However, France's intense opposition to the U.S. attack on Iraq in 2003 provoked widespread anti-French sentiment in the U.S.

France and the United States have a history of uneasy relations. For example, when Charles de Gaulle led French Resistance forces during World War II and when he served as president in the Fifth Republic, he often challenged American leadership. More recently, French public opinion was highly critical of President George W. Bush. Public opinion polls reveal that the French are "apprehensive about the United States acting as world leader, fearful of its hegemony, and mistrustful of its alleged ambitions and its motives. They, moreover, dislike many of America's social policies and are critical of our values."[11] The French tend to equate globalization with Americanization—and to regard both as a threat to French autonomy.

Yet France and the United States are not simply at loggerheads. American films, television programs, and music are enormously popular in France. France and the United States have close economic ties. For example, the United States is the largest foreign investor in France. American companies with operations in France employ 550,000 workers, and French-owned companies with operations in the United States employ 600,000 American workers.

The French "Non"—Now or Forever?

Ever since the creation of the European Union (EU), the organization that presently includes twenty-seven European countries, France has been a leader promoting closer European cooperation. In 2005, the French again influenced the shape of the EU, but this time in a very different way. After two years of difficult negotiations, an EU commission chaired by former French president Valéry Giscard d'Estaing produced a draft EU constitution. It streamlined decision-making, increased the influence of the European parliament, and created the offices of president and foreign minister. The draft constitution was intended to represent a giant step forward in the process of European integration.

EU regulations require unanimous support from all member states to approve changes in its organization and powers. By May 2005, ten member states had approved the draft constitution; none had rejected it. However, in a **referendum** in May 2005, French voters defeated the treaty by 55 to 45 percent. The referendum's defeat precipitated a grave crisis in the EU. Two factors explain why the referendum was rejected. First, polls suggested that opponents feared that it would further increase France's already high unemployment rate. An astonishingly high 81 percent of blue collar workers and 60 percent of lower-middle-class voters opposed the treaty. Second, a split in the Socialist Party (PS), one of France's major governing parties and a traditional supporter of the EU, contributed to the referendum's defeat. Although most PS leaders supported the referendum, several opposed it. Exit polls revealed that 59 percent of the PS electorate voted "no" in the referendum—enough to tip the balance toward rejection.[12] The vote highlighted a gulf between mainstream political leaders—most of whom campaigned for a yes vote—and the majority of French voters.

The Sarkozy Presidency: The Same Old, Same Old—Or a New Beginning?

Did a new era begin in 2007 with the election of Nicolas Sarkozy and a pro-Sarkozy majority in parliament? According to a French political scientist, Nicolas Sarkozy was elected because France is "anxious, questioning its being open to Europe and the world, and losing strong political and social foundations. Based on this analysis, the conservative candidate elaborated a political project articulated around values of authority, morality, national identity, respect, hard work, and achievement."[13] Will the Sarkozy presidency constitute a critical juncture or the "same old, same old," that is, a continuation of the age-old gulf between the French state and civil society?

President Sarkozy was elected in large part because he advocated bold new approaches to dealing with an ailing economy, high unemployment, undocumented immigration, crime, and threats to social cohesion and national identity. President Sarkozy's first initiatives after his election suggested a new beginning. For example, he appointed several prominent Socialist politicians to positions in his administration, including Bernard Kouchner to the key cabinet position of foreign minister. (Kouchner is cofounder of Médecins Sans Frontières—Doctors Without Borders—the humanitarian organization awarded the Nobel Peace Prize in 1999.) However, Sarkozy soon lived up (or down!) to his reputation for being erratic and short-tempered. He announced reform proposals without consulting even his own advisers, changed course without warning, and failed to pursue a coherent vision. Economic instability originating in the United States in 2006 quickly spread to Europe and limited Sarkozy's margin of maneuver. He had a highly visible divorce, quickly followed by a much photographed romance. As a result, his initially high popularity ratings (above 60 percent) plummeted to around 40 percent a year after his election.

Themes and Implications

Our analysis of the evolution of French development has identified some key turning points in French history. It is useful to highlight the distinctive ways that

France has addressed the four key themes that provide our framework for analyzing comparative politics.

Historical Junctures and Political Themes

Analyzing the four themes that frame *Introduction to Comparative Politics* reveals dramatic changes in French politics in the past few decades.

France in a World of States. For over a century following Napoleon's defeat in 1815, the country displayed an inward-looking, isolationist orientation. At the same time, France aggressively increased its colonial possessions. In the long run, this exploitative relationship was harmful not only to the colonies but to the French economy as well because it sheltered France from international competition, and stifled technological and industrial development. France's integration in the EU and participation in the global economy have enabled the French economy to become more modern and efficient.

France's tortured relationship with Germany—the two countries fought three devastating wars in less than a century—has weighed heavily on state development. The fact that France and Germany have had cordial relations since the end of World War II, thanks to the EU and the expansion of the European and world economies, has provided France with vastly increased security. The alliance between the two countries has been vital in promoting European economic and political integration.

Although a middle-rank power, France remains an important player on the world stage. For example, it has developed nuclear weapons and sophisticated military technology. France is among the world's leading arms exporters. It is a major participant in the Western alliance led by the United States. But, in contrast to Britain and Germany, it has often been a gadfly to the United States.

The French state has been a powerful, capable instrument, helping the country adapt to the challenges posed by global economic competition. In recent decades, the state has promoted internationally acclaimed high-tech industrial projects, including rapid rail travel (the TGV, that is, *train à grande vitesse*);

leadership in the European consortium that developed the Airbus wide-bodied airplane; and relatively safe and cheap nuclear-powered electricity.

France's high-tech achievements rank among the world's best. For example, TGVs carry passengers from one end of France to the other at average speeds of nearly 200 miles an hour! In 2004, the tallest and longest multispan bridge in the world was built in central France. These projects were sponsored by France's powerful and well-financed state. But they may also be among the last major state-sponsored innovations. International economic competition, EU and other treaty commitments, ideological shifts, and citizens' demands for more autonomy have challenged France's **statist** tradition.

Governing the Economy. The heyday of statism followed World War II, when state leadership enabled the French economy to soar. However, the postwar style of state direction, useful in an era when France was relatively underdeveloped, is problematic in the current period, when rapidly changing technology and economic globalization put a premium on flexibility.

At the same time, citizens fiercely resist the state's attempt to retrench because they judge that it will reduce living standards. Government initiatives to reduce state spending on medical care, pensions, and unemployment insurance have provoked popular explosions that perpetuate the chasm between the state and citizens.

The Democratic Idea. France has a complex relationship to the democratic idea. On the one hand, France's strong statist tradition opposes popular participation and decision-making because they hamper rational direction by qualified, objective leaders. On the other hand, France has passionately promoted two quite different democratic currents. The first, inspired by philosopher Jean-Jacques Rousseau in the eighteenth century, stipulates that citizens should participate directly in political decisions rather than merely choose leaders. This idea nourishes protests, like those of May 1968, that challenge established institutions. A second democratic current, identified with republican values, rejects direct democracy in

The world's longest and tallest multispan bridge, Millau, France. *Source:* © Chris Hellier/Corbis.

favor of representative or parliamentary government. Opponents of de Gaulle regarded him as trampling on representative democracy and exercising *le pouvoir personnel* (personal power).

France's democratic theory and institutions face important challenges. The no vote in the 2005 referendum on the EU constitution highlights that French citizens fear entrusting their fate to distant and, in their view, undemocratic institutions. Another chronic problem involves reconciling state autonomy and democratic participation within France.

Politics of Collective Identity. French national identity has always been closely linked to state formation. The Revolution championed an inclusive assimilationist orientation that welcomed newcomers into the political system—as long as they accepted dominant republican values. The French approach stresses that shared political values rather than inherited racial or ethnic characteristics are what bind the French together; ethnic, racial, religious, or gender identities should remain confined to the private sphere and play no role in the public arena.

Nevertheless, France can hardly be considered a unified society. French national identity has been destabilized recently by ethnic conflict and globalization. Jean-Marie Le Pen and the FN gained widespread support by charging that unemployment, crime, and urban decay are caused by Muslim immigrants and their children. At the same time, most native-born citizens whose parents are Muslim immigrants consider themselves fully French, but are often treated as second-class citizens. French national identity has been further jostled by French participation in the EU and globalization.

Implications for Comparative Politics. The study of French politics offers rich lessons for the study of comparative politics. Scholars have coined the term French exceptionalism to highlight that French politics is distinctive. Factors include a strong statist tradition and intense ideological conflict, which in turn has fueled political instability, reflected in frequent regime change. Does the exceptional character of French politics rule out comparison? Quite the contrary! For without comparison, we cannot identify and explain what is exceptional about France.

Because France has continually tried to reshape its destiny by conscious political direction, it provides a natural laboratory to test the importance of variations in institutional design. At a more general level, the French have often expected the state to pursue important economic and political goals. In countries without a strong statist tradition (for example, the United States and Britain), private groups must rely on their own efforts. What can we learn from comparing the two approaches? What are the strengths and weaknesses of statism?

A place to begin our analysis of current French politics is with France's political economy, for the way that a country organizes economic governance deeply influences the functioning of its political system.

SECTION 2 Political Economy and Development

France's gross national product (GNP) makes it the world's eighth-largest economy. It has accomplished this feat by a combination of skillful state management, a highly educated population, and favorable historical and geographic circumstances. (France is centrally located in one of the world's richest regions.) Prior to the 1980s, the state played a key role in shaping and steering the economy. Since then, there has been a sharp increase in the importance of markets, a decline in the state's role, and a shift from an inward-looking economic posture to an export orientation that has transformed France into a major participant in the global economy.

Yet the French economic record is not simply one of success. Unemployment has hovered around 10 percent for decades, although it has declined somewhat in the past few years. France has slipped from having the world's fourth-largest economy in the 1990s to the eighth today, and from having the sixth-largest per capita income to the eighteenth. A good place to start our analysis of French economic development is the period following World War II, when the French economy began a rapid ascent.

The New French Revolution

The Third Republic's humiliating failure to meet the Nazi threat in 1940, in part because of France's lagging economic performance, proved a turning point. When France was liberated and the Fourth Republic was created in 1946, influential groups active in the Resistance concluded that economic and social modernization was essential. "After the war," Richard Kuisel observes, "what was distinctive about France was the compelling sense of relative economic backwardness. This impulse was the principal stimulus for economic renovation and set France apart from other countries."[14] The modernizers were enormously successful. One study described the postwar shift as "a new French Revolution. Although peaceful, this has been just as profound as that of 1789 because it has totally overhauled the moral foundations and social equilibrium of French society."[15]

State and Economy

The new French Revolution involved sweeping changes in the economy, society, and values. As a result of its statist tradition of economic management, France was potentially able to develop the institutional capacity to steer the economy—once the goal shifted from economic protection to economic expansion. From guardian of the established order, the state became the sponsor of social and economic progress, an approach often described as *dirigisme.* The project was brilliantly successful.

French-Style Economic Management

The French developed a variety of techniques to foster economic modernization. In the French model of economic management, the state was a (indeed, *the*) chief player.

Planning. After World War II, the French developed the technique known as **indicative planning**. A national Planning Commission of senior civil servants established broad national economic and social priorities for the next four or five years. Unlike the coercive style of Soviet planning, indicative planning was developed and implemented by democratic procedures. Successive plans established maximum feasible rates of economic growth, proposed crash programs for the development of specific industries and regions, and identified social priorities such as educational targets.

De Gaulle's Leadership. Planning began in the Fourth Republic, but the process was given a shot in the arm in 1958 when Charles de Gaulle, the most influential politician in twentieth-century French history, returned to power. De Gaulle was a faithful representative of traditional France, deeply attached to the values of order and hierarchy, which earned him the enmity of the left. Yet he was also a rebel: he believed that if France was to play a leading role on the world stage, shock therapy was needed to strengthen the French economy.

Dirigisme. Under de Gaulle's leadership, the state financed favored industrial sectors and firms, and it encouraged the creation of large firms, which were dubbed "national champions." Key economic decisions were made in governmental ministries and the planning agency. State leadership compensated for the relatively weak role played by private entrepreneurs. The state provided a hefty proportion of the financing for industrial development, in the form of subsidies, loans, and tax write-offs. Some state-created and state-managed firms were in the vanguard of technological progress. For example, the state reduced France's dependence on imported petroleum by developing safe and reliable nuclear energy. About four-fifths of France's electricity nowadays is produced by nuclear reactors, and France is a world leader in the nuclear power industry.

France's Economic Miracle. During the period that a French economist called "the thirty glorious years" (1945–1975), the planners and their allies were remarkably successful. French economic growth was among the world's highest during this period—a striking contrast to the 1930s, when the French economy declined at the rate of over 1 percent annually (see Table 3.2). Average yearly income nearly tripled between 1946 and 1962. After a century of

Table 3.2

Average Growth Rates in Gross National Product, 1958–1973

Japan	10.4%
France	5.5
Italy	5.3
West Germany	5.0
Belgium	4.9
Netherlands	4.2
Norway	4.2
Sweden	4.1
United States	4.1
United Kingdom	3.2

Source: Reprinted by permission of the State University of New York Press, from *The Fifth Republic at Twenty* by William G. Andrews and Stanley Hoffmann (Eds). © 1981 State University of New York. All rights reserved.

economic stagnation, France leapfrogged into the twentieth century.

May 1968 and Beyond: Economic Crisis and Political Conflict

And yet, despite the dramatic economic growth of the 1950s and 1960s—or because of the way that economic restructuring was carried out—economic change generated political conflict. The Gaullist regime was superbly equipped to direct change. But its arbitrary style and refusal to consult widely eventually provoked an explosive reaction.

The most dramatic challenge was a massive wave of strikes and demonstrations in May 1968, which immobilized the entire country for weeks. What united diverse groups—students, workers, artists, and professionals—was anger at the high-handed style of authority in universities, political institutions, and workplaces. Other European countries were also modernizing during this period. But, with the exception of Italy, no other country experienced such intense opposition movements.

The May movement was followed by years of intense labor mobilization. A rapid increase in female employment, beginning in the early 1970s (see Figure 3.2), also provoked some important strikes by women protesting unequal treatment.

France

Students and workers unite in a mass demonstration on the Left Bank of Paris, May 27, 1968. *Source:* AP Images.

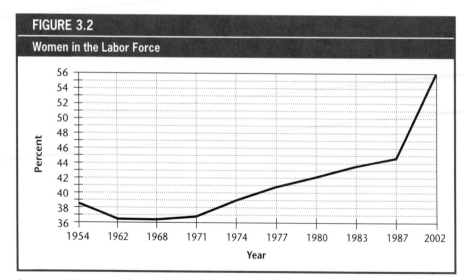

FIGURE 3.2

Women in the Labor Force

Source: INSEE, in Louis Dirn, *La Société française en tendances* (Paris: PUF, 1990), p. 108; 2002 data from INSEE, *Tableaux de l'Économie Française, 2003–2004* (Paris: INSEE, 2003), p. 77.

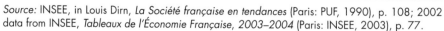

Economic Instability

Economic growth slowed in the mid-1970s when the shift of workers out of agriculture and from rural to urban areas began to reach its limit. France was affected by steep increases in petroleum prices. When developing nations, including Taiwan, South Korea, and Brazil, industrialized, French industrial jobs were eliminated and entire regions were devastated. At the same time, advanced industrialized nations outstripped France in high-tech sectors like microelectronics, bioengineering, and robotics.

The postwar state-centered approach helped promote crash programs for industrial reconstruction and modernization. But it was poorly suited to helping the French economy to decentralize decision-making and compete effectively in the global economy. Moreover, the succession of conservative governments in the 1960s and 1970s stubbornly rejected demands by workers for a greater share of material benefits and political political power.

French Socialism in Practice—and Conservative Aftermath

After right-wing governments failed to meet the economic challenges of the 1970s, the left finally got the chance to try. A new era began when, after twenty-three years of conservative governments, Socialist candidate François Mitterrand defeated incumbent president Valéry Giscard d'Estaing in the 1981 presidential election. Mitterrand's government quickly sponsored an array of radical reformist measures, including:

- Sharp increases in social benefits, including hikes in the minimum wage, family allowances, old-age pensions, rent subsidies, and state-mandated paid vacations.
- The creation of public sector employment.
- State assistance to develop cutting-edge technologies (in the biotech, telecommunications, and aerospace industries).
- The **nationalization** of many firms in the industrial and financial sectors. Following the nationalization measures, public sector firms accounted for 28 percent of France's gross domestic production, 23 percent of

French exports, and 36 percent of investments.[16] Thirteen of France's twenty largest industrial firms and most banks were integrated into the public sector.

The Socialist approach extended the postwar *dirigiste* approach to economic governance, expanded social benefits, and promoted participation by rank-and-file workers and labor unions in economic decision-making. Many citizens achieved significant gains from the Socialist program, and many of the newly nationalized firms were strengthened by the infusion of government subsidies. The Socialist reform agenda helped modernize the French economy, society, and state in the long run. However, in the short run, it drove France to the brink of bankruptcy. Business interests in France bitterly opposed the government's socialist policy orientation, and international investors avoided France like the plague. Further, an international economic recession in the early 1980s reduced the demand for French exports, just when the government's increased social spending enabled French consumers to buy foreign imports. France's international currency reserves were rapidly exhausted. Something had to give—and fast.

The crisis cruelly demonstrated how limited was the margin of maneuver for a medium-rank power like France. Mitterrand reluctantly ordered an about-face in economic policy in 1983. France's failure to achieve autonomous state-sponsored development in the early 1980s has often been cited as demonstrating the futility of nationally based radical or democratic socialist reforms. Within France, it helped discredit the traditional *dirigiste* pattern.

France's Neoliberal Modernization Strategy

Although the state has continued to play an important role in economic governance since 1983, it has scaled back its commanding role and often defers to private decision makers. The major elements in this market-friendly "**neoliberal** modernization strategy" are privatization, deregulation, and liberalization.[17]

Privatization. Since 1983, governments of left and right alike have sponsored a sweeping privatization program. The decision to support privatization was especially wrenching for the Socialists, who had long championed nationalization and, as we have seen, had sponsored an extensive increase in public sector firms when elected in 1981.

Although privatization in France has involved a drastic shift from public to private control, the change is less substantial than meets the eye. For example, there is considerable continuity in managerial ranks when firms are privatized.

Deregulation and Liberalization. A key element in the Socialists' right turn, extended by governments of the left and right since then, was the **deregulation** of commodity, financial, and labor markets. Price controls have been largely eliminated. Government controls have been dismantled in the financial sector, where market forces, not ministry of finance officials, now determine the allocation of loans and investments. Labor markets have become more flexible, in that employers have greater freedom to hire, promote, deploy, and fire workers. Yet critics charge that deregulation has not gone far enough and that French labor markets remain overly rigid. Some claim that this contributes to France's high unemployment rate because employers are reluctant to hire new workers.

Impact of the European Union. France's participation in the EU has further reduced the state's role in economic management. The Single European Act in 1987, the Maastricht Treaty in 1991, and the Growth and Stability Pact in 1997 have tied France more tightly to its European neighbors and limited state discretion.

EU directives encountered stiff popular resistance in France beginning in the 1990s. In 1995, when Prime Minister Alain Juppé proposed spending cutbacks to trim the budget deficit, the initiative provoked massive strikes by public sector workers that threatened the Juppé government's very existence. In 2003 and 2007, pension reforms that increased the retirement age for private and public sector workers were implemented despite massive strikes and demonstrations. In the 2005 referendum, popular opposition to the EU helped tip the balance toward a no vote. (See "Global Connection: France and the European Union.")

The End of Dirigisme? Although for over two decades French governments have sponsored reforms to free market forces, they have done so in a distinctively French manner. For better or worse, statism is alive and well in France. Political scientist Vivien Schmidt observes that France has not "abandoned its statist model. . . . Governments have not stopped seeking to guide business . . . even as they engineer the retreat of the state."[18]

Global Connection

France and the European Union

France has been a charter member and one of the most powerful states in the European Union since it was founded in 1958. (The EU was originally known as the European Economic Community.) After three devastating wars in less than a century between France and Germany, both countries decided there was no alternative but to cooperate. The EU has been resoundingly successful in fostering close ties between the two countries and the other member states of the organization. (The number of members steadily increased to twenty-seven by 2007.)

The EU enjoyed widespread support in France during the first decades of its existence because it was credited with contributing to economic prosperity and political stability. French farmers received the largest share of the EU's lavish program of agricultural subsidies. France has developed close economic relations with other countries in West Europe.

Yet French participation in the EU became increasingly controversial. Many French citizens fear that France's distinctive culture and identity, as well as extensive welfare state programs, are threatened by membership in the EU. Some key EU decisions involve the need for sacrifice, notably, a requirement to limit government deficits and public debt. As was described above, President Chirac's decision to hold a referendum to ratify the draft European constitution backfired.

President Sarkozy helped end the stalemate produced by the French veto by proposing a scaled-back version of the draft Constitution. However, conflicts persist among EU members, for example, whether to admit Turkey to membership.

Assessing French Economic Performance

The French economy faces daunting problems. For starters, during President Chirac's second term, economic growth was less than 2 percent annually, second only to Portugal within the EU, and it remains anemic under President Sarkozy. France has not been adept in shifting from an industrial society based on manufacturing to a postindustrial economy geared to the production of services. France's slippage is reflected in a decline in competitiveness, as measured by France's export performance.

A key problem is unemployment, especially for older and younger age groups. Whereas 49 percent of Germans and 58 percent of British between 55–64 years old are employed, the comparable figure for French workers is 38 percent. Whereas 15 percent of Germans and 14 percent of British under age 25 are unemployed, the comparable figure for young French is 21 percent.[19]

Social Policy

An extensive network of social programs provides most French citizens with an unusually high quality of life. Cradle-to-grave social services begin before birth, with pregnant women entitled to free prenatal care. Preschool facilities, supported by public subsidies, are excellent. Students that pass the baccalauréat, a stiff high school graduation exam, are entitled to attend a public university, at which tuition costs several hundred dollars a year. Housing is affordable for most citizens because of extensive public housing and rent subsidies. The minimum wage is far higher than the level prevailing in the United States, and employers are legally required to provide their employees with six weeks of paid vacation annually. Those who lose jobs receive substantial unemployment insurance benefits and job retraining. The long-term unemployed are eligible to participate in a minimum income program for two years. Many citizens are eligible to retire at age 62, with pensions close to the wage or salary levels of employed workers.

A key element of the social security system, as social programs are known in France, is health insurance, financed mostly by payroll taxes. In return for modest co-payments, most French have free prescription drugs as well as outpatient, specialized, and hospital care. In 2000, the World Health Organization ranked the French health care system first in the world. And the results speak for themselves. Infant mortality rates are about half those in the United States. Life expectancy is 81 years. No wonder that Michael Moore's 2007 documentary film, *Sicko,* that compared medical treatment in several countries, praised the French public health care system so lavishly!

A *New York Times* journalist described the French system of social provision "as a global ideological rival" to the American model.[20] Many of the social benefits described here—guaranteed as a right either to all citizens or (depending on the particular program) to employed workers—would be the envy of most people in the world.

However, despite its popularity, the social security system has been under great stress recently. The principal reason is cost: social expenditures account for nearly one-third of France's gross domestic product, second only to Sweden among EU countries.[21] Tax revenues and contributions to finance social programs are outstripped by soaring medical costs, high levels of unemployment, and a demographic imbalance between retired workers and actively employed workers. The result is that the state must borrow to close the gap.

Critics charge that high social costs have contributed to employers' reluctance to create jobs. Socialist Prime Minister Lionel Jospin (1995–2002) sought to boost employment by reducing the legal workweek from thirty-nine to thirty-five hours. Employers were limited from ordering employees to work overtime and were required to pay higher wages for overtime work. Business groups strongly opposed the reform and through the years conservative governments have relaxed restrictions on overtime work. By 2007, the average workweek for full-time workers was 39 hours. President Sarkozy made a centerpiece of his presidential campaign the promise to put the French to work. He promoted an increase in the workweek by eliminating payroll taxes on overtime work. Over the vehement opposition of unions, he sponsored an increase in the years that many workers must work before retiring.

A major problem with social programs is that benefits are distributed quite unequally. Two groups of citizens are highly organized and have obtained the lion's share of benefits: full-time, stably employed workers, especially civil servants, and older citizens. At the other extreme, younger citizens and people of color tend to be shortchanged. Historian Timothy B. Smith claims that "French public policy, despite its rhetoric of solidarity, creates or aggravates as many inequalities as it corrects."[22]

Environmental Policy

France has a mixed record on ecology. The state has traditionally given higher priority to industrial development and economic growth than to environmental concerns. While the powerful state was quite indifferent to environmental concerns, so too was the general public: ecology ranked low on the list of issues that captured public attention. To illustrate: although France has more nuclear power plants than any other country in the world, the French antinuclear movement is far weaker than its German counterpart. The French Green Party (or, rather, parties, since there are several) is far weaker than the German Greens.

In recent years, the issue of environmental protection has gained increased importance. Among the reasons are the growing evidence of climate change, the high price of petroleum, and fears concerning the safety of the food supply, in part linked to concerns about genetically modified organisms (GMOs). President Chirac sponsored a constitutional amendment in 2005 that integrated into the constitution a Charter of Environmental Protection. A key provision is the "precautionary principle," which authorizes the introduction of genetically modified changes in living organisms only if there is convincing evidence that they are safe.

President Sarkozy proclaimed the need to link environmental protection and economic growth. He created a superministry of ecology and sustainable development in 2007 that integrated formerly separate government departments. He organized a major conference of public and private organizations to generate proposals for balancing environmental concerns and economic growth. Among the reforms that his government sponsored are a phasing out of incandescent light bulbs and stiff taxes on large, gas-guzzling automobiles. However, to the disappointment of many French, Sarkozy bowed to EU pressure and relaxed restrictions on the use of GMOs in French agriculture.

Society and Economy

French economic performance has traditionally been hindered by stormy relations between management and labor, a major cause of France's economic difficulties. Typically, employers refused to bargain collectively with unions, and workers in turn resorted to strikes and pressured the state to mandate gains. French labor unions have long had a beleaguered existence. For example, they obtained the legal right to organize at the plant level only after the May 1968 uprising. Employers were not legally required to bargain collectively with unions over wages and hours until the Socialist government passed reform legislation in 1982. The labor movement was further weakened when economic growth slowed in the 1970s and economic restructuring destroyed labor's traditional industrial bastions. Currently, less than 10 percent of the wage-earning population belongs to a labor union.

Inequality and Ethnic Minorities

In the postwar period, when labor was scarce, French business and government agencies actively sought to recruit immigrants, mostly from North Africa, to do the heavy lifting in the booming construction and industrial sectors. Since the 1980s, however, unskilled jobs have disappeared and these immigrants and their offspring, most of whom are Muslim, are often the object of hostility. Two specialists observe that "Many of the challenges of integration [involving those of Muslim background]—perhaps most of them—have nothing to do with Islam. . . . And everything to do with the poor social conditions and lack of educational capital of recent immigrants and their children and grandchildren."[23]

A dramatic illustration of widespread discrimination toward immigrants and second-generation French citizens was provided by a recent study. When researchers mailed several thousand applications for job openings using fictitious names and identical CVs, "Thomas Lecomte" and "Guillaume Dupont" (the names of "traditional" Frenchmen) received one invitation to a job interview for every nineteen applications that were sent. However, "Youssuf Belkacem" and "Karim Brahimi" (obviously, Muslim names), who possessed identical qualifications, received only one invitation to an interview for every fifty-four applications.[24]

Inequality and Women

Women's economic position is double-edged. On the one hand, France has adopted a number of family-friendly social policies. Mothers are entitled to four to six months of paid maternity leave; fathers to two weeks of paid paternity leave. A sliding scale of family allowances eases the financial cost of parenting. Women find it easier to work outside the home because all children above age three are guaranteed a place in public, low-cost daycare facilities staffed by highly qualified teachers.[25] As a result, over four-fifths of mothers have paid employment.[26]

On the other hand, French women are far from achieving economic and social equality. France ranks tenth among countries on the 2008 UN Gender-Related Development Index. The proportion of female managers and administrators in France is among the lowest of industrialized countries. More broadly, the gender wage gap is a hefty 20 percent.

The Generation Gap

France's extensive welfare state arrangements, coupled with France's low growth rate, have penalized younger workers. The difficulty of dismissing stably employed workers limits job creation. The burden falls heavily on the young, who are over twice as likely to be unemployed as older French.

Recent government measures to deregulate labor markets have proved a mixed blessing. Although managers enjoy greater flexibility in scheduling work, two-thirds of new hires fill temporary or low-wage part-time jobs. Whereas in the past twenty years the number of secure, full-time jobs has increased by 12 percent, the number of part-time jobs has increased by 400 percent and the number of fixed-term jobs by 600 percent.[27] In brief, it does not pay to be young in France: one-fifth of all households headed by those under twenty-five years old have incomes below the poverty line—double the proportion in 1979.[28]

One response by young people to this disturbing situation is to emigrate in search of jobs. The most popular destination is London, home to 86,000 French expatriates.[29]

The Dilemmas of European Integration

A government-commissioned study observes, "[EU] legislation has assumed an increasingly important place in French economic and social life."[30] EU membership has been an important factor in forcing France to curtail *dirigisme*. The weight of the EU is evident in such varied domains as the organization and governance of business firms, labor relations, food and medicines, and even cultural life, all of which are the object of EU regulations.

EU membership has fundamentally altered France's trade orientation. Whereas the bulk of France's international trade and investment in the postwar period were with its former colonies in Asia and Africa, over 60 percent of its imports and exports are currently with other member states of the EU. Membership in the EU has contributed to French economic growth and assisted many sectors of the French economy. For example, French farmers receive more subsidies than any other group in the EU. (However, EU reforms will involve a substantial reduction of these benefits in coming years.) Although the EU has provided many benefits, popular opposition has increased because, rightly or wrongly, the EU is blamed for many of the economic and social strains of recent years.

France in the Global Economy

France is highly integrated in the global economy and has benefited enormously from globalization. Imports and exports have steadily increased and now account for half of French GDP.

Foreign investors, especially American pension funds, own nearly half of all shares traded on the French stock exchange. About one-third of all French workers are employed in firms that are at least partly foreign-owned. Contrary to the stereotype of France as a bucolic, rural economy, only about 3 percent of the population is employed in agriculture. At the same time, the agricultural sector is highly productive; France is the world's third-largest agricultural exporter. France boasts a large number of world-class industrial, banking, and high-tech firms. In 2003, the business magazine *Forbes* compiled a list of the world's four hundred best-performing companies. France was second only to the United States in the number of companies on the list.[31]

Yet French participation in the global economy, as well as the performance of the French economy more generally, has caused intense political strains. We analyze this issue in the next two sections.

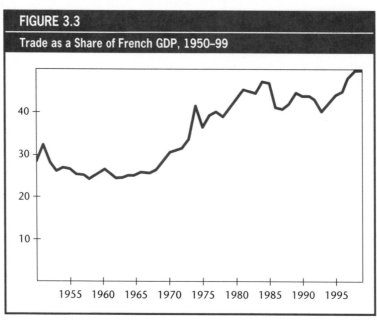

FIGURE 3.3
Trade as a Share of French GDP, 1950–99

Source: Penn World Tables and World Bank, *World Development Indicators*, 2001 (CD-ROM).

SECTION 3 | Governance and Policy-Making

Charles de Gaulle, founding father of the Fifth Republic, did his work well—too well, many now believe. Although he designed the Fifth Republic to enable a strong executive to govern relatively free of parliamentary and other restraints, this very success created a design flaw in the institutional architecture of the Fifth Republic. Ever since the creation of the new republic in 1958, there has been criticism that the executive is overly powerful and not sufficiently accountable.

At the same time, there have been four significant changes in the distribution of power among political institutions within the Fifth Republic. The first change involves the centralized state. Article 2 of the French constitution specifies, "France is a Republic, *indivisible*, secular, democratic and social." For many years, an indivisible state meant a highly centralized state. However, reforms since the 1980s have transferred substantial governmental powers to local, departmental, and regional authorities. The changes involve a reinterpretation of what it means to be "indivisible." A broad consensus has developed that the French state is stronger and more effective when subnational governments share governmental responsibilities. At the same time, France remains a **unitary system**, as opposed to a **federal system**. (In a unitary system, the state possesses virtually all constitutional powers; in a federal system, the constitution grants subnational governments significant independent powers.)

Second, as described in Section 2, the state's relation to the economy has shifted. Although the state continues to have an exceptionally important role, it now consults and persuades more—and commands less.

The third change involves constitutional mechanisms that limit state action. Until recently, a nation that emphasizes the importance of formalized legal codes and that boasts the modern world's second-oldest written constitution (after the United States) did not consider that the constitution should be scrupulously respected. French democratic theory held that the elected government should have a free hand to govern without hindrance by constitutional texts or the unelected judiciary. This too has changed. The constitution of the Fifth Republic has come to be regarded as the authoritative source for allocating power among political institutions, and the Constitutional Council has gained the vital power of **judicial review**: that is, the power to nullify legislation and sanction executive actions that it judges to violate the constitution.

Fourth, an important bundle of constitutional reforms was passed in 2008 that aimed to achieve greater balance among political institutions. They imposed term limits on the president such that he or she is henceforth limited to a maximum of two five-year terms; reduced the executive's power over the judiciary; and moderately strengthened parliament's powers (in particular, the powers of the parliamentary opposition). It is too soon to assess the significance of these reforms. However, the four sets of changes identified here require analyzing French political institutions with a fresh eye.

Organization of the State

The Fifth Republic is usually described as a semi-presidential system. In a presidential system, such as in the United States, the executive and the legislature are elected separately, and the two branches have independent powers, although they also share responsibility in important areas, for example, regarding the passage of legislation. Neither branch selects the other, is directly accountable to the other, or controls the other's agenda. Moreover, both institutions have fixed terms in office, and neither one can force the other to resign and face new elections. The one exception in a presidential system is that the legislature can impeach and force the president to resign when it deems that he or she has committed treason or other grave misdeeds. A similar impeachment procedure exists in the French Fifth Republic, although it has never been used: an absolute majority of both houses of parliament must vote articles of impeachment. The president's case is then judged by a High Court of Justice made up of twelve members apiece from the two legislative chambers.

In a parliamentary system, the executive and legislature are linked organically. The government is elected by parliament and accountable to it: the government must resign if parliament passes a motion of no confidence. At the same time, the government has substantial control over the parliamentary agenda and can dissolve parliament, thereby necessitating new elections.

In the Fifth Republic, both the president and parliament are popularly elected. In contrast to both presidential and parliamentary systems, the French system provides for a dual executive: the president appoints a prime minister and government. As in parliamentary systems, the parliament can force the government (but not the president) to resign by voting a motion of no confidence—what the French call a *motion of censure*.

Why is the Fifth Republic considered a *semipresidential* (and not a *semiparliamentary*) system? Because whenever the Fifth Republic deviates from a purely parliamentary or presidential model, the result is to strengthen the executive. The fusion of executive and legislative powers characteristic of parliamentary regimes enables the executive to control the parliamentary agenda and dissolve parliament. Yet the French parliament cannot vote censure of the president, in contrast to parliamentary regimes. Thus, the president—the key office within the dual executive—is not answerable to parliament. This feature reflects the separation of powers found in presidential systems.

Ever since the creation of the Fifth Republic, many have criticized the imbalance between the executive and parliament and, more generally, the absence of checks and balances restraining the exercise of presidential power. Although several reforms have partially redressed the balance, it continues to this day. At the same time, the Fifth Republic has proved among the most stable regimes in modern French history. Support for the regime has been bolstered by France's economic prosperity and a peaceful international context.

Since the early 1980s, the Fifth Republic has overcome two daunting political challenges. The first was a shift in political control (alternation) between opposing partisan coalitions. When François Mitterrand defeated incumbent president Valéry Giscard d'Estaing in 1981, despite widespread fears the institutions of the Fifth Republic proved quite adequate to the challenge. Since then, alternation between left and right coalitions has occurred several times.

The second challenge arose when the president led one political coalition and a rival political coalition elected a majority in parliament. The French call this situation *cohabitation*, or power sharing. For decades, the Gaullist party dominated both the presidency and parliament, thus preventing a test from occurring. However, the unthinkable finally came to pass during the presidency of François Mitterrand, when parliamentary elections in 1986 produced a right-wing majority in the National Assembly. President Mitterrand immediately bowed to political realities by appointing Jacques Chirac, leader of the conservative coalition, to be prime minister. The event proved to be the mouse that roared. The two seasoned politicians quickly devised workable solutions to governing, and despite a few tremors the regime held firm. As with alternation, cohabitation has occurred several times since then.

The most recent experience of cohabitation, in 1997–2002, provoked an important institutional reform designed to minimize the chances of it recurring. When the Socialists and their allies won the 1997 parliamentary elections, Jacques Chirac, who had been elected president only two years earlier, was forced to name Socialist leader Lionel Jospin as prime minister. The long period of cohabitation—five full years—proved highly unpopular. In an attempt to prevent a repeat performance, major parties agreed to reduce the president's term from seven to five years, the same length as that of the National Assembly, and to hold elections for the two branches at about the same time. Doing so greatly increases the chance that the same political coalition will win both elections. The 2007 presidential and parliamentary elections completely fulfilled these expectations.

The Executive

How is a semipresidential system organized? In parliamentary regimes, the head of state—either a president or a monarch—is mostly a figurehead who symbolizes the unity of the nation and exercises purely ceremonial duties. The bulk of executive power, involving the making and implementation of policy, is wielded by the prime minister and cabinet (collectively known as the government). In France, the president combines the two roles to a large extent. He (there has never been a female president) is head of state. But he also has important formal and informal power to direct the executive and shape policy. At the same time, he shares executive power with the prime minister and cabinet—who are appointed by the president but are accountable to parliament. The complex relationship between the president and prime minister will be analyzed below.

France was the first major country to adopt a semipresidential system. After the Soviet Union crumbled and communism was abandoned, Russia and many newly independent countries formerly part of the Soviet Union, as well as Bulgaria, Poland, and Romania in East Central Europe, were inspired by France's example to adopt the semipresidential system. Other countries with a semipresidential system include Austria, Finland, Iceland, Pakistan, Portugal, Sri Lanka, and (most recently) Iraq. There are now over 40 semipresidential systems in the world.[32] According to Gianfranco Pasquino, an Italian political scientist, the reason that semipresidential systems have become so popular is that they "appear endowed with both more governmental capabilities and more institutional flexibility than parliamentary and presidential systems."[33] According to Pasquino, the semipresidential system combines the best of both worlds, since it permits energetic governmental action while delivering the flexibility of a parliamentary system. It might be noted, however, that this claim clashes with the French experience, where the semipresidential system favors an unduly powerful president.

The President

When both the executive and the legislature are controlled by the same party coalition—what we will term *united control*—the French president combines the powers of the U.S. president—notably, command of the executive branch and independence from the legislature—with the powers that the government possesses in a parliamentary regime—namely, control of parliament's agenda and the ability to dissolve parliament.

The presidency is such a powerful position because of (1) the ample powers that the constitution has conferred on the office; (2) the towering personalities of Charles de Gaulle, the founder and first president of the Fifth Republic, and François Mitterrand, the Socialist president from 1981 to 1995; and (3) political practices of the Fifth Republic.

The Constitutional Presidency. The president is the only political leader directly elected by the entire French electorate. This provides an immense source of personal support. In order to be eligible to run, a candidate must be a French citizen and at least twenty-three years old. The constitutional reform of 2008 limits the president to two consecutive terms. The office of vice president does not exist in France; if a president dies in office, the president of the Senate (the upper house of parliament) acts as interim president, and a new election is held within a short time.

In order to run for president, a candidate must be nominated by 500 mayors and other local elected officials. Because there are about 40,000 such officials, it is not too difficult to qualify; thus, many candidates typically compete in presidential elections; for example, there were twelve candidates in 2007.

A two-ballot system of election is used for presidential elections. To win on the first ballot, a candidate must obtain an absolute majority of those voting. If no candidate receives a first-ballot majority, the case in every presidential election to date, a runoff election is held two weeks later between the two front-runners.

Although only candidates nominated by major political parties stand a realistic chance of winning, minor-party candidates can affect which candidates make it to the runoff ballot. As described in Section 1, the most dramatic example occurred in 2002, when Lionel Jospin, the Socialist party candidate, came in third, behind Jacques Chirac and far-right candidate Jean-Marie Le Pen.

The constitution of the Fifth Republic endows the president with the ceremonial powers of head of state. He resides in the resplendent Élysée Palace, in a fashionable section of Paris, and represents France at international diplomatic gatherings. The constitution also grants the president important political powers. The president:

- names the prime minister, chooses or approves the prime minister's choice

of cabinet officials, and nominates high-ranking civil, military, and judicial officials. Among the constitutional reforms of 2008 was the requirement that presidential nominations can be rejected by a vote of three-fifths of the members of the commissions in the two houses of parliament that have jurisdiction over the nominations.

- presides over meetings of the Council of Ministers (the government). Note that the constitution charges the president, not the prime minister, with this responsibility.
- conducts foreign affairs, through the power to negotiate and ratify treaties, as well as to name French ambassadors and accredit foreign ambassadors to France.
- directs the armed forces, bolstered by a 1964 decree that grants the president exclusive control over France's nuclear forces. Although the president can order French troops into combat, the constitutional reform of 2008 requires that he must obtain parliamentary approval if armed forces are involved in hostilities longer than four months.
- is empowered to dissolve the National Assembly and call for new elections.
- appoints three of the nine members of the Constitutional Council, including its president, and can refer bills passed by parliament to the council to determine if they conform to the constitution.
- is authorized to address parliament in person. This will occur in the majestic (indeed, monarchic) setting of the Palace of Versailles. President Sarkozy sponsored this possibility in the package of constitutional reforms passed in 2008. The

amendment stipulates that, following the president's appearance, parliament can debate the presidential message but not vote. Thus, the president remains unaccountable vis-à-vis parliament.

Four other constitutional grants of power strengthen the president's position. Article 5 directs the president "to ensure, by his arbitration, the regular functioning of the governmental authorities, as well as the continuance of the State." This clause bolsters the president's authority by making him or her the sole official responsible for arbitrating among state institutions and guaranteeing national independence.

Article 16 authorizes the president to assume emergency governing powers when, in his or her judgment, France's independence is threatened. It is unthinkable that a president would invoke Article 16 except in a grave crisis. (The only time it has occurred was in 1962, when President de Gaulle assumed emergency powers in response to the threat of a military coup linked to the war in Algeria.)

Article 89 authorizes the president, with the approval of the prime minister, to propose constitutional amendments. Each chamber of parliament must approve the amendment. It must then be ratified either by a national referendum or by a three-fifths vote of both houses of parliament meeting together as a congress. The amendment procedure has been used with increasing frequency in recent years. President Chirac sponsored fourteen amendments in the twelve years of his presidency, more than any other president.

Article 11, which was amended in 1995, authorizes the president to organize a referendum to approve important policy initiatives or reorganize political institutions, provided that the proposed change is first approved by the government. (This procedure is distinct from the use of the referendum to amend the constitution.) With the memory of the 2005 no vote on the European constitution relatively fresh, President Sarkozy will probably avoid calling a referendum.

Presidential Personalities. The constitution grants the president extensive powers—on paper. But the president's use of these powers depends in large part on leadership skills. Charles de Gaulle, the first president in the Fifth Republic, made full use of his constitutional

Table 3.3	
Presidents of the Fifth Republic	
Charles de Gaulle	1958–1969
Georges Pompidou	1969–1974
Valéry Giscard d'Estaing	1974–1981
François Mitterrand	1981–1995
Jacques Chirac	1995–2007
Nicolas Sarkozy	2007–Present

power and set the standard for his successors. (Table 3.3 lists the Fifth Republic's presidents and their terms of office.)

De Gaulle was the most influential politician in modern French history. As first president in the Fifth Republic, he created the precedent that presidents could define the country's goals, dominate the policy-making process, direct France's foreign relations, and supervise the government and bureaucracy.

The two presidents following de Gaulle—Georges Pompidou and Valéry Giscard d'Estaing—were not highly influential, in part because they did not have as clear a vision of what they hoped to accomplish. The next president to make full use of presidential powers was François Mitterrand, who defeated incumbent President Giscard for re-election in 1981. Mitterrand was re-elected in 1988 and remained in office until 1995, the longest presidential term in the history of the Fifth Republic. Despite his criticism of de Gaulle's autocratic style, Mitterrand ruled in a manner that was strikingly similar. However, he was also the first president forced to swallow the bitter pill of cohabitation, after conservative forces won the 1986 parliamentary elections.

On his retirement in 1995, Mitterrand was succeeded as president by Jacques Chirac, a decades-long fixture on the French political scene. Chirac served two terms as president, retiring in 2007. He proved more adept at gaining power than in pursuing bold goals. Rather than noteworthy achievements, his presidency will be remembered for some major political blunders, discussed in Section 5. When he left office in 2007, the French newspaper *Le Monde* commented, "The French have the impression that the country was immobilized for the twelve years of Chirac's presidency."[34]

Nicolas Sarkozy, Chirac's successor, has relished wading into the thick of the political fray. He has frequently intervened in the everyday business of government and has dominated media coverage to an unprecedented extent. According to a French political scientist, Sarkozy's election "marked a new phase in the history of the Fifth Republic," one marked by an "absolutist presidency."[35] For example, François Fillon, Sarkozy's prime minister, has functioned more as his chief of staff than as chief of government. President Sarkozy has sponsored a flurry of policy initiatives: reducing income, corporate, wealth, and estate taxes; increasing the workweek; limiting public sector strikes; reducing pension benefits; reducing the size of the civil service; and reforming

political institutions. Yet few rate Sarkozy's presidency a success. In his first year in office, his achievements fell considerably short of his campaign promises: he failed to achieve his major goals of reducing unemployment and increasing citizens' purchasing power. Several reforms have provoked widespread demonstrations and strikes. And his governing style alienated many voters. One disillusioned former supporter expressed a widely shared sentiment: "He hasn't achieved a quarter of what he promised. He's on TV every day but he hasn't changed a thing."[36] After a honeymoon period in which President Sarkozy enjoyed unprecedentedly high levels of public support, his poll standings in 2008 plummeted to an unprecedentedly low level.

Leaders

Nicolas Sarkozy

Source: © Horacio Villalobos/epa/Corbis.

Nicolas Sarkozy is an audacious and controversial figure. He is the first French president from an immigrant background. Although he was born in Paris, his father was Hungarian, his mother of Greek Jewish background. His parents migrated to France following Hungary's communist takeover after

World War II. Nicolas Sarkozy was not a child of privilege. He attended the University of Paris, not one of France's selective elite schools (described below).

Sarkozy decided at an early age to pursue a political career. In his youth, he reportedly boasted that one day he would be elected president. He has few interests other than politics—and living well! While a teenager, Sarkozy joined the conservative party that became the UMP and was soon chosen leader of the party's youth organization. At a UMP meeting in 1975, he was allotted two minutes to make a speech. Instead, he spoke for ten minutes. Jacques Chirac, prime minister at the time, was so impressed that he took Sarkozy under his wing.

Chirac's help was invaluable in Sarkozy's rapid political rise: he was elected mayor of a Paris suburban town at age twenty-eight, and elected to parliament five years later. Appointed a junior minister and official spokesperson for the government at age thirty-three, he quickly established a political reputation for making waves. Conservative supporters loved—and liberal opponents detested—his blunt talk about crime and immigration.

Throughout his career, he reveled in breaking taboos and making headlines. When he was appointed minister of the interior, responsible for law and order within France, he organized a drive to deport undocumented immigrants. He also ordered a

(continued)

Leaders

Nicolas Sarkozy (*continued*)

crackdown on crime that, according to critics, encouraged the police to harass youth, especially those from immigrant backgrounds. In 2005, when visiting a crime scene in a shabby suburban neighborhood near Paris, he described criminals as "scum" and later recommended that run-down neighborhoods should be "disinfected." When youths from these neighborhoods went on a rampage several weeks later, they hurled his insults back at him.

At the same time, President Sarkozy has been among the few mainstream politicians to support affirmative action programs that aim to assist immigrants to achieve social and economic mobility. And he was the first French president to appoint men and women of color to cabinet positions.

Sarkozy made no secret of his presidential ambitions. In 2005, he gained control of the UMP, France's most powerful political party, ran a brilliant presidential campaign, including the all-important televised debate with Ségolène Royal that opened this chapter, and gained a decisive victory in the presidential election.

In his first years in office, Sarkozy proved more successful at capturing the presidency than at governing. Not long after his election, he suffered a steep drop in popularity. One reason was that many French (especially his conservative supporters) found his behavior offensive and unpresidential. For example, soon after separating from his second wife in late

2007, he was photographed touring Disneyland-Paris hand-in-hand with Carla Bruni, a wealthy heiress who is a former model and highly successful pop singer. Several weeks later (and before their subsequent marriage), the couple took a highly public vacation to the Egyptian pyramids. Nor did his poll standings improve when, thanks to his Ray-Ban sunglasses and Rolex watch, he became known as "President Bling-Bling" — slang for someone who loves flashy jewelry!

Sarkozy's bad temper further contributed to his difficulties. For example, while he was touring an agricultural fair, he was filmed snarling a vulgar insult at someone who snubbed him. His impulsive behavior has extended to the realm of policy. On several occasions, he announced a proposal—often without consulting his advisers—only to reverse himself soon after. And last—but not least—despite his campaign promise to put France back to work and boost people's purchasing power, there was little evidence of either occurring in the first years of his presidency.

On the other hand, Sarkozy has learned from his mistakes. After the incidents just described, he retreated from public view and assumed a more dignified demeanor. Further, his popularity increased when he sponsored institutional changes reviewed below and took a leading international role during the economic crisis in late 2008, while occupying the rotating presidency of the EU.

The Political President. The most important political factor that affects the extent of presidential power is whether the president's party coalition has a parliamentary majority. A president that can rely on majority support in parliament enjoys a commanding position. For example, in addition to the constitutional power to designate prime ministers, presidents have successfully claimed the ability to dismiss them. During periods of unified control, presidents have exercised the power, assigned to the government by the constitution, to shape policy in virtually any domain they choose.

The Prime Minister and Government

Although the constitution provides the president with ample powers, the prime minister and government are

authorized to make many key policy decisions. The constitution designates the government, not the president, as the preeminent policy-making institution. Article 20 states that the government "shall determine and direct the policy of the nation. It shall have at its disposal the administration and the armed forces." And Article 21 authorizes the prime minister to "direct the action of the government. He [the prime minister] is responsible for national defense. He assures the execution of the laws." Thus, when prime ministers accept presidential leadership, as they invariably do during periods of unified control, it is because of *political dynamics* rather than *constitutional directive.*

The constitution authorizes the president to appoint the prime minister. Most prime ministers have been leaders of the major party in the dominant coalition in

Institutional Intricacies: Of Presidents and Prime Ministers

The relationship between the president and prime minister is a key element in the Fifth Republic. There are two possible situations: 1) periods of unified control, when the president and prime minister are political allies; and 2) periods of cohabitation, when the two are political opponents. The first situation is characterized by undisputed presidential supremacy. Presidents select as prime minister an ally who is leader of the majority party coalition. For example, in 2007, newly elected President Sarkozy's choice was François Fillon, a former cabinet minister and close friend. Loyal and effective prime ministers provide the president with parliamentary support for the government's policies, sympathetic media treatment, and firm control of the government and state bureaucracy. A competent prime minister frees the president to conduct international affairs and focus on important policy questions.

Prime ministers also serve as lightning rods to protect the president. By taking the heat for controversial decisions, they partially shield the president from criticism. Political scientist Robert Elgie describes the prime minister's thankless position: "When things go well, the President often receives the credit. When things go badly, the Prime Minister usually takes the blame. If things go very badly and the President starts to be criticized, then the Prime Minister is replaced. If things go very well and the Prime Minister starts to be praised, then the Prime Minister is also replaced." *

Serving as prime minister is regarded as a stepping stone to the presidency. This dynamic explains why presidents generally dismiss prime ministers after several years and name a fresh replacement. Indeed, when a prime minister loses popularity and is not replaced, the president's standing suffers.

The second situation is cohabitation, when the president and prime minister are political rivals. At these times, the balance shifts from cooperation to competition. Moreover, the prime minister has some powerful resources: he or she controls the government, parliament, and the bureaucracy. As a result, the president is forced to beat a dignified retreat although he retains major responsibility for foreign and defense policy.

The constant sniping between the president and prime minister that occurred during the seemingly endless period of cohabitation between 1997 and 2002 proved highly unpopular. It provoked a constitutional reform in 2000 designed to avoid cohabitation in the future. The reform reduced the president's term to five years, the same length as that of deputies in the National Assembly. Holding presidential and parliamentary elections within two months of each other, and making the terms of the two offices identical, nearly guaranteed that the same political coalition would win both elections. It worked. In 2002 and 2007, conservatives swept the presidential and parliamentary elections. Unified control will doubtless endure until at least 2012, when the next presidential and parliamentary elections are scheduled. Thus, cohabitation has become a distant memory. Few lament its passing.

*Robert Elgie, *The Role of the Prime Minister in France,* 1981–91 (New York: St. Martin's Press, 1993), p. 1.

the National Assembly (the powerful lower house of parliament). This ensures parliamentary support for the prime minister and government. (The boxed feature on institutional intricacies further explores the complex relationship of presidents and prime ministers.)

During periods of unified control, the president formulates the state's overall policy direction, while the prime minister is responsible for translating general policies into specific programs, securing parliamentary support, and supervising the implementation of policy. Presidents retain predominant responsibility for overall defense and foreign policy, but the prime minister determines the government's specific policy orientation and legislative timetable. The prime minister is also responsible for coordinating and supervising the work of the cabinet, as well as arbitrating conflicts among cabinet ministers over policy and budget priorities.

The prime minister nominates, and the president appoints, members of the cabinet or government, a collective body under the prime minister's direction. Most cabinet members, also known as ministers, are senior politicians from the parties in the dominant parliamentary coalition. Cabinet positions are allotted in rough proportion to parties' strength in the majority parliamentary coalition.

Until President Sarkozy's election, most cabinet ministers were white men. Sarkozy broke precedent by appointing women to half the senior cabinet positions in Prime Minister François Fillon's first government. Most noteworthy was Minister of Justice Rachida Dati, daughter of North African immigrants of humble circumstances.

Presidents and prime ministers shape the cabinet to convey political messages. For example, President Sarkozy made waves by appointing several Socialists to Prime Minister Fillon's government, including Bernard Kouchner, cofounder of Doctors Without Borders, who was named foreign minister.

Cabinet ministers direct government departments and propose policy initiatives in their domain. Cabinet positions differ widely in power. Key ministries include Finance, Defense, Foreign Affairs, and Interior.

The prime minister and other cabinet ministers are assisted by a personal staff, known as a *cabinet*, to help them supervise departments and provide policy assistance. (Note that the *cabinet*, italicized here, is a different body from the cabinet or government, composed of government ministers.) Members of *cabinets* are usually drawn from the ranks of the most talented civil servants—graduates of elite schools described below. Their mission is to serve as the minister's eyes and ears. *Cabinets* enable cabinet ministers to wield considerable power.

Even more than is the case for cabinets in other political regimes, the French cabinet is not a forum for searching policy debate or collective decision-making. The cabinet meets to fulfill constitutional requirements, for example, to authorize the appointment of key administrative officials. Important policies are shaped at a higher level—at the Élysée or Matignon (the official residence of the prime minister)—or by interministerial committees, that is, informal working groups of ministers and high administrators.

Bureaucracy and Civil Service

Although France is often described as having a dual executive, the bureaucracy is a third important element of the executive. The most powerful administrators in the French state are found in the Élysée, Matignon, and ornate government ministries in Paris. The day-to-day work of the state, however, is performed by an army of civil servants, including 2.3 million in the state administration and another 2.7 million who staff public hospitals, semipublic agencies, and subnational governmental bureaucracies. The Fifth Republic bolstered the bureaucracy's already formidable influence by limiting parliament's power and authorizing the government to issue binding administrative regulations with the force of law.

The top administrative positions are highly coveted. Recruitment is limited to graduates of elite educational institutions known as **grandes écoles**. While there are over 1 million students in higher education, mostly at public universities, only 40,000 students attend a *grande école*, and only 3,000 are enrolled in the most selective *grandes écoles*.[37] Although French political discourse emphasizes the importance of meritocracy, children from culturally and economically favored milieux have an immense advantage in the fierce competition for admission to the *grandes écoles*.

Despite the small size of the elite schools, they receive nearly one-third of all public expenditures on higher education. Meanwhile, universities are starved for funds, bursting at the seams, and often unable to provide adequate education. Students who graduate at the top of their class at a *grande école* are admitted into an even more select fraternity: a **grand corps**, small, cohesive networks with particular specialties, such as the financial inspectorate or diplomatic service. Membership in a *grand corps* is for life and guarantees a fine salary, high status, and considerable power. Recently, members of the *grands corps* have also filled top executive positions in public and private corporations and banks. Many members run for parliament and are named to the cabinet. Over half of all prime ministers in the Fifth Republic have been members of *grands corps*, as were presidents Giscard d'Estaing and Chirac.

The state and bureaucracy have recently experienced a loss of prestige, power, and morale because of the diminished scope of state activity, the increased power of the private sector, ideological changes, and the growing importance of the EU. President Sarkozy criticized what he described as France's bloated bureaucracy and ordered it to be trimmed in certain sectors, for example, the military and education.

Public and Semipublic Institutions

In the past two decades, many important state-owned industrial enterprises have been privatized, such as the Renault auto company, as well as large firms in banking, transportation (for example Air France), energy, and telecommunications. Large and powerful semipublic agencies remain—for example, Electricity of France, the agency that monopolizes the distribution of electricity throughout France, has been described as a state within the state. But like the civil service, semipublic agencies no longer enjoy the prestige and power of yesteryear.

Other State Institutions

Given the far-flung reach of the French state, many state institutions warrant close attention. We focus here on those with great power or that are described in the constitution.

The Military and the Police

In all countries, the military and police are the executive agencies that employ coercion to enforce law and order. The armed forces have traditionally played only a minor role in politics.

France is a middling-rank power nowadays. But unlike Britain and Germany, for example, generally loyal members of the military alliance led by the United States, France has maintained a studied distance. For example, when De Gaulle returned to power in 1958, he soon ordered the United States to close military bases in France created after World War II, and he announced that France was withdrawing from the integrated command structure of the North Atlantic Treaty Organization (NATO). De Gaulle and his successors sponsored an independent French nuclear striking force, with sophisticated delivery systems. France is among the world's major arms exporters. However, in an attempt to reduce tension with the United States, President Sarkozy ordered France to rejoin NATO's command structure in 2008.

Although France lost its far-flung colonial empire after World War II, Africa has been the one region outside Europe where France retains major influence. For decades, French troops were dispatched to prop up friendly dictators in former French colonies that became nominally independent in the 1960s. France has sponsored extensive assistance programs in the countries of francophone Africa (that is, former African colonies, where French is spoken). France's influence in the region has been waning recently, however.

In recent years, France has participated in United Nations–sponsored peacekeeping operations in post-conflict situations, such as in Bosnia, Afghanistan, and Lebanon. It has committed more troops to peacekeeping forces than any other country in the world.

Within France, the police operate with considerable freedom—too much, according to critics. Alongside police forces under the control of local governments, there is a national police force, directed by the ministry of defense and garrisoned throughout France. Judges and executive officials have rarely reined in the police. The "forces of order," as they are called in France, have a reputation for engaging in brutal tactics, illegal surveillance, arbitrary actions, and racism. Racial profiling of young Arab men targeted for identity checks and strip searches has produced ugly confrontations. (Section 5 describes uprisings in 2005 and 2007 involving widespread torching of buildings and cars.)

The Judiciary

Traditionally the French judiciary possessed little autonomy and was considered an arm of the executive. In the past two decades, however, this condition has changed dramatically. The Constitutional Council has assumed central importance and independent administrative regulatory authorities have been created in such varied sectors as broadcasting, stock market transactions, and commercial competition.

The Constitutional Council. Two scholars observe, "Originally an obscure institution conceived to play a marginal role in the Fifth Republic, the Constitutional Council has gradually moved toward the center stage of French politics and acquired the status of a major actor in the policy-making system."[38]

The nine members of the council are appointed for staggered nine-year nonrenewable terms. The president of the republic and the presidents of the National Assembly and Senate each appoint three members. The president of the republic names the council's president. Those named to the Constitutional Council are generally distinguished jurists or elder statesmen. Ex-presidents are entitled to sit on the council. The first woman ever named to the council was appointed in 1992.

Four factors contributed to the Constitutional Council's increased power.

- Broadening the council's jurisdiction to include the power of judicial review—that is, the power to invalidate legislation if the council judges that it violates the constitution. In most cases, the council can only strike down recently enacted legislation in the brief period before the law is officially implemented. (An exception will be noted below.) If it fails to so, the legislation can never be reviewed. But it is unprecedented in France that a judicial body can overrule the legislature, and the council now exercises this sweeping power in a bold and continuous fashion. If a major innovation of the Fifth Republic in the first years of the republic was to establish the dominance of the executive over the legislature, a major development since then has been to establish the primacy of the constitution, as interpreted by the Constitutional Council, over both the legislature and executive.

- Broadening access to the Constitutional Council. At first, only the president of the republic and the presidents of the two houses of the legislature could bring cases to the council. A constitutional amendment passed in 1974 authorized sixty deputies or sixty senators to bring suit. As a result, the council now rules on most important new legislation. Access to the Council was further increased by a measure included in the constitutional reform package of 2008. It authorizes citizens who are defendants in trials to allege that a law violates their fundamental rights. The Constitutional Council is responsible for reviewing the case and can declare the law unconstitutional. (In such cases, the Council can invalidate past laws.)

- Transferring the power to appoint judges from the executive to magistrates elected from among the ranks of judges. This change required a constitutional amendment in 1993. The same amendment created a new Court of Justice of the Republic to try cases against government ministers accused of crimes committed while in office. The court comprises six deputies and six senators, elected by the two chambers of the legislature, and three senior judges. The autonomy of the judiciary was further strengthened in 2008. Until then, the president directed the *Conseil supérieur de la magistrature*, the highest judicial governing body. The constitutional reform of 2008 transferred this power to an independent judge. However, critics charge that the judiciary continues to be unduly subject to political influence. For example, the minister of justice, a political appointee, exercises important power over judges.

The French judicial system of Roman law, codified in the Napoleonic Code and similar codes governing industrial relations and local government, differs substantially from the pattern prevailing in Britain, the United States, and other nations inspired by the common law system. French courts accord little importance to judicial precedent; what counts is legislative texts and the codification of legislation in specific subfields. The trial system also differs from that in the United States. French judges play an active role in questioning witnesses and recommending verdicts to juries. A judicial authority, the *juge d'instruction*, prepares the prosecution's case. Criminal defendants enjoy fewer rights than in the U.S. or British system of criminal justice.

State Council. France has about thirty administrative courts that try cases alleging administrative misconduct, an important safeguard given the bureaucracy's power and the wide scope of administrative regulations. The most important administrative court is the *Conseil d'État* (State Council). Members of the State Council belong to one of the most powerful *grands corps.* The State Council provides advice to the government about the constitutionality, legality, and coherence of proposed laws.

The Economic, Social and Environmental Council

The constitution designates the Economic, Social and Environmental Council as a consultative body composed of representatives from business, agriculture, labor unions, social welfare organizations, and consumer groups, as well as distinguished citizens from cultural and scientific fields. The council has issued influential reports on important public issues, including job discrimination toward immigrants and reorganization of the minimum wage system. However, it has no legislative power and occupies a relatively modest role within the regime.

Subnational Government

There are three layers of subnational elected governments in France: municipal, departmental, and regional. With 36,000 municipalities, France has more local governments than all other Western European countries combined! Although the system seems unusually cumbersome, citizens are deeply attached to local government and local politicians command great respect.

Until the 1980s, local governments were quite weak. For example, state agents, called **prefects**, directed the 100 departments (roughly equivalent to counties) into which France is divided. At that time, the Socialist government sponsored a fundamental overhaul of local government. The national government's supervision of local governments was reduced, regional governments were created, and localities were authorized to levy taxes and sponsor economic, social,

and cultural activities. A constitutional amendment in 2003 further extended the scope of decentralization, enshrined the principle of decentralization in the constitution, and required the national government to provide local governments with adequate funds.

The decentralization reforms have enabled regional, departmental, and city governments to gain significant responsibility for education, transportation, social welfare, and cultural activity. Subnational governments have sponsored public transportation facilities that link cities in the provinces, thereby modifying the characteristic wheel-and-spokes pattern by which all French roads and railroads formerly led to Paris! The reforms have brought government closer to citizens.

Yet decentralization has provided tempting opportunities for corruption. Many local officials have been convicted of taking kickbacks in return for authorizing questionable land development schemes and for granting contracts for public works projects. The reforms have also increased economic inequalities among localities and regions.

The Policy-Making Process

The policy-making process differs substantially between periods of unified control and cohabitation. When control is united, the president formulates most major policy initiatives, usually after consulting with the prime minister and powerful cabinet ministers. Government ministers, assisted by top civil servants, develop legislative proposals and administrative regulations that translate broad policy into concrete action. The parliament usually approves the government's initiatives without significant modifications.

There are fewer opportunities in France, compared with most other democratic regimes, for public and private actors outside government to influence policy-making or hold government accountable. The constitution enshrines executive dominance at the expense of the legislature and popular participation. The bureaucracy is large, expert, and often domineering. Private interests have less access than in most democratic regimes.

The position of the executive and the French state more generally have been deeply affected by France's participation in the global economy. EU commitments have limited France's freedom of action, although EU membership has also enabled France to leverage its power by gaining a leading voice in this influential multilateral organization. EU membership has also redistributed power among the political institutions of the French state. Executive agencies have gained power relative to the French parliament, since the executive represents France in EU decision-making and parliament has little choice but to accept the results. The Constitutional Council and State Council have gained an authoritative role in interpreting and applying EU treaty commitments and directives. They have ruled that EU directives trump the French constitution. As a result of the close integration of France in the EU, it is difficult to unravel where the "EU" begins and "France" leaves off.

As France has become more integrated within the EU and the wider global arena, the gulf has widened between political decision-makers and ordinary citizens. This has created additional stress on the system of political representation. Despite reforms described above, including limiting the president's term to five years and strengthening the autonomy of the judiciary, as well as reforms strengthening parliament described in Section 4, France's institutional structure remains the target of widespread criticism.

SECTION 4 Representation and Participation

The construction of the Fifth Republic was inspired by Charles de Gaulle's belief that political parties and parliament had overstepped their proper role in the Third and Fourth Republics and had thereby prevented vigorous executive leadership. Although de Gaulle did succeed in limiting parliament's role, he completely failed to curb political parties. Ironically, however, the development of strong, well-organized, centralized parties early in the Fifth Republic—squarely contrary to de Gaulle's intentions—has helped provide decisive leadership and political stability, which were de Gaulle's highest priorities.

What explains this curious turn of events? De Gaulle's decision to provide for popular election of the presidency powerfully contributed to the development of strong parties. He failed to anticipate that, in order to win the all-important presidential contest, the formerly decentralized parties of the Fourth Republic would become centralized, unified organizations. The result facilitated strong executive leadership. However, because parties have not helped foster popular participation and representation, France's centuries-old tradition of popular protest against state authority persists.

The Legislature

Parliaments everywhere have been described as ceding power to the executive. But in the Third and Fourth Republics, parliament enjoyed more power than most other legislative bodies. In the Fifth Republic, its powers were substantially reduced. For decades, the political system was criticized for the strong imbalance between the executive and legislature. Sweeping constitutional reforms enacted in 2008 were designed to address this basic problem.

The French parliament is bicameral and consists of the National Assembly and the Senate. For reasons to be discussed, the National Assembly is the more powerful of the two houses. In France's semipresidential system, parliament lacks the independence that legislatures enjoy in presidential systems. Moreover, since the president is not responsible to parliament, it cannot hold the executive fully accountable. Parliament in the Fifth Republic has lost power to the president, government, bureaucracy, judiciary, television, subnational governments, and the EU!

Article 34 of the constitution, which defines the scope of parliament's legislative jurisdiction, was a revolution in French constitutional law. Rather than authorizing parliament to legislate in all areas except those explicitly designated as off-limits—true to France's tradition of parliamentary sovereignty—the constitution enumerates those areas in which parliament *is* authorized to legislate and prohibits legislation on other matters. Furthermore, in areas outside parliament's jurisdiction, the executive can issue legally binding regulations and decrees. Even within the domain of parliamentary competence, the government can request parliament to authorize it to issue ordinances with the force of law. The procedure enables the government to save time, avoid extensive parliamentary debate, or limit unwelcome amendments. Yet another procedure by which the executive can bypass parliament is by calling a referendum.

Within the limited area of lawmaking, the constitution grants the government extensive powers to control legislative activity. The government is mostly responsible for establishing the parliamentary agenda. As in other parliamentary regimes, the government, not backbenchers or the opposition, initiates most bills that eventually become law—about 90 percent in a typical legislative session.

Parliament has especially limited control over the budgetary process. Members of parliament are prohibited from introducing budget amendments that will raise expenditures or lower revenues. Furthermore, parliament must approve the budget within seventy days after it has been submitted, or the government can enact it by decree (although this has never occurred in the Fifth Republic).

The executive can dissolve the National Assembly before its normal five-year term ends, which necessitates new elections. (The executive cannot dissolve the Senate, but this matters little since the Senate lacks some vital powers enjoyed by the National Assembly.) If the executive dissolves the National Assembly, it cannot do so again for a year.

The government's control over parliament's legislative and other activity is bolstered by Article 44, by which the government can call for a single vote— known as the *vote bloqué* ("blocked vote," or package vote)—on all or a portion of a bill. The government can select which amendments to include with the text. Governments have used—or, according to the opposition, abused—the package vote procedure to restrict debate on many key legislative texts.

The government can further curb parliament by calling for a confidence vote on either its overall policies or a specific piece of legislation (Article 49, clause 3). This provision applies only to the National Assembly; the Senate is not authorized by the constitution to pass a motion of no confidence (that is, censure). When the government calls for a confidence vote on a text, the measure is considered approved unless the National Assembly passes a censure motion by an absolute majority of all deputies within twenty-four hours. (Members of the National Assembly are known as deputies; members of the Senate are known as senators.) In effect, deputies who abstain are counted as voting with the government. If an absolute majority of deputies

does vote against the measure, it is defeated and— more significant—the government is required to resign. However, no government has ever been brought down by a confidence vote of this kind. (The National Assembly did vote to censure General de Gaulle's hand-picked government in 1962 by another route, forcing it to resign. This was the only time in the Fifth Republic that a censure motion has passed.)

Article 49 (3) has been among the most hotly contested and criticized features of the Fifth Republic. The 2008 constitutional reform limited its usage by the government.

Deputies can also submit motions to censure the government (and thereby force it to resign) on their own initiative. A motion must be signed by one-tenth of all deputies in the National Assembly. The procedure for passing this kind of censure motion is the same as the one called by the government. However, deputies who sign a censure motion of this kind cannot do so again during the life of the legislature. This limits the number of parliament-initiated censure motions.

Since the government normally commands majority support in the National Assembly, there is little chance that a censure motion will pass. In fact, as mentioned above, only one no-confidence vote has ever passed in the fifty-year history of the Fifth Republic.

Because of the severe restrictions under which parliament functions, and its quite limited power, it is widely perceived as a rubber stamp. Because opposition parties cannot air grievances effectively, discontented groups often prefer taking to the streets rather than channeling demands through parliament.

Voting in the National Assembly is generally along party lines, and there is strong party discipline: that is, deputies from each party usually vote as a bloc. This means that the government can generally count on obtaining majority support for proposed legislation.

In some parliamentary systems, parliamentary committees—the French term them commissions— play a vital role. But not in the Fifth Republic. There are six permanent commissions: Foreign Policy; Finances, Economy, and Planning; Defense and Armed Forces; Constitutional Changes, Legislation, and General Administration; Cultural, Family, and Social Affairs; and Economic, Environmental, and Territorial Affairs. Commissions are responsible for reviewing proposed legislation and reporting back to the full house.

The constitution also authorizes parliament to create commissions of inquiry to investigate the executive, but the few that have been created were ineffective.

In recent years, parliament has modestly increased its role. For example, the number of sessions a week when members of parliament can pose oral questions to the government was increased from one to three by a constitutional amendment in 1995. A 1990 reform slightly increased the opportunity for members of parliament to initiate legislation. Several constitutional reforms adopted in 2008 modestly strengthened parliament's powers. For example, after parliamentary commissions examine a legislative proposal, parliament thereupon debates and votes upon the text amended in commission. In the past, the government's original text was the basis for parliamentary debate. Further, the 2008 reform granted opposition parties the right to control a portion of the parliamentary agenda, and it reserved part of each parliamentary session for evaluation of the government's activity (as opposed to considering new legislative proposals). Although these reforms should have a significant impact, the imbalance between executive and legislature remains a fundamental weakness of the Fifth Republic.

How a Bill Becomes a Law

Following a bill's introduction, the bill is reviewed by a parliamentary commission in the chamber where it was introduced and is then debated and possibly amended by the full chamber. If it receives majority support, it goes to the second chamber, where the same procedure is followed. Most bills that receive priority scrutiny are introduced by the government.

If a bill is passed in identical form by the two houses, it becomes law (unless subsequently struck down by the Constitutional Council). If the two houses vote different versions of a bill, the process of deliberation and voting is repeated. If the two houses pass a different version twice—or after one reading, if the government declares the bill a priority matter—a joint commission composed of members from both houses seeks to negotiate a compromise. If the commission reaches agreement, the text is voted on by both houses. If the Senate fails to pass the text at this reading, the government can request the National Assembly to have the last word. If the National Assembly

passes the bill, the measure is considered approved. The National Assembly is the more powerful house both because it can pass a law opposed by the Senate and because it alone can vote censure and force the government to resign.

Once a bill has been voted into law, the constitution authorizes the president of the republic, president of either chamber of the legislature, or sixty deputies or senators to request the Constitutional Council to review the text. The council can strike down the entire text of a law or only those provisions that it judges to violate the constitution. The council must be asked to rule within one month after a bill is passed. After this period, the bill becomes law and can never be reviewed by the council.

In 2008, the constitution was amended to authorize citizens who are on trial to request that the Constitutional Council strike down the law under which they are charged if the Council judges that the law violates citizens' basic rights.

Electing the Legislature

Elections to select deputies to the 577 single-member districts of the National Assembly are held according to a two-ballot plurality election procedure, similar in most respects to the one for presidential elections. To be elected at the first ballot, a candidate must receive a majority of votes in the district. Because many candidates compete in most districts, few candidates are elected at the first round. If no candidate receives a majority at the first ballot, a runoff election is held the following week. Whereas in presidential elections, only the two front-runners may compete at the runoff, in runoff elections to the National Assembly all candidates receiving at least 12.5 percent of the votes of registered voters can compete. While most runoff elections pit one candidate on the left against one on the right, some "triangular" runoffs occur, in which three candidates compete.

Since party alliances typically reflect the left-right divide, the system used to elect the National Assembly contributes to polarization within French politics. Because a cohesive coalition usually gains a majority in parliament, this strengthens political stability in the entire political system. Political scientist Jean Charlot claimed that the two-ballot electoral system "has proved . . . one of the most solid underpinnings of the Fifth Republic."[39]

There are 343 members of the Senate. Most are elected for six-year terms by mayors and town councilors from France's 100 *départements* (administrative districts into which mainland and overseas France is divided) as well as from several overseas territories. A strong rural over-representation ensures that the Senate will be particularly conservative.

Political Parties and the Party System

France has a multiparty system: that is, more than two parties capture a significant share of the popular vote. We have described how powerful parties have facilitated stable leadership and political alternation in office. In recent years, there has been a decline in the ideological distance between the major parties on the center-left and center-right. Although this has reduced tensions between these parties, many French citizens consider that these governing parties do not represent their interests. As a result, voters have gravitated to fringe parties.

The result of this development is that one can identify two different axes of electoral competition in contemporary France. The first involves competition in presidential and parliamentary elections between a center-left and center-right party that are regarded as having the capacity to govern. These two parties have won the presidency and the lion's share of seats in parliament most of the time.

The second axis pits the two major governing parties against small, fringe parties, often located at the extremes of the political spectrum, that is, pro-system parties against parties calling for radical change of one kind or another. This logic was evident in the 2005 referendum on the EU draft constitution, when the center-left and center-right parties recommended approval of the referendum while fringe parties campaigned for a no vote.

Nicolas Sarkozy performed effectively on both dimensions in his 2007 presidential election campaign. As the candidate of France's major center-right party, and a long-time cabinet minister, he represented order, stability, and continuity. At the same, he presented himself as an outsider and advocated a "rupture" (his term) with the established system, in part by embracing themes championed by Le Pen: the value of work, patriotism, and law and order.

The Major Parties

The *Union pour un mouvement populaire* (UMP) and the *Parti socialiste* (PS) currently vie for national dominance. For the past several decades, each one has led a coalition that includes smaller, allied parties. The UMP has led a center-right coalition, the PS a center-left coalition. The two coalitions have alternated control of key political institutions in the Fifth Republic, with the UMP-led alliance generally enjoying the advantage.

The UMP and PS are continually challenged by smaller parties. Several ally with one or the other major party; others oppose both parties. We review here the UMP and PS and, more briefly, two of the most important small parties.

Union pour un Mouvement Populaire (UMP). After de Gaulle returned to power in 1958, a new party was created to support his leadership that melded many smaller parties on the center-right. Largely thanks to de Gaulle's popularity, what later became known as the UMP was the keystone of the Fifth Republic in the early years. Although the party lost its commanding position in the mid-1970s, it has re-established its dominance in the current period.

The UMP was created to support de Gaulle's personal leadership and his goals of championing France's national independence, while providing strong political leadership, modernizing French society and economy, and preserving the country's distinctive cultural heritage. The party has never had a precise program, and its positions have frequently changed.

Beginning in the mid-1970s, the UMP slipped from first place. Jacques Chirac, who became leader of the party in 1974, lost presidential bids in 1981 and 1988. With Chirac still in control, the UMP regained its premier role in the 1990s. Chirac was elected president in 1995 and re-elected president in 2002, while Nicolas Sarkozy, who became leader of the party in 2002, was elected president in 2007 and his popularity contributed to the UMP's victory in elections to the National Assembly held a month after the presidential elections. Thus, the UMP has controlled the presidency since 1995, and the National Assembly and government since 2002. Since the next presidential and parliamentary elections are not scheduled to occur until 2012—and, as will be described in a moment, the PS is in severe disarray—the UMP's future looks bright.

The UMP's social base generally reflects its conservative orientation. It enjoys strong support from business executives, shopkeepers, professionals, farmers, the elderly, the wealthy, and the highly educated. Its popularity with elderly voters provides the party with an additional edge, particularly as the population is becoming increasingly composed of older people.

Parti Socialiste (PS). The PS was created well over a century ago. In the early years of the Fifth Republic, it was a perpetual and ineffective opposition party. However, in the 1970s, François Mitterrand helped make the party into a modern, attractive alternative to the ruling conservative coalition. When Mitterrand was elected president in 1981, and the PS swept parliamentary elections, it played a key role in shaping present-day France by embracing the institutions of the Fifth Republic (many on the left opposed the legitimacy of the Fifth Republic in the early years) and sponsoring sweeping reforms in the 1980s and 1990s that have helped modernize the economy and society.

However, as described in Section 2, the party lost its ideological bearings after the right turn of 1983 and has yet to define a coherent new identity. It lost legislative elections in 2002 and 2007, as well as the last three presidential elections. The PS is deeply divided by ideological and personal conflicts. When Ségolène Royal ran for president in 2007, she failed to unite the party's warring factions. The party was further weakened after the election when President Sarkozy appointed several leading PS politicians to positions in Prime Minister Fillon's government and other public agencies, and when party leaders engaged in a bitter struggle to fill the position of party chair. More generally, the PS has failed to fulfill the role of an effective opposition in the face of President Sarkozy.

Despite its electoral setbacks, the PS remains a powerful force in French politics. It is the largest opposition party in the National Assembly (and the number of PS deputies elected to the legislature in 2007 increased by fifty-five). It scored solid advances in the 2008 municipal and regional elections, and now controls the Paris city hall, many other urban governments, and twenty of France's twenty-two regional governments. However, much work remains if the party is to regain national dominance: it must unify around a new and attractive program, mount a credible opposition to the Sarkozy administration, and renew its leadership. Thus far, none of these developments has occurred.

The PS draws support from public sector workers, notably teachers and civil servants, and members of the liberal professions. Although there are differences between the electorates of the PS and UMP, both parties tend to represent the more secure strata of French society. The most vulnerable and excluded groups, including unskilled workers, the unemployed, and school dropouts, have been especially likely either to support fringe parties or to remain on the political sidelines.

Small Parties

Although the UMP and PS have consolidated the center-right and center-left of the spectrum, many voters believe that neither party is responsive to their concerns. These voters support an array of small parties (sometimes known as splinter parties). The extreme case occurred in the 2002 presidential election, when Jospin and Chirac, the PS and UMP candidates, received only 36 percent of the first ballot vote. In 2007, although Royal and Sarkozy received over half the first ballot votes, candidates from smaller parties received a hefty 43 percent of the vote.

Splinter parties contribute to the diversity, vitality—and confusion—of French political life. Among the most significant are *les Verts* (Greens), several ultra-left Trotskyist parties, and the *Parti communiste français* (PCF). Special mention should be made of the PCF, which was the largest party in France for several years after World War II. It has steadily declined to near-insignificance. In 2007, the PCF presidential candidate received less than 2 percent of the vote, although the party rebounded in the 2008 municipal elections and continues to control a significant number of towns and cities. Given space limitations, we limit our analysis to the two largest splinter parties.

Front National (FN). The FN was among the first political parties in Western Europe since World War II to promote racist themes. The party's fortunes have been tied to the popularity of its founder, Jean-Marie Le Pen, a flamboyant orator whose speeches blend folksy humor and crude attacks. Le Pen's first success in the 1980s came from targeting immigrants, primarily those of Algerian background, as the cause of France's problems. His answer was to deport them or, at the least, deprive them of social benefits.

In recent years, Le Pen and the FN increased its support by appealing to voters' discontent about crime, the corruption of mainstream politicians, economic insecurity, and European integration. Le Pen has proposed protectionism, pulling France out of the EU, eliminating the income tax, and outlawing abortion. In the 1990s, he added Jews to his list of scapegoats, repeatedly characterizing the Holocaust as a "historical detail" and making crude anti-Semitic jokes. Le Pen has been convicted several times of violating anti-racist laws.

Le Pen's biggest breakthrough occurred in 2002. By nosing out Socialist candidate Lionel Jospin and coming in second at the first round, he qualified to compete in the runoff ballot against frontrunner Jacques Chirac. Le Pen gained only 10 percent of the vote in the 2007 elections, and came in fourth, in part because (as described above) Nicolas Sarkozy appropriated Le Pen's principal campaign themes. Le Pen's advanced age (he was seventy-nine during the 2007 election) also contributed to his poor showing.

Although the FN has apparently passed its peak, and Le Pen has largely withdrawn from political life, his greatest achievement was not winning elections but reshaping France's political agenda by highlighting issues like immigration and crime. For this reason, the editor of an influential newsweekly described Le Pen's movement as "the most important political phenomenon of the last 25 years. . . ."[40]

Nouveau Centre (NC) and Mouvement Démocratique (MoDem). Two new parties—the Nouveau Centre (NC), and the Mouvement Démocratique (popularly known as MoDem)—are the modest remnants of major centrist and Christian Democratic political parties in the Fourth and Fifth Republics. Centrist parties maintained a separate existence from the Gaullist party in the beginning of the Fifth Republic because they rejected de Gaulle's opposition to European integration. In the 1970s, Valéry Giscard d'Estaing, a young centrist politician who was originally an ally of de Gaulle, helped consolidate centrist parties into a large party, the *Union des démocrates pour la France* (UDF). Giscard was elected president in 1974, but in 1981 he was defeated for re-election by François Mitterrand.

In 2002, the UMP attempted to persuade the UDF to merge, but François Bayrou, the party leader who had replaced the aging Giscard, refused. In 2005, Bayrou became increasingly critical of the UMP. He ran for president in 2007 on a platform that advocated transcending left-right cleavages in favor of a centrist position that would unite moderates on both sides. The fact that with 18.6 percent of the vote he came in third produced the greatest surprise of the election.

In the parliamentary elections that followed the 2007 presidential elections, most UDF deputies running for re-election threw in their lot with the UMP in order to gain the UMP's support. (Without it, they would not have been re-elected.) At this point, the UDF renamed itself the Nouveau Centre and elected twenty-two deputies to the National Assembly. Bayrou continued to oppose the UMP and he formed another party, the Mouvement Démocratique (MoDem). MoDem candidates in the 2007 parliamentary elections received a meager 8 percent of the vote, and only three MoDem deputies were elected. However, Bayrou seeks to preserve the MoDem as a centrist alternative to the UMP and PS, probably because his sights are fixed on running for president again in 2012.

Elections

French voters go to the polls nearly every year to vote in a referendum or in elections for municipal, departmental, or regional councilor, deputy to the European Parliament or National Assembly, and president. The most important elections are the legislative and presidential elections (see Tables 3.4 and 3.5). Turnout is usually high. For example, 84 percent of registered voters cast a ballot in the 2007 presidential elections.

After the Socialist Party's right turn and the PCF's decline in the 1980s, scholars identified a trend toward the "normalization" and "Americanization" of French

France

Table 3.4

Electoral Results, Elections to National Assembly, 1958–2007 (percentage of those voting)

	1958	1962	1967	1968	1973	1978	1981	1986	1988	1993	1997	2002	2007
Far Left	2%	2%	2%	4%	3%	3%	1%	2%	0%	2%	2%	3%	2%
PCF	19	22	23	20	21	21	16	10	11	9	10	5	4
Socialist Party/ Left Radicals	23	21	19	17	22	25	38	32	38	21	26	25	26
Ecology	—	—	—	—	—	2	1	1	1	12	8	4	3
Center	15	15	18	10	16	21*	19*		19*	19*	15*		8
Center-Right	14	14	0	4	7			42*				5*	4
UNR-RPR-UMP	18	32	38	44	24	23	21	—	19	20	17	34	40
Far Right	3	1	1	0	3	0	3	10	10	13	15	12	
Abstentions	23	31	19	20	19	17	30	22	34	31	32	36	40

*Number represents the percentage of combined votes for center and center-right parties.

Sources: Françoise Dreyfus and François D'Arcy, *Les Institutions politiques et administratives de la France* (Paris: Economica, 1985), p. 54; *Le Monde*, March 18, 1986; *Le Monde, Les élections législatives* (Paris: Le Monde, 1988); Ministry of the Interior, 1993, 1997; *Le Monde*, June 11, 2002; www.electionresources.org/fr/deputies.php?election=2007&region=fr (accessed June 18, 2007).

politics. This involved a trend toward a two-party system, with the UMP on the center-right; the PS on the center-left. In most elections, the UMP and PS were the frontrunners at the first ballot. Smaller parties that were formerly independent tended to ally with one of the two major parties. The Americanization of French politics also involved a tendency to elevate the personalities of political leaders over ideological issues.

Despite these trends, France's political style remains quite different from that found in American politics. It is far from having a two-party system: In the 2007 presidential election, only 57 percent of voters chose Sarkozy and Royal at the first ballot; the remaining 43 percent cast their votes for ten other candidates. And recall the presidential debate between Sarkozy and Royal that opened this chapter, when the two candidates went head to head debating details of their policy differences for over two hours—persuasive evidence that France has resisted the sound-bite style of American political discourse!

Yet recent developments have caused scholars to speak of a crisis in the French party system:

- There is ample support for fringe parties not part of the select "cartel" of governmental parties. Recall the 2005 referendum on the European constitution, when 55 percent of the electorate opposed the "yes" vote advocated by the two major parties. In the 2007 presidential election campaign, when voters were asked whether they trusted the left or the right to govern the country, three-fifths of respondents replied that they trusted neither camp.[41]

- Voting patterns have been increasingly unstable. Political scientist Pascal Perrineau notes, "A new type of voter is emerging, less docile to social and territorial allegiances, less faithful to a party or political camp, and less involved in the act of voting. . . . Voters are likely to change their minds from one election to another, or even from one ballot to another in the same election."[42] In all six legislative elections held between 1981 and 2002, the governing majority swung between the center-left and center-right parties. In

Table 3.5

Presidential Elections in the Fifth Republic (percentage of those voting)

	December 1965		June 1969		May 1974		April–May 1981		April–May 1988		April–May 1995		April–May 2002		April–May 2007	
	Candidate	Ballot Percentage	Candidate	Ballot Percentage	Candidate	Ballot Percentage	Candidate	Ballot Percentage	Candidate	Ballot Percentage	Candidate	Ballot Percentage	Candidate	Ballot Percentage	Candidate	Ballot Percentage
Extreme Right									Le Pen (FN)	14.4	Le Pen (FN)	15.0	Le Pen (FN)	17.0 (17.9)	Le Pen (FN)	10
															De Villiers	2
Center Right de Gaulle (Center-Right)	de Gaulle (UNR)	43.7 (54.5)	Pompidou (UNR)	44.0 (57.6)			Chirac (RPR)	18.0	Chirac (RPR)	19.9 (46.0)	Chirac (RPR)	20.8 (52.6)	Chirac (RPR)	19.9 (82.1)	Sarkozy (UMP)	31 (53)
Center Lecanuet (Opposition-Center)	Lecanuet (Center)	15.8	Poher (Center)	23.4 (42.4)	Giscard	32.9 (50.7)	Giscard	28.3 (48.2)	Barre	16.5	Balladur (UDF)	18.9	Bayrou (UDF)	6.8	Bayrou (UDF)	19
													Saint-Josse (CNPT)	4.3	Nihous (CNPT)	1
													Madelin (PR)	3.9		
Center Left Mitterrand (Socialist-Communist)	Mitterrand (PS)	32.2 (45.5)	Defferre (PS)	5.1	Mitterrand (PS)	43.4 (49.3)	Mitterrand (PS)	25.8 (51.8)	Mitterrand (PS)	34.1 (54.0)	Jospin (PS)	23.3 (47.4)	Jospin (PS)	16.1	Royal (PS)	26 (47)
													Chevèrement	5.3	Voynet (Greens)	2
													Mamère (Greens)	5.3		
Left			Duclos (PCF)	21.5			Marchais (PCF)	15.3	Lajoinie (PCF)	6.8	Hue (PCF)	8.6	Hue (PCF)	3.4	Buffet (PCF)	2
													3 candidates (Extreme Left)	10.6	4 candidates (Extreme Left)	7
Abstentions		15.0 (15.5)		21.8 (30.9)		15.1 (12.1)		18.9 (14.1)				20.6		27.9 (19.9)		16 (16)

Note: Numbers in parentheses indicate percentage of vote received in second ballot. Percentages of votes for candidates do not add to 100 because of minor party candidates and rounding errors.

Sources: John R. Frears and Jean-Luc Parodi, *War Will Not Take Place: The French Parliamentary Elections of March 1978* (London: Hurst, 1976), p. 6; *Le Monde, L'Élection présidentielle: 26 avril–10 mai 1981* (Paris: *Le Monde*, 1981), pp. 98, 138; *Le Monde*, April 28 and May 12, 1998; *Journal officiel*, May 14, 1995; *Le Monde*, May 5–6, 2002; *Le Monde*, May 7, 2002; www.electionresources.org/fr/president.php?election=2007&region=fr (accessed on June 18, 2007).

the 2007 presidential elections, half the electorate remained undecided until the closing weeks of the campaign.

- Senior politicians from across the political spectrum, including former prime ministers, cabinet ministers, a president of the Constitutional Council, and prominent mayors, have been accused and in some cases convicted of corruption. Most notably, there is sworn testimony that when former President Jacques Chirac served as mayor of Paris between 1977 and 1994, he received illicit political contributions and kickbacks from companies doing business with the Paris city government.

Allegations of corruption by President Chirac.
Source: © Phillipe Wojazer/Reuters/Corbis Reuters.

Political Culture, Citizenship, and Identity

For decades after World War II, a predominantly working-class subculture, structured by the strong grip of the PCF, faced a subculture of religiously observant and politically and socially conservative French people linked to the Catholic Church. Both subcultures comprised a network of organizations: sports, culture, mutual aid, and professional activities. Since the 1980s, these subcultures have declined in importance. The PCF has become a small and insignificant splinter party, and nowadays only 12 percent of French Catholics attend mass weekly.[43] The decline of the communist and Catholic subcultures has produced a vacuum that helps explain increased volatility in electoral behavior. We analyze here the changing forms of French political and social identity.

Social Class

For centuries, France was among the countries in which class cleavages periodically fueled intense political conflict. Under the impact of economic change and ideological reorientation, however, there was a rapid decline of class identification in the 1970s, especially among manual workers (see Table 3.6). One reason is the downsizing since the 1970s of basic industries, including steel, shipbuilding, automobiles, and textiles. This has produced a drastic reduction in

Table 3.6
Proportion of French Citizens Identifying Themselves as Members of a Social Class

	1976	1983	1987
Total	68%	62%	56%
Occupation of respondents:			
Higher executives, professionals	68%	67%	60%
Middle executives, school teachers	57%	66%	63%
Office workers	64%	62%	59%
Manual workers	74%	71%	50%

Source: L'Expansion, March 20–April 27, 1987, in Louis Dirn, *La Société française en tendances* (Paris: PUF, 1990), p. 63.

the size of the industrial workforce. Another reason is the decline of the trade union movement, a traditionally important source of working-class identity and activity.

Citizenship and National Identity

France has a double-edged approach to citizenship and national identity, described as the "republican model," that dates back to the Revolution of 1789. On the one hand, an inclusionary aspect specifies that any immigrant who accepts French political values and culture is entitled to citizenship. On the other hand, what has been described as the French republican model informally demands that citizens support the core republican values of liberty, equality, fraternity, and secularism. It dictates that religious, cultural, ethnic, and other social identities should remain private and should play no role in the public sphere.

The French often criticize the American conception of multiculturalism (the French call it communitarianism) because, in their view, it reduces politics to conflicts among social identities, fragments the political community, and erodes common ties of citizenship. Although stiff laws prohibit racial and religious discrimination, hate crimes, and incitement to racist violence, political scientist Robert Lieberman notes that the republican model "has not gone beyond the color-blind frame and the model of individual discrimination to embrace a more collective approach that attempts to compensate for inequalities between groups."[44] However, as described in Section 2, the color-blind approach masks striking economic and political inequalities. The unemployment rate among Muslims is twice that of the overall population. Virtually no citizens of North African or Black African background have been elected to municipal councils or parliament, or appointed to the Constitutional Council or upper reaches of the administration.[45] President Sarkozy's appointment of several people of color to cabinet positions in 2007 was a dramatic innovation.

A recent controversy highlights the powerful influence of the republican model. In 2004, parliament passed a law by a lopsided majority banning "conspicuous signs of religious affiliation" in public schools. Although the law banned the wearing of the Jewish yarmulka (skullcap) and large Catholic crosses, the principal target was the hidjab (headscarf—or *foulard,* in French). A government agency estimated that about 1,250 of nearly 1 million Muslim schoolgirls wore the headscarf in school.[46] Nonetheless, the law was defended as necessary to preserve religious neutrality in public schools, and as a way to combat Muslim **fundamentalism** and protect Muslim girls from intimidation, since the headscarf allegedly symbolizes their inferior status. That there was overwhelming support for the ban—about 80 percent of the French—suggests a widespread fear of Islam as well as a strong consensus for a militant version of the secular republican model. Yet this approach serves to divide the body politic by stigmatizing Muslims. As historian Joan Scott comments, the policy reflected "the impotence and/or unwillingness of the government to . . . adjust national institutions and ideologies . . . to the heterogeneity of [France's] current population. . . ."[47]

Race, Religion, and Ethnicity

Issues of race, religion, and ethnicity in France are intertwined with immigration. France has traditionally attracted large numbers of immigrants. Indeed, in 1930, the proportion of immigrants was higher than in the United States.[48] According to political sociologist Charles Tilly, France has "served as Europe's greatest melting pot."[49] Today, one French person in four has at least one parent or grandparent who is foreign-born. The most prominent example is President Sarkozy.

In the past half-century, most immigrants came from the Maghreb, France's three former North African colonies of Algeria, Morocco, and Tunisia. Other recent immigrants come from sub-Saharan (Black) Africa, Portugal, and Turkey. The majority of recent immigrants are Muslim; about half are of Arab background. Although the categories of immigrants, Muslims, and Arabs overlap, the three groups are not identical.

There are 5 million Muslims in France, one-third of all Muslims in West Europe. About three-quarters of Muslims in France migrated from the Maghreb or have parents or grandparents who did. The remainder hail from over 100 countries. About half the Muslims in France are French citizens.

Muslims differ widely in political and religious beliefs and practices. While many fast on religious holidays, relatively few adhere to strict practices, such as praying five times daily. Nor do many support reshaping French society and public policies to conform to Muslim religious doctrine (what is called an Islamist approach).

What many Muslims do share is poverty. Large numbers live in dilapidated public housing projects located on the outskirts of Paris, Marseille, and Lyon. For example, about one-quarter of Marseille's residents are Muslim. These uninviting low-income neighborhoods (the French call them *cités*) are desolate places.

There is widespread anti-immigrant sentiment in France. One poll reported that a majority of respondents believe that there are too many immigrants in France. This attitude is linked to racism. Over 60 percent of respondents in another poll claimed that racist reactions are sometimes justified.[50]

In response to anti-immigrant and anti-Muslim attitudes, governments have sponsored measures like the headscarf ban, described above, and have limited new immigration to France. In 1998, the requirements for obtaining French citizenship were tightened. When he was interior minister, Nicholas Sarkozy sponsored reforms in 2003 and 2006 to further restrict immigration. During the 2007 presidential campaign, he promised to create a ministry of immigration and national identity, a linkage implying that immigrants are responsible for France's social unrest. (Sarkozy created the ministry after his election.)

Gender

France was the birthplace of modernist feminist thought. Philosopher and novelist Simone de Beauvoir's *The Second Sex,* published after World War II, is a landmark analysis of women's subordinate position that analyzed how gender differences are socially constructed. In the 1960s and 1970s, French feminist theorists played a major role in reshaping literary studies around the world. However, there is considerable gender inequality in France, and women's movements, like many other French social movements, have been relatively weak.

Women, the largest "minority"—in reality, 53 percent of the population—are highly underrepresented in the French political system. For example, France has been at the low end of EU countries with respect to women's legislative representation. There has never been a female president of the republic and only one prime minister. Ségolène Royal was the first woman to be a major presidential contender.

France took a giant step toward increasing women's representation by a constitutional amendment of 1999 and legislation passed in 2000 mandating gender equality, that is, **parity**, in many political institutions. How did this occur in a country that opposes quotas and affirmative action? The short answer is that advocates of the measure defended it not as rectifying women's unequal representation but as a way to ensure that the political class accurately reflected the sexual composition of the electorate, that is, as a way to achieve true universalism.[51]

The **parity law** requires political parties to nominate an equal number of male and female candidates in legislative bodies whose members are elected by a list system. These include municipal councils, regional councils, and the European Parliament. Parties that violate the law may be disqualified. The parity law has been enormously effective in rectifying the traditional gender imbalance in these important institutions. Roughly equal numbers of men and women now serve on these elected bodies.

However, the glass ceiling is far from shattered. For example, the law is much less demanding for positions filled by elections in single-member districts such as the National Assembly: parties that fail to respect parity in these elections receive reduced public campaign subsidies. Thus, only 19 percent of deputies elected to the National Assembly in 2007 were women—up from the 12 percent of female deputies in the previous legislature, but a far cry from parity.

Further, the parity law does not apply to executive offices, including president, prime minister, and cabinet ministers, and men continue to monopolize these powerful positions. For example, although female membership on regional councils soared after the 2004 regional elections, only one of twenty-two regional councils elected a female president—Ségolène Royal.

If the parity law has not produced full gender equality, it has been a first step. Moreover, it doubtless helped Ségolène Royal obtain the PS nomination for president in 2007. Indeed, four of the twelve candidates running for president that year were women. And President Nicolas Sarkozy appointed an unprecedented number of women to Prime Minister François Fillon's government.

Interests, Social Movements, and Protest

The political party system represents one arena for citizen participation and representation. Citizens also pursue their interests by collective action and protest.

Organized Interests

Nearly two centuries ago, social theorist Alexis de Tocqueville lamented that France's centralized state discouraged the development of a vibrant civil society. This generally remains the case. For example, France has fewer voluntary associations, including civic groups, foundations, and think tanks, than are found in other industrialized democracies. Further, those associations that do exist are heavily dependent on the state for financial support. One study found that public subsidies constitute over half of all associations' resources.[52]

The state bureaucracy has typically been reluctant to consult with interest groups when developing and implementing policy. There are exceptions. The farm lobby (the FNSEA) and umbrella business group (Medef) participate in consultative commissions and have easy access to policy-makers. Yet most interest groups have little influence. (See boxed feature: "Citizen Action: French Trade Unions.")

Citizen Action

French Trade Unions

The character of the French trade union movement explains much about protest in France. French unions never organized as large a proportion of workers as did unions in other Western European countries, and they have steadily declined in strength from their postwar high: from a high of over 30 percent in the postwar period, the proportion of the active labor force belonging to a union has plummeted to under 10 percent nowadays—the lowest figure of any industrialized democracy. Most union members are found among public sector workers. Moreover, the trade union movement is highly fragmented. There are five umbrella trade unions that compete with each other for members and influence. In the past, most confederations were loosely allied with one or another political party. The confederations have severed such ties, but their rivalry continues. Consequently, save for exceptional moments, such as when the government proposes a cutback in social benefits that all unions oppose, organized labor rarely speaks with one voice.

France's economic difficulties have often been linked to the conflictual state of industrial relations. As opposed to the situation in Germany, for example, French unions and employers do not cooperate to negotiate wage levels, working conditions, and retirement arrangements. Instead, they engage in running battles on these issues, which often end in state-imposed solutions.

This description gives the impression that unions are a weak force in French politics and society. But in some respects, unions are quite powerful. First, they play a key role in some public and private institutions. For example, union nominees often win elections to company works councils. Unions help manage the social security, health, pension, and unemployment insurance funds. Second, when unions challenge government proposals, they often mobilize large numbers of members, other workers, and the general citizenry. When union-directed strikes and demonstrations bring France to a halt, employers and the state are forced to negotiate in order to restore order.

Thus, during normal periods, French employers and the state often ignore unions, calculating that they are not a significant force. But in times of crisis, employers and state officials must court union leaders. At such times, feverish all-night negotiations take place. The outcome often includes wage gains and other benefits, after which the cycle of "normalcy" resumes—until the next explosion.

In part as a result of the decentralization reforms described in Section 2, and the shift to a more modest state, the number of voluntary associations has soared recently. Whereas 5,000 new associations were created each year in the 1950s, that figure doubled in the 1960s, more than doubled again in the 1970s, increased to 40,000 in the 1980s, reached 68,000 in 2001, and has continued to increase since then. The total number of associations in 2001 was 700,000.[53] What is not known is whether associations' influence has increased proportionately.

Social Movements and Protest

Although the institutions of the Fifth Republic were designed to discourage citizens from acting autonomously, France's centuries-old tradition of direct protest persists. According to the World Values Survey, France is second only to Italy in the proportion of citizens who have participated in demonstrations. Groups engaging in strikes and demonstrations in recent years include farmers, fishing interests, postal workers, high school and university students and professors, truckers, railway workers, health care workers, the unemployed, retired workers, homeless, those from immigrant backgrounds, research workers, and actors—to provide a partial list! Such turbulence is explained by the fact that, when institutional channels of representation are inadequate, French citizens take to the streets.

To sum up the last two chapters, there is a sharp imbalance in the Fifth Republic between institutions of policy-making and implementation versus mechanisms for participation and representation. The result may be to weaken the state's capacity to address current challenges.

SECTION 5 French Politics in Transition

Two recent social upheavals demonstrate the troubled state of French politics and society. Both demonstrate widespread distrust of political institutions.

Two Upheavals

In November 2005, France erupted in flames following a tragic accident in a shabby Paris suburb. Two young Frenchmen of Algerian background, fleeing from the police, were accidentally electrocuted after entering an electrical power substation. Critics charged that the police pursued the young men in order to carry out another of the identity checks to which Arab youth are frequently subjected. The police claimed that they had done nothing to provoke the boys' flight.

News of the incident triggered riots in *cités* throughout France. For three weeks, bands of young men roamed nightly and torched cars, schools, and public buildings. (Ten thousand cars were burned.) The carnage ended when heavy police reinforcements were dispatched to the turbulent neighborhoods.

Why did the deaths of two young men provoke such widespread destruction? A major cause is France's persistently high rate of unemployment among young Muslim men, as described in Section 2. A contributing factor was that, shortly before the accident, then-Minister of the Interior Nicolas Sarkozy publicly denounced juvenile delinquents as scum.

After the riots ended, the government announced (yet another) crash program of assistance for low-income neighborhoods. However, the underlying problems that caused the crisis persist. In fact, a repeat performance occurred nearly two years to the day after the riots. Right after two Muslim youths riding a motorbike were killed in a collision with a police car in November 2007, youths went on a rampage, setting fire to a local police headquarters, several private buildings, and dozens of cars. A *New York Times* reporter noted that "A chilling new factor makes it, in some sense, more menacing [than the 2005 disturbances]. The one-time rock throwers and car burners have taken up hunting shotguns and turned them on the police."[54] More than 130 police officers were injured during the riots, including 30 hit by buckshot and shotgun pellets. In yet another case of *déjà vu* all over again, the government announced a plan to beef up security and provide more assistance to neighborhoods with high levels of poverty and violence.

The two crises highlight a particularly acute political challenge in present-day France. Both call attention to the difficulties of young Muslims. As we review here, there are other unresolved issues on the French political agenda.

Political Challenges and Changing Agendas

The incidents in 2005 and 2007 are extreme but not unique events. They belong to a tradition of popular protest in France that originated in the French Revolution of 1789 and has flourished for centuries. Recall the May 1968 protest movement. More recently, when the government tried to trim social benefits in 1995, strikes shut down railroads, buses, the Paris *métro* (subway), the postal system, and trash collection. After 2 million people throughout France turned out to demonstrate solidarity with the strikers, the government abandoned many of the proposed changes. Other important strikes and demonstrations have occurred in the trucking industry in 2002, the health care sector in 2003 and 2004, the cultural sector in 2003, in opposition to pension reforms in 2003 and 2005, the electrical power industry in 2004, in opposition to a youth employment program in 2006, and in opposition to pension cuts and a reduction in teachers in 2007. Yet another protest may be making news while you read this book!

Oui to Roquefort Cheese, Non to Genetically Engineered Products

The issue of globalization has generated a durable opposition movement among far-leftists, intellectuals, farmers, environmentalists, and ordinary citizens. The movement's best-known leader is José Bové, a sheep farmer sporting a handlebar mustache who comes from southwestern France, where Roquefort cheese is produced. Bové helped found a small farmers movement that opposes standardized methods of farming by agribusiness corporations (including the use of genetically modified seed), as well as farmers' loss of autonomy when large corporations centralize food processing and distribution. He became a media hero when he ransacked a McDonald's construction site near his home in 1999, for which he was sentenced

to a six-week prison term. Bové received wide support across the political spectrum for his action. He also traveled to Seattle, Washington, in 1999, to join the protests against the World Trade Organization (WTO), an international financial institution that promotes global trade and investment. In the years since then, Bové was sentenced to four additional prison terms (most recently in 2007) for destroying genetically modified crops. . However, his popularity as a folk hero has not translated into electoral support: when he ran for president in 2007, he garnered a meager 1.3 percent of the vote.

The French antiglobalization movement, which Bové helps lead, claims that it is not trying to stop globalization. It designates itself as the *mouvement altermondialiste*—that is, a movement seeking another kind of globalization than presently exists. The movement has wide appeal in France. Many French fear that globalization, as presently organized, is eroding the benefits associated with the "French social

Globalization. This cartoon appeared when José Bové traveled to the Seattle meeting of the World Trade Organization in 1999. *Source:* Plantu, Cartoonists and Writers Syndicate, from Cassettes, Mensonges et Vidéo (Paris: Le Seuil, 2000), p. 36.

model." They are also concerned that the invasion of American companies, products, and values will decimate France's distinctive culture and cherished way of life. At the same time, France is a major participant in the global economy, and, while many French are disdainful of American culture and public policy, American movies are box office hits!

One of the major organizations leading opposition to globalization is Attac, which stands for the Association in Support of the Tobin Tax. (Nobel economics prize laureate James Tobin first proposed the idea of a tax on short-term capital movements in order to deter international financial speculation.) Attac has been a sponsor of the World Social Forum, an annual assembly of antiglobalization activists from around the world.

The Challenge of Le Pen and the FN

The antiglobalization movement is one response to France's position in a changing world. Le Pen's Front National is another. Political sociologist Pierre Birnbaum observes, "What the National Front proposes to the French people . . . is a magical solution to their distress, to their loss of confidence in grand political visions of the nation."[55]

The FN's success may be due less to the substance of its ideas than to its position as critic of the established system. Polls suggest that many of the party's supporters do not share its positions but vote for the FN as a way to challenge the established system of parties and politicians. In the 2002 presidential elections, one-third of Le Pen's supporters were unemployed; more workers voted for Le Pen than for any other candidate.[56] Nicolas Sarkozy stole Le Pen's thunder in 2007 by stressing themes popular among Le Pen supporters, including patriotism, law and order, and conservative social values.

Muslim–Jewish Tensions

France has the largest number of both Muslims (5 million) and Jews (600,000) of any country in Europe. Although tensions between Jews and Muslims existed for years, the second Palestinian Intifada against Israel and Israel's occupation of the West Bank in 2002 provoked a wave of anti-Semitic attacks on Jews and synagogues, Jewish cemeteries, schools, kosher restaurants, and sports clubs. While these attacks peaked in 2004, a particularly horrific anti-Semitic crime occurred in 2006, when a Jewish man was kidnapped, tortured, and burned to death.

Anti-Semitic violence is especially common in lower-class neighborhoods with significant numbers of Jews and Muslims. Jewish children are often harassed in schools in these neighborhoods. According to one specialist, these "incidents are linked to some very real social problems in France, where many Arabs who are having a hard time or are frustrated with what is going on in Palestine are taking it out on Jews."[57]

Not all anti-Semitic violence is committed by Muslims. Skinheads and neo-Nazis have also attacked Jews, and they have targeted Muslims as well. For example, in 2007, skinheads desecrated Jewish and Muslim tombstones in several cemeteries in northern cities.

France Falling?

The French have not minimized the challenges they face. Indeed, the country has been wracked by self-doubt in recent years, as illustrated by a cottage industry of books by French authors with titles like *France Falling* and *France's Disarray*. For example, *France Falling,* a relentless critique of France's political and economic system, which found absolutely nothing to praise, was on a best-seller list for months.[58] A public opinion poll in 2006 found that three-fourths of the French believe that the next generation will have fewer opportunities than their elders. Another poll reported that 63 percent of the French believe their country is in decline. Indeed, one political analyst chides the French for being unduly self-critical![59]

A balanced assessment requires taking account not only of France's problems but of the many aspects of France's society, economy, and political system that are admirable. For example, France's formerly hierarchical pattern of state-society relations has shifted toward a more pluralist pattern. Local governments have greater freedom to experiment. Citizens have greater freedom of choice in areas like television programming and telephone service.

A reform enacted in 1999 further enlarged citizens' freedom of choice. The civil solidarity pact (*pacte civil de solidarité*, or PACs) involves civil union between unmarried couples of the same or opposite sex. The PACs provides many of the legal rights formerly enjoyed only by married couples. These days, about one-quarter of couples choose the PACs over traditional marriage. The innovation reflects a liberalization of French cultural attitudes. It is also a reflection of the weakening of the institution of traditional marriage. For example, the government's official statistical agency reported that 47 percent of all French children in 2004 were born out of wedlock; this compares with 6 percent in 1965.[60]

Socioeconomic and Institutional Reforms

France's high unemployment rate, declining international competitiveness, and daunting deficit in financing social programs have provoked intense debate over the causes of these problems and what should be done to resolve them. To what extent are cherished social benefits to blame, such as the thirty-five-hour work week, ample paid vacations, universal health coverage, the relatively young retirement age, generous pensions, and legal protections for stably employed workers? How significant is inadequate public funding of R & D? How important is the government's failure to reshape the educational system to meet the needs of a high-tech postindustrial society? What is the impact of the poor quality of what the French call social dialogue, that is, consultation and negotiation between organized business groups and labor unions?

French politics has been dominated for decades by the issue of how to reverse France's relative economic decline. French voters elected President Sarkozy in 2007 because they judged that he possessed the energy and vision needed to break the logjam in French politics. At the same time, the election did not signify a desire for a wholesale elimination of the French social model. Soon after Sarkozy's election, Olivier Roy, a French scholar, pointed out that "Americans misunderstand what a 'conservative' France could be: it does not mean a drastic shift toward a free market . . . but a balance between a welfare (and strong) state and a more flexible labor market."[61] Among President Sarkozy's first reforms were restrictions on the right to strike; reducing income, business, and estate taxes; and providing tax incentives to encourage employees to work longer hours. How history evaluates his presidency will in large part hinge on whether these changes promote greater economic growth and competitiveness.

France's political institutional framework— described by *Le Monde* as being in a state of "profound crisis"—is another arena that has been in urgent need of reform.[62] Polls reveal that citizens hold political leaders and institutions in pitifully low esteem. Between 1977 and 2006, the proportion of the French who judged that politicians "are very little or not at all concerned" with what ordinary citizens think increased from 42 to 69 percent. Fewer than half of those polled during the 2007 presidential campaign judged that the election results would improve living conditions in France. And 61 percent reported not trusting either major party to govern the country.[63]

Another indication of the need for reform is the frequency of antigovernment demonstrations. While the tendency to engage in direct and widespread protest has deep roots in French political culture, design flaws in the institutional structure of the Fifth Republic, notably, the imbalanced relations of executive and legislature, worsened this situation. Scholars generally agree that the Fifth Republic's semipresidential system endows the executive with far too much power and the legislature with too little.

As described in Section 3, President Sarkozy sponsored a substantial overhaul of France's political institutions in 2008. The most important changes include:

1. Limiting the president's tenure to two terms and authorizing the president to address parliament directly.
2. Parliament's powers are somewhat increased. The legislative texts that form the basis for parliamentary debate and vote are those recommended by parliamentary commissions (rather than, as before, the government). Further, the government no longer completely controls the legislative agenda; it shares

control with the leaders of parties represented in parliament. Parliament has gained a limited right to veto presidential appointments.

3. Opposition parties in parliament gain increased rights to propose laws and control parliamentary debate.
4. For the first time, citizens may bring suit in the Constitutional Council alleging that a law violates their fundamental rights.
5. The judiciary has gained greater autonomy.

Although political scientists differ on the extent and importance of the changes, they may create some checks and balances that will provide greater balance between the executive and parliament, between the government and the opposition, and between leadership and representation in the Fifth Republic. If successful, they may rank among President Sarkozy's greatest achievements.

French Politics, Terrorism, and France's Relation to the United States

France has a very different relationship to terrorism than does the United States. The first and only times that the United States was the site of foreign terrorist attacks occurred in 1993 and 2001. By contrast, France was the target of numerous domestic and international terrorist attacks long before, as well as after, 9/11.

Two movements with no relation to radical Islam have launched attacks in France for decades. One movement seeks independence for the Basque region in Southwestern France; the other movement seeks independence for the Mediterranean island of Corsica, an integral part of the French state. In 2004, two-thirds of the 361 people incarcerated in French prisons for terrorist activity were members of these separatist movements.[64]

France's troubled relationship to Algeria, the former colony that gained independence in 1964 after a brutal war with France, has been another source of terrorism dating back to the 1950s. Before France granted Algeria independence in 1962, France was targeted by militants seeking Algerian independence. Later it was attacked by disaffected French military officers and *colons* (settlers) from Algeria who opposed France's decision to grant Algeria independence. In the 1990s, radical Islamists of Algerian background launched attacks in retaliation for the French government's support for the anti-Islamist Algerian government.

Although French intelligence services dismantled these terrorist networks, the growth of Al Qaeda and other radical Islamic-based organizations in the last several years has posed a new threat. France has reacted vigorously, expelling radical imams (preachers), engaging in extensive surveillance, and conducting identity checks and sweeps to dismantle terrorist networks.

France's intelligence agencies, located in the ministries of defense, interior, and justice, are reputed to be among the most effective in the world. However, they have also been criticized for human rights abuses. One study points to "preventive roundups [often targeting Muslims] and the associated indiscriminate detention of suspects; and the broad powers given to the magistrates to conduct the sweeps and detentions with very little oversight."[65]

France has been a close partner with the United States in the international antiterrorist campaign. The two helped form a multilateral antiterrorist apparatus based in Paris. However, more generally, the two countries remain "troubled allies"—to quote the title of a book about their relationship published one half century ago![66]

A low point in French–American relations came in the months before the United States attack on Iraq in 2003, when President Chirac threatened to veto a U.S.-sponsored resolution seeking UN authorization for the impending war and the French prime minister blasted the United States in a speech at the UN.

A significant change in French–U.S. relations followed the election of Nicolas Sarkozy. In an election-night speech in 2007, he called for an end to French–American tensions. He alluded to France's "American friends" and declared, "France will always be at [the Americans'] side when they need her." But France continues to chafe at American power. The two countries will doubtless remain "troubled allies" for the foreseeable future.

The Challenges of European Integration

The EU and globalization pose particular challenges for French national identity and political, economic, and cultural autonomy. It is no coincidence that support for fringe parties of the left and right—which are uniformly critical of France's participation in the EU—has increased with the deepening of European integration in the past two decades.

An important reason why voters rejected the European draft constitution in 2005 was because they feared that it would require cuts in French social benefits, as well as because of its democratic deficit and its alleged threat to French independence and identity. The coalition opposing the EU constitution stretched from Le Pen's FN through the *altermondistes* to far-left parties. However, immediately after his election, President Sarkozy proposed a compromise. The streamlined text that he sponsored, with Angela Merkel of Germany, promises to revive the process of European integration.

A key question, to which a satisfactory answer has not yet been found, is whether French national identity can be refashioned just when the French republican values of liberty, equality, and fraternity have become widely shared, and when its dominant model of cultural assimilation is widely questioned.

French Politics in Comparative Perspective

France has long provided a fascinating case for comparative analysis. A few of the many issues involving the study of France that comparativists have analyzed include:

- French exceptionalism. What is the character and extent of French exceptionalism? Is French politics becoming less exceptional? In what ways? Why or why not?
- One reason some scholars claim that political patterns in France are becoming less exceptional is that *dirigisme* and ideological conflict, two of the central features of the exceptionalist model, have declined in recent years. On the other hand, we have described how *dirigisme* has been transformed but not abandoned. Further, if "classic" left-right divisions have declined, new cleavages have developed.
- What can we learn from analyzing the tensions between the French social model and economic constraints? What are the strengths and weaknesses of the French welfare state? What is the desirable balance for French citizens between time devoted to work and other spheres of social life (family, leisure, and so forth)? Must France curtail relatively extensive social protections in order to remain competitive internationally and to assure equity between younger and older French? Might economic performance be improved without substantial cutbacks in social programs? How?
- What are the strengths and weaknesses of France's semipresidential system? We have stressed the difficulties caused by an imbalance between executive and legislature. Are the recent reforms sufficient to provide an adequate balance?
- What does the rise of fringe parties tell us about the relationship between political parties, and social and ideological cleavages? Does France's multiparty system provide a model to be emulated—or avoided?
- How significant has been the Le Pen phenomenon? What does it say about the functioning of the French political system?
- How adequately does the French political system reconcile the conflicting values of

cohesion and national unity versus toleration, indeed celebration, of diversity? How does the secular, republican model of integration compare with other modes of social integration?

- France provides an exciting opportunity to study the extent to which public policy can reduce gender inequality. What are the pros and cons of the parity law?

- French school children are taught to revere the Declaration of the Rights of Man and the Citizen of 1789 and to take pride in the fact that France has championed the values of liberty, equality, and fraternity. However, the fact that these values are now the heritage of people throughout the world means that they no longer serve as markers to identify what is distinctively French. How well has France managed the dilemma of preserving national identity at the same time that the country has become part of the European Union and a participant in the global economy? How well do French political culture and institutions equip the country to confront the challenges?

These issues will shape the French political agenda in coming years—and provide ample opportunities for comparative analysis! In brief, more than four decades after youthful French protesters chanted in May 1968, "The struggle continues," the words have lost none of their relevance.

Key Terms ≫≫

conservative
socialist
decentralization
ancien régime
revolution
republic
secularism
civil society
authoritarian
proportional representation
referendum
statist
dirigisme
indicative planning

nationalization
neoliberal
privatization
deregulation
unitary system
federal system
judicial review
cohabitation
grandes écoles
grands corps
prefects
fundamentalism
parity law

Suggested Readings ≫≫

Bell, David A. *The Cult of the Nation in France: Inventing Nationalism,* 1680–1800. Cambridge: Harvard University Press, 2001.

Birnbaum, Pierre. *The Idea of France.* New York: Hill & Wang, 2001.

Bleich, Erik. *Race Politics in Britain and France: Ideas and Policymaking since the 1960s.* Cambridge: Cambridge University Press, 2003.

Bowen, John. *Why the French Don't Like Headscarves: Islam, the State, and Public Space.* Princeton: Princeton University Press, 2007.

Brubaker, Rogers. *Citizenship and Nationhood in France and Germany.* Cambridge: Harvard University Press, 1992.

Elgie, Robert. *Political Institutions in Contemporary France.* New York: Oxford University Press, 2003.

Gopnik, Adam. *Paris to the Moon.* New York: Random House, 2000.

Gordon, Philip H., and Sophie Meunier. *The French Challenge: Adapting to Globalization.* Washington, D.C.: Brookings Institution, 2001.

Hall, Peter A. *Governing the Economy: The Politics of State Intervention in Britain and France.* New York: Oxford University Press, 1986.

Kastoryano, Riva. *Negotiating Identities: States and Immigrants in France and Germany.* Princeton: Princeton University Press, 2002.

Knapp, Andrew. *Parties and the Party System in France: A Disconnected Democracy?* Hampshire: Palgrave Macmillan, 2004.

Laurence, Jonathan, and Justin Vaisse. *Integrating Islam: Political and Religious Challenges in Contemporary France.* Washington, D.C.: Brookings Institution Press, 2006.

Lebovics, Herman. *Bringing the Empire Back Home: France in the Global Age.* Durham, N.C.: Duke University Press, 2004.

Levy, Jonah. *Tocqueville's Revenge: State, Society, and Economy in Contemporary France.* Cambridge: Harvard University Press, 1999.

Lewis-Beck, Michael S., ed. *The French Voter: Before and After the 2002 Elections.* London: Palgrave and Macmillan, 2004.

Noiriel, Gérard. *The French Melting Pot: Immigration, Citizenship, and National Identity.* Minneapolis: University of Minnesota Press, 1996.

Pierce, Roy. *Choosing the Chief: Presidential Elections in France and the United States.* Ann Arbor: University of Michigan Press, 1995.

Robb, Graham. *The Discovery of France: A Historical Geography from the Revolution to the First World War.* New York: Norton, 2007.

Rosanvallon, Pierre. *The Demands of Liberty: Civil Society in France since the Revolution.* Cambridge: Harvard University Press, 2007.

Sa'adah, Anne. *Contemporary France: A Democratic Education.* Lanham, Md.: Rowman & Littlefield, 2003.

Schmidt, Vivien A. *From State to Market? The Transformation of French Business and Government.* Cambridge: Cambridge University Press, 1996.

Scott, Joan W. *Parité!: Sexual Equality and the Crisis of French Universalism.* Chicago: University of Chicago Press, 2005.

Scott, Joan W. *The Politics of the Veil (The Public Square).* Princeton: Princeton University Press. 2007.

Smith, Timothy B. *France in Crisis: Welfare, Inequality and Globalization since 1980.* Cambridge: Cambridge University Press, 2004.

Tiersky, Ronald. *François Mitterrand: The Last French President.* New York: St. Martin's Press, 2000.

Tilly, Charles. *The Contentious French: Four Centuries of Popular Struggle.* Cambridge: Harvard University Press, Belknap Press, 1986.

Treacher, Adrian. *French Interventionism: Europe's Last Global Player?* Brookfield, Vt.: Ashgate, 2003.

Suggested Websites >>

Embassy of France in the United States
www.ambafrance-us.org
French Ministry of Foreign and European Affairs
www.diplomatie.gouv.fr/en/
French National Assembly
www.assemblee-nationale.fr/english/index.asp
French President
www.elysee.fr/elysee/english/welcome.2.html

French Prime Minister
www.premier-ministre.gouv.fr/en
Le Monde newspaper
www.lemonde.fr
Libération, a center-left newspaper
www.liberation.fr
Le Figaro, a conservative newspaper
www.lefigaro.fr

Endnotes >>

[1] *Le Monde*, March 20, 2007.

[2] Simon Schama, *Citizens: A Chronicle of the French Revolution* (New York: Knopf, 1989), p. 62.

[3] Perry Anderson, *Lineages of the Absolutist State* (London: New Left Books, 1974), p. 111. See also Theda Skocpol, *States and Social Revolutions: A Comparative Analysis of France, Russia, and China* (New York: Cambridge University Press, 1979).

[4]Lynn Hunt, *Politics, Culture, and Class in the French Revolution* (Berkeley and Los Angeles: University of California Press, 1984), pp. 15, 56.

[5]Joan B. Landes, *Women and the Public Sphere in the Age of the French Revolution* (Ithaca, N.Y.: Cornell University Press, 1988), pp. 171–172.

[6]Tocqueville's two landmark studies, where he contrasts the United States and France, are the two-volume *Democracy in America* (Garden City: Anchor Books, 1969) and *The Old Régime and the French Revolution* (Garden City: Anchor Books, 1955).

[7]William H. Sewell Jr., *Work and Revolution in France: The Language of Labor from the Old Regime to 1848* (Cambridge: Cambridge University Press, 1980), p. 199.

[8]Richard F. Kuisel, *Capitalism and the State in Modern France* (Cambridge: Cambridge University Press, 1981), pp. 15–16.

[9]Suzanne Daley, "As French Campaign Ends, Many Focus on Next Round," *New York Times*, April 20, 2002.

[10]*Le Monde,* April 23, 2002.

[11]Richard Kuisel, "What Do the French Think of Us? The Deteriorating Image of the United States, 2000–2004," *French Politics, Culture, and Society* 22, no. 3 (Fall 2004): 107.

[12]*Le Monde*, May 30, 2005.

[13]Pascal Perrineau, "Analyse de l'Election présidentielle des 22 avril et 6 mai et des élections législatives des 10 et 17 juin 2007: une rupture politique?" *French Politics, Culture and Society* 25, no. 3 (Winter 2007), p. 80.

[14]Richard F. Kuisel, *Capitalism and the State in Modern France* (Cambridge: Cambridge University Press, 1981), p. 277.

[15]Henri Mendras with Alistair Cole, *Social Change in Modern France: Towards a Cultural Anthropology of the Fifth Republic* (Cambridge: Cambridge University Press, 1991), p. 1.

[16]Laurent Ménière, *Bilan de la France, 1981–1993* (Paris: Hachette, 1993), p. 18.

[17]Peter A. Hall described the new economic orientation since the mid-1980s as a "neo-liberal modernization strategy." Hall, "From One Modernization Strategy to Another: The Character and Consequences of Recent Economic Policy in France" (paper presented to the Tenth International Conference of Europeanists, Chicago, March 15, 1996).

[18]Vivien A. Schmidt, *From State to Market? The Transformation of French Business and Government* (Cambridge: Cambridge University Press, 1996), p. 442.

[19]Eurostats, *Le Monde*, March 13, 2007.

[20]Roger Cohen, "Paris and Washington Speak Softly," *International Herald Tribune*, October 20, 1997.

[21]INSEE, *Tableaux de l'Economie Française, 2003–2004* (Paris: INSEE, 2003), p. 103.

[22]Timothy B. Smith, *France in Crisis: Welfare, Inequality and Globalization since 1980* (Cambridge: Cambridge University Press, 2004), pp. 6.

[23]Jonathan Laurence and Justin Vaisse, *Integrating Islam: Political and Religious Challenges in Contemporary France* (Washington, D.C.: Brookings Institution Press, 2006), p. 10.

[24]*Metro*, March 15, 2007. Also see Laurence and Vaisse, *Integrating Islam*, op. cit., p. 62.

[25]Kimberly J. Morgan, *Working Mothers and the Welfare State: Religion and the Politics of Work-Family Policies in Western Europe and the United States* (Stanford: Stanford University Press, 2005), chs. 3–4.

[26]Commissariat général du plan, *Rapport sur les perspectives de la France* (Paris: La Documentation Française, 2000), p. 54.

[27]Jacques Rigaudiat, "A propos d'un fait social majeur: la montée des précarités et des insécurités sociales et économiques," *Droit Social*, no. 3, March 2005.

[28]Fondation Abbé Pierre pour le logement des Défavorisés, "L'Etat du mal logement en France," Paris, rapport annuel 2006.

[29]*New York Times*, June 2, 2006.

[30]*Rapport sur les perspectives de la France*, p. 45.

[31]Sophie Meunier, "Free-Falling France or Free-Trading France?" *French Politics, Culture and Society* 22, no. 1 (Spring 2004): 98–107.

[32]Robert Elgie, ed., *Semi-Presidentialism in Europe* (Oxford: Oxford University Press, 1999).

[33]Gianfranco Pasquino, "Semi-presidentialism: A Political Model at Work," *European Journal of Political Research*, 31 (1997), pp. 136–37.

[34]Editorial, "Chirac, sans Regret," *Le Monde*, May 16, 2007.

[35]Gérard Grunberg, "Les Elections Françaises de 2007," *French Politics, Culture & Society* 25, No. 3 (Winter 2007), p. 66.

[36]Luc Bronner et al, "Un an après . . . ." *Le Monde*, May 9, 2008.

[37]Ezra Suleiman, "Les élites de l'administration et de la politique dans la France de la Ve République: Homogénéité, puissance, permanence," in Ezra Suleiman and Henri Mendras, eds., *Le recrutement des élites en Europe* (Paris: La Découverte, 1995), p. 33.

[38]John T. S. Keeler and Alec Stone, "Judicial-Political Confrontation in Mitterrand's France: The Emergence of the Constitutional Council as a Major Actor in the Policy-making Process," in Stanley Hoffmann, George Ross, and Sylvia Malzacher, eds., *The Mitterrand Experiment: Continuity and Change in Mitterrand's France* (New York: Oxford University Press, 1987), p. 176.

[39]Jean Charlot, *La Politique en France* (Paris: Livre de Poche, 1994), p. 21.

[40]*L'Express*, September 14, 2006.

[41]*Le Monde*, March 14, 2007.

[42]Pascal Perrineau, "Election Cycles and Changing Patterns of Political Behavior in France," *French Politics and Society* 13, no. 1 (Winter 1995): 53.

[43]*New York Times*, April 19, 2005.

[44]Robert C. Lieberman, "Weak State, Strong Policy: Paradoxes of Race Policy in the United States, Great Britain, and France?" *Studies in American Political Development* 16 (Fall 2002): 139.

[45]*Le Monde*, March 26, 2008.

[46]Laurence and Vaisse, *Integrating Islam*, op. cit., p. 80.

[47]Joan Wallach Scott, *The Politics of the Veil* (Princeton: Princeton University Press, 2007), p. 40.

[48]Patrick Weil, *La France et ses étrangers* (Paris: Gallimard, 1991), p. 28.

[49]Charles Tilly, Foreword to Gérard Noiriel, *The French Melting Pot: Immigration, Citizenship, and National Identity* (Minneapolis: University of Minnesota Press, 1996), p. vii.

[50]*Le Monde*, March 22, 2006.

[51]Joan W. Scott, *Parité!: Sexual Equality and the Crisis of French Universalism* (Chicago: University of Chicago Press, 2005), ch. 3.

[52]Cited in Pierre Rosanvallon, *The Demands of Liberty: Civil Society in France Since the Revolution* (Cambridge: Harvard University Press, 2007), p. 257.

[53]Ibid., pp. 261–62.

[54]Elaine Sciolino, "In French Suburbs, Same Rage, but New Tactics," *New York Times*, November 28, 2007.

[55]Pierre Birnbaum, *The Idea of France* (New York: Hill & Wang, 2001), pp. 278–279.

[56]*Le Monde,* April 30, 2002.

[57]*New York Times,* February 26, 2002.

[58]Nicolas Baverez, *La France qui tombe* (Paris: Perrin, 2003); Alain Duhamel, *Le Désarroi français* (Paris: Plon, 2003).

[59]The first poll was reported in Académie des Sciences Morales et Politiques, *La France prépare mal l'avenir de sa jeunesse* (Paris: Editions du Seuil, 2007), p. 9; the second in Sophie Meunier, "Free-Falling France or Free-Trading France?"

[60]*Le Monde*, February 16, 2005. The figure of one quarter is reported in *Le Monde*, October 10, 2007.

[61]Olivier Roy, "Friend or Faux?" *New York Times*, May 15, 2007.

[62]*Le Monde*, March 14, 2007.

[63]*Le Monde*, March 26–27, 2006.

[64]Jonathan Laurence and Justin Vaisse, *Integrating Islam*, p. 245.

[65]Ibid., p. 262.

[66]Edgar S. Furniss, *France, Troubled Ally* (New York: Praeger, 1960).

Christopher S. Allen

Chapter 4 »GERMANY

Official Name: **Federal Republic of Germany (Bundesrepublik Deutschland)**

Location: **Central Europe**

Capital City: **Berlin**

Population (2008): **82.3 million**

Size: **357,021 sq. km.; slightly smaller than Montana**

1806–1871
Nationalism and
German Unification

1871–1918
Second Reich

1919–1933
Weimar Republic

1933–1945
Third Reich

1939–1945
World War II

SECTION 1   The Making of the Modern German State

Politics in Action

May Day in Europe—and most of the world—is usually a day of traditional protests and celebratory parades by organized labor movements and democratic left wing political parties, but in Hamburg in 2008 there was a sharper edge to the demonstrations. Challenging the social forces of the democratic left were groups of far right-wing nationalists who provoked the most radical of the left to engage in sometimes violent clashes in the streets. The German weekly *Der Spiegel* reported that 1,100 neo-Nazis and members of the extreme right-wing National Democratic Party (NPD) confronted over 7,000 anti-fascist left wing groups in a day-long series of demonstrations, barricades, and fires.

When such street protests lead to violence in Germany, they usually cause observers to raise the spectre of the turbulent Weimar Republic years in the 1920s, when Nazis and Communists had much larger conflicts as Germany's first experiment in democracy gave way to Hitler's Third Reich. These contemporary conflicts are but a pale image of those events. However, they are a disturbing indicator of significantly increased fragmentation of German democratic politics in the early 21st century compared to the more consensual politics in the years since the end of the World War II in 1945.

For almost all of the post–World War II period, the Federal Republic of Germany (FRG) admirably developed a stable, democratic government run by two large parties, the Social Democratic Party (*Sozialdemokratische Partei Deutschlands*, SPD) on the moderate left, the Christian Democratic Union and its sister party the Christian Social Union (CDU/CSU) on the moderate right, and one smaller party in the center, the pro-free market but socially liberal Free Democratic Party (FDP). In what came to be called a "two and a half party system" the FDP, depending on the issues, would join one of the two larger parties to form stable governments for the first forty-plus years of the FRG.

The emergence of the environmental Green Party, gaining seats in the *Bundestag* for the first time in 1983, was one harbinger of change. The other was the increasing growth of the Left Party (*die Linke*), once a mostly eastern German former communist party that began to develop considerable strength in the west in 2004. The 2005 election confirmed that the days of the "two and a half party" system were long gone, as the FDP and the two new parties received almost 26 percent of the total vote.* The electoral arithmetic had become much more complicated because the three smaller parties won enough seats to prevent one of the two large parties coalescing with only one of the smaller ones. The only other possible

---

*Significantly, no far right party has ever achieved the 5 percent threshold for winning seats in the *Bundestag,* but the NPD has recently surpassed 5 percent of the vote and won seats in two eastern German state parliaments.

1945–1990
A Divided Germany

1990–1998
The Challenge of German
Unification

1998–2001
Germany in the Euro Era

2001–
Germany after September 11

result—other than a three-party coalition—was what in fact occurred: a "Grand Coalition" between the SPD and CDU/CSU. Since 2005, however, this compromise coalition has produced considerable disagreement, ineffective governance, and enabled the three smaller parties—as the only opposition—to increase their support in opinion polls to almost 35 percent of the electorate by mid-2008.

The increasing fluidity of the party system has made coalition possibilities much more difficult. The longer that the SPD and CDU/CSU remained in a coalition in which agreement on major issues was difficult, the more support increased for the three smaller parties. Since the 2005 election, the "natural" coalitions

of CDU/CSU and FDP on the moderate right, and SPD and Greens (who comprised the government from 1998–2005) on the moderate left, have been unable to form because neither potential coalition controlled 50 percent of the seats. The Left Party's 8.7 percent share of the vote in 2005—and its increasing popularity to between 12 percent and 14 percent in opinion polls in mid-2008—made coalition possibilities difficult: none of the other parties wanted to join in coalition with the Left due to its status as a former communist party.

By the third year of the SPD-CDU/CSU Grand Coalition, German politics had become more stable, thanks to a popular chancellor in Angela Merkel and

FIGURE 4.1

The German Nation at a Glance

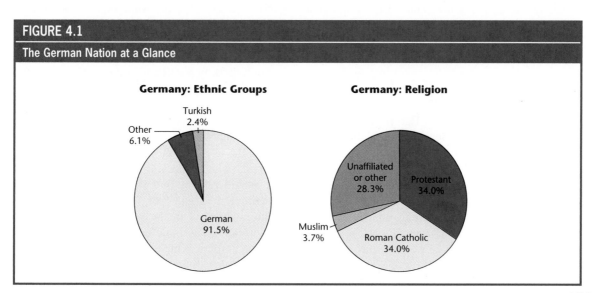

159

Germany

Table 4.1

Political Organization

Political System	Parliamentary democracy.
Regime History	After the Third Reich's defeat, Germany was partitioned and occupied by Allies in 1945. In 1949 the Federal Republic of Germany (FGR) was established in the west, and the German Democratic Republic (GDR) was established in the east. The two German states unified in 1990.
Administrative Structure	Federal, with 16 states. Germany does not have sharp separation between levels of government.
Executive	Ceremonial president is the head of state, elected for a five-year term (with a two-term limit) by the Federal Convention. Chancellor is head of government and is a member of the *Bundestag* and a leader of the majority party or coalition.
Legislature	Bicameral. *Bundestag* (614 members at 2005 federal election) elected via dual-ballot system combining single-member districts and proportional representation. Upper house (*Bundesrat*) comprised 69 members who are elected and appointed officials from the 16 states.
Judiciary	Autonomous and independent. The legal system has three levels: Federal High Court, which is the criminal-civil system; Special Constitutional Court, dealing with matters affecting Basic Law; and Administrative Court, consisting of Labor, Social Security, and Finance courts.
Party System	Multiparty. Major parties are Social Democratic Party (SDP), the Greens, Christian Democratic Union (CDU), Christian Social Union (CSU), Free Democratic Party (FDP), and Left Party (*die Linke*. PDS).

modest economic growth. But it had also become more unpredictable than it had been during most of its democratic history since the end of WWII. While Germany was certainly not about to descend again into the pre–Third Reich chaos of the 1920s, German democracy faced some of its sharpest challenges and unpredictable outcomes in decades.

Geographic Setting

Germany is located in central Europe and has been as much a western European nation as an eastern European one. It has a total area of 137,803 square miles (slightly smaller than the state of Montana). Its population of 82 million, comprising over 85 percent ethnic Germans, all of whom speak German as the primary language, is roughly evenly divided between Roman Catholics and Protestants. It has the largest population of any country in western Europe and is second only to Russia in all of Europe. Germany has been relatively homogeneous ethnically; however,

ethnic diversity has been increased by the presence of several million Turks in Germany, first drawn to the Federal Republic in the 1960s as **Gastarbeiter** (guest workers)—foreign workers who had no citizenship rights. Furthermore, increased migration across borders by EU citizens is further decreasing cultural homogeneity.

For a densely populated country, Germany has a surprisingly high proportion of its land in agricultural production (54 percent). It is composed of large plains in northern Germany, a series of smaller mountain ranges in the center of the country, and the towering Alps to the south at the Austrian and Swiss borders. It has a temperate climate with considerable cloud cover and precipitation throughout the year. For Germany, the absence of natural borders in the west and east has been an important geographic fact. For example, on the north, it borders both the North and Baltic seas and the country of Denmark, but to the west, south, and east, it has many neighbors: the Netherlands,

Germany

Belgium, Luxembourg, France, Switzerland, Austria, the Czech Republic, and Poland. Conflicts and wars with its neighbors were a constant feature of German life until the end of World War II.

Germany's lack of resources—aside from iron ore and coal deposits in the Ruhr and the Saarland—has shaped much of the country's history. Since the Industrial Revolution in the nineteenth century, many of Germany's external relationships, both commercial and military, have revolved around gaining access to resources it lacks within its national borders. Germany is divided into sixteen **federal states** (*Bundesländer*), many of which correspond to historic German kingdoms and principalities (such as Bavaria, Saxony, and Hesse) or medieval trading cities (such as Hamburg and Bremen).

Critical Junctures

Nationalism and German Unification (1806–1871)

The first German "state" (or more accurately, entity) was the Holy Roman Empire, founded by Charlemagne in 800 A.D. (sometimes referred to as the First Reich). But this loose and fragmented "*Reich*" (empire) bore little resemblance to a modern nation-state; it was composed of up to 300 sovereign entities including the territories of present-day Germany, Austria, and the Czech Republic.

Two main factors hindered German state formation: uncertain geographic boundaries and religious (Protestant vs. Catholic) division.[1] As a result of these divisions, the German language, as well as German physical and cultural traits, played a larger role in defining national identity than such features did in other European states. For many nineteenth-century Germans, the lack of political unity stood in sharp contrast to the strong cultural influence of such literary and religious figures as Goethe, Schiller, and Luther.

The victories of the French emperor Napoleon against Prussia and Austria brought an end to the Holy Roman Empire in 1806. But the defeat and occupation aroused strong German nationalist sentiment, and in 1813–1814 the Prussians—the largest and most powerful of the German-speaking states—led an alliance in a "War of Liberation" against Napoleon's France, culminating in a new German confederation created in 1815.

In 1819, authoritarian Prussian leaders confidently launched a tariff union with fellow German states that by 1834 encompassed almost all of the German Confederation except Austria, greatly expanding Prussian influence. But free-market capitalism and democracy did not take root in the Prussian-dominated Germanic principalities. Instead, there surfaced qualities such as a strong state, the dominance of a reactionary group of noble landlords in eastern Prussia called **Junkers,** a patriotic military, and a political culture dominated by honor, duty, and service to the state.

The European revolutions of 1848 sparked many prodemocracy uprisings, including those of Berlin and Vienna, respectively, the Prussian and Austrian capitals. But these revolutionary democratic movements in Germany and Austria were violently and quickly suppressed. Germany was united instead by a "revolution from above" led by Count Otto von Bismarck, who became minister-president of Prussia in 1862.[2] A *Junker* who reflected the values and authoritarian vision of his class, Bismarck realized that Prussia needed to industrialize and modernize its economy to compete with Britain, France, and the United States. He created an unlikely and nondemocratic coalition of northeastern rural *Junker* lords and northwestern Ruhr Valley iron industrialists, known as the "marriage of iron and rye." Unlike the French and American revolutionaries, the coalition leaders relied on the support of wealthy elites rather than on the democratic working class and peasant/farmers. Very simply, Bismarck was contemptuous of democracy, preferring "blood and iron" as his primary political tools. He was also as good as his word, launching three short wars—against Denmark (1864), Austria (1866), and France (1870)—that culminated in the unification of Germany. The so-called Second Reich, excluding Austria and with the King of Prussia as *Kaiser* (emperor), was proclaimed in 1871.

The Second Reich (1871–1918)

The Second Reich was an authoritarian regime controlled by industrial and landed elites. It was symbolically democratic in that the Iron Chancellor allowed for universal male suffrage for the lower house (*Reichstag*) of the bicameral legislature, but real decision-making authority lay in the hands of the upper house (*Landtag*), which Bismarck controlled.

The primary goal of the Second Reich was rapid industrialization, supported by state power and a powerful banking system geared to foster large-scale industrial investment rather than by the trial-and-error methods of free markets.[3] This path was so successful that Germany had become a leading industrial power by 1900, emphasizing such industries as coal, steel, railroads, dyes, chemicals, industrial electronics, and machine tools. The state pushed the development of such heavy industries at the expense of those producing consumer goods. Lacking a strong domestic consumer-goods economy, Germany had to export a substantial portion of what it produced on world markets.

Rapid transformation from a largely agrarian society in the 1850s to an industrial one by the turn of the twentieth century created widespread social dislocation and growing opposition to the conservative regime. A small middle class of professionals and small-business owners with rising expectations pressured the government—mostly unsuccessfully—to democratize and provide basic **liberal** (that is, free-market) rights. Industrialization also promoted the growth of a manually skilled working class and the corresponding rise of a militant Social Democratic Party (*Sozialdemokratische Partei Deutschlands*, SPD). The Social Democrats' primary goals were economic rights in the workplace and democratization of the political system. The party was greatly influenced by the founders of socialism, the Germans Karl Marx and Friedrich Engels. Socialist philosophy argues that workers, as producers of society's goods and services, should possess the country's economic and political power.

As German **chancellor** (head of government) from 1871 to 1890, Bismarck alternately persecuted and grudgingly tolerated the democratic and socialist opposition. He banned the Social Democratic Party yet created the beginnings of the first welfare state as a way to blunt the effects of rapid economic growth. Social welfare benefits included health insurance and the first forms of state-sponsored old-age pensions. This combination of welfare with political repression is sometimes referred to as Bismarck's "iron fist in a velvet glove."

Bismarck also significantly influenced German political culture by creating a strong and centralized German state. The *Kulturkampf* (cultural struggle) he initiated was a prime example of Prussian and Protestant dominance. Essentially a movement against the Catholic Church, it sought to remove educational and cultural institutions from the church and place them under the state. This action, which alienated the church and many Catholic Germans, left a powerful political legacy.

By 1900, Germany's primary economic challenge consisted of obtaining necessary raw materials and accessing world markets to sell its finished goods, in order to sustain rapid economic growth. Germany then embarked on an imperial adventure sometimes called "the scramble for Africa." However, as a latecomer on this continent, Germany could colonize only resource-poor southwestern and eastern Africa. From 1871 until World War I, Germany tried and failed to extend its colonial and economic influence. This failure inflamed German nationalists and pushed German leaders to rapidly develop the shipbuilding industry and a navy to secure German economic and geopolitical interests.

An undemocratic domestic political system, the lack of profitable colonies, an exposed geopolitical position in central Europe, and increasingly inflamed nationalism heightened Germany's aggression toward other nations and ultimately prompted it to declare war in 1914.

German leaders expected World War I to be brief and victorious. It turned into a protracted conflict, however, and cost Germany both its few colonial possessions and its imperial social order. The Second Reich collapsed in November 1918, leaving a weak foundation for the country's first attempt to establish a parliamentary democracy.

The Weimar Republic (1918–1933)

Kaiser Wilhelm II abdicated after Germany's defeat in World War I, and the Weimar Republic (the constitution was drafted in that eastern German city) replaced the Second Reich. The SPD, the only remaining party not discredited by the failed war, found itself in charge of Germany's first democracy. Its first unwelcome task was to surrender to the Allies—an action that was later used to discredit the party.

The new government was a **procedural democracy** (formal political institutions without broad public support), holding regular elections and comprising multiple parties from the far left to the far right. Yet it had a fatal flaw: the many right-wing political parties and social forces, as well as the Communists on the left, refused to accept the legitimacy of democratic government.

From the beginning, the SPD leadership was on shaky ground: it foolishly asked the undemocratic military to guarantee order and stability. Because SPD leaders signed the Treaty of Versailles and its onerous reparations payments for war costs that the victorious Allied coalition demanded from Germany, the right accused the government of having "stabbed Germany in the back." Further, the SPD-led government failed to address the ruinous inflation of 1923, when the government was forced to print worthless *Reichmarks* to pay the huge war reparations.

Into this turmoil stepped Adolf Hitler, a little-known, Austrian-born former corporal in the German army, who became the leader of the Nazi Party in 1920 (**Nazi** is a German abbreviation for National Socialist German Workers' Party). Taking advantage of a deepening economic crisis, the Nazis mobilized large segments of the population by preaching hatred of the left and of "inferior, non-Aryan races"—especially Jews, whom Hitler accused of defiling racial purity, betraying German patriotism, and enjoying illegitimate economic privilege.

After the Great Depression spread to central Europe in 1931, Germany became more unstable, with none of the major parties able to win a majority or even form durable government coalitions. Frequent elections produced ever-shakier minority governments, party fragmentation and lack of a stable majority. The Nazis relentlessly pressed for political power from a population that continued to underestimate Hitler's real intentions and viewed his hate-filled speeches as merely political rhetoric. The Nazis were rewarded in early 1933 when they and their conservative allies maneuvered President Paul von Hindenburg, a former World War I general, into appointing Hitler chancellor in a Nazi-Nationalist coalition government sworn in on January 30. Once in power, the Nazis began to ban political parties and took advantage of a fire at the Reichstag that they tried to blame on the Communists to engage in sweeping repression of the opposition. Hitler then pressured President Hindenburg to grant—by "emergency" executive order—broad, sweeping powers to the Nazi-dominated cabinet. This act made the Reichstag irrelevant as a representative political body and enabled the Nazi regime to consolidate its hold on power.

The Third Reich (1933–1945)

After the Nazis had obtained the chancellorship, establishing social control was their next major priority. This took the form of banning political parties and then all civic and religious institutions.

Ultimately, the Nazis employed propaganda and demagoguery—along with the military, paramilitary, and police through arbitrary and brutal suppression of the opposition—to mobilize large segments of the German population. Using mesmerizing speeches and a relentless propaganda ministry led by Joseph Goebbels, Hitler exercised total control of political power and the media to reshape German politics to his party's vision. This vision allowed no opposition, even within the party.

Initial Nazi domestic policy was focused on two major areas: centralization of political power and the rebuilding of an economy devastated by the depression of the early 1930s. The Nazis concentrated all political authority in Berlin, removing any regional political autonomy. The main purpose of this top-down system was to ensure the repression of political opposition, Jews and other minorities.

The Nazis' economic program was also autocratic in design and implementation. Because free trade unions had been banned, both private and state-run industries forced workers, including slave laborers during World War II, to work long hours for little or no pay. The program emphasized heavier industries that required massive investment from the large manufacturing cartels, the banking system, and the state itself. Although some segments of big business had initially feared Hitler before he took power, most of German industry eventually endorsed Nazi economic policies. The Nazis also emphasized massive public works projects, such as building the *Autobahn* highway system, upgrading the railroad system, and constructing ostentatious public buildings. Almost all favored Nazi industries had direct military application.

During the Third Reich, Hitler fanned the flames of German nationalism by glorifying the warrior tradition in German folklore and exulting in imperial Germany's nineteenth-century victories. Extolling a mythically glorious and racially pure German past, he made scapegoats out of homosexuals, ethnic minorities, and, especially, Jews. Anti-Semitism proved an important political force that Hitler deployed to blame any political problems on this "external" international minority and to target them as enemies who should be relentlessly persecuted and suppressed. Thus, in the first years of Nazi rule, Jews were excluded from professions, including teaching, law, medicine, and the

Hitler strides triumphantly through a phalanx of Nazi storm troopers (SA) in 1934.   *Source:* Ullstein Bilderdienst.

civil service, and prohibited from marrying non-Jews. As described below, much worse was yet to come.

The Nazis refused to abide by the provisions of the Treaty of Versailles. Germany began to produce armaments in large quantities, and remilitarized the Rhineland. The Nazis also rejected the territorial divisions of World War I, since Hitler claimed that a growing Germany needed increased space to live (*Lebensraum*) in eastern Europe. He engineered a union (*Anschluss*) with Austria in March 1938 and the occupation of the German-speaking Sudetenland section of Czechoslovakia in September 1938. The Third Reich's attack on Poland on September 1, 1939, finally precipitated World War II.

Hitler's grandiose visions of world domination were dramatically heightened by the German conquests of much of Europe during 1939 and 1940. In 1941, Hitler attacked the Soviet Union, assuming that defeating the Soviet Union would be as easy as his other conquests. The attack was an enormously costly failure, and foreshadowed the Third Reich's defeat almost four bloody years later.

The most heinous aspect of the Nazi regime was the systematic extermination of 6 million Jews and the imprisonment in concentration camps of millions of other civilians. Concentration camps were first created in 1933 for Jews, political opponents, homosexuals, and gypsies. Prisoners were treated with extreme

"Enemies of the Third Reich" *Source:* Courtesy of the Trustees of the Boston Public Library, Rare Books and Manuscripts. Reproduced with the permission of Alexandra Szyk Bracie, daughter of Arthur Szyk, in cooperation with The Arthur Szyk Society/Historicana, www.szyk.com.

brutality and large numbers were shot or died from starvation, disease, or overwork. Several years later, the Nazis created extermination camps in occupied countries like Poland, equipped with gas chambers to murder the Jews and other inmates. Hitler had explicitly stated in *Mein Kampf* (*My Struggle*), written in 1925 while he was imprisoned for leading a failed insurrection, that the Germans were the master race and all those of non-Aryan ethnicity, especially Jews, were inferior. But as with many of his statements during his rise to power, many Germans chose to ignore the implications of this hatred or thought it was mere exaggeration. The magnitude of Nazi plans for other races, religions, opposing political views, gays, and gypsies, among others, became apparent after Hitler came to power, but by then any chance of domestic opposition had passed. Persecution of Jews and other racial and ethnic minorities grew steadily more atrocious until Germany's defeat in 1945.

A Divided Germany (1945–1990)

Germany was occupied by the victorious Allied powers from 1945 to 1949. However, cold war tensions soon led to the formal division of Germany: the Federal Republic of Germany (FRG) in the west, run by the Allies (Britain, France, and the United States), and the communist German Democratic Republic (GDR), directed by the Soviet Union in the east. This division was not expected in 1945, but postwar Germany soon took on the respective postwar visions of the two victorious sides. The major German cold war focal point was the city of Berlin, like Germany itself, divided between Allied- and Soviet-supported governments.

During the years of occupation in West Germany (1945–1949), German and Allied officials reduced the powers of the central state in domestic politics; some of these powers were assumed by regional governments. Western German reformers also rebuilt the party system, helping to create parties with more broad-based interests and ideological considerations. The most significant political development was the merger for the first time in 1946 of Roman Catholic and Protestant interests into the Christian Democratic Party. The result was the emergence of a large center-right party that ruled the FRG, alone or in coalition, for the first twenty years of the new republic.

Formal nation-statehood was restored to the two Germanys in 1949, and the Occupation ended, but neither half of divided Germany was fully sovereign. The FRG deferred to the United States in matters of international relations, as did the GDR to the Soviet Union. Neither of the two Germanys joined the cold war's international alliances—NATO (North Atlantic Treaty Organization) and the Warsaw Pact, respectively—until 1955.

In 1949, the Federal Republic became a democracy, characterized by constitutional provisions for free elections, civil liberties and individual rights, and an independent judiciary. The Federal Republic's democratic system produced rapid economic growth and remarkable political stability for the first forty years of its existence. Alternation from a moderate center-right government to a moderate center-left one, and back again, produced high standards of living and a genuine democratic regime. Under Christian Democratic chancellors Konrad Adenauer (1949–1963) and Ludwig Erhard (1963–1966), the FRG saw the establishment of a new parliamentary regime, an extensive system of social welfare benefits, a politically regulated market economy, and the re-establishment of strong regional governments.

Under Social Democratic chancellors Willy Brandt (1969–1974) and Helmut Schmidt (1974–1982), the FRG first enjoyed robust full employment and a large increase in social services. The SPD also advocated a more equal distribution of income. But later in the 1970s, two economic recessions produced increased unemployment and forced Chancellor Schmidt to introduce moderate cutbacks in social services. Unlike many Western capitalist countries in the 1980s, however, West Germany retained many of the social programs of the postwar welfare state, a stance that enjoyed wide public support.

The Christian Democrats returned to power in 1982 under the leadership of Chancellor Helmut Kohl, who formed a center-right coalition with the Free Democratic Party (FDP), a moderate centrist party that had allied with both of the two major parties in most governments since 1949. The 1949–1990 period established the viability of constitutional democracy in the Federal Republic, as the country maintained a firm commitment to parliamentary government and political stability.

In the meantime, the German Democratic Republic was established in Soviet-occupied East Germany in 1949. The GDR was a one-party state under the control of the Communist Party, which was known as the Socialist Unity Party (SED, *Sozialistische Einheits Partei*). Although the state provided full employment, housing, and various social benefits to its citizens, it was a rigid, bureaucratic, Stalinist regime that tightly controlled economic and political life under the leadership of party chairmen Walter Ulbricht, Willi Stoph, and finally Eric Honnecker. The East German regime stressed the desirability of communism and suppressed public dissent as deviationist and undermining the "true path of socialism." The infamous *Stasi*, or secret police, was an extensive system of surveillance that kept tabs on all German citizens and ruthlessly dealt with those suspected of opposing the regime. East Germans caught trying to escape to the West were executed on the spot. In August 1961, East Germany erected the Berlin Wall to keep its citizens from fleeing to West Germany.

For more than forty years, the international role of the two Germanys was limited. Because of NATO's

geopolitical restrictions, West German energies were focused on rebuilding the economy and pursuing European economic integration. East Germany was similarly restricted. Although it became the strongest of the Warsaw Pact's economies, it also loyally toed the Soviet line in international affairs.

The Challenge of German Unification (1990–1998)

Germany's unification in 1990 took place rapidly. When Soviet rule over Germany and other communist regimes in East Central Europe loosened, and the Berlin Wall was opened in November 1989, the two German states envisioned a slow process of increased contacts and cooperation while maintaining separate sovereign states for the short term. Yet a currency reform provided East Germans with valuable West German deutsche marks and fueled massive migration westward in the summer of 1990. The process of German unification proceeded much faster than anyone could have imagined. After a referendum on unification and intense negotiations in the late summer, the former East Germany was incorporated into the FRG as five new West German states (*Länder*).

Formal unification took place in the fall of 1990 as Helmut Kohl, the "unification chancellor," won a strong re-election victory for his center-right Christian Democratic–Free Democratic coalition. But unification euphoria did not last, as its costs strained Germany's budget and democratic institutions. The process proved much more difficult than expected. The communist-planned economy (sometimes called a *command economy*) was much weaker than had been recognized. The production of goods was determined more by rigid government dictates than by real consumer needs, and what was produced was of shoddy quality. The East German level of technology was decades behind, and the unified German government spent huge sums just to rebuild communication networks.

Incorporating the disadvantaged East Germany into the FRG had an adverse impact on a wide range of public policies, including unemployment expenses, structural-rebuilding funds, and the large tax increases necessary to pay for it all. Because the production apparatus in eastern Germany was so deficient, unemployment soared. The proportion of the unemployed in eastern Germany—approximately 20 percent, more than twice the figure in the prosperous west—helped fuel scattered ultra-right-wing political movements. Skinheads and others targeted foreigners (often Turks) as scapegoats, and there were several vicious attacks on minority groups beginning in the 1990s.

The difficulties of unification were complicated by the Kohl government throughout the 1990s. In order to win the support of eastern Germans, he sugarcoated the enormity of the unification process as well as its duration. In order to win the support of western Germans, he had to convince them that the 7.5 percent "unification tax" imposed on them in the early 1990s would be sufficient to achieve economic integration. Unfortunately for Kohl, the longer the unification process remained incomplete, the less willing the German electorate was to give him continued support.

By 1998, Kohl's center-right coalition had run out of both gas and ideas. Successfully convincing Germans that a change was necessary, newly elected SPD Chancellor Gerhard Schröder, a generation younger than Kohl, formed a coalition government with the environmentalist Green Party for the first time in the nation's history. Significant too was the continued high support for the former Communist Party (now called *die Linke*) in eastern Germany (over 20 percent), which enabled it to gain more than 5 percent of the total German vote. With almost 54 percent of the electorate voting for parties of the left, clearly a new era had arrived in Germany.

Germany in the Euro Era (1998–2001)

Germany's leaders—from Konrad Adenauer, the first postwar chancellor, through Schröder—were all strong supporters of European integration. Germany is the economic anchor of the EU, and its membership in the EU has enabled it to do things and to take on needed political responsibilities that it would be unable to carry out alone. Former chancellor Kohl (1982–1998) realized this and was a firm advocate of all measures that would assist in a smooth, stable, and comprehensive EU.

The accelerating pace of European integration, however, produced movement toward a common monetary policy, a European central bank, and a single (virtual) currency in 1999. This, followed by the replacement of eleven European national currencies in favor of the euro on January 1, 2002, placed additional pressures on the Federal Republic. Many Germans wondered whether the EU would provide the same stability as the redoubtable deutsche mark (DM) and the inflation-fighting Deutsche Bundesbank. The fall in value of the euro by some 25 percent in relation to the dollar in 1999 and 2000—and its subsequent rise to more than 50 percent greater than the dollar eight years later—was worrisome to Germans long accustomed to a stable and predictable DM. So too was the loss of domestic control of monetary and fiscal policies, due to the EU requirement that member states not run deficits greater than 3 percent of GDP.

With respect to open borders and seemingly free-flowing immigration, Germans also feared that Europeanization threatened to erode what it meant to be German. At the same time that immigration and political asylum increased in Germany during the 1990s, the birth rate, particularly in the former GDR, dropped precipitously. Far-right and even some moderate right-wing politicians used these demographic changes to whip up nationalist support for decreasing the flow of migrants to the FRG. Ironically, these demographic changes also coincided with the inability of the highly regarded secondary educational system to produce enough skilled workers for the information age. Germany's vocational educational system and integrated apprenticeship system, described in Section 2, have worked exceptionally well for traditionally strong German industries, but they have been less effective in producing highly qualified workers for the information sector. Finally, the issue of democratic governance was an additional European challenge. With fiscal and monetary policy essentially determined by either Brussels or the European Central Bank, where does democratic governance really lie?

Germany after September 11 (2001–)

The terrorist attacks on the United States had several significant effects on German domestic and international politics. Among the most significant were immigration/globalization, antiterrorist measures, and Germany's relationship with the United States.

The enlargement of the EU with the addition of twelve central and eastern European countries since 2004 highlighted the challenge that immigration poses for Germany, since there are no restrictions on movement by citizens of member states to other EU member states. During the *Gastarbeiter* period after World War II, immigration to Germany was comparatively straightforward. Workers came from southern Europe and Turkey, supposedly for limited periods, and would return home when economic conditions no longer required their services. Of course, several generations of Turkish-Germans remain in the Federal Republic. But in the first decade of the twenty-first century, in addition to migrants coming for economic opportunities in a globalizing world, a wave of migrants arrived from unstable and repressive countries in Africa and East Europe seeking political asylum.

The discovery that some of the 9/11 terrorists had lived in Hamburg prior to the attacks only added to the tension. Germany's sensitivity after World War II to the excesses of the Nazi regime was responsible for the liberal asylum laws; postwar German governments viewed with pride the country's openness to oppressed people facing repression. Yet the discovery that several of the terrorists belonged to an Al Qaeda cell in Hamburg before going to the United States created uneasy discussion in Germany on the issue of freedom versus security. In the wake of 9/11, the Schröder and Merkel governments increased domestic surveillance to locate additional terrorist cells, and made a series of arrests and detentions. While such aggressive actions by police and security forces helped identify potential threats to domestic and international security, they rested uneasily with considerable segments of the German population, creating tension between Germany and the United States

Germany's opposition to the Iraq war also drove a large wedge between the United States and the Federal Republic. The tension was exacerbated by the conduct of Gerhard Schröder during his 2002 reelection campaign. His leading issue in the final weeks of the campaign—largely reflecting the preferences of the German public—was in direct opposition to the Bush administration's Iraq policy in the months before the war in early 2003. Although the campaign never degenerated to the level of American–French acrimony regarding the Iraq war, the long-standing strong relationship between Germany and the United States took a significant hit because of this dispute. Further exacerbating these tensions were the acquittals of two Moroccan alleged terrorists in Germany in February 2004. Because the Bush Administration refused to release witnesses—who were being held in detention in the United States—who could potentially exonerate the two Moroccan suspects in Germany, the judges in the two German courts were forced to release the two defendants because they could not present a proper defense.

Themes and Implications

Historical Junctures and Political Themes

Because of the historic importance of militarism and a corresponding authoritarian political culture, Germany's role in the world of states is contentious. For all states, military strength is a basic tool used to shape and consolidate. But in Germany, late unification propelled by war created a state that caused tremendous fear among Germany's neighbors. The conduct of World War I and the crimes of the Third Reich during World War II intensified this fear. Although more than fifty years have passed since the end of World War II and although Germany's independent political actions are constrained by the EU, many Europeans remain wary of Germany's international role.

The second theme, governing the economy, has been colored profoundly by Germany's late unification and the issue of state building. Delayed unification and industrialization in Germany prevented it from embarking on the race for empire and raw materials until the late nineteenth century. The pursuit of fast economic growth and an awakened sense of German nationalism in the late nineteenth century produced an aggressive, acquisitive state in which economic and political needs overlapped. The fusion of state and economic power enabled Hitler to build the Third Reich. Consequently, policy-makers and political leaders after World War II desired to remove the state from actively governing the economy. Thus, the postwar period saw the development of *Modell Deutschland* (the German model), a term often used to describe the Federal Republic of Germany's distinctive political and socioeconomic features. While amazingly successful for decades after World War II, it remains an open question whether these economic institutions will continue to function well in a unified Europe.[4]

The democratic idea, our third theme, is one that developed much later in Germany than in most other advanced industrialized countries. It was not until 1918 and the shaky Weimar Republic that Germany attained democracy at all. Despite a formal democratic constitution, Weimar was a prisoner of forces bent on its destruction. Unlike stable multiparty political systems in other countries, the Weimar Republic was plagued by a sharp and increasing polarization of political parties. And of course Germany's descent into authoritarianism in the 1930s destroyed every vestige of democracy.

The constitution of the Federal Republic in 1949 was designed to overcome Weimar's shortcomings. A system of federalism, constitutional provisions to encourage the formation and maintenance of coalitions, and a streamlined political party system proved solid foundations for the new democracy. Electoral turnout of 80 to 90 percent for almost all elections since 1949 further suggests that Germans have embraced democracy, although skeptics once argued that Germans voted more out of duty than anything else.[5] However, four peaceful electoral regime changes in the past fifty years, in which both the government and the opposition functioned more smoothly than in most other democratic regimes, have finally put doubts about German democracy to rest. The remaining uncertainties involve how fully the democratic culture will penetrate formerly communist eastern Germany and how successfully Germany's politics will adapt to a five-party system since the Left Party now appears to be a permanent fixture.

As for the fourth theme, the politics of collective identity, more than in other democratic countries, German political institutions, social forces, and patterns of life emphasize collective action rather than the individualism characteristic of the United States. This does not imply that German citizens have less personal freedom compared to those in other developed democracies or that there is no conflict in Germany. It means that political expression, in both the state and civil society, revolves around group representation and cooperative spirit in public action.

Certainly, Germany's history from Prussian militarism through Nazism has led many observers to believe that collectivist impulses should be eradicated. However, to expect Germany to embrace an individualistic democracy like that of the United States is misguided. Germany's development of a collective identity since 1945 has relied on a redefinition of Germany in a European context. For example, one of the first provisions of the SDP-Green coalition agreement was to ease Germany's restrictive immigration law to enable those who had lived in Germany for decades to obtain citizenship. German collective identity is changing.

Implications for Comparative Politics

Germany differs from other developed countries in substantial ways. Germany—like Japan—was late to industrialize and late to democratize. But the most significant difference between Germany and other western European states is, of course, the Nazi period and the destruction that the Third Reich wrought. Concerns about this period, however, have been somewhat allayed by Germany's stable democratic experience since 1949.

Germany's significance for the study of comparative politics lies in several areas: the contrast between its nationalistic history and democratization in an integrating Europe; its unique form of organized capitalism that is neither state-led nor laissez-faire; its successful form of representative democracy that combines widespread participation and representation of the entire electorate in a stable parliamentary regime; and a politics of identity that builds on existing collectivities in an increasingly multifaceted political culture.

Political Economy and Development

State and Economy

Germany's capitalist economy relies on a coordinated network of small and large businesses working together. Most German banks—especially local and regional ones—see their primary role as providing long-term investments to support Germany's internationally competitive manufacturing industries. German banks have been the prime foundation for the country's economic pattern of stable, long-term relationships among economic partners rather than the short-term deals common among banks, investors, and firms in the United States. Although these practices have eroded somewhat among the largest banks (e.g., Deutsche Bank, Dresdner Bank) in the face of globalization, deregulation, and Europeanization, the core principles of this arrangement remain, particularly among small and medium-sized firms and financial institutions.

The Role of the State Before 1945

In the years before unification in 1871, many of Germany's regional governments played a strong role in promoting economic growth and development. They worked directly and indirectly with private economic interests, thus blurring distinctions between the state and the market. The foundations for economic growth were established, and the most spectacular early leaps of industrial modernization happened, before Germany's unification in 1871. The creation of a customs union (*Zollverein*) in 1834 from eighteen independent states with a population of 23 million people propelled industrial modernization by greatly facilitating trade among these states after centuries of economic stagnation.

Bismarck became the dominant symbol for Prussia's hegemonic position in brokering the interests of grain-growing *Junkers* in the east with those of the coal and steel barons in the Ruhr. Bismarck used the development of the railroad as a catalyst for this "marriage of iron and rye."[6] He astutely realized that although railroads were a primary consumer of coal and steel, they also provided an effective way to transport the *Junkers*' grain to market from the relatively isolated eastern part of Germany. The image of Prussian-led, rapid, state-enhanced industrial growth is important, but small-scale agricultural production remained in many parts of the southern states, particularly in Bavaria, and small-scale craft production continued in Württemberg and many other regions.

By 1871, a unified Germany was forced to compete with a number of other countries that had already developed industrialized capitalist economies. German business and political elites realized that a gradual, small-firm-oriented economy would face ruinous competition from countries such as Britain, France, and the United States. To become competitive, the German state became a powerful force in the German economy. The most influential analysis of German industrial growth during the nineteenth century was by economic historian Alexander Gerschenkron. He maintained that Germany's transformation from a quasifeudal society to a highly industrialized one during the latter two-thirds of the nineteenth century was made possible by explicit coordination among government, big business, and a powerful universal banking system (with a given bank handling a variety of financial transactions as opposed to separate banks for savings and commercial activities).

A severe economic crisis in 1923, caused largely by Germany's payment of massive reparations to the Allies as required by the Versailles Treaty that ended World War I, destabilized the economy and produced massive hyperinflation. After the 1929 stock market crash, Hitler used demagoguery and hatred to claim that his leadership could produce the solution for all of Germany's problems. During the Third Reich, between 1933 and 1945, the state worked hand in glove with German industry to repress workers, employ slave labor, and produce military armaments. As a result, a number of leading industrialists, notably those of the Krupp steel works and the IG Farben chemical complex, were tried and convicted of war crimes after the Allied victory.

The Social Market Economy

Unlike Anglo-American laissez-faire policies, or heavy-handed state-led economic policies, German economic policies after World War II were indirect and supportive rather than clumsy and overly regulatory. Although the government sets broad guidelines, it encourages the formation of voluntary associations to coordinate negotiations among employers, banks, trade unions, and regional governments in order to reach the government's policy objectives. Its economic policy-making is flexible in two ways.

First, German regulation establishes a general framework for economic activity rather than providing detailed standards. The government sets broad licensing and performance standards for most professions and industries. Government policy-makers believe that once their core requirements are met and their general objectives known, private actors can be trusted to pursue government goals without detailed regulation. Violating government standards can result in fines or, in some criminal cases, imprisonment. In contrast, the United States has no such core requirements. Instead, it often produces many layers of detailed—and sometimes contradictory—regulations in the wake of banking failures and financial abuses.

Second, among the major European economies, Germany has the smallest share of industry in national government hands; but it allows state governments to have considerable power. This is called cooperative federalism, which delegates to the states (*Länder*) the administrative powers to oversee the implementation of laws and regulations passed at the federal level.

Postwar policy-makers avoided a dominating role for the state in the Federal Republic's economic life. Unlike the French and the Japanese states, which have intervened much more in the economy, the German state has evolved a careful balance between the public and private sectors. Germany has avoided the opposite pattern as well: the frequently antigovernment, free-market policies of Britain and the United States since the 1980s.

In other words, the relationship between state and market in Germany is neither free market nor state dominant. Rather, the state sets clear general ground rules, acknowledged by the private sector, but then allows market forces to work relatively unimpeded within the general framework of government supervision. For example, the Federal Bank Supervisory Office encourages banks to have slightly more capital reserves than the international standard and it certifies

the competency of senior management. The German system of **framework regulations** has enabled German economic policy to avoid the sharp lurches between laissez-faire and state-led economic policy that have characterized Britain since World War II. This system often appears externally rigid but internally flexible (in the sense that large institutions and firms are often surprisingly flexible in adapting applied technologies to produce specialized goods). In short, this system regulates not the details, but the general rules of the game under which all actors must play.

Some would criticize such a system as being too cumbersome and inflexible. However, supporters praise its ability to generally produce agreement on major policy direction without major social dislocation. For example, the banks are legally allowed to develop close financial ties with firms in other industries, including owning their stock, granting them long-term loans, having representatives on their boards of directors, and voting as stockholders. The end result is that much private investment is based on "patient capital" geared toward long-term economic success rather than quick profits in the short term. Once agreement has been informally worked out among all the major parties, it is easier to move forward with specific policies and/or legislation. Since the time of the first postwar chancellor, Christian Democrat Konrad Adenauer, the Germans have referred to this approach as the **social market economy** (*Sozialmarktwirtschaft*).

But the contemporary period has been much more stressful for this model. Among the many social components of the German economy once considered bedrocks, but now under pressure, are such diverse public benefits as health care, workers' rights, public transportation, and financial support for the arts. In some respects, these benefits are similar to those provided by other European governments. However, the provision of some public benefits through organized private interests (such as the quasipublic "sickness funds" that provide for health insurance) makes the German social market economy a blend of public and private actions that support and implement public policies. The social market economy blurs state/market distinctions in the hope of producing a socially responsible capitalism. The social component of the social market economy is distinctive to Germany. Several programs, such as savings subsidies and vocational education, contribute to the production of income. The former contributes to a stable pool of investment capital, while the latter helps create a deep pool of human capital that has enabled Germany to produce high-quality goods throughout the postwar period. But as we see below, these programs face daunting challenges.

Germany, for most of its postwar history, has been a high-wage, high-welfare nation that has maintained its competitive world position far better than have most other advanced industrialized states since the oil crises of the 1970s. An emphasis on high skills in key export-oriented manufacturing industries was the special path that German economic policy took to maintain its competitive position. An elaborate vocational education system combined with apprenticeship training underlay this policy, which was implemented through the **works councils,** firm-level institutions elected by every worker in all German companies with five or more employees. This system of training workers in advanced skills enabled Germany for many years to resist the postindustrial service sector emphasis pursued by countries such as the U.S. and Britain.

Relying extensively on its elaborate apprenticeship program, Germany maintained a competitive position in such traditional manufacturing industries as automobiles, chemicals, machine tools, and industrial electronics. By relying on its highly skilled work force, Germany resisted for many years the claim that it must lower its wage costs to match those of newly industrializing countries. Germany's record suggests that a developed country in a globalized world economy can still compete in manufacturing by raising product quality rather than by lowering wage costs. Despite a lack of natural resources, Germany has maintained a trade surplus with a large working-class population that historically has spurned protectionism. With one in every three jobs devoted to exports (one in two in the four manufacturing industries just mentioned), protectionism would be self-defeating for German unions. The skills and productivity of its workers have helped German industry acquire natural resources and pay high wages. This has enabled Germany's highly skilled blue-collar workers to drive expensive German automobiles, obtain high-quality medical care, and enjoy six weeks of paid vacation each year.

Germany's research and development strategy has enhanced these economic policies. Rather than push for specific new breakthroughs in exotic technologies or invent new products that might take years to commercialize, the strategy is to adapt existing technologies to traditional sectors and refine already competitive sectors. This was the exact opposite of U.S. research and development strategy. During the postwar years, this policy has enabled Germany to maintain a favorable balance of trade and a high degree of competitiveness. However, German unification and European integration have forced German industry and policy-makers to reexamine and perhaps modify this model. Taking others' core discoveries and quickly applying them to production requires coordinated policies among all producer groups. The primary challenge since the 1990s has been trying to integrate into this system former GDR workers raised in an industrial culture that encouraged workers to follow orders rather than apply skill and initiative. One of the major tasks for early twenty-first century governments has been to improve Germany's vocational education system, particularly in the five eastern states.

Other than the government, the German institution that, until recently, was most responsible for shaping economic policy was the very independent *Bundesbank* (central bank). *Bundesbank* policy produced low inflation, both because this was a traditional demand of all central bankers and because of Germany's history of ruinous inflation during the Weimar Republic. However, when the government wished to expand the economy by increasing spending or reducing taxes, the *Bundesbank* preferred policies that favored monetary restrictions over fast economic growth. As a result, the government and the *Bundesbank* disagreed on economic policy repeatedly in the years since after unification. Since the introduction of the euro, however, the European Central Bank (ECB) has usurped the *Bundesbank*'s role. Although the ECB is modeled on the *Bundesbank* (and is also located in Frankfurt), it signifies a change in German economic policy from the national to the European level.

Despite the long success of the German model, the early twenty-first century ushered in a period of deep introspection concerning economic stagnation. Upon its election in 1998, the SPD-Green government led by Gerhard Schröder pledged to maintain the core features of the *Sozialmarktwirtschaft*. But it too found each of these traditionally successful policies facing mounting challenges from Europeanization, globalization, and a powerful deregulatory free enterprise ideology. However, the presence of the environmental Greens in the cabinet for the first time gave added weight and attention to climate change and environmental policies.

The expansion of the EU to twenty-seven countries in 2007 had an important impact on German-specific organized capitalist institutions. Now, German firms could go to lower-cost eastern and southern European countries to find the best deals rather than maintain the kind of long-standing business relationships that were the lynchpin of the German model. Continued globalization meant that lower-cost but high-quality goods, such as automobiles from East Asia, threatened the strength of Germany's auto producers such as BMW and Daimler-Chrysler. More fundamentally, the German organized capitalist model was increasingly attacked at the ideational level. For many years, free-market adherents from abroad criticized the German model for its "clubby" relationships among what the Germans called the "social partners" (business associations, labor unions, and federal and state governments). Yet, as long as Germany's economy thrived, German officials could slough off the criticism. As the German economy's troubles mounted, policy-makers had no effective answers to such criticism. Yet as the American financial crisis associated with deregulation and free-market policies spread to Europe in early 2008, some began to wonder whether the German organized capitalist model might still be appropriate after all.

Welfare Provision

Welfare policies can be described as the social part of the social market economy. Although the Federal Republic's social welfare expenditures are not as extensive as those in Scandinavia, public services in the Federal Republic dwarf those in the United States. From housing subsidies to savings subsidies, health care, public transit, and the rebuilding of the destroyed cities and public infrastructure of the former GDR, the Federal Republic is remarkably generous in its public spending. Even under the moderately conservative rule of the CDU-led Adenauer coalition during the 1950s and early 1960s, there was a strong commitment to provide adequate public services. This strategy recalls Bismarck's efforts to use public services to forestall radical demands in the late nineteenth century. For antidemocratic conservatives like Bismarck and for democratic conservatives like Adenauer, comprehensive welfare benefits were attempts to blunt and soften the demands of the Social Democratic Party and the trade unions. Welfare in Germany has never been a gift but a negotiated settlement, often after periods of conflict between major social forces.

During the mid-1970s, when unemployment grew from 1 or 2 percent to roughly 4 percent and when some social welfare measures were capped (but not reduced), citizens of the Federal Republic spoke of the crisis of the welfare state. Yet non-German observers were hard-pressed to find indications of crisis. Clearly, contraction of substantial welfare state benefits in no way approximated the cutbacks of the United States and Britain in the 1980s and 1990s.

Since the 1980s, continued high unemployment (by German standards) and the costs of support for workers who had depleted their benefits presented difficult dilemmas for the welfare state. German jobs tend to be highly paid, so employers have tried to avoid creating part-time jobs, preferring to wait to hire until the need for employees is sustainable. During times of recession, the number of new jobs created can be minuscule.

Current Strains on the Social Market Economy

Throughout the postwar period, unemployment was virtually nonexistent—hovering around 1 percent. Since the onset of economic strains in the 1980s, however, unemployment has not dropped below 6 percent. One persistent problem facing successive German governments has been shouldering the cost of sustaining the long-term unemployed. An even more serious challenge involved devising a way for the Federal Republic's elaborate vocational education and apprenticeship system to absorb all the new entrants into the labor market. This problem could have undermined one of the strengths of the German economy: the continued supply of skilled workers. Despite these threats in the mid-1980s, both the

A cynical western German view of money spent to rebuild eastern Germany.
Source: © Janusz Majewski/Cartoonists and Writers Syndicate, from *Frankfurter Allgemeine Zeitung.*

unemployment compensation system and the vocational education and apprenticeship system survived. However, the issue resurfaced with the large increase in the unemployment rate following unification in 1990, particularly in the eastern German states.

In the early 1990s, the smoothly functioning German economic juggernaut faltered. First, the Kohl government badly misjudged the costs of unification. In 1992, Kohl finally acknowledged that the successful integration of the eastern economy into the western one would cost much more and take longer than originally predicted. Second, the structural challenges that the German political economy faced in the mid-1990s proved far more extensive than anything the Federal Republic had encountered since the 1950s. The amount budgeted in the early 1990s for reconstruction of eastern Germany's infrastructure was approximately 20 percent of the entire national budget. Yet even these huge sums were not enough to help smooth the assimilation process, and a large gap in productivity levels still exists between the two regions. Third, western German democratic corporatist institutions, composed of employers and trade unions with a long history of cooperation, were difficult to transfer to eastern Germany since they had to be created from scratch. In their absence, the *Treuhandanstalt* (the government reconstruction agency—*Treuhand,*

for short) took the path of least resistance and simply privatized some 7,000 of the total of 11,000 firms that it had inherited from East Germany. One of the most significant costs of this transition from state to private ownership was high unemployment in the eastern sector. Some 1.2 million workers were officially unemployed, and in the early 1990s, another 2 million enrolled in a government-subsidized short-term program combined with job training (this program's funds were later slashed as part of an austerity budget).

The costs of the social market economy, particularly following unification, stretched the upper limits of Germany's capacity to pay. Massive budget cuts became imperative by the early and mid-1990s. The completion of the EU's single market placed additional strains on the German government. More significant for the German government, the EU has begun to disturb the intricate, mutually reinforcing pattern of government and business self-regulation. In addition, the growing push for deregulation in European finance threatens Germany's distinctive finance-manufacturing links, which depend on long-term relationships between the two parties, not on short-term deals.[7] Thus, the trend toward Europeanization may be incompatible with the consensus-oriented and coordinated nature of Germany's political and social institutions as shown by the worldwide financial crisis in late 2008.

Tensions have also flared up between former East and West Germans. The East German economy was strong by communist standards and provided jobs for virtually all adults who wanted one. But East German industry, as in most other former communist countries, was inefficient by Western standards, and most firms were not able to survive the transition to capitalism. Among the most serious problems were overstaffing and inadequate quality controls. Consequently, many easterners lost their jobs when newly privatized firms had to compete in a capitalist economy.

In short, the magnitude of the problems in eastern Germany threatened to overwhelm the institutional capacity to handle them. It certainly helped defeat Helmut Kohl's CDU/CSU-FDP center-right coalition government in 1998. Some pessimistic observers began to suggest that these stresses placed the German political economy in a precarious position. Germany's economic prowess has depended on certain manufacturing industries that produce eminently exportable goods but whose technologies must constantly be upgraded and whose labor costs continue to rise. Complicating the demands on Germany's economic institutions is the obligation to align Germany's economic policies with those of its European neighbors.

Thus, early in the twenty-first century, the prospects for the German political economy seem dimmer than in previous decades. Poor economic performance created the *Wirtschaftsstandort* debate (literally, location for economic growth), which argued that the combination of domestic and international factors had made Germany a much less attractive place for investment by either international or German capital. In response to this challenge, the Schröder government passed a tax reform package in 2000, followed in 2003 by Schröder's Hartz IV reform package of personal and corporate tax cuts that challenged many traditional labor market institutions to become more "flexible" along Anglo-American lines. These contentious issues helped precipitate the early election (one year ahead of schedule) in September 2005 that produced the SPD's defeat. Although the reforms seemed to mollify the equities markets, they were bitterly opposed by the left-leaning rank and file of Schröder's Red-Green coalition. For many, his programs represented an abandonment of fundamental principles and directly led some SPD members, most notably former

SPD Finance Minister Oskar Lafontaine, to join with the former Communist Party of Democratic Socialism (PDS) from eastern Germany to form the new Left Party just before the 2005 election. Schröder's policies divided the left-of-center parties and saw the CDU/CSU emerge as the largest party, forcing Schröder into retirement and leaving the SPD as only the junior partner in the Grand Coalition government.

Society and Economy

Booming economic growth after WWII provided a sound foundation for social development. The social market economy of the Christian Democrats was augmented by governments led by Social Democrats from 1969 to 1982, when the social programs of the 1950s and 1960s were extended and enhanced. The expansion of social policies provided Germany with a solid foundation for forty years. Until the 1990s, Germany provided generous benefits to almost all segments of the population, including support for public transit, subsidies for the arts, virtually free higher and vocational education, and a comprehensive welfare state. There was also a general tolerance for a wide variety of political and artistic opinion. But the costs of unification, adjustment to the EU, and globalization have begun to undercut Germany's perception of itself as a prosperous country with a high standard of living and a well-paid work force. The strong role of trade unions and the consequent unwillingness of employers to confront workers on wage and workplace, once indicators of pride and success, have become sources of criticism. Higher unemployment and social service cutbacks have somewhat increased stratification of the society and the workplace. The primary workplace fault line lies between the core of mostly male, high-skilled blue-collar workers in the largest competitive industries and less-skilled workers, often employed in smaller firms with lower wages and not always full-time work. A significant number of women and immigrants are among the less-skilled workers.

Ethnicity and Economy

The most controversial social issue for German society since the 1990s has been race and ethnicity, with profound implications for Germany's ideology and political culture. Racist attacks against Turkish immigrants and other ethnic minorities have forced Germans to confront the possibility that almost fifty years of democracy have not tamed the xenophobic aspects of their political culture. The issue of ethnic minorities was exacerbated in the 1990s and 2000s by unification and European integration. Nationalism apparently has not disappeared. East Germans were raised in a society that did not celebrate, or even value, toleration or dissent and in which official unemployment did not exist. East Germany was a closed society, as were most other communist regimes, and many of its citizens had little contact with foreign nationals before 1989. In contrast, since the 1960s, West Germany has encouraged the migration of millions of guest workers (*Gastarbeiter*) from southern Europe. The Federal Republic has also provided generous provisions for those seeking political asylum, in an effort to overcome—to some degree at least—the legacy of Nazi persecution of non-Germans from 1933 to 1945.

The *Gastarbeiter* program originated after 1961 when the construction of the Berlin Wall caused a labor shortage because East Germans could no longer emigrate to the West. Thus, temporary workers were recruited from southern Europe with the stipulation that they would return to their native countries if unemployment increased. However, the economic boom lasted so long that by the time the economy did turn down in the mid-1970s, it was difficult for these so-called guests to return to homes in which they had not lived for a decade or more. These foreign workers produced heightened social strain in the 1970s and 1980s, a time of increasing unemployment. Because German citizenship was not granted to the guest workers or their children, the problem remained unresolved. The clash between German and *Gastarbeiter* cultures increased in intensity into the 1980s, particularly in areas where Turkish workers were highly concentrated. However, in a significant departure from past practice, the Schröder-led SPD-Green government in 1999 adopted a slightly easier immigration policy, allowing some second-and third-generation *Gastarbeiter* to obtain German citizenship or maintain dual citizenship.

Upon unification, few former GDR citizens were able to respond positively. Instead of guaranteed lifetime employment, they faced a labor market that did not always supply enough jobs, one where structural unemployment idled up to 25 percent of the work force. And they were expected to embrace completely and immediately a much more open and ethnically diverse society than they had ever known. Thus, immigrants and asylum seekers became scapegoats for the lack of employment, and Germans who were falling through the cracks of the welfare state were susceptible to racist propaganda blaming ethnic minorities for the rapid upheaval that had occurred. Events like these helped precipitate the—still relatively small—growth of the far-right NPD in the mid-2000s.

Germany's changing economy produced a "tech shortage" in the early 2000s that forced the Schröder government to recruit software specialists from India who would be granted "green cards" (that is, permanent residency status) upon their arrival! In other words, a new wave of *Gastarbeiter* was arriving precisely when some Germans were increasingly agitated about the immigration boom. The problem, however, was that the speed with which the German economy needed to embrace the information sector could not wait. The country needed both to increase Germany's presence in this complex sector and enable its traditionally strong industries to adapt to new forms of international competition. The economic pressures did not allow the luxury of waiting for the German secondary educational system to get up to speed.

Gender and Economy

Until the late 1970s, men traditionally dominated all positions of authority in management and the union movement. The union movement has made greater strides than management in expanding leadership opportunities for women, but men still hold the dominant positions in most unions. More than half of all German women were in the work force by the late 1970s, but their participation only reached 66.8 percent in the 1990s, while the male participation rate remained steady at 80 percent (see Table 4.2). Beyond the workplace, the differences between the laws of the former East and West Germany have created a firestorm of controversy. In the East, women had made far greater social and economic progress than in the West, and both women and men had received generous government support for childcare and family leave. During the last Kohl government, one of the

Table 4.2				
Labor Force Participation Rates (Ages 15–65)				
	1997	*1999*	*2001*	*2003*	*2005*
Male	80.3%	80.9%	80.1%	79.2%	80.4%
Female	62.8%	63.5%	64.9%	65.1%	66.8%

Source: Federal Statistical Office, Germany, 2007.

most heated debates concerned the cancellation of the more liberal East German policies toward women (including abortion) in favor of the more conservative and restrictive ones of the Federal Republic. In the 2005 election, Angela Merkel's weakness among women voters, especially in the east where she grew up, was due to her changing positions on the abortion issue. Once favoring the liberal eastern policy, she changed her position as she rose within the CDU, a switch that may have helped her gain the chancellorship in 2005.

Perhaps the most significant obstacle that German women have to overcome is not so much the benefits that they receive but the premise on which women's role in German society is defined.[8]

Women's benefits in German society have been tied more to their roles as mothers and wives than as autonomous individuals. This means that within the context of the labor market, individual German women face discrimination and assumptions about their career patterns that American women have largely overcome. As increasing numbers of women enter the German work force, it is harder for them to achieve positions of power and responsibility as individuals than it is for their American counterparts.

A final social cleavage is the generation gap, which has two dimensions. The first of these is the so-called postmaterialist social movement, which focuses on lifestyle concerns rather than bread-and-butter economic issues. It has not hinged on class, since many within this group tend to be university-educated children of the middle class. This group has not, however, been able to create an identity strong enough to challenge the highly skilled working class's dominance in the structure of the Federal Republic. The still-dominant working-class culture of the Federal Republic has acted as a barrier to the postmaterialist social movement's attaining further influence.

The second aspect of the generation gap comprises pensioners and older workers. The German birthrate fell markedly in the last decade of the twentieth century, particularly in the former GDR. This placed great demographic pressure on the German welfare state because the low birthrate and the increasing age of the baby boom generation meant that fewer younger workers now contribute to the welfare and retirement benefits of an increasing elderly population. This time bomb is just hitting German politics in the early 21st century, largely because the Kohl government during the 1980s and 1990s essentially ignored it. Pensions are one of many unresolved issues with which the Angela Merkel-led CDU/CSU-SPD Grand Coalition struggles.

Germany in the Global Economy

Germany's relationship to the regional and international political economy is shaped by two factors: the EU and globalization.

The European Union

The EU was embraced by most Germans and by the political and industrial establishment, especially in the first few years after unification. As Europe's leading economic power, Germany has benefited greatly from European integration. Many actions and policies that might once have been viewed by its neighbors as German domination have become more acceptable when seen as Germany's active participation as a member of the EU. But the cost for Germany was that it had to adapt to an unfamiliar free-market economic model quite different from the organized capitalism that had developed after World War II.

Several difficult issues confront Germany's international position in the early twenty-first century. One concern is whether German-specific institutional arrangements, such as its institutionalized system of worker (and union) participation in management, tightly organized capitalism, and elaborate system of apprenticeship training, will prove adaptable or durable in wider European and global contexts.[9] Before the worldwide economic crisis in late 2008, most observers thought that Germany's institutional, political, or cultural patterns may not successfully transfer beyond

Global Connection

The EU and the Euro

One of the Federal Republic's most lasting legacies at the end of the twentieth century was its commitment to European integration. As early enthusiasts of European unity, Germany's postwar political leaders realized the positive opportunity that a more formally united continent would present. In its relations with other states after World War II, Germany faced two different kinds of criticism. First was the fear of a too-powerful Germany, a country that had run roughshod over its European neighbors for most of the first half of the twentieth century. Second was the opposite problem: what was often described as an economic giant–political dwarf syndrome in which Germany was accused of benefiting from a strong world economy for fifty years while taking on none of the political and military responsibilities. The fact that these are mutually contradictory positions did not spare Germany from criticism. Yet Chancellors Kohl, Schröder, and Merkel since the 1990s hoped that an integrated Europe might solve both problems simultaneously. Germany remains the economic anchor of the EU, while Germany's membership in the EU has enabled it to take on political responsibilities that it would be unable to assume on its own, such as UN peacekeeping operations in eastern Europe. Until then, Germany's aggressive militarist history prevented Germany—and its neighbors—from developing a strong military.

The euro was a crucial part of this broader European goal. Although the deutsche mark (DM) was the very foundation of postwar German economic performance and contributed mightily to German self-confidence, it remained only one currency among many in Europe, thereby giving German and Europe an economic disadvantage in relation to both North America and East Asia. Kohl, Schröder, and now Merkel realized that economic success for both Germany and Europe depended on creating a stronger economic foundation, which is where the euro came in.

The euro was introduced in most countries of the EU in 2002. Gone was the redoubtable DM in favor of a currency that had no human beings on the notes, only nonspecific buildings, bridges, and arches. In the first few months of the "physical" euro, the currency traded below the value of the dollar. Considerable uncertainty among Germans mounted as to whether adopting the new currency was a good idea. Yet by the middle of 2002, financial scandals in the United States caused the euro to rise in value and achieve parity with the dollar. However, its continued rise since then against a sharply weakening dollar raised a different set of concerns: the higher-valued euro now made it more difficult for the export-oriented German economy to sell its goods in the United States.

the Federal Republic. Since then, the idea of a more stable form of capitalism received a second look.

Germany in a Globalizing World

Issues such as trade, economic competition with East Asia and North America, the introduction of the euro, the general pace of economic integration, climate change, and patterns of financial regulation have challenged the German postwar policies of finding a stable balance between state and market.

As a goods-exporting nation, Germany has always favored an open trading system. Management and unions realize that exports represent both profits and

jobs, and that seeking refuge in protectionism would be self-defeating. Yet international competition has caused unemployment to remain persistently high in the early twenty-first century (near 10 percent). With respect to banking regulation, the Schröder government sponsored a law (since endorsed by the Merkel government) that enabled banks to sell their large ownership shares in German companies. This altered the prevailing postwar policy of encouraging banks to maintain equity holdings in other firms as a form of investment oriented toward the long term. This took the German model perilously close to the Anglo-American world of highly mobile capital investment. Many large German banks now see themselves more as international players than as German ones. Some have suggested that the pressures of competing in a globalized world economy have made the German-specific patterns of the country's political economy more of a liability than an asset. Similar criticisms have occurred since the mid-1970s, but the challenges to the German model in the early twenty-first century seem the most fundamental yet.

However, the worldwide economic crisis of 2008 that originated in the American housing and financial sectors has exploded into western Europe. Many wonder whether the more traditionally regulated form of continental European organized capitalism might be far more preferable than American-style deregulation after all.

SECTION 3 Governance and Policy-Making

The primary goals at the Federal Republic's founding in 1949 were to work toward eventual unification of the two Germanys and, more important, to avoid repeating the failure of the Weimar Republic that resulted in Hitler reaching power and the laying to rest of the legacy of the Nazi regime. When unification was blocked indefinitely, the founders instituted the **Basic Law** (*Grundgesetz*) as a compromise. They preferred to wait until Germany could be reunited before using the term *constitution* (*Verfassung*). After unification in 1990, however, the term *Basic Law* was retained because of the FRG's unqualified success after World War II. In addition, the institutional framework spelled out by the basic law for the FRG was simply applied to the five *Länder* of the former GDR.

The other goal, ensuring a lasting democratic order, presented a more complicated problem. Two fundamental institutional weaknesses had undermined the Weimar government: (1) provisions for emergency powers enabled leaders to arbitrarily centralize authority and suspend democratic rights, and (2) the fragmentation of the political party system prevented stable majorities from forming in the *Reichstag*. This second weakness, instability, encouraged the first: the use of emergency powers to break legislative deadlocks. It was, of course, Weimar's weakness that made possible the Nazi takeover, and so the primary motivation of state rebuilding after World War II was to minimize the risk of extremism. The attempt to deal with these problems involved introducing federalism and a weak presidency to curb the risk of arbitrary power, and instituting reformed electoral procedures and what was named the constructive vote of no confidence to curb instability.

Organization of the State
The Basic Law and Promoting Stability

Under Allied guidance during the occupation, the builders of the postwar government sought to inhibit centralized power by establishing a federal system with significant powers for the states (*Länder*). It is paradoxical that a document that owes so much to the influence of foreign powers has proved so durable. Under the Basic Law of the Federal Republic, many functions that had formerly been centralized during the imperial, Weimar, or Nazi periods, such as the educational system, the police, and the radio networks, now became the responsibility of the states. Although the federal *Bundestag* (lower house) became the chief lawmaking body, the implementation of many laws fell to the state governments. Moreover, the state governments sent representatives to the *Bundesrat* (upper house), which was required to approve bills passed in the *Bundestag*.

There was little opposition from major actors within the Federal Republic to this shift from a centralized to a federal system. The Third Reich's arbitrary abuse of power had created strong sentiment for curbing the state's repressive capacities. Further, the development of a federal system was not a departure but a return to form. Prior to the unification of Germany in 1871, the various regions of Germany had formed a decentralized political system with such autonomous institutions as banks, universities, vocational schools, and state administrative systems.

Several methods were used to surmount party fragmentation and the inability to form working majorities.

The multiplicity of parties, a characteristic of the Weimar Republic, was partly controlled in the FRG by the **5 percent rule:** a political party must receive at least 5 percent of the national vote to obtain seats in the *Bundestag* (and 5 percent of the vote in state or municipal elections for representation in those governments). Under the 5 percent rule, smaller parties have tended to fade, with most of their members absorbed by the three major parties. However, the Green Party in the early 1980s and the former Communist Party of East Germany, reformed as the Party of Democratic Socialism, in the 1990s, now *die Linke* (the Left Party), surpassed the threshold and appear likely to remain in the *Bundestag*. No extreme right-wing parties, however, have ever achieved 5 percent of the national vote to attain seats in the *Bundestag* (although three have won seats in *Länder* governments in the past ten years).

The *Bundestag* has achieved working majorities for several other reasons. Because the interval between elections is set at four years (except under unusual circumstances), and does not have easy provisions for "snap" elections as in Weimar, governments have a fair opportunity to implement their programs and take responsibility for success or failure. The electoral system was also changed from a pure proportional representation system under the Weimar government to a combination of proportional representation and single-member electoral districts. New constitutional provisions limited the possibility for the *Bundestag* to vote a government from office. Under the Weimar constitution, majorities of disparate forces could be mustered to unseat the chancellor but were unable to agree on the choice of a replacement. To overcome the weakness of the cabinet governments of Weimar, the Federal Republic's founders added a twist to the practice familiar in most other parliamentary systems, in which a prime minister is brought down by a vote of no confidence. In the Federal Republic, a no-confidence vote must be "constructive," meaning that a chancellor cannot be removed unless the *Bundestag simultaneously* elects a new chancellor (usually from an opposition party).

This constitutional provision, called the **constructive vote of no confidence,** strengthens the chancellor's power in two ways. First, it means that chancellors can more easily reconcile disputes among cabinet officials because the dispute does not threaten the chancellor's position. Second, it forces the opposition to come up with concrete and specific alternatives to the existing government and prevents them from fostering opposition for its own sake. In other words, to vote out one chancellor, the *Bundestag* must simultaneously vote in another.

The one time a constructive vote of no confidence occurred was in 1982, when Helmut Kohl replaced Helmut Schmidt. However, in 2005 Gerhard Schröder called for a new election a year ahead of schedule when his SPD party lost a major *Land* election. In a maneuver subsequently ruled legal by the federal president and the Constitutional Court, Schröder intentionally lost a vote of confidence in order to hold an early election. He argued that the loss in the *Land* election, thereby changing the balance of power in the *Bundesrat*, or upper house (see below for details), required a new election to clarify his coalition's mandate.

Another element that strengthens political stability involves increasing the chancellor's powers. As the leader of the dominant party or coalition of parties, the chancellor now has control over the composition of the cabinet, so that the federal president is merely the ceremonial head of state. Under the Weimar Constitution, the president could wield emergency powers, but FRG presidents have been stripped of such broad power.

The principles of the Federal Republic's government contained in the Basic Law give the nation a solid foundation, one that appeared capable of assimilating the five *Länder* of the former GDR when unification occurred in 1990. After surviving for over a half-century, the Federal Republic has clearly attained its most important goals. It has permitted successful alternations in power and has encouraged the Left Party (i.e., the former Communist Party in the east) to democratize. In addition, undemocratic right-wing parties have received only miniscule support, despite occasional neo-Nazi threats and some incidents of racist violence.

Government Institutions

Germany is organized as a federal system, with sixteen *Länder* (states), each with considerable powers (see Figure 4.2). As a parliamentary democracy, the

---

Germany

FIGURE 4.2

Constitutional Structure of the German Federal Government

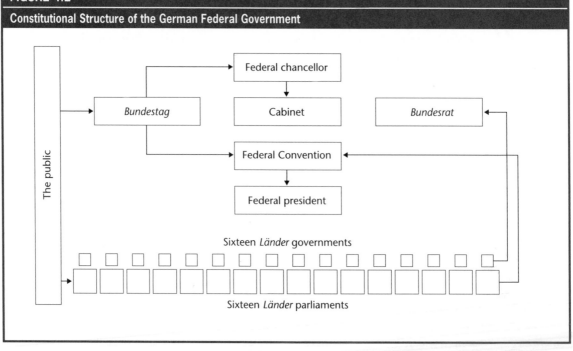

German government resembles the parliamentary systems of Britain and Japan: there is a fusion of powers in that the chancellor, the executive or head of government, is also the leader of the leading party (or coalition) in the *Bundestag.* This contrasts with the separation of powers in the United States, in which the president and cabinet officials cannot simultaneously serve in the Congress. Generally, the executive dominates the legislature in the Federal Republic. Most members of the governing parties support the chancellor at all times, since their own positions depend on a successful government.

The Executive

The division between the head of government (the chancellor) and the head of state (the president) is firmly established in the Federal Republic, with major political powers delegated to the chancellor. Responsibilities and obligations are clearly distinguished between the two offices. For example, the chancellor can be criticized for the government's policies without the criticism being perceived as an attack against

the state itself. This division of power in the executive branch was essential to establish respect for the new West German state after Hitler assumed both offices as the *Führer.*

The President

The German president is the head of state, a much weaker position than that of the chancellor. Like constitutional monarchs in Britain, for example, German presidents stand above the political fray, which means that their role is more ceremonial than political. Among the most common functions are signing treaties, presiding at formal state functions, and overseeing *Bundestag* protocols. German presidents are almost always senior politicians who are moderates within their respective parties and thus broadly acceptable to the electorate. However, if there were a political crisis affecting the chancellor, the president would remain as a caretaker of the political process, thus providing continuity in a time of national uncertainty.

For example, should a parliamentary crisis arise and no candidate could command the support of an absolute majority of *Bundestag* members, the president could provide stability. He or she could decide whether the country is to be governed by a minority administration under a chancellor elected by a plurality of deputies or whether new elections should be called.[10]

The Federal Convention (*Bundesversammlung*), an assembly of all *Bundestag* members and an equal number of delegates elected by the state legislatures (the equivalent of an electoral college), chooses the president according to the principle of proportional representation. Horst Köhler, sponsored by the opposition CDU/CSU and FDP, defeated Gesine Schwann, sponsored by the governing SPD/Green coalition, in a narrow vote of 604 to 598 in 2004. Schwann would have been the first female Federal president. The term of office is five years and, since 1969, only one president has served a second term. But in May 2008, Köhler announced that he wanted to run for a second term beginning in 2009.

The Chancellor

The chancellor is elected by a majority of the members of the *Bundestag*. In practice, this means that the chancellor's ability to be a strong party leader (or leader of a coalition of parties) is essential to the government's success. A government is formed after a national election or, if the chancellor leaves office between elections, after a majority of the *Bundestag* has nominated a chancellor in a constructive vote of no confidence. The new leader consults with other party (and coalition) officials to make up the cabinet. These party leaders have considerable influence in determining which individuals receive ministries. In the event of a coalition government, party leaders often designate during the election campaign who will receive certain ministries. Negotiations on which policies a coalition will pursue can often become heated, and the choice of ministers for particular ministries is made on policy as well as personal grounds.

The most significant cabinet ministries are those of finance, economics, justice, interior, and foreign policy (the Foreign Ministry). Decision-making within the cabinet meetings is often pro forma, since many of the important deliberations are conducted beforehand. In many cases, chancellors rely on strong ministers in

key posts, but some chancellors have taken ministerial responsibility themselves in key areas such as economics and foreign policy. The economics and finance ministries always work closely with the European Central Bank (ECB).

Once the cabinet is formed, the chancellor has considerable authority to govern, thanks to the power of the Federal Chancellery (*Bundeskanzleramt*). This office is a kind of super ministry with wide-ranging powers in many areas. It enables the chancellor to oversee the entire government as well as to mediate conflicts among the other ministries.

The office of the chancellor has played a pivotal role in the Federal Republic. Perhaps the most significant source of the chancellor's powers is the constructive vote of no confidence, mentioned above, along with the fact that he or she is usually the leader of the largest party in parliament. Chancellors also face significant limits on their power. As discussed in Section 4, the *Bundesrat* (upper house) must ratify all legislation passed in the *Bundestag* (lower house) unless overridden by a two-thirds vote. In addition, since the *Bundesrat* generally implements most legislation, chancellors have to consider the position of the upper house on most issues. Although Germany did not get its first female president in 2004, more significantly it got its first chancellor in Angela Merkel in 2005. She had a generally successful first few years despite dealing with a difficult coalition government.

The Bureaucracy

An essential component of the executive is the national bureaucracy. In Germany, it is very powerful and protected by long-standing civil service provisions. Firing or otherwise removing a bureaucrat is very difficult. **Civil servants** strongly believe that their work is a profession, not just a job.

Surprisingly, the federal government employs only about 10 percent of civil servants, with the remainder employed by state and local governments. Today, most civil servants either are graduates from major German universities or come from positions within the political parties. The federal bureaucrats are primarily policy-makers who work closely with their ministries and the legislature. The bureaucrats at the state and local levels are the predominant agents of policy implementation because the states must administer most policies determined at the national level. This overlapping and coordinating of national, regional, and local bureaucracies is supported by the importance that Germans give to the provision of public services. The ongoing institutionalized relationship among the various levels of the bureaucracy has produced more consistent and effective public policies than are found in most other countries, where federal and state governments are often at odds with one another. **Overlapping responsibilities** on policy issues make it difficult to demarcate specifically the responsibility of federal institutions from the national to the regional level and from the regional to the local level.

During the Second and Third Reichs, German civil servants had a reputation for inflexibility and rigidity. The modern German bureaucracy has won high, if grudging, respect from the population. It is generally seen as efficient, although sometimes arcane. German bureaucrats enjoy a well-deserved reputation for competence. Some bureaucrats, mostly top federal officials, are appointed on the basis of party affiliation, following the traditional German pattern of proportionality, namely, allowing all major political groupings to be represented in the society's institutions, in this case the bureaucracy. However, in the 1970s, the Social Democratic Brandt government attempted to purge the bureaucracy of suspected left-wing radicals by issuing the so-called Radicals Decree, a move that tarnished its reputation for impartiality and fairness. The majority of civil servants are chosen on the basis of merit, with elaborate licensing and testing for those in the highest positions.

Semipublic Institutions

In the late 1940s, the idea of a strong central state in Germany was discredited for two reasons: the excesses of Nazism and the American occupation authorities' preference for the private sector. West German authorities faced a dilemma. How could they rebuild society if a strong public sector role were prohibited? The answer was to create modern, democratic versions of those nineteenth-century institutions that blurred the differences between the public and private sectors. These semipublic institutions have played a crucial role in the German political economy, one that has long been unrecognized.

Semipublic institutions (called quasigovernmental institutions in the U.S.) are powerful, efficient, and responsible for much national policy-making. The most influential include the *Bundesbank* (until some powers were usurped by the European Central Bank—ECB), the health insurance funds that administer the national health care system, and the vocational education system (which encompasses the apprenticeship training system). These are part of the integrated system of **democratic corporatism** in which national (and state) governments delegate certain policy-making authority to these institutions, which engage in continuous dialogue with all relevant participants in the policy community to develop appropriate policies.

In countries that had a guild system in the Middle Ages, such as Germany, an inclusionary, democratic corporatist form of representation is common. Here, various professions or organized groups represent the interests of their members. In return for access to deliberation and power, these groups are expected to aggregate the interests of their members and act responsibly. Semipublic institutions, with their democratic corporatist membership, combine aspects of both representation and implementation. German semipublic institutions differ greatly from pluralist representation in countries such as the United States, where interest groups petition public authority for redress of grievances while keeping at arm's length from the implementation process. The democratic corporatist interest groups are also closely intertwined with the Federal Republic's semipublic agencies. For example, implementation of the health care system requires an intricate set of negotiations among many semipublic institutions. These institutions are an apparent seamless web that shapes, directs, implements, and diffuses German public policy.

The political scientist Peter Katzenstein has described semipublic agencies as *detached institutions*.[11] He sees them as primarily mediating entities that reduce the influence of the central state. Katzenstein finds that they have tended to work best in areas of social and economic policy. Among the most important semipublic agencies are the Chambers of Industry, the Council of Economic Advisors (known colloquially as the Five Wise Men), and the institutions of worker participation (co-determination and the works councils). Even areas of the welfare system are semipublic because welfare benefits are often distributed by organizations not officially part of the state bureaucracy. The most significant examples of this are the **health insurance funds** (*Krankenkassen*), which bring all major health interests together to allocate costs and benefits through an elaborate system of consultation and group participation.

Another important set of semipublic institutions is the unions, which participate in industrial relations through the system known as co-determination (*Mitbestimmung*) (see "Citizen Action: Co-Determination"). This group of institutions is discussed here because **co-determination** legally gives workers opportunities to shape public policy.

Another German institution, the works councils (*Betriebsräte*), gives German workers access to the policy implementation process. In contrast to code-termination, which gives trade unions a voice outside the plant (that is, on the board), the works councils represent workers inside the workplace and address shop-floor and plant-level affairs. The trade unions have historically addressed collective bargaining issues, whereas the works councils have concentrated on social and personnel matters. With the trend to more flexible workplaces since the late 1980s, these lines of demarcation have blurred.

The unions are a countrywide, multi-industry organization representing 6.41 million diverse workers. The works councils, on the other hand, owe their primary allegiance to their local plants and firms. Despite an 85 percent overlap in personnel between unions

Citizen Action

Co-Determination

Co-determination is a government-sanctioned institutional relationship between organized labor and business that gives labor movements the right to participate in major decisions that affect their firms and industries. Often seen as a specific organizational form of **democratic corporatism**, co-determination is found in northern Europe, including the Netherlands and Scandinavia, but best known in the Federal Republic of Germany. Co-determination (*Mitbestimmung*) allows representatives of workers and trade unions to obtain voting seats on the supervisory boards of directors of firms with 2,000 or more employees.

German co-determination has two official forms: one for the coal and steel industries and one for all other industries. The former provides full parity for worker representatives in all decisions on the supervisory board, whereas the latter provides a representative of management with the tie-breaking vote. Post–World War II roots of co-determination sprang from the anger of German workers toward the complicity of German industrialists with the Nazi war machine. This was especially true of the coal and steel barons; hence, the full parity in those industries. The idea of placing

workers and union representatives on the boards of directors of these firms was seen by many as a way to ensure accountability from German capitalism.

The laws governing co-determination, first passed in the early 1950s and expanded in the 1970s, reflect the powerful role of the trade unions in the politics of the Federal Republic. They give the workers—and indirectly their unions for those firms so organized—a form of institutionalized participation through membership on the supervisory boards of German firms. Rather than making German firms uncompetitive, this system actually has had the opposite effect. Workers and unions can comprehend, if not unilaterally determine, corporate decisions regarding investment and the introduction of new technologies. Co-determination has allowed German workers a broader and deeper knowledge of the goals and strategies of the firms for which they work. In addition, it has boosted worker-management cooperation. The most pressing challenge for co-determination in the future will be whether these German-specific institutional patterns will spread to other European countries or whether they will be overtaken by European-wide labor relations policies that are more deregulatory and market oriented.

and works councils and despite a structural entanglement between these two major pillars of labor representation in the Federal Republic, these divisions can produce tensions among organized labor. A period of general flux and plant-related, management-imposed flexibility beginning in the mid- and late 1980s and sporadically continuing since, particularly in eastern Germany, has exacerbated these tensions. Until the early twenty-first century the unions were usually able to avoid the proliferation of any serious plant-level divisions among workers that might have eroded their stature in the German economy. However, in the wake of the Hartz IV reforms during Schröder's second term that merged the unemployment and welfare systems reforms and required the unemployed to take jobs either outside their home region or outside their chosen profession, the unions' privileged position in Germany had begun to erode.

Other State Institutions

In addition to the institutions discussed so far, the military, the judiciary, and subnational governments are essential institutions for governance and policy-making.

The Military and Police

From the eighteenth century (when Prussian and other military forces in German-speaking regions dominated pre-unified Germany) through World War II, the German military was powerful and aggressive. After World War II, the military was placed completely under civilian control and tightly circumscribed by law and treaty. The end of the cold war produced two other important changes in German military policy: the reduction in U.S. armed forces stationed in Germany and payments made to Russia for removal of soldiers and materiel from the former East Germany.

Germany has a universal service arrangement requiring all citizens over the age of eighteen to perform one year of military or civilian service. In 1990, Germany had about 600,000 men and women in the military, but in 1994 after unification and the end of the Cold War, the Federal Government fixed the figure at approximately 340,000 as the costs of unification rose. Germany spends approximately 1.5 percent of its GDP on the military. Germany's armed forces have been legally proscribed from extra-national activity, first by the Allied occupation and later by the German Basic Law. Under the provisions of the Basic Law, the German military is to be used only for defensive purposes within Europe, and then in coordination with NATO authorities. Only very limited military activity under tightly circumscribed approval (via NATO) has altered the general prohibition. German participation in the UN peacekeeping mission in Bosnia was one example. Agreeing to participate in opposition to Serbian aggression in Kosovo in 1999, a decision made by the Red-Green government, was another, and sending troops to Afghanistan—even forming a joint Franco-German brigade—was a third. Thus, the post–World War II opposition to deployment of the German army is gradually eroding.

Discussion of the German police involves focusing on three areas. The first is the postwar experience in the FRG, where police powers have been organized on a *Land* basis and, after the excesses of the Third Reich, have been constitutionally circumscribed to ensure that human and civil rights remain inviolate. To be sure, there have been exceptions. For example, during the dragnets for the Red Army *Faktion* terrorists in the late 1970s, many critics argued that German police forces were compromising civil liberties in their desire to capture the terrorists.

The second area is that of the GDR's notorious secret police, the *Stasi*. The Ministry for State Security (the *Stasi*'s formal name) included some 91,000 official employees; moreover, in 1989, more than 180,000 East Germans and perhaps 4,000 West Germans worked as informants for the *Stasi*.[12] In proportion to the 16 million GDR citizens, the *Stasi* was more encompassing than was the Gestapo during Nazi rule. The *Stasi* spied on virtually the entire society and arbitrarily arrested and persecuted thousands of citizens. Since unification, *Stasi* archives have been open to all because the East Germans and later the FRG believed that full and open disclosure of *Stasi* excesses was essential in a democratic state. In so doing, however, names of informants were made public, which created bitter confrontations among former friends and neighbors.

The third area is the heightened concern for security in Germany in the wake of 9/11. Germany is particularly concerned about terrorism since numerous members of the Al Qaeda terrorist organization, including several of the 9/11 bombers, lived for years in Hamburg and other German cities. Germany will need to balance the pressing demand for terrorist surveillance with the preservation of civil liberties.

The Judiciary

The judiciary has always played a major role in German government because of the state's deep involvement in political and economic matters. During the Nazi regime, the judiciary was induced to issue a wide range of antidemocratic, repressive, and even criminal decisions, including banning non-Nazi parties, allowing the seizure of Jewish property, and sanctioning the deaths of millions.

The Federal Republic's founders were determined that the new judicial system would avoid these abuses. One of the first requirements was that the judiciary explicitly safeguard the democratic rights of individuals, groups, and political parties. In fact, the Basic Law contains a more elaborate and explicit statement of individual rights than exists in either the U.S. Constitution or in British common law.

However, the Federal Republic's legal system differs from the common law tradition of Britain and its former colonies (including the United States). The common law precedent-based system is characterized by adversarial relationships between contending parties, in which the judge (or the court itself) merely provides the arena for the struggle. In continental Europe, including France and Germany, the legal system is based on a codified legal system with roots in Roman law and the Napoleonic code.

In the Federal Republic, the judiciary is an active administrator of the law rather than solely an arbiter. While the task of the state is to create the laws to attain specified goals, the judiciary should safeguard their implementation. In both defining the meaning of complex laws and in implementing their administration, German courts go considerably beyond those in the United States and Britain, which supposedly have avoided political decisions. The German judiciary is an independent institution. In 2001, there were over 21,000 judges in Germany, with approximately 25 percent of them female. The German judiciary remains outside the political fray

on most issues. However, a ruling in 1993 that limited access to abortion for many women, in direct opposition to a more liberal law in East Germany, was a clear exception to the general pattern. The judiciary was also criticized in the 1990s for showing too much leniency toward perpetrators of racist violence.

The court system in the Federal Republic is three-pronged. One branch consists of the criminal-civil system, which has as its apex the Federal High Court. It is a unified rather than a federal system and tries to apply a consistent set of criteria to cases in the sixteen states. The Federal High Court reviews cases that have been appealed from the lower courts, including criminal and civil cases, disputes among the states, and matters that would be viewed in some countries as political, such as the abortion ruling.

The Special Constitutional Court deals with matters directly affecting the Basic Law. A postwar creation, it was founded to safeguard the new democratic order. Precisely because of the Nazis' abuses of the judiciary, the founders of West Germany added a layer to the judiciary, basically involving judicial review, to ensure that the democratic order was maintained. However, several subsequent rulings have caused concern about the judiciary's commitment to protecting civil liberties from arbitrary executive actions.

The **Administrative Court** system is the third branch of the judiciary. Consisting of the Labor Court, the Social Security Court, and the Finance Court, the Administrative Court system has a much narrower jurisdiction than the other two branches. Because the state and its bureaucracy have such a prominent place in the lives of German citizens, this level of the court system acts as a check on the arbitrary power of the bureaucracy. Compared to Britain, where much public policy is determined by legislation, German public policy is more often determined by the administrative actions of the bureaucracy. Citizens can use these three courts to challenge bureaucratic decisions, for example, with respect to labor, welfare, or tax policies.

In the 1990s, the courts came under great pressure to resolve the intractable policy issues that unification and European integration brought about. As they were drawn deeper into the political thicket, their decisions came under increased scrutiny. Clandestine searches for terrorists in the late 1970s left many observers believing that the rights of citizens were compromised. Many critics wish that today's courts would show the same diligence and zeal in addressing the crimes of neo-Nazism, not to mention potential Al Qaeda terrorists, as the courts did in the 1970s, when Germany was confronted with violence from small ultra-leftist groups. The judicial system as a whole now must walk a fine line between maintaining civil rights in a democratic society and providing security from various sources of extremist violence.

Subnational Government

There are sixteen *Länder* (states) in the Federal Republic; eleven constituted the old West Germany and five the former East Germany. Unlike the weakly developed regional governments of Britain and France, German state governments enjoy considerable autonomy and independent powers. Each state has a regional assembly (*Landtag*), which functions much as the *Bundestag* does at the federal level. The governor (*Minister-Präsident*) of each *Land* is the leader of the largest party (or coalition of parties) in the *Landtag* and forms a government in the *Landtag* in much the same way as does the chancellor in the *Bundestag*. Elections for each of the sixteen states are held on independent, staggered four-year cycles, which generally do not coincide with federal elections and only occasionally coincide with elections in other *Länder*. Like the semipublic institutions, subnational governments in Germany are powerful, important, and responsible for much national policy implementation.

Particularly significant is Germany's "marble-cake" federalism—the interaction among state and federal governments that sees the former implement many of the laws passed by the latter. In fact, from its hybrid beginnings, German federalism has become one of the most imitated systems in the world among newly democratized countries. A good way to show how German federalism works in a specific policy arena is to cite the example of **industrial policy** (*Ordnungspolitik*). Regional governments are much more active than the national government in planning and targeting economic policy and therefore have greater autonomy in administering industrial and environmental policies. Since the *Länder* are constituent states, they are able to develop their own regional versions of public policies. Because the different regions have different economic needs and industrial foundations, most voters see these powers as legitimate and appropriate.

The state governments encourage banks to make direct investment and loans to stimulate industrial development. They also encourage cooperation among regional firms, many in the same industry, to spur international competition. State governments also invest heavily in vocational education to provide the skills needed for manufacturing high-quality goods, the core of the German economy. Organized business and organized labor have a direct role in shaping curricula to improve worker skills through the vocational education system. These *Land* governments have improved industrial adaptation by shaping the state's competitive framework rather than by adopting a heavy-handed regulatory posture. The states do not pursue identical economic policies, and there are various models of government involvement in economic policy.

In the Federal Republic, state politics is organized on the same political party basis as the national parties. This does not mean that national politics dominates local politics. However, the common party names and platforms at all levels let voters see the connection among local, regional, and national issues. Because parties adopt platforms for state and city elections, voters can see the ideological differences among parties and not be swayed solely by personalities. This does not mean that personalities do not play a role in German regional politics. Rather, the German party system encourages national political figures to begin their careers at the local and state levels. Regional and local party members' careers are tied closely to the national, regional, and local levels of the party. Thus, ideological and policy continuity across levels is rewarded. Some observers suggest that this connection in the Federal Republic among national, regional, and local politics may be one reason that voter turnout in German state elections far exceeds that of equivalent U.S. elections.

Local governments in the Federal Republic can raise revenues by owning enterprises, and many do. This has partly resulted from the historical patterns of public sector involvement in the economy but also from the assumption that these levels of government are the stewards of a collective public good. By operating art museums, theater companies, television and radio networks, recreational facilities, and housing complexes and by providing various direct and indirect subsidies to citizens, local governments promote the quality of life in modern society. Even during the various recessions since the early 1980s, there have been relatively few cutbacks in ownership of public enterprises or in social spending.

The Policy-Making Process

The chancellor and the cabinet have the principal responsibility for policy-making, but their power cannot be wielded in an arbitrary fashion. The policy-making process in Germany is largely consensus-based, with contentious issues usually extensively debated within various public, semipublic, and private institutions. Although the legislature has a general role in policy-making, the primary driving forces are the respective cabinet departments and the experts on whom they call.

Policy implementation is similarly diffuse. Along with corporatist interest groups and various semipublic organizations, the *Bundesrat* (upper house) also plays a significant role. Among the areas of policy most likely to be shaped by multiple actors are vocational education, welfare, health care, and worker participation. Germany's status as a federal state, one populated by a broad range of democratic corporatist groups and parapublic institutions, means that policy implementation has many participants. Even in such areas as foreign and security policy, the federal cabinet departments sometimes rely on business interests in policy implementation. EU policy is shaped by both national and regional governments, as well as by private sector interests that use corporatist institutions to participate in the process.

Both unification issues and the increasing significance of the EU changes have put this informal style of policy-making under tremendous pressure. Among the issues that proved most intractable at the domestic level are those of political asylum, racist violence, and scandals that tarnished the reputations of major public figures in the political system and in major interest groups. At the European level, issues involving the euro and counterterrorism remain difficult. Moreover, for all of its system-maintaining advantages, the German consensual system contains a certain intolerance of dissent. Among examples are the structure of the party system that forces politicians to work slowly through the organization, the 5 percent threshold for party representation, and judicial banning of political parties. This intolerance helps to explain the protest from outside the parties that started in the 1960s and has continued on and off ever since.

Representation and Participation

In the aftermath of unification and European integration, Germany continues to strive for democratic participation that is both inclusive and representative. The nation still struggles with issues surrounding collective identities. Incorporating disparate political cultures (east and west, for example) is a dilemma for any society. The key issue for Germany is how to develop a system of democratic participation that encompasses both extra-institutional groups and organized political institutions.

Legislature

The legislature occupies a prominent place in the political system, with both the lower house (*Bundestag*) and the upper house (*Bundesrat*) holding significant and wide-ranging powers. The Federal Republic is similar to other parliamentary regimes that have a fusion of power in which the executive branch derives directly from the legislative branch. In other words, there is not a sharply defined separation of powers between cabinet and legislature.

The process for choosing members of the two houses differs substantially. The *Bundestag* elects its members directly; voters choose both individual district representatives and the political parties that represent their interests. The *Bundesrat*'s members, on the other hand, are officials who are elected or appointed to the regional (*Länder*) governments. Both branches of the legislature are broadly representative of the major interests in German society, although some interests such as business and labor are somewhat overrepresented, whereas ecological and noneconomic interests are somewhat underrepresented.

Germany's two-ballot electoral system for the *Bundestag* has produced two significant outcomes. First, the proportional representation electoral system produces multiple parties. Second, the 5 percent hurdle ensures that only parties with significant support obtain seats in the *Bundestag*. This has helped Germany avoid the wild proliferation of parties that plagues some democracies, such as Italy and Israel, where coalitions are extremely difficult to form.

The German parliamentary system represents a synthesis between the British and U.S. traditions of a single legislator representing one district and the European tradition of proportional representation in which the percentage of the vote is equal to the percentage of the parliamentary seats (see "Institutional Intricacies: Proportional Representation and the Story of the German 'Double Ballot'"). The German hybrid system, known as **personalized proportional representation,** requires citizens to cast two votes on each ballot: the first for an individual candidate in the local district

and the second for a list of national/regional candidates grouped by party affiliation (see Figure 4.3).

At the same time, however, seats in the *Bundestag* are allocated among parties by proportional representation. Specifically, the percentage of total seats won per party corresponds strongly with the party's percentage of the popular vote. For example, if a party's candidate wins a seat as an individual member, his or her party is allotted one less seat from the party's slate elected via list voting. In practice, the two large parties, the Social Democrats and the Christian Democrats, win most of the district seats because they are elected by a plurality system of winner-take-all in each district. The smaller parties' representatives are almost always elected through the party lists. Thus, the list system creates stronger, more coherent parties.

The *Bundestag*

The lower house of the legislature, the *Bundestag*, consists of 614 seats. *Bundestag* members almost always vote with their parties. This party unity contributes to consistency in the parties' positions over the course of a four-year legislative period and enables the electorate to identify each party's stance on

Institutional Intricacies: Proportional Representation and the Story of the German "Double Ballot"

Proportional representation is a method of electing legislative representatives in parliamentary democracies. In the more commonly used list form, proportional representation involves allocating seats in the legislature among political parties in the same proportion as the parties' share of the popular vote. For example, if a political party received 20 percent of the vote in an election, under proportional representation this party would receive 20 percent of the seats in the legislative body. Germany uses a combination of single-member districts and proportional representation (see the sample ballot in Figure 4.3), but the allocation of seats in the *Bundestag* still depends on the proportion of the vote that the parties obtain in the votes by party list. The advantage of this system is

that every voter has his or her "own" local representative, yet the entire *Bundestag* comprises members who reflect the respective share of each party's total vote.

This system has the effect of personalizing list voting because voters have their own local representative, but they also can choose among several parties representing various ideologies. To ensure that only major parties are represented, only those that get 5 percent of the vote or that have three candidates who directly win individual seats can gain representation in the *Bundestag*.

Sources: The Oxford Companion to Politics of the World, edited by Joel Krieger. Copyright 2001 by Oxford University Press, Inc. Used by permission of Oxford Press, Inc.

FIGURE 4.3

Bundestag Election Ballot

Stimmzettel

für die Wahl zum Deutschen Bundestag im Wahlkreis 136 Kreisfreie Stadt Wiesbaden am 2. Dezember 1990

Sie haben 2 Stimmen

hier 1 Stimme	hier 1 Stimme
für die Wahl	für die Wahl
eines/einer Wahlkreis-	einer Landesliste (Partei)
abgeordneten	- maßgebende Stimme für die Verteilung der Sitze insgesamt auf die einzelnen Parteien -
Erststimme	**Zweitstimme**

With their "first vote," voters from the Bonn electoral district can choose a candidate by name from the lefthand column. The "second vote" in the righthand column is cast for a party list at the federal level.

a range of issues. Consequently, all representatives in the *Bundestag* can be held accountable, based on their support for their parties' positions. Party discipline, in turn, helps produce more stable governments.

The tradition of strong, unified parties in the *Bundestag* has some drawbacks. The hierarchy within parties relegates newer members to a comparatively long stint as backbenchers. Since party elders and the Federal Chancellery control the legislative agenda and key policy decisions, individual legislators have few opportunities to make an impact. Some of the most prominent national politicians preferred to serve their

political apprenticeship in state or local government, where they would have more visibility. Chancellors Gerhard Schröder and Helmut Kohl took this route as governors of Lower Saxony and Rhineland Palatinate, respectively.

The executive branch introduces legislation in accordance with the Basic Law, which requires that the executive initiate the federal budget and tax legislation. Although most bills are initiated by the cabinet, this does not diminish the influence of *Bundestag* or *Bundesrat* members. In fact, because the chancellor is the leader of the major party or coalition of parties, no sharp division exists between the executive and legislative branches. There is generally strong consensus within parties and within coalitions about what legislation should be introduced. Parties and coalitions, which depend on party discipline to sustain majorities, place a high value on agreement regarding major legislation.[13]

When the chancellor and the cabinet propose a bill, it is sent to a relevant *Bundestag* committee. Most of the committee deliberations take place privately so that the individual committee members can have considerable latitude to shape details of the legislation. The committees will call on their own expertise as well as that of relevant government ministries and testimony from pertinent interest groups. This arrangement may appear to be a kind of insiders' club. However, the committees generally call on a wide range of groups, both pro and con, that are affected by the proposed legislation. By consulting the corporatist interest groups, a more consensus-oriented outcome is achieved. In contrast, legislative sessions in countries with a more pluralist (less inclusive) form of lobbying, such as Britain and the United States, tend to be contentious and less likely to produce agreement. Under pluralism, it is relatively easy for groups to articulate issues; however, without a coordinated institutional structure, policy-making is more haphazard.

After emerging from committee, the bill has three readings in the *Bundestag*. The debate in the *Bundestag* often produces considerable criticism from the opposition and sharp defense by the governing parties. The primary purpose of the debate is to educate the public about the major issues of the bill. Following passage in the *Bundestag*, the *Bundesrat* must approve the bill.

Most members of the national legislature are male, middle-class professionals, even in the supposedly working-class Social Democratic Party, which had a much greater proportion of blue-collar deputies in the 1950s. There were few women lawmakers until the 1980s and 1990s, when the Greens elected an increasing number of female *Bundestag* members, and women began to gain slots on the Social Democrats' electoral lists.[14] Fewer than 10 percent of *Bundestag* members were women through the 1983 election, but since 1987, the number of women has increased substantially, reaching 31.6 percent with the 2005 election (see Table 4.3). The addition of newer parties such as the worker-oriented ex-communist Left Party and the continued presence of the Greens with their counterculture lifestyles has increased the variety of backgrounds among *Bundestag* members. In fact, the proportional representation system used in Germany increases the number of women and minorities elected to the *Bundestag*. Many parties, particularly the Social Democrats, the Greens, and the Left, select candidates for their electoral lists based on gender and diversity.

The *Bundesrat*

The *Bundesrat* has a different role from the U.S. Senate or the British House of Lords. The *Bundesrat* is the mechanism that makes the federal system work. It is responsible for the distribution of powers between national and state governments and grants to the states the right to implement federal laws. It is the point of

intersection for the national and the state governments and is made up of sixty-nine members from the sixteen state governments. Each state sends at least three representatives to the *Bundesrat,* depending on its population. States with more than 2 million residents have four votes, and states with more than 6 million people have five votes.

The political composition of the *Bundesrat* at any given time is determined by which parties are in power in the states. Each state delegation casts its votes on legislation in a bloc, reflecting the views of the majority party or coalition. Consequently, the party controlling the majority of state governments can have a significant effect on legislation passed in the *Bundestag*. And because state elections usually take place between *Bundestag* electoral periods, the *Bundesrat* majority can shift during the course of a *Bundestag* legislative period.

The *Bundesrat* must approve all amendments to the constitution as well as all laws that address the fundamental interests of the states, such as taxes, territorial integrity, and basic administrative functions. It exercises a **suspensive veto;** that is, if the *Bundesrat* votes against a bill, the *Bundestag* can override the *Bundesrat* by passing the measure again by a simple majority. If, however, a two-thirds majority of the *Bundesrat* votes against a bill, the *Bundestag* must pass it again by a two-thirds margin. In usual practice, the *Bundesrat* has not acted to obstruct. When the legislation is concurrent—that is, when the state and national governments share administrative responsibilities for implementing the particular policy—there is almost always easy agreement between the two houses. Also, a party or coalition that has achieved a stable majority in the *Bundestag* can overcome any possible obstruction by the *Bundesrat*.

The *Bundesrat* introduces comparatively little legislation, but its administrative responsibilities are considerable. Most of the members of the *Bundesrat* are also state government officials, well experienced in the implementation of particular laws. Their expertise is frequently called on in the committee hearings of the *Bundestag*, which are open to all *Bundesrat* members. This overlapping is a unique feature of the Federal Republic. Many U.S. observers make the mistake of equating German and U.S. federalism; however, Germany has a qualitatively different relationship between national and state governments.

Table 4.3			
Percentage of Women Members of the *Bundestag*			
Year	*Percentage*	*Year*	*Percentage*
1949	6.8	1980	8.5
1953	8.8	1983	9.8
1957	9.2	1987	15.4
1961	8.3	1990	20.5
1965	6.9	1994	26.3
1969	6.6	1998	30.2
1972	5.8	2002	32.2
1976	7.3	2005	31.8

Source: Bundeszentrale für Politische Bildung, 2005.

The *Bundesrat*'s strong administrative role is a key component of the government. For example, the *Bundesrat* administers a major television network (ARD) and coordinates the link between regional and national economic policies and vocational education systems. The *Bundesrat*'s structure positions it close to the concerns and needs of the entire country and provides a forum for understanding how national legislation will affect each of the states.

Although the *Bundesrat* was originally envisioned to be more technocratic and less politically contentious than the popularly elected *Bundestag*, debates in the *Bundesrat* became strongly politicized beginning in the 1970s. The most common occurrence was the conflict that emerged when regional elections caused a change in control of the *Bundesrat*, especially when this change gave more influence to the party, or group of parties, that was in opposition to the *Bundestag*. For example, part of Helmut Kohl's difficulty in his last term (1994–1998) resulted from the Social Democrats' controlling a majority of state governments, where they occasionally blocked national legislation. After Schröder's narrow victory in the 2002 federal elections and the CDU victory in several *Land* elections since then, similar conflict occurred in the remainder of the SPD-Green second term.

With the increasing significance of the European Union (EU), the *Bundesrat* has a role to play here as well. It promotes representation for the *Länder* in EU institutions, most notably in the Council of Regions. It also gained a veto power over certain German positions on EU decisions.

Political Parties and the Party System

Germany has often been called a **party democracy** because its parties are so important in shaping state policy. Its multiparty system has proved quite stable for most of the period since World War II. Until the early 1980s, Germany had a "two-and-a-half" party system, composed of a moderate-left Social Democratic Party (SPD), a moderate-right Christian Democratic grouping (CDU in all of West Germany except Bavaria, where it is called the CSU), and a small centrist Free Democratic Party (FDP). During their time as the only parties on the political landscape

(1949–1983), these groups presided over a stable, growing economy and a broad public consensus on economic and social policies.

During the 1980s and 1990s, two new parties emerged to challenge the "two-and-a-half" major parties and to complicate Germany's comparatively tidy political landscape.[15] These were the Greens/*Bündnis* '90, generally of the left and favoring ecological, environmental, and peace issues; and the Party of Democratic Socialism (PDS), the former Communist Party of East Germany. In 2005, the latter merged with a group of former left-wing Social Democrats who believed Schröder's reforms undermined social democracy and formed *die Linke* (Left Party). Two other small right-wing parties, the National Democratic Party (*Nationaldemokratische Partei Duetschlands*, NPD) and the German People's Union (*Deutsche Volksunion*, DVU), also emerged. Much more conservative than the CDU/CSU, they emphasized nationalism and intolerance toward immigrants and ethnic minorities. Neither of these two right-wing parties has yet won seats in the *Bundestag* because of the 5 percent rule. Both have occasionally exceeded 5 percent in regional elections, however, and have won seats in those bodies.

The five main parties have clearly identifiable social bases. The traditional Christian Democratic bases are moderate conservative Protestants and Catholics, but in recent years religion has played a much less significant role in their policies. Social Democrats represented the traditional working class for the first half of the twentieth century, but since then have tried to catch more middle-class voters in the center. The Free Democrats are a secular party that favors small government and individual freedoms. The Greens focus on ecological issues, and the new Left Party's social bases are eastern Germans who feel left behind by unification and western German former Social Democrats who believe their former party has moved too far toward the center.

The Christian Democrats

The Christian Democrats combine the Christian Democratic Union (CDU, in all *Länder* except Bavaria) and the Christian Social Union (CSU, the affiliated Bavarian grouping). Unlike the older parties

FIGURE 4.4

Distribution of Seats

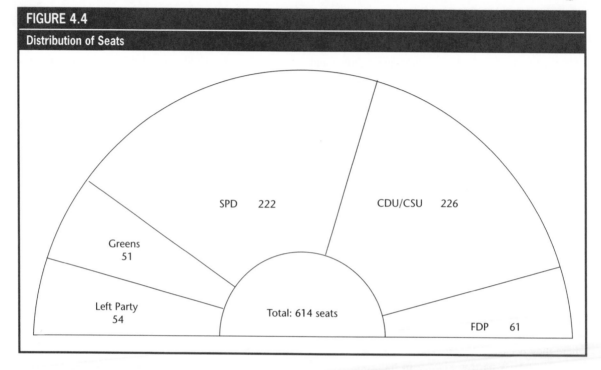

SPD 222

CDU/CSU 226

Greens 51

Left Party 54

Total: 614 seats

FDP 61

(SPD and FDP) of the Federal Republic, the CDU/CSU was founded immediately after World War II and united Catholics and Protestants in one confessional (Christian) party and served as a catchall party of the center-right. During Weimar, the two Christian denominations were divided politically with the former in the Catholic Center Party and the latter in several other parties.

Programmatically, the CDU/CSU stressed the social market economy, involving procapitalist elements as well as a paternalistic sense of social responsibility.[16] Under chancellors Adenauer and Erhard, the Christian Democrats held political power for almost twenty years. Its social policies during this period were paternalistic and moderately conservative. The CDU/CSU even explicitly codified this approach with the phrase *Kinder, Kirche, Kuche* (children, church, and kitchen), which defined the Christian Democrats' view of women's primary roles and was originally a motto of the last Kaiser's wife.

After the SPD and FDP established their center-left coalition in 1969, the CDU/CSU spent thirteen years as the opposition party. Returning to power in 1983 under the leadership of Helmut Kohl, the CDU/CSU with their FDP coalition partners retained power through four elections until 1998. The most significant and historic accomplishments—truly twin legacies—of the long Kohl regime are German unification and Germany's integration into the EU.

Although Angela Merkel became Germany's first female chancellor after the 2005 election, the circumstances of her victory were much less glorious than either she or her Christian Democratic colleagues originally expected. Instead of the preferred coalition with the FDP, their traditional coalition partner, the CDU/CSU was forced into a "Grand Coalition" with the SPD for only the second time in the Federal Republic's history. Merkel only emerged as chancellor three weeks after the election, after the CDU/CSU and SPD contentiously negotiated their agreement. It came at a heavy price for the Christian Democrats; in return for Gerhard Schröder stepping aside as the SPD's chancellor candidate, the Christian Democrats agreed to take only six of the fourteen cabinet seats, leaving the remaining eight to the SPD. Essentially the "Grand Coalition" is what Americans call "divided

Leaders

Angela Merkel

Source: © Jens Buettner/epa/Corbis

Angela Merkel, fifty-one years old when she became the first female chancellor in 2005, has had a remarkable road to the pinnacle of German politics. A minister's daughter, a physicist by profession, a latecomer to political life, an eastern German, a Protestant in a party dominated by Catholics, and a woman who has eschewed feminist positions, Merkel surprised many Germans when she finally became Germany's head of government after the most inconclusive election in the fifty-six-year history of the Federal Republic of Germany.

She was actually born in western Germany, but her family moved to eastern Germany when her father was offered the ministry of a Lutheran church in Brandenburg (eastern Germany). She showed no interested in politics in communist East Germany, preferring to study science. She earned a degree in physics and obtained a research position in East Berlin when Germany was still divided. Like many East Germans, she acquired her political awakening in 1989 when she took part in pro-democracy protests as the Berlin wall came down. When free political parties emerged, Merkel was drawn to the Christian Democrats, perhaps because of her father's professional religious background.

A quick political learner, Merkel rose through the ranks of the Christian Democrats, particularly since western parties that wanted to establish a presence in eastern Germany desired skilled and astute easterners who would help these parties establish a political foundation there. She held several regional Christian Democratic Party positions and soon caught the political eye of four-time CDU chancellor Helmut Kohl. She won a seat in the *Bundestag* and was named the environment minister in 1994. After the Christian Democrats were defeated in the 1998 election, Merkel rapidly moved into the political vacuum in the wake of Helmut Kohl's departure from the Christian Democratic leadership.

In the 2005 election, she failed to develop two potential advantages, namely her gender and her background in eastern Germany. She pointedly avoided feminist positions, perhaps necessary in the male-dominated CDU/CSU. However, she lost considerable political support from women when she chose to support the much more restrictive West German abortion law instead of the more liberal law that had prevailed in East Germany. She also has not been effective in recruiting large numbers of women from her party to run for seats in the *Bundestag*. In fact, the three parties of the left (SPD, Greens, and Left) have 41.2 percent women among their deputies while the parties of the right (Christian Democrats and FDP) have only 20.9 percent women in the *Bundestag*. She also failed to use her background to alleviate the fears of eastern Germans, who suffer from much higher unemployment (20 to 25 percent) than do the states of the former West Germany (8 percent). In numerous campaign appearances in eastern Germany, she would address the crowds using the pronoun "you" instead of "we." The CDU finished third in the five eastern German states behind the SPD and the Left parties. Merkel's achievement in becoming the first female chancellor was most impressive, but she faced formidable obstacles as she began her historic political journey.

In her first several years leading the "Grand Coalition" she did well in managing international issues and the economy began to rebound in 2007. But because the Christian Democrats and Social Democrats disagree on fundamental issues (immigration, the nature of structural economic reform, and foreign policy), they were unable to achieve significant progress.

government." When things go well, both take credit; when they don't, each blames the other. This can impede political accountability, which can sometimes result in lower support for both parties in subsequent elections since there are now three other options besides the CDU/CSU and the SPD.

The Social Democratic Party

As the leading party of the left in Germany, the *Sozialdemokratische Partei Deutschlands* (SPD) has had a long and durable history. The SPD was founded in 1875 in response to rapid industrialization and Bismarck's authoritarian role. After surviving Bismarck's attempts in the 1880s to outlaw it, it grew to be the largest party in the *Reichstag* by 1912.[17] Following World War I, it became the leading party—but without a majority—of the Weimar Republic during its early years.

Despite being the second-largest party in postwar Germany from 1945 to 1948, the SPD was able to obtain only about 30 percent of the popular vote from 1949 until the early 1960s. In an attempt to broaden its constituency, it altered its party program at a 1959 party conference in Bad Godesberg. Deemphasizing its primary reliance on Marxism and its working-class base, its new goal was to broaden its appeal to recruit voters from throughout the social structure and

become what the political scientist Otto Kirchheimer has called a "catchall party."[18] The Bad Godesberg conference transformed the SPD into a party similar to other western European social democratic parties.

In 1969, the SPD was finally elected to office as the leading member of a majority coalition, with the FDP. It remained in power for thirteen years under chancellors Willy Brandt and Helmut Schmidt. The SPD brought to the coalition a concern for increased welfare and social spending.[19] This was due partly to pressure by left-wing extra-parliamentary opposition groups and student demonstrations in 1968. The FDP brought support for increased individual freedom of expression at a time when youths in all industrialized societies were seeking a greater voice. The principal factor cementing these two dissimilar parties for such a long time was the strong performance of the economy. The coalition finally broke up in the early 1980s, when an economic recession prevented the increased social spending demanded by the SPD left wing.

During the 1980s and 1990s when it was out of power, the SPD failed to formulate clear alternative policies to make itself attractive to its members, supporters, and voters. In 1998, the Kohl regime was exhausted and the SPD was able to form an unexpected coalition with the Greens and formed a government that lasted until 2005. The seven years

High Point of the Summer Concert Season. "Egon, when is the coal miners' choir finally coming out?" The sign on the tree says, "Bono, Geldof, Groenemeyer proudly present SPD-AID: Your Voice Against Low Poll Numbers." (Groenemeyer is a German rock musician.)
Source: © Greser & Lenz from *Frankfurter Allgemeine Zeitung* June 24, 2007.

of the second SPD-led regime were initially successful, but divisions within the party about the nature of structural reform—and the direction of Social Democracy in Germany—brought the second term of the SPD-Green government to an early end.

The Greens

The Greens entered the political scene in 1979 and have won seats at national and regional levels ever since. It is a heterogeneous party that first drew support from several different constituencies in the early 1980s: urban-based **Citizens Action Groups,** environmental activists, farmers, anti–nuclear power activists, the remnants of the peace movement, and small bands of Marxist-Leninists. After overcoming the 5 percent hurdle in the 1983 *Bundestag* elections, the Green Party went on to win seats in most subsequent state elections by stressing noneconomic quality-of-life issues. The electoral successes of this "antiparty party" generated a serious division within the party. The *realos* (realists) believed that it was important to moderate the party's positions in order to enter political institutions and gain access to power; the *fundis* (fundamentalists) opposed any collaboration with existing parties, even if this meant sacrificing some of their goals and damaging their chances of gaining power.

Although the realists gained the upper hand, the party failed to benefit because all the other parties began to include environmental and quality-of-life issues in their party programs. Until merging with the eastern German Bündnis '90 in 1993, the Greens' position looked bleak. The squabbling between *fundis* and *realos* undercut the party's credibility. The Greens' failure to motivate its own core constituency during the early 1990s greatly hampered the party. The unexpected death of a popular former party leader—the American-born Petra Kelly, a *fundi*—and the moderation of a former party leader (and former foreign minister), Joschka Fischer, signaled the transformation of the Greens into a dependable, innovative coalition partner.

The persistent ecological problems of the former East German states have presented the Greens with a tremendous opportunity. After several years in which the party's fortunes were uncertain, it increased its share of the vote to 8.6 percent in 2002 by pressing anti-nuclear, anti-genetic modification and climate change issues and now appears to be a permanent fixture in the *Bundestag*. Following the 2005 election, the Greens returned to the opposition benches in the *Bundestag* when its share of the vote dropped to 8.1 percent after briefly flirting with the idea of entering a coalition with the Christian Democrats and FDP. However, Green party members rebelled against the idea of coalition with pro-business parties. Yet in 2008 in Hamburg following its *Land* election, the Greens agreed to join the CDU in the regional government. This is yet another sign of possible increased party volatility in Germany.

The Free Democratic Party

The FDP's major influence is its role as a swing party because it has allied with each of the two major parties (SPD and CDU/CSU) at different periods since 1949. Regularly holding the foreign and economics ministries in coalition with the Christian Democrats, the FDP's most notable leaders were Walter Scheel, Count Otto Lambsdorff, and Hans-Dietrich Genscher.

The FDP's perspective encompasses two ideologies, broadly characterized here as economic liberalism (*liberal* in the European sense of *laissez-faire* individualism) and social liberalism (namely individual personal freedoms). During the postwar period, the FDP relied on two philosophies to align itself with the two major political groupings, the CDU/CSU and the SPD. The party was a member of almost all governing coalitions from 1949 to 1998, but with its strategy of cogoverning with first one major party and then the other, the FDP has occasionally been accused of lacking strong political convictions.

During the years of the SPD-Green governments (1998–2005), the FDP became much more explicitly a free-market party, emphasizing deregulation and privatization. After winning 9.8 percent of the vote in 2005, it hoped to join the Christian Democrats in a right-wing coalition, but the latter's poor showing prevented it from forming a majority. The growth of both the Green and the Left Parties has diminished the former fifty-year "kingmaker" status of the FDP and its role with the two large parties. There are more options for all of the parties now.

The Left Party (*die Linke*)

In June 2005, the former eastern German Communist Party (Party of Democratic Socialism) merged with a breakaway faction of the SPD that called itself the *Wahlalternative Arbeit und Soziale Gerechtigkeit* (WASG, or "electoral alternative for labor and social justice") to form the Left Party. The PDS was concentrated in the five states of the former East Germany, and although it received as much as 25 percent of the vote in some regional and local elections, it always drew well under the 5 percent mark in elections in the *Länder* of the former West Germany. While it was officially a new party concentrated in the former East Germany, it has had a long and volatile history. It formed from the Communist Party of Germany (*Kommunistische Partei Deutschlands*, KPD), which was founded after World War I. In the late 1940s, the Communist Party flourished in the Soviet zone and was renamed the Socialist Unity Party (*Sozialistische Einheits Partei*, SED). It dominated all aspects of life in East Germany and was considered the most Stalinist and repressive regime in eastern Europe.

After unification in 1990, the SED demonstrated considerable tactical agility by changing its name and program, and it received considerable support in the five *Länder* of the former East Germany. Throughout the 1990s, the difficulties of unification helped boost the strength of the PDS. It gained over 20 percent of the vote in the five new German states in the *Bundestag* elections of 1994, 1998, and 2002 and won seats in the *Bundestag* in four consecutive elections.

The WASG, composed of left-wing dissident former SPD members and led by former finance minister Oskar Lafontaine, offered an attractive option for the PDS. Based primarily in western Germany, the WASG provided electoral support for the PDS precisely where the latter was weakest. Polling as high as 12 percent nationwide prior to the election, it obtained 8.7 percent of the vote in September 2005 and represented an intriguing complication for the other parties.

In fact, the Left Party's strong showing, largely due to its opposition against budget cuts, is the main reason why neither the SPD and Greens, nor the CDU/CSU and FDP, were able to form either a left-wing or right-wing coalition. With a growing base in the west (4.9 percent) and traditional eastern support (nearly 25 percent) it seems solidly entrenched as the fifth party. However, all other parties have ruled out dealing with the Left—including the SPD and Greens—even though the three left-of-center parties won 51.1 percent of the votes and had a potential 21 seat majority. Since its breakthrough in the 2005 *Bundestag* election, the Left Party has won seats in four western *Länder* parliaments (now ten of the sixteen German *Länder*) and had regularly attained between 12 to 14 percent in opinion polls by mid-2008.

While the Left Party is still finding its way as a parliamentary party on the opposition benches, it is performing an important task in eastern Germany. The FRG is one of the few countries in western Europe that has not had a far-right and/or neo-fascist party gain seats in its national legislature. Because the primary support for the Left Party in the east comes from marginalized and/or unemployed people in German society, it has provided a left-wing alternative to those who, under other circumstances, might turn to the far right.

The Far Right

There have been various splinter-group right-wing parties throughout the Federal Republic's history, but with the exception of the neo-Nazi National Democratic Party of Germany (*Nationaldemokratische Partei Deutschland*, NPD), which received 4.3 percent of the vote in 1969, they had never seriously threatened to win seats in the *Bundestag*. There are two far-right political parties[20] that have won seats in regional parliaments since 2000: the German People's Union (*Deutsche Volksunion*, DVU), and the NPD. None, however, have come close to winning seats in the *Bundestag*. The latter two parties have won *Land* government seats in 2006.

Elections

For nearly fifty years in the Federal Republic, voting participation rates averaging 80 to 90 percent at the federal level matched or exceeded those in all other western European countries There have been five major periods of party dominance (plus the 1966–69 Grand Coalition) between 1949 and the present:

1. CDU/CSU-FDP coalition (1949–1966; CDU/CSU majority, 1957–1961)

2. Grand Coalition (CDU/CSU–SPD) interregnum (1966–1969)
3. SPD–FDP coalition (1969–1982)
4. CDU/CSU–FDP coalition (1982–1998)
5. SPD-Green coalition (1998–2005)
6. Grand Coalition (CDU/CSU–SPD) (2005–)

As Table 4.4 suggests, Germany has enjoyed relatively stable electoral allegiance, despite unification, European integration, and the introduction of two new parties in the *Bundestag* during the decade of the 1990s. The electorate appears to be divided into relatively stable party followings, but as recent support for the two large parties has waned, to the benefit of the three smaller parties, voter volatility is increasing.

Political Culture, Citizenship, and Identity

With political parties representing such a broad ideological spectrum, there is wide-ranging political debate in Germany. This diversity is reflected in the media, where newspapers appeal to a broad range of political opinion. There is a wide variety of private TV cable and satellite channels, but the three main public channels (two national, one a series of regionals) provide a balance of major party positions. Until the late 1990s, most public channels prohibited paid TV campaign commercials during the two-month electoral campaigns.

There is a strong participatory ethic among the democratic left, fostered by the many opportunities for participation at the workplace through co-determination and the works councils. Moreover, one of the primary appeals of the Greens has been their emphasis on **grass-roots democracy**—that is, rank-and-file participation. The strength of the Greens, and now the Left Party, has forced the traditional parties to focus on mobilizing their supporters and potential supporters. The presence of the Greens and the Left Party has also helped dispel some of the old stereotypes about the country's legendary preference for consensus, order, and stability.

Germany's educational system has also changed since the Federal Republic was created, particularly in terms of the socialization of German citizens. The catalyst was the student movement of the 1960s. At that time, the university system was elitist and restrictive and did not offer sufficient critical analysis of Germany's bloody twentieth-century history. Not only did the student mobilizations of the 1960s open up the educational system to a wider socioeconomic spectrum, they also caused many of the so-called '68 Generation (1968 was the year of the most significant student demonstrations) to challenge their parents about attitudes shaped by the Nazi period and before.

However, anti-ethnic and anti-immigrant violence in the late 1980s, mid-1990s, and early 2000s raised questions among some observers regarding the genuineness of German toleration. Given Germany's persecution of Jews, homosexuals, and political opponents during the first half of the twentieth century and the unimaginable horrors of the Holocaust, such concerns must be taken extremely seriously. Although Germany is not alone among industrialized nations in racist violence, its history imposes a special burden to overcome any display of intolerance if it is to gain the world's respect.

The Schröder Red-Green government began to change the rules on citizenship, democracy, and participation in Germany. Until 1998, German citizenship was based on blood, that is, German ethnicity. Unlike many European nations, Germany made it difficult for residents without native ethnicity to be naturalized, and it denied citizenship even to the children of noncitizens who were born and brought up in Germany. Ethnic Germans whose ancestors had not lived in Germany for centuries were allowed to enter Germany legally and to become citizens immediately. One of the first acts of the Schröder government was to allow expedited citizenship for long-time foreign residents.

Perhaps the most contentious citizenship/identity problem has surrounded the political asylum question. Following World War II, Germany passed one of the world's most liberal political asylum laws, in part to help atone for the Nazis' political repression of millions. With the end of the cold war and the opening up of east European borders, the trickle of asylum seekers turned into a flood. This influx drove the Kohl government to curtail drastically the right of political asylum. Germany's commitment to democratic rights appeared to contain some new conditions, and many

Table 4.4

FRG Election Results, 1949–2005

Year	Party	Percentage of Vote	Government	Year	Party	Percentage of Vote	Government
1949	Voter turnout	78.5	CDU/CSU–FDP	1983	Voter Turnout	89.1	CDU/CSU
	CDU/CSU	31.0			CDU/CSU	48.8	
	SPD	29.2			SPD	38.2	
	FDP	11.9			FDP	7.0	
	Others	27.8			Greens	5.6	
1953	Voter turnout	86.0	CDU/CSU–FDP		Others	0.5	
	CDU/CSU	45.2		1987	Voter turnout	84.3	CDU/CSU
	SPD	28.8			CDU/CSU	44.3	
	FDP	9.5			SPD	37.0	
	Others	16.7			FDP	9.1	
1957	Voter turnout	87.8	CDU/CSU		Greens	8.3	
	CDU/CSU	50.2			Others	1.3	
	SPD	31.8		1990	Voter turnout	78.0	CDU/CSU
	FDP	7.7			CDU/CSU	43.8	
	Others	10.3			SPD	33.5	
1961	Voter turnout	87.8	CDU/CSU–FDP		FDP	11.0	
	CDU/CSU	45.3			Greens	3.8	
	SPD	36.2			PDS	2.4	
	FDP	12.8			Bündnis '90	1.2	
	Others	5.7			Others	3.5	
1965	Voter turnout	86.8	CDU/CSU–SPD	1994	Voter turnout	79.0	CDU/CSU
	CDU/CSU	47.6	Grand		CDU/CSU	41.5	
	SPD	39.3	Coalition		SPD	36.4	
	FDP	9.5			FDP	6.9	
	Others	3.6			Greens	7.3	
1969	Voter turnout	86.7	SPD–FDP		PDS	4.4	
	CDU/CSU	46.1			Others	3.5	
	SPD	42.7		1998	Voter turnout	82.3	SPD-Greens
	FDP	5.8			CDU/CSU	35.1	
	Others	5.4			SPD	40.9	
1972	Voter turnout	86.0	SPD–FDP		FDP	6.2	
	CDU/CSU	44.9			Greens	6.7	
	SPD	45.8			PDS	5.1	
	FDP	9.5			Others	6.0	
	Others	16.7		2002	Voter turnout	79.1	SPD-Greens
1976	Voter turnout	90.7	SDP–FDP		SPD	38.5	
	CDU/CSU	48.2			CDU/CSU	38.5	
	SPD	42.6			Greens	8.6	
	FDP	7.9			FDP	7.4	
	Others	0.9			PDS	4.0	
1980	Voter Turnout	88.6	SPD–FDP		Others	3.0	
	CDU/CSU	44.5		2005	Voter turnout	77.7	
	SPD	42.9			CDU/CSU	35.2	
	FDP	10.6			SPD	34.2	
	Others	0.5			FDP	9.8	
					Left Party	8.7	
					Greens	8.1	

Source: German Information Center, 2005.

Current Challenges

The Complicated Politics of Immigration

Germany, like virtually all other western European nations, has discovered that it has become an immigrant country. To be sure, a nation-state that did not achieve unity until 1871 faced calamitous questions of immigration and nationality. In fact, the nationalism unleashed in the late nineteenth century in the wake of economic and political upheaval caused catastrophe for nonethnic Germans. Because of that late-nineteenth- and early-to-mid-twentieth-century oppression of racial and ethnic minorities, the Federal Republic realized in the postwar period that it had a special obligation to both Jews and other ethnic minorities whom the Nazis had persecuted and killed. It was this history that caused the new FRG government to pass generous asylum laws, allowing those who faced political persecution to obtain residency, if not citizenship, in a democratic Germany.

Citizenship was a more difficult proposition for immigrants to Germany. The 1913 Immigration Law (until liberalized by the SPD/Green Schröder government in 1999) stipulated that citizenship was based on blood (*jus sanguis*) and not naturalization (*jus solis*). This meant that German citizenship was easy to obtain for "ethnic" Germans who had lived in Russia or eastern Europe for generations and did not speak German, but difficult for the *Gastarbeiter* (guest workers) who had lived in Germany since the 1960s.

In fact, the tension between cultural conceptions of citizenship and the economic demands of both Germany and the EU lie at the heart of the complicated politics of immigration. On the one hand, some Germans and Europeans are fearful of what immigration will do to traditional conceptions of what being a "German" actually is. Racist violence is an extreme manifestation of this sentiment. On the other hand, globalization and Europeanization have opened up the Continent to increasing migration, which, to some, is the very point of the process. Adding to the economic pressures on European countries to increase immigration is the demographic time-bomb that affects almost all western European countries: a population decrease of the "native" or "ethnic" portions of their population, fueling the fears of some among this population. Yet this aging population is also relying on a welfare and pension system that demands that there be a young work force to pay for it. Western European policy-makers now realize that a partial solution to the fiscal obligations that an aging population represents is new, young, immigrant workers who will both revitalize economic growth and help fund the pension and welfare obligations. To do so, however, requires that Germany—and many of its neighbors—fundamentally reconsider what it means to be a citizen.

involved a definition of identity that looked remarkably insular in a Europe that was becoming more international and global.

Gender did not appear to be a politically significant cleavage in Germany until the 1960s, since women had remained politically marginalized for most of the first half of the Federal Republic's history. Taking to heart the admonition *Kinder, Kirche, Küche* (children, church, and kitchen), many German women were socialized into believing that their status as second-class citizens was appropriate. Until the social explosions of the 1960s, very few women held positions in society outside the home.

Even with the spread of feminism since the 1970s, German women have generally lagged slightly behind

their American counterparts in business and in civil society. However, as the data in Table 4.3 show, German women have quadrupled their representation in the *Bundestag* from approximately 8 percent in 1980 to almost 32 percent in 2005; and of course Angela Merkel is the first female chancellor.

The differences between East and West Germany on social policy affecting women provoked great controversy after unification. Women in the former East Germany had far more presence and influence in public life and in the workplace than did their counterparts in West Germany. In the former East Germany, women had made far greater social and economic progress (relatively speaking) and enjoyed greater government provision for such services as childcare and family leave. In fact, one of the hottest items of contention in Germany during the early 1990s was whether to reduce East German–style benefits to women (including abortion) in favor of the more conservative and restrictive ones of the Federal Republic. The West German law prevailed after unification, to the consternation of many.

Interests, Social Movements, and Protest

Germany remains a country of organized collectivities: major economic producer groups such as the BDI (Federal Association of German Industry), BDA (Federal Association of German Employers), and DGB (German Trade Union Confederation); political parties (in which authentic participatory membership remains higher than in most other countries); and social groups.

From the descriptions of organized business and organized labor in Section 3, it is clear that interest groups in Germany operate differently than they do in the United States and Britain. In the Federal Republic, interest groups are seen as having a societal role and responsibility that transcend the immediate interests of their members. Germany's codified legal system specifically allows private interests to perform public functions, albeit within a clearly specified general framework. Thus, interest groups are seen as part of the fabric of society and are virtually permanent institutions. This view places a social premium on their adaptation and response to new issues.

Strikes and demonstrations do occur on a wide range of economic and noneconomic issues. Political institutions sometimes are mistakenly seen as fixed structures that are supposed to prevent or repress dissent. A more positive way to analyze strikes and other conflicts is to interpret them as mechanisms pressuring institutions and policies to be responsive.[21] Rather than being detrimental to democratic participation, such bottom-up protests embody its essence.

Such a system does not encourage fractious competition; instead, it creates a framework within which interest groups can battle yet eventually come to an agreement on policy. Moreover, because they aggregate the interests of all members of their group, they often take a broader, less parochial view of problems and policy solutions. How does the German state mediate the relationship among interest groups? Peter Katzenstein observes that in the Federal Republic, "the state is not an actor but a series of relationships," and these relationships are solidified in what he has called "parapublic institutions."[22] The parapublics encompass a wide variety of organizations, among which the most important are the *Bundesbank* (although many of its powers now reside with the European Central Bank, ECB), the institutions of codetermination, the labor courts, the social insurance funds, and the employment office. Katzenstein notes that the parapublics have been assigned the role of "independent governance by the representatives of social sectors at the behest of or under the general supervision of the state."[23] In other words, organizations that would be regarded as mere interest groups in other countries work with certain quasigovernment agencies to fill a parapublic role in the Federal Republic. These organizations assume a degree of social responsibility, through their roles in policy implementation that go beyond what political scientist Arnold Heidenheimer has called the "freewheeling competition of 'selfish' interest groups."[24] For example, through the state, the churches collect a church tax on all citizens born into either the Protestant or Roman Catholic churches. This provides the churches with a steady stream of income, ensuring them institutional permanence while compelling them to play a major role in the provision of social welfare and aid to the families of foreign workers.

Interest groups and parapublic agencies limit social conflict by regular meetings and close coordination. However, this system is subject to the same problems that have plagued corporatism in more centralized industrial societies such as Sweden and France. If the system fails and conflicts are allowed to go unresolved, the effectiveness of the institutions is questioned, and some elements of society may go unrepresented. A partial failure of certain interest groups and institutions led to a series of social movements during the 1960s and 1970s, particularly around university reform, wage negotiations, and foreign policy. The rise of the Green Party in the 1980s and 1990s is a prime example of a movement that responded to the inability of existing institutions to address, mediate, and solve certain contentious issues. Likewise the growth of the Left Party to represent some 25 to 30 percent of the voters in eastern Germany who did not feel represented by the traditional western parties is another.

Until recently, most conflicts and policy responses were encompassed within this system. Yet not all individuals found organizations to represent their interests. Those who are outside the organized groups fall into several categories. Political groups that fail to meet the 5 percent electoral threshold, such as the NPD and the German People's Union (DVU), belong in this category, along with smaller right-wing groups. The substantial Turkish population, comprising 2.3 percent of Germany's inhabitants, might be included here. Many Turks have resided in Germany for decades, but unlike workers from EU countries like Italy and Spain, Turkish residents have few rights in Germany. Finally, the once-active leftist community of revolutionary Marxists still retains a small presence, mostly in large cities and university towns. Some of these left-wing parties contest elections, but they never get more than 1 percent of the vote.

Since the student mobilizations of the late 1960s, Germany has witnessed considerable protest and mobilization of social forces outside established channels. Among the most significant have been feminists, the peace movement, the antinuclear movement, and the peaceful church-linked protests in East Germany in 1989 that were a catalyst for the breakdown of the communist regime. All four groups, in different ways, challenged fundamental assumptions about German politics and highlighted the inability of the institutional structure to respond to their needs and issues. Opposition to a restrictive abortion law in the 1970s, demonstrations against the stationing of nuclear missiles on German soil in the 1980s, regular protests against nuclear power plants since the 1970s, and courageous challenges to communism have shown the vibrancy of German protest.

Since the 1990s, there has been less protest from the left than from the right. Illegal neo-Nazi groups were responsible for racist attacks. Significantly, all of these attacks by the right-wing fringe provoked spontaneous, peaceful marches of 200,000 to 500,000 people in various cities. This reaction suggests that social protest, as a part of an active democratic political discourse, has matured. In the early twenty-first century, the issue of the Iraq war has produced an increase in social protest, largely among forces on the left of the governing SPD-Green coalition. There have also been smaller right-wing protests against continued immigration, such as the May Day Hamburg riot in 2008, but these have not approached the violent episodes of the 1990s.

German Politics in Transition

Political Challenges and Changing Agendas

The announcement by Federal President Horst Kölher in May 2008 that he wanted to serve a second term would normally not be surprising. He was a popular figure in this largely ceremonial office and had performed the head of state function well. However, this announcement complicated further the increasingly uneasy relationship between the Grand Coalition partners, the CDU/CSU and SPD. Köhler won in 2004 by narrowly defeating the SPD candidate Gesine Schwann. After Köhler's announcement, the SPD promptly announced that it would nominate Schwann again for this presidential contest to be decided by the *Bundestag* and *Bundesrat* in May 2009.

This decision by Köhler and the CDU/CSU has exacerbated the tensions among the German parties in several ways. First, the two Grand Coalition partners are running competing candidates for head of state. Second, the SPD's backing down to Köhler and the Christian Democrats by not running their own candidate would cause even more Social Democratic voters to desert the SPD and vote for the Left Party in the *Bundestag* election in September 2009. Third, the only way that Schwann could win would be with the support of the

SPD, Greens, and the Left Party, which the SPD was fearful of doing (the FDP supports Köhler). Fourth, the Left Party would be forced to take on a "kingmaker" status for which neither the party nor the country may be ready.

By mid-2008 there were both encouraging and discouraging political developments in Germany. Despite predictions to the contrary, Germany's economy had avoided the most severe effects of the credit crisis that had hit countries like the U.S. and U.K. with their emphasis on deregulation and unconstrained markets. Germany, with some degree of pride, could look to its more organized economic policy model with improved economic growth and a drop in unemployment to 8.5 percent, the lowest in half a decade, and be thankful that it had—for the most part—avoided deregulatory, housing, and financial crises.

On the other hand, Angela Merkel's chancellorship seemed to signify a refreshing change from the strife-ridden second Schröder term. Three years after her narrow election, Merkel was personally popular and seemed ahead of the curve by stressing climate change and human rights as major international issues. But the reality of contemporary German politics is more complicated. The five-party system, with the three smaller parties representing 35 percent of the electorate, does not auger well. Merkel would either have to form a complicated three-party coalition with two of the small parties, or organize another Grand Coalition with the SPD—which would only increase the strength of the three smaller parties over the longer term. And the strains of disagreement with her SPD coalition partner on economic and foreign policy did not bode well with an election looming in a year. Moreover, Merkel still faces the challenges that bedeviled Schröder: (1) the still-formidable uncompleted tasks in eastern Germany associated with unification; (2) the rapid expansion of the European Union (EU) and its free-market–style policy focus that is at odds with the institutionally based, organized-capitalist German economy; and (3) the intense pace of globalization that threatens Germany's competitive edge. Even more alarming was a May 2008 government report that showed that 25 percent of Germans were classified as poor or relied on welfare benefits. The 64,000-euro question is whether Germany can deploy the institutional and political skills to recover its formerly strong position.

The path taken by German politics will be determined by the resolution of the four core themes identified in Section 1. The more hopeful outcome would be for Merkel to negotiate a genuine compromise with the SPD and bridge the formidable gaps between these two large parties. Only with a sound and effective foundation of domestic policy will Germany be able to successfully address the larger issue of European integration and the challenge of globalization and a more volatile international climate in the wake of the Iraq war. By finding common ground to address such problems as economic competitiveness, unemployment, and the still gaping East–West divide, among many others, the Grand Coalition could develop the patience and sound institutional foundation to accomplish a great deal. To her credit, Merkel has been very good at fostering incremental change.

The more pessimistic outcome would see unresolved major issues as dividing the coalition partners and producing a continued stalemate. One result would be an increased share of the vote going to the three opposition parties. Democracies need both a government and an opposition, but if the Grand Coalition has major fissures, finding stable new coalitions may be difficult. Can Germany's organized society and institutional political structure muster the increased cooperation necessary to maintain a vibrant democracy? And what of Germany's high-wage economy and welfare structure in the face of increased economic competition from lower-wage countries in East Asia and elsewhere? Will using the euro enable Germany to thrive, or will it undermine the previous strengths of the German economy? And what is the state of the German economy in the face of domestic structural challenges, as well as globalization of the international economy? It remains to be seen whether the Grand Coalition can implement significant economic and political reforms such as Schröder's policy that merged the unemployment and welfare systems reforms and required the unemployed to take jobs outside their home region or outside their chosen profession.

For many years, Germany was held up as a model for other industrialized societies to emulate. But there have been significant changes in Germany since unification. The expansion of the EU since the 1990s has enabled more European citizens to live and work outside their home countries. What will happen to

German collective identity given this fluidity and the change in German citizenship laws by the SPD-Green government, and the subsequent criticism by some far-right forces? Can the elaborate and long-effective institutional structure that balances private and public interests be maintained? Will the EU augment or challenge Germany's position in Europe? Will these challenges threaten Germany's enviable position in the face of increased globalization of the world economy?

The future of German politics depends on how the country addresses the four primary themes identified in this analysis of the Federal Republic. For much of the period after World War II, Germany enjoyed a spiral of success that enabled it to confront these issues with confidence and resolve. For example, problems of collective identities were handled in a much less exclusionary way as women, nonnative ethnic groups, and newer political parties and movements began to contribute to a stable and healthy diversity in German politics. Democratic institutions effectively balanced participation and dissent, offsetting the country's turbulent and often racist past by almost fifty years of a stable multiparty democracy. Germany's economic success has been significant and unique. The country is a stronghold of advanced capitalism yet supports an extensive state welfare program and mandates worker/trade union/works councils' participation in managerial decision-making. These successes have helped Germany participate more effectively on the international scene. Since the late 1980s, Germany has confidently, and with the support of its neighbors and allies, taken a leading role in European integration. It is firmly anchored in western Europe but is uniquely positioned to assist in the transition of the former communist central and eastern European states toward economic and political modernization and EU membership.

However, close examination of the four themes reveals that Germany's path is not yet certain. In the area of collective identities, Germany faces many unresolved challenges. Turkish and other non-German guest workers remain essential to Germany's economy, and some will now be able to obtain German citizenship. Their long-term acceptance by the CDU/CSU, not to mention the smaller ultra-right parties, will likely be the key to a fundamental change in the concept of who is a German. The influx of refugees and asylum seekers has placed great strains on German taxpayers

and increased ethnic tensions. German nationalism, suppressed since the end of World War II, has shown some signs of resurgence. Two generations after the end of World War II, some younger Germans are asking what being German actually means. The change in citizenship laws will complicate this issue, for although this search for identity can be healthy, various extremist groups still preach exaggerated nationalism and hatred of foreigners and minorities. Such tendencies are fundamentally incompatible with Germany's playing a leading role in a unifying Europe.

Democracy in Germany appears well established after almost sixty years of the Federal Republic. It features high voter turnout, a stable and responsible multiparty political system, and a healthy civic culture. Despite the inconclusive election, German politicians have negotiated an interim solution, and they have done so via constitutional principles common to all multiparty parliamentary systems.[25]

Many observers believe that broad-based participation is part of the fabric of German political life. The overriding challenge for Germany's political institutions is the assimilation of the five eastern states. Can eastern Germans who have lost jobs and benefits in the transition to capitalism understand that ethnic minorities are not the cause of their plight? Can tolerance and understanding offset a right-wing fringe that preaches hatred and targets scapegoats to blame for the costs of unification? Also, what is the legacy of a bureaucratic state that as recently as the 1970s, under a Social Democratic-led government, purged individuals alleged to have radical tendencies? In other words, if social tensions continue to grow, how will the German state respond?

There is reason for optimism. Eastern Germans have shown that they understand and practice democracy amazingly well. After years of authoritarian communist rule, many East Germans initially regarded dissent not as political participation but as treason. However, the evolution of the Left Party into an effective political force that articulates the interests of its voters—now in the West as well as the East—offers considerable promise. In the recent elections, the Left Party has been considered unsuitable as a potential coalition partner because of its communist origins. However, when the Greens first obtained seats in the *Bundestag* in 1983, it was often viewed as an irresponsible party and not appropriate as a coalition partner. Yet fifteen years later, the Greens joined the SPD in the first left-wing majority government in German history. The lesson to be learned from the Greens' transformation from a motley crew of *alternativen* (counterculture) to a governing coalition partner is that continued participation in democratic institutions can have positive results for both the party and the institutions.

Germany's approach to governing the economy also faces challenges in the early twenty-first century. For many years, the German economy was characterized as "high everything," in that it combined high-quality manufacturing with high wages, high fringe benefits, high worker participation, and high levels of vacation time.[26] Critics insisted that such a system could not last in a competitive world economy. Nevertheless, the German economy has remained among the world's leaders. But the huge costs of unification, the globalization of the world economy, and the strong emphasis on laissez-faire principles in many neighboring countries challenge the German model anew.[27]

German Politics in Comparative Perspective

Germany offers important insights for comparative politics. First, how successfully has Germany remade its political culture and institutions in the wake of a fascist past? Countries such as Japan, Italy, and Spain, among developed states, also bear watching on this point. To what extent has Germany's impressive democratic experience during the first fifty years of the Federal Republic exorcised the ghosts of the Third Reich? To what extent have the educational system, civil service, and the media addressed the Nazi past? To what extent do these institutions bear some responsibility for the recent rise of right-wing violence? Have the reforms in the educational system since the 1960s provided a spirit of critical discourse in the broad mainstream of society that can withstand right-wing rhetoric? Can judges effectively sentence those who abuse the civil rights of ethnic minorities? Will the news media continue to express a wide range of opinion and contribute to a healthy civic discourse? Or will strident, tabloid-style journalism stifle the more reasoned debate that any democracy must have to survive and flourish?

Second, Germany's historical development provides important material for comparative analysis. It was late to achieve political unity and late to industrialize. These two factors, combined with an unfavorable institutional mix, eventually helped produce a catastrophic first half of the twentieth century for Germany and the whole world. Yet the country's transition to a successful, developed economy with an apparently solid democratic political system would seem to provide more positive lessons for other countries. Those that might derive the most benefit may be industrializing nations as they also attempt to achieve economic growth and develop stable democracies.

Third is the role of organized capitalism. Germany offers a distinctive model for combining state and market. Germany's organized capitalism, together with its social market economy, has blurred the distinction between the public and private sectors. The German state pursues development plans based on its cooperative interaction with a dense network of key social and economic participants, particularly in such areas as climate change. Despite Germany's prominence as a powerful, advanced, industrialized economy, this model remains surprisingly understudied.

Germany offers a fourth insight, one that relates to the issues of tolerance and respect for civil rights for ethnic minorities. The Schröder government modified Germany's immigration policies to provide a path for long-time foreign workers to gain citizenship. Can residual ethnic tensions be resolved in a way that enhances democracy? Clearly, the issue of collective identities offers both powerful obstacles and rich opportunities to address one of the most crucial issues that Germany faces in the new century.

Finally, what is the role of a middle-rank power as the potential leader of a regional world bloc of some 450 million people? Germany is facing intense pressures from within its borders, such as conflict among ethnic groups, and from a complex mix of external influences. Its role as both a western and an eastern European power pulls it in opposite directions. Should the country emphasize the western-oriented EU and build a solid foundation with its NATO allies? Or should it turn eastward to step into the vacuum created by the demise and fragmentation of the former USSR? Can Germany's twentieth-century history permit it to play a leading geopolitical role? What an ironic but inspiring twist if Germany, the country whose virulent nationalism caused the most widespread destruction and destabilization in the twentieth century, took the lead at the head of the supranational EU in promoting democracy, creativity, and stability in the twenty-first century.

Key Terms >>>

Gastarbeiter (guest workers)
federal state
Junkers
liberal
chancellor
Kulturkampf
procedural democracy
Nazi
Zollverein
framework regulations
social market economy
works councils
Basic Law
5 percent rule

constructive vote of no confidence
civil servants
overlapping responsibilities
democratic corporatism
health insurance funds
co-determination
Administrative Court
industrial policy
personalized proportional representation
suspensive veto
party democracy
Citizens Action Groups
grass-roots democracy

Suggested Readings >>>

Allen, Christopher S., ed. *Transformation of the German Political Party System: Institutional Crisis or Democratic Renewal?* New York: Berghahn, 2001.

_____, "Ideas, Institutions and the Exhaustion of *Modell Deutschland?*" *German Law Journal* 5, no. 9 (September 2004): 1133–1154.

Braunthal, Gerard. *The Federation of German Industry in Politics.* Ithaca: Cornell University Press, 1965.

_____. *Parties and Politics in Modern Germany.* Boulder: Westview Press, 1996.

Craig, Gordon. *The Politics of the Prussian Army.* Oxford: Oxford University Press, 1955.

Dahrendorf, Ralf. *Society and Democracy in Germany.* Garden City: Anchor, 1969.

Deeg, Richard. *Finance Capital Unveiled: Banks and Economic Adjustment in Germany.* Ann Arbor: University of Michigan Press, 1998.

Eley, Geoff. *Reshaping the German Right: Radical Nationalism and Political Change After Bismarck.* New Haven: Yale University Press, 1980.

Esping-Anderson, Gøsta. *Three Worlds of Welfare Capitalism.* Princeton: Princeton University Press, 1990.

Gerschenkron, Alexander. *Bread and Democracy in Germany.* 2d ed. Ithaca: Cornell University Press, 1989.

Hirschman, Albert O. *Exit, Loyalty, and Voice: Responses to Decline in Firms, Organizations, and States.* Cambridge: Harvard University Press, 1970.

Inglehart, Ronald. *Culture Shift in Advanced Industrial Society.* Princeton: Princeton University Press, 1990.

Jacoby, Wade. *Imitation and Politics: Redesigning Modern Germany.* Ithaca: Cornell University Press, 2001.

Katzenstein, Peter, ed., *Industry and Politics in West Germany: Toward the Third Republic.* Ithaca: Cornell University Press, 1989.

Katzenstein, Peter. *Policy and Politics in West Germany: The Growth of a Semi-Sovereign State.* Philadelphia: Temple University Press, 1987.

_____. *Tamed Power: Germany in Europe.* Ithaca: Cornell University Press, 1997.

Kemp, Tom. *Industrialization in Nineteenth Century Europe.* 2d ed. London: Longman, 1985.

Markovits, Andrei S., and Reich, Simon. *The German Predicament: Memory and Power of the New Europe.* Ithaca: Cornell University Press, 1997.

Moore, Barrington. *Social Origins of Dictatorship and Democracy.* Boston: Beacon Press, 1965.

Piore, Michael, and Sabel, Charles. *The Second Industrial Divide.* New York: Basic Books, 1984.

Rein, Taagepera, and Shugart, Matthew Soberg. *Seats and Votes: The Effects and Determinants of Electoral Systems.* New Haven: Yale University Press, 1989.

Richter, Michaela. "Continuity or *Politikwechsel?* The First Federal Red-Green Coalition." *German Politics and Society* 20:1 (Spring 2002), 1–48.

Röpke, Wilhelm. "The Guiding Principle of the Liberal Programme." In H. F. Wünche, ed., *Standard Texts on the Social Market Economy.* New York: Gustav Fischer Verlag, 1982.

Rueschemeyer, Dietrich, Stephens, Evelyne Huber, and Stephens, John D. *Capitalist Development and Democracy.* Chicago: University of Chicago Press, 1992.

Schmitter, Philippe C., and Lembruch, Gerhard, eds. *Trends Toward Corporatist Intermediation.* Beverly Hills: Sage, 1979.

Shirer, William. *The Rise and Fall of the Third Reich.* New York: Simon & Schuster, 1960.

Steinmo, Sven, Thelen, Kathleen, and Longstreth, Frank, eds. *Structuring Politics: Historical Institutionalism in Historical Perspective.* New York: Cambridge University Press, 1992.

Streeck, Wolfgang. "Introduction: Explorations into the Origins of Nonliberal Capitalism in Germany and Japan." In Wolfgang Streeck and Kozo Yamamura, eds., *The Origins of Non-Liberal Capitalism* (Ithaca: Cornell University Press, 2002), pp. 1–38.

Thelen, Kathleen. *How Institutions Evolve: The Political Economy of Skills in Germany, Britain, the United States and Japan.* Cambridge: Cambridge University Press, 2004.

Tilly, Charles, ed. *The Formation of National States in Western Europe.* Princeton: Princeton University Press, 1975.

Turner, Lowell, ed. *Negotiating the New Germany: Can Social Partnership Survive?* Ithaca: Cornell University Press, 1997.

Yamamura, Kozo, and Streeck, Wolfgang. *The End of Diversity? Prospects for German and Japanese Capitalism.* Ithaca: Cornell University Press, 2003.

Suggested Websites ≫

American Institute for Contemporary German Studies, Johns Hopkins University
www.aicgs.org/
German Embassy, German Information Center
www.germany-info.org/relaunch/index.html
German News (in English) 1995–Present
www.germnews.de/dn/

German Studies Web, Western European Studies Section
www.dartmouth.edu/~wess/
Max Planck Institute for the Study of Societies, Cologne
www.mpi-fg-koeln.mpg.de/index_en.html
WZB, Social Science Research Center, Berlin
www.wz-berlin.de/default.en.asp

Endnotes ≫

[1]Charles Tilly, ed., *The Formation of National States in Western Europe* (Princeton: Princeton University Press, 1975).

[2]Barrington Moore, *Social Origins of Dictatorship and Democracy* (Boston: Beacon Press, 1965).

[3]Tom Kemp, *Industrialization in Nineteenth Century Europe*, 2d ed. (London: Longman, 1985).

[4]Richard Deeg, "The Comeback of *Modell Deutschland*? The New German Political Economy in the EU," *German Politics* 14 (2005): 332–353.

[5]Ralf Dahrendorf, *Society and Democracy in Germany* (Garden City: Anchor, 1969).

[6]Alexander Gerschenkron, *Bread and Democracy in Germany*, 2d ed. (Ithaca: Cornell University Press, 1989).

[7]Richard Deeg, *Finance Capital Unveiled: Banks and Economic Adjustment in Germany* (Ann Arbor: University of Michigan Press, 1998).

[8]Joyce Mushaben, "Challenging the Maternalist Presumption: Gender and Welfare Reform in Germany and the United States," in Ulrike Liebert and Nancy Hirschman, eds., *Women and Welfare: Theory and Practice in the U.S. and Europe* (Rutgers: Rutgers University Press, 2001).

[9]For an excellent understanding of the dynamics of institutional adaptation, see: Albert O. Hirschman, *Exit, Voice, and Loyalty: Responses to Decline in Firms, Organizations, and States* (Cambridge: Harvard University Press, 1970).

[10]http://eng.bundespraesident.de/en/-,11167/The-role-of-the-Federal-Presid.htm.

[11]Peter Katzenstein, *Policy and Politics in West Germany: The Growth of a Semi-Sovereign State* (Philadelphia: Temple University Press, 1987).

[12]John O. Koehler, *Stasi: The Untold Story of the East German Secret Police* (Boulder: Westview Press, 1999).

[13]Michaela Richter, "Continuity or Politikwechsel? The First Federal Red-Green Coalition." *German Politics & Society* 20, no. 1 (Spring 2002): 1–48.

[14]Frank Louis Rusciano, "Rethinking the Gender Gap: The Case of West German Elections," *Comparative Politics* 24, no. 3 (April 1992): 335–358.

[15]Christopher S. Allen, ed., *Transformation of the German Political Party System: Institutional Crisis or Democratic Renewal?* (New York: Berghahn, 2001).

[16]Aline Kuntz, "The Bavarian CSU: A Case Study in Conservative Modernization" (Ph.D. diss., Cornell University, 1987).

[17]Carl E. Schorske, *German Social Democracy, 1905–1917: The Development of the Great Schism* (Cambridge: Harvard University Press, 1983).

[18]Otto Kirchheimer, "The Transformation of Western European Party Systems," *Political Parties and Political Development* (Princeton: Princeton University Press, 1966), pp. 177–200.

[19]Gerard Braunthal, *The German Social Democrats Since 1969: A Party in Power and Opposition*, 2nd ed. (Boulder: Westview Press, 1994).

[20]Hans-Georg Betz, *Radical Right-Wing Populism in Western Europe* (New York: St. Martin's Press, 1994).

[21]Wolfgang Streeck and Kathleen Thelen, eds., *Beyond Continuity: Institutional Change in Advanced Political Economies* (New York: Oxford University Press, 2005).

[22]Katzenstein, *Policy and Politics in West Germany.*

[23]Peter J. Katzenstein, ed., *Industry and Politics in West Germany: Toward the Third Republic* (Ithaca: Cornell University Press, 1989), p. 333.

[24]Arnold J. Heidenheimer, *Comparative Public Policy: The Politics of Social Choice in America, Europe and Japan*, 3d ed. (New York: St. Martin's Press, 1990).

[25]Gabriel A. Almond and Sidney Verba, eds., *The Civic Culture Revisited* (Newbury Park: Sage, 1989).

[26]Lowell Turner, ed., *Negotiating the New Germany: Can Social Partnership Survive?* (Ithaca: Cornell University Press, 1997).

[27]Gary Herrigel, "The Crisis in German Decentralized Production," *European Urban and Regional Studies* 3, no. 1 (1996): 33–52.

Shigeko N. Fukai and Haruhiro Fukui

Chapter 5 ≫ JAPAN

Official Name: **Japan**

Location: **Eastern Asia**

Capital City: **Tokyo**

Population (2008): **127.3 million**

Size: **377,835 sq. km.; slightly smaller than California**

1867
Meiji Restoration inaugurates rapid Japanese industrialization and modernization.

1889
Constitution of the Great Empire of Japan establishes a bicameral legislature, the Imperial Diet.

1900–1901
Constitutional Party of Political Friends (Seiyukai) formed.

1912–1926
Taisho Democracy period.

1925
Universal Manhood Suffrage Law promulgated. Japan Trade Union Council formed.

1931–1932
Japanese army takes control of Chinese Manchuria without orders from the government in Tokyo.

1932
Military officers attempt but fail to take over government.

1937
Japan invades China.

1941
Japan attacks U.S. naval base in Pearl Harbor. United States declares war on Japan.

1945
Atomic bombs dropped on Hiroshima and Nagasaki. Soviet Union declares war on Japan. Japan surrenders. Allied occupation and reform of Japan begin.

1947
New Constitution of Japan promulgated in 1946 comes into effect featuring a democratic government and a peace clause (Article 9) renouncing the right to make war.

1951
Japanese Peace Treaty and United States–Japan Mutual Security Treaty signed in San Francisco.

1955
Socialist parties unite to form Japan Socialist Party (JSP); conservative parties merge into Liberal Democratic Party (LDP).

1976
Lockheed scandal and arrest of former Prime Minister Tanaka Kakuei: the first of the major scandals that will rock the Japanese government.

The Making of the Modern Japanese State

SECTION 1

Politics in Action

In the July 2007 elections for the House of Councilors, the upper chamber of Japan's bicameral parliament (the Diet), the Liberal Democratic Party (LDP), which had long dominated the nation's politics, suffered a crushing defeat. For the first time in its history, the LDP did not gain a majority or plurality position in the house. The largest share of vote (39.5 percent) went to the main opposition party, the Democratic Party of Japan (DPJ). This was a dramatic reversal of the LDP's landslide victory in the lower chamber (House of Representatives) elections held less than two years before. That spectacular victory had been won by the party when it was led by Koizumi Junichiro,* a third-generation Diet member with a reputation as a tough, nationalist, populist, reformist, and maverick politician. The spectacular defeat of the LDP in 2007 was suffered when the party was led by Abe (pronounced ah-bay) Shinzo, another third-generation Diet member,

but unlike Koizumi, a prickly, aloof, and traditional politician. The victorious DPJ was led by Ozawa Ichiro, a second-generation Diet member and reform-minded politician who was also a former member of the LDP and a veteran of its intense factional politics.

The House of Councilors is a much less powerful part of the Japanese parliament than the House of Representatives, which chooses the country's prime minister, who, in turn, forms the government. Nevertheless, the defeat of the LDP in the upper house elections introduced a new and important "twist" in Japanese politics. For the first time in Japan's postwar history, the lower and upper houses of the Diet are controlled by different parties. The LDP and its coalition partner, the Clean Government Party (CGP), hold well over two-thirds of the seats in the more powerful lower house, while a majority of seats in the upper house is controlled by the DJP and other opposition parties. This has created a situation that is literally called a "twisted" Diet. Under the rules spelled out in the Constitution of Japan, the LDP-led government is still able to have most of its cabinet-sponsored bills enacted, even if they are rejected by the opposition-dominated upper house, by having the bills passed a second time with a

---

*In Japanese, the family name (Koizumi) comes before the given name (Junichiro). The same is true in other East Asian (Confucian) cultures, including China, Korea, and Vietnam.

1985
Telecommunications and tobacco industries privatized. Equal Employment Law enacted.

1989
Showa emperor, Hirohito, dies. LDP loses in House of Councilors election.

1990
Prince Akihito ascends throne as Heisei emperor.

1992
Japan New Party (JNP) founded by LDP dissidents.

1993
LDP loses in House of Representatives general election; first non-LDP government since 1955 formed by coalition centered on the JNP.

1994
New House of Representatives election law passed. LDP returns to power in coalition with the JSP.

1996
LDP forms first single-party cabinet since 1993.

1997
Asian financial crisis shakes Japanese stock market and economy.

1998
LDP cabinets implement a series of measures to resuscitate stagnant economy, but to no significant effect. Japan's economy remains depressed into the first

years of the twenty-first century.

2001
National government ministries and agencies reorganized. Self-Defense Force ships dispatched to Indian Ocean to assist U.S. Navy in its antiterrorism operations.

2004
SDF troops sent to Iraq to assist U.S. postwar mission.

2005
LDP led by Koizumi Junichiro wins landslide victory in House of Representatives election.

2007
LDP led by Abe Shinzo loses to opposition Democratic Party of Japan (DPJ) in House of Councilors election.

In the divided Diet following the 2007 upper house election, the LDP led by Fukuda Yasuo in control of the lower house, and the DPJ led by Ozawa Ichiro in control of the upper house, are constantly engaged in a tug-of-war over all important bills and personnel matters on the parliamentary agenda. *Source:* © Asahi Shimbun, November 29, 2007.

ねじれ鉢巻き

針 すなお

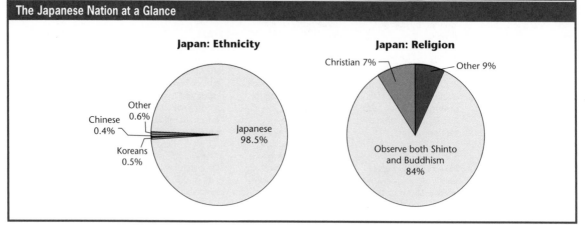

FIGURE 5.1

The Japanese Nation at a Glance

Japan: Ethnicity

- Japanese 98.5%
- Other 0.6%
- Chinese 0.4%
- Koreans 0.5%

Japan: Religion

- Observe both Shinto and Buddhism 84%
- Christian 7%
- Other 9%

two-thirds majority in the lower house. The passage of a bill to amend the constitution, however, requires the concurrence of two-thirds or more members of *both* houses. This becomes a virtual impossibility when more than a third of the seats are controlled by the opposition in the upper house as it is now.

Six weeks after the disastrous upper house election, Abe resigned as LDP president and prime minister (the two positions went together) and was succeeded by yet another second-generation Diet member, this time an unassuming and unambitious moderate, Fukuda Yasuo. In September 2008, or within a year of his election as

Table 5.1

Political Organization

Political System	Parliamentary democracy and constitutional monarchy, in which the emperor is merely a symbol of national unity.
Regime History	Current constitution promulgated in 1946 and in effect since 1947.
Administrative Structure	Unitary state, 47 units of intermediate-level subnational government "prefectures," and 1,790 lower-level units designated as city, town, or village.
Executive	Prime minister selected by legislature; a cabinet of about twenty ministers appointed by prime minister.
Legislature	Bicameral. The upper house (House of Councilors) has 242 members elected for six-year terms. Half of the members are elected every three years. One hundred forty-six are elected from multiple-seat prefecture-wide districts; 96 are elected nationally by a party list proportional representation method. The lower house (House of Representatives) has 480 members elected for four-year terms, which may be shortened by the dissolution of the house. Three hundred lower house members are elected from single-seat constituencies; 180 are elected by party list proportional representation from eleven regional electoral districts.
Judiciary	Supreme Court has fifteen judges appointed by the cabinet, except the chief judge who is nominated by the cabinet and appointed by the emperor; all are eligible to serve until seventy years of age, subject to popular review.
Party System	One-party dominant (Liberal Democratic Party) since mid-1950s; has become more competitive since early 1990s. Major parties: Liberal Democratic Party, Democratic Party of Japan, Clean Government Party, Social Democratic Party, Japan Communist Party.

Abe's successor, Fukuda abruptly resigned and was succeeded by another heir of a well-known political family and a fifth-generation Diet member, Aso Taro. In a nation mired in a seemingly endless economic stagnation and political instability, the game of musical chairs went on at the top of its power structure.

Recent political developments in Japan thus highlighted the extent to which the leadership of the nation's two dominant parties, and therefore its parliament and government itself, has become "hereditary" and a virtual heirloom of entrenched political families. They also highlighted how uncertain and uneasy the Japanese electorate is about the state of the nation's politics and economy under the stewardship of the entrenched ruling party and, as a result, how volatile Japanese electoral politics, at both the national and local levels, have become.

Geographic Setting

The nation of Japan is a group of 6,852 islands lying off the northeastern coast of Asia. With a territory of about 145,900 square miles, Japan is slightly smaller than California, slightly larger than Germany, and one twenty-fifth the size of China. All but four of its islands—Honshu, Hokkaido, Kyushu, and Shikoku—are less than 500 square miles in size.

Japan is the tenth most populous country in the world, with about 127 million people. With about 870 people per square mile, it is the eighth most densely populated nation with a population of 1 million or more. It has about eleven times the population density of the United States. Japan is a very urbanized country, where about two-thirds of the total population lives in cities with 10,000 or more people per square mile. Well over 80 percent of the Japanese people live in 780 or so large cities, most with a population of 50,000 or more.

Japan is poorly endowed with natural resources. The only exception is water from the normally plentiful rainfall that feeds the paddy fields and ensures an adequate supply of the nation's dietary staple, rice. Consequently, Japan heavily depends on imports from abroad for virtually all natural resources required by its people and industry. Moreover, only about 13 percent of land in Japan is arable, compared to about 20 percent in the United States, 25 percent

in Britain, and well over 30 percent in Germany and France. As a result of its need to import natural resources and foodstuffs, modern Japan has been a natural trading state. Japan's closest neighbors are Korea and China. Ancient and medieval Japan imported not only large amounts of material goods from these neighbors, but also wide-ranging forms of culture, such as religion, literature, law, architecture, and fine arts. Medieval Japan also developed trading and diplomatic relationships with peoples who lived in what would be today's Vietnam, Thailand, Malaysia, Indonesia, and the Philippines. Starting in the mid-nineteenth century, Japan developed extensive contacts—and sometimes serious conflicts—with Russia and the United States.

Critical Junctures

Ancient and Medieval Japan

Archeological evidence shows that hunters and gatherers inhabited the Japanese archipelago as early as 30,000 B.C.E. By about 7,000 B.C.E., some inhabitants began to build and live in small settlements and raise livestock. By the end of the fourth century B.C.E., rice, which would soon become the Japanese staple crop, began to be grown in the southwestern regions of the country. By the middle of the third century A.D., several tribal states had emerged in the same regions. A century or so later, they came under the control of a leader—possibly an immigrant member of a Korean aristocratic family—described in the oldest extant Japanese books dating back to the early eighth century as a "heavenly king" descended from the primeval deity, the Sun Goddess, of the animistic Japanese religion, Shinto (the Way of the Gods).

The early rulers of this insular kingdom frequently sent representatives to Korea and China who returned with products of these more advanced cultures. These included the teachings of the Chinese philosopher, Confucius (551–479 B.C.E.), about a political and social order based on reverence for one's ancestors and deference to authority, ideas that have had an enduring effect on Japanese society. Buddhism from India, too, reached Japan via China and Korea in the middle of the sixth century. Commingled with the native

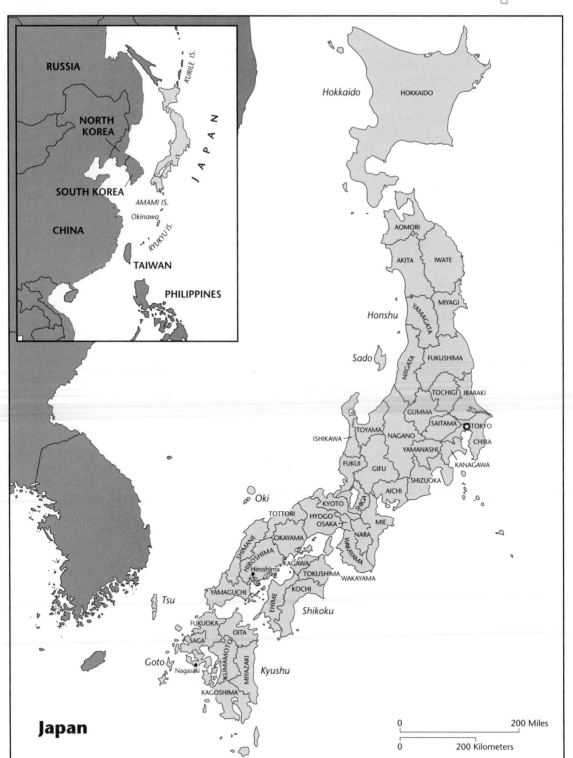

RUSSIA

NORTH
KOREA

SOUTH KOREA

CHINA

TAIWAN

PHILIPPINES

KURILE IS.

JAPAN

AMAMI IS.

Okinawa

RYUKYU IS.

Hokkaido HOKKAIDO

AOMORI

AKITA IWATE

Honshu YAMAGATA MIYAGI

Sado NIIGATA FUKUSHIMA

TOCHIGI IBARAKI

GUMMA

TOYAMA NAGANO SAITAMA TOKYO

ISHIKAWA CHIBA

YAMANASHI KANAGAWA

FUKUI GIFU

SHIZUOKA

AICHI

Oki KYOTO SHIGA

TOTTORI HYOGO MIE

OSAKA NARA

SHIMANE OKAYAMA WAKAYAMA

HIROSHIMA KAGAWA

Hiroshima TOKUSHIMA WAKAYAMA

KOCHI

YAMAGUCHI EHIME

Tsu *Shikoku*

FUKUOKA

SAGA OITA

Goto KUMAMOTO

Nagasaki MIYAZAKI *Kyushu*

KAGOSHIMA

Japan

0   200 Miles

0   200 Kilometers

religion, Shinto, Confucianism and Buddhism continue to shape everyday life in today's Japan.

For the greater part of the last fifteen centuries, Japan has existed as a unified and independent state. Up to the late twelfth century, it was ruled first by shifting coalitions of tribal groups, and then by those claiming the title of heavenly king, or emperor, and their regents, who founded the world's longest reigning—and still surviving—monarchy. In the late twelfth century, however, the emperor yielded effective rule of the country to a powerful military leader, called the *shogun*.[1]

The Tokugawa Shogunate (1603–1867)

In the early seventeenth century, the shogun, Tokugawa Ieyasu, founded a dynasty that came to bear his name. The Tokugawa Shogunate was a feudal autocracy that ruled Japan for 265 years from their seat of government in the city of Edo, today's Tokyo. A figurehead emperor resided in the city of Kyoto.

For the duration of its iron-fisted despotic rule, Tokugawa Japan was closed nearly completely to regular contacts with foreign governments and citizens. The country was divided into lands administered by the central government that included all the major cities and mining towns and 270 or so mostly rural fiefdoms governed by local lords. Roughly half of these local lords were related to or family friends of the Tokugawa rulers. Their fiefdoms were deliberately located near lands owned by other lords, so that Tokugawa's close allies could keep an eye on potential rebels. All local lords were required to visit Edo to pay homage to the shogun every few years and to contribute both funds and labor to a variety of public works undertaken by the central government. These mandatory requisitions kept the local lords sufficiently poor and weak to remain subservient to the shogunate.

Social classes in Tokugawa Japan were strictly segregated, living and working separately, each within officially demarcated neighborhoods. There was a minuscule class of nobles at the imperial court in Kyoto. There were also six officially ranked classes— warriors, farmers, artisans, merchants, "filthy hordes," and "nonhumans." Warriors, called *bushi* or samurai in Japanese, accounted for about eight percent of the population. "Filthy hordes" and "nonhumans" were "outcaste" categories, whose members were barred from "normal" occupations and made a living by collecting horse and cattle carcasses and working on their hides or by begging.[2] Women were treated as inherently inferior and subordinate to men and denied participation in public affairs even at the village level.

As a rule, boys from samurai families—and increasingly those from the families of well-to-do farmers and merchants—received elementary school education. In addition to reading, writing, and simple arithmetic, these children were taught the Confucian precepts of the correct social order and proper personal behavior.[3]

Japan in the Meiji-Taisho Era (1868–1925)

The Tokugawa regime was toppled in 1868 by an armed revolt, known as the Meiji Restoration. This revolt had its roots in the forcible entry in 1853 and 1854 of a small flotilla of American warships into the Bay of Shimoda, some 100 miles southwest of Edo, in defiance of the centuries-old official ban on unauthorized foreigners entering into Japanese territory. The arrival of U.S. Navy Commodore Matthew C. Perry's squadron and the shogun's capitulation to his demand that Japan open its ports to American naval and merchant ships, followed in quick succession by similar demands by other Western powers, gave samurai estranged from the Tokugawa and their followers an excuse to rebel against the shogunate in order, they claimed, to defend the honor of the nation.

The rebellion ushered in a period of great political and social turmoil, verging on a full-fledged civil war, but in a little over a decade, led to the fall of the Tokugawa regime and establishment of a new government by the triumphant rebel leaders in 1868. They installed a young heir to the imperial throne as the nation's new emperor, arguing that they were "restoring" the throne to Japan's true sovereign rulers, whose power had been usurped by the Tokugawa shoguns and their predecessors. All Japanese emperors took for themselves a reign title to mark their period of rule. The young emperor's reign title was Meiji ("enlightened rule"), and this important period in Japanese history came to be known as the Meiji Restoration. Over the next fifty years, Japan's government was led by an oligarchy of the leaders of the anti-Tokugawa rebellion, who ruled in the emperor's name and spearheaded a "revolution from above" that transformed a feudal country into one of the world's major industrial and military powers.

The opening of Japan to the outside world was both sudden and complete. The new Meiji government let foreigners enter the country for all legitimate purposes and sent Japanese nationals abroad to seek the knowledge and technology deemed necessary for modernizing the nation. In 1871, for example, a 107-member mission was sent to the United States and Europe, where they spent twenty months in a dozen different countries, visiting government offices, military academies, banks, factories, shipyards, and other modern institutions.[4]

As part of its modernization drive, the Meiji government replaced the six-class system of the Tokugawa period with a three-class system. The samurai class was retained, but farmers, artisans, and merchants were lumped into a single "commoner" class and the two outcaste groups were combined into a "new commoner" class. This change of names, however, did not lead to a significant change in either the social status or the economic conditions of members of each class. Those of the new commoner class, in particular, continued to face discrimination and harassment. Meiji Japan remained quite similar to Tokugawa Japan in its basic social structure. One significant difference, however, was that, in principle, all children in the country now had access to free and compulsory elementary school education, and many did take advantage of it to improve their job and life prospects.

Meiji Japan imported not only economic models and cultural forms but also political ideas from the West. The introduction of the democratic idea to Japan at this time gave rise to a "freedom and people's rights" movement led by two new political groups respectively named the Liberal and the Reform parties. Both parties called for the adoption of parliamentary government and other democratic institutions. The Meiji oligarchy responded in 1889 by promulgating a constitution modeled after that of Prussia (later Germany), another rapidly modernizing nation, and instituting a bicameral legislature, the Imperial Diet (a term that was also derived from the Prussian model).

The 1889 "Constitution of the Great Empire of Japan" formalized the leading role of the Meiji oligarchy. The charter guaranteed civil rights and freedoms to the people "subject to the limitations imposed by law" and required every law to be enacted with the consent of the Imperial Diet. But the emperor retained the prerogative to sanction and promulgate all laws; open, close, and adjourn the Diet; and declare war, make peace, and conclude international treaties. In practice, however, the ruling oligarchs exercised the emperor's powers. They dominated the powerful non-elective institutions of government, such as the Privy Council, the House of Peers (the upper chamber of the Imperial Diet), and the civil and military services. The elected representatives of the people spoke through the less powerful lower chamber of the Diet, the House of Representatives, and a few legally recognized political parties. The House of Representatives could block legislation, but the oligarchy could, if necessary, have laws enacted by imperial fiat.

Nonetheless, there was some progress toward political liberalization in Japan during an era known as **Taisho Democracy** (roughly 1912–1926). "Taisho" was the reign title of the Meiji emperor's son, who succeeded to the throne in 1912. The two original political parties, now renamed respectively Seiyukai (Constitutional Party of Political Friends) and Kenseito (Constitutional Government Party), alternately formed a government through limited electoral competition.[5]

The most important political event in the Taisho Democracy period was the 1925 revision of the House of Representatives Election Law, better known as the Universal Manhood Suffrage Law. This event represented the culmination of a tortuous campaign that had been launched in the last years of the nineteenth century but gathered momentum only in the "democratic twenties." The revision removed the requirement that a male citizen must have paid a prescribed amount of national taxes in order to be able to vote. It did not extend the suffrage to women.

Despite some important political changes, Taisho Democracy was fundamentally superficial and fragile. Class inequalities continued to divide and destabilize Japanese society. Rural Japan was dominated by a small class of wealthy landlords and urban Japan by a few giant industrial and financial conglomerates, known as *zaibatsu*, while the government bureaucracy was controlled by graduates of a single government-run university. As the Japanese economy became mired in a protracted recession after World War I and then devastated by the Great Depression in the early 1930s, the upper- and middle-class advocates of democracy at home and peace abroad faced savage attacks by the military and right-wing groups, who enjoyed the support of the increasingly restless urban and rural poor.

Japan under Military Rule and in War

Buoyed by Japanese victories in the 1894–1895 Sino-Japanese War and the 1904–1905 Russo-Japanese War, the military's political power and influence grew steadily throughout the Meiji-Taisho eras. A new emperor, Hirohito, came to the throne in 1926 and began a reign period with the title Showa ("enlightened peace"), which lasted until 1989. The military continued to become increasingly autonomous from the civilian government and started to pursue its own defense and foreign policy goals

The expansionist policy of the military was given an important boost when an army general and Seiyukai party leader, Tanaka Giichi, was appointed prime minister in 1927. The announcement by the new government of a "resolute" policy toward China, especially its northeastern region, known as Manchuria, which absorbed 70 percent of Japan's exports at the time, triggered a series of events and eventually led to the Japanese invasion and occupation of the region and the creation of a puppet state called Manchukuo in 1932.[6]

In that same year, a band of young naval officers attacked several government offices in Tokyo in an abortive coup d'état and shot to death the prime minister, Inukai Tsuyoshi, who had opposed the military's growing political power. In a similar attempt in February 1936, army troops led by radical officers invaded a number of government offices, murdered the finance minister and several others, and occupied a whole block in central Tokyo for four days.[7] Neither action immediately led to the formation of a military government, but both helped to intimidate opponents of the military inside and outside the government. All political parties were effectively silenced, then disbanded by government order in 1941. Japan had entered a period of military rule.

By that time, Japan was also in a period of a militaristic foreign policy. When the League of Nations had condemned the Japanese invasion of China in 1933, Japan walked out of the organization. Faced with growing international criticism, Japan entered an ostensibly defensive military alliance with Nazi Germany in 1936, which fascist Italy joined the following year. In the summer of 1937, Japanese army units in China used a skirmish between Japanese and Chinese troops at Lugouqiao (Marco Polo) Bridge outside Beijing as an excuse to embark on a full-scale invasion of China proper. From December of the same year to February of next year, the Japanese army unleashed a murderous rampage against civilians in the then capital city of China, an incident that has come to be known as the "Rape of Nanking." When the United States terminated its trade agreement with Japan in 1939, thus blocking Japanese access to a major source of raw materials, the government in Tokyo decided to seek an alternative source of supplies in Southeast Asia. In July 1941, Japan moved its troops into French Indochina (present-day Vietnam). In response, Washington froze Japanese-owned assets in the United States and banned the sale of oil to Japan.

Faced with the prospect of exhausting its limited fuel supplies, the Japanese government, now led by General Tojo Hideki, made the fateful decision to start a war against the United States. On December 7, 1941, Japanese naval air units executed a carefully planned surprise attack on the U.S. naval base at Pearl Harbor in Hawaii. The United States immediately declared war on Japan.

Japan had some notable military successes at the outset of the war, but it soon began to lose one major battle after another. By late 1944, its effort was reduced to a desperate defense of its homeland from increasingly frequent and devastating air raids by American bombers. In early August 1945, Japan's resistance was finally broken by the nearly total destruction of two major cities, Hiroshima and Nagasaki, by the first atomic bombs used in war. By then, virtually all major Japanese cities, including Tokyo, had been reduced to rubble by a series of relentless American bombing raids. On August 15, Emperor Hirohito gave an unprecedented radio address to the nation in which he announced Japan's unconditional surrender.

The Allied Occupation (1945–1952)

The Allied Occupation of Japan following World War II transformed an authoritarian state into a democracy.[8] The occupation, which lasted from 1945 to 1952, was formally a joint operation by the major Allies: the United States, Britain, the Soviet Union, and China. In practice, the United States, represented by General Douglas MacArthur, who held the position of **Supreme Commander for the Allied Powers (SCAP)**, played the overwhelmingly predominant role.

During the first year and a half of the occupation, SCAP pursued two major goals: the complete demilitarization and democratization of Japan. The Japanese armed forces were swiftly dismantled, troops were demobilized, military production was halted, and wartime leaders were either arrested or purged from their positions in the government. Seven of them, including General Tojo, were executed for war crimes. Militaristic and antidemocratic political, legal, economic, and social institutions and practices were abolished. At the same time, the workers' right to organize was recognized, women were given the vote, and major *zaibatsu* were dissolved. However, much of the Japanese government bureaucracy was left intact. Its most powerful and nationalistic constituent, the Ministry of Home Affairs, was divided into smaller and weaker ministries and agencies; but the national bureaucracy as a whole not only survived but even gained in power and prestige during the occupation as the de facto interpreter and implementer of SCAP directives and policies. The enormous power of Japan's bureaucracy outlasted the occupation and continued to be felt for the greater part of the postwar period.

The most important step taken toward the democratization of Japan during the Occupation was the promulgation of a new constitution. Based on a draft prepared in 1946 by a handful of American lawyers at General MacArthur's behest, it was a thoroughly democratic and uniquely pacifist constitution, although it inherited its basic format from the imperial Japanese constitution. The new constitution relegated the emperor to a purely symbolic role, while naming the people as the sovereign of the state. It also elevated the bicameral Diet to the position of the state's highest and sole law-making organ with all its members, including those in the reorganized and renamed upper house, the House of Councilors, directly elected by the people. More power was given to the lower house, the House of Representatives.

The preamble to the Japanese constitution states: "We, the Japanese people, desire peace for all time and are deeply conscious of the high ideals controlling human relationship, and we have determined to preserve our security and existence, trusting in the justice and faith of the peace-loving peoples of the world." This is followed by a "peace clause" in Article 9, which reads:

> Aspiring sincerely to an international peace based on justice and order, the Japanese people forever renounce war as a sovereign right of the nation and the threat or use of force as means of settling international disputes.
>
> In order to accomplish the aim of the preceding paragraph, land, sea, and air forces, as well as other war potential, will never be maintained. The right of belligerency of the state will not be recognized.

Contrary to the spirit, if not the letter, of this provision, a military force, euphemistically called the **Self-Defense Forces (SDF),** was created in the early 1950s, ironically at the insistence of the United States government, and has since grown into one of the largest and best-equipped military forces in the world. But the pacifist spirit that the article represents lives on in the political values of the majority of Japanese people.

Contemporary Japan (1952 to the Present)

Competitive party politics also revived after the war. The prewar Seiyukai reemerged as the Japan Liberal Party, which dominated Japanese politics for much of the occupation period. The Liberals' major rival, the Japan Socialist Party (JSP), won a slim plurality in the Diet elections in 1947 and formed a coalition government with the Japan Progressive Party (later called the Democratic Party), which was descended from the prewar Kenseito. But the Liberals returned to power a year and a half later and thereafter steadily consolidated their hold on the Diet. The Liberal and the Democratic parties merged into the Liberal

Democratic Party (LDP) in 1955, which would effectively monopolize control of government until the early 1990s. Despite its name, the LDP was, and remains, a conservative political party.

From 1955 to 1993, the LDP won every Diet election and formed every government. Japan's political system was what is called a **predominant-party regime.** But this long and generally stable era of unbroken LDP rule was not uneventful. A major political crisis occurred in 1960 over the revision of the U.S.–Japan Mutual Security Treaty that had been signed at the end of the occupation in 1951. The LDP government's proposal to revise and strengthen the treaty provoked fierce opposition both in the Diet and in the streets of Tokyo and other major cities. Hundreds of thousands of protesters, led by JSP Diet members and leaders of the General Council of Trade Unions of Japan (**Sohyo**) and the National Federation of Students' Self-Government Associations (*Zengakuren*), marched against the treaty and Prime Minister Kishi

Demonstrators against renewal of U.S.–Japan Mutual Security Treaty in front of Diet Building in Tokyo, May 1960. *Source:* AP Images.

Nobusuke's government. The protesters warned that the treaty would make Japan a semi-permanent dependent military ally of the United States and an enemy of Japan's closer neighbors, China and the Soviet Union. Nonetheless, the government pushed the revised treaty through the Diet, where the LDP had a strong majority.

The government's action provoked such a violent public reaction with an anti-American tinge that President Eisenhower's scheduled state visit to Japan was canceled, and Prime Minister Kishi and his cabinet were forced to resign. The Japan Socialist Party, which led the protest movement, split amid the turmoil, and a group of moderates formed a separate party. This split caused considerable long-term damage to the JSP and its major trade union ally, *Sohyo,* while helping the LDP and *Sohyo*'s conservative rival, the Japanese Confederation of Labor (**Domei**).

The experience of the 1960 political crisis led Kishi's successors to avoid tackling controversial constitutional and security policy issues and concentrate on economic problems. This change in the LDP's strategy ushered in two decades of political stability and phenomenal economic growth for Japan.

The country was jolted, however, by the "oil shock" of 1973, when the Organization of Petroleum Exporting Countries (OPEC) announced its decision to drastically raise the price of crude oil sold by its members and, in some cases, to suspend exports altogether. The decision was intended to pressure importers of Middle Eastern oil to support the Arab states in their conflict with Israel. OPEC's action caused a widespread panic and a sharp economic downturn in Japan, which was heavily dependent on oil imports. A second oil shock followed in 1979 in the wake of the Islamic revolution in Iran, although it did not have as devastating an impact on the Japanese economy as did the earlier crisis. Nevertheless, after these shocks and in an increasingly competitive international trade and investment environment, the Japanese economy never regained the vigor it had boasted in the preceding two decades.

Despite the weaker performance of the Japanese economy, the LDP maintained its majority position in the Diet through the 1980s. The socialist parties, on the other hand, continued to suffer a decline in electoral performance, due largely to the declining influence of organized labor, particularly left-wing unions affiliated with *Sohyo*, in an increasingly middle-class society. The leftist *Sohyo* was the largest national federation of Japanese labor in 1960, but by 1967 it was second to the more conservative *Domei*. In 1987, a new national labor federation, the Japanese Trade Union Confederation (**Rengo**), was formed under *Domei*'s leadership. *Sohyo* joined *Rengo* two years later, which worked against the political interests of the JSP and to the advantage of the LDP.

In the 1970s and 1980s, Japan was rocked by a series of political scandals involving many top LDP leaders. In 1976, a former prime minister, Tanaka Kakuei, was found guilty of accepting bribes from the Lockheed Corporation for brokering the purchase of Lockheed planes by a Japanese airline. In the "Recruit" scandal of 1988, more than a dozen LDP leaders and senior bureaucrats were charged with receiving gifts and contributions from a job-placement company.

Such scandals hurt the LDP's electoral fortunes, but not to the extent of threatening its control of government until Japan fell into a protracted economic downturn in the late 1980s and 1990s. The economic troubles were blamed on the LDP government's poor judgment and incompetence. Its critics charged that the government made it much too easy for businesses to borrow money in the second half of the 1980s; this led, in turn, to a "bubble economy," a situation in which speculative borrowing produces overpriced real estate, overvalued stocks, and other bubbles that are liable to "pop" and cause a sharp economic downturn when investor confidence is shaken. The LDP government responded to Japan's popped economic bubble with an excessively tight financial and tax policy, which gave rise to a deep and protracted recession. As a result, for the first time since it was founded in 1955, the party lost its majority position in the House of Councilors in 1989. It then suffered an even more serious defeat in the 1993 House of Representatives election. This led to the formation of two short-lived coalition governments without the participation by the LDP that gave way to a "politics-makes-strange-bedfellows" governing coalition made up of the LDP and its long-time principal rival, the Japan Socialist Party—which by then had been renamed the Social Democratic Party (SDP).[9] Since then, the LDP has remained the senior partner in a series of coalition governments in which one of its leaders has been the country's prime minister.

Themes and Implications

Historical Junctures and Political Themes

Japan joined the modern world of states in the late nineteenth century after two and a half centuries of self-imposed isolation. To its leaders and people, the world then appeared divided between powerful, arrogant, and self-aggrandizing states, on the one hand, and powerless and often conquered states, on the other. It clearly saw itself as part of the latter group.

To survive in such a world, a state must either be independently powerful both economically and militarily, as Japan tried to be before World War II, or seek a powerful ally's protection, as it has done in the postwar period. Wartime experiences, particularly the horror of the atomic bombings, led most Japanese to abandon faith in military force as a guarantee for national security. The only alternative was cooperation with other nations, particularly the most powerful ones. For Japan, this has meant a close relationship with the United States. Postwar Japan has thus been an avowed internationalist state, committed to an active role in global organizations, but with a degree of realist cynicism in its view that national power is what truly matters in international relations.

In the wake of the September 11, 2001, terrorist attacks on the United States, Japanese public opinion was overwhelmingly in favor of participating in the war on terrorism. When the war turned out to be a military campaign against the Taliban in Afghanistan, however, the Japanese public reaction turned more cautious and, when the war was expanded to include the invasion of Iraq in the spring of 2003, Japanese public opinion became overwhelmingly negative. Nonetheless, the Japanese government continued, at persistent U.S. insistence, to support American-led military actions in Afghanistan and Iraq with the dispatch of Self-Defense Force troops, arms, and equipment to the conflict areas.

Japan's entry into the modern world also exposed its citizens to the democratic idea. By the 1890s, though still an autocratic oligarchy, Meiji Japan had formally become a constitutional monarchy with a partially elected parliament and vocal political parties. Its government was faced with persistent popular demands for more democracy and greater citizen participation in government. Before World War II, however, Japan remained far more committed to rapid industrialization and military buildup than to democratization. Nonetheless, the experiment with democratic politics in prewar Japan, albeit half-hearted and ultimately unsuccessful, prepared the Japanese for the democracy that was introduced after the war. The democratic idea is an integral element of political culture in today's Japan.

Meiji Japan developed an industrial economy in a country that had neither the natural resources nor the technologies needed for successful modernization in the late nineteenth and early twentieth centuries. Meiji-era development therefore involved extensive and systematic intervention by the state in the management of the national economy, an approach that later came to be known as **industrial policy.** This model of economic growth was spectacularly successful in both prewar and postwar Japan and was emulated by many other nations, especially those in East Asia. Industrial policy, however, ceased to work as effectively in the late twentieth century as globalization challenged the sanctity of national boundaries and the role of the state in governing the economy significantly declined. For more than a decade from the early 1990s onward, the Japanese economy was mired in a protracted recession that seemed to defy any remedy based on industrial policy.

The Japanese began to develop a strong sense of national identity early in their history, and among members of its small elite, as early as the late seventh century. Following the failed attempt by Mongolian forces to invade the country in the late thirteenth century, a nationalist ideology was deliberately constructed and propagated with the aid of a divine-land myth. On the other hand, regional, communal, and class-based identities were suppressed and failed to grow strong enough to compete with national identity. The nationalist ideology was subsequently systematically cultivated by leaders of Meiji and early Showa Japan and successfully harnessed to their aggressive foreign and military policies, which eventually led to the Pacific War (1941–1945). The ideology appeared to die with Japan's defeat in the war, but there are some signs of its revival, though in a much weaker form, in the first decade of the twenty-first century.

Implications for Comparative Politics

Japan is a hybrid nation in several senses. It is geographically and ethnically an Asian nation with a very homogeneous population, but the historical pattern of its political and economic development has more in common with some European nations than with its Asian neighbors. Japanese modernization and economic development came late, in comparison with western Europe and the United States, but Japan was an early developer compared with much of the rest of the world. Once one of the most aggressive militarist nations in the world, it has been a pacifistic democracy since World War II. Its hybrid character in these and other aspects makes Japan an exceptionally interesting and rich case for multifaceted comparison with other advanced industrial democracies, as well as with newly industrialized and developing nations.

Japan's geographical, historical, and cultural attributes make it particularly interesting to compare its politics with those of other Asian nations, especially those in the Confucian cultural zone of Northeast Asia: China, including Taiwan, and North and South Korea. Japan also shares the rice paddy culture with these countries and those in Southeast Asia, with which it also has close historical ties. Rice paddy culture encouraged, on the one hand, early development of sophisticated water management, irrigation, and hydraulic engineering technologies necessary for the successful cultivation of rice and, on the other hand, a certain humility and deference to the forces and whims of nature that often verged on fatalism. In the view of some scholars, rice paddy culture, with its emphasis on the importance of water and control of water, was also conducive to the development of an autocratic state. According to this view, whoever gained control of water in such a society would likely gain control of the economy and often even the reins of the state. Aspects of this culture still influence not only religion, festivals, and art, but also a variety of government practices and politics throughout the region.

The evident ethnic and cultural similarities and affinities between Japan and other East Asian nations should also encourage us to try to understand and explain the many important differences between them.[10] Why, for example, did Japan begin to modernize its political system and social institutions and industrialize its economy so much earlier than its Asian neighbors? Why has postwar Japan had a stable democratic system, while most Asian nations have experienced authoritarian government, unstable multiparty politics, or extensive political violence, including revolution? Is there anything that other East Asian nations can learn from the Japanese experience with modernization, industrialization, and democratization?

Japan's geographical, historical, and cultural attributes are certainly markedly different from those of Western nations. Yet there are many fruitful comparisons to be made between Japan and the West. Why, for example, did Japan develop a national unity and identity, and unite the nation, earlier than most Western nations? How has Japan adopted institutions, ideas, and values from the West in the modernization of its economy and the democratization of its politics while still maintaining fundamental aspects of its unique culture and national identity?

Comparisons between modern Japan and modern Germany are particularly interesting. These nations entered the modern world about the same time in the nineteenth century, pursued rapid economic development, became major military powers by the early twentieth century, started and lost World War II, were occupied and transformed by their wartime enemies, and reemerged in the postwar world as two of the world's most economically powerful and politically stable democracies. How can we explain such remarkable similarities between these two very different countries? What political lessons might be learned from the Japanese and German experiences, particularly in their transition from autocracy to democracy?

Japan thus lends itself, as few other nations do, to very interesting and enlightening comparisons with nations in quite different geographic regions and cultural areas of the world.

SECTION 2 Political Economy and Development

Modern Japan has been an interventionist state throughout most of its history, meaning that the government has played a large and active role in the nation's economic development. At its birth during the Meiji Restoration in the mid-nineteenth century, the early leaders of modern Japan were determined to build a "rich nation with a strong army." Japan thrived in the subsequent decades as long as its economy grew at a rapid and steady pace. But after World War I, as its economy fell into a serious and protracted slump, the Japanese state began to face domestic political turmoil. The devastation of its economy by the worldwide depression a decade later set Japan on a course of increasingly harsh authoritarian rule at home and militarist expansionism abroad. The course of events led eventually to a fatal war with the United States and its allies.

After World War II, Japan abandoned the "strong army" part of the earlier national agenda to concentrate on the "rich nation" part. This policy generated a long period of economic growth and political stability under the seemingly permanent rule of the Liberal Democratic Party. The good times came to an end, however: the economic bubble burst in the early 1990s and Japan has since been beset with deep and pervasive political and economic uncertainties.

Politics and economics in Japan have long been closely and causally related to each other. This section looks in some detail at how they interact, in what institutional and cultural contexts, and with what significant effects on citizens' lives and Japanese society.

State and Economy

Wars and Japanese Economic Development

The rapid growth of the Japanese economy in the late 1950s through the early 1970s has rightly been called an economic miracle. The impressive performance of the Japanese economy, however, did not begin after World War II. The economy had grown steadily by an average of about 3 percent per year from the Meiji Restoration in 1868 through the early twentieth century, and accelerated to more than 5 percent per year in the 1930s.

The worldwide depression of the early 1930s devastated the Japanese economy, especially its agrarian sector. The sharp drops in the prices of rice and raw silk—the two products on which most Japanese farmers depended for income—caused widespread and severe poverty and suffering among them. Unlike most other industrial nations of the period, however, Japan recovered remarkably quickly from the worst effects of the depression, thanks initially to vastly increased public spending by the government, especially military expenditures following the beginning of the Japanese invasion of northern China in the fall of 1931, and subsequently to rapidly growing exports of industrial goods. Over the five-year period between 1932 and 1937, the total value of Japanese exports tripled. Driven by the thriving export trade, the production of industrial goods also increased very rapidly: between 1935 and 1940, the production of metals, chemicals, and machinery increased by, respectively, 46, 57, and 170 percent.[11] On the eve of World War II, Japan was already one of the world's fastest-growing and most competitive economies.

The rapid growth of the Japanese economy was due to a combination of domestic factors, such as government policy, the entrepreneurial talent and initiative of business leaders, and a motivated, literate, and increasingly skilled work force. International factors, including wars, were also important. The Sino-Japanese War (1894–1895) and the Russo-Japanese War (1904–1905) significantly contributed to the growth of Japanese heavy industry. World War I was a windfall for Japanese business, even though, or rather because, Japan was not directly involved as a combatant. Taking advantage of the disruption of the existing European-dominated trade networks caused by the war, especially in Asia, Japanese textile, steel, machine tool, chemical, and shipping industries quickly expanded. The wartime boom left Japan's international trade balance with a surplus for the first time in the nation's history.[12]

Even World War II, which devastated Japan physically and psychologically, was in a sense a blessing in disguise for its economy. As successful as it had been, the prewar Japanese economy had been hobbled with a structural problem that impeded growth and development: the grossly uneven distribution of income and wealth. Extensive poverty not only generated considerable social tension, but also prevented the formation of a sufficiently large domestic market for Japan's own manufactures, not to mention imports from abroad. The post-World War II Occupation-sponsored reforms significantly reduced the concentration of wealth and economic power in Japan. The assets and control of the largest *zaibatsu* corporations were divided up into several new and independent firms. Well over half of Japan's urban workers were unionized by the end of the 1940s. Most of the landlord-owned farmland was redistributed among poor tenant farmers, which reduced the latter's population from nearly 30 percent to about 5 percent of Japanese farmers.[13] This reform transformed rural farmers from an important source of prewar political radicalism into one of the most reliable blocs of conservative (that is, LDP) voting in postwar Japan. Altogether, these changes vastly expanded Japan's middle class and its domestic consumer markets.

Furthermore, the Occupation's demilitarization program forced Japan not only to disarm but also to quit the arms trade. This freed Japan from the burden of military spending, which had swallowed up about one-third of the total budget in the early 1930s and three-quarters at the beginning of World War II. As a result, Japan was able to devote its capital, labor, and technology almost exclusively to the production of goods and services for civilian consumption. This shift soon facilitated Japan's emergence as one of the most productive, competitive, and wealthiest nations in the postwar world.

The Korean War of the 1950s and the Vietnam War of the 1960s were also highly beneficial for the Japanese economy. Japanese factories were the main suppliers of the goods and services required by the U.S. military during both wars, which triggered a series of long economic booms. By the time these war-induced booms ended in the early 1970s, Japan had become the second-largest market economy in the world.

The Cold War contributed to the Japanese economic miracle, too. The U.S.–Soviet rivalry led to a dramatic shift in American policy toward both Japan and Germany. By 1948, Washington's primary objectives were no longer the total demilitarization and democratization of the two occupied nations, but their swift economic recovery and incorporation into the U.S.-led anticommunist ideological and military bloc. After China came under communist rule in 1949 and the Korean War broke out in 1950, Japan's new role as a key ally of the United States in Asia became even more evident.

From 1947 to 1951, the United States helped Japan rebuild its war-devastated economy by providing aid, including food, worth about $1.8 billion. The Occupation authorities also helped the Japanese government overcome postwar economic chaos, especially rampant inflation, by balancing the government budget, raising taxes, imposing price and wage freezes, and resuming limited foreign trade. After Japan regained its independence in 1952, the United States continued to help by opening its markets to Japanese exports and granting Japanese firms access to advanced industrial technology developed by U.S. firms. The United States supported Japan's admission to the United Nations, the International Monetary Fund (IMF), the World Bank, and the General Agreement on Tariffs and Trade (GATT). Membership in such international organizations enabled Japan to gain access to overseas raw materials, merchandise and capital markets, and advanced industrial technology and scientific information. All these factors helped Japan turn itself into a formidable export machine that began producing large trade surpluses by the mid-1960s.

The State's Role in the Economy

Government has played a key role in the development of the modern Japanese economy from the very beginning. In the mid-nineteenth century, the Meiji state founded and operated munitions factories, mines, railroads, telegraph and telephone companies, and textile mills. Within a decade and a half, most of these businesses were sold at token prices to private entrepreneurs, some of whom subsequently emerged as heads of *zaibatsu* conglomerates.[14] During the rest of the nineteenth century and the first forty years of the twentieth century, these corporate empires dominated Japanese industry. They spearheaded the rapid expansion of the economy in cooperation with a fervently nationalistic and disciplined state bureaucracy.[15] The

bureaucracy provided *zaibatsu*-affiliated firms direct subsidies, tax breaks, tariff protection, and roads, railroads, port facilities, and communications networks built with tax money.

The state's role as the patron and protector of domestic industry continued after the post-World War II Allied Occupation. In fact, no sooner had the Occupation ended in 1952 than the Japanese government began to devise and implement policies and programs to jump-start the war-ravaged economy. Under its so-called industrial policy, the government provided investment funds, tax breaks, foreign exchange, and foreign technologies to specifically targeted strategic industries, including electric power, steel, transportation, and coal mining. Subsequently added to this package of special favors for the chosen industries was a system of informal government counsel known as **administrative guidance.** Such counsel often led to mergers and the formation of cartels, which gained significant advantages in competing with domestic rivals and foreign competitors.

Over the years, the benefits of industrial policy shifted to the semiconductor, computer, aerospace, and other high-tech industries. The forms of government pro-business favors also changed. The new strategies included **nontariff barriers (NTBs)** against foreign imports, public funds for corporate research and development projects, and joint public–private projects to promote cutting-edge technologies.[16]

By the 1980s, surging Japanese exports had made Japan the world's largest creditor nation and the United States began to view Japanese trade as a serious threat to its own industries. This led to a series of policies aimed at slowing the growth of Japanese imports. Of particular importance among them was the joint decision made in September 1985 at The Plaza Hotel in New York—thus subsequently known as the Plaza Accord—by representatives of the U.S., Japanese, and European financial authorities to force the dollar to depreciate against other major currencies, the yen in particular, so as to blunt the competitiveness of Japanese exports. In other words, the dollar was worth fewer yen, which had the effect of making Japanese exports more expensive for Americans to buy. Alarmed by the spectre of an impending depressive impact that the multilateral decision threatened to have on the Japanese economy in general, and export-dependent small businesses in particular, the

Bank of Japan (BOJ) drastically cut interest rates, inadvertently triggering a hyperinflation (a "bubble") of stock and real estate prices. Toward the end of 1989, the Japanese government belatedly and abruptly tightened lending regulations in a panic and the BOJ raised the interest rates. This sudden policy reversal burst the bubble and subsequently touched off a protracted recession.

Most critics blame inept monetary and fiscal policies for hatching both the economic bubble and the protracted recession. Some, however, point also to the "**iron triangle**" of politicians, bureaucrats, and business leaders (discussed in the next section, "Governance and Policy-Making") for letting the bubble grow as large as it did and then, when it burst, delaying the implementation of much-needed policy responses. Still others criticize the LDP government's rush in the late mid-1980s to integrate Japan into the global economy, which made the country more vulnerable to external economic trends.

Until the early 1990s, Japan had maintained a nearly total ban on the import of foreign rice. A sudden shortage caused by an exceptionally poor crop in 1993 led the nation to import a limited amount of foreign rice for the first time. As a result of multilateral trade negotiations held in the same year, the Japanese government agreed to increase its annual rice import to 8 percent of domestic consumption by 2000. Angry farmers were mollified by the payment of generous compensation. At the end of 1998, the Japanese government decided, with the farmers' acquiescence, to replace the import quotas with tariffs at prohibitive rates of about 1,000 percent. As a result, Japan imports only about 8 percent of the approximately 9.3 million tons of rice annually consumed in the country.

Notwithstanding such fastidious protection of its rice farming and farmers, the degree of Japan's self-sufficiency in food supply, calculated in calorie terms, decreased from 79 percent in 1960 to 40 percent in 2003, compared to Britain's 70 percent, Germany's 84 percent, France's 122 percent, and the United States' 128 percent. Japan thus ranks 29th in food independence today among the 30 OECD member states. This is, to an important extent, a result of the protectionism focused on rice and a few other crops, which has weakened domestic agriculture by depriving farmers of incentives to diversify their crops to keep up with changing consumer preferences. This concentration on rice farming was adopted immediately after the end of World War II when the government embraced wide-ranging protectionist policies, including highly restrictive regulations governing farmland ownership and the distribution and marketing of rice, as well as subsidies for construction of rural roads, irrigation works, and other farm-related infrastructure. These policies gave birth to a gigantic national network of another kind of iron triangle, this time farmers, politicians, and bureaucrats, joining together to successfully resist and prevent any effective reform of a long-outdated food-supply system.

The inability of Japan's domestic agriculture to meet the nation's food needs has become a serious and growing concern for the Japanese public. In a December 2006 government poll, about 80 percent of respondents expressed worries about the problem and nearly half of respondents believed that domestic supply should meet at least 60 percent of the nation's needs.

Japan's financial sector has also remained under strong state control and protection. Administrative guidance has led the nation's major banks and securities firms to form tight networks of mutual cooperation and assistance, backed by an implicit government commitment to bail out their members in trouble, if necessary. In other words, the state has assumed the role of an implicit lender of last resort to the banks and securities firms, which has helped weak and internationally uncompetitive financial institutions survive. Nevertheless, in the hard times of the 1990s and early 2000s, many of these institutions—saddled with bad loans accumulated in the bubble economy of the preceding decade—went bankrupt. Those that survived stopped lending, especially to small businesses, thus effectively starving them of investment funds and aggravating the recession.

The Japanese government set up the Financial Services Agency in 2001 with a view to helping the banks and securities firms rid themselves of bad loans and begin to lend again. The agency has since mediated a series of bank mergers to create some of the largest financial institutions in the world, such as the Mitsubishi-Tokyo-UFJ Bank conglomerate. The creation of these giant banks, however, has not helped create new jobs, spark new demand, or lift Japan out of the long recession. Banking thus remains one of the weakest sectors of the Japanese economy.

Japan's financial sector has also suffered from the presence of a monopolistic public service organization, Japan Post, which, in addition to being the national postal system, served both as the primary savings bank for most Japanese and as the largest provider of life insurance for their households. In recent years, the personal savings and life insurance premiums in Japan Post's accounts accounted for a quarter of the personal financial assets in the country. The bulk of this enormous fund was invested in "safe" government bonds that financed a wide range of public and semipublic corporations and public works, such as highways and bridges. But, once built, many of these were hardly used due to either insufficient demand or high tolls. Japan Post's operations thus tended not only to suppress competition in Japan's banking and insurance markets, but also to divert huge amounts of funds away from truly needed and productive investments.

Japan Post was officially privatized and divided into four separate companies in the fall of 2007, thanks largely to the single-minded campaign waged by a maverick LDP Diet member and prime minister (April 2001–September 2006), Koizumi Junichiro. While underway, Koizumi's campaign met and survived fierce and persistent opposition from his fellow LDP Diet members, whose success at the ballot box depended on the votes of Japan Post's 270,000 or so civil service employees. It was opposed just as fiercely by the bureaucrats in various government ministries who counted on postretirement jobs at public corporations financed by government bonds, which were in turn backed by the postal savings and life insurance policy premiums collected by Japan Post. The four officially private corporate heirs to the Japan Post monopoly still remain under the control of a holding company, one-third of which is owned by the government. The group continues to threaten to overwhelm not only financial institutions in the private sector but even the public regulations that govern the operations of the financial industry. The case of Japan Post thus illustrates just how difficult it is even for an exceptionally strong-willed reformist prime minister to bring about a much-needed change in the country's economy in the face of widespread and determined opposition by vested interests inside the government and ruling party.

Society and Economy

The Private Sector

The private industrial sector of the Japanese economy is characterized by interdependence and networking among a small number of giant firms, on the one hand, and a vast number of small firms, on the other. In 2004, about 97 percent of some 576,400 companies in the manufacturing sector were small businesses with fewer than one hundred employees per firm. Most big businesses are affiliated with one or another of several huge business alliances, commonly known as *keiretsu.* Each *keiretsu* is composed of a major bank, and several large manufacturing, trading, shipping, construction, and insurance companies that are of comparable size and horizontally linked with one another in their economic activities. There are also more than a dozen similar but smaller business alliances, including those built around the major automobile manufacturers, notably Toyota and Nissan. These, too, are usually called *keiretsu,* but they are characterized more by vertical ties that link several large firms to numerous smaller ones, which serve as subcontractors to their bigger partners.

The Mitsubishi Group is a good example of a horizontally organized *keiretsu.* Although it is a descendant of a pre-World War II *zaibatsu* with the same name, today's Mitsubishi Group is no longer owned or controlled by a single family. It is composed of about thirty formally independent, coequal corporations whose presidents form an informal executive committee called the Friday Club, which, as its name suggests, meets once a week as a rule. Each of the member corporations is a leading firm in its own line of business, including Mitsubishi Motors, Nikon Corporation, and Kirin Brewery, as well as the Bank of Tokyo-Mitsubishi UFJ financial institution noted above.

By contrast, the Toyota Group, led by the world's largest automaker, Toyota Motor Corporation, represents a vertically organized *keiretsu.* Under the automobile maker's direct control are a dozen large corporations that maintain subcontracting relationships with about 250 small firms. In turn, many of these subcontractors hand down some of their work to even smaller firms. In other words, the Toyota Group is a huge pyramid made up of several hundred legally independent but operationally interdependent firms.

The subcontracting system provides Japan's small businesses with jobs and access to both markets and some of the advanced technologies in the possession of the big businesses within their group. The big businesses benefit from cost-cutting made possible by the use of subcontractors' employees on an as-needed basis rather than those on their own regular payroll. During an economic downturn, the big firms protect themselves by reducing orders placed with their subcontractors or delaying payment for orders already filled.

Both types of *keiretsu* are now faced with the threat posed by the rapidly increasing acquisition of large ownership shares of Japanese firms by foreign investors. As Japanese businesses have struggled to survive hard times by restructuring themselves, many have come under foreign control through mergers and acquisitions. A U.S. investment company, Ripplewood Holdings, acquired a Japanese bank, the Tokyo-based Shinsei Bank, in 2000, the first example of a Japanese bank coming under a foreign firm's management and control. In the meantime, the leading U.S. automobile manufacturer, Ford, has gained equity in half a dozen Japanese companies, including Mazda, the nation's fourth-ranked car maker, while the French company, Renault, now owns 44 percent of its Japanese counterpart, Nissan, and the British telecommunications giant, Vodafone, owns two-thirds of Japan Telecom's shares. Faced with slumping stock prices and their depressive effects on the worth of many Japanese firms, an increasing number of companies have begun to take steps to reinforce *keiretsu*-type ties among themselves in order to protect themselves against hostile takeovers by foreign investors.

Women account for about 50 percent of Japan's labor force. Their ranks have grown in recent decades for several reasons, including their increasing level of education. Between 1990 and 2006, the percentage of female high school graduates who continue on to junior college or university increased more than

15 percent, from 37.4 percent to 52.5 percent.[17] Women with college diplomas tend to work outside the home before, and increasingly after, they marry. Another factor in the increasing rate of female employment is the diffusion of home appliances, such as refrigerators and washing machines, which have freed married women from many traditional housekeeping chores and permitted them to seek part-time jobs. Furthermore, Japan's two-decade-long economic downturn has made it hard for many families to make ends meet with one income. Especially since the 1990s, the growing number of women seeking jobs for additional income has been matched by the increasing need of service industries for low-paid temporary and part-time employees. The average female worker's pay in the manufacturing sector was 59.7 percent of the average male worker's in Japan in 2003, compared to 80.6 percent in Britain and 91.0 percent in Sweden.[18] Japanese women also lag considerably behind their counterparts in most other advanced industrial nations in making inroads into management ranks. Women accounted for only 10 percent of management-level personnel at Japanese companies in 2003, compared to 46 percent in the U.S. and more than 30 percent in Britain, France, Germany, and Sweden.

Another important characteristic of the Japanese economy is the close, and normally cooperative, relationships between labor unions and management. As discussed in Section 1, several labor federations merged in the late 1980s into a larger national organization, the Japanese Trade Union Confederation (*Rengo*). This merger was a result of the growing weakness of the labor movement, which had seen a decline in the proportion of unionized labor in Japan's industrial work force from about 35 percent in 1970 to 25 percent in 1990, and well below 20 percent in 2006. While the larger unions continue to participate in the nationally coordinated annual wage negotiations with employers, known as the **spring labor offensive,** the radicalism and militancy that once characterized labor's position in such negotiations have steadily diminished.

By the time Japan's economic miracle ended around 1990, the country had become virtually free of violent labor disputes and there was no longer a sharp awareness of class divisions among its people. Thanks to a relatively egalitarian pattern of income

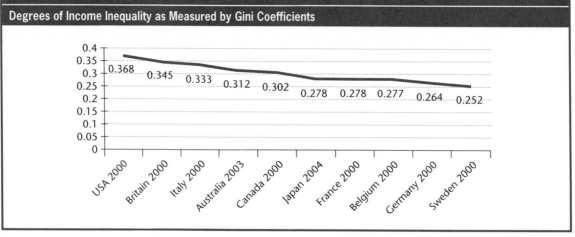

FIGURE 5.2

Degrees of Income Inequality as Measured by Gini Coefficients

Source: Honkawa Data Tribune, *Shakai jitsujo deta zuroku* (Graphic presentations of data on social conditions), http://www2. ttcn.ne.jp/honkawa/4660.html.

distribution (see Figure 5.2), most Japanese had come to identify themselves as members of the middle class and as economically well off as most other Japanese. This popular perception, however, began to change in the late 1990s as the Japanese economy not only ceased to grow, but actually shrank. According to the 2006 OECD economic survey of the country, Japan's rate of relative poverty is now one of the highest among the organization's member states, due partly to the rapidly increasing age of its population, but, more importantly, to an increase in the number of part-time, or nonregular, workers, which has reached 30 percent of the nation's total labor force. The situation is aggravated by the relatively low level of overall government spending on social welfare and a pattern of public benefits (such as social security) distribution that does not give due advantage to those with lower incomes. Young workers—especially those who work part-time or have temporary jobs—are in a particularly difficult situation in the current period of slow economic growth.

Employment, Social Security, and Taxation

Japanese workers earn wages comparable to those of most North American and western European workers, although they are paid in a somewhat different way. The typical Japanese wage or salary consists of relatively low basic monthly pay, substantial semi-annual bonuses, and several allowances of variable amounts. Allowances are paid, for example, for dependents, housing, and commuting costs, and the midsummer and year-end bonuses usually amount to about one-third of the basic annual wage. Retirement benefits for most employees consist of lump-sum severance pay equal to about thirty-five months' salary and, for those who satisfy the age and length-of-service requirements, a contribution-based pension. Many employees of large firms are provided with company-subsidized housing and access to company-owned recreational, sporting, and vacationing facilities.

While Japan's postwar economy was expanding, the demand for young and cheap labor continued to grow. But the country's population growth rates began to level off in the mid-1950s and then decline in the mid-1970s. The result was a perennially tight labor market and low unemployment rate. In order to attract and keep skilled workers under these circumstances, many employers guaranteed such employees, explicitly or implicitly, job security until retirement, which was usually at about age fifty-five. This practice, which almost exclusively benefited male workers, was known as the **lifetime employment** system and became a

Current Challenges

The Protracted Recession

Economic conditions changed radically in Japan in the early 1990s as the economy fell into a protracted recession. The hard times forced many firms to abandon the traditional practices of lifetime employment and virtually automatic annual pay raises. Some firms began to pay their employees on the basis of performance ("merit"), transfer them to lower-paying positions, often in subsidiary firms, or force them to retire at much younger ages than previously required. As has happened in the United States, increasing numbers of people of all ages started to work on a part-time, consulting, work-on-call, or work-at-home basis.

These changes caused considerable hardships to many families, particularly because the Japanese social security system is relatively undeveloped compared to its counterparts in most Western nations. It was not until after World War II that the Japanese government made a systematic effort to provide a minimum level of social security for all citizens. The development of a comprehensive national social security system was mandated by the 1947 Constitution, which says that "In all spheres of life, the State shall use its endeavors for the promotion and extension of social welfare and security, and of public health." During the four decades following the Allied Occupation, a number of state-sponsored and wholly or partially state-financed social security programs were established. But in the wake of the 1973 oil crisis, the government began to attempt to shift the major burden of financing the rapidly expanding social security system to the private sector.

This so-called Japanese-style welfare society approach failed to restrain the growth of either public or private welfare expenditures in subsequent years. Today, social security claims a little over a quarter of the annual government budget and is the largest public expenditure item in Japan. The tax-financed pension, medical insurance, unemployment insurance, and workers' compensation programs provide virtually all Japanese citizens with some social security benefits. However, the amounts of the benefits are hardly sufficient to meet the needs of most citizens.

Like people in most other developed countries, Japanese pay both direct and indirect taxes. The former include income, corporate, inheritance,

and land-value taxes; the latter include consumption (sales), alcohol, tobacco, petroleum, and stock exchange taxes. A capital gains tax was introduced in 1989. The maximum rates of national and local income taxes are, as of 2008, 37 percent and 13 percent, respectively. The average Japanese taxpayer pays about 23 percent of his or her annual income in national and local taxes. This is only a little lower than the rate paid by the average U.S. taxpayer, but considerably lower than that paid by the average western European taxpayer. The average Japanese, however, does not enjoy as many tax-supported social welfare benefits and public amenities as does the average western European. This makes most Japanese wary about making nonessential purchases, an attitude that collectively has helped to suppress consumer spending and prolong the recession.

In the last few decades of the twentieth century, Japan was one of the most expensive countries in the world in which to live or travel. Since mid-1999, however, the nation has experienced a steady decline in consumer prices, including housing costs. The trend toward lower prices should be a boon to Japanese citizens and foreign visitors alike. But that is not necessarily the case when the declining prices result from a protracted recession with its unpleasant, often devastating, consequences for the economy. The current Japanese recession, which began with the bursting of the bubble economy of the 1980s, has depressed not only consumer prices, but also investment and employment. The decline in private investments reflects in large measure a decline in funds available from banks and other lending institutions that are saddled with nonperforming loans. The decline in the amount of private money available for investment was mostly made up for by public funds generated not by tax revenue, which has also declined, but by government bonds regularly issued by both the national and local governments. As a result, the outstanding balance of long-term public bonds, to be eventually repaid by the taxpayers of either this or future generations, now amounts to about 770 trillion yen (about $6.7 trillion), or 150 percent of Japan's GDP. How this mounting public debt will be repaid is one of the biggest challenges faced by the Japanese government and people.

distinctive trait of the Japanese economic miracle. Despite the fact that the ratio of temporary or part-time workers has increased from 16 percent in 1985 to 33 percent in 2006, in part because of Japan's continuing economic difficulties, lifetime employment for a significant share of the workforce has remained an important feature of the Japanese economy.[19]

Japan in the Global Economy

The Trading State

Since the Meiji Restoration of 1868, Japan's government and business leaders have pursued rapid industrialization, initially by exporting relatively cheap products of labor-intensive industries, such as textiles, and then by exporting higher-value-added products of more capital-intensive industries, including iron and steel, shipbuilding, and machinery. Since the 1960s a number of developing nations have followed this strategy. The best-known examples are the **newly industrialized countries (NICs)** in East Asia: South Korea, Taiwan, and Singapore. By the early 1990s they had been joined by other Asian nations, such as Thailand, Malaysia, Indonesia, and China.

By the mid-1970s, Japan's export-led development strategy had paved the way for the country to become an economic superpower, with the second-largest GNP after the United States.[20] By the early 1990s, Japan was the leading source of official development assistance (ODA) to the Third World (a position it held until 2001), the third-largest source of foreign direct investments after the United States and Britain, and the third-largest trading nation after the United States and Germany.

Nearly 98 percent of Japan's $647 billion exports in 2006 consisted of industrial goods, especially machinery and automobiles, and 43 percent of its $579 billion imports in the same year consisted of fuels, industrial raw materials, and foodstuffs. Japan continues to import raw materials, turn them into industrial products, and sell them back to the rest of the world, often at large profits. However, Japanese imports of industrial goods such as machinery, equipment, and textiles from neighboring Asian nations have vastly increased as industrialization has progressed in the region.

Japan continues to have chronic deficits (imports exceeding exports) in its trade balances with nations that export fuels, raw materials, and food, including most Middle Eastern nations, some South American nations such as Brazil and Chile, Australia, and New Zealand. These deficits are more than made up for by chronic and larger surpluses (exports exceeding imports) in Japan's trade with the United States, some European nations such as Britain and the Netherlands, and, above all, most nations in Asia, with the exception of China and Malaysia. In 2006, Japan's overall trade surplus (exports minus imports) amounted to about $68 billion. For a long time, the United States was by far the largest of Japan's trading partners. In 2007 the U.S. lost that position to China (see Figure 5.3). But the U.S. is still the largest contributor to Japan's trade surplus because of the huge amount of Japanese products it purchases. The U.S. contribution to Japan's trade surplus in 2002 was about $61 billion, or about 77 percent of the total; by 2006 it had risen to $77.6 billion, or 114 percent of Japan's total surplus. In other words, without the U.S. contribution, Japan's trade balance in 2006 would have been a $9.6 billion deficit.

Washington used to charge Tokyo with unfair trade practices of one kind or another, and the two governments have engaged in trade disputes and negotiations. In the 1950s, Japan was accused of adopting a protectionist policy of high tariffs on foreign manufactured goods. After tariffs were substantially lowered in the 1960s, the U.S. criticism shifted to a variety of nontariff barriers, such as import quotas, discriminatory application of safety and technical standards against imports, and a government procurement policy favoring domestic products.[21] In the 1980s, Japan was accused of creating and maintaining structural impediments to foreign imports and investments, including a complex domestic distribution system, collusive business practices among *keiretsu* companies, and exorbitant rents in metropolitan areas. According to U.S. critics, these practices made it virtually impossible for U.S. and other foreign companies to enter Japan's domestic markets and successfully compete with Japanese producers. Japanese companies were also charged with engaging in predatory trade practices, such as dumping (selling goods abroad at prices lower than those charged at home).

Over the years, Japan has become increasingly sensitive and responsive to such criticisms, and it

FIGURE 5.3

Japan's Trade Balances with the U.S., China, and the World

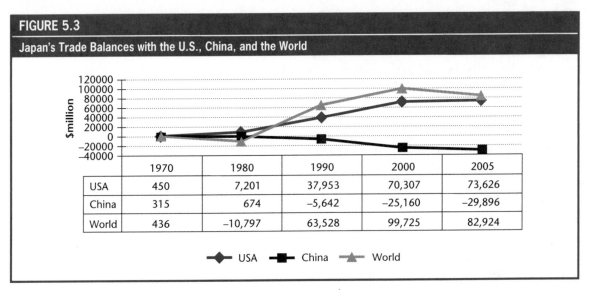

	1970	1980	1990	2000	2005
USA	450	7,201	37,953	70,307	73,626
China	315	674	−5,642	−25,160	−29,896
World	436	−10,797	63,528	99,725	82,924

◆ USA   ■ China   ▲ World

Note: Dollar values converted from yen values at each year's average exchange rate.

Sources: Yano Tsuneta kinenkai, ed., *Suji de miru nihon no 100-nen*, 3rd ed. [Japan's 100 years in numbers] (Tokyo: Kokuseisha, 1991), pp. 325–326; Keizai kikakucho chosakyoku [Research Bureau, Economic Planning Agency], ed., *Keizai yoran (Heisei 6-nen ban)* [Economic handbook, 1994 edition] (Tokyo: Ministry of Finance Printing Office, 1994), pp. 188–189, 192–193; Somucho tokeikyoku [Bureau of Statistics, Management and Coordination Agency], ed., *Sekai no tokei* [Statistics of the World] (Tokyo: Ministry of Finance Printing Office, 1998), pp. 202, 220–221; Somusho tokei kenshujo [Statistical Research and Training Institute, Ministry of Internal Affairs and Communications Statistics Institute], eds., *Sekai no tokei 2007* [Statistics of the World 2007] (Tokyo: Ministry of Finance Printing Office, 2007), pp. 234–235, Table 9-6.

has removed or significantly reduced the tariff and nontariff import barriers and abandoned many of the alleged predatory trade practices. Meanwhile, China has replaced Japan as the trading partner of the United States with the largest bilateral trade surplus and with the largest foreign exchange reserves in the world. Fueled by surging foreign investments that flow into the country—lured by its huge market, low production costs, highly skilled labor, and ample and cheap land—China has become the "world factory" and a formidable competitor to Japanese industry.

The increasing international competition has led many Japanese manufacturers to relocate their plants to China and other developing countries, especially those in Southeast and South Asia. Some Japanese firms have begun to invest in development of oil, natural gas, and other energy-related resources abroad, while still others are increasingly involved in the mergers and acquisitions of foreign firms. As a result, Japan's income account surplus (net income from

Japanese overseas investments) has been larger than its trade account surplus since 2004. Japan has thus become more dependent on returns from overseas investment than on earnings from export trade for its income from international transactions, a change that signals a major transition in Japan's engagement with the world economy.

On the other hand, foreign direct investment (FDI) in Japan and merchandise imports relative to GDP, as well as the proportion of foreign workers in its labor force, remain the lowest among the OECD member states. The Japanese economy is therefore seen as still relatively closed. This does not, however, make it immune to impacts of accelerating globalization. The increasing amount of Japanese FDI abroad contributes to domestic unemployment. Japan also faces a serious challenge due to its continued dependency on importing raw materials and foodstuffs, which have experienced rapidly rising prices because of the increased demand from emerging economies, particularly China.

Japan in International Organizations

Japan is a leading member of the United Nations and most of its specialized agencies, as well as the International Monetary Fund (IMF) and the World Bank. It joined these latter two international financial institutions a few months after the end of the Allied Occupation in 1952 and is today the second-largest subscriber, after the United States, to each organization's equity and operating funds. Since each of the five largest subscribers has the right to appoint its own representative to the board of executive directors, Japan effectively has a permanent seat on the boards of the IMF and the World Bank.

Japan did not join the UN until 1956, mainly because of the initial opposition of the Soviet Union to the admission of a major U.S. ally at the height of the cold war. Japan is now the second-largest contributor to the UN budget. Since the mid-1990s, it has been seeking, so far unsuccessfully, to join the United States, Britain, France, Russia, and China as a permanent member of the Security Council. Japan has been very active and visible in Asian and Pacific economic organizations. It is not only the largest contributor to the **Asian Development Bank (ADB)** but has also provided all its past governors. It is a founding member and a major promoter of the **Asia-Pacific Economic Cooperation (APEC)** forum and actively supports the **Association of Southeast Asian Nations (ASEAN).**

The Asia-Pacific region has been of special economic and strategic interest to Japan since long before World War II. But, in contrast to its earlier efforts to dominate the region through military power, Japan now tries to play the role of a constructive partner in the development of regional cooperation. The rising tide of regionalism around the world in recent years, highlighted by the expansion of the European Union (EU), the conclusion of the North American Free Trade Agreement (NAFTA), and, above all, China's increasingly active involvement in the East Asian regional political economy, has reinforced Japan's interest in enhancing regional cooperation in its own backyard.

The debilitating currency crisis that swept the region in 1997 gave birth to a sense of shared "Asian identity" among leaders of many nations in the region and triggered a move to expand economic cooperation among them. With a view to promoting financial cooperation among governments in the region so as to prevent a recurrence of a similar crisis, a series of agreements has since been concluded, such as the currency-swap arrangement known as the Chiang Mai Initiative—named after the northern Thai city where it was agreed to in 2000. Japan has concluded economic partnership agreements (EPAs) so far with five ASEAN member states and is now trying to integrate and expand them into a comprehensive regional EPA.

In the meantime, steadily intensifying trading and investment activities by private firms in the region, notably Japanese firms, have stimulated the emergence and development of multiple networks of intraregional economic cooperation characterized by, above all, cross-border exchanges in intermediate, or producer, goods such as steel and plywood. Intra-regional trade now accounts for nearly 60 percent of the combined total of foreign trade by the thirteen "ASEAN Plus Three" nations, namely, the ten ASEAN members plus China, Japan, and South Korea. This percentage of intraregional trade is higher than NAFTA's and approaches that of the EU.

SECTION 3 Governance and Policy-Making

Governance and policy-making in contemporary Japan is dominated by informal coalitions of leading members of the long-ruling Liberal Democratic Party (politicians) and national civil servants (bureaucrats). The bureaucrats, as a rule with the help of advisory groups of academic and professional experts, develop the majority of new policies and draft the majority of new bills to be debated and voted into law by the politicians, whose party controls the House of Representatives (the lower house) of the parliament (the Diet). The policies approved and laws enacted by legislators are then implemented by civil servants, and elicit diverse reactions from citizens and especially from organized special interests. Their reactions in turn lead bureaucrats and politicians to develop new policies, revise existing laws, and enact new laws. This section discusses various aspects of this cyclical process among bureaucrats, politicians, and citizens, including its major participants, institutional setting and cultural environment, and significant consequences.

Organization of the State

Japan is divided into forty-seven prefectures (provinces), which are, in turn, subdivided into about 1,790 municipalities (as of April 2008), ranging from large cities like Yokohama, with about 3.6 million residents, to half a dozen villages with no more than a few hundred inhabitants. It is a unitary state in which the prefectures and municipalities are subordinate, both economically and politically, to the central government and enjoy much more limited decision-making power than their counterparts in federal states, such as the United States and Germany.

Under the 1947 Constitution, Japan is a constitutional monarchy and a parliamentary democracy, much like Britain and Sweden. The monarch (the emperor) is the symbolic head of state, but the Japanese people exercise sovereign power through their elected representatives in the Diet. The Diet elects the prime minister, who then forms a cabinet. By law, at least half of the cabinet positions must be filled by members of either house of the Diet; in practice, all but a very few are filled by Diet members. Laws enacted by the Diet are implemented by the executive branch of government, which is led by the prime minister and the cabinet and operates through a national civil service. The cabinet is constitutionally subordinate and collectively answerable to the Diet. The national civil service operates under the direction of the cabinet and is therefore indirectly answerable to the Diet.

The constitution invests the Diet with the power to nominate the prime minister, enact laws, approve the government budget, ratify international treaties, and audit the financial transactions of the state. The Diet is bicameral, consisting of an upper chamber, the House of Councilors, and a lower chamber, the House of Representatives. Both houses consist exclusively of popularly elected members. The lower house is the larger and more powerful of the two, with the power to override the opposition of the upper house in votes on the budget, ratification of international treaties, and the nomination of a new prime minister.

An ordinary bill already passed by the lower house, then rejected by the upper house, may be voted on again and into law by a two-thirds majority of lower house members present and voting. Because the LDP effectively controlled both houses of the Diet, this provision had not been invoked since the late 1950s. But in January 2008, the ruling coalition of the Liberal Democratic Party (LDP) and Clean Government Party (CGP) had to resort to it to pass a bill authorizing the Japanese Maritime Self-Defense Force to resume refueling foreign ships in the Indian Ocean in support of the U.S.-led anti-terrorism activities in and around Afghanistan. The bill had failed in the upper house because, as discussed in Section 1, the opposition parties, which felt that the Indian Ocean operations violated the Peace Clause of the Japanese constitution, had gained a majority in the July 2007 House of Councilors election. In the next several months, the ruling coalition resorted to this provision twice to reinstate road-related bills rejected by the oppositions in the Upper House.

The Diet also has the power to investigate any matter of national interest, whereas the prime minister and the cabinet have the obligation to report to the Diet on the state of the nation and its foreign relations. In fulfilling this obligation, cabinet ministers regularly attend meetings of Diet committees and answer members' questions.

As in other parliamentary systems, the prime minister and the cabinet ("the government") serve only as long as they have the confidence of the Diet. If the House of Representatives passes a motion of no confidence against a cabinet, the government must either dissolve the lower house within ten days or resign. This leads either to the formation of a new cabinet or to a new lower house general election. For example, in 1993, a motion of no confidence against an LDP cabinet passed with the support of a dissident LDP faction. This led to splits in the ruling party and the birth of two splinter parties, which in turn led to the LDP's historic defeat in the general election that followed and the formation of the first non-LDP coalition government since the powerful conservative party was founded in 1955.

Nevertheless, it is the cabinet rather than the Diet that initiates most legislation and in effect makes laws. This is mostly because members of the Diet have virtually no legislative staff of their own, whereas cabinet ministers enjoy easy access to the substantial staff and resources of the civil service. During the LDP's long one-party rule, civil servants drafted the majority of bills. Most of these bills then passed the Diet with the support of ruling party members. By comparison, bills introduced by individual Diet members, especially those sponsored by opposition members alone, were few in number and far less successful; only those receiving nonpartisan support, and usually sponsored by a whole standing or ad hoc committee, enjoyed a good chance of passage. This style of governance was, however, suspended, if not ended for good, by the defeat of the LDP-CGP ruling coalition in the 2007 upper house election: cabinet-sponsored bills passed by the lower house may now be frequently voted down in the upper house by opposition members in control of that house, forcing the cabinet to have it passed for a second time in the lower house by a two-thirds majority vote, as happened with the Maritime Self-Defense Force anti-terrorism operations bill in January 2008.

The Japanese Monarchy and the Royal Family

Japan has the oldest surviving monarchy in the world with the reign of the first legendary emperor dating back to the mid-7th century B.C.E. and that of the first documented emperor to the late 7th century A.D. According to tradition, Akihito, the present occupant of Japan's Chrysanthemum Throne—so-called after the flower chosen as the crest of the imperial family in 1868—is the 125th in an unbroken line of emperors and empresses. His ancestors were Japan's actual rulers from the late seventh through the early tenth centuries and thereafter remained the nation's titular rulers until shortly after the end of World War II. Under the Meiji Constitution (1889–1947), the emperor was not only Japan's sovereign ruler but also a demigod whose person was considered sacred and inviolable. The 1947 Constitution relegated the emperor to the status of a symbol of the Japanese state in which the people were sovereign. The Japanese monarchy has

both survived and been transformed by the country's devastating defeat in World War II and the far-reaching postwar reforms, and it continues to thrive as an important national symbol.

Compared to his aloof and enigmatic father, Hirohito, who at least figuratively led Japan into and out of the disastrous world war and whose role in that war remains controversial,[22] Emperor Akihito is a far more modern and cosmopolitan monarch. An eleven-year-old boy at war's end, he lived through the austere early postwar years as an impressionable young man, mingled freely with classmates from commoner families, learned English from an American Quaker woman, and married a businessman's daughter (née Shoda Michiko). Nonetheless, the Japanese royal family remains sheltered and hidden from public view to a much greater extent than most of its counterparts in the rest of the world. In this sense, the Japanese monarchy remains an extraordinarily tradition-bound institution.

The Executive

The Prime Minister and the Cabinet

The prime minister, who is the chief executive of the government, is elected by the Diet, usually the leader of the party that has a majority or plurality of seats in the House of Representatives. The House of Representatives and the House of Councilors separately elect a candidate for prime minister by a simple majority during a plenary session. If different candidates are elected by the two houses, the one elected by the lower house becomes prime minister. The person chosen to be the prime minister must be a current Diet member, and retains his or her seat in the Diet while serving as head of the executive branch.

Since the LDP was formed in 1955, all but three of Japan's 25 prime ministers have been the president of that party; the three non-LDP prime ministers served from April 1994–January 1996. Although its formal rules called for election by vote at a party convention, traditionally, the LDP selected its president by consensus often forged through backdoor negotiations among faction leaders. This process tended to produce "everybody's second choice" as party president/prime minister, someone who held important cabinet and/or party positions in previous governments, usually in accordance with a seniority promotion system built on the intraparty factional balance. (Factions are discussed in Section 4).

This tradition was briefly broken by Koizumi Junichiro, who successfully shored up his initially weak support base within the party with broad popular support, which many thought would be beneficial to the party's electoral fortune. Koizumi also broke with tradition in making his cabinet and party executive appointments by completely ignoring seniority and factional balance. This Koizumi experiment in bucking tradition seemed to end with the sudden resignation in September 2007 of his unpopular successor, Abe Shinzo, after only one year in office. The LDP leadership selection process returned to "normalcy" with the selection of Fukuda Yasuo as prime minister to succeed Abe. Fukuda proved to be no more popular than Abe with approval ratings of around 25 percent in mid-2008, due largely to public unhappiness about Japan's continuing economic difficulties.

Once elected, the Japanese prime minister has nearly absolute authority to appoint or dismiss any member of his cabinet. The appointment of members of an LDP cabinet is usually dictated mainly by the need to maintain a balance of power among the several intraparty factions and keep them happy. The coalition cabinets that have governed the nation since August 1993, the first two of which did not include the LDP, have been composed of representatives of the coalition parties chosen on the basis of the same principle of balance among the several parties.

The prime minister has the constitutional right to submit bills to the Diet in the name of the cabinet; to exercise control and supervision of the national civil service; and in rare cases, to suspend a cabinet member's constitutionally guaranteed immunity from an adverse legal action during his or her tenure in office. The prime minister is also the nation's commander in chief and may order, subject to the Diet's consent, the Self-Defense Forces to take appropriate action in a national emergency.

As in other parliamentary systems, the prime minister and the cabinet are responsible to the lower house of the legislature. If the House of Representatives passes a motion of "no confidence" against the prime minister and his cabinet, they must either resign or dissolve the House of Representatives and call a new general election. A new prime minister and cabinet are then chosen based on the results of the election. Prime ministers have also resigned in Japan for other reasons, including corruption scandals, loss of support from important elements of his party, or ill health. In fact, the average tenure in office of prime ministers in postwar Japan has been just a little over two years, with several serving for less than a year. This tendency is reinforced by the tradition of making the prestige and perquisites of the top government offices, including that of prime minister, available to as many Diet members of the ruling party or parties as possible.[23] Although the almost uninterrupted rule of the LDP since 1955 has given Japanese politics a deserved reputation for stability, the frequent turnover of prime ministers has led some observers to become cynical about the importance of that office to the functioning of the Japanese government, terming it a "karaoke democracy," with different prime ministers taking turns performing for a short time at the "microphone" while the professional civil service conducts the real ongoing business of governing the country.[24]

The executive powers and responsibilities of the Japanese cabinet are wide-ranging. In addition to those common to the executive branch of government in most other representative democracies, they include the following:

- advising and taking responsibility for any of the emperor's ceremonial actions that are of concern to the state, such as the promulgation of laws and international treaties, convocation of the Diet, dissolution of the House of Representatives, and receiving foreign ambassadors and ministers
- designating the chief justice of the Supreme Court, who is formally appointed by the emperor
- appointing all other judges of the Supreme Court and those of the lower courts

- calling the Diet into extraordinary session and the upper house into emergency session
- approving expenditure of the state's reserve funds

In a sweeping reorganization of the national civil service in 2001, many ministries and agencies were either consolidated or abolished, and, as a result, the membership of the cabinet underwent a significant change. According to the 2001 reform law, the cabinet is limited to eighteen members, including the prime minister. The composition of the Japanese cabinet as of early 2008 is shown in Table 5.2. In the Fukuda cabinet re-formed in August 2008, two members were women, the Minister of State for Consumer Affairs and the Minister of State for Population and Gender Equality Issues. No woman has ever held the office of prime minister in Japan.

Table 5.2
Cabinet Positions (Early 2008)
Prime Minister
Minister of Internal Affairs and Communications
Minister of Justice
Minister of Foreign Affairs
Minister of Finance
Minister of Education, Culture, Sports, Science, and Technology
Minister of Health, Labor, and Welfare
Minister of Agriculture, Forestry, and Fisheries
Minister of Economy, Trade, and Industry
Minister of Land, Infrastructure, and Transport
Minister of the Environment
Minister of Defense
Minister of State: Okinawa and Affairs Related to the Northern Territories
Minister of State: Financial Services, Administrative and Regulatory Reforms
Minister of State: Economic and Fiscal Policy
Minister of State: Population and Gender Equality Issues
Chief Cabinet Secretary
Chairman of the National Public Safety Commission

The National Bureaucracy

At the core of the contemporary Japanese state are a dozen central government ministries, each with more or less exclusive jurisdiction over a specific area or areas of public policy. Each ministry's mandate, as defined by law and practice, includes both regulatory and custodial powers over individuals, corporations, and other organizations. The regulatory power is exercised mainly through the enforcement of legal and quasi-legal requirements for licenses, permits, or certificates for virtually any kind of activity with actual or potential effects on the public interest. The custodial power is used to provide various types of public assistance to private citizens and groups, such as subsidies and tax exemptions for particular industries.

Japan's central government ministries are all very much alike in organization and behavior. Each is headed by a minister and one or two senior vice ministers, one to three parliamentary secretaries, one vice minister, and one or two deputy ministers. The first three offices are held by members of the Diet, as a rule, while the last two are held by career officials of the ministry concerned. The core organization of a ministry consists of a minister's secretariat; several staff bureaus, which are concerned mainly with broad policy issues; and several line bureaus, responsible for the implementation of specific policies and programs. The bureaus are each subdivided into divisions and departments. These core components are supplemented, as a rule, by several auxiliary agencies, commissions, committees, and institutes. For example, staff bureaus of the Ministry of Economy, Trade, and Industry (METI) devise policies and programs in areas such as industrial policy, international trade, and international economic cooperation, while its line bureaus are responsible for the development and implementation of policies for all major manufacturing industries, including chemicals, industrial machinery, automobiles, and aircraft. METI's work is aided by its auxiliary organizations, the Natural Resources and Energy Agency, the Small and Medium Enterprise Agency, the Nuclear and Industrial Safety Agency, the Japan Patent Office, and eight regional bureaus and their local offices. METI's predecessor, the Ministry of International Trade and

Institutional Intricacies: Vicissitudes of Bureaucratic Power and Pride

In the 1970s and 1980s, Japan's government bureaucracy, epitomized by the Ministry of Finance (MOF) and the Ministry of International Trade and Industry (MITI), was greatly admired, both within the nation and abroad, as the uniquely intelligent, energetic, and dedicated architect of the nation's post-World War II economic success. Its policy-making prowess was acclaimed in books such as Ezra Vogel's *Japan as Number One* (1979) and Chalmers Johnson's *MITI and the Japanese Miracle* (1982).

By the end of the 1990s, however, the enviable reputation of these institutions had completely dissipated. For example, a poll taken in March 1998 by the *Asahi Shimbun*, a prominent Japanese newspaper, found that only 1 percent of respondents trusted ministry bureaucrats very much and 25 percent did so to some extent, while 50 percent did not trust them much and 21 percent not at all. What caused this dramatic turnaround in the image of Japan's professional civil servants?

First and foremost, the depressed state of the Japanese economy was blamed on the bureaucrats. Second, a series of headline-grabbing scandals involving ministry bureaucrats tainted the public image of not only the individual ministries directly involved but also the entire national bureaucracy. Third, politicians began to claim a greater share of policy-making power at the expense of bureaucrats. Fourth, diminishing tax revenue and tighter spending discipline spelled a shrinking war chest for the bureaucrats to tap into for greasing their relationships with politicians and special interest groups, thus seriously eroding their influence. Finally, largely as a result of these developments, the bureaucrats themselves began to lose much of their sense of mission and purpose, which had guided their bold, and often innovative, decisions and actions in the better times.

Industry (MITI), played a central role in the rehabilitation and development of the Japanese economy after World War II by providing wide-ranging policy guidance and assistance to the nation's war-ravaged industries.[25]

Ministerial autonomy has often verged on ministerial chauvinism and has often seriously interfered with cooperation among ministries. Its **vertically divided administration** has been a defining characterization of the way the Japanese civil service operates. For example, in the aftermath of the devastating earthquake that hit Kobe City in January 1995, ministerial egoism and parochialism were widely blamed for long delays, often with tragic consequences, in the central government's response to the disaster.

During most of the postwar period, the high prestige of Japan's national bureaucracy attracted a large number of university graduates to the annual civil service entrance examinations and ensured that only the best performers were appointed to fast-track positions in the central ministries and auxiliary organizations, especially the most prestigious among them, such as the Ministry of Finance (MOF), Ministry of International Trade and Industry (MITI; later reorganized and renamed METI), and Ministry of Foreign Affairs (MOFA). As Japan grew richer, the attraction of careers in the private sector, especially in one of the conglomerate-affiliated giant corporations, rose rapidly, while the relative popularity of civil service careers declined. During the late 1980s, the number of applicants taking the civil service entrance examination in the most competitive fast-track category, officially called Class I, decreased by nearly one-third. Still, entry remains very competitive: In 2007, only about one out of fourteen applicants passed the exam in this category.

The mandatory retirement age for Japan's national civil servants is 60, but, by custom, most retire at a younger age, usually about fifty-five, with fairly modest retirement benefits. This leads them to seek new jobs upon retirement. Many find high-paying positions in public or semipublic corporations or in the major private firms. This way of gaining postretirement employment is known as *amakudari,* or "descent from heaven." The "descent" is usually arranged in advance between the ministry ("heaven") from which the official is retiring and one of the public, semipublic, or private enterprises with which the ministry has a close relationship. The Japanese civil service law forbids employment of a retired civil servant within two years of his or her retirement by a private enterprise that has had a close relationship with the government office where the retired official was employed in the last five years. This restriction, however, may be lifted at the National Personnel Authority's discretion, which is routinely done for several dozen retiring senior bureaucrats each year. Moreover, there are no legal restrictions on the "descent" of a retired official to a public or semipublic organization.

In 2005, Japan's national government, including its auxiliary organizations, employed about 610,000 people, or a little more than 1 percent of the approximately 60 million gainfully employed people. The Japanese central government budget (2005) claimed a larger percentage share of the nation's gross national product (GNP) than did the United States' federal government budget (2004), but a somewhat smaller share than Germany's and considerably smaller than France's or Britain's (2005). The percentage share of GNP of the total spending by Japan's national, prefectural, and municipal governments and other governmental bodies was equal to the United States' and both were substantially smaller than that of Britain, Germany, and France (see Figure 5.4). It is difficult to compare the efficiency of different nations' public bureaucracies, but it is probably reasonable to call Japan's civil service relatively lean and thrifty. However, as noted in the Institutional Intricacies box, the traditional image of Japanese bureaucrats as a group of unselfish, public-minded, and incorruptible mandarins—as their scholar-official antecedents in Imperial China were called—was seriously compromised in the 1990s and early 2000s by a series of corruption scandals involving officials in some of the traditionally most powerful and prestigious ministries and agencies, including the ministries of Finance and Foreign Affairs.

In addition to the central government ministries and agencies, there were, as of 2007, about eighty public and semipublic enterprises funded wholly or substantially by the central government. Their activities ranged from energy resource development to international cooperation to publicly managed gambling.

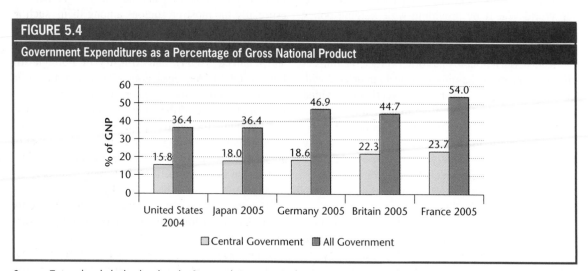

FIGURE 5.4

Government Expenditures as a Percentage of Gross National Product

Source: Zaimusho shukeikyoku chosaka [Research Division, Budget Bureau, Ministry of Finance], *Zaiseikankei shoshiryo 2007* [Assorted Financial Data, 2007]; http://www.mof.go.jp/jouhou/syukei/siryou/sy1909l.pdf.

Other State Institutions

The Military

Japan's military establishment was totally dismantled by the Allied Occupation authorities after World War II, and, as mentioned in Section 1, the nation was forbidden to rearm by the peace clause of the 1947 Constitution. Nonetheless, the outbreak of the Korean War in 1950 led the Japanese government, with American encouragement, to launch a rearmament program. Initially, a so-called police reserve force was created, to avoid provoking controversy over its constitutionality. By 1954, this force had evolved into the Self-Defense Forces (SDF) under the authority of the Japan Defense Agency. In 1959, the Supreme Court ruled that Article 9 allowed Japan to take necessary measures to defend itself as an independent nation. The SDF have since grown into a substantial armed force, and the majority of Japanese people have come to accept it as a legitimate component of the Japanese state. In 2007, the Japan Defense Agency was elevated to the status of a ministry.

Following the September 11, 2001, terrorist attacks on the United States, the Japanese government dispatched, with little overt public or media opposition, half a dozen warships to the Indian Ocean to assist the U.S. forces in their military operations in and around Afghanistan. This was soon followed by Diet passage of a Special Anti-Terrorism Measures Bill and the adoption by the cabinet of a Basic Plan of Special Anti-Terrorism Measures, which authorized the SDF to assist American and British forces in Afghanistan—including the refueling of the warships of the United States and its allies—and later in Iraq. The 2001 law expired in November 2007, but was succeeded by a new law, despite its rejection by the opposition-dominated upper house, as mentioned above. The National Defense Program approved by the cabinet earlier in 2004 explicitly upheld the SDF's right to participate in international peace-keeping missions.

Nevertheless, Japan continues to rely heavily on the United States for its security. This arrangement is based on the 1960 Treaty of Mutual Cooperation and Security between Japan and the United States. By virtue of the treaty and the Agreement on the Status of U.S. Armed Forces, which stipulates detailed rules for the implementation of the treaty, the United States still maintains an extended network of military bases and facilities and about 47,000 troops in Japan.

The Judiciary

The judicial branch of the Japanese government operates according to the rules set by the Supreme Court and is theoretically free from interference by the other two branches of government. The Supreme Court consists of the chief judge and fourteen other judges. All judges are appointed by the cabinet, except for the chief judge of the Supreme Court, who is nominated by the cabinet and formally appointed by the emperor. Supreme Court judges are subject to popular review and potential recall in the first House of Representatives election following their appointment and every ten years thereafter. Otherwise, judges of all courts may serve until the mandatory retirement ages of seventy for Supreme Court and small claims court judges and sixty-five for all others. In the twenty popular reviews of Supreme Court judges held through 2005, no judge received a negative vote from more than about 15 percent of the voters.

The Supreme Court, eight higher (regional) courts, and fifty district (prefectural) courts are invested with, and occasionally use, the constitutional power of judicial review. But the Supreme Court has been extremely reluctant to declare an existing law unconstitutional. For example, lower courts have twice found the Self-Defense Forces in violation of the war-renouncing Article 9 of the 1947 Constitution. On each occasion, the Supreme Court reversed the lower court's verdict on the grounds that the issue was too political to be amenable to judicial review. During the half-century of its existence up to 2007, the Supreme Court upheld lower court verdicts on the unconstitutionality of existing laws in only five cases, none of which involved a controversial political issue.

The reluctance of the Japanese Supreme Court to use its power of judicial review may be attributed to several factors. First, there is an influential legal opinion in Japan that holds that the judiciary should not intervene in decisions of the legislative or executive branches of government, which represent the people's will more directly than the judiciary. Second, Japan has a much weaker case law tradition than either the

Institutional Intricacies: Japan's Self-Defense Forces

In the first decade of the twenty-first century, Japan's Self-Defense Force (SDF) is roughly equal—in operational capability if not in physical size—to the armed forces of a major western European nation. In 2006, Japan's defense budget of $41.1 billion was ranked sixth in military spending in the world, after the United States, China, Russia, Britain, and France.

From Washington's point of view, however, Japan's defense spending is too small relative to its overall economic power. Japan spends less than 1 percent of its GNP on defense, while for the U.S., the comparable figure is about 4 percent (about $536 billion in 2006, or thirteen times as much as Japan). Not surprisingly, U.S. leaders have persistently demanded a larger defense effort by Tokyo, and Japan has responded not by large increases in defense spending, which would be financially difficult as well as politically unpopular, but by, among other things, expanding the scope of its participation in UN-sponsored peacekeeping operations in various regions of the world.

Beginning with the dispatch of three civilian election watchers to Angola in 1992, Japanese, including SDF troops in an increasing number of cases, have participated during the past decade in peacekeeping activities in Cambodia, Mozambique, El Salvador, Rwanda, Syria/Golan Heights, Bosnia/Herzegovina, East Timor, and Iraq. Under the Koizumi government's rule, in particular, Japan significantly expanded its paramilitary role in cooperation with UN- or U.S.-led actions around the world. Its successors, led by Abe Shinzo and Fukuda Yasuo, began to seek replacement of the existing temporary laws authorizing overseas dispatch of SDF troops for strictly limited purposes by a permanent law, which would permit deployment of troops on more open-ended and flexible terms. The move gained support of many DPJ Diet members, including its leader, Ozawa Ichiro.

These government actions, however, have not won the support of public opinion. For example, a January 2003 *Asahi Shimbun* poll found 27 percent of respondents approving and 62 percent opposing Japanese participation in a U.S.-led war against Iraq. A November 2005 poll by the same newspaper similarly found 22 percent in favor of and 69 percent against the continuing stationing of SDF troops in Iraq. A January 2008 poll by another major Japanese newspaper, *Nikkei Shimbun*, found 35 percent supporting and 46 percent opposing the proposed permanent law on the overseas dispatch of SDF troops. It thus seems that the LDP-led governments have been attempting to oblige "international public opinion" at the expense of domestic public opinion, a dangerous game to play in a democracy.

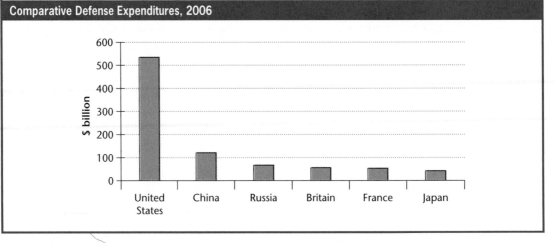

FIGURE 5.5A

Comparative Defense Expenditures, 2006

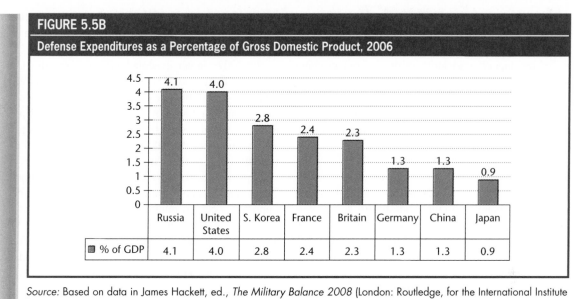

FIGURE 5.5B

Defense Expenditures as a Percentage of Gross Domestic Product, 2006

	Russia	United States	S. Korea	France	Britain	Germany	China	Japan
▣ % of GDP	4.1	4.0	2.8	2.4	2.3	1.3	1.3	0.9

Source: Based on data in James Hackett, ed., *The Military Balance 2008* (London: Routledge, for the International Institute for Strategic Studies, 2008), pp. 443–445.

United States or Britain. This makes judges more inclined to follow precedents rather than propounding new interpretations. Third, judicial passivity may reflect the traditional reluctance of the Japanese people to resort to litigation to settle disputes. Finally, Japan lacks a tradition of judicial review: under the Meiji Constitution, the emperor was above the law, and the courts did not have the power to deny the legality of any executive act taken in his name.

Since the Allied Occupation, professional judges alone have decided the outcome of cases brought to court. But in May 2009, Japan will begin to use a quasijury system for major criminal cases. Guilt or innocence of the accused—and, if convicted, the sentence—will be determined by a judicial panel composed of three professional judges and six laypersons. Many consider the introduction of this **"Lay Judge System"** (*saibanin-seido*) to be one of the most radical government reforms in post–Occupation Japan and a major step toward putting the country's democratic ideals into practice in its legal system.

The Police

From early 1948 to mid-1954, local municipalities held direct control over about three-quarters of the Japanese police force (with the national government controlling the rest). Since then, the Japanese police have operated under the direct control of prefectural governors and prefectural public safety commissions. There are forty-seven prefectural police headquarters and safety commissions directly responsible for the maintenance and activities of all Japanese police officers, although the National Police Agency exercises supervisory authority and has coordinating power over the prefectural organizations and their personnel. This relatively decentralized structure reflects, in part, a reaction against the much dreaded coercive power associated with the prewar and wartime Japanese police.

Until the 1980s, the Japanese police enjoyed a reputation, both at home and abroad, as the highly disciplined, efficient, and effective guardian of the nation's peace and the citizens' safety. Since then, however, that enviable reputation has been replaced with one of mediocre performance, low motivation, and even widespread corruption. According to the National Police Agency's annual white paper, the incidence of criminal offenses reported in the country increased more than 50 percent between 1980 and 2003, from about 1,160 to about 1,780 per 100,000 citizens; but the rate at which criminals were apprehended fell by more than 50 percent, from about 60 percent to 29 percent, in the same period. The change is attributable partly to the increasing cultural and behavioral heterogeneity of the Japanese society, resulting from growing generational gaps and a slow but steady increase in the number of resident and visiting foreigners. It is also due partly to a decline in the number of applicants for police jobs and the resulting decline in the police/crime ratio.

Nonetheless, Japan remains a relatively safe society, with only about half as many criminal offenses per population reported in 2004 as the U.S., less than one-third as many as France, one-fourth as many as Germany, and one-fifth as many as Britain. When it comes to the percentage of offenders apprehended, Japan's record of a little under 26 percent in 2004 was higher than those of the United States and Britain, but about five percent lower than France's and only about half of Germany's. Once a case comes to trial, Japan boasts a conviction rate of 99.9 percent.

The criminal justice system in Japan, however, has been criticized for abuse of prisoners and suspects, and the arbitrary and often inhumane way the prison system is run. The astoundingly high conviction rate is achieved by prosecutors' heavy reliance on confessions. Confessions are often coerced by abusive interrogations in the "substitute prisons" where suspects can be detained for up to 23 days by police and prosecutors, and are given very restricted access to their lawyers—in violation of constitutional guarantee (Article 34) of the right to counsel and *habeas corpus*, which directs that a person either be charged before a judge or released. Under international pressure, a few reforms were under way in mid-2008, including the introduction of guidelines for conducting interrogations. The scheduled introduction in May 2009 of a quasijury system may help to open the judicial system to greater public scrutiny and raise concerns for human rights abuses in the system.

Japan is, along with the United States, one of the very few developed countries that still practice capital punishment. Executions in Japan are carried out by hanging and conducted in great secrecy. Neither the person awaiting execution nor the prisoner's family are informed of the exact date or time the sentence is to be carried out. The prisoner is informed only that morning that the execution order has been issued; the family is told only after the execution has taken place.

In 2007, Japan executed nine people; the U.S. executed forty-two. The two countries thus have a roughly comparable rate of execution per murder case. According to a 2004 government public opinion poll, 81.4 percent of respondents supported the death penalty on the grounds that it serves to prevent personal vendettas and to deter future crimes. Only 6 percent of the respondents were against capital punishment. There was a nonpartisan group of 72 Diet members opposed to capital punishment, including the former chief of the National Police Agency, in mid-2008. This number, however, represented a sharp drop from 120 of such lawmakers found two years earlier, a drop apparently due to the weight of public opinion in favor of the death penalty.

Subnational Government

Japanese prefectures and their subdivisions have long been under the administrative and financial control of the central government and enjoy only limited decision-making authority. In this respect, Japan (like France) differs from most other industrial democracies, where subnational levels of government have greater autonomy.

The lopsided distribution of decision-making power in the Japanese political system has been sustained by an equally lopsided division of taxation power. The central government collects nearly two-thirds of the taxes levied by all levels of governments and provides the funds for nearly one-third of local government expenditures through extensive grants-in-aid and subsidies programs. The obviously weak and inferior status of local government vis-à-vis national government tends to discourage citizens from participating in government and politics at the grass-roots level and thus impedes the development of democracy.

Decentralization of decision-making power was an important plank in the ambitious reform agenda of the government of Prime Minister Koizumi when it took office in April 2001. A special advisory panel was appointed in the same year to investigate the issue and recommend a plan of action to empower local government, both politically and economically. The panel submitted its final report to the prime minister in 2004. However, the only tangible result of this widely publicized exercise was the transfer of tax sources worth about $30 billion from central to local control in exchange for abolition of the central government's subsidies for local government projects worth about $50 billion. The net result of this "reform" was thus a drastic reduction in the income of local governments with little effect on their actual decision-making power. Moreover, the Fukuda government, which took office in September 2007, decided to nationalize the collection of about half of the local corporate taxes in order to redistribute the revenue from the affluent urban areas, where opposition parties tend to do better at the ballot box, to the poorer rural areas, which happen to be the LDP's key electoral base. This decision has effectively reversed what little had been accomplished by the Koizumi government's "fiscal decentralization initiative" campaign.

The Policy-Making Process

The majority of bills passed by the Diet originate in the national civil service. When the Liberal Democratic Party was in power alone, draft bills were reviewed and approved by a party committee called the Policy Research Council. When the LDP has shared power in a coalition government, as has been the case since the mid-1990s, bills are also reviewed and approved by its partner parties.

The LDP's Policy Research Council operates through a dozen standing committees, each corresponding to a government ministry and, as of 2007,

As Prime Minister Fukuda Yasuo helplessly looks on, the grabby Budget Monster goes roaring down the slippery slope of Mt. Mounting Government Debt. *Source:* © Asahi Shimbun, December 26, 2007.

「欲しがり怪獣」は大借金坂を転がり落ちていく

山田　紳

about eighty-five ad hoc committees. Some of these ad hoc committees are concerned with broad, long-term policy issues, such as revision of the constitution, fiscal policy, and the educational system. Others deal with more specific matters, such as government assistance to depressed industries, treatment of foreign workers, and problems related to U.S. military bases in the country. Their recommendations are presented to the Council's executive committee and then to the party's Executive Council. If approved at both levels, the recommendations usually become LDP policies to be implemented through legislative actions of the Diet or administrative actions of the bureaucracy.

Most LDP policy committees are led by veteran Diet members who are experienced and knowledgeable in specific issue areas. Over the years, they have formed close personal relationships with senior civil servants and leaders of special interest groups. These LDP legislative leaders, who form among themselves what are popularly known as *zoku* (tribes), work through so-called "iron triangles" with their bureaucratic and business allies. Such tribes and iron triangles dominate policy-making in all major policy areas, but especially agriculture, construction, education, telecommunications, and transportation.

Many of the bills drafted by bureaucrats and introduced in the Diet by an LDP cabinet originate in a tribe, as do many administrative measures implemented by a government ministry.

The iron triangles promote special interests favored by politicians and bureaucrats. Bureaucrats have their turfs protected and often expanded by sympathetic politicians, and politicians have their campaign war chests filled with contributions from the interest groups that they support. The LDP tribes are thus the principal actors in Japan's ubiquitous **pork-barrel politics** and the major sources of political corruption and scandals that have frequently rocked the country. Big businesses, small shop owners, farmers, builders, insurers, and doctors are all represented by their own tribes that protect them against those who threaten their interests, whether they are Japanese consumers, insurance policy holders, patients, or foreign producers and exporters.

The resistance and obstruction by powerful entrenched interests, determined to hang on to and perpetuate the status quo, have stymied reformist efforts in virtually all major policy areas, giving Japanese politics an appearance of a downtown intersection in a perennial gridlock. This political paralysis makes it extremely difficult to change old policies, practices, and procedures in any significant or timely way. This paralysis aggravates already bad situations, such as the protracted economic slump and the mounting public debt that have dogged the nation for more than a decade and a half. In light of the long history of failed reform projects—announced with great fanfare but left unfulfilled by a succession of prime ministers and cabinets—Japan is yet to find leadership strong enough to overcome, or skillful enough to get around, vested interests, both inside and outside government, that continue to block the many political and economic changes that the nation badly needs. In the final analysis, it may take a more truly competitive democracy, where rival parties alternate in power with a degree of predictability and certainty, for such leadership to emerge.

SECTION 4   Representation and Participation

The most important official forums through which Japanese citizens express their interests are the parliament (the Diet) and local legislatures. The principal actors who represent them are therefore Diet members, most of whom are affiliated with political parties, and members of prefectural and municipal assemblies, the majority of whom are independents. Citizens exercise some control over the legislators' conduct and performance through periodic elections. There are, however, other organizations and activities that represent citizens' interests and opinions outside the legislatures, such as interest groups and social movements.

The Legislature

According to the postwar Japanese constitution, the Diet is the highest and sole law-making organ of the state. How the Diet is constituted and how it operates are therefore critical questions in assessing the current state of democracy in Japan. The method by which Diet members are elected will be discussed below.

The House of Representatives, the lower and more powerful house of the Diet, currently has 480 members. The full term of office for its members is four years, but the actual term served by a member in the last quarter century has averaged about three years. As in other parliamentary systems, this is because the lower house may be dissolved by the cabinet when the House passes a motion of no confidence against the cabinet. When this happens, the cabinet must either resign or dissolve the lower house and call a new election. The cabinet may also voluntarily choose to dissolve the lower house when the ruling party believes it is to its advantage to call a new general election.

The House of Councilors, the upper house of the Diet, currently has 242 members. Their term of office is six years. Their terms are staggered, as is the case with U.S. senators, so that half of the 242 members are elected every three years.

The presiding officers of the House of Representatives are the speaker and vice speaker; those of the House of Councilors are the president and vice president. Unlike their counterparts in the U.S. Congress, the presiding officers of the Japanese Diet are expected to be nonpartisan in discharging their duties. When a member of the Diet is elected to any of these four positions, the member gives up his or her party affiliation and becomes a nominal independent.

An ordinary session of the Diet sits for 150 days each year, beginning in mid-January. If necessary, it may be extended once. An extraordinary session may be called at any time by the cabinet or by one-quarter of the members of either house. As in the U.S. Congress, a good deal of business is conducted in the standing and ad hoc committees of each house. In 2007, there were seventeen standing and seven ad hoc committees in the lower house and seventeen standing and five ad hoc committees in the upper house. A simple majority is required for the passage of a bill or a resolution by either house or a committee, unless it is a proposal to revise the constitution, which requires the consent of two-thirds or more of all members in each house and then is put to the vote for final approval in a national referendum.

A bill may be introduced in either house of the Diet, but must be considered and approved by both houses in order to become a law. In practice, an overwhelming majority of bills have been introduced first in the House of Representatives and later referred to the House of Councilors. A bill may be introduced by the cabinet, the house as a whole, a committee of the house, or a member or members of the house. In all cases, it is first submitted to the presiding officer of the relevant house, then referred by him or her to an appropriate committee for initial consideration, unless the introducer requests for special reasons that the bill be immediately sent to and considered by the entire house. A member's bill that does not require a budget appropriation must be cosigned by twenty or more lower house members or ten or more upper house members; one that requires a budget appropriation must be cosigned by fifty or more lower house or twenty or more upper house members.

A bill approved by a committee of either house is referred to and debated by the whole house and, if approved, transmitted to the other house, where the same process is repeated. A bill that has been approved by both houses is signed by the speaker of the lower house or the president of the upper house, whichever has approved it last, and presented to the emperor for *pro forma* promulgation.

As mentioned in Section 3, if a bill approved by the House of Representatives is then rejected by the House of Councilors, the measure may still become law by being passed again by a two-thirds majority in the lower house. The annual government budget must be introduced to the lower house and may be passed by that house alone, regardless of the upper house's action or opinion. The same applies to international treaties. Unlike members of the U.S. Congress, but like legislators in other parliamentary democracies, Japanese Diet members normally vote strictly along party lines.

The overwhelming majority of Japanese legislators are men. As of January 2008, only 9.3 percent of

On February 29, 2008, the 2008 budget was passed by the LDP-led majority in the House of Representatives plenary session boycotted by all members of the opposition parties except the Japan Communist Party. *Source:* © 2008 The Yomiuri Shimbun.

the lower house and 18.2 percent of the upper house members were women. On a list compiled in late 2007 by the Inter-Parliamentary Union, Japan tied with Gambia and Georgia for 96th place among 189 ranked nations in the percentage of women among those elected in the country's most recent election to either a unicameral parliament or the more powerful lower house of a bicameral parliament. Rwanda was first, with 48.8 percent for lower house and 34.6 percent for upper house members, followed by unicameral Sweden, with 47.3 percent.

When an incumbent retires or dies, he or she is often succeeded by a relative, typically a son, or a senior aide. Thanks to the campaign organization and personal networks bequeathed by the predecessor, such a successor has significant advantage over rival candidates in winning, first, the nomination of his or her party and, then, the election. In the 2005 House of Representatives general election, such "hereditary" candidates accounted for 31 percent of all winners and 41 percent of the LDP-affiliated winners. All but one of the nine LDP politicians who served as prime minister between 1990 and 2008 were "hereditary" lower house members.

In the Japanese Diet, as in the U.S. Congress, committee deliberations, where interest groups can exert their influence most effectively, play the central role in the legislative process. By comparison, sessions of the whole chamber seldom lead to substantial changes in a bill that has already been approved by a committee. As a result, entrenched special interests, represented by tribes and iron triangles in committee deliberations, are likely to have their cases heard far more sympathetically than newer and less organized interests, such as women and youth that are not so represented.

Political Parties and the Party System

For nearly forty years, from its founding in the mid-1950s to the early 1990s, the Liberal Democratic Party dominated the Diet, a situation which lent the Japanese party system and party politics an air of extraordinary stability and predictability. By the end of the 1980s, however, a series of corruption scandals had begun to take heavy tolls on the party. One such scandal, in which a top LDP leader was charged with taking a bribe from a trucking company, led in 1992 to the passage of an opposition-sponsored nonconfidence vote against the cabinet, followed by defections of dozens of LDP Diet members to form several splinter parties, the LDP's crushing defeat in the June 1993 lower house general election, and the sudden rise and as sudden fall of an anti-LDP coalition cabinet in the wake of that election. These events marked the beginning of a new era of uncertainty and unpredictability in Japanese party and electoral politics.

At the end of the 1980s, there were five parties regularly contesting Diet elections: the LDP, the Japan Socialist Party (JSP), the Clean Government Party (CGP), the Democratic Socialist Party (DSP), and the Japan Communist Party (JCP). The LDP, the JSP, and the JCP were descendants of pre-World War II parties that had been disbanded (banned in the JCP's case) before World War II and later revived. The DSP was formed in 1960 by defectors from the JSP. The CGP was founded in 1964 as the political arm of a lay Buddhist association, *Sokagakkai* (Value Creation Academy).

As mentioned above, more than fifty LDP Diet members, most of them self-proclaimed anticorruption reformists, defected and formed splinter parties in the early 1990s. One group led by a former prefectural governor, Hosokawa Morihiro, was named the Japan New Party (JNP); another group led by another former prefectural governor, Takemura Masayoshi, was named the New Party Sakigake (NPS); and a third and largest group led by a future prime minister, Hata Tsutomu, and a future opposition leader, Ozawa Ichiro, was named the Japan Renewal Party (JRP). A loose coalition of these offshoots of the LDP and the existing opposition parties, such as the JSP, the DSP, and the CGP, defeated the LDP in the 1993 lower house election and formed the first non-LDP government since 1955 with the JNP's Hosokawa serving as prime minister.

The Hosokawa coalition government undertook and accomplished a major and long overdue reform of the House of Representatives members' election law, which is discussed below. The coalition government, however, lasted for only a little over eight months and was succeeded in June 1994 by a "grand coalition" cabinet formed by the LDP, the JSP, and the NPS, and led by the first socialist prime minister, Murayama Tomiichi, since the early post-World War II period. The grand coalition fell in January 1996, but the LDP has since stayed in power without an interruption, albeit only in coalition with one or more other parties. The JSP was renamed the Social Democratic Party (SDP) following the fall of the Murayama cabinet, then lost about half of its Diet members to the newly formed Democratic Party of Japan (DPJ). It has since suffered a steady decline in its parliamentary representation, and retained only half a dozen seats in either house of the Diet in early 2008. The majority of JNP Diet members also joined the DPJ in 1996, leaving the JNP virtually defunct.

In the fall of 2007, there were still five major parties: the LDP, the DPJ, the CGP, the JCP, and the SDP (see Table 5.3). Ideologically, the LDP is a conservative party and stands at the right end of the political party spectrum; the JCP and SDP are at the left end; and the DPJ and CGP are centrist, but both lean toward the conservative end. Japanese politics has not been intensely ideological since the end of the 1970s, but the revision of the constitution and expansion of the international role of the Self-Defense Forces, both increasingly vigorously pushed by the LDP, now loom as potentially highly divisive issues.

Since its founding in 1955, the LDP has been divided into several entrenched rival factions, each led by a veteran Diet member. Until the late 1980s, the boss of each faction and his followers used to be bound by close **clientelist** ties of mutual help and dependence. The boss helped his followers with campaign funds at election time and sponsored their appointment to Diet, cabinet, and party offices. His followers reciprocated by pledging support for the boss's bid for the office of the LDP president, which was, given the LDP's control of the Diet, virtually synonymous with the office of prime minister.

In recent years, the ties between a leader and his followers in an LDP faction and among faction members in general have substantially loosened, and the factions' influence on Diet members' legislative and electoral behavior has declined. On the other hand, groups of Diet members that are formed around specific policy issues, often crossing factional and party lines, have increased in number and gained in influence. The intraparty and cross-party opposition to many of the reform plans pushed by the former prime minister Koizumi, such as the privatization of the postal services and the decentralization of taxing and spending power, is a case in point.

Table 5.3

Japanese Political Parties, September 2007

Ideological Tendency	Party Name	Year Founded	Diet Seats, September 28, 2007	
			HR	HC
Right	Liberal Democratic Party (LDP)	1955	305	84
Center	Democratic Party of Japan (DPJ)	1998	113	115
	Clean Government Party (CGP)	1964	31	21
Left	Social Democratic Party (SDP)	1955	7	5
	Japan Communist Party (JCP)	1945	9	7
Others and Independents			15	10
Vacancies			0	0
Totals			480	242

Note: HR = House of Representatives; HC = House of Councilors

Source: Kikuoka Nobuko, ed. *Kokkai Binran [Diet Handbook]*, 121st edition (Nihon Seikei Shimbunsha, October 10, 2007), pp. 70, 102.

As of early 2008, the LDP remains the dominant party in the lower house of the Diet, but it has suffered a substantial decline in electoral support since the late 1980s and faces the looming prospects of yielding its position as the most successful parliamentary party to either the DPJ, now led by the former LDP politician, Ozawa Ichiro, or a coalition led by the DPJ in the near future. Should that happen, however, Japanese government policies on key domestic and foreign policy issues are unlikely to change significantly, considering the close ideological affinity between the two major parties.

The DPJ and the SDP (formerly JSP) have also been host to entrenched intraparty factions. In fact, theirs have been, in some ways, more disruptive than their LDP counterparts. While LDP factions have been concerned primarily with fundraising and the distribution of government and party offices among its Diet members, the factions in the DPJ and the SDP have been divided primarily along ideological and policy lines. For example, some are more willing than others to have SDF units participate in collective self-defense actions abroad, revise the 1947 Constitution, or join the LDP in a coalition government. Both parties have been seriously handicapped by the factional divisions among their leaders and members in competing with the LDP and other parties both in the legislature and at the ballot box.

Elections

Elections to the House of Representatives must be held at least once every four years. But, as in other parliamentary systems, there is no specified date for election, and they most often take place before the four-year limit is reached. New elections are called if the House is dissolved by the prime minister following the passage of a vote of no confidence in the government. The cabinet may also voluntarily choose to dissolve the lower house when the ruling party believes it to be to its advantage to call a new general election in order to extend its mandate to govern.

The system by which members of the House of Representatives are elected was drastically changed in 1994. Under the old system, which had been in place since the mid-1920s, all lower house members, as well as some of the House of Councilors, were elected in multimember districts by the **Single Non-Transferable Vote (SNTV)** method. This system tended to lead candidates of the same party to compete against each other within a district by high-lighting their qualifications and strengths in matters other than their views on policy issues. This tendency toward personal politics was reinforced by the rule common to all Japanese parties that their Diet members must support the party line on all major policy issues. As a result, many candidates tried to win an election by offering their constituents a variety of highly personal services, ranging from finding jobs for constituents or their children to lobbying for government subsidies for local firms. Constituency service activities were carried out primarily by the candidate's personal campaign organization, known as *koenkai* (support association).

The *koenkai* mobilized local community groups, such as agricultural cooperatives and shopkeepers' associations, for their candidates. It took large amounts of money and hard work to set up and maintain a viable *koenkai* organization. The funds were provided mainly by local businesses. The LDP's long rule depended on the extensive and sturdy networks of clientelist relationships between LDP politicians, their *koenkai* organizations, and local businessmen and farmers.

This highly personalized, *koenkai*-centered style of campaigning and fundraising was blamed, rightly or wrongly, for widespread political corruption. Many critics, including some LDP leaders, called for changes in the electoral system, but their efforts were thwarted by the opposition of both LDP and opposition party politicians until the pressure of public opinion for reform became irresistible in the early 1990s.

In the 1994 reform, the SNTV system as the electoral system for the House of Representatives was replaced by a **Mixed Member Proportional (MMP)** system that combines a **single-member district (SMD)** and **proportional representation (PR)** system. MMP was first used in West Germany after World War II and adopted by a number of other countries in the 1990s, including Italy, Hungary, Mexico, and New Zealand, as well as Japan. Those who championed this system in Japan argued that it would help rid lower house elections of money politics and corruption by replacing competition for votes among individual candidates based on promises of local services and personal favors by competition among the parties based on policy ideas and commitments.

As a result of the 1994 electoral reforms, the existing 129 multimember districts that elected 511 lower house members under the SNTV system were replaced with 300 single-member districts and 11 regional multimember districts that would elect an additional 200 members through a PR method based on party lists. The number of members elected from the PR districts was reduced to 180 in 2000 and, as a result, the House of Representatives today has 480 seats.

In the 300 single-member districts, winners are decided on a "first-past-the-post" system: in other words, whichever candidate gets the most votes wins. This is much like the way members of the U.S. House of Representatives are elected. The other180 members of House of Representatives are elected according to what is called a *party list* system of proportional representation (PR) from eleven regional electoral districts that have between six and thirty seats to fill depending on size. To qualify for a place on the ballot a party must hold at least five current Diet seats, have won at least 2 percent of the vote in the most recent Diet election, or have at least ten candidates running in the current election. Each qualified party submits a ranked list of its candidates in that regional district to the election management committee in advance of the voting. Voters mark ballots for their preferred political party. Seats in the House of Representatives are then allocated to the parties in numbers proportionate to their shares of the total vote, and those seats are, in turn, given to the candidates according to their rank on the party's list. In sum, each voter casts two ballots in a lower house election, one for a particular candidate in the single member district and one for a party in the multimember regional district.

The 242 members of the House of Councilors are elected to six-year terms. As noted above, Councilors' terms are staggered, so half of the members (121) are elected every three years. Unlike the House of Representatives, the House of Councilors cannot be dissolved and elections occur regularly every three years. But like the lower house, upper house elections are also carried out according to a two-track parallel system. Ninety-six members (forty-eight in each triennial upper house election) are elected by a party list proportional representation (PR) method, like that described above for the House of Representatives,

Table 5.4

Percentage Shares of Seats and Proportional Representation Votes by Party

| | Lower House | | | | Upper House | | | |
| | Seats | | Votes | | Seats | | Votes | |
	2003	2005	2003	2005	2004	2007	2004	2007
Liberal Democratic Party	49.4%	61.6%	35.0%	38.2%	40.5%	30.6%	30.0%	28.1%
Democratic Party of Japan	37.2	23.5	37.4	31.0	41.3	49.6	37.8	39.5
Clean Government Party	7.1	6.4	14.8	13.3	9.1	7.4	15.4	13.2
Japan Communist Party	1.9	1.9	7.8	7.3	3.3	2.5	7.8	7.5
Social Democratic Party	0.8	1.5	5.1	5.5	1.6	1.7	5.3	4.5
Other parties & independents	10.4	3.5	—	4.7	4.1	8.3	3.6	6.3

Sources: Asahi Shimbun, November 10, 2003, p. 1; July 13, 2004, p. 1; September 13, 2005, p. 6; July 30, 2007, p. 5.

except it is done on a *nationwide* basis rather than by regional districts. The remaining 146 (or 73 every three years) upper house members are elected from districts, which elect between two and ten representatives, by the single nontransferable vote (SNTV) system that was formerly used to elect all members of the House of Representatives.

As Table 5.4 suggests, the LDP remained the dominant party in the lower house under the new electoral system during the first decade following its introduction. In terms of the *shares of the vote*, as opposed to those of the *seats*, however, the party lost to the DPJ in the 2003 general election. In upper house elections, moreover, the DPJ beat the LDP both in votes and seats in both the 2004 and, more decisively, the 2007 elections, when it won the plurality party position in the house. The LDP may well have lost for good its hegemonic status among Japan's parliamentary parties, probably due more to the public dissatisfaction with the economic and social policies of the succession of LDP-centered governments than to the changes in the House of Representatives' election laws.

Until the late 1980s, voter turnout in postwar Diet elections fluctuated between 68 and 77 percent in lower house elections and 57 and 75 percent in upper house elections. As a result of voter disgust with politicians, turnout hit low points in the mid-1990s, at about 60 percent for the House of Representatives and

45 percent for the House of Councilors. The turnout rates subsequently recovered to 67 percent in the 2005 lower house election and 59 percent in the 2007 upper house election.

Political Culture, Citizenship, and Identity

Compared to most other countries in today's world, Japan is an ethnically and culturally homogeneous country, and its citizens have a very well-developed sense of national identity. This identity was molded into a strong and aggressive nationalist ideology in the period before World War II, when Japan attempted to build a colonial empire in East Asia on the model of those erected by European powers around the world. Japan's defeat in World War II put an end to aggressive nationalism and dreams of empire building. The strong sense of national identity, however, survived the war and remains an important feature of Japanese political culture.

On the other hand, religion has not been an important factor in modern Japanese politics or society. The postwar Japanese constitution, like its U.S. model, provides for the separation of state and religion. Most Japanese are nominally Buddhist and/or Shintoist, but many are not sure, nor do they care, whether they are Buddhist or Shintoist, and are in fact counted as both.

For example, in 2000, when the total Japanese population was about 125 million, there were about 106 million Japanese Shintoists, nearly 96 million Buddhists, 1.7 million Christians, and a little over 10 million followers of other faiths.

In prewar Japan, a combination of Confucian and Shinto precepts nurtured the idea of a unique family-nation ruled and protected by descendants of its original divine creator. In postwar Japan, the nation as the object of personal loyalty has been largely replaced by a smaller organization or group, such as a firm, but the group-centered rather than individualistic view of life and society continues to prevail.

The Japanese are among the best-schooled people in the world. Six-year elementary and three-year lower secondary school education is compulsory, and virtually all children finish. Moreover, over 95 percent of lower secondary school graduates go to three-year upper secondary schools, and nearly half of upper secondary school graduates go to two-year junior colleges or four-year universities. Schools are predominantly public, and private schools differ little from public schools in either organization or curriculum. All schools use similar textbooks in all subject areas, thanks to a national textbook certification system. All drafts of textbooks must be submitted to the Ministry of Education, Science, Sports, and Culture for inspection, often resulting in extensive revisions, and certification before they can be used in schools. Due to this de facto censorship system, Japanese textbooks tend to avoid detailed discussion of controversial issues, such as the role of the emperor in the series of wars fought by Japan in the nineteenth and twentieth centuries, the atrocities committed by Japanese troops in China and elsewhere in World War II, the controversy over the constitutionality of the Self-Defense Forces, or the causes and consequences of corruption in Japanese government and society.

The most important function of the school in contemporary Japan is to prepare students for entrance into either the job market or higher-level schools. The preparatory mission common to all Japanese schools absorbs the bulk of students' time and energy, leaving little of either for acquiring knowledge for its own sake, learning to enjoy art, or developing critical faculties. The centralized and rigidly controlled educational system produced a literate and hard-working labor force during the period when the modern Japanese economy grew rapidly in the late nineteenth century through the late twentieth century.[26] Recent international surveys have revealed, however, the inability of Japanese students, when compared to their counterparts in other advanced industrial nations, to think creatively and critically.

Japan boasts one of the highest per person newspaper circulation rates among the major industrial nations. This is also true for books and magazines: some 80,000 new books per year and nearly 3,000 monthly magazines are published. Virtually every Japanese household owns at least one television set. The Japanese are thus exposed to a huge amount of media-purveyed information.

Japan's mainstream mass media tend to be politically and socially conservative by American standards, due mainly to the indirect but pervasive influence of the government and corporate management. Such influence is a function of two characteristic features of the news business in contemporary Japan: the influence of the "press club" and the importance of advertising as a revenue source. A press club consists of one or more reporters from each accredited member newspaper, television station, radio station, or news service agency. Each club is provided with office space by the organization it covers, and its members gather information mainly from the organization's official spokespersons. A reporter who seeks unofficial information risks losing good standing with the host organization and even club membership. The system works to suppress publication of news critical of the organizations concerned, such as a government ministry or a major firm.[27] Moreover, all major Japanese newspapers and privately owned television and radio stations depend heavily on advertisements for the bulk of their income and tend to avoid publishing information that could embarrass or offend their advertisers, unless such information is published first by nonmainstream Japanese or foreign media.

The ethnic and cultural homogeneity of Japanese society has been gradually eroded by its increasing contact with the outside world, especially since the late twentieth century when the process of globalization significantly intensified. Compared with the developed nations of North America and western Europe, however, Japan remains far less exposed to and penetrated by foreign influences. The number of resident foreigners in Japan in 2005, for example, was only about 2 million, or about 1.5 percent of Japan's total population. Moreover, about a third of these foreigners were Koreans, a little over a quarter were Chinese, and about 15 percent were Japanese Brazilians. In other words, about 70 percent of them were those with ethnic and cultural backgrounds shared with or very similar to the Japanese. This was even truer of foreign students studying at Japanese universities: in 2004 there were about 91,000 of them, of whom about 66 percent were Chinese, 13 percent were Koreans, and the majority of the remainder were other Asians.

Interests, Social Movements, and Protest

Apart from the flag-bedecked sound trucks of various extreme right-wing nationalist groups that drive noisily around the streets of major cities, today's Japan is basically a politically quiescent society whose citizens grumble privately rather than protest publicly.

Energy and Environmental Issues

Japan's rapid industrialization and urbanization gave rise to intense conflicts over a number of domestic environmental issues in the 1950s and 1960s. In fact, a series of extremely severe cases of industrial pollution, such as often-fatal mercury poisoning known as **Minamata disease,** made Japan one of the world's best-known victims of environmental hazards resulting from reckless industrialization. A set of stiff antipollution laws passed by the Diet in the early 1970s has helped prevent a recurrence of such devastating disasters and has contributed greatly to a cleaner environment in Japan.

Today, many Japanese citizens are deeply concerned about the unpredictable and often violent changes in the climate and weather they experience with increasing frequency, which many attribute to global warming. Neither the Japanese government nor the average Japanese citizen, however, has been actively involved in domestic or international actions, much less movements, to stop or slow down the potentially catastrophic phenomenon.

Japan was the host for the December 1997 Conference of the Parties to the United Nations Framework Convention on Climate Change (UNFCCC), which adopted the Kyoto Protocol that aimed to get governments to commit to reducing greenhouse gases. However, Japan has in fact been the worst laggard among advanced industrial nations in the concerted global effort to reduce greenhouse gasses and arrest the climate change. This has been widely and loudly condemned as such, for example by an international coalition of environmental nongovernment organizations (NGOs) at the December 2007 UNFCCC conference held in Bali, Indonesia. There has nonetheless been little visible official or public reaction to such criticisms, much less constructive response, in Japan.

The same has been true of Japanese behavior and attitude on the whaling issue. The nation's fishermen have been annually slaughtering nearly 1,000 whales since 1987, ostensibly for research purposes. Whale meat has been sold in many neighborhood fish stores and supermarkets around the country, in defiance of widespread and intense international criticisms. According to the results of a January 2008 poll jointly conducted by Greenpeace Japan and Nippon Research Center, 71 percent of respondents supported suspension of Japanese whaling in international waters, although 66 percent were in favor of continuing whaling in Japan's own coastal waters. Besides, demand for whale meat has been in decline in recent years, especially among the young, and an increasing amount has been left unsold. The above-mentioned poll, however, also indicated that more than three-quarters of respondents had heard about neither the international regulations on whaling nor the fact that the whales caught and sold in Japan with government sanction routinely included several dozen members of species on the World Conservation Union's "Red List of Threatened Species."

Japanese public opinion on the issue of nuclear reactors has been somewhat more active and articulate. The electric power industry and the LDP leadership have been vigorously pushing the increasing use of nuclear power as an alternative to imported fuels, especially oil from the Middle East. Japan is already one of the world's major users of nuclear energy, with fifty-five reactors supplying about 18 percent of the electric power used in the country in 2005. Still, a number of local communities and governments strongly object to the construction of reactors in their own backyards. The opposition intensified in the wake of accidents, in 1997 and 1999, at one of Japan's major nuclear power plant sites, **Tokai Village**. In the last several years, however, the concern about hazards associated with nuclear reactors has been increasingly overshadowed by a number of other headline events, including the 2001 terrorist attacks on the United States and the Iraq War.

In the wake of 9/11, the Japanese public was as powerfully gripped by the fear of international terrorism as the American public, according to polls on the subject conducted by the major Japanese newspapers at the time. Two weeks after the events in the United States, 81 percent of respondents in an *Asahi Shimbun* poll believed that similar terrorist attacks might occur in Japan. When it comes to military action in Afghanistan and, especially, Iraq, however, Japanese public opinion was overwhelmingly negative from the beginning: In a January 2003 *Asahi Shimbun* poll, 69 percent of respondents opposed and 20 percent supported the U.S. invasion of Iraq, even if Iraq were in possession of weapons of mass destruction, as alleged. However, no organized actions or movements emerged in Japan against international terrorism or the wars in Afghanistan and Iraq. As on most international environmental issues, the Japanese public has remained passive, if not inarticulate, on the issue of international terrorism.

The Former Outcaste Class

The segregation of Japan's outcaste class dates back to the pre–Tokugawa era and survived until after World War II. For centuries, members of the class were condemned to pariah status associated with particular residential areas, known in recent times as "discriminated hamlets" or "unliberated hamlets," and were forced to do types of work once regarded as unclean, such as disposing of carcasses and working with hides and leather. The Japanese caste system was not as complex as the Hindu caste system in India and was more like the systems found in early medieval Europe and in premodern and early modern

China and Korea. As in the other places, the system was legally abolished long ago, but the prejudice it nurtured for centuries has persisted.

In the 1970s, a series of laws was passed to help eliminate the approximately 4,600 discriminated hamlets that still existed and integrate the more than 1 million people who lived there into the broader national community. Since then, considerable improvement has been made in the economic conditions of former outcaste communities, but complete equality and full integration into the national community remain unfulfilled goals.

The Women's Movement

The movement to improve the social and political status of women in Japan has a long history, dating back to the early part of the Meiji period. The movement had its origins in the democratic ideas imported from the West in the nineteenth century and was an important part of the "freedom and people's rights" movement in the 1880s. Japan's first major women's organization was the Tokyo Women's Temperance Union, founded in 1886, which campaigned mainly for the abolition of prostitution. The Bluestocking Society, formed in 1911 by a group of younger women writers, attacked the traditional patriarchal family system and called for the expansion of educational and professional opportunities for women.

The Taisho Democracy era after World War I saw the birth of women's organizations more explicitly committed to achieving gender equality in politics. The Society of New Women founded in 1920 successfully lobbied the Imperial Diet to amend the Peace and Police Law, which prohibited women's participation in political parties and other political organizations. This was followed by the formation of Japan's first suffragist organization in 1924 and its first openly socialist women's organization in 1929. In the militarist climate of the 1930s, however, all of these liberal women's organizations were disbanded and replaced by organizations promoting the traditional status and role of women as good homemakers, wives, and mothers.

The emancipation of women was one of the most important goals of the postwar reforms undertaken during the Allied Occupation. Japanese women were enfranchised for the first time and began to participate actively in politics as voters. Numerous women's organizations were founded, including the League of Japanese Women Voters, the Women's Democratic Club, and the Federation of Women's Organizations. Their presence and activities have improved Japanese women's social status and political roles. Discrimination against women, however, remains a conspicuous characteristic of contemporary Japanese society and politics.

The Equal Employment Law enacted in 1985, for example, requires employers to make efforts to prevent gender-based discriminatory practices, but does not provide penalties for violations. Although the law was revised in 1999, discrimination against women employees continues in the form of the so-called two-track hiring system, under which women are hired on a clerical and men on a managerial track. Prohibition of discrimination against pregnant women, which is commonplace in most other advanced industrial nations, has only begun to be seriously discussed in Japan. According to the 2007/2008 edition of the United Nations *Human Development Report* (HDR), Japan ranked eighth and the United States twelfth in the Human Development Index (HDI), which measures overall quality of economic and physical life, among 177 nations. But according to the 2007 edition of the World Economic Forum's *Global Gender Gap Report*, which measures degrees of gender equality in the areas of economic participation, educational attainment, political empowerment, and health and survival, Japan ranked ninety-first, as compared with the United States, which was thirty-first, among 128 nations. Thus, among advanced industrial societies, Japan has a particularly long way to go to achieve gender equality.

Ethnic Minorities: Ainu, Okinawans, Koreans, and New Immigrants

Japan is a relatively homogeneous society, but it does have serious identity problems, although they are neither as widespread nor as intense as those found in a number of other nations that are wracked by ethnic or religious conflict. Identity issues are of particular concern to the ethnic minority known as the Ainu,

those from Japan's southernmost island prefecture, Okinawa, formerly known as the Kingdom of the Ryukyus, and Koreans and other resident foreigners in Japan.

The Ainu are descendants of the ancient hunter-gatherers believed to have once inhabited the greater part of the northern regions of Japan, especially today's prefecture of Hokkaido. With their distinct language and culture, they were treated as a quasiforeign community before the Meiji Restoration. They traditionally had no concept or institution of private property and, during the Meiji period, when they began to be treated as integral members of the Japanese nation, they lost their communally owned land to immigrants from other regions of the country. They were also forced to abandon hunting by government decree. Most Ainu fell into extreme poverty. As the number of non-Ainu immigrants in their home territories grew, intermarriage increased. Today, about 30,000 Japanese citizens are known to have some Ainu ancestry, but the number of full-blooded Ainu is estimated to be no more than a few hundred.

Until the late 1990s, the Ainu were, in theory, protected by a nineteenth-century Law to Protect Former Native Inhabitants of Hokkaido. In practice, the impoverished Ainu community was afflicted with a high incidence of alcoholism, tuberculosis, and venereal disease. Their plight was almost completely ignored by the Japanese government and public until the mid-1980s. In 1986, a prime minister's reference to Japan as a homogeneous nation led leaders of the Ainu community to protest publicly and the prefectural government of Hokkaido to propose a new law to protect Ainu human rights, improve their social and economic conditions, and preserve and promote their traditional culture. An Ainu scholar-author, Kayano Shigeru, was the runner-up on the Japan Socialist Party proportional representation list in the 1992 upper house election; two years later, he filled a vacancy left by a deceased JSP member and became the first Ainu ever to serve in the Diet. He was instrumental in the enactment of the 1997 Law to Promote Ainu Culture, which replaced the archaic Meiji law.

The pre–Meiji status of the people in Japan's southernmost island chain, the prefecture of Okinawa, was somewhat similar to the Ainu's. They were subjects of the Kingdom of the Ryukyus, a state under Chinese suzerainty until the early seventeenth century, when the kingdom was invaded and occupied by a military force sent by the lord of a Japanese feudal domain in southern Kyushu and came under ambiguous dual suzerainty of Qing China and Tokugawa Japan. The Meiji government incorporated the island kingdom into the newly created system of local administration as one of three dozens or so prefectures in 1879.

Like the Ainus, Okinawans, with their own distinctive language and culture, have faced prejudice and discrimination. Throughout its history since the Meiji period to the present day, Okinawa has remained the poorest prefecture in the country. In the three-month-long Battle of Okinawa, by far the bloodiest fought between Japanese and U.S. forces within Japanese territory at the end of World War II, about 120,000, or nearly two-thirds, of the approximately 190,000 Japanese killed or missing were Okinawans and nearly 94,000, or 80 percent, of the latter were civilians, including many who committed suicide explicitly or implicitly by order of the local Japanese commanders. An attempt by nationalist scholars and Ministry of Education officials to revise secondary school history textbooks so as to absolve the Imperial Japanese Army of its responsibility for the mass suicides committed by many Okinawans during the Battle of Okinawa provoked in early 2008 the largest protest demonstration, with some 110,000 participants, in the islands' history. The island-wide protest forced the ministry to rescind most of the objectionable revisions proposed.

After the war ended with Japan's unconditional surrender in August 1945, Okinawa was administratively separated from the rest of the country, placed under U.S. military rule, and turned into a key outpost of U.S. forces in the cold war. The island prefecture was returned to Japanese administration in 1972, after 27 years of military occupation, and yet it remains host to three quarters of the U.S. military bases in Japan. These bases take up 10 percent of its entire land area, which accounts for only 0.6 percent of Japan's territory. Moreover, it still ranks at the bottom of the nation's forty-seven prefectures in per capita income, despite the influx of a large number of immigrants and

an even larger amount of capital from the rest of the country since its reversion to Japan's jurisdiction. The Okinawan identity as an ethnic minority has considerably weakened over the years, but not completely disappeared.

After the Meiji Restoration and especially after Japan annexed Korea in 1910, many Koreans migrated to Japan. Initially, most came to Japan voluntarily. By the 1930s, however, they were increasingly brought by force to work in some of the nation's most poorly equipped and accident-prone factories and mines. At the end of World War II, more than 2 million Koreans were living in Japan. A majority of them returned to South or North Korea, but a significant number stayed in Japan.

Unlike some countries, such as the United States, that grant citizenship, as a rule, to any person born within their territories regardless of their parents' citizenship status, based on the *jus soli* ("right of the soil") principle, Japan grants citizenship to anyone born of a parent who is a Japanese citizen regardless of where he or she is born, but to nobody else except through naturalization, based on the *jus sanguinis* ("right of blood") principle. Moreover, Japan does not permit dual citizenship. Most of the million or so ethnic Koreans who currently live in Japan were born of Korean parents and therefore were denied Japanese citizenship at birth. A minority of them have applied for and acquired Japanese citizenship after they reached the legally required age of 20. The majority, estimated to be about 600,000 at the present time, remain resident aliens, either because they have not reached the age required for naturalization application or because they choose not to give up their Korean citizenship for one reason or another. Like other alien residents, these Koreans cannot vote in Japanese elections, nor qualify to receive publicly funded social security or pension benefits, and often face discrimination in their personal lives, no matter whether they were born in Japan or how long they have lived in the country.

Today, there is substantial public support for allowing resident foreigners in general and Koreans in particular to vote and run as candidates in local elections, though not in Diet elections. By the end of 2005, more than half of the approximately 2,000 municipalities that existed at that time had adopted resolutions in favor of granting Korean residents the right to vote in local elections. The Supreme Court decided in 1995 that such a move would be constitutional. But the LDP and the government continue to oppose the move and have so far blocked it.

The most important and difficult problem related to ethnic minorities is no longer the physical hardships or material deprivations inflicted on them by deliberate government policy. In fact, many former minority enclaves have received generous financial assistance from both the national and local governments during the last three decades and today enjoy greatly improved community facilities, such as paved roads, well-equipped schools, public libraries, and community centers. The core issue facing the minorities in Japan is the social and cultural discrimination that they continue to experience, especially in employment and marriage.

Like many other advanced industrial societies, contemporary Japan attracts foreign workers who legally enter the country but often overstay their visa. As of late 2004, about 800,000 foreign workers, mainly from Asia and Brazil (virtually all Brazilians of Japanese descent), were employed in Japan, nearly 20 percent of them illegally. A large majority had come to Japan in search of jobs and ended up employed in menial and often exploitative jobs, including the "sex industry," that still paid them much higher wages than jobs available in their own countries. These immigrant workers are increasingly indispensable to many Japanese businesses suffering from chronic shortages of young and cheap labor, but these workers are also feared and resented by some Japanese, who see them as a threat to their own wages, pensions, free medical care, and even jobs. Unlike the situation in some European countries with much higher percentages of foreign workers and much higher unemployment rates, no organized violence against foreign workers by Japanese citizens has yet been reported.

SECTION 5 Japanese Politics in Transition

Political Challenges and Changing Agendas

Despite the sorry state of the economy, Japan remains an affluent and socially stable nation by international standards. Despite the protracted recession and the mounting public debts, the Japanese standard of living remains among the highest in the world. Although rocked by a particularly heinous crime from time to time, Japan's crime rate is still considerably lower than that of other major industrial nations. Absenteeism from school, defined as absence for more than three months per year, at the compulsory elementary and lower secondary education levels remains at, respectively, one-third of 1 percent and 2.7 percent. Besides, nearly all lower secondary school graduates enroll at and finish voluntary upper secondary school

The rapid aging, or "graying," of the nation's population is a social problem of great concern to the Japanese government and people today. Japan has the world's second longest average life expectancy: 78.7 years for men and 85.6 for women in 2007. At the same time, the country's current birthrate of about 1 percent is among the lowest in the world. As a result of these two trends, Japan is expected to have the highest percentage (22.5 per 1,000) of citizens over sixty-five years of age in the world by the year 2010. This will inevitably lead to a sharp rise in the cost of health care for elderly people and a significant shortfall in the number of younger, productive workers. Alarmed by these trends, some municipalities in Japan now offer monetary rewards to parents with new babies. But this has made little difference to the overall picture of steadily declining birthrates in the country as a whole.

In the area of foreign policy, the Japanese government's top priority remains the maintenance of the closest possible relationship with the United States, a goal set shortly after World War II and, by and large, successfully achieved by a long succession of

LDP-led governments. The United States has consistently been chosen as the most likable foreign country by a large plurality of respondents in every major public opinion poll taken in Japan during the past decade. It is small wonder, then, that the United States has long been the favorite overseas destination of Japanese tourists: 3.9 million Japanese visited the U.S. in 2005, compared with 3.4 million who visited China, including Hong Kong, and 2.4 million who went to South Korea.

Until about a decade ago, the United States-Japan Mutual Security Treaty was routinely condemned as being in violation of the peace clause of the 1947 Japanese Constitution, not only by the Communist and Socialist parties but also by many others, especially in academia and the labor movement. According to the results of recent public opinion polls, however, an overwhelming majority of Japanese now consider the treaty beneficial to Japanese national interests. Moreover, Japanese are increasingly receptive to the long-standing U.S. demand that Japan participate more willingly and extensively in both bilateral and multilateral peacekeeping operations, especially those undertaken under United Nations auspices, as discussed in Section 3. But growing opposition to the LDP-led coalition government's support of the American war in Iraq, which has included sending SDF troops to assist in the nation-building effort, reflects a seemingly widening gap between government action and the Japanese public's views of the war and, especially, of Japanese involvement in it. This threatens to erode the Japanese people's longstanding affection for and trust in the United States, particularly their approval of the military alliance between the two nations.

Next to its relationship with the United States, contemporary Japan has given high priority to the cultivation of friendly ties with its immediate neighbors in East Asia. Its effort on that score has been generally successful, with its relationships with China, South Korea, and all the Southeast Asian nations considerably improving during the last quarter century. The progress, however, has been disrupted, and often even reversed, by disputes over two highly charged and closely related issues.

First, every summer from the end of World War II to the end of Koizumi's prime-ministerial tenure in 2006, usually on August 15 (the date of Japan's surrender in World War II) after the mid-1970s, Japanese prime ministers and most cabinet members made it a rule to visit the controversial Yasukuni ("Nation at Peace") Shinto Shrine in Tokyo to pay their respects to the souls of the nearly 2.5 million "heroes" killed in the wars fought by Japan since the Meiji Restoration of the mid-nineteenth century. The Japanese leaders' visits are objectionable to many in the neighboring nations, mainly for two reasons. First, the overwhelming majority (86 percent) of the "war heroes" enshrined are those killed in World War II, including the seven top wartime government and military leaders who were executed for commission of war crimes. Second, the exhibitions and inscriptions at the museum attached to the shrine cling steadfastly to the position that the war, which it calls the "Greater East Asia War," was fought by Japan for its self-defense and that the postwar trials of the Japanese leaders and soldiers were totally arbitrary, biased, and unjustified. Faced with the outcries of the governments and citizens of the neighboring nations, especially China and both Koreas, the two latest prime ministers, Abe and Fukuda, but not some members of their cabinets, have refrained from visiting the shrine. Their successors, however, may resume the long established practice and rekindle the neighboring nations' criticisms.

The second controversy involves the official authorization of secondary school history textbooks that subscribe to a nationalistic ideology similar to that espoused by the Yasukuni Shrine. In a recent round of this decades-old controversy, a history textbook compiled by a group of right-wing historians was approved in the spring of 2001 by Ministry of Education reviewers for use in lower secondary schools. The news provoked instant and angry outcries among government leaders and intellectuals in China, South and North Korea, and several Southeast Asian nations. They charged that the textbook either completely ignored or papered over the Japanese aggression and brutalities committed by Japanese military and civilian personnel in their countries before and during World War II.

The Yasukuni Shrine and textbook episodes point to the presence and, in some quarters, expansion of a nationalistic, and potentially chauvinistic, ideology and movement in contemporary Japanese society. Prime Minister Koizumi's insistence on his right to make a ritual visit to the controversial Shinto shrine, no matter how much it might shock and anger many foreign governments and citizens, was emblematic of this aspect of Japanese political culture at the turn of the new millennium. So too is the immense popularity of Tokyo's governor and a well-known nationalist ideologue, Ishihara Shintaro. His recent remark—no doubt made tongue-in-cheek, but highly inflammable all the same—that if China kept bullying Japan, then Japan should threaten to arm itself with nuclear weapons—provoked little public and media attention or criticism in Japan. These are very disconcerting episodes to those who treasure the reputation of post-World War II Japan as a genuinely democratic and pacifist nation.

It would, however, be rash to jump to the conclusion that the nationalists, especially the more chauvinistic among them, are taking over Japan. Koizumi's visits to the Yasukuni Shrine were, in large measure, an obligatory gesture dictated by a promise he had made to war-bereaved families at the time of his election as LDP president. The controversial history textbook has been actually adopted and used by less than 1 percent of Japan's 11,000 or so lower secondary schools, forcing the publisher in 2007 to stop issuing the original version of the textbook (at a substantial loss).

Japan's role in the world, including its security policy, is undergoing notable, but often confusing, changes in other ways, too. The events of September 11, 2001, had a powerful impact on Japanese public opinion: in an October 2001 poll by Japan's largest newspaper, the *Yomiuri Shimbun,* antiterrorism measures ranked at the top of the list of the most urgent policies for the government to act on. Nonetheless, as mentioned already, Japanese public opinion remains opposed to the use of military force in antiterrorist, or any other, operations abroad. Polls taken by the *Asahi Shinbun* at the same time found those opposed to the deployment of SDF troops abroad outnumbering, 46 percent to 42 percent, those approving such actions. Those opposed to relaxing restrictions on the use of arms by SDF troops, too, outnumbered those who approved it, 51 percent to 39 percent.

Another factor affecting Japan's role in the world is the sharp decline of the country's global economic power during the past decade. Once touted as the world's most dynamic industrial economy, Japan ranked only twenty-fourth on a fifty-five-nation relative economic competitiveness list, compiled in 2007 by the International Institute for Management Development of Lausanne, Switzerland. Japan was the largest donor of official development assistance (ODA) funds throughout the 1990s, but yielded pride of place to the United States in 2001 and fell to the third rank below Britain in 2006.

Japanese Politics in Comparative Perspective

Postwar Japan's economic success inspired many other Asian nations to adopt the Japanese model of development. Like Japan, these countries used an assortment of government policies and institutions to facilitate human capital formation (especially education), high savings and investment rates, efficient resource allocation, and export expansion to stimulate the rapid growth of their national economies. But today's Japan is no longer an economic miracle or model.

Japan thus presents a model of state-led development that worked successfully for more than a century but faltered badly in the last decade of the 1990s and first years of the 2000s. This experience raises some interesting questions about the state's role in governing the economy:

- Why did the Japanese model of economic development work for so long, but then prove unable to adapt to changing domestic and international circumstances? In particular, what role did the state play in both the successes and failures of Japan's development model?
- Will state-led development ever work again in Japan and, if so, under what conditions? How would the role of government have to change in order to help revive the Japanese economy?

- Might the Japanese model still work successfully in other nations and, if so, under what domestic or international conditions and at what stages of national development?

Japan has also often been cited as a model of so-called East-Asian-style democracy. The Western model of democratic government emphasizes active citizen participation in the affairs of the state, the role of independent political parties and interest groups, and the periodic alternation of power among competing political parties. The Japanese model is said to rely on a passive and compliant citizenry and monopoly of power by one party or the government bureaucracy. Until recently, Japan and most of its Asian neighbors in fact tended to place far greater emphasis on economic growth and political stability than on citizen participation in politics or the protection of individual citizens' political and human rights. This emphasis is particularly agreeable to those who believe in the Confucian ideal of an orderly, hierarchical, harmonious society governed by a wise and benevolent ruler or ruling elite with the support of a loyal and obedient citizenry. This model has often been used to justify authoritarian and repressive governments in post-World War II Asia, but it has significantly weakened as individualistic democratization has spread to formerly authoritarian "Confucian" states, including South Korea and Taiwan.

The instability of Japanese politics since the LDP's electoral defeats in the 1990s also calls into question the long-term viability of such a model of governance in contemporary East Asia. Where there are deep economic, social, or ideological divisions in society, democracy inevitably gives rise to political contention. Japan experienced just such intense political conflict during the formative period of its postwar democracy (1947–1960). In fact, it took a major political crisis caused by a massive popular protest against the undemocratic and high-handed manner in which the government pursued the 1960 revision of the U.S.-Japanese Mutual Security Treaty to usher in a period of compromise and consensus that lasted for the next three decades and helped produce stability and prosperity.

In other words, it took Japan a decade and a half of intense political conflict—and several more decades if one considers the struggle for democracy in prewar Japan—to learn to practice democracy in peace. After the traumatic experience of 1960, the ruling LDP began to take the opposition's opinions on policy matters seriously. Long before its unchallenged dominance of Japanese politics ended in the early 1990s, the LDP had begun to co-opt and incorporate into its own programs many of the interests of organized labor, though not necessarily of unorganized workers or consumers, through informal consultations and deals made with the opposition, if only to avert another political crisis.[28]

The democratic idea thus did not become established in Japan in the absence of political conflict but rather through conflict, just as happened in western Europe and the United States. The rupture of consensus and return of open conflict that led to the change of government in 1993 did not mean a breakdown of democracy. On the contrary, it reflected the strength and maturity of Japanese democracy by proving the ability of Japanese citizens to "throw the rascals out" (the LDP) through the ballot box. Moreover, this changing of the guard gave the opposition an opportunity to participate in governing and the LDP a chance to learn how to be the opposition within the framework of democratic government.

While this first change of government in Japan in nearly forty years did not last long, it has helped to reduce oligarchic influences and increase democratic elements in contemporary Japanese politics. The succession of coalition governments that have governed the nation since 1993 have proven, by and large, more sensitive to public opinion and less beholden to special interests than earlier LDP one-party governments.

Nevertheless, nearly a decade into the twenty-first century, the first order of business for the Japanese government remains the real and effective reform of its many moribund political, economic, and social institutions, for the sake not only of its own people but also for the other nations in the Asia-Pacific region and, indeed, in the increasingly interdependent world, all of which have a stake in a politically stable and economically vibrant Japan.

Japan

Key Terms ≫

bushi (samurai)
Taisho Democracy
zaibatsu
Supreme Commander for the Allied Powers (SCAP)
Self-Defense Forces (SDF)
predominant-party regime
Sohyo
Domei
Rengo
industrial policy
administrative guidance
nontariff barriers (NTBs)
iron triangles
keiretsu
spring labor offensive
lifetime employment
newly industrialized countries (NICs)

Asian Development Bank (ADB)
Asia-Pacific Economic Cooperation (APEC)
Association of Southeast Asian Nations (ASEAN)
vertically divided administration
amakudari
"Lay Judge System" (*saibanin-seido*)
zoku
pork-barrel politics
clientelist
Single Non-Transferable Vote (SNTV)
koenkai
Mixed Member Proportional (MMP)
single-member district (SMD)
proportional representation (PR)
Minamata disease
Tokai Village

Suggested Readings ≫

Amyx, Jennifer A. *Japan's Financial Crisis: Institutional Rigidity and Reluctant Change*. Princeton, N.J.: Princeton University Press, 2004.

Barnhard, Michael A. *Japan Prepares for Total War: The Search for Economic Security, 1919–1941*. Ithaca, N.Y.: Cornell University Press, 1987.

Calder, Kent E. *Crisis and Compensation: Public Policy and Political Stability in Japan, 1949–1986*. Princeton, N.J.: Princeton University Press, 1988.

Callen, Tim, and Ostry, Jonathan D., eds. *Japan's Lost Decade: Policies for Economic Revival*. Washington, D.C.: International Monetary Fund, 2003.

Colignon, Richard A., and Usui, Chikako. *Amakudari: The Hidden Fabric of Japan's Economy*. Ithaca, N.Y., and London: Cornell University Press, 2003.

Dower, John. *Embracing Defeat: Japan in the Aftermath of World War II*. London: Penguin Books, 1999.

Francks, Penelope. *Japanese Economic Development: Theory and Practice*. London: Routledge, 1992.

Gluck, Carol. *Japan's Modern Myths: Ideology in the Late Meiji Period*. Princeton, N.J.: Princeton University Press, 1985.

Hall, John Whitney, et al., eds. *The Cambridge History of Japan*, 6 vols. Cambridge: Cambridge University Press, 1988–1993.

Hook, Glenn D., et al. *Japan's International Relations: Politics, Economics and Security*. London: Routledge, 2001.

Kohno, Masaru. *Japan's Postwar Party Politics*. Princeton, N.J.: Princeton University Press, 1997.

Leonardsen, Dag. *Japan as a Low-Crime Nation*. Houndmills, UK: Palgrave Macmillan, 2004.

Lockwood, William W. *The Economic Development of Japan: Growth and Structural Change, 1868–1938*. Princeton, N.J.: Princeton University Press, 1954.

McVeigh, Brian J. *Nationalisms of Japan: Managing and Mystifying Identity*. Lanham, Md.: Rowman and Littlefield, 2004.

Mulgan, Aurelia George. *Japan's Failed Revolution: Koizumi and the Politics of Economic Reform*. Canberra: Asia Pacific Press, 2002.

Pempel, T. J. *Regime Shift: Comparative Dynamics of the Japanese Political Economy*. Ithaca, N.Y.: Cornell University Press, 1998.

Samuels, Richard J. *"Rich Nation, Strong Army": National Security and the Technological Transformation of Japan*. Ithaca, N.Y.: Cornell University Press, 1994.

Stockwin, J. A. A. *Governing Japan: Divided Politics in a Resurgent Economy*. 4th ed. Oxford: Blackwell, 2008.

Upham, Frank K. *Law and Social Change in Postwar Japan*. Cambridge: Harvard University Press, 1987.

Wright, Maurice. *Japan's Fiscal Crisis: The Ministry of Finance and the Politics of Public Spending, 1975–2000*. Oxford: Oxford University Press, 2002.

Suggested Websites ≫

Asahi Shimbun, a newspaper
www.asahi.com/english
Daily Yomiuri Online, a newspaper
www.yomiuri.co.jp/dy
Japan Guide
jguide.stanford.edu
Japan Politics Central
jpcentral.virginia.edu

The Library of Congress
www.loc.gov/rr/international/asian/japan/resources/
japan-government.html
The Mainichi Daily News, a newspaper
http://mdn.mainichi.jp
Nikkei Net International, economic news
www.nni.Nikkei.co.jp

Endnotes ≫

[1]George Sansom, *A History of Japan, 1334–1615* (Stanford, Calif.: Stanford University Press, 1961); A. L. Sadler, *A Short History of Japan* (Sydney: Angus and Robertson, 1963), ch. 4–6.

[2]George De Vos and Hiroshi Wagatsuma, eds., *Japan's Invisible Race: Caste in Culture and Personality* (Berkeley: University of California Press, 1966); Frank K. Upham, *Law and Social Change in Postwar Japan* (Cambridge: Harvard University Press, 1987), ch. 3.

[3] Ronald P. Dore, *Education in Tokugawa Japan* (London: Athlone, 1965).

[4]W. G. Beasley, *Japan Encounters the Barbarian: Japanese Travellers in America and Europe* (New Haven, Conn.: Yale University Press, 1995), ch. 9.

[5]Peter Duus, *Party Rivalry and Political Change in Taisho Japan* (Cambridge, Mass.: Harvard University Press, 1968).

[6]Sadako N. Ogata, *Defiance in Manchuria: The Making of Japanese Foreign Policy, 1931–1932* (Berkeley: University of California Press, 1964), Pt. II.; Yoshihisa Tak Matsusaka, *The Making of Japanese Manchuria, 1904–1932* (Cambridge, MA, Harvard University Asia Center, distributed by Harvard University Press, 2001).

[7]Ben-Ami Shillony, *Revolt in Japan: The Young Officers and the February 26, 1936 Incident* (Princeton, N.J.: Princeton University Press, 1973).

[8]Robert E. Ward and Sakamoto Yoshikazu, eds., *Democratizing Japan: The Allied Occupation* (Honolulu: University of Hawaii Press, 1987); John Dower, *Embracing Defeat: Japan in the Aftermath of World War II* (London: Penguin Books, 1999).

[9]Haruhiro Fukui and Shigeko N. Fukai, "The End of the Miracle: Japanese Politics in the Post–Cold War Era," in *The Rise of East Asia: Critical Visions of the Pacific Century,* ed. Mark T. Berger and Douglas A. Borer (New York: Routledge, 1997), pp. 37–60.

[10]Charles C. Ragin, *The Comparative Method: Moving Beyond Qualitative and Quantitative Strategies* (Berkeley: University

of California Press, 1987), ch. 3; Adam Preworski and Henry Teune, *The Logic of Comparative Social Inquiry* (New York: Wiley-Interscience, 1970).

[11]Hugh Patrick and Henry Rosovsky, "Japan's Economic Performance: An Overview," in *Asia's New Giant: How the Japanese Economy Works,* ed. Hugh Patrick and Henry Rosovsky (Washington, D.C.: Brookings Institution, 1976), pp. 7–9; Takafusa Nakamura, " 'Yakushin nihon' no uraomote" [The Appearance and Reality of the "Advancing Japan"], in *Showa keizaishi* [*An Economic History of the Showa Period*], ed. Hiromi Arisawa (Tokyo: Nihon *Keizai Shimbunsha,* 1976), pp. 108–11; Hugh Borton, *Japan's Modern Century: From Perry to 1970,* 2nd ed. (New York: Ronald Press Co., 1970), p. 305, Table 5.

[12]William W. Lockwood, *The Economic Development of Japan: Growth and Structural Change, 1868–1938* (Princeton, N.J.: Princeton University Press, 1954), pp. 38–39.

[13]Ronald P. Dore, *Land Reform in Japan* (London: Oxford University Press, 1959), 176, Table 9.

[14]Lockwood, *The Economic Development of Japan,* pp. 14–15.

[15]Hidemasa Morikawa, *Zaibatsu: The Rise and Fall of Family Enterprise Groups in Japan* (Tokyo: University of Tokyo Press, 1992).

[16]Daniel I. Okimoto, *Between MITI and the Market: Japanese Industrial Policy for High Technology* (Stanford, Calif.: Stanford University Press, 1989), ch. 2.

[17]Nippon tokei kyokai, ed., *Toukei de miru nippon 2008* (Tokyo: Nippon tokei kyokai, 2007), p. 118.

[18]Somusho tokeikyoku and tokei kenkyujo [Statistics Bureau and Statistical Research and Training Institute, Ministry of Internal Affairs and Communications], eds., *Sekai no tokei* [*Statistics of the World*] (Tokyo: Ministry of Finance Printing Office, 2007), pp. 311, 313, Table 12–10.

[19]Nippon Tokei Kyokai, *Tokei de miru Nippon 2008,* pp. 178–179.

[20]Richard Rosecrance, *The Rise of the Trading State* (New York: Basic Books, 1986).

[21]Stephen D. Cohen, *Cowboys and Samurai: Why the United States Is Losing the Industrial Battle and Why It Matters* (New York: Harper Business, 1991).

[22]Herbert P. Bix, *Hirohito and the Making of Modern Japan* (New York: HarperCollins, 2000); Stephen S. Large, *Emperor Hirohito and Showa Japan: A Political Biography* (London: Routledge, 1992).

[23]Shigeko N. Fukai, "The missing leader: the structure and traits of political leadership in Japan," in Ofer Feldman, ed. *Political Psychology in Japan: Behind the Nails that Sometimes Stick Out (and Get Hammered Down)* (Hauppauge, NY: Nova Science Publishers, 1999.)

[24]Purnendra Jain and Takashi Inoguchi, eds. *Japanese Politics Today: Beyond Karaoke Democracy?* (New York: St. Martin's Press, 1997).

[25]Chalmers Johnson, *MITI and the Japanese Miracle: The Growth of Industrial Policy, 1925–1975* (Stanford, Calif.: Stanford University Press, 1982).

[26]Thomas P. Rohlen, *Japan's High Schools* (Berkeley: University of California Press, 1983). For an overview of contemporary Japanese school education, see Thomas P. Rohlen and Chris Björk, eds., *Education and Training in Japan,* 3 vols. (London: Routledge, 1998).

[27]Laurie Anne Freeman, *Closing the Shop* (Princeton, N.J.: Princeton University Press, 2000).

[28]Kent E. Calder, *Crisis and Compensation* (Princeton, N.J.: Princeton University Press, 1991).

Atul Kohli and Amrita Basu

Chapter 6 >> INDIA

Official Name: **Republic of India (Bharat)**

Location: **South Asia**

Capital City: **New Delhi**

Population (2008): **1.1 billion**

Size: **3,287,590 sq. km.; slightly more than one-third the size of the United States**

1526
Mughal dynasty founded.

1612–1690
British East India Company establishes trading stations at Surat, Bombay, and Calcutta.

1757
Britain establishes informal colonial rule.

1857
Britain establishes formal colonial rule in response to Sepoy Rebellion.

1885
Indian National Congress is created.

SECTION 1

The Making of the Modern Indian State

India is experiencing two revolutions, alongside and in opposition to one another. The first is the revolution in technology, industry, and trade that is celebrated in special issues of *Time*, *The Economist*, and *Foreign Affairs*. For the last twenty-five years or so, the Indian economy grew between 5 and 6 percent annually. Today, inspite of the global financial crisis that began in late 2008, India, along with China, is expected to remain one of the world's fastest growing and potentially largest economies. Unfortunately, India's growing wealth has exacerbated inequalities along regional, rural–urban, and class lines. Thus the second revolution is of the rising expectations of the poor and the dispossessed. Those who have not benefited from the technological revolution express their dissatisfaction in various arenas, anywhere from voting a party of the lowest strata into power, as in India's largest state, Uttar Pradesh, to waging violent insurgency in thirteen out of twenty-eight states. India's prime minister, Dr. Manmohan Singh, has characterized the "Maoist rebels" as India's major "law and order problem." And yet, with over a billion people, many of them very poor, India has maintained democratic institutions since gaining independence after World War II. How India can ensure economic growth while moderating inequalities within the frame of a democracy is one of its most pressing political challenges.

Politics in Action

Millions of Indians went to the polls in May 2004 and elected the Congress Party. The next general elections in India are expected in 2009. The current ruling party, The Congress is no longer a hegemonic ruling force. It has continued to rule only with the support of various other parties, including India's main communist party, the Communist Party of India, Marxist (or CPM). (The CPM, a parliamentary party, is entirely distinct from the Communist Party Maoist, an underground party engaged in guerilla activity.) The departure from old patterns of single party rule by The Congress also introduced some novel developments for Indian democracy. Sonia Gandhi, Rajiv Gandhi's widow, and heir to the Gandhi dynasty, stepped aside and passed the mantle of power to Manmohan Singh. For the first time ever, a man who was neither a leader of his own party nor that of the ruling alliance ruled India. Instead, he was a scholar, a civil servant, and a member of the Sikh minority community.

National elections in India are dramatic moments that reveal salient themes of contemporary Indian politics. The 2004 elections underline at least three such themes. First and foremost is a fairly obvious observation that nevertheless raises a significant question: India continues to elect its rulers through regular elections. With over a billion people of diverse cultural

1947
India achieves independence from Britain; India and Pakistan are partitioned; modern Indian state is founded.

1947–1964
Jawaharlal Nehru is prime minister.

1966–1984
Indira Gandhi is prime minister (except for a brief period from 1977 to 1980).

1999–2004
Bharatiya Janata Party government in power.

2004
Congress Party–dominated coalition government; the United Progressive Alliance comes to power.

Sonia Gandhi elected in the 2004 national elections. *Source:* © Amit Bhargava/Corbis.

backgrounds, many of them very poor, how has India managed to maintain democratic institutions since gaining independence after World War II?

Second, competition for power in India continues to be intense, with no political party enjoying a position of unchallenged dominance. (This represents a strong contrast with the period of several decades following independence, when the Congress Party won every election.) Neither of the two major electoral contenders, the Congress or the Bharatiya Janata Party (BJP), is at present able to muster anything close to a majority of parliamentary seats to form a government. As a centrist party, the Congress stands for secularism, economic liberalization, and mild redistribution of wealth. The BJP, by contrast, has championed religious nationalist and antiminority positions. In addition to these two main contenders, other major competitors include the all-India CPM and nearly thirty regional parties with a presence in the parliament. The CPM, though communist in name and organization, has evolved into a social democratic party that accepts the limits of a market economy and of democracy, but nevertheless seeks greater benefits for India's numerous poor. The last national elections that put Congress back at the helm, albeit supported by the communists, have been rightly interpreted as a victory—though quite possibly a temporary victory—for the forces of secularism and limited redistribution over the more conservative politics of the religious nationalists.

FIGURE 6.1

The Indian Nation at a Glance

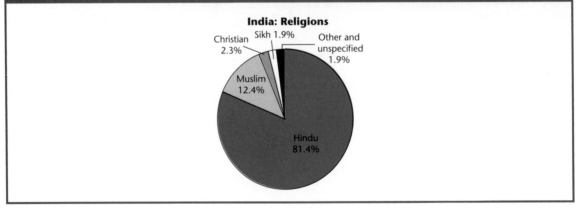

Geographic Setting

India is a populous and geographically and culturally diverse country. Its large size, approximately 2,000 miles in both length and width, is rivaled in Asia only by China. Its rich geographic setting includes three diverse topographic zones (the mountainous northern zone, the basin formed by the Ganges River, and the peninsula of southern India) and a variety of climates (mountain climate in the northern mountain range; dry, hot weather in the arid, northern plateau; and subtropical climate in the south).

Along with its neighbors Pakistan and Bangladesh, the region is physically isolated from the rest of Asia by the Himalayas to the north and the Indian Ocean to the east, south, and west. The northwest frontier is the only permeable frontier, and it is the route that successive invaders and migrants have used to enter this region.

With over 1 billion people, India is the country with the second largest population in the world, after its neighbor China. It is the world's largest democracy and the oldest democracy among the developing countries of Asia, Africa, and Latin America. India

---

Table 6.1

Political Organization

Political System	Parliamentary democracy and a federal republic.
Regime History	In 2004, the government was formed by the United Progressive Alliance; the Congress Party is the single largest party in the government and Manmohan Singh is prime minister.
Administrative Structure	Federal, with twenty-eight state governments.
Executive	Prime minister, leader of the party with the most seats in the parliament.
Legislature	Bicameral, upper house elected indirectly and without much substantial power; lower house, the main house, with members elected from single-member districts, winner-take-all.
Judiciary	Independent constitutional court with appointed judges.
Party System	Multiparty system. The Congress Party is the dominant party; the Bharatiya Janata Party (BJP) is the major opposition party.

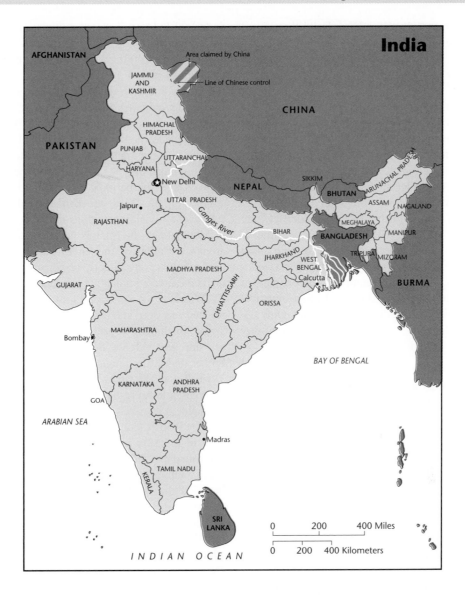

has functioned as a democracy with full adult suffrage since 1947, when it emerged as a sovereign nation-state, following the end of British colonial rule. The durability of Indian democracy is especially intriguing considering the diversity of Indian society. Some fourteen major languages and numerous dialects are spoken. India contains many different ethnic groups, a host of regionally concentrated tribal groups, as well as adherents of virtually every major religion. In addition to the majority Hindu population, India includes Muslims, **Sikhs**, Jains, Buddhists, Christians, and even several tiny Jewish communities. Furthermore, Indian society, especially Hindu society, is divided into myriad caste groupings. Although these are mainly based on occupation, they also tend to be closed social groups in the sense that people are born into, marry, and die within their caste. India is still largely an agrarian society; 70 percent of the population lives in far-flung villages in the rural areas. The major cities, Bombay (renamed Mumbai),

Calcutta (renamed Kolkata), and New Delhi, the national capital, are densely populated.

Critical Junctures

India's recorded history dates back to the Indus Valley Civilization of the third millennium B.C.E. The subcontinent, comprising Pakistan, India, and Bangladesh, has witnessed the rise and fall of many civilizations and empires. The invasion of northwestern India by Alexander the Great in 326 B.C.E. introduced the development of trade and communication with western Asia. Shortly after Alexander left, the Maurya dynasty (322–185 B.C.E.) under Emperor Ashoka united the kingdoms of northern India into a single empire. The Mughal dynasty (early sixteenth century to mid-nineteenth century) further expanded its kingdom to include most of the Indian subcontinent and parts of what is now Afghanistan. Only the most recent legacies that have shaped present-day politics are reviewed here.

The Colonial Legacy (1757–1947)

Motivated by a combination of economic and political interests, the British started making inroads into the Indian subcontinent in the late seventeenth and early eighteenth centuries. Since 1526, large sections of the subcontinent had been ruled by the Mughal dynasty, which hailed from Central Asia and was Muslim by religion. As the power of the Mughal emperors declined in the eighteenth century, lesser princely contenders vied with one another for supremacy. In this environment, the British East India Company, a large English trading organization with commercial interests in India and strong backing from the British Crown, was able to play off one Indian prince against another, forming alliances with some, subduing others, and thus strengthening its control through a policy of divide and rule. After a major revolt by an alliance of Indian princes against growing British power, known as the Sepoy Rebellion or the Mutiny of 1857, the British Crown assumed direct control of India and retained it until 1947.

In order to consolidate their political and economic hold, the British created three main varieties of ruling arrangements. First, the British allowed the **Maharajas**,

traditional Indian princes, to continue to rule as many as 500 small- to medium-sized states—covering an area equal to two-fifths of the subcontinent—throughout the colonial period. In exchange for accepting British rule, these Indian princes were allowed a relatively free hand within their realms. Second, in other parts of India, such as Bengal (currently Bihar, West Bengal, and Bangladesh), the British practiced indirect rule by transforming traditional Indian elites with large land holdings into legal landlords, the *zamindars,* in exchange for periodic payments to the colonial administration. Third, the British established direct rule in the remaining regions of India, for example, in Mumbai and the Madras presidencies (large areas around the cities of the same name), where British civil servants were directly responsible for collecting land taxes and adjudicating law and order.

Whatever its particular forms, British rule seldom reached very deep into Indian society, especially in rural areas, which were organized into countless relatively self-sufficient villages. Social life within villages was further divided by religiously sanctioned caste groups. Typically, a few landowning castes dominated many other castes lower in the ritual, occupational, and income hierarchies.

The British sought to create a semblance of coherence in India by creating a central government that controlled and led these various territories and indigenous authority structures. Important instruments included the creation of an all-India civil service, police force, and army. Although at first only British nationals could serve in these institutions, with the introduction of modern educational institutions, some educated Indians were incorporated into government services. Unlike many other colonies, particularly in Africa, the British helped create a relatively effective state structure in India. When India emerged from British rule in 1947, it inherited, maintained, and expanded colonial institutions. The contemporary civil administration, police, and armed services continue to be organized along the principles the British established in the last century.

The Nationalist Movement (1885–1947)

Two centuries of British colonial rule witnessed growing intellectual and cultural ferment in India. The

British colonial rulers and traditional Indian elites had become allies of sorts, squeezing from the poor Indian peasantry resources that they simultaneously used to maintain the colonial bureaucratic state and support the conspicuous lifestyles of a parasitic landlord class. With the growth of commerce, education, and urbanization, groups of urban, educated upper-caste Indian elites emerged as the new Indian leaders. They observed and closely interacted with their colonial rulers and resented being treated as second-class citizens. It was not long before Indian nationalists opposed these arrangements through the Indian National Congress (INC), which was actually formed by an Englishman in 1885. In its early years, the INC was mainly a collection of Indian urban elites who periodically met and petitioned British rulers, invoking liberal principles of political equality and requesting greater Indian involvement in higher political offices. The British largely ignored these requests, and over time, the requests turned into demands, pushing some nationalists into militancy and others into nonviolent mass mobilization.

World War I was an important turning point for Indian nationalists. After the war, as great European empires disintegrated, creating new sovereign states in Europe and the Middle East, the principle of self-determination for people who considered themselves a nation gained international respectability. Indian nationalists were also inspired by the Russian revolution of 1917, which they viewed as a successful uprising against imperialism.

Mohandas Karamchand Gandhi, one of the most influential and admirable leaders of the twentieth century, was primarily responsible for transforming the INC from a narrow, elitist club to a mass nationalist movement. After becoming INC leader in the 1920s, Gandhi successfully mobilized the middle classes, as well as a segment of the peasantry, into an anticolonial movement that came to demand full sovereignty for India. The more successful the INC became, the more the British either had to repress it or make concessions— and they tried both. However, World War II consumed Britain's energies, and made the political, economic, and symbolic costs of colonization extremely onerous. In order to gain Indian support for its war efforts, the British promised Indians independence. Soon after the war, India became a sovereign state in August 1947.

Three characteristics of the nationalist movement greatly influenced state building and democracy in India. First, the INC came to embody the principle of unity within diversity, which served India well in creating and maintaining a relatively stable political system. Because the INC became a powerful political organization committed to establishing an Indian nation, many conflicts could play themselves out within the INC without undermining its unity.

Second, the nationalist movement gave rise to lasting divisions between Hindus and Muslims. A segment of the Indian Muslim elite refused to accept the leadership of Gandhi and the INC, demanded separate political rights for Muslims, and called for an independent Muslim state when the INC refused. The resulting division of the subcontinent into two sovereign states in 1947—the Muslim state of Pakistan and the secular state of India, most of whose citizens were Hindu—was turbulent and bloody. Millions of Muslims fled from India to Pakistan, and millions of Hindus fled the other way; more than 10 million people migrated and nearly a million died in inter-ethnic violence. The euphoria of independence in India was thus tempered by the human tragedy that accompanied the subcontinent's Partition. India and Pakistan have fought three wars since Partition and, although there have been some significant recent initiatives to defuse tensions, relations between them remain frosty. Especially in the aftermath of the terrorist attacks in Mumbai in late 2008.

Third, the nationalist movement laid the foundations for democracy in India. Although Gandhi pioneered the use of civil disobedience to challenge British laws that he regarded as unjust, he did so on the basis of profound ethical commitments and nonviolent means. Many of the INC's prominent leaders, like Jawaharlal Nehru, were educated in England and were committed democrats. Moreover, the INC participated in limited elections allowed by the British, ran democratic governments with limited powers in various British-controlled Indian provinces, and chose its own leaders through internal elections. These preindependence democratic tendencies were valuable assets to Indian democracy.

The Nehru Era (1947–1964)

At independence, India was confronted with major political problems, including a massive inflow of refugees, war with Pakistan over the disputed state of

Leaders

Mohandas Karamchand Gandhi

Mohandas Karamchand Gandhi (called "Mahatma," great soul, by his followers) was born in 1869 in western India. He studied law in London for two years and worked in Durban, South Africa, as a lawyer and an activist for twenty-one years, developing the political strategies of nonviolence, or *satyagraha* (grasp of truth). On his return to India in 1915, he set about transforming the Indian National Congress into a mass party by reaching out to the urban and rural poor, non-Hindu religious groups, and the scheduled castes, who he called *Harijans*, or Children of God. Following the British massacre of unarmed civilians gathered in protest in the Punjab (at Jallianwala Bagh, a location well known in Indian history) in April 1919, Gandhi and Jawaharlal Nehru proposed a noncooperation movement. This required a boycott of British legal and educational institutions as well as British merchandise in favor of *swadeshi*, or indigenous varieties. (The image of Gandhi weaving his own cloth is familiar to many.) Gandhi believed that mass civil disobedience could succeed only if people were truly committed. The involvement of some Congress workers in a violent incident in 1922 greatly disturbed him, causing him to call off the noncooperation movement. Gandhi was strongly opposed to the partition of India along religious lines in 1947, but because he had resigned from Congress in 1934, his protests were ignored. Nevertheless, he dominated India's nationalist movement for more than two decades until he was assassinated in January 1948, five months after India achieved its goal of self-rule, or *swaraj*, by a Hindu extremist who thought Gandhi was overly sympathetic to Muslim interests.

Mahatma Gandhi, the leader of India's independence movement as he appeared at the head of a 200-mile march, staged in defiance of the statute establishing a government salt monopoly by the British colonial government in 1930. *Source:* UPI/Bettmann.

Kashmir situated between the two countries, and the need to consolidate numerous Indian princely states into a coherent national state. Nehru used the governmental machinery that India had inherited to accomplish these tasks.

After independence, India adopted a democratic constitution and established a British-style democracy with full adult suffrage. Because political power now required winning elections, the INC had to transform itself from an opposition movement into a political party, the Congress Party. It was highly successful in doing so, in part by establishing a nationwide patronage system. The Indian constitution defines India as a federal system.

Another important change in the decade following independence was the linguistic reorganization of states. Hindi is the most widely spoken Indian language; however, most Hindi speakers are concentrated in the north-central part of the country. Indians living in the south, east, and parts of the west speak a variety of other languages. Concerned about domination by Hindi speakers, many of these non-Hindi groups demanded a reorganization of the Indian union into linguistically defined states. Initially, Nehru resisted this demand, worried that linguistic states within a federation might become secessionist and demand sovereignty. As demands for linguistic states mounted, especially from south Indian groups, Nehru compromised in 1956: the new Indian union was organized around fourteen linguistically defined states. In the years that followed, additional states were carved out of existing ones, and there are now twenty-eight major states within India.

Jawaharlal Nehru was an internationalist who wanted India to play a global role. Together with other postcolonial leaders of Asia and Africa, Nehru initiated what became known as the nonaligned movement, which united those countries wishing to maintain a distance from the two superpowers. India and many other developing countries viewed both Western capitalism and Soviet communism with suspicion. Under Nehru, India played a leadership role among nonaligned developing countries while pursuing mixed economic policies at home that were neither fully capitalist nor fully socialist (see Section 2).

Nehru's initiatives put India firmly on a stable, democratic road. However, the colonial state's tendency to favor landowning Indian elites carried over into the Nehru era. Powerful groups in the society, including elite bureaucrats, wealthy landowners, entrepreneurs, and leaders of well-organized ethnic movements, enjoyed a favored position. While Nehru and the Congress Party continued to maintain a pro-poor, socialist rhetoric, they generally failed to deliver on their promises.

The Indira Gandhi Era (1966–1984)

When Nehru died in 1964, the Congress Party was divided over the choice of a successor and hurriedly selected mild-mannered Lal Bahadur Shastri as prime minister. When he died of a heart attack in 1966 and rivalry again broke out over his successor, party elites found a compromise candidate in Nehru's daughter, Indira Gandhi. They chose her to capitalize on the fact that as Nehru's daughter, she would help the Congress Party garner the electoral support it needed to remain in power. They also calculated that she would be a weak woman who could be manipulated by competing factions within the party. They were right about the first point, but decisively wrong about the second.

As prime minister from 1966 to 1984, except for the brief period of 1977 to 1980, Indira Gandhi's rule had several long-term legacies for contemporary Indian democracy. First, Indian politics became more personalized, populist, and nationalist. During the late 1960s, the Bengali-speaking eastern half of Pakistan, which was separated from its western half by nearly 1,000 miles of Indian territory, demanded sovereignty. As violence escalated within Pakistan and refugees from East Pakistan began pouring into India, Gandhi ordered Indian forces to intervene. This led to the creation of the sovereign state of Bangladesh. Because the United States sided with Pakistan in that conflict (and the Soviet Union backed India), Indira Gandhi was able to mobilize Indian nationalist sentiment against both Pakistan and the United States. India's victory increased Indira Gandhi's popularity. She soon consolidated her leadership over the Congress Party, forcing out leaders who opposed her and replacing them with loyal allies. She thereby created a new Congress Party in her own image and portrayed the old Congress elite as conservative defenders of the status quo. Gandhi's populist rhetoric won her the support of India's poor. From 1971 to 1984, she dominated Indian politics as much as Mahatma Gandhi or her father ever had.

A second legacy of Indira Gandhi's rule was to further centralize the Indian political system. During the Nehru era, local elites had helped select higher political officeholders, but in the 1970s, Indira Gandhi directly appointed officeholders at both the national and regional levels. Although this strategy enabled her to gain a firm grip over the party, it isolated her from broader political forces and eroded the legitimacy of regional leaders.

Leaders

The Nehru–Gandhi Dynasty

Jawaharlal Nehru

Jawaharlal Nehru was a staunch believer in liberal democratic principles. Along with Gandhi and others, he was at the forefront of India's nationalist movement. When India became independent in 1947, Nehru became prime minister, as head of the Congress Party, and retained that position until his death in 1964. Nehru, a committed nationalist and social democrat, sought to strengthen India's autonomy and national economy and improve the lives of the Indian poor. He established India as a socialist, democratic, and secular state in theory, if not always in practice. On the international front, he helped found the nonaligned movement, a forum for expressing the interests and aspirations of developing countries that did not want to ally with the United States or the Soviet Union during the cold war. Nehru attempted to set India on a rapid road to industrialization by establishing heavy industry. He was equally committed to redistributing wealth through land reform and to democratic and individual rights, including the right to private property. Upon his death, India inherited a stable polity, a functioning democracy, and an economy characterized by a large public sector and an intricate pattern of state control over the private sector.

Indira Gandhi

Indira Gandhi (no relation to Mahatma Gandhi) became prime minister shortly after the death of her father, Jawaharlal Nehru, and dominated the Indian political scene until her assassination in 1984. Her years in power strengthened India's international position, but her domestic policies weakened democratic institutions. Her tendencies toward centralization and the personalization of authority within the Congress and the concomitant use of demagogic rhetoric in electoral campaigns contributed to the erosion of the Congress Party. By defining the regional conflict in the Punjab and tensions with Pakistan as Hindu–Sikh and Hindu–Muslim problems, respectively, she contributed to further erosion of the party's secular base and to rising religious violence. Her decision to send troops into the holiest of the holy Sikh temples in Amritsar, in order to root out Sikh militants using the temple as a sanctuary, deeply alienated Sikhs, a small but important religious group in India. The ensuing bloodshed culminated in her assassination by one of her Sikh bodyguards in 1984. Her death ushered in a new generation of the Nehru–Gandhi dynasty, as her son Rajiv Gandhi served as prime minister until 1989.

A third important legacy of Indira Gandhi's rule was her failure to translate populist rhetoric into real gains for India's poor. She was unable to redistribute agricultural land from large landowners to those who worked the land or to generate employment, provide welfare, or improve access by the poor to education and medical services.

Indian politics became increasingly turbulent under Indira Gandhi, a fourth legacy of her rule. As her popularity soared, so did opposition to her. The old Congress elite denounced her demagogic political style, arguing that her government was corrupt; they began organizing mass demonstrations and strikes to press their case. In 1974, the political situation in India became quite unstable; with the opposition organizing general strikes, Indira Gandhi declared a national **Emergency**, suspended many democratic rights, and arrested most opposition leaders. The Emergency lasted nearly two years, the only period since 1947 when India was not a fully functioning democracy.

In 1977, Indira Gandhi rescinded the Emergency and called for national elections, confidently expecting that she would be reelected. To her surprise, she was soundly defeated, and for the first time since independence, a non-Congress government came to power. Various groups that had opposed Gandhi hastily joined together in a loosely organized party (the Janata Party) that was able to unite India's fragmented opposition groups and achieve electoral success. However, soon after the elections, Janata leaders became factionalized, and the Janata government collapsed. Indira Gandhi exploited the situation to regain power in the 1980 parliamentary elections.

Indira Gandhi's tenure in power between 1980 and 1984 was marked by a personal and populist political style, an increasingly centralized political system, failure to implement antipoverty policies, and growing political turbulence. However, she departed from her previous approach in two ways. The first was in the realm of the economy. During the 1970s, India's industrial establishment grew relatively slowly because the government spent too much on buying political support and too little on investment; incomes of the poor were not improving, and therefore demand for new products was limited. Excessive rules and regulations were counterproductive, both for domestic entrepreneurs and for integrating India into the world economy. With few means to rechannel government spending or improve the spending capacity of the poor, Gandhi started changing the rules that governed India's economy, especially embracing India's private sector as a means to improve economic performance.

The second important change concerns the strategy Indira Gandhi employed to achieve electoral support. Given her weakening commitment to socialism and secularism, which both she and her father had championed since the 1950s, Indira Gandhi needed to devise an alternative platform. In the early 1980s, she began to use religious appeals to mobilize India's Hindu majority. By introducing religion into politics, the Congress Party sowed the seeds for the growth of the Hindu nationalist BJP.

Another way that religious conflicts began to reenter Indian politics in the early 1980s involved the growing conflict between the Sikh religious minority, based in the Punjab, and the national government. During the course of the conflict, Indian security forces invaded and extensively damaged the holiest Sikh shrine, the Golden Temple in the city of Amritsar, to attack Sikh militants besieged there. In 1984, Gandhi was killed by one of her Sikh bodyguards. Immediately after Gandhi's assassination, rampaging mobs of Hindus brutally murdered Sikhs in New Delhi, Kanpur, and other north Indian cities. Most of the 3,700 Sikh victims were poor. Some leading figures within the Congress Party orchestrated anti-Sikh violence. In this respect, it resembled the anti-Muslim violence organized by the BJP in the following decade.

Indira's son, Rajiv Gandhi, won a landslide victory in the subsequent national elections as a result of the sympathy that his mother's assassination generated. He came to office promising clean government, a high-tech economy that would carry India into the next century, and reduced ethnic conflict. He was somewhat successful in ameliorating tensions in the state of Punjab. But Rajiv Gandhi inflamed tensions between Hindus and Muslims by sponsoring a law that placed Muslim women under the purview of the family. His leadership was marred by allegations of corruption concerning an arms deal between the Indian government and the Swedish Bofors company.

With Indira Gandhi's death, the tradition of powerful and populist prime ministers came to an end. India has since been facing poverty and governmental instability that began during the Indira Gandhi era. This was evident in increasing factionalism within the Congress Party, India's dominant party since independence. Moreover, other secular political parties proved unable to fill the vacuum in government caused by the Congress Party's disintegration.

Coalition Governments (1989 to the Present)

In not one of the six parliamentary elections since 1989 has a single party won an absolute majority of seats. Between 1998 and 2004, a BJP-led coalition government with Atal Behari Vajpayee as prime minister ruled India. A coalition government, the United Progressive Alliance (UPA), headed by the Congress Party with Manmohan Singh as prime minister, won the 2004 elections. Coalition governments at the national level and in most states have generally been hurriedly arranged and poorly conceived. The cement that binds coalitions together has been more negative than positive. For example, opposition to Congress brought the Janata government to power in 1977. Opposition to the BJP played a major role in the election of the UPA in 2004 (see Table 6.2).

Politics in India today is characterized by precarious coalition governments, weakened political

Table 6.2

Prime Ministers of India, 1947–Present

	Years in Office	Party
Jawaharlal Nehru	1947–1964	Congress
Lal Bahadur Shastri	1964–1966	Congress
Indira Gandhi	1966–1977	Congress
Morarji Desai	1977–1979	Janata
Charan Singh	1979–1980	Janata
Indira Gandhi	1980–1984	Congress
Rajiv Gandhi	1984–1989	Congress
V. P. Singh	1989–1990	Janata
Chandra Shekhar	1990–1991	Janata (Socialist)
Narasimha Rao	1991–1996	Congress
Atal Bihari Vajpayee	1996 (13 days)	BJP & allies
H. D. Deve Gowda	1996–1997	United Front
I. K. Gujral	1997–1998	United Front
Atal Bihari Vajpayee	1998–1999, 1999–2004	BJP & allies
Manmohan Singh	2004–	Congress & allies

institutions, periodic electoral violence, and considerable political activism along class and ethnic lines. These developments have generated policies that range from limited action on the economic front to nationalist outbursts on the political front. Whether any party or charismatic leader capable of unifying the country across the salient cleavages will emerge remains to be seen.

India after September 11

The tense relations between India and the United States during the cold war began to improve under the Clinton administration, after the Soviet Union's demise deprived India of its former ally. Since September 11, 2001, the United States has greatly increased its military presence in Asia and seeks to gain greater access to the Indian Ocean and Persian Gulf, for which it needs India's cooperation. The United States has become increasingly involved in trying to resolve regional conflicts within South Asia. It sought to negotiate Indo-Pakistan tensions over Kashmir, the civil war in Sri Lanka, and armed conflict between the monarchy and Maoist militants in Nepal, and most recently, Indo-Pak tensions created by the terrorist attacks on Mumbai.

In a striking departure from past practice, political and military relations between India and the U.S. have continued to improve. India strongly supported the U.S. intervention in Afghanistan. With the overthrow of the Taliban and the establishment of the Hamid Karzai government, India established close diplomatic, civil, and commercial ties to the new Afghan government. Tensions between India and the United States resurfaced in 2003 when India opposed the U.S. war against Iraq, on the grounds that it did not have UN backing. Yet strong forces continue to favor close ties between the two countries. The United States is India's largest trading partner, and U.S.-based investment in the Indian economy has substantially increased. India has sought to retain its prominent place in Washington's security strategy. The U.S. and India formalized a pact in 2008 that would allow India to acquire nuclear materials globally while integrating India into a closer alliance with the U.S. The challenge for India will be how to strengthen ties with the United States without compromising its own regional ambitions and submitting to all of Washington's preferences.

Themes and Implications

Historical Junctures and Political Themes

India in a World of States.   India's domestic difficulties reflect and influence its changing status in the world of states. In an increasingly interdependent global political and economic system, India's attainment of nuclear weapons signaled the dawn of a new era. As a result, simmering historical tensions over territories such as Kashmir will need to be managed very carefully. India shares borders with two nuclear powers, China and Pakistan, and has engaged in wars and periodic border skirmishes with both. India and Pakistan have a history of hostilities, and their politicians have exploited the tensions between them during domestic political crises. An important challenge facing the Indian state is how to simultaneously improve relations with the U.S.A. and China.

Governing the Economy.   Successful economic performance is necessary for India to fulfill its national and global ambitions. Indian policymakers initially sought economic self-sufficiency through a policy of state-led industrialization focused on meeting the needs of its large internal market. This protectionist economic strategy had mixed results. Although it resulted in the development of some important basic industries, it also generated extensive inefficiencies and did little to alleviate the country's severe poverty. Like many other developing nations, India must adjust its economic strategy to meet the demands of increasingly competitive and interdependent global markets. Since about 1980, India's leaders have consistently sought to reform the Indian economy, with some favorable results. During the 1980s, these reforms consisted mainly of government incentives to India's established private sector to increase production. Since 1991, the reforms have opened the Indian economy to the outside world. The results include a growing economy but also growing inequalities. Among the daunting challenges facing Indian leaders is how to ensure sustained growth while sponsoring measures to reduce economic inequalities.

The Democratic Idea.   India has sustained the democratic idea for over half a century, barring a short period of authoritarianism between 1975–1977. India can boast of a vibrant and vigilant civil society, periodic elections, unfettered media, and relatively autonomous courts and bureaucracy. However, these institutions have been corroded over the years. Since the late 1980s, political parties have deployed electoral strategies that have exacerbated ethnic tensions. One challenge that India faces is how to balance an increasingly divided society with the demands of social, economic, and political citizenship for all. Further, since the vast majority of India's citizens are Hindu, political parties may be tempted to play the Hindu card to the detriment of India's minority religious communities.

India has recently become more democratic in some ways but less so in others. More groups with more diverse identities are participating in politics than ever before. They are joining a larger range of political parties from more diverse regions of the country. The Indian political class can no longer be identified with a single region, caste, and class. However, India's business groups are also well organized and wield considerable influence on the decision-making of Indian governments; this tends to negate some of the popular gains of identity politics. Moreover, a key ingredient of democracy is the protection of minority rights, and on this count India is also less democratic than in the past. India's Muslims are especially insecure about their well-being in India.

The Politics of Collective Identity.   That there are intense conflicts around the issue of collective identity is not surprising in multicultural India. However, parties and the state have mobilized the electorate along ethnic lines in elections, with dangerous consequences. Democracy should provide a level playing field for a tussle between different interests and identities. India faces the challenge of reconciling domestic electoral strategies of ethnic mobilization to capture power with the moderation that is demanded in the exercise of such power, all the while coping with the demands of multiethnic and multiclass groups and sustaining economic growth.

Implications for Comparative Politics

Certain exceptional features of the Indian state have great significance for the study of comparative politics. First, India is a poor yet vibrant democracy. Despite widespread poverty and illiteracy, most Indians value their citizenship rights and exercise them vigorously. India belies theories of modernization that posit that democracy and economic growth are conjoined. At independence, the country was struggling with problems of nation building, poverty, and poor human development indicators, and was managing a transition to democracy. Against all odds, India became and remains a thriving democracy, an especially striking achievement given the authoritarian fate of most other newly independent colonies in Asia and Africa.

Second, the Indian state has managed to remain fairly cohesive and stable—although this must be qualified by the turmoil at various times in the states of Punjab, Gujarat, and especially Kashmir. Indian politics thus offers a case study of the tempering influence of democracy on ethnic cleavages. Contrast the BJP's exclusionary rhetoric when it was in opposition with its rhetorical shift toward moderation after becoming India's ruling party in 1999. In an attempt to stabilize a fractious multiparty coalition government, the BJP was forced to put contentious religious issues such as the temple in Ayodhya on a back burner.

Third, as home to over a billion people with diverse cultural, religious, and linguistic identities, Indian democracy offers an arena for testing and studying various theories and dilemmas of comparative politics. For instance, one dilemma is how multiethnic democracies can develop a coherent institutional system that provides representation to diverse interests without degenerating into authoritarianism or total collapse.

Fourth, theorists dealing with recent transitions to democracy in Latin America and Eastern Europe have puzzled over the question of what constitutes a consolidated democracy and how one achieves such consolidation. Here, a comparison between India and Pakistan is instructive. Whereas India has functioned as a democracy for all but two years since 1947, Pakistan has functioned as an authoritarian state with military rule for most of the same period. Why should this be so? Moreover, the Indian experience with authoritarianism during the Emergency era in the late 1970s and the resurgence of democratic norms when Indira Gandhi was voted out by an angry citizenry show the importance of elections. It also shows that the existence of democratic institutions and procedures can lead to the diffusion of democratic norms throughout the society.

Fifth, comparativists have explored whether democracy and social equity can be achieved simultaneously in poor countries. The case of Kerala, a state in southern India, suggests an affirmative answer. Although it is one of the poorest states in India, Kerala has achieved near-total literacy, long life expectancy, low infant mortality, and high access to medical care. Kerala's development indicators compare favorably with the rest of India, other low-income countries, and even wealthy countries like the United States. Why should Kerala perform so much better than many other Indian states?

Finally, there is a lively debate in comparative politics concerning the impact of democracy on economic growth. While cross-national evidence remains inconclusive, India's record of steady growth of 6 percent annually for nearly twenty-five years suggests the tantalizing possibility of successful economic management within the framework of a democracy. What can other emerging democracies learn from India's recent experience in growth promotion?

This discussion of critical junctures in Indian history highlights the central challenge of contemporary Indian politics: how to establish a coherent, legitimate government that will use its power to facilitate economic growth and equitable distribution. The former requires the formation of durable electoral coalitions without exacerbating political passions and ethnic conflicts. The latter requires careful implementation of policies that simultaneously help entrepreneurs produce goods and ensure a fair distribution of national income.

SECTION 2 Political Economy and Development

At the time of independence, India was largely a poor, agricultural economy. Although a majority of Indians, especially India's poor, still work and live in the countryside, India today also has a substantial industrial base and a vibrant middle class. Since the introduction of economic liberalization policies under Narasimha Rao's Congress government in 1991, all Indian governments have supported economic reform. Before discussing what liberalization entails, why it has become a priority, and what its implications are for Indian politics, we review the historical evolution of the Indian economy.

State and Economy

The Economy under British Rule

During the colonial period, the Indian economy was largely agricultural, with hundreds of millions of poor peasants living in thousands of small villages, tilling the land with primitive technology, and producing at a low level of efficiency. The British, along with Indian landlords, extracted extensive land revenues, taxes, and tributes from Indian princes. However, they reinvested only a small portion of this surplus into improving agricultural production. As a result of this mismanagement, Indian agricultural productivity mostly stagnated in the first half of the twentieth century. For example, productivity in India was considerably lower in 1950 than in Japan or even China.

Some industry developed under colonial rule, but its scope was limited. The British sold manufactured goods to India in exchange for Indian raw materials. Because the British economy was more advanced, it was difficult for Indians to compete successfully. Indigenous manufacturing, especially artisanal production, was ruined by the forced opening of the Indian market to British goods. Thus, the Indian economy at independence in 1947 was relatively stagnant, especially in agriculture. Some private sector industry did develop, but it constituted only a small proportion of the national economy.

The Economy after Independence

One of the central tasks facing Indian leaders after 1947 was to modernize the sluggish economy. During Nehru's rule, India adopted a model of development based largely on private property, although there was extensive government ownership and guidance of private economic activity. Nehru created a powerful planning commission that, following the Soviet model, made five-year plans for the Indian economy, outlining government investment priorities. Unlike the plans in communist party states, however, the Indian plans also indicated priority areas for private entrepreneurs, who remained a powerful force in the Indian economy.

The Indian government levied high tariffs on imports, arguing that new Indian industries, so long disadvantaged under colonial rule, required protection from foreign competitors. The government tightly regulated the start-up and expansion of private industries under the presumption that the government was the best safeguard of the public interests. This government-planned private economy achieved mixed results. It helped India create an impressive industrial base but did little to help the poor, and its protected industries were quite inefficient by global standards.

Nationalist in temperament, Nehru and other Congress Party leaders were suspicious of involving foreign investors in India's economic development. The government thus undertook a series of coordinated economic activities on its own. It made significant public sector investments to create such heavy industries as steel and cement; protected Indian entrepreneurs from foreign competition; where possible, further subsidized these producers; and finally, created elaborate rules and regulations controlling the activities of private producers. As a result, India developed a substantial industrial base over the next few decades.

Congress leaders promised to redistribute land from landowners to tenants in order to weaken the former supporters of the colonial government and motivate the tillers of the land to increase production. Although it eliminated some of the largest landowners in the early 1950s, it allocated poor tenants and agricultural laborers very little land. Unlike the communist government in China, India's nationalist government had neither the will nor the capacity to undertake radical property redistribution. Instead, most of the land remained in the hands of medium- to large-sized landowners. Many became part of the Congress political machine in the countryside. This development further weakened the Congress Party's capacity to assist the rural poor and undermined its socialist commitments.

The failure of land reforms led to a new agricultural strategy in the late 1960s known as the **green revolution**. Instead of addressing land redistribution, the state sought to provide landowners with improved seeds and access to subsidized fertilizer. Because irrigation was essential for this strategy to succeed and because irrigation was assured only to larger farmers in some regions of India, the success of the green revolution was uneven. Production increased sharply in some areas, such as the Punjab, but other regions (and especially the poorer farmers in these regions) were left behind. Nevertheless, as a result of this strategy, India became self-sufficient in food (and even became a food exporter), thus avoiding the mass starvation and famines that had occurred in the past.

Between 1950 and 1980, the Indian government promoted what has been described as **state-led economic development**. This development policy consisted of an expansion of the public sector, protection of the domestic sector from foreign competition, and rules and regulations to control private sector activity. Political leaders hoped to strengthen India's international position by promoting self-sufficient industrialization.

To a great extent, the Indian government succeeded in achieving this goal. By 1980, India was a major industrial power able to produce its own steel, airplanes, automobiles, chemicals, military hardware, and many consumer goods. On the agricultural side, although land reforms had failed, the revised agricultural strategy had improved food production.

State-led development insulated the Indian economy from global influences. The strategy resulted in modest economic growth—not as impressive as that of Brazil, Mexico, or the Republic of Korea, but better than that of many less developed countries. The main beneficiaries were the business classes, medium and large landowning farmers, and political and bureaucratic elites. A substantial urban middle class also developed during this phase. However, state-led development was associated with a number of problems. First, given the lack of competition, much industry was inefficient by global standards. Second, the elaborate rules and regulations controlling private economic activity encouraged corruption, as entrepreneurs bribed bureaucrats to get around the rules. And third, the focus on heavy industry directed a substantial portion of new investment into buying machinery rather than creating jobs. As a result, 40 percent of India's population, primarily poor tenant farmers and landless laborers, did not share in the fruits of this growth. And because population growth continued, the number of desperately poor people increased substantially during these decades.

Economic Liberalization

India moved toward **economic liberalization** beginning in the 1980s and accelerating after 1991. Throughout the world, socialist models of development came under attack. Within India, political and economic elites were increasingly dissatisfied with India's relatively sluggish economic performance, especially compared with dynamic East Asian economies. For example, during the 1970s, whereas India's economy grew at the rate of 3.4 percent per year, South Korea's grew at 9.6 percent. India's business and industrial classes increasingly found government intervention in the economy more of a hindrance than a help. Realizing that poverty limited the possibility for expanding domestic markets, they increasingly sought to export their products.

India's economy has done relatively well since the 1980s, growing at an average of 6 to 7 percent per year, a record especially noteworthy when compared to the dismal performance of many debt-ridden Latin American and African economies, such as Brazil and Nigeria. Some of this improved performance resulted from domestic liberalization that, since the 1980s, has enabled Indian entrepreneurs to operate with fewer government restrictions, and since 1991 from external liberalization that has further integrated India into the global economy. Economic performance has also been improved by public loans to small factory owners and farmers and by public investments in their enterprises. However, a large part of economic growth in the 1980s was based on increased borrowing from abroad, which represented a shift from a conservative fiscal policy. This expansionary fiscal policy, largely funded by foreign loans, was risky because India's exports to other countries did not grow very rapidly. For example, its exports during the 1980s grew at approximately 6 percent per year in comparison to 12 percent per year for both South Korea and China. As a result, the need to repay foreign loans put enormous pressure on the government toward the end of the decade. India was forced in the early 1990s to borrow even more from such international agencies as the International Monetary Fund (IMF) and the World Bank. In return for fresh loans, these international organizations required the Indian government to reduce its deficit through such controversial measures as reducing subsidies to the poor and selling government shares in public enterprises to the private sector. Critics allege that the government sold some public enterprises at prices well below their market value.

Liberalization has both a domestic and an international component. The government has sought to dismantle controls over private sector economic activities, especially in industry. More recently, new industries have been created, including oil and natural gas, transportation infrastructure, telecommunications, and power generation. The government has provided a variety of incentives to industry, including tax breaks, eliminating customs duties on the import of equipment, and underwriting losses.

Alongside government reforms aimed at opening up and privatizing the economy have been policy moves to cut the workforce in public enterprises in order to reduce public spending and deficits. The government has announced measures to reduce the size of the work force by not filling vacancies when employees retire. The goal is to reduce the labor force in public enterprises by 2 percent a year, or 10 percent over five years. In 2002, the government sponsored a voluntary early retirement scheme for government employees. The government has also sought to reduce workers' legal protections. Industrialists have demanded that the government revise a law requiring government authorization before firms can lay off workers or close factories that employ a minimum of a hundred workers; industry has demanded that the threshold be raised to a thousand. Industry has also called for easing restrictions on hiring temporary workers.

Reforms in Agriculture

India's agricultural production made modest progress during the 1990s, helped by good rains during the decade. Government policies, however, focused on improving urban industry and services. The higher rates of growth in the cities have created growing inequalities between the city and the countryside. Weather patterns, especially the timeliness of seasonal rains (the monsoons), also continue to significantly affect Indian agriculture. Drought hit large parts of the countryside and affected agricultural production and employment opportunities in 2002. Unable to find work or buy food, people faced starvation and suicide, and mass migration occurred in Rajasthan, Madhya Pradesh, and other states. The victims were invariably from the poorest, lowest-caste segments of the rural population.

The impact of economic liberalization on agriculture has been growing. With the goal of reducing subsidies, the central government excluded millions of impoverished families just above the poverty line from receiving publicly subsidized food supplies. Furthermore, the government sharply increased the price of food sold under the public distribution system. The government's decision to remove restrictions on imports to conform to World Trade Organization (WTO) rules has important implications for the agrarian sector. Agricultural producers, such as coffee farmers in south India, are being harmed by increased imports. Just when prices of primary commodities are

falling worldwide, and the United States and other industrialized countries have maintained trade barriers on agricultural products and subsidized their domestic farmers, India's agriculture economy is being opened up to global forces without safety nets in place.

To summarize, India's economy has grown at a relatively impressive annual growth rate since 1980, averaging between 6 and 7 percent (see Figure 6.2). India's foreign exchange reserves are much higher than they were in the past. Some industries, such as information technology, have taken off. The service sector is expanding and contributing significantly to India's economic growth. Liberalization policies have succeeded in their intentions of accelerating industrial growth. The significant growth of the Indian economy is most likely propelled by a number of other factors: the share of the slower-growing agricultural economy in the overall economy continues to decline steadily, both the knowledge and the stock of modern technology continues to grow, and the closer relationship between government and business has increased the share of private investment in overall investment, thereby increasing production.

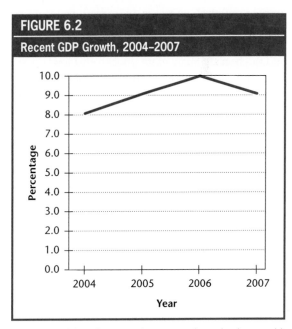

FIGURE 6.2

Recent GDP Growth, 2004–2007

Source: World Bank National Accounts data, devdata.world-bank.org/data-query/SMChartExp.asp.

Social Welfare Policy

India's poor are a diverse, heterogeneous, and enormous group constituting more than one-third of the population. Since independence, the percentage of the poor has been cut in half. However, because of India's rapid population growth, this advance has not been sufficient to reduce the absolute numbers of the poor, which increased from around 200 million in the 1950s to about 300 million in the new millennium. India has the sad distinction of having the largest number of poor people in the world. Nearly two-thirds of the Indian population and three-fourths of the poor live in rural areas. Urban poverty accounts for only one-fourth of the poor population, but the number of poor urban people, more than 70 million, is still staggering.

India's poorest people are illiterate women and children and untouchables and tribals. They include peasant farmers who own little land, agricultural tenants, landless laborers in villages, and those without regular jobs in cities who eke out a living on society's margins, often huddled into shantytowns that lack sanitary facilities and electricity or living on the streets of cities like Kolkata and Mumbai.

Although most poor people are unorganized, they exercise political influence in several ways. First, their sizable numbers impel many Indian politicians to adopt populist or socialist electoral platforms. Second, because many of the poor share a lower-caste status (especially within specific states), they can have a considerable impact on electoral outcomes. In some states, notably West Bengal and Kerala, there is a long history of radical politics; the poor in these states are well organized by communist or socialist parties and periodically help elect left-leaning governments. Third, the anger and frustration of the poor provide the raw material for many social movements in India.

Over the years, Indian governments have undertaken various poverty alleviation programs. Some have been partly successful, but most have not. In some Indian states, such as West Bengal and Kerala, elected communist governments have been somewhat successful in land redistribution. Overall, however, land reforms have proved to be nearly impossible in India's democracy.

India has very few Western-style welfare programs such as unemployment insurance, comprehensive public health programs, or guaranteed primary education. The size of the welfare problem is considerable and would tax the resources of any government. No Indian government has ever attempted to provide universal primary education, although there has been considerable internal and external pressure to do so.

One set of welfare-enhancing programs that has had modest success in India is public employment programs. They enable the national and state governments to sponsor the construction of roads and bridges and the cleaning of agricultural waterways. Because the rural poor are unemployed for nearly half the year when agricultural jobs are not available, public employment programs have become an important source of off-season jobs and income. Many surveys have demonstrated that such programs help the poor, though mostly in the short run, and the programs rarely benefit the poorest citizens. The present government is undertaking a reform of the employment guarantee scheme to provide employment to India's rural poor. Many respected observers have repeatedly stated that development spending, public investment, and bank credit to the rural sector were crucial to economic growth in the 1980s and remain critical today.

Society and Economy

Wealth and income present stark contrasts in Indian society. At the top, a small number of incredibly affluent Indians have made fortunes in business and industry. The wealth of the Ambanis, Tatas, and Birlas rivals that of the richest corporate tycoons in the world. Below them, a much larger group, nearly 100 million Indians (approximately 10 percent) are relatively well off and enjoy a standard of living comparable to that of the middle classes in many developed countries. India has a sophisticated, technologically developed industrial sector that produces a variety of consumer products, military technologies, nuclear energy, computers, and computer software. For instance, India's nuclear explosions were the product of indigenous scientific and technological research.

India's lower middle classes, about half of all Indians, are mainly small farmers or urban workers. Relatively poor by global standards, they barely eke out a living. Finally, at the bottom of the class structure, between a quarter and a third of the population is extremely poor and is concentrated mostly in India's thousands of villages as landless laborers and as the urban unemployed in city slums. Low levels of literacy, poverty, and primitive technology characterize a good part of India's rural society.

India's large population continues to grow at a relatively rapid pace, and India will surpass China as the world's largest country in a few years. Since India already has more labor than it can use productively, rapid population growth hinders economic growth. Simply put, the more people, the more mouths there are to feed, and the more food and economic products must be produced simply to maintain people's standard of living.

Why does India's population continue to grow at such a rapid pace? The comparison with China provides part of the explanation. The communist-led Chinese government has pursued strict birth control policies of one child per family since the late 1970s. In part, coercion was used to implement these policies. The result was to reduce birthrates dramatically. India's democratic government, by contrast, has found it difficult to implement population control policies.

Coercion is not the only means of reducing population growth rates, however. By 2005, the national rate of population growth was around 1.68 percent per year, a figure that Kerala had achieved many years earlier. An important reason was that Kerala has one of the highest literacy rates, especially female literacy rates, in India. Whereas the average literacy rate in India is around 48 percent for females (and 70 percent for males), Kerala's female literacy rate is 90.92 percent. Literate women are more likely to marry later in life, exercise options in the work force, have some power in personal relationships, and practice birth control.

India is one of the few countries in the world that has a lower percentage of females than men; the ratio is 1.06 males to females. Indian society favors boys over girls, as evidenced by all social indicators, from lower female literacy and nutrition rates to lower survival of female versus male infants. Prejudice against girls is reinforced through such traditions as the dowry system (the Hindu custom of giving the groom and his family assets at the time of a daughter's wedding). Although giving and receiving a dowry is illegal, it

continues to be practiced, and the sums involved have grown alongside increased materialism and aspirations for upward social mobility, particularly among the urban middle and lower middle classes.

India also has the world's largest population of child labor. Children are employed widely, not only in agricultural labor but also in such urban enterprises as match making and rug weaving and selling tea or sweets at train stations. Children usually work long hours at low wages. They cannot receive an education and consequently lose the chance for upward social mobility. The issue of child labor is closely related to India's failure to provide universal primary education (see Figure 6.3). Many Indian elites argue that in their poor country, compulsory primary education is an unaffordable luxury. However, this argument is not persuasive; many poor African countries have higher rates of primary school enrollments than does India (and recall the example of Kerala, among India's poorer states). The more likely obstacle to universal primary education is poverty and caste inequality. Many upper-caste elites do not see lower-caste children as their equals and do not consider educating lower-caste children a priority. Child labor is directly linked to poverty and survival, since many poor families see large families as a form of insurance. For most poor

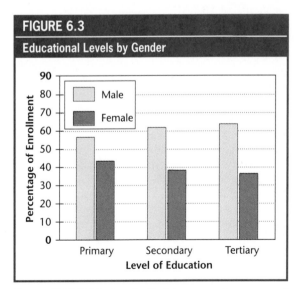

FIGURE 6.3

Educational Levels by Gender

Source: UNESCO Institute for Statistics, www.uis.unesco.org/en/stats/stats.

families, a larger family also means not being able to invest in each child's education as they depend on their children's labor for survival.

Caste issues pervade many other aspects of India's political and economic life (see "Institutional Intricacies: The Caste System"). First, by assigning people to specific occupations, it impedes the free movement of labor and talent. Although the link between caste and occupation has been weakening in India, especially in urban areas, it remains an important organizing principle for employment. Second, in the political arena, caste is a powerful force around which political groups and voting blocs coalesce. Because caste is usually organized at the local level, Indian politics often takes on a local and segmented quality. Related to this, caste cuts across class, making it difficult for labor and lower rural classes in India to act in a politically cohesive manner. Third, the Indian government often uses caste as a basis for **reservations**, the Indian version of affirmative action. The government reserves some jobs, admissions into universities, and similar privileges for members of specific underprivileged castes. This has become a highly contentious issue in Indian politics. And last, those who suffer the most in India's **caste system** are those at the bottom of the caste hierarchy: the untouchables. Nearly 10 percent of India's population, or some 90 million people, are categorized by the Indian census as belonging to the untouchables, or **scheduled castes**, as they are officially known. Notwithstanding considerable government efforts, the social stigma that members of this group suffer runs deep.

Institutional Intricacies: The Caste System

Originally derived from the Portuguese word *castas*, today the word *caste* inevitably evokes images of a rigid hierarchy that characterizes Hindu society. In reality, some Christians and Muslims also observe caste distinctions. While caste continues to be more significant in the rural than the urban areas, the caste system is less immutable and timeless than is often assumed.

In addition to traditional religious doctrines, political mobilization has shaped and influenced the character of the modern caste system.

Historically, the **caste system** compartmentalized and ranked the Hindu population of the Indian subcontinent through rules governing various aspects of daily life, such as eating, marriage, and prayer. Sanctioned by religion, the hierarchy of caste is based on a conception of the world as divided into realms of purity and impurity. Each hereditary and endogamous group (that is, a group into which one is born and within which one marries) constitutes a *jati*, which is itself organized by *varna*, or shades of color. The four main *varna* are the **Brahmin**, or priestly, caste; the Kshatriya, or warrior and royal, caste; the Vaishyas, or trading, caste; and the Shudra, or artisan, caste. Each of these *varna* is divided into many *jatis* that often approximate occupational groups (such as potters, barbers, and carpenters). Those who were not considered members of organized Hindu society because they lived in forests and on hills rather than in towns and villages, or were involved in "unclean" occupations such as sweepers and leather workers, were labeled **untouchables**, outcastes, or **scheduled castes**. Because each *jati* is often concentrated in a particular region, it is sometimes possible to change one's *varna* when one moves to a different part of the country by changing one's name and adopting the social customs of higher castes, for example, giving up eating meat.

Even though the British colonial government disapproved of the caste system, it hardened caste identities by employing rigid systems of classification. The post–Independence Indian government outlawed caste discrimination but strengthened caste identities by making caste the basis for positive discrimination in education and employment. Scheduled castes, which constitute about 16 percent of the population, or 160 million, and scheduled tribes, 7 percent of the population, or 70 million, were eligible for government quotas in the aftermath of independence. Amidst enormous controversy, the government extended reservations to the so-called "other backward classes," who are estimated to constitute between 32 to 52 percent of the population; the exact figures are contested.

India in the Global Economy

Not long after the liberalization of the domestic economy began in the 1980s, the government sponsored a significant shift toward integrating India into the international economy. Embracing globalization quickly bore fruit. Foreign investment soared from $100 million a year between 1970 and 1991 to nearly $4 billion annually between 1992 and 1998, to nearly $8 billion in 2006–2007. However, the level of foreign direct investment in India remains relatively low by global standards; China and Brazil receive several times that volume each year.[1] Furthermore, because foreign investment focuses on the domestic market, it has not always facilitated export promotion, potentially a major benefit in poor countries.

One high-tech sector in which India has excelled is computer software. Indian firms and multinational corporations with operations in India take ample advantage of India's highly skilled and poorly paid scientific and engineering talent to make India a world leader in the production of software. India can boast the equivalent of the Silicon Valley in the boom area around Bangalore in southern India, home to a large number of software firms. Furthermore, within the past few years, transnational corporations have taken advantage of the fact that India's large numbers of scientifically trained graduates are fluent English-speakers.

When Americans have a problem in operating their computer, cable television, or appliance, their call for help these days is likely to be answered by a technician in New Delhi or Bangalore.

Considerable pressure is being brought to bear on the Indian government to ease restrictions on banking, insurance, and other services as part of the World Trade Organization's (WTO) agreement on trade in services. More than forty foreign banks operate independently in India, and the government is now allowing foreign holdings in Indian banks. It has also opened up the insurance sector to private and foreign investment. The result can be a mixed blessing. For example, foreign banks have focused on retail banking in profitable urban areas, ignoring less lucrative areas of lending. Small borrowers in agriculture and small-scale industrialists have found their access to bank lending curtailed. Loans to rural areas and poorer regions have fallen.

A significant component of India's performance in the international political economy concerns its regional context. India is a giant among the South Asian countries of Pakistan, Bangladesh, Sri Lanka, Nepal, and Bhutan, although its northern neighbor, China, is an even bigger and more powerful giant. However, levels of regional economic integration are low because of troubled relations between these countries. Figure 6.4 compares exports as a percentage of gross national product (GNP) for India and its major

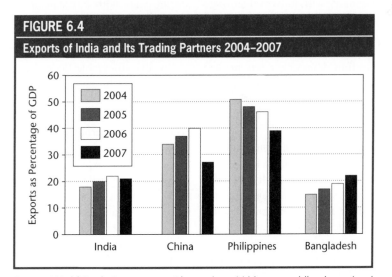

FIGURE 6.4

Exports of India and Its Trading Partners 2004–2007

Source: World Bank Country at a Glance, http://ddp-ext.worldbank.org/ext/DDPQQ/member.do?method=getMembers&userid=1&queryId=135.

trading partners; India's export quantity and rate of growth are relatively low. As nations increasingly look to their neighbors for trade and investment, the pressure on India and its neighbors to increase economic contact is likely to grow. Some movement in this direction was already evident in the first half of the 1990s, especially toward China, but there is still a long way to go before South Asia develops an integrated zone of economic activity.

In conclusion, economic globalization has had a powerful and complex impact on India's economy and politics. India is a potential economic superpower of the twenty-first century. It is well positioned to reap the benefits of a large, well-trained, highly skilled population willing to work for low wages, and a growing number of world-class corporations. Globalization has promoted the rapid expansion of a large middle class, whose members eagerly participate in the world's consumer culture. At the same time, however, globalization has increased economic inequality by generating more benefits for those in the middle and upper ranks of the income pyramid than for the rural and urban poor. The challenge for the current Congress-dominated coalition is to devise ways for globalization to work for all.

SECTION 3 Governance and Policy-Making

Organization of the State

India is a democratic republic with a parliamentary and federal system of government. The constitution adopted in 1950 created this system, and, although there have been many profound changes since then in the distribution and use of power, the basic character of India's political system has remained unchanged. For much of this period, India has been a stable, democratic country with universal suffrage and periodic elections at local, state, and national levels. This continuity and democratic stability are remarkable among developing countries. To simplify a complex reality, Indian democracy has proved so resilient because its political institutions, while always under pressure, have been able to accommodate many new power challenges and to repress the most difficult ones.

India's constitution is lengthy. In contrast to the British constitution on which it is modeled, it is a written document that has been periodically amended by legislation. Among its special features, three are worth noting. First, unlike many other constitutions, the Indian constitution directs the government to promote social and economic equality and justice. The constitution thus goes beyond stipulating formal procedures of decision-making and allocating powers among political institutions, and outlines policy goals.

Although the impact of these constitutional provisions on government policies is limited, the provisions ensure that issues of welfare and social justice are not ignored. Second, the Indian constitution, like the U.S. Constitution, provides for freedom of religion and defines India as a secular state. And third, the constitution allows for the temporary suspension of many democratic rights under emergency conditions. These provisions were used, somewhat understandably, during wars with Pakistan or China. But they have also been invoked, more disturbingly, to deal with internal political threats, most dramatically during the national Emergency from 1975 to 1977, when a politically vulnerable Indira Gandhi suspended many democratic rights and imprisoned her leading political opponents.

India's federal system is relatively centralized. The central government controls the most essential government functions such as defense, foreign policy, taxation, public expenditures, and economic planning, especially industrial planning. State governments formally control such policy areas as agriculture, education, and law and order within the states. Because they are heavily dependent on the central government for funds in these policy areas, however, the power of the states is limited.

India is a parliamentary democracy designed on the British model. The Indian parliament, known as the *Lok Sabha*, or House of the People, the lower chamber of parliament, is the most significant political institution. The leader of the political party with the most seats in the *Lok Sabha* becomes the prime minister, who nominates a cabinet, mostly from the ranks of other members of parliament belonging to the ruling coalition. The prime minister and the cabinet, along with permanent civil servants, control much of the government's daily functioning. The prime minister is the lynchpin of the system because effective power is concentrated in that office, where most of the country's important policies originate. By contrast, the office of the president is largely ceremonial. In periodic national elections, 544 members of the *Lok Sabha,* the lower house of the bicameral parliament, are elected. The *Lok Sabha* is much more politically significant than the *Rajya Sabha*, the upper house. The prime minister governs with the help of the cabinet, which periodically meets to discuss important issues, including any new legislation that is likely to be initiated. Individually, cabinet members are the heads of various ministries, for example, Foreign Affairs or Industry, that direct the daily work of the government and make up the permanent bureaucracy.

The Executive

The President and the Prime Minister

The president is the official head of the state and is elected indirectly every five years by an electoral college composed of elected representatives from the national and state governments. In most circumstances, the president acts on the advice of the prime minister and is thus not a very powerful political figure. The presidency is a ceremonial office, symbolizing the unity of the country, and it is supposedly above partisan politics. Under exceptional circumstances, however, especially when the selection of a prime minister becomes a complex issue, the president can play an important political role. For example, in the 1998 election, there was a hung parliament, with no party gaining a clear majority. The president then requested the party with the largest percentage of votes, the BJP, to show that it could muster enough allies to form a government.

The prime minister and other cabinet ministers are the most powerful political figures in India. Because they represent the majority party coalition in parliament, the passage of a bill is not as complicated a process as it can be in a presidential system, especially one with a divided government. The prime minister and the cabinet also head various ministries, so that after legislation is passed, they oversee its implementation. In practice, the permanent bureaucracy, especially the senior- and middle-level bureaucrats, are responsible for policy implementation. Nevertheless, as in most other parliamentary systems, such as those in Britain, Germany, and Japan, there is considerable overlap in India between the executive and the legislative branches of the government, creating a greater degree of centralization of power than is initially evident. The duration of the prime minister's tenure in office has become steadily truncated over time. Between 1947 and 1984, except for a few brief interludes, India had only two prime ministers: Nehru and Indira Gandhi (see Table 6.2). This is nearly unique among democracies; it underlines the powerful hold that the Nehru–Gandhi family had on India's political imagination. Since then, there has been a more rapid turnover.

The method of selecting a prime minister in India is fairly complex. The original choice of Nehru was a natural one, given his prominent position in the nationalist movement and his relationship to founding father Mohandas Karamchand Gandhi. The choice of Indira Gandhi was less obvious. She was chosen to head the Congress Party by a group of prominent second-tier party leaders because of her national name, which they calculated would reap handsome electoral rewards. A similar logic prevailed when Rajiv Gandhi was chosen by party elites to succeed his mother. Rajiv Gandhi benefited from the wave of sympathy generated by his mother's assassination, and he led the Congress Party back to power in 1984 with a handsome electoral majority.

Following Rajiv Gandhi's assassination, the Nehru–Gandhi family line appeared to have reached an end, since Rajiv Gandhi's wife, Sonia Gandhi, was of Italian background, and their children were too young to enter politics. In 1991, Narasimha Rao was brought back as an elder statesman who was nonthreatening and acceptable to competing factions within the

Congress Party. Both subsequent United Front prime ministers were compromise candidates who lacked the personality and power to manage their disparate coalitions. In 1998, the Congress Party attempted to resurrect its fortunes by choosing Sonia Gandhi to head the party, creating the possibility that the political rule of the Nehru–Gandhi family would continue. The gamble paid off in 2004 when Congress, headed by Sonia Gandhi, narrowly edged the BJP out of power. Although she declined to be prime minister, mainly to avoid controversy about her Italian origins, as head of the Congress Party, she wields significant power over the government. Her son, Rahul Gandhi, became general secretary of the Congress Party in 2007.

The Cabinet

The prime minister chooses the cabinet, mostly from among the party's members elected to parliament. Seniority, competence, and personal loyalty are the main criteria that a prime minister takes into account when choosing cabinet ministers. Regional and caste representation at the highest level of government must also be considered. During Indira Gandhi's rule, personal loyalty was critical in the choice of senior ministers. Rajiv Gandhi, by contrast, put a high premium on competence, which unfortunately he equated with youth and technical skills, at the expense of political experience. Since Vajpayee was able to form a government only with the help of many smaller parties in 1999, the heads of these parties had to be accommodated, producing a vast, eclectic, and disparate cabinet.

The Bureaucracy

The prime minister and cabinet ministers run the government in close collaboration with senior civil servants. Each senior minister oversees what is often a sprawling bureaucracy, staffed by some very competent, overworked, senior civil servants and by many not-so-competent, underworked, lowly bureaucrats.

The **Indian Administrative Service (IAS)**, an elite corps of top bureaucrats, constitutes a critical but relatively thin layer at the top of India's bureaucracy. The competence of the IAS is a central reason that India is moderately well governed. Because political

leaders come and go, whereas senior civil servants stay, many civil servants possess a storehouse of knowledge and expertise that makes them very powerful. Higher-level civil servants in India reach their positions after considerable experience within the government. They are named to the IAS at a relatively young age, usually in their early twenties, by passing a highly competitive entrance exam. Some of India's most talented young men and women were attracted to the IAS during the 1950s and 1960s, reflecting the prestige that service in national government used to enjoy in Indian society. The attraction of the IAS has declined, however, and many talented young people now go into engineering or business administration, or leave the country for better opportunities abroad. Government service has become tainted as areas of corruption have developed and the level of professionalism within the IAS has eroded, mainly because politicians prefer loyalty over merit and seniority when making promotions. Nevertheless, the IAS continues to recruit very talented young people, many of whom become dedicated senior civil servants who still constitute the backbone of the Indian government.

Below the IAS, the level of talent and professionalism drops rather sharply. Within each ministry at the national level and in many parallel substructures at the state level, the bureaucracy in India is infamous for corruption and inefficiency. These problems contribute to the gap between good policies made at the top and their poor implementation at the local level.

Other State Institutions

The Military and the Police

Unlike the militaries in many other developing countries, the Indian military has never intervened directly in politics. The Indian military, with more than 1 million well-trained and well-equipped members, is a highly professional organization. Over the years, the continuity of constitutional, electoral politics and a relatively apolitical military have come to reinforce and strengthen each other. Civilian politicians provide ample resources to the armed forces and, for the most part, let them function as a professional organization. The armed forces, in turn, obey the orders of democratically elected leaders, and although they lobby to preserve their own interests, they mostly stay out of the normal tumble of democratic politics.

Since the 1970s, two factors have weakened this well-institutionalized separation of politics and military. First, during Indira Gandhi's rule, loyalty to political leaders became the key criterion for securing top military jobs. This policy tended to politicize the military and narrow the separation between politics and the military.

Second, there were growing regional and ethnic demands for secession (see Section 4). As these demands became more intense in some states, notably in Kashmir, and as militants began to resort to armed conflict, occasionally with the help of India's often-hostile neighbor Pakistan, the Indian government called in the armed forces. However, soldiers are not trained to resolve political problems; rather, they are trained to use force to secure compliance from reluctant political actors. As a result, not only have democratic norms and human rights been violated in India, but the distance between politics and the military has narrowed.

A similar trend toward politicization and deprofessionalization has occurred in India's sprawling police services, but with a difference. The Indian police organization has never been as professionalized as the armed forces, and the police services come under the jurisdiction of state governments, not the central government. Because state governments are generally less well run than the national government, the Indian police are not apolitical civil servants. State-level politicians regularly interfere in police personnel issues, and police officers in turn regularly oblige the politicians who help them. The problem is especially serious at lower levels. The police are easily bribed and often allied with criminals or politicians. In some states, such as Bihar and Uttar Pradesh, police often take sides in local conflicts instead of acting as neutral arbiters or enforcers of laws. When they take sides, they tilt the power balance in favor of dominant social groups such as landowners or upper castes or the majority Hindu religious community.

In addition to the regular armed forces and the state-level police forces, paramilitary forces, controlled by the national government, number nearly half a million men. As Indian politics became more turbulent in the 1980s, paramilitary forces steadily expanded.

Because the national government calls on the regular armed forces only as a last resort in the management of internal conflicts and because state-level police forces are not very reliable, paramilitary forces are viewed as a way to maintain order. A large, sprawling, and relatively ineffective police service remains a problematic presence in Indian society.

The Judiciary

An independent judiciary is another component of India's state system. But unlike Britain, where the judiciary's role is limited by parliamentary sovereignty, a fundamental contradiction is embedded in the Indian constitution between the principles of parliamentary sovereignty and judicial review. Over the years, the judiciary and the parliament have often clashed, with the former trying to preserve the constitution's basic structure and the latter asserting its right to amend the constitution (see "Institutional Intricacies: The Executive versus the Judiciary"). The judiciary comprises an apex court, atop a series of national courts, high courts in states, and lower courts in districts.

The supreme judicial authority is the Supreme Court, comprising a chief justice and seventeen other judges. Judges are appointed by the president, but, as in most other matters of political significance in India, only on the advice of the prime minister. Once appointed, judges cannot be removed from the bench until retirement at age sixty-five. The caseload on the Supreme Court, as on much of the rest of the Indian legal system, is extremely heavy, with a significant backlog.

The main political role of the Supreme Court is to ensure that legislation conforms to the intent of the constitution. Because the Indian constitution is very detailed, however, the need for interpretation is not as great as in many other countries. Nevertheless, there are real conflicts, both within the constitution and in India's political landscape, that often need to be adjudicated by the Supreme Court. For example, the constitution simultaneously protects private property and urges the government to pursue social justice. Indian leaders have often promulgated socialist legislation, for example, requiring the redistribution of agricultural land. Legislation of this nature is considered by the

Institutional Intricacies: The Executive versus the Judiciary

Over the years, the Supreme Court has clashed head to head with the parliament as a result of the contradiction between principles of parliamentary sovereignty and judicial review that is embedded in India's constitution. For instance, during the early years of independence, the courts over-turned state government laws to redistribute land from landlords (*zamindars*), saying that the laws violated the *zamindars'* fundamental rights. In retaliation, the parliament passed the first of a series of amendments to the constitution to protect the executive's authority to promote land redistribution. But matters did not end there. The Supreme Court responded by passing a judgment stating that the parliament did not have the power to abrogate fundamental rights. In 1970, the court also invalidated the bank nationalization bill and a presidential order abolishing privy purses (including titles and privileges of former rulers of India's princely states). In retaliation, the parliament passed a series of amendments that undercut the Supreme Court's rulings, thus moving the power balance toward parliamentary sovereignty. The Supreme Court responded that the court still reserved for itself the discretion to reject any constitutional amendments passed by parliament on the grounds that the amendments could not change the constitution's basic structure. During the Emergency period, the parliament passed yet another amendment that limited the Supreme Court's judicial review to pro-cedural issues. The Janata government in the post–Emergency era, however, reversed these changes, thus reintroducing the tension between the executive and judiciary.

Since the 1980s, the courts have increasingly functioned as a bulwark for citizens by protecting their civil liberties from state coercion. For instance, since 1993, it has enforced a policy of compensating victims of violence while in police custody. In 1985, the Supreme Court upheld a verdict finding two people guilty of murdering their wives on the grounds that the dowry was insufficient and sentenced them to life imprisonment. In the mid-1980s, the Supreme Court clashed with parliament on its interpretation of personal law over the Shah Bano case. In India, personal law falls under the purview of religion; a woman married under religious law cannot seek divorce or alimony under secular law. Neither Muslim nor Hindu personal law entitles women to alimony. The British colonial gov-ernment had passed a law that required divorced men to provide maintenance to their ex-wives. Shah Bano, a destitute seventy-five-year-old woman abandoned and later divorced by her husband, filed for mainte-nance under this law. The Supreme Court upheld Shah Bano's right to maintenance on the grounds that secular laws transcended personal law (religious law). The parliament, however, succumbing to pressures from re-ligious leaders, passed a bill excluding Muslim women from the purview of secular laws.

The battle between the executive and the judiciary has compromised the autonomy of the courts. The judiciary has been affected by the general malaise of institutional decay that has affected Indian politics over the years. The backlog of cases has grown phe-nomenally, while expeditious judgment of cases has declined dramatically.

Supreme Court because it potentially violates the right to private property. Many Supreme Court cases have involved the conflict between socialistically inclined legislation and constitutional rights. Cases involving other politically significant issues, for instance, rights of religious minorities such as Muslims and the rights of women, also periodically reach the Supreme Court.

Like many other Indian political institutions, the Supreme Court lost much of its autonomy in the 1980s. The process began during Indira Gandhi's rule, when she argued that the court was too conservative

and an obstacle to her socialist program. To remedy this shortcoming, she appointed many pliant judges, including the chief justice. The Supreme Court itself more or less complied with her wishes during the two years of Emergency (1975–1977), when the political and civil rights of many Indians were violated. No such dramatic instance of a politicized Supreme Court has recurred since the late 1970s.

The Supreme Court often functions as a bulwark for citizens against state invasiveness, as is evident from many landmark civil rights judgments. The

Court introduced a system of public interest litigation that enabled bonded laborers, disenfranchised tribal people, the homeless, and indigent women to redress their claims. In recent years, the Supreme Court has defended environmental causes. To protect the Taj Mahal, India's most treasured national monument, from damage by air pollution, it ordered the closure of 212 nearby businesses that had chronically violated environmental regulations. It similarly shut down almost 200 polluters along the Ganges River. The Court enforced clean water and air laws in New Delhi in 1996–1997 by ordering that polluting cars and buses be removed from the roads and by shutting down polluting enterprises. It required central and state governments to prevent starvation by releasing food stocks and to promote education by providing school lunches and daycare facilities.

Compared to other large, multiethnic democracies, India has generally shown great respect for the pillars of civil rights: a free and lively press, legal protections for citizens' rights, and an independent judiciary. India's media, especially its newspapers and magazines, are as free as any in the world. They represent a wide variety of viewpoints, engage in vigorous investigative reporting and analysis, and maintain pressure for public action. The combination of a vocal intellectual stratum and a free press is a cherished element in India's democracy.

Nevertheless, India's tradition of a strong, interventionist state has enabled the government to violate civil liberties. Global events conjoined with national ones resulted in a restriction of civil liberties in the aftermath of September 11. The Indian parliament passed the Prevention of Terrorism Act (POTA). Its definition of terrorism was extremely vague, and a citizen could be charged under POTA without having committed a specific act: conspiring, attempting to commit, advocating, abetting, advising, or inciting such acts were punishable with penalties ranging from stiff prison sentences to death. Confessions made to police officers were admissible as evidence in courts, contrary to ordinary law, and confessions were brutally extracted in Indian police stations.

The government made charges under POTA in a highly discretionary and political manner. The largest number of arrests took place in India's newest state, Jharkhand, where members and supporters of Marxist-Leninist groups were incarcerated under POTA. The BJP-led government depicted pro-independence groups in Kashmir and Muslim groups throughout India as terrorists. It banned the Students Islamic Movement of India (SIMI), the students' wing of the radical Islamic Jamaat-e-Islami political party in Pakistan, but did not ban the Bajrang Dal, the militant organization with ties to the Visva Hindu Parisad that has repeatedly organized anti-Muslim violence, including in Gujarat in 2002.

Shortly after Manmohan Singh became prime minister, the cabinet repealed POTA on grounds that it had been misused, and instead amended existing laws to tackle terrorism. Whereas POTA placed the burden of proof on the accused, the amended act shifts it back to the prosecutor.

Subnational Government

Under India's federal system, the balance of power between the central and state governments varies by time and place. In general, the more powerful and popular the central government and prime minister, the less likely states can pursue an independent course. During the rule of Nehru and especially under Indira Gandhi, the states were often quite constrained. By contrast, weaker central governments, like the BJP-led alliance that took office in 1999, or the Congress-led alliance that took office in 2004, enlarge room for state governments to maneuver. When state governments are run by political parties other than the national ruling party—and this is often true in contemporary India—there is considerable scope for center-state conflict. For example, a popular communist government in West Bengal has often disagreed with the national government in New Delhi, charging it with discriminatory treatment in the allocation of finances and other centrally controlled resources.

While the political parties at the national and the state levels may differ, the formal structure of the twenty-eight state governments parallels that of the national government. The chief minister of each state heads the state government. The chief minister is the leader of the majority party (or the party with most seats) in the lower house of the state legislature. The chief minister appoints cabinet ministers who head various ministries staffed by a state-level, permanent bureaucracy.

The quality of government below the national level is often poor, contributing to regional and ethnic conflicts.

In lieu of a president, each state has a governor, appointed by the national president. The governors, like the president, are supposed to serve on the advice of the chief minister, but in practice, they often become independently powerful, especially in states where the national government is at odds with the state government or where state governments are unstable. Governors can dismiss elected state governments and proclaim temporary presidential rule if they determine state governments to be ineffective. When this happens, the elected government is dissolved, and the state is governed from New Delhi until fresh elections are called and a new government is elected. Although this provision is intended to be a sensible constitutional option, an intrusive national government has often used it for partisan purposes.

The power struggle between the central government and the states is ongoing. With many Indian states inhabited by people with distinctive traditions and cultures, including language, and with conflicting political parties in power at the national and state levels, central-state relations can be fueled by substantial political and ethnic conflicts.

Indian politics has become increasingly regionalized in recent years. Three new states were formed in 2000 out of existing states. Furthermore, states have become increasingly autonomous economically and politically. As a result of economic liberalization, states have acquired rights and opportunities to seek out investors independent of the national government. One consequence is that regional inequalities are widening as states like Haryana, Punjab, Maharashtra, Gujarat, Andhra Pradesh, Karnataka, and Tamil Nadu have aggressively sought investments while some of the largest and poorest states in the north and east—such as Bihar and U.P.—have fallen behind.

The twenty-eight states of India's federal system have also come to play an increasingly important role in national governance. In each of the national elections since 1989, parties based in a single state have been key to the success of coalition governments. According to the Election Commission's classification of parties, in the five national elections between 1991 and 2004, the vote share of national parties (those with a base in many states) dropped from 80.91 percent in 1991 to 67.98 percent in 1998 and the proportion of seats they controlled went from 86 percent in 1991 to 72 percent in 1998. By contrast, parties based in single states increased their percentage share of the votes from 17 to 27 percent and their seats from 16 to 29 percent. Since 1989, every coalition government has depended on regional parties for its survival. This development has double-edged implications for democracy. On the one hand, governing coalitions that are established by disparate parties with little ideological or programmatic cohesion are likely to be unstable. On the other hand, national governments are less likely than they were in the past to seek the dismissal of state governments because national governments are likely to be composed of regional political parties.

The *panchayats,* which function at the local, district, and state levels, represent the most important attempts at the devolution of power. The *panchayats* were responsible in the precolonial era for adjudicating conflicts and presiding over community affairs in the rural areas. In 1959, the Indian government introduced a three-tier model of *panchayats,* linked together by indirect elections. However, it gave the *panchayats* meager resources, for members of parliament and the legislative assembly saw them as potential rivals to their authority. By the mid-1960s, the *panchayats* were stagnating and declining.

Some states revived the *panchayats* on their own initiative. In 1978, the communist government of West Bengal overhauled the *panchayat* system by providing for direct elections and giving them additional resources and responsibilities. Other states followed suit. In 1992, the national government amended the constitution to enable all states to strengthen the *panchayats,* although states were free to create their own models. It envisaged the *panchayats'* primary role as implementing development programs and encouraging greater local involvement in government. The amendment stipulated that *panchayat* elections would be held every five years and made provisions for reserving 33 percent of the seats for women and seats proportional to the population for scheduled castes and tribes. In the first elections held under the new framework (in 1993), 700,000 women were elected to office. Most states met and several exceeded the 33 percent women's reservations at all three levels.

The abilities of women who were elected to the *panchayats* varied widely. Women who had a prior history of political activism were most likely to use the *panchayats* to benefit women. Some were responsible for the *panchayats'* sponsoring important local development projects. Others sought *panchayat* action on behalf of women over issues like marriage, divorce, and alcoholism. However, most women elected to the *panchayats* had no prior history of activism and became tokens who were silenced, marginalized, and, in extreme situations, even harassed and attacked. Many women ran for election in order to represent the interests of powerful men. In some cases, when women threatened male candidates, they were accused of sexual immorality. Women were often ignorant about the functions of the *panchayats* and relied on their husbands for advice.

The resources and planning capabilities of the *panchayats* remain relatively limited. State legislatures determine how much power and authority the *panchayats* can wield. Most *panchayats* are responsible for implementing rural development schemes but not devising them. Policy is made at the national and state levels. Although considerable resources pass through them, local governments have little discretion over how they are allocated. Local political elites, bureaucrats, and influential citizens often siphon off a large share of public funds and determine where projects will be located, who gets a contract, and who is hired on public projects. Thus, many local governments in India tend to be corrupt, ineffective, and wasteful. City streets are not kept clean, potholes are not repaired, irrigation canals are not properly maintained, and rural schools are so poorly built that they leak as soon as the monsoons start.

The Policy-Making Process

Major policies in India are made by the national government, in New Delhi. The prime minister and senior cabinet ministers are generally responsible for initiating policies. Behind the scenes, senior civil servants in each ministry, as well as in cross-ministry offices like the prime minister's secretariat and the planning commission, play a critical role in identifying problems, synthesizing data, and presenting to political leaders alternative solutions and their implications. After decisions have been made at the highest level, many require new legislation. Because the prime minister usually has a clear majority in parliament, passage of most legislation is ensured, except in extremely controversial areas.

The real policy drama in India occurs early on, when major bills are under consideration, and during the process of implementation. Consider economic liberalization policies, which represented a major policy change. The new course was formulated at the highest level of government, involving only a handful of senior ministers and bureaucrats. To reach the decision, however, a fairly complex set of political activities took place. Decision-makers consulted some of the most important interest groups, such as associations of Indian businessmen and representatives of international organizations like the World Bank and the IMF. Others, including those who might be adversely affected, expressed themselves; organized labor, for example, called a one-day general strike to warn the government that any attempt to privatize the public sector would meet considerable resistance. Newspapers, magazines, and intellectuals expressed both support and opposition. Political parties got into the act. Members of the ruling party, the Congress in this case, did not necessarily support the political thinking of their own leaders at the early stage; rather, they worried about the political implications of policies for intraparty power struggles and future elections. Opposition parties, in turn, worried about the interests of their constituents. These pressures modified the policy that the government eventually adopted.

After policies have been adopted, their implementation is far from assured. Continuing with the liberalization example, some aspects of the new policy package proved easier to implement than others. Changing the exchange rate (the value of the Indian rupee in relation to the U.S. dollar) was relatively easy to implement because both the policy decision and its implementation require the actions of only a handful of politicians and bureaucrats. By contrast, the attempts to simplify the procedures for Indian or foreign business executives to create new business enterprises proved far more complicated. Implementation of such policies involves layers of bureaucrats, most of whom benefit from the control they already exercise. When forced to relinquish power, many dragged their feet and, where possible, sabotaged the newly simplified procedures.

Another example is the policies aimed at improving the standard of living for the Indian poor. Since the 1960s, the national government has attempted to redistribute agricultural land and create public works programs to help India's rural poor. The national government set the broad outlines for land reforms and allocated funds for public works programs but left refinement of these policies, as well as their implementation, to state governments. State governments differ with respect to social classes in the state, ruling party coalitions, and quality of their bureaucracies. The result is that the implementation of antipoverty policies within India has been quite uneven.

Attempts to generate extra employment for the rural poor through public works projects (such as road construction and canal cleaning) have been somewhat more successful than land redistribution policies because they do not involve any direct confiscation of property. The main issues in the implementation of these policies are the quality of projects chosen, whether they target the poor, and how honestly they are completed. Because the quality of local governments in implementing national policies varies (although it is rarely very high), many of the funds spent on poverty alleviation programs have been wasted. Public works policies have been most effectively implemented in the states of Maharashtra and West Bengal, where there is considerable political pressure from caste or class politics, and in some southern states, where the local bureaucracy is more efficient.

To review, the policy-making process in India, though relatively centralized, takes into account various interests and frequently produces well-developed policies. By contrast, the process of implementation is quite decentralized and relatively ineffective. Sound policy ideas and positive intentions do not reach fruition because policies are diluted at the state and local levels and because of lackluster implementation.

SECTION 4 Representation and Participation

Over the years, India has become a participatory democracy, as previously excluded social groups such as the poor, the landless, and backward castes entered the political arena and used their influence to shape the political process. In the early years after independence, the Congress Party mobilized most groups. However, in recent years, there has been a proliferation of political parties that have appealed to the Indian masses on ethnic grounds (particularly caste and religion), a trend initiated by Indira Gandhi. Simultaneously, the adoption of the democratic idea in the institutional sphere led to an explosion of social movements in civil society. Poor women have marched on the streets of Andhra Pradesh demanding prohibition of the sale of liquor (because of the economic toll it inflicts and its role in domestic violence), while poor tribals in Maharashtra have protested their displacement by the construction of large dams. The democratic idea is so deeply rooted that today thousands of nongovernmental organizations function in the country, representing causes ranging from welfare issues, to the environment, to human rights. Some social movements have transformed themselves into political parties, while others militantly oppose the established political system. Thus, ironically, while Indian democracy has become more truncated in some respects as it has experienced institutional decline and decay, it has flourished in other respects through the growth of popular participation within and outside the party system.

The Legislature

A good place to begin the discussion of representation and participation in a democracy is with the legislature. The Indian parliament is bicameral, consisting of the *Rajya Sabha* and the *Lok Sabha*. Although the government dominates the parliament, election to the *Lok Sabha* is of vital importance. First, the outcome of parliamentary elections determines which party coalition will control the government. Second, although members of parliament are unable to influence policies directly, they enjoy considerable status, personal access to resources, and influence over allocations of government monies and contracts within their constituencies.

Elections to the *Lok Sabha* must be held at least every five years, but, as in other parliamentary systems, the prime minister may choose to call elections earlier. India is divided into 544 electoral districts of roughly equal population, each of which elects and sends one representative to the national parliament by a first-past-the-post electoral system. The major political parties nominate most candidates. Elections in India are won or lost mainly by parties, especially by party leaders, so most legislators are beholden to party leaders for securing a party ticket. Success in elections therefore does not depend on having an independent power base but on belonging to a party whose leader or whose programs are popular. Given the importance of the party label for nominations, members of parliament maintain strong voting discipline in the *Lok Sabha.* The main business of the *Lok Sabha* is to pass new legislation as well as to debate government actions. Although members sometimes introduce bills, the government introduces most new legislation. After bills are introduced, they are assigned to parliamentary committees for detailed study and discussion. The committees report the bills back to the *Lok Sabha* for debate, possible amendment, and preliminary votes. They then go to the *Rajya Sabha,* the upper house, which is not a powerful chamber; it generally approves bills passed by the *Lok Sabha.* Most members of the *Rajya Sabha* are elected indirectly by state legislatures. After any final modifications by the *Rajya Sabha,* bills return to the *Lok Sabha* for a third reading, after which they are finally voted on in both houses and forwarded to the president for approval.

To understand why the *Lok Sabha* does not play a significant independent role in policy-making, keep in mind that (1) the government generally introduces new legislation; (2) most legislators, especially those belonging to the Congress Party, are politically beholden to party leaders; and (3) all parties use party whips to ensure voting along party lines. One implication of parliament's relative ineffectiveness is that routine changes in its social composition do not have significant policy consequences. Whether members of parliament are business executives or workers, men

or women, or members of upper or lower castes is not likely to lead to dramatic policy shifts. Nevertheless, groups in society derive satisfaction from having one of their own in the parliament, and dramatic shifts in social composition are bound to influence policy.

The typical member of parliament is a male university graduate between forty and sixty years old. Over the years, there have been some changes in the social composition of legislators. For example, legislators in the 1950s were likely to be urban men and were often lawyers and members of higher castes. Today, nearly half the members of parliament come from rural areas, and many have agricultural backgrounds. Members of the middle castes (the so-called backward castes) are also well represented today. These changes reflect some of the broad shifts in the distribution of power in Indian society. By contrast, the proportion of women and of poor, lower-caste individuals in the parliament remains low. The representation of women in parliament has not increased much from the 4.4 percent (or 22 women) in the first parliament (1952–1957) to 8.8 percent (48 women) in the 1998 elections, to 8.3 percent (45 women) in the lower house of parliament and 11.57 percent in the upper house of parliament in 2004 (see Figure 6.5).

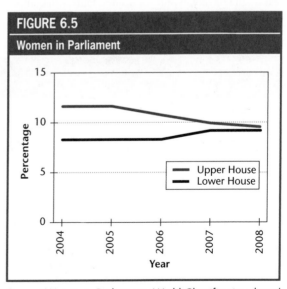

FIGURE 6.5

Women in Parliament

Source: Women in Parliaments World Classification. http://www.ipu.org/wmn-e/arc/classif300908.htm.

Successive governments since 1996 have supported a constitutional amendment guaranteeing at least 33 percent reserved seats for women in parliament and the legislative assemblies. However, although most political parties have endorsed the bill in their election manifestos, they have not supported its passage in parliament. It was defeated in December 2000, when a range of parties expressed either ambivalence or opposition to it. Parties that represent the lower middle castes opposed the reform because it made no provision for reservations on a caste basis. As a compromise measure, then Home Minister L. K. Advani supported the chief election commissioner's proposal to require all political parties to reserve 33 percent of their nominations for women contestants. Critics fear that political parties will nominate women in unwinnable constituencies. Thus far, parties' records in nominating women candidates have been poor. In the 1996 parliamentary elections, for example, political parties allotted less than 15 percent of the total number of tickets to women. Women constitute only 10 to 12 percent of the membership of political parties.

Political Parties and the Party System

Political parties and elections are where much of the real drama of Indian politics occurs. Parties in control of a majority of seats in the national or state parliaments form the national and state governments and control government resources. Parties thus devote substantial political energy to contesting and winning elections. Since independence, the party system has evolved from being dominated by the Congress Party to one in which Congress is among the major parties but far from dominant (see Table 6.3). Thus, what began as virtually a one-party system has evolved into a real multiparty system, with three main political tendencies: centrist, center-left, and center-right. Within this framework, there are at least four potentially significant national parties and countless regional parties competing for power. The four parties with significant national presence are the Congress, the Janata Party, the BJP, and the Communist Party of India Marxist; (CPM). Whereas the CPM is a left-leaning party and the BJP is a religious, right-leaning one, both Congress and the Janata are more or less centrist parties. Furthermore, coalitions among these parties have occurred in the past. For example, the Janata Party joined forces with the CPM and other smaller parties in the 1996 elections to form the United Front and was able to form two short-lived, left-leaning governments. For the most part the CPM supported the United Progressive Alliance government, which came to power in 2004. Further, the major parties are unable to form a government on their own but must stitch together coalitions that include many small, usually regionally based parties. As one would expect,

Table 6.3										
Major Party Election Results										
	1991		1996		1998		1999		2004	
	%	Seats	%	Seats	%	Seats	%	Seats	%	Seats
Congress	37.3	225	29	143	25.4	140	28.4	112	26.69	145[a]
BJP & Allies	19.9	119	24	193	36.2	250	41.3	296	35.91	189
Janata	10.8	55	Joined with UF		Joined with UF		1	1	Joined with Congress	
United Front	—	—	31	180	20.9	98	—	—	—	—
Communists[b]	—	48	Joined with UF		Joined with UF		5.4	32	7.0	53
Others							23.9	107	19.9	78

[a]The more relevant figures in 2004 for Congress and allies were 35.82 and 219, respectively.
[b]Includes both the CPM and the CPI.

Source: India Today, July 15, 1991, March 16, 1998; *Economic Times* website, economictimes.indiatimes.com; and *The Hindu,* May 20, 2004.

there are feverish negotiations among coalition parties over the allocation of cabinet positions and the policies that the governing coalition will pursue.

The Congress Party

The Congress Party was India's premier political party until the 1990s. Many aspects of this party have already been discussed because it is impossible to analyze Indian politics without referring to its role. To summarize briefly, the Congress Party built its electoral network by creating patrons who would mobilize electoral support for the party during elections.

Once in power, the Congress Party would channel government resources to these people, further enhancing their local position and ensuring their support. This patronage system (some call it machine politics) worked quite well for the Congress Party for nearly two decades. Nevertheless, even when the party was electorally successful, this strategy generated internal contradictions. The propoor Congress Party of India had a socialist shell, but came to be internally dominated by high-caste, wealthy Indians.

By the early 1950s, with Nehru at its helm, Congress was the unquestioned ruling party of India. Over the years, especially since the mid-1960s, this hegemony came to be challenged. By the time Indira Gandhi assumed power in 1966, the old Congress Party had begun to lose its political sway, and anticolonial nationalism was fading. The spread of democratic politics mobilized many poor, lower-caste citizens who depended less and less on village big men for political guidance. As a result, numerous regional parties started challenging Congress's monopoly on power. Weather-related food shortages in the mid-1960s also hurt the Congress Party in the 1967 elections.

Indira Gandhi sought to reverse the decline in the Congress's electoral popularity through mobilizing India's vast majority, the poor, by promising poverty alleviation as the core of her political program. This promise struck a popular chord, propelling Indira Gandhi to the top of India's political pyramid. Her personal success, however, came at a cost to the party. The old Congress split into two parties, with one branch, the Congress (O), becoming moribund and leaving the other, Congress (I) (the "I" stands for Indira) to inherit the position of the old undivided

Congress. Nevertheless, the Congress Party formed all governments from independence to 1989, with just one interlude, when the Janata Party formed the government (1977–1980). Since 1989, Congress headed governments from 1991 to 1996 and returned to power again in 2004.

Prior to Indira Gandhi's prime ministership, rank-and-file party members elected the lowest-level Congress Party officers, who in turn elected officers at higher levels of the party organization, up to the position of the party leader, who was the prime minister during the long period when the Congress formed the government. Indira Gandhi reversed this bottom-up party structure with a top-down structure in which leaders appointed party officers. With some modifications, including some limited internal party elections, this is basically how the contemporary Congress Party is organized. The top-down structure enables the leaders to control the party, but it is a major liability when grassroots support is necessary. As the nation's oldest party, the Congress continues to attract substantial electoral support. If this support ever declined sharply, most likely the party rank and file would demand its reorganization.

Whereas Congress during the 1970s had a left-of-center, propoor political platform, beginning in 1984 it moved toward the ideological center under Rajiv Gandhi (see Section 2). For much of the 1980s and the 1990s, the Congress Party tilted right of center, championing issues of economic efficiency, business interests, and limited government spending over the rights of the poor and the working people and over social questions of health, education, and welfare. However, under Sonia Gandhi's leadership, Congress has moved somewhat to the left.

As a nationalist party, the Congress Party is intimately associated with the stability of the Indian nation and the state. Regardless of its economic program, therefore, the Congress has always attracted support from diverse social groups: rich and poor, upper and lower castes, Hindus and Muslims, northerners and southerners.

The Janata Party

The Janata Party, India's other centrist party, formed short-lived national governments in 1977, 1989, and together with other parties through the United Front in 1996 and 1997. The Janata Party, however, is not so much a political party as an umbrella for various parties and factions that change with political circumstances. The Janata Party was created in 1977 when several small parties that opposed Indira Gandhi's Emergency hurriedly united to contest her and, much to their own surprise, won the national elections. This loose coalition lasted only a little over two years, when conflicting leadership ambitions tore it apart.

During the late 1980s, the Janata Party enjoyed another brief term as a national government under the leadership of a breakaway Congress leader, V. P. Singh (who passed away in late 2008). With these appeals, the party won enough seats in the national parliament to form a minority government in 1989. Once again, factionalism overwhelmed any attempt at a stable government, and this second attempt with a non-Congress-led government collapsed after a little over two years. Since then, the Janata Party has been able to survive only under the umbrella of the United Front, which is a collection of smaller parties, including the CPM. The Janata Party has a very weak organizational structure and lacks a distinctive, coherent political platform. To distinguish itself from Congress, it claims that it is more Gandhian, a reference to Mahatma Gandhi's vision that modern India should be more decentralized and village oriented, and less pro-Brahmin. Although most of its efforts at political self-definition have not been very successful, V. P. Singh undertook one major policy initiative while in power that identified the Janata Party with a progressive cause. This was the acceptance of the Mandal Commission's recommendation that India's **other backward classes**, generally, the middle, rural castes that constitute a near majority in the Indian countryside, be provided substantial reservations (or reserved access) to government jobs and educational institutions. The government's acceptance of this recommendation produced a nationwide outburst of riots and violence led by upper castes, who felt threatened. The uproar eventually contributed to the downfall of V. P. Singh's government. How strongly backward castes will continue to identify with this party in the future is unknown. For now, the Janata Party is viewed, especially in north-central India, as a party of small, rural agriculturalists who generally fall somewhere in the middle of the rigid caste hierarchy between Brahmins and untouchables.

The Bharatiya Janata Party (BJP)

The BJP, one of the major political parties in contemporary India, is a direct descendant of the Jana Sangh Party, which entered the Indian political scene in 1951. The Jana Sangh joined the Janata Party government in 1977 but then split off and formed the BJP in 1980. The BJP is a right-leaning, Hindu-nationalist party, and the first major party to mobilize explicitly on the basis of religious identity and adopt an anti-Muslim stance. In comparison to both the Congress and the Janata, the BJP is better organized; it has disciplined party members, who after a prolonged apprenticeship become party cadres, and the authority lines within the party are relatively clear and well respected.

The party is closely affiliated with many related organizations, the most significant of which is Rashtriya Swayam Sevak Sangh (RSS), which recruits young people (especially educated youth in urban areas) through a disciplined set of cultural activities, including the study of a chauvinistic reinterpretation of India's "great Hindu past." These young people, uniformed in khaki shorts and shirts, can often be seen in Indian cities doing group exercises in the mornings and evenings and singing songs glorifying India's Sanskritic civilization (Sanskrit is the classical language in which some of the ancient Hindu scriptures are written). Recalling the pursuits of right-wing fascist groups of interwar Europe, the activities of these youth groups dismay many non-Hindu minorities and Indian liberals, who fear the havoc that this cultural politics can produce.

Those traditionally attracted to the Jana Sangh and the BJP were mainly urban, lower-middle-class groups, especially small traders and commercial groups. As long as this was its main source of support, the BJP remained a minor actor on the Indian political scene. Since the mid-1980s, however, the BJP has widened its base of support appreciably by appealing to Hindu nationalism, especially in north-central and western India, as well as in the southern state of Karnataka. The decline in the Congress Party's popularity created a vacuum that the BJP was well positioned to fill. Moreover, the BJP found in Indian Muslims a convenient scapegoat for the frustrations of various social groups and successfully mobilized Hindus in an attempt to create a religiously oriented political force where none had existed before. The electoral success of the BJP in 1989 and 1991 and its formation of the government in 1999 underscore the party's rapid rise to power. The BJP's early efforts resulted in its ruling four states from 1991 to 1993, although it lost power in three of the four in 1993. During the 1999 parliamentary elections, the BJP scored a major success and formed the national government, only to lose power again in 2004.

The BJP's growth in the 1980s and 1990s represented a break with past traditions. In the aftermath of independence, the RSS and its affiliated organizations were widely regarded as divisive, anti-Muslim organizations. The *Bharatiya Jana Sangh* responded to its stigmatization by adopting a relatively moderate, centrist position, which the BJP upheld through the 1984 elections, when it won only two seats in parliament. The BJP's fortunes began to rise after the 1989 elections, when it emerged as the third-largest party after the Congress and Janata parties. In 1991, the BJP held the second-largest number of seats in parliament. To capitalize on the Hindu support it had been mobilizing, the BJP joined the RSS and VHP in a campaign questioning the legitimacy of the Babri Masjid (a Muslim mosque) in Ayodhya that was designed to shore up anti-Muslim sentiments. BJP leaders argued that the mosque at Ayodhya, a place of worship for India's Muslims, had been built on the birthplace of the Hindu god Rama. On December 6, 1992, thousands of Hindus, encouraged by the BJP, stormed and demolished the mosque. Seventeen hundred people were killed in the accompanying riots.

Six years later, as a result of the failures of other parties to lead effective governments, the BJP formed a governing coalition, the National Democratic Alliance, led by Prime Minister Atal Behari Vajpayee. However, its mismanagement of the economy soon generated a popular backlash against the BJP. The BJP government collapsed in 1999, just thirteen months after taking power.

However, the BJP formed a new electoral coalition, again headed by Atal Behari Vajpayee; it was elected in 1999 and lasted a full term, until 2004. It was more broadly based than previous BJP-led coalition governments because it attracted the support of regionally based political parties in various states. The result not only strengthened the BJP's hold on power

but also strengthened trends toward the regionalization of Indian politics.

Another reason for the greater strength of the BJP-led government in 1999 was its cultivation of a more moderate, centrist stance. In 1996, most political parties shunned an alliance with the BJP, for it was tainted by its militant identity. Even in 1998, the BJP put together a governing coalition with great difficulty. In 1999, the BJP went to great lengths to project Atal Behari Vajpayee as a moderate, centrist leader. Moreover, the National Democratic Alliance platform shelved contentious issues that identified it with the interests of Hindus over and against those of religious minorities. None of this, however, proved sufficient for the BJP to maintain power in the 2004 elections.

The BJP has never fully swung to the political center or abdicated its militance, even when in power. It continues to retain strong ties to the RSS and periodically demonstrates its commitment to constructing a temple in Ayodhya. The most striking evidence of this was the BJP's role in fomenting violence against Muslims in Gujarat in 2002 and its reluctance to act decisively to bring the guilty to trial in their aftermath.

The riots in Gujarat in early 2002 were among the worst that India has experienced in the post–independence period. The BJP claimed that the catalyst for the violence was an attack on a trainload of Hindu pilgrims returning from Ayodhya, in which fifty-nine Hindus were killed. Although it alleged that Muslims, with possible links to transnational terrorist organizations, were responsible for the arson, there is substantial evidence that the fire was in fact an accident. In the weeks that followed, Hindu groups engaged in a campaign of terror against the Muslim population of Gujarat in which approximately 2,000 people were killed. The violence was sanctioned by leading political officials of the BJP state government in Gujarat. Unlike riots of the past, which were an urban phenomenon, this one spread to the villages and gained the support of scheduled castes and tribals and included extensive sexual assaults on women. However, with tacit support from the national government, the BJP government in Gujarat called for early elections in 2002 and won by capitalizing on the electoral support of Hindus that it had mobilized during the riots. It won the 2007 elections in Gujarat once again with a landslide victory.

A number of factors have prevented the BJP from moving in a wholly centrist direction. The first and most important concern is its close ties to the RSS and the Hindu religious organization, the *Visva Hindu Parishad* (VHP). Since its formation in 1964, the VHP has sought to strengthen Hindu identity in a chauvinist and exclusionary fashion. In the 1960s, its activities centered on converting Muslims, who, it claimed, had been forcibly converted to Hinduism. In the 1980s, it became active around the construction of the temple in Ayodhya.

There are clearly some important differences in the orientation of these organizations. The RSS is committed to economic nationalism, the BJP to liberalization. The VHP has been implicated in violence, whereas the BJP has promised stability. Despite these differences, the BJP has maintained a close relationship to the RSS and the VHP. The RSS has intervened to mend rifts within the party in various states. It has helped ensure that the BJP, unlike most Indian political parties, has never split. Moreover, it is hard to imagine a complete rupture between the RSS and the BJP: the highest-ranking BJP members are of RSS backgrounds, and many have continuing ties to the RSS. The BJP's relationship to the VHP, though conflictual at times when the BJP is in office, has also been close. RSS and VHP activists have regularly participated in the electoral campaigns of the BJP in state and general elections. Moreover, the riots that the VHP has engineered have polarized the electorate along Hindu-Muslim lines in a way that has benefited the BJP.

The BJP's continuing commitment to privileging the interests of the Hindu majority, evident in response to the Gujarat riots, the temple construction in Ayodhya, and policies in Kashmir, has increased the vulnerability of the Muslim community. Although the BJP has consistently proclaimed its attachment to secular principles, it has taken steps to undermine the conditions under which secularism flourishes. Its promises of providing clean, honest governance have been marred in recent years by charges of corruption by high-ranking officials, in the discriminatory distribution of relief after a massive earthquake in Gujarat in 2001, in evidence that the army engaged in corruption after a border clash with Pakistan in 1999, and in patterns of bribery in defense procurement in 2001.

The Communist Party of India (CPM)

The CPM is an offshoot of the Communist Party of India, which was formed during the colonial period and has existed nearly as long as the Congress Party. Although the contemporary CPM has a national presence in that it nearly always elects representatives to the *Lok Sabha*, its political base is concentrated in two of India's states, West Bengal and Kerala, where it has repeatedly been elected to power, most recently in the 2006 Assembly elections. These states often elect *Lok Sabha* members who run on a CPM ticket.

The CPM is a disciplined party, with party cadres and a hierarchical authority structure. Other than its name and internal organization, however, there is nothing communist about the CPM; rather, it is a social democratic party like the British Labour Party or the German Social Democratic Party. Within the national parliament, CPM members often strongly criticize government policies that are likely to hurt the poor. Where the CPM runs state governments, for example, in West Bengal and Kerala, it has provided a relatively honest and stable administration and pursued a moderate but effective reform program, ensuring the rights of agricultural tenants (such as preventing their evictions), providing services to those living in shantytowns, and encouraging public investments in rural areas.

However, the CPM was the target of extensive controversy and criticisms in its actions around special economic zones (SEZs), which it and other state governments have created by acquiring land where they lower taxes to attract foreign and domestic investment. In January 2007, villagers protested the government's acquisition of a large tract of land in Nandigram for a special economic zone. The police, under orders from the state government, fired on the protesters. Following a debate in parliament, Manmohan Singh decided to continue to support the creation of SEZs, but the CPM's reputation was marred in the process.

Elections

Elections in India are a colossal event. Nearly 500 million people are eligible to vote, and close to 300 million do so. The turnout rate in the 1990s of more than 60 percent was considerably higher than in the United States,

Election Rally   *Source: Danish Small/Reuters/ Corbis.*

India's electoral system, like the British system, is a first-past-the-post system. A number of candidates compete in an electoral district; the candidate with the most votes wins. This system privileges the major political parties. It also generates considerable pressure for opposition parties to ally against the government. In practice, however, given the differences among opposition parties and the considerable clash of leadership ambitions, many parties compete, favoring the candidates of the larger parties.

One of the pillars of Indian democracy is its system of open, honest elections. Credit for this goes in part to the Election Commission, a constitutionally mandated central body that functions independently of the executive. Particularly since 1991, with the appointment of a respected chief, the Election Commission has defended free and fair elections.

Political Culture, Citizenship, and Identity

The only generalization that can be made about Indian political culture is that in such a large and culturally diverse country, no single set of cultural traits is shared by the entire population. Nevertheless, three important tendencies are worth noting. These political cultural traits reflect India's hybrid political style, as a rigid, hierarchical, and village-oriented old civilization adapts itself to modern socioeconomic changes, especially to democratic politics.

One important tendency is that India's political and public spheres are not sharply divided from personal and private spheres of activity. The idea that public office is not a legitimate means for personal enrichment or for furthering the interests of family members or of personal associates is not yet fully accepted in India. As a result, there is fairly widespread misuse of public resources for personal gain, that is, widespread corruption in political life. The positive aspect of this tendency is the high level of political involvement by the citizenry in public life.

Second, the Indian elite is extremely factionalized. The roots of such behavior are complex, reflecting India's fragmented social structure. Although some important exceptions exist, generally the personal political ambitions of Indian leaders prevent them

although it declined to 58 percent in 2004. The level of technology used in both campaigning and the conduct of elections is fairly low. Television plays an increasingly important role, but much campaigning still involves face-to-face contact between politicians and the electorate. Senior leaders fly around the country, making speeches to millions of potential supporters at political rallies held in tiny villages and district towns. Lesser politicians and thousands of party supporters travel the dusty streets, accompanied by blaring music and political messages from loudspeakers.

Given the high rate of illiteracy, pictures of party symbols are critical: a hand for the Congress (I); a lotus for the BJP; a hammer and sickle for the CPM. Illiterate voters signify their vote for a candidate in the polling booth by putting thumb marks on one of these symbols. During the campaign, therefore, party representatives work very hard to associate certain individuals and election platforms with specific symbols. A typical election slogan is, "Vote for the hammer and sickle because they stand for the rights of the working people."

from pursuing such collective goals as forming cohesive political parties, running a stable government, or focusing on problems of national development. In contrast to many East Asian countries, where the norms of consensus are powerful and political negotiation is often conducted behind closed doors, politics in India veers toward the other extreme, and open disagreements and conflicts are the norm.

The third and possibly most important tendency concerns the fragmentation of political life in India. Indian society is highly segmented. Different regions have different languages and cultures; within regions, villages are poorly connected with each other; and within villages, different castes often live in isolation from one another. Politics is often fragmented along caste lines, but even caste grievances tend to remain local rather than becoming national or even regional. Some observers of India find this segmented quality of Indian politics a blessing because it localizes problems, facilitating political stability, but others find it a curse because it stymies the possibility of national reforms to improve the lot of the poorest members of society.

Democracy is relatively well established in India. Most Indians value their citizenship rights and, in spite of poverty and illiteracy, exercise them with vigor. However, the spread of democratic politics can simultaneously fuel political conflicts. The spread of democracy is undermining many of India's political givens, including some of the most rigid hierarchies, and has begun to produce new political patterns.

The most significant of these recent developments concerns identity politics. Region, language, religion, and caste all help Indians define who they are. Such differences have generated political cleavages in India, underlining the importance and yet the malleability of collective identities. Some of these identity conflicts remained dormant when Nehru's secular nationalism and Indira Gandhi's poor-versus-rich cleavage defined the core political issues. In the 1980s and 1990s, however, with the relative decline of the Congress Party and with developments in telecommunications and transportation that have made people more aware of each other's differences, identity-based political conflicts have mushroomed in India.

Two of the more significant conflicts deserve mention. First, caste conflicts, formerly confined to local

and regional politics, have taken on a national dimension in recent years. For example, groups of backward castes had made a political mark in many states, but prior to Mandal, they were seldom a cohesive factor in national politics. V. P. Singh hoped to create a powerful support base out of these disparate groups. However, the move backfired. The threatened upper castes reacted sharply with demonstrations, riots, and political violence. Not only did this disruption contribute to the downfall of Singh's government, but it also converted the conflict between castes from a local and regional issue to a divisive national issue.

The second identity-based political conflict that has reemerged has pitted Hindus and Muslims against each other. For most of the post independence period, Hindu-Muslim conflicts have been triggered by tensions between the two communities on the local level. However, political circumstances, especially political machinations by ambitious leaders, can inflame these tendencies and instigate overt conflict. This has happened since the mid-1980s, as the BJP has whipped up anti-Muslim sentiments in an effort to unite disparate Hindu groups into a political force. The resulting aggression against Muslims illustrates the dangers of identity-based political passions.

There are many poor or otherwise frustrated social groups in India whose anger is available for political mobilization. Whether the BJP will succeed in tapping this anger in the longer term cannot be predicted. What can be said is that democracy and large pockets of social frustration provide a combustible mix that will continue to generate unexpected outcomes in Indian politics.

Interests, Social Movements, and Protest

India has a vibrant tradition of political activism that has both enriched and complicated the workings of democracy. Social movements, nongovernmental organizations (NGOs), and trade unions have put pressure on the state to address the interests and needs of underprivileged groups and check its authoritarian tendencies.

Among the groups that are politically active, labor has played a significant but not leading role. Labor unions are politically fragmented, particularly at the national level. Instead of the familiar model of one factory/one union, several political parties often organize within a single factory. Above the factory level, several labor organizations compete for labor's support. The government generally stays out of labor-management conflicts. India's industrial relations are thus closer to the pluralist model practiced in Anglo-American countries than to the corporatist model of Mexico. The political energies of unions are channeled into frequent local battles involving strikes, demonstrations, and a peculiarly Indian protest technique called *gherao,* which entails workers' encircling and holding executives of the firm hostage until their demands are met.

Social movements, the most important form of civil society activism, date back to the mid-1970s. During the period of the national Emergency (1975–1977) when the government imprisoned members of the opposition, activists came together to form political parties and social movements, often with close ties to one another. In 1977, the Gandhian Socialist leader Jai Prakash Narain organized the movement for total democracy that ultimately brought about the downfall of Congress and the election of the Janata Party. A decade later, V. P. Singh resigned from Congress and formed the *Jan Morcha* (Peoples' Front), an avowedly nonpolitical movement that brought new groups into politics and helped bring the National Front to power in 1989.

Social movements and NGOs continued to grow and assume new organizational forms in the 1980s. Until the early 1980s, when Indira Gandhi was prime minister, the state was distrustful of what is commonly known in India as the voluntary sector and sought to restrict its activities. When Rajiv Gandhi came to power, he cultivated a closer relationship with NGOs, recognizing their potential for taking over some of the development work that the state had traditionally performed. Over the years, the government's financial support for NGOs has steadily increased. During the seventh five-year plan (1985–1990), the federal government spent about US $11 million each year through NGOs; by 2002 this had increased to more than $44 million annually. Today, there are 20,000 voluntary organizations listed with the Ministry of Home Affairs, and the actual number is much higher. The most significant social movements include the

women's movement, the environmental movement, the farmers' movement, and the *dalit* movement. (The term dalit is derived from the Indo-Aryan root, "dal," which means suppressed or crushed. The Arya Samaj, a reform movement among Hindus that began in 1875, first used the term. It is widely used today in preference to the terms "scheduled castes" or "untouchables" to call attention to the discrimination the community has experienced and its dignity in fighting it.) In recent years, there has also been a growth of antinuclear and civil liberties activism. The large number and extensive activities of social movements make India quite distinctive among developing countries.

The environment movement has been spurred by the magnitude of the country's environmental crisis and the ineffectiveness of its environmental laws. India suffers from severe air pollution in large cities and contaminated lakes and rivers. The shortage of drinking water is worsened by salinization, water overuse, and groundwater depletion. The emission of carbon dioxide has contributed to the greenhouse effect, leading to an increase in temperature, a rise in the sea level, and the destruction of coastal croplands and fisheries. Commercial logging, fuel wood depletion, and urbanization have caused serious problems of deforestation, which is associated with droughts, floods, and cyclones.

Successive governments have promoted increased production at the expense of environmental protection. Effective enforcement of environmental laws and policies would put many firms out of business and slow down economic growth. Moreover, it would be very time-consuming and difficult for the government to monitor and control all small-scale industries. Although the Congress Party sponsored most of India's environmental laws, it also catered to the interest of big business at the expense of environmental protection. The United Front has been a strong supporter of environmental issues but has tended to target only big business rather than small businesses. The BJP has explicitly favored business interests over environmental concerns. Social movements and NGOs have been the major supports of environmental protection.

The Chipko movement against deforestation in the Himalayas, which emerged in the early 1970s, has been one of the longest-lasting movements against deforestation and has influenced similar forms of activism in other regions of the country. Large-scale protest at the 1984 Union Carbide disaster in Bhopal demanded greater compensation for victims of the gas leak, as well as more environmental regulations to prevent similar disasters in the future. This resulted in the creation of the Central Pollution Control Board in 1986 and a series of environmental statutes, regulations, and protocols.

The largest and most significant environmental movement in India has protested the construction of the Sardar Sarvodaya Dam in western India. The Narmada Bachao Andolan (NBA) has organized opposition to the construction of the dam on grounds that it will benefit already prosperous regions to the detriment of poor regions, lead to the large-scale displacement of people, and put in place vastly inadequate resettlement schemes. A large proportion of those who would be displaced are tribals who do not possess land titles. The movement has galvanized tens of thousands of people to engage in nonviolent protest to oppose the construction of the dam. The protest caused the World Bank to rescind promised loans, but the Indian government is still pursuing the project.

Women and questions of gender inequality have been at the forefront of environmental struggles like the Chipko and Narmada movements. The 1980s also witnessed the formation of a number of autonomous urban women's organizations. They campaigned around rape in police custody, dowry murders, *sati* (the immolation of widows on their husbands' funeral pyres), female feticide (through the use of amniocentesis), media misrepresentation of women, harmful contraception dissemination, coercive population policies, and, most recently, the adverse impact of the economic reforms.

The *dalit* movement looks back to Dr. Balasaheb Ambedkar, the *dalit* author of the Indian constitution, as the founding father of the movement. He created the Republican Party in the late 1960s. The disintegration of the party gave rise to the emergence of the Dalit Panthers. The movement demanded that *dalits* be treated with dignity, and provided better educational opportunities. Today, the *dalit* movement reflects *dalits*' growing aspirations for electoral power and public office.

Kanshi Ram formed the Bahujan Samaj Party (BSP) in 1989 with the goal of achieving political power for the *dalits*. The BSP experienced significant growth in the 1990s. Its strength is mainly confined to

Placards protesting the construction of the Sardar Sarvodaya Dam.
Source: © Tom Pietrasik/ Corbis.

Uttar Pradesh, where it has oscillated between playing ally and enemy to the BJP. In 2002, the BJP became a minority coalition partner to the BSP in UP in order to broaden its support base among lower-caste Hindus. However, this alliance collapsed by the following year. The BSP returned to power in UP in 2007 with a comfortable majority under the leadership of the enigmatic Mayawati. Amidst its aspirations to exercise power in India's largest state, the BSP has forsaken its earlier commitments to social justice and the eradication of class inequality, often focusing instead in the skilful use of symbolic politics.

Other small lower-caste parties and movements have been active in Maharashtra and Tamil Nadu. However, none of these parties is able to play a national role. Moreover, these parties have confined themselves to seeking political power for *dalits* and lack a broader vision of social transformation. Tensions have emerged within the *dalit* community. Some of the poorer and lower-status *dalits* feel that the better-off, higher-status *dalits* have benefited from reservations at their expense. Radical sections within the *dalit* movement argue that *dalits* ought not to depend entirely on reservations or the state, but should initiate a mass movement of their own that highlights issues of employment, education, and landlessness.

Three important developments have influenced the character and trajectory of social movements in recent years. First, many social movements have developed closer relationships to the state and to electoral politics. In the past, social movements tended to be community based and issue-specific. Once they had achieved some success, around the felling of forest trees, the construction of a dam, or higher prices for agricultural subsidies, the movement would subside. Although many social movements continue to be confined by their focus, duration, and geographic reach, some of them have sought to overcome these difficulties by engaging in electoral politics. The *dalit* movement and Hindu nationalism are two of the most important examples. Other movements have sought to work with particular branches of the state. The women's movement, for example, has worked closely with the bureaucracy and the courts. In part because of the closer relationship between social movements and the state, an enduring broad left-wing formation

consisting of left-wing parties and social movements has not emerged. By contrast, Hindu nationalists, particularly under the auspices of the VHP, have sustained their strong connections to the BJP.

Second, the growth of the religious right has confronted left-wing social movements with a serious challenge and dilemma. Unlike some regions of the world where the religious right and the secular left disagree on most issues, the situation in India is more complex. Segments of the religious right, like parts of the left, oppose economic liberalization and globalization. For example, both feminists and Hindu nationalists oppose the commodification of women's bodies. Similarly, the women's movement has put on the back burner its demand for a uniform civil code that would provide equal treatment of men and women of all religious communities under the law because the BJP has made this very demand, albeit for very different reasons. Furthermore, several social movements have abandoned a commitment to poverty alleviation and embraced the state-initiated shift toward the market.

Third, many NGOs and social movements have developed extensive transnational connections. The consequences for social movements have been double-edged. On the positive side, funding from foreign sources has been vital to the survival of NGOs and social movements. India lacks a tradition of donating to secular-philanthropic causes, and corporate funding is limited and tightly controlled. However, organizations receiving foreign funding are often viewed with suspicion and have difficulty establishing their legitimacy. Moreover, foreign funding has created a sharp division between activists with and without access to foreign donors.

If these developments have complicated the agendas of social movements, there is also a potential for NGOs and social movements to grow stronger. There are greater opportunities than ever for social movement and NGO activists to avail themselves of the resources that the state is making available. Some groups have already done this by putting candidates up for elections at the local level, as we have seen in the case of the *panchayats*. Furthermore, the BJP's defeat in the 2004 elections, coupled with the relatively strong performance of left-of-center parties, may well revitalize movements of the most underprivileged groups.

To review, political participation over the years in India has broadened in scope and deepened in intensity. A single-party system dominated by the Congress Party has slowly been supplanted by a multiparty system of parties on the left and the right. Similarly, caste hierarchies have eroded in Indian society, and upper castes cannot readily control the political behavior of those below them. The result is that many groups in society increasingly feel empowered and seek to translate this new consciousness and sense of efficacy into material gains by influencing government policies.

SECTION 5 Indian Politics in Transition

India has become the site of extensive terrorist violence in recent years. In the 1990s most of these attacks were related to regional conflicts in the Punjab, Jammu and Kashmir, and the Northeast. Attacks have continued in Jammu and Kashmir (October 2001, May 2002). However starting with a bomb explosion at the Indian Parliament on December 13, 2001, in which fifteen people were killed, bombings have become more widespread and their targets more diverse. They have taken place in New Delhi (October 2005, July 2008), Kolkata (January 2002), Varanassi (March 2006), Jaipur (May 2008), and Ahmadabad (July 2008). The worst incidents have occurred in Mumbai, India's cosmopolitan financial capital: in August 2003, August 2005, and July 2006. But in an even more deadly assault in November 2008, more than 170 Americans, British and Indians were killed in shootings, arson and bombings. While the source of terrorist attacks in recent years varies and is often unclear, militant Hindu organizations have organized some and militant Islamic organizations have planned more of them. Domestic organizations have participated but international organizations have played more important roles. The target of the most recent attacks is as much the U.S. and global forces as the Indian state; the political consequences for India and its relationship with Pakistan are devastating.

Political Challenges and Changing Agendas

As a large country with a legitimate government and sizable armed forces, India's policies toward Kashmir and Pakistan were not deeply influenced by the United States in the past. However, in an increasingly interdependent global economic context, India has become far more vulnerable to global pressures. India's foreign and domestic policies are significantly influenced by the much closer ties it has developed to the United States.

Kashmir within a World of States

Of all the challenges that India has faced since independence, among the most enduring and intractable is its relationship to Kashmir, the state located in northern India on the border with Pakistan. The roots of conflict within Kashmir have often been attributed to the ethnic and religious diversity of the state, which is roughly 65 percent Muslim and 35 percent Hindus and other minorities. The non-Muslim minorities—Hindus, Sikhs, and Buddhists, who are concentrated in the areas of the state called Jammu and Ladakh—largely wish to live under Indian sovereignty. The Kashmir Valley, which is predominantly Sunni Muslim, is mostly in favor of Kashmir's becoming an independent country or part of Pakistan. However, ethnic differences do not explain separatist sentiments.

With a majority Muslim population, Kashmir should logically have become part of Pakistan. However, Kashmir's Maharajah was sympathetic to India and decided to cede to it. Britain agreed on condition that the wishes of the Kashmirs would be taken into account. At independence, Nehru promised that a referendum on Kashmir would decide the status of the region. However, the Indian government has never honored this pledge, mainly because it has feared a pro-independence vote.

With the partial exceptions of 1947–1953 and 1977–1984, Kashmir has been directly ruled from New Delhi. This has hindered democratic participation and institutional development in the state. As demands for independence grew, so too did the repressive actions of the Indian state, leading to spiraling cycles of insurgent militance and state-sanctioned violence. The Indian government enacted the Armed Forces Special Powers Act (Jammu and Kashmir) of 1990 to grant military and other security forces extensive powers in conducting counterinsurgency operations. Under this legislation, security forces have often engaged in extensive extra-judicial killings.

The national government has ruled Kashmir undemocratically through a combination of repression, direct control, and manipulation to install unrepresentative governments. The constant rigging of elections has prevented the development of free and autonomous competition among political parties. While elections were held in most parts of the country from 1952 onward, in Kashmir elections to the legislative assembly were held only in 1962 and to parliament only in 1967. Most elections in Jammu and Kashmir have been fraudulent. The elections in 2002 and 2004 were partial exceptions. Although the police and army forced people to vote, in part in response to the separatists' call for an electoral boycott, they were more open and inclusive than previous elections.

More than any other conflict, the Kashmir dispute is triggered and sustained by the international context. Since the early 1990s, Pakistan has provided Kashmiri militants with weapons and support. Superpower rivalry in the cold war deterred India and Pakistan from reaching an agreement on the status of Kashmir. Tensions between India and Pakistan are one of the important reasons for the two countries' high military expenditures (see Figure 6.6). Relations between the two countries have periodically swung from terrible to moderately good—only to decline again. In May 1999, Muslim separatists, widely believed to be backed by Pakistan, seized Indian-controlled territory in Jammu and Kashmir. India engaged in a military campaign against the separatists until Pakistan secured their withdrawal. Two years later tensions escalated again.

In October 2001 there was an exchange of fire on the border between the two countries. Relations plummeted further after an attack on the Jammu and Kashmir legislative assembly and, what was far more serious, an attack on the Indian parliament in December of that year. India charged that Pakistan had orchestrated the attacks and prepared for war by

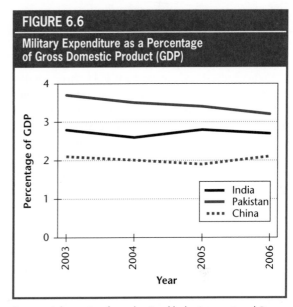

FIGURE 6.6

Military Expenditure as a Percentage of Gross Domestic Product (GDP)

Source: Information from the Stockholm International Peace Research Institute (SIPRI), Military Expenditure Database, first. sipri.org/index.php?page=step3&compact=true.

amassing over one million troops near the Pakistani border. Pakistan responded in kind, and for several weeks, nuclear conflagration seemed a distinct possibility. Intense intervention by the United States helped defuse the situation, and Pakistan and India withdrew most of their troops and declared a cease fire along the Jammu and Kashmir border. Since then, the United States has worked behind the scenes to pressure Pakistan to restrain terrorists within its borders. In a symbolically important move, in 2005 the Indian and Pakistani governments initiated a bus service across the cease-fire line for the first time in fifty years. Violence in Kashmir has abated since 2007. Pakistan's support for the insurgency has waned, and the major insurgent groups have lost support among the Kashmiris.

Nuclear Power Status

Soon after the BJP first came to power in May 1998, it fulfilled an electoral promise by gate crashing the nuclear club. Although it cited regional threats from China and Pakistan as the key reason to develop nuclear weapons, its decision can also be traced to electoral considerations. Electoral mobilization in an atmosphere of economic turmoil and poverty prompted political parties to mobilize Indians' national pride, thereby deflecting attention from domestic economic and political problems.

When India set off a nuclear test, Pakistan responded in kind, triggering fears of a nuclear arms race in South Asia. Worldwide condemnation swiftly followed and many countries, including the United States, imposed economic and technology sanctions on both India and Pakistan. The Vajpayee and the Clinton administrations engaged in several rounds of arms control talks in which Clinton tried to persuade India to sign the Comprehensive Test Ban Treaty (CTBT) and the Nuclear Non-Proliferation Treaty (NPT) in exchange for lifting U.S. sanctions. In 1998, India announced its intention to sign the CTBT if talks with the United States ended successfully and also signaled its willingness to join other nuclear control groups. In 1999, India and Pakistan agreed to continue a moratorium on further nuclear tests and signed the Lahore Declaration, which committed them to improving relations with each other.

The Manmohan Singh government took a dramatic step toward defusing tensions from the nuclear issue after its election in 2004. While emphasizing that decisions about India's nuclear programs must be made domestically and should not be subject to externally imposed sanctions, Singh highlighted India's nonproliferation record and its commitment to preventing the proliferation of weapons of mass destruction. Parliament voted to propose a stricter regime of external transfers and tighter controls to prevent international leakages. When Manmohan Singh and George W. Bush met in Washington, D.C., in September 2004, they issued a joint statement emphasizing the commitment of the two countries to work together to stop the proliferation of weapons of mass destruction. In July 2005 they agreed that India could secure international help for its civilian nuclear reactors while retaining its nuclear arms. This agreement paved the way for removing a U.S. ban on nuclear technology sales to India.

The Indo–U.S. nuclear treaty allows the two countries to cooperate on nuclear issues despite India's violation of nonproliferation norms. There has been considerable opposition to the nuclear agreement within India. Initially, the BJP spearheaded the opposition,

but the CPM's opposition has been more far-reaching and significant. In spite of these challenges, the Indo-U.S. nuclear treaty was finally ratified by both the U.S. and India in 2008.

The Challenge of Ethnic Diversity

The future of Indian democracy is closely bound up with how the country confronts the growing politicization of ethnic identities. Mobilized ethnic groups seeking access to state power and state-controlled economic resources are a basic component of the contemporary Indian political scene. Caste, language, and religion all provide identities around which political mobilization can be galvanized. Identification with a group is heightened by the democratic context, in which parties and leaders freely choose to manipulate such symbols. When studying Indian politics, it is difficult to separate interest- and identity-based politics. For example, caste struggles in India are simultaneously struggles for identity, power, and wealth. Identity politics in India is likely to be characterized by two trends: considerable political ferment, with a variety of dissatisfied groups making demands on parties and governments; and pressure on political parties to broaden their electoral appeal to disadvantaged groups, especially those belonging to the middle and lower strata, many of whom are very poor. India's political leaders will thus continue to experience pressures to expand their support base by promising economic improvements or manipulating nationalist symbols. Under what conditions will such political forces engage in constructive rather than destructive actions? Will democracy succeed in merely tempering the effect of such forces, or will it in the long run promote a positive channeling of identity politics? Answers to these questions partly hinge on India's economic performance.

Economic Performance

India's economic experience is neither a clear success nor a clear failure. If many African countries have done poorly economically and many East Asian countries (prior to 1997) have had dramatic successes, India falls somewhere in the middle. Three conditions may explain this outcome. The first is the relationship between political governance and economic growth. In this, India has been fortunate to have enjoyed relatively good government since independence: its democratic system is mostly open and stable, its most powerful political leaders are public spirited, and its upper bureaucracy is well trained and competent.

The second condition concerns India's strategy for economic development. India in the 1950s chose to insulate its economy from global forces, limiting the role of trade and foreign investment and emphasizing the role of government in promoting self-sufficiency in heavy industry and agriculture. The positive result of this strategy was that India now produces enough food to feed its large and growing population and produces a vast range of industrial goods. This strategy, however, was not without costs. Most of India's manufactured goods are produced rather inefficiently by global standards. India sacrificed the additional economic growth that might have come from competing effectively in global markets and by selling its products abroad. It also gave up another area of potential economic growth by discouraging foreign investment. And last, during the phase of protective industrialization, India did little to alleviate its staggering poverty: land redistribution failed, job creation by heavy industries was minimal, and investment in the education and health of the poor was minuscule in relation to the magnitude of the problem. The poor also became a drag on economic growth because they were unable to buy goods and stimulate demand for increased production; because an uneducated and unhealthy labor force is not a productive labor force.

Yet despite this sluggish past, India's economy over the last quarter of a century has grown handsomely. As discussed earlier, the main forces propelling this change have been a closer relation between respective Indian governments and Indian business groups, liberalization of the economy, and integration in the global economy. This steady growth, however, is not without problems. A variety of inequalities are growing. As a result, India's numerous poor are not benefiting as much from growth as they might. The reduction in public spending has hurt the poor by limiting their access to publicly funded education and health services. Reconciling continuing growth with rapid poverty alleviation remains a pressing challenge,

especially in light of the fact that the global economic slowdown in the late 1980s is likely to impact India's growth adversely.

Indian Politics in Comparative Perspective

Given its large size, diversity, and vibrant social and political system, India is an exceptionally good case study for analyzing themes of general significance in comparative politics. In this concluding section, we first examine the implications of the study of India for comparative politics and then assess how India's politics and its economy will influence developments in a regional and global context.

Some comparative scholars suggest that citizens' widespread desire to exercise some control over their government is a potent force encouraging democracy. This assumption is clearly illustrated in India. Although democracy was introduced to India by its elites, it has established firm roots within society. A clear example is when Indira Gandhi declared Emergency rule (1975–1977) and curtailed democratic freedoms. In the next election, in 1977, Indian citizens decisively voted Indira Gandhi out of power, registering their preference for democratic rule. Most Indians value democracy and use its institutions to advance their claims.

Comparativists debate whether democracy or authoritarianism is better for economic growth. In the past, India did not compare well with the success stories of East Asian and Chinese authoritarian-led countries. India's impressive economic growth in recent years reopens these old debates. Moreover, the collapse in the late 1990s of several East Asian economies and the subsequent rise of instability within those societies makes a study of Indian democracy more relevant to understanding the institutional and cultural factors underpinning economic stability in the long run.

Another theme concerns the implications of establishing democracy in multiethnic societies. The rising tide of nationalism and the breakup of the Soviet Union and Yugoslavia, among others, have prompted closer examination of how and why India continues to exist as a cohesive entity. By studying India's history, particularly the post–1947 period, comparativists could explore questions of how cleavages of caste, religion, and language in India balance one another and cancel the most destructive elements in each. Comparativists have also puzzled over the conditions under which multiple and contradictory interests could be harnessed within a democratic setup to generate positive economic and distributional outcomes. Here, the variable performance of different regions in India can serve as a laboratory. For instance, two communist-ruled states, Kerala and West Bengal, have (to a certain extent) engaged in land redistribution policies. An examination of factors such as the role of the mobilizing parties and the interaction between the landless poor and the entrenched landed elite could provide answers. The main elements of the Kerala model are a land reform initiative that abolished tenancy and landlord exploitation, effective public food distribution that provides subsidized rice to low-income households, protective laws for agricultural workers, and pensions for retired agricultural laborers, and a high rate of government employment for low-caste communities.

Another question engaging comparativists is whether success in providing education and welfare inevitably leads to success in the economic sphere. Again, the case of Kerala provides pointers for further research. Kerala scores high on human development indicators such as literacy and health, and its economy has also grown in recent years.

What are the international and domestic challenges that India faces at the dawn of the twenty-first century? How will it cope with its new-found status as a nuclear power? How can it prevent further escalation of conflict in the region that could end in a nuclear conflagration? A worst-case scenario would be a conventional war with Pakistan that could escalate into a nuclear war. Domestically, both countries are wracked with ethnic tensions, one with a military dictatorship and the other with an elected coalition government. In an attempt to hold on to power, the leaders of each country could try to divert attention toward a national security threat from its neighbor, a ploy that has been used effectively in the past by politicians in both countries. The history of three wars between India and Pakistan, the simmering tensions over Kashmir, and both countries' possession of nuclear arms could prompt a nuclear war. The challenge for India is to establish a stable relationship with its nuclear neighbors, Pakistan and China, that would eschew proliferation of their nuclear and ballistic missiles arsenals and engage in constructive diplomatic and economic cooperation. India's history of wars with both countries is not an encouraging starting point, but the engagement of Western powers in generating a dialogue between these countries is a portent for the future. The recent initiation of people-to-people contacts and resumption of talks among leaders provides grounds for optimism. Whether such overtures will result in fruitful negotiations on Kashmir and on economic cooperation in the region remains to be seen. Answers to these questions depend at least in part on domestic political developments.

For over sixty years, democracy in India has been a double-edged sword. Winning elections involves attracting votes. While avoiding authoritarianism, the practice of democracy, particularly electoral politics, has worsened ethnic relations between Hindus and Muslims, upper and lower castes, and north and south. With the spread of democracy, many dissatisfied groups are finding their voices and becoming politically mobilized. The challenge for Indian politics is how to repair the divide within a democratic framework. Current voter emphasis on good governance and sound economic management rather than on religious or nationalistic issues might transform electoral platforms in the twenty-first century. Will India be able to manage its domestic tensions and enlarge social, political, and economic rights for its citizens?

Another challenge for India is how to combine its global ambitions of becoming a strong power with its program for economic liberalization. The increasing interdependence of global economies as manifested in global effects of the 1997 East Asian crisis and the dependence of developing countries on investor confidence and external aid should not be underestimated. While India was protected from the East Asian debacle because of the partially closed nature of its economy, it nevertheless suffered some economic blows in the aftermath of becoming a nuclear state when economic sanctions resulted in the loss of billions of dollars in foreign aid. However, the Indian economy recovered relatively quickly. Even with modest liberalization, India is now attracting considerable foreign investment and growing at an impressive rate. The Indian case nevertheless embodies the tensions inherent in combining democracy with economic liberalization. Political parties in India face pressures to expand their support base by promoting contradictory economic improvements or by manipulating nationalist symbols. But simultaneously, these promises clash with the task of economic liberalization. The challenge faced by Indian governments is how to combine the task of economic liberalization with the conflicting demands of electoral politics.

How India reconciles its national political ambitions, domestic political demands for greater economic redistribution, and global pressures for an efficient economy will affect its influence on regional and global trends. Will India be able to capitalize on some of its positive achievements, such as the longstanding democratic ethos framed by functioning institutions, a vibrant civil society and media, and a growing middle class imbued with the desire to succeed economically? Or will it be crippled by ethnic hostility resulting in inaction at best and total disintegration of the country at worst? The current trends indicate a scenario of two-party rule, with either a BJP-led or a Congress-led coalition ruling at the center. There also seems to be some room for optimism with regard to voter needs and interests on the international and domestic fronts. Public opinion polls show an overwhelming number of people in India and Pakistan want improved relations between the two countries. On the domestic side, the preoccupation of voters with secularism, equitable distribution, and economic management was evident from the results of the 2004 national elections. Of course, balancing the demands of simultaneously achieving equity and efficiency generates its own problems. Understanding the ways in which India meets these challenges will be of enormous interest to students of comparative politics in the years to come.

Key Terms 》》

Sikhs
Maharajas
zamindars
Emergency (1975–1977)
green revolution
state-led economic development
economic liberalization
reservations
caste system

Brahmin
untouchables
scheduled castes
Lok Sabha
Rajya Sabha
Indian Administrative Service
panchayats
other backward classes

Suggested Readings 》》

Bardhan, Pranab. *The Political Economy of Development in India.* New Delhi: Oxford University Press, 1984.

Basu, Amrita. *Two Faces of Protest: Contrasting Modes of Women's Activism in India.* Berkeley: University of California Press, 1992.

———, and Kohli, Atul, eds. *Community Conflicts and the State in India.* New Delhi: Oxford University Press, 1998.

Bayly, C. A. *The New Cambridge History of India: Indian Society and the Making of the British Empire.* Vol. 2, no. 1. Cambridge: Cambridge University Press, 1988.

Brass, Paul R. *The New Cambridge History of India: The Politics of India Since Independence.* Vol. 4, no. 1. Cambridge: Cambridge University Press, 1990.

———. *The Production of Hindu-Muslim Violence in Contemporary India.* Madison: University of Wisconsin Press, 2005.

Carras, Mary C. *Indira Gandhi: In the Crucible of Leadership.* Boston: Beacon Press, 1979.

Chatterjee, Partha, ed. *State Politics in India.* New Delhi: Oxford University Press, 1997.

Dreze, Jean, and Amartya, Sen, eds. *Economic Development and Social Opportunity.* New Delhi: Oxford University Press, 1995.

Frankel, Francine. *India's Political Economy, 1947–2004: The Gradual Revolution.* New Delhi: Oxford University Press, 2005.

Gopal, Sarvepalli. *Jawaharlal Nehru: A Biography.* Vols. 2 and 3. New Delhi: Oxford University Press, 1984.

Graham, Bruce. *Hindu Nationalism and Indian Politics.* Cambridge: Cambridge University Press, 1990.

Hardgrave, Robert L., Jr., and Kochanek, Stanley A. *India: Government and Politics in a Developing Nation.* 4th ed. New York: Harcourt Brace Jovanovich, 1986.

Hasan, Zoya. *Quest for Power: Oppositional Movements and Post-Congress Politics in Uttar Pradesh.* Delhi: Oxford University Press, 1998.

Jaffrelot, Christophe. *The Hindu Nationalist Movement and Indian Politics, 1925 to the 1990s: Strategies on Identity Building, Implantation and Mobilization.* New York: Columbia University Press, 1996.

Jalal, Ayesha. *Democracy and Authoritarianism in South Asia.* Cambridge: Cambridge University Press, 1995.

Jalan, Bimal. *India's Economic Crisis: The Way Ahead.* New Delhi: Oxford University Press, 1991.

Jenkins, Rob. *Regional Reflections: Contemporary Politics Across India's States.* New Delhi: Oxford University Press, 2004.

Kohli, Atul. *Democracy and Discontent: India's Growing Crisis of Governability.* Cambridge: Cambridge University Press, 1991.

———. *State Directed Development: Political Power and Industrialization in the Global Periphery.* Cambridge: Cambridge University Press, 2004.

———. *The State and Poverty in India: The Politics of Reform.* Cambridge: Cambridge University Press, 1987.

———, ed. *The Success of India's Democracy.* Cambridge: Cambridge University Press, 2001.

Misra, B. B. *Government and Bureaucracy in India: 1947–1976.* New Delhi: Oxford University Press, 1986.

Nayar, Baldev Raj. *India's Mixed Economy.* Bombay: Popular Prakashan, 1989.

Ray, Raka, and Katzenstein, Mary, eds. *Social Movements in India: Poverty, Power and Politics.* Lanham, MD: Rowman and Littlefield, 2005.

Rothermund, Dietmar. *An Economic History of India: From Pre-Colonial Times to 1986.* London: Croom Helm, 1988.

Rudolph, Lloyd, and Rudolph, Susanne. *In Pursuit of Lakshmi: The Political Economy of the Indian State.* Chicago: University of Chicago Press, 1987.

Sarkar, Sumit. *Modern India: 1885 to 1947.* Madras: Macmillan, 1983.

Varshney, Ashutosh. *Ethnic Conflict and Civic Life: Hindus and Muslims in India.* New Haven,: Yale University Press, 2002.

———, ed. *India and the Political Economy of Developing Countries: Essays in Honor of Myron Weiner.* New Delhi: Sage Publishers, 2004.

Weiner, Myron. *The Child and the State in India.* Princeton, N.J.: Princeton University Press, 1992.

———. *The Indian Paradox: Essays in Indian Politics.* New Delhi: Sage, 1989.

Wilkinson, Steven. *Votes and Violence: Electoral Competition and Ethnic Riots in India.* Cambridge: Cambridge University Press, 2004.

Suggested Websites ➤➤

Bharatiya Janata Party (BJP)
www.bjp.org
Economic and Political Weekly, a good source of information on Indian politics
www.epw.org.in
Frontline, a magazine with coverage of Indian politics
www.flonnet.com
The Hindu, an English daily paper in India
www.hinduonnet.com

Hindustan Times
www.hindustantimes.com
Directory of Indian government websites
goidirectory.nic.in
Sabrang Communications, providing coverage of human rights issues in India
www.sabrang.com

Endnotes ➤➤

1*Times of India*, September 7, 2002.

Louis DeSipio

Chapter 7 »» THE UNITED STATES

Official Name: **United States of America**

Location: **North America, between Canada and Mexico**

Capital City: **Washington, D.C.**

Population (2008): **303.8 million**

Size: **9,826,630 sq. km.; about half the size of South America; slightly larger than China**

1776
Independence from Great Britain declared

1788
U.S. Constitution replaced Articles of Confederation

1803
Supreme Court establishes judicial review in *Marbury v. Madison*

1803
Louisiana Purchase

1830s
Mass political parties emerge, and electorate expands to include a majority of white men

1861–1865
U.S. Civil War

1865–1876
Reconstruction era: the United States establishes but fails to guarantee voting rights for freed slaves

1896
Voter turnout in elections begins century-long decline

1933–1940
The New Deal responds to the economic distress of the Great Depression

The Making of the Modern American State

SECTION 1

Politics in Action

In Spring 2006, as many as five million immigrants, their family members, and advocates of immigrant rights marched in 150 cities nationwide. What unified these protestors? They opposed legislation passed in the U.S. House of Representatives criminalizing immigrant presence in the United States without an immigrant visa. This legislation passed in response to outrage among many in the United States that 12 million unauthorized immigrants resided in the United States, that their numbers were growing, and that they were perceived to be changing the national culture. These advocates of immigration restriction did not, for the most part, protest in the streets as did the immigrant rights advocates. Instead, they used the media, particularly new forms of media such as talk radio and Internet blogs, to build a social movement to pressure Congress to add new barriers to unauthorized migration, to criminalize unauthorized status, and, perhaps, to reduce legal immigration, which is also at historic highs.

The high level of immigration-related popular organization seemed to signal substantial changes in policy. In the years since the protests, however, policy has changed little. The Senate rejected the criminalization provisions passed by the House, largely removing this from the popular debate. The House and Senate did agree to build a fence along as much as 700 of the 1,950 miles of the U.S.–Mexican border and to add staffing and resources to Immigration and Customs Enforcement, the agency responsible for policing the border. The core of U.S. immigration policy has changed little in this period.

Why did popular concern and fear (among immigrants and their supporters) and outrage (among those seeking restriction) not translate into major policy change? Several explanations are possible, but each speaks to the design of the U.S. national government. Like the U.S. public, Congress is divided on immigration. Some seek restriction and criminalization, others want to ensure that employers have a sufficient labor supply and are willing to expand immigration to achieve this goal, and still others want to ensure that unauthorized immigrants have the opportunity to transition to a legal status. None of these positions represents a majority and each can block the others. The U.S. presidency is a weak executive compared to leaders in parliamentary systems. President Bush's leadership was weakened by his lack of popular support in the electorate and his lame-duck status. So, the president and the executive branch were largely irrelevant to the immigration debate. Ultimately, the electorate in a democratic system should be able to influence legislators. In the current era, however, most incumbent members of Congress face little risk of electoral defeat, which reduces their incentive to compromise on immigration or other highly conflictual issues.

1941–1945
U.S. participates in World War II

1964
Tonkin Gulf Resolution authorizes military actions in Vietnam

1974
Richard Nixon resigns the presidency in the face of certain impeachment

1978
California passes Proposition 13

1996
Federal government ends the guarantee of social welfare programs to the poor established during the New Deal

1998–1999
U.S. House of Representatives impeaches and the U.S. Senate acquits President Clinton

2000
George W. Bush (R) defeats Al Gore (D) in a disputed election resolved by a ruling from the U.S. Supreme Court

2001
The World Trade Center and the Pentagon are targets of terrorist attacks using hijacked civilian airliners

So, despite deep-seated concerns in the American public about many aspects of immigration policy, little has changed. A compromise will eventually be reached, but in the interim many more unauthorized immigrants will join U.S. society, many millions of unauthorized immigrants will live in U.S. society without legal protections, and U.S. citizens concerned about the cultural and economic impact of immigrants will become further alienated from U.S. politics.

Geographic Setting

The 3.79 million square miles of the United States occupy approximately half of the North American continent and represent an area about half of the size of the Russian Federation and slightly larger than China. Its population, approximately 304 million people, is dwarfed by the populations of China and India.

The United States has only two neighbors, Mexico and Canada, which do not present a military threat and are linked in a comprehensive trade agreement: the **North American Free Trade Agreement (NAFTA)**. U.S. territory is rich in natural resources (such as coal, oil, and metals), arable land, navigable rivers, and protected ports. The abundance of land and natural resources has engendered a national ethos that there will always be enough resources to meet national needs. This abundance explains in part the low support for environmental protection laws in the United States. Finally, the United States has always had low

"The decision to build a fence along parts of the U.S. border with Mexico appeared to many as a metaphor for the barriers that the U.S. was establishing with other nations in other policy arenas." *Source:* TOLES © 2006 The Washington Post. Reprinted with permission of UNIVERSAL PRESS SYNDICATE. All rights reserved.

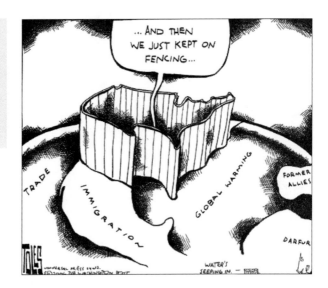

315

The United States

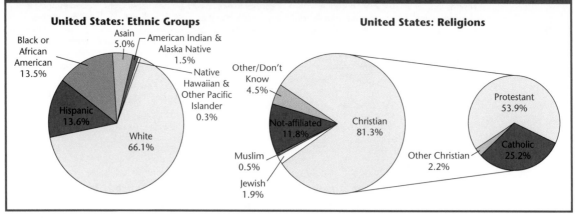

FIGURE 7.1

The American Nation at a Glance

United States: Ethnic Groups

- Black or African American 13.5%
- Asain 5.0%
- American Indian & Alaska Native 1.5%
- Native Hawaiian & Other Pacific Islander 0.3%
- Hispanic 13.6%
- White 66.1%

United States: Religions

- Other/Don't Know 4.5%
- Not-affiliated 11.8%
- Christian 81.3%
- Muslim 0.5%
- Jewish 1.9%
- Protestant 53.9%
- Catholic 25.2%
- Other Christian 2.2%

population densities and has served as a magnet for international migration. In 2006, for example, the United States had approximately 84 people per square mile. This compares to 611 people per square mile in Germany, 968 in India, and 17,060 in Singapore.[1]

European colonization led to the eventual unification of the territory that became the United States under one government and the expansion of that territory from the Atlantic to the Pacific Oceans. This process began in the early 1500s and reached its peak in

Table 7.1

Political Organization

Political System	Presidential system.
Regime History	Representative democracy, usually dated from the signing of the Declaration of Independence (1776) or the Constitution (1787).
Administrative Structure	Federalism, with powers shared between the national government and the fifty state governments; separation of powers at the level of the national government among legislative, executive, and judicial branches.
Executive	President, "directly" elected (with Electoral College that officially elects president and vice president) for four-year term; cabinet is advisory group of heads of major federal agencies and other senior officials selected by president to aid in decision-making but with no formal authority.
Legislature	Bicameral. Congress composed of a lower house (House of Representatives) of 435 members serving two-year terms and an upper house (Senate) of 100 members (two from each state) serving six-year terms; elected in single-member districts (or, in the case of the Senate, states) by simple plurality (some states require a majority of voters).
Judiciary	Supreme Court with nine justices nominated by president and confirmed by Senate, with life tenure; has specified original and appellate jurisdiction and exercises the power of judicial review (can declare acts of the legislature and executive unconstitutional and therefore null and void).
Party System	Essentially two-party system (Republican and Democrat), with relatively weak and fractionalized parties; more than in most representative democracies, the personal following of candidates remains very important.

the nineteenth century, when rapid population expansion was reinforced by an imperialist national ideology **(manifest destiny)** to push the westward boundary of the country from the Appalachians to the Pacific. The indigenous residents of the western territories were pushed aside in the process of expansion. The United States experimented with colonialism at the turn of the twentieth century, leading to the annexation of Hawaii, Guam, the Northern Marianas Islands, and Puerto Rico. Hawaii became a state in 1959.

The United States faces little challenge to its territorial boundaries today. Although some in Puerto Rico seek independence, most want either a continuation of Commonwealth or statehood. Commonwealth status for Puerto Rico reflects something of a semantic compromise; Puerto Rico is a colony of the United States that has been granted autonomy in local governance, but has limited autonomy in trade and foreign policy. Puerto Ricans are U.S. citizens by birth and can travel freely to the United States. Guam is an "unincorporated territory" (a U.S. territory that is not on the road to statehood and does not have all of the protections of the U.S. Constitution).

Critical Junctures

The first four critical junctures in U.S. political history appeared at points when mass discontent became sufficiently organized to alter governing institutions or relationships. Each of these junctures challenged dominant paradigms of who should have a voice in democratic government and what the relationship between government and citizen should be. Four periods of focused popular demand are explored here: the period from the beginning of the American Revolution through the ratification of the U.S. Constitution, the Civil War and Reconstruction, the New Deal, and a contemporary period of routinely divided national government that began with the 1968 national elections. This last period, which is ongoing, is somewhat less focused than the other three because we cannot know its ultimate outcome. It was into this ongoing period of divided national government that the United States experienced the attacks of September 11, 2001, the final critical juncture analyzed here.

The Revolutionary Era (1773–1789)

The American Revolution was sparked by mass and elite discontent with British colonial rule that resulted in the signing of the **Declaration of Independence** on July 4, 1776. The Revolution itself was only the beginning of a process of creating a new form of government. Mass interests sought to keep government close to home, in each colony, and wanted each colony to have substantial autonomy from the others. Elite interests advocated a national government with control over foreign policy, national assumption of state Revolutionary War debts, and the ability to establish national rules for commerce.

Mass interests won this battle initially. From 1777 to 1788, the **Articles of Confederation** governed the nation. The Articles' weaknesses, specifically the inability of the national government to implement foreign or domestic policy, to tax, or to regulate trade between the states without the acquiescence of the individual governments of each of the states, allowed elite interests to gain support for their replacement with the Constitution. The limited powers of the national government under the Articles rested in a legislature, but the states had to ratify most key decisions. In this period, states established their own foreign policies, which were often divergent from each other. They also established their own fiscal policies and financed state budgets through extensive borrowing.

The Constitution maintained most power with the states but granted the federal (or national) government authority over commerce and foreign and military policy. It also provided the federal government with a source of financing independent of the states. And, most important, it created an executive officer, the president, who had powers independent of the legislature. Initially, the U.S. presidency was quite weak, but its power grew in the twentieth century. The Constitution delegated specific, but limited, powers to the national government. These included establishing post offices and roads, coining money, promoting the progress of science, raising and supporting an army and a navy, and establishing a uniform rule of naturalization. These powers can be found in Article I, Section 8 of the Constitution and tend to vest the federal government with the power to create a national economy. Finally, the Constitution sought to limit the citizenry's voice in government. Presidents were elected indirectly, through the Electoral College. Members of the Senate were elected by state legislatures. Only the members of the House of Representatives were elected by the people, but regulation of who could vote for members of the House was left to the states. (See "Institutional Intricacies: The Electoral College.") In the nation's early years, only property-holding men held the vote in most states. By the 1840s, most white adult men were enfranchised. Women did not receive voting rights nationally until 1920.

As popular support for ratification of the Constitution began to rise, many who had supported the Articles of Confederation made a new demand: that the newly drafted U.S. Constitution include enumerated protections for individuals from governmental power. Meeting this demand for a **Bill of Rights**, a specific set of prohibitions on the new national government was necessary to ensure the ratification of the Constitution. Although the specific rights guaranteed in the Bill of Rights had little substantive meaning for Americans in the 1790s, over time they came to offer protections against the excesses of national and state government. Interpretation of the meaning of these rights ensured that the federal courts would play an increasingly significant role in U.S. national government, particularly in the twentieth century.

The Civil War and Reconstruction (1861–1876)

The second critical juncture in U.S. political history was the Civil War. While the morality of slavery convulsed the nation prior to the war, the war itself began over the question of whether the states or the national government should be dominant. Despite the seeming resolution of this question during the Revolutionary era, many states still believed they could reject specific federal laws. Any time Congress threatened to pass legislation that would restrict slavery in the South, the legislation would be met by a threat by one or more southern state legislatures to nullify the law. From the perspective of most in the North and some in the South, the potential for any state to nullify federal laws put the union at risk (and would return the United States to the system of governance under the Articles of Confederation). The Civil War resolved this issue in favor of the indivisibility of the union. A second long-term consequence was to establish an enforceable national citizenship to supplement the state citizenship that had predated the ratification of the Constitution.[2] This establishment of a national citizenship began a slow process that culminated in the New Deal, as the nation's citizens looked to the federal government to meet their basic needs in times of national crisis.

Institutional Intricacies: The Electoral College

Until votes started to be counted in the 2000 election, most Americans did not realize that voters do not directly elect the president or the vice president. Instead, they learned, the president and vice president are elected by the Electoral College, which in turn is elected by the voters on Election Day.

The framers of the Constitution designed the Electoral College to act as a check on the passions of the citizenry. Like the indirect election of senators by state legislatures that survived until 1913, the Electoral College was a device to place elites between voters and the selection of leaders. Senators are now elected directly, but the Electoral College remains. On Election Day, voters elect a slate of electors who are pledged to vote for a particular candidate. The number of electors in a state is equal to the state's number of Representatives plus its two senators. With the ratification of the Twenty-Third Amendment to the Constitution in 1961, the District of Columbia also has three electors, although it has no voting representation in Congress. To win, a candidate must earn half the total number plus one, or 270, of the Electoral College votes.

The electors, who are not named on the ballot, are selected by the state parties. They are usually state party leaders who are named as an honor for past service. As a result, they are very likely to support the candidate to whom they are pledged when the electors meet in each state capital early in December. Most states also require (by law) that an elector vote for the candidate to whom he or she is pledged. But there are examples, as recently as the 2004 election, where electors did not vote for their pledged candidate.

Such "faithless" electors have not affected the outcome of any election so far. What would happen in a close election if a handful of electors did not vote for the candidate to whom they were pledged? Congress, under the Constitution, would have to count their votes as reported. Thus, in this hypothetical close election, a few stray electors could deny the winner a majority by voting for a third candidate. This would throw the election into the House of Representatives. More unlikely, the electors could vote for the losing candidate and give him or her the presidency.

As the 2000 election demonstrated, the Electoral College system can make a winner out of the person who places second in the popular vote. Al Gore won the popular vote by more than 500,000 votes, but he lost the Electoral College by a vote of 271 to 266 (one faithless elector from the District of Columbia did not vote for Al Gore, who had won a majority of the District of Columbia's popular vote). All but two states award electoral votes on a winner-take-all basis. This practice maximizes the influence of their voters and increases the likelihood that candidates will campaign in that state; no large state is likely to sacrifice this practice unless all do. Thus, the candidate who receives the most votes in these winner-take-all states wins all of the state's Electoral College votes. In races with three or more serious candidates, these votes can be awarded to candidates who received far less than a majority of the state's votes.

As part of the process of establishing full citizenship for the freed slaves after the war, Congress revisited the question of individual liberties and citizenship for the first time since the debate over the Bill of Rights at the end of the Revolutionary era. These post–Civil War debates on the relationship of citizens to the national government established several important principles in the Fourteenth Amendment to the Constitution (1868) that shape citizenship today. First, it extended the protections of the Bill of Rights to cover actions by states as well as by the federal government (the courts slowed the implementation of this provision). Second, it extended citizenship to all persons born in the United States. This made U.S. citizens of freed slaves (a legal necessity because an 1857 Supreme Court ruling, *Dred Scott* v. *Sanford,* had held that all blacks, slave or free, were not and could never be U.S. citizens) but also guaranteed that U.S.-born children of the tens of millions of immigrants who migrated after 1868 would become U.S. citizens at birth. Without this constitutional protection, the children of immigrants could have formed a legal underclass—denied citizenship but with no real tie to a foreign land. (This kind of excluded status characterized the children of many immigrants to Germany until 2000.) Third, Congress sought to establish some federal regulation of voting and to grant the vote to African Americans (these provisions were strengthened in the Fifteenth Amendment, ratified in 1870). Failure of the federal government to continue to enforce black voting rights meant that African Americans, particularly in the South, could not routinely exercise the vote until the passage of the Voting Rights Act in 1965. These fundamental guarantees that ensure electoral opportunities today limit prerogatives recognized as the states' responsibilities in the Constitution. The Voting Rights Act and subsequent nationalization of voting rights and voting procedures would have likely been found to be unconstitutional without these Civil War–era amendments.

The New Deal Era (1933–1940)

The third critical juncture in U.S. political development was the New Deal, the Roosevelt administration's response to the economic crisis of the Great Depression. The federal government tapped its constitutional powers to regulate interstate commerce in order to vastly expand federal regulation of business. It also established a nationally guaranteed safety net, which included such programs as **Social Security** to provide monthly payments to the elderly who had worked, housing programs to provide housing for the working poor, and food subsidies for children in poor households. Finally, the federal government subsidized the agricultural sector and to offer farmers protections against the cyclical nature of demand. These programs, which had been understood as being within the purview of the states to the extent that they existed at all, expanded dramatically in the fifty years after the New Deal. The legislative and judicial battles to establish such policies are direct outcomes of the New Deal and represent a fundamental expansion of the role of the federal government in the lives of individual Americans.

This juncture also saw the federal government assert dominance over the states in delivering services to the people that gave substantive meaning to the national citizenship that was established during the critical juncture of the Civil War and Reconstruction. Equally important, the critical juncture of the New Deal saw the presidency assert dominance over the Congress in terms of policy-making. The U.S. president during the New Deal, Franklin D. Roosevelt, found powers that no previous president had exercised and permanently changed the office of the presidency. Despite many changes in U.S. politics since 1933, all post–New Deal presidents remain much more powerful than any of their predecessors, except perhaps for Abraham Lincoln, who served during the Civil War. Beginning in the 1960s, however, Congress began to challenge growth in executive power.

The expanded role of the federal government in the 1930s should be seen in the context of demands for even more dramatic changes. Unemployment rates as high as 40 percent, a worldwide decline in demand for U.S. manufactures, and ecological changes that made much agricultural land unproductive spurred widespread demand for wealth redistribution and centralization of power in the federal government that had not been seen either before or after in American politics. Although the New Deal programs represented a significant change from the policies that preceded the Great Depression, they also reflected underlying American political values (see Section 4) relative to other visions for the U.S. government that were discussed in the era. Even in the New Deal era, class-based politics was kept to a minimum.

As the Depression came to a close, the United States geared up for its involvement in World War II. Although the United States had previously been involved in an international conflict beyond its borders, the experience of World War II was different at the inception of U.S. involvement and at the conclusion. The United States entered the war after U.S. territory was attacked (the Japanese bombing of Pearl Harbor). After the war, the United States was at the center of a multilateral strategy to contain the Soviet Union. This newly internationalist foreign policy enjoyed wide popular support.

Divided Government and Political Contestation of the Scope of Government (1968 to the Present)

The fourth critical juncture, which began with the 1968 presidential election, is ongoing today. This critical juncture has two dimensions. First, the national government has been routinely divided between the two political parties. Division such as this cannot exist in parliamentary systems. This division exacerbates the inefficiency that was designed into the American constitutional order and increases popular distrust of government (see Section 3).

The 1968 election saw the election of Richard Nixon (a California Republican) to the presidency. Through Nixon's term and that of his Republican successor, Gerald Ford, the Democrats maintained control of both houses of Congress. In the period since 1968, one of the parties has controlled the presidency, the U.S. Senate, *and* the U.S. House of Representatives only five times. The Democrats controlled all three from 1977 to 1981, from 1993 to 1995, and beginning in 2009. The Republicans controlled all three from late January to early June 2001 and again from January 2003 to January 2007. This division of the federal government between the parties and the emergence by the end of the 1990s of a near equal division between parties in the electorate in the 2000 and 2004 elections

slow the government's ability to respond to controversial policy issues.

The second ongoing dimension of the contemporary critical juncture began a few years later but emerges from the apparent inefficiency caused by divided government. Many in the United States began to question the steady increase in the scope of governmental services that was ongoing throughout the twentieth century, and particularly since the New Deal. The electoral roots of this popular discontent can be found in the passage of Proposition 13 by California voters in 1978. California allows citizens to propose ballot initiatives—legislation that appears on the state ballot. If passed by the voters, it cannot be reversed by the legislature. This is one of the few forms of direct democracy in the U.S. system. Proposition 13 limited California's ability to increase **property taxes**. The dissatisfaction expressed by Californians with the cost of government soon spread to other states. The passage of Proposition 13 began an era that continues today, in which many citizens reject the expansion of government and its role in citizens' lives that began with the New Deal.

Popular discontent in the contemporary era is not limited to taxes; it also focuses on the scope of government. This period saw popular mobilization to reshape government's involvement in "values" issues, such as abortion, gay marriage, and the role of religion in U.S. life. It is considerably more difficult for policymakers to find middle-ground compromise positions on issues such as these. Advocates on all sides of these issues seek to use government to protect their interests, while condemning government for allegedly promoting the interests of groups with alternative positions. The U.S. government offers individuals and groups with differing positions the opportunity to influence policy in different (governmental) arenas. Ultimately, the courts—the unelected branch of the U.S. government—become the venue to shape government policies on social issues.

While divided government had become the norm in 1968, the division became even more razor thin in the late 1990s. Each election raises the possibility of a switch in partisan control of the Senate or the House and the intense focus of both parties and **interest groups** on winning the handful of seats that could switch from one party to the other. This nearly even legislative division makes judicial nominations more contentious as well.

September 11, 2001, and Its Aftermath

It is in this environment—one of routinely divided government and national and local debates about the size and scope of government—that the United States responded to the September 11, 2001 terrorist attacks. Initially, Congress and the populace rallied behind the president to increase the scope of federal law enforcement powers and to provide financial assistance for New York City, the families of the victims of the attack, and the airlines. Quickly, however, partisan divisions and concerns about the powers the president was seeking for the federal government (a concern related to the size and scope of government) began to appear. With Congress so closely divided and neither side actively seeking compromise, the United States soon saw the consequences of the structure and scope of government in the period of the fourth critical juncture. These divisions were exacerbated by the preparations that the Bush administration made in 2002 and early 2003 to invade Iraq and by its willingness to pursue domestic tax cuts and dramatically increase the size of the federal budget deficit.

In the weeks after September 11, 2001, the United States experienced a rare period of national consensus and international support. Domestically, President Bush's popularity surged to 90 percent. Largely without debate (or significant dissent), Congress passed a dramatic expansion of government's ability to conduct surveillance, to enforce laws, to limit civil liberties, and to fight terrorism—the United and Strengthening America by Providing Appropriate Tools to Intercept and Obstruct Terrorism Act (or **USA PATRIOT Act**) of 2001. Just 65 of the 435 members of the U.S. House of Representatives and 1 of the 100 members of the U.S. Senate voted against this bill.

Popular support for President Bush and his administration's initial efforts to respond to the challenges of September 11 continued as the administration prepared for an invasion of Afghanistan. Bush justified this military action with evidence that the September 11 hijackers were trained in Afghanistan and that the Al Qaeda network received protection from the Taliban

regime that ruled Afghanistan. At the beginning of the war, nearly nine in ten Americans supported military action in Afghanistan.

The United States also experienced a period of international support immediately following the September 11, 2001 attacks. In addition to immediate offers of humanitarian assistance, initial U.S. military responses to the attacks won widespread backing around the world. U.S. allies joined the United States in what President Bush characterized as a "war against international terrorism." When the United States invaded Afghanistan in October 2001, the coalition included forty nations, including all NATO member states. Popular support in other countries was also high to create an international coalition to remove the Taliban government in Afghanistan. Support for participation of their own governments exceeded 65 percent among Danes, the French, Indians, Italians, the Dutch, and the British. Nearly two-thirds of Germans supported U.S. military action in Afghanistan.

The initial domestic cohesion and international support for the United States in the months after September 11, 2001 dissipated quickly in 2002 and 2003. Although the causes were numerous and differed domestically and internationally, U.S. efforts to extend the war on terrorism to Iraq became the focus of many of the objections to growing U.S. power and unilateralism in international affairs.

Domestically, Bush saw steadily declining popular support. It dropped below 50 percent in 2005 and below 30 percent in 2008. Why did his support slip so dramatically? A sizeable minority of the U.S. population opposed the U.S. invasion of Iraq without the support of the United Nations or other international bodies. This opposition grew in the period after the military phase of the war ended when it became evident that the peace would be harder fought than the war. U.S. and coalition force casualties in Iraq, for example, numbered 173 in March and April 2003, the period of combat. U.S. causalities had grown to 4,000 by March 2008. Bush's support also declined when he advocated strongly partisan positions on contentious domestic issues such as tax cuts that benefited high-income earners, the partial privatization of Social Security, and support for the social conservative agenda. While

A jet crashes into the World Trade Center on September 11, 2001.
Source: AP Images/Moshe Bursuker

these positions did not differ from those taken prior to September 11, 2001, many expected that Bush would govern more consensually during a period of national crisis. The Bush administration also paid a political price for the multiple failures in the federal government's response to Hurricane Katrina's destruction of New Orleans and the Gulf Coast. Bush's policies and overall stridency in domestic and foreign policy returned the country to the near-even partisan division that had characterized the country in the 1990s. The switch of one state in the Electoral College (Ohio—which President Bush won by 119,000 votes) would have given the presidency to John Kerry in 2004.

The United States also faced significant opposition from its allies. Germany and France, in particular, opposed U.S. intervention in Iraq and prevented both United Nations and NATO support for U.S. military activities. The growing opposition to U.S. unilateralism in international affairs resulted in a dramatic decline in positive feelings for the United States among residents of other countries. In the summer of 2002, 75 percent of UK residents and 61 to 63 percent of French, Germans, and Russians had a favorable view of the United States. Just two years later, the share reporting favorable views of the United States declined to 58 percent in the United Kingdom, 37 percent in France, 38 percent in Germany, and 47 percent in Russia.[3]

In the years immediately after the September 11, 2001 attacks on the United States, the United States won and squandered international support, and the Bush administration lost some of the domestic support that it enjoyed in the months after the attack. In retrospect, neither of these outcomes is surprising. Allies of the United States have increasingly sought multilateral solutions to international affairs and are suspicious of U.S. unilateralism. Domestically, the electorate was largely divided prior to 2001, and these divisions reappeared as the shock of the 2001 attacks diminished and other, largely domestic issues returned to their traditional spot at the top of most citizens' policy agendas. In the era of divided government and political contestation of the scope of government, national unity will be the exception rather than the rule.

Themes and Implications

Historical Junctures and Political Themes

The conflict between the president and Congress, the centralization of federal power in the twentieth century, and the growing concern about the cost and scope of government represent ongoing themes in U.S. politics. These are not quickly or easily resolved because the Constitution slows resolution by creating a system of **federalism** and **separation of powers** (see Section 3). As will be evident, the period of consensus after the September 11, 2001 attacks was an exceptional moment in American politics. When the Constitution was drafted in 1787, its framers were wary of allowing the federal government to intervene too readily in matters of individual liberties or states' prerogatives, so they created a governing system with multiple powers. These limits remain today even as the United States has achieved sole superpower status, and other countries, as well as U.S. citizens, expect the United States to lead.

In the modern world, the United States may be at a disadvantage with such a system relative to other governing systems that can react more quickly and decisively to societal needs and shifts in public opinion. Leadership in parliamentary systems changes when leaders lose support from the legislature. In parliamentary systems, even when they are burdened by the compromises necessary to maintain coalition governments, prime ministers can exercise power in a way that a U.S. president or Congress can never expect to do. When a prime minister loses the support of his or her party on key issues, elections are called. In the United States, elections are held on a regular cycle, regardless of the popularity of the president. The presidency and Congress are routinely controlled by the two opposing parties. In addition to the differences between the parliamentary and the presidential systems, federalism (a division of governing responsibilities between the national government and the states) further slows government action.

The tensions inherent in a system designed to impede governmental action are seen in each of the cross-national themes explored in this book: a world of states, governing the economy, the democratic idea, and the politics of collective identity.

Until the New Deal era and World War II, the United States pursued a contradictory policy toward the rest of the world of states: it sought isolation from international politics but unfettered access to international markets. World War II changed the first of these stances, at least at elite levels (see Section 2): the United States sought to shape international relations through multilateral organizations and military force. It designed the multilateral organizations so that it could have a disproportionate voice (for example, in the United Nations Security Council). The United States used military force to contain communism around the world. With the decline of communism and the end of the cold war, this postwar internationalism has declined; some now call for a reduced role of the U.S. government in the world of states or, at a minimum, a greater willingness to use a unilateral response to international military crises. This willingness to move unilaterally manifested itself in the shallow coalition that supported the United States in the Iraq War. This decline in interest in the U.S. role in the world among some in U.S. society reflects the fact that foreign policy has never been central to the evolution of U.S. politics and governance.

The federal government and the states have sought to manage the economy by building domestic manufacturing, exploiting the nation's natural resources, and regulating the banking sector, while interfering little in the conduct of business (see Section 2). Thus, the United States has governed the economy only selectively. This hands-off attitude toward economic regulation can come at a price. The global credit crisis of 2008 was the result of dramatic increases in home lending to borrowers in the United States who were very unlikely to be able to repay the loans unless housing prices continued to increase. These "subprime" loans often trapped borrowers with low initial payments that would rapidly grow to levels that they could not pay.

To build industry and exploit resources, the government built roads and other infrastructure, educated citizens, and opened its borders to guarantee a workforce. It also sought access to international markets. Only in exceptional circumstances has it limited the operations of business through antitrust or environmental regulation. Yet its ability to continue to promote the nation's commerce is today limited by the challenge to the size and scope of government.

The democratic idea inspired the American Revolution and all subsequent efforts to secure and increase freedom and liberty. The democratic idea in the U.S. context was one of an indirect, representative democracy with checks on democratically elected leaders. The emergence of a strong national government after the New Deal era meant that national coalitions could often focus their demands on a single government. The decline in mediating institutions that can channel these demands reduces the ability of individual citizens to influence the national government (see Section 4).

A continuing challenge in U.S. governance is the politics of collective identities. As a nation of immigrants, the United States must unite immigrants and descendants of immigrants from Europe, Africa, Latin America, and Asia with the established U.S. population. Previous waves of immigrants experienced only one to two generations of political and societal exclusion based on their differences from the larger society. Whether today's immigrants (particularly those who enter the United States without legal immigrant status) experience the same relatively rapid acculturation remains an open question (See "Current Challenges: Incorporating Immigrants."). Preliminary evidence indicates that the process may be even quicker for immigrants who possess skills and education but slower for those who do not.[4] National economic decline or the rise of a virulent anti-immigrant sentiment could slow or even stop the acculturation process. Despite the acculturation of previous waves of immigrants and their children, the United States has never fully remedied its longest-lasting difference in collective identities with full economic and political incorporation of African Americans.

Implications for Comparative Politics

Scholars of U.S. politics have always had to come to terms with the idea of American exceptionalism—the idea that the United States is unique and cannot easily be compared to other countries. In several respects, the United States *could* be considered exceptional: its geography and natural resources offer it advantages that few other nations can match; its experience with mass representative democracy is longer than that of other nations; it has been able to expand the citizenry beyond the descendants of the original members; and U.S. society has been much less divided by class than have the societies of other states.[5]

The United States has influenced other nations both because of its success and because it sometimes imposes its experiences on others. The U.S. Constitution, for all of its limitations, has served as the model for the constitutions of many newly independent nations. Some form of separation of powers (see Section 3) has become the norm in democratic states. Similarly, district-based and **single-member-plurality (SMP) electoral systems** (see Section 4) have been widely adapted to reduce conflict in multiethnic states, of which the United States was the first large-scale example. Through its active role in multilateral institutions such as the United Nations (UN) and international financial institutions such as the International Monetary Fund (IMF), the United States also attempts to impose its will on other nations. Thus, for all of its strengths and weaknesses, it is necessary to know about the U.S. experience to understand more fully the shape of modern democracies throughout the world.

SECTION 2 # Political Economy and Development

State and Economy

When national leaders present the accomplishments of the United States, they often hold its economy up as an example of what the nation offers to the world and what it offers to its citizens. By governing the economy less, the United States allows the private economy to thrive. In this simplified version of this story, the private sector is the engine of national growth, and this private sector is most successful when left alone by government. Economic success, then, is tied to the **free market**—the absence of government regulation and the opportunity for entrepreneurs to build the nation's economy.

Relative to other advanced democracies, the U.S. economy is much less regulated. The U.S. government has traditionally taken a **laissez-faire** attitude toward economic actors. This absence of regulation allowed for the creation and expansion of many new types of production that subsequently spread throughout the world, such as the assembly line early in the twentieth century, industrialized agriculture at mid-century, and Internet commerce at its end, but also can come at a cost. U.S. policymakers cede power to private actors who are not concerned with the impact of their activities on the broader economy, such as the mortgage lenders who built the subprime lending industry or the investment banks that bought the subprime loans. As the number of borrowers who could not pay their monthly mortgage payments grew, the U.S. economy slid toward recession and the global economy slowed.

The Constitution reserves for the federal government authority to regulate *inter*state commerce and commerce with foreign nations. As a result, state and local governments are limited in their ability to shape the economy. When states have tried to regulate commerce, their efforts have been ruled unconstitutional by the Supreme Court. Over time, however, states have established the ability to regulate workplace conditions as part of their **police powers** or of jurisdiction over public health and safety.

With the exception of agriculture, higher education, and some defense-related industries, the size of various sectors of the economy is almost entirely the result of the free market. The federal government does try to incubate some new industries, but it primarily uses grants to private agencies—often universities—to accomplish this end. This stimulation of new economic activity makes up a very small share of the nation's gross national product. The United States also occasionally supports ailing industries. While these account for more in terms of federal expenditures than does stimulation for new industries, political support for propping up ailing industries usually dies quickly. With limited government intervention, the shape of the economy is determined largely by market forces.

Agriculture is an exception to this pattern. Since the New Deal, the federal government has guaranteed minimum prices for most agricultural commodities and has sought to protect agriculture by paying farmers to leave some land fallow. It has also considerably reduced the costs of production and risks associated with agriculture by providing subsidized crop insurance, canals and aqueducts to transport water, and flood control projects. It has subsidized the sale of U.S. agricultural products abroad and purchased some surplus agricultural production for storage and distribution in the United States. Although a less explicit form of subsidy, weak regulation of U.S. immigration laws has ensured a reliable, inexpensive labor supply.

The federal government has also limited its own ability to regulate the economy. With the formation of the **Federal Reserve Board** in 1913, it removed control of the money supply from democratically elected officeholders. Today, unelected leaders on the Federal Reserve Board, many with ties to the banking industry, control the volume of money in the economy and the key interest rates that determine the rates at which banks lend money to businesses and individuals. As the United States slid toward recession in 2008, the Federal Reserve was the central U.S. policy-making agency seeking to avert recession. Its decisions to lower interest rates gave financial markets confidence, but is outside of the control of the electorate. In other words, the Federal Reserve's decision to end the interest rate cuts out of fears of inflation cannot be reversed by Congress or the president. The Federal Reserve also assumed new responsibilities that may signal an expansion of its role in U.S. society. It worked with investment bank J.P. Morgan so that it could absorb another investment bank, Bear Stearns, that otherwise would have collapsed and potentially damaged the global economy. The Federal Reserve accepted as collateral as much as $30 billion in mortgage-related loans that had been made to borrowers with poor credit records that ultimately may not be repaid. Without the Federal Reserve guarantees, Bear Stearns would have collapsed, forcing other ailing investment firms and banks into bankruptcy and damaging the U.S. economy as a whole.

The U.S. government does not regulate the flow of capital. As a result, many large U.S.-based firms have evolved into multinational corporations, removing themselves from a great deal of U.S. government regulation and taxation.

While the United States has taken a more laissez-faire approach to its economy than have other advanced democracies, it is important to recognize that from the nation's earliest days, the federal government promoted agriculture and industry, spurred exports, and (more recently) sought to stabilize the domestic and international economy. These promotional efforts included tariffs, which sought to disadvantage products that competed with U.S. manufactures; roads and canals, so that U.S.-produced goods could be brought to market cheaply and quickly; the distribution of federally owned lands in the West to individuals and to railroads, so that the land could contribute to national economic activity; and large-scale immigration, so that capital would have people to produce and consume goods (see Section 3).

Efforts to promote U.S. industry often came at the expense of individual citizens, who are less able to organize and make demands of government. Tariffs, for example, kept prices high for domestic consumers, and the enhanced road system and consequent cheap transportation forced native producers to compete in a world economy where their locally produced goods might be more expensive than the same goods produced elsewhere in the United States or abroad.

Through much of the nation's history, the United States used its diplomatic and military resources to establish and maintain markets for U.S.-produced commodities and manufactures abroad. The United States, for example, uses its position in the world economy and on multilateral lending institutions to open markets, provide loans for nations facing economic distress, and protect some U.S.-produced goods from foreign competition. In sum, despite national rhetoric to the contrary, the United States has consistently promoted economic development, though not by regulating production or spurring specific industries.

The U.S. economy has increasingly come to rely on two unintentional forms of international subsidy. First, it has built up a steadily increasing international trade deficit. In other words, the United States has bought much more abroad than it has sold. In 2007, for example, the United States imported $709 billion more in goods and services than it exported. Although some aspects of these trade deficits could well reflect a strength in the U.S. economy (for example, being able to purchase goods produced inexpensively abroad), continuing deficits of this level will act as a downward pressure on the U.S. dollar in the long run (see Figure 7.2). Slowing this downward pressure for the time being is the second form of international subsidy: the U.S. dollar is the international reserve currency. This means that many nations and individual investors keep their reserves (their savings) in dollars. By doing this, they keep demand for the dollar up, reducing the downward pressure that comes from trade deficits. By buying U.S. government bonds, they are lending the United States money. The European common currency, the euro, is increasingly serving as a reserve currency, leading to a decline in the value of the dollar relative to the euro (and other currencies) and increasing the cost to U.S. consumers of goods produced abroad. Between 2001 and 2007, the share of total foreign exchange reserves held in euros increased from 18 to more than 25 percent; the share held in dollars decreased from 73 to 64 percent. The long-term stability of the U.S. economy and the value of the dollar as a reserve currency are being challenged by an increasing national debt (which is discussed later in this chapter) and market concerns about unfunded liabilities in federal and state pension, health care, and insurance programs.

The government, both federal and state, regulates aspects of the economy and employer-labor relations. Beginning in 1890, the United States enacted

The United States

FIGURE 7.2

U.S. Trade Deficit, 1994–2007

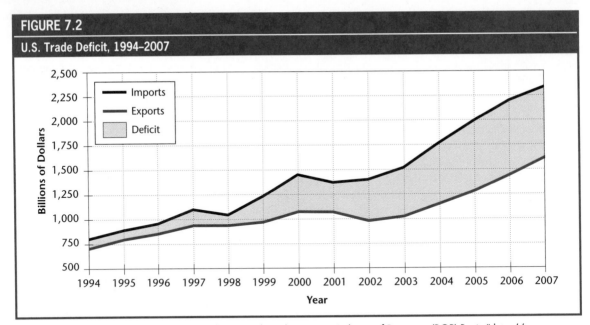

Source: U.S. Bureau of the Census, "U.S. Trade in Goods and Services—Balance of Payments (BOP) Basis," http://www.census.gov/foreign-trade/statistics/historical/gands.pdf (accessed on March 26, 2008).

antitrust legislation that gave it the ability to break up large businesses that could, by the nature of their size, control an entire market. These antitrust powers have been used sparingly. Antitrust legislation gives the government a power that is very much at odds with a laissez-faire ideology, but its unwillingness to use this authority except in the most egregious cases (and the courts' occasional rejection of government antitrust initiatives) reflects the underlying hands-off ideology.

In the twentieth century, the U.S. government took on new responsibilities to protect citizens and to tax businesses, in part, to provide government-mandated services for workers. The government also expanded regulation of workplace safety, pension systems, and other worker-management relations issues that limit the ability of industry to operate in a free market relative to its workforce (see Section 3). Despite this expansion of the government role in providing protections to workers, the United States offers fewer guarantees to its workers than do other advanced democracies.

The public sector has traditionally been smaller in the United States than in other advanced democracies. Nevertheless, the U.S. government and the states conduct activities that many believe could be better conducted by the private sector. The federal government operates hospitals for veterans (through the Veterans Administration), provides water and electrical power to Appalachian states (through the Tennessee Valley Authority), manages lands in the West and Alaska (through the Department of Interior), runs the civilian air traffic control system (through the Federal Aviation Administration), and, after September 11, manages passenger and luggage screening at commercial airports (with increasing support from private contractors). Roads have traditionally been built and maintained by the state and federal governments, and waterways have been kept navigable (and open to recreational use) by the federal government.

The U.S. government privatized some activities in recent years. The postal service, for example, became a semi-independent corporation in 1970. The federal government is trying to end subsidies for Amtrak that it inherited when the company's private sector owners went bankrupt in 1971.

Often left out of the story of the development of the U.S. economy is the role of its natural resources and the environment. The nation's territory is diverse in terms of natural resources and environments, stretching from tropical to arctic. The territory includes arable land that can produce more than enough year round for the domestic market as well as for extensive exports. These lands have not been subject to invasion for much of the nation's history. Land has become increasingly concentrated in a few hands, but in the past, it was held in small plots tilled at least in part by the owners. This tradition of equitable land distribution (encouraged by government policies in the nineteenth century that distributed small plots to resident landholders) dampened the class tensions that appeared in societies with entrenched landholding elites. Not all Americans were eligible for this land giveaway, however. Recently freed slaves could not obtain free lands in the West, and some share of the gap in wealth between whites and blacks today can be attributed to the access that whites had to western lands in the last century.[6]

The United States has been advantaged in terms of trade. It has protected ports and navigable rivers and few enemies that can challenge U.S. control over these transportation resources. For more than a century, it was able to expand trade while not investing in a large standing military to defend its trade routes. This long history of safety in U.S. territory made the events of September 11 all the more unnerving for Americans. The symbolic importance of the name of one of the September 11 targets, New York's World Trade Center, raised for many Americans questions about whether the buildings were targeted in part because they represented the increasing presence of American commerce abroad.

One area in which the United States has taken a limited role in regulating the activities of private actors in the American economy is environmental regulation. When the environment first became an issue in international politics, the United States took aggressive action to clean the air and the nation's oceans and navigable waterways. In each of these regulatory areas, federal legislation had dramatic impacts. Emissions standards have made the air much healthier, even in the nation's most car-focused cities. Waterways that were dangerous to the touch are now open to swimming. New lands were added to the national park system.[7] The visible successes of the early environmental **regulations** reduced the salience of environmental issues, particularly those that would have impact in areas where few people live. As the environment has diminished as a popular concern, traditional laissez-faire attitudes toward governmental regulation have allowed presidents and Congress to trade economic gains for environmental losses.

These 1970s-era environmental regulations have not been followed by a continuing national commitment to environmentalism. President Ronald Reagan opened federal lands to further commercial exploitation. President George W. Bush proposed opening the Arctic National Wildlife Refuge (ANWR) to oil exploration, an effort that was blocked by a Democratic-led filibuster in the U.S. Senate. Presidents of both parties reduced auto fuel efficiency standards for cars and light trucks, a pattern that may have been reversed in 2007 with the passage of legislation requiring steady increases in average auto and light truck fuel economy between 2008 and 2020.

The United States has fewer environmental regulations than other advanced democracies and has been less willing to engage in multilateral agreements on environmental issues than on issues such as international security and economic cooperation. The United States, for example, is a signatory to the Kyoto Protocols to limit climate change (primarily through the reduction of greenhouse gases), but the treaty was never sent to the U.S. Senate for ratification and is, consequently, nonbinding on the United States. Among the reasons offered by President Bush for his failure to send the treaty to the Senate for ratification was the strain that he believed that it would put on the U.S. economy. Under Kyoto, the United States would have been obliged to cut greenhouse gas emissions by 7 percent between 2008 and 2012. The comparable requirement for European Community states was an 8 percent cut in this period (on average, people in the United States produce twice the volume of greenhouse gases as do Europeans, a function of differing levels of regulation and different costs for consuming energy). Nine U.S. states and 740 U.S. cities have passed emissions caps that broadly follow Kyoto guidelines (though often less rapidly than Kyoto would mandate). Unlike an international treaty, however, these state and city efforts can be amended with a majority vote in a legislature and are more difficult to enforce.

Society and Economy

The United States adheres more strictly to its laissez-faire ideology in terms of the outcomes of the economic system. The distribution of income and wealth is much more unequal in the United States than in other advanced democracies. In 2006, for example, the richest fifth of families earned approximately 50.5 percent of the nation's income. The poorest fifth, on the other hand, earned just 3.4 percent (see Figure 7.3). The top 5 percent alone earned more than 22.3 percent of the total amount earned. Wide differences exist between women and men and between racial groups. Women, on average, earned $12,000 annually less than men in 2005. Non-Hispanic whites earned

an average of $29,000 in 2005 compared to $26,000 for Asian Americans, $17,000 for blacks, and $14,000 for Hispanics.

The United States has always tolerated these conditions and sees them as an incentive for people at the lower end of the economic spectrum. Wealth and income have become more skewed since 1980 (when the top 20 percent of households earned approximately 44 percent of what was earned), a phenomenon that has not been an issue of national political concern. In fact, the mere mention in an election of the class implications of a policy, particularly tax policy, will usually lead to the charge of fomenting class warfare.

Federal income taxation of individuals is progressive, with higher-income people paying a higher share of their income in taxes. Rates range from 0 percent for individuals with incomes less than $8,950 to 35 percent for individuals with incomes exceeding approximately $363,000. The progressive nature of federal taxes is reduced considerably by two factors. Upper-income taxpayers receive a much higher share of their income from investments, which are taxed at

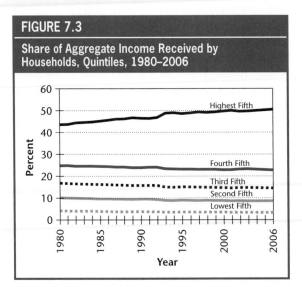

FIGURE 7.3

Share of Aggregate Income Received by Households, Quintiles, 1980–2006

Source: U.S. Bureau of the Census, Historical Income Data, "Table H-1. Income Limits for Each Fifth and Top 5 Percent of Households All Races: 1967 to 2007," http://www.census.gov/hhes/www/income/histinc/h01AR.html (accessed on October 17, 2008).

lower rates. Second, all taxpayers with salary income are subject to a regressive tax for Social Security and disability benefits. The tax for Social Security and Medicare is currently 7.65 percent paid by the worker and 7.65 percent paid by the employer. The Social Security share of this tax is imposed only on the first $102,000 of income and not at all on higher incomes. This is a regressive tax: higher-income taxpayers pay a lower share of their income for Social Security than do lower-income taxpayers.

State and local taxes tend to be much less progressive. Most states levy a sales tax. This is a flat tax, ranging between 2.9 and 8.75 percent depending on the state, on most consumption; some states exempt food and other items from sales taxation. For lower-income people, sales taxes act as a flat tax on most or all of their income. Upper-income people pay a smaller share of their income because they do not have to dedicate all of their income to consumption. Not all states have income taxes. Among those that do, no state has an income tax that is as progressive as the federal income tax. The final major form of individual taxation is property taxes. All people pay these in one way or another. Property owners pay them directly and can deduct the tax payment from their federal and, in some cases, state income taxes. Renters pay them as part of their rent payment but do not directly get any tax benefits. Governments in the United States have increasingly supplemented taxes with user fees charged for the provision of specific services.

Thus, the vast gap between rich and poor in the United States is not remedied by progressive taxation. This gap might well have led to the emergence of class-based political movements, but immigration policy, which also promoted economic development, focused workers' attention away from class and toward cultural differences that reduced the salience of class divisions in U.S. society. Unions, which could also have promoted class-based politics and focused workers' attentions on income inequalities, have traditionally been weak in the United States. This weakness reflects individual-level antipathy toward unions, but also state and federal laws that limit the abilities of unions to organize and collectively bargain. Today, approximately 12 percent of American workers are unionized; this rate steadily

declined in the twentieth century, but is slowly edging upwards.

Agriculture and industry could not have grown in the United States without the importation of this immigrant labor. With only a few exceptions, the United States has sought to remedy labor shortages with policies that encouraged migration. Today, the United States is one of just four countries that allow large-scale migration of those who do not already have a cultural tie to the receiving nation. (The others—Canada, Australia, and New Zealand—share a colonial history with the United States.) Contemporary immigration to the United States numbers approximately 1,100,000 people annually, who immigrate under the provisions of the law to a permanent status that allows for eventual eligibility for U.S. citizenship (see Figure 7.4).[8] Another 500,000 migrate without legal status each year and stay (many more who migrate as undocumented immigrants come and go during any year).[9]

Although the United States tolerates the unequal distribution of income and wealth, in the twentieth century, it intervened directly in the free market to establish protections for workers and, to a lesser degree, to guarantee the welfare of the most disadvantaged in the society. The programs for workers, which are primarily distributive policies, receive much more public support than do programs to assist the poor, which are primarily redistributive policies. **Distributive policies** allocate resources into an area that policymakers perceive needs to be promoted without a significant impact on income or wealth distribution. **Redistributive policies** take resources from one person or group in society and allocate them to a more disadvantaged group in the society. It should be noted that most worker benefits, such as health insurance, childcare, and pensions, are provided by private employers, if they are provided at all, but are regulated by the government.

In 2006, approximately 44 million people, or about one in seven Americans, did not have health insurance. Many poor families are eligible for a needs-based health insurance program, Medicaid, provided by the federal government. In the mid-1990s, Congress and President Bill Clinton sought to craft a policy solution to insure the uninsured; their efforts collapsed around questions of cost and

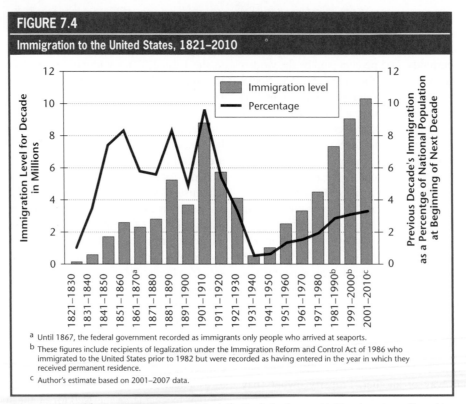

FIGURE 7.4

Immigration to the United States, 1821–2010

a Until 1867, the federal government recorded as immigrants only people who arrived at seaports.

b These figures include recipients of legalization under the Immigration Reform and Control Act of 1986 who immigrated to the United States prior to 1982 but were recorded as having entered in the year in which they received permanent residence.

c Author's estimate based on 2001–2007 data.

Source: Adapted from DeSipio, Louis, and Rodolfo O. de la Garza, *Making Americans/Remaking America: Immigration and Immigrant Policy* (Boulder, Colo.: Westview Press, 1998), Table 2.1.

the role of government in allocating and regulating health insurance.

Employers and the health care industry are again looking to government for assistance in providing insurance, and the uninsured (and the potentially uninsured) will demand government action. The cost of insurance and fears among the insured that they may lose their insurance have placed health care issues among the top issues in U.S. elections. The proposals of major candidates, however, reflect ongoing debates about the size and scope of government. Republican candidates generally favor subsidies so that individuals can buy insurance from private providers. Few Democrats advocate a single government-managed insurance program like those of other advanced democracies.

Despite these many concerns, it seems even less likely today than it did in the early 1990s that the federal government will assume a responsibility for providing health insurance to the American populace. The cost, estimated to be at least $176 billion annually, is too high, and there is no consensus in Congress as to who should manage such a program: the public or private sectors. Finally, subsequent presidents learned a lesson from the Clinton administration's experience with trying to reform health care: that there is little to be gained because the financial cost of successful health care reform is very high and any reform would require new taxes that would generate much opposition in the electorate.

Best known among the federal programs aimed toward workers is Social Security, which taxes workers and their employers to pay for benefits for retired and disabled workers (and nonworker spouses). In the past, retirees almost always received more than they had paid into the system (a form of intergenerational redistribution), but it will take some reform to guarantee that this outcome continues when today's workers reach retirement age. Actuarial estimates indicate that the Social Security Trust Fund will be exhausted in 2041. Of more immediate importance, Medicare—the government health plan for the elderly—will begin run out of funds in 2019. The U.S. government faces the dilemma of having to lower benefits for each of these programs, raising taxes, or paying benefits out of general revenues. Changing the tax basis of Social Security and Medicare now (or lowering benefits now) would delay this point of reckoning, but there is little incentive for Congress to act in this area and suffer the political consequences in an era of divided government.

The government also established a minimum wage and a bureaucratic mechanism to enforce this wage. Some states and localities have established higher minimum wages than the federal minimum wage. Citizen groups in several cities nationwide over the past decade have promoted a further expansion of the idea of a minimum wage to a "living wage," a wage sufficient to live in high-cost cities and often double the federal minimum wage. These living wage campaigns seek to force cities and municipal contractors to pay such wages.

The states regulate worker–employer relations through unemployment insurance and insurance against workplace injuries. Benefits and eligibility requirements vary dramatically by state, although the federal governmental mandates that all workers be eligible for twenty-six weeks of benefits (assuming the worker has been employed for more than six months).

Beginning in the 1930s, the United States also established social welfare programs to assist the economically disadvantaged. As one would expect in a system organized around the free market, these programs have never been as broad-based or as socially accepted as in other economies. The states administered these programs—which provide food, health care, housing assistance, some job training, and some cash assistance to the poor—with a combination of federal and state funds. They establish benefit levels, and are responsible for moving recipients off the programs. Eligibility and benefit levels varied dramatically from state to state. Prior to 1996, there was a federal guarantee of some food and cash assistance for everyone who met eligibility thresholds. This guarantee disappeared in 1996 when recipients were limited in the duration of their eligibility and states were entrusted with developing programs to train recipients for work and to find jobs for them. Although enacted separately from the 1996 welfare reform, the federal government also reduced the availability of federally managed housing for the poor and expanded subsidies for the poor to secure housing in the private market.

In today's economy, public benefits and public employment are increasingly limited to U.S. citizens. Over time, these policies could enhance differences between the non-Hispanic white and black populations, on the one hand, and ethnic groups with large shares of immigrants, such as Latinos and Asian Americans, on the other.

The federal and state governments have one final recurring impact on the national economy that is more indirect but will likely be of increasing importance in the coming years: both the federal and state governments are entering a period of high deficit spending. Current estimates suggest that the federal government will spend $410 billion more than it raised in 2008. Projections indicate that half of the states will face budget deficits in 2009 with a total deficit of at least $37 billion. Most states will be required to close this deficit very quickly by raising taxes or cutting services. The federal government, on the other hand, can continue to run a large annual deficit. The sum of these deficits—the national debt—totals nearly $9.5 trillion.

Deficits can have a salutary effect on the national economy during weak economic times because the federal government can more easily borrow and then spend this money to stimulate the economy and support individuals who are out of work. In the long run, however, this federal debt absorbs money that could be invested in private sector activities and will slow national economic growth. In 2008, the federal government will pay approximately $443 billion in interest on its debt.

The United States in the Global Economy

Since colonial times, the United States has been linked to world trade. By the late twentieth century, the United States had vastly expanded its role in international finance and was an importer of goods produced abroad (often in low-wage countries that could produce goods less expensively than U.S. factories) as well as an exporter of agricultural products.

After World War II, the United States reversed its traditional isolationism in international politics to take a leading role in the regulation of the international economy. The increasing interdependence of global economies was the result, in part, of conscious efforts by world leaders at the end of World War II, through the Bretton Woods Agreement, to establish and fund multinational lending institutions. These were to provide loans and grants to developing economies in exchange for their agreement to reduce government regulation of their economies and open their domestic markets to internationally produced goods. Chief among these institutions were the World Bank and the International Monetary Fund. Since their establishment in the 1940s, they have been supplemented by a network of international lending and regulatory agencies and regional trading agreements. The Group of Eight (G-8), for example, conducts annual meetings of the leaders of the eight largest industrial democracies (the United States, Japan, Germany, Britain, France, Italy, Canada, and Russia).

The United States is also part of regional trading networks, such as NAFTA with Canada and Mexico. NAFTA did not initially have extensive support in Congress, but President Clinton used all the powers of the presidency to win the support of members of his own party, and the treaty narrowly passed. After its passage, the United States entered into an agreement with neighboring countries in the Caribbean to reduce tariffs on many goods (the Caribbean Basin Initiative).

NAFTA and the Caribbean Basin Initiative are likely the precursors of other regional trading agreements in the Americas. In 2002, Congress passed, and the president signed into law, authority for the president to negotiate an expansion of regional trading alliances along the lines of NAFTA. This legislation allowed the president to circumvent constitutional limits on the powers of the office. Congress agreed that it would review any trade agreement negotiated by the president with a yes or no vote that precluded amendment. Advocates of expanded trade agreements argue that this presidential authority is necessary so that other nations entering into the agreement with the United States can be assured that what they negotiate will become the law. Critics note that such treaty authority circumvents constitutional mandates that the Congress have a role in shaping policy and limits the ability of labor and environmental interests (or other groups who might oppose freer trade) to shape trade relations. This authority expired in 2007 after Democrats took control of the House and Senate and President Bush's popularity ebbed, but will likely be reauthorized for President Obama. Over time, the United States will likely enter into a free trade area of the Americas that could potentially include as many as thirty-four nations and would serve as a counterweight to the European Community (and currency zone).

The U.S. government plays a central role in the international political economy. It achieves this through its domination of international lending agencies and regional defense and trade organizations. Although these international organizations reflect a desire by policymakers to address some international financial issues multilaterally (at least with the other advanced democracies), these efforts are ultimately limited by domestic politics. Some in Congress and a significant minority of the citizenry oppose U.S. involvement in multilateral organizations. Thus, while presidents may promote an international agenda, Congress often limits the funding for international organizations. The United States then appears to many outside the country as a hesitant and sometimes resentful economic leader.

In recent years, another multilateral institution has emerged that can potentially challenge U.S. economic dominance. The European Union (EU) is much more than a trading alliance. It is an organization of twenty-seven European nations with growing international influence. Fifteen EU members share a common currency, the euro. As the euro comes into widespread use, the dollar has faced its first challenge in many years as the world's dominant trading currency.

In addition to contributing to multilateral institutions, the United States funds binational international lending through such agencies as the Export-Import Bank and the Overseas Private Investment Corporation. These agencies make loans to countries and private businesses to purchase goods and services from U.S.-owned businesses. The United States also provides grants and loans to allies to further U.S. strategic and foreign policy objectives or for humanitarian reasons.

The new role of the United States in multilateral economic and defense organizations and the growth in bilateral aid reflect a change in the nation's approach to its role in the world economy. The United States has slowly, and grudgingly, adapted to a world where it can no longer rest on its exceptionalism or simply assert its central role. Its economy and the larger society feel the effects of economic changes abroad. Thus, the U.S. government and, more slowly, the American people have seen their problems and needs from a global perspective. This incorporation into the larger world is certainly not complete. The separation of powers between the executive and legislative branches, and the local constituencies of members of Congress, ensures continuing resistance to this new international role.

The role of the United States in the international economy may be tested in coming years in a way that it has not been since the formation of the multilateral organizations after World War II. The strength of these international organizations is inherently limited by the increasing presence of multinational corporations that are able to transfer capital and production across national boundaries with little control by governments. While this change in the political economy is a political problem that all countries will face in the twenty-first century, the United States is and will be central to this problem. As the domestic U.S. economy is increasingly shaped by these international forces, U.S. citizens will demand economic stability from their government. The U.S. government was designed to be weak (see Section 3), so it will not be able to respond easily. The seeming lack of response will lead to strengthened calls by some in U.S. society to isolate the United States from the regulation of the international economy that it has helped shape. If these voices become dominant, the United States may find itself at odds with the international organizations that it helped create and that promote U.S. trade internationally.

SECTION 3 **Governance and Policy-Making**

Organization of the State

The governing document of the United States is the Constitution. It was drafted in 1787 and ratified by the necessary nine states the following year (all thirteen colonies had ratified it by 1790). The Constitution was not the first governing document of the United States. It was preceded by the Articles of Confederation, which concentrated most power in the states. The revision of the Articles established a central government that was independent of the states but left the states most of their pre-existing powers (particularly police powers and public safety, the most common area of interaction between citizens and government). Although it had limited powers, the new U.S.

government exercised powers over commerce and foreign policy that were denied to the states.

The Constitution has been amended twenty-seven times since 1787. The first ten of these amendments (ratified in 1791) make up the Bill of Rights, the set of protections of individual rights that were a necessary compromise to ensure that the Constitution was ratified. The remaining seventeen amendments have extended democratic election practices and changed procedural deficiencies in the original Constitution that came to be perceived as inconsistent with democratic practice. Examples of amendments to extend democratic election practices would be the extension of the vote to women and to citizens between the ages of eighteen and twenty (the Nineteenth and Twenty-Sixth Amendments, respectively) or the prohibition of poll taxes, a tax that had to be paid before an individual could vote (the Twenty-Fourth Amendment). Changes to procedural deficiencies in the Constitution included the linking of presidential and vice-presidential candidates on a single ticket, replacing a system where the candidate with the most votes in the Electoral College won the presidency and the second-place candidate won the vice presidency (the Twelfth Amendment), and establishing procedures to replace a president who becomes incapacitated (the Twenty-Fifth Amendment).

Each amendment requires three-quarters of the states to agree to the change. Although the Constitution allows states to initiate amendments, all twenty-seven have resulted from amendments initially ratified by Congress. When Congress initiates an amendment to the Constitution, two-thirds of senators must vote in favor of the amendment before it is sent to the states. States set their own procedures for ratifying constitutional amendments. In some, a simple majority in the legislature is sufficient, while others require support from a higher share of the legislature (such as two-thirds of those voting). Some require that a special convention be called to review the amendment.

Understanding two principles is necessary to understand American constitutional government: federalism and separation of powers. Federalism is the division of authority between multiple levels of government. In the case of the United States, the division is between the federal and state governments. Separation of powers is an effort to set government against itself by vesting separate branches with independent powers so that any one branch cannot permanently dominate the others.

These two characteristics of American government—federalism and separation of powers—were necessary compromises to guarantee the ratification of the Constitution. They should not, however, be viewed simply as compromises. On the contrary, they reflect a conscious desire by the constitutional framers to limit the federal government's ability to control citizens' lives. To limit what they perceived as an inevitable tyranny of majorities over numerical minorities, the framers designed a system that set each part of government against all the other parts. Each branch of the federal government could limit the independent action of the other two branches, and

the federal government and the states could limit each other. Although the potential for tyranny remained, the framers hoped that the individual ambitions of the members of each branch of government would cause each branch to fight efforts by other branches to undermine individual liberties.[10]

Federalism and separation of powers have a consequence that could not be fully anticipated by the framers of the Constitution: U.S. government is designed to be inefficient. Because each part of government is set against all others, policy-making is difficult. Inefficiencies can be partly overcome through extragovernmental mediating institutions such as political parties, but no single leader or branch of government can unequivocally dominate policy-making as the prime minister can in a parliamentary system. Although a consensus across branches of government can sometimes appear in times of national challenge, such as in the period immediately after the September 11 attacks, this commonality of purpose quickly dissolves as each branch of government seeks to protect its prerogatives and position in the policy-making process. As an example, the USA PATRIOT Act passed Congress with few dissenting voices, but there was much more dissent four years later to renew provisions of the bill set to expire or to pass new legislation expanding the powers granted to the executive branch.

Federalism is the existence of multiple sovereigns. A citizen of the United States is simultaneously a national citizen and a citizen of one of the states. Each citizen has responsibilities to each of these sovereigns and can be held accountable to the laws of each. Over the country's 200-year history, the balance of power between the two principal sovereigns has shifted, with the federal government gaining power relative to the states, but to this day, states remain responsible for many parts of citizens' lives and act in these areas independently of the federal government.

Over time, many powers traditionally reserved to the states have shifted to the federal government. The period of the most rapid of these shifts was the New Deal, when the federal government tapped its commerce regulation powers to create a wide range of programs to address the economic and social needs of the people.

The second organizing principle of American government is separation of powers. While each of the states has adopted some form of separation of powers, its purest form exists at the federal level. Each of the three branches of the federal government—the executive, the legislature (see Section 4), and the judiciary—shares in the responsibilities of governing and has some oversight over the other two branches. In order to enact a law, for example, Congress (the legislative branch) must pass the law, and the president (the executive branch) must sign it. The president can block the action of Congress by vetoing the law. Congress can override the president's veto through a two-thirds vote in both houses of Congress. The courts (the judiciary) can review the constitutionality of laws passed by Congress and signed by the president. Congress and the states acting in unison, however, can reverse a Supreme Court ruling on the constitutionality of a law by passing a constitutional amendment by a two-thirds vote that is subsequently ratified by three-quarters of the states. The Senate (the legislative branch) must ratify senior appointments to the executive branch, including members of the cabinet, as well as federal judges. The president nominates these judges, and Congress sets their salaries and much of their jurisdiction (except in constitutional matters). In sum, separation of powers allows each branch to limit the others and prevents any one branch from carrying out its responsibilities without the others' cooperation. It also allows for the phenomenon of divided government in which different political parties control the executive and legislative branches of government, which has been the norm for the federal government since 1968.

Federalism and separation of powers create a complexity in U.S. government that cannot be found in other advanced democracies. This complexity encourages an ongoing competition for political power. The states traditionally played a greater role in these battles but are relatively less important now than they were before the 1930s.

The Executive

The Presidency

The American presidency has grown dramatically in power since the nation's first days. The president, who is indirectly elected, serves a fixed four-year term and

is limited to two terms by a constitutional amendment ratified in 1951. The president is both head of state and head of government. The roots of presidential power are found in these roles more than in the powers delegated to the presidency in the Constitution.

Through much of the political history of the United States, the president was not at the center of the federal government. Quite the contrary: the Constitution established Congress as the central branch of government and relegated the president to a much more poorly defined role whose primary responsibilities are administering programs designed and funded by Congress. Although twentieth-century presidents found new powers and exercised powers unimaginable to earlier presidents, the structural weaknesses of the presidency remain. The president must receive ongoing support from Congress to ensure the implementation of his agenda. But the president cannot control Congress except to the degree that public opinion (and, to a much lesser degree, party loyalty) encourages members of Congress to support the president. As a result, U.S. presidents are far weaker than prime ministers in parliamentary systems; they can, however, stay in office long after they have lost popular support.

The president is the commander in chief of the military and may grant pardons, make treaties (which are ratified with the approval of two-thirds of the Senate), and make senior appointments to the executive branch and to judicial posts (again with the Senate's concurrence). The president is required to provide an annual state of the union report to Congress and may call Congress into session. Finally, the president manages the bureaucracy, which at the time of the Constitution's ratification was small but has subsequently grown in size and responsibility. Thus, in terms of formal powers, the president is far weaker than Congress is.

With one exception, presidents until the turn of the twentieth century did not add considerably to the delegated powers. The exception among nineteenth-century presidents was Abraham Lincoln, who dominated Congress during the Civil War. His example was one that twentieth-century presidents followed. He became a national leader and was able to establish his own power base directly in the citizenry. Lincoln realized that each member of Congress depended on a local constituency (a district or state) and was able to label their activities as being local or sectional. Lincoln created a national power base for the presidency by presenting himself as the only national political leader, an important position during the Civil War. He had an advantage in being commander in chief during wartime; however, the foundation of his power was not the military but his connection to the people.

In the twentieth century, presidents discovered that they had a previously untapped resource. Beginning with Theodore Roosevelt, twentieth-century presidents used the office of the president as a bully pulpit to speak to the nation and propose public policies that met national needs. No member of Congress or the Senate could claim a similar national constituency. Roosevelt began a trend that has been tapped by each of his successors. He used the mass media (in his case, newspapers) to present a national agenda to the American people.

Later in the twentieth century, presidents found a new power. As the role of the federal government expanded, they managed a much larger federal bureaucracy that provided goods and services used by nearly all citizens. Thus, a program like Social Security connects almost all citizens to the executive branch. Although Congress appropriates the funds for Social Security and played a significant role in its design, the executive branch sends the checks each month. Beginning with the New Deal, presidents proposed programs that expanded the federal bureaucracy and, consequently, the connection between the people and the president. In 2003, for example, President Bush proposed and Congress passed an expansion to the Medicare program, providing prescription drug insurance for Medicare recipients. Estimates indicate that this program will cost the government $1.2 trillion over its first decade. The 2008 downturn in the U.S. economy led the president to propose (and Congress to pass) a stimulus package made up largely of tax rebates for individuals with incomes up to $87,000 in 2007. The total cost to the government of this stimulus bill was $152 billion.

Finally, twentieth-century presidents learned an important lesson from the experience of Abraham Lincoln. The president has an authority over the military that places the office at the center of policy-making in military and international affairs. This centrality is particularly evident in times of war when immediate decisions may have to be made. Thus, in the period from World War II to the collapse of the Soviet Union, the presidency gained strength from the widely perceived need for a single decision-maker. After September 11, the president assumed direction of the U.S. response, although Congress quickly sought to reestablish its prerogatives.

Even as Congress balked at some presidential initiatives in the post-9/11 period, the public looked to the executive branch, and more specifically to President Bush, to lead. Bush used these popular expectations strategically in 2002 to support Republican candidates in close races. Republicans won control of the Senate and gained several seats in the House of Representatives and added to these margins in 2004. Gains such as these by the incumbent party in an off-year election and at the beginning of a second presidential term are unusual.

Although the presidency gained powers in the twentieth century, the office remains structurally weak relative to Congress. Despite popular expectations for presidential leadership in the period after 9/11, presidential dominance in policy-making has declined relative to the period between World War II and the end of the cold war. Presidential power is particularly undercut by the norm of divided government: presidents have little power over Congresses controlled by the other party. The bureaucracy is a weak link on which to build institutional power. Congress has significant powers to shape it. Congress has become increasingly restive about ceding power in international affairs to the president. Since Congress retains the power to appropriate funds, the president must ultimately yield to its will on the design and implementation of policy.

Until the election of Barack Obama in November 2008, all presidents had been white men. All but one (John F. Kennedy) have been Protestant.

While being a former general was once a stepping-stone to the presidency, in today's politics having served as a governor works to a candidate's advantage. Presidents from 1976 to 2003 included four former governors (Georgia's Jimmy Carter, California's Ronald Reagan, Arkansas's Bill Clinton, and Texas's George W. Bush). Despite a common assumption, only four vice presidents have been elected to the presidency immediately at the end of their terms. It is more

Leaders

Barack Obama

Barack Obama's 2008 election to the presidency surprised many observers of U.S. society and politics. Obama self-identifies as, and is understood to be, African American in a society that has persistently discriminated against blacks. His African roots come from his father, who migrated to the United States as a student in the early 1960s, which makes him unique on another dimension. No previous President is the child of an immigrant to the United States. His mother was white and, as his campaign often repeated, traced her roots to Kansas (and through her ancestors to England and Ireland). Obama is the first person of African descent to win the presidency. Many observers felt that this would prevent many white Americans from supporting his candidacy. In the end, the majority of white voters did oppose Obama, but his victory was sealed by strong support from African Americans, Latinos, and Asian Americans.

Obama's victory over John McCain was sizeable in the electoral college (365 to 173), including victories in southern and western states that have not voted for Democratic candidates in recent elections. Obama's victory was more narrow in the popular vote—53 percent to 46 percent.

Obama's preparation for his candidacy and for the presidency included service as a community organizer and later as a civil rights attorney. His community organizing work included job training, educational mentoring, electoral mobilization, and tenants' rights organizing on the South Side of Chicago. His organization used Catholic parishes as the locus of its organizing efforts.

On many other dimensions, Obama shared characteristics with people recently elected to the Presidency. He is trained as a lawyer, is married, and held elective office at the time of his candidacy. After seven years' service in the Illinois legislature, Obama was elected to the U.S. Senate in 2004. Although few sitting United States Senators have been elected to the presidency is recent years, this did not work to Obama's disadvantage since his 2008 Republican opponent was also a U.S. Senator (as was his primary challenger for the Democratic presidential nomination, Senator Hillary Rodham Clinton). Obama's short service in the U.S. Senate precluded him from developing much of a reputation as a legislator. He served as the primary Democratic sponsor of two major pieces of legislation, on nuclear nonproliferation and on the creation of a website to track federal spending.

President Obama began his administration facing greater challenges than most of his predecessors. The United States was engaged in two ground wars abroad as well as the war on terrorism that began with the September 11, 2001 attacks on the United States. Obama's resources to address these international challenges were limited by a collapse in the global economy that worsened throughout 2008. Structuring the U.S. response, rebuilding strategic relations with U.S. allies, and meeting the growing demands in the U.S. for change faced the new administration and the new president. Obama's nontraditional background and rapid rise to the U.S. presidency created hope for many that he would be able to overcome these challenges.

common for vice presidents to move to the presidency on the death (or, in one case, the resignation) of the president.

The Cabinet and the Bureaucracy

To manage the U.S. government, the president appoints (and the Senate confirms) senior administrators to key executive branch departments. The chief officers at each of the core departments make up the president's cabinet. These senior officers include heads of prominent departments such as the secretary of state, the attorney general, and the secretary of defense, as well as lesser-known officials such as the secretary of veterans affairs. Contrary to the case in parliamentary systems, the U.S. cabinet has no legal standing, and presidents frequently use it only at a symbolic level. The president is also free to extend membership to other senior appointed officials (such as the U.S. ambassador to the United Nations), so the number of cabinet members fluctuates from administration to administration.

The senior officers of the executive branch agencies manage a workforce of approximately 1.7 million civilian civil servants (the bureaucracy). Although formally part of the executive branch, the bureaucracy must also be responsive to Congress. Under certain circumstances, it operates independently of both elective branches and, rarely, under the direction of the courts. The presidential appointees establish broad policy objectives and propose budgets that can expand or contract the responsibilities of executive-branch offices. Congress must approve these budgets, and it uses this financial oversight to encourage bureaucrats to behave as their congressional monitors wish. Although the size of the federal bureaucracy had been in steady decline since the early 1980s, the new federal military and security responsibilities established after the September 11 attacks have reversed this trend. The federalization of airport baggage screening alone added approximately 43,000 workers to the federal bureaucracy (approximately three times the size of the U.S. Environmental Protection Agency).

September 11 also spurred a challenge to the protections traditionally guaranteed to the federal bureaucracy that would not have been politically possible prior to the attacks. When the Department of Homeland Security was formed to unite many federal agencies responsible for domestic security, Congress exempted the approximately 170,000 federal workers in the twenty-two agencies from civil service protections. President Bush argued that this change would ensure the agency would be more responsive to public security threats. Opponents expressed concern that presidents could use the Department of Homeland Security to reward political supporters with patronage appointments, which would impede its mission of homeland security.

Arguably, the inability of either Congress or the president to control the bureaucracy fully should give it some independence. Although this may be true in the case of policy areas that are of little interest to the elected branches, the bureaucracy as a rule does not have the resources to collect information and shape the laws that guide its operations. Interest groups have steadily filled this informational role, but the information comes at a cost. Bureaucracies often develop symbiotic relations with the interests that they should be regulating. The interest groups have more access to Congress and can shape the operations of the regulatory agencies. These **iron triangle relationships** (among a private interest group, a congressional committee or subcommittee overseeing the policy in question, and a federal agency implementing the policy) often exclude new players who represent alternative views on how policies should be implemented. Thus, without an independent source of authority, the bureaucracy is dependent not just on the elected branches, but also on interest groups.

Other State Institutions

Besides the presidency and the Congress (see Section 4), several other institutions are central to the operation of U.S. government: the military, national security agencies, the judiciary, and state and local governments.

The Military

The U.S. Army, Navy, Marine Corps, Coast Guard, and Air Force are made up of approximately 1.4 million active-duty personnel plus an additional 1.3 million reserve and national guard troops. The president is commander in chief of the U.S. military, but on a day-to-day basis, U.S. forces serve under the command of a nonpolitical officers' corps made up of graduates of the nation's military academies and officer candidate training programs at civilian universities and from the ranks of the military services.

Because of the unique geographic advantages of the United States, the military has had to dedicate few of its resources to defending U.S. territory. In the nineteenth century, its primary responsibilities were to defend U.S. shipping on the high seas and to colonize the West. Beginning with the new U.S. geopolitical role after World War II, the military was given new responsibilities to support U.S. multilateral and regional defense agreements. In the 1990s, the U.S. military was committed to multilateral military operations and United Nations peacekeeping efforts, but these diminished in response to a lack of interest on the part of the Bush administration and concerns that the military was overextended in Iraq and Afghanistan.

The United States increasingly looks to its allies to support U.S. military objectives abroad. In preparation for war with Iraq, U.S. military leaders designed an invasion force of 130,000, with 100,000 ground troops and the remainder in support positions abroad. These 100,000 U.S. military ground troops were supported by at least 15,000 British ground troops. By the middle of 2008, this force had grown to 158,000 U.S. troops and 10,500 allied troops (approximately 45 percent from the UK). These group forces were supplemented by the labors of approximately 160,000 contractors.[11]

As the United States extended its military role in Afghanistan and Iraq, it sought to expand the size of the military, but it faced difficulties in meeting its recruitment goals. By increasing recruitment bonuses and educational benefits for veterans, lowering the educational standards for new recruits and, in some cases, waiving prohibitions based on previous criminal convictions of recruits, the military was able to expand slowly.

Many of the traditional responsibilities of the military, such as support of troops and specialized technical activities, have been transferred to reserve units and to private firms who work under contract to the Defense Department. Reserve troops are now called to active duty more frequently. They have been required to serve multiple long-term commitments in Iraq and Afghanistan and have been prohibited from leaving the reserves at the end of their commitments.

The repeated deployment of troops since the beginning of the U.S. military presence in Afghanistan has led to concerns that the U.S. military is stretched too thin and would not be able to respond if the U.S. faced a new military challenge. A related concern about the military in the Bush era focused on training. The abuse of prisoners in Iraq's Abu Ghraib prison by Army troops led to concerns that the military chain of command was decaying in wartime.

With the increased expectations for the military came increased reliance on defense technologies. U.S. nuclear weapons, intelligence technologies, and space-based defense technologies, as well as the maintenance of conventional weaponry and troop support, have significantly raised the cost of maintaining the military. This has led to ongoing national debates about the cost of the military and whether defense resources should

be expended for technology or for troops. Industries have emerged to provide goods and services to the military. Proposals to cut defense spending often face opposition from these industries.

National Security Agencies

The September 11, 2001, attacks focused the attention of policy-makers on domestic security to an unprecedented degree. Agencies with responsibility in this area that had been dispersed throughout the federal government were united in the Department of Homeland Security under a single cabinet secretary. Responsibility for airport screening was federalized, and funding for border enforcement increased dramatically. Although it took somewhat longer, intelligence-gathering agencies were placed under the administrative control of a director of national intelligence (see Section 4). Funding for domestic security and international intelligence gathering increased by approximately one-third.

Legislation passed in the months after September 11, 2001, also subjected U.S. citizens and permanent residents to greater levels of government scrutiny and to potential violations of civil rights. The Bush administration asserted (and the courts rejected) a position that suspected terrorists could be seized and held indefinitely, without charges.

The Judiciary

Of the three branches of federal government, the courts are the most poorly defined in the Constitution. Initially, it was unclear what check the courts had on other branches of government. Equally important, the courts were quite dependent on the president, who appointed judges, and on Congress, which approved the nomination of judges and set the jurisdictional authority for the courts. The early days of the federal courts confirmed this weakness. Judges often had to travel from city to city to hear cases; the judiciary saw a higher turnover in the early years than in any subsequent period of American history.

In 1803, the Supreme Court established the foundation for a more substantial role in federal policy-making. It ruled in **Marbury** v. **Madison** that the courts inherently had the right to review the constitutionality of the laws. This ruling, though used rarely in the nineteenth century, gave the judiciary a central place in the system of **checks and balances**. The Court that ruled in *Marbury* v. *Madison* recognized the weakness of the federal courts in this era. While asserting their power to review the constitutionality of a piece of federal legislation, the substantive effect of the ruling was to give a political victory to the sitting president, Thomas Jefferson, against the partisan and ideological interests of a majority of the members of the Court. The majority of the Court at the time had been nominated to the judiciary by political opponents of Jefferson. Had the same justices ruled against President Jefferson, he would likely have disregarded this ruling and demonstrated the fundamental weakness of the federal courts.

Even with the power of judicial review, the judicial branch remained weaker than the other branches. In addition to Congress's ability to establish court jurisdiction in nonconstitutional cases and the president's ability to fill the courts with people of his choosing, the courts have other weaknesses. They must rely on the executive branch to enforce their decisions. Enforcement proves particularly difficult when a court's rulings are not in line with public opinion, such as when the courts ruled that organized prayer did not belong in the public schools or that busing should be used as a tool to accomplish racial integration in the schools. The courts' own rules have also limited their powers. Traditionally, the courts limit standing—the ability to bring suits—to individuals who saw their rights directly challenged by a law, policy, or action of government.

Beginning in the second half of the twentieth century, the federal courts gained power relative to the other branches of government. In part, this was accomplished by expanding the rules of standing so that groups as well as individuals could challenge laws, policies, or government actions and by maintaining longer jurisdiction over cases as a tool to establish limited enforcement abilities. The courts also gained relative power because of the expansion of federal regulatory policy. Unclear laws and regulations, often requiring technical expertise to implement, placed the courts at the center of many policy debates. The courts have also gained power because they became a venue for individuals and groups in society whose interests were neglected by the democratically elected institutions but who could make claims based on constitutional guarantees of civil rights or civil liberties. African Americans, for example, received favorable rulings from federal courts before Congress and the president responded to their demands. Since the September 11 attacks, the executive branch and majorities in Congress manifested a willingness to limit individual rights in a search for collective security. Courts—including the Supreme Court—have been more cautious. In 2004, the Supreme Court rejected administration assertions that it could seize and hold suspected terrorists indefinitely. Instead, the court ruled that U.S. citizens and foreign nationals detained as terrorists can challenge their status in the federal courts.

The steady increase in judicial power in the twentieth century should not obscure the fundamental weaknesses of the courts relative to the elected branches. Although courts in some cases have been able to establish connections with the citizenry around specific issues, the courts are more dependent on the elected branches than the elected branches are on them.

Subnational Government

State governments serve as an important part of government in the United States. Their responsibilities include providing services to people more directly than does the federal government. Most important among these is education, which has always been a state and local responsibility in the United States.

States and localities serve a critical function in contemporary U.S. governance. They are able to experiment with new policies. If a policy fails in a single state, the cost is much lower than if the entire country had undertaken a new policy that eventually failed. Successes in one state can be copied in others or nationally.

In addition to state governments, citizens pay taxes to, and receive services from, local governments that include counties, cities, and districts for special services such as water and fire protection, and townships. These local entities have a different relationship to the states, however, than do states to the federal government. The local entities are statutory creations of the state and can be altered or eliminated by the state (and are not a form of federalism).

Local governments are nevertheless very important in the system of American governance. They provide many of the direct services that the citizenry receives from the government. Because states and localities have different resources (often based on local property taxes) and different visions of the responsibilities of government, people in the United States may receive vastly different versions of the same government service, depending simply on where they live. Education provides an example. Property tax–poor areas may spend only a few thousand dollars per year educating students, while property tax–rich areas may spend $15,000 to $20,000 per student. Some states try to equalize education spending within the state.

The Policy-Making Process

Separation of powers and constitutional limits on each branch of government create a federal policy-making process with no clear starting or ending point. Instead, citizens and organized interests have multiple points of entry and can contest outcomes through multiple venues. There is little centralization of policy-making except in a few areas where there is consensus among national leaders. Without centralization, policies often conflict with each other (for example, the United States currently subsidizes tobacco cultivation but seeks to hamper tobacco companies from selling cigarettes through high taxes, health warnings, and limits on advertising). Federalism further complicates policy-making. Each of the states sets policy in many areas, and states often have contradictory policies. State policy-making institutions are often used strategically to shape the debate around an issue or to influence other states or the federal government. In sum, policy advocates have many venues in which to propose new policies or change existing policies: congressional committees, individual members of Congress, executive branch regulatory agencies, state governments, and, in some states, direct ballot initiatives.

With so many entrance points, there are equally many points at which policies can be blocked. Once Congress passes a law, executive branch agencies must issue regulations to explain specifically how the law will be implemented. Subtle changes can be inserted as part of this process. On controversial issues, senior political appointees set policy for the writing of regulations. Laws that must be implemented by several agencies raise a possible role for the cabinet to craft government-wide solutions to policy needs, but recent presidents have not used the cabinet as a whole to structure policy-making in this way.

Furthermore, people or interest groups that feel disadvantaged by the regulations can contest regulations in the courts. They also can contest the law itself, if the assertion can be made that the law is unconstitutional or conflicts with another law or with state government responsibilities. Once a policy is in place, it can be opposed or undermined by creating a competing policy in another agency or at the state level.

The Constitution gives no guidance about the origins and outcomes of policy initiatives. The president is directed to present an annual report to Congress on the state of the nation. Over time, this has evolved into an organized set of policy proposals. In the absence of presidential leadership in policy-making, Congress partially filled the void. Enumerated powers in the Constitution direct Congress to take action in specific policy areas, such as establishing a post office or building public roads. Once Congress established committees to increase its efficiency (see Section 4), these committees offered forums for discussion of narrow policy areas of importance to society. These committees, however, are not mandated in the Constitution and are changed to reflect the policy needs of each era. Thus, while presidents can propose policies (and implement them), only Congress has the ability to deliberate about policy and pass it into law.

The courts provide a forum for debating the outcome of policy decisions, but have rarely initiated policies. Beginning in the 1970s, however, some federal courts experimented with initiating policy as a way of maintaining jurisdiction in cases brought before them. These efforts, such as court-mandated control over state prison or mental health care systems, spurred much national controversy and caused the judiciary to decline in public opinion. Today, the courts are much more likely to block or reshape policies than to initiate them.

Because there is no clear starting point for initiating policies, individual citizens have great difficulty when they seek to advocate a new policy. Into this void have come extragovernmental institutions, some with narrow interests and some promoting collective interests. Prominent or wealthy individuals or groups can get Congress's or the president's attention through campaign contributions and other types of influence in support for their candidacies and the causes they support.

Mediating institutions have also emerged to represent mass interests. Political parties, organized on a mass basis in the 1830s, organize citizen demands and channel them to political leaders. The parties balance the needs of various interests in society and come as close as any other group in society to presenting comprehensive policy proposals (often summarized in the parties' platforms). Group-based interests also organize to make narrow demands. Veterans are an early example of a group in society that made a group-specific demand on federal policy-making. In the twentieth century, as both federal and state governments began to implement more widespread distributive and redistributive policies, more organized interest groups appeared. These interest groups have become the dominant form of mediating institution in U.S. politics (see Section 4). Unlike political parties, however, interest groups represent only a single issue or group of narrowly related issues. Thus, the complexity of policy-making in the United States has created an equally complex structure of making demands.

SECTION 4 Representation and Participation

The Legislature

Of the three branches in the federal government, the founders envisioned that Congress would be at the center and would be the most powerful. They concentrated the most important powers in it and were most explicit about its responsibilities. For most of the nation's history, their expectations for the powers of Congress have been met.

One of the most important compromises of the Constitutional Convention involved the structure of Congress. States with large populations wanted seats in the national legislature to be allocated based on population. Small states feared they would be at a disadvantage under this system and wanted each state to have equal representation. The compromise was a **bicameral** system with two houses, one allocated by population—the House of Representatives—and the other with equal representation for each state—the Senate. This compromise has remained largely uncontested for the past 200 years despite the growing gap in population between large and small states. Today, for example, the 515,000 residents of Wyoming elect two senators, the same number elected by the more than 36.5 million residents of California. The senatorial vote of each resident of Wyoming has seventy-one times the impact of each Californian. In this pattern, the U.S. Senate is unique among legislatures in the world's democracies.

The two legislative bodies are structured differently. The House has 435 members (a number fixed since 1910) and is designed to be more responsive to the popular will. Terms are short (two years), and the districts are smaller than Senate seats except in the smallest states. After 2010, the average House seat will have approximately 722,000 constituents and will continue to grow. The Senate has 100 members and is designed to be more deliberative, with six-year, staggered terms. Although unlikely, it is possible every two years to vote out an entire House of Representatives; the Senate could see only one-third of its members unseated during any election year.

Membership in the U.S. Congress is slightly more diverse than the people who have held the presidency, although most members of Congress are white male Protestants. In the 110th Congress (2007–2008), approximately 16 percent of officeholders were women, 8 percent were African American, 5 percent were Latino, and 1 percent were Asian American. Most members of Congress, regardless of gender, race, or ethnicity, are highly educated professionals. Law is the most common profession. The Senate is less racially diverse but has a comparable share of women to the House: three Latinos, two Asian Americans, one African American, and 16 women served in the Senate in 2008. The election of a Democratic majority in 2006 changed the gender and racial composition of the House leadership considerably. Nancy Pelosi (D-CA) was elected as the House of Representative's first woman Speaker (the senior position in the House and the second in line to presidency after the vice president). Five African American members were elected to committee chairs (including the powerful Ways and Means Committee and Judiciary Committee).

The two central powers of Congress are legislation and oversight. For a bill to become law, it must be passed in the same form by both the House and the Senate and signed by the president. Equally important, Congress has the ability to monitor the implementation of laws that it passes. Since it continues to control the appropriation of funds for programs each year, Congress can oversee programs being administered by the executive branch and shape their implementation through allocations of money or by rewriting the law.

Congress has organized itself to increase its efficiency. Discussion and debate take place primarily in committees and subcommittees. The committee system permits each member to specialize in specific areas of public policy. Committees are organized topically, and members often seek to serve on committees that are of particular interest to their constituencies—for instance, a member of Congress from a rural area may seek to serve on the Agriculture Committee. All members seek to serve on committees that have broad oversight of a wide range of government activities, such as the Appropriations Committee, through which all spending bills must pass. Specialization allows each member to have some influence while not requiring that she or he know the substance of all facets of government.

For a bill to become law, it must be reviewed by the committee and subcommittee that have responsibility for the substantive area that it covers. When a member proposes a bill, it is referred to a committee based on the subject matter of the legislation and usually never gets any further. In each session, relatively few bills are given hearings before a subcommittee or committee. The House and Senate leadership (the Speaker of the House, the Senate Majority Leader, and committee chairs) are central to deciding which

bills receive hearings. If the bill receives support from the committee, it must then be debated by the body as a whole. In the House, this may never occur because that institution has another roadblock: the Rules Committee, which determines what can be debated on the floor and under what terms. Only in the Senate can debate be unlimited (although it can be limited by cloture, a vote of sixty senators to limit debate). These hierarchical structures strengthen the powers granted to the House and the Senate in the Constitution because they allow Congress to act efficiently and to use its powers to investigate federal programs, even though it does not administer them. As a result, Congress places itself at the center of the policy-making process. Although congressional power waned somewhat in the late twentieth century, Congress remains the foremost branch of American government. This specialization and hierarchy ensure that congressional leaders are more central to the design and oversight of policy than are members of European parliaments.

This tension between the constitutional powers of Congress and the national focus on the president as the national leader became evident in the federal government's response to the September 11 attacks. Initially, President Bush shaped the public policy response, including a large emergency appropriation that included financial assistance for New York City, grants and loans to the airlines, an increase in defense and intelligence spending, and military action against Afghanistan. Congress quickly followed the presidential lead and appropriated funds, federalized airport security screening, and supported military action in Afghanistan that targeted the Al Qaeda movement that took responsibility for the September 11 attacks and the Taliban government that provided a safe haven for Al Qaeda.

As Bush administration policies evolved and the response came to focus on structural changes in the federal government, however, Congress began to reassert its constitutional prerogatives. Congressional concern about the growth in executive power after September 11 was probably most evident in its reaction to the Bush administration's reorganization of more than fifty federal agencies into the cabinet-level Department of Homeland Security. The selection of federal agencies with security responsibilities to exclude from the new department (most notably the Federal Bureau of Investigation) reflected White House sensitivities to agencies with strong support in Congress that would, though logically placed in the new agency, make the Department of Homeland Security less likely to receive congressional approval.

Congress also asserted itself to ensure that the National Commission on Terrorist Attacks on the United States, unofficially known as the 9/11 Commission, would be formed, funded, and given sufficient time to conduct its investigation and write its report. Initially, the Bush administration opposed the formation of such an investigative commission and, once it relented in the face of strong congressional opposition to its position, sought to limit the scope, funding, and longevity of the commission. The commission documented executive branch intelligence-gathering failures and provided the political pressure necessary to force the Bush administration to create a new federal official—the Director of National Intelligence—who would oversee most U.S. intelligence-gathering agencies.

As the Bush administration moved toward war with Iraq, Congress also forced the president to seek and obtain congressional approval for any U.S. military action against Iraq and for the costs of conducting the war. The president also has to seek annual congressional approval for war-related expenditures. These totaled more than $520 billion by 2008. This annual appropriation process has allowed Congress to investigate the conduct of the wars and reconstructions and hold administration officials accountable for their previous assurances to Congress. As public concern about the Iraqi reconstruction grew, Congress increasingly used the supplemental appropriation bill debates as venues for criticism of the Bush administration and to amend the appropriations bills to shape unrelated federal programs.

Congressional oversight of presidential leadership in the U.S. response to September 11 and the wars in Afghanistan and Iraq should demonstrate that Congress has not yielded as the president gained power. It passed legislation to undermine presidential power and, equally important, applied its authority to investigate federal programs to weaken the presidency. Beginning with Watergate (the Nixon administration scandals in which Nixon and his aides used the institutions of the federal government to investigate

and intimidate Nixon's political opponents), Congress has directly investigated presidents. These investigations of presidents and their senior appointees weaken the connection between the presidency and the people (regardless of the specific charges being investigated or the outcome of the investigation). Investigations of modern presidents weaken not just the presidents as individuals, but also the presidency as an office.

Political Parties and the Party System

Electoral politics in the United States is organized around two political parties. The roots of two-party politics can be found both in the nation's political culture and in the legal structures that govern elections. Today, the two major parties are the Democrats and the Republicans. The Democrats can trace their origins to the 1800 election, while the Republicans first appeared in 1856. Despite the fact that today's parties have consistently competed against each other, the coalitions that support them (and which they, in turn, serve) have changed continually.

Today, the Republicans depend on a coalition of upper-income voters, social conservatives, small-business owners, residents of rural areas, and evangelical Christians. They receive more support from men than from women and are strongest in the South and the Mountain West. In 2004, voters identifying "moral values" as the most important issue facing the country were particularly important to President Bush's victory in several states, including Ohio. Bush won nearly four out of five votes of those voters who identified moral values as the most important issue facing the nation.

The Republicans have tried to make inroads in minority communities but have been largely unsuccessful, with the exception of Cuban Americans and some Asian American groups (see Table 7.2). President Bush sought to bring a higher share of the Latino vote into the Republican fold and succeed relative to other Republican candidates, but these inroads were lost as the United States debated immigration policy in the mid-2000s. For Republicans to win Latino (or African American) votes on a wider scale, the party would have to be willing to alienate some core Republican constituencies.

Table 7.2

Candidate Vote in Presidential Elections, by Race and Ethnicity, 1976–2008 (in percentages)

	Whites	Blacks	Hispanics	Asian Americans
1976				
Carter (D)	47	83	76	n.a.
Ford (R)	52	16	24	n.a.
1980				
Reagan (R)	56	11	33	n.a.
Carter (D)	36	85	59	n.a.
Anderson (I)	7	3	6	n.a.
1984				
Reagan (R)	64	9	37	n.a.
Mondale (D)	35	90	62	n.a.
1988				
Bush (R)	59	12	30	n.a.
Dukakis (D)	40	86	69	n.a.
1992				
Clinton (D)	39	83	61	31
Bush (R)	40	10	25	55
Perot (I)	20	7	14	15
1996				
Clinton (D)	43	84	72	43
Dole (R)	46	12	21	48
Perot (I)	9	4	6	8
2000				
Bush (R)	54	8	31	41
Gore (D)	42	90	67	54
Nader (I)	3	1	2	4
2004				
Bush (R)	58	11	43	44
Kerry (D)	41	88	56	58
2008				
Obama (D)	43	95	67	62
McCain (R)	55	4	31	35

Note: Data not collected on Asian Americans until 1992. Data do not always add up to 100 because of votes for other candidates.

Source: New York Times. 2008. "Election Results 2008." New York Times, [November 9]. http://elections.nytimes.com/2008/results/president/national-exit-polls.html [accessed November 10, 2008].

The contemporary Democratic coalition includes urban populations, the elderly, racial and ethnic minorities, workers in export-oriented businesses, unionized labor, and, increasingly, working women. Suburban voters have increasingly joined the Democratic coalition. Today's Democrats are concentrated in the Northeast and on the West Coast. The Democrats have built a steady advantage among women voters. This is a double advantage for the Democrats: women have higher turnout rates than do men, and men split their votes more evenly.

Democratic partisanship grew steadily over the Bush years. In 2007, Democrats made up 33 percent of the electorate, Republicans 28 percent, and Independents 39 percent. These Independents, who were more likely to lean toward the Democrats than the Republicans, become the focus of state and national general election campaigns. Generally, Democrats, who are more likely to be poor, less educated, and younger than Republican voters, are less likely to turn out on Election Day. After the 2008 election, the Democrats controlled governorships in 29 states, and the Republicans controlled 21. The Democrats won a majority of members of the House of Representatives in 2008 (257 to 178) and a one-vote majority in the Senate.

As is evident from the Democratic U.S. Senate and House majorities won in the 2008 elections, the relative Republican advantage in holding federal offices in the last two decades of the twentieth century is changing. Internal conflicts in the Democratic Party in the 1970s and 1980s limited its ability to present a cohesive message and reach out to new constituencies. These conflicts—particularly disputes over the size and scope of government, affirmative action (programs designed to redress past discrimination against racial and ethnic minorities and women) and other race-sensitive programs, and taxation and the deficit—subsided during the Clinton presidency and have remained quiet since he completed his term. Beginning in the 1990s, internal conflicts grew in the Republican Party that President Bush was able to soothe. Moral conservatives and fiscal conservatives each wanted the party to focus on their interests and jettison the others' issues as a way of expanding the party's base of support.

Democrats used the contested 2008 presidential primary to increase dramatically the number of new registrants and voters. The Democrats, building on the excitement of the Obama and Clinton candidacies, saw particular gains in registration among young voters. The Republicans did not see similar gains in registration or turnout.

These party divisions lead to speculation that new parties might emerge. The political culture of the United States dampens the likelihood that a faction of one of the parties (such as the religious right from the Republicans) will break off and form a party that competes in election after election. Instead, two coalitional parties are the norm, an unusual pattern among advanced democracies.

Electoral law reinforces this situation. Most U.S. elections are conducted under a single-member-plurality election system in district-based elections. Single-member district-based elections reward coalitional parties and diminish opportunities for single-issue parties or narrowly focused parties, such as the Green Party, in today's politics. Broad coalitional parties can contest seats in election after election, while smaller parties in the United States are likely to dissolve after several defeats. Finally, since the existing parties have written the electoral laws in each of the states, they have made it difficult for new parties to get on the ballot.

Geography reinforces the difficulty faced by small and single-issue parties in an SMP system. There are more than 600,000 elected offices in the United States. To compete regularly in even a small percentage of these, a party must have a national presence and a national infrastructure. Most third parties fail long before they are able to compete in more than a few hundred of these 600,000 races. The Green Party, for example, fielded only 370 candidates in 2004, or just 6 of every 10,000 elective offices. Green Party candidates won 58 of these offices.

Finally, the heterogeneity of the U.S. population and the range of regional needs and interests rewards parties that can form coalitions prior to elections, as does a system with just two political parties. The Constitution-driven inefficiency of the U.S. government would become all the more dramatic if multiple parties (rather than two that must, by their nature, be coalitions) were competing in legislatures to shape outcomes.

Elections

The United States takes pride in its long practice of democracy. As an example of its commitment to democratic norms, it points to the frequency of elections and the range of offices filled through elections. As is not the case in parliamentary systems, these elections are conducted on a regular schedule: presidential elections every four years, Senate elections every six years, House of Representatives elections every two years. States and localities set the terms of state and local offices, but almost all have fixed terms. General elections for federal offices are held the first Tuesday after the first Monday in November. States and localities establish dates for primary elections and for general elections for nonfederal offices. Thus, while elections are regularly scheduled, there are frequently multiple elections in the same year.

Fundamental to understanding U.S. elections is federalism. States set the rules for conducting elections and for who can participate and how votes are counted. When the country was founded, this authority was almost complete, since the Constitution said little about elections. At the country's founding, most states limited electoral participation to white male landholders. By the 1830s, many states had eliminated the property-holding requirement, in part in response to the emergence of competitive political parties that sought to build membership.

Further expansion of the U.S. electorate required the intervention of the federal government and amendment of the Constitution to reduce state authority in determining voter eligibility. The first of the efforts to nationalize electoral rules was initially a failure. This was the effort to extend the franchise to African Americans after the Civil War through the Fourteenth and Fifteenth Amendments. More successful was the Nineteenth Amendment, ratified in 1920, which extended the vote to women.[12] The Civil War amendments finally had an impact with the passage of the Voting Rights Act (VRA) in 1965, which secured African Americans access to the ballot box. In 1975, Congress extended the VRA to other ethnic and racial groups who had previously seen their right to vote abridged because of their origin or ancestry—Hispanics, Asian Americans, Native Americans, and

Alaskan Natives. The Twenty-Sixth Amendment gave the vote to all citizens aged eighteen and older in 1971.

States continue to regulate individual participation in elections through their control of voter registration. In most advanced democracies, the national government is responsible for voter registration rather than the individual. Individual registration prescreens potential voters to ensure they meet the state's requirements for voting: residence in the jurisdiction for a set amount of time and, in many states, the absence of felony convictions. While this may appear minimal and necessary to prevent voter fraud such as an individual's voting multiple times in the same election, the requirement to register in advance of the election prevents many from being able to vote.[13]

There is a second consequence of federalism on U.S. elections: the responsibility for holding elections, deciding which nonfederal offices are filled through elections, and determining how long nonfederal officeholders will serve before again having to be elected is the responsibility of the states and, if the states delegate the power, to localities. Thus, a local office that is elected in one state could be an appointed office in another. Terms for state and local offices, such as governors, vary. Elections are held at different points throughout the year.

Finally, federalism shapes elections by delegating to the states responsibilities for determining how votes are collected and how they are counted, even in elections to national office. This became evident as a result of the controversy that followed the 2000 elections. Florida allowed local jurisdictions to design ballots, select voting machines, and establish rules for counting the ballots. One of the most controversial design decisions was Palm Beach County's "butterfly ballot," which led many voters who thought they were casting their vote for Al Gore actually to vote for Pat Buchanan. The several legal challenges filed by the Gore and Bush campaigns in state and federal courts after the elections focused on questions of the legality and constitutionality of ballot designs, counting rules, and deadlines established by Florida counties and the state.

What are the consequences of this federalist system of elections? At a minimum, it leads to confusion and burnout among potential voters. Many voters are unaware of elections that are not held on the same schedule as national elections. Others who are aware become overloaded with electoral responsibilities in jurisdictions that have frequent elections and so choose not to vote in local races.

One result of this decentralized system with a legacy of group-based exclusion is that increasing numbers of citizens do not vote. In the late 1800s, for example, turnout in national elections exceeded 80 percent of those eligible to vote, and the poor participated at rates comparable to the rich. By 1996, turnout in the presidential election dropped below 50 percent (returning to 61 percent in the 2008 election). In state and local races, turnouts in the range of 10 to 20 percent are the norm. Perhaps more important, turnout varies dramatically among different groups in society. The poor are less likely to vote than the rich, the young less likely than the old, and the less educated less likely than the more educated.[14] Because blacks and Hispanics are more likely to be young, poor, and have lower levels of formal education, they are less likely to vote than are whites. Hence, political institutions are less likely to hear their demands and respond to their needs.

These class- and age-driven differences in participation are not entirely the result of federalism and variation in the rules for individual participation and the conduct of elections. Declining party competitiveness at the state level also plays a role. Nevertheless, it is important to observe that the steady elimination of formal group-based exclusion has been replaced by the marginalization of the majority of some groups, such as Asian Americans and Hispanics. Thus, despite the expansion of the electorate to almost all adults, the United States has yet to live up to its democratic ideals.

This declining participation should not obscure the dramatic changes in leadership and issues addressed that result from elections. The 1994 elections saw an unprecedented increase in Republican members of the House of Representatives that allowed Republicans to take control of the House for the first time in forty years (see Figure 7.5). Republicans also took control of the Senate in that year and were able to pass legislation that dramatically changed the nation's welfare

The confusing design of the presidential ballot of Palm Beach, Florida, appears to have caused more than 3,000 Gore supporters to vote for Pat Buchanan. Had Gore won these votes, he would have won the presidency. *Source:* Gary Rothstein/Getty Images.

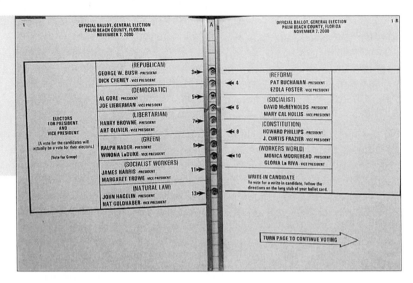

system and slowed the growth of the federal government. In 1998, Democrats unexpectedly gained seats in the sixth year of a presidential term by a member of their party for the first time since 1822. This victory ensured the Senate's acquittal of President Clinton in his impeachment trial. In 2006, the Democrats regained control of the Senate and House of Representatives and elected the first woman to serve as Speaker of the House (Nancy Pelosi).

Political Culture, Citizenship, and Identity

The United States is a large country with distinct regional cultures, ongoing immigration leading to distinct languages and cultures, class divisions, and a history of denying many Americans their civil rights. Despite these cleavages, the United States has maintained almost from its first days a set of core political values that has served to unify the majority of the citizenry. These values are liberty, equality, and democracy.

Liberty, as it is used in discussions of U.S. political culture, refers to liberty from restrictions imposed by government. A tangible form of this notion of liberty appears in the Bill of Rights, which provides for the rights of free speech, free assembly, free practice of religion, and the absence of cruel and unusual punishment. Support for liberty takes a second form: support for economic liberty and free enterprise. Property and contract rights are protected at several places in the Constitution. Furthermore, Congress is empowered to regulate commerce.

Clearly, these liberties are not mutually exclusive. Protections of the Bill of Rights often conflict with

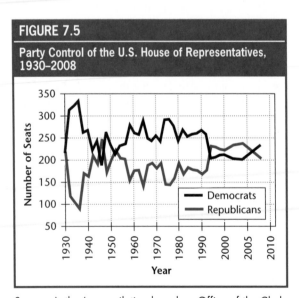

FIGURE 7.5

Party Control of the U.S. House of Representatives, 1930–2008

Source: Author's compilation based on Office of the Clerk, U.S. House of Representatives, http://clerk.house.gov/member_info/electionInfo/2006/2006Stat.htm (accessed on April 7, 2008).

Despite a steady liberalization of rules on who can vote, voting rates in the United States have declined for the past 100 years. *Source:* By permission of Gary Varvel and Creators Syndicate, Inc.

each other: economic liberties reward some in the society at the cost of economic opportunities for others. Nevertheless, the idea that citizens should be free to pursue their beliefs and their economic objectives with only limited government interference has been a unifying element in U.S. political culture.

Equality is the second unifying American political value. In the Declaration of Independence, it is "self-evident" that "all men are created equal." Nevertheless, at various times in the nation's history, women, Native Americans, African Americans, Mexican Americans, Chinese Americans, Japanese Americans, and immigrants have been excluded from membership in the polity and, consequently, from access to this equality. But each of the excluded groups, such as African Americans during the civil rights movement, has used the widespread belief in equality to organize and demand that the United States live up to its ideals.

It is important to observe what this belief in equality is not. The equality that has long been sought is equality of opportunity, not equality of result, such as that sought in the communist states. There is support for the notion that people should have an equal opportunity to compete for economic rewards, not that they should end up at the same point.

The final unifying value is representative democracy. Throughout the nation's history, there has been a belief that government is legitimate only to the degree that it reflects the popular will. As with the notion of equality, the pool of citizens whose voices should be heard has changed over time, from white male property holders at the time of the founding to most citizen adults today (convicted felons are excluded from the franchise in many states). Nevertheless, excluded populations have continually sought to influence the polity.

The United States has never had a national religion and, at times in the nation's history, conflicts between Protestants and Catholics have been divisive. In contemporary society, division over religion is more between those for whom religion provides routine guidance in politics and social interactions and those for whom religion is a more private matter that does not shape political activities.

In 2006, 52 percent of U.S. adults were Protestant, 25 percent were Roman Catholic, and 2 percent were Jewish. Nearly 17 percent of U.S. adults reported no religious preference. Despite the fact that there is no national religion in the United States, religion plays a more central role in U.S. politics than it does in the politics of European democracies. Church attendance is higher in the United States and church membership is growing. Moral issues—such as abortion and gay rights—guide the votes of a sizeable minority of the population. Many elected leaders are overt in their religiosity to a degree that would not be acceptable in European politics (and would not have been in U.S. politics as recently as twenty-five years ago).

Values are very much at the heart of contemporary political debates. Leaders have marshaled these values throughout the nation's history to reduce potential cleavages in U.S. society. Since the United States cannot look to a common ethnicity of its people (as, for example, Germany can), to a sovereign with a historical tie to the citizenry (as in a monarchy like the United Kingdom), or to a purported common religion or ideology among its citizens (as does Iran or Cuba), the belief in these values has been used to unify the diverse peoples of the United States.[15] Voluntary membership based on belief in this creed serves to unify the disparate peoples of the United States.

Interests, Social Movements, and Protest

In the United States, political participation has long included activities other than elections and party politics. In the nation's story about its origins, protest proves central; the Revolution was spurred by acts of civil disobedience such as the Boston Tea Party. Similarly, protest and social movements repeatedly forced the United States to live up to its democratic ideals. From the woman's suffrage movement of the nineteenth century to the civil rights movement of the 1950s and 1960s, people defined as being outside the democratic community organized to demand that they be included. The success of these movements was enhanced by their ability to tap the political values discussed in the previous section.

These protest movements have also been able to tap the willingness of Americans to become involved in collective action. First chronicled by a visitor from France in the 1830s, Alexis de Tocqueville, this voluntarism and civic involvement have long been identified as stronger in the U.S. democracy than in other advanced democracies.

In recent years, however, observers of U.S. politics have noted a decline in civic involvement, a decline that has also appeared in the other advanced democracies. Although social movements remain, they have become much more driven by elites than were their predecessors. At the same time, voluntarism and civic involvement have declined, and the likelihood of participation has followed the patterns of voting, with the more educated, wealthier, and older generally more likely to volunteer and be civically engaged.[16] This decline in civic involvement in U.S. politics has serious long-term implications for society. As civic involvement declines, Americans talk about politics less with their peers and have a lessened sense that they can shape political outcomes. They are less likely to be part of networks that allow for collective political action. Political scientist Robert Putnam has identified this as the "bowling alone" phenomenon in which social capital—the networks of relationships with norms of behavior, trust, and cooperation that increase the likelihood that society will function effectively—is in decline.[17] Americans traditionally had many social venues, such as bowling leagues, where they had an outlet to talk about politics and, potentially, to organize when they were frustrated with political outcomes. There are fewer of these today (people are busier, have more job responsibilities, and spend more time watching television), and the decline in civic engagement has led to reduced political efficacy and greater frustration with the course of politics.

Protest, of course, remains an option for people who feel neglected by the political order. In 2006, for example, as many as 5 million immigrants, their families, and their supporters took to the streets to protest anti-immigrant legislation in the U.S. House of Representatives. Mass protests such as these are very much the exception. Despite the fact that many in the United States oppose immigration at current levels, the social movement organizations that have formed to promote this cause—most notably the Minuteman organization—have rarely been able to generate much mass participation. Large-scale mass opposition to U.S. military involvement in Iraq has not spurred mass protest (as did U.S. involvement in Vietnam, for example).

The decline in social movements and other ways to organize the politically marginalized (such as labor unions), however, has shifted the focus of protest from organized collective actions to more isolated and, often, violent protests (such as the 1995 bombing of the federal building in Oklahoma City or the antiglobalization protests in Seattle in 1999) that fail to build more support for the demands of the people organizing the protest. Militia movements— organizations of individuals willing to take up arms to defend their own notion of U.S. political values and the Constitution, for example—represent the concerns of some in today's society, but few support their activities.

The twentieth century saw the rise of a new form of organized political activity: interest groups (see Citizen

Citizen Action

Environmental Defense Fund

The dramatic expansion in the territory and population of the United States over its more than 200-year history frequently came at the cost of the nation's natural resources. U.S. timber, coal, and oil fueled the growth of the global economy. U.S. farms produced a bounty that reduced the cost of grains and foodstuffs worldwide, but that often exhausted the soil, requiring the use of fertilizers and pesticides that cause long-term environmental damage. Rivers and lakes were manipulated to ensure that they could serve as transportation routes and sources of energy. Fossil fuels consumed at rates higher than most other nations have sped the production of greenhouse gases, which lead to a global warming. These challenges to the natural environment have spurred steadily increasing citizen action to ensure that government protects the environment.

In 1970, Congress established the Environmental Protection Agency (EPA) to centralize government efforts to protect the environment. In this period, Congress also passed legislation to protect endangered species (the Endangered Species Act, 1973), to reduce air pollution (the Clean Air Act, 1963), and to limit water pollution (the Clean Water Act, 1977), among other environmental regulation. For these legislative efforts to be effective, the EPA and other government agencies must be willing to enforce the law and to identify gaps in government's environmental protections that would provide the foundation for new congressional action. As the protection of the environment is often seen as coming at the expense of economic growth (and is often opposed by economic interests who profit from the product of challenges to the natural environment), the executive branch resists exercising its statutory responsibilities. Environmentally focused interest groups advocate before the EPA, before Congress, and in the federal courts to fill this gap to represent people concerned with the environment.

The Environmental Defense Fund (EDF), founded in 1967, is one of the oldest environmental interest groups in the United States and has one the largest memberships (500,000 dues-paying members). The EDF seeks to use the power of science to protect the environment, with a recognition that in the context of policy-making in the United States, economic interests will have a voice in environmental debates regardless of the science. Its staff includes more scientists and economists than any environmental interest group. Their strategy is twofold. The first step is to create alliances with the corporate sector and landholders. When these cooperative efforts fail, they litigate. This willingness to work with polluters alienates some in the environmental movement, but represents an advocacy strategy representative of U.S. political values. EDF can, however, look to tangible successes in banning dangerous pesticides, reducing acid rain, protecting fisheries so that fish can spawn, removing lead from gasoline, and establishing collaborations with large corporations to reduce greenhouse gas emissions. The use of the federal courts as cudges increased the incentives for the cooperative efforts to form.

Why the courts and not Congress or the EPA? More than the legislative or executive branches, the courts have the independence to evaluate whether the law is being violated. They are less directly influenced by short-term economic or business considerations. Some judges have resisted the notion that the federal government has the constitutional authority to regulate the environment, but Supreme Court rulings have established precedents for judicial intervention. Thus, environmental interest groups—like the interest groups representing many in the United States who have the power of numbers, but not economic power—see the courts as the branch of the federal government most likely to respond to demands based on law and, in the case of the environment, science.

Action: Environmental Defense Fund). Like political parties and candidates for office, these organizations try to influence the outcome of public policy by influencing policy-makers. They differ, however, in that they are usually organized to influence a single issue or a tightly related group of issues. Also unlike social movements, they rely on money and professional staff rather than on committed volunteers. Interest groups increased in prominence as the federal and state governments increasingly implemented distributive and redistributive policies. Beginning in the 1970s, a specialized form of interest group, the **political action committee (PAC)**, appeared to evade restrictions on corporations and organized labor to make financial contributions to political candidates and political parties.

Interest groups are so numerous in U.S. politics that it is not possible to even venture a guess as to their number. To show their diversity, however, it is important to realize that they include national organizations, such as the National Rifle Association, as well as local groups, such as associations of library patrons who seek to influence city council appropriations. They include mass organizations, such as the American Association of Retired Persons, which claims to represent the interests of more than 35 million people over the age of fifty, and very narrow interests, such as oil producers seeking to defend tax protections for their industry.

Although interest groups and PACs are now much more common than social movements in U.S. politics, they do not replace one key function traditionally fulfilled by the social movements, which seek to establish accountability between citizens and government. Interest groups by definition are organized to protect the needs of a cohesive group in the society and to make demands that government allocate resources in a way that benefits the interests of that group. Thus, they tend to include as members people who already receive rewards from government or are seeking new benefits. Their membership, then, tends to include more socially, financially, and educationally advantaged members of U.S. society. There is no place in the network of interest groups for individuals who are outside the democratic community or whose voices are ignored by the polity. The key role that social movements and protest have played in U.S. politics is being replaced by a more elite and more government-focused form of political organization. This is not to say that social movements and collective protest will not reappear in the future, but such a reappearance would require that the insider-focused strategy employed by interest groups could no longer ensure the outcomes that their members seek from government.

United States Politics in Transition

Political Challenges and Changing Agendas

The United States today faces some familiar and some new challenges that result from the nation's new place in the world of states. Primary among the continuing challenges is the need to live up to its own definition of the democratic idea and to balance this goal of representative government elected through mass participation with the divergent economic outcomes that result from its laissez-faire approach to governing the economy. As it has throughout its history, the United States must address these challenges with a system of government that was designed to impede the actions of government and a citizenry that expects much of government but frequently does not trust it to serve popular needs.

Although challenges to achieving the democratic idea are not new to U.S. political life, the circumstances in which they are debated are new for several reasons. Most important, the United States has assumed a relatively new role and set of responsibilities in the world of states, at least new as far as the past sixty years; U.S. governing institutions must now respond not just to their own people, but more broadly to an international political order that is increasingly interconnected and seeks rapid responses to international security, political, and economic crises. The institutional arrangements of U.S. government reduce the potential for quick responses and increase the likelihood of parochial responses that the rest of the world can hear as isolationism or unilateralism. These institutional arrangements are reinforced by a citizenry that for the most part cares little about foreign policy (except when war threatens), expects quick and often painless solutions to international crises, and has little respect, and sometimes open animosity, for multinational political and economic institutions such as the U.N. and the I.M.F. Despite the citizenry's continued focus on domestic concerns, U.S. jobs and national economic well-being are increasingly connected to international markets and to the willingness of governments and individuals to buy U.S. bonds. Over time, many in the United States may come to resent this economic integration.

Economics is not the only role that the United States plays in the world of states, as has been brought home in the period since the September 11 attacks. Its military, bilateral, and multilateral defense arrangements guarantee that the U.S. military will have a global presence. Again, this represents a substantial change from the nation's historical role prior to World War II. Although the citizenry has demonstrated a willingness to pay the financial cost of a global military, it has been much less willing to sacrifice the lives of members of the military. As a result, U.S. leaders must continually balance their military objectives and responsibilities to allies and international organizations with an inability to commit U.S. forces to conflicts that might lead to substantial casualties.

This tension between U.S. reliance on a global economic order among developed nations and a willingness to pursue a unilateral military and defense policy appeared repeatedly after the September 11 attacks. The initial approach of national leaders as well as the citizenry was to pursue military actions against Afghanistan and Iraq alone if necessary. Although alliances formed for each military engagement, this threat of unilateral action made the building of long-term multilateral alliances all the more difficult.

In addition to its economic and military roles in the world of states, the United States exports its culture and language throughout the world. Certainly, this process contributes to economic development in the United States; equally important, it places the United States at the center of an increasingly homogenizing international culture. The process also can generate hostile reactions in defense of national and local cultures.

The substantial changes in the U.S. connections to the world of states have not been matched by equally dramatic changes in the U.S. role in governing the economy. The laissez-faire governance that has characterized the United States from its earliest days continues. The United States tolerates income and wealth disparities greater than those of other advanced democracies. Equally important, business is less regulated and less taxed in the United States than in other democracies. Few in the polity contest this system of economic regulation.

Since the Great Depression, the United States has seen an expansion of redistributive programs to assist the poor. In the period of divided government, however, the U.S. has reduced its commitment to assisting the poor and has established time limits for any individual to collect benefits. Based on this history, it seems highly unlikely that the United States will develop targeted programs to assist citizens in need that compare to those of other advanced democracies.

Distributive programs targeted to the middle class, such as Social Security, Medicare, and college student loans, have also been implemented in the twentieth century. These have much more support among voters and are harder to undermine, even if they challenge traditional laissez-faire approaches to the U.S. role in governing the economy. The costs of these programs, however, are putting an increasing long-term burden on the federal budget and, because of deficit spending, on the national economy. A political will to deal with these long-term costs is absent.

Regardless of whether the focus is domestic or international policy, the U.S. government faces a challenge to its sense of its own democratic idea that is more dramatic than that faced by other advanced democracies. The 61 percent of the electorate who turned out in 2008 was high by recent standards, but it's not clear that this pattern will continue if the relatively even partisan balance in the electorate shifts toward an advantage for one of the parties. Turnout in non-presidential-year elections is even lower: this was approximately 40 percent of registered voters in 2006. Participation is not spread evenly across the population: older, more affluent, and more educated citizens are much more likely to vote than are the young, the less educated, and the poor. Thus, elected representatives are simultaneously receiving less guidance from a narrower subset of the people. Contributing to this process is the increasing cost of campaigns in the United States and the burdensome need to raise ever-increasing sums of money.

The breadth of nonelectoral politics is also narrowing. Previous study of the United States found rich networks of community-based organizations, voluntary organizations, and other forms of nonelectoral political activity. Community politics in the United States, however, began to decline in the 1950s (roughly when electoral turnout began to decline) and appears to be at record lows today. This is the "bowling alone" phenomenon discussed above.

This decline in electoral and nonelectoral politics magnifies a final dilemma that the United States faces

as it looks to the future. The politics of collective identities has always been central to U.S. politics because the country has been a recipient of large numbers of immigrants through much of its history. Each wave of immigrants has differed from its predecessors in terms of culture and religion. These differences forced the country to redefine itself in order to live up to its democratic idea. The "old" group of each era also perceived the "new" group as a threat to the political values of the nation. Today, Asian and Hispanic immigrants are seen as a challenge by the descendants of European immigrants.

The United States has experienced a long period of sustained high levels of immigration since 1965. The current period of high immigration has seen higher levels of overall immigration than the previous period of sustained high immigration (beginning after the Civil War and extending to the 1920s). In this previous

Current Challenges

Incorporating Immigrants

That the United States is a nation of immigrants is a truism. What is often overlooked, however, is that the flow of immigrants to the United States is not evenly spread across its history. Instead, some periods, such as the current one, see high levels of immigration, and others see much more moderate levels. As each of these periods of high immigration reaches maturity, the United States has to relearn how to ensure that the new immigrants achieve the same levels of success as the children of previous periods of immigration.

In 2006, approximately 38 million residents of the United States were born abroad. These foreign-born residents make up nearly 13 percent of the U.S. population. Although the number of foreign-born residents in the United States is at a historic high, they make up a lower share of the national population than in previous periods of high immigration because the national population is so much larger. Today's immigrants overwhelmingly trace their origins to Latin America and to Asia, two regions that sent few immigrants to the United States prior to the current immigrant wave (which began when U.S. immigration law was reformed in 1965).

Immigrants are generally more educated and better skilled than the average person from their countries of origin, but they have less education and fewer professional skills than the U.S. workforce. While some immigrants are at the top of the U.S. workforce and many can be found in positions in the technology industry, the average immigrant works in service, administrative, agriculture, or manufacturing jobs.

The experience of previous waves of immigrants offers a partial lesson for immigrant incorporation today. Immigrants bring with them a drive that facilitates economic advance. Immigrants, on average, work more hours and have more jobs than do the U.S.-born. Immigrant households have more workers than do households headed by the U.S.-born. This economic drive allows immigrant households in part to overcome the low salaries associated with the sectors of the economy in which they work. Even with this drive, however, immigrant households tend to earn less than those headed by the U.S.-born. This gap is particularly large for recent immigrants and those without legal status in the United States.

The U.S. economy is much changed from a century ago. Manufacturing and agriculture have declining labor needs, and the number of low-skill jobs that have absorbed immigrants over the past three decades is not growing. There are few job-training resources to prepare low-skill immigrants for the needs of the U.S. economy. Thus, economic gains seen in immigrant populations over the past several decades may not continue in the future.

Immigrants are demonstrating a steady development of political ties to the United States, although they are slower to make these connections formal through naturalization. Survey data demonstrate that immigrants quickly develop ties to the political values of the United States (liberty, equality, and democracy), sometimes at levels greater than those of the U.S.-born. Immigrants show only moderate interest in the politics of their native lands. When disputes arise between the United States and the nation of origin, immigrants most often agree with the U.S. government's position on the issue. Immigrants, however, are somewhat slow to naturalize. Slightly more than one-third of immigrants have naturalized. While this may reflect a failure among immigrants to choose to become citizens, a more likely explanation is that some immigrants are ineligible (those who are undocumented and those who immigrated legally within the past five years) and others are interested but find the

application requirements too onerous or too expensive. With time, most eligible immigrants naturalize, although most do only a few years after they become eligible (after five years of legal residence).

A final measure supplements economic and political incorporation to assess whether immigrants are becoming full members of U.S. society, and, in this area, there is much less evidence. For the current wave of immigration to be successful, their children—the second generation—must have opportunities comparable to those of other Americans. These children start with a structural disadvantage: they overwhelmingly reside in urban and suburban areas with poor tax bases and, hence, poor schools. It was schooling that allowed previous generations of immigrant children to improve their position in U.S. society. If equal educational opportunities are denied to today's children of immigrants, these past successes will likely not be repeated. Perhaps the greatest domestic challenge that the United States faces in the coming years is ensuring that its commitment to large-scale immigration is matched by a commitment to ensuring that those immigrants and the second generation become equal participants in the opportunities and political responsibilities of membership in the American polity.

period, however, the final fifteen years were characterized by increasingly vitriolic national debates about limiting the volume of immigration and limiting immigration from parts of Europe (southern and eastern) that had only recently begun to send large numbers of immigrants to the United States. Many in Congress today are proposing legislation to further deter undocumented migration, but there have been few proposals to reduce the opportunities for legal immigration. In sum, it seems likely that sustained high levels of immigration, quite diverse in terms of its origins, will continue well into the future.

The absence of strong political parties, mediating institutions, and nonelectoral community politics may dampen the political integration of these immigrants and their children. The preliminary evidence is that naturalization rates are increasing, but that naturalized citizens vote and participate in other forms of politics at lower levels than comparably situated U.S.-born citizens. If these patterns continue, the United States faces a risk that has not come to pass

in its long history of high levels of immigration: contemporary immigrants and their children may not be represented in the political order, even when these immigrants achieve formal political equality by naturalizing as U.S. citizens.

In the past, the weaknesses of the U.S. constitutional system could be overcome in part through institutional arrangements and mediating institutions. In terms of institutions, Congress dominated the executive until the New Deal era, after which the president dominated Congress until Watergate. This institutional dominance reflected the framers' intent through the Great Depression and after, at least in terms of the dominance of one branch. It is unclear that the framers envisioned a system where two, and occasionally all three, branches of government would compete for dominance and where the Congress and the presidency would be routinely controlled by different political parties.

Mediating institutions also played a role in the past that they are incapable of addressing today. Once they formed as mass institutions in the 1830s, the parties served a necessary role in unifying popular opinion and forcing elite compromise. Today, parties are in decline and have been replaced by a distinct type of mediating institution that does not seek compromise across issues and instead promotes narrow interests. Interest groups connect the citizenry to political institutions, as did parties, but the purpose of this connection is to advance a narrow agenda.

Thus, the United States faces the challenges that it has confronted throughout its history and continues to be limited by a governing system that seeks to inhibit government activity. In the past, it has been able to overcome these challenges through active citizen participation, often channeled through mediating institutions and the mobilization of new groups to active political participation. With citizen participation becoming more selective and mediating institutions less broadly based, the United States is more poorly situated to face challenges. As it is now centrally positioned in the international economic and political order, the country's ability to overcome challenges has implications not just for its people but also for people throughout the world.

United States Politics in Comparative Perspective

From the perspective of the study of comparative politics, the United States may well remain an enigma. Its size, wealth, unique experiences with immigration, history of political isolation from the world, and reliance on separation of powers and federalism do not have clear parallels among other advanced democracies. This distinctness comes through perhaps most clearly in the way the United States engages its international political responsibilities. While the president has traditionally directed the scope of U.S. foreign policy, Congress, as it reasserts power relative to the president, will likely play an increasing role. Members of Congress, who represent narrow geographic districts and are more directly connected to mass interests, are less likely to take an internationalist perspective than is the president. When Congress speaks on international issues, it is often with multiple voices, including some that oppose U.S. involvement

in multilateral organizations. This conflict over control and direction of foreign policy has become more evident since the end of the cold war. An example would be tensions over U.S. payments to support the United Nations. The objections of one, admittedly well-placed, senator, Jesse Helms, chair of the Senate Foreign Relations Committee, and his perceptions of excessive bureaucracy at the United Nations caused the United States to slow its support payments to the organization and risk its voice in the activities of U.N. agencies. Because Helms controlled the actions of the Foreign Relations Committee, which had to authorize the U.S. payments, he was able to alter U.S. policy and ultimately force the United Nations to change its policies. Most nations, let alone individual legislators, do not have this sort of power. Only in the United States can a senator have more power than a president.

The impact of the constitutionally mandated structural and institutional weaknesses of U.S. government is not limited to the American people. The United States plays a dominant role in the world economy, as well as a central political role in international organizations. Thus, the inefficiencies and multiple entry points into U.S. policy-making shape the ability of the United States to respond to crises and develop coherent long-term policies in conjunction with its allies. In 1998, for example, as the world economy declined, the president, with the support of the chair of the Federal Reserve, proposed that the United States increase its contribution to the IMF by $18 billion. Congress initially balked at this request for several reasons, none of which were apparent to the U.S. allies. Some opposed the new appropriations because of concerns about international organizations in general. Others sought to block presidential initiatives because of the president's political weaknesses. Others, likely the majority of those who opposed the initiative, thought that they could bargain with the president to earn his support for initiatives that they sought to pass. While the power of intransigence and horse trading makes sense to analysts of U.S. politics, analysts abroad cannot so easily understand the seeming failure of the United States to act in a time of crisis. Eventually Congress passed the added IMF appropriation.

In sum, despite its central role in the international economic system and in multilateral organizations, the United States often remains reluctant to embrace fully the international system that it helped shape. This hesitancy appears despite the active role of U.S. economic interests abroad and the importance of international trade to the U.S. economy. The United States does not hesitate to impose its will abroad when it perceives its security threatened, as was evident in the period leading up to the Iraq war, or when it perceives that the rules made by the international organizations undermine its economic or political interests, as was evident in President Bush's refusal to submit the Kyoto protocols to the Senate for ratification. Thus, despite its central role in the world of states, the United States is sometimes a hesitant leader. While this has been the case since the emergence of the United States as a global political leader in the post–World War II era, the new challenges of the post-9/11 world make this a much more difficult position to sustain. The challenge of the contemporary era is not states—as it was in the Cold War era—but instead international non-state-based networks. These cannot so easily be controlled through economic dominance and multilateral political alliances. As the United States faces the new challenges of a post–9/11 world, it must again reexamine the degree to which it is willing to act unilaterally and to pay the price for global concern about its occasional unilateralism.

Key Terms 》》

North American Free Trade Agreement (NAFTA)
manifest destiny
Declaration of Independence
Articles of Confederation
Bill of Rights
Social Security
property taxes
interest group
USA PATRIOT Act
federalism
separation of powers
single-member-plurality (SMP) electoral system

free market
laissez-faire
police powers
Federal Reserve Board
regulations
distributive policies
redistributive policies
iron triangle relationships
Marbury v. *Madison*
checks and balances
bicameral
political action committee (PAC)

Suggested Readings 》》

Amar, Akhil Reed. *The Bill of Rights: Creation and Reconstruction.* New Haven, Conn.: Yale University Press, 1998.

Burns, Nancy, Schlozman, Kay Lehman, and Verba, Sidney. *The Private Roots of Public Action: Gender, Equality, and Political Participation.* Cambridge, Mass.: Harvard University Press, 2001.

Dawson, Michael C. *Black Visions: The Roots of Contemporary African-American Political Ideologies.* Chicago: University of Chicago Press, 2002.

Deering, Christopher J., and Smith, Steven S. *Committees in Congress.* 3d ed. Washington, D.C.: Congressional Quarterly Books, 1997.

DeSipio, Louis. *Counting on the Latino Vote: Latinos as a New Electorate.* Charlottesville: University Press of Virginia, 1996.

Elkins, Stanley, and McKitrick, Eric. *The Age of Federalism.* New York: Oxford University Press, 1993.

The Federalist Papers. Edited by Clinton Rossiter. New York, Mentor, 1961.

Fenno, Jr., Richard F. *Home Style: House Members in Their Districts.* Glenview, Ill.: Scott, Foresman, 1978.

Hartz, Louis. *The Liberal Tradition in America.* New York: Harvest/ HBJ, 1955.

Judis, John B., and Teixeira, Ruy. *The Emerging Democratic Majority.* New York: Scribner, 2002.

Kupchan, Charles. *The End of the American Era: U.S. Foreign Policy and the Geopolitics of the Twenty-First Century.* New York: Knopf, 2002.

Levinson, Sanford. *Constitutional Faith.* Princeton, N.J.: Princeton University Press, 1988.

Lowi, Theodore J. *The End of Liberalism: The Second Republic of the United States.* 2d ed. New York: Norton, 1979.

Nye, Joseph, Jr. *The Paradox of American Power: Why the World's Only Superpower Can't Go It Alone.* New York: Oxford University Press, 2002.

Sniderman, Paul, and Piazza, Thomas. *The Scar of Race.* Cambridge: Harvard University Press, 1993.

Verba, Sidney, Schlozman, Kay Lehman, and Brady, Henry. *Voice and Equality: Civic Voluntarism in American Politics.* Cambridge, Mass.: Harvard University Press, 1995.

Wilson, Woodrow. *Congressional Government: A Study in American Politics.* Baltimore: Johns Hopkins University Press, 1885.

Wolfinger, Raymond, and Rosenstone, Steven. *Who Votes?* New Haven, Conn.: Yale University Press, 1980.

Zaller, John. *The Nature and Origins of Mass Opinion.* New York: Cambridge University Press, 1992.

Zolberg, Aristede. *A Nation By Design: Immigration Policy in the Fashioning of America.* Cambridge, Mass: Harvard University Press, 2006.

Suggested Websites ⟩⟩

The 9/11 Commission Report
http://www.gpoaccess.gov/911/
FindLaw—Cases and Codes: U.S. Constitution
findlaw.com/casecode/constitution/
The New York Times
www.nytimes.com
Thomas—Legislative Information from the Library of Congress
thomas.loc.gov

U.S. Census Bureau
www.census.gov
White House
www.whitehouse.gov

Endnotes ⟩⟩

[1] U.S. Census Bureau, *Statistical Abstract of the United States: 2008* (Washington, D.C.: U.S. Bureau of the Census, 2007), Table 1298.

[2] Rogers Smith, *Civic Ideals: Conflicting Visions of Citizenship in U.S. History* (New Haven, Conn.: Yale University Press, 1997).

[3] The Pew Research Center for the People & the Press, *A Year After the Iraq War: Mistrust of America and Europe Ever Higher, Muslim Anger Persists* (Washington, D.C.: The Pew Research Center for the People & the Press, 2004).

[4] Ramakrishnan, S. Karthick. *Democracy in Immigrant America: Changing Demographics and Political Participation* (Stanford, CA: Stanford University Press, 2005).

[5] Louis Hartz, *The Liberal Tradition in America* (New York: Harvest/HBJ, 1955).

[6] Randall Robinson, *The Debt: What America Owes to Blacks* (New York: Plume, 2001).

[7] Bryner, Gary C., *Blue Skies, Green Politics: the Clean Air Act of 1990 and its Implementation* (Washington, D.C.: CQ Press, 1995).

[8] U.S. Department of Homeland Security, *U.S. Legal Permanent Residents: 2007* (Washington, D.C.: Office of Immigration Statistics, 2008).

[9] Passel, Jeffrey S. *The Size and Characteristics of the Unauthorized Migrant Population in the U.S.: Estimates Based on the March 2005 Current Population Survey* (Washington, D.C.: Pew Hispanic Center, 2006).

[10] See *The Federalist Papers,* ed. Clinton Rossiter (New York: Mentor, 1961), particularly *Federalist* Nos. 10 and 51.

[11] Avant, Deborah, *The Market for Force: The Consequences of Privatizing Security* (New York: Cambridge University Press, 2005).

[12] Kristi Anderson, *After Suffrage: Women in Partisan and Electoral Politics Before the New Deal* (Chicago: University of Chicago Press, 1996).

[13] Ruy A. Teixeira, *The Disappearing American Voter* (Washington, D.C.: Brookings Institution, 1992).

[14] Raymond Wolfinger and Steven Rosenstone, *Who Votes?* (New Haven, Conn.: Yale University Press. 1980).

[15] Sanford Levinson, *Constitutional Faith* (Princeton, N.J.: Princeton University Press, 1988).

[16] Sidney Verba, Kay Lehman Schlozman, and Henry Brady, *Voice and Equality: Civic Voluntarism in American Politics* (Cambridge: Harvard University Press, 1995).

[17] Robert D. Putnam, *Bowling Alone: The Collapse and Revival of American Community* (New York: Simon and Schuster, 2000).

Part 3 >> Developing Democracies

Darren Kew and Peter Lewis

Chapter 8 »NIGERIA

Section 1 The Making of the Modern Nigerian State
Section 2 Political Economy and Development
Section 3 Governance and Policy-Making
Section 4 Representation and Participation
Section 5 Nigerian Politics in Transition

Official Name: **Federal Republic of Nigeria**

Location: **Western Africa**

Capital City: **Abuja**

Population (2008): **146.2 million**

Size: **923,768 sq. km.;** slightly **more than twice the size of California**

1960
Independence. Nigeria consists of three regions under a Westminster parliamentary model. Abubakar Tafawa Balewa, a northerner, is the first prime minister.

January 1966
Civilian government deposed in coup. General Aguiyi Ironsi, an Igbo, becomes head of state.

July 1966
Countercoup is led by General Yakubu Gowan (an Anga, from the Middle Belt) with aid from northern groups.

1967–1970
Biafran civil war

July 1975
Military coup deposes Gowan; led by General Murtala Muhammed, a northerner.

February 1976
Murtala Muhammed assassinated in failed coup led by Middle Belt minorities. Muhammed's second-in-command, General Olusegun Obasanjo, a Yoruba, assumes power.

September 1978
New constitution completed, marking the adoption of the U.S. presidential model in a federation with 19 states.

October 1979
Elections held. A majority in both houses is won by NPN, led by northern/Hausa-Fulani groups. Alhaji Shehu Shagari

is elected Nigeria's first executive president.

December 1983
Military coup led by General Muhammadu Buhari, a northerner.

August 1985
Buhari is overthrown by General Ibrahim B. Babangida, a Middle Belt Muslim, in a palace coup. Babangida promises a return to democracy by 1990, a date he delays five times before being forced from office.

June 12, 1993
Moshood Abiola wins presidential elections, but Babangida annuls the election eleven days later.

August 1993
Babangida installs Ernest Shonekan as "interim civilian president" until new presidential elections could be held later that autumn.

November 1993
Defense Minister General Sani Abacha seizes power in a coup. Two years later he announces a three-year transition to civilian rule, which he manipulates to have himself nominated for president in 1998.

July–Sept. 1994
Prodemocracy strike by the major oil union, NUPENG, cuts Nigeria's oil production by an estimated 25 percent. Sympathy strikes ensue, followed by arrests of political and civic leaders.

SECTION 1 # The Making of the Modern Nigerian State

Politics in Action

April 2007 marked an important landmark in Nigerian democracy. For the first time, one Nigerian civilian president was scheduled to hand power to another after elections that month. Yet the event was troubled by political intrigues created by President Obasanjo, who wished to extend his stay in office beyond his constitutional limit of two terms by provoking the electorate into crisis through blatant electoral fraud. The savvy Nigerian public, however, refused to take the bait. The mood was summed up when an international election monitor in Kaduna asked people waiting in line to vote whether they thought the election would be rigged by Obasanjo and the ruling People's Democratic Party. "Oh yes, they will definitely rig this election," came the response. Stunned, the monitor then asked why they were planning to vote if they knew the election was rigged. "Because," one voter explained, "we do not want to

give Obasanjo a reason to annul the election and stay in power." Despite massive electoral violations across the country, the nation remained calm and Obasanjo had little choice in May 2007 but to hand power to his hand-picked successor, Umaru Musa Yar'Adua.

The moment captured two central, yet contradictory, trends in Nigeria's current political development. On the one hand, democratization in Nigeria—nearly a decade after the exit of the military from power—has yet to produce good governance. Instead, authoritarian rule has given way to competitive oligarchy, in which an increasingly greedy, oil-rich political elite fight to expand their power at all costs, while more than 90 percent of Nigerians struggle to survive on less than two U.S. dollars per day. Despite the machinations of the irresponsible elite, however, the Nigerian public—like the Kaduna voters—has grown increasingly frustrated with the slow pace of change and the intrigues of its leaders, and has begun to take matters into its

June 1998
General Abacha dies; succeeded by General Abdulsalami Abubakar, a Middle Belt Muslim from Babangida's hometown. Abubakar releases nearly all political prisoners and installs a new transition program. Parties are allowed to form unhindered.

1999
Former head of state Olusegun Obansanjo and his party, the PDP, sweep the presidential and National Assembly elections, adding to their majority control of state and local government seats. The federation now contains thirty-six states.

November 1999
Zamfara state in the north is the first of twelve to institute the *shari'a* criminal code.

That same month, President Obasanjo sends the army to the Niger Delta town of Odi to root out local militias, leveling the town in the process.

2000
Communal conflicts erupt in Lagos, Benue, Kaduna, and Kana states at different times over localized issues.

Spring 2002
The Supreme Court passes several landmark judgments, overturning a PDP-biased 2001 electoral law, and ruling on the control of offshore oil and gas resources. In November the Court opens the legal door for more parties to be registered.

August 2002
The National Assembly begins impeachment proceedings against President Obasanjo over budgetary issues. The matter ends by November, with the president apologizing.

July 2003
Rogue police units stage a coup in Anambra State, temporarily arresting the governor. The putsch soon collapses, but Anambra becomes a war zone between the governor and the state's political kingpin, who has family ties to the president.

May 2006
President Obasanjo tries to amend the constitution to allow himself a third term in office, but is defeated by the National Assembly, reflecting

an unprecedented public outcry against Obasanjo.

April–May 2007
The ruling PDP again takes a vast majority of election victories across the nation amid a deeply compromised process. Umaru Musa Yar'Adua, picked from obscurity by President Obasanjo, becomes president. Yar'Adua promises reform, but spends his first year trying to solidify his tenuous hold on power.

December 2008
The Supreme Court upholds President Yar' Adua's election in a narrow 4–3 decision.

own hands, demanding a greater share of the nation's wealth and a greater say in political decisions.

In addition, the young democracy faces the challenge of managing the country's contentious ethnic and religious diversity in conditions of scarcity and weak institutions. Furthermore, years of widespread poverty and political corruption despite skyrocketing oil revenues have left most Nigerians with little patience to wait for President Yar'Adua's fragile, internally divided government to deliver significant progress. Nigeria encapsulates many characteristics that more broadly identify Africa. These opposing forces are rooted in the constant struggle in Nigeria between **authoritarian** and democratic governance, the push for development amidst persistent underdevelopment, the burden of public corruption, and the pressure for accountability. Nigeria, like all other African countries, has sought to create a viable nation-state out of the social incoherence created by its colonial borders. More than 250 competing ethnic groups, crosscut by two major religious traditions, have repeatedly clashed over economic and political resources, as well

as issues of administrative and legal identity. All of these factors combine to produce the political entity known as Nigeria with low levels of popular **legitimacy** and **accountability**, and a persistent inability to meet the most basic needs of its citizens. Against this background, Nigeria today remains essentially an **unfinished state** characterized by instabilities and uncertainties. The last military takeover occurred in 1983, when elections were so flawed and civilian rule so corrupt that the public welcomed a coup. The 1999 and 2003 elections were also deeply flawed, and the 2007 elections were decried by international observers as a "farce." Will Nigeria return to the discredited path of authoritarianism and greater underdevelopment, or will the civilian leadership rise to achieve a consolidated democracy and sustainable growth?

Geographic Setting

Nigeria, with 130 million people inhabiting 356,669 square miles, ranks as the most populous nation in Africa and among the ten largest in the world. A cen-

FIGURE 8.1

The Nigerian Nation at a Glance

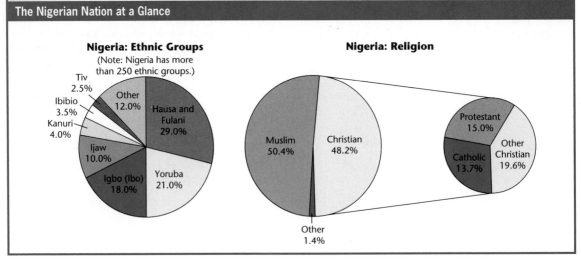

Nigeria: Ethnic Groups
(Note: Nigeria has more than 250 ethnic groups.)

Tiv 2.5%
Ibibio 3.5%
Kanuri 4.0%
Other 12.0%
Hausa and Fulani 29.0%
Ijaw 10.0%
Igbo (Ibo) 18.0%
Yoruba 21.0%

Nigeria: Religion

Muslim 50.4%
Christian 48.2%
Other 1.4%
Protestant 15.0%
Other Christian 19.6%
Catholic 13.7%

Table 8.1

Political Organization

Political System	Federal republic
Regime History	Democratic government took office in May 1999, after sixteen years of military rule. The most recent national elections were held in 2007.
Administrative Structure	Nigeria is a federation of thirty-six states, plus the Federal Capital Territory (FCT) in Abuja. The three tiers of government are federal, state, and local. Actual power is centralized under the presidency and the governors.
Executive	U.S.-style presidential system, under Umaru Musa Yar'Adua
Legislature	A bicameral civilian legislature was elected in April 2007. The 109 senators are elected on the basis of equal representation: three from each state, and one from the FCT. The 360 members of the House of Representatives are elected from single-member districts.
Judiciary	Federal, state, and local court system, headed by the Federal Court of Appeal and the Supreme Court, which consists of fifteen appointed associate justices and the chief justice. States may establish a system of Islamic law (*shari'a*) for cases involving only Muslims in customary disputes (divorce, property, etc.). Most Nigerian states feature such courts, which share a Federal *Shari'a* Court of Appeal in Abuja. Non-Muslim states may also set up customary courts, based on local traditional jurisprudence. Secular courts retain supreme jurisdiction if conflict arises between customary and secular courts.
Party System	Nearly fifty parties have been registered by the Nigerian electoral commission since 2002. The largest are the People's Democratic Party (PDP), the All Nigerian People's Party (ANPP), the Action Congress (AC), and the All Progressive Grand Alliance (APGA). PDP won the presidency, majorities in both houses of the National Assembly, as well as a majority of governorships, state assemblies, and local governments.

ter of West African regional trade, culture, and military strength, Nigeria is bordered by four countries—Benin, Niger, Chad, and Cameroon, all of them Francophone—and by the Gulf of Guinea in the Atlantic Ocean to the south. The modern country of Nigeria, however, like nearly all the other contemporary states in Africa, is not even a century old.

Nigeria was a British colony from 1914 until its independence on October 1, 1960, although foreign domination of much of the territory had begun in the mid-nineteenth century. Nigeria's boundaries had little to do with the borders of the precolonial African societies in the territory that the British conquered. Instead, these boundaries merely marked the point where British influence ended and French began. Britain ruled northern and southern Nigeria as two separate colonies until 1914, when it amalgamated its Northern and Southern Protectorates. In short, Nigeria was an arbitrary creation reflecting British colonial interests. The consequences of this forced union of myriad African cultures and ruling entities under one political roof remain a central feature of Nigerian political life today.

Nigeria's location in West Africa, its size, and its oil-producing status have made it a hub of regional activity. Demographically, it overwhelms the other fifteen countries in West Africa, with a population that is nearly 60 percent of the region's total. Moreover, Nigeria's gross domestic product (GDP) typically represents more than half of the total GDP for the entire subregion.

Nigeria's ethnic map can be divided into six inexact areas or "zones." The northwest (or "core North") is dominated by Nigeria's single largest ethnic group, the Hausa-Fulani, two formerly separate groups that over the past century have largely merged. The northeast is a minority region, the largest of whom are the Kanuri. Both regions in the north are predominantly Muslim. A large swath of territory stretching across the center of the country, called the Middle Belt, is also home to a wide range of minority groups of both Muslim and Christian faiths. The southwest (referred to as the Western Region in the First Republic) is dominated by the country's second largest ethnic group, the Yoruba, who are approximately 40 percent Muslim, 50 percent Christian (primarily Protestant), and 10 percent practitioners of Yoruba traditional

beliefs. The southeast (which formed the hub of the First Republic's Eastern Region) is the Igbo homeland, Nigeria's third largest group, who are primarily Christian, and where Protestant evangelical movements have become popular. Between the Yoruba and Igbo regions of the south is the southern minority zone, which stretches across the Niger Delta areas and east along the coast as far as Cameroon.

Critical Junctures

A number of critical junctures have shaped the character of the Nigerian state and illustrate the difficult path that the country has taken during the past half-century. Nigeria's recent history reflects influences from the precolonial period, the crucial changes wrought by British colonialism, the postcolonial alternation of military and civilian rule, and the economic collapse from 1980 to 2000, precipitated by Nigeria's political corruption and its overreliance on the petroleum industry, which has been reinforced by the post–2003 oil boom.

The Precolonial Period (800–1900)

In contrast to the peoples of the forest belt to the south, the more open terrain in the north, with its need for irrigation, encouraged the early growth of centralized states. Such states from the eighth century included Kanem-Bornu in the northeast and the Hausa states in the northwest. Another attempt at state formation led to the emergence of a Jukun kingdom, which by the end of the seventeenth century was a tributary state of the Bornu Empire.

A major element that shaped developments in the savanna areas of the north was trade across the Sahara Desert with northern Africa. Trade brought material benefits as well as Arabic education and Islam, which gradually replaced traditional spiritual, political, and social practices. In 1808, the Fulani, who came from lands west of modern Nigeria through a holy war (*jihad*), established an Islamic empire, the Sokoto Caliphate. The Sokoto Caliphate used Islam and a common language, Hausa, to forge unity out of the disparate groups in the north. The Fulani Empire held sway until British colonial authority was imposed on northern Nigeria by 1900.

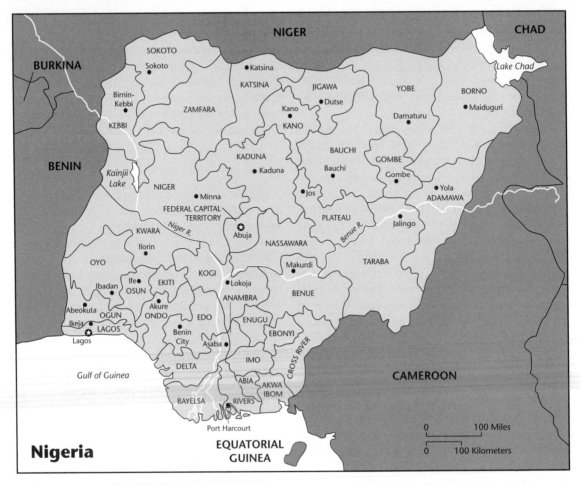

Nigeria

Toward the southern edge of the savanna politics was generally conducted along kinship lines. Political authority was diffuse, such that later Western contacts described them as "stateless," or **acephalous societies**. Because such groups as the Tiv lacked complex political hierarchies, these societies escaped much of the upheaval experienced under colonialism by the centralized states, and retained much of their autonomy.

Southern Nigeria included the highly centralized Yoruba empires and the kingdoms of Oyo and Ife; the Edo kingdom of Benin in the Midwest; the acephalous societies of the Igbo to the east; and the trading city-states of the Niger Delta and its hinterland, peopled by a wide range of ethnicities.

Several precolonial societies had democratic elements that scholars speculate might have led to more open and participatory polities had they not been interrupted by colonialism. Governance in the Yoruba and Igbo communities involved principles of accountability and representation. Among the Islamic communities of the north, political society was highly structured, reflecting local interpretations of Qur'anic principles. Leadership structures were considerably more hierarchical than those of the south, dominated educated and women were typically consigned to a subordinate political status. The Islamic Fulani Empire was a confederation in which the rulers, emirs, owed allegiance to the sultan, who was the temporal and spiritual head of the empire. The sultan's powers, in turn, were circumscribed by the obligation to observe Islamic principles.

Precolonial Polities and Societies
Source: K. Michael Barbour, Julius Oguntoyinbo, J.O.C. Onyemelukwe, and James C. Nwafor, *Nigeria in Maps* (New York: Africana Publishing Company, 1982), 37.

Colonial Rule and Its Impact (1860–1945)

Competition for trade and empire drove the European imperial powers further into Africa after 1860. Colonial rule deepened the extraction of Nigeria's natural resources and the exploitation of Nigerian labor, according to the economic and political requisites of Britain, the governing power. Colonialism left its imprint on all aspects of Nigeria's existence, bequeathing political and economic systems that have left enduring imprints on development and governance.

Where centralized monarchies existed in the north, the British ruled through a policy known as **indirect rule**, which allowed traditional structures to persist as subordinates to the British governor and a small administrative apparatus. Where more dispersed kingships ruled, as among the Yoruba, or where acephalous societies existed, particularly among the Igbo and other groups in the southeast,

the colonizers either strengthened the authority of traditional chiefs and kings or appointed **warrant chiefs** (who ruled by warrant of the British Crown), weakening the previous practices of accountability and participation.

The British played off ethnic and social divisions to keep Nigerians from developing organized political resistance to colonial rule, and where resistance did develop, the colonizers were not afraid to employ repressive tactics, even as late as the 1940s. Yet the British also promoted the foundations of a democratic political system before they left in 1960. This dual standard left a conflicted democratic idea: formal democratic institutions yet an authoritarian political culture. Colonialism also strengthened the collective identities of Nigeria's multiple ethnic groups by fostering political competition among them, primarily among the three largest: the Hausa-Fulani, Yoruba, and Igbo.

Divisive Identities: Ethnic Politics under Colonialism (1945–1960)

Based on their experience under British rule, leaders of the anticolonial movement came to regard the state as an exploitative instrument, and its control as an opportunity to pursue personal and group interests rather than broad national interests. Thus, when the British began to negotiate a gradual exit from Nigeria, the semblance of unity that had existed among the anticolonial leaders prior to the 1950s soon evaporated, and intergroup political competition became increasingly fierce.

Nigerian leaders quickly turned to ethnicity as the preferred vehicle to pursue competition and mobilize public support. The three largest ethnic groups, the Hausa-Fulani, Igbo, and Yoruba, though each a minority, together comprise approximately two-thirds of Nigeria's population. They have long dominated the political process. By pitting ethnic groups against each other for purposes of divide and rule and by structuring the administrative units of Nigeria based on ethnic groups, the British ensured that ethnicity would be the primary element in political identification and mobilization.

Initially, ethnically based associations were concerned with nonpolitical issues: promoting mutual aid for housing and education, as well as sponsoring cultural events. With the encouragement of ambitious leaders, however, these groups took on a more political character. Nigeria's first political party, the National Council of Nigeria and the Cameroons (later the National Convention of Nigerian Citizens, NCNC), initially drew supporters from across Nigeria. As the prospects for independence increased, however, indigenous elites began to divide along ethnic lines to mobilize support for their differing political agendas.

Recognizing the multiethnic character of their colony, the British divided Nigeria into a federation of three regions with elected governments in 1954. Each of the regions soon fell under the domination of one of the major ethnic groups and their respective parties. The Northern Region came under the control of the Northern People's Congress (NPC), dominated by Hausa-Fulani elites. In the southern half of the country, the Western Region was controlled by the Action Group (AG), which was controlled by Yoruba elites. The Igbo,

the numerically dominant group in the Eastern Region, were closely associated with the NCNC, which became the ruling party there. Thus, ethnic and regional distinctions of modern Nigeria were reinforced in divisive ways during the transition to independence.[1]

Chief Obafemi Awolowo, leader of the AG, captured the sentiment of the times when he wrote in 1947, "Nigeria is not a nation. It is a mere geographical expression. There are no 'Nigerians' in the same sense as there are 'English,' 'Welsh,' or 'French.' The word 'Nigerian' is merely a distinctive appellation to distinguish those who live within the boundaries of Nigeria from those who do not."[2]

The First Republic (1960–1966)

The British granted Nigeria independence in 1960 to an elected parliamentary government. Nigerians adopted the British Westminster model at the federal and regional levels, with the prime minister chosen by the majority party or coalition. Northerners came to dominate the federal government by virtue of their greater population. The ruling coalition for the first two years quickly turned into a northern-only grouping when the NPC achieved an outright majority in the legislature. Having benefited less from the economic, educational, and infrastructural benefits of colonialism, the northerners who dominated the First Republic set out to redistribute resources to their benefit. This NPC policy of "northernization" brought them into direct conflict with their southern counterparts, particularly the Yoruba-based AG and later the Igbo-dominated NCNC.

When an AG internal conflict led to a political crisis in the Western regional assembly in 1962, the NPC-led national government seized the opportunity to subdivide the Western (largely Yoruba) Region in two—diluting Yoruba political power. Violence escalated among the Yoruba factions in the West as the NPC-dominated government engaged in extensive political corruption. A fraudulent census, falsified ballots in the general elections, widespread violence, and intimidation of supporters and candidates alike ensured the NPC a tarnished victory in 1965.

Rivalries intensified as the NPC sat atop an absolute majority in the federal parliament with no need for its former coalition partner, the NCNC. Nnamdi Azikiwe, the NCNC leader who was also president in

Nigeria in 1955: Divided into three federated regions. The administrative division of Nigeria into three regions later became the basis for ethnoregional conflicts. (Note: At the time of independence, the southeastern part of the country, which had been governed as a trust territory, opted to become part of independent Cameroon; two northern trust territories opted to become part of independent Nigeria.) *Source:* K. Michael Barbour, Julius Oguntoyinbo, J.O.C. Onyemelukwe, and James C. Nwafor, *Nigeria in Maps* (New York: Africana Publishing Company, 1982), 39.

Nigeria, 1955

Lake Chad

To Nigeria 1961

NORTHERN REGION

Niger River

Benue River

WESTERN REGION

To Nigeria 1961

EASTERN REGION

To Cameroon 1961

0   100 Miles

0   100 Kilometers

the First Republic (then a largely symbolic position), and Tafawa Balewa, the NPC prime minister, separately approached the military to ensure that if it came to conflict, they could count on its loyalty. Thus, "in the struggle for personal survival both men, perhaps inadvertently, made the armed forces aware that they had a political role to play."[3]

Civil War and Military Rule (1966–1979)

With significant encouragement from contending civilian leaders, a group of largely Igbo officers seized power in January 1966. Aguiyi Ironsi, also an Igbo, who became head of state by dint of being the highest-ranking officer rather than a coup plotter, was killed in a second coup in July 1966, which brought Yakubu Gowon, a Middle Belt Christian, to power as a consensus head of state among the non-Igbo coup plotters.[4]

Because many northern officials had been killed in the initial coup, a tremendous backlash against Igbos flared in several parts of the country. Ethnic violence sent many Igbos fleeing to their home region in the east. By 1967, the predominantly Igbo population of eastern Nigeria attempted to secede and form its own independent country, named Biafra. Gowon built a military-led government of national unity in what remained of Nigeria (the north and

west) and, after a bloody three-year war of attrition and starvation tactics, defeated Biafra in January 1970. The conflict exacted a heavy toll on Nigeria's populace, including at least a million deaths.

After the war, Gowon presided over a policy of national reconciliation, which proceeded fairly smoothly with the aid of growing oil revenues. Senior officers reaped the benefits of the global oil boom in 1973–1974, however, and corruption was widespread. Influenced by the unwillingness of the military elite to relinquish power and the spoils of office, Gowon postponed a return to civilian rule, and was overthrown in 1975 by Murtala Muhammad, who was assassinated before he could achieve a democratic transition. General Olusegun Obasanjo, Muhammad's second-in-command and successor, peacefully ceded power to an elected civilian government in 1979, which became known as the Second Republic. Obasanjo retired but would later reemerge as a civilian president in 1999.

The Second and Third Republics, and Predatory Military Rule (1979–1999)

The president of the 1979–1983 Second Republic, Shehu Shagari, and his ruling National Party of Nigeria (NPN, drawn largely from the First Republic's

General Olusegun Obasanjo was the Nigerian head of state who supervised the transition to civilian rule from 1976 to 1979. In 1995 he was arrested and convicted in a secret trial in connection with an alleged attempt to overthrow the regime of General Abacha. After his release, he won the presidency in 1999 as a candidate for the PDP.
Source: Bettmann/Corbis.

When General Buhari refused to pledge a rapid return to democratic rule and failed to revive a plummeting economy, his popular support wavered, and in August 1985 General Ibrahim Babangida seized power. Although Babangida quickly announced a program of transition to democratic rule, he and his cohort engaged in an elaborate series of stalling tactics in order to extend their tenure in office and then annulled the presidential election of June 1993. In stark contrast to all prior elections, the 1993 election was relatively fair, and was evidently won by Yoruba businessman Chief Moshood Abiola. The annulment provoked angry reactions from a population weary of postponed transitions, lingering military rule, and the deception of rulers. Babangida could not resist public pressures to resign, but he did manage to handpick his successor, Ernest Shonekan, to head a weak civilian caretaker government. General Sani Abacha, who had been installed by Babangida as defense minister, soon seized power. He prolonged the now established tradition of military dominance, combining repression with frequent public promises to restore constitutional democracy. Like Babangida, Abacha announced a new program of transition to civilian rule and regularly delayed the steps in its implementation. He cracked down on political opposition, severely constricted civil liberties and political rights, and fomented corruption on a massive scale. Only Abacha's sudden death in June 1998 saved the country from certain crisis. General Abdulsalami Abubakar, Abacha's successor, quickly established a new transition program and promptly handed power to an elected civilian government led by President Olusegun Obasanjo and the People's Democratic Party (PDP) in May 1999.

The Fourth Republic (1999 to the Present)

Obasanjo was called out of retirement by the leaders of the PDP to run for president. Obasanjo, although a Yoruba, handed over power as military head of state in 1979 to the northerner Shehu Shagari at the dawn of the Second Republic. The northern political establishment then concluded that Obasanjo was a Yoruba candidate they could trust. In addition, many perceived that an ex-military leader could better manage the thorny task of keeping the armed forces in the barracks once they left power.

northern-dominated NPC), did little to reduce the mistrust between the various parts of the federation, or to stem rampant corruption. The NPN captured outright majorities in the 1983 state and national elections through massive fraud and violence. The last vestiges of popular tolerance dissipated, and a few months later the military, led by Major General Muhammadu Buhari, seized power.

General Sani Abacha, a prominent member of Nigerian military regimes since December 1983, took over the government in November 1993, disbanded all elective institutions, and suppressed opposition forces. His death in June 1998 was celebrated in the streets; he and his close supporters looted billions of U.S. dollars from the nation's coffers.
Source: AP Images.

Yet Obasanjo was initially unpopular among his own people, and he assumed the presidency in 1999 with few Yoruba votes in an election marred by irregularities at the polls. Nonetheless, he claimed a broad mandate to arrest the nation's decline by reforming the state and economy. Within weeks, he electrified the nation by retiring all the military officers who had held positions of political power under previous military governments, seeing them as the most likely plotters of future coups.

Obasanjo targeted the oil sector for new management and lobbied foreign governments to forgive Nigeria's massive debts. The minimum wage was raised significantly, a "truth and reconciliation" commission was set up to address past abuses, and commissions were formed to fight corruption and channel oil revenues back to the impoverished and environmentally ravaged Niger Delta region, where oil is extracted. Civil society groups thrived on renewed political freedom, and the media grew bold in exposing corrupt

practices in government. Despite this ambitious reform agenda, however, Obasanjo had political debts to his party, and his political survival, notably his bid for re-election in 2003, required that the anticorruption campaign left entrenched interests unscathed and corrupt politicians in place. Having surrounded himself with politicians he didn't trust, Obasanjo largely kept his own counsel. He was openly disdainful of the National Assembly and eventually faced three motions to impeach him. Avoiding impeachment, Obasanjo secured renomination from his party (the PDP) in the 2003 elections through a series of political accommodations with key party barons. The PDP political machinery engaged in widespread electoral malpractices, including rigged elections in the states of the Niger Delta and the southeast. Political deals and sharp election practices saved the president's second term and secured the PDP's dominance, but public confidence plummeted. Faced with increasing political turmoil and social conflict, the president called a National Political Reform

Conference in early 2005, ostensibly to review the constitution and the structure of the federation, with the unstated goal of shoring up his government's sagging legitimacy.

As the conference debated a variety of national issues, the media seized upon a document being circulated that quietly proposed the idea of amending the Constitution to remove the two-term limit on the president. This ploy provoked widespread outrage, leading to its collapse. Yet the following year another ploy to extend his term was submitted to the National Assembly, buried in a package of more than 100 constitutional amendments. Under enormous media scrutiny and public outcry, the Senate rejected the amendment package in May 2006. Even President Obasanjo, who had always maintained in public that he had nothing to do with the effort, felt compelled ironically to hail the defeat as a "victory for democracy."

Stymied by the legislature, the president's supporters moved to Plan B. A massively fraudulent election was planned for April 2007, with sufficiently blatant rigging and confusion to provoke the public into the streets in order to declare a state of emergency and allow President Obasanjo to stay in office. PDP dominance in the National Assembly, state legislatures, and governorships would also be assured. Meanwhile, the president chose a little-known, reclusive governor from the north with health problems to be his successor: Umaru Musa Yar'Adua of Katsina State, the younger brother of Obasanjo's (deceased) deputy head of state when he had been military leader (1976–1979). Obasanjo also had himself named "chairman for life" of the PDP's ruling board with the power to remove anyone from the party. If he could not extend his stay, as his supporters hoped, then he could at least try to manipulate the seemingly docile Yar'Adua from the background.

Yet Obasanjo misjudged both the Nigerian people and Yar'Adua. Despite local and international condemnation of the April 2007 polls, the public did not erupt, and Obasanjo had little choice but to hand power over to Yar'Adua in May 2007. President Yar'Adua, for his part, quickly demonstrated his independence and set out to gain control of the PDP and to restrain Obasanjo, reversing a number of Obasanjo's controversial decisions. The National Assembly soon instigated investigations into

Obasanjo and his associates, unearthing extensive corruption allegations against his administration, though he has yet to be prosecuted.

President Yar'Adua, however, remained burdened with a legitimacy gap from the sham 2007 polls, helped only partly by a split 4–3 decision of the Supreme Court in December 2008 upholding his election. Yar'Adua's first year and a half in office saw little action on the ambitious policy promises he made during the campaign; instead, he focused on solidifying his control of the PDP and on winning the court challenge to his election. As he gains success in both these objectives, it remains to be seen if he will then pursue the economic development, election reform, and rule of law agendas he promised at the outset of his term, or whether his administration will remain largely adrift amid infighting and continuing concerns about the president's health.

Themes and Implications
Historical Junctures and Political Themes

Federalism and democracy have been important strategies in Nigeria for realizing "unity in diversity" (the national motto), with the goals of building a coherent nation-state out of more than 250 different ethnic groups and blending democratic values with accountable government. In reality, the legacy of colonial rule and many years of military domination have yielded a unitary system in federal guise: a system with an all-powerful central government surrounded by weak and economically insolvent states.

When the military returned to the barracks in 1999, it left an overdeveloped executive arm at all levels of government—federal, state, and local—at the expense of weak legislative and judicial institutions. Unchecked executive power under the military, and a dominant executive under the civilians, has encouraged the arbitrary exercise of authority, accompanied by patronage politics, which sap the economy of its vitality, prevent accountability, and undermine the rule of law.

Since the return of democratic rule, the state governments, the National Assembly, and the judiciary have been whittling away at the powers of the national executive. The president, however, remains the dominant figure in Nigerian politics.

Nigeria in the World of States. Although Nigeria enjoys economic and military power within the West African region, on a global level, it is marginalized and vulnerable. Nigeria, with its natural riches, has long been regarded as a potential political and economic giant of Africa. Nigerian leaders have long aspired to regional leadership, undertaking several peacekeeping operations and an ambitious diplomatic agenda—through the United Nations, the African Union, and on its own—to broker peace initiatives and to foster democracy in some instances. Recent efforts include Sudan's troubled Darfur region, Cote D'Ivoire, and Zimbabwe. Yet the World Bank lists Nigeria among the poorest 20 percent of the countries of the world, with a GDP per capita of just over $300. Instead of independent growth, today Nigeria depends on unpredictable oil revenues, sparse external loans, and aid—a victim of its leaders' bad policies and poor management. Owing to neglect of agriculture, Nigeria moved from self-sufficiency in the production of basic foodstuffs in the mid-1960s to heavy dependence on imports less than twenty years later. Manufacturing activities, after a surge of investment by government and foreign firms in the 1970s, suffered from inefficiency and disinvestment in subsequent decades, sagging to levels not seen since independence.

Nigeria's economy remains dependent on oil. Years of predatory military rule made Nigeria a political and economic pariah in the 1990s, and deteriorating political institutions made the country a way station for international drug trafficking to the United States and for international commercial fraud. Although the most recent accession of democratic government ended the nation's political isolation, its economy remains subject to the vicissitudes of the international oil market. The government has been favored since 2003 by high oil prices and increasing U.S. consumption of Nigerian oil and gas, but there has been little effective restructuring or diversification of the petroleum monoculture so far. Nigeria is now again suffering the consequences of not addressing its oil dependence, as its projected oil revenues have dropped more than half as oil prices fell in late 2008 under global recession pressures.

Governing Nigeria's Economy. Nigeria's oil dependence is a symptom of deeper structural problems.

The very concept of the state was introduced into the colony in large part to restructure and subordinate the local economy to European capitalism. The Nigerian colonial state was conceived and fashioned as **interventionist**, with broad license to intrude into major sectors of the economy and society. The principal goals of the British colonial enterprise were to control the Nigerian economy and to marshal the flow of resources from the colonies to the metropole. A secondary concern was the creation of an economy hospitable to free markets and private enterprise. Nigeria's interventionist state extended its management of the economy, including broad administrative controls and significant ownership positions in areas as diverse as agriculture, banking, commerce, manufacturing, transportation, mining, education, health, employment, and, eventually, oil and natural gas.

After independence in 1960, Nigeria's civilian and military rulers alike expanded the interventionist state, which came to dominate all facets of the nation's economic life. Successive governments began in the late 1980s to reverse this trend, but privatization and economic reform have been piecemeal at best. President Obasanjo promised to sell off government interests in the telephone, power, and oil sectors, although the state remains by far the largest source of economic activity. His efforts to promote better macroeconomic management and to root out endemic corruption bore some results, but unemployment and poverty remain virtually unchanged, or worse in some sectors.

Democratic Ideas amid Colonialism and Military Rule. Colonialism introduced a cultural dualism—a clash of customs, values, and political systems—between the traditions of social accountability in precolonial society, and emerging Western ideas of individualism. These pressures weakened indigenous democratic bases for the accountability of rulers and responsibility to the governed, along with age-old checks on abuses of office. Although the colonial rulers left Nigeria with the machinery of parliamentary democracy, they largely socialized the local population to be passive subjects rather than responsive participants. Even as colonial rule sought to implant democracy in principle, in practice it bequeathed an authoritarian legacy to independent Nigeria. Military rule continued this pattern from 1966 to 1979 and again from 1983 to 1999, as juntas promised democratization yet governed with increasing severity.

This dualism promoted two public realms to which individuals belonged: the communal realm, in which people identified by ethnic or subethnic groups (Igbo, Tiv, Yoruba, and others), and the civic realm under the colonial administration and its successors in which citizenship was universal.[5] Because the colonial state and its "civic" realm began as an alien, exploitative force, Nigerians came to view the state as the realm from which rights must be extracted, duties and taxes withheld, and resources plundered (see Section 4), whereas morality was reserved for the ethnic or communal realm. Military regimes in the postcolonial era continued this pattern, and when they left in 1999, the democratic government faced the task of governing amid strong communal loyalties and an amoral civic realm.

In addition to suffering the burden of two public realms, the democratic idea in Nigeria has also been filtered through deep regional divisions. The British policy of indirect rule had profoundly different effects on the northern and southern regions. The south experienced both the benefits and burdens of colonial occupation. The coastal location of Lagos, Calabar, and their regions made them important hubs for trade and shipping activity, around which the British built the necessary infrastructure—schools (promoting Christianity and Western education), roads, ports, and the like—and a large African civil service to facilitate colonialism. In northern Nigeria, where indigenous hierarchical political structures were better established, the British used local structures and left intact the emirate authorities and Islamic institutions of the region. The north consequently received few infrastructural benefits, little Christian missionary activity, and its traditional administration was largely preserved.

A pattern of uneven development resulted, with the south enjoying the basis for a modern economy and exposure to democratic institutions and the north remaining largely agricultural and monarchical. These disparities between northern and southern Nigeria propelled northern leaders in the First and Second Republics to secure control of the federal government in order to redistribute resources to the north, while military rulers selectively colluded with northern elites

and manipulated their fears and weathered southern resentments.

Despite these setbacks, the democratic idea remained vibrant across Nigeria throughout even the darkest days of military rule, and it remains strong even as frustrations rise over the imperfections of the current democratic government. Nigeria's incredible diversity continually demands constant processes of negotiation and protections of interests that democracy promises, albeit after a difficult period of transition.

Nigeria's Fragile Collective Identity. This division between north and south is overlaid with hundreds of ethnic divisions across the nation, which military governments and civilians alike have been prone to manipulate for selfish ends. Four decades after the Biafran civil war, Nigeria often seems as divided as it was in the prelude to that conflict. Fears of another civil war rose during the mid-1990s.

These many cultural divisions have been continually exacerbated by the triple threats of **clientelism**, corruption, and unstable authoritarian governing structures, which together foster ethnic group competition and hinder economic potential.[6] Clientelism is the practice by which particular individuals or segments receive disproportionate policy benefits or political favors from a political patron (called "godfathers" in Nigeria), usually at the expense of the larger society. In Nigeria, patrons are often linked to clients by ethnic, religious, or other cultural ties, and these ties have generally benefited only a small elite. By fostering political competition along cultural lines, clientelism tends to undermine social trust and political stability, which are necessary conditions for economic growth. Clientelism thus reduces the state to an arena of struggle over distribution of the "national cake" among primarily ethnic clients rather than serving as a framework of governance.

Despite the prevalence of ethnicity as the primary form of political identity and the accompanying scourge of ethnic-based clientelism, the idea of Nigeria has taken root among the country's ethnic groups almost 50 years after independence. Most Nigerians enjoy many personal connections across ethnic and religious lines, and elites in both the north and the south have significant business activities throughout the country. Nevertheless, ethnicity remains a critical flashpoint that has led to localized ethnic violence on many occasions, and politicians continue to use ethnic identification to forward their political objectives, often divisively.

Implications for Comparative Politics

The saying that "as Nigeria goes, so goes the rest of sub-Saharan Africa" may again be relevant. With a population of more than 140 million growing at nearly 3 percent annually, Nigeria is by far the largest country in Africa and among the ten most populous countries in the world. One out of every five black Africans is Nigerian. Unlike most other countries on the continent, Nigeria has the human and material resources to overcome the vicious cycle of poverty and **autocracy**. Hopes for this breakthrough, however, have been regularly frustrated over five decades of independent rule. Moreover, smaller neighbors like Ghana and Botswana have managed to consolidate democracy and grow their economies. If Nigeria, with its vast resources, cannot succeed in breaking

this cycle, what does that mean for the rest of sub-Saharan Africa?

Nigeria remains the oldest surviving federation in Africa, and it has managed through much travail to maintain its fragile unity. That cohesion has come under increasing stress, and a major challenge is to ensure that Nigeria does not ultimately collapse. Nigeria's past failures to sustain democracy and economic development also render it an important case for the study of resource competition and the perils of corruption, and its experience demonstrates the interrelationship between democracy and development. Democracy and development depend on leadership, political culture, institutional autonomy, and the external economic climate; Nigeria has much to teach us on all these topics.

At this stage, it is uncertain whether Nigeria will return to the path of autocracy, underdevelopment, and fragmentation or continue on a course toward democratic consolidation and national construction. In the following sections, we will explore these issues and evaluate how they may shape Nigerian politics in the years ahead.

SECTION 2 Political Economy and Development

We have seen how colonialism bequeathed Nigeria an interventionist state and how governments in the postindependence period continued this pattern. The state became the central fixture in the Nigerian economy, stunting the private sector and encumbering industry and commerce. As the state began to unravel in the late 1980s and 1990s, leaders grew more predatory, plundering the petroleum sector, the nation's remaining source of revenues, and preventing the nation's vast economic potential from being realized.

State and Economy

Through direct ownership of industry and services or through regulation and administrative control, the Nigerian state plays the central role in making decisions about the extraction, deployment, and allocation of scarce economic resources. Any major economic activity involves the state in some way, whether

through licenses, taxes, contracts, legal provisions, trade and investment policy, or direct involvement of government agencies. The state's premier role in the economy arises from control of the most productive sectors, particularly the oil industry. Most of the nation's revenues, and nearly all of its hard currency, are channeled through the government. The discretion of leaders in spending those earnings, known as **rents**, forms the main path for channeling money through the economy. Consequently, winning government contracts—for supplies, construction, services, and myriad functions connected to the state—becomes a central economic activity, and those who control the state become the gatekeepers for many lucrative arrangements.[7] In most societies, access to the state and its leadership confers some economic advantages, but it can literally be a matter of life and death in impoverished countries like Nigeria. Those left out of these rent-seeking opportunities—perhaps seventy percent of Nigerians—must try to survive on petty trade and subsistence agriculture (the so-called informal sector of the economy) where taxes and regulation rarely reach. This informal sector accounts for about one-fifth of the entire Nigerian GDP, much of it earned through cross-border trade.

Origins of Economic Decline

In the colonial and immediate postcolonial periods, Nigeria's economy was centered on agricultural production for domestic consumption as well as for export. Despite the emphasis on exports, Nigeria was self-sufficient in food production at the time of independence. Vital to this effort was small-scale, local production of sorghum and maize in the north and cassava and yams in the south. Some rice and wheat were also produced. It was not until later in the 1960s that emphasis shifted to the development of nonfood export crops through large-scale enterprises.

Nearly exclusive state attention to large-scale, nonfood production meant that small farmers were left out and received scant government support. Predictably, food production suffered, and food imports were stepped up to meet the needs of a burgeoning population. Despite such government neglect, agriculture was the central component of the national economy in the First Republic. A combination of three factors effectively undermined the Nigerian agricultural sector.[8] The first was the Biafran War (1967–1970), which drastically reduced palm oil production in the east, where the war was concentrated. Second, severe drought in 1969 produced a famine from 1972 through 1974. Finally, the development of the petroleum industry caused a total shift in economic focus from agriculture to petroleum production. Agricultural export production plummeted from 80 percent of exports in 1960 to just 2 percent by 1980. To compensate for widening food shortfalls, food imports surged by 700 percent between 1970 and 1978.

With the 1970s boom in revenues from oil, Nigeria greatly increased its expenditures on education, defense, and infrastructure. The university system was expanded, roads and ports were built, and industrial and office buildings were constructed. Imports of capital goods and raw materials required to support this expansion rose more than seven-fold between

1971 and 1979. Similarly, imports of consumer goods rose dramatically (600 percent) in the same period as an increasingly wealthy Nigerian elite developed a taste for expensive imported goods.[9] By 1978, the Nigerian government had outspent its revenues and could no longer finance many of its ambitious projects; consequently, the government was forced to borrow money to make up the deficit, causing external debt to skyrocket.

The acceleration in oil wealth spurred increasing corruption, as some officials set up joint ventures with foreign oil companies and others stole public funds. Other officials simply stole public funds for their own benefit. The economic downturn of the 1980s created even greater incentives for government corruption, and the Babangida and Abacha administrations became infamous for avarice. Within three years of seizing power in 1993, General Abacha allowed all of Nigeria's oil refineries to collapse, forcing this giant oil-exporting country into the absurd situation of having to import refined petroleum. Abacha's family members and friends, who served as fronts, shamelessly monopolized the contracts to import this fuel in 1997. Elsewhere, outside the oil sector, small-time scam artists proliferated such that by 2002, Internet scams had become one of Nigeria's top five industries, earning more than $100 million annually.

In sum, the oil boom was a double-edged sword for Nigeria. On the one hand, it generated tremendous income; on the other, it became a source of external dependence and badly skewed the Nigerian economy. Since the early 1970s, Nigeria has relied on oil for more than 90 percent of its export earnings and about three-quarters of government revenues, as shown in Table 8.2. Hasty, ill-managed industrial and infrastructural expansion under both military and civilian regimes, combined with the neglect of the agricultural sector, further weakened the Nigerian economy. As a result, the economy was unable to compensate for the sharp fall in world oil prices after 1981 and descended into crisis.

From 1985 to the Present: Deepening Economic Crisis and the Search for Solutions

Structural Adjustment.   The year 1985 marked a turning point for the Nigerian state and economy. It

Table 8.2

Oil Sector Statistics, 1970–2008

	Annual Output (million barrels)	Oil Exports as Percent of Total Export	Government Oil Revenue (Naira millions)	Percent of Total Revenue
1970	396	58	166	26
1974	823	93	3,726	82
1979	840	93	8,881	81
1980	753	96	12,353	81
1981	525	97	8,563	70
1985	544	97	10,915	75
1987	464	93	19,027	76
1989	614	95	41,334	82
1993	720	91	162,102	84
1994	733	85	160,192	79
1998	700	90	248,500	70
2001	2,083	98	1,668,000	79
2002	2,068	94	1,884,000	80
2003	2,291	91	2,194,000	78
2007	2,166	95	6,734,000 ($56.12 billion)	80
2008 (est.)	2,010	95	9,637,000 ($80.31 billion)	80

Sources: Output is from *Petroleum Economist* (1970–1989); price index and exports are from IMF, *International Financial Statistics* (1970–1984), and from Central Bank of Nigeria, *Annual Reports* (1985–1989); revenues are from Central Bank of Nigeria, *Annual Reports* (various years). From Tom Forrest, *Politics and Economic Development in Nigeria* (Boulder: Westview Press, 1993), 134. 1990s statistics are from the Nigerian Federal Office of Statistics, *Annual Abstract of Statistics: 1997 Edition*, from the 1998 IMF *Annual Report*, and from Vision 2010, *Report of the Vision 2010 Committee: Main Report* (Abuja: Federal Government of Nigeria, September 1997). Nigerian Economic Summit Group, *Economic Indicators* (Vol. 8, no. 2, April–June 2002). Compilation and some calculations by Darren Kew.

ushered in Ibrahim Babangida's eight-year rule and revealed the economy's precarious condition. Within a year of wresting power from General Buhari in August 1985, the Babangida regime developed an economic **structural adjustment program (SAP)** with the active support of the World Bank and the IMF (also referred to as the **international financial institutions**, or **IFIs**). The decision to embark on the SAP was made against a background of increasing economic constraints arising from the continued dependence of the economy on waning oil revenues, a growing debt burden, **balance of payments** difficulties, and lack of fiscal discipline.[10]

The large revenues arising from the oil windfall enabled the state to increase its involvement in direct production. Beginning in the 1970s, the government created a number of parastatals (state-owned enterprises; see Section 3), including large shares in major banks and other financial institutions, manufacturing, construction, agriculture, public utilities, and various services. Although the government has since sold many of its parastatals, the state remains the biggest employer as well as the most important source of revenue, even for the private sector. By the 1980s, the public bureaucracy in Nigeria had swollen to more than 3 million employees (most employed by the federal and state governments), representing more than 60 percent of employment in the modern, formal sector of the economy.

Privatization, which is central to Nigeria's adjustment program, means that state-owned businesses would be sold to private (nonstate) investors, domestic or foreign. Privatization is intended to generate revenue, reduce state expenditures for loss-making operations, and improve efficiency. Expectations that privatization would encourage Nigerian and foreign investments in manufacturing have been largely disappointed. On a domestic level, Nigerian entrepreneurs have found that trading, government contracting, and currency speculation offer more reliable yields than manufacturing. Potential foreign investors remain hesitant to risk significant capital in an environment characterized by political and social instability, unpredictable economic policies, and endemic corruption. Only a few attractive areas such as telecommunications, utilities, and oil and gas are likely to draw significant foreign capital.

Economic Planning. Beginning in 1946, when the colonial administration announced the ten-year Plan for Development and Welfare, national plans have been prepared by the ministries of finance, economic development, and planning. Five-year plans were the norm from 1962 through 1985, when their scope was extended to fifteen years. The national plan, however, has not been an effective management tool. The reasons are the absence of an effective database for planning and a great lack of discipline in plan implementation. The state strives to dictate the pace and direction of economic development, but lacks the tools and political will to deliver on its obligations.

Nigerian and foreign business leaders revived dialogue with government on economic direction with the 1994 establishment of the annual Nigerian Economic Summit Group (NESG). This differed from previous planning efforts in that it was based on the coequal participation of government and private sector representatives. Two years later, General Abacha initiated the Vision 2010 process (see "Global Connection: From Vision 2010 to NEEDS"). Participants in Vision 2010 advocated reductions in government's excessive role in the economy with the goals of increasing market efficiency and reducing competition for control of the state. The Obasanjo administration accepted much of the Vision 2010 agenda at the outset of its first term, although it did not say so publicly because of the plan's association with General Abacha's predatory regime. Many of the private sector participants in Vision 2010 continue to meet regularly through the Economic Summit. Advice from the NESG continues to influence the economic policies of both the Yar'Adua administration and the National Assembly.

President Obasanjo opened his second term in office in 2003 with a renewed focus on economic reform and development. His appointment of a bold, reformist economic team won the praise of international financial institutions. Nigeria stabilized its macroeconomic policy, restructured the banking sector, and established a new anticorruption agency, the Economic and Financial Crimes Commission (EFCC). Since its foundation in 2003, the EFCC has indicted a cabinet minister, the inspector general of the police (the head of the nation's police force), and several governors. In addition, Obasanjo's finance minister fostered growth-oriented policies and other reformist ministers battled the federal government's notoriously corrupt bureaucracy to improve performance.

Unfortunately, many of these ambitious goals were followed by lackluster implementation, and President Obasanjo's efforts to extend his tenure in office soon absorbed much of his attention and a growing share of public funds. President Yar'Adua has also made little progress on continuing this agenda during his first year in office. Many problems must still be overcome in the economy: low investment, low capacity utilization, dysfunctional power supply, unreliable distribution, stifling corruption, and overregulation. Average annual GDP growth rates were negative from 1981 through 1987 and rose only moderately above the rate of population growth for the first five years that President Obasanjo was in office. Consumption and investment have also recorded negative growth (see Table 8.3). Buoyant oil revenues have helped to spur the economy higher since 2005, but poverty has not significantly diminished, and there remain basic questions about the sustainability of growth without a more diversified productive foundation, especially as the price of oil plummeted in late 2008. Plans under the NEEDS framework to spur growth outside the oil sector began to show promise after 2006, but it remains to be seen if this will be sustained.

Global Connection

From Vision 2010 to NEEDS

In the early 1990s, concerned with the nation's economic decline, a number of the larger Nigerian businesses and key multinational corporations decided to pursue new initiatives. With the involvement of then head of state Ernest Shonekan, they arranged the first Economic Summit, a high-profile conference that advocated numerous policies to move Nigeria toward becoming an "emerging market" that could attract foreign investment along the lines of the high-performing states in Asia.

Shortly after the first Economic Summit, however, General Abacha took control and continued the ruinous economic approach of Babangida's later years. The Economic Summit, meanwhile, continued to meet annually. After his flawed 1994 budget sent the Nigerian economy into a tailspin, Abacha was ready to listen to the summit participants. He accepted several of their recommendations, and by 1996 the economy began to make modest gains. Therefore, when key members of the summit proposed Vision 2010, General Abacha seized the opportunity presented and endorsed it in September 1996. Chief Shonekan was named the chair.

Through Vision 2010, the government pledged to adopt a package of business-promoting economic reforms, while business pledged to work toward certain growth targets consistent with governmental priorities in employment, taxation, community investment, and the like. Along with government and business leaders, key figures were invited to participate from nearly all sectors of society, including the press, nongovernmental organizations, youth groups, marketwomen's associations, and others. Government-owned media followed Vision 2010's pronouncements with great fanfare, while the private media reviewed them with a healthy dose of skepticism regarding Abacha's intentions and the elitist nature of the exercise. Vision 2010's final report called for:

- restoring democratic rule
- restructuring and professionalizing the military
- lowering the population growth rate
- rebuilding education
- meaningful privatization
- diversifying the export base beyond oil

- supporting intellectual property rights
- central bank autonomy

Whatever its merits, Vision 2010 was imperiled because of its association with Abacha. When the new Obasanjo administration took office in 1999 lacking a comprehensive economic plan of its own, however, it quietly approached Shonekan for the detailed recommendations and data produced by Vision 2010. Consequently, the general economic strategy and objectives of Vision 2010 are largely echoed in those of the current government. The Economic Summit, meanwhile, continues to provide annual assessments of the Nigerian economy and critical economic advice to policy-makers.

President Obasanjo repackaged and developed many of these goals into a new economic initiative for his second term, the National Economic Empowerment and Development Strategy (NEEDS). NEEDS lists several ambitious objectives for restructuring the Nigerian economy. First is government reform, particularly in terms of anticorruption, greater transparency, rule of law, and contract enforcement, which are all important political institutional supports for a properly functioning economy. Second, NEEDS seeks to spur private sector development through a renewed privatization effort, infrastructure development, agricultural support, and industrial expansion. In addition, NEEDS targets the development concerns of the nation's poor majority, through government assistance for Nigeria's ailing health, education, unemployment, and antipoverty programs. After announcing these efforts in 2003, the Obasanjo administration undertook some efforts to achieve them, fueled with annual GDP growth of 6 percent from the recent oil boom. Overall, however, NEEDS fell victim to the president's all-absorbing intent to stay in power, and he paid it little attention. Upon taking office in 2007, President Yar'Adua announced his intention to continue the thrust of the policy goals of NEEDS and Vision 2010, announcing his own Vision 2020.

Source: Vision 2010 Final Report, September 1997; Federal Government of Nigeria, the *National Economic Empowerment and Development Strategy*, March 2004.

Nigeria

Table 8.3

Selected Economic Indicators, 1980–2007

	Real GDP (Naira billions) (1993 = 100)	GDP (% Growth)	Manufacturing Capacity Utilization (%)*	Inflation Rate (%)
1980	96.2	5.5	70.1	9.9
1985	68.9	9.4	37.1	5.5
1990	90.3	8.1	40.3	7.4
1993	100.0	2.7	37.2	57.2
1995	103.5	2.2	29.3	72.8
1997	111.1	3.9	–	8.5
1999	114.4	1.0	–	6.7
2000	118.8	3.8	–	6.9
2001	123.5	4.0	–	18.9
2002	127.7	3.4	–	16.9
2003	133.1	4.2	–	13.5
2005	466.6	7.2		19.8
2007	789.0	6.3		4.8
GDP % Growth				
1976–1986	–1.3			
1987–1997	1.6			
1997–2007	3.98			

*Manufacturing capacity utilization is the average (across the economy) percentage of full production capabilities at which manufacturers are producing.

Sources: Vision 2010. *Report of the Vision 2010 Committee: Main Report.* Abuja: Federal Government of Nigeria, September 1997; World Bank, "Nigeria at a Glance," 1998 (www.worldbank.org), the 1998 IMF *Annual Report.* Nigerian Economic Summit Group, *Economic Indicators* (Vol. 8, no. 2, April–June 2002).

Perhaps Obasanjo's greatest economic achievement was paying off most of Nigeria's heavy foreign debt, which had exacerbated the nation's economic stagnation (see Table 8.4). President Obasanjo made debt relief one of his highest priorities on taking office in 1999 and promptly undertook numerous visits to the capitals of Europe, Asia, and the United States to urge the governments of those countries to forgive most of Nigeria's obligations. For a long time, his pleas fell largely on deaf ears as Nigeria's National Assembly showed little inclination to spend within the nation's means and the president himself showered funds on wasteful projects such as a half-billion-dollar soccer stadium. After persistent international lobbying, however, along with progress on economic reforms during Obasanjo's second term, Nigeria eventually secured an agreement for a substantial reduction of the country's

debt. In June 2005, the Paris Club of official creditors approved a package of debt repayments, repurchases, and write-offs that would effectively reduce Nigeria's external debt by 90 percent within two years.

President Yar'Adua has vowed to continue President Obasanjo's reforms, promising to declare a "state of emergency" on the power sector in particular, in order to address this most basic infrastructural need. He has also pledged to be the "rule of law" president to crack down on corruption, and has reversed some of the last-minute privatization deals that President Obasanjo awarded himself and his allies. Yar'Adua has also quietly allowed the National Assembly to investigate a host of corruption allegations against the Obasanjo administration, including more than $10 billion that was intended to improve the electricity supply. Yet he also hobbled the EFCC's anticorruption efforts and relies on

Table 8.4

Nigeria's Total External Debt (millions of US$; current prices and exchange rates)

Nigeria's Debt Compared to its Earnings:

	1976	1986	1996	1997	1999
Total Debt/GDP	3.7	109.9	72.0	63.1	83.8
Total Debt Service/Exports	3.7	28.4	15.2	15.9	204
		2000	2001	2002	2003
Total Debt/GDP		97.3	86.9	76.5	72.6
Total Debt Service/Exports		147.6	147	177.5	159.5
					2007
Total Debt/GDP					4.8
Total Debt Service/Exports					15.8

Sources: UNDP, World Bank, *African Development Indicators* (Washington, D.C.: World Bank, 1992), 159; UNDP *1998 Human Development Report;* World Bank, "Nigeria at a Glance," 1998 (www.worldbank.org). Nigerian Economic Summit Group, *Economic Indicators* (Vol. 8, no. 2, April–June 2002).

a number of corrupt figures to run his government, including one under investigation for money-laundering in Britain.

Social Welfare. Given the continued decline in its economic performance since the early 1980s, it is not surprising that Nigeria's social welfare has suffered greatly as well. Since 1986, there has been a marked deterioration in the quantity and quality of social services, complicated by a marked decline in household incomes (see Table 8.5). The SAP program and subsequent austerity measures emphasizing the reduction of state expenditures have forced cutbacks in spending on social welfare.

Budgetary austerity and economic stagnation have hurt vulnerable groups such as the urban and rural poor, women, the young, and the elderly. Indeed, Nigeria performs poorly in meeting basic needs: life expectancy is barely above forty years, and infant mortality is estimated at more than 80 deaths per 1,000 live births. Nigeria's provision of basic education is also inadequate. Moreover, Nigeria has failed to develop a national social security system, with much of the gap filled by family-based networks of mutual aid. President Obasanjo took an important step in meeting basic needs when he raised the minimum

wage nearly tenfold in 1999. Since wage levels had hardly been raised in years despite the inflation of the previous decade, the gains for workers with formal sector jobs were more meager than the increase suggests. Moreover, most Nigerians do not have access to formal sector jobs, and roughly 70 percent of the population must live on less than a dollar per day, while 92 percent of Nigerians live on less than two dollars per day.

The provision of health care and other social services—water, education, food, and shelter—remains woefully inadequate in both urban and rural areas. Beyond the needless loss of countless lives to preventable and curable maladies, Nigeria's neglect of the health and social safety nets will likely bear more bitter fruit. The nation stands on the verge of an AIDS epidemic of catastrophic proportions. The United Nations estimates that HIV infection rates are at 8.6 percent of the population and are likely to spread to 10 percent by the end of the decade, dooming perhaps 15 million Nigerians. Some states in Nigeria have already surpassed the 10 percent mark. The government has made AIDS a secondary priority, leaving much of the initiative to a small group of courageous but underfunded nongovernmental organizations. The Obasanjo administration began providing subsidized

Table 8.5

Index of Real Household Incomes of Key Groups 1980/81–1986/87, 1996, 2001 (Rural self-employed in 1980/81 = 100)

	1980/81	1981/82	1982/83	1983/84	1984/85	1985/86	1986/87	1996*	2001*
Rural self-employed	100	103	95	86	73	74	65	27	32
Rural wage earners	178	160	147	135	92	95	84	48	57
All rural households	105	107	99	89	74	84	74	28	33
Urban self-employed	150	124	106	94	69	69	61	41	48
Urban wage earners	203	177	164	140	101	101	90	55	65
All urban households	166	142	129	109	80	80	71	45	53

*Estimated, based on 1980/81 figures adjusted for a 73 percent drop in per capita GDP from 1980 to 1996, and an 18 percent increase in per capita GDP from 1996 to 2001. The FOS lists annual household incomes for 1996 as $75 (N 6,349) for urban households and $57 (N 4,820) for rural households, suggesting that the gap between urban and rural households is actually 19 percent closer than our estimate.

Sources: National Integrated Survey of Households (NISH), Federal Office of Statistics (FOS) consumer price data, and World Bank estimates. As found in Paul Collier, *An Analysis of the Nigerian Labour Market,* Development Economics Department Discussion Paper (Washington, D.C.: World Bank, 1986). From Tom Forrest, *Politics and Economic Development in Nigeria* (Boulder: Westview Press, 1993), 214. 1996 data from FOS *Annual Abstract of Statistics: 1997 Edition,* p. 80.

antiretroviral medications in 2002, but the UN estimates that these are reaching only about 17 percent of Nigerians who are HIV positive.

Society and Economy

Because the central government in Nigeria controls access to most resources and economic opportunities, the state has become the major focus for competition among ethnic, regional, religious, and class groups.[11] A partial explanation for the failure of economic strategies can be found within Nigerian society itself—a complex mix of contending ethnic, religious, and regional constituencies.

Ethnic and Religious Cleavages

Nigeria's ethnic relations have generated tensions that sap the country's economy of much-needed vitality.[12] Competition among the largest groups is centered on access to national economic and political resources. The dominance of the Hausa-Fulani, Igbo, and Yoruba in the country's national life, and the conflicts among political elites from these groups, distort economic affairs. Religious cleavages have also affected economic and social stability. Some of the federation's states in the north are populated mainly by Muslims, whereas others, particularly in the middle and eastern parts of the south, are predominantly Christian.

Government ineptitude (or outright manipulation), and growing Islamic and Christian assertion, have heightened conflicts between adherents.[13] Christians have perceived past northern-dominated governments as being pro-Muslim in their management and distribution of scarce resources as well as in their policy decisions, some of which jeopardized the secular nature of the state. These fears have increased since 1999, when several northern states instituted expanded versions of the Islamic legal code, the *shari'a.* For their part, Muslims feared that President Obasanjo, a born-again Christian, tilted the balance of power and thus the distribution of economic benefits against the north. The decline in the Nigerian economy also contributed to the rise of Christian and Muslim fundamentalisms, which have spread among unemployed youths and others in a society suffering under economic collapse. Disputes over economic and political issues have sometimes escalated into physical attacks on Christians, Muslims, and members of ethnic groups residing outside their ethno-religious homelands.

Since the return of democracy in 1999, many ethnic-based and religious movements have taken advantage of renewed political freedoms to organize around their interests and to press the government to address their grievances. Some mobilization has been peaceful, but many armed groups have also formed, at times with the encouragement or complicity of the mainstream political movements. In the oil-producing regions, these militias live off the pay they receive in providing security for oil "bunkering": illegal criminal networks (often including individuals in the oil industry, political leaders, and the military) that tap into pipelines, siphon oil, and resell it on the black market.

Youths from the Niger Delta minorities, primarily the Ijaw, have occupied Shell and Chevron facilities on several occasions to protest their economic marginalization. One spectacular incident on an offshore oil platform in 2002 saw a group of local women stage a peaceful takeover using a traditional form of protest: disrobing in order to shame the oil companies and local authorities. Some of these protests have ended peacefully, but since 2003 the number and firepower of the militias have increased, making the region increasingly militarized. The Obasanjo government periodically responded to these incidents and other disturbances with excessive force. After Ijaw militias killed several policemen in the village of Odi in late 1999, the military subsequently flattened the village, raping and killing many innocent people. Army units committed similar retaliatory atrocities in 2001 among villages in the Middle Belt state of Benue, when ethnic militias apparently killed several soldiers engaged in a peacekeeping mission during an interethnic dispute.

In the Niger Delta, the struggle of the minority communities with the federal government and multinational oil corporations has been complicated by clashes among the minority groups themselves over control of land and access to government rents. Fighting among the Ijaws and the Itsekiris near Warri in 2003 claimed more than 100 lives. Ethnic-based mobilization, including the activities of militias and vigilante groups, has increased across the country since the transition to civilian rule. Political leaders have sometimes built alliances with such groups and are increasingly using them to harass and even kill political opponents. These practices have reached a dangerous threshold in the Niger Delta, where an ethnic militia attacked a state capital in late 2004 and

forced the flight of the governor, who was originally instrumental in organizing the militia and used them to rig his reelection in 2003. Since that time, a host of new militant groups have arisen, engaging in oil bunkering and kidnapping to make money, and occasionally attacking oil installations. The largest such group, the Movement for the Emancipation of the Niger Delta (MEND), has repeatedly threatened to drive out foreign oil interests if their demands for a greater share of oil revenues are not met. The activities of MEND and other militants have forced more than a quarter of Nigeria's onshore oil operations to shut down through persistent attacks on offshore and onshore installations.

These divisive practices overshadow certain positive aspects of sectional identities. For example, associations based on ethnic and religious affinities often serve as vehicles for mobilizing savings, investment, and production, such as informal credit associations. Sectional groups such as the Igbo *Ohaneze* or the Yoruba *Afenifere* have also advocated more equitable federalism and continued democratic development. These groups, which form an important foundation of civil society, have continued to provide a vehicle for political expression while also reflecting the divisive pressures of Nigeria's cultural pluralism.

Gender Differences

Although the Land Use Act of 1978 stated that all land in Nigeria is ultimately owned by the government, land tenure in Nigeria is still governed by traditional practice, which is largely patriarchal. Despite the fact that women, especially from the south and Middle Belt areas, have traditionally dominated agricultural production and form the bulk of agricultural producers, they are generally prevented from owning land, which remains the major means of production. Trading, in which women feature prominently, is also controlled in many areas by traditional chiefs and local government councilors, who are overwhelmingly male.

Women have not succeeded in transforming their economic importance into political clout, but important strides are being made in this direction. Their struggle to achieve access to state power is a reflection of several factors. Women's associations in the past tended to be elitist, urban based, and mainly concerned with issues of trade, children, household welfare, and religion.[14] The few that did have a more political orientation have been largely token appendages of the male-dominated political parties or instruments of the government. An example of the latter was the Better Life Program, directed by the wife of Babangida, and its successor, the Family Support Program, directed by Abacha's wife. Women are grossly underrepresented at all levels of the governmental system; only 8 (of 469) national legislators are women.

Reflecting the historical economic and educational advantages of the south, women's interest organizations sprouted in southern Nigeria earlier than in the north. Although these groups initially focused generally on nonpolitical issues surrounding women's health and children's welfare, organizations like Women in Nigeria began to form in the 1980s with explicit political goals, such as getting more women into government and increasing funds available for education.

As in the south, northern women's NGOs at first focused on less politicized issues, but by the end of the 1990s, explicitly political organizations emerged such as the 100 Women Groups, which sought to elect 100 women to every level of government. Northern groups also showed tremendous creativity in using Islam to support their activities, which was important considering that tenets of the religion have been regularly used by Nigerian men to justify women's subordinate status. Women's groups in general have been more dynamic in developing income-generating projects to make their organizations and constituents increasingly self-reliant, compared with male-dominated NGOs that depend heavily on foreign or government funding.

Nigeria in the Global Economy

At the international level, the Nigerian state has remained comparatively weak and dependent on Western industrial and financial interests. The country's acute debt burden was dramatically reduced in 2005, but Nigeria is still reliant on the developed industrial economies for finance capital, production and information technologies, basic consumer items, and raw materials. Mismanagement, endemic corruption, and the vagaries of international commodity markets have largely squandered the country's economic potential. Apart from its standing in global energy markets, Nigeria has receded to the margins of the global economy.

Nigeria and the Regional Political Economy

Nigeria's aspirations to be a regional leader in Africa have not been dampened by its declining position in the global political economy. Nigeria was a major actor in the formation of the **Economic Community of West African States (ECOWAS)** in 1975 and has carried a disproportionately high financial and administrative burden for keeping the organization afloat. Under President Obasanjo's initiative, ECOWAS voted in 2000 to create a parliament and a single currency for the region as the next step toward a European Union–style integration. These lofty goals will take years of concerted efforts from the region's troubled governments to become a reality, and the lackluster results of past integration efforts do not bode well for success.

Nigeria was also the largest contributor of troops to the West African peacekeeping force, the ECOWAS Monitoring Group (known as ECOMOG). Under Nigerian direction, the ECOWAS countries dispatched ECOMOG troops to Liberia from 1990 to 1997 to restore order and prevent the Liberian civil war from destabilizing the subregion. Ironically, despite military dictatorship at home, Nigerian ECOMOG forces invaded Sierra Leone in May 1997 to restore its democratically elected government, a move generally endorsed by the international community. The United Nations assumed leadership of the operation in 1999, but Nigeria continues to contribute troops. Nigeria under President Obasanjo also sought to mediate crises in Guinea-Bissau, Togo, and Ivory Coast, and in Darfur (Sudan), Congo, and Zimbabwe outside the ECOWAS region.

Because it is the largest economy in the West African subregion, Nigeria has at times been a magnet for immigration. At the height of the 1970s oil boom, many West African laborers, most of them Ghanaians, migrated to Nigeria in search of employment. When the oil-based expansion ceased and jobs became scarce, Nigeria sought to protect its own workers by expelling hundreds of thousands of West Africans in 1983 and 1985. Many Nigerians now flock to the hot Ghanaian economy for work and to countries across the continent, including far-off South Africa.

Nigeria and the Political Economy of the West

Nigeria's global influence peaked in the 1970s at the height of the oil boom. Shortly after the 1973–1974 global oil crisis, Nigeria's oil wealth was perceived by the Nigerian elite as a source of strength. In 1975, for example, Nigeria was selling about 30 percent of its oil to the United States and was able to apply pressure to the administration of President Gerald Ford in a dispute over Angola.[15] By the 1980s, however,

the global oil market had become a buyers' market. Thereafter, it became clear that Nigeria's dependence on oil was a source of weakness, not strength. The depth of Nigeria's international weakness became more evident with the adoption of structural adjustment in the mid-1980s. Given the enormity of the economic crisis, Nigeria was compelled to seek IMF/World Bank support to improve its balance of payments and facilitate economic restructuring and debt rescheduling, and it has had to accept direction from foreign agencies ever since.

In addition to its dependence on oil revenues, Nigeria remains dependent on Western technology and expertise for exploration and extraction of its oil reserves. Nevertheless, oil can be an important political resource. For example, after General Babangida cancelled presidential elections in 1993, pressure by

Despite being sub-Saharan Africa's largest crude oil exporter, Nigeria faces chronic fuel shortages. General Abacha allowed the nation's four refineries to collapse, forcing the country into the absurd situation of importing fuel—through middlemen who gave enormous kickbacks to Abacha and his family. Shortages have resurfaced periodically since 1999. *Source: Jay Oguntuwase-Asope, The Guardian (Lagos), August 12, 1998.*

U.S. and European oil companies on their home governments ensured that severe economic sanctions on Nigeria were not imposed. The United States is now turning toward Nigerian oil to diversify its supply base beyond the Middle East, which should improve Nigerian government revenues but may not significantly alter the overall dependency of the economy.

Nigeria remains a highly visible and influential member of the Organization of Petroleum Exporting Countries (OPEC), selling on the average more than 2 million barrels of petroleum daily (although militancy in the Niger Delta has reduced this figure) and contributing approximately 8 percent of U.S. oil imports. Britain, France, and Germany each have more than $1 billion in investments. Nigeria's oil wealth and its great economic potential have tempered the resolve of Western nations in combating human rights and other abuses, notably during the Abacha period from 1993 to 1998.

The West has been supportive of the return of Nigerian leadership across Africa. Together with President Thabo Mbeki of South Africa, President Obasanjo was instrumental in convincing the continent's leaders to transform the OAU into the African Union (AU) in

2002, modeled on European-style processes to promote greater political integration across the continent. The AU's first item of business, largely promoted by Mbeki and Obasanjo, was to endorse the New Partnership for Africa's Development (NEPAD), through which African governments committed to good governance and economic reforms in return for access to Western markets and financial assistance. NEPAD remains a central element in Nigerian and South African foreign policy, but their hesitancy to apply pressure for reforms in important countries, such as Zimbabwe, has led to significant ambivalence toward NEPAD among Western governments.

Despite its considerable geopolitical resources, Nigeria's economic development profile remains harsh. Nigeria is listed very close to the bottom of the UNDP's Human Development Index (HDI), 142 out of 174, behind India and Haiti. Gross national product (GNP) per capita in 2001 was $300, less than 2 percent of which was recorded as public expenditures on education and health, respectively. These figures compare unfavorably with the $860 per capita GNP for China and $390 per capita for India.

SECTION 3   Governance and Policy-Making

The rough edges of what has been called the "unfinished Nigerian state" can be seen in its institutions of governance and policy-making. What seemed like an endless political transition under the Babangida and Abacha regimes was rushed through in less than a year by their successor, Abdulsalami Abubakar. President Obasanjo thus inherited a government that was close to collapse, riddled with corruption, unable to perform basic tasks of governance, yet facing high public expectations to deliver rapid progress. He delivered some important economic reforms over his eight years as president, but he gradually succumbed to the "Big Man," prebendal style of increasingly corrupt military rule, establishing his own clientistic networks and seeking to change the Constitution to allow himself to stay in power indefinitely. The Nigerian public, however, rejected his ambitions, providing his political opponents, civil society, and the media a

strong base to mobilize and force him to leave in May 2007. President Yar'Adua, like Obasanjo, came to power without a client network of his own and faced the same dilemma of whether he needed to build one in order to govern.

Organization of the State

The National Question and Constitutional Governance

After almost five decades as an independent nation, Nigerians are still debating the basic political structures of the country, who will rule and how, and in some quarters, if the country should even remain united. They call this fundamental governance issue the "national question." How is the country to be governed given its great diversity? What should be the institutional form of the government? How can all sections of the country work in harmony and none feel excluded or dominated by the others? Since independence, Nigeria has stumbled between democracy and constitutionalism, on the one hand, and military domination on the other. The May 2006 rejection of President Obasanjo's third-term gambit suggests that Nigeria may have turned a corner in terms of a growing respect for constitutional rule.

Since the amalgamation of northern and southern Nigeria in 1914, the country has drafted nine constitutions—five under colonial rule (in 1922, 1946, 1951, 1954, and 1960) and four after colonial rule: the 1963 Republican Constitution, the 1979 Constitution of the Second Republic, the 1989 Constitution intended for the Third Republic, and the current 1999 Constitution of the Fourth Republic, which essentially amended the 1979 version. Nigerian constitutions have suffered under little respect from military or civilian leaders, who have often been unwilling to observe legal and constitutional constraints. Governance and policy-making in this context are conducted within fragile institutions that are swamped by personal and partisan considerations. Perhaps sensing this shift in Nigerian political culture, Umaru Yar'Adua came to office promising to be the "rule of law" president. We will discuss these key elements of recent periods of military rule, their continued influence in the present, and the young institutions of the Fourth Republic.

Federalism and State Structure

Nigeria's First Republic experimented with the British-style parliamentary model, in which the executive (the prime minister) is chosen directly from the legislative ranks. The First Republic was relatively decentralized, with the locus of political power in the three federal units: the Northern, Eastern, and Western Regions. The Second Republic constitution, which went into effect in 1979, adopted a U.S.-style presidential model. The Fourth Republic continues with the presidential model: a system with a strong executive who is constrained by a system of formal checks and balances on authority, a bicameral legislature, and an independent judicial branch charged with matters of law and constitutional interpretation.[16]

Like the United States, Nigeria also features a federal structure comprising 36 states and 774 local government units empowered, within limits, to enact their own laws. Together, these units constitute a single national entity with three levels of government. The judicial system also resembles that of the United States, with a network of local and appellate courts as well as state-level courts. Unlike the United States, however, Nigeria also allows customary law courts to function alongside the secular system, including *shari'a* courts in Muslim communities.

In practice, however, so many years of military rule left a pattern of governance—a political culture—that retains many authoritarian strains despite the formal democratization of state structures. The control of oil wealth by this centralized command structure has further cemented economic and political control in the center, resulting in a skewed federalism in which states enjoy nominal powers, but in reality are nearly totally dependent on the central government. Another aspect of federalism in Nigeria has been the effort to arrive at some form of elite accommodation to moderate some of the more divisive aspects of cultural pluralism. The domination of federal governments from 1960 to 1999 by northern Nigerians led southern Nigerians, particularly Yoruba leaders, to demand a "power shift" of the presidency to the south in 1999, leading to the election of Olusegun Obasanjo. Northerners then demanded a shift back to the north in 2007, propelling Umaru Yar'Adua, a northern governor, into office, and southerners expect a return back by 2015, but to a different southern ethnic group than Obasanjo's. This ethnic rotation principle is not formally found in the constitution, but all the major political parties recognize it as a necessity so that Nigeria's many ethnic communities can feel that they have a stake in the federal government. Moreover, the parties practice ethnic rotation at the state and local levels as well, rotating those offices among local ethnic groups and subgroups in a similar fashion.[17]

This informal norm of ethnic rotation has built upon an older, formal practice, known as "federal character." Federal character calls for ethnic quotas in government hiring practices, and was introduced into the public service and formally codified by the 1979 constitution, although the armed forces have long observed such quotas. Although this principle is regarded by some as a positive Nigerian contribution to governance in a plural society, its application has also

Current Challenges

Federalism in Nigeria

The federal system has historically enjoyed wide support within Nigeria. With the "national question" unanswered, however, the federal structure endures increasing strain. At the conclusion of the civil war in 1970, many assumed that the question of national unity had been finally settled. Attempts to include clauses on the right to secede in the constitutions of 1979 and 1989 were roundly rejected by the drafting committees. Yet the most recent transition period featured a number of public debates about partition, particularly among the Yoruba and more recently in the Niger Delta, while other groups have continually lamented their political marginalization. Questions have also been raised as to whether Nigeria will continue to be a secular state and persist as a federation if it is to accommodate the country's ethnic, cultural, and religious heterogeneity.

To resolve these issues, some Nigerians have called for a national conference to review the basis of national unity and even to consider the restructuring of Nigeria into a loose confederation of autonomous states, perhaps along the lines of the First Republic. Such calls were ignored by the military, which foreclosed any debate on the viability of a united Nigeria, thus maintaining the geographic status quo. After resisting pressures for a national conference, President Obasanjo surprised the public by convening the National Political Reform Conference in early 2005, but it soon became clear that the president's primary intent was to amend the constitution to allow himself additional terms in office rather than to address ethnic self-determination concerns.

The establishment of the ethnic rotation principle—a "power shift"—by the end of the Obasanjo years, however, was a tremendously positive development in moving toward addressing the national question. Some critics have argued that a power shift is antidemocratic, meaning that it is antimajoritarian and encourages elite bargaining at the expense of public votes. Yet it also encourages elite accommodation and introduces greater predictability in the system, reducing the perception that control of political offices is a zero-sum game.

intensified some intergroup rivalries and conflicts. In recent years, there have been calls for the use of merit over federal character in awarding public sector jobs. (See "Current Challenges: Federalism in Nigeria.")

The Executive

Evolution of the Executive Function

In the Second Republic, the earlier parliamentary system was replaced by a presidential system based on the American model. The president was chosen directly by the electorate rather than indirectly by the legislature, based on a widespread belief that a popularly elected president could serve as a symbol of national unity. The framers of the Second Republic's constitution believed that placing the election of the president in the hands of the electorate, rather than parliament, would mitigate a lack of party discipline in the selection of the executive. The Second Republic's experiment with presidentialism lasted for only four years before it was ended by the 1983 coup. Although some Nigerian intellectuals call for a return to parliamentarism, the presidential model has become entrenched in the nation's political arena.

The Executive under Military Rule

The leadership styles among Nigeria's seven military heads of state varied widely. The military regime of General Gowon (1966–1975) was initially consensual, with major national decisions made by a council of officers from across the federation, but the head of state clung to power for several years after the war. His authority declined while he increasingly relied on a small group of advisers. Generals Muhammad and Obasanjo (during his first stint as head of state as a military ruler, 1976–79) governed through expanded collegial institutions, though their executive control was strengthened in practice. General Buhari, after ousting the civilian Second Republic, made no pretense of political transition, and instituted stern authoritarian control.

After a few years of relatively consensual governance, the Babangida regime (1985–1993) drifted into a more personalized and repressive mode of governance. Abacha (1993–1998) exceeded his predecessors in his harsh autocratic rule. General Abubakar, in contrast, moved quickly to relax political controls, institute a rapid democratization program, and curb the abuses of the security services. Nearly all military leaders talked of "transitions to democracy," though only Generals Obasanjo and Abubakar fulfilled the pledge of yielding power to an elected government.

Under military administrations, the president, or head of state, made appointments to most senior government positions.[18] Since the legislature was disbanded, major executive decisions (typically passed by decrees) were subject to the approval of a ruling council of high-level military officers. By the time of Abacha's Provisional Ruling Council (PRC), however, this council had become virtually a rubber stamp for the ruler. Given the highly personalistic character of military politics, patron-client relationships flourished during this period. The military pattern of organization, with one strongman at the top and echelons of subordinates below in a pyramid of top-down relationships, spread throughout Nigerian political culture and subcultures.

Having been politicized and divided by these patron-client relationships, the military was structurally weakened during its long years in power. Under Babangida and Abacha, the military was transformed from an instrument that guarantees national defense and security into another predatory apparatus, one more powerful than political parties. Four decades after the first military coup of January 1966, most Nigerians now believe that the country's political and economic development has been profoundly hampered by military domination and misrule. Within days of his taking office in 1999, President Obasanjo retired more than ninety military officers who had held political offices (such as military governorships) under the previous military juntas, seeing them as the most likely plotters of future coups. While there have been media reports of several coup plots, the military establishment has so far remained loyal and generally within its constitutional security roles.

In addition, President Obasanjo paid close attention to keeping the military professionally oriented—and in the barracks. U.S. military advisers and technical assistance were invited to redirect the Nigerian military toward regional peacekeeping expertise—and to keep them busy outside of politics. So far, this strategy has been effective, but the military remains a threat. President Yar'Adua entered office with a deep legitimacy gap after the botched 2007 elections, and although members of the officer corps were known to be angry over the debacle, they did not stage a coup. Public sentiments against military rule certainly helped to restrain such officers in 2007. If President Yar'Adua cannot deliver improved governance and economic performance, however, military entrepreneurs may be emboldened to take "corrective actions."

The Obasanjo Administration

President Obasanjo's first six months in office were marked by a number of initiatives to reform the armed forces, revitalize the economy, address public welfare, and improve standards of governance. Prominent among these priorities, the president sought to root out misconduct and inefficiency in the public sector. His initial appointments to manage the oil industry drew early praise for their clean management and contracting policies, and the persistent fuel scarcities of the Abacha years abated. Soon, however, familiar patterns of clientelism and financial kickbacks for oil licenses resurfaced. Obasanjo proposed an anticorruption commission with sweeping statutory powers to investigate and prosecute public officials. Delayed in its establishment, the commission had little impact, and was accused by detractors of being a political tool of the presidency. A second anticorruption commission founded in 2003, the Economic and Financial Crimes Commission (EFCC), has had an impressive record of indictments, as discussed in Section 2.

A major impediment to reform, however, came from the ruling party itself. The PDP is run by a collection of powerful politicians from Nigeria's early governments, many of whom grew rich from their complicity with the Babangida and Abacha juntas. With a difficult reelection bid in 2003, these fixers again delivered a victory for the president and the PDP, accomplished through massive fraud in a third of Nigeria's states and questionable practices in at least another third of the country.

The fraud in the 2003 elections undermined the PDP government's legitimacy and signaled to "Big Men" across Nigeria that any method to achieve power was acceptable in Nigerian politics. Shortly after the governor of Anambra state was "elected" in a race that was by all accounts rigged—President Obasanjo himself later publicly admitted as much—the governor sought to distance himself from the "godfather" who had rigged the election for him. After the governor was abducted and released by rogue police officers, Anambra was reduced to a war zone between supporters of the governor and those of his patron. Obasanjo and other PDP leaders sought to mediate, but, tellingly, the president refused to give the governor police protection or to arrest his political adversary.

President Obasanjo also appeared to have come out of the 2003 election convinced that he needed to build his own prebendal network if he were to govern and if he were to pursue his ambition to stay in office past two terms. He and his supporters soon moved to gain control of the PDP, offering benefits for loyalty and removing allies of rival Big Men in the party, particularly those of Vice President Abubakar Atiku. The president then signaled the EFCC to investigate his rivals, arresting some and forcing others to support his plans. When Obasanjo's third-term amendment was quashed by the National Assembly in May 2006, the president then had himself named "Chairman for Life" of the PDP, with the power to eject anyone from the party, even his successor as president.

Not surprisingly, President Yar'Adua spent much of his first year in office trying to gain some control over the PDP. He halted many of the last-minute privatizations of state assets into the hands of Obasanjo loyalists and replaced the chairman on the EFCC. The Yar'Adua administration also did nothing to prevent the National Assembly from instigating a series of investigations into the Obasanjo administration that unearthed massive corruption, including the discovery that more than $10 billion had been sunk into the power sector that had produced no results. President Yar'Adua has also assisted many of the PDP governors—ten of whom have so far had their elections overturned by the courts—to

retain their seats in rerun elections, thus building important alliances. By mid-2008, Yar'Adua appeared to have greater control of the PDP and Obasanjo seemed on the decline.

These developments demonstrated the continuing deficits of legitimacy for the government as well as the democratic system. As Nigeria's political elites continue to flout the rules of the system, it is inevitable that patronage, coercion, and personal interest will drive policy more than the interests of the public. President Yar'Adua has so far utilized the rule of law to strengthen his position, although his assistance for many of the governors has raised some questions. Will he too seek to be a "Big Man" and play prebendal power politics, or will he seek to strengthen the rule of law and democratic development?

The Bureaucracy

The bureaucracy touches upon all aspects of Nigerian government. The colonial system relied on an expanding bureaucracy to govern Nigeria. As government was increasingly "Africanized," the bureaucracy became a way to reward individuals in the patrimonial system (see "Current Challenges: Prebendalism"). Bureaucratic growth was no longer determined by function and need; increasingly, individuals were appointed on the basis of patronage, ethnic group, and regional origin rather than merit.

It is conservatively estimated that federal and state government personnel increased from a modest 72,000 at independence to well over 1 million by the mid-1980s. The salaries of these bureaucrats presently consume roughly half of government expenditures, which leaves less for the other responsibilities of government, from education and health care to building the roads. Several of President Obasanjo's progressive ministers undertook extensive reforms within their ministries, with some successes, but which the bureaucracy fought at every turn. President Yar'Adua has promised to continue civil service reforms, but has yet to undertake any systematic effort.

Semipublic Institutions

Among the largest components of the national administration in Nigeria are numerous state-owned enterprises,

Current Challenges

Prebendalism

Prebendalism is the disbursing of public offices and state rents to one's ethnic clients.* It is an extreme form of clientelism that refers to the practice of mobilizing cultural and other sectional identities by political aspirants and officeholders for the purpose of corruptly appropriating state resources. Prebendalism is an established pattern of political behavior that justifies the pursuit of and the use of public office for the personal benefit of the officeholder and his clients. The official public purpose of the office becomes a secondary concern. As with clientelism, the officeholder's clients comprise a specific set of elites to which he is linked, typically by ethnic or religious ties, and this linkage is key to understanding the concept. There are thus two sides involved in prebendalism, the officeholder and the client, and expectations of benefits by the clients (or supporters) perpetuate the prebendal system in a pyramid fashion with a "Big Man" or "godfather" at the top and echelons of intermediate Big Men and clients below.

As practiced in the Babangida and Abacha eras, when official corruption occurred on an unprecedented scale, prebendalism deepened sectional cleavages and eroded the resources of the state.

It also discouraged genuinely productive activity in the economy and expanded the class of individuals who live off state patronage.

As long as prebendalism remains the norm of Nigerian politics, a stable democracy will be elusive. These practices are now deeply embedded in Nigerian society and are therefore more difficult to uproot. The corruption resulting from prebendal practices is blamed for the enormous overseas flight of capital into private accounts. It seems that the lion's share of the $12.2 billion windfall of the early 1990s was pocketed by Babangida and senior members of his regime. General Abacha continued this pattern and diverted at least $5 billion from the Nigerian central bank, and President Obasanjo and members of his administration are now being questioned for the disappearance of more than $10 billion into the power sector alone. Transparency International regularly lists Nigeria among the most corrupt countries.

*Richard Joseph, *Democracy and Prebendal Politics in Nigeria: The Rise and Fall of the Second Republic* (Cambridge: Cambridge University Press, 1987), 55–68.

---

usually referred to as **parastatals**. In general, parastatals are established for several reasons. First, they furnish public facilities, including water, power, telecommunications, ports, and other transportation, at lower cost than private companies. Secondly, they were introduced to accelerate economic development by controlling the commanding heights of the economy, including steel production, petroleum and natural gas production, refining, petrochemicals, fertilizer, and certain areas of agriculture. Thirdly, there is a nationalist dimension that relates to issues of sovereignty over sectors perceived sensitive for national security.

Parastatals such as agricultural commodity boards and the Nigerian National Petroleum Corporation (NNPC) have been used to co-opt and organize business and societal interests for the purpose of politically controlling the economy and dispensing state largesse. It is not surprising, therefore, that one of the major requirements of the economic structural adjustment program discussed in Section 2 was the privatization of most of these enterprises.

Privatizing the parastatals was a central plank of the reform strategy under the Obasanjo administration. The telecommunications and power industries were put up for sale, and the administration promised to sell parts of the oil industry and privatize part or all of the NNPC. Open licensing in the telecommunications sector after 1999 ushered in a cellular phone boom that has revolutionized Nigerian society and made the country the fastest growing cellular market in the world. Privatization of the national landline network and the power industries, however, became patronage boondoggles rife with corruption, which the Yar'Adua administration is now investigating. President Yar'Adua also reversed the sales of oil refineries to Obasanjo cronies during his last days in office. Yar'Adua has also announced a plan to break the NNPC into smaller units, but he has to implement this plan. He did, however, appoint his brother, Abubakar Yar'Adua, as the NNPC's managing director.

Other State Institutions

Other institutions of governance and policy-making, including the federal judiciary and subnational governments (incorporating state and local courts), operate within the context of a strong central government dominated by a powerful chief executive.

The Judiciary

At one time, the Nigerian judiciary enjoyed relative autonomy from the executive arm of government. Aggrieved individuals and organizations could take the government to court and expect a judgment based on the merits of their case. This situation changed as each successive military government demonstrated a profound disdain for judicial practices, and eventually it undermined not only the autonomy but also the very integrity of the judiciary as a third branch of government.

The Buhari, Babangida, and Abacha regimes, in particular, issued a spate of repressive decrees disallowing judicial review. Through the executive's power of appointment of judicial officers to the high bench, as well as the executive's control of judicial budgets, the government came to dominate the courts. In addition, what was once regarded as a highly competent judiciary was undermined severely by declining standards of legal training as well as by bribery. The decline of court independence reached a new low in 1993 when the Supreme Court, in what some analysts labeled "judicial terrorism," endorsed a government position that literally placed all actions of the military executive beyond the pale of judicial review. The detention and hanging of Ken Saro-Wiwa and eight other Ogoni activists in 1995 (see Section 2) underscored the politicization and compromised state of the judicial system.

With the return of civilian rule in 1999, however, the courts have slowly begun to restore some independence and credibility. In early 2002, for instance, the Supreme Court passed two landmark judgments.

The first struck down a 2001 election law that would have prevented new parties from contesting the national elections in 2003—a decision that contravened the wishes of the president and the ruling party. The Court also decided against the governors of Nigeria's coastal states over control of the vast offshore gas reserves, declaring these to be under the jurisdiction of the federal government. Since the farcical 2007 elections, the courts have overturned ten gubernatorial races and a host of legislative contests, and the Supreme Court is reviewing the presidential election as well.

State and Local Judiciaries. The judiciaries at the state level are subordinate to the Federal Court of Appeal and the Supreme Court. Some of the states in the northern part of the country with large Muslim populations maintain a parallel court system based on the Islamic **shari'a** (religious law). Similarly, some states in the Middle Belt and southern part of the country have subsidiary courts based on customary law (See Table 8.1). Each of these maintains an appellate division. Otherwise, all courts of record in the country are based on the English common law tradition, and all courts are ultimately bound by decisions handed down by the Supreme Court.

How to apply the *shari'a* has been a source of continuing debate in Nigerian politics. For several years, some northern groups have participated in a movement to expand the application of *shari'a* law in predominantly Muslim areas of Nigeria, and some even have advocated that it be made the supreme law of the land. Prior to the establishment of the Fourth Republic, *shari'a* courts had jurisdiction only among Muslims in civil proceedings and in questions of Islamic personal law. In November 1999, however, the northern state of Zamfara instituted a version of the *shari'a* criminal code that included cutting off hands for stealing, and stoning to death for those (especially women) who committed adultery. Eleven other northern states adopted the criminal code by 2001, prompting fears among Christian minorities in these states that the code might be applied to them and creating a divisive national issue. Two thousand people lost their lives in Kaduna in 2000 when the state installed the *shari'a* criminal code despite a population that is half Christian.

Although the *shari'a* criminal code appears to contradict Nigeria's officially secular constitution, President Obasanjo refused to challenge it, seeing the movement as a "fad" that would burn out if left alone. The president was wrong about it burning out, but his refusal to challenge the *shari'a* proved wise in that it saved the nation from a deeply divisive policy debate, while the political and legal systems of the northern states have had time to adjust and adapt to the criminal code. In fact, although the *shari'a* systems in these states have created more vehicles for patronage, they have also opened up new avenues for public action to press government for accountability, policy action, and reform. In addition, women's groups mobilized against several questionable local *shari'a* court decisions to challenge them at the appellate level, winning landmark decisions that helped to extend women's legal protections under the code.

State and Local Government

State governments are generally weak and dependent on federally controlled revenues, as shown in Table 8.6. Nigeria's centralization of oil revenues has fostered intense competition among local communities and states for access to national patronage. Most of them would be insolvent and unable to sustain themselves without substantial support from the central government because of the states' weak resource and tax base. About 90 percent of state incomes are received directly from the federal government, which includes a lump sum based on oil revenues, plus a percentage of oil income based on population. The states and local governments, however, must generate more resources of their own to increase the efficiency of both their administrations and private economic sectors. In all likelihood, only

Table 8.6

Percentage Contribution of Different Sources of Government Revenue to Allocated Revenue, 1980–2009

	Oil Revenue Petroleum Profits Tax	Mining Rents and Royalties	Nonoil Revenue Customs and Excise Duties	Others
1980	58.1	25.7	12.3	3.9
1981	55.5	19.6	20.4	4.5
1983	35.7	33.4	18.9	12.0
1985	47.8	30.0	14.7	7.5
1987	50.6	25.4	14.3	9.7
	Oil Revenues (Combined)		Nonoil Revenue	Other
1992	86.2		8.4	5.4
1994	79.3		9.1	11.6
1995	53.2		8.1	38.7*
1996	51.1		10.6	38.3*
2001	79.7		17.6	2.7
2002	78.6		19.4	2.0
2003	78.1		19.9	2.0
2007	80.1		16.9	3.0
2009 (est.)	57.3		38.4	4.3

*Beginning in 1995, the Nigerian government began including surplus foreign exchange as federally collected revenue in its accounting.

Sources: Federal Ministry of Finance and Economic Development, Lagos. From Adedotun Phillips, "Managing Fiscal Federalism: Revenue Allocation Issues," *Publius: The Journal of Federalism,* 21, no. 4 (Fall 1991), p. 109. Nigerian Federal Office of Statistics, *Annual Abstract of Statistics: 1997 Edition.* Nigerian Economic Summit Group, *Economic Indicators* (Vol. 8, no. 2, April–June 2002).

the states of Lagos, Rivers, and Kano could survive without federal subsidies.

Major reforms in 1988 sought to strengthen the local government system and foster their independence from state governments. In practice, however, the federal government disburses state and local government funds directly to the state governors, who have utilized this fiscal control to force state legislatures and local governments into submission. Across Nigeria, most local governments have degenerated into prebendal patronage outposts for the governors to dole to loyalists, such that for the most part, they do little to address their governance responsibilities.

The federal, state, and local governments have the constitutional and legal powers to raise funds through taxes. However, Nigerians share an understandable unwillingness, especially those in self-employment, trade, and other informal sector activities, to pay taxes and fees to a government with such a poor record of delivering basic services. The result is a vicious cycle: government is sapped of resources and legitimacy and cannot adequately serve the people. Communities, in turn, are compelled to resort to self-help measures to protect these operations and thus withdraw further from the reach of the state. Because very few individuals and organizations pay taxes, even the most basic government functions are starved of resources,

and the states become more dependent upon federal oil wealth in order to function (see Table 8.7).

The return of democratic rule has meant the return of conflict between the state and national governments, much like during the Second Republic (1979–1983). The primary vehicle for conflict since 1999 has been a series of "governors' forums," one for the seventeen southern governors, one for the nineteen northern governors, one for each of the six zones, and one for all thirty-six governors. Ad hoc committees on specific issues have also arisen. Southern governors, and south-south zonal governors in particular, have been especially active in asserting greater legal control over the resources in their states (such as oil) and over the offshore oil and gas reserves.

A number of governors have turned to armed militias and vigilante groups to provide security in their states and to intimidate political opponents. Many of these groups were initially local responses to the corrupt and ineffective police force, or enforcers of the new *shari'a* codes in the north, but the governors have sensed the larger political usefulness of these groups. Consequently, political assassinations and violence increased as the 2003 and 2007 elections approached. Some of these militias in the Niger Delta or political thugs in other parts of the country have

Table 8.7											
Share of Total Government Expenditure (%)											
	1961	*1965*	*1970*	*1975*	*1980*	*1987*	*1992*	*1996*	*2001*	*2002*	*2008*
Federal Government	49	53	73	72	66	75	72	74	57	52.3	52.7
State Government	51	47	27	28	34	25	28*	26*	24	26	26.7
Local Government**	–	–	–	–	–	–	–	–	20	21.7	20.6
Total Expenditure (millions Naira)	336	445	1,149	10,916	21,349	29,365	128,476	327,707	1,008,780	1,111,950	2,748,000

*Note that 67% of state spending in 1992 and 49% of it in 1996 came from federal government oil earnings, part of which are allocated annually to all the states roughly in proportion to their population size.

**Local government expenditures are included in state government figures in 1961 and 1965, and federal figures from 1970 through 1996.

Sources: Central Bank of Nigeria, Annual Report and Statement of Accounts; Federal Office of Statistics, Abstract of Annual Statistics (Lagos: Federal Government Printer, 1961, 1965, 1970, 1975, 1980, 1987, and 1997). From Izeubuwa Osay-imwese and Sunday Iyare, "The Economics of Nigerian Federalism: Selected Issues in Economic Management," *Publius: The Journal of Federalism*, 21, no. 4 (Fall 1991), p. 91. Nigerian Economic Summit Group, Economic Indicators (Vol. 8, no. 2, April–June 2002). 1990s percentage calculations by Darren Kew.

grown independent and turned on their former masters, raising the spectre of local warlords that have ruined other African nations.

The Policy-Making Process

Nigeria's prolonged experience with military rule has resulted in a policy process based more on top-down directives than on consultation, political debate, and legislation. A decade of democratic government has seen important changes, as the legislatures, courts, and state governments have begun to force the presidency to negotiate its policies and work within a constitutional framework.

Military rule has left indelible marks on policy-making in Nigeria. Because of their influence in recruitment and promotions, as well as through their own charisma or political connections, senior officers often developed networks of supporters of the same or lower rank, creating what is referred to as a "loyalty pyramid."[19] Once in power, the men at the top of these pyramids in Nigeria gained access to tremendous oil wealth, passed on through the lower echelons of the pyramid to reward support. Often these pyramids reflect ethnic or religious affiliations (see the discussions of corruption in Section 2 and **prebendalism** in Section 3) such as the "Kaduna Mafia" of northern elites, but pyramids like the "Babangida"

or "Abacha Boys" included a patchwork of officers beyond their ethnic circle.

Because the military dominated Nigeria for three-quarters of its independent existence, civilian politics bears a strong resemblance to the politics of loyalty pyramids among the military.[20] Many of the current civilian politicians belonged to the loyalty pyramids of different military men—as bureaucrats, members of military cabinets, business partners to exploit Nigeria's oil wealth, and so on. Now that the politicians are in power, some of them former military officers, they are taking up the reins of the civilian portions of these pyramids, while they undoubtedly retain some influence with military figures.

Civilian policy-making in present-day Nigeria centers largely on presidential initiative in proposing policies, which are then filtered through the interests of the "Big Men." Invariably, their agendas conflict with those of the president and with each other, and policies are consequently blocked or significantly altered. Frequently, the reformist agenda is stalled or ineffectual. President Obasanjo's reforms took a back seat to his own concern for reelection in 2003 and then tenure elongation in 2006–2007. President Yar'Adua has promised his own reform agenda, but he has spent his first year primarily seeking to navigate and control the competition of interests among the Big Men of the political class.

SECTION 4 Representation and Participation

Representation and participation are two vital components in modern democracies. Nigerian legislatures have commonly been sidelined or reduced to subservience by the powerful executive, while fraud, elite manipulation, and military interference have marred the party and electoral systems. Consequently, Nigerian society has found modes of participation outside the official structures. An important focus of this section will therefore be unofficial (that is, extra-governmental) methods of representation and participation through the institutions of **civil society**. Formal representation does not necessarily enhance participation. In fact, there are situations in which the most important modes of political participation are

found outside institutional channels such as elections and legislatures—or even in opposition to them.

The Legislature

Not surprisingly, Nigeria's legislature has been a primary victim of the country's political instability. Legislative structures and processes historically suffered abuse, neglect, or peremptory suspension by the executive arm. Until the first coup in 1966, Nigeria operated its legislature along the lines of the British Westminster model, with an elected lower house and a smaller upper house composed of individuals selected by the executive. For the next thirteen years of military rule, a Supreme Military Council performed legislative functions by initiating and passing decrees at will. During the second period of civilian rule, 1979–1983, the bicameral legislature was introduced similar to the U.S. system, with a Senate and House of Representatives (together known as the National Assembly) consisting of elected members.

Election to the Senate is on the basis of equal state representation, with three senators from each of the thirty-six states, plus one senator from the federal capital territory, Abuja. The practice of equal representation in the Senate is identical to that of the United States, except that each Nigerian state elects three senators instead of two. Election to the Nigerian House of Representatives is also based on state representation but weighted to reflect the relative size of each state's population, again after the U.S. example. Only eight women were elected in 1999 to sit in the Fourth Republic's National Assembly. This reflects the limited political participation of Nigerian women in formal institutions, as discussed in Section 2.

Nigerian legislatures under military governments were either powerless or nonexistent. Even under civilian administrations, however, Nigerian legislatures were subjected to great pressure by the executive and have never assumed their full constitutional role. Since independence, the same party that won the executive has almost always managed to win the majority in the National Assembly and state assemblies—through coalitions at the federal level in the First and Second Republics, and outright majorities for the People's Democratic Party (PDP) since 1999. Consequently, the executive has been consistently able to influence legislators through executive powers, party machines, and even outright bribery.

This is the critical difference between the Nigerian and U.S. systems: in Nigeria, the president controls and disburses public revenues, which the Assembly only influences by its right to pass the budget. The U.S. Congress, by contrast, controls the public purse. The Nigerian constitution says that the National Assembly is supposed to control the public purse. In practice, however, the presidency receives the oil revenues first, and has consistently refused to place all of those revenues directly into the Federation Account as it is constitutionally obliged. Instead, the presidency typically disburses funds as it wishes, paying little attention to the budgets passed by the National Assembly. So far, the Assembly has yet to mount a sufficient challenge to take back its full constitutional prerogatives.

Given this history of executive dominance, the National Assembly that took office in 1999 began its work with great uncertainty over its role in Nigerian politics. With both the House and the Senate controlled by the PDP, along with the presidency, the familiar pattern of executive dominance of the legislature through the party structures continued. Legislators spent most of their time clamoring for their personal spending funds to be disbursed by the executive and voted themselves pay praises. Other legislators tested the waters for the first time with a variety of radical bills that never emerged from committee, including one that would have asked the United States to invade Nigeria if the military staged another coup. The president, meanwhile, referred to legislators as "small boys" and rarely accorded them the respect of an equal branch of government.

Gradually, however, the National Assembly began to fight back and gain some relevance. In annual budget negotiations, Assembly leaders struggled to resist presidential dominance. In August 2002, the House and the Senate, led by members of Obasanjo's own party, began impeachment proceedings against the president for refusing to disburse funds as agreed in that year's budget. However, the president continued to ignore budgets, leading to two subsequent—and unsuccessful—attempts to impeach him.

Perhaps the greatest victory for the National Assembly was when it rejected President Obasanjo's constitutional amendments in May 2006 that would have allowed him additional terms in office. The president, however, ensured that these victories for the institution came at a heavy price for its members: Nearly 80 percent of legislators elected in 1999 were not returned in 2003, and another 80 percent did not return in 2007—not because their constituents voted them out, but because they were removed in the PDP primaries, a process that President Obasanjo and the governors largely controlled. President Yar'Adua has so far shown greater respect for the National Assembly, refusing to intervene in its early leadership struggles and working within the budget passed by the legislature. Legislatures at the state level face a similar imbalance of power with the governors, who control large local bureaucracies and control the funds received from the federally shared revenues.

The Party System and Elections

An unfortunate legacy of the party and electoral systems after independence was that political parties were associated with particular ethnic groups.[21] The three-region federation created by the British, with one region for each of the three biggest ethnic groups (Hausa-Fulani, Yoruba, and Igbo), created strong incentives for three parties—one dominated by each group—to form. This in turn fostered a strong perception of politics as an ethnically zero-sum (or winner-takes-all) struggle for access to scarce state resources, which encouraged the political and social fragmentation that ultimately destroyed the First Republic and undermined the Second Republic. Unlike Ghana, Cote D'Ivoire, Mexico and, to some extent, India, Nigeria did not develop an authoritarian dominant-party system after independence, which might have transcended some of these social cleavages. Instead, multiple ethnic-based parties deepened existing social divisions.

In addition to the three-region structure of the federation at independence, Nigeria's use of a first-past-the-post plurality electoral system produced legislative majorities for these three parties with strong ethnic identities. During subsequent democratic experiments, many of the newer parties could trace their roots to their predecessors in the first civilian regime. Consequently, parties were more attentive to the welfare of their ethnic groups than to the development of Nigeria as a whole. Control of the center, or special political access, assured claims to substantial financial resources. In a polity as potentially volatile as Nigeria, these tendencies intensified political polarization and resentment among the losers.

In the Second Republic, the leading parties shared the same ethnic and sectional support, and often the same leadership, as the parties that were prominent in the first civilian regime. In his maneuvering steps toward creating the civilian Third Republic, General Babangida announced a landmark decision in 1989 to establish only two political parties by decree.[22] The state provided initial start-up funds, wrote the

constitutions and manifestos of these parties, and designed them to be "a little to the right and a little to the left," respectively, on the political–ideological spectrum. Interestingly, the elections that took place under these rules from 1990–1993 indicated that the two parties cut across the cleavages of ethnicity, regionalism, and religion, demonstrating the potential to move beyond ethnicity.[23] The Social Democratic Party (SDP), which emerged victorious in the 1993 national elections, was an impressive coalition of Second Republic party structures, including elements of the former UPN, NPP, PRP, and GNPP. The opposing National Republican Convention (NRC) was seen as having its roots in northern groups that were the core of the National Party of Nigeria (NPN).

Table 8.8 shows historical trends in electoral patterns and communal affiliations. As clearly outlined, northern-based parties dominated the first and second experiments with civilian rule. Given this background, it is significant that Moshood Abiola was able to win the presidency in 1993, the first time in Nigeria's history that a southerner electorally defeated a northerner. Abiola, a Yoruba Muslim, won a number of key states in the north, including the hometown of his opponent. Southerners therefore perceived the decision by the northern-dominated Babangida regime to annul the June 12 elections as a deliberate attempt by the military and northern interests to maintain their decades-long domination of the highest levels of government.

Old Roots and New Alignments: The PDP and the Other Parties of the Fourth Republic

Nigerians generally reacted with anger to General Abacha's 1993 coup and his subsequent banning of the SDP and NRC. With the unions crushed and Abiola in jail by the end of 1994, democracy deteriorated. In late 1996, the Abacha government registered only five parties, most of whose members had no public constituency and little political experience. During 1997, the five parties, branded by the opposition as "five fingers of a leprous hand," began to clamor for General Abacha to run for president. The presidential election scheduled for August 1998 was reduced to a mere referendum, endorsed by the chief justice of the

Table 8.8

Federal Election Results in Nigeria, 1959–2007

Presidential Election Results, 1979–2003

	Victor (% of the vote)	**Leading Contender** (% of the vote)
1979	Shehu Shagari, NPN (33.8)	Obafemi Awolowo, UPN (29.2)
1983	Shehu Shagari, NPN (47.3)	Obafemi Awolowo, UPN (31.1)
1993	M.K.O. Abiola, SDP (58.0)	Bashir Tofa, NRC (42.0)
1999	Olusegun Obasanjo, PDP (62.8)	Olu Falae, AD/APP alliance (37.2)
2003	Olusegun Obasanjo, PDP (61.9)	Mohammadu Buhari, ANPP (31.2)
2007	Umaru Yar'Adua, PDP (69.8)	Mohammadu Buhari, ANPP (18.7)

Parties Controlling the Parliament/National Assembly (Both Houses) by Ethno-Regional Zone, First to Fourth Republics

		Northwest	North-Central	Northeast	Southwest	South-South	Southeast
First	1959	**NPC**	**NPC** (NEPU)	**NPC**	*AG*	*AG*	NCNC*
	1964–65	**NPC**	**NPC**	**NPC**	NNDP* (AG)**	NNDP* (AG)**	NCNC
Second	1979	**NPN**	PRP **(NPN, UPN)**	GNPP **(NPN)**	*UPN* **(NPN)**	**NPN** *(UPN)*	NPP*
	1983	**NPN**	**NPN** (PRP)	**NPN**	*UPN* **(NPN)**	**NPN**	NPP**
Third	1992	**NRC**	*SDP* **(NRC)**	*SDP* **(NRC)**	*SDP*	**NRC** *(SDP)*	**NRC**
Fourth	1999	**PDP** *(APP)*	**PDP**	**PDP** *(APP)*	AD **(PDP)**	**PDP** *(APP)*	**PDP**
	2003	*ANPP* **(PDP)**	*ANPP* **(PDP)**	**PDP** *(ANPP)*	**PDP** AD	**PDP** *(ANPP)*	**PDP** (APGA)
	2007	*ANPP* **(PDP)**	**PDP** *ANPP*	**PDP** *ANPP*	**PDP** AC	**PDP**	**PDP** PPA

Boldfaced: Ruling party

Italicized: Leading opposition

*: Coalition with ruling party

**: Coalition with opposition

National Assembly and State-Level Elections

Senate	1999	2003
PDP	63	73
APP/ANPP	26	28
AD	20	6

House	1999	2003
PDP	214	213
APP/ANPP	77	95
AD	69	31
Other		7

Table 8.8 (continued)

Federal Election Results in Nigeria, 1959–2007

Governorships	1999	2003
PDP	21	28
APP/ANPP	9	7
AD	6	1
State Houses of Assembly	*1999*	*2003*
PDP	23	28
APP/ANPP	8	7
AD	5	1

2007 election results:

Parties	House of Representatives		Senate	
	Votes %	Seats	Votes %	Seats
People's Democratic Party	54.5	223	53.7	76
All Nigeria People's Party	27.4	96	27.9	27
Action Congress	8.8	34	9.7	6
Others	2.8	7	2.7	–

Governorships		State Assemblies	
26	PDP	28	PDP
5	ANPP	5	ANPP
2	PPA	1	PPA
2	AC	2	AC
1	APGA		

List of Acronyms Used in Table 8.8

AC	Action Congress	NPN	National Party of Nigeria
AG	Action Group	NPP	Nigerian People's Party
AD	Alliance for Democracy	NRC	National Republican Convention
ANPP	All Nigerian People's Party (formerly APP)	PPA	Progress People's Alliance
APGA	Alll People's Grand Alliance	PRP	People's Redemption Party
APP	All People's Party	PDP	People's Democratic Party
GNPP	Great Nigerian People's Party	SDP	Social Democratic Party
NAP	Nigerian Advance Party	UPN	Unity Party of Nigeria
NCNC	National Convention of Nigerian Citizens (formerly National Council of Nigeria and the Cameroons)		
NEPU	Northern Elements Progressive Union		
NNDP	Nigerian National Democratic Party		
NPC	Northern People's Congress		
NPF	Northern Progressive Front		

Supreme Court as legally permissible. The "transition" process had become a travesty.[24] Once Abacha's plan to be certified as president became a certainty, domestic opposition increased. A group of former governors and political leaders from the north (many former NPN and PRP members) publicly petitioned Abacha not to run for president and human rights and prodemocracy groups protested. Even General Babangida voiced his opposition to Abacha's continuing as president. The only real obstacle to Abacha's plan for "self-succession" was whether the military would allow it.

Although there had been frequent rumors of Abacha's ill health, his death on June 8, 1998, was still a great surprise. The following day, General Abubakar, chief of Defense Staff, was sworn in as head of state. Shortly afterward, he promised a speedy transition to democracy and began releasing political prisoners. There were immediate calls for Chief Abiola's release and his appointment to head an interim government of national unity. Abiola's fatal heart attack a month after Abacha's death raised considerable suspicion. New parties quickly formed, and even Yoruba political leaders agreed to participate, although they insisted that the next president should be a Yoruba to compensate their people for having been robbed of their first elected presidency.

Once again, political associations centered on well-known personalities, and intense bargaining and mergers took place. The G-34, the prominent group of civilian leaders who had condemned Abacha's plans to perpetuate his power, created the People's Democratic Party (PDP) in late August, minus most of their Yoruba members, who joined the Alliance for Democracy (AD). At least twenty more parties applied for certification to the electoral commission (INEC); many of them were truly grass-roots movements, including a human rights organization and a trade union party.

To escape the ethnic-based parties of the First and Second Republics, INEC required that parties earn at least 5 percent of the votes in twenty-four of the thirty-six states in local government elections in order to advance to the later state and federal levels. This turned out to be an ingenious way of reducing the number of parties, while obliging viable parties to broaden their appeal. The only parties to meet INEC's requirements were the PDP, AD, and the All People's Party (APP). In order to assuage the Yoruba over Abiola's lost 1993 mandate, the Big Men of the PDP turned to retired General Obasanjo, who went on to defeat an AD/APP alliance candidate in the presidential contest in February 1999.

The parties of the Fourth Republic are primarily alliances of convenience among Big Men from across Nigeria. Their sole purpose is to gain power. They have no ideological differences or policy platforms that distinguish them, such that politicians who lose in one party will frequently shift to another. Yet these parties do feature one terribly important innovation that distinguishes them from those of the First and Second Republics: the PDP, APP (now ANPP), and other leading parties of the Fourth Republic are multiethnic. They rely on elite-centered structures established during previous civilian governments and transition programs, and demonstrate the cross-ethnic alliances that developed over the last quarter-century, particularly through the two mega-parties of the Third Republic. The PDP includes core members of the northern established NPN, the northern progressive PRP, and the Igbo-dominated NPP of the Second Republic, as well as prominent politicians from the Niger Delta. The APP (now ANPP) is also a multiethnic collection, drawing from the Second Republic's GNPP, a party dominated by the northeastern-based Kanuri and groups from the Middle Belt, and also features politicians who had prominent roles in the Abacha-sponsored parties. The ANPP also includes northwestern politicians of royal lineage, Igbo business moguls, and southern minority leaders. The AD, however, was as Yoruba-centered as its predecessors, the UPN in the Second Republic and the AG in the First Republic. The party would later pay at the polls for its lack of national appeal, however, and would join with breakaway factions of the PDP to form the Action Congress (AC—see below).

This rise of multiethnic political parties is one of the most significant democratic developments of the Fourth Republic. In multiethnic parties there is a strong incentive for politicians to bargain and bridge their ethnic differences *within* the party, so that they may then compete with the other parties in the system, which would preferably be multiethnic as well.[25] In Nigeria, ethnic divisions—supported by prebendal networks—still dominate national politics, but the multiethnic parties have at least done fairly well at bridging these many divides during election periods and at fostering a climate of compromise during particularly divisive national debates. Greasing the wheels of these compromises among the elites, however, are preferential treatment in access to public offices, government contracts, and the corrupt spoils of oil wealth. In short, multiethnic parties have widened the circle of corruption, allowing the biggest politicians to build vast patronage networks across ethnic lines and diluting—but not erasing—the ethnocentric aspects of the prebendal system. Lower ethnic tensions have come at the price of greater elite corruption, which may be seen as progress if compared to the ethnically charged political climate that led to the 1967–1970 civil war, but which must transition to more accountable party politics if the 92 percent of Nigerians who live on less than $2 per day are to share in the nation's great wealth.

The main vehicle whereby other African countries like Ghana have begun to rise out this elite corruption trip is through the rise of a unified, viable political opposition, which has not developed in Nigeria. With tight control of government and its largess, the PDP extended its majorities in the largely compromised elections of 2003 and the farcical elections of 2007. Thus, the Fourth Republic has enjoyed no real opposition movement at the national level and in most of the states.

Complicating matters has been an explosion in the number of political parties. Late in 2002, the Supreme Court overruled the INEC's restrictive policies on registering parties, and dozens of new parties were permitted to contest the 2003 elections. By 2007, more than forty parties were contesting offices across Nigeria, leading to a confusing presidential ballot for the nation's voters, half of whom are illiterate. The two main opposition parties, the ANPP and AD, never organized a working relationship or a serious policy challenge to the PDP, except in the weeks prior to elections. ANPP leaders generally preferred to work with the PDP in order to gain access to government largesse, and some of its leaders joined the PDP as the 2007 elections approached. The AD was more outspoken in its opposition to the PDP, but did little for most of its constituents in the six Yoruba states it won in 1999. AD declined to nominate a 2003 presidential candidate

in exchange for a PDP promise not to mount serious challenges against other AD candidates in the Yoruba region. The PDP, however, reneged on the backroom deal and defeated the AD at all levels in five of the six southwestern states in 2003. With seven ANPP governors, one AD governor, and a small number of National Assembly legislators among them, many of whom were willing to strike personal deals with the PDP, opposition parties in Nigeria were reduced to the margins of national politics.

Hopes for a viable opposition initially revived as the 2007 elections approached. Vice President Abubakar Atiku, who led one of the largest factions within the PDP, fell out with President Obasanjo. The president moved quickly to remove Atiku allies from leadership roles in the PDP. The Vice President then played an important role in rallying his allies in the National Assembly to reject Obasanjo's term extension amendments in May 2006. Thereafter, Obasanjo relentlessly pursued Atiku to ensure that he would not become president in 2007, hounding Atiku and his supporters with the EFCC through endless corruption investigations and court battles that kept Atiku off the ballot until it was far too late for him to mobilize a serious campaign. Extraordinarily, Obasanjo and Atiku even leveled specific allegations of massive corruption at each other, backed with evidence submitted to the courts.

As it became clear that President Obasanjo would never allow Atiku to gain the 2007 PDP nomination for president, Atiku and many of his PDP supporters defected to a new party that merged with the remnants of the AD, called the Action Congress (AC). Initially, it appeared that as many as 15 PDP governors might bolt for the AC, forming a mighty opposition party, especially if it allied with the ANPP. Soon thereafter, however, the EFCC announced that it was investigating a stunning thirty-one of the nation's thirty-six governors—a clear message that Obasanjo was ready to go after anyone that opposed him or supported Atiku. Given the massive rigging of the election and the fact that Vice President Atiku was never allowed to mount a serious campaign effort, we have no idea what the public's true preferences may have been. The Nigerian opposition is weak and divided.

The PDP thus took power again in 2007 with a massive majority across Nigeria, controlling the presidency, twenty-seven governorships and state assemblies, and more than two-thirds of the seats of the National Assembly. Yet it was also a party in disarray. With Obasanjo out of the presidency, his enemies soon moved to undermine his new position as Chairman for Life of the Board of Trustees of the PDP, from which Obasanjo fought back. With ten PDP governorships annulled by election tribunals and reruns required, meanwhile, local PDP factions returned to feuding. Amid this infighting, President Yar'Adua moved quietly to assert control of the party, helping many of the new governors to "win" their election reruns through an unreformed INEC, and methodically removing Obasanjo allies from leadership positions.

Political Culture, Citizenship, and Identity

Military rule left Nigeria with strong authoritarian influences in its political culture. Most of the younger politicians of the Fourth Republic came of age during military rule and naturally learned the business of politics from Abacha, Babangida, and their military governors. Nigeria's deep democratic traditions discussed in Section 1 remain vibrant among the larger polity, but they are in constant tension with the values imbibed during years of governance when political problems were often solved by military dictate, power, and violence rather than by negotiation and respect for law. This tension was manifest in the irony that the leading presidential contenders in 2003 were all former military men, one of whom—Buhari—was the ringleader of the 1983 coup that overthrew the Second Republic. Perhaps symbolic of a growing shift in Nigerian political culture away from its authoritarian past, however, Umaru Yar'Adua is the nation's first university graduate to become president.

Modernity versus Traditionalism

The terrain of political culture, citizenship, and identity is a contested arena within Nigeria. The interaction of Western (colonial) elements with traditional (precolonial, African) practices has created the tensions of a modern sociopolitical system that rests uneasily on traditional foundations. Nigerians straddle two worlds, each undergoing constant evolution. On one hand, the strong elements in communal societies that promoted accountability have been weakened by the intrusion of Western culture oriented toward individuality, and exacerbated by urbanization. On the other hand, the modern state has been unable to free itself fully from rival ethnic claims organized around narrow, exclusivist constituencies.

As a result, exclusivist identities continue to dominate Nigerian political culture and to define the nature of citizenship.[26] Individuals tend to identify with their immediate ethnic, regional, and religious (or subethnic, subregional, and subreligious) groups rather than with state institutions, especially during moments of crisis. Entirely missing from the relationship between state and citizen in Nigeria is a fundamental reciprocity—a working social contract—based on the belief that there is a common interest that binds them.

Religion

Religion has been a persistent source of comfort and a basis for conflict throughout Nigerian history. Islam began to filter into northeast Nigeria in the eleventh and twelfth centuries, spread to Hausaland by the fifteenth century, and greatly expanded in the early nineteenth century. In the north, Islam first coexisted with, then gradually supplanted, indigenous religions. Christianity arrived in the early nineteenth century, but expanded rapidly through missionary activity in the south. The amalgamation of northern and southern Nigeria in 1914 brought together the two regions and their belief systems. The nation is now evenly divided between Muslims and Christians.

These religious cultures have consistently clashed over political issues such as the secular character of the state. The application of the *shari'a* criminal code in the northern states has been a focal point for these tensions. For many Muslims, the *shari'a* represents a way of life and supreme (personal) law that transcends secular and state law; for many Christians, the expansion of *shari'a* law threatens the secular nature of the Nigerian state and their position within it. The pull of religious versus national identity becomes even stronger in times of economic hardship, as today, despite the massive oil revenues.

The Press

The plural nature of Nigerian society, with the potential to engender a shared political culture, can be seen in virtually all aspects of public life. The Nigerian press has long been one of the liveliest and most irreverent in Africa. The Abacha regime moved to stifle its independence, as had Babangida. In addition, members of the media are sometimes regarded as captives of ethnic and regional constituencies, which has weakened their capacity to resist attacks on their rights and privileges. Significantly, much of the Nigerian press has been based in a Lagos-Ibadan axis in the southwestern part of Nigeria and has frequently been labeled "southern." Recently, however, independent television and radio stations have proliferated around the country, and forests of satellite towers now span Nigerian cities to support the boom in Internet cafés and telecommunications. Internet-based investigative journalists such as www.saharareporters.com have utilized the uncensored medium of the Internet to print stories that the mainstream newspapers have been afraid to publish, exposing the corrupt activities of some of Nigeria's biggest politicians.

Interests, Social Movements, and Protest

Because the political machinery was in the hands of the military over the 1980s and 1990s, Nigerians sought alternative means of representation and protest. Historically, labor has played a significant role in Nigerian politics, as have student groups, women's organizations, and various radical and populist organizations. Business groups have frequently supported and colluded with corrupt civilian and military regimes. In the last year of the Abacha regime, however, even the business class, through mechanisms like Vision 2010, began to suggest an end to such arbitrary rule. The termination of military rule has seen civil society groups flourish across Nigeria.

Labor

Organized labor has played an important role in challenging governments during both the colonial and postcolonial eras in several African countries, Nigeria among them. Continuous military pressure throughout the 1980s and 1990s forced a decline in the independence and strength of organized labor in Nigerian politics. The Babangida regime implemented strategies of **state corporatism** designed to control and co-opt various social forces such as labor. When the leadership of the Nigerian Labour Congress (NLC), the umbrella confederation, took a vigorous stand against the government, the regime sacked the leaders and appointed conservative replacements. Prodemocracy strikes in mid-1994 by the National Petroleum Employees Union (NUPENG) and other sympathetic labor groups significantly reduced oil production and nearly brought the country to a halt, whereupon the Abacha regime arrested and disbanded its leadership.

The Nigerian labor movement has been vulnerable to reprisals by the state and private employers. The government has always been the biggest single employer of labor in Nigeria, as well as the recognized arbiter of industrial relations between employers and employees. Efforts by military regimes to centralize and co-opt the unions caused their militancy and impact to wane. Moreover, ethnic, regional, and religious divisions have often hampered labor solidarity, and these differences have been periodically manipulated by the state. Nevertheless, labor still claims an estimated 2 million members across Nigeria and remains one of the most potent forces in civil society. The unions have a great stake in the consolidation of constitutional rule in the Fourth Republic and the protections that allow them to organize and act freely on behalf of their members. Given the strength of the NLC, the PDP has sought to break it into its constituent unions to dilute its impact, but has so far been unsuccessful.

The Business Community

Nigeria has a long history of entrepreneurialism and business development. This spirit is compromised by tendencies toward rent-seeking and the appropriation of state resources. Members of the Nigerian business class have been characterized as "pirate capitalists" because of the high level of corrupt practices and collusion with state officials.[27] Many wealthy individuals have served in the military or civilian governments, while others protect their access to state resources by sponsoring politicians or entering into business arrangements with bureaucrats.

Private interests have proven surprisingly resilient, as organized groups have emerged to represent the interests of the business class and to promote general economic development. There are numerous associations throughout Nigeria representing a broad variety of business activities and sectoral interests. National business associations, such as the Nigerian Association of Chambers of Commerce, Industry, Mines, and Agriculture (NACCIMA), the largest in the country, have taken an increasingly political stance, expressing their determination to protect their interests by advocating for better governance.

Other Social Groups

Student activism continues to be an important feature of Nigerian political life. Since the 1990s, many universities have seen the rise of what are called "cults"—gangs of young men who are typically armed and sometimes do have cultish rituals associated with their groups. Many of these cultists "graduated" to join the militias and thugs of the politicians in this decade, while the cults are also often employed by elites for their power plays. In partial response to the cult phenomenon, religious movements have proliferated across Nigerian universities, providing students with an alternative way of life to these violent groups. Yet the religious groups on campuses have also provided vehicles for encouraging and recruiting both Christian and Muslim fundamentalists.

Growing restiveness over economic hardship and military oppression led to a sharp increase in the number of human rights groups and other nongovernmental organizations (NGOs) since the 1990s.[28] Greater funding for NGOs from foreign governments and private foundations assisted the growth of this sector, most notably in the south but gradually in the north as well. They have generally focused on such issues as civil protection (and since 2000, on a Freedom of Information Act), gender law, health care, media access, and public housing. Most are urban based, although efforts to develop rural networks are underway.

The movement to resist President Obasanjo's third-term bid in May 2006 resurrected some of civil society's previous level of alliance building, as did some of the labor-led protests to Obasanjo's many—and often successful—efforts to raise the price of fuel. Civil society groups also condemned Obasanjo's efforts to provoke an election crisis in 2007, but faced a quandary: if they organized protests to the flawed elections, they might give Obasanjo the excuse he needed to declare a state of emergency. Consequently, few groups resisted the election outcomes, preferring to accept Yar'Adua in order to get rid of Obasanjo, and to fight the more flagrant election violations at the tribunals.

Overall, civil society groups are making substantial contributions to consolidating democracy in Nigeria. In particular, many groups have built good working relationships with the National Assembly and state legislatures, from which both sides have benefited. Their relationships with the political parties, however, remain distant. Nigeria's prospects for building a sustainable democracy during the Fourth Republic will depend, in part, on the willingness of many of these advocacy groups to increase their collaboration with the political parties, while avoiding cooptation and maintaining a high level of vigilance and activism.

SECTION 5 Nigerian Politics in Transition

Despite the slow progress of the Fourth Republic, Nigerians overwhelmingly favor democratic government over military rule. About 70 percent of respondents in a recent survey said that they still prefer democracy to any other alternative, although popular frustration is growing with the slow pace of reform and continued corruption in politics.[29] Will democracy in Nigeria be consolidated sufficiently to meet minimal levels of public satisfaction, or will the nation again succumb to destructive authoritarian rule?

Nigerian politics must change in fundamental ways for democracy to become more stable and legitimate. First and foremost, the nation must turn from a system of politics dominated by "Big Men"—for all intents and purposes, a competitive oligarchy—to a more representative mode of politics that addresses the fundamental interests of the public. Second, Nigerians must conclusively settle the national question and commit to political arrangements that accommodate the nation's diversity. In short, Nigeria's Fourth Republic must find ways of moving beyond prebendal politics and develop a truly national political process in which mobilization and conflicts along ethnic, regional, and religious lines gradually diminish, and which can address Nigeria's true national crisis: poverty and underdevelopment.

Political Challenges and Changing Agendas

Nigeria's fitful transition to democratic rule between 1985 and 1999 was inconclusive, largely because it was planned and directed from above. This approach contrasts sharply with the popular-based movements that unseated autocracies in Central and Eastern Europe. The military periodically made promises for democratic transition as a ploy to stabilize and legitimate their governments. General Abubakar dutifully handed power to the civilians in 1999, but only after ensuring that the military's interests would be protected under civilian rule and creating an overly powerful executive that reinforces **patrimonialism**, a system of power in which authority is maintained through patronage. The military's rapid transition program produced a tenuous, conflicted democratic government that faces daunting tasks of restoring key institutions, securing social stability, and reforming the economy. The continuing strength and influence of collective identities, defined on the basis of religion or ethnicity, are often more binding than national allegiances. The parasitic nature of the Nigerian economy is a further source of instability. Rent-seeking and other unproductive, often corrupt, business activities remain accepted norms of wealth accumulation.

Nonetheless, Nigerians are sowing seeds of change in all of these areas. Attitudes toward the military in government have shifted dramatically. The decline in the appeal of military rule can be attributed to the abysmal performances of the Babangida and Abacha regimes in economic oversight and governance. Many now recognize that the military,

apart from its contributions to national security, is incapable of promoting economic and social progress in Nigeria. With the armed forces discredited for the moment, the nature of the struggles among civilian political elites will decide the direction of political and economic change. Thus, democratic development may be advanced in the long run if stable coalitions appear over time in a manner that balances the power among contending groups, and if these key elites adapt to essential norms and rules of the political game.

Initially, members of the new political class confined their struggles within the constraints of the democratic system: using the courts, media, legislatives struggles, and even legal expediencies such as impeachment. Political actors largely worked through formal institutions, contending openly and offsetting the power of a single group or faction. Since the 2003 elections, however, the political elite have also shown a growing willingness to use extra-systemic measures to forward their interests through election rigging, corruption, and militia-led violence. The Niger Delta has grown particularly violent, with increasingly well-armed militias that in some cases have shown a measure of independence from their political patrons.

The next critical step down the long road of democratic development for Nigeria is the creation of a viable, multiethnic opposition party that is also loyal, meaning that it plays by the rules of the system. Opposition parties help to reduce corruption in the system because they have an interest in exposing the misconduct of the ruling party, which in turn pressures them to restrain their own behavior. Furthermore, in order to unseat the ruling party and win elections, opposition parties need to engage the public to win their votes. In this manner, issues of interest to the public are engaged by the parties. This is the basis of the social contract: elites gain the privilege of power so long as they use it to promote the public interest.

The introduction of so many new parties since 2002 has hurt the development of a viable, loyal opposition, further diluting it and allowing the PDP to govern largely unchecked. Worse, several minor parties have managed to win only narrow ethnic constituencies, raising the specter that Nigeria may return to the ruinous ethnic party politics of the past. Yet the larger of these opposition parties could also provide the building blocks of a viable opposition party or coalition if the PDP implodes along its strong internal divisions, as it nearly did in 2007 when PDP splinter factions formed the AC.

The project of building a coherent nation-state out of competing nationalities remains unfinished. Ironically, because the parties of the Fourth Republic generally do not represent any particular ethnic interest—indeed, they do not represent anyone's interests except those of the leaders and their clients—ethnic associations and militias have risen to articulate ethnic-based grievances. Ethnic consciousness cannot—and should not—be eliminated from society, but ethnicity cannot be the main basis for political competition. If current ethnic mobilization can be contained within ethnic associations arguing over the agenda of the parties, then it can be managed. If, however, any of the ethnic associations captures one of the political parties or joins with the militias to foment separatism, instability will result. The Niger Delta has gone furthest down this road, with a number of militias that have voiced ethnonationalist demands, some of which verge on separatism.

Democratic development also requires further decentralization of power structures in Nigeria. The struggle on the part of the National Assembly and the state governors to wrest power from the presidency has advanced this process, as has the growing competence and role of the judiciary. Privatization of government parastatals could also reduce the power of the presidency over time, since it will no longer control all the primary sectors of the economy. A more decentralized system allows local problems to be solved within communities rather than involving national institutions and the accompanying interethnic competition. Decentralization also lowers the stakes for holding national offices, thereby reducing the destructive pressures on political competition and political office. The devolution of power and resources to smaller units, closer to their constituents, can substantially enhance the accountability of leaders and the transparency of government operations.

Civil society groups are the final link in democratic consolidation in Nigeria. These groups are critical players in connecting the Nigerian state to the Nigerian people. They aggregate and articulate popular interests into the policy realm, and they provide advocacy on behalf of their members. If the political parties are to reflect anything more than elite interests and clientelist rule, the parties must reach out and build alliances with the institutions of civil society. For opposition parties to become a viable opposition movement capable of checking the power of the PDP, they will have to build alliances with civil society groups in order to mobilize large portions of the population. Foreign pressure also plays an important role in maintaining the quest for democracy and sustainable development. In recent years, major external forces have been more forthright in supporting civil society and democratization in Nigeria. The United States, Britain, and some member states of the European Union quite visibly exerted pressure on Babangida and Abacha to leave and applied modest sanctions in support of democracy. This has been made possible, in part, by a changing international environment, especially the willingness of the major industrial countries and the international financial institutions to support democracy around the world.

Nevertheless, the Western commitment to development and democracy in Africa is limited by the industrial powers' addiction to oil, which has blunted the impact of such pressure on Nigeria, and is now exacerbated by growing competition for energy resources from China. Much of the initiative for Africa's growth therefore needs to emerge from within. In Nigeria, such initiatives will depend on substantial changes in the way Nigerians do business. It will be necessary to develop a more sophisticated and far less corrupt form of capitalist enterprise and the development of entrepreneurial, particularly middle class interests within Nigeria who will see their interests tied to the principles of democratic politics and economic initiative. The middle class is beginning to grow under democratic rule, but it remains small and vulnerable to economic and political instability.

Nigerian politics has been characterized by turmoil and periodic crises ever since the British relinquished colonial power. Almost fifty years later, the country is still trying to piece together a fragile democracy, while per capita incomes are scarcely higher than at independence. Despite a number of positive trends, the nation continues to wrestle with overdependence of its economy on oil, enfeebled infrastructure and institutions, heightened sociopolitical tensions, an irresponsible elite, and an expanding mass culture of despondency and rage. Only responsible government combined with sustained civil society action can reverse this decline and restore the nation to what President Obasanjo called "the path to greatness."

Nigerian Politics in Comparative Perspective

The study of Nigeria has important implications for the study of African politics and, more broadly, of comparative politics. The Nigerian case embodies a number of key themes and issues that can be generalized. We can learn much about how democratic regimes are established and consolidated by understanding Nigeria's pitfalls and travails. Analysis of the historical dynamics of Nigeria's ethnic conflict helps to identify institutional mechanisms that may be effective in reducing ethnic conflict in other states. We can also learn much about the necessary and sufficient conditions for economic development, and the particular liabilities of oil-dependent states. Each of these issues offers comparative lessons for the major themes explored in this book: the world of states, governing the economy, the democratic idea, and the politics of collective identities.

A World of States

Nigeria exists in two "worlds" of states: one in the global political economy and the other within Africa. We have addressed at length Nigeria's position in the world. Economically, Nigeria was thrust into the world economy in a position of weakness, first as a British colony and later as an independent nation. Despite its resources and the potential of oil to provide the investment capital needed to build a modern economy, Nigeria has grown weaker. It has lost much of its international clout, and in place of the international respect it once enjoyed as a developing giant within Africa, the country became notorious throughout the 1990s for corruption, human rights abuses, and failed governance. The return of democracy and soaring oil prices have restored some of Nigeria's former stature, but its economic vulnerability and persistent corruption keep it a secondary player in the world of states.

This chapter has remarked, "As Nigeria goes, so goes the rest of sub-Saharan Africa." The future of democracy, political stability, and economic renewal in other parts of Africa, and certainly in West Africa, will be greatly influenced for good or ill by unfolding events in Nigeria. Beyond the obvious demonstration effects, the economy of the West African subregion could be buoyed by substantial growth in the Nigerian economy. In addition, President Obasanjo conducted very active public diplomacy across Africa, seeking to resolve major conflicts, promote democracy, and improve trade. President Yar'Adua has so far been far less active in foreign policy, but global priorities remain similar to his predecessor's. Thus far, however, international political and business attention has shifted elsewhere on the continent, focusing on such countries as South Africa, Botswana, and Ghana. Growing insurgency in the Niger Delta has also meant that Nigeria has even fallen behind Angola as the largest oil producer on the continent. This portends a danger of greater marginalization, reflecting the expanding patchwork of Africa among areas of stability and growth, contrasted with areas of turmoil and decay.

Governing the Economy

Nigeria provides important insights into the political economy of underdevelopment. At independence in 1960, Nigeria was stronger economically than its Southeast Asian counterparts Indonesia and Malaysia. Independent Nigeria appeared poised for growth, with a wealth of natural resources, a large population, and the presence of highly entrepreneurial groups in many regions of the country. Today, Nigeria is among the poorest countries in the world in terms of per capita income, while many of its Asian counterparts have joined the ranks of the newly industrializing countries. One critical lesson Nigeria teaches is that a rich endowment of resources is not enough to ensure economic development. In fact, it may encourage rent-seeking behavior that undermines more productive activities.[30] Sound political and institutional development must come first.

Other variables are critically important, notably democratic stability and a capable developmental state. A developmentalist ethic, and an institutional structure to enforce it, can set limits to corrupt behavior and constrain the pursuit of short-term personal gain at the expense of national economic growth.

Institutions vital to the pursuit of these objectives include a professional civil service, an independent judiciary, and a free press. Nigeria has had each of these, but they were gradually undermined and corrupted under military rule. The public "ethic" that has come to dominate Nigerian political economy has been prebendalism. Where corruption is unchecked, as in Nigeria, the Philippines under Ferdinand Marcos, or Latin American countries such as Ecuador and Venezuela, economic development suffers accordingly.

Nigeria also demonstrates that sustainable economic development requires sound economic policy. Without export diversification, commodity-exporting countries are buffeted by the price fluctuations of one or two main products. This situation can be traced back to overreliance on primary commodity export-oriented policies bequeathed by the British colonial regime. Yet other former colonies, such as Malaysia and Indonesia, have managed to diversify their initial export base. Nigeria, by contrast, has substituted one form of commodity dependence for another, and it has allowed its petroleum industry to overwhelm all other sectors of the economy. Nigeria even became a net importer of products (for example, palm oil and palm nuts) for which it was once a leading world producer. Nigeria is even in the absurd position of being unable to feed itself, despite rich agricultural lands. In comparative perspective, we can see that natural resource endowments can be tremendously beneficial. The United States, for example, has parlayed its endowments of agricultural, mineral, and energy resources into one of the world's most diversified modern economies. Meanwhile Japan, which is by comparison poorly endowed with natural resources, has one of the strongest economies in the world, achieved in large part through its unique developmental strategies. Each of these examples illustrates the primacy of sound economic policies implemented through consolidated political systems.

The Democratic Idea

Many African countries have experienced transitions from authoritarian rule.[31] With the end of superpower competition in Africa and the withdrawal of external support for Africa's despots, many African societies experienced a resurgence of popular pressures for greater participation in political life and more open forms of governance. Decades of authoritarian, single-party, and military rule in Africa have left a dismal record of political repression, human rights abuses, inequality, deteriorating governance, and failed economies. A handful of elites have acquired large fortunes through wanton corruption. Consider Nigeria's "missing" $12.2 billion windfall in oil revenues after the Gulf War in 1991 or the fact that former Zairian president Mobutu Sese Seko's personal wealth was estimated to be several billion dollars—perhaps as much as the country's entire external debt. Kenya's former president Daniel arap Moi is considered among the richest men in Africa, a group to which Ibrahim Babangida and the late Sani Abacha of Nigeria have belonged, and which former President Obasanjo may well have joined as well. The exercise of postcolonial authoritarian rule in Africa has contributed to economic stagnation and decline. The difficulties of such countries as Cameroon, Togo, and Zimbabwe in achieving political transitions reflects, in large part, the ruling elites' unwillingness to cede control of the political instruments that made possible their self-enrichment.

Nigeria exemplifies the harsh reality of authoritarian and unaccountable governance. Nigerians have endured six military regimes, countless attempted coups, and a bloody civil war that claimed more than 1 million lives. They have also seen a once-prospering economy reduced to a near shambles. Today, democracy has become a greater imperative because only such a system provides the mechanisms to limit abuses of power and render governments accountable.

Collective Identities

Nigeria presents an important case in which to study the dangers of communal competition in a society with deep cultural divisions. How can multiethnic countries manage diversity? What institutional mechanisms can be employed to avert tragedies such as the 1967–1970 civil war or the continuing conflicts that have brought great suffering to Rwanda and the former Yugoslavia? This chapter has suggested institutional reforms such as multiethnic political parties, decentralization, and a strengthened federal system that can contribute to reducing tensions and minimizing conflict.

Insights from the Nigerian experience may explain why some federations persist, while identifying factors that can undermine them. Nigeria's complex social map, and its varied attempts to create a nation out of its highly diverse population, enhances our understanding of the politics of cultural pluralism and the difficulties of accommodating sectional interests under conditions of political and economic insecurity. Federal character in Nigeria has become a form of ethnic and regional favoritism and a tool for dispensing patronage. Yet the country has benefited in some ways from the attention devoted to creating state and local governments, and from giving people in different regions a sense of being stakeholders in the entity called Nigeria.

Nigeria's challenges reflect the frustrated hopes of its people for a better life, stable government, and a democratic political order, while suggesting the potential contributions that this country could make to the African continent and the wider international arena. The quest for responsive and capable democratic governance leads in one direction, while another direction presents the specter of military entrepreneurs, or ethnic and religious extremists, plunging Nigeria into another cycle of coups, decline, and possibly collapse.

Key Terms ⟫

authoritarian
legitimacy
accountability
unfinished state
jihad
acephalous societies
emirs
indirect rule
warrant chiefs
interventionist
clientelism
autocracy
rents

structural adjustment program (SAP)
international financial institutions (IFIs)
balance of payments
privatization
Economic Community of West African States (ECOWAS)
parastatals
shari'a
prebendalism
civil society
state corporatism
patrimonialism

Suggested Readings ⟫

Aborisade, Oladimeji, and Mundt, Robert J. *Politics in Nigeria,* 2nd ed. New York: Longman, 2002.

Achike, Okay. *Public Administration: A Nigerian and Comparative Perspective.* London: Longman, 1978.

Adamolekun, L. *Politics and Administration in Nigeria.* London: Hutchinson, 1986.

Agbaje, Adigun. *The Nigerian Press: Hegemony and the Social Construction of Legitimacy, 1960–1983.* Lewiston, N.Y.: Edwin Mellen Press, 1992.

———. "Twilight of Democracy in Nigeria." *Africa Demos* 3, no. 3:5. Atlanta: The Carter Center of Emory University, 1994.

Beckett, Paul A., and Young, Crawford, eds. *Dilemmas of Democracy in Nigeria.* Rochester, N.Y.: University of Rochester Press, 1997.

Bienen, Henry. *Political Conflict and Economic Change in Nigeria.* London: Frank Cass, 1988.

Diamond, Larry. *Class, Ethnicity and Democracy in Nigeria: The Failure of the First Republic.* London: Macmillan, 1988.

———. "Nigeria: The Uncivic Society and the Descent into Praetorianism." In Larry Diamond, J. Linz, and S. M. Lipset, eds., *Politics in Developing Countries: Comparing Experiences with Democracy,* 2nd ed. Boulder, Colo.: Lynne Rienner Publishers, 1995, 417–491.

Decalo, Samuel. *Coups and Army Rule in Africa,* 2nd ed. New Haven: Yale University Press, 1990.

Dudley, Billy. *An Introduction to Nigerian Government and Politics.* Bloomington: Indiana University Press, 1982.

Ekeh, Peter P., and Osaghae, Eghosa E., eds. *Federal Character and Federalism in Nigeria.* Ibadan: Heinemann, 1989.

Falola, Toyin. *Violence in Nigeria: The Crisis of Religious Politics and Secular Ideologies.* Rochester, N.Y.: University of Rochester Press, 1999.

Forrest, Tom. *Politics and Economic Development in Nigeria.* Boulder, Colo.: Westview Press, 1993.

Horowitz, Donald L. *Ethnic Groups in Conflict.* Berkeley: University of California Press, 1985.

Joseph, Richard A. *Democracy and Prebendal Politics in Nigeria: The Rise and Fall of the Second Republic.* Cambridge: Cambridge University Press, 1987.

Kew, Darren. "Political Islam in Nigeria's Transition Crisis," *Muslim Politics Report* (Council on Foreign Relations: New York), May–June, 1996.

Kirk-Greene, Anthony, and Rimmer, Douglas. *Nigeria Since 1970: A Political and Economic Outline.* London: Hodder and Stoughton, 1981.

Lewis, Peter M. "Endgame in Nigeria? The Politics of a Failed Democratic Transition." *African Affairs* 93 (1994): 323–340.

Lewis, Peter M., Rubin, Barnett R., and Robinson, Pearl T. *Stabilizing Nigeria: Pressures, Incentives, and Support for Civil Society.* New York: Century Foundation, for the Council on Foreign Relations, 1998.

Lubeck, Paul. *Islam and Urban Labor in Northern Nigeria.* Cambridge: Cambridge University Press, 1987.

Luckham, Robin. *The Nigerian Military: A Sociological Analysis of Authority and Revolt, 1960–67.* Cambridge: Cambridge University Press, 1971.

Melson, Robert, and Wolpe, Howard, eds. *Nigeria: Modernization and the Politics of Communalism.* East Lansing: Michigan State University Press, 1971.

Nyang'oro, Julius, and Shaw, Tim, eds. *Corporatism in Africa: Comparative Analysis and Practice.* Boulder, Colo.: Westview Press, 1989.

Olukoshi, Adebayo, ed. *The Politics of Structural Adjustment in Nigeria.* London: James Currey Publishers, 1993.

Osaghae, Eghosa. *Crippled Giant: Nigeria Since Independence.* Bloomington: Indiana University Press, 1998.

Oyediran, Oyeleye, ed. *Nigerian Government and Politics Under Military Rule.* London: Macmillan, 1979.

Reno, William. *Warlord Politics and African States.* Boulder, Colo.: Lynne Rienner Publishers, 1998.

Sklar, Richard L. *Nigerian Political Parties: Power in an Emergent African Nation.* New York: NOK Publishers, 1983.

Soyinka, Wole. *Open Sore of a Continent.* Oxford: Oxford University Press, 1996.

Suberu, Rotimi. *Federalism and Ethnic Conflict in Nigeria.* Washington, D.C.: U.S. Institute of Peace, 2001.

Watts, Michael, ed. *State, Oil, and Agriculture in Nigeria.* Berkeley: University of California Press, 1987.

Wunsch, James S., and Olowu, Dele, eds. *The Failure of the Centralized State: Institutions and Self-Governance in Africa.* Boulder, Colo.: Westview Press, 1990.

Young, Crawford. *The Rising Tide of Cultural Pluralism: The Nation-State at Bay?* Madison: University of Wisconsin Press, 1993.

Suggested Websites ≫

British Broadcasting Corporation: A 2002 interview with President Obasanjo
news.bbc.co.uk/2/hi/talking_point/1800826.stm
Gamji: A collection of news stories from Nigerian newspapers, as well as opinion pieces and other news links
www.gamji.com
The Guardian, Nigeria's leading daily newspaper

www.ngrguardiannews.com
Human Rights Watch reports
hrw.org/doc/?t=africa&c=nigeri
International Institute for Democracy and Electoral Assistance
archive.idea.int/frontpage_nigeria.htm
Stanford University's Center for African Studies
www.stanford.edu/dept/AFR/

Endnotes ≫

[1] Much of this context is recounted in James S. Coleman, *Nigeria: Background to Nationalism* (Berkeley: University of California Press, 1958).

[2] Obafemi Awolowo, *Path to Nigerian Freedom* (London: Faber and Faber, 1947), pp. 47–48.

[3] Billy Dudley, *An Introduction to Nigerian Government and Politics* (Bloomington: Indiana University Press, 1982), p. 71.

[4] Robin Luckham, *The Nigerian Military: A Sociological Analysis of Authority and Revolt 1960–67* (Cambridge: Cambridge University Press, 1971).

[5]Peter Ekeh, "Colonialism and the Two Publics in Africa: A Theoretical Statement," *Comparative Studies in Society and History* 17, no. 1 (January 1975).

[6]Richard A. Joseph, *Democracy and Prebendal Politics in Nigeria: The Rise and Fall of the Second Republic* (Cambridge: Cambridge University Press), pp. 55–58.

[7]Gavin Williams and Terisa Turner, "Nigeria," in John Dunn, ed., *West African States: Failure and Promise* (Cambridge: Cambridge University Press, 1978), pp. 156–157.

[8]Michael J. Watts, *State, Oil and Agriculture in Nigeria* (Berkeley: University of California Press, 1987), p. 71.

[9]Watts, *State Oil and Agriculture in Nigeria,* p. 67.

[10]Tom Forrest, *Politics and Economic Development in Nigeria,* 2nd ed. (Boulder, Colo.: Westview Press, 1995), pp. 207–212.

[11]Dele Olowu, "Centralization, Self-Governance, and Development in Nigeria," in James S. Wunsch and Dele Olowu, eds., *The Failure of the Centralized State: Institutions and Self-Governance in Africa* (Boulder, Colo.: Westview Press, 1991), p. 211.

[12]Robert Melson and Howard Wolpe, *Nigeria: Modernization and the Politics of Communalism* (East Lansing: Michigan State University Press, 1971).

[13]Toyin Falola, Violence in Nigeria: *The Crisis of Religious Politics and Secular Ideologies* (Rochester, N.Y.: University of Rochester Press, 1998).

[14]Pat A. Williams, "Women and the Dilemma of Politics in Nigeria," in Crawford Young and Paul Beckett, eds., *Dilemmas of Democracy in Nigeria* (Rochester, N.Y.: University of Rochester Press, 1997), pp. 219–241.

[15]Anthony Kirk-Greene and Douglas Rimmer, *Nigeria Since 1970: A Political and Economic Outline* (London: Hodder and Stoughton 1981), p. 49.

[16]Rotimi Suberu, *Federalism and Ethnic Conflict in Nigeria* (Washington, D.C.: U.S. Institute of Peace, 2001).

[17]Suberu, *Federalism and Ethnic Conflict in Nigeria,* pp. 119–120.

[18]Henry Bienen, *Armies and Parties in Africa* (New York: Africana Publishing, 1978), pp. 193–211.

[19]Samuel DeCalo, *Coups and Army Rule in Africa* (New Haven, Conn.: Yale University Press, 1976), p. 18.

[20]Joseph, *Democracy and Prebendal Politics in Nigeria,* pp. 52–53.

[21]Richard Sklar, *Nigerian Political Parties* (Princeton: Princeton University Press, 1963).

[22]Babafemi Badejo, "Party Formation and Party Competition," in Larry Diamond, Anthony Kirk-Greene, and Oyeleye Oyediran, eds., *Transition Without End: Nigerian Politics and Civil Society Under Babangida* (Boulder, Colo.: Lynne Rienner Publishers, 1997), p. 179.

[23]Eghosa Osaghae, *Crippled Giant: Nigeria Since Independence* (Bloomington: Indiana University Press 1999), pp. 233–239.

[24]Peter M. Lewis, Barnett Rubin, and Pearl Robinson, *Stabilizing Nigeria: Pressures, Incentives and Support for Civil Society* (New York: Council on Foreign Relations, 1998), p. 87.

[25]Donald L. Horowitz, "Making Moderation Pay: The Comparative Politics of Ethnic Conflict Management," in Montville, ed., *Conflict and Peacemaking in Multiethnic Societies* (New York: Lexington Books, 1991), chapter 25.

[26]Rotimi Suberu, *Public Policies and National Unity in Nigeria,* Research Report No. 19 (Ibadan: Development Policy Centre, 199), pp. 9–10.

[27]Sayre Schatz, " 'Pirate Capitalism' and the Inert Economy of Nigeria," *Journal of Modern African Studies* 22, no. 1 (March 1984): 45–57.

[28]Adebayo Olukoshi, "Associational Life," in Diamond, Kirk-Greene, and Oyediran, *Transition Without End,* pp. 385–86.

[29]Peter Lewis, Etannibi Alemika, and Michael Bratton, *Down to Earth: Changes in Attitudes to Democracy and Markets in Nigeria,* Afrobarometer Working Paper No. 20, Michigan State University, August 2002.

[30]See Terry Lynn Karl, *The Paradox of Plenty* (Berkeley: University of California Press, 1997); and Michael Ross, "The Political Economy of the Resource Curse," *World Politics* 51 (January 1999), 297–322.

[31]Michael Bratton and Nicolas van de Walle, *Democratic Experiments in Africa* (Cambridge: Cambridge University Press, 1997).

Alfred P. Montero

Chapter 9 ≫ BRAZIL

Official Name: **Federative Republic of Brazil (Republica Federativa do Brasil)**

Location: **Eastern South America**

Capital City: **Brasília**

Population (2008): **196.3 million**

Size: **8,511,965 sq. km.; slightly smaller than the United States**

1822
Dom Pedro I declares himself emperor of Brazil, peacefully ending three hundred years of Portuguese colonial rule.

1824
Constitution drafted

1888
Abolition of slavery

1889
Dom Pedro II, who assumed throne in

1840, is forced into exile; landowning elites establish an oligarchical republic

1891
A new constitution establishes a directly

elected president

1930
Getúlio Vargas gains power after a coup led by military and political leaders. His period of dictatorship (1937–1945)

is known as the New State.

1945
Vargas calls for general elections. General Eurico Dutra of the Social Democratic Party wins.

1950
Vargas is elected president. Scandals precipitate his suicide in 1954.

1956
Juscelino Kubitschek becomes president.

1960
Jânio Quadros becomes president.

SECTION 1 The Making of the Modern Brazilian State

Politics in Action

In January 2007, President Luiz Inácio Lula da Silva of Brazil walked onto the stage of the World Economic Forum in Davos, Switzerland. Facing an audience of a few hundred of the most important leaders of business, financial, and government leaders, Lula began his address by recalling his first visit to the Forum four years earlier in which he announced the inauguration of several social policies aimed at reducing poverty and hunger in Brazil. As in 2003, Lula came to Davos after winning a decisive victory in the second round of the presidential contest the previous autumn. If the first victory had been the result of widespread hope that the leader of the Workers' Party (*Partido dos Trabalhadores*, PT), an erstwhile vanguard of the political left in Brazil, could bring new hope to the poor and dispossessed, the second electoral victory was the result of having achieved some success in engineering social change. For the first time in contemporary Brazilian history, aggregate indicators of inequality were slowly reversing themselves. The best known of these—the GINI coefficient—had long registered Brazil as one of the most unequal countries in the world. Now, for the first time, President Lula could claim that even this stubborn indicator of Brazil's social problems was showing some movement in the right direction.

That Lula, once again, chose Davos as the place to most publicly champion the achievements of his first term and lay out the goals of his second term is itself indicative of how much change Brazil has seen in the past decade. Only ten years before Lula's second appearance at the World Economic Forum, protesters led by the PT and union activists were marching outside the stock exchange in Rio de Janeiro protesting the auctioning of *Companhia Vale do Rio Doce* (CVRD), a mining conglomerate that was Brazil's largest public firm. The sale of Vale was the latest in a series of **privatization** moves that began in the early 1990s with the sale of Brazil's steel mills, fertilizer firms, and utility companies. Fifty-two state enterprises had already been sold, and now it was Vale's turn. The activists gathered outside the stock exchange could not imagine that only five years later, they would support Lula's candidacy, one based on not only social reform but a continuation of the very economic policies that led to Vale's sale. Many of these activists would claim that the chief beneficiaries of such policies were the very people in the audience at Davos.

This capacity for mixing market-oriented economic reform with socially conscious welfare policies that focus on alleviating poverty, reducing hunger, and improving the lives of most Brazilians is a talent that Lula has demonstrated continually. Like his predecessor, Fernando Henrique Cardoso (1994–2002), Lula da Silva has been able to consolidate a new Brazil that embraces the market but is also aware of the great social debt borne by the government. Such an approach is appropriate for a country of numerous contradictions.

1961
Quadros resigns. João Goulart gains presidency despite an attempted military coup.

1964
A military coup places power

in the hands of successive authoritarian regimes.

1984
Diretas Já!, a mass mobilization campaign, calls for direct elections.

1985
Vice-presidential candidate José Sarney becomes president on the sudden death of elected president Tancredo Neves.

1988
A new constitution grants new social and political rights.

1989
Fernando Collor is elected president.

1992
Collor is impeached; Vice President Itamar Franco assumes presidency.

1994
Fernando Henrique Cardoso is elected president after his Real Plan controls inflation.

1998
Cardoso is reelected.

1999
The Real Plan weathers a financial crisis.

2002
Lula da Silva is elected president.

FIGURE 9.1

The Brazilian Nation at a Glance

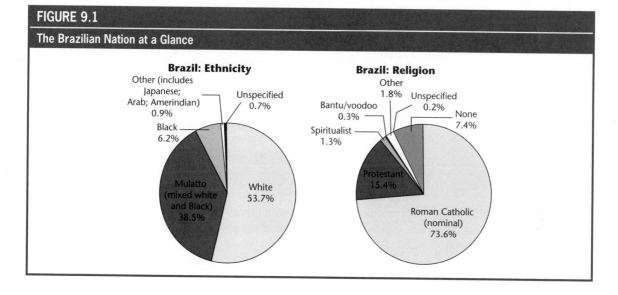

Brazil: Ethnicity
Other (includes Japanese; Arab; Amerindian) 0.9%
Unspecified 0.7%
Black 6.2%
Mulatto (mixed white and Black) 38.5%
White 53.7%

Brazil: Religion
Other 1.8%
Bantu/voodoo 0.3%
Unspecified 0.2%
Spiritualist 1.3%
None 7.4%
Protestant 15.4%
Roman Catholic (nominal) 73.6%

While it stands as the tenth largest economy in the world, Brazil is also one of the most unequal countries on the globe. The political system has remained democratic for more than twenty years, yet getting things done in congress and making elites more accountable to the people and to one another remain ongoing challenges. Democracy coexists with corruption just as growth coexists with poverty and inequality in Brazil.

Geographic Setting

Brazil is larger than the continental United States and occupies two-thirds of South America. It borders all the other countries of South America except Ecuador and Chile. The population of 183 million is concentrated in the urban southern and southeastern regions, with more than 19 million inhabitants in Greater São Paulo alone. This density contrasts with the northern, sparsely populated rain forest regions of the Amazon. Overall, Brazil's 18 inhabitants per square kilometer makes it less densely populated than the United States, France, or Britain.

The physical geography of Brazil is diverse, including thick rain forest in the Amazon valley, large lowland swamps known as the *pantanal* in the central western states, and vast expanses of badlands known as the *sertão* in the north and northeast. The country is rich in natural resources and arable land.

Table 9.1

Political Organization

Political System	Federal republic, presidential with separation of powers.
Regime History	Democratic since 1946 with periods of military authoritarianism, especially 1964–1985.
Administrative Structure	Federal, with twenty-six states plus the Federal District, which also functions as a state. Subnational legislatures are unicameral. State governments have multiple secretariats, the major ones commonly being economy, planning, and infrastructure. The states are divided into municipalities (more than 5,500), with mayors and councilors directly elected.
Executive	President, vice president, and cabinet. The president and vice president are directly elected by universal suffrage in a two-round runoff election for four-year terms. Since 1998, the president and vice president may run for a second term.
Legislature	Bicameral: The Senate is made up of three senators from each state and from the Federal District, elected by plurality vote for an eight-year term; the Chamber of Deputies consists of representatives from each state and from the Federal District, elected by proportional vote for a four-year term.
Judiciary	Supreme Court, High Tribunal of Justice, regional courts, labor courts, electoral courts, military courts, and state courts. Judiciary has financial and administrative autonomy. Most judges are appointed for life.
Party System	Multiparty system including several parties of the right, center-left, and left. Elections are by open-list proportional representation. There is no restriction on the creation and merging of political parties.

The Amazon has an abundance of tropical fruit and minerals; the central and southern regions provide most of the country's iron ore and coal; offshore and onshore sources of petroleum in Rio de Janeiro and the northeast coastline are also significant. Brazil's farmlands are particularly fertile, including large soy-producing areas, coffee in Rio de Janeiro and in São Paulo, and sugar and other agriculture along the narrow stretch off the northeast coast. The Amazon's climate is wet, the *sertão* is dry, and the agricultural areas of the central, southeastern, and southern regions are temperate.

Centuries of voluntary and involuntary immigration of Europeans and Africans contributed to the emergence of an ethnically mixed society. Although this complexity makes any classification scheme precarious, the National Brazilian Institute of Geography and Statistics (IBGE) claims that 49.7 percent of the population is white, 42.6 percent is *pardo* (brown or mulatto), 6.9 percent is black, and 0.5 percent is Asian.[1] These numbers probably ignore people of mixed race,

from indigenous and white parents, who are known as *mestizos* but are sometimes classified erroneously as being white or *pardo*. The indigenous people who live in the vast Amazon basin are estimated to number 250,000.[2] The Asian population is dominated by people of Japanese descent who immigrated, mostly to São Paulo, from 1908 through the 1950s to seek improved economic conditions. Numbering more than 1.5 million, this community of Japanese descendants is the largest outside Japan.

Like other ethnically plural societies such as India, Mexico, Nigeria, Russia, Iran, and the United States, Brazil is a unique blend of distinct cultural influences. Portuguese as the common language helps keep Brazilians united, and, unlike the people of India, Iran, and Nigeria, Brazilians are not greatly divided over religious differences. Roman Catholicism was imposed by Portuguese colonial rule, and then reinforced by immigration from Catholic Italy, Spain, and Portugal at the end of the nineteenth century. In recent years, evangelical Protestants have made

inroads, especially those in the Pentecostal churches. Protestants now compose about 12 percent of the population. Afro-Brazilian and indigenous religions also operate alongside the Catholic liturgy throughout Brazil.

Critical Junctures

The Brazilian Empire (1822–1889)

Europeans first arrived in Brazil in 1500 with an expedition led by the Portuguese explorer Pedro Alvares Cabral. Unlike the other countries of Latin America, Brazil was a Portuguese colony, not a Spanish one. So it was spared the violent wars of independence that coincided with the comparatively more spasmodic collapse of the Spanish colonial system during the 1810s and 1820s. Brazilian independence was declared peacefully by the Crown's own agent in the colony.

In 1808, when Napoleon Bonaparte invaded Spain and Portugal, the Portuguese king, João VI, and his court escaped to Brazil. After the defeat of Napoleon, Dom João returned to Portugal to reclaim his throne, but he left his son, Dom Pedro, behind in Rio de Janeiro as prince regent. In September 1822, Dom Pedro declared Brazil independent and took the new title of emperor of Brazil. In 1824, a constitution was drafted, making Brazil the only constitutional monarchy in the Americas. In 1840, Dom Pedro I's son, Dom Pedro II, assumed the throne.

To control such a sprawling territory, the empire centralized authority in the emperor, who acted as a **moderating power** (*poder moderador*), mediating conflicts among the executive, legislative, and judicial branches of government and powerful landowning elites, known as the landed **oligarchy**. This centralization of authority provided a contrast with the other postcolonial Latin American states, which suffered numerous conflicts among territorially dispersed strongmen called *caudillos*.

In contrast with its neighbors, imperial Brazil enjoyed several features of a functioning representative democracy: regularity of elections, the alternation of parties in power, and scrupulous observation of the constitution. In substance, however, liberal institutions only regulated political competition among the rural, oligarchical elites, reflecting the interests of a privileged minority and not the larger Brazilian population.

The Old Republic (1889–1930)

The next critical juncture in Brazilian history occurred in 1889 with the peaceful demise of the empire, the exile of Dom Pedro II, and the emergence of a republic ruled by the landowning oligarchy (the Old Republic). The decline of slavery and the rise of republicanism were the main forces that ended the empire. Britain's ban of the slave trade in 1850 and Brazil's abolitionist movement gradually wore away slavery as an institution until it was abolished in 1889. Socioeconomic changes also paved the way for abolition. The impressive growth of the coffee economy, which was concentrated in the state of São Paulo, reduced the demand for slaves. Unlike the plantation sugar economy of the northeast, coffee did not require slaves. By this time, too, liberal political values in opposition to the centralization of political authority had taken root among the coffee oligarchy.

The Old Republic (1889–1930) consolidated the political rise of the coffee oligarchy and a small urban industrial class and commercial elite linked to the coffee trade. The constitution of 1891, which was inspired by the U.S. model, established a directly elected president as the head of government, guaranteed the separation of church and state, and expanded the franchise to include all literate males (about 3.5 percent of the population before 1930). The **legitimacy** of the republican political system was established on governing principles that were limited to a privileged few, but no longer determined by the hereditary rights of the emperor. Power was decentralized to the states, which gained greater authority to formulate policy, spend money, levy taxes, and maintain their own militias.

Although the republican elite went further than the empire's elite in expressing liberal ideas in the constitution, most Brazilians continued to reside in rural areas where the landed oligarchy vigorously suppressed dissent. As in the southern United States and in Mexico, landed elites manipulated local political activity. The colonels, as these elites were called in Brazil, assumed extensive extralegal authority to gather their poor workers and "vote them" (use their votes to guarantee the election of officials favored by the local colonels). This process became widely known as *coronelismo*.

The ties that developed between the patron (the landowner) and the client (the peasant) during the Old Republic became the basis of modern Brazilian politics. In return for protection and occasional favors, the client did the bidding of the patron. As urbanization and the growth of the state's administrative and bureaucratic agencies proceeded, the process of trading favors and demanding action was transformed and became known as **clientelism**. *Coronelismo* in rural areas and clientelism in urban areas were extended to the politics of the national state. In this way, the state was dominated by **patrimonialism**—the injection of private interests into public policymaking.

In contrast to the centralization of power during the empire, the Old Republic consecrated the power of local elites. The **politics of the governors** empowered regional elites, mainly from the coffee and cattle regions, who dominated national politics. Three states in particular emerged as key players: São Paulo (coffee), Minas Gerais (coffee and ranching), and Rio Grande do Sul (ranching). The presidency alternated so regularly among them that this period of Brazilian political history is referred to as the rule of *café com leite* ("coffee with milk"), reflecting the dominance of the São Paulo coffee and Minas Gerais cattle elites.

The 1930 Revolution

The Great Depression of the 1930s upset the economic and political base of the Old Republic. As world

Leaders

Getúlio Dornelles Vargas

etúlio Dornelles Vargas (1883–1954) came from a wealthy family in the cattle-rich southernmost state of Rio Grande do Sul. Vargas's youth was marked by political divisions within his family between federalists and republicans, conflicts that separated Brazilians during the Old Republic and particularly in Rio Grande do Sul, which had a strong regional identity. Political violence, which was common in the state's history, also affected Vargas's upbringing. His two brothers were each accused of killing rivals, one at the military school in Minas Gerais that Getúlio attended with one of his older siblings. After a brief stint in the military, Vargas attended law school in Porto Alegre, where he excelled as an orator. Like many others in his generation, his university education was incomplete. He supplemented his studies by reading many books published in other countries.

After graduating in 1907, he began his political career as a district attorney. Later, he served as majority leader in the state senate. In 1923, Vargas was elected federal deputy for Rio Grande do Sul, and in 1924 he became leader of his state's delegation in the Chamber of Deputies. In 1926, he made another political career change when he was named finance minister for the Washington Luis administration (1926–1930). He served for a year before winning the governorship of his home state. Never an ideologue, Vargas embraced a highly pragmatic style of governing that made him one of Brazil's most popular politicians by the end of the 1920s.

Vargas's powerful political position as governor of Rio Grande do Sul catapulted him into national prominence in 1929. The international economic crisis compelled several regional economic oligarchies to unite in opposition to the coffee and financial policies of the government. The states, including the state of São Paulo, divided their support between two candidates for the presidency: Julio Prestes, who was supported by President Luis, and Vargas, head of the opposition. The two states of Minas Gerais and Rio Grande do Sul voted as a bloc in favor of Vargas, but he lost the 1930 election. Immediately after this loss, a

Getúlio Vargas as president in 1952. *Source:* Hulton/Getty Archive/ Getty Images.

conspiracy among discontented military and political leaders led to the coup of October 1930, which installed Vargas in power.

No other figure in Brazilian political history has ever affected the country as much as Getúlio Vargas. His New State launched a series of reforms that established the terms on which Brazilian society would be linked to the state for decades. Even today, his political legacy continues in the form of state agencies and laws protecting workers.

Source: For more on Vargas's life, see Robert M. Levine, *Father of the Poor? Vargas and His Era* (New York: Cambridge University Press, 1998).

demand for coffee plummeted, the coffee and ranch elites faced their worst crisis. Worker demonstrations and a resurgent Brazilian Communist Party challenged the legitimacy of the Old Republic. Among the ranks of discontented political elites, a figure emerged who would change the shape of Brazilian politics for the rest of the century: Getúlio Vargas (see "Leaders: Getúlio Dornelles Vargas").

After a disputed presidential campaign in 1930, Vargas came to power as the head of what he called a new "revolutionary government." He moved swiftly to crush middle-class and popular dissent and built a political coalition around a new economic project of industrialization led by the central government and based on central state resources. In contrast to the Old Republic, Vargas insisted on controlling the regional governments by replacing all governors (except in Minas Gerais) with handpicked allies (*interventores*). The center of gravity of Brazilian politics swung back to the national state.

Vargas believed he could win the support of these groups by answering their demands in a controlled way. They would be allowed to participate in the new political order, but only as passive members of state-created and state-regulated unions and associations. This model of government was **state corporatism**. It rejects the idea of competition among social groups by having the state arbitrate all conflicts. For instance, when workers requested increases in their wages, state agencies would determine to what extent such demands were answered and how business would pay for them.[3]

By 1937, Vargas had achieved a position of virtually uncontested power. During the next eight years, Vargas consolidated his state corporatist paradigm with labor codes, the establishment of public firms to produce strategic commodities such as steel and oil, and paternalistic social policies. Packaged with nationalist fervor, these policies were collectively called the **New State** (*Estado Novo*).

The New State was decidedly authoritarian. Vargas, who was called *pai do povo* (father of the people), could not be upstaged by competing political images and organizations. Brazilian society would be linked directly to the state and to Vargas as the state's primary agent. Although the New State's constitution had fascist overtones, Vargas's policies were as much inspired by the New Deal of U.S. President Franklin D. Roosevelt as by fascist Italy or Nazi Germany.[4] The new regime expanded the existing rudimentary social insurance and pension programs into a broad welfare and health care system for urban workers. Although unemployment insurance was not envisaged by the new laws, workers were provided with insurance against occupational accidents, illness, and death. Vargas created a Ministry of Labor and labor courts to regulate and solve conflicts between employers and labor. After World War II, the armed forces experienced marked improvements in professional standards of promotion and conduct through the establishment of the Superior War College (*Escola Superior de Guerra*).[5]

The Populist Republic (1945–1964)

The ever-growing mobilization of segments of the working and middle classes as well as U.S. diplomatic pressure forced Vargas, in 1943, to call for full democratic elections to be held in December 1945. Three political parties emerged to contest the election: the Social Democratic Party (PSD) and the Brazilian Labor Party (PTB) were pro-Vargas, while the National Democratic Union (UDN) stood against him. The PSD and the PTB, which operated in alliance, were both creations of the state, while the UDN brought together various regional forces committed to a return to liberal constitutionalism. By October 1945, the bitterness of the campaign led the military to force Vargas's resignation, two months before the general election.

The turn to democracy in 1946 fell far short of breaking with the past. The new 1946 constitution guaranteed periodic elections, but the most important economic and social policies were still decided by the state bureaucracy and not by the national legislature.

Populism, not democracy, became the defining characteristic of the new political order. In Brazil, the terms *populist* and *populism* refer to politicians, programs, or movements that seek to expand citizenship to previously disenfranchised sectors of society in return for political support. Populist governments tend to grant benefits to guarantee support, but they discourage lower-class groups from creating autonomous organizations. Populists also do not regard themselves as accountable to the people.

Vargas returned to power after he was elected in 1950. Brazilian workers supported him for his promises to improve the social insurance system. However, economic limitations and opposition claims that he was preparing a new dictatorship made Vargas politically vulnerable.[6] Vargas was soon swept up in a bizarre scandal involving the attempted assassination of a popular journalist. The crisis drove Vargas to take his own life on August 24, 1954.

Under Vargas's democratic successor, Juscelino Kubitschek (in office from 1956 to 1960), the economic picture improved. Brazilian industry expanded tremendously in the 1950s. Kubitschek was a master of political symbolism and **nationalism**. His administration promoted images of a new and bigger Brazil, capable of generating "fifty years of development in five." Chief among these symbols of the new Brazil was Kubitschek's decision to move the country's capital from Rio de Janeiro to a planned city called Brasília. The building of this utopian city acted as a political symbol to rally support among Brazil's business popular classes for Kubitschek's developmentalist policies.

The presidents who followed Kubitschek's term proved much less competent.[7] Jânio Quadros, elected in 1960, resigned months later with little explanation. His successor, João Goulart, embarked on an ill-fated campaign for structural reforms, mainly of the educational system and agrarian reform. But he faced an increasingly polarized situation as peasant league movements, students, and professional organizations organized protests, strikes, and illegal seizures of land. As right-wing organizations battled leftist groups in the streets of the capital, the military's distrust of Goulart convinced them to end Brazil's experiment with democratic populism in March 1964.

The Rise of Bureaucratic Authoritarianism (1964–1985)

The military government that came to power in 1964 installed what the Argentine sociologist Guillermo O'Donnell termed **bureaucratic authoritarianism (BA)**.[8] These authoritarian regimes emerge in response to severe economic crises and are led by the armed forces and key civilian allies, most notably professional economists, engineers, and administrators. Repression in Brazilian BA varied from combinations of mild forms that constricted civil rights and other political freedoms and harsher forms that included wholesale censorship of the press through institutional acts, torture of civilians, and imprisonment without trial. The first and the last two military rulers, Castelo Branco (1964–1967), Ernesto Geisel (1974–1979), and João Figueiredo (1979–1985), presented less violent forms of authoritarianism, whereas the rule of Artur Costa e Silva (1967–1969) and of Emilio Médici (1969–1974) encompassed the worst forms of physical repression.

Initially, the military government envisioned a quick return to civilian rule and even allowed the continuation of democratic institutions, though in a limited form. After being purged in 1964 of the BA's opponents, the national congress continued to function and direct elections for federal legislators and most mayors (but not the president or state governors) were held at regular intervals. In November 1965, the military abolished all existing political parties and replaced them with only two: the National Renovation Alliance, or ARENA, and the Brazilian Democratic Movement, or MDB. ARENA was the military government's party, and MDB was the "official" party of the opposition. Former members of the three major parties joined one of the two new parties.[9]

Although these democratic institutions were more than pro forma, their powers were severely limited. The military government used institutional decrees to legislate the most important matters, thereby stopping the congress from having an important voice. Few civilian politicians could speak out directly against the military for fear of being removed from office.

In economic policy, the military reinforced the previous pattern of state interventionism. The government actively promoted **state-led development** by creating hundreds of state corporations and investing millions in established public firms such as Vale. Under military leadership, Brazil implemented one of the most successful economic development programs among newly industrialized countries. Often called the "Brazilian miracle," these programs demonstrated

Brazil's capital, Brasília. The planned city was designed by the world-famous Brazilian architect Oscar Niemeyer. *Source:* Georges Holton/Photo Researchers.

that, like France, Germany, and Japan in earlier periods, a developing country could create its own economic miracle.

The Transition to Democracy and the First Civilian Governments (1974–2001)

After the oil crisis of 1973 set off a wave of inflation around the world, the economy began to falter. Increasing criticism from Brazilian business led Geisel and Figueiredo to sustain a gradual process of democratization.[10] Initially, these leaders envisioned only a liberalizing, or opening (*abertura*), of the regime that would allow civilian politicians to compete for political office. As was later the case with Gorbachev's *glasnost* in the Soviet Union, however, control over the process of liberalization gradually slipped from their hands and was captured by organizations within civil society. In 1974, the opposition party, the MDB, stunned the military government by increasing its representation in the Senate from 18 to 30 percent and in the Chamber of Deputies from 22 to 44 percent. These numbers did not give it a majority, but the party did capture a majority in both chambers of the state legislatures in the most important industrialized southern and southeastern states.[11]

Abertura accelerated in the following years. The opposition made successive electoral gains and used them to get concessions from the government. The most important of these concessions was the reestablishment of direct elections for governors in 1982, political amnesty for dissidents, the elimination of the government's power to oust legislators from political office, and the restoration of political rights to those who had previously lost them. The gubernatorial elections of November 1982 sealed the fate of promilitary candidates as opposition gubernatorial candidates won landslide victories in the major states.

The military, which wanted to maintain as much control over the succession process as possible, preferred to have the next president selected within a restricted electoral college. Mass mobilization campaigns sought the right to elect the next president directly. The *Diretas Já!* ("Direct Elections Now!") movement, comprising an array of social movements, opposition politicians, and labor unions, expanded in size and influence in 1984.[12] Their rallies exerted tremendous pressure on the military at a moment when the question of who would succeed General Figueiredo was not clear. The military's fight to keep the 1984 elections indirect alienated civilian supporters of the generals, many of whom broke with the regime and backed an alliance (the Liberal Front) with Tancredo Neves, the candidate of the opposition PMDB, or Party of the MDB. Neves's victory in 1984, however, was marred by his sudden death on the eve of the inauguration. Vice President José Sarney became the first civilian president of Brazil since 1964.

The sequence of events that led to Sarney's presidency was a keen disappointment to those who had hoped for a clean break with the authoritarian past. Most of the politicians who gained positions of power in the new democracy hailed from the former ARENA or its misleadingly named successor, the Democratic Social Party (PDS). Most of these soon joined Sarney's own PMDB or its alliance partner, the Party of the Liberal Front (PFL).[13]

A chance for fundamental change appeared in 1987 when the national Constituent Assembly met to draft a new constitution. Given the earlier success of the opposition governors in 1982, state political machines became important players in the game of constitution writing. The state governments petitioned for the devolution of new authority to tax and spend. Labor groups also exerted influence through their lobbying organization. Workers demanded constitutional protection of their right to strike and called for an extension of the right to public employees, who had previously been prohibited from engaging in such activism. The constitution also granted workers the right to create their own unions without authorization from the Ministry of Labor.[14] As a whole, the constitution guaranteed a rich array of social and political rights, yet it also left vestiges from the corporatist past, including protection of public firms in petroleum (Petrobrás) and telecommunications from foreign investment and privatization.

The other primary issue of the day was inflation. Soon after Sarney's rise to power, annual rates of inflation began to skyrocket. The government invoked several stabilization plans to stop the explosion of prices, but to no avail. By the presidential elections of 1989, the first since the 1960s to be held as direct elections for that post, Brazilian society was calling for a political leader who would remedy runaway inflation and remove corrupt and authoritarian politicians from positions of power.

Rising from political obscurity, an ex-governor from Alagoas, a small state in the poor northeast, Fernando Collor de Mello, became president. Collor and his small party, the Party of National Reconstruction (PRN), had fought a grueling campaign against Lula da Silva, the popular left-wing labor leader and head of the Workers' Party (*Partido dos Trabalhadores,* or PT) (see "Citizen Action: The Workers' Party" in the "Political Parties and the Party System" section later in this chapter). To counteract Lula's appeal among the Brazilian people, Collor's campaign rhetoric appealed to the poor, known as the *descamisados* ("shirtless ones"), who were attracted by his attacks against politicians and the social problems caused by bureaucratic inefficiency.

The Collor presidency was a critical juncture as the government's economic team began the privatization of state enterprises, deregulation of the economy, and the reversal of decades of policies that had kept Brazil's markets closed to the rest of the world. Yet Collor failed to solve the nagging problem of inflation and, ironically, was soon accused of bribery and influence peddling and was impeached in September 1992, an ignominious end for the first directly elected president since the 1960s.

Collor's impeachment brought to the presidency Itamar Franco, a well-known politician in Minas Gerais who was less well known at the national level as Collor's vice president. Despite a high level of uncertainty during Franco's first year, including rumors of a military coup that was allegedly in the works in 1993, his government played an important stabilizing role. Perhaps his most important decision was to support his minister of finance, Fernando Henrique Cardoso, a sociologist and senator from São Paulo, in a plan to conquer inflation. In July 1994, Cardoso implemented the Real Plan, which created a new currency, the real. Monthly inflation fell from 26 percent to 2.82 percent in October 1994 (see Section 2).

Cardoso rode the success of the Real Plan to the Brazilian presidency, beating out Lula and the PT in 1994 and again in 1998 to become the first Brazilian president to be reelected. After his inauguration in January 1995, Cardoso proved adept at keeping inflation low and consolidating some of the structural reforms of the economy. As the story of Vale suggests, privatization moved forward. Other reforms, however, remained stuck in congress, including crucial reforms of the tax system. Brazil's budget and trade deficits increased, and financial crises in Asia and Russia in 1997 and 1998 eventually led to a crisis in the Real Plan. In January 1999, after weeks of foreign investors taking money out of the country, the value of the *real* collapsed. The currency soon stabilized, and hyperinflation did not return. Although a systemic reform of the tax system remained a distant goal, the Cardoso administration was able to pass the Law of Fiscal Responsibility in 2000, which addressed many of the pernicious effects of runaway spending by state and municipal governments.

After September 11, 2001

The events of September 11 and the collapse of the Argentine economy that same year produced a fundamental crisis of confidence in Brazil. The fate of the economy now hinged on events across the border and in the United States. As one of Brazil's top three export markets and as its chief partner in the common market of the south (MERCOSUL, see Section 2), Argentina's crisis threatened to destabilize the recovery of the *real*. Meanwhile, the economic and diplomatic repercussions from

Washington's war on terror threatened to displace social and economic priorities in Brazil's relations with the United States. Diplomacy with Washington became particularly embittered over the Bush administration's insistence on going to war with Iraq and its heavy-handed approach to dealing with foreigners, Brazilians included, who had to go through demeaning checks at American airports.

The election of Lula da Silva as president in October 2002 reflected a response to the need to put the social agenda ahead of the American focus on security. Lula claimed frequently in international meetings that "poverty is the most devastating weapon of mass destruction." Lula's election also reflected the maturation of democracy. Once a proponent of socialism, Lula embraced Cardoso's reform agenda. He passed major social security reforms in 2003 and 2004, but then suffered from the same inefficiencies of his predecessor when his reforms became stuck in congress during the run-up to municipal elections in late 2004. In 2005, Lula's government became mired in a widening corruption scandal involving Workers' Party leaders accused of bribing legislators for their votes on reform. Worse still, PT governments, once the example of good governance in Latin America, were accused of procuring kickbacks to fund electoral activities. The crisis threatened Lula's presidency and its lofty aspirations, but Lula won reelection in 2006 anyway and he continued to garner high presidential approval ratings well into his second term.

Themes and Implications

Historical Junctures and Political Themes

In the world of states, both international and domestic factors have influenced the Brazilian state's structure, capacity, and relations with society. During the days of the empire, international opposition to slavery forced powerful oligarchs to turn to the state for protection. The coffee and ranch economies that provided the material base for the power of the Old Republic were intricately tied to Brazil's economic role in the world. Even the *Estado Novo,* with its drive to organize society, was democratized by the defeat of fascism in Europe. The return to democracy during the 1980s was also part of a larger global experience, as authoritarian regimes gave way all over Latin America, Eastern Europe, southern Europe, and the Soviet Union.

Within Brazil, the state adjusted to changes in the distribution of power; the rise of new, politically active social classes; and the requirements of development. The federal state saw power shift regularly between the central and subnational governments. These swings between centralizing periods, such as the empire and the *Estado Novo*, to decentralizing experiences, such as the Old Republic and the more recent transition to democracy, punctuated many of the critical junctures of Brazilian politics.

The inclusion of new political actors such as the working and middle classes reshaped the Brazilian state during the twentieth century. Vargas's New State provided mechanisms for mobilizing and organizing workers and professionals. Populist democracy later provided these social segments protection from unsafe working environments, the effects of eroding wages, and the prohibitive expense of health care. Public firms such as Vale employed hundreds of thousands of Brazilians and dramatically altered the development possibilities of the country. Not surprisingly, during the 1980s and 1990s, neoliberal reforms dramatically altered the role of the Brazilian state and its relations with society (see Section 2).

State-led growth established the essential foundation for the governing of the economy. Developmentalism transformed Brazil from a predominantly agrarian economy into an industrialized economy. To be sure, growth was poorly distributed, and the social problems that emerged from it remain at the heart of the country's ongoing struggles with democracy.

Regarding the democratic idea, Brazil certainly has the institutions of a democracy, but in many ways, decades of patrimonialism, populism, corporatism, and corruption undermine these institutions. Brazilian politicians typically cultivate personal votes (they are known as **personalist politicians**) and avoid following the rule of parties or alliances. Many switch parties several times in a political career. As a result, Brazilian political parties are extremely weak.

Personalism in Brazilian politics persists because it is well rewarded.

Even with these enduring shortcomings in democracy, Brazilians prefer this form of government. They appreciate that democracy gives them more say in public policymaking. Thousands of new political groups, social movements, civic networks, and economic associations have emerged in recent years. The Brazilian state is highly decentralized into twenty-six states, a federal district, and 5,564 municipalities. Each of these centers of power has become a locus of demand-making by citizens and policymaking by elites. Under these circumstances, centralized rule following the model of the New State or the bureaucratic authoritarian period is impossible and undesirable today.

Collective identities remain uncertain in Brazil, although Brazilians are now more commonly linked through their place in the democratic order. Who are the Brazilians? This has always been a vexing question, no less so now that Brazil's borders are becoming obsolete in a world of heavy flows of international commerce, finance, and ideas. One common response to the question is that the symbols of the Brazilian nation continue to tie Brazilians together: carnival, soccer, samba, and bossa nova. Yet even as these symbols have become more prevalent, they have also lost some of their meaning because of commercialization and export as part of a tourist-attracting image of Brazil. Catholicism is a less unifying force today as Pentecostalism and evangelism have eaten into the church's membership. Women have improved both their social position and their political awareness as gender-based organizations have become a more important resource of civil society. Yet even here, Brazil remains an extremely patriarchal society: women are expected to balance motherhood and other traditional roles in the household, even while they are pressured by economic need to produce income.

Perhaps race, more than any other form of identity, remains the most difficult issue to understand in Brazilian politics and society. Racial identity continues to divide Brazilians, but not in the clear-cut manner it divides blacks and whites in the United States. These categories are multiple and often they coalesce due to racial mixing in ways that defy the kind of stark, black–white segregation in the United States.

Like race, class continues to separate Brazilians. Economic reforms and the erosion of populist redistribution have caused social gaps to widen further, making Brazil a highly fragmented society. Although it is one of the world's ten wealthiest economies, with a nominal gross domestic product of US$1 trillion, that wealth is poorly distributed. Like India, Brazil's social indicators such as income distribution, infant mortality, and nutrition consistently rank near the bottom in the world of states, though these indicators are improving. Income disparities mirror racial differences since the poor are represented by mostly blacks and mulattos, and the rich are almost invariably white. The poverty of the north and northeast also contrasts with the more industrialized and prosperous southeastern and southern states.

Implications for Comparative Politics

As a large, politically decentralized, and socially fragmented polity, Brazil presents several extraordinary challenges to the study of comparative politics. First, the Brazilian state is an anomaly. It has been both highly centralized and decentralized during different periods of its history. In each of these periods, the state produced lasting political legacies that have both strengthened and weakened its capacity for promoting development, democracy, and social distribution. Although political centralization has been an important factor in making the French state strong, decentralized states such as the United States and German federations have also proven to be successful formulas for government. The Brazilian case is a laboratory for evaluating which approach is likely to be more successful in other large, decentralized states in the developing world, such as China and India and, until recently, Russia.

While the complexity of the Brazilian state represents one problem area, the weakness of the country's democratic institutions suggests another, and perhaps more troubling, concern. Along with Russia, Brazil demonstrates how the lack of coherent party systems and electoral institutions can endanger democracy. In contrast to the highly organized polity of Germany and the strength of parties in parliamentary democracies like the United Kingdom and Japan, Brazil's experience highlights how anemic representative institutions can weaken democracy.

Paradoxically, as Brazil developed economically and made its way back to democracy in the 1980s, it also became a more socially unequal country. Established democracies like India and transitional democracies like Mexico and Russia have also experienced the reality that democratization does not improve the distribution of wealth. Finally, the complex divisions afflicting Brazilians' collective identities challenge all attempts to address the country's problems. Yet even today, Brazilians and outside observers continue to treat the country as a singular unit. In this regard, Brazil presents a puzzle for theories about collective identities: How has such a socially fragmented society remained a coherent whole for so long?

SECTION 2 Political Economy and Development

Like most other countries in the developing world, Brazil's politics has always been shaped by the country's quest for economic and social development. Two processes in particular have left enduring legacies: the pattern of state intervention in the domestic market and the effects of external economic change. Historically, these two factors have influenced each other. External economic crises—world depressions, fluctuations in the price of exported goods such as coffee, upsurges in the prices of imported goods—have compelled the Brazilian state to intervene in the domestic economy through protection, subsidies, and even the production of goods that it previously imported. During the twentieth century, these policies made Brazil one of the newly industrialized countries of the world, alongside Mexico, India, and

China. But globalization in recent years has made the Brazilian economy once again highly dependent upon the country's strategic position in world markets. Without the benefit of the state-led development that guided Brazil during much of the last half century, the country faces a crossroads in its model of economic growth. This section explores the state-led model of development in Brazil and the forces of dependency and globalization that have shaped the country's economic development.

State and Economy

Like its Latin American neighbors, Brazil's economic development prior to the New State was based on **export-led growth**, that is, on the export of agricultural products such as sugar, cotton, coffee, and, for a short time in the early 1900s, rubber. In the nineteenth century, coffee emerged as the engine of growth in the Brazilian economy. By the time of the Old Republic, a strong demand for Brazilian coffee in Europe and North America gave the country a virtual monopoly in the global market. Cotton, sugar, and cereals continued to be important export products too, but they were secondary to coffee. By 1919, coffee composed 56 percent of Brazil's total exports. Only five years later, that figure jumped to 75 percent.[15]

The dominance of coffee ensured that the Old Republic would keep Brazil active in the world market with minimal state involvement. Export receipts provided a reservoir of capital to build railroads, power stations, and other infrastructure. These investments, in turn, spurred the growth of some light industries, mostly in textiles, footwear, and clothing. With ample domestic capital, public finance was relegated to a minor role.

The Brazilian state's involvement in the economy became far more **interventionist** during the 1930s when the Great Depression caused international demand for coffee to decline. As exports fell, imports of manufactured goods also declined. The incentives that were produced by the crisis led Brazilian manufacturers to replace these goods with domestically produced ones. These forces prompted **import substitution industrialization (ISI)**, a model of development that promoted domestic industrial production of previously imported manufactured goods. Initially, large doses of

state intervention were not necessary. The initial phase of ISI—the so-called light, or easy, phase—focused on manufactured products that required little capital or sophisticated technology. Most of these industries, such as textiles and food processing, were labor intensive and created jobs. Although these conditions did not require large infusions of state capital, Vargas's New State provided limited subsidies and tariff protection to nascent ISI sectors.

At the end of World War II, new ideas about Third World development came to be popular among various international agencies. The new goal was to "deepen" the ISI model by promoting heavy industry and capital-intensive production. In Brazil, as in Argentina, Mexico, and India, a new generation of **state technocrats**—experts in economic development—took an active role in designing new policies. Inspired by the texts of the United Nations Economic Commission for Latin America (ECLA), these technocrats targeted particular industrial sectors as strategic.[16] Then, through the use of industrial policies including planning, subsidies, and financial support, state agencies promoted the quick growth of these sectors.

Brazil was the epitome of ECLA-style **developmentalism**, the ideology and practice of state-sponsored growth, during the 1950s in Latin America. More than any other Latin American state, the Brazilian state was organizationally capable of implementing industrial policies to deepen ISI. New bureaucratic structures, such as a national development bank and national public firms, were created during the first and second Vargas governments to produce as well as to regulate industrial growth. The producer state promoted private investment by extracting and distributing raw materials for domestic industries at prices well below the international market level. These lower prices were in effect subsidies to domestic industry. Other firms linked to sectors of the economy receiving these supports would benefit in a chain reaction.

Although growth rates achieved impressive levels during the 1950s and early 1960s and even higher levels in the 1970s (see Table 9.2), it was during this period that the first serious contradictions of ISI emerged.[17] Protection fostered noncompetitive, inefficient production because it removed incentives for competition. Although industries grew, they did so by depending too heavily on public subsidies. ISI

Table 9.2	
Governing the Economy: GDP Growth Rates	
1940–1949	5.6%
1950–1959	6.1%
1960–1969	5.4%
1970–1979	12.4%
1980–1989	1.5%
1990–1996	2.1%
1997–2000	0.8%
2001–2003	1.0%
2004–2007	3.2%

Source: Brazilian Institute of Geography and Statistics (IBGE), *Anuario Estatístico Brasilero* (Rio de Janeiro: IBGE, various years).

also became import-intensive. Businesses used subsidized finance to import technology and machinery. The government helped these firms by overvaluing the currency to make import prices cheaper. This overvaluation of the currency hurt export earnings, which were necessary to pay for imports. As a result, the export sector could not supply the state with much-needed revenues to sustain growth, prompting the government to print money, which in turn led to inflation. Under the Goulart government (1961–1964), the economy's capacity to import and export dwindled, and stagnation set in. The economic crisis that soon followed contributed to the coup of 1964 and Goulart's fall.

The failures of ISI during the 1960s inspired new thinking about development, at least in Brazilian and other Latin American academic circles. The so-called dependency school, whose adherents were known as *dependencistas,* emerged in the social sciences around the idea that underdeveloped or "peripheral" countries faced tremendous obstacles to achieving sustained levels of industrialization and growth in a world dominated by "core" economies in North America and Western Europe. ISI's failures, the *dependencistas* argued, were due to the ill-fated attempt to adjust marginally the inherently exploitative structure of world markets. Pursuing capitalist development only favored the core economies, so the *dependencistas* advocated (vaguely) de-linking Brazil from the world economy. This early attack on what we today call globalization inspired a new generation of progressive

thinkers, among them the sociologist and future president Fernando Henrique Cardoso, who became one of the preeminent proponents of a variant of the dependency argument. The fall of Brazilian democracy, however, would provide little opportunity for these groups to take their ideas out of the universities.

The rise of the military governments in 1964 led to reform but eventually to an attempt to deepen ISI through state-led development methods. From 1964 to 1985, the state continued to promote industrialization, especially the production of consumer durable goods such as automobiles, televisions, refrigerators, and machinery for the domestic market. Multinational firms also invested and transferred technology to these and other new industries. Table 9.3 highlights the important contribution of industry to the Brazilian gross domestic product.

Para-statals, also known as public or state firms, played an important role in the military's development model. Large-scale projects in shipbuilding, mining, steel, oil, bauxite, and aluminum were financed and managed by bureaucratic agencies and state firms, and often included foreign companies. Peter Evans, an American political economist, insightfully characterized these complex relations among the state, foreign investors, and domestic capitalists as a "triple alliance."[18] The state, however, remained the dominant partner.

In the 1970s, Brazil's military leaders realized that, in order to finance the huge public expenditures

Table 9.3			
Governing the Economy: Sector Composition of the GDP, 1970–2007			
Year	Agriculture	Industry	Services
1970	11.6%	35.9%	52.6%
1980	10.2%	41.0%	48.8%
1990	9.3%	34.2%	56.5%
2000	9.0%	29.0%	62.0%
2007	5.1%	30.8%	64.0%

Source: IBGE and Werner Baer, *The Brazilian Economy: Growth and Development,* 4th ed. (New York: Praeger, 1994), pp. 382–383. © 1995 by Werner Baer. Reprinted by permission of Greenwood Publishing Group, Inc. All rights reserved.

of national industrial policy, international financial markets would have to play a role. The military also began to emphasize primary exports such as coffee, iron ore, cereals, and other agricultural products. Policies designed to increase agricultural productivity and technological modernization were expanded. The export of agricultural surplus and the sale of food products in the internal market were facilitated by a growing agribusiness sector. Spurred on by state subsidies, agribusiness supplied new resources and management for previously inefficient agricultural subsectors. One of the most unusual agribusiness ventures occurred in the 1970s, when the military government introduced a plan to use sugarcane alcohol as a fuel source. Northeast agribusiness boomed during these years as the sugar economy became tied to the dynamic industrial economy of the southern and southeastern regions. In recent years, the Brazilian government has promoted exports of this energy resource as an alternative to fossil fuels.

The Environmental Costs of State-Led Growth

The impressive growth of industry and agriculture was concentrated in the central and southern regions of Brazil. Centers of growth in the states of São Paulo, Minas Gerais, Rio de Janeiro, and Rio Grande do Sul became the locomotives of the country's development and sites of environmental degradation. As capital-intensive industries became more common in Brazil, ecologically destructive technologies were used without much regulation. Before the mid-1970s, Brazilian policymakers were unconcerned with the emission of toxic waste into the ground at major industrial zones, air pollution in overgrown urban areas, or pesticide and chemical fertilizer use in agricultural regions.

The environmental costs of these attitudes became clear in the 1970s. Guanabara Bay and the Paraiba do Sul River basin, both in Rio de Janeiro state, were brought to the brink of biological death. Urban pollution in São Paulo devastated the Tietê River, which runs through the city, making it no better than a toxic waste dump in some areas and threatening the health of millions. By far the worst tragedy was in Cubatão, an industrial city 60 kilometers east of metropolitan São Paulo. There, petrochemical industries and steel mills wreaked havoc on the environment, pumping 1,102 tons of pollutants into the surrounding ecological system each day. The conditions in the residential area of Cubatão became so bad that by 1981, one city council member reported that he had not seen a star in twenty years.[19] Thousands reported becoming afflicted with tuberculosis, pneumonia, bronchitis, emphysema, asthma, and cancer. Forty of every one thousand babies in Cubatão were stillborn.

Big development projects reached the forests of the Amazon River basin in the 1970s with Vale do Rio Doce's Carajás mining work in the eastern Amazon. This and other industrial projects threatened the tropical forests, as did cattle ranching, timber extraction, and slash-and-burn agriculture by poor farmers, a practice that allowed frequent rains to leech nutrients from the soil and prevent the return of tropical habitats. By the 1980s, it was clear that the primary result of these practices was the deforestation of the Amazon.

Brazil's worsening environmental problems received official attention after 1972, when the United Nations held its Conference on the Human Environment. Soon afterward, Brazil created an environmental secretariat, and in 1981 the government established the National Environmental Council (CONAMA), which included officials from national and state government, and representatives from business, professional, and environmental groups. State governments also established their own environmental agencies and passed important legislation.[20] In 1975, São Paulo passed a comprehensive antipollution law. The cleanup of Cubatão began in 1983.

Partly as a result of the return to democracy in 1984, new environmental movements within and outside Brazil began to influence official and public opinion on the costs of resource degradation. Much attention was brought to these problems at the United Nations Conference on the Environment in Rio de Janeiro in 1992, a follow-up to the 1972 meeting. Hundreds of **nongovernmental organizations**, many who attended the 1992 earth summit, have since worked diligently to underscore the unique importance of Brazil in the growing global concern surrounding climate change.[21] The Amazon, which represents one of the major mechanisms for absorbing excess CO_2, suffered deforestation during the 1990s at an alarming rate. By 2004, logging, farming, and development had destroyed 20 percent of it. Though the Brazilian government backed away from making sweeping commitments to reduce CO_2 emissions after the third international UN conference on the environment, held in Kyoto, Japan, in 1997, it has since renewed efforts to reduce deforestation. Since 2004, the rate of deforestation has declined noticeably, though every year Amazonian territory the size of the state of Massachusetts is deforested and developed despite the government's efforts. Part of the problem lies with the government's reluctance to underutilize the country's vast natural resources for development and to be seen as taking orders from foreigners who many Brazilians see as having designs on appropriating the Amazon basin for their own interests.

The Fiscal System

In developed countries such as the United States, Germany, France, and Britain, governments can use tax policy to punish polluters. In Brazil, however, tax collection has been notoriously weak, making this a less useful instrument to regulate business or individuals. As the Brazilian economy became more complex after the 1960s, new opportunities for evading taxes emerged. An **informal economy** of small firms, domestic enterprises, street vendors, and unregistered employees proliferated, virtually outside the domain of the taxable economy. In some cases, these enterprises grew to a substantial size, accounting for the distribution of everything from artisans' goods to professional services. Legally registered companies began to subcontract unregistered professionals to render services beyond the reach of the tax system. Although reliable information is lacking, economists estimate that the informal economy could be as large as a third of Brazil's gross domestic product ($300 million) and it may employ about 30 million to 45 million people. Figures on tax evasion in both the formal and informal sectors estimate that federal coffers lose more than $70 billion a year.

Other problems developed for the tax system after the transition to democracy. The new constitution of 1988 decentralized the fiscal structure by allowing the states and municipalities to expand their collection of taxes and to receive larger transfers of funds from Brasília. Significant gaps emerged in tax collection responsibilities and public spending as a result of these changes. Although the central state spent less than it collected in taxes between 1960 and 1994, Brazil's 5,564 municipal governments spent several times more than they collected. Subnational governments also gained more discretion over spending since the destination of most of these funds was not predetermined by the federal government. The governors also used public banks held by the state governments to finance expenditures, thus expanding their debt.

The Collor administration began to reverse some of the adverse effects by threatening to cut off federal debt servicing and to close down regional banks. Efforts to increase tax receipts to 25 percent of GDP helped to stave off a fiscal meltdown.[22] But it was the Cardoso administration's efforts at recovering federal tax revenues and reducing the fiscal distortions produced by Brazil's federal structure that made the greatest difference. Tax evasion was slowed, as the federal tax collection agency was expanded and its surveillance powers enhanced. Legislation in 1994, 1998, and 2000 allowed the federal government to employ more discretion over transfers of funds constitutionally earmarked for the state and municipal governments and to cap the states' ability to acquire debt. The most important reform, the Fiscal Responsibility Law, passed in 2000, set strict limits on federal, state, and municipal expenditures, but its enforcement is still in doubt. Given still large civil service payrolls (often these constitute more than 70 percent of state and municipal revenues), governments are hard-pressed to implement the law. The National Confederation of Municipalities estimates that 80 percent of Brazil's mayors and sixteen of twenty-seven states are not in compliance with the law's strict requirements. These problems have been at the center of Brazil's mounting public debt, which rose to over 50 percent of GDP at the end of Cardoso's administration in 2002 (see Figure 9.2).

In 2003, Lula's government passed a tax reform that permitted increases in seven federal taxes and

FIGURE 9.2

Governing the Economy: Brazilian Public Sector Debt as a Percentage of GDP, 1995–2007

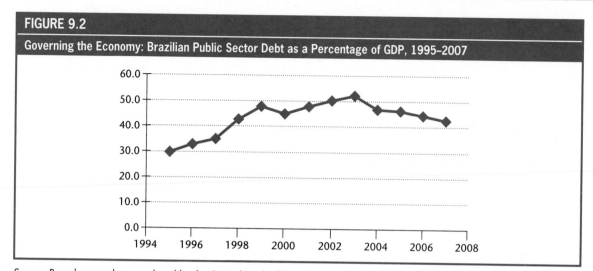

Source: Based on numbers produced by the Central Bank of Brazil.

simplified the tax code. Other aspects of tax reform, however, remained unfulfilled. Legislation to address fiscal competition among the states, the simplification and unification of the states' value-added tax, and efforts to reduce the overall tax burden on business (currently 35 percent) were postponed. The government also failed to do something about the weight of taxes, such as sales taxes, that fall more heavily on the poor. Still, the Lula government has been able to reduce the public sector debt modestly, as Figure 9.2 illustrates.

The Problem of Inflation

Inflation deserves special mention in Brazil, for in no other country, with the possible exceptions of Germany and Argentina, has this phenomenon had such a lasting impact on a country's politics. In Brazil, inflation accompanied state-led development, especially after 1974. The Brazilian state, business, and unions all distorted the value of goods and services by manipulating prices, interest rates, and wages. After the transition to democracy, successive attempts to control inflation fell apart as different interest groups attempted to retain these controls. No fewer than seven "stabilization" plans designed to control prices between 1985

and 1994 fell apart, sometimes generating "hyperinflation" (600 percent or more annual inflation). Figure 9.3 illustrates this terrible track record.

The Sarney, Collor, and Franco governments sought to control the growth in prices by setting the

FIGURE 9.3

Governing the Economy: Annual Rates of Inflation, 1989–2003

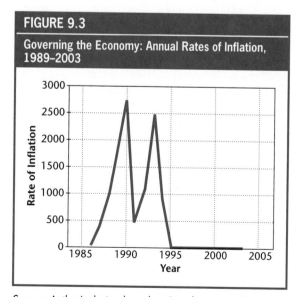

Source: Author's design based on Brazilian Central Bank figures, 2005.

value of some basic products and freezing wages while the government reduced spending. The plans all failed. Once fixed prices could not be maintained or government spending could not be restrained or wages were increased in accordance with monthly inflation rates, the inflationary spiral would heat up.

Only Cardoso's Real Plan proved successful in reining in inflation. The Real Plan anchored the real, the new currency, to the dollar. Unlike a similar plan in Argentina, the Real Plan did not fix the real to the dollar strictly but allowed it to float within bands, thus achieving more flexibility in the exchange rate. This is one of the main reasons that the real was able to weather the kind of financial turmoil that led the Argentine economy to ruin in 2001–2002.

Paradoxically, the Real Plan's formula for success proved to be a source of weakness. Soon after the Mexican peso crisis of December 1994, Central Bank managers in Brasília became convinced that the real was overvalued, just as the *peso* had been before its crash. Overvaluation made exports more expensive abroad, raised the costs of production, and made imports cheaper. Brazil's trade deficit rose by more than 140 percent after 1995 and foreign investors became antsy following financial crises in Asia and Russia in 1997–1998. Even Cardoso's signing of a US$42 billion bailout sponsored by the International Monetary Fund (IMF) in November 1998 could not avoid a crisis. The real fell by more than 50 percent against the dollar in January 1999. Despite the devaluation, hyperinflation did not return, and the government was successful in moderating the growth in public spending through reforms such as the Law of Fiscal Responsibility. Renewed growth and good fiscal management by the Lula administration have begun to reduce the massive public debt.

Society and Economy

Brazil's astounding levels of industrialization during the 1950s, 1960s, and 1970s had lasting effects on the urban population. In 1950, 35 percent of the population lived in urban areas. By 1980, that number had increased to 68 percent. During the same period, employment in industry jumped from 14 percent to 24 percent, while employment in agriculture declined from 60 percent to 30 percent. Import substitution had

created these jobs by expanding the size of both the working and the middle classes. Service-sector professionals like lawyers, doctors, and private teachers soon found clients as the domestic consumer market grew along with the working class.

Nevertheless, the number of jobs created in the industrial sector did not begin to absorb the huge number of unemployed Brazilians. Many of the new jobs required skilled and semiskilled specialized labor. Metallurgy, automobile production, and mining did not provide many opportunities for the large numbers of unskilled workers in the Brazilian labor market. In the late 1980s and 1990s, even skilled workers faced losing their jobs because of intense industrial restructuring. During the 1990s, manufacturing jobs fell by 48 percent and unemployment in metropolitan areas rose above 18 percent. Service-sector employment increased, but not enough to make up for industrial job losses. These jobs also paid less and offered fewer protections from arbitrary dismissal.

Industrialization also failed to eradicate the racial inequalities inherited from slavery. Despite the impressive industrial development of Brazil, Afro-Brazilians continued to make less than their white colleagues and had fewer opportunities for upward mobility. According to one study, nonwhite men and women in Brazil have made real gains in their income because of improvements in education and occupation, but the gap separating nonwhite income from white income remains significant.[23] On average, blacks make 41 percent and mulattos make 47 percent of what whites make.

Women constitute 28 percent of the economically active population in Brazil and continue to enter the labor market in record numbers. In 2003, more than half of all women were in the work force as compared with 73 percent of all men. Brazil also ranks second only to the United States in the percentage of women in top management positions (44 percent to 46 percent in the United States). Working women typically have more years of schooling than men, but they still receive lower salaries for the same job. Women make 57 percent of what men make. Afro-Brazilian women, who are doubly disadvantaged by race and gender, are more likely to have underpaid and menial work. For example, more than 90 percent of domestic servants are black women.

The uneven effects of industrialization patterns and other demographic and policy factors discussed below have all worked against the equalization of income distribution in Brazil. Income is more maldistributed in Brazil than it is in most other developing countries, including Mexico, India, China, and Nigeria (see Table 9.4).

The Welfare System

In a country of startling social inequalities, welfare policy plays a remarkably minor role in the lives of most Brazilians. Although welfare and education expenditures constitute about 11 percent of the GDP, among the highest levels in the world, the money has not improved Brazil's mediocre welfare state. Unlike the systems in Britain, France, Germany, and Japan, Brazil's welfare system has not reduced the high level of poverty or helped the majority of the poor.

Brazil supports a public school system as well as a health, retirement, and social assistance system that includes funds for unemployment relief. Salaried workers are entitled to benefits such as health care, worker's compensation, retirement pensions, paid vacations, and overtime pay, yet only an estimated 15 percent of the Brazilian population qualify for

these benefits. Workers in the informal sector, who are normally undocumented, cannot collect welfare since technically the federal government does not consider them employed. Corruption, clientelism, and outright waste make the welfare system incapable of delivering benefits to the people who need them the most.[24]

Part of the problem is that more people need welfare than actually contribute to the welfare state. Today, only half of the 70 million people who are economically active contribute to the welfare system. That means that the government must finance the shortfall with debt.

Between 1960 and 2000, while the population doubled, the number of retired people multiplied elevenfold. As a result, retirement benefits and pensions currently exceed the salaries of working employees by 30 percent. The average retirement age for public employees is fifty-seven for men and fifty-four for women, though pension reforms passed in 2003 will raise the age to sixty for men and fifty-five for women by 2010. The fiscal problems of the pension system fall most heavily on the public system. While developed economies spend just 1.7 percent of GDP on public pensions, Brazil spends almost three times that number, and its retirement-age population is only 40 percent that of the developed economies. More than 70 percent of all income transfers are retirement benefits that go to middle-class and upper-class individuals, including politicians, judges, and military officers. The indigent receive only 1.5 percent of these monies. Such imbalances deepen the social disparities evident in Brazil.

Some of the groundwork for reversing poverty and inequality was established during the Cardoso administration. In addition to several cash transfer programs meant to provide grants directly to poor families to enhance their health and the education of their children, Cardoso initiated programs targeting the rural poor. One example is the Family Health Program which, since 1995, provides teams of community health workers to areas of the country that have historically been underserved. By 2006, more than 60 percent of all of Brazil's municipalities participated in the program. Some studies have shown that this program has accelerated the decline in infant mortality and, along with other programs, has improved prenatal care and family reproductive medicine, including reductions in the rates of HIV/AIDS.[25]

Table 9.4				
Governing the Economy: Brazilian Income Distribution in Comparative Perspective				
Country	10% Richest	20% Richest	20% Poorest	10% Poorest
Brazil	46.9	63.2	2.4	0.7
Mexico	43.1	59.1	3.1	1.0
Chile	47.0	62.2	3.3	1.2
China	33.1	50.0	4.7	1.8
Nigeria	40.8	55.7	4.4	1.6
India	28.5	43.3	8.9	3.9
United States	29.9	45.8	5.4	1.9
United Kingdom	28.5	44.0	6.1	2.1
France	25.1	40.2	7.2	2.8
Russia	23.8	39.3	8.2	3.3

Source: World Bank, *World Development Indicators 2005* (Washington, D.C.: World Bank, 2005), Table 2.7.

The Lula administration has been even more focused on social reform. In the fall of 2003, the government passed a social security reform that raised the minimum retirement age, placed stricter limits on benefit ceilings, reduced survivor benefits, and taxed pensions and benefits. Issues including the taxation of social security benefits for judges and military officers and the reduction of survivor benefits for the latter group became stumbling blocks in cross-party negotiations. These and other issues became the basis for government concessions, including reducing proposed cuts, so that the total annual savings produced by the reform were less than half of the original target.

Some of Lula's other bold new social reforms have captured headlines. The most notable is *Bolsa Família* (the School Grant Program), a conditional cash transfer program that consolidated three programs that were initiated under the Cardoso government. Lula expanded the funding of *Bolsa Família*, which grants modest monthly sums to families that keep their children in school and see the doctor for regular vaccinations and check-ups. Since 2003, 11.1 million families or 20 percent of the Brazilian population (46 million people) have benefited from *Bolsa Família*.[26] Both Cardoso's and Lula's sustained efforts in social welfare have generated some aggregate results in that poverty rates have fallen since 1994 and other improvements in human development indicators such as reduced illiteracy, particularly in the poorest regions of the north and northeast, have been recorded in recent years.

Agrarian Reform

Landownership in Brazil remains concentrated in the hands of only 1 percent of the landowning class. The arable land held by this small group of owners (about 58,000) is equal to the size of Venezuela and Colombia combined. Over 3 million other farmers survive on only 2 percent of the country's land. An additional 4.5 million Brazilians are farm laborers or squatters who own no land. In the 1980s and 1990s, several landless peasant movements grabbed headlines by sanctioning illegal land invasions and coming to blows with rural landowners and police. Among the most important of these groups, the Landless

Workers' Movement (*Movimento dos Sem-Terra*, or MST) attracted the most attention by seizing some 1.38 million acres.

The Cardoso administration responded to these problems by expropriating some unproductive estates and settling 186,000 families on them. Perhaps sensing that the Lula government would be more sympathetic, the MST dramatically increased the rate of land invasions in 2003–2005. Lula promised to resettle 60,000 families, but budgetary realities made actual redistributions fall well short of this target. MST rhetoric and direct action will continue to escalate tensions and test the Lula government's commitment to fiscal probity and modest social reform.

Any serious effort to address rural poverty will affect urban poverty. Through rural-to-urban migration, the landless poor have swelled the rings of poverty that surround Brazil's major cities. During the 1950s and 1960s, the growth of industry in the south and southeast enticed millions to migrate to the states of São Paulo, Minas Gerais, and Rio de Janeiro in the hopes of finding new economic opportunities. The rapidity of rural-to-urban migration was striking. More than 31 million people migrated to these cities during the 1960s and 1970s. By 1991, 75 percent of Brazil's population was living in urban areas.

The flood of migrants to urban areas and the growth of urban populations created terrible social problems. The pressures on Brazilian cities for basic services such as sanitation, education, and transportation soon overwhelmed the budgets of municipalities and state governments. Poor people were left to their own devices. Squatters soon took government land, settling on the outskirts of the major cities. They built huge shantytowns called *favelas* around cities like Rio and São Paulo.

Regional disparities in income worsened during this period. The military governments addressed this problem by transferring revenues from the industrialized south and southeast to the poor north and northeast, where many of their supporters were based. The federal government subsidized communication and transportation in the poorer regions and created new state agencies to implement regional developmental projects. These policies had mixed results. The contribution of poor regions to GDP increased.

The growth rate of the central and western regions was spurred on by agribusiness activities, mineral exploration, and financial services. The economic gap between regions narrowed, but social and income disparities within the underdeveloped regions increased. Industrialization in the poorer regions was capital intensive and therefore labor saving but did not create jobs. Only the most skilled workers in these regions benefited from these changes. Poor agricultural management, ecological destruction, the murder of native Brazilians due to the need to expropriate land for mining and agriculture, and corruption all weakened the distributive effect of these policies.

Favelas in Rio de Janeiro.   *Source:* Marc Valdecantos

Today, the northern and northeastern regions remain much poorer than those in the south and southeast. Whereas 15 percent of the population in the southeast subsist under the poverty line, more than 50 percent of the inhabitants of the northeast are below that marker. The life expectancy of a northeasterner—fifty-eight years—is nine years below that of a resident of São Paulo state (sixty-seven years) and fifteen years below that of a resident of Rio Grande do Sul (seventy-three years).[27]

Brazil in the Global Economy

As the financing needs of state-led industrialization outstripped the resources of the national development bank and domestic bankers, the deepening of ISI required Brazil to pursue international sources of credit. During the late 1960s and the 1970s, private lenders were eager to provide loans to Brazil and other fast-growing countries. As a result, Brazil became the largest single debtor country in the developing world.

External events had a hand in creating and then managing Brazil's external debt. By the end of the 1970s, the world economy had been hit with two oil price shocks that sent inflation rates soaring in the United States and other industrialized countries. Many of these countries also held Brazilian debt. As the central banks in Europe and the Federal Reserve in the United States ratcheted interest rates upward to force prices back down, Brazil's interest payments soared.[28]

After Mexico declared a moratorium on interest payments in 1982, private investors began to shun Brazil and other Latin American debtors. During the 1980s, the so-called "Lost Decade" of slow growth and debt crisis, the IMF and the World Bank became important suppliers of badly needed credit. But only debtors who promised to take concrete steps to reduce inflation, open their domestic markets to foreign competition, promote exports, and privatize state industries were eligible for help.

Brazil, along with Argentina and Peru, rejected these conditions. The Sarney government refused to implement the free-market policies demanded by the international financial institutions. In 1987, his government took the ultimate gamble in resisting creditors by declaring a moratorium on debt repayment, a move that sent a signal to investors that Brazil would control its own reform agenda on its own terms. The moratorium, however, did not last. It was lifted a few months later under intense pressure from the international financial community. Opposition to the moratorium within the country was also great in the business community, which feared that such aggressive action would scare off foreign investors and ruin the country's already tattered credit rating.

Collor reversed course. Partly in response to pressure from international creditors and partly in recognition that Sarney's alternative policies had failed, he agreed to put Brazil on the path of free-market policies with reforms that included the privatization of state enterprises and the deregulation of the economy. These domestic changes were reflected externally as Collor began to normalize relations between Brazil and the multilateral agencies, especially the IMF.

The liberalization of markets opened Brazilian industry to higher degrees of foreign competition. As a result, the competitiveness of domestic firms emerged as a core problem. One 1997 study showed that the overall productivity of Brazilian industry runs at only 27 percent of the U.S. level.[29] Inefficiencies caused by poor infrastructure, untrained labor, and lack of access to technology and capital continue as key obstacles. The average Brazilian worker has only six years of schooling, half as much as the average worker in Japan or the United States.

How Brazil will fare in an increasingly interconnected and competitive global marketplace will also depend on its external political relations. Brazil's trade relations with the United States have been particularly conflictual. Both countries tangled over Brazilian exports of steel, soy, orange juice, and other products during the 1980s and especially in recent years. The political climate was less charged during the 1990s when international free-trade accords, such as the North American Free Trade Agreement (NAFTA), received the support of both Washington and most Latin American governments. But relations soured during years preceding the World Trade Organization (WTO) meeting in Cancún, Mexico, in 2003. In a battle with developed economies over agricultural subsidies, Brazil, along with China, South Africa, and India, led an alliance of 21 countries to pressure the European Union and the United States to negotiate the phasing out of these subsidies. The subsequent walkout of the Brazilian and other developing country representatives set the stage for subsequent conflicts. Presently, negotiations to establish the Free Trade Area of the Americas (FTAA) have slowed to a crawl. Brazil wishes to negotiate with the U.S. with the added leverage of its subhemispheric block, MERCOSUL, behind it (See "Global Connection: Governing the Economy in a World of States: MERCOSUL.") The Americans have agreed reluctantly, but refusal to discuss agricultural policies remains a sticking point.

Brazil's degree of commitment to the international free-trade system will likely expand in the coming years with the growing importance of its export sector. Due to increased prices for commodities such

Global Connection

Governing the Economy in a World of States: MERCOSUL

After several years of negotiating the Treaty of Asunción, Brazil, Argentina, Paraguay, and Uruguay inaugurated MERCOSUL, a regional common market group, in January 1995. Under MERCOSUL (Mercosur in Spanish), Brazil and its trade partners agreed to reduce tariffs on imports from signatories gradually until 2006, when the 10,000 items

that make up the tariff listings of all four countries must conform to a common external tariff (CET) regime.

During the negotiations over the Treaty of Asunción between March 26, 1991, and MERCOSUL's inauguration, trade among the partners increased from 8 to 20 percent, making the case for a subhemispheric common market stronger. After a rough start due to the

Mexican *peso* crisis, the signatories reaffirmed their commitment to forge the common market. Efforts to remove gradually tariff protections and nontariff protections, such as regulations that slow the flow of trade, proceeded with few disruptions.

At the center of MERCOSUL's evolution is the long list of products that the CET targets. However, the signatories are allowed to exclude up to 300 items (399 in Paraguay) as exceptions to the CET. The partners also agreed to numerous dispute-resolution mechanisms to avoid conflicts that might threaten the free-trade group.

MERCOSUL is only the latest in a list of common market schemes in Latin America. In 1960, the Latin American Association of Free Trade (ALALC) initiated a process for forming a common market in twelve years. Although this goal was unfulfilled because of persistent differences among the group's members, intraregional trade increased from 7.7 percent in 1960 to 13.8 percent in 1980. Subhemispheric common market groups unconnected to ALALC also emerged as the Andean Group in 1969 (Bolivia, Colombia, Ecuador, and Venezuela) and the Central American Common Market in 1960 (Costa Rica, Guatemala, El Salvador, Honduras, and Nicaragua). ALALC was replaced in 1980 with the Latin American Integration Association (ALADI). Unlike ALALC's mission of forming a common market, ALADI's goal was to foster the formation of preferential trade agreements among subhemispheric groups. These efforts received their most important boost soon after the administration of George H. W. Bush delivered its Enterprise for the Americas Initiative (EAI) in 1990, a plan of lofty goals for hemispheric economic integration, which are being implemented now through the Free Trade Area of the Americas (FTAA). Soon after the EAI was announced, the existing regional groups and a new wave of other groups formed preferential organizations. Besides MERCOSUL, the most important of these was the North American Free Trade Agreement (NAFTA), initiated on January 1, 1994.

MERCOSUL differs from NAFTA in several ways. First, it is designed to be a common market among developing countries and not, as NAFTA is, a tripartite free-trade area organized to reduce tariffs primarily across the U.S.–Mexico border. Second, MERCOSUL can evolve in ways unimagined in NAFTA, such as the creation of a common currency. Finally, MERCOSUL can and has negotiated free-trade agreements with other global blocks such as the European Union (EU). This gives these four developing countries more leverage on the international level. Mexico's interests as a developing country are arguably not given the same priority by its trade partners in NAFTA.

MERCOSUL also differs markedly from the EU. Because the EU is a supranational organization, its members shift important sovereign areas of policy such as commercial; competition; increasingly justice and home affairs; and for the members of the euro zone, monetary policy to Brussels. The signatories of MERCOSUL do not envision more than a commercial and perhaps monetary agreement, and all this is negotiated multilaterally. MERCOSUL does not have an executive body such as the EU Commission that regulates the behavior of members. It has dispute resolution mechanisms, but nothing like the European Court of Justice whose, decisions are binding on EU members.

Like its predecessors, MERCOSUL was a product and a cause of increased commercial integration among its signatories. Since its creation, MERCOSUL has contributed to a threefold increase in trade among its members, but with an upsurge in world prices for soya, grains, and minerals, trade with the rest of the world has increased more rapidly than inter-MERCOSUL trade since 2004. MERCOSUL is also at a diplomatic crossroads regarding the role it will play in the continuing FTAA process. President Lula da Silva has used Brazil's leadership within MERCOSUL to extract concessions from Washington on the type and pacing of trade liberalization in the hemisphere, but the results have not substantially deepened the level of regional integration as originally envisioned in the Treaty of Asunción.

Source: Lia Valls Pereira, "Tratado de Assunção: Resultados e Perspectivas," in Antônio Salazar P. Brandão and Lia Valls Pereira, eds., *Mercosul: Perspectivas da Integração* (Rio de Janeiro: Fundação Getúlio Vargas, 1996), p. 11; *The Economist,* July 5, 2007.

as soy, oranges, wheat, coffee, and other products that Brazil exports, the country's account enjoyed a healthy surplus of $36.5 billion in February 2008. Trade has grown with developing countries such as China and India as fast as it has with Europe and the United States, suggesting that Brazil is becoming one of the major manufacturing and agrindustry nodes in the globalized system of production and consumption.

Domestic and international opposition to globalization might constrain the Lula presidency from pursuing further integration into global markets. But the commodity boom and its effects on Brazilian growth levels in recent years suggests will likely motivate the government to stick to its commitments to expand the country's position in global markets. On the fiscal side, Lula's embrace of good fiscal management and modest social reforms has generated results that have satisfied the IMF's requirements and pleased many looking for meaningful social change. Lula has even found ways of making Brazil's relations with the international financial institutions work in favor of his administration's social justice goals. During his two terms in office, Lula has signed several agreements with the World Bank and the Inter-American Development Bank to create and fund new social assistance programs. *Bolsa Família* has become a showcase program for developing countries, and that has made the international financial institutions very interested in making it as successful as possible in Brazil itself.

SECTION 3 Governance and Policy-Making

Organization of the State

The institutions of the Brazilian state have changed significantly since independence. Even so, a number of institutional legacies have endured and continue to shape Brazilian politics. The most important is the centralization of state authority in the executive. Paradoxically, a second legacy is the decentralized federal structure of the Brazilian state. The constitution of 1988 attempted to construct a new democratic order but left these contradictory tendencies in place. The president retained the authority to legislate on social and economic matters, but new powers governing the implementation of these policies were devolved to the state and municipal governments. As a result, the 1988 constitution was simultaneously the focus of much hope and intense attack. It was to be the governing document for the new democracy, but it became an instrument used to confound political and economic reform. Since it was the result of the bargaining of many different groups, it failed to provide a coherent vision of how institutions should be structured and what functions they should have. The separation of powers remains ill-defined, allowing ad hoc and informal arrangements to determine the boundaries of official authority.

Some generalizations about the organization of the Brazilian state can be made. First, the church and state are officially separated. The Catholic Church never controlled any portion of the state apparatus or directly influenced national politics as it did in other Catholic countries, including Spain. This does not mean, however, that the Catholic Church plays no role in Brazilian politics (see Section 4).

Second, Brazil has a presidential system of government. The directly elected president is the head of state, head of government, and commander in chief of the armed forces. The Brazilian state has traditionally placed vast power in the hands of the executive. Although the executive is one of three branches of government (the legislature and the judiciary being the other two), Brazilian presidents have traditionally been less bound by judicial and legislative constraints than their European or North American counterparts. Brazilian constitutions have granted the executive more discretion than the other branches in enforcing laws or in making policy. The legislature and the judiciary historically have played secondary roles.

The Brazilian state does not have the checks and balances of the U.S. government system. It differs also from the semipresidentialism of France. Brazil's executive and the bureaucracy manage most of the policymaking and implementation functions of government. Both the federal legislature and the state governments look to the president and, in economic matters, to the minister of the economy for leadership on policy. The heads of the key agencies of the economic bureaucracy—the ministers of the economy and of planning, the president of the Central Bank, and the head of the national development bank—have more discretion over the details of policy than the president does. Although some Brazilian presidents have delegated less to bureaucratic agencies, recent presidents have had little choice but to delegate, given the growing complexity of economic and social policy. Ultimate authority nevertheless remains in the hands of the president, who may replace the cabinet ministers.

Although the Brazilian president is the dominant player among the three branches of government, the powers of the legislature and the judiciary are becoming stronger. Since the transition to democratic rule in 1985, these institutions have become critical to democracy. The 1988 constitution gave many oversight functions to the legislature and judiciary, so that much presidential discretion in economic and social policy is now subject to approval by either the legislature or the judiciary, or both. This gives these branches of government some independence and leverage over the presidency, although this power is not often employed effectively. Centralizing traditions are still strong in Brazil, making the obstacles to the deconcentration of executive power enormous.

A third generalization that may be offered on the Brazilian state is that it is decentralized. Like Germany, Mexico, India, and the United States, the Brazilian state has a federal structure. The country's twenty-six states are divided into 5,564 municipal governments. Most of the country's presidents have relied on subnational bases of power to stay in office. The presidents of the Old Republic and even Getúlio Vargas counted on the support of local clientelist political machines led by self-interested governors and mayors.

With the transition to democracy, these "barons of the federation," as one study calls them, became a crucial source of political support for legislators as well as presidents.[30] By controlling indispensable reservoirs of patronage through their powers of appointment and spending, governors and even some mayors can wield

extraordinary influence.[31] In recent years, attempts to mollify this subnational constituency have watered down key pieces of reform legislation.

Seen as a whole, political decentralization, which was accelerated with the constitution of 1988, has further fragmented the Brazilian polity. At the same time, some subnational governments have become an important source of innovative policymaking.[32] Average Brazilian citizens have more access to their municipal and state governments than they do to their federal representatives, which suggests that decentralization may eventually strengthen democracy by making political elites more accountable to their local constituencies.

The Executive

A majority of delegates to the 1987 National Constituent Assembly that drafted the new democratic constitution favored the creation of a parliamentary system. President Sarney, who did not want to see his powers reduced, used his support among the governors to lobby against the parliamentary option. The best he could do was force the members of the assembly to defer the issue to a plebiscite in 1993. Yet the plebiscite, envisioned by the Constitution's Framers as the climactic event that would determine Brazil's political structure, ended by giving a stamp of approval to the existing presidential system.

In 1993, the campaign to retain presidentialism succeeded in convincing people that the parliamentary option was little more than a trick to "take the right to vote away from the people." The concept of a parliamentary system that would allow a prime minister to be elected by legislative elites and not directly by the citizenry seemed contrary to what Brazilians had fought for during the long struggle for democracy. Brazilians did not want to lose the ultimate check on the presidency: direct elections by voters every four years. Popular elections will now present a crucial test for presidents wishing to pursue their agendas for another four years.

If parliamentary government seemed a far-off goal, rules designed to rein in the power of the federal executive still found their way into the 1988 constitution. In part as a reaction to the extreme centralization of executive authority during military rule, the delegates restored some of the congressional prerogatives that existed prior to 1964, and they granted new ones. Among the new ones were oversight over economic policy and the right of consultation on executive appointments. Executive decrees, which allowed the president to legislate directly, were replaced by "provisional measures" (MPs) (also known as "emergency measures"). MPs preserved the president's power to legislate for thirty days, at the end of which congress can pass, reject, or allow the provisional law to expire. President Sarney and his successors got around this restriction by reissuing their "provisional measures" indefinitely; yet to become law, they would need to survive a two-thirds vote of both houses of the congress. Finally, the 1988 constitution limited the president to a single term, a provision common to Latin American constitutions. In 1997, however, Cardoso succeeded in passing a constitutional amendment that removed the one-term rule, allowing him and twenty-two governors to run again in 1998. This expansion of presidential power was later met with a restriction on the power to reissue provisional measures, which both houses of Congress passed in 2001.

Despite these new constraints, Brazilian presidents were still able to use emergency measures with considerable success because of the sorry state of the economy. Given crisis conditions, how could Congress deny the president the right to railroad through much-needed reform legislation? Some presidents articulated such arguments with great frequency. Collor, for example, severely abused these powers. In his first year in office, Collor handed down 150 emergency measures. Technically, this meant that the country experienced a crisis situation every forty-eight hours.[33] Worse still, the Supreme Tribunal, the highest court in Brazil, did little to curb this obvious abuse of constitutional authority by the president. The use of presidential discretionary power has only reinforced the powers of the executive to legislate.[34] Even with restrictions passed in 2001, more than 80 percent of all legislation originates in the executive branch.

The president also retains extremely valuable powers of appointment over the huge Brazilian bureaucracy, particularly at the ministerial level. Among them are broad powers to select and dismiss close associates and select ministers for the armed forces according to the merit system prevailing in their respective branches. For most other positions, the president usually appoints ministers from groups of his long-time cronies and collaborators, or from any of the existing parties. Although these appointees are not as cohesive a group as the presidential *camarillas* in Mexico, the close-knit and often personal networks binding the Mexican president and his chief ministers and advisors, this comparison illustrates the importance of personal ties to the president in Brazil. Under the 1988 constitution, the president must negotiate with congress and some powerful groups (such as business associations, labor unions, bar associations) over certain positions in the cabinet, mainly those responsible for economic policymaking. Presidential appointments are also often crafted to reward or entice the leaders of parties in Congress to support the executive's reform agenda.

Among the chief cabinet posts, the ministries of economy (also called finance during certain administrations) and planning have had extraordinary influence. Since the beginning of the military governments, the ministry of economy has had more authority than any other executive agency of the state. These powers grew in response to the economic problems of the 1980s and 1990s. As a result of their control of the federal budget and the details of economic policy, recent ministers of the economy have had levels of authority typical of a prime minister in a parliamentary system. For example, the success of Cardoso in the 1994 presidential campaign was due in large part to his effective performance as Itamar Franco's minister of economy.

The Bureaucracy: State and Semipublic Firms

Bureaucratic agencies and public firms have played key roles in Brazilian economic and political development during the twentieth century. After 1940, the state created a large number of new agencies and public enterprises. Many of these entities were allowed to accumulate their own debt and plan development projects without undue influence from central ministries or politicians. Public firms became a key part of the triple alliance of state, foreign, and domestic capital that governed the state-led model of development. Yet it was the state that dominated this alliance. By 1981, ten of the top twenty-five enterprises in Brazil were owned by the federal government, and eight others were owned by state governments. Public expenditures as a share of GDP increased from 16 percent in 1947 to more than 32 percent in 1969, far higher than in any other Latin American country except socialist Cuba.[35]

Much of this spending (and the huge debt that financed it) was concentrated on development projects, many of gigantic proportions. Key examples include the world's largest hydroelectric plant, Itaipú; Petrobrás's petroleum processing centers; steel mills such as the gargantuan National Steel Company in Volta Redonda, Rio de Janeiro; and Vale do Rio Doce, which maintains interests in sectors as diverse as mining, transport, paper, and textiles. Under the past three military governments (Médici, Geisel, and Figueiredo), dozens of other projects were completed, including the trans-Amazonian highway, the Tucuruí hydroelectric plants, the Niteroi bridge, the Açominas metallurgy park, and the National Nuclear Reactor Program. These and hundreds of more modest projects accounted for much of the country's industrial production. On the eve of the debt crisis in 1982, the top thirty-three projects, including those just listed, absorbed US$88 billion in external debt, employed 1.5 million people, and added $47 billion to the GDP.

Managing the planning and finance of these projects required enormous skill. Several public agencies were responsible, but the National Bank for Economic and Social Development (*Banco Nacional de Desenvolvimento Economico e Social,* or BNDES) stands out as an important coordinator. Founded by Vargas in the early 1950s, the BNDES played a key role in channeling public funds to industrial projects. Among the bank's greatest achievements was the creation of an automobile sector based on subsidized public steel; foreign assemblers such as Ford, General Motors, and Volkswagen; and domestic suppliers of parts and labor. Under President Juscelino Kubitschek, the BNDES implemented an industrial policy in automobiles called the Plan of Goals (*Plano de Metas*), which coordinated domestic and international resources to create the largest automobile industry in Latin America.[36]

The experience of the BNDES demonstrated that despite Brazil's clientelist legacies, the Brazilian bureaucracy could function effectively. Meritocratic advancement and professional recruitment granted these agencies some autonomy from political manipulation. Such agencies were considered islands of efficiency in a state apparatus characterized by patronage and corruption.[37]

Other state and semipublic firms, however, were rife with clientelism. Civilian and military leaders often appointed their supporters as the heads of these enterprises, positions with quite generous salary and retirement packages. Many public firm managers took advantage of their positions to dole out government contracts to associates and even to their own companies in the private sector.

The fiscal crisis of the 1980s put severe strains on the entire economic bureaucracy, but some things failed to change. The 1988 constitution did not alter significantly the concentration of power in the economic bureaucracy that made developmentalism with clientelism possible. In fact, the new constitution reinforced certain bureaucratic monopolies by codifying them as rights. For example, the state's control over petroleum, natural gas, the exploration of minerals, nuclear energy, and telecommunications was protected constitutionally. These sectors could not be privatized, much less sold to foreign governments or multinational companies.

What the writers of the new constitution did do in response to the fiscal crisis was place new restraints on the activity of state-directed industries. The fiscal independence of state firms was curtailed with restrictions on the amount of debt they could incur. The constitution imposed additional obstacles to the creation of public firms, including the requirement that congress approve any new state enterprises proposed by the executive branch.

Some of the constitutional protections of the public firms lasted only a few years. After his election in 1989, Fernando Collor began a sweeping reform of Brazil's public bureaucracy, beginning with the privatization of large public firms in steel, chemicals, and mining. In 1990, his government launched the National Destatization Program (*Programa Nacional de Destatização,* PND). Under the PND, more than US$39 billion in public firms were sold ($8.5 billion in the steel sector alone) by 2004. Although the program slowed under the Franco administration, the Cardoso administration went even further. The government convinced the Congress to amend the constitution to remove the public monopoly on petroleum refining, telecommunications, and infrastructure, making these sectors available for auction. Electricity distribution, cellular phone bands, and the octopus-like structure of Vale were put up for privatization. In 1998, much of the public telecommunications sector was privatized, bringing in about $24 billion.

Paradoxically, the agency at the center of the privatization process in Brazil is the BNDES, which is also the agency most responsible for developmentalism. Faced with the fiscal crisis of the 1980s, BNDES managers adopted a new perspective on the state's role in the economy. Instead of targeting industries and spending large sums to promote them, its new mission was to provide financing to productivity-enhancing investments such as new technology and labor retraining. As a result, the economic bureaucracy in Brazil continues to play a crucial role in the country's development.

The Military and the Police

The military is another significant arm of the state. Like many other South American militaries, the Brazilian armed forces retain substantial independence from civilian presidents and legislators. Brazil has suffered numerous coups; those in 1930 and 1964 were critical junctures, while others brought in caretaker governments that eventually ceded to civilian rule. Although the military's grip on power was never as tight as in Argentina during the murderous "Dirty War" governments (1976–1983), the generals have maintained influence in Brazilian politics, blocking policies they do not like and lobbying on behalf of those they favor.

The military's participation in Brazilian politics became more limited, if still quite expansive, following the transition to democracy. Several laws governing areas of policymaking affecting the armed forces gave the military broad prerogatives to "guarantee internal order" and to play a "tutelary role" in civilian government. During the Sarney administration, members of the armed forces retained cabinet-level rank in areas of importance to the military, such as the ministries of the armed forces and the nuclear program. Military officers also kept middle- and lower-level positions in public firms and bureaucratic agencies. Most important, the armed forces were successful in securing amnesty for human rights abuses committed during the preceding authoritarian regime. In an effort to professionalize the armed forces and keep them in the barracks, the Collor government slashed the military budget, which reduced the resource autonomy the military enjoyed during the authoritarian period. Collor also replaced the top generals with officers who had few or no connections to the authoritarian regime and were committed to civilian leadership. Collor's reforms were helped by the decline of the country's arms industry, which lost key markets for ordnance, tanks, and guns in the Middle East during the 1980s. The collapse and privatization of these military industries gave civilians more control over the generals.[38] One example of civilian authority was the successful removal of the commandant of the Brazilian Air Force, Brigadier Walter Werner Bräuer, for alleged involvement in drug trafficking, money laundering, and organized crime activities. Despite public demonstrations by air force officers supporting Bräuer, congressional investigations continued, and the general was dismissed at the end of 1999.

The military police are only nominally controlled by state governors; they are trained, equipped, and managed by the armed forces, which also maintain a separate judicial system to try officers for wrongdoing. The state police consists of two forces: the civil police force, which acts as an investigative unit and is not completely uniformed, and the uniformed military police force, which maintains order.

During the 1990s, economic crisis and press coverage made urban crime one of the most important political issues facing the country. Perhaps the most telling indicator of the rising level of violence is the fact that more than fifty mayors were assassinated in Brazil between 1990 and 2000. Murders, kidnappings, rapes, and violent robberies are the talk of nightly news programs, and these subjects often dominate citizens' lists of chief concerns.

The specter of criminal violence has shocked Brazilians into voting for politicians who promise them better police security. Yet as more attention has focused on the use of police resources, Brazilians have learned that these forces themselves are often part of the problem. Despite official oversight of police authorities, in practice the military and civil police forces in many cities of the northeast, in São Paulo, and in Rio de Janeiro often act abusively. Cases of arbitrary detention, torture, corruption, and systematic killings by Brazilian police have received much international attention. Human rights investigations have found that off-duty police officers are regularly hired by merchants and assorted thugs to kill street urchins whom they accuse of theft. One study in Rio de Janeiro between 1993 and 1996 showed that police officers shoot to kill rather than to disable.[39] The majority of victims were shot in the shoulders or the head; in 40 of the 697 cases, the victims were shot in the back of the head in gangland execution style. The victims were mostly young black men and boys, and had no criminal records whatsoever. Other studies have shown that at least 10 percent of the homicides in Rio de Janeiro and São Paulo are committed by the police.[40] Recently released data show that such acts occur regularly throughout Brazil.[41]

The federal police force is a small unit of approximately 3,000 people. It operates like a combined U.S. Federal Bureau of Investigation, Secret Service, Drug Enforcement Agency, and Immigration and Naturalization Service. Under the authority of the executive, the federal police are responsible for providing security to public officials, cracking down on drug rings, administering customs regulations, and investigating federal crimes. The demands placed on this single agency have caused some Brazilian politicians to propose that the federal police be split up into more specialized units, as in the U.S. system.

Other State Institutions

The Judiciary

The Brazilian judiciary is composed of a network of state courts, which have jurisdiction over state matters, and a federal court system, not unlike the one in the United States, which maintains jurisdiction over federal crimes. A supreme court (the Supreme Federal Tribunal), similar in jurisdiction to the U.S. Supreme Court but lacking a clear judicial review authority over the other branches of government, acts as the final arbiter of court cases. The eleven justices are appointed by the president and confirmed by an absolute majority of the Senate. The Superior Court of Justice, with thirty-three sitting justices, operates under the Supreme Federal Tribunal as an appeals court. Matters requiring interpretation of the Constitution go to the Supreme Federal Tribunal. The military maintains its own court system. Most judges in the Brazilian judicial system serve for life.

The judiciary is designed to adjudicate political conflicts as well as civil and social conflicts. The Electoral Supreme Tribunal (*Tribunal Supremo Electoral,* TSE) has exclusive responsibility for the organization and oversight of all issues related to voting. The seven-member TSE is composed of three justices elected from the members of the Supreme Federal Tribunal, two from the Superior Court of Justice, and two nominated by the president from a group of six attorneys of notable ability who are selected by the Supreme Federal Tribunal. The seven justices on the TSE serve for two years, and they have the power to investigate charges of political bias by public employees, file criminal charges against persons violating electoral laws, and scrutinize and validate electoral results. In addition to these constitutional provisions, under electoral law and its own regulations, the TSE monitors the legal compliance of electoral campaigns and executive neutrality in campaigns. The integrity of the tribunal in the conduct of elections has remained very high, making fraud relatively rare in national elections. The TSE is assisted in this process by a system of regional electoral courts that oversee local elections.

As in the rest of Latin America, penal codes established by legislation govern the powers of judges. This makes the judiciary less flexible than its North American counterparts, which operate on case law, but it provides a more effective barrier against judicial activism—the tendency of the courts to render broad interpretations of the law. The main problem in the Brazilian system has been the lack of judicial review. Lower courts are not obliged to follow the precedents of the STF or STJ. The judicial branch is independent from politics, but its various courts can be too independent of one another, making for an ambiguous structure of judicial oversight.

In recent years, the judiciary has been severely criticized for its perceived unresponsiveness to Brazil's social problems and the persistent corruption in the lower courts. These problems are particularly apparent in rural areas, where impoverished defendants are often denied the right to a fair trial by powerful landowners, who have undue influence over judges and procedures. Children are especially victimized; courts have refused to hear cases prosecuting those who profit from child prostitution, pornography, and murder of street urchins.

Official corruption in the judiciary is an important and high-profile issue. The federal police initiated "Operation Anaconda" in São Paulo in 2003 to root out corrupt judges who sold writs of habeas corpus and other "services" to defendants. The operation exposed a crime ring implicating eleven federal judges, police officers, and other agents of the court system. Such events escalated tensions between the presidency and the judiciary. Lula retained the upper hand in that struggle as opinion surveys showed that the judiciary is considered the most corrupt and least reliable of institutions in Brazil. But the president's fortunes changed in 2005 when allegations by one political party leader associated with the government accused leaders of the PT, many with offices in the presidential palace, of bribing legislators for their votes in Congress.

A more everyday indicator of systemic corruption is the difficulty that citizens face in prosecuting the police. In the state of Rio de Janeiro, between January 1996 and July 1997, 68 percent of cases in military court involving the police were withdrawn without a hearing because of insufficient evidence (which is often destroyed by the police) or because of the police's favorite excuse: that the defendant was injured or killed "while resisting arrest." Although federal legislation in 1996 granted civil courts jurisdiction over such matters, paradoxically the power to investigate these crimes was left in the hands of the police.

The Supreme Tribunal's reluctance to act on these matters leaves little hope for change in the short term. Judicial reform has thus far focused on beefing up the Supreme Tribunal's judicial review functions, avoiding the more difficult question of restructuring the judiciary to eliminate corruption.

Restructuring of the judiciary continues to receive attention. Proposals for reform include subjecting judges to external control through periodic elections.

Members of the judiciary deeply resent and fear such a prospect. They argue that it would push the institution into the kind of partisanship that has marred policy debates on key social and political issues. Others view the structure of the judiciary and its approach to interpreting and implementing laws as the central obstacles to accomplishing policy goals. Like the Brazilian bureaucracy, the judiciary has a complex structure, with multiple jurisdictions at different levels of government. The problems inherent in this complex network of adjudication were made clear during the privatization of Vale, when opposition groups in different states and jurisdictions were able to use the local courts to create numerous obstacles to the sale.

Subnational Government

The structure of subnational politics in Brazil consists of a governor; his chief advisers, who also usually lead key secretariats such as economy and planning; and a unicameral legislature, which is often dominated by the supporters of the governor. Governors are elected to four-year terms and, under the 1997 amendment of the 1988 constitution, may run for a second term.

State and municipal governments wield tremendous influence in Brazilian politics. Since the days of the Old Republic, governors and mayors have been essential sources of support for presidents and federal legislators. This "politics of the governors" expanded with the transition to democracy. The 1982 elections created the first opportunity since the inauguration of the military regime for Brazilians to elect their governors directly, which made these subnational politicians crucial standard-bearers of the transition. This lent legitimacy to the governors' campaign to decentralize fiscal resources in the form of taxes and federal transfers.

The 1988 constitution provided much of what the governors and mayors wanted. First, the states and municipalities were promised a larger share of tax revenues. At the same time, however, the governors and mayors were successful in deflecting Brasília's attempts to devolve additional spending responsibilities to subnational government, particularly in the areas of education, health, and infrastructure. The governors also proved successful in protecting state banks from a major overhaul, which was greatly needed, given that these financial institutions continued to fund irresponsible subnational spending by accumulating huge debts that the federal government agreed to roll over.

During the Collor administration, the federal government began to regain much of the fiscal authority it had lost to the states and municipalities. The Central Bank made good on its threats to intervene in bankrupt state banks and to privatize them. The federal government also refused to roll over state debt without a promise of reform, including the privatization of money-losing utility companies. The Cardoso administration required states and municipalities to finance a larger share of social spending, including education and health care. At the same time, new legislation empowered Brasília to claim more discretionary authority over fiscal transfers and tax revenues that had previously devolved to subnational governments.

Despite these efforts, Brazilian presidents must continue to negotiate the terms of reform with governors as much as with the congress. Lula met with the twenty-seven governors repeatedly during 2003 and 2004 to work out the details of fiscal reform. One of the reasons why the supposed savings his reform created were limited was that the president had to concede shares of new taxes and cede control of some state revenues that might otherwise have been used to contain spending and reduce the mounting federal debt.

Although most subnational politics are still preoccupied with the distribution of political favors in return for fiscal rewards, certain governors and mayors have devised innovative solutions to Brazil's social and economic problems. One study of the state of Ceará in the poor northern region has demonstrated that even the most underdeveloped subnational governments can produce important policies to promote industrial investment, employment, and social services.[42] Mayors affiliated with Lula's PT have had much electoral success (more than doubling their number between 2000 and 2004 to lead 411 cities) based on a solid record of effective local government. Such examples are a reminder that the quality of political leadership matters greatly in determining how well subnational governments are run.

The Policy-Making Process

Although policy-making continues to be fluid and ambiguous in Brazil, certain domains of policy are clearly demarcated. Foreign policy, for example, is exclusively within the purview of the executive branch. Political parties and the Congress in general still have only inconsistent power over investment policies. Because most legislation originates in the executive branch, bureaucratic agencies retain command over the details of social and economic policies.

The process of making policy in Brazil can be characterized by one common quality: the tendency of clientelism to inject itself at every stage, from formulation and decision-making to implementation. Established personal contacts often shape who benefits from policy-making, a hallmark of clientelistic practice. Quid pro quos, nepotism, and other kinds of favoritism, if not outright corruption, regularly obstruct or distort policy-making.[43] The most salient recent example is the scandal involving municipal PT politicians who regularly received kickbacks (the so-called "second cash box" or *caixa dois* affair). This will have lasting effects since the scandal has tarnished the reputation of the leftist party with the most erstwhile credentials as a proponent of clean government.

Complex formal and informal networks linking the political executive, key agencies of the bureaucracy, and private interests tend to be the chief players in clientelist circles. One of Cardoso's contributions to sociology before he became involved in Brazilian politics was his characterization of these clientelistic networks as **bureaucratic rings**. For Cardoso, the Brazilian state is highly permeable, fragmented, and therefore easily colonized by private interests that make alliances with mid-level bureaucratic officers. By shaping public policy to benefit these interests, bureaucrats gain the promise of future employment in the private sector. While in positions of responsibility, bureaucratic rings are ardent defenders of their own interests. Because they are entrenched and well connected throughout the Brazilian bureaucracy, few policies can be implemented without the resources and support of the most powerful bureaucratic rings. These rings represent one of the most enduring forms of established clientelistic exchange in the Brazilian state.

One example of the role of bureaucratic rings is the creation of large development projects. The politics surrounding these decisions were often intense. Governors and mayors wanted lucrative public projects to be placed in their jurisdictions; private contractors yearned for the state's business; and politicians positioned themselves for all the attendant kickbacks, political and pecuniary.[44] Although the days of huge development projects are over, the public sector still formulates policy and allocates resources under the influence of bureaucratic rings.

Among the key sources of influence external to the state is organized business. Unlike business associations in some Asian and West European countries, Brazilian business groups have remained independent of corporatist ties to the state. There is no Brazilian version of the French agricultural association *Fédération Nationale des Syndicats d'Exploitants Agricoles* (FNSEA) or the parapublic institutions of the Federal Republic of Germany. Business associations have also remained aloof from political parties. Brazil has nothing akin to Mexico's National Action Party (*Partido Acción Nacional,* or PAN), a party that claims to represent a large portion of the business class. That does not mean, however, that Brazilian business interests are not organized. Lobbying by Brazilian entrepreneurs is common, and their participation in bureaucratic rings is legendary. Few major economic policies are passed without the input of the Federation of São Paulo Industries (*Federação das Industrias do Estado de São Paulo,* or FIESP). Other business groups, some that have broken off from FIESP, continue to defend their interests energetically as Brazil reforms its economy.

The country's labor confederations and unions have had less consistent access to policymaking. Although unions were once directly organized and manipulated by the corporatist state, they gained autonomy in the late 1970s and the 1980s. From then on, they sought leverage over policymaking through outside channels, such as the link between the *Central Única dos Trabalhadores* (CUT, Workers' Singular Peak Association) and Lula da Silva's Workers' Party. Attempts to bring labor formally into direct negotiations with business and the state have failed. Shortly after assuming power, Sarney initiated talks among business, government, and representatives of the major labor federations. These talks quickly broke down. Widening cleavages within the Brazilian union movement tended to split sectors of organized labor, causing some segments to refuse to be bound by any agreement. Later, during the Collor administration, a second attempt at tripartite negotiation, called the "sectoral chambers," took place in the São Paulo automotive sector. These talks produced some noteworthy accords, but the chambers did not last because of opposition from the Ministry of Economy and other agencies. These experiences contrast sharply with the legacy of codetermination in Germany and other formulas for maintaining collective bargaining with state mediation in West European countries.

Policy implementation is also highly politicized. Debate and lobbying do not stop in Brazil once laws are enacted. Policy implementation is a subject of perpetual bargaining. One popular phrase, *o jeito brasileiro* ("the Brazilian way"), captures this aspect of Brazilian politics.[45] The Brazilian way is to scoff at the law and find a way around it. If one wants to get something without really paying for it, one asks for a *jeito*—a momentary suspension or exception to the rules. Paradoxically, *jeito* can be the source of great efficiency in Brazilian society, but it carries a heavy price in that the rule of law is not respected. Therefore, reform of the policy-making process will require more than restrictions on clientelism and legislative and judicial oversight of suspected bureaucratic rings. It will require a shift in thinking about the role of law in Brazilian society.

Representation and Participation

The most enduring aspect of contemporary Brazilian political institutions is the capacity of minority interests to block institutional change. The fragmentation of legislative politics, the weaknesses of political parties, and the interests of particular politicians and their clientelistic allies make enacting reform on behalf of the national interest extremely difficult. Getting things done involves the political use of public resources. Politicians and parties that are most capable of dispensing patronage and cultivating clientele networks are the most successful in the Brazilian system. While this benefits some voters who are the periodic recipients of these favors and resources, more often than not, the main beneficiaries are a small number of elite economic and political interests who develop ongoing relationships with legislators, governors, and presidents. Representation, therefore, is weak in Brazil.

The transition to democracy, however, coincided with an explosion of civil society activism and mobilization. The expansion of voting rights and the involvement of gender and ethnic groups, urban social movements, and environmental and religious organizations in Brazilian politics expanded greatly the range of political participation. Nonetheless, political institutions up to this point in Brazilian political history have failed to reconcile these contradictory forces between the deficiencies of representation and the expansion of political participation.

The Legislature

The 594-member national legislature is bicameral, consisting of an upper house, the Senate, with 81 members, and a lower house, the Chamber of Deputies, with 513 members. Each state and the federal district elect three senators by simple majority. Senators serve for eight-year terms and may be reelected without limits. Two-thirds of the Senate is elected at one time, and the remaining one-third is elected four years later. Senatorial elections are held concurrently with those for the Chamber of Deputies, which places all of its seats up for election after each four-year cycle. Federal deputies may be reelected without limits. The number of members in the Chamber of Deputies is, in theory, proportional to the population of each state and the federal district. Each state is allowed a minimum of eight and a maximum of seventy deputies, regardless of population.

Both houses of the legislature have equal authority to make laws. In all cases, each chamber can propose or veto legislation passed by the other. Bills go back and forth between houses without going through a conference committee of the two chambers, as in the United States. Once the bill is passed by both houses, the president may sign it into law, reject it as a whole, or reject it in part. The legislature can override a presidential

veto with a majority of the vote in both houses during a joint session, but such instances are rare. Constitutional amendments must be passed twice by three-fifths of the votes in each house of congress. Amendments may also be passed by an absolute majority in a special unicameral constituent assembly proposed by the president and created by both houses of congress. The Senate retains authority to try the president and other top officials, including the vice president and key ministers and justices, for impeachable offenses. It also has the power to approve appointments to high offices, including justices of the high courts, heads of diplomatic missions, and the directors of the Central Bank.

Complex constitutional rules for determining representation in the legislature favor sparsely populated states, especially in the north. Because these states are the most numerous in the federal system, voters from small states tend to be overrepresented in the legislature by as much as 33 times more per voter than are voters in São Paulo. If seats were allocated on a strictly proportional order, then São Paulo should have 114 seats and Roraima would have one. Instead, São Paulo has seventy and Roraima has eight. The least populated states are also the poorest and most rural in Brazil. Typically, they have been political bases for conservative landowning interests and, more recently, agribusiness. After 1964 the military cultivated support among conservative rural groups by granting statehood to sparsely populated territories in the north and northeast, reinforcing their overrepresentation in the Chamber. These precedents continued into the democratic period and largely explain why conservative landowners and agribusiness elites maintain positions of great influence in the Brazilian congress.

In contrast to the presidency, the Brazilian legislature has rarely played a dominant role in the country's politics. In part, that is due to the ability of the president to impose policy through corporatism and populism. However, the congress must accept some of the blame. Many senators and deputies are more interested in cultivating and dispensing patronage than in representing and being accountable to the voters. As a result, representatives have never organized their parties or large segments of the population in support of national policy. Only the rarest of exceptions exist to this rule of Brazilian congressional politics.

Legislators view their service primarily as a means to enhance their own income with generous public pensions and through kickbacks earned in the dispensing of political favors. Election to the federal legislature is often used as a steppingstone to even more lucrative, especially executive, posts.[46] After the presidency, the governorships of the industrialized states are the most coveted positions. Appointment to head any of the premier ministries and state firms also ranks high, since these are choice positions from which to distribute and receive favors. Although many members of Congress are independently wealthy, most come from the middle or upper middle classes; most of these have much to gain from appointment to well-paid posts in the executive and the para-statal enterprises. Ethnic minorities and women are poorly represented in their ranks. A mere 3 percent of seats in Congress are held by Afro-Brazilians. Only 6 percent of the seats in the Chamber and 7 percent of those in the Senate are held by women. Lula's cabinet includes three women from the PT.

The Congress has largely failed to use the expanded powers granted by the 1988 constitution. Lack of a quorum to vote is a frequent problem, and recently acquired powers have provided greater opportunities for some legislators to practice corruption and backroom dealing, conditions that have helped to break down party loyalties and reinforce the self-serving nature of congressional politics. The many deficiencies of the Brazilian legislature were magnified in recent years by several corruption scandals. Before 2005, the most serious case involved a handful of senators and deputies who were accused of embezzling from regional development projects or directly from the national treasury. Now that the Lula government has been targeted for corrupt dealings with legislators, Congress has once again been criticized for its lack of accountability.

One response to legislative corruption has been to use parliamentary commissions of inquiry to review cases of malfeasance by elected officials. Testimony before a congressional commission by the party leader making the most sweeping accusations of bribery against the Lula government enraptured the nation during the summer of 2005. Although these temporary committees have demonstrated some influence, most notably the parliamentary commission of inquiry that investigated Collor and recommended his impeachment, they have not always produced results. The temporary committees work alongside sixteen permanent legislative committees that treat issues as diverse as taxation and human rights. These committees, however, are not nearly as strong as the major committees in the U.S. Congress. Due to the self-interested focus of Brazilian politicians and the related weakness of political parties, legislative committees, both temporary and permanent, often fail to conclude an investigation or find solutions to persistent dilemmas in policy.

Political Parties and the Party System

The Brazilian political party system is one of the most mercurial in the world. Party names, affiliations, and the structure of party alliances are constantly in flux. This is nothing new in Brazilian political history. Like many of the country's current problems, party instability stretches back to the New State of Getúlio Vargas and the centralization of politics in the Brazilian state. State corporatism and populism were hostile to the development of independent party organizations. Political parties, when they did emerge, were created by state managers. Populist redistribution reinforced these tendencies, as workers and the middle class became accustomed to asking what they would receive from a politician in return for support. Except for members of the Communist Party and other extreme organizations, Brazilian voters did not develop a strong sense of political identity linked to established parties.

Many of the traditional weaknesses of the party system were reinforced after the transition to democracy, making parties even more anemic. The rules governing the party system made it easier for politicians to switch parties, virtually at will. A distinguished analyst of Brazilian politics, Scott Mainwaring, found that the 559 representatives of the 1987–1991 legislature had belonged to an average of over three parties during the five years of the legislature.[47] Politicians switched parties to increase their access to patronage. The rules of the electoral system even created incentives for politicians to ignore party labels. Brazil's experience with **proportional representation (PR)**, which is used to elect federal and state deputies, is particularly important in this regard. (See "Institutional Intricacies: Proportional Representation.")

Brazil's mix of presidentialism and multiparty democracy creates other problems for the country's system of representation. Given the political fragmentation of the legislature and the weakness of the party system, presidents are unable to maintain majority alliances in Congress, a requirement for stability in a multiparty system. In parliamentary systems, the party in power has an absolute majority or stands at the head of an alliance of parties that compose a majority. As a result, the ruling party or alliance can implement a programmatic approach to legislation. By contrast, in Brazil the president has never been able to maintain a supraparty alliance in congress. More often, Brazilian

Institutional Intricacies: Proportional Representation

Proportional representation was introduced in Brazil in 1932 and was later reaffirmed by the military governments. Unlike Mexico, Britain, and the United States, but like many of the European parliamentary democracies, Brazil is divided into electoral districts that choose more than one representative. The ability to choose more than one representative means that a broader range of voices may be heard in elected offices.

Minority parties can make alliances to pass the threshold of votes needed to achieve representation. Proportional representation may be based on either a closed-list or an open-list system. In a closed-list PR, the party selects the order of politicians, and voters cannot cross party lines. Because voters are effectively choosing the party that best represents them, this system encourages party loyalty among both the electorate and individual politicians. In an open-list PR system, the voters have more discretion and can cross party lines. Brazil's PR system is open-list. Voters cast single ballots for either a party label, which adds to the party's total for determining representation, or for individuals. No names appear on Brazilian ballots, so voters must write in their choices.

Electoral districts for the election of state and federal deputies are entire states in Brazil. In any given election, there may be between six and seventy federal deputies and from twelve to eighty-four state deputies running for office. With few limits on how many individuals and parties may run in the same electoral district, crowded fields discourage party loyalty and emphasize the personal qualities of candidates, who must stand out in the minds of voters. Party affiliations do little to reduce the confusion of the average Brazilian voter as he or she is confronted with dozens of names for each position. Worse still, the open-list PR system creates incentives for politicians to ignore party labels, because voters can cross party lines with ease. That even leads to politicians from the same party running against each other for the same position within a district.

Open-list proportional representation explains why there are so many parties in Brazil. With so much emphasis on the personal qualities of politicians, ambitious individuals can ignore the established party hierarchies while achieving elected office. They need only create their own parties or form alliances to get on the ballot and gain enough votes to qualify for representation. As a result, Brazil has the most fragmented party system in Latin America and one of the most fragmented in the world.

As if the open-list PR system were not distorting enough, Brazilian electoral law also allows incumbents to keep their party affiliation and remain on the ballot for the next election. This provision strips political parties of any control over their members: an incumbent may ignore the party's interests while in office but still must be kept on the ballot during the next contest.

Brazil's electoral system differs from other open-list proportional representation systems in that state, not national, parties select legislative candidates. In most cases, Brazilian governors exert tremendous influence over who can be elected. This further weakens national party leaders, who remain beholden to governors who can reward them with supportive nominees or rivals.

Source: Scott Mainwaring, "Brazil: Weak Parties, Feckless Democracy," in Scott Mainwaring and Timothy R. Scully, eds., *Building Democratic Institutions: Party Systems in Latin America* (Stanford, Calif., Stanford University Press, 1995), p. 375.

presidents have attempted to govern above parties, dispensing favors to key congressional politicians to get legislation approved. Alternatively, presidents have not been shy about railroading reform through congress by using their discretionary authorities. As Timothy Power, a scholar of presidential authority in Brazil, has noted, "The [presidential] pen is mightier than the congress."[48]

In the midst of Brazil's confusing party system, a number of political organizations have emerged over the last few years. These parties can be defined ideologically, although the categories are not as internally consistent or as cut and dry as they might seem (see Table 9.5). Brazilian political parties are internally eclectic.

Table 9.5

The Democratic Idea: The Major Parties in Brazil

Conservative/Right-Wing Parties

PFL/DEM	*Partido da Frente Liberal* (Party of the Liberal Front) (refounded as the *Democratas* (Democrats) in March 2007)
PL	*Partido Liberal* (Liberal Party)
PPB	*Partido Progressista Brasileiro* (Brazilian Progressive Party)

Centrist Parties

PMDB	*Partido do Movimento Democrático Brasileiro* (Party of the Brazilian Democratic Movement)
PSDB	*Partido da Social Democracia Brasileira* (Party of Brazilian Social Democracy)
PTB	*Partido Trabalhista Brasileiro* (Brazilian Labor Party)

Populist/Leftist Parties

PT	*Partido dos Trabalhadores* (Workers' Party)
PSB	*Partido Socialista Brasileiro* (Brazilian Socialist Party)
PCdoB	*Partido Comunista do Brasil* (Communist Party of Brazil)
PDT	*Partido Democrático Trabalhista* (Democratic Labor Party)
PPS	*Partido Popular Socialista* (ex-Partido Comunista Brasileiro) (Popular Socialist Party)

Political parties on the right currently defend neoliberal economic policies designed to shrink the size of the public sector. They support the reduction and partial privatization of the welfare state. A majority advocate a liberal trade policy and support MERCOSUL, but a substantial minority press for protectionism and the continuation of subsidies, particularly in agriculture. No party of the right has yet emerged as a solid defender of neoliberal restructuring of the economy, although scholars have detected a significant trend in favor of these policies among the parties on the right. On constitutional reform, right-wing parties are fairly united in favor of rolling back social spending; they also advocate electoral reform—specifically, the establishment of a majority or mixed, rather than purely proportional, district voting system, although this is contentious within the rightist cohort.

A loose set of conservative parties currently struggles for the mantle of the right. In front of the pack is the PFL (Party of the Liberal Front), which was refounded in March 2007 as the Democrats (DEM). PFL/DEM is one of the largest parties in the Senate and the Chamber and an organization that generally is in opposition to President Lula. Many small parties with low to moderate levels of representation in congress ally themselves with right-wing and center-right parties or advocate right-wing issues; the Brazilian Labor Party (PTB), the Brazilian Progressive Party (PPB), and the evangelistic Liberal Party (PL) are examples.

The two other large parties in congress are the PMDB (Party of the Brazilian Democratic Movement, the successor to the old MDB) and the PSDB (the Party of Brazilian Social Democracy, originally an offshoot of the PMDB and Cardoso's party). These parties, while having disparate leftist and rightist elements, tend to dominate the center and center-left segment of the ideological spectrum. Along with the PFL/DEM, these have been the key governing parties during the democratic era. Some scholars argue that these parties formed a disciplined pro-reform bulwark in congress for Cardoso especially; hence, they are "government parties."[49] Other scholars argue that although these parties seem to vote coherently in favor of reform, these votes are infrequent and, more important, they are the product of the president's dispensing large amounts of patronage to particular politicians to manufacture a coherent vote.[50] Yet there is agreement that these parties have become ideologically more cohesive in favor of neoliberal reform, and hence they can be characterized as being on the right or center-right.[51]

Political parties on the left advocate reducing deficits and inflation but also maintaining the present size of the public sector and improving the welfare state. Left-oriented parties want to expand the state's role

Citizen Action

The Workers' Party

Luiz Inácio "Lula" da Silva, founder of the Workers' Party and Brazilian president (2002–2006). *Source:* © Jornal do Brasil, August 19, 1998.

Source: Margaret Keck, *The Workers' Party and Democratization in Brazil* (New Haven, Conn.: Yale University Press, 1992), pp. 219–220.

The creation of the Workers' Party (PT) in the early 1980s was a remarkable development in Brazilian history. The PT was founded by workers who had defied the military government and engaged in strikes in São Paulo's metalworking and automobile industries in 1978 and 1979. Although the PT began with a working-class message and leftist platform, its identity broadened during the 1980s and early 1990s. The party and its leader, Luiz Inácio "Lula" da Silva, increasingly campaigned for the support of the middle class, the rural and urban poor, and even segments of business and the upper classes. Unlike previous populist parties in Brazil, the PT aimed both to bring previously excluded groups into the political arena and to change the status quo substantively.

Lula da Silva ran for the presidency five times: in 1989, 1994, 1998, 2002, and for reelection in 2006. In 1989, he qualified for, but lost, the runoff to Collor. In 1994 and 1998, he was beaten during the first round by Cardoso. In 1998, the PT forged an electoral alliance with other leftist parties, but despite a unified leftist ticket, Lula captured 31.7 percent of the vote to Fernando Henrique Cardoso's 53.1 percent. Lula did much better in 2002, beating Cardoso's designated successor, José Serra, in the second round with 61.3 percent, the largest share for any presidential winner in the democratic period. In 2006, Lula beat the PSDB's candidate, Geraldo Alckmin, in the second round with a commanding 60.8 percent of the vote.

The party's electoral success is a product of its demonstrated capacity for clean and effective government at all levels in Brazil's federal system, though that has been tested recently by repeated scandals involving municipal corruption and vote-buying. Still, unlike most other Brazilian parties, the PT actively seeks to represent workers and the poor and it tries to maintain a high degree of internal democracy. Grassroots organizations still maintain a strong voice inside the PT, so any solutions to a leadership crisis must involve these members of the base.

Brazil

in promoting and protecting domestic industry. On constitutional reform, they support the social rights guaranteed by the 1988 constitution.

On the left, the most important party continues to be the Workers' Party (PT). (See "Citizen Action: The Workers' Party."). Since 1985 the PT has occupied much of the left's political space, marginalizing already peripheral parties such as the Brazilian Socialist Party (PSB), the Brazilian Communist Party (PCB—renamed the Popular Socialist Party, or PPS, in 1992), and the Communist Party of Brazil (PCdoB). The Democratic Labor Party (PDT), a populist organization, advocates Vargas-era nationalism and state-led development. The PSB is led by Ciro Gomes, a former finance minister (under Itamar Franco) and former governor of Ceará. Gomes ran for president in 1998 and 2002 but did not make it to the second round in either contest. In 2003, Lula appointed him minister of national integration, a position that the president hoped would keep Gomes's party on the government's side in congress. When the PPS (then Gomes' party) left the government in 2004, Gomes remained in his cabinet post, effectively leaving the PPS for the PSB. In 2006, he won the largest vote total of any person running for a seat in the Chamber of Deputies. He remains a favorite to replace Lula in 2010.

As might be expected, the proliferation of political parties has only added to the incoherence of legislative politics. Currently, no party has more than 23 percent of the seats in either house of congress (see Figures 9.4 and 9.5). Cardoso's multiparty alliance of the PSDB-PFL-PTB-PPB controlled 57 percent of the vote in the lower house and 48 percent in the upper house. Lula's presently has no similar "governing coalition," though his government depends on enticing centrist and center-right parties to vote for his legislation. Though party switching has now been limited by law, party merging and routine clientelism still make the loyalty of so-called "pro-government" parties remarkably soft. Consistency of support is difficult to maintain as turnover in the Chamber is high, with 50 to 60 percent of the members being replaced with each election. This reality has reinforced the common claim of the executive to be the only source of political order in the Brazilian democratic system.

FIGURE 9.4

Share of Seats of the Major Parties in the Chamber of Deputies, Based on October 2006 Election Results

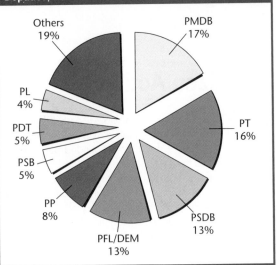

Source: Data from final TSE numbers.

FIGURE 9.5

Share of Seats of the Major Parties in the Senate, Based on October 2006 Election Results

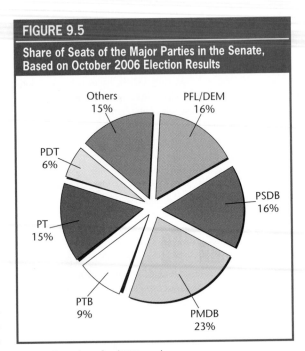

Source: Data from final TSE numbers.

Lula's rise to power initially changed some aspects of the dominant alliance patterns, but fundamental problems with legislative coherence continued. Lula's PT forged a somewhat stable congressional alliance during the first term, including parties on the right and center-right (PL, PTB) and on the left (PSB, PPS, PCdoB) in favor of his reform agenda. For example, the passage of the first phases of social security reform in 2003 reflected relatively coherent support among the progovernment parties during the roll-call votes on these reform packages. Even the fractious PMDB, which increased its interests in acquiring cabinet positions and working with Lula in congress, voted for the government's policies. These votes also reflected the weakness of the opposition parties. More than 43 percent of the opposition PFL and PSDB deputies voted for the social security reforms. Yet Lula's first "victories" also underscored the Achilles heel of relying on the support of undisciplined parties. Defections from the government parties, including four notable PT members who were expelled from the party in December 2003, made congressional support unreliable. For example, the roll-call votes on the first phase of social security reform in the Chamber suffered over 56 defections out of approximately 350 deputies from the government coalition parties. The reforms would not have passed the required three-fifths majority threshold without PFL and PSDB votes, parties that nominally are not allied to the government. Even after securing broad support in one house, legislation can fail by not garnering similar support in the other chamber. The government's attempt to renew a financial transactions tax that finances social programs in 2007–2008 ran aground in the upper house after failing to get the same support it garnered in the Chamber.

Elections

Because of urbanization and economic modernization, the Brazilian electorate grew impressively after 1945. Improved literacy and efforts by political parties to expand voter registration increased the number of citizens eligible to vote. All illiterates were given the right to vote in 1985, the voting age was reduced from eighteen to sixteen in 1988, and voting was made compulsory for those eighteen and older, except for illiterates and citizens over seventy. The Brazilian electorate stands at 106 million and regularly votes (for example, turnout in the October 2006 presidential vote was 83.2 percent in both rounds).

The expansion of the Brazilian electorate coincided with the proliferation of political organizations and movements dedicated to marshaling popular support. Mass appeal became an important element in campaigns and political alliances. With the return to democracy in the 1980s, newly independent labor unions and special-interest organizations emerged, making new alliances in civil society possible. Nevertheless, the richness of political organization was restrained by the legacies of state-centered structures of social control.

Contests for public office in Brazil are dominated by the rules of proportional representation (PR), which distort democratic representation as well. Everything, from federal legislative to municipal council positions, is distributed to ensure proportionality among political parties. In addition to its effects on the party system, open-list PR (see "Institutional Intricacies: Proportional Representation") weakens the incentives for politicians to listen to the electorate. Given the multiplicity of parties, the unbalanced apportionment of seats among the states, and the sheer size of some electoral districts (which are the 27 states themselves), candidates often have few incentives to be accountable to their constituencies. In states with hundreds of candidates running in oversized electoral districts, the votes obtained by successful candidates are often scattered, limiting the accountability of those elected. In less populated states, there are more seats and parties per voter; the electoral and party quotients are lower. As a result, candidates often alter their legal place of residence immediately before an election in order to run for a safer seat, compounding the lack of accountability.

As in all other modern nations, the media play a key role in Brazilian political campaigns. With the *abertura,* political parties gained the right to air electoral propaganda on radio and television. All radio stations and TV channels are required to broadcast, at no charge, two hours of party programming each day during a campaign season. The parties are entitled to an amount of time on the air proportional to their number of votes in the previous election.

In recent years, elections, particularly presidential contests, have become touchstones of the country's progress in building democracy. The 1989 presidential election gave Brazilians their first opportunity to elect the president directly. Collor's (PRN) selection became an important precedent that further strengthened Brazilian democracy. Ironically, his impeachment two years later also promoted democracy because it reinforced the rule of law and enhanced the oversight functions of the congress. Fernando Henrique Cardoso's election in 1994 and reelection in 1998 repeated and reinforced the 1989 precedent of direct elections for the presidency. Although elections cannot guarantee democracy, recent contests have shown how far Brazilian democracy has come in little over a decade.

Seen from the perspective of average Brazilians, however, the situation is a bit more complex. Although most Brazilians are suspicious of authoritarianism and wary of the return of the military or any other form of dictatorship, they seem to be disappointed with the results of democracy. The weakness of political parties, coupled with the persistence of clientelism and accusations of corruption even against previously squeaky clean parties such as the PT, have disillusioned average Brazilians with their country's politics. According to opinion polls, support for democracy as a viable system of government is under 50 percent nationwide. Brazilians vote, but they disparage politics and politicians regularly. For example, in the October 2006 presidential elections, 6 million voters turned in blank or spoiled ballots, a common indicator of voter discontent in Brazil. It is even more indicative of disapproval since Brazil moved to electronic voting after 2002. It should also be noted that these characteristics of the voters pervade all class, ethnic, and gender groups. Those who vote and those who return spoiled ballots come from every walk of life. Lula's voters in 2002 were generally those who voted for Cardoso in 1994 and 1998.

Political Culture, Citizenship, and Identity

The notion of national identity describes a sense of national community that goes beyond mere allegiance to a state, a set of economic interests, regional loyalties, or kinship affiliations. The cultivation of a national identity occurs through a process of nation building during which a set of national symbols, cultural terms and images, and shared myths consolidates around historical experiences that define the loyalties of a group of people.

Several developments made Brazilian nation building possible. Unlike nation formation in culturally, linguistically, and geographically diverse Western Europe, Africa, and Asia, Brazil enjoyed a homogeneous linguistic and colonial experience. As a result, Brazilian history largely avoided the ethnic conflicts that have become obstacles to nation building in Eastern Europe, Nigeria, and India. Immigrants added their ideas and value systems at the turn of the century, but they brought no compelling identities that could substitute for an overarching national consciousness. Regional secessionist movements were uncommon in Brazilian history and were short-lived episodes when they did emerge in the twentieth century.

Despite Brazil's rich ethnic makeup, racial identities in Brazil have seldom been the basis for political action. In part, this was the result of the historical myth that the country was racially mixed. Therefore, a singular racial consciousness emerged around the spurious idea that Brazil was a racial democracy. Even in the face of severe economic and political oppression of native peoples, Afro-Brazilians, and Asians, the myth of racial democracy has endured in the national consciousness. As a result, the unique contributions of different ethnic groups were appropriated into the national consciousness of the "Brazilian."

Brazilian literature, political discourse, and history textbooks reinforced the myth of racial democracy. For example, the famous Brazilian historian Gilberto Freyre, in his book *The Masters and the Slaves,* described the evolution of social relations among blacks and whites since colonial times, but he treated the underlying reality of racial conflict as an issue of secondary importance.[52] For such intellectuals, miscegenation had diminished racial differences and made conflict unlikely. This thinking buttressed the false belief that prejudice and discrimination were lacking among whites, blacks, indigenous peoples, and mulattos.

Like the myth of racial democracy, the major collective political identities in Brazilian history have sought to hide or negate the real conflicts in society. For example, the symbols and images of political nationalism tended to boost the quasi-utopian visions of the country's future development. Developmentalists under the military governments and democratic leaders such as Kubitschek espoused optimism that "Brazil is the country of the future." In the face of severe fiscal, social, and political problems, Brazilians continue to have faith in their country, even when their confidence in their politicians and democratic institutions has been shaken.

Gendered identities are another significant dimension of Brazilian politics. And as with racial identities, socioeconomic realities belie the widely perceived view that women have equal citizenship with men. Brazilian women make only 70 percent of what men make and black women do even worse at 40 percent. Only 7 percent of women with university degrees earn more than twenty times the minimum wage (about $75 per month), as compared to 28 percent of men. In rural areas, women are substantially disadvantaged in the granting of land titles. Female heads of families are routinely passed over by official agencies distributing land titles to favor oldest sons, even when these are minors. Thirty-four percent of illiterate women earn the minimum wage or less, versus 5 percent of illiterate males. Despite women's improved economic, social, and political importance, progress on women's issues is slow. This situation has sparked more women's activism, but more commonly, it has led to feelings of pervasive disempowerment.

The persistence of optimistic myths about the country in the face of socioeconomic and political realities often sets the stage for angry disengagement from politics. This reflects a weak system of political socialization. Pervasive corporatism and populism in twentieth-century Brazilian politics, and the current crisis in these forms of mobilizing popular support, have limited Brazilians' avenues for becoming more involved in politics. The weakness of political

Carnival in Brazil, the world's largest floor show, is also an insightful exhibition of allegories and popular myths about the country, its people, and their culture.   *Source:* Bettmann/Corbis.

parties is one problem. But an underfunded primary and secondary educational system and a largely uncritical media leave most Brazilians without the resources to become more politically aware. Brazil's illiteracy rate of 16.7 percent remains one of the highest in Latin America and is a key obstacle to mobilizing the electorate. The frenetic nature of political change in Brazil has confused the citizenry, further breaking down whatever continuous political identities might emerge. Perhaps the ultimate reflection of these distressing tendencies is the cynical joke among Brazilians that "Brazil is the country of the future and *always will be.*"

The political sentiments of Brazilian society are actually quite static because most Brazilians feel powerless to change their fates. Brazilians have always considered liberal democratic institutions, particularly individual rights, as artificial or irrelevant. Although this view may appear cynical, it is a deeply ingrained notion in Brazilian political culture. Since the end of the nineteenth century, Brazilians have made a distinction between the "legal" Brazil—that is, the formal laws of the country—and the "real" Brazil—what actually occurs. A prime example was the turn-of-the-twentieth-century liberal democracy, which concealed the patronage-ridden interior of Brazilian politics. Brazilian intellectuals developed the phrase *para ingles ver* ("for the English to see") to describe the notion that liberal democracy had been implanted to impress foreign observers, hiding the fact that real politics would be conducted behind the scenes. As Brazil struggles to balance the interests of foreign investors with those of its own people, many Brazilians continue to believe that much of the politics they observe is really "for the English to see."

One of the key outcomes of the sense of powerlessness among the majority of Brazilians was the belief that the state should organize society. This idea helped to justify both the Vargas dictatorship in 1937 and the military rule that followed the coup of 1964. The primacy of the state manifested itself in Brazilian political culture. The notion that the state had a duty to provide for its citizens' welfare placed the state at the center of the Brazilian polity and put the president at the center of the state. It should be clear, based on this analysis, that both society and the state in Brazil developed a set of core ideas that favored the establishment of a strong central government with an overbearing presidentialism. These ideas were not just imposed on Brazilians by savvy politicians; they were the product of many decades of social and political conflict.

During the redemocratization process, new trends in Brazilian political culture emerged. Most segments of Brazilian society came to embrace "modernization with democracy," even if they would later raise doubts about its benefits. The Catholic Church played an important role in promoting democracy. During the transition, a number of Catholic political organizations and movements aided by the church organized popular opposition to the military governments. After the transition, archbishops of the Catholic Church helped assemble testimonials of torture victims. The publication of these depositions in the book *Nunca Mais* (*Never Again*) fueled condemnation of the authoritarian past. In this way, an establishment that previously had been associated with social conservatism and political oppression became a catalyst of popular opposition to authoritarianism.

Another trend that developed during and after the transition to democracy was the growth of a profound distrust of the state. Brazilians began to doubt the ability of the state to find solutions to the country's economic and social problems. Business groups assailed the failures of state-led development, while labor unions claimed that corporatist management of industrial relations could not satisfy the interests of workers. As a result, Brazilians became increasingly receptive to fringe voices that promised to eradicate the previous economic-political order. By 1989, most Brazilians were willing to trust a little-known politician, Fernando Collor, who told the electorate what they wanted to hear. Collor swore to go to war against indolent state employees, corrupt politicians, and inefficient state enterprises. The results were, at least in part, disastrous. By ceding their authority to an untested figure like Collor, Brazilians failed one of the most important tests of democracy: ensuring that elected officials will be accountable to the electorate.

A third trend in Brazilian political culture can be seen among the most elite segments of society. Soon after the transition to democracy, many journalists, economists, politicians, intellectuals, and entrepreneurs began to embrace the notion that national institutions could be adjusted incrementally to strengthen democracy and promote economic growth. Constitutional, administrative, and economic reform became priorities of politicians such as Fernando Henrique Cardoso.

For average Brazilians, the dynamics of institutional tinkering are virtually unintelligible. The electorate must feel substantial change, primarily in their pocketbooks. Cardoso was able to deliver in 1994 when his Real Plan reduced inflation and increased the buying power of most Brazilians. That success gave him the popular support he needed to become president and launch an array of institutional reforms. In 1998, facing another presidential contest and with his reforms stuck in congress, Cardoso barely beat out Lula. Although his poll ratings make Lula the most popular president in recent memory, the progress of his reform agenda will also ultimately dictate how voters will remember him and whether they will support a successor he endorses in 2010.

The task of selling even the most complex sets of policies to a population with weak political socialization and poor general education has become central to gaining and maintaining political power in Brazil. This problem has placed a premium on the adept management of the media, particularly radio and television. The Brazilian media are free to criticize the government, and most of the broadcast businesses are privately owned. Although there is significant government influence over the resources necessary for media production and the advertising revenue from government campaigns, there is no overt government censorship, and freedom of the press is widely and constitutionally proclaimed. The largest media organizations are owned by a small group of conglomerates. The Globo network is Brazil's preeminent media empire and one of the five largest television networks in the world. It has been formidable in shaping public opinion; some believe it played a prominent role in Collor's election in 1989. Conglomerates like Globo play favorites and, in return, they expect licensing concessions from their political friends.

Unlike the situation in the United States, the events of 9/11 did not fundamentally change Brazilian political culture or its views of the nation's sense of security or vulnerability. Having fought against the military regime's torture and arbitrary killings—a kind of state terrorism—in their own country, Brazilians are very aware that democracy and decency have enemies capable of the greatest cruelty. Many Brazilians also live with a number of everyday terrors—poverty, hunger, disease, and violence—that they regard as far more dangerous than terrorism. In this context, American insistence that Brazil toe Washington's foreign policy line on Iraq and the war on terror often backfires. Brazilians resent such overtures, which only spark the people's nationalism.

Interests, Social Movements, and Protest

Despite the growing disengagement of most Brazilians from politics and the country's legacy of state corporatism, autonomous collective interests have been able to take positions of importance in the political landscape. The role of business lobbies, rural protest movements, and labor unions, particularly those linked to the Workers' Party, are all examples of how Brazilian civil society has been able to break through the vise of state corporatism and social control.

As noted, the Catholic Church was actively engaged in organizing grass-roots movements during and after the transition to democracy. After the profound changes in Catholic doctrine brought about by the Second Vatican Council in the early 1960s, the church in Brazil became more active in advocating social and political reform. The Brazilian church, through the National Conference of Brazilian Bishops (CNBB), produced an array of projects to improve literacy, stimulate political awareness, and improve the working and living conditions of the poor. Although some conservative segments of the Brazilian church reacted violently against the church's "messing in politics," the CNBB pressed on.

One well-known outcome of these changes was the development of liberation theology, a doctrine that argued that religion had to free people at the same time from their sins and from social injustice. In Brazil, this thinking was associated with the Franciscan theologian Leonardo Boff. During the *abertura,* this doctrinal shift sought to relate theology to Brazilian reality by having priests become directly involved in improving the lot of poor Brazilians by defending their social and political needs.[53] By organizing community-based movements to press for improved sanitation, clean water, basic education, and, most important, freedom from oppression, Catholic groups mobilized millions of citizens. Among the Brazilian church's most notable accomplishments was the development of an agrarian reform council in the 1970s, the Pastoral Land Commission. The commission called for the extension of land tenure to poor peasants. The Brazilian church also created ecclesiastical community movements to improve conditions in the *favelas.*

In the mid-1970s, Brazil witnessed a historic awakening of social and political organization: grass-roots popular movements; new forms of trade unionism; neighborhood movements; professional associations of doctors, lawyers, and journalists; entrepreneurial associations; and middle-class organizations. At the same time, a host of nongovernmental organizations (NGOs) became more active in Brazil; among them were Amnesty International, Greenpeace, and native Brazilian rights groups. Domestic groups active in these areas increasingly turned to the NGOs for resources and information, adding an international dimension to what was previously an issue of domestic politics.

Women's organizations played a significant role in popular urban social movements during the 1970s. By the 1980s, women were participating in and leading popular initiatives on a wide variety of issues related to employment and the provision of basic services. Many of these organizations enlisted the support of political parties and trade unions in battles over women's wages, birth control, rape, and violence in the home. Although practically absent in employers' organizations, women are highly active in rural and urban unions. Out of the country's 5,324 urban unions, 14.8 percent have elected women directors. Fewer women are leaders of rural unions (6.6 percent), but they compose 78 percent of active membership. In recent years, Brazilian women have created more than 3,000 organizations to address their issues. Included in this total are special police stations (*delegacias de defesa da mulher,* DDMs) dedicated to addressing crimes against women. The DDMs have emerged in major Brazilian cities, and particularly in São Paulo, where their performance has been mixed.

Women's groups have seen their power increase as more women have joined the work force: 39 percent of women now work outside the home. That figure is higher than in Mexico (22 percent) and Argentina (33 percent). More than 20 percent of Brazilian families are supported exclusively by women. The share of domestic servants in the female work force has declined from 32 percent to 20 percent over the past ten years, suggesting that traditional roles for women have not absorbed the increase in the female work force.

Women have also made some strides in representative politics and key administrative appointments. Ellen Gracie Northfleet became the first woman to head the Supreme Court recently while Lula appointed the second woman to the court, Carmen Lúcia Antunes Rocha, in 2006. A woman also sits on the board of directors of the Central Bank. Women in formal politics have in recent years become mayors of major cities such as São Paulo, and a woman, Roseanna Sarney, sustained a major candidacy for president in 2002 until it was derailed by corruption allegations. The number of women with seats in congress nearly doubled following the election of October 2002, but the rate remains one of the lowest in Latin America nonetheless.

In contrast to the progress of women's movements, a politically significant organization to address racial discrimination has not emerged. This fact is especially surprising because Brazil is one of the world's most racially mixed countries. Only during the 1940s did some public officials and academics acknowledge that prejudice existed against blacks. At that time, the problems of race were equated with the problems of class. Given the absence of legally sanctioned discrimination since the abolition of slavery in 1888, prejudice came to be viewed as class based, not race based. Attacking class inequality was thus considered a way to address prejudice against blacks. This belief seemed plausible because most poor Brazilians are either *pardo* (mulatto) or black. But it might be just as logical to suggest that they are poor because they are black. In any case, the relationship between race and class in Brazil is just as ambiguous as it is in the United States and other multiethnic societies.

Some analysts believe that a gradual and peaceful evolution of race relations is possible. Others argue that as a consequence of white domination, blacks lack the collective identity and political organization necessary to put race relations on the political agenda. Both sides seem to agree, however, that although poverty and color are significantly correlated, overt confrontation among races is uncommon. Ironically, this may explain why no serious national discussion of race relations has ever emerged in Brazil.

The rights of Brazil's indigenous peoples, the Indians of the Amazon, remain at the center of the debate on the country's most pressing social problems. Over the past half-century, the development of the Amazon has threatened the cultures and lives of Indians. For example, members of the Ianomami, a tribe with one of the largest reserves in Brazil, are frequently murdered by miners so they can gain access to mines in Indian territory. During the military government, the national Indian agency, FUNAI, turned a blind eye to such abuses with its claim that indigenous cultures represented "ethnic cysts to be excised from the body politic."[54] With the *abertura,* many environmental NGOs defended the human rights of indigenous people as part of their campaign to defend the Amazon and its people. The end of military rule and the economic crisis of the 1980s slowed exploitation of the Amazon.

The 1988 constitution recognized the rights of indigenous peoples for the first time, creating large reserves for tribes like the Ianomami. Yet these protections were eroded when President Cardoso, under pressure by landowning conservative allies from the northeast, implemented a policy to allow private interests to make claims on over half of all indigenous lands. Miners, loggers, and land developers invade native lands, often with destructive consequences for the ecology and indigenous people. Allied against these interests are members of the Workers' Party, a coalition of indigenous groups known as COIAB, and church-based missionary organizations. The Kayapó and their resistance to large-scale development projects in the Amazon are a key example of how environmental, labor, and indigenous issues are melding together to form a powerful grassroots campaign. Members of the Kayapó tribe have been successful in politically disrupting damming and mining projects through mass media campaigns.[55] Their struggle continues, but without more federal protection, Amazonian Indians will continue to be threatened.

The sprouting of movements, associations, and interest groups may seem impressive, but they represent specific constituencies. Most Brazilians do not bother to participate in parties, movements, and unions because the basic functions of government such as security, justice, education, and health care simply do not reach them. When confronted with immediate deprivations, many Brazilians avoid organized and peaceful political action, often taking to the streets in sporadic riots. These events are usually sparked by changes in utility and transport prices, but they do not last for more than a few hours. Such events demonstrate that many Brazilians feel they have only two choices in the face of unresponsive political and state organizations: violent protest or passivity.

SECTION 5 Brazilian Politics in Transition

Political Challenges and Changing Agendas

As the financial and monetary crisis that began in Asia in late 1997 continued to scare foreign investors throughout the developing world, Fernando Henrique Cardoso appeared on a Cable News Network (CNN) business show in December. The Brazilian president proclaimed his country a safe place for foreign money, a stable and growth-oriented economy sure to remain immune from the economic difficulties afflicting Asia. Ten years later, after his convincing reelection as

Brazil's president in the October 2006 presidential elections, Lula da Silva appeared at the World Economic Forum in Davos, Switzerland, the most important meeting of the major economic decision-makers in the world. Lula repeated many of the ideas Cardoso once espoused on CNN: Brazil is ready to take off as a major economy and a global power. This was striking since Lula had previously been known as a representative of the trade unions and an ardent critic of "neoliberal reform." What explained this transformation?

The investors gathered at Davos knew something that the viewers of Cardoso on CNN did not know back in 1997. In the years between Cardoso's interview and Lula's reelection, Brazil had weathered its own economic crisis in January 1999 and emerged with relatively low inflation and otherwise good economic fundamentals. Continued dedication to fiscal stability and modest social reforms had also produced good returns in these areas. If, in his first visit to Davos, Lula appeared as if a representative from another world, a leftist politician with no real track record of market-oriented reform under his belt, his 2007 appearance confirmed his acceptance by the international community as a reformer who had embraced his predecessor's vision of change but had deepened these commitments, particularly in the social area. For those assembled in Davos in 2007, Lula symbolized the new twenty-first century capitalism with a human face.

Lula achieved this level of support in the international financial community through his sustained dedication to meeting and exceeding IMF deficit targets, his government's strategic but nonetheless positive engagement with the United States on trade issues, and the partnering of Brazil's new social policies with the resources of multilateral agencies. These are all testament to Lula's belief that Brazil must engage the global marketplace rather than turn away from it.

At the same time, there are serious costs to the presidential strategy of reforming the Brazilian political and economic structure in order to become more competitive in global markets. To curry center-right support, the Brazilian president has had to embrace the very mechanisms of clientelism that are at the heart of many of the inefficiencies that create a deadlock on the country's democratic institutions. Given a weak party system and constitutional requirements that all amendments must be passed twice by 60 percent majorities in both houses of congress, clientelism has become the presidency's most powerful mechanism for cultivating support in order to piece together large, fractious majorities needed to pass particular reform bills. It is not surprising then that some party officials affiliated with the PT and other government parties stepped over the line and employed corrupt practices to guarantee support for legislation.

This strategy created serious paradoxes for the Lula presidency. Despite his criticism of Cardoso's tendency to kowtow to clientelistic interests, many of them in the conservative parties and in the poorest regions of Brazil where opposition to agrarian reform and social distribution is strongest, Lula has also depended upon the support of some of these forces to pass reform legislation. While Lula has not gone to the expensive lengths Cardoso did in buying the support of governors and political machines in congress with promises of spending, his reforms have suffered the watering down effect that comes with making politically expedient concessions to secure passage. And like his predecessor, Lula has done little to reinforce the discipline of political parties or reduce the fragmentation of the legislature. The expulsion of rebel members of his own PT demonstrates his commitment to partisan discipline in his own party, but the absence of electoral reform reflects Lula's pragmatic realization that his party must work with much less-disciplined allies on the center-left and center-right. In Lula's second term, electoral reform will re-emerge as an area for reform, but the president will tackle it while reforming his own party's battered image.

Despite the heady rhetoric of Cardoso's 1994 presidential campaign and the rising expectations of long-frustrated social democrats inside and outside Brazil, his administration offered little in the way of changing Brazilian politics for the long haul. Cardoso made only token progress on the country's persisting social inequalities. The Real Plan reduced the eroding effect of hyperinflation on the incomes of the poor, boosting consumption for millions of Brazilians. But other policies were less effective. Economic liberalization caused thousands of Brazilian firms to shave their labor costs, putting hundreds of thousands out of work. Privatization, for example, put an estimated 546,000 out of work as sold-off firms downsized to become viable market actors. As urban unemployment has increased, so too have urban violence and crime. The government distributed more land to poor people in rural areas, but these efforts failed to make a dent in Brazil's concentrated system of land tenure. Some innovations in health reform and education emerged regarding improving the availability of anti-HIV drugs and state-level experiments, respectively, but wider reforms received only lip service from the administration. The Lula presidency's mixture of modest social reform with a sustained commitment to fiscal probity and open markets will continue to build on Cardoso's accomplishments, but like his predecessor, Lula will not be able to generate vast social and political structural change. Pragmatism in the face of mounting problems seems to be the theme of both the Cardoso and Lula presidencies.

Both the fiscal and the environmental limits to Brazil's economic development have been stretched almost to their breaking points. Even without a significant downturn in the global economy, the fate of the Brazilian economy is being threatened by the state's high indebtedness, the difficulty of cutting public spending, especially in the area of entitlements such as pensions, and the social and ecological costs of the maldistribution of income and the abuse of natural resources. The tendency to see solutions to Brazil's economic problems in terms of promoting exports and enlarging the economy deepens these problems. Considering that many of Brazil's exports are still extractive (such as iron ore and lumber), or agricultural commodities, these recommendations place ever more pressure on the country's ecology. Deforestation of the Amazon and international climate change are intricately linked, and as a new American president assumes power in January 2009, a renewed commitment at the international level may be possible to address the problem. Brazil is situated to be a leader in this field in international diplomacy, but it must balance its domestic interests with its international commitments skillfully.

The fragile ecosystem of the Amazon is in particular danger. Despite all of the attention the Amazon's natural value is given in the international media, in Brazil, "Amazonian defense"—the securing of the porous and vegetation-covered borders of Brazil's north from the encroachment of drug cartels and illegal miners—gets more attention than the "defense of the Amazon." The work of Brazilian and international NGOs in the Amazon is still relatively a recent—since the democratic transition—phenomenon, while development and security concerns are much older. And the work of these groups inevitably confronts the popular, nationalist sentiment that international actors cannot tell Brazilians what to do with "their Amazon basin."

The challenges facing Brazil and the way that the country's political leaders have chosen to deal with them are similar to experiences elsewhere. The Brazilian state lacks the resources to promote development as it did during the days of Vargas, Kubitschek,

and military rule. With the advent of the Real Plan, the priorities have been to attract foreign capital, boost export earnings, and favor the highest bidders in the privatization of public firms. The developmentalist state lives on only in some BNDES policies. Like former state-led industrializers India, Mexico, and France, Brazil has turned in the neoliberal direction, limiting the state's role in the economy. This shift in the state's organization reminds us of the importance of our theme of highlighting critical junctures in state formation.

In contrast to the corporatist and populist role of the state, the moderating power in Brazilian history, the central state has become a far more passive agent in society. Brazilian workers no longer negotiate labor issues with state mediation, as they still do in Germany. Instead, labor unions, when they are capable, negotiate directly with business. In most cases, given high urban unemployment, the interests of business usually prevail. Urban workers receive little or no compensation from the state when they suffer layoffs or reductions in their salaries and workplace benefits. Most rural workers, the millions in the informal sector, and minorities are in an even more precarious position, as they lack the few benefits and protections enjoyed by salaried urban workers. The weakness of the judiciary, human rights violations by police and security forces, and the tendency to vigilantism and class conflict in poor, rural areas reinforce the anemia of a civil society that increasingly discounts its role in politics.

In this context, Brazilian democracy has suffered greatly, the importance of which we highlighted in our theme of the democratic challenge. The poor feel doubly divorced from politics, both socially and politically disenfranchised from a process they view as unresponsive to their needs. Over time, this sense of disengagement has turned into open doubt about the utility of democracy itself. Stories of official corruption and the popular assumption that politicians' priority is their own pocketbook reinforce the idea that representatives are unaccountable to their constituencies. The weakness of political party loyalties and well-documented instances of corruption involving organizations such as the PT compound the problem of accountability. By contrast, much stronger democracies such as Germany, the United States, France, and Britain rely on well-defined rules that force political leaders to be accountable to other branches of government and to their own constituencies. Brazil's example has shown how difficult it is to embrace the democratic idea without these structures.

Although some of Brazil's problems are unique, many take the same form as they do elsewhere. Like all other major economies in the world, Brazil's is well integrated into the global economy. Despite the country's current problems with monetary stability and debt, Brazil is one of the world's key platforms for agricultural production and manufacturing. Brazil's share of the world market in iron ore, textiles, footwear, steel, machine parts, and autos makes it an important hub in the multinational production of several industrial products. It is a crucial supplier of raw materials as well as a large market for multinational producers. It has advantages few other developing countries enjoy. This also means, however, that Brazilian firms and workers (not to mention the public sector itself) must be able to adapt to greater competition from abroad and the needs of foreign capital. Given the speed with which technology outpaces itself, the pressure to train workers, boost productivity, and enhance research and development has grown tremendously. Brazil is struggling just to keep pace with globalization.

As globalization and democratization have made Brazilian politics less predictable, older questions about what it means to be Brazilian have re-emerged. Brazil highlights the point made in the Introduction about our theme on political identities, the point that such identities are often reshaped in changed circumstances. What it means to be Brazilian has become a more complex question given the way that Brazil, like the rest of the world, has been bombarded by foreign consumer images. Democracy has given ordinary Brazilians more of a voice, and they have used it to express and shape their own understandings, but mostly on local issues, not at the national level. Women, nongovernmental organizations, Catholics, Pentecostals, blacks, landless peasants, and residents of *favelas* have all organized in recent years around social and cultural issues. On the one hand, these movements have placed additional pressure on an already weakened state to deliver goods and services. On the other hand, these groups have supplied alternatives to the state by providing their own systems of social and cultural support. Because the domain of the state in other countries is constrained by the need to compete in the global economy, space is created for nonstate actors to provide goods and services that were previously produced by the state. What is missing in all of this is a sense of the "national question." How are all these disparate groups linked? Do they have a common, national interest?

One very recent development involves the way that Brazilian elites see the role of the country in forging a counterweight to the hegemonic power of the United States. In both Brazil's engagement with the United States in trade policy (in the FTAA and the WTO) as well as in security and other diplomatic relations, Lula's approach has been summed up by his foreign minister, Celso Amorim, as "benign restraint." Following this policy, Brazil opposes the United States on issues such as the war in Iraq and American agricultural subsidies, but it cooperates with Washington in the war against terrorism and regional integration. Lula's government is committed to fighting terrorism but it is unwilling to ignore social justice or to bend to the security policies of the United States. It remains to be seen whether this strategy will produce a coherent Brazilian self-image of the country's role in the world of states.

Brazilian Politics in Comparative Perspective

The most important lesson that Brazil offers for the broader study of comparative politics is that fragmented polities threaten democracy, social development, and nation building. The Brazilian political order is fragmented on several levels. The central state is fragmented by conflicts between the executive and the legislature, divided alliances and self-interested politicians in congress, decentralized government, and an indecisive judiciary with a complicated structure and an uncertain mission. Political parties are fragmented by clientelism and electoral rules that create incentives for politicians and voters to ignore party labels. Finally, civil society itself is fragmented into numerous, often conflictual, organizations, interest groups, professional associations, social movements, churches, and, most important, social classes and ethnic identities.

In some societies that are similarly fragmented, such as the United States and India, institutions have been more successful in bridging the gaps between individualistic pursuits and the demand of the people for good government. Rich systems of social organization and reciprocity that are linked to the state through political parties, parliaments, and even informal associations strengthen democracy in these countries. Where these systems are faulty, as they are in Brazil, fragmentation reinforces the weakness of the state and the society.

Recent Brazilian politics shows that a weak state deepens the citizenry's sense that all politics is corrupt. Although corruption is present in all polities to some degree, it does not by itself produce the angry disengagement from politics that has emerged in Brazil. Much more is wrong with the Brazilian political order. Police brutality, human rights violations, judicial incompetence, and the inability of bureaucratic agencies to respond to social demands have just as powerful an effect in legitimizing civic disengagement.

These problems only reinforce the importance of creating systems of accountability to reduce the corruption, police abuse, and bureaucratic incompetence that have given rise to these doubts. Unfortunately, the English word *accountability* has no counterpart in either Portuguese or Spanish. Given Brazil's (and Latin America's) long history of oligarchical rule and social exclusion, the notion of making elites accountable to the people is so alien that the languages of the region lack the required vocabulary. Systems of accountability must be built from the ground up; they must be nurtured in local government and in community organizations and then in the governments of states and the central state. The judiciary, political parties, the media, and organizations of civil society must be able to play enforcement and watchdog roles. These are the building blocks of accountability, and the accountability of political elites is the fulcrum of democracy.

Without a system of elite accountability, representation of the citizenry is impossible. The 60 percent of the Brazilian population that is classified as poor or close to poor has few autonomous organizations to pressure government. More than business, labor, or professional groups, the poor depend on their elected officials to find solutions to their problems. Brazilian politicians have shown that through demagoguery and personalism, they can be elected. But being elected is not the same as guaranteeing a constituency its right to be represented. For this to occur, institutions must make political elites accountable to the people who elected them. When that condition is met, genuine representation of citizens' interests becomes possible.

Lula's success in reducing hunger, poverty, and inequality—the most important goals of his presidency—has produced a laudable record thus far with implications for democracy. *Bolsa Família* has not only made a substantial change in the lives of millions of poor Brazilians, it might even begin to cut the ties of dependency, especially in the countryside, that make rural workers and their families dependent on landowners and local political barons. This might lead these people to vote without concern for what the erstwhile local *coroneis* prefer, an outcome that would change 500 years of Brazilian history.

Part of the problem is that sustaining even these successful reform efforts requires great political unity, but Brazil's experience confirms that political fragmentation can have a virulent effect on a country's sense of national purpose. Collective identities, by definition, require mechanisms that forge mutual understandings among groups of people. Fractured societies turn to age-old ethnic identities that, as the India-Pakistan and Nigerian experiences demonstrate, can produce destructive, internecine conflict. In Brazil, such extreme conflict has been avoided, but the divisive effects of a fragmented polity on collective identities are serious nonetheless. Divided by class, poor Brazilians continue to feel that politics holds no solutions for them, so they fail to mobilize for their rights. Blacks, women, and Indians share some of the same interests because they are paid less than white men are for the same kind of work. Yet few national organizations have been able to unite a coalition of interest groups to change business practices in this regard. Finally, all Brazilians should be concerned with the clearing of rain forests, the pollution of rivers and lakes, and the destruction of species, yet the major political parties and the congress seem incapable of addressing these issues on behalf of future generations. Such national concerns continuously take a back seat to the self-interests of politicians in Brazil.

Perhaps the most serious effect of political fragmentation on Brazil has involved the struggle to achieve the country's interests in an increasingly competitive, global marketplace. While globalization forces all countries, and particularly developing countries, to adapt to new technology, ideas, and economic interests, it also lets states take advantage of the opportunity to attract investment. Given the weakness of the Brazilian state, the social dislocation produced by industrial restructuring (such as unemployment), and the current instability of the international investment climate, Brazil maintains only an ambiguous vision of its role in the global capitalist order. Although Brazilian business, some unions, and key political leaders speak of the need to defend Brazil's interests in the international political economy, the country has few coherent strategies. Such questions are inherently complex and politically difficult, perhaps no less so in Brazil than in France. But dealing with these issues requires a somewhat consistent policy created by a political leadership with clear ideas about the interests of the country. In Brazil's fragmented polity, developing such unambiguous strategies is difficult.

Acting now on behalf of Brazil's interests in the world of states must be a priority of the Lula presidency. In the world since September 11, 2001, issues of security are outpacing matters of equity and development. Lula's government is committed to fighting terrorism, but it is unwilling to ignore social justice or to bend to the security policies of the United States. The fact in 2003 that the Brazilians began to fingerprint Americans traveling to the country in response to the Bush administration's policy of doing the same to foreigners with visas traveling through American airports is evidence that the Lula government retains its autonomy and remains committed to its policy of "benign restraint." But Lula also believes in more than a purely reactive policy. His appearance at Davos and in the international media is an attempt to improve the image of Brazil as an increasingly fair and just nation, concerned with international issues such as poverty, hunger, and disease. That his ideas are also being championed by the World Bank and the

International Monetary Fund is ironic, but surely not contradictory.

Finally, Brazil's experience with economic restructuring and democratization will continue to influence countries undergoing similar transformations in Latin America and the rest of the developing world. As a large and resource-rich country, Brazil presents a useful case for comparison with other big developing countries such as Mexico, Russia, India, and China. Its evolving federal structure, as well as its efforts to manage its resources while dealing with environmental costs, can inform similar processes in these countries.

As a transitional democracy, Brazil can provide insights into which governance systems work better than others. As a negative example, Brazil's ongoing experiment with presidentialism, multiparty democracy, and open-list PR may well confirm the superiority of alternative parliamentary systems in India and Germany or presidentialism in France and the United States. As a positive example, Brazil's experiences with keeping a diverse country united through trying economic times will have much to teach Russia and Nigeria, since these countries too are weighed down by the dual challenges of economic reform and nation building.

Within Latin America, Brazil continues to consolidate its position as the preeminent economy of the region. Through MERCOSUL, Brazil exerts authority on commercial questions, and with its continued dominance of the Amazon basin, the country's political elite retains the world's attention when they speak on environmental issues in the developing world. Brazil's experiences with balancing the exigencies of neoliberal economic adjustment with the sociopolitical realities of poverty will keep it at center stage as the World Bank and the IMF and the region's political, economic, and academic leaders discuss the possibilities for a new model of development.

Brazil may not be "the country of the future," but it is a country with a future. None of the maladies of Brazilian politics and social development are immune to improvement. If political reform is consolidated in the next few years, the groundwork will have been laid for transforming Brazil into a country that deserves the respect of the world.

Key Terms ⟫⟫

privatization

moderating power

oligarchy

legitimacy

clientelism

patrimonialism

politics of the governors

interventores

state corporatism

New State

populism

nationalism

bureaucratic authoritarianism (BA)

state-led development

abertura

personalist politicians

export-led growth

interventionist

import substitution industrialization (ISI)

state technocrats

developmentalism

para-statals

nongovernmental organizations

informal economy

favelas

bureaucratic rings

proportional representation (PR)

Suggested Readings ⟫⟫

Alvarez, Sonia. *Engendering Democracy in Brazil.* Princeton, N.J.: Princeton University Press, 1990.

Ames, Barry. *The Deadlock of Democracy in Brazil: Interests, Identities, and Institutions in Comparative Politics.* Ann Arbor: University of Michigan Press, 2001.

Evans, Peter B. *Dependent Development: The Alliance of Multinational, State, and Local Capital in Brazil.* Princeton, N.J.: Princeton University Press, 1979.

Furtado, Celso. *The Economic Growth of Brazil: A Survey from Colonial to Modern Times.* Berkeley: University of California Press, 1963.

Goldstein, Donna M. *Laughter Out of Place: Race, Class, Violence, and Sexuality in a Rio Shantytown.* Berkeley, CA: University of California Press, 2003.

Hochstetler, Kathryn and Margaret Keck. *Greening Brazil: Environmental Activism in State and Society.* Durham, N.C.: Duke University Press, 2007.

Keck, Margaret. *The Workers' Party and Democratization in Brazil.* New Haven, Conn.: Yale University Press, 1992.

Kingstone, Peter R., and Power, Timothy J., eds. *Democratic Brazil: Actors, Institutions, and Processes.* Pittsburgh: University of Pittsburgh Press, 2000.

Mainwaring, Scott. *Rethinking Party Systems in the Third Wave of Democratization: The Case of Brazil.* Stanford: Stanford University Press, 1999.

Matta, Roberto da. *Carnivals, Rogues, and Heroes: An Interpretation of the Brazilian Dilemma.* Notre Dame, Ind.: University of Notre Dame Press, 1991.

Samuels, David J. *Ambition, Federalism, and Legislative Politics in Brazil.* New York: Cambridge University Press, 2003.

Scheper-Hughes, Nancy. *Death Without Weeping: The Violence of Everyday Life in Brazil.* Berkeley: University of California Press, 1992.

Schneider, Ben Ross. *Politics Within the State: Elite Bureaucrats and Industrial Policy in Authoritarian Brazil.* Pittsburgh: University of Pittsburgh Press, 1991.

Sheriff, Robin E. *Dreaming Equality: Color, Race, and Racism in Urban Brazil.* New Brunswick: Rutgers University Press, 2001.

Skidmore, Thomas E. *Black into White: Race and Nationality in Brazilian Thought.* Durham, N.C.: Duke University Press, 1993.

———. *The Politics of Military Rule in Brazil, 1964–85.* New York: Oxford University Press, 1988.

Stepan, Alfred. *Rethinking Military Politics: Brazil and the Southern Cone.* Princeton, N.J.: Princeton University Press, 1988.

———, ed. *Democratizing Brazil: Problems of Transition and Consolidation.* New York: Oxford University Press, 1989.

Tendler, Judith. *Good Government in the Tropics.* Baltimore: Johns Hopkins University Press, 1997.

Weyland, Kurt. *Democracy Without Equity: Failures of Reform in Brazil.* Pittsburgh: University of Pittsburgh Press, 1996.

Suggested Websites »

LANIC database, University of Texas-Austin, Brazil Resource page
lanic.utexas.edu/la/brazil/
YouTube, President Lula da Silva's 2007 address at Davos
http://www.youtube.com/watch?v=RqsDMU3ASgo
The U.S. Library of Congress Country Study Page for Brazil
lcweb2.loc.gov/frd/cs/brtoc.html

SciELO Brazil, Searchable Database of Full-Text Articles on Brazil
www.scielo.br
National Development Bank of Brazil, Searchable Database of Documents on Brazilian Economy and Development (many in English)
www.bndes.gov.br/english/default.asp

Endnotes »

[1]IBGE (Instituto Brasileiro de Geografia e Estatística), *PNAD–Pesquisa Nacional por Amostra de Domicílios 2006* Vol 27 (Rio de Janeiro: IBGE, 2006). For more on Brazil's multiclassification system, see George Reid Andrews, *Blacks and Whites in São Paulo, Brazil, 1888–1988* (Madison: University of Wisconsin Press, 1991).

[2]See Bertha K. Becker and Claudio A. G. Egler, *Brazil: A New Regional Power in the World Economy: A Regional Geography* (New York: Cambridge University Press, 1992), p. 5; and Terence Turner, "Brazil: Indigenous Rights vs. Neoliberalism," *Dissent* (Summer 1996): 67.

[3]For a complete treatment of state corporatism in Brazil during this period, see Ruth Berins Collier and David Collier, *Shaping the Political Arena: Critical Junctures, the Labor Movement, and Regime Dynamics in Latin America* (Princeton, N.J.: Princeton University Press, 1991), pp. 169–195.

[4]Robert M. Levine, *Father of the Poor? Vargas and His Era* (New York: Cambridge University Press, 1998), pp. 8–9.

[5]For an analysis of this "new professionalism," see Alfred Stepan, *The Military in Politics: Changing Patterns in Brazil* (Princeton, N.J.: Princeton University Press, 1971).

[6]Thomas E. Skidmore, *Politics in Brazil, 1930–1964: An Experiment in Democracy* (New York: Oxford University Press, 1967), p. 101.

[7]Maria do Carmo Campello de Souza, *Estado e Partidos Políticos no Brasil (1930 a 1964)* (São Paulo: Editora Alfa-Omega, 1975).

[8]Guillermo O'Donnell, *Modernization and Bureaucratic-Authoritarianism: Studies in South American Politics* (Berkeley: Institute of International Studies, University of California, 1973).

[9]Thomas E. Skidmore, *The Politics of Military Rule in Brazil, 1964–85* (New York: Oxford University Press, 1988), p. 49.

[10]Leigh A. Payne, *Brazilian Industrialists and Democratic Change* (Baltimore: Johns Hopkins University Press, 1994), ch. 4.

[11]For an analysis of these critical elections, see Bolivar Lamounier, "Authoritarian Brazil Revisited: The Impact of Elections on the Abertura," in Alfred Stepan, ed., *Democratizing Brazil: Problems of Transition and Consolidation* (New York: Oxford University Press, 1989).

[12]Margaret Keck, *The Workers' Party and Democratization in Brazil* (New Haven, Conn.: Yale University Press, 1992), pp. 219–220.

[13]Timothy J. Power, *The Political Right in Postauthoritarian Brazil: Elites, Institutions, and Democratization* (University Park: Pennsylvania State University Press, 2000).

[14]Margaret Keck, "The New Unionism in the Brazilian Transition," in Stepan, *Democratizing Brazil,* 284.

[15]See Celso Furtado, *The Economic Growth of Brazil: A Survey from Colonial to Modern Times* (Berkeley: University of California Press, 1963).

[16]For a more complete treatment of how developmentalist ideas cultivated in ECLA affected policy choices in Brazil, see Kathryn Sikkink, *Ideas and Institutions: Developmentalism in Brazil and Argentina* (Ithaca, N.Y.: Cornell University Press, 1991).

[17]More complete treatment of the ISI experience can be found in Albert O. Hirschman, *A Bias for Hope: Essays on Development and Latin America* (New Haven, Conn.: Yale University Press, 1971).

[18]Peter B. Evans, *Dependent Development: The Alliance of Multinational, State, and Local Capital in Brazil* (Princeton, N.J.: Princeton University Press, 1979).

[19]These and other examples of ecological destruction are analyzed in Werner Baer and Charles C. Mueller, "Environmental Aspects of Brazil's Development," in Werner Baer, ed., *The Brazilian Economy: Growth and Development,* 4th ed. (New York: Praeger, 1995).

[20]For more on state environmental efforts, see Barry Ames and Margaret E. Keck, "The Politics of Sustainable Development: Environmental Policy Making in Four Brazilian States," *Journal of Interamerican Studies and World Affairs* 39, no. 4 (Winter 1998): 1–40.

[21]Kathryn Hochstetler and Margaret Keck, *Greening Brazil: Environmental Activism in State and Society* (Durham, N.C.: Duke University Press, 2007).

[22]Alfred P. Montero, "Devolving Democracy? Political Decentralization and the New Brazilian Federalism," in Peter

R. Kingstone and Timothy J. Power, eds., *Democratic Brazil: Actors, Institutions, and Processes* (Pittsburgh: University of Pittsburgh Press, 2000).

[23]Peggy A. Lovell, "Race, Gender, and Development in Brazil," *Latin American Research Review* 29, no. 3 (1994), pp. 7–35.

[24]Kurt Weyland, *Democracy Without Equity: Failures of Reform in Brazil* (Pittsburgh: University of Pittsburgh Press, 1996).

[25]Morsch, E., N. Chavannes, M. van den Akker, H. Sa, G.J. Dinant, "The Effects of the Family Health Program on Child Health in Ceará State, Northeastern Brazil," *Arch Public Health* 59 (2001):151–65.

[26]Kathy Lindert, Anja Linder, Jason Hobbs, and Benedicte de la Briere, "The Nuts and Bolts of Brazil's *Bolsa Família* Program: Implementing Conditional Cash Transfers in a Decentralized Context," Social Protection Discussion Paper No. 0709, May 2007, pp. 18–19.

[27]Leonardo Guimarães Neto, "Desigualdades Regionais e Federalismo," in Rui de Britto Álvares Affonso and Pedro Luiz Barros Silva, eds., *Desigualdades Regionais e Desenvolvimento* (São Paulo: FUNDAP, 1995).

[28]Jeffry A. Frieden, *Debt, Development, and Democracy: Modern Political Economy and Latin America, 1965–1985* (Princeton, N.J.: Princeton University Press, 1991), pp. 54–65.

[29]Diana Jean Schemo, "The ABC's of Business in Brazil," *New York Times,* July 16, 1998, pp. B1, 7.

[30]Fernando Luiz Abrúcio, *Os Barões da Federação: O Poder dos Governadores no Brasil Pós-Autoritário* (São Paulo: Editora HUCITECU, 1998).

[31]David Samuels, *Ambition, Federalism, and Legislative Politics in Brazil,* (New York: Cambridge University Press, 2003).

[32]Alfred P. Montero, *Shifting States in Global Markets: Subnational Industrial Policy in Contemporary Brazil and Spain* (University Park: Pennsylvania State University Press, 2002).

[33]Timothy J. Power, "Politicized Democracy: Competition, Institutions, and 'Civic Fatigue' in Brazil," *Journal of Interamerican Studies and World Affairs* 33, no. 3 (Fall 1991): 75–112.

[34]Argelina Figueiredo and Fernando Limongi, "O Congresso e as Medidas Provisórias: Abdicação ou Delegação?" *Novos Estudos CEBRAP* 47 (1997): 127–154.

[35]Thomas J. Trebat, *Brazil's State-Owned Enterprises: A Case Study of the State as Entrepreneur* (New York: Cambridge University Press, 1983).

[36]Helen Shapiro, *Engines of Growth: The State and Transnational Auto Companies in Brazil* (New York: Cambridge University Press, 1994).

[37]Peter B. Evans, "Predatory, Developmental, and Other Apparatuses: A Comparative Political Economy Perspective on the Third World State," *Sociological Forum* 4, no. 4 (1989): 561–587.

[38]Wendy Hunter, *Eroding Military Influence in Brazil: Politicians Against Soldiers* (Chapel Hill: University of North Carolina Press, 1997).

[39]Paulo Sérgio Pinheiro, "Popular Responses to State-Sponsored Violence in Brazil," in Chalmers et al., eds., *The New Politics of Inequality in Latin America.*

[40]Human Rights Watch, *Police Brutality in Urban Brazil* (New York: Human Rights Watch, 1997), 13.

[41]Ronald E. Ahnen, "The Politics of Police Violence in Democratic Brazil," *Latin American Politics and Society* 49:1 (Spring, 2007), 141–64.

[42]Judith Tendler, *Good Government in the Tropics* (Baltimore: Johns Hopkins University Press, 1997).

[43]For a study of how these exceptions have emerged in Brazil, see Barbara Geddes, *Politician's Dilemma: Building State Capacity in Latin America* (Berkeley: University of California Press, 1994).

[44]Ben Ross Schneider, *Politics Within the State: Elite Bureaucrats and Industrial Policy in Authoritarian Brazil* (Pittsburgh: University of Pittsburgh Press, 1991).

[45]Lívia Neves de H. Barbosa, "The Brazilian Jeitinho: An Exercise in National Identity," in David J. Hess and Roberto A. DaMatta, eds., *The Brazilian Puzzle: Culture on the Borderlands of the Western World* (New York: Columbia University Press, 1995).

[46]Barry Ames, *The Deadlock of Democracy in Brazil: Interests, Identities, and Institutions in Comparative Politics* (Ann Arbor: University of Michigan Press, 2001).

[47]Scott Mainwaring, "Brazilian Party Underdevelopment in Comparative Perspective," *Political Science Quarterly* 107 (1993).

[48]Timothy J. Power, "The Pen Is Mightier Than the Congress: Presidential Decree Power in Brazil," in John M. Carey and Mathew S. Shugart, eds., *Executive Decree Authority: Calling Out the Tanks or Just Filling Out the Forms* (New York: Cambridge University Press, 1998).

[49]See Argelina C. Figueiredo and Fernando Limongi, "Presidential Power, Legislative Organization, and Party Behavior in Brazil," *Comparative Politics* 32 (January 2000): 151–170.

[50]See Ames, *Deadlock of Democracy.*

[51]See Power, *The Political Right in Postauthoritarian Brazil.*

[52]See especially Gilberto Freyre, *The Mansions and the Shanties: The Making of Modern Brazil* (New York: Knopf, 1963), ch. 12.

[53]Ralph Della Cava, "The 'People's Church,' the Vatican, and Abertura," in Stepan, *Democratizing Brazil.*

[54]Turner, "Brazil: Indigenous Rights vs. Neoliberalism," p. 67.

[55]William H. Fisher, "Megadevelopment, Environmentalism, and Resistance: The Institutional Context of Kayapó Indigenous Politics in Central Brazil," *Human Organization* 53, no. 3 (1994): 220–232.

Merilee S. Grindle

Chapter 10 ≫ **MEXICO**

Official Name: **United Mexican States (Estados Unidos Mexicanos)**

Location: **Southern North America**

Capital City: **Mexico City**

Population (2008): **109.9 million**

Size: **1,972,550 sq. km.; slightly less than three times the size of Texas**

1521
Spaniards led by
Hernán Cortés capture
the Aztec capital,
initiating three centuries
of colonial rule

1810–1821
War of independence
from Spain

1876–1911
Dictatorship of Porfirio
Diaz

1910–1920
Mexican Revolution

1917
Mexican
Constitution

1929
Plutarco Elías Calles
founds PRI

1934–1940
Presidency of Lázaro
Cárdenas; entrench-
ment of corporatist state

1968
Massacre of Tlaltelolco;
hundreds of protesting
students killed

1978–1982
State-led development
reaches peak with
petroleum boom
and bust

SECTION 1

The Making of the Modern Mexican State

Politics in Action

On December 1, 2006, Felipe Calderón Hinojosa* became president of Mexico. Yet only ten days earlier, his political rival, Andrés Manuel López Obrador, had declared himself the "legitimate" president of Mexico. Members of López Obrador's Party of the Democratic Revolution (PRD) vowed to prevent Calderón from taking the oath of office. Members of Calderón's National Action Party (PAN) staged a sit-in on the main floor of the lower house of congress to ensure that the swearing-in ceremony could take place as scheduled. Before Calderón entered through a side door for a rushed, ten-minute ceremony, lawmakers from the two opposing parties had engaged in fistfights and thrown chairs at each other. Calderón gave his inauguration speech later in the day at the National Auditorium.

These events symbolized one of the most bitter and polarizing elections in recent Mexican history. On July 2, 2006, Mexicans had gone to the polls to choose a new president and new members for the Chamber

---

*In most Spanish-speaking countries, people usually have two surnames (family names), their father's and their mother's. The father's surname is written before the mother's and is the name by which they are formally known. For examples, the full name of the president of Mexico is Felipe Calderón Hinojosa, and he is known as President Calderón.

of Deputies and the Senate. The election was so close and the allegations of fraud by all sides so intense that it was not until September 5 that the Federal Electoral Tribunal (IFE) was able to declare Calderón the winner. In the end, he won with 35.89 percent of the vote. López Obrador won 35.31 percent and Roberto Madrazo of the Institutional Revolutionary Party (PRI) won 22.26 percent. The Chamber of Deputies and the Senate were equally divided. In the Chamber of Deputies, for example, the PAN won 206 seats, the PRD 127, and the PRI 106.

Although the events surrounding the 2006 elections represented a challenge for Mexico's fragile democracy, they also demonstrated the profound political changes that Mexico has experienced in the past twenty years. In 1986, the PAN was the most important opposition party in the country and the PRD did not exist. The IFE had not yet been created and all elections were administered by the federal government, which had been ruled by the PRI without interruption or serious opposition since 1929.

The PRI government of Mexico was sometimes called "the perfect dictatorship" and under its regime, political conflict was largely limited to internal party struggles and quiet repression. For several decades this system produced political stability and economic growth. Yet, increasingly during the 1980s and 1990s, Mexicans began to press for fairer elections and more responsive public officials. They demanded the right of

1982 Market reformers come to power in PRI	**1989** First governorship is won by an opposition party	**1996** Political parties agree on electoral reform	**2000** PRI loses presidency; Vicente Fox of PAN becomes president, but without majority support in congress	**2006** Felipe Calderón Hinojosa of PAN is elected president; no party has a majority of seats in congress
1988 Carolos Salinas is elected amid charges of fraud	**1994** NAFTA goes into effect; uprising in Chiapas; Colosio assassinated	**1997** Opposition parties advance nationwide; PRI loses absolute majority in congress for first time in its history		

opposition parties to compete for power on an equal basis with the PRI. They argued that the president had too much power and that the PRI was riddled with corruption. By 2000, a significant number of the country's 100 million citizens wanted political change. In that year, Vicente Fox Quesada of the PAN was able to defeat the PRI. He won the election largely because the old civil-authoritarian system could no longer ensure political stability, economic progress, and responsiveness to the demands of a society that was increasingly characterized by inequality.

Today, political and economic dissatisfaction continues to characterize Mexico. For elites, the opportunities of globalization have provided unprecedented wealth and cosmopolitan lifestyles. Yet indicators of increased poverty are everywhere. At least a quarter of the population lives on less than two dollars a day. The public education and health systems struggle to meet demand. In the countryside, the peasant population faces destitution. In urban areas, the poor are forced to find meager sources of income however they can.

The recent, polarizing election was a result not only of Mexico's increasing democratization but also of Fox's inability to promote greater economic growth or political progress during his presidency. The 2006 election drew attention to the ongoing and interrelated challenges of Mexico's development:

- Would a country with a long tradition of authoritarian government be able to sustain a democratic political system in the face of increasing demands and high expectations?

- Would a country that had long sought economic development through government activism and the domestic market be able to compete effectively in a competitive, market-driven global economy?

- Would a country long noted for severe inequalities between the rich and the poor be capable of providing better living standards for its growing population?

Geographic Setting

Mexico is one of the most geographically diverse countries in the world, encompassing snow-capped volcanoes, coastal plains, high plateaus, fertile valleys, rain forests, and deserts within an area slightly less than three times the size of Texas. To the north, it shares a 2,000-mile-long border with the United States; to the south, a 600-mile-long border with Guatemala and a 160-mile-long border with Belize. Two imposing mountain ranges run the length of Mexico: the Sierra Madre Occidental to the west and the Sierra Madre Oriental to the east. As a result, the country is noted for peaks, plateaus, and valleys that produce an astonishing number of microclimates and a rich diversity of plants and animals. Mexico's varied geography has historically made communication and transportation between regions difficult and

FIGURE 10.1

The Mexican Nation at a Glance

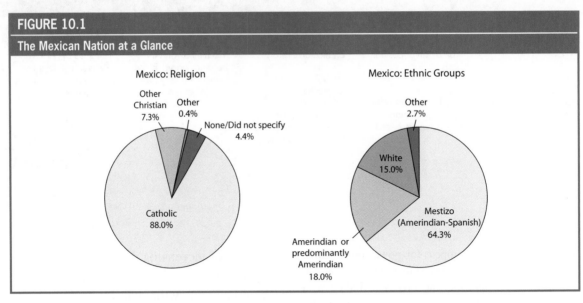

Mexico: Religion

- Other Christian 7.3%
- Other 0.4%
- None/Did not specify 4.4%
- Catholic 88.0%

Mexico: Ethnic Groups

- Other 2.7%
- White 15.0%
- Mestizo (Amerindian-Spanish) 64.3%
- Amerindian or predominantly Amerindian 18.0%

infrastructure expensive. The mountainous terrain tends to limit large-scale commercial agriculture to irrigated fields in the northern part of the country, while the central and southern regions produce a wide variety of crops on small farms. Soil erosion and desertification are major problems because of the steep terrain and unpredictable rainfall in many areas. The country is rich in oil, silver, and other natural resources, but it has long struggled to manage those resources wisely.

The human landscape is equally dramatic. With some 107 million inhabitants, Mexico is the world's

Table 10.1

Political Organization

Political System	Federal republic
Regime History	Current form of government since 1917
Administrative Structure	Federal with thirty-one states and a federal district
Executive	President, elected by direct election with a six-year term of office; reelection not permitted
Legislature	Bicameral Congress. Senate (upper house) and Chamber of Deputies (lower house); elections held every three years. There are 128 senators, 3 from each of the thirty-one states, 3 from the federal (capital) district, and 32 elected nationally by proportional representation for six-year terms. The 500 members of the Chamber of Deputies are elected for three-year terms from 300 electoral districts, 300 by simple majority vote and 200 by proportional representation.
Judiciary	Independent federal and state court system headed by a Supreme Court with eleven justices appointed by the president and approved by the Senate
Party System	Multiparty system. One-party dominant (Institutional Revolutionary Party) system from 1929 until 2000. Major parties: National Action Party, Institutional Revolutionary Party, and the Democratic Revolutionary Party.

eleventh most populous country—the second-largest nation in Latin America after Portuguese-speaking Brazil and the largest Spanish-speaking nation in the world. Sixty percent of the population is *mestizo,* or people of mixed **Amerindian** and Spanish descent. About 30 percent of the population claims indigenous (Amerindian) descent, although only about 6 percent of the population speaks an indigenous language rather than Spanish. The rest of the population is made up of Caucasians and people with other backgrounds. The largest **indigenous groups** are the Maya in the south and the Náhuatl in the central regions, with well over 1 million members each. There are also dozens and perhaps hundreds of smaller linguistic and social groups throughout the country. Although Mexicans pride themselves on their Amerindian heritage, issues of race and class divide the society.

Mexico was transformed from a largely rural to a largely urban country in the second half of the twentieth century, with more than 75 percent of the population now living in urban areas. Mexico City has become one of the world's largest cities, with about 20 million inhabitants.[1] Annual population growth has slowed to about 1.4 percent, but society continues to adjust to the baby boom of the 1970s and early 1980s as these twenty- to thirty-year-olds seek jobs and form families. Migration both within and beyond Mexico's borders has become a major issue. Greater economic opportunities in the industrial cities of the north lead many men and women to seek work there in the *maquiladoras*, or assembly industries. As a result, border cities like Tijuana and Ciudad Juárez have experienced tremendous growth in the past twenty years. Many job seekers continue on to the United States, lured by a larger job market and higher wages. The problem repeats itself in reverse on Mexico's southern border, with many thousands of Central Americans looking for better prospects in Mexico and beyond.

Mexico

Critical Junctures

Mexicans are deeply affected by the legacies of their collective past, including centuries of colonialism and decades of political instability after the end of Spanish rule. The legacies of the distant past are still felt, but the most formative event in the country's modern history was the Revolution of 1910. Mexico experienced the first great social revolution of the twentieth century, a conflict that lasted for more than a decade and claimed the lives of as many as 1 million people. The revolution was fought by a variety of forces for a variety of reasons, which made the consolidation of power that followed as significant as the revolution itself. The institutions and symbols of the current political regime emerged from these complex conflicts.

Independence and Instability (1810–1876)

Spain ruled Mexico for three centuries, administering a vast economic, political, and religious empire in the interests of the imperial country, its kings, and its representatives in North America (see "Global Connection: Conquest or Encounter?"). Colonial policy was designed to extract wealth from the territory then known as New Spain and to limit the possibilities for Spaniards in the New World to benefit from agriculture, commerce, or industry without at the same time benefiting the mother country. It was also designed to ensure commitment to the Roman Catholic religion and the subordination of the Amerindian population.

In 1810, a parish priest in central Mexico named Miguel Hidalgo called for an end to Spanish misrule. At the head of a motley band of insurgents, he began the first of a series of wars for independence that pitted rebels against the Spanish Crown for eleven years. Although independence was gained in 1821, Mexico struggled to create a stable and legitimate government for decades after. Liberals and conservatives, federalists and centralists, those who sought to expand the power of the church and those who sought to curtail it, and those who wanted a republic and those who wanted a monarchy were all engaged in the battle for Mexico's soul during the nineteenth century. Between 1833 and 1855, thirty-six presidential administrations came to power.

Adding insult to injury during this disorganized period, Mexico lost half its territory to the United States. Its northern territory of Texas proclaimed and then won independence in a war ending in 1836. Then the Lone Star Republic, as Texas was called at the time, was annexed by the United States in 1845, and claims on Mexican territory north of the Rio Grande were increasingly heard from Washington. On the basis of a dubious claim that Mexico had invaded U.S. territory, the United States declared war on its southern neighbor in 1841. In 1847, the U.S. army invaded the port city of Veracruz. With considerable loss of civilian lives, U.S. forces marched toward Mexico City, where they engaged in the final battle of the war at Chapultepec Castle. An 1848 treaty gave the United States title to what later became the states of Texas, New Mexico, Utah, Nevada, Arizona, California, and part of Colorado for about $18 million, leaving a legacy of deep resentment toward the United States, which many Mexicans still consider to be the "Colossus of the North."

The loss in this war did not make it any easier to govern Mexico. Liberals and conservatives continued their struggle over issues of political and economic order and, in particular, the power of the Catholic Church. The Constitution of 1857 incorporated many of the goals of the liberals, such as a somewhat democratic government, a bill of rights, and limitations on the power of the church. The constitution did not guarantee stability, however. In 1861, Spain, Great Britain, and France occupied Veracruz to collect debts owed by Mexico. The French army then continued on to Mexico City, where it subdued the weak government, and established the rule of Emperor Maximilian (1864–1867). Conservatives welcomed this respite from liberal rule. Benito Juárez returned to the presidency in 1867 after defeating and executing Maximilian. Juárez, a Zapotec Indian from Oaxaca who came to be a liberal hero, is still hailed in Mexico today as an early proponent of more democratic government.

The Porfiriato (1876–1911)

Over the next few years, a popular retired general named Porfirio Díaz became increasingly dissatisfied

Global Connection

Conquest or Encounter?

The year 1519, when the Spanish conqueror Hernán Cortés arrived on the shores of the Yucatán Peninsula, is often considered the starting point of Mexican political history. But the Spanish explorers did not come to an uninhabited land waiting to be excavated for gold and silver. Instead, the land that was to become New Spain and then Mexico was home to extensive and complex indigenous civilizations that were advanced in agriculture, architecture, and political and economic organization—civilizations that were already more than a thousand years old. The Mayans of the Yucatán and the Toltecs of the central highlands had reached high levels of development long before the arrival of the Europeans. By 1519, diverse groups had fallen under the power of the militaristic Aztec Empire, which extended throughout what is today central and southern Mexico.

The encounter between the Europeans and these indigenous civilizations was marked by bloodshed and violence. The great Aztec city of Tenochtitlán—the site of Mexico City today—was captured and largely destroyed by the Spanish conquerors in 1521. Cortés and the colonial masters who came after him subjected indigenous groups to forced labor; robbed them of gold, silver, and land; and introduced flora and fauna from Europe that destroyed long-existing aqueducts and irrigation systems. They also brought alien forms of property rights and authority relationships, a religion that viewed indigenous practices as the devil's work, and an economy based on mining and cattle—all of which soon overwhelmed existing structures of social and economic organization. Within a century, wars,

savage exploitation at the hands of the Spaniards, and the introduction of European diseases reduced the indigenous population from an estimated 25 million to 1 million or fewer. The Indian population took 300 years just to stop decreasing after the disaster of the conquest.

Even so, the Spanish never constituted more than a small percentage of the total population, and massive racial mixing among the Indians, Europeans, and to a lesser extent Africans produced a new *raza*, or *mestizo* race. This unique process remains at once a source of pride and conflict for Mexicans today. What does it mean to be Mexican? Is one the conquered or the conqueror? While celebrating Amerindian achievements in food, culture, the arts, and ancient civilization, middle-class Mexico has the contradictory sense that to be "Indian" nowadays is to be backward. Many Amerindians are stigmatized by mainstream society if they speak a native dialect. But perhaps the situation is changing, with the upsurge of indigenous movements from both the grassroots and the international level striving to promote ethnic pride, defend rights, and foster the teaching of Indian languages.

The collision of two worlds resonates in current national philosophical and political debates. Is Mexico a Western society? Is it colonial or modern? Third or First World? Southern or Northern? Is the United States an ally or a conqueror? Perhaps most important, many Mexicans at once welcome and fear full integration into the global economy, asking themselves: Is globalization the new conquest?

with what he thought was a "lot of politics" and "little action" in Mexico's government. After several failed attempts to win and then take the presidency, he finally succeeded in 1876. His dictatorship lasted thirty-four years and was at first welcomed by many because it brought sustained stability to the country.

Díaz imposed a highly centralized authoritarian system to create political order and economic progress. Over time, he came to rely increasingly on a

small clique of advisers, known as *científicos* (scientists), who wanted to adopt European technologies and values to modernize the country. Deeply disdainful of the vast majority of the country's population, Díaz and the *científicos* encouraged foreign investment and amassed huge fortunes. During this period, known as the *Porfiriato*, this small elite group monopolized political power and reserved lucrative economic investments for itself. Economic and political opportunities were closed off for new generations of middle- and upper-class Mexicans, who became increasingly resentful of the greed of the Porfirians and their own lack of opportunities.

The Revolution of 1910 and the Sonoran Dynasty (1910–1934)

In 1910, conflict broke out as reformers sought to end the dictatorship. Díaz had pledged himself to an open election for president, and in 1910, Francisco I. Madero, a landowner from the northern state of Coahuila, presented himself as a candidate. The slogan "Effective Suffrage, No Reelection" summed up the reformers' goals in creating opportunities for a new class of politically ambitious citizens to move into positions of power. When this opposition swelled, Díaz jailed Madero and tried to repress growing dissent. But the clamor for change forced Díaz into exile. Madero was elected in 1911, but he was soon using the military to put down revolts from reformers and reactionaries alike. When Madero was assassinated during a **coup d'état** in 1913, political order in the country virtually collapsed.

At the same time that middle-class reformers struggled to displace Díaz, a peasant revolt that focused on land claims erupted in the central and southern states of the country. This revolt had roots in legislation that made it easy for wealthy landowners and ranchers to claim the lands of peasant villagers. Encouraged by the weakening of the old regime and driven to desperation by increasing landlessness, villagers armed themselves and joined forces under a variety of local leaders. The most famous of these was Emiliano Zapata, who amassed a peasant army from Morelos, a state in southern Mexico. Zapata's manifesto, the Plan de Ayala, became the cornerstone of the radical agrarian reform that would be incorporated into the Constitution of 1917.

In the northern part of the country, Francisco (Pancho) Villa rallied his own army of workers, small farmers, and ranch hands. He presented a major challenge to the national army, now under the leadership of Venustiano Carranza, who inherited Madero's middle-class reformist movement and eventually became president. Villa's forces recognized no law but that of their chief and combined military maneuvers with

In 1914, Pancho Villa (right) met with Emiliano Zapata in Mexico City to discuss the revolution and their separate goals for its outcome.
Source: Robert Freck/Odyssey/Chicago.

banditry, looting, and warlordism in the territories under their control. In 1916, troops from the United States entered Mexico to punish Villa for an attack on U.S. territory. Although this badly planned, poorly executed military operation failed to locate Villa, the presence of U.S. troops on Mexican soil resulted in increased public hostility toward the United States, against which feelings were already running high because of a 1914 invasion of Veracruz.

The Mexican Constitution of 1917 was forged out of the diverse and often conflicting set of interests represented by the various revolutionary factions. The document established a formal set of political institutions and guaranteed citizens a range of progressive social and economic rights: agrarian reform, social security, the right to organize in unions, a minimum wage, an eight-hour workday, profit sharing for workers, universal secular education, and adult male suffrage. Despite these socially advanced provisions, the constitution did not provide suffrage for women, who had to wait until 1953 to vote in local elections and 1958 to vote in national elections. In an effort to limit the power of foreign investors, the constitution declared that only Mexican citizens or the government could own land or rights to water and other natural resources. It also contained numerous articles that severely limited the power of the Roman

Catholic Church, long a target of liberals who wanted Mexico to be a secular state. The signing of the document signaled the formal end of the revolution and the intent of the contending parties to form a new political regime. Despite such noble sentiments, violence continued as competing leaders sought to assert power and displace their rivals. By 1920, a modicum of stability had emerged, but not before many of the revolutionary leaders—including Zapata and President Carranza—had been assassinated in struggles over power and policy.

Despite this violence, power was gradually consolidated in the hands of a group of revolutionary leaders from the north of the country. Known as the Sonoran Dynasty, after their home state of Sonora, these leaders were committed to a capitalist model of economic development. Eventually, one of the Sonorans, Plutarco Elías Calles, emerged as the *jefe máximo,* or supreme leader. After his presidential term (1924–1928), Calles managed to select and dominate his successors from 1929 to 1934. The consolidation of power under his control was accompanied by extreme **anticlericalism**, which eventually resulted in warfare between the government and the conservative leaders of the Catholic Church and their followers.

In 1929, Calles brought together many of the most powerful contenders for leadership, including many regional warlords, to create a political party. The bargain he offered was simple: contenders for power would accommodate each other's interests in the expectation that without political violence, the country would prosper and they would be able to reap the benefits of even greater power and economic spoils. They formed a political party, whose name was changed in 1938 and again in 1946, to consolidate their power; and for the next seven decades, Calles's bargain was effective in ensuring nonviolent conflict resolution among elites and the uninterrupted rule of the Institutional Revolutionary Party (PRI) in national politics.

Although the revolution was complex and the interests contending for power in its aftermath were numerous, there were five clear results of this protracted conflict. First, the power of traditional rural landowners was undercut. But in the years after the revolution, wealthy elites would again emerge in rural areas, even though they would never again be so powerful in national politics nor would their power be so unchecked in local areas. Second, the influence of the Catholic Church was strongly curtailed. Although the church remained important in many parts of the country, it no longer participated openly in national political debates. Third, the power of foreign investors was severely limited; prior to the revolution, foreign investors had owned much of the country's land as well as many of its railroads, mines, and factories. Henceforth, Mexican nationalism would shape economic policy-making. Fourth, a new political elite consolidated power and agreed to resolve conflicts through accommodation and bargaining rather than through violence. And fifth, the new constitution and the new party laid the basis for a strong central government that could assert its power over the agricultural, industrial, and social development of the country.

Lázaro Cárdenas, Agrarian Reform, and the Workers (1934–1940)

In 1934, Plutarco Elías Calles handpicked Lázaro Cárdenas, a revolutionary general and former state governor, as the official candidate for the presidency. The *jefe máximo* fully anticipated that Cárdenas would go along with his behind-the-scenes management of the country and that the new president would continue the economic policies of the postrevolutionary coalition. To his great surprise, Cárdenas executed a virtual coup that established his own supremacy and sent Calles packing to the United States for an "extended vacation."[2] Even more unexpectedly, Cárdenas mobilized peasants and workers in pursuit of the more radical goals of the 1910 revolution. He encouraged peasant associations to petition for land and claim rights promised in the Constitution of 1917. During his administration, more than 49 million acres of land were distributed, nearly twice as much as had been parceled out by all the previous postrevolutionary governments combined.[3] Most of these lands were distributed in the form of *ejidos* (collective land grants) to peasant groups. *Ejidatarios* (those who acquired *ejido* lands) became one of the most enduring bases of support for the government. Cárdenas also encouraged workers to form unions and demand higher wages and better working conditions. He established his nationalist credentials in 1938 when he wrested the petroleum industry from foreign investors and placed it under government control.

During the Cárdenas years (1934–1940), the bulk of the Mexican population was incorporated into the political system. Organizations of peasants and workers, middle-class groups, and the military were added to the official party, and the voices of the poor majority were heard within the councils of government, reducing the risk that they would become radicalized outside them. In addition, the Cárdenas years witnessed a great expansion of the role of the state as the government encouraged investment in industrialization, provided credit to agriculture, and created infrastructure.

Lázaro Cárdenas continues to be a national hero to Mexicans, who look back on his presidency as a period when government was clearly committed to improving the welfare of the country's poor. His other legacy was to institutionalize patterns of political succession and presidential behavior that continue to set standards for Mexico's leaders. He campaigned extensively, and his travels took him to remote villages and regions, where he listened to the demands and complaints of humble people. Cárdenas served a single six-year term, called a *sexenio*, and then relinquished full power to his successor—a pattern of presidential succession that still holds in Mexican politics. Cárdenas's conduct in office created hallowed traditions of presidential style and succession that all subsequent national leaders have observed.

The Politics of Rapid Development (1940–1982)

Although Cárdenas had directed a radical reshuffling of political power in the country, his successors were able to use the institutions he created to counteract his reforms. Ambitious local and regional party leaders and leaders of peasants' and workers' groups began to use their organizations as pawns in exchange for political favors. Gradually, the PRI developed a huge patronage machine, providing union and *ejido* leaders with jobs, opportunities for corruption, land, and other benefits in return for delivering their followers'

political support. Extensive chains of personal relationships based on the exchange of favors allowed the party to amass far-reaching political control and limit opportunities for organizing independent of the PRI. These exchange relationships, known as **clientelism**, became the cement that built loyalty to the PRI and the political system.

This kind of political control enabled post-Cárdenas presidents to reorient the country's development away from the egalitarian social goals of the 1930s toward a development strategy in which the state actively encouraged industrialization and the accumulation of wealth. Initially, industrialization created jobs and made available a wide range of basic consumer goods to Mexico's burgeoning population. Economic growth rates were high during the 1940s, 1950s, and 1960s, and Mexicans flocked to the cities to take advantage of the jobs created in the manufacturing and construction industries. By the 1970s, however, industrial development policies were no longer generating rapid growth and could not keep pace with the rapidly rising demand for jobs.

The country's economy was in deep crisis by the mid-1970s. Just as policy-makers began to take actions to correct the problems, vast new amounts of oil were discovered in the Gulf of Mexico. Soon, rapid economic growth in virtually every sector of the economy was refueled by extensive public investment programs paid for with oil revenues. Based on the promise of petroleum wealth, the government and private businesses borrowed huge amounts of capital from foreign lenders, who were eager to do business with a country that had so much oil. Unfortunately for Mexico, international petroleum prices plunged sharply in the early 1980s, and Mexico plunged into a deep economic crisis that affected many other countries around the world.

Crisis and Reform (1982–2001)

This economic crisis led two presidents, Miguel de la Madrid (1982–1988) and Carlos Salinas (1988–1994), to introduce the first major reversal of the country's development strategy since the 1940s. New policies were put in place to limit the government's role in the economy and to make it easier for Mexican producers to export their goods. This period clearly marked the beginning of a new effort to integrate Mexico more fully into the global economy. In 1993, by signing the **North American Free Trade Agreement (NAFTA)**, which committed Mexico, the United States, and Canada to the elimination of trade barriers among them, Mexico's policy-makers signaled the extent to which they envisioned that the future prosperity of their country would be linked to that of its two neighbors to the north.

The economic reforms of the 1980s and 1990s were a turning point for Mexico and meant that the country's future development would be closely tied to international economic conditions. A major economic crisis at the end of 1994, in which billions of dollars of foreign investment fled the country, was indicative of this new international vulnerability. The peso lost half of its value against the dollar within a few days, and the government lacked the funds to pay its debt obligations. The Mexican economy shrank by 6.2 percent in 1995, inflation soared, taxes rose while wages were frozen, and the banking system collapsed. The United States orchestrated a $50 billion bailout, $20 billion of which came directly from the U.S. Treasury. Faced with limited options, the administration of Ernesto Zedillo (1994–2000) implemented a severe

and unpopular economic austerity program, which restored financial stability over the next two years.

Economic crisis was exacerbated by political concerns. On January 1, 1994, a guerrilla movement, the Zapatista Army of National Liberation (EZLN), seized four towns in the southern state of Chiapas. The group demanded land, democracy, indigenous rights, and an immediate repeal of NAFTA. Many citizens throughout the country openly supported the aims of the rebels, pointing out that the movement brought to light the reality of two different Mexicos: one in which the privileged enjoyed the fruits of wealth and influence and another in which citizens were getting left behind because of poverty and repression. The government and the military were also criticized for inaction and human rights abuses in the state.

Following close on the heels of rebellion came the assassination of the PRI's presidential candidate, Luis Donaldo Colosio, on March 23, 1994, in the northern border city of Tijuana. The assassination shocked all citizens and shook the political elite deeply. The murder opened wide rifts within the PRI and unleashed a flood of speculation and distrust among the citizenry. Many Mexicans were convinced that the assassination was part of a conspiracy of party "dinosaurs," political

Mexican presidential candidates are expected to campaign hard, traveling to remote locations, making rousing campaign speeches, and meeting with citizens of humble origins. Here, presidential candidate Vicente Fox Quesada is on the campaign trail. *Source:* R. Kwiotek/ Zeitenspiegel/Corbis/Sygma.

hardliners who opposed any kind of democratic transformation.[4] Although this allegation has never been proved, speculation about who was behind the assassination has continued to this day. Fear of violence helped provide the PRI with strong support in the August 1994 elections.

The PRI was able to remain in power, but these shocks provoked widespread disillusionment and frustration with the political system. Many citizens, especially in urban areas, decided that there was no longer any reason to support the PRI. Buoyed by a 1996 electoral reform, the opposition made important gains in the legislative elections the following year. For the first time in modern Mexican history, the PRI lost its absolute majority in the Chamber of Deputies, the lower house of the national legislature. Since then, the congress has shown increasing dynamism as a counterbalance to the presidency, blocking executive decisions, demanding unrestricted information, and initiating new legislation. In addition, opposition parties have won important governorships and mayorships. The 2000 election of Vicente Fox as the first non-PRI president in seven decades was the culmination of this electoral revolution.

After September 11

Vicente Fox found it difficult to bring about the changes that he had promised to the Mexican people. The difficulties he faced as he attempted to implement his ambitious agenda arose in part because he and his administration lacked experience in addressing the challenges of governance on a national scale. However, a bigger problem for Fox was that he lacked the compliant congressional majority and the close relationship with his party that his PRI predecessors had enjoyed. Proposals for a reform of the tax code and for restructuring the government-controlled electricity corporation went down to defeat, and the president was subjected to catcalls and heckling when he made his annual reports to the congress.

With his legislative agenda stalled, Fox hoped that achievements in international policy would enhance his prestige at home. He was particularly hopeful that a close personal connection with the U.S. president,

George W. Bush, would facilitate an agreement under which a greater number of Mexicans would be able to migrate to the United States and work there. Bush had indicated that building a partnership with Mexico would be an important component of his foreign policy program, and the two governments initiated talks on a possible migration accord in 2001.

The terrorist attacks on September 11, 2001, dramatically changed the outlook, however. Top U.S. officials immediately turned their attention away from Mexico and Latin America and toward Afghanistan and the Middle East, diminishing the prospects for significant breakthroughs in U.S.–Mexican relations. It did not help that some in Washington felt that Mexico had been slow to express its solidarity with the United States in the wake of the attacks. The possibility of an agreement on migration disappeared as Washington moved to assert control over its borders and to restrict access to the United States. In the months that followed, Mexican officials cooperated with their U.S. counterparts in efforts designed to improve security at border crossings between the two nations, but many in Mexico City were frustrated that no progress was being made on issues like migration that were important to their country.

In 2002, Mexico began a two-year term as a member of the United Nations Security Council. The Fox administration intended the country's return to the council after a twenty-year absence to signal the desire of a democratic Mexico to play a larger role in international affairs. However, deliberations at the UN headquarters in New York focused increasingly on U.S. proposals for the use of force against Iraq. The Bush administration, aware of Mexico's close economic ties with the United States, believed that Mexico could be convinced to support its position on the issue. Public opinion in Mexico was so deeply opposed to an invasion of Iraq, however, that Fox's government decided to reject U.S.-sponsored resolutions on the subject. The U.S. officials who had counted on Mexican support were bitterly disappointed, but failed to realize that memories of past U.S. invasions and occupations still made questions involving national sovereignty very sensitive in Mexico and that any Mexican government that effectively sponsored a U.S. attack on a smaller, weaker country would have to confront a tremendous backlash.

Due to his ineffective government, Fox's standing within his own party was sufficiently diminished that he was unable to promote the candidacy of his chosen heir, the secretary of the interior, Santiago Creel. Instead, the PAN turned to Felipe Calderón Hinojosa, the former secretary of energy. His main opponent in the presidential race was the former mayor of the Federal District, Andrés Manuel López Obrador of the PRD. The presidential race was bitterly fought and deeply polarized the electorate. López Obrador accused Calderón of favoring the rich at the expense of Mexico's poor; Calderón argued that López Obrador had authoritarian tendencies that imperiled Mexico's democracy and that his economic policies would threaten Mexico's stability.

When Calderón won by a small margin, López Obrador refused to concede defeat and alleged that his opponent had gained office through fraud. Nonetheless, Calderón's victory was ratified by the country's electoral authorities and he assumed office on December 1, 2006. Ten days earlier, López Obrador held a shadow inauguration in which he declared himself Mexico's "legitimate" president. These developments raised the fear among many Mexicans that Calderón's presidency would be marked by political anarchy. However, López Obrador's actions seem to have had the unintended effect of dividing the opposition and allowing Calderón to consolidate his hold on power. The new president also benefited from a general perception that his administration was more competent and more politically savvy than the previous Fox administration. As a consequence, his approval ratings remained high in the initial years of his administration.

Calderón faced a series of challenges. He had to deal with rising corn prices that were making the cost of tortillas—the main staple in the diet of most Mexicans—increasingly expensive. He was able to achieve major legislative goals, however. First, his government passed a political reform bill that changed the way political campaigns were financed. Second, he pushed through a fiscal reform bill that raised corporate taxes.

By far the greatest challenge Mexico faced, however, was the increasing cost of fighting the war on drugs. Calderón relied on the army and federal police to launch military offensives against drug cartels throughout the country. Within weeks of taking office, he had deployed thousands of troops and police to states plagued by the drug trade, such as Baja California, Michoacán, and Guerrero. It is still too soon to tell how successful the military offensive against the drug trade will be or its consequences for Mexico's future. But this military offensive against drug traffickers engaged in the export of illegal drugs to the United States is yet another demonstration of how closely Mexico and the United States are linked.

Themes and Implications

Historical Junctures and Political Themes

The modern Mexican state emerged out of a popular revolution that proclaimed goals of democratic government, social justice, and national control of the country's resources. In the chaotic years after the revolution, the state created conditions for political and social peace. By incorporating peasants and workers into party and government institutions, and by providing benefits to low-income groups during the 1930s, it became widely accepted as legitimate. In encouraging considerable economic growth in the years after 1940, it also created a belief in its ability to provide material improvements in the quality of life for large portions of the population. These factors worked together to create a strong state capable of guiding economic and political life in the country. Only in the 1980s did this system begin to crumble.

In its external relations, Mexico has always prided itself on ideological independence from the world's great powers. For many decades, its large population, cultural richness, political stability, and front-line position regarding the United States prompted Mexico to consider itself a natural leader of Latin America and the developing world in general. After the early 1980s, however, the government rejected this position in favor of rapid integration into a global economy. The country aspired to the status enjoyed by the **newly industrialized countries (NICs)** of the world, such as South Korea, Malaysia, and Taiwan. While the reforms of the 1980s and 1990s, and especially NAFTA, have advanced this goal, many citizens are concerned that the government has accepted a position of political, cultural, and economic subordination to the United States.

Mexico enjoyed considerable economic advancement after the 1940s, but economic and political crises after 1980 shook confidence in its ability to achieve its economic goals and highlighted the conflict between a market-oriented development strategy and the country's philosophical tradition of a strong and protective state. The larger questions of whether a new development strategy can generate growth, whether Mexican products can find profitable markets overseas, whether investors can create extensive job opportunities for millions of unemployed and part-time workers, and whether the country can maintain the confidence of those investors over the longer term continue to challenge the country.

Politically, after the Revolution of 1910, the country opted not for true democracy but for representation through government-mediated organizations within a **corporatist state**, in which interest groups became an institutionalized part of state structure rather than an independent source of advocacy. This increased state power in relation to **civil society**. The state took the lead in defining goals for the country's development and, through the school system, the party, and the media, inculcated in the population a broad sense of its legitimate right to set such goals. In addition, the state had extensive resources at its disposal to control or co-opt dissent and purchase political loyalty. The PRI was an essential channel through which material goods, jobs, the distribution of land, and the allocation of development projects flowed to increase popular support for the system or to buy off opposition to it.

This does not mean that Mexican society was unorganized or passive. Indeed, many Mexicans were actively involved in local community organizations, religious activities, unions, and public interest groups. But traditionally, the scope for challenging the government was very limited. At the same time, Mexico's strong state did not become openly repressive except when directly challenged. On the contrary, officials in the government and the party generally worked hard to find ways to resolve conflicts peacefully and to use behind-the-scenes accommodation to bring conflicting interests into accord.

By the 1980s, cracks began to appear in the traditional ways in which Mexican citizens interacted with the government. As the PRI began to lose its capacity to control political activities and as civic groups increasingly insisted on their right to remain independent from the PRI and the government, the terms of the state-society relationship were clearly in need of redefinition. The administration of President Zedillo signaled its willingness to cede political power to successful opposition parties in fair elections, and electoral reform in 1996 and competitive elections in 1997 were significant steps that led to the defeat of the PRI in 2000. Mexico's future stability depends on how well a more democratic government can accommodate conflicting interests while at the same time providing economic opportunities to a largely poor population.

Implications for Comparative Politics

The Mexican political system is unique among developing countries in the extent to which it managed to institutionalize and maintain civilian political authority for a very long time. In a world of developing nations wracked by political turmoil, military coups, and regime changes, the PRI regime established enduring institutions of governance and conditions for political stability. Other developing countries have sought to emulate the Mexican model of stability based on an alliance between a dominant party and a strong development-oriented state, but no other government has been able to create a system that has had widespread legitimacy for so long. Among developed nations, perhaps Japan comes closest to this model. The PRI's revolutionary heritage, as well as its ability to maintain a sense of national identity, were important factors in accounting for its political continuity.

Currently, Mexico is a country undergoing significant political change without widespread violence, transforming itself from a corporatist state to a democratic one for the first time in its long history. At the same time, it struggles to resolve the conflicts of development through integration with its North American neighbors. Mexico has been categorized as an upper-middle-income developing country, and its per capita income is comparable to countries such as Latvia, Malaysia, South Africa, and Chile.[5]

It has made significant strides in industrialization, which accounts for about 27.2 percent of the country's gross domestic product (GDP). Agriculture contributes about 4.0 percent to GDP, and services contribute some 68.9 percent.[6] This structure is very similar to the economic profiles of Argentina, Brazil, Poland, and Hungary. But unlike those countries, Mexico is oil rich. The government-owned petroleum industry is a ready source of revenue and foreign exchange, but this commodity also makes the economy extremely vulnerable to changes in international oil prices.

Mexico's industrial and petroleum-based economy gives the country a per capita income higher than those of most other developing nations. If income were spread evenly among all Mexicans, each would receive $6,230 annually—far more than the per capita incomes of Nigeria ($320), India ($530), and China ($1,100), but considerably less than those of France ($24,770), Germany ($25,250), Britain ($28,350), and Mexico's wealthy neighbor, the United States ($37,500).[7] Of course, income is not spread evenly. Mexico suffers from great inequalities in how wealth is distributed, and poverty continues to be a grim reality for millions of Mexicans. The way the country promoted economic growth and industrialization is important in explaining why widespread poverty has persisted and why political power is not more equitably distributed.

SECTION 2 Political Economy and Development

State and Economy

During the years of the Porfiriato (1876–1911), Mexico began to produce some textiles, footwear, glassware, paper, beer, tiles, furniture, and other simple products. At that time, however, policy-makers were convinced that Mexico could grow rich by exporting its raw materials to more economically advanced countries. Their efforts to attract domestic and international investment encouraged a major boom in the production and export of products such as henequin (for making rope), coffee, cacao (cocoa beans), cattle, silver, and gold. Soon, the country had become so attractive to foreign investors that large amounts of land, the country's petroleum, its railroad network, and its mining wealth were largely controlled by foreigners. Nationalist reaction against the power of these foreign interests played a significant role in the tensions that produced the Revolution of 1910.

In the postrevolutionary Mexican state, this nationalism combined with a sense of social justice inspired by popular revolutionary leaders such as Zapata. Mexicans widely shared the idea that the state had the responsibility to generate wealth for all its citizens. As a result, the country adopted a strategy in which the government guided the process of industrial and agricultural development. Often referred to as **state capitalism**, this development strategy relied heavily on government actions to encourage private investment and reduce risks for private entrepreneurs. In the twenty years following the revolution, many of those concerned about the country's development became convinced that economic growth would not occur unless Mexico could industrialize more fully. They argued that reliance on exports of agricultural products, minerals, and petroleum—called the agro-export model of development—forced the country to import manufactured goods, which, over the long term, would always cost more than what was earned from exports. Mexico, they believed, should begin to manufacture the goods that it was currently importing.

Import Substitution and Its Consequences

Between 1940 and 1982, Mexico pursued a form of state capitalism and a model of industrialization known as import substitution, or **import substituting industrialization (ISI)**. Like Brazil and other Latin American countries during the same period, the government promoted the development of industries to supply the domestic market by encouraging domestic and international investment; providing credit and tax incentives to industrialists; maintaining low rates of inflation; and keeping wage demands low through subsidized food, transportation, housing, and health care for workers. It also fostered industrialization by establishing state-owned steel mills, electric power generators, ports, and petroleum production and by using tariffs and import licenses to protect Mexican industries from foreign competition. These policies had considerable success. Initially, the country produced mainly simple products like shoes, clothing, and processed foods. But by the 1960s and 1970s, it was also producing consumer durables (refrigerators, automobiles, trucks), intermediate goods (steel, petrochemicals, and other products used in the manufacturing process), and capital goods (heavy machinery to produce manufactured items).

Mexican agriculture was also affected by this drive to industrialize. With the massive agrarian reform of the 1930s (see Section 1), the *ejido* had become an important structure in the rural economy, accounting for half the cultivated area of the country and 51 percent of the value of agricultural production by 1940. After Cárdenas left office, however, government policy-makers moved away from the economic development of the *ejidos*. They became committed instead to developing a strong, entrepreneurial private sector in agriculture. For them, "the development of private agriculture would be the 'foundation of industrial greatness.'"[8] They wanted this sector to provide foodstuffs for the growing cities, raw materials for industry, and foreign exchange from exports. To encourage these goals, the government invested in transportation networks, irrigation projects, and agricultural storage facilities. It provided extension services and invested in research. It encouraged imports of technology to improve output and mechanize production. Since policy-makers believed that modern commercial farmers would respond better to these investments and services than would peasants on small plots of land, the government provided most of its assistance to large landowners.

The government's encouragement of industry and agriculture set the country on a three-decade path of sustained growth. Between 1940 and 1950, GDP grew

at an annual average of 6.7 percent, while manufacturing increased at an average of 8.1 percent. In the following two decades, GDP growth rates remained impressive, and manufacturing growth continued to outpace overall growth in the economy. In the 1950s, manufacturing achieved an average of 7.3 percent growth annually and in the 1960s, 10.1 percent annually. Agricultural production grew rapidly as new areas were brought under cultivation and **green revolution** technology (scientifically improved seeds, fertilizers, and pesticides) was extensively adopted on large farms. These were years of great optimism as foreign investment increased, the middle class grew larger, and indicators for health and welfare steadily improved. Even the poorest Mexicans believed that their lives were improving. Table 10.2 presents data that summarize a number of advancements during this period. So impressive was Mexico's economic performance that it was referred to internationally as the "Mexican Miracle."

While the government took the lead in encouraging industrialization, it was not long before a group of domestic entrepreneurs developed a special relationship with the state. Government policies protected their products through high tariffs or special licensing requirements, limiting imports of competing goods. Business elites in Mexico received subsidized credit to invest in equipment and plants; they benefited from cheap, subsidized energy; and they rarely had to pay taxes. These protected businesses emerged as powerful players in national politics. In the 1940s and 1950s, they led a set of industry-related interest groups that worked to promote and sustain favorable policies. With this organizational foundation, groups like the chambers of industry, commerce, and banking began to play increasingly important roles in government policy-making. They were able to veto efforts by the government to cut back on their benefits, and they lobbied for even more advantages. The government remained the source of most policy initiatives, but generally it was not able to move far in the face of opposition from those who benefited most from its policies.

Workers also became more important players in Mexico's national politics. As mentioned in Section 1, widespread unionization occurred under Cárdenas, and workers won many rights that had been promised

Table 10.2

Mexican Development, 1940–2006

	1940	1950	1960	1970	1980	1990	2006
Population (thousands)	19,815	26,282	38,020	52,771	70,416	88,598	104,200
Life expectancy (years)[a]	–	51.6	58.6	62.6	67.4	68.9	74.5
Infant mortality (per 1,000 live births)	–	–	86.3	70.9	49.9	42.6	35.3
Illiteracy (% of population age 15 and over)	–	42.5	34.5	25.0	16.0	12.7	8.4
Urban population (% of total)	–	–	50.7	59.0	66.4	72.6	76.0
Economically active population in agriculture (% of total)	–	58.3	55.1	44.0	36.6	22.0	18.0[b]

	1940–1950	1950–1960	1960–1970	1970–1980	1980–1990	1990–2003	2004–2005
GDP growth rate (average annual percent)	6.7	5.8	7.6	6.7	1.6	1.3	3.0
Per capita GDP growth rate	–	–	3.7	3.7	–0.7	–0.2	1.9

[a]Five-year average.
[b]2001

Sources: Statistical Abstract for Latin America (New York: United Nations, Economic Commission for Latin America, various years); Roger Hansen, *The Politics of Mexican Development* (Baltimore, Md.: Johns Hopkins University Press, 1971); *Statistical Bulletin of the OAS.* World Bank Country Data for Mexico, http://www.worldbank.org/data/countrydata/countrydata. html; World Bank, World Development Indicators.

in the Constitution of 1917. Cárdenas organized the unions into the Confederation of Mexican Workers (CTM), which became the most powerful voice of organized labor within the PRI. The policy changes initiated in the 1940s, however, made the unions more dependent on the government for benefits and protection; the government also limited the right to strike. Despite the fact that unions were closely controlled, organized workers continued to be an elite within the country's working classes. Union membership meant job security and important benefits such as housing subsidies and health care. These factors helped compensate for the lack of democracy within the labor movement. Moreover, labor leaders had privileged access to the country's political leadership and benefited personally from their control over jobs, contracts,

and working conditions. In return, they guaranteed labor peace.[9]

In agriculture, those who benefited from government policies and services were primarily farmers who had enough land and economic resources to irrigate and mechanize, as well as the capacity to make technological improvements in their farming methods and crops. By the 1950s, a group of large, commercially oriented farmers had emerged to dominate the agricultural economy.[10] Like their urban counterparts in business, they became rich and powerful. These rural landowners also became firm supporters of the continuation of government policies that provided them with special advantages.

There were significant costs to this pattern of economic and political development. Most important, government policies eventually limited the potential for further growth.[11] Industrialists who received extensive subsidies and benefits from government had few incentives to produce efficiently. High tariffs kept out foreign competition, further reducing reasons for efficiency or quality in production. Importing technology to support industrialization eventually became a drain on the country's foreign exchange. In addition, the costs of providing benefits to workers increased beyond the capacity of the government to generate revenue, especially because tax rates were kept low as a further incentive to investors. Mexico's tax rates, in fact, were among the lowest in the world, and opportunities to avoid payment were extensive. Eventually, the ISI strategy became less effective in generating new jobs, as industrialists moved from investing in labor-intensive industries such as processed foods and textiles to capital-intensive industries such as automobiles, refrigerators, and heavy equipment.

Moreover, as the economy grew, and with it the power of industrial, agricultural, and urban interests, many were left behind. The ranks of the urban poor grew steadily, particularly from the 1960s on. Mexico developed a sizable **informal sector**—workers who produced and sold goods and services at the margin of the economic system and faced extreme insecurity. By 1970, a large proportion of Mexico City's population was living in inner-city tenements or squatter settlements surrounding the city.[12]

Also left behind in the country's development after 1940 were peasant farmers. Their lands were often the least fertile, plot sizes were minuscule, and access to markets was impeded by poor transportation and exploitive middlemen who trucked products to markets for exorbitant fees. Farming in the *ejido* communities, where land was held communally, was particularly difficult. Because *ejido* land could not be sold or (until the early 1980s) rented, *ejidatarios* could not borrow money from private banks because they had nothing to pledge as collateral if they defaulted on their payments. Government banks provided credit, but usually only to those who had political connections. The government invested little in small infrastructure projects throughout the 1960s, and agricultural research and extension focused on the large-farm sector. Not surprisingly, the *ejido* sector consistently reported low productivity.

Increasing disparities in rural and urban incomes, coupled with high population growth rates, contributed to the emergence of rural guerrilla movements and student protests in the mid- and late 1960s. The government was particularly alarmed in 1968, when a student movement openly challenged the government on the eve of the Mexico City Olympic Games. Moreover, by the early 1970s, it was becoming evident that the size of the population, growing at a rate of some 3.5 percent a year, and the structure of income distribution were impeding further industrial development. The domestic market was limited by poverty; many Mexicans could not afford the sophisticated manufactured products the country would need to produce in order to keep growing under the import substitution model.

The Mexican government had hoped that industrialization would free the economy from excessive dependence on the industrialized world, and particularly on the United States, making the country less subject to abrupt swings in prices for primary commodities. Industrialization, however, highlighted new vulnerabilities. Advanced manufacturing processes required ever more foreign investment and imported technology. Concern grew about powerful multinational companies, which had invested heavily in the country in the 1960s, and about purchasing foreign technology with scarce foreign exchange. By the late 1960s, the country was no longer able to meet domestic demand for basic foodstuffs and was forced to import increasingly large quantities of food, costing the government foreign exchange that it could have used for better purposes. By the 1970s, some policymakers had become convinced that industrialization had actually increased the country's dependence on advanced industrial countries and particularly on the United States.

Sowing the Oil and Reaping a Crisis

In the early 1970s, Mexico faced the threat of social crisis brought on by rural poverty, chaotic urbanization, high population growth, and the questioning of political legitimacy. The government responded by increasing investment in infrastructure and public industries, regulating the flow of foreign capital, and increasing social spending. It was spending much

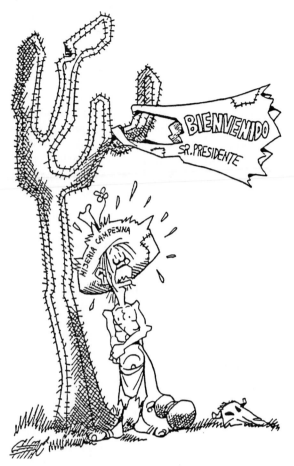

A farmer with a hat labeled "rural misery" hangs his shirt on a cactus: "Welcome, Mr. President." Among those who benefited least from the government's development policies are the rural poor. *Source: Ausencias y Presencias Gente de Ayer y Hoy en su Tinta: Problemática Política, Social, Vista por un Cartoonista Potosino by Luis Chessal, Universidad Autonoma de San Luis Potosí, Mexico, 1984.*

sustained, the government devalued the peso in 1976 to encourage exports and discourage imports. It also signed a stabilization agreement with the International Monetary Fund (IMF) to reduce government spending, increase tax collection, and control inflation. Little progress was made in changing existing policies, however, because just as the seriousness of the economic situation was being recognized, vast new finds of oil came to the rescue.

Between 1978 and 1982, Mexico was transformed into a major oil exporter. As international oil prices rose rapidly, from $13.30 per barrel in 1978 to $33.20 per barrel in 1981, so too did the country's fortunes, along with those of other oil-rich countries such as Nigeria, Iran, Indonesia, and Venezuela. The administration of President José López Portillo (1976–1982) embarked on a policy to "sow the oil" in the economy and "administer the abundance" with vast investment projects in virtually all sectors and major new initiatives to reduce poverty and deal with declining agricultural productivity. Oil revenues paid for much of this expansion, but the foreign debt also mounted as both public and private sectors borrowed heavily to finance investments and lavish consumer spending.

By 1982, Mexico's foreign debt was $86 billion, and the peso was seriously overvalued, making Mexican products more expensive on the world market. Oil accounted for 77.2 percent of the country's exports, causing the economy to be extremely vulnerable to changes in oil prices. And change they did. Global overproduction brought the international price for Mexican petroleum down to $26.30 a barrel in 1982 and to even lower levels in the years that followed. Revenues from exports declined dramatically. At the same time, the United States tightened its monetary policy by raising interest rates, and access to foreign credit dried up. Wealthy Mexicans responded by sending vast amounts of capital out of the country just as the country's international creditors were demanding repayment on their loans. In August 1982, the government announced that the country could not pay the interest on its foreign debt, triggering a crisis that reverberated around the world. The impact of these conditions on the Mexican economy was devastating. GDP growth in 1982 was –0.6 percent and fell to –4.2 percent the following year.

more than it generated, causing the public internal debt to grow rapidly and requiring heavy borrowing abroad. Between 1971 and 1976, inflation rose from an annual average of 5.3 percent to almost 16 percent, and the foreign debt more than tripled. In response to mounting evidence that its policies could not be

The economic crisis had several important implications for structures of power and privilege in Mexico. First, faith in the import substitution policy was destroyed. The crisis convinced even the most diehard believers that import substitution created inefficiencies in production, failed to generate sufficient employment, cost the government far too much in subsidies, and increased dependency on industrialized countries. In addition, the power of interest groups and their ability to influence government policy declined. Bankruptcy and recession exacted their toll on the fortunes of even large entrepreneurs. As economic hardship affected their members, traditional business organizations lost their ability to put strong pressure on the government.

Similarly, the country's relatively privileged unions lost much of their bargaining power with government over issues of wages and protection. Union leaders loyal to the PRI emphasized the need for peace and order to help the nation get through tough times, while inflation and job loss focused many of the country's workers on putting food on the table. A shift in employment from the formal to the informal economy further fragmented what had once been the most powerful sector of the party. Cuts in government subsidies for public transportation, food, electricity, and gasoline created new hardships for workers. The combination of these factors weakened the capacity of labor to resist policy changes that affected the benefits they received.

In addition, new voices emerged to demand that the government respond to the crisis. During the recession years of the 1980s, wages lost between 40 and 50 percent of their value, increasingly large numbers of people became unemployed, inflation cut deeply into middle-class incomes, and budgets for health and education services were severely cut back. A wide variety of interests began to organize outside the PRI to demand that government do something about the situation. Massive earthquakes in Mexico City in September 1985 proved to be a watershed for Mexican society. Severely disappointed by the government's failure to respond to the problems created by death, destruction, and homelessness, hundreds of communities organized rescue efforts, soup kitchens, shelters, and rehabilitation initiatives. A surging sense of political empowerment developed, as groups long accustomed to dependence on government learned that they could solve their problems better without government than with it.[13]

Moreover, the PRI was challenged by the increased popularity of opposition political parties, one of them headed by Cuauhtémoc Cárdenas, the son of the country's most revered president, Lázaro Cárdenas. The elections of 1988 became a focus for protest against the economic dislocation caused by the crisis and the political powerlessness that most citizens felt. Carlos Salinas, the PRI candidate, received a bare majority of 50.7 percent, and opposition parties claimed widespread electoral fraud.

New Strategies: Structural Reforms and NAFTA

Demands on the Salinas administration to deal with the economic and political crisis were extensive. At the same time, the weakening of the old centers of political power provided the government with a major opportunity to reorient the country's strategy for economic development. Between 1988 and 1994, the mutually dependent relationship between industry and government was weakened as new free-market policies were put in place. Deregulation gave the private sector more freedom to pursue economic activities and less reason to seek special favors from government. A number of large government industries were reorganized and sold to private investors. A constitutional revision made it possible for *ejidatarios* to become owners of individual plots of land; this made them less dependent on government but more vulnerable to losing their land. In addition, financial sector reforms that changed laws about banking and established a stock exchange encouraged the emergence of new banks, brokerage firms, and insurance companies.

Salinas pursued, and Zedillo continued, an overhaul of the federal system and the way government agencies worked together. Called the New Federalism in the Zedillo administration, it was an attempt to give greater power and budgetary responsibilities to state and local governments, which had been historically very weak in Mexico. Beginning with education and health, the presidents hoped decentralization would make government more efficient and effective. Additionally, the central bank, the institution responsible for making national monetary policy, became independent from the government in 1994, although exchange rates are still determined by the finance ministry.

Among the most far-reaching initiatives was NAFTA. This agreement with Canada and the United States created the basis for gradual introduction of free trade among the three countries. These changes were a major reversal of import substitution and economic intervention that had marked government policies in the past. However, the liberalization of the Mexican economy and opening of its markets to foreign competition increased the vulnerability of the country to changes in international economic conditions. These factors, as well as mismanaged economic policies, led to a major economic crisis for the country at the end of 1994 and profound recession in 1995. NAFTA has meant that the fate of the Mexican economy is increasingly linked to the health of the American economy. For example, the economic strength of Mexico's northern neighbor sheltered the country from the contagion of the 1997–1998 Asian financial crisis, while the economic cooldown in the United States slowed growth in Mexico in the early 2000s.

Society and Economy

Mexico's economic development has had a significant impact on social conditions in the country. Overall, the standard of living rose markedly after the 1940s. Rates of infant mortality, literacy, and life expectancy have steadily improved. Provision of health and education services expanded until government cutbacks on social expenditures in the early 1980s. Among the most important consequences of economic growth was the development of a large middle class, most of whom live in Mexico's numerous large cities. By the 1980s, a third or more of Mexican households could claim a middle-class lifestyle: a steady income, secure food and shelter, access to decent education and health services, a car, some disposable income and savings, and some security that their children would be able to experience happy and healthy lives.

These achievements reflect well on the ability of the economy to increase social well-being in the country. However, the impressive economic growth through the early 1970s and between 1978 and 1982 could have produced greater social progress. In terms of standard indicators of social development—infant mortality, literacy, and life expectancy—Mexico fell behind a number of Latin American countries that grew less rapidly but provided more effectively for their populations. Costa Rica, Colombia, Argentina, Chile, and Uruguay had lower overall growth but greater social development in the period after 1940. These countries paid more attention to the distribution of the benefits of growth than did Mexico. Moreover, rapid industrialization has made Mexico City one of the most polluted cities in the world, and in some rural areas, oil exploitation left devastating environmental damage.

Mexico's economic development also resulted in a widening gap between the wealthy and the poor and among different regions in the country. Although the poor are better off than they were in the early days of the country's drive toward industrialization, they are worse off when compared to middle- and upper-income groups. In 1950, the bottom 40 percent of the country's households accounted for about 14 percent of total personal income, while the top 30 percent had 60 percent of total income.[14] In 2000, it is estimated, the bottom 40 percent accounted for about 10.3 percent of income, while the top 40 percent shared 78.1 percent.[15] As the rich grew richer, the gap between the rich and the poor increased.

Among the poorest are those in rural areas who have little or no access to productive land. Harsh conditions in the countryside have fueled a half-century of migration to the cities. Nevertheless, some 25 million Mexicans continue to live in rural areas, many of them in deep poverty. Many work for substandard wages and migrate seasonally to search for jobs in order to sustain their families. Among rural inhabitants with access to land, almost half have five hectares (about twelve acres) or less. This land is usually not irrigated and depends on erratic rainfall. It is often leached of nutrients as a result of centuries of cultivation, population pressure, and erosion. The incidence of disease, malnutrition, and illiteracy is much higher in Mexico's rural areas than in urban areas. When the rebels in Chiapas called for jobs, land, education, and health facilities, they were clearly reflecting the realities of life in much of the country.

Poverty has a regional dimension in Mexico. The northern areas of the country are significantly better off than the southern and central areas. In the north, large commercial farms using modern technologies grow fruits, vegetables, and grains for export. The U.S. border, the principal destination of agricultural products, is close at hand, and transportation networks are extensive and generally in good condition. Moreover, industrial cities such as Monterrey and Tijuana provide steady jobs for skilled and unskilled labor. Along the border, a band of *maquiladoras* (manufacturing and assembly plants) provides many jobs, particularly for young women who are seeking some escape from the burdens of rural life or the constraints of traditional family life.

In the southern and central regions of the country, the population is denser, the land poorer, and the number of *ejidatarios* eking out subsistence greater. Transportation is often difficult, and during parts of the year, some areas may be inaccessible because of heavy rains and flooding. Most of Mexico's remaining indigenous groups live in the southern regions, often in remote areas where they have been forgotten by government programs and exploited by regional bosses for generations. The conditions that spurred the Chiapas rebellion are found throughout the southern states.

The economic crisis of the 1980s had an impact on social conditions in the country as well. Wages declined by about half, and unemployment soared as businesses collapsed and the government laid off workers in public offices and privatized industries. The informal sector expanded rapidly. Here, people manage to make a living by hawking chewing gum, umbrellas, sponges, candy, shoelaces, mirrors, and a variety of other items in the street; jumping in front of cars at stoplights to wash windshields and sell newspapers; producing and repairing cheap consumer goods such as shoes and clothing; and selling services on a daily or hourly basis. While the informal sector provides important goods and services, conditions of work are often dangerous, and uncertainty as to where the next peso will come from is endemic.

The economic crisis of the 1980s also reduced the quality and availability of social services. Expenditures on education and health declined after 1982 as the government imposed austerity measures. Salaries of primary school teachers declined by 34 percent between 1983 and 1988, and many teachers worked second and even third jobs in order to make ends meet. Per capita health expenditures declined from a high of about $19 in 1980 to about $11 in 1990. Although indicators of mortality did not rise during this troubled decade, the incidence of diseases associated with poverty—malnutrition, cholera, anemia, and dysentery—increased. The crisis began to ease in the early 1990s, however, and many came to believe that conditions would improve for the poor. The government began investing in social services. When a new economic crisis occurred in the mid 1990s, however, unemployment surged, and austerity measures severely limited investments. Despite considerable recovery in the late 1990s, wages remain low for the majority of workers while taxes and the cost of living have increased.

Mexico in the Global Economy

The crisis that began in 1982 altered Mexico's international economic policies. In response to that crisis, the government relaxed restrictions on the ability of foreigners to own property, reduced and eliminated tariffs, and did away with most import licenses. Foreign investment was courted in the hope of increasing the manufacture of goods for export. The government also introduced a series of incentives to encourage the private sector to produce goods for export. In 1986, Mexico joined the General Agreement on Tariffs and Trade (GATT), a multilateral agreement that sought to promote freer trade among countries and that later became the basis for the World Trade Organization (WTO). In the 1990s and early 2000s, Mexico signed trade pacts with many countries in Latin America, Europe, and elsewhere.

The government's effort to pursue a more outward-oriented development strategy culminated in the ratification of NAFTA in 1993, with gradual implementation beginning on January 1, 1994. This agreement is important to Mexico. In 2000, 89 percent of the country's exports were sent to the United States, and 74 percent of its imports came from that country.[16] Access to the U.S. market is essential to Mexico and to domestic and foreign investors. NAFTA signaled a new period in U.S.–Mexican relations by making closer integration of the two economies a certainty.

NAFTA also entails risks for Mexico. Domestic producers worry about competition from U.S. firms. Farmers worry that Mexican crops cannot compete effectively with those grown in the United States; for example, peasant producers of corn and beans have been hard hit by the availability of lower-priced U.S.-grown grains. In addition, many believe that embracing free trade with Canada and the United States indicates a loss of sovereignty. Certainly, Mexico's economic situation is now more vulnerable to the ebb and flow of economic conditions in the U.S. economy. Some are also concerned with increasing evidence of "cultural imperialism" as U.S. movies, music, fashions, and lifestyles increasingly influence consumers. Indeed, for Mexico, which has traditionally feared the power of the United States in its domestic affairs, internationalization of political and economic relationships poses particularly difficult problems of adjustment.

On the other hand, the United States, newly aware of the importance of the Mexican economy to its own economic growth and concerned about instability on its southern border, hammered together a $50 billion economic assistance program composed of U.S., European, and IMF commitments to support its neighbor when crisis struck in 1994. The Mexican government imposed a new stabilization package that contained austerity measures, higher interest rates, and limits on wages. Remarkably, by 1998, Mexico had paid off all of its obligations to the United States.

Globalization is also stripping Mexico of some of the secrecy that traditionally surrounded government decision-making, electoral processes, and efforts to deal with political dissent. International attention increasingly focuses on the country, and investors want clear and up-to-date information on what is occurring in the economy. The Internet and e-mail, along with lower international telephone rates, are increasing the flow of information across borders. The government can no longer respond to events such as the peasant rebellion in Chiapas, alleged electoral fraud, or the management of exchange rates without considering how such actions will be perceived in Tokyo, Frankfurt, Ottawa, London, or Washington.

SECTION 3 Governance and Policy-Making

Mexico, like the United States and Canada, is a federal republic, although until the 1990s, state and local governments had few resources and a limited sphere of action when compared with the national level. Under the PRI, the executive branch held almost all power, while the legislative and judiciary branches followed the executive's lead and were considered rubber-stamp bodies. During the years of PRI hegemony, the government was civilian, authoritarian, and corporatist. Currently, Mexico has multiparty competitive elections, and power is less concentrated in the executive branch and the national government. Since the mid-1980s, great efforts have been made to reinvigorate the nation's laws and institutions and to make the country more democratic.

Organization of the State

According to the supreme law of the land, the Constitution of 1917, Mexico's political institutions resemble those of the United States. There are three branches of government, and a set of checks and balances limits the power of each. The congress is composed of the Senate and the Chamber of Deputies. One hundred twenty-eight senators are elected, three from each of the country's thirty-one states; three from the Federal District, which contains the capital, Mexico City; and another thirty-two elected nationally by **proportional representation (PR)**. The 500 members of the Chamber of Deputies are elected from 300 electoral districts—300 by simple majority vote and 200 by proportional representation. State and local governments are also elected. The president, governors, and senators are elected for six years, and deputies (representatives in the lower house) and municipal officials are elected for three.

In practice, the Mexican system is very different from that of the United States. The constitution is a long document that can be easily amended, especially when compared to that of the United States. It lays out the structure of government and guarantees a wide range of human rights, including familiar ones such as freedom of speech and protection of the law, but also economic and social rights such as the right to a job and the right to health care. Economic and social rights are acknowledged but in practice do not reach all of the population. Although there has been some decentralization of power, the political system is still much more centralized than that of the United States. Congress is now more active as a decision-making arena and as a check on presidential power, but the executive remains central to initiating policy and managing political conflict.

The Executive

The President and the Cabinet

The presidency is the central institution of governance and policy-making in Mexico. Until the 1990s, the incumbent president always selected who would run as the PRI's next presidential candidate, appointed officials to all positions of power in the government and the party, and often named the candidates who almost automatically won elections as governors, senators, deputies, and local officials. Even with a non-PRI incumbent, as is currently the case, the president continues to set the broad outlines of policy for the administration and has numerous resources to ensure that those policy preferences are adopted. Until the mid-1970s, Mexican presidents were considered above criticism in national politics and revered as symbols of national progress and well-being. While economic and political events of the 1980s and 1990s diminished presidential prestige and politicians are showing an increasing willingness to stand up to the chief executive in today's multiparty system, the extent of presidential power remains a legacy of the long period of PRI ascendance.

Mexican presidents have a set of formal powers that allows them to initiate legislation, lead in foreign policy, create government agencies, make policy by decree or through administrative regulations and procedures, and appoint a wide range of public officials. More important, informal powers provide them with the capacity to exert considerable control. The president manages a vast patronage machine for filling positions in government and initiates legislation and policies that were, until recently, routinely approved by the congress.

Mexican presidents, though powerful, are not omnipotent. They must, for example, abide by a deeply held constitutional norm, fully adhered to since 1940, by stepping down at the end of their six-year term, and they must adhere to tradition by removing themselves from the political limelight to allow their successors to assume full presidential leadership. All presidents, regardless of party, must demonstrate their loyalty to the myths and symbols of Mexican nationalism, such as the indigenous roots of much of its culture and the agrarian origins of the revolution, and they must make a rhetorical commitment to social justice and sovereignty in international affairs.

Moreover, in the 1990s, President Zedillo relinquished a number of the traditional powers of the presidency. He announced, for example, that he would not select his PRI successor but would leave it up to the party to determine its candidate. In doing so, however, he created considerable conflict and tension as the PRI had to take on unaccustomed roles and as politicians sought to fill the void left by the "abandonment" of presidential power. Vicente Fox and Felipe Calderón inherited a system in which the president is expected to set the policies and determine the priorities for a very wide range of government activity, yet needs a strong party in congress and experienced people in his administration to make this happen.

Under the PRI, presidents were always male and almost always members of the outgoing president's cabinet. Four of the five presidents who served between 1946 and 1976 had previously been ministers of the interior, with responsibility for the maintenance of law and order in the country. With the expansion of the government's role in economic development, candidates in the 1970s and 1980s were selected from the ministries that managed the economy. José López Portillo (1976–1982) had been minister of finance, and Miguel de la Madrid (1982–1988) and Carlos Salinas (1988–1994) had served as ministers of planning and budgeting. The selection of Luis Donaldo Colosio, who had been minister of social development and welfare, was thought by political observers to signal renewed concern with social problems. When Colosio was assassinated in 1994, the selection of Ernesto Zedillo, who had first been minister of planning and budgeting and then minister of education, was interpreted as reflecting an ongoing concern with social issues and as an effort to maintain the policies of economic liberalization that Salinas had introduced. With the victory of the PAN in 2000, this long tradition came to an end. Prior to running for president, Vicente Fox had been in business and had served as the governor of the state of Guanajuato. Calderón, although he had served briefly as Fox's secretary of energy, was not his chosen successor. Fox had hoped to be succeeded by his secretary of the interior, Santiago Creel. In this respect, Calderón's victory in 2006 continued a trend toward greater independence of parties from presidential preferences.

Mexican presidential candidates since the mid-1970s have had impressive educational credentials and have tended to be trained in economics and management rather than in the traditional field of law. Presidents since López Portillo have had postgraduate training at elite institutions in the United States. By the 1980s, a topic of great debate in political circles was the extent to which a divide between *políticos* (politicians) and *técnicos* (**technocrats**) had emerged within the national political elite. Among the old guard of the PRI, there was open skepticism about the ability of young technocrats like Carlos Salinas and Ernesto Zedillo to manage political conditions in the country. During the presidential campaign of 1994, considerable efforts were made to stress the more humble origins of Colosio and Zedillo and the fact that they had had to work hard to get an education. Under Fox and Calderón, the ties of the PAN to business elites have raised similar fears that the government would not respond to the concerns of everyday citizens.

Once elected, the president moves quickly to name a cabinet. Under the PRI, he usually selected those with whom he had worked over the years as he rose to political prominence. He also used cabinet posts to ensure a broad coalition of support; he might, for example, appoint people with close ties to the labor movement, business interests, or some of the regional strongholds of the party. Only in rare exceptions were cabinet officials not active members of the PRI. When the PAN assumed the presidency in 2000, the selection of cabinet members and close advisers became more difficult. Until then, PAN had elected officials only to state and local governments and to congress. As a consequence, the range of people with executive experience to whom Fox could turn was limited. He

appointed U.S.-trained economists for his economic team and business executives for many other important posts. Few of these appointees had close ties to the PAN, and few had prior experience in government. His powers were curtailed to some degree by a more forceful congress and his administration's lack of experience in governing. Whereas Fox preferred technocrats with limited political experience, Calderón filled his cabinet positions with longtime members of the PAN who have a longer history of political engagement. His administration consequently has shown a greater capacity to carry out its agenda despite lacking a majority in congress. Over the years, few women have been selected for ministry-level posts—there are a handful of examples in recent administrations—and thus far they have only presided over agencies with limited influence over decision-making, like the ministries of tourism, ecology, and foreign relations.

The president has the authority to fill numerous other high-level positions, which allows him to provide policy direction and keep tabs on what is occurring throughout the government. The range of appointments that a chief executive can make means that the beginning of each administration is characterized by extensive turnover of positions, and as a result, progress on the president's policy agenda can be slow during his first year in office as newly appointed officials learn the ropes and assemble their staff. The president's power to make appointments provides him with the capacity to build a team of like-minded officials in government and ensure their loyalty to him. This system traditionally served the interests of presidents and the PRI well; under the PAN, given the limited number of its partisans who have experience at national levels, the system has not guaranteed the president as much power over the workings of the executive branch.

The Bureaucracy

Mexico's executive branch is large and powerful. Almost 1.5 million people work in the federal bureaucracy, most of them in Mexico City. An additional 1 million work in state-owned industries and semiautonomous agencies of the government. State and local governments employ over 1.5 million people.

Officials at lower levels in the bureaucracy are unionized and protected by legislation that gives them job security and a range of benefits. At middle and upper levels, most officials are called "confidence employees"; they serve as long as their bosses have confidence in them. These officials have been personally appointed by their superiors at the outset of an administration. Their modest salaries are compensated for by the significant power that they can have over public affairs. For aspiring young professionals, a career in government is often attractive because of the challenge of dealing with important problems on a daily basis. Some employees also benefit from opportunities to take bribes or use other means to promote their personal interests.

The Para-Statal Sector

The **para-statal** sector—composed of semiautonomous or autonomous government agencies, many of which produce goods and services—was extremely large and powerful in Mexico prior to the 1990s. Because the government provided significant support for the development of the economy as part of its post–1940 development strategy, it engaged in numerous activities that in other countries are carried out by the private sector. Thus, until the Salinas administration, the country's largest steel mill was state-owned, as were the largest fertilizer producer, sugar mills, and airlines. In addition, the national electricity board still produces energy and supplies it at subsidized prices to industries. The state-owned petroleum company, PEMEX, grew to enormous proportions in the 1970s and 1980s under the impact of the oil boom. NAFIN, a state investment corporation, provides a considerable amount of investment capital for the country. At one point, a state marketing board called CONASUPO was responsible for the importation and purchase of the country's basic food supplies, and in the 1970s, it played a major role in distributing food, credit, and farm implements in rural areas.

This large para-statal sector was significantly trimmed by the economic policy reforms that began in the 1980s. In 1970, there were 391 para-statal organizations in Mexico. By 1982, their number had grown to 1,155, in part because of the expansion of government activities under presidents Echeverría and López Portillo and in part because of the nationalization of private banks in 1982. Shortly afterward, concerted efforts were made to privatize many of these industries, including the telephone company, the national airlines, and the nationalized banks. By 1994, only 215 state-owned industries remained, and efforts continued to sell or liquidate many of them. However, some core components of the para-statal sector will likely remain in government hands for the foreseeable future because an influential bloc of nationalist political actors insists on the symbolic importance of public ownership of key industries. The Fox government, a partisan of the private sector, raised the possibility of privatizing PEMEX and the electricity board, but quickly retreated to very partial measures in the face of extensive opposition to private ownership of the "national patrimony." The Calderón administration is also committed to the introduction of greater reforms aimed at liberalizing the economy. However, to date the administration's main economic proposals have centered on the need to maximize governmental revenue by reforming the tax code.

Other State Institutions

The Military

Mexico is one of only a few countries in the developing world, particularly in Latin America, to have successfully marginalized the military from centers of political power. Although former military leaders dominated Mexican politics during the decades immediately after the Revolution of 1910, Calles, Cárdenas, and subsequent presidents laid the groundwork for civilian rule by introducing the practice of rotating regional military commands so that generals could not build up geographic bases of power. In addition, post-revolutionary leaders made an implicit bargain with the military leaders by providing them with opportunities to engage in business so that they did not look to political power as a way of gaining economic power. After 1946, the military no longer had institutional representation within the PRI and became clearly subordinate to civilian control. No military officer has held the presidency since that time.

This does not mean that the military has existed outside politics. It has been called in from time to time to deal with domestic unrest: in rural areas in the 1960s, in Mexico City and other cities to repress student protest movements in 1968, in 1988 in the arrest of a powerful labor leader, in 1989 to break a labor strike, in 1990 to deal with protest over electoral fraud, in Chiapas beginning in late 1994, and to manage the Mexico City police in 1997. The military was also called in to deal with the aftermath of the earthquake in Mexico City in 1985, but its inadequate response to the emergency did little to enhance its reputation in the eyes of the public.

In recent years, the military has been heavily involved in efforts to combat drug trafficking, and rumors abound about deals struck between military officials and drug barons. Such fears were confirmed when General Jesús Gutierrez Rebollo, the head of the antidrug task force, was arrested in 1997 on accusations of protecting a drug lord. When the PAN government made it possible for citizens to gain greater access to government information, it was discovered that the military had been involved in political repression, torture, and killing in the 1970s and 1980s. The scandal created by such revelations further lowered its reputation.

Despite these scandals, the military continues to be used to fight drug traffickers. Within weeks of taking office, Calderón had deployed thousands of military troops to Michoacán and Baja California to combat criminal organizations engaged in the drug trade. When the president dressed in military fatigues to address the troops in Michoacán in late January 2006—marking the first time in postrevolutionary history that a Mexican president had donned military garb—it was a dramatic manifestation of the increased role the military would play under his administration in the fight against crime. Another sign of the military's increased importance in fighting the drug trade was that Calderón called for an increase in the pay of military personnel, even while ordering a 10 percent cut in pay for himself and all members of his cabinet.

Whenever the military is called in to resolve domestic conflicts, some Mexicans become concerned that the institution is becoming politicized and may come to play a larger role in political decision-making. Thus far, such fears have not been realized, and many believe that as long as civilian administrations are able to maintain the country's tradition of stability, the military will not intervene directly in politics. The fact that the country successfully observed the transfer of power from the PRI to the PAN also has increased a sense that the military will remain subordinate to civilian control.

The Judiciary

Unlike Anglo-American legal systems, Mexico's law derives from the Roman and Napoleonic tradition and is highly formalized and explicit. The Constitution of 1917 is a lengthy document that has been amended many times and contains references to a wide range of civil rights, including items as broad as the right to a healthy environment. Because Mexican law tends to be very explicit and because there are no punitive damages allowed in court cases, there are fewer lawsuits than in the United States. One important exception to this is the *amparo* (protection), whereby individual citizens may ask for a writ of protection, claiming that their constitutional rights have been violated by specific government actions or laws.

There are federal and state courts in Mexico. The federal system is composed of the Supreme Court, which decides the most important cases in the country; circuit courts, which take cases on appeal; and district courts, where all cases enter the system. As in the United States, Supreme Court justices are nominated by the president and approved by the Senate. Since most of the important laws in Mexico are federal, state courts have played a subordinate role. However, this is changing. As Mexican states become more independent from the federal government, state law has been experiencing tremendous growth. In addition, there are many important specialized federal courts, such as labor courts, military courts, and electoral courts.

Like other government institutions in Mexico, the judiciary was for many decades politically, though not constitutionally, subordinate to the executive. The courts occasionally slowed the actions of government by issuing *amparos*; however, in almost every case in which the power of government or the president was at stake, the courts ruled on the side of the government. The Zedillo administration tried to change this by emphasizing the rule of law over that of powerful individuals. Increasing interest in human rights issues by citizens' groups and the media added pressure to the courts to play a stronger role in protecting basic freedoms. Zedillo's refusal to interfere with the courts' judgments also strengthened the judiciary. This trajectory continued under Fox and Calderón.

Although the judicial system remains the weakest branch of government, reforms continue to be proposed. In February 2008, the lower house of congress approved amendments to the constitution that would result in a major overhaul of the judiciary by introducing public trials with oral testimony and the presumption of innocence. If approved by the Senate and ratified by seventeen of the thirty-one states, the reforms would be one of the most significant changes to the judiciary in modern Mexican history.

Subnational Government

As with many other aspects of the Mexican political system, regional and local government in Mexico is quite different from what is described in the constitution. Under Mexico's federal system, each state has its own constitution, executive, unicameral legislature, and judiciary. Municipalities (equivalent to U.S. counties) are governed by popularly elected mayors and councils. But most state and municipal governments are poor. Most of the funds they command are transferred to them from the central government, and they have little legal or administrative capacity to raise their own revenue. States and localities also suffer greatly from the lack of well-trained and well-paid public officials. As at the national level, many jobs are distributed as political patronage, but even officials who are motivated to be responsive to local needs are generally ill equipped to do so. Since the early 1990s, the government has made several serious efforts to decentralize and devolve more power to state and local governments. At times, governors and mayors have resisted such initiatives because they meant that regional and local governments would have to manage much more complex activities and be the focus of demands from public sector workers and their unions. Local governments were also worried that they would be unable to acquire the budgetary resources necessary to carry out their new responsibilities.

There are exceptions to this picture of regional and local government impoverishment and lack of capacity. The governments of some northern states, such as Nuevo León, have been more responsive to local needs and better able to administer public services. In such states, local municipalities have become famous for the extent to which they differ from the norm in most of Mexico. The city of Monterrey, for example, has a reputation for efficient and forward-looking municipal government. Much of this local capacity can be credited to a regional political tradition that has stressed independence from—and even hostility to—Mexico City and the PRI. In addition, states and localities that have stronger governments and a tradition of better service tend to be areas of greater wealth, largely in the north of the country. In these cases, entrepreneurial groups and private citizens have often invested time and resources in state and local government.

Until 1988, all governors were from the PRI, although many believe that only electoral fraud kept two governorships out of the hands of an opposition party in 1986. Finally, in 1989, a non-PRI governor assumed power in Baja California, an important first. By late 2005, thirteen states and the Federal District were governed by parties other than the PRI. Also, municipalities have increasingly been the focus of authentic party competition. As opposition parties came to control these levels of government, they were challenged to improve services such as police protection, garbage collection, sanitation, and education. PRI-dominated governments have also tried to improve their performance because they are now more threatened by the possibility of losing elections.

The Policy-Making Process

The Mexican system is very dependent on the quality of its leadership and on presidential understanding of how economic and social policies can affect the development of the country. As indicated throughout this chapter, the six-year term of office, the *sexenio,* is an extremely important fact of political life in Mexico. New presidents can introduce extensive change in positions within the government. They are able to bring in "their" people, who build teams of "their" people within ministries, agencies, and party networks. This generally provides the president with a group of high- and middle-level officials who share a general orientation toward public policy and are motivated to carry out his goals. When the PRI was the dominant party, these officials believed that in following presidential leadership, they enhanced their chances for upward political mobility. In such a context, even under a single party, it was likely that changes in public policies could be introduced every six years, creating innovation or discontinuity, or both. As indicated, the limited experience of the PAN in executive office and the increasing role of congress in policy-making meant that the influence of the president on government became less strong after 2000. Nevertheless, Mexicans continue to look to the president and the executive branch for policy leadership.

Together with the bureaucracy, the president is the focal point of policy formulation and political management. Until 1997, the legislature always had a PRI majority and acted as a rubber stamp for presidentially sponsored legislation. Since then, the congress has proven to be a more active policy-maker, blocking and forcing the negotiation of legislation, and even introducing its own bills. The president's skills in negotiating, managing the opposition, using the media to acquire public support, and maneuvering within the bureaucracy can be important for ensuring that his program is fully endorsed.

Significant limits on presidential power occur when policy is being implemented. In fact, in areas as diverse as the regulation of working conditions, antipollution laws, tax collection, election monitoring, and health care in remote rural areas, Mexico has extremely advanced legislation on the books. Yet the persistence of unsafe factory conditions, pollution in Mexico City, tax evasion, electoral fraud, and poor health care suggests that legislation is not always translated into practice. At times, policies are not implemented because public officials at the lower levels disagree with them or make deals with affected interests in order to benefit personally. This is the case, for example, with taxes that remain uncollected because individuals or corporations bribe officials to overlook them. In other cases, lower-level officials may lack the capacity or skills to implement some policies, such as those directed toward improving education or rural development services. For various reasons, Mexican presidents cannot always deliver on their intentions. Traditionally, Mexican citizens have blamed lower-level officials for such slippage, but exempting the president from responsibility for what does or does not occur during his watch has become much less common since the 1970s.

Representation and Participation

How do citizen interests get represented in Mexican politics, given the high degree of centralization, presidentialism, and, until recently, PRI domination? Is it possible for ordinary citizens to make demands on government and influence public policy? In fact, Mexico has had a relatively peaceful history since the revolution, in part because the political system offers some channels for representation and participation. Throughout this long history, the political system has emphasized compromise among contending elites, behind-the-scenes conflict resolution, and distribution of political rewards to those willing to play by the formal and informal rules of the game. It has also responded, if reluctantly and defensively, to demands for change.

Often, citizens are best able to interact with the government through a variety of informal means rather than through the formal processes of elections, campaigns, and interest group lobbying. Interacting with government through the personal and informal mechanisms of clientelism usually means that the government retains the upper hand in deciding which interests to respond to and which to ignore. For many interests, this has meant "incorporation without power."[17] Increasingly, however, Mexican citizens are organizing to alter this situation, and the advent of truly competitive elections has increased the possibility that citizens who organize can gain some response from government.

The Legislature

Students in the United States are frequently asked to study complex charts explaining how a bill becomes a law because the formal process of lawmaking affects the content of legislation. Under the old reign of the PRI in Mexico, while there were formal rules that prescribed such a process, studying them would not have been useful for understanding how the legislature worked. Because of the overwhelming presence of this political party, opposition to presidential initiatives by Mexico's two-chamber legislature, the Senate and the Chamber of Deputies, was rarely heard. If representatives did not agree with policies they were asked to approve, they counted on the fact that policy implementation was flexible and allowed for after-the-fact bending of the rules or disregard of measures that were harmful to important interests.

Members of the Mexican congress are elected through a dual system of "first past the post" (that is, the candidate with the most votes wins) and proportional representation. Each state elects three senators. Two of them are determined by majority vote, and the third is determined by whichever party receives the second highest number of votes. In addition, thirty-two senators are determined nationally through a system of proportional representation that awards seats based on the number of votes cast for each party. Senators serve six-year terms. The same type of electoral system works in the Chamber of Deputies, with 300 selected on the basis of majority vote and 200 additional representatives chosen by proportional representation. Deputies are elected for three-year terms. Representation in congress has become somewhat more diverse since the end of the 1980s. A greater number of political parities are now represented; women have begun to be elected to more positions; and some representatives also emerged from the ranks of community activists who had participated in activities such as urban popular movements.

Since 1988, the PRI's grip on the legislature has been steadily weakened to the point where in 2006 they became, for the first time ever, the minority party in congress. In large part because of the decline of the PRI's power, the role of congress in the policy process has been strengthened considerably since the late 1990s.[18] The cost of greater power sharing between the executive and the legislature, however, has been a slow-down in the policy process. This was especially true under the Fox administration, when relations with congress became very confrontational. And although Calderón has been able to negotiate more effectively

with congress, he too has found himself constrained by a lack of a clear majority. The biggest change, therefore, has been that congress has evolved from a rubber-stamp institution to one that must be negotiated with by the executive branch.

Political Parties and the Party System

Even under the long reign of the PRI, a number of political parties existed in Mexico. By the mid-1980s, some of them were attracting more political support, a trend that continued into the 1990s and 2000s. Electoral reforms introduced by the López Portillo, de la Madrid, Salinas, and Zedillo administrations made it easier for opposition parties to contest elections and win seats in the legislature. In 1990, an electoral commission was created to regulate campaigns and elections, and in 1996 it became fully independent of the government. Now all parties receive funding from the government and have access to the media. Furthermore, in 2008 Calderón successfully pushed through congress an electoral reform law that changed how political campaigns were financed.

The PRI

Mexico's Institutional Revolutionary Party (PRI) was founded by a coalition of political elites who agreed that it was preferable to work out their conflicts within an overarching structure of compromise than to continue to resort to violence. In the 1930s, the forerunner of the PRI (the party operated under different names until 1946) incorporated a wide array of interests, becoming a mass-based party that drew support from all classes in the population. Over seven decades, its principal activities were to generate support for the government, organize the electorate to vote for its candidates, and distribute jobs and resources in return for loyalty to the system.

Until the 1990s, party organization was based largely on the corporate representation of class interests. Labor was represented within party councils by the Confederation of Mexican Workers (CTM), which included industry-based unions at local, regional, and national levels. Peasants were represented by the National Peasant Confederation (CNC), an organization

FIGURE 10.2

Congressional Representation by Party, 2006

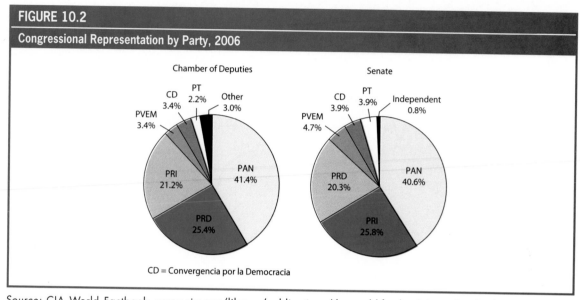

CD = Convergencia por la Democracia

Source: CIA World Factbook, www.cia.gov/library/publications/the-world-factbook/geos/mx.html#Govt; see also www.senado.gob.mx and www.camaradediputados.gob.mx.

of *ejido* and peasant unions and regional associations. The so-called popular sector, comprising small businesses, community-based groups, and public employees, had less internal cohesion but was represented by the National Confederation of Popular Organizations (CNOP). Of the three, the CTM was consistently the best organized and most powerful. Traditionally, the PRI's strongest support came from the countryside, where *ejidatarios* and independent small farmers were grateful for and dependent on rewards of land or jobs. As the country became more urbanized, the support base provided by rural communities remained important to the PRI, but produced many fewer votes than were necessary to keep the party in power.

Within its corporate structures, the PRI functioned through extended networks that distributed public resources—particularly jobs, land, development projects, and access to public services—to lower-level activists who controlled votes at the local level. In this system, those with ambitions to public office or to positions within the PRI put together networks of supporters from above (patrons), to whom they delivered votes, and supporters from below (clients), who traded allegiance for access to public resources. For well over half a century, this system worked extremely

well. PRI candidates won by overwhelming majorities until the 1980s (see Figure 10.3). Of course, electoral fraud and the ability to distribute government largesse are central explanations for these numbers, but they also attest to an extremely well-organized party.

Within the PRI, power was centralized, and the sector organizations (the CTM, the CNC, and the CNOP) responded primarily to elites at the top of the political pyramid rather than to member interests. Over time, the corporate interest group organizations, particularly the CTM and the CNC, became widely identified with corruption, bossism, centralized control, and lack of effective participation. By the 1980s, new generations of voters were less beholden to patronage-style politics and much more willing to question the party's dominance. When the administrations of de la Madrid, Salinas, and Zedillo imposed harsh austerity measures, the PRI was held responsible for the resulting losses in incomes and benefits. Simultaneously, as the government cut back sharply on public sector jobs and services, the PRI had far fewer resources to distribute to maintain its traditional bases of support. Moreover, it began to suffer from increasing internal dissension between the old guard—the so-called dinosaurs—and the "modernizers" who wanted to reform the party.

Mexico

FIGURE 10.3

PRI Support in Congressional Elections, 1946–2006

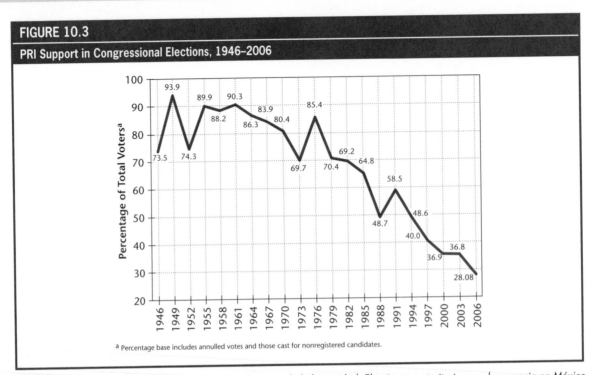

[a] Percentage base includes annulled votes and those cast for nonregistered candidates.

Source: For 1946–1988: Juan Molinar Horcasitas, *El tiempo de la legtimidad: Elecciones, autoritarismo y democracia en México* (México, D.F.: Cal y Arena, 1991). For 1991: Secretaría Nacional de Estudios, Partido Acción Nacional, *Análisis del Proceso Federal Electoral 1994, 1995.* For 1994: Instituto Federal Electoral, *Estadístca de las Elecciones Federales de 1994, Compendio de Resultados* (Mexico, D.F., 1995). For 1997: www.ife.org.mx/ww-worge/tablas/mrent.htm. For 2000, 2003, and 2006: Instituto Federal Electoral, www.ife.org.mx. In 2003 and 2006, the PRI formed the senior partner in the *Alianza para Todos* (Alliance for Everyone), which brought the PRI and the much smaller PVEM together on a single ticket in some states in 2003 and at the national level in 2006. In 2006, the PRD formed the senior partner of the *Coalición por el Bien de Todos* (Coalition for the Good of All), which was formed with the *Partido del Trabajo* (Labor Party) and *Convergencia* (Convergence).

In the late 1980s, the PRI began to be challenged by parties to the right and left, and outcomes were hotly contested by the opposition, which claimed fraudulent electoral practices.

As the PRI faced greater competition from other parties and continued to suffer from declining popularity, efforts were made to restructure and reform it. The CNOP was replaced by an organization that sought to incorporate a wide array of non-class-based citizen and neighborhood movements. In 1990, membership rules were altered to allow individuals and groups not identified with its corporate sector organizations to join. In addition, regional party organizations gained representation at the national level. Party conventions were introduced in an effort to democratize the internal workings of the party, and some states and localities

began to hold primaries to select PRI candidates, a significant departure from the old system of selection by party bosses.

The PRI continues to face a difficult future. Mexico's voters are younger, better educated, more middle class, and more likely to live in urban areas than they were in the days of the PRI's greatest success—the 1940s, 1950s, and 1960s. The 1988 presidential elections demonstrated the relevance of changing demographic conditions when only 27.3 percent of the population of Mexico City voted for the PRI candidate and only 34.3 percent of the population in other urban areas supported him. By 2006, support for the party had fallen so far in the nation's capital that only 11.68 percent of voters in the Federal District cast their ballots for PRI congressional candidates. With the vast

Table 10.3

Voting in Presidential Elections, 1934–2006

Year	Votes for PRI Candidate[a]	Votes for PAN Candidate	Votes for PRD	Turnout (% Voters Among Eligible Adults)[b]
1934	98.2	—	—	53.6
1940	93.9	—	—	57.5
1946	77.9	—	—	42.6
1952	74.3	7.8	—	57.9
1958	90.4	9.4	—	49.4
1964	88.8	11.1	—	54.1
1970	83.3	13.9	—	63.9
1976[c]	93.6	—	—	29.6
1982	71.0	15.7	—	66.1
1988	50.7	16.8	30.95[d]	49.4[e]
1994	50.1	26.7	16.59	77.16
2000	36.1	42.5[f]	16.64[g]	64.0
2006	22.26[h]	35.89	35.31[i]	58.55

[a]From 1958 through 1982, includes votes cast for the *Partido Popular Socialista* (PPS) and the *Partido Auténtico de la Revolución Mexicana* (PARM), both of which regularly endorsed the PRI's presidential candidate. In 1988, they supported opposition candidate Cuauhtémoc Cárdenas.

[b]Eligible population base for 1934 through 1952 includes all males ages twenty and over (legal voting age: twenty-one years). Both men and women ages twenty and over are included in the base for 1958 and 1964 (women received the franchise in 1958). The base for 1970–1988 includes all males and females ages eighteen and over (the legal voting age was lowered to eighteen, effective 1970).

[c]The PRI candidate, José Lopez Portillo, ran virtually unopposed because the PAN failed to nominate a candidate. The only other significant candidate was Valentín Campa, representing the Communist Party, which was not legally registered to participate in the 1976 election. More than 5 percent of the votes were annulled.

[d]These are the totals for the "*Frente Democrático Nacional*" that endorsed Cuauhtémoc Cárdenas. Part of this coalition went on to become the PRD.

[e]Estimated using data from the Federal Electoral Commission. However, the commission itself has released two different figures for the number of eligible voters in 1988. Using the commission's larger estimate of eligible population, the turnout would be 44.9 percent.

[f]Votes cast for *Alianza por el Cambio* (Alliance for Change), formed by the *Partido Acción Nacional* (PAN) and the *Partido Verde Ecologista de Mexico* (PVEM).

[g]Votes cast for the *Alianza por México* (Alliance for Mexico), formed by the PRD, the *Partido del Trabajo* (Labor Party), the *Partido de la Sociedad Nacionalista* (Party of the Nationalist Society), *Convergencia por la Democracia* (Convergence for the Democracy), *Partido Acción Social* (Party of Social Action).

[h]Votes cast for the *Alianza para Todos* (Alliance for Everyone), formed by the PRI and the PVEM.

[i]Votes cast for the *Coalición por el Bien de Todos* (Coalition for the Good of All), formed by the PRD, the *Partido del Trabajo* (Labor Party), and *Convergencia* (Convergence).

Sources: From *Comparative Politics Today: A World View,* 4th ed., Gabriel Almond and G. Bingham Powell, Jr. © 1988. Reprinted by permission of Addison-Wesley Educational Publishers, Inc. For 1988: *El Universal,* "*Resultados Electorales,*" graficos.eluniversal. com.mx/tablas/presidente/presidentes.htm. For 1994: Instituto Federal Electoral, *Estadística de las Elecciones Federales de 1994, Compendio de Resultados* (Mexico, D.F., 1995). For 2000 and 2006: Instituto Federal Electoral, www.ife.org.mx.

majority of the country's population now living in cities, the PRI will have to win the support of more urban voters in order to remain a relevant political force. Nonetheless, the PRI continues to be one of the most important political parties in the country. It did not, as some predicted, dissolve once it lost the ability to control the presidency. It is still the only party that has a presence in every region of the country. And even now that its numbers in congress have dwindled to an all-time low, it continues to be a major political actor.

Since no one party controls congress, and since relations between the PAN and the PRD are so acrimonious, the PRI often holds the balance of power.

The PAN

The National Action Party (PAN) was founded in 1939 to represent interests opposed to the centralization and anticlericalism of the PRI. It was founded by those who believed that the country needed more than one strong political party and that opposition parties should oppose the PRI through legal and constitutional actions. Historically, this party has been strongest in northern states, where the tradition of resistance to Mexico City is also strongest. It has also been primarily an urban party of the middle class and is closely identified with the private sector. The PAN has traditionally campaigned on a platform endorsing greater regional autonomy, less government intervention in the economy, reduced regulation of business, clean and fair elections, rapprochement with the Catholic Church, and support for private and religious education. When PRI governments of the 1980s and 1990s moved toward market-friendly and export-oriented policies, the policy differences between the two parties were significantly reduced. Nevertheless, a major difference of perspectives about religion continued to characterize the two parties. The PAN has always favored a closer relationship with the Catholic Church.

For many years, the PAN was able to elect only nine to ten percent of all deputies to the national congress and capture control of a few municipal governments. Beginning in the 1980s and 1990s, it was able to take advantage both of the economic crises (and the PRI's subsequent weakened ability to control the political process) and political reforms to increase its power. By 2006, the PAN controlled the governorships of eight states and held a plurality of seats in congress.

In 2000, the party took the unusual step of nominating Vicente Fox for the presidency, despite the fact that he was not a longstanding member of the party. Many party insiders considered him to be an opportunistic newcomer to the party, and they worked to limit his ability to run for office, forcing him to look for other sources for financing his campaign. Starting

in 1997, the "Friends of Fox" organization began to raise funds and promote his candidacy for president. Fox gained in popularity throughout the country, and in 1999, the party had little option but to nominate him as its candidate. The Friends of Fox continued to provide the most important source of campaign support, however, and when Fox won the presidential election, the PAN organization was weak and not at all united in backing him. His inability to capitalize on his electoral victory and push forward a more ambitious package of reforms allowed the party insiders to regain control of the nominating process and advance the candidacy of Felipe Calderón in 2006. Unlike Fox, he was a lifelong member of the PAN and was the son of one of the PAN's founding members.

The PRD

Another significant challenge to the PRI has come from the Democratic Revolutionary Party (PRD), a populist, nationalist, and leftist alternative to the PRI. Its candidate in the 1988 and 1994 elections was Cuauhtémoc Cárdenas, the son of Mexico's most famous and revered president. He was a PRI insider until party leaders virtually ejected him for demanding internal reform of the party and a platform emphasizing social justice. In the 1988 elections, Cárdenas was officially credited with winning 31.1 percent of the vote, and his party captured 139 seats in the Chamber of Deputies. He benefited from massive political defection from the PRI and garnered support from workers disaffected with the boss-dominated unions, as well as from peasants who remembered his father's concern for agrarian reform and the welfare of the poor.

Even while the votes were being counted, the party began to denounce widespread electoral fraud and claim that Cárdenas would have won if the election had been honest. The PRD challenged a number of vote counts in the courts and walked out on the inaugural speech given by the PRI's Salinas. Considerable public opinion supported the party's challenge. After the 1988 elections, then, it seemed that the PRD was a strong contender to become Mexico's second most powerful party. It was expected to have a real chance in future years to challenge the PRI's "right" to the presidency.

Nevertheless, in the aftermath of these elections, the party was plagued by internal divisions over its platform, leadership, organizational structure, and election strategy. By 1994, it still lagged far behind the PRI and the PAN in establishing and maintaining the local constituency organizations needed to mobilize votes and monitor the election process. In addition, the PRD found it difficult to define an appropriate left-of-center alternative to the market-oriented policies carried out by the government. While the claims that such policies ignored the need for social justice were popular, policies to respond to poverty that did not imply a return to unpopular government intervention were difficult to devise. In the aftermath of the assassination of the PRI candidate for president, Luis Donaldo Colosio, citizens also became more alarmed about violence, and some were concerned that the level of political rivalry represented by the PRD threatened the country's long-term political stability. In the 1994 elections, Cárdenas won only 17 percent of the votes, although the PRD elected seventy-one deputies and eight senators.

Thanks to the government's continued unpopular economic policies and the leadership of a successful grassroots mobilizer named Andrés Manuel López Obrador, who was elected to head the party in 1996, the PRD began to stage a remarkable turnaround. Factional bickering was controlled, and organizational discipline increased. In addition, the PRD proved successful in moving beyond its regional strongholds and established itself as a truly national party. In 1997, the party increased its share of seats in the Chamber of Deputies and in the Senate. Most important, Cárdenas became the first popularly elected mayor of Mexico City, providing him and the party with an opportunity to demonstrate their ability to govern. By this time, the PRD had managed to shed some of its reputation as a "one-horse show" and had won two governorships. In 2000, López Obrador was elected mayor of Mexico City with 39.5 percent of the vote, signaling again the political importance of the capital city. In the presidential race, Cárdenas ran again, but he was able to garner only 16.5 percent of the vote. The party's performance in the legislative race was equally disappointing.

The party's fortunes improved somewhat in 2003, when the size of its delegation in the Chamber of Deputies rose to 97. Although the problem of factional infighting had still not been completely resolved by 2005, by then four states and the Federal District were governed by the PRD. Another governor had been elected as the representative of a coalition between the PRD and the PAN, which put aside their divergent ideologies and worked together on the local level to unseat the PRI in the rural, traditional state of Chiapas.

Thanks largely to its control over the capital city and the existence of PRD administrations on the municipal level in parts of the country, the party was able to boast that about a quarter of the country's population lived under a PRD government. Furthermore, under the leadership of López Obrador, the PRD's prospects for the 2006 elections looked good. Indeed, for most of 2005, polls indicated that López Obrador was the clear favorite to win the presidency. In early 2006, however, Calderón was able to shift the focus of his campaign and raise fears that a López Obrador presidency would threaten the stability of Mexico's economy. The election was hard fought and characterized by growing animosity. In the end, Calderón was able to win by a narrow margin. López Obrador refused to concede defeat and staged several protests, including a shadow inauguration where he declared himself the "legitimate" president of Mexico. Despite these protests and although the PRD emerged as the second most powerful party in congress, Calderón has been able to work effectively with congress. This is because the PAN and the PRI have been able to form an alliance that effectively excludes the PRD.

Other Parties

There are a number of smaller parties that contest elections in Mexico. In 2006, the most important small parties were: *Convergencia* (Convergence); *Partido del Trabajo* (PT, Labor Party); *Partido Verde Ecologista Mexicana* (PVEM, Green Party); *Partido Nueva Alianza* (New Alliance Party); *Partido Alternativa Socialdemócrata y Campesina* (Social Democratic and Peasant Alternative Party). Since Mexican law requires parties to receive at least 2.5 percent of the vote to be able to compete in future elections, the long-term viability of some of these organizations is very doubtful. Small parties usually do win a few of the seats in the Chamber of Deputies and the Senate that are filled by proportional representation. Also, these groups sometimes wield influence on national politics by forming alliances with the larger parties, either endorsing their candidates for president or governor in national and state elections or backing a single slate of candidates for congress. For example, in 2006, Convergence and the PT formed an alliance—the Coalition for the Good of All—with the PRD, while the Green Party joined with the PRI in the Alliance for Mexico. Some of these small parties appear to have clear agendas. For example, the Social Democratic Alternative Party was founded by Patricia Mercado, a prominent feminist leader, and promotes not only women's rights but also an alternative left-of-center economic strategy that contrasts with the PRD. However, many of these small parties often appear to be opportunistic in the shifting alliances they make. Because a few of the most insignificant parties apparently exist only to tap into the public funding that finances election campaigns in Mexico, many Mexicans have a low regard for some of these organizations.

Elections

Each of the three main political parties draws voters from a wide and overlapping spectrum of the electorate. Nevertheless, a typical voter for the PRI is likely to be from a rural area or small town, to have less education, and to be older and poorer than voters for the other parties. A typical voter for the PAN is likely to be from a northern state, to live in an urban area, to be a middle-class professional, to have a comfortable lifestyle, and to have a high school or even a university education. A typical voter for the PRD is likely to be young, to be a political activist, to have an elementary or high school education, to live in one of the central states, and to live in a small town or an urban area. As we have seen, the support base for the PRI is the most vulnerable to economic and demographic changes in the country. Voting for opposition parties is an urban phenomenon, and Mexico continues to urbanize at the rate of 3 percent per year. This means that in order to stay competitive, the PRI will have to garner more support from urban areas. It must also be able to appeal to younger voters, especially the large numbers who are attracted to the PRD and the PAN.

Electoral reforms introduced by the López Portillo, de la Madrid, Salinas, and Zedillo administrations made it easier for opposition parties to contest elections and win seats in the legislature. In 1990, an electoral commission was created to regulate campaigns and elections, and in 1996 it became fully independent from the government. Now all parties receive government funding and have guaranteed access to the media. These and other laws that limit campaign spending and campaign contributions were a response to demands that the government level the playing field between the PRI and the other parties. Beginning in 1994, elections have been more competitive and much fairer, and subsequent congressional, state, and municipal elections reinforced the impression that electoral fraud is on the wane in many areas. The PAN's victory in 2000 substantially increased this impression. But in 2006, López Obrador claimed that Calderón's victory was fraudulent. Because of the polarized nature of the election, the legitimacy of the federal electoral authorities was questioned, although no evidence of wide-scale fraud or election tampering was ever uncovered.

Political Culture, Citizenship, and Identity

Most Mexicans have a deep familiarity with how their political system works and the ways in which they might be able to extract benefits from it. They understand the informal rules of the game in Mexican politics that have helped maintain political stability despite extensive inequalities in economic and political power. Clientelism has long been a form of participation in the sense that through their connections, many people, even the poorest, are able to interact with public officials and get something out of the political system. This kind of participation emphasizes how limited resources, such as access to health care, can be distributed in a way that provides maximum political payoff. This informal system is a fundamental reason that many Mexicans continued to vote for the PRI for so long.

However, new ways of interacting with government are emerging, and they coexist along with the clientelistic style of the past. An increasing number of citizens are seeking to negotiate with the government on the basis of citizenship rights, not personal patron-client relationships. The movements that emerged in the

1980s sought to form broad but loose coalitions with other organizations and attempted to identify and work with reform-oriented public officials. Their suspicion of traditional political organizations such as the PRI and its affiliates also led them to avoid close alliances with other parties, such as the PAN and the PRD.

As politics and elections became more open and competitive, the roles of public opinion and the mass media have become more important. Today, the media play an important role in public opinion formation in Mexico. In the past, it was not easy for newspapers, magazines, or radio and television stations to be openly opposed to the government. For many years, the government used access to newsprint, which it controlled, to reward sympathetic news coverage and penalize coverage it considered hostile.

As with other aspects of Mexican politics, the media began to become more independent in the 1980s, enjoying a "spring" of greater independence and diversity of opinion.[19] There are currently several major television networks in the country, and many citizens have access to CNN and other global networks. The number of newspapers is expanding, as is their circulation, and several news magazines play the same role in Mexico that *Time* and *Newsweek* do in the United States. Citizens in Mexico today clearly hear a much wider range of opinion and much greater reporting of debates about public policy and criticism of government than at any time previously.

Interests, Social Movements, and Protest

The Mexican political system has long responded to groups of citizens through pragmatic **accommodation** to their interests. This is one important reason that political tensions among major interests have rarely escalated into the kind of serious conflict that can threaten stability. Where open conflict has occurred, it has generally been met with efforts to find some kind of compromise solution. Accommodation has been particularly apparent in response to the interests of business. Mexico's development strategy encouraged the growth of wealthy elites in commerce, finance, industry, and agriculture (see Section 2).

Labor has been similarly accommodated within the system. Wage levels for unionized workers grew fairly consistently between 1940 and 1982, when the economic crisis caused a significant drop in wages. At the same time, labor interests were attended to in terms of concrete benefits and limitations on the rights of employers to discipline or dismiss workers. Union leaders controlled their rank and file in the interest of their own power to negotiate with government, but at the same time, they sought benefits for workers who continued to provide support for the PRI. The power of the union bosses has declined, in part because the unions are weaker than in the past, in part because union members are demanding greater democratization, and in part because the PRI no longer monopolizes political power. Likewise, in the countryside, rural organizations have gained greater independence from the government. Indigenous groups have also emerged to demand that government be responsive to their needs and respectful of their traditions. Since 1994, the rebels in Chiapas have become a focal point for broad alliances of those concerned about the rights of indigenous groups (ethnic minorities) and rural poverty.

Despite the strong and controlling role of the PRI in Mexico's political history, the country also has a tradition of civic organizations that operate at community and local levels with considerable independence from politics. The economic crisis of 1982 combined with this civic tradition to heighten demands for assistance from the government. In October 1983, as many as 2 million people participated in a civic strike to call attention to the economic crisis and demand a forceful government response. In urban areas, citizen groups demanded land rights in squatter settlements, as well as housing, infrastructure, and urban services, as rights of citizenship rather than as a reward for loyalty to the PRI.[20] In the aftermath of the 1985 earthquake, citizen groups became especially dynamic in demanding that government respond to the needs of citizens without reference to their history of party loyalty.[21] Many also became active in groups that share concerns about quality-of-life issues such as clean air and safe neighborhoods (see "Citizen Action: Urban Popular Movements").

In subsequent years, a variety of groups in Mexico have continued to organize around middle-class and urban issues. Women, with a strong cultural role as caretakers of the home, have begun to mobilize in many cities to demand community services, equal pay,

Citizen Action

Urban Popular Movements

In October 1968, hundreds of students and working-class people took to the streets of Mexico City to protest high unemployment and the authoritarianism of the government. What began as a peaceful rally in Tlatelolco Plaza ended in a tragedy when government troops opened fire on the crowd and killed more than 200 people. The political activism of the students heralded the birth of urban popular movements in Mexico. The massacre in Tlatelolco became a symbol of a government that was unwilling or unable to respond to citizen demands for economic and political equity. The protest movements sparked by the events of 1968 sought to transcend class boundaries and unite voices around a range of urban issues, from housing shortages to inadequate public services to lack of land to centralized decision-making. Such social movements forged new channels for poor and middle-class urban residents to express their needs. They also generated forums for demanding democratic government that the traditional political system was not providing. In May 1980, the first national congress of urban movements was held in Monterrey in northern Mexico.

Urban popular movements, referring to activities of low- and modest-income (popular) groups, gained renewed vitality in the 1980s. When the economic crisis resulted in drastic reductions of social welfare spending and city services, working- and middle-class neighborhoods forged new coalitions and greatly expanded the national discussion of urban problems. The Mexico City earthquake of 1985 encouraged the formation of unprecedented numbers of grassroots movements in response to the slow and poorly managed relief efforts of the government. Turning to each other, earthquake victims organized to provide shelter, food, and relocation. The elections of 1988 and 1994 provided these groups with significant opportunities to press parties and candidates to respond to their needs. They insisted on their rights to organize and protest without fear of repression or co-optation by the government or the PRI. As the opposition parties expanded rapidly, some leaders of urban movements enrolled as candidates for public office.

Urban popular movements bring citizens together around needs and ideals that cut across class boundaries. Neighborhood improvement, the environment, local self-government, economic development, feminism, and professional identity have been among the factors that have forged links among these groups. As such identities have been strengthened, the need of the political system to negotiate and bargain with a more independent citizenry has increased.

---

legal equality, and opportunities in business traditionally denied to them.[22] Furthermore, political issues that are commonly discussed in the United States, such as abortion and gay rights, have recently begun to be debated publicly in Mexico. Previously, parties of the left focused most of their attention on questions of economic redistribution, but this has recently begun to change. In April 2007, the PRD-controlled legislature of Mexico City voted to decriminalize abortions in the first trimester (in the rest of Mexico abortion continues to be illegal except in cases of rape or severe birth defects, although in fact gaining access to a legal abortion even under these circumstances is exceedingly difficult). And in November 2006, the PRD voted to legalize gay civil unions. The PAN remains vehemently opposed to these measures. For example, in 2000 the PAN-dominated legislature of

Mexicans demonstrate for better housing in Mexico City's central plaza. *Source:* Robert Freck/ Odyssey/Chicago.

Guanajuato voted to ban abortion even in the case of rape, and established penalties of up to three years in prison for women who violated the law.

Although President Vicente Fox was opposed to abortion, he did attempt to distance himself from the Guanajuato law and for the most part avoided discussing contentious social and cultural subjects. But under his administration condom use was encouraged and a campaign against homophobia—featuring radio ads that portrayed gay relationships sympathetically—was

launched. In 2004, he caused a furor within his own party when his administration approved the distribution of the morning after pill in public clinics. These policies were denounced by Calderón, who vowed in his 2006 campaign to ban the use of this pill and openly expressed his opposition to abortion and gay rights. It is unclear at this point how strongly these issues resonate with the Mexican public or how important they will be in years to come in defining the differences between the major political parties.

SECTION 5   Mexican Politics in Transition

Political Challenges and Changing Agendas

Mexico confronts a world of increasing interdependence among countries. For all countries, economic integration raises issues of national sovereignty and identity. Mexicans define themselves in part through a set of historical events, symbols, and myths that focus on the country's troubled relationship with the United States. Among numerous national heroes and martyrs are those who distinguished themselves in confrontations with the United States. The myths of the Revolution of 1910 emphasize the uniqueness of the country in terms of its opposition to the capitalists and militarists of the northern country. In the 1970s, Mexicans were encouraged to see themselves as leading Third World countries in arguing for enhanced bargaining positions in relation to the industrialized countries of the north. This view stands in strong contrast to more recent perspectives touting the benefits of

an internationally oriented economy and the undeniable post-NAFTA reality of information, culture, money, and people flowing back and forth across borders.

The country's sense of national identity is affected by international migration. Of particular importance in the Mexican case is labor migration. Every year, large numbers of Mexicans enter the United States as workers. Many return to their towns and villages with new values and new views of the world. Many stay in the United States, where Hispanics have become the largest ethnic minority population in the country. Most continue to believe that Mexican culture is preferable to American culture, which they see as excessively materialistic and violent. Although they believe that Mexico is a better place to nurture strong family life and values, they are nevertheless strongly influenced by U.S. mass culture, including popular music, movies, television programs, fast food, and consumer goods (see "Global Connection: Mexican Migration to the United States").

Global Connection

Mexican Migration to the United States

The contrast between the poverty of much of the developing world and the prosperity of industrialized nations is nowhere on more vivid display than it is along the 2,000-mile-long border between Mexico and the United States. Because of the economic disparities that exist between the two

neighboring countries, Mexicans with limited opportunities at home have long been venturing north of the border in search of jobs and a higher standard of living. The money that these migrants send back to Mexico helps to sustain not just their own families but entire regions that have been left behind by the

(continued)

Global Connection

country's uneven pattern of growth and development. As the number of Mexican migrants seeking opportunities abroad has grown in recent years, their presence in the United States has come to have profound ramifications for the politics of both nations.

Mexicans began moving to the United States in substantial numbers late in the nineteenth century, and their ranks grew as many fled the chaotic conditions that had been created by the Revolution of 1910. Although some of these early migrants found work in northern industrial centers such as Chicago, most settled in the border states of California and Texas, where they joined preexisting Mexican communities that had been there since the days when the American southwest had been part of Mexico. Even greater numbers of migrants began to arrive during World War II, when the U.S. government allowed Mexican workers, known as *braceros*, to enter the country to help provide much-needed manpower for strategic production efforts. The *bracero* program remained in place after the war, and under it, a predominantly male Mexican workforce provided seasonal labor to U.S. employers, mostly in the agricultural sector.

After the *bracero* program came to an end in 1964, Mexicans continued to seek work in the United States, despite the fact that most then had to enter the country illegally. To a large extent, the U.S. government informally tolerated the employment of undocumented migrants until the 1980s, when policy-makers came under pressure to assert control over the border. The 1986 Immigration Reform and Control Act (IRCA) allowed migrants who had been in the United States for a long period of time to gain legal residency rights, but it called for tighter controls on immigration in the future.

However, rather than cutting off the movement of Mexicans into the United States, IRCA and subsequent efforts to deter illegal immigration simply turned a pattern of seasonal migration into a flow of migrants that settled permanently north of the border. Before 1986, most Mexican migrant workers left their families at home and worked in the United States for only a few months at a time before returning to their country with the money they had earned. But many of the seasonal migrants who gained amnesty under IRCA then sent for their families to join them, creating a more permanent immigrant community. Also, with increased vigilance and new barriers making the crossing of the border more difficult, more of the migrants who arrived in the United States decided to remain there rather than risk apprehension by traveling back and forth between the two countries. High-profile efforts to patrol the border around urban areas such as San Diego and El Paso led migrants to use more remote crossing points, and although the number of Mexicans who died trying to reach the United States rose as many attempted to travel through the desolate deserts of Arizona, the overall rate of illegal immigration was not affected by the government's crackdown.

In the 1990s and 2000s, growing Mexican communities in the United States spread into areas such as North Carolina, Georgia, Arkansas, and Iowa, where few Mexicans had lived before. They also became increasingly mobilized politically as they organized to resist anti-immigrant voter initiatives such as Proposition 187 in California in 1994 and Proposition 200 in Arizona in 2004, both of which threatened to cut off social services for undocumented migrants. At the same time, their political importance in Mexico has reached unprecedented heights as officials at all levels of government there recognize the critical importance to the Mexican economy of the $16.6 billion that the country receives each year in remittances from migrants working in other countries. Mexican governors, mayors, and federal officials now regularly visit representatives of migrant groups in the United States, often seeking their support and funding for projects at home. Moreover, a 1996 law allowing Mexicans to hold dual citizenship could allow many Mexican migrants to have a voice in the governance of both the country of their birth as well as the country where they now reside. In 2005, Mexican legislators finally approved a system under which registered Mexican voters living abroad could participate in federal elections using mail-in ballots, and it is easy to imagine that this huge group could play a decisive role in future electoral contests.

The inability of the Mexican economy to create enough jobs pushes additional Mexicans to seek work in the United States, and the cash remittances that migrants abroad send home to their families and communities are now almost as important a source of income for Mexico as PEMEX's oil sales. However, the issues surrounding migration have become even more complex since the attacks of September 11, 2001. Hopes for a bilateral accord that would permit more Mexicans to enter and work in the United States legally evaporated after U.S. officials suddenly found themselves under greatly increased pressure to control the country's borders. Illegal immigration has not abated, however, and Mexican officials continue to try to convince their counterparts in Washington that allowing more migrants to cross the border legally would actually enhance U.S. security by reducing the number of unauthorized crossings. Whether or not the U.S. government approves, the difference in wages between the United States and Mexico will persist for a long time, which implies that migration will also persist.

There is disagreement about how to respond to the economic challenges that Mexico faces. Much of the debate surrounds the question of what integration into a competitive international economy really means. For some, it represents the final abandonment of Mexico's sovereignty. For others, it is the basis on which future prosperity must be built. Those who are critical of the market-based, outward-oriented development strategy are concerned about its impact on workers, peasants, and national identities. They argue that the state has abandoned its responsibilities to protect the poor from shortcomings of the market and to provide for their basic needs. They believe that U.S. and Canadian investors have come to Mexico only to find low-wage labor for industrial empires located elsewhere, and they argue that those investors will not hesitate to abandon Mexico for even lower-wage countries such as China when the opportunity arises. They see little benefit in further industrial development based on importation of foreign-made parts, their assembly in Mexico, and their export to other markets. This kind of development, they argue, has been prevalent in the *maquiladoras,* or assembly industries, many of which are located along the U.S.–Mexico border. Those who favor closer integration with Canada and the United States acknowledge that some foreign investment does not promote technological advances or move the work force into higher-paying and more skilled jobs. They emphasize, however, that most investment will occur because Mexico has a relatively well-educated population, the capacity to absorb modern technology, and a large internal market for industrial goods.

In addition to the economic challenges it faces, Mexico provides a testing ground for the democratic idea in a state with a long history of authoritarian institutions. The democratic ideas of citizen rights to free speech and assembly, free and fair elections, and responsive government are major reasons that the power of the PRI came under so much attack beginning in the 1980s. Currently, Mexico is struggling with opening up its political institutions to become more democratic. However, efforts to bring about greater transparency in the Mexican political system often run up against obstacles as government ministries resist pressures to release sensitive documents and as investigations into the repressive activities of the PRI regime in decades past have been stymied. These setbacks left some Mexicans skeptical of claims that a truly open, democratic political culture is being forged.

Centralization of power and decision-making is another legacy that Mexico is trying to revise. Countries around the globe increasingly recognize that the solutions to many policy problems lie at regional and local levels. While the government has introduced the decentralization of a number of activities and services, state and municipal governments are struggling to meet the demands of citizens who want competence, responsiveness, and accountability from their local and regional public officials.

Improving social conditions is an important challenge for Mexico. While elites enjoy the benefits of sumptuous lifestyles, education at the best U.S. universities for their children, and luxury travel throughout the world, large numbers of Mexicans remain ill-educated, poorly served with health care, and distant from the security of knowing that their basic needs for food, shelter, and employment can be met. The Chiapas rebellion of 1994 made the social agenda a topic of everyday conversation by reminding Mexicans that some people lived in appalling conditions with little hope for the future.

Current Challenges

Human Rights in Mexico

The government of Vicente Fox (2000–2006) committed itself to opening up government and improving the state of human rights in Mexico. In the past, the government had been able to limit knowledge of its repressive actions, use the court system to maintain the political peace, and intimidate those who objected to its actions. Fox appointed human rights activists to his cabinet and ordered that secret police and military files be opened to public scrutiny. He instructed government ministries to supply more information about their activities and the rights that citizens have to various kinds of services. Fox also invited the United Nations to open a human rights office in Mexico. He encouraged the ratification of the Inter-American Convention on Enforced Disappearance of Persons. The government also sought to protect the rights of Mexicans abroad, and the United States and Mexico established a working group to improve human rights conditions for migrants.

The results of these actions have been dramatic. For the first time, Mexicans learned of cases of hundreds of people who had "disappeared" as a result of police and military actions. In addition, citizens have come forward to announce other disappearances, ones they were unwilling to report earlier because they feared reprisals. In 2002, former president Luis Echeverría was brought before prosecutors and questioned about government actions against political dissent in 1968 and 1971, a kind of accountability unheard of in the past. The National Human Rights Commission has been active in efforts to hold government officials accountable and to protect citizens nationally and abroad from repetitions of the abuses of the past.

Yet challenges to human rights accountability remain. Opening up files and setting up systems for prosecuting abusers needs to be followed by actions to impose penalties on abusers. The Mexican judicial system is weak and has little experience in human rights cases. In addition, action on reports of disappearances, torture, and imprisonment has been slowed by contention about civil and military jurisdictions. In an embarrassing revelation to the government, Amnesty International reported several cases of disappearances that occurred after Fox assumed leadership of the country. There were also reports of arbitrary detentions and extrajudicial executions. In October 2001, Digna Ochoa, a prominent human rights lawyer, was shot. In the aftermath of this assassination, the government was accused of not doing enough to protect her, even when it was widely known that she had been targeted by those opposed to her work. Human rights activists claimed that police and military personnel, in particular, still had impunity to the laws. The strength of the Fox administration was tested in these events, and although human rights were much more likely to be protected than in the past, the government still had a long way to go in safeguarding the rights of indigenous people, political dissidents, migrants, gays and lesbians, and poor people whose ability to use the judicial system is limited by poverty and lack of information.

As in the United States, some argue that the best solutions to these problems are economic growth and expanded employment. They believe that the achievement of prosperity through integration into the global economy will benefit everyone in the long run. For this to occur, however, they insist that education will have to be improved and made more appropriate for developing a well-prepared work force. They also believe that improved education will come about when local communities have more control over schools and curricula and when parents have more choice between public and private education for their children. From their perspective, the solution to poverty and injustice is fairly clear: more and better jobs and improved education.

For those critical of the development path on which Mexico embarked in the 1980s and 1990s, the problems of poverty and inequity are more complex. Solutions involve understanding the diverse causes of poverty, including not only lack of jobs and poor education but also exploitation, geographic isolation, discriminatory laws and practices, as well as the disruptive impact of migration, urbanization, and the tensions of modern life. In the past, Mexicans looked to government for social welfare benefits, but their provision was deeply flawed by inefficiency and political manipulation. The government consistently used access to social services as a means to increase its political control and limit the capacity of citizens to demand equitable treatment. Thus, although many continue to believe that it is the responsibility of government to ensure that citizens are well educated, healthy, and able to make the most of their potential, the populace is deeply suspicious of the government's capacity to provide such conditions fairly and efficiently.

Finally, Mexico is confronting major challenges in adapting newly democratic institutions to reflect ethnic and religious diversity and provide equity for women in economic and political affairs. The past decade has witnessed the emergence of more organized and politically independent ethnic groups demanding justice and equality from government. These groups claim that they have suffered for nearly 500 years and that they are no longer willing to accept poverty and marginality as their lot. The Roman Catholic Church, still the largest organized religion in the country, is losing members to Protestant sects that appeal particularly to the everyday concerns of poor Mexicans. Women, who make up 32 percent of the formal labor force but 40 percent of professional and technical workers, are becoming more organized, but they still have a long way to go before their wages equal those of men or they have equal voice in political and economic decisions.

Mexican Politics in Comparative Perspective

Mexico faces many of the same challenges that beset other countries: creating equitable and effective democratic government, becoming integrated into a global economy, responding to complex social problems, and supporting increasing diversity without losing national identity. Indeed, these were precisely the challenges that the United States faced at the millennium, as did India, Nigeria, Brazil, Germany, and others. Mexico confronts these challenges within the context of a unique historical and institutional evolution. The legacies of its past, the tensions of the present, and the innovations of the future will no doubt evolve in ways that continue to be uniquely Mexican.

What will the future bring? How much will the pressures for change and the potential loss of national identity affect the nature of the political system? In 1980, few people could have foreseen the extensive economic policy reforms and pressures for democracy that Mexico would experience in the next two decades. Few would have predicted the defeat of the PRI in the elections of 2000 or the electoral outcome of 2006. In considering the future of the country, it is important to remember that Mexico has a long tradition of relatively strong institutions. It is not a country that will easily slip into sustained political instability. A tradition of constitutional government, a strong presidency, a political system that has incorporated a wide range of interests, little military involvement in politics, and a deep sense of national identity: these are among the factors that need to be considered in predicting the political consequences of democratization, economic integration, and greater social equality in Mexico.

Mexico represents a pivotal case of political and economic transition for the developing world. If it can successfully bridge the gap between its past and its future and move from centralization to effective local governance, from regional vulnerability to global interdependence, and from the control of the few to the participation of the many, it will set a model for other countries that face the same kind of challenges.

Key Terms ≫

mestizo	coup d'état
Amerindian	anticlericalism
indigenous groups	*ejidos*
maquiladoras	*ejidatarios*

sexenio

clientelism

North American Free Trade Agreement (NAFTA)

newly industrializing countries (NICs)

corporatist state

civil society

state capitalism

import substituting industrialization (ISI)

green revolution

informal sector

proportional representation (PR)

technocrats

para-statal

accommodation

Suggested Readings ⟩⟩

Babb, Sarah L. *Managing Mexico: Economists from National-ism to Neoliberalism.* Princeton, N.J.: Princeton University Press, 2001.

Bethell, Leslie, ed. *Mexico Since Independence.* Cambridge: Cambridge University Press, 1991.

Castañeda, Jorge G. *Perpetuating Power: How Mexican Presidents Were Chosen.* New York: New Press, 2000.

Chand, Vickram K. *Mexico's Political Awakening.* Notre Dame, Ind.: University of Notre Dame Press, 2001.

Collier, Ruth Berins. *The Contradictory Alliance: State-Labor Relations and Regime Change in Mexico.* Berkeley: University of California Press, 1992.

Cook, Maria Lorena, Middlebrook, Kevin J., and Molinar, Juan (eds.). *The Politics of Economic Restructuring in Mexico.* San Diego: Center for U.S.-Mexican Studies, University of California, 1994.

Cornelius, Wayne A. "Nation-Building, Participation, and Distribution: The Politics of Social Reform Under Cárdenas." In Gabriel A. Almond, Scott Flanagan, and Robert J. Mundt (eds.), *Crisis, Choice, and Change: Historical Studies of Political Development.* Boston: Little, Brown, 1973.

Cornelius, Wayne A., Eisenstadt, Todd A., and Hindley, Jane (eds.). *Subnational Politics and Democratization in Mexico.* San Diego: Center for U.S.-Mexican Studies, University of California, 1999.

Davidow, Jeffrey. *The U.S. and Mexico: The Bear and the Porcupine.* Princeton, N.J.: Markus Wiener Publishers, 2004.

Dominguez, Jorge I., and Lawson, Chappell H. (eds.). *Mexico's Pivotal Democratic Election: Candidates, Voters, and the Presidential Campaign of 2000.* Stanford, Calif.: Stanford University Press, 2004.

Durand, Jorge, Douglas S. Massey, and Emilio A. Parrado. "The New Era of Mexican Migration to the United States," *The Journal of American History* 86: 2 (September 1999).

Foweraker, Joe, and Craig, Ann L. (eds.), *Popular Movements and Political Change in Mexico.* Boulder, Colo.: Lynne Rienner, 1990.

Grindle, Merilee S. *Challenging the State: Crisis and Innovation in Latin America and Africa.* Cambridge: Cambridge University Press, 1995.

Harvey, Neil. *The Chiapas Rebellion: The Struggle for Land and Democracy.* Durham, N.C.: Duke University Press, 1998.

Krauze, Enrique. *Mexico, Biography of Power: A History of Modern Mexico, 1810–1996.* Trans. by Hank Heifetz. New York: HarperCollins, 1997.

Lawson, Chappell H. *Building the Fourth Estate: Democratization and the Rise of a Free Press in Mexico.* Berkeley: University of California, 2002.

Levy, Daniel C., and Bruhn, Kathleen. *Mexico: The Struggle for Democratic Development.* Berkeley: University of California Press, 2001.

Lustig, Nora. *Mexico: The Remaking of an Economy.* 2nd ed. Washington, D.C.: Brookings Institution, 1998.

Meyer, Michael C., Sherman, William L., and Deeds, Susan M. *The Course of Mexican History.* 7th ed. New York: Oxford University Press, 2002.

Paz, Octavio. *The Labyrinth of Solitude: Life and Thought in Mexico.* New York: Grove Press, 1961.

Preston, Julia, and Dillon, Samuel. *Opening Mexico: The Making of a Democracy.* New York: Farrar, Straus and Giroux, 2004.

Salinas de Gortari, Carlos. *México: The Policy and Politics of Modernization.* Trans. by Peter Hearn and Patricia Rosas. Barcelona: Plaza & Janés Editores, 2002.

Suárez-Orozco, Marcelo, ed. *Crossings: Mexican Immigration in Interdisciplinary Perspective.* Cambridge: Harvard University Press, 1998.

Ugalde, Luis Carlos. *The Mexican Congress: Old Player, New Power.* Washington, D.C.: Center for Strategic and International Studies, 2000.

Womack, John, Jr. *Zapata and the Mexican Revolution.* New York: Vintage Books, 1968.

Suggested Websites ≫

Office of the President (in Spanish and English)
www.presidencia.gob.mx
Secretariat of Foreign Relations (in Spanish and English)
www.sre.gob.mx
El Universal newspaper (in Spanish and English)
estadis.eluniversal.com.mx/noticiash.html
The Mexico Project, National Security Archive
www2.gwu.edu/~nsarchiv/mexico

Washington Post (registration required, free)
www.washingtonpost.com/wp-dyn/world/americas/
  northamerica/mexico
Federal Electoral Institute (in Spanish only)
www.ife.org.mx/portal/site/ifev2/

Endnotes ≫

[1]This figure represents an estimate of the metropolitan area of Mexico City, which extends beyond the official boundaries of the city.

[2]An excellent history of this event is presented in Wayne A. Cornelius, "Nation-Building, Participation, and Distribution: The Politics of Social Reform Under Cárdenas," in Gabriel A. Almond, Scott Flanagan, and Robert J. Mundt (eds.), *Crisis, Choice and Change: Historical Studies of Political Development* (Boston: Little, Brown, 1973).

[3]Michael C. Meyer and William K. Sherman, *The Course of Mexican History*, 5th ed. (New York: Oxford UP, 1995), pp. 598–599.

[4]Although the self-confessed "lone gunman" was jailed, the ensuing investigation raised concerns about a possible conspiracy involving party and law enforcement officials as well as drug cartels. Rumors circulated about a cover-up scandal. Eventually, skepticism about the integrity of the inquiry was so great that President Salinas called for a new investigation. At this point, little remains known about what exactly happened in Tijuana and why.

[5]United Nations Development Programme, *Human Development Report* (2006), http://hdr.undp.org/en/media/hdr_20072008_tables.pdf.

[6]World Bank, *World Development Indicators* database, August 2004, http://www.worldbank.org/data/countrydata/countrydata.html.

[7]World Bank, *World Development Report, 2001* (New York: Oxford University Press, 2001).

[8]Merilee S. Grindle, *State and Countryside: Development Policy and Agrarian Politics in Latin America* (Baltimore: Johns Hopkins University Press, 1986), p. 63, quoting President Avila Camacho (1940–1946).

[9]Kevin J. Middlebrook (ed.), *Unions, Workers, and the State in Mexico* (San Diego: Center for U.S.-Mexican Studies, University of California Press, 1991).

[10]Grindle, *State and Countryside*, pp. 79–111.

[11]For a description of this process, see Carlos Bazdresch and Santiago Levy, "Populism and Economic Policy in Mexico," in Rudiger Dornbusch and Sebastian Edwards (eds.), *The Macroeconomics of Populism in Latin America* (Chicago: University of Chicago Press, 1991), p. 72.

[12]For an assessment of the mounting problems of Mexico City and efforts to deal with them, see Diane E. Davis, *Urban Leviathan: Mexico City in the Twentieth Century* (Philadelphia: Temple University Press, 1994).

[13]Joe Foweraker and Ann L. Craig (eds.), *Popular Movements and Political Change in Mexico* (Boulder, Colo.: Lynne Rienner, 1989).

[14]Roger Hansen, *The Politics of Mexican Development* (Baltimore: Johns Hopkins University Press, 1971), p. 75.

[15]World Bank, *World Development Indicators, 2004*, p. 61.

[16]Economist Intelligence Unit, *Country Commerce, Mexico* (London: EIU, September 2001), p. 43.

[17]Daniel Levy and Gabriel Székely, *Mexico: Paradoxes of Stability and Change* (Boulder, Colo.: Westview Press, 1983), p. 100.

[18]See Luis Carlos Ugalde, *The Mexican Congress: Old Player, New Power* (Washington, D.C.: Center for International and Strategic Studies, 2000).

[19]See Chapell H. Lawson, *Building the Fourth Estate: Democratization and the Rise of a Free Press in Mexico* (Berkeley: University of California Press, 2002).

[20]Susan Eckstein (ed.), *Power and Popular Protest: Latin American Social Movements* (Berkeley: University of California Press, 1989).

[21]Wayne A. Cornelius and Ann L. Craig, "Politics in Mexico," in Gabriel Almond and G. Bingham Powell (eds.), *Comparative Politics Today,* 5th ed. (Boston: Scott Foresman, 1992), p. 502.

[22]Foweraker and Craig, *Popular Movements and Political Change in Mexico.*

Joan DeBardeleben

Chapter 11 ≫ RUSSIA

Section 1 The Making of the Modern Russian State
Section 2 Political Economy and Development
Section 3 Governance and Policy-Making
Section 4 Representation and Participation
Section 5 Russian Politics in Transition

Official Name: **Russian Federation (Rossiyskaya Federatsiya)**

Location: **Eastern Europe/ Northern Asia**

Capital City: **Moscow**

Population (2008): **141.4 million**

Size: **17,075,200 sq. km.; approximately 1.8 times the size of the United States**

1917
The Bolshevik seizure of power

1918–1928
Civil war, war communism, and the New Economic Policy

1929–1953
Stalin in power

1929–1938
Collectivization and purges

1953–1955
Leadership change after Stalin's death

1941–1945
Nazi Germany invades Soviet Union; "Great Patriotic War"

1956–1964
The Khrushchev era and de-Stalinization

1965–1982
The Brezhnev era and bureaucratic consolidation

1982–1985
Leadership change after Brezhnev's death

1985–1991
The Gorbachev era and *perestroika*

SECTION 1 The Making of the Modern Russian State

Politics in Action

On April 15, 2008, just before the end Vladimir Putin's final term as president of the Russian Federation, delegates of the dominant political party, United Russia, gathered in Moscow for a party congress. In a show of overwhelming enthusiasm, the party delegates unanimously approved the creation of the custom-made post for Putin as party chairman. Termed by some as a party of the "political establishment" of the Russian elite, United Russia enjoyed a meteoric rise during Putin's presidency. Up to 2008, Putin had refused membership or a formal role in any political party, including United

Russia, which had, de facto, been a vehicle for realizing his political dominance. But now Putin relented; he agreed to serve as chairman of the party but without party membership. At the same time Dmitry Medvedev, Putin's hand-picked newly elected successor as Russian president, the post having the strongest constitutional power, was also invited to join United Russia. But he declined. Both Putin and Medvedev maintained that a partisan president was a poor idea, but that Putin, as prime minister, should accept. As Putin said, "The fact that the head of a party occupies the position of prime minister is a perfectly civilized, natural, and traditional practice for democratic states."

FIGURE 11.1

The Russian Nation at a Glance

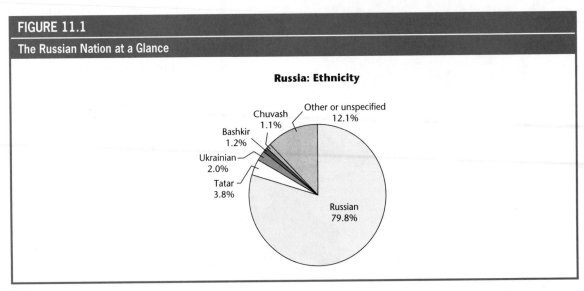

Russia: Ethnicity

Chuvash 1.1%
Other or unspecified 12.1%
Bashkir 1.2%
Ukrainian 2.0%
Tatar 3.8%
Russian 79.8%

That Putin would chair a party without membership in it is certainly unusual. To many, this seemed the logical outcome of the informal symbiotic relationship with United Russia that had undergirded Putin's ever-increasing control over political appointments and elite career mobility. Other observers saw the move as a way for Putin to cement his continuing political dominance after vacating the post of president. At a most fundamental level, however, this extraordinary arrangement, while in some ways mimicking structures present in Western parliamentary democracies, highlights the degree to which individual leaders dominate over institutions in the Russian context, as well as the readiness of the active public to accede authority to powerful figures, with few instruments to call them to account. Some scholars called this "democratic backsliding," while others mince no words and label it "authoritarian." However, this designation may be too simple, for while

Table 11.1

Political Organization

Political System	Constitutionally a federal state, presidential system
Regime History	Re-formed as an independent state with the collapse of communist rule in December 1991; current constitution since December 1993
Administrative Structure	Federal system, originally with eighty-nine subnational governments including twenty-one republics, fifty-five provinces (*oblast'*, *krai*), eleven autonomous districts or regions (*okrugs* or autonomous *oblast'*), and two cities of federal status. As of March 2008, the number of subnational governments was reduced to eighty-three, through a merger of regions.
Executive	Dual executive (president and prime minister). Direct election of president; prime minister appointed by the president with the approval of the lower house of the parliament (*State Duma*).
Legislature	Bicameral. Upper house (Federation Council) appointed by heads of regional executive and representative organs. Lower house (*State Duma*) is chosen by direct election, since 2007 by a proportional representation system for all 450 deputies. Prior to that, half of the 450 deputies were chosen through a proportional representation system and half from single-member constituencies. Powers include proposal and approval of legislation, approval of presidential appointees.
Judiciary	Independent constitutional court with nineteen justices, nominated by the president and approved by the Federation Council, holding twelve-year terms with possible renewal.
Party System	Multiparty system with a dominant party (United Russia)

power is increasingly centralized and elections are weak vehicles of democratic control, no doubt public support for Putin is real; whether it will be transferred to his presidential successor remains to be seen. Russia remains a polity in transformation, with no assured outcome and a potentially unstable trajectory. For these reasons, in *ICP,* we locate Russia in the transitional democracy category of our typology (see Chapter 1).

Geographic Setting

After the Soviet Union broke up in 1991, fifteen newly independent states emerged on its territory. This section focuses on the Russian Federation, the largest successor state and the largest European country in population (about 142 million in 2007) and, in area, the largest country in the world, spanning eleven time zones.

Russia underwent rapid industrialization and urbanization under Soviet rule. Only 18 percent of Russians lived in urban areas in 1917; 73 percent do now. Less than 8 percent of Russia's land is arable, while 45 percent is forested. Russia is rich in natural resources, concentrated in western Siberia and northern Russia. These include minerals (even gold and diamonds), timber, and oil and natural gas exports, which now form the basis of Russia's economic wealth.

The tsarist empire extended east to the Pacific, south to the Caucasus Mountains and the Muslim areas of Central Asia, north to the Arctic Circle, and west into present-day Ukraine, eastern Poland, and the Baltic states. Unlike the empires of Western Europe, with their far-flung colonial possessions, Russia's empire bordered its historic core. With its unprotected location spanning Europe and Asia, Russia had been repeatedly invaded and challenged for centuries. This exposure to outside intrusion encouraged an expansionist mentality among the leadership; some historians argue that this factor, combined with Russia's harsh climate, encouraged Russia's rulers to craft a centralizing and autocratic state.[1]

In the USSR, the Russian Republic formed the core of a multiethnic state. Russia's ethnic diversity and geographic scope have made it a hard country to govern. Currently Russia faces pockets of instability on several of its borders, most notably in Tajikistan and Afghanistan in Central Asia, and in Georgia and Azerbaijan on the southern border. Russia's western neighbors include Ukraine, Belarus, and several EU member states (Finland, Estonia, Latvia, Lithuania, and Poland). Located at a critical juncture between Europe, the Islamic world, and Asia, Russia's regional sphere of influence is now disputed.

Critical Junctures

The Russian Revolutions and the End of the Russian Tsarist State

Until the revolution of 1917, an autocratic system headed by the tsar ruled Russia. The historian Richard Pipes explains that before 1917, Russia had a **patrimonial state** that not only ruled the country but also owned the land.[2] The majority of the population (peasants) was tied to the nobles (through serfdom), the state, or the church. The serfs were emancipated in 1861 as a part of the tsar's efforts to modernize Russia and to make it militarily competitive with the West. Emancipation did not, however, destroy the traditional communal peasant organization in the countryside, and individual peasant farming did not develop in Russia on a significant scale.

A Russian bourgeoisie, or entrepreneurial class, also failed to emerge in Russia as it had in Western Europe. The key impetus for industrialization came from the Russian state and from foreign capital. As Russia industrialized, large factories emerged alongside small, private workshops. Trade unions were illegal until 1906, and even then their activities were carefully controlled. In the wake of the defeats in the Russo-Japanese war and continued tsarist repression, workers became increasingly discontented, alongside liberal intellectuals, students, and, later, peasants. Revolution broke out in 1905, involving widespread strikes in the cities and rural uprisings. The regime, however, maintained control through repression and economic reforms, until its collapse in 1917.

The Bolshevik Revolution and the Establishment of Soviet Power (1917–1929)

In March 1917, at the height of World War I, two revolutions occurred in Russia. The March revolution threw out the tsar (Nicholas II) and installed a moderate provisional government. In November,

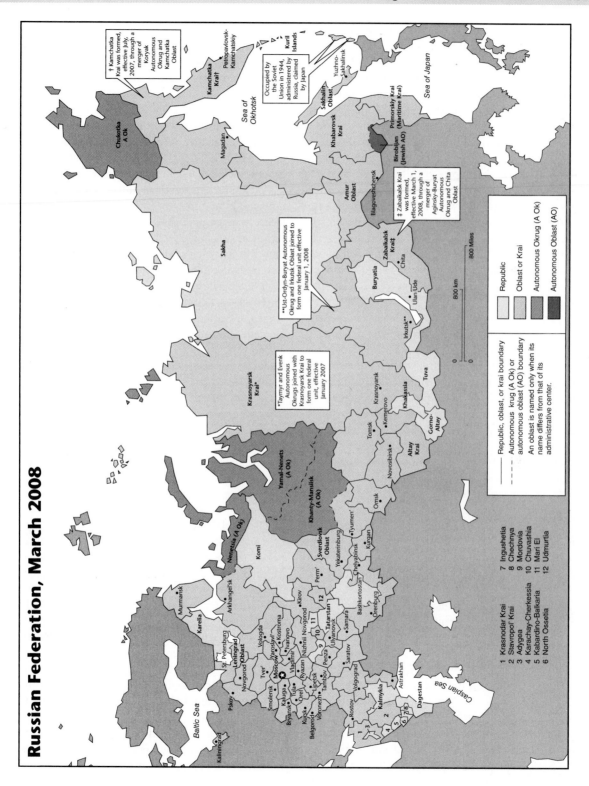

Russian Federation, March 2008

Legend:
- Republic
- Oblast or Krai
- Autonomous Okrug (A Ok)
- Autonomous Oblast (AO)

Republic, oblast, or krai boundary
Autonomous krug (A Ok) or autonomous oblast (AO) boundary

An oblast is named only when its name differs from that of its administrative center.

† Kamchatka Krai was formed, effective July, 2007, through a merger of Koryak Autonomous Okrug and Kamchatka Oblast

‡ Zabaikalsk Krai was formed, effective March 1, 2008, through a merger of Aginsky-Buryat Autonomous Okrug and Chita Oblast

**Ust-Ordyn-Buryat Autonomous Okrug and Irkutsk Oblast joined to form one federal unit effective January 1, 2008

*Taymyr and Evenk Autonomous Okrugs joined with Krasnoyarsk Krai to form one federal unit, effective January 2007

Occupied by the Soviet Union in 1944, administered by Russia, claimed by Japan

1 Krasnodar Krai
2 Stavropol' Krai
3 Adygea
4 Karachay-Cherkessia
5 Kabardino-Balkaria
6 North Ossetia
7 Ingushetia
8 Chechnya
9 Mordovia
10 Chuvashia
11 Mari El
12 Udmurtia

800 km
800 Miles

the Bolsheviks, led by Vladimir Lenin, overthrew that government. This second revolution marked a major turning point in the history of Russia. Instead of trying to imitate Western European patterns, the Bolsheviks applied a dramatically different blueprint for economic, social, and political development.

The Bolsheviks were a particular brand of Marxists; they believed their revolution reflected the political interests of a specific social class, the proletariat (working class). Most of the revolutionary leaders, however, were not themselves workers but came from a more educated and privileged stratum, the intelligentsia. But in 1917, the Bolsheviks' slogan, "Land, Peace, and Bread," appealed to both the working class and the discontented peasantry, which made up more than 80 percent of Russia's population.

The Bolsheviks formed a tightly organized political party based on their unique understanding of Marxism. Their strategy was founded on two key ideas: democratic centralism and vanguardism. **Democratic centralism** mandated a hierarchical party structure in which leaders were elected from below, but strict discipline was required in implementing party policy once a decision was made. Over time, the centralizing elements of democratic centralism took precedence over the democratic elements, as the party tried to insulate itself first from informants of the tsarist forces and later from both real and imagined threats to the new regime. The concept of a **vanguard party** governed the Bolsheviks' relations with broader social forces: party leaders claimed that they understood the interests of the working people better than the people did themselves. Over time, this philosophy was used to rationalize virtually all actions of the Communist Party and the state it dominated. Neither democratic centralism nor vanguardism emphasized democratic procedures or accountability of the leaders to the public. Rather, these concepts focused on achieving a "correct" political outcome that would reflect the "true" interests of the working class, as defined by the leaders of the party.

In 1922 the Bolsheviks formed the Union of Soviet Socialist Republics (USSR), henceforth referred to as the Soviet Union. The Bolsheviks took extraordinary measures to ensure the survival of the regime. The initial challenge was an extended civil war (1918–1921) for control of the countryside and outlying regions. The Bolsheviks introduced war communism to ensure the supply of materials necessary for the war effort. The state took control of key economic sectors and forcibly requisitioned grain from the peasants. The *Cheka,* the security arm of the regime, was strengthened, and restrictions were placed on other political groups, including other socialist parties. By 1921, the leadership recognized the political costs of war communism. In an effort to accommodate the peasantry, the New Economic Policy (NEP) was introduced in 1921 and lasted until 1928. State control over the economy was loosened so that private enterprise and trade were revived. The state, however, retained control of large-scale industry.

Gradually, throughout the 1920s, the authoritarian strains of Bolshevik thinking eclipsed the democratic elements. Lacking a democratic tradition and bolstered by the vanguard ideology of the party, the Bolshevik leaders were plagued by internal struggles following Lenin's death in 1924. These conflicts culminated in the rise of Joseph Stalin and the demotion or exile of prominent party figures such as Leon Trotsky and Nikolai Bukharin. Many observers saw Stalin as moving the Soviet Union definitively away from some of the original ideas of Lenin, while others saw Stalinism as a logical outcome of Lenin's vanguard concept. By 1929, all open opposition, even within the party itself, had been silenced.

The Bolshevik revolution also initiated a period of international isolation. To fulfill their promise of peace, the new rulers had to cede important chunks of territory to Germany under the Brest-Litovsk Treaty (1918), which was partially returned to Russia only after Germany was defeated by Russia's allies (the United States, Britain, and France). However, these countries were hardly pleased with Russia's revolution, which led to the expropriation of foreign holdings and which represented the first successful challenge to the capitalist order. The former allies sent material aid and troops to oppose the new Bolshevik government during the civil war. Lenin had hoped that successful working-class revolutions in Germany and other Western countries would bolster the fledgling Soviet regime. When this did not occur, Stalin developed the idea of building "socialism in one country," which defined Soviet state interests as synonymous with the promotion of socialism. To survive in such isolation, the new Soviet state pursued a policy of rapid industrialization and increased political control.

The Stalin Revolution (1929–1953)

From 1929 until his death in 1953, Stalin consolidated his power as Soviet leader by establishing the basic characteristics of the Soviet regime that substantially endured until the collapse of the communist system in 1991. Stalin brought changes to virtually every aspect of Soviet life. The state became the engine for rapid economic development, with state ownership and control of virtually all economic assets (land, factories, housing, and stores). By 1935, more than 90 percent of agricultural land had been taken from the peasants and made into state or collective farms. This **collectivization** campaign was justified as a means of preventing the emergence of a new capitalist class in the countryside, but it actually targeted the peasantry as a whole, leading to widespread famine and the death of millions. Survivors who resisted were arrested or exiled to Siberia. In the industrial sector, a program of rapid industrialization favored heavy industries (steel mills, hydroelectric dams, machine building); production of consumer goods was neglected. Economic control operated through a complex but inefficient system of central economic planning, in which the state planning committee (Gosplan) set production targets for every enterprise in the country. Under the influence of rapid industrialization, people were uprooted from their traditional lives in the countryside and catapulted into the rhythm of urban industrial life. Media censorship and state control of the arts strangled creativity as well as political opposition. The party/state became the authoritative source of truth; anyone deviating from the authorized interpretation could be charged with treason.

In the early 1920s, the Communist Party was the only political party permitted to function, and by the early 1930s, open opposition or dissent within the party was eliminated. Gradually, the party became subject to the personal whims of Stalin and his secret police. Party bodies ceased to meet on a regular basis, and they no longer made important political decisions. Party ranks were periodically cleansed of potential opponents, and previous party leaders as well as citizens from many other walks of life were violently purged (arrested, sentenced to labor camps, sometimes executed). Overall, an estimated 5 percent of the Soviet population was arrested at one point or another under the Stalinist system, usually for no apparent cause. The arbitrary and unpredictable terror of the 1930s left a legacy of fear. Only among trusted friends and family members did people dare to express their true views. Forms of resistance, when they occurred, were evasive rather than active: peasants killed their livestock to avoid giving it over to collective farms; laborers worked inefficiently, and absenteeism was high.

Isolation of the Soviet citizen from interaction with the outside world was a key tool of Stalinist control. Foreign news broadcasts were jammed; travel abroad was highly restricted; and contacts with foreigners brought citizens under suspicion. The economy was isolated from interaction with the international economic system. Although this policy shielded Soviet society from the effects of the Great Depression of the 1930s, which shook the capitalist world, it also allowed an inefficient system of production to survive in the USSR. Protected from foreign competition, the economy failed to keep up with the rapid pace of economic and technological transformation in the West.

In 1941, Nazi Germany invaded the Soviet Union, and Stalin had little choice but to join the Allied powers. Wartime casualties were high, about 27 million people, including 19 million civilians. Therefore, it is no wonder that even today those wartime sacrifices and losses are frequently recalled, since World War II had such a profound impact on the outlook of an entire generation of Soviet citizens. Soviet propaganda dubbed it the Great Patriotic War, evoking images of Russian nationalism rather than of socialist internationalism; the sacrifices and heroism of the war period remained a powerful symbol of Soviet pride and unity until the collapse of communist power. The war period was marked by support for traditional family values and a greater tolerance for religious institutions, whose support Stalin sought for the war effort. Among the social corollaries of the war effort were a declining birthrate and a long-lasting gender imbalance as a result of high wartime casualties among men. The war also affected certain minority ethnic groups that were accused of collaborating with the enemy during the war effort and were deported to areas farther east in the USSR. These included Germans, Crimean Tatars, and peoples of the northern Caucasus regions such as the Chechens, Ingush, and Karachai-Balkar. Their later rehabilitation and resettlement caused renewed disruption and conflict, contributing to the ethnic conflicts of the post–Soviet period.

The Soviet Union was a major force in the defeat of the Axis powers in Europe. After the war, the other Allied powers allowed the Soviet Union to absorb new territories into the USSR itself (these became the Soviet republics of Latvia, Lithuania, Estonia, Moldavia, and portions of western Ukraine), and they implicitly granted the USSR free rein to shape the postwar governments and economies in eastern Germany, Poland, Hungary, Czechoslovakia, Yugoslavia, Bulgaria, and Romania. American offers to include parts of the region in the Marshall Plan were rejected under pressure from the USSR. With Soviet support, local communist parties gained control of all of these countries; only in Yugoslavia were indigenous communist forces sufficiently strong to gain power largely on their own and thus later to assert their independence from Moscow.

Following World War II, the features of Soviet communism were largely replicated in those areas newly integrated into the USSR and in the countries of Eastern Europe. The Soviet Union tried to isolate its satellites in Eastern Europe from the West and to tighten their economic and political integration with the USSR. The Council for Mutual Economic Assistance (CMEA) and the Warsaw Treaty Organization (a military alliance) were formed for this purpose. With its developed industrial economy, its military stature bolstered in World War II, and its growing sphere of regional control, the USSR emerged as a global superpower. But the enlarged Soviet bloc still remained insulated from the larger world of states. Some countries within the Soviet bloc, however, had strong historic links to Western Europe (especially Czechoslovakia, Poland, and Hungary), and in these areas, domestic resistance

to Soviet dominance forced some alterations or deviations from the Soviet model. Over time, these countries served not only as geographic buffers to direct Western influence on the USSR but also as conduits for such influence. In the more Westernized Baltic republics of the USSR itself, the population firmly resisted assimilation to Soviet rule and eventually spearheaded the disintegration of the Soviet Union in the late 1980s.

Attempts at De-Stalinization (1953–1985)

Stalin's death in 1953 triggered another critical juncture in Soviet politics. Even the Soviet elite realized that Stalin's system of terror could be sustained only at great cost to the development of the country. The terror destroyed initiative and innovation, and the unpredictability of Stalinist rule inhibited the rational formulation of policy. The period from Stalin's death until the mid-1980s saw a regularization and stabilization of Soviet politics. Terror abated, but political controls remained in place, and efforts to isolate Soviet citizens from foreign influences continued.

Nikita Khrushchev, who succeeded Stalin as the party leader from 1955 until his removal in 1964, embarked on a bold policy of de-Stalinization. Although his specific policies were only minimally successful, he initiated a thaw in political and cultural life, an approach that planted the seeds that ultimately undermined the Stalinist system. Khrushchev rejected terror as an instrument of political control and revived the Communist Party as a vital political institution. The secret police (KGB) was subordinated to party authority, and party meetings were resumed on a regular basis. However, internal party structures remained highly centralized, and elections were uncontested. In the cultural sphere, Khrushchev allowed sporadic liberalization, with the publication in the official media of some literature critical of the Stalinist system.

Leonid Brezhnev, Khrushchev's successor, who headed the party from October 1964 until his death in 1982, partially reversed the de-Stalinization efforts of the 1950s and early 1960s. Controls tightened again in the cultural sphere. Individuals who expressed dissenting views (members of the so-called dissident movement) through underground publishing or publication abroad were harassed, arrested, or exiled. However, unlike in the Stalinist period, the political repression was predictable: people knew when they were transgressing permitted limits of criticism. The Brezhnev regime could be described as primarily bureaucratic and conservative, seeking to maintain existing power structures rather than to introduce new ones.

During the Brezhnev era, a **tacit social contract** with the population governed state-society relations.[3] In exchange for political compliance, the population enjoyed job security; a lax work environment; low prices for basic goods, housing, and transport; free social services (medical care, recreational services); and minimal interference in personal life. Wages of the worst-off citizens were increased relative to those of the more educated and better-off portions of the population. The intelligentsia was allowed more freedom to discuss publicly issues that were not of crucial importance to the regime.

From the late 1970s onward, an aging political leadership was increasingly ineffective at addressing the mounting problems facing Soviet society. Economic growth rates fell, living standards improved only minimally, and opportunities for upward career mobility declined. To maintain the Soviet Union's superpower status, resources were diverted to the military sector, gutting the capacity of the consumer and agricultural spheres to satisfy popular expectations. The costs of exploiting new resource deposits (mostly in Siberia) soared. High pollution levels affected health through higher morbidity rates and declining life expectancy. At the same time, liberalization in some Eastern European states and the telecommunications revolution made it increasingly difficult to shield the population from exposure to Western lifestyles and ideas. Among a certain critical portion of the population, aspirations were rising just as the capacity of the system to fulfill them was declining.

Perestroika and Glasnost (1985–1991)

Mikhail Gorbachev took office as a Communist Party leader in March 1985 at the relatively young age of fifty-three. He endorsed a reform program that centered around four important concepts intended to spur economic growth and bring political renewal without undermining Communist Party rule. These were *perestroika, glasnost, demokratizatsiia,* and "new thinking." ***Perestroika*** (restructuring) involved decentralization and rationalization of economic structures to enable individual enterprises to increase efficiency and take initiative. The central planning system was to be reformed, but not disbanded. To counteract the resistance of entrenched central bureaucracies, Gorbachev enlisted the support of the intelligentsia, who benefited from his policy of *glasnost*. ***Glasnost*** (openness) involved relaxing controls on public debate and allowing diverse viewpoints to be aired. ***Demokratizatsiia*** was an effort to increase the responsiveness of political organs to public sentiment, both within and outside the party, introducing some elements of competitive elections and the formation of public interest groups. Finally, "***new thinking***" referred to a foreign policy approach involving integration of the USSR into the global economy and emphasizing the common challenges facing East and West, such as the cost and hazards of the arms race and environmental degradation.[4] Gorbachev's reform program was designed to adapt the communist system to new conditions rather than to usher in its demise.

Gorbachev's policies triggered a fundamental change in the relationship between state and society in the USSR. Citizens pursued their interests and beliefs through a variety of newly created organizations at the national and local levels. These included ethnonationalist movements, environmental groups, groups for the rehabilitation of Stalinist victims, charitable groups, new or reformed professional organizations, political clubs, and many others. The existence of these groups implicitly challenged the Communist Party's monopoly of power. By March 1990, pressures from within and outside the party forced the Supreme Soviet (the Soviet parliament) to rescind Article 6 of the Soviet constitution, which provided the basis for single-party rule. Embryonic political parties challenged the Communist Party's monopoly of political control. In the spring of 1989, the first contested elections since the 1920s were held for positions in the Soviet parliament. These were followed by elections at the republic and local levels in 1990, which, in some cases, put leaders in power that pushed for increased republic and regional autonomy.

The most divisive issues facing Gorbachev were economic policy and demands for republic autonomy. Only 50.8 percent of the Soviet population was ethnically Russian in 1989. In several of the fourteen non-Russian republics that made up the USSR, popular front organizations formed. First in the three Baltic republics (Latvia, Lithuania, and Estonia) and then in other union republics (particularly Ukraine, Georgia, Armenia, Moldovia [later renamed Moldova], and Russia itself), demands for national autonomy and, in some cases, for secession from the USSR, were put forth. Gorbachev's efforts failed to bring consensus on a new federal system as popular support and elite self-interest took on an irreversible momentum, resulting in a "separatism mania."

Gorbachev's economic policies failed as well. Half-measures sent contradictory messages to enterprise directors, producing a drop in output and undermining established patterns that had kept the Soviet economy functioning, albeit inefficiently. To protect themselves, regions and union republics began to restrict exports to other regions, despite planning mandates. In a "war of laws," regional officials openly defied central directives. In response, Gorbachev issued numerous decrees; their number increased as their efficacy declined.

Gorbachev achieved his greatest success in foreign policy. Just as his domestic support was plummeting, he was awarded the Nobel Peace Prize in 1991, reflecting his esteemed international stature. Under his "new thinking", the military buildup in the USSR was halted, important arms control agreements were ratified, and many controls on international contacts were lifted. In 1989, Gorbachev refused to prop up unpopular communist governments in the East European countries. First in Hungary and Poland, then in the German Democratic Republic (East Germany) and Czechoslovakia, pressure from below pushed the communist parties out of power, and a process of democratization and market reform ensued. To Gorbachev's dismay, the liberation of Eastern Europe fed the process of disintegration in the Soviet Union itself. Politicians in both East and West declared the cold war over.

Collapse of the USSR and Establishment of the Russian Federation (1991 to the Present)

In 1985 Mikhail Gorbachev drafted Boris Yeltsin into the leadership team as a nonvoting member of the USSR's top party organ, the Politburo. Little did he know the pivotal role that Yeltsin would play in bringing about the final demise of the Soviet Union. In 1991, Yeltsin became president of the Russian Republic through direct popular vote, establishing his democratic credentials. Shortly after, in August 1991, a coalition of conservative figures attempted a coup d'état, and temporarily removed Gorbachev from the Soviet leadership post. While Gorbachev was held captive at his summer house (*dacha*), Boris Yeltsin climbed atop a tank loyal to the reform leadership and rallied opposition to the attempted coup. Yeltsin declared himself the true champion of democratic values and Russian national interest. In December 1991, Yeltsin joined the leaders of Ukraine and Belorussia (later renamed Belarus) to declare the end of Soviet rule and formation of a loosely structured entity, called the Commonwealth of Independent States.

With this move, the Russian Federation stepped out as an independent country. As its leader, Yeltsin took a more radical approach to reform than Gorbachev had done. He quickly proclaimed his commitment to Western-style democracy and market economic reform. However, that program was controversial and proved hard to implement. Yeltsin's economic reform program presented Russians with an increasingly uncertain future, declining real wages, and high inflation. The Russian parliament, elected in 1990, mirrored popular skepticism, producing a political stalemate. The executive and legislative branches of the government failed to reach consensus on the nature of a new Russian constitution; the result was a bloody showdown in October 1993, after Yeltsin disbanded what he considered to be an obstructive parliament and laid siege to its premises, the Russian White House. The president mandated new elections and a constitutional referendum in December 1993. The constitution, adopted by a narrow margin, put in place a set of institutions marked by a powerful president and a relatively weak parliament. Even with enhanced powers, Yeltsin was unable to halt rising levels of corruption, crime, and social decline.

Yeltsin's initial popularity was also marred by an extended military conflict to prevent Chechnya, a southern republic of the Russia, from seceding from the federation. Several times earlier, both prior to incorporation into the Russian Empire in 1859 and again after the Bolshevik revolution in 1917, local forces had fought unsuccessfully to maintain the independence of this largely Muslim area. During World War II, following an anti-Soviet uprising, Stalin deported hundreds of Chechens to Soviet Central Asia. In response to Chechen separatist efforts, Russian military forces intervened in December 1994, apparently fearing that sentiment could spread to other regions. The costly and poorly managed war drew widespread criticism and became an important issue in the 1996 presidential campaign. A cease-fire agreement signed in May 1996 only temporarily abated the conflict but did help to assure Yeltsin's electoral victory. In 1999, terrorist bombings, attributed to Chechen rebels, occurred in apartment buildings in Moscow and two other Russian cities, causing about 300 deaths. The second war in Chechnya was launched, this time with greater popular support.

In August and September 1998, a major financial crisis triggered a political one. Plagued by poor health and an increasingly evident alcohol problem, in 1999 Yeltsin nominated a surprise candidate to the post of prime minister of Russia. Vladimir Putin, a little-known figure from St. Petersburg, was a former KGB operative in East Germany. His political advance was swift, and the rise in his popularity was equally meteoric. In December 1999, Yeltsin resigned as president of the Russian Federation. In the March 2000 elections, Putin won a resounding victory.

After September 11, 2001

Putin's tenure as president, which continued until May 2008, benefited from auspicious conditions, as high international gas and oil prices fed tax dollars into the state's coffers. In 1999, the economy experienced its first real growth in over a decade, a trend that has continued into the new millennium but which could be threatened by the financial crisis that developed in 2008. Putin recorded consistently high levels of popular support throughout his tenure and in 2008 successfully managed the transition of his handpicked successor, Dmitry Medvedev, to president. However, despite these positive signs, since 2000 Russia has been characterized by a drift to authoritarianism, categorized by many observers as a "democratic backslider."[5]

Since 2000, Russia has become increasingly self-assertive in the international sphere, facilitated by the country's economic recovery and energy wealth. Following the attacks on the World Trade Center and the Pentagon on September 11, 2001, President Putin expressed solidarity with the U.S. in the struggle against terrorism. Terrorist attacks in Russia reinforced a sense of common purpose. However, unanimity with the United States quickly unraveled, as Russia withheld its support for the American incursion into Iraq and as Russian leaders became concerned about increasing American influence in neighbouring Georgia and post–Soviet Central Asia, and about the American proposal to install an antimissile defense system in Poland and the Czech Republic. Western support for Kosovo's independence from Serbia and the American support for NATO membership for Ukraine and Georgia emerged as other conflict points. A turning point was the 2004 Orange Revolution in Ukraine, a successful popular protest against a fraudulent election. The Russian press emphasized the role of foreign financial support for the protestors, who advocated a more pro-Western orientation for Ukraine. A further crisis point occurred in August 2008 when Russian forces intervened militarily to prevent the Georgian government from attempting to regain control of the regions of South Ossetia and Abkazia, which, although formally part of Georgia, were effectively in the Russian orbit of influence through the presence of Russian peacekeepers.

Russia itself has suffered a string of terrorist attacks since 1999 that had initially been related to the Chechen separatist movement but later developed stronger international ties. Several serious incidents occurred following 9/11. On October 23, 2002, more

Russia

Current Challenges

Terrorism: The Russian Case

Over the past several years the threat of terrorism has been a reality for Russians. Among the most disturbing instances were bombings of several residential apartment buildings in Moscow and Volgodonsk in 1999, a hostage-taking in a popular Moscow theatre in 2002, bombings in and outside the Moscow subway, and a school hostage-taking in the southern town of Beslan in 2004.

Unlike the terrorist threat facing the United States, attacks in Russia initially had indigenous roots in the separatist region of Chechnya. Terrorism became a tool of Chechen militants in the face of Russian military efforts to defeat separatist forces. In several terrorist incidents, female suicide bombers, the so-called "black widows" of fallen Chechen militants, played a visible role.

Because Russia is a multiethnic state with several Muslim population groups, Russian authorities have had to be careful not to give anti-terrorist rhetoric an anti-Muslim tone. As President Putin noted in 2004, "it is obvious that . . . to vent anger towards terrorists against people of different beliefs or ethnicities is absolutely unacceptable, and in a country with such a diversity of religions and ethnicities it is completely destructive." Furthermore, he emphasized that it is a goal of terrorists themselves to undermine Russian unity not only by pushing for Chechen separatism, but also by driving a wedge of distrust and hostility between diverse ethnic and religious groups. According to Putin, the battle against the terrorist threat is "truly a fight for the unity of the country."[1] Over time, linkages between Russian terrorist groups and international Islamic fundamentalist organizations have taken on increasing importance.

It has been difficult for Russian authorities to isolate terrorist elements because of the indigenous roots of the grievances that initially triggered the attacks. Ethnic profiling has in fact tainted both government actions and popular sentiments. Individuals with a south Caucasian appearance have felt themselves subject to various forms of harassment, including complaints of arbitrary identity checks, planting of drugs and weapons, and obstruction of registration for residence permits.[2] On the other hand, more recently the Russian government has attempted to undermine the terrorist appeal in Chechnya and surrounding areas by offering a general amnesty for former rebels who had never been convicted of crimes and who agreed to lay down their arms.

In terms of policy, recent amendments to a 1998 anti-terrorism law place restrictions on the media in disseminating information that might hinder or prevent counter-terrorist measures, some critics view these measures as potentially placing restrictions on freedom of speech. Efforts to combat terrorism have become increasingly centralized since the Beslan crisis. In 2006, the FSB (the Federal Security Service, successor to the KGB) was granted the main coordinating role in the form of a "National Anti-terrorist Committee." The Beslan tragedy also led to a broadened legal definition of terrorism that critics felt could be used to ban antigovernment meetings or demonstrations.

[1] Speech at a meeting of the Presidential Council for Coordination with Religious Organisations, Sept. 29, 2004, website of the President of Russia http://www.kremlin.ru/appears/2004/09/29/1659_type63374type63376type63378type82634_77347.shtml.

[2] Human Rights Watch Briefing Paper, "On the Situation of Ethnic Chechens in Moscow," February 24, 2003, http://www.hrw.org/backgrounder/eca/russia032003.htm.

than 700 hostages were held by bomb-laden terrorists in a Moscow theater; at least 120 died, including the hostage-takers. In August 2004, two Russian passenger planes crashed simultaneously, killing at least eighty-nine passengers. Other attacks targeted schools, apartment buildings, and public transport. A galvanizing event was the hostage-taking in the town of Beslan in southern Russia on September 1, 2004. On the first day of school, terrorist forces herded 1,000 children and family members into the gymnasium. Not permitting the victims food or water, the hostage-takers made demands that were unacceptable

Following the presidential election of March 2008, the new Russian president, Dmitry Medvedev, nominated the highly popular former president, Vladimir Putin, to serve as his prime minister. *Source:* AP Images/ITAR-TASS, Presidential Press Service, Vladimir Rodionov.

to the Russian government: the removal of Russian troops from neighboring Chechnya and the release of Chechen rebels held by the government. On Friday, September 3—fifty-two hours later—in response to an explosion inside the school, Russia special forces stormed the building in an effort to release the victims. More than 300 of the 1,000 hostages—the majority children—were dead.

Meanwhile, in March 2003, Russian authorities tried to set Chechnya on a track of normalization, holding a referendum that would confirm Chechnya's status within the Russian Federation. However, the president of Chechnya, elected with Russian support, was killed by Chechen rebels. In March 2005 and July 2006, former Chechen president Aslan Maskhadov and the radical insurgent leader Shamil Basayev were killed by Russian forces. In 2008, a tenuous stability characterized the republic, badly damaged by more than a decade of violent conflict.

Terrorist incidents provided Putin with an added justification for a radical recentralization of political power. Following the Beslan tragedy, Putin announced reforms that eliminated elections of regional governors, making them more dependent on the president; new legislation presented obstacles to nongovernmental organizations with foreign connections. A counterterrorism law made

it easier to restrict press freedom and civil liberties in the face of alleged terrorist threats.

Just as economic growth revived, worries about security increased. While Western experts debated whether authoritarian tendencies might yet be reversed, many Russians were just hoping that the enhanced powers would help ensure a secure and stable way of life.

Themes and Implications

Historical Junctures and Political Themes

Following the collapse of the USSR in 1991, international support for the new reform-oriented government in Russia surged, with the proliferation of aid programs and international financial credits. In the 1990s, Russia's status as a world power waned, and the expansion of Western organizations (NATO, EU) to Russia's western border undermined its sphere of influence in Central and Eastern Europe. Russia's eastern neighbors, except Belarus, looked more to Europe than to Russia as a guidepost for the future. But Russia's economic recovery, the rise of energy prices, and Europe's dependence on imports of Russian natural gas and oil provided an important basis for Russia's renewed international influence. No longer simply a supplicant in its relationship to the West, Russia reasserted its role as a major European power under Putin's leadership. However, Russia's defense of a disputed presidential election outcome during Ukraine's Orange Revolution in November 2004 suggested the primacy of Russian national interest over democratic values. With its "near abroad," Russia has had difficulties establishing itself as a respected regional leader. At the same time, by 2008 tensions between Russia and the West had reached a level unprecedented in the post-communist period.

For nearly a decade after the collapse of the Soviet system, the Russian Federation seemed mired in a downward spiral of economic collapse and political paralysis. By the late 1990s, the Russian public was disillusioned and distrustful of its leaders, and resentment remained over the dismal results of the Western-inspired reform program.

After 1998, however, growth rates recovered, budget surpluses became routine, and the population experienced marked increase in economic confidence. Questions arose, however, about the depth of the apparent economic recovery, reinforced by the 2008 financial crisis and ensuing global recession. Some experts attribute the economic turnaround to high oil prices rather than to effective government policy, global economic trends will likely push Russia back into a renewed slump. At the same time, wide disparities in wealth and income, as well as important regional inequalities, continue to plague the system. Although many important policy problems have been addressed, others remain unresolved, including inadequate levels of foreign investment, capital flight, continuing high levels of inequality, the decline in the agricultural sector, and corruption. Furthermore, in 2005, reforms of the welfare system elicited broad public protest, as vulnerable groups feared a collapse of the social safety net they rely on for basic subsistence. The public remains skeptical of many features of a market economic system, which feeds suspicions that public optimism could easily turn sour in the face of a new economic jolt, such as occurred in 1998 and was developing in 2008.

Concerns about the fate of Russian democracy have also become widespread in the West as well as among certain groups inside Russia. On the positive side, the constitution adopted in 1993 has gained a surprising level of public acceptance, even as observers express intensifying concern that key reforms adopted after 2000 may be undermining real political competition. The regime justifies these changes as necessary to ensure state capacity to govern and to secure continuing economic growth, but critics see the Russian desire for order as leading the country down an authoritarian path with only the trappings of political democracy, under the tutorship of a dominant establishment political party, United Russia.

Finally, Russians continue to seek new forms of collective identity. The loss of superpower status, the dominance of Western economic and political models in the 1990s, and the absence of a widely accepted ideology have all contributed to uncertainty about what it means to be Russian and where Russia fits into the world as a whole. Meanwhile, Russia itself suffers from internal divisions. Although overt separatism has been limited to the Republic of Chechnya, differing visions of collective identity have emerged in some of Russia's ethnic republics, particularly in Muslim areas. A revival of Russian nationalism, directed partly at the West and partly at non-Christian ethnic minority groups, is a phenomenon of increasing concern. Other aspects of identity, including social class and gender roles, are also being reconsidered.

Implications for Comparative Politics

Many countries in the world today are attempting a transition from authoritarian rule to democratic governance. In Russia's case, one of the most important factors affecting this process is the tradition of strong state control, stretching from tsarist times through the Soviet period, and now influencing present developments. In addition, the intertwined character of politics, economics, and ideology in the Soviet Union has made democratization and economic reform difficult to realize at the same time. In effect, four transition processes were initiated simultaneously in the early 1990s: democratization, market reform, a redefinition of national identity, and integration into the world economy. Whereas other democratizing countries may have undergone one or two of these transitions, Russia initially tried to tackle all four at once. The difficulties of extricating political from economic power are particularly stark. Because the former communist elites had no private wealth to fall back on, corrupt or illegal methods were sometimes used to maintain former privileges—methods taken over by Russia's new capitalist class. Citizens, confronted with economic decline and an ideological vacuum, have been susceptible to appeals for strong state control, as well as nationalist appeals. No doubt economic uncertainty has made the Russian public willing to accept strong leadership and limits on political expression that would be resisted in many Western countries. Russia's current "backsliding" from democratic development may, in part, reflect the difficulties of pursuing so many transitions at once.

Political Economy and Development

The collapse of the Soviet system in late 1991 ushered in a sea change, radically reducing the state's traditionally strong role in economic development and opening the Russian economy to foreign influence. However, the process of market reform that the Russian government pursued after 1991 brought with it a dramatic decline in economic performance as well as fundamental changes in social relationships. To respond, the Russian government struggled to create tools to regulate the new market forces and to manage impacts of global economic forces. Since 1999, after experiencing an unprecedented period of economic depression from 1991 to 1998, Russia has experienced renewed economic growth, but this growth has been built largely on the country's wealth of energy and natural resources. Extreme levels of social inequality and corruption remain, so that the relative costs and benefits of Russia's transition from a state-run economy to some form of quasimarket system are still contested.

State and Economy

Under the Soviet command economy, land, factories, and all other important economic assets belonged to the state. Short- and long-term economic plans defined production goals, but these were frequently too ambitious to be fulfilled. Productivity and efficiency were low in Soviet enterprises, and innovation was not rewarded. Except in the illegal black market and peasant market, prices were controlled by the state. Firms and individuals were not permitted to develop direct links to foreign partners; these were all channeled through the central economic bureaucracy. This international isolation shielded the economy from economic recessions and depressions that plagued Western economies, but lacking foreign competition, the quality of many Russian consumer goods was low by international standards. Both producers and consumers were denied access to many advances available in Western industrial societies.

Because enterprises were weakly motivated by the need to turn a profit, they had neither the incentives nor the resources to increase production of goods in short supply or to respond to consumer demand. Retail stores piled up stocks of unwanted goods, while goods in high demand were often unavailable. Shortages forced citizens to wait in line for basic items.

Environmental quality deteriorated under Soviet rule because ecological goals were subordinate to production quotas. Large nature-transforming projects (hydroelectric dams, huge factory complexes) were glorified as symbols of Soviet power. Energy intensity was among the highest in the world, and many priority industries (metallurgy, machine building, chemicals, energy production) were highly polluting, resulting in a visibly higher incidence of respiratory and other ailments. Inadequate technological safeguards and an insufficient regulatory structure led to the disastrous nuclear accident at Chernobyl (in Ukraine) in 1986, which contaminated immense areas of agricultural land in Ukraine and Belorussia (now Belarus), as well as some areas of Russia.

Despite these weaknesses, the Soviet economic model registered some remarkable achievements: rapid industrialization, provision of social welfare and mass education, relatively low levels of inequality, and advances in key economic sectors such as the military and space industries. Nonetheless, over time, the top-heavy nature of Soviet planning and the isolation of the Soviet economy could no longer deliver increased prosperity at home and competitive products for export. These inadequacies spurred Mikhail Gorbachev to initiate his program of restructuring (*perestroika*). However, Gorbachev's efforts to reform the economic system were halting and contradictory. The results were declining economic performance, increasing regionalism, and an uncertain economic environment. Only after the collapse of the USSR in 1991 did a concerted effort at fundamental economic change take place.

State and Economy in the Russian Federation

In 1992, Boris Yeltsin immediately endorsed radical **market reform**, sometimes referred to as **shock therapy**. The changes were to be rapid and thorough, jolting the Russian economy into a new mode of operation. Although shock therapy would inevitably throw large parts of the economy into a downward spin, reformers hoped that the recovery would be relatively quick and that citizens would accept short-term economic sacrifices, including rising unemployment and higher prices, in order to achieve longer-term economic benefits.

Four main pillars of reform were lifting price controls, encouraging small private businesses, privatizing most state-owned enterprises, and opening the economy to international influences. According to the concept underlying the reforms, economic decision-making would be turned over to new private owners, who would be forced to respond to consumer demands and to increase efficiency and quality by exposure to a competitive economic environment governed by market prices. The more open economic environment would attract foreign investment capital, eliminating the need for state subsidies, and helping to make firms internationally competitive. However, in practice the policies had dramatically negative consequences for most Russian citizens. The consumer price index increased by about 2,500 percent between December 1991 and December 1992, and real wages (after controlling for the effects of inflation), on average, declined by an estimated 50 percent between late 1991 and January 1993. International lenders, most notably the International Monetary Fund (IMF), placed strict conditions on Russian loans in order to try to control inflationary tendencies, but the restrictions on the money supply that these policies implied produced their own problems.[6]

Some private business activity was allowed even in the late Soviet period, but private entrepreneurs were more actively encouraged by the new Russian leadership. However, these new ventures faced a number of obstacles, which included confusing regulations, high taxes, lack of capital, and a poor infrastructure (transport, banking, communications) for doing business. With the breakdown of the Soviet distribution system, trade became the most lucrative arena for upstart businesses. These included thousands of small kiosks on city streets; over time, the most successful moved into permanent quarters, alongside a wide range of restaurants, cafes, and entertainment establishments. Although the number of small businesses increased quickly in the early 1990s, they have provided a smaller proportion of employment and GNP, compared to most European countries.

Another important component of the government's program was rapid privatization of the state sector. In 1992, a privatization law was passed, and by early 1994, an estimated 80 percent of medium-sized and large state enterprises in designated sectors of the economy had been transformed into **joint-stock companies**. The most widely adopted method for privatizing state enterprises gave managers and workers of the enterprise (jointly) the right to acquire a controlling packet (51 percent) of enterprise shares at virtually symbolic prices. Each citizen of Russia was issued a **privatization voucher** with a nominal value of 10,000 rubles (about ten U.S. dollars). This privatization method allowed workers to use these vouchers to acquire shares in the enterprises where they worked. Many experts consider that this approach, called **insider privatization**, placed substantial obstacles to reform of business operations because it made managers reluctant to increase efficiency by firing excess labor, which kept work discipline lax. Some managers extracted personal profit from enterprise operations rather than investing available funds to improve production. In addition, many managers did not have the necessary skills to restructure enterprise operations effectively, and some resisted badly needed outside investment that might threaten insider ownership. This path also did not bring real workers' control; protection of shareholder rights was weak, so that savvy managers found ways, over time, to buy out worker shares or prevent workers from having a real impact on decision-making. In August 2001, legislation strengthening shareholder rights was signed by the president.

In 1995, the second stage of privatization was launched. At that point, firms could sell remaining shares for cash or investment guarantees. However, this phase of privatization proceeded much more slowly than expected. Many enterprises were unattractive to potential Russian and foreign investors because they were white elephants with backward technology that would require massive infusions of capital for restructuring. Some of the more attractive enterprises (in sectors such as oil and gas production, telecommunications, mass communications, and minerals) fell into the hands of developing finan-cial-industrial conglomerates that had acquired their wealth through positions of power or connections in the government. The loans-for-shares program of 1996 was a particularly controversial approach and is credited by some observers with helping to secure the position of Russia's wealthy and powerful busi-ness elite. Under this program, favored businessmen were granted control of lucrative enterprises (through control of state shares) in exchange for loans to the cash-strapped Russian government. When the govern-ment could not repay the loans, the favored businesses gained ownership of the shares. In other cases, securi-ties auctions gave advantages to large business inter-ests that became an increasingly powerful force on the Russian political scene in the late 1990s as politicians tried to win their favor, particularly before elections, to secure sources of campaign financing.

The pace and scope of privatization in Russia were rapid and thorough compared to other postcom-munist countries. However, the new joint-stock com-panies did not meet expectations. Productivity and efficiency did not increase significantly; unprofitable firms continued to operate; investment was weak; and the benefits of ownership were not widely or fairly distributed. The government continued to subsidize ineffective operations through various means, making most Russian firms uncompetitive and unattractive to potential investors. Renationalization of some enter-prises came under discussion and was, for the most part, rejected. However, in certain key sectors, such as energy, the government has reasserted its owner-ship, for example as majority shareholder in the large natural gas monopoly Gazprom.

Reform of agriculture produced even less sat-isfactory results than industrial privatization. Large joint-stock companies and associations of individual households were created on the basis of former state and collective farms. These privatized companies operated inefficiently, and agricultural output declined through-out the 1990s. Foreign food imports (including meat and a whole range of processed goods) also undercut domestic producers, contributing to a downward spiral in agricultural investment and production. In 2003, a new Land Code took effect, allowing the sale of agricul-tural land for agricultural purposes, with some restric-tions, including the exclusion of foreigner buyers.

By the late 1990s, it appeared that the govern-ment's reform program had not achieved most of its underlying goals (see Figure 11.2). Russia was in the grip of a severe depression, more sustained than the Great Depression of the 1930s in the United States and Western Europe. Industrial production was less than half the 1990 level. Basic industrial sectors such as machine building, light industry, construction materials, and wood products were the worst off. The depression fed on itself, as declining capacity in one sector deprived other sectors of buyers or suppliers. Consumer purchasing power dropped with the decline in real wages. Firms were unable to pay their sup-pliers, were in arrears to their employees, and owed taxes to the government. Even the state was behind in its wage, social benefit, and pension payments. Under these conditions, barter arrangements, often involving intertwined linkages of several enterprises or organi-zations, became common.

A key obstacle to the success of the market reform agenda in the 1990s was the weakness of state institutions. This may seem ironic, since one of the

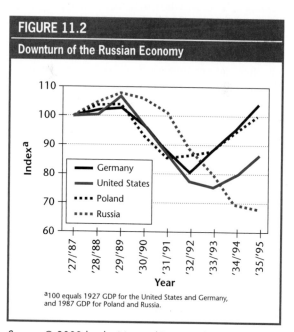

FIGURE 11.2

Downturn of the Russian Economy

Legend:
— Germany
— United States
···· Poland
▪▪▪▪ Russia

Y-axis: Index[a] (60, 70, 80, 90, 100, 110)

X-axis: Year ('27/'87, '28/'88, '29/'89, '30/'90, '31/'91, '32/'92, '33/'93, '34/'94, '35/'95)

[a]100 equals 1927 GDP for the United States and Germany, and 1987 GDP for Poland and Russia.

Source: © 2002 by the National Bureau of Asian Research. Reprinted from Millar, James, R. "Normalization of the Rus-sian Economy: Obstacles and Opportunities for Reform and Sustainable Growth," *NBR Analysis 13*, no. 2, April 2002, by permission of the National Bureau of Asian Research.

main ideas underlying market economic reform is to reduce state control of the economy. However, a well-functioning state apparatus is essential to carry out law-enforcement functions, to assure tax collection, to regulate key sectors such as banking, and to assure adherence to health, environmental, and labor standards. Without an effective tax collection system, for instance, the state cannot acquire revenues needed to pay its own bills on time, to provide essential services to the population, and to ensure a well-functioning economic infrastructure (such as transportation, energy, public utilities). Since the Russian government was not able to provide many of these services efficiently, businesses have often taken matters into their own hands, for example, by hiring private security services, turning to the **mafia** for protection, or by paying bribes. Weak government capacity feeds corruption and criminality, producing risks both to business and to the population at large.

The central state had difficulty exerting its authority in relation to the regions of the Russian Federation and in the face of increasing power of **oligarchs**, wealthy individuals who had benefited from the privatization process and who often held significant political influence as well.[7] These new Russian capitalists were able to gain control of important economic assets but often did not reinvest their profits to spur business development; rather, wealth was siphoned off through capital flight, in which money was removed from the country and deposited in foreign accounts or assets. Diverse methods of laundering money to avoid taxes became widespread. Corruption involving government officials, the police, and operators abroad fed a rising crime rate, which spilled over into many Western countries. Rich foreigners, Russian bankers, and outspoken journalists became targets of the Russian mafia. Rather than controlling these abuses, policies of the Russian government itself had contributed to the creation of this new group of financial and business oligarchs.

A financial crisis in August 1998 brought the situation to a head. Underlying the crisis was the Russian government's inability to pay its many creditors. The government successively took on new loans at progressively higher rates of interest in order to pay off existing debts. Following a sharp upturn in 1996–1997, in August 1998 the Russian stock market lost more than 90 percent of its value, and the government defaulted on its bonds. Many Russian banks, holders of the Russian government's short-term bonds, were facing imminent bankruptcy. The government began to print more of the increasingly valueless rubles, threatening to undermine the ruble's value further and thus intensify the underlying financial crisis.

The government was finally forced to allow a radical devaluation of the overvalued ruble. Within a two-week period, the ruble lost two-thirds of its value against the U.S. dollar, banks closed or allowed only limited withdrawals, supplies of imported goods decreased, and business accounts were frozen—forcing some firms to lay off employees and others to close their doors. In retrospect, despite its immediate disastrous effects, the 1998 financial crisis ushered in positive changes. First, the devalued ruble led to a sharp reduction in imports of Western commodities, making Russian producers competitive. Firms were able to improve their products, put underused labor back to work, and thus increase productivity. The state budget benefited from improved tax revenues; barter declined, as did payment arrears. Economic growth registered 5.4 percent in 1999 and remained at around 6 to 7 percent between 2003 and 2008.[8] Other developments fueled optimism about Russia's economic future. A budget surplus replaced a deficit, and the foreign debt load declined from 90 percent of GDP in 1998 to 31 percent in 2006.[9] (See Figure 11.3)

A second trigger for the economic upturn was rising international oil and gas prices, making Russian economic success heavily dependent on its natural resources. Tax proceeds from oil and gas revenues also have spilled into government tax coffers, making up as much as 20 to 30 percent of the budget.[10] A "Stabilization Fund," created by the Russian government to hold excess income from high oil and gas prices, reached about $117 billion in mid-2007.[11] The fund is intended to protect the country from the shock of a possible future decline in energy prices (such as occurred in October 2008) and also prevent the government from establishing expenditure levels that might not be sustainable. However, critics suggest that the government should be using some of the budget surplus to deal with pressing issues such as

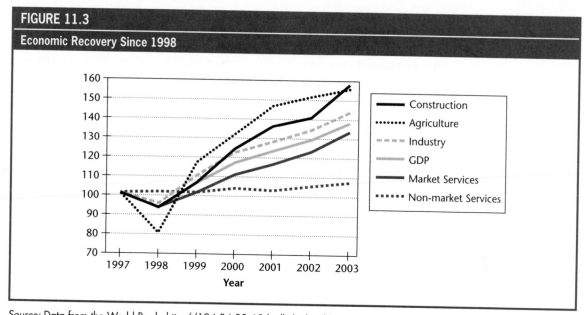

FIGURE 11.3

Economic Recovery Since 1998

Construction
Agriculture
Industry
GDP
Market Services
Non-market Services

Source: Data from the World Bank; http://194.84.38.65/mdb/upload/PAR_020805_eng.pdf.

shoring up the pension fund or increasing investment in critical infrastructure and industrial capacity of the country.

To be sure, when he came to office, Putin took some measures to improve the state's ability to manage the economy. After a sluggish first year, an active legislative program emerged under Putin's leadership in 2001 and 2002. A new Ministry for Economic Development and Trade was charged with developing the underlying concept. One of the first steps was a simplification of the tax system, intended to increase tax compliance and facilitate enforcement. A 13 percent flat income tax was one very visible aspect of the package, and adjustments were also made to corporate taxes as well. Under Putin, other government initiatives included amendments to the corporate governance law to protect shareholders' rights; legislation to control money laundering; provision for the sale of land to both domestic and foreign buyers (in the first instance, commercial and urban land only); a new labor code that tightened conditions for trade union organization; a new system governing the distribution of authority and of tax revenues among the center, the regions, and local organs; a new customs code; pension reform; amendments to the bankruptcy law;

and initiatives to reduce subsidization of housing and communal services. Efforts to secure Russia's membership in the World Trade Organization, another project of the government that has fueled optimism about Russia's trade growth, was still on the table in 2008. However, beginning in 2005, criticism was again emerging that the government was sluggish in pushing forward further reforms, that the economic bubble could be burst by falling energy prices, and that the exchange rate for the ruble was again reaching levels that could undermine the competitiveness of domestic production.

Another important feature of Putin's policy involved efforts to rein in the power of the economic oligarchs, while still retaining important powers in the hands of those loyal to the Kremlin. There is no indication that a fundamental change in this approach will occur under Medvedev's leadership as president, and Medvedev has given some indication that he may try to promote small and medium businesses more assertively. Putin made it clear that oligarchs who attempted to use their financial positions to affect political outcomes would suffer sanctions. Several attacks on media moguls were the first stage in this process, as business magnates Vladimir

Gusinsky and Boris Berezovsky were targeted. Gusinsky's NTV was nearly the sole TV critic of the Kremlin's military action against the secessionist Republic of Chechnya; Gusinsky also had close ties to President Vladimir Putin's political rival, Moscow mayor Luzhkov. Berezovsky was also a thorn in the Kremlin's side, threatening to broadcast controversial charges on TV-6 alleging government links to 1999 apartment bombings that had been attributed to terrorists. Charges of tax evasion and fraud were brought against both men, presented as part of the government's campaign to assure proper business practices by business oligarchs. Berezovsky fled to self-imposed exile in the United Kingdom, while Gusinsky fled to Spain.

A particularly prominent case has involved Mikhail Khodorkovsky, the chief executive officer and major shareholder of the giant Russian oil company, Yukos. In October 2003, Khodorkovsky was placed under arrest for fraud and tax evasion, and in May 2005, he was sentenced by a Russian court to nine years in prison. Critics of the government charged that the process was motivated by political considerations because Khodorkovsky had provided financial support to opposition political parties and had proposed radical changes in political structures that would weaken the power of the Russian presidency. The attack on Yukos at least temporarily undermined investor confidence (including foreign investors) among shareholders who feared government pretexts for other economic takeovers.

Corruption is another major obstacle to effective economic management in Russia. Transparency International, an independent civil society organization, produces an annual Corruption Perceptions index, based on a compilation of independent surveys. In 2006, Russia received a poor ranking, 2.5 on a 10-point scale, with 10 being the least corrupt.[12] This gave Russia a rank of 121 (along with countries like Gambia, Honduras, and Rwanda) out of the 163 countries surveyed. Putin's failure to reduce both the reality and perception of corruption marred Russia's image abroad while also causing clear damage domestically. While petty corruption may help to compensate for inefficiencies in the economic system or in state services, one form of corruption, often referred to as "**state capture**," is particularly detrimental to economic development.

Hellman and Kaufmann define Russia as a high "state capture economy," referring to "the efforts of firms to shape the laws, policies, and regulations of the state to their own advantage by providing illicit private gains to public officials."[13] Vladimir Popov concludes that the inability to maintain law and order undermines good economic performance, particularly when combined with rapid democratization.[14]

Society and Economy

Economic Reform and Russian Society

Experience prior to the formation of the Russian Federation in 1991 led Russians to expect a broad range of social welfare support such as free higher education and health care, and low-cost access to essential goods and services. Citizens received some benefits, such as housing, access to vacation facilities, and subsidized meals, through their place of employment, thus making the Soviet workplace a social as well as an economic institution. Participation in the labor market was high: almost all able-bodied adults, men and women, worked outside the home. The full-employment policy made unemployment compensation unnecessary. The retirement age was fifty-five for women and sixty for men, although in the early 1980s about one-third of those beyond retirement age continued to work. Modest pensions were guaranteed by the state, ensuring a stable but minimal standard of living for retirement. As a matter of state policy, wage differentials between the best- and worst-paid workers were lower than in Western countries. Although reflecting cultural values, this approach reduced the incentive for outstanding achievements and innovation. Due to state ownership, individuals could not accumulate wealth in real estate, stocks, or businesses. Privileges that did exist were modest by Western standards. Although political elites had access to scarce goods, such as high-quality heath care, travel, and vacation homes, these privileges were hidden from public view.

Many goods and services, although in the economic reach of every citizen, were in short supply in the Soviet period, so queues were a pervasive part of everyday life. Housing shortages restricted mobility and forced young couples and their children to share small apartments with parents. An irony of the system was that labor in many sectors was in constant short supply, reflecting the inefficient use of the work force. Labor productivity was low by international standards and work discipline weak: drunkenness and absenteeism were common. A Soviet saying of the time captured this element of the tacit social contract: "We pretend to work, they pretend to pay us." Whereas the lax work atmosphere reduced the likelihood and frequency of labor conflicts, it also kept production inefficient. Alcoholism was also a significant source of low labor productivity.

With a declining economy in the 1990s, the state could not meet the traditional social expectations of Russian citizens. In the 1990s, budget constraints necessitated cutbacks in state welfare programs at a time when there was a growing need for them. Pensions had less and less buying power, and state services proved inadequate to deal with increasing problems of homelessness and poverty. In line with the new market ideology, tuition fees for postsecondary education were introduced in many cases, and although a system of universal health care remained in place, higher-quality health care was made more obviously dependent on an ability to pay. The cost of medicine rose beyond the reach of many citizens. Benefits provided through the workplace were cut back, as even viable businesses faced pressures to reduce costs and increase productivity.

Some groups have benefited from the reform process, while others have suffered sharp declines. Wage rates are highest for highly skilled employees in the natural resource sectors (such as oil and gas), in banking and finance, and for individuals with marketable skills such as knowledge of English or German. At the extreme end, the wealthiest enjoy a standard of living luxurious even by Western standards. These people, many of them multimillionaires with Western bank accounts, were able to take advantage of the privatization process to gain positions in lucrative sectors like banking, finance, oil, and gas.

On the other side, in the 1990s, the number of homeless and beggars skyrocketed, especially in large cities like Moscow, a magnet for displaced persons and refugees from war zones on Russia's perimeter. Furthermore, as a result of low wage levels, the majority of those in poverty were, and continue to be,

the working poor. Consumer price inflation gradually declined over the 1990s but still has an important impact on incomes, spiking again with the 1998 financial crisis; at the end of 1999 the rate of inflation was 36.5 percent, falling to an acceptable 9 percent by the end of 2006.[15] In 2008, however, rising world food prices also had an impact in Russia.

Unemployment was lower than expected in the 1990s because many enterprises kept underemployed staff on their rolls, at low wages or with temporary layoffs. Official unemployment estimates were about 9.8 percent in 2000 and between 6 and 8 percent in 2004 to 2006, but actual rates are probably higher.[16] These figures also hide short-term layoffs, workers who are still employed but only sporadically paid, or people who have shifted to partial employment. On the other hand, employment in the shadow economy goes unreported. Levels of unemployment are particularly high in some regions, including republics and regions with high ethnic minority populations. Aboriginal groups in Russia's far north have suffered especially adverse effects as a result of the economic decline. Northern regions depend on the maintenance of a fragile transport and communications system for deliveries of basic necessities such as fuel and food. Social impacts of economic stress included higher rates of crime, suicide, and mortality; alcoholism continues to be a significant problem, particularly for males. All of these factors increase the likelihood of dysfunctional family structures, producing a particularly marked impact on children.

Even with the economic upturn following 1999, large differentials in income and wealth remain, but the portion of the population living below the subsistence level has declined noticeably (from 27.3 percent of the population in 2001 to 15.3 percent in 2006).[17] Overall, since 2000, levels of personal consumption have grown following years of decline, but many individuals (particularly men) keep two to three jobs just to make ends meet. A particularly contentious issue, which led to massive street demonstrations in several Russian cities in early 2005, involved changes to social welfare policy. Referred to as the "monetarization of social benefits" (Federal Law 122), the reforms include rescinding or reducing the provision of certain services (such as public transport and medicine) free of charge to a wide range of previously entitled groups (pensioners, veterans, the disabled), and their replacement by a modest monetary payment, lower than the cost people would have to pay for the services. Subsidies for public utilities and housing were also reduced. Viewed as part of the liberal market reform process, these reforms were intended to increase the role of the market and reduce the direct financial burden on local governments. Research does indicate that those groups receiving these benefits were not necessarily the most needy, so the reform also involved an effort to better target state support. However, many Russians viewed the changes as a direct reduction in social welfare for those who had served the country through years of hardship. Following large-scale demonstrations throughout the country, the government agreed to accompany the reforms by a modest increase in pensions, to restore subsidized transport, and to allow individuals some choice in how they receive state subsidies.

In 2005, Putin announced a new program of National Projects intended to address inadequacies in the social sector and to reverse Russia's decline in population.

The Projects focus on four priority areas: health care, education, housing, and agriculture. Opinion surveys indicate that most Russians are split on whether these policies are likely to have a positive impact, with higher hopes for education and health care than for agricultural and housing.[18] The National Projects were put under the stewardship of First Deputy Prime Minister Dmitry Medvedev, who was subsequently supported by Putin as his successor as president, and elected to the post in March 2008. Whether these reforms will be pushed more assertively and effectively during Medvedev's presidency might be affected by the level of world oil prices and their impact on tax revenues, the source of potential reinvestment in the areas targeted by the National Projects, as well as in pensions and social welfare and employment programs. Medvedev's previous involvement with these policy areas and some increased investments in 2008 indicates that the Putin-Medvedev team may realize their critical importance for the Russian public. However, the fashioning of policies that are effective in reaching the average citizen may require increased involvement of interest groups

Moscow protest against cuts in social benefits in 2005. *Source:* © Smolsky Sergei/ITAR-TASS/Corbis.

Russians line up at the money exchange kiosk. The longer line wants to receive social benefits rather than money, whereas the shorter line is happy to give up social benefits in exchange for money. *Source: Courtesy Rossiiskie vesti.*

representing the public (such as trade unions and professional associations, nongovernmental organizations, and citizens' groups at the local level) in the formation of social priorities and policy instruments.

Women still endure many of the same hardships faced in the Soviet period. Official Soviet ideology advocated gender equality and was highly successful in achieving virtual equality of educational opportunity and in integrating women into the labour force. However, women continue to occupy lower status and lower-paid positions than men, particularly in sectors such as retail trade, education, health, culture, and administration. In the Soviet period, demands on women were high due to their triple burden (employee, wife, mother). These patterns continue today; however, the growth of the service sector and improved access to consumer goods has eased the situation for those who can take advantage of these benefits. Women have access to a three-year maternity leave, which is only partially paid. Fathers play

a relatively small role in child rearing; many women rely on grandparents to help out. Employers are sometimes reluctant to hire women of childbearing age, since the exercise of maternity leave is often viewed as disruptive in the workplace. Some data suggest, however, that while women are more likely to register with unemployment offices and take longer to find new jobs, levels of actual unemployment are about equal for men and women.[19] Furthermore, in general, women have proven more adaptable to change than men, as evidenced in life expectancy rates. Life expectancy for Soviet men fell from 66 years in 1966–1967 to under 59 for Russian males in 2003 (from 74 to 72 for women), rising to 60.4 and 73.2 years, for men and women respectively, in 2006.[20]

Alongside reduced life expectancy, a low birth rate in Russia has produced an impending demographic crisis. The birthrate fell from 16.6 births per 1,000 people in 1985, down to 8.9 in 1996, rising again to a rate of 10.4 in 2006; in 2006 the death rate was

15.2.[21] These figures underlie a progressive decline in the population of the country. The decline in population has been tempered only by the immigration of ethnic Russians from other former Soviet republics (see Figure 11.4). Although declining birth rates are a common corollary of economic modernization, in the 1990s many couples in Russia were especially reluctant to have children because of daily hardships, future uncertainty, a declining standard of living, and continuing housing shortages. The National Projects, mentioned above, have been credited with a small reversal in this trend, but the demographic situation remains troubling.

Russian Political Culture and Economic Change

Alongside more objective factors, culture affects processes of economic change. Several aspects of Russian culture may have inhibited adaptation to a market economy. These include a weak tradition of individual entrepreneurship, a widespread commitment to egalitarian values, and a reliance on relations of personal trust rather than written contracts. Profit, as a measure of success, is less important to many Russians than is support for friends and coworkers. Selection of business partners or recruitment of personnel may be strongly influenced by personal contacts and relationships rather than by merit. Incentive structures of the Soviet period also have been internalized by older population groups, including features that encourage risk avoidance, low productivity, poor punctuality, absenteeism, lack of personal responsibility and initiative, and a preference for security over achievement.[22] However, young people in Russia are being socialized in a new cultural environment and, when offered appropriate incentives, Russian employees tend to operate at high levels of efficiency and, after a period of time, adopt work habits rewarded by the employing organization. A continuing problem is resignation in the face of a culture of bribes and special favors. Legal measures to control these practices may not be effective without a cultural change that stigmatizes bribes and other illegal mechanisms to gain advantage.[23]

Younger Russians are better equipped to adapt to the new economic conditions. Not only are they more flexible due to their age, but they also have different expectations. Consequently, they are more supportive of the market transition and are more oriented toward maximizing self-interest and demonstrating initiative. Thus, generational change is an important factor in understanding Russia's economic development. Nevertheless, a significant portion of Russians of all age groups still question values underlying the market reform process, preferring an economy that is less profit driven and more oriented to equality and the collective good. Survey data suggest that although Russians support the idea of democracy and appreciate the freedom they have gained since the collapse of communism, they are much less enamored with the basic notions underlying the capitalist economic system.[24]

Russia in the Global Economy

Right up to the end of the Soviet period, the economy remained relatively isolated from outside influences. Most of the USSR's trade (53 percent of imports, 51 percent of exports in 1984) was carried out with

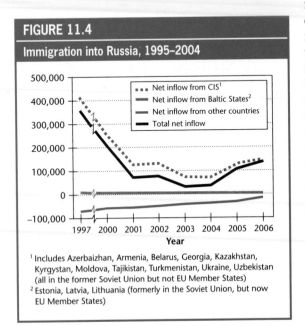

FIGURE 11.4

Immigration into Russia, 1995–2004

- Net inflow from CIS[1]
- Net inflow from Baltic States[2]
- Net inflow from other countries
- Total net inflow

[1] Includes Azerbaizhan, Armenia, Belarus, Georgia, Kazakhstan, Kyrgystan, Moldova, Tajikistan, Turkmenistan, Ukraine, Uzbekistan (all in the former Soviet Union but not EU Member States)
[2] Estonia, Latvia, Lithuania (formerly in the Soviet Union, but now EU Member States)

Source: Russian Annual Statistical Report 2003; Current Statistical Survey, no. 1 (48) 2004; and website of the Federal Statistical Agency of the Russian Federation, www.gks.ru.

the countries of Eastern Europe.[25] The ruble was non-convertible, meaning that its exchange rate was set by the state and did not fluctuate freely in response to economic forces. All foreign trade was channeled through central state organs, so individual enterprises had neither the possibility nor the incentive to seek external markets. Accounts in Western currencies (so-called hard currency) were under state control. Russia's rich natural resource base, particularly oil and gas, provided an important source of hard currency income. Gorbachev sought to integrate the USSR into the global economy by permitting some foreign investment through joint ventures and by reducing barriers to foreign contacts. In the 1990s, restrictions on foreign investment were further reduced; the value of the ruble was allowed to respond to market conditions, and firms were permitted to conclude agreements directly with foreign partners.

During the 1990s, Western governments (with Germany at the top of the list) made fairly generous commitments of technical and humanitarian assistance. The World Bank, the International Monetary Fund (IMF) and the European Union (EU) contributed substantial amounts of economic assistance, often in the form of repayable credits. Release of IMF credits, issued to stabilize the ruble, was made contingent on Russia's pursuing a strict policy of fiscal and monetary control and lifting remaining price controls. The Russian government had difficulties in meeting these conditions, and thus the funds were released intermittently. After the August 1998 crisis, the Russian government defaulted first on the ruble-denominated short-term debt and then on the former Soviet debt. Since then, debt repayments have been made on time. In 2001, the Russian government decided to forgo additional IMF credits. By 2004, it had paid off its IMF debt and, bit by bit, has cut its remaining debt obligation.

Russia has had problems attracting foreign investment, even in its improved economic circumstances since 1999, and levels still remain low, but rising, compared to other East European countries. In 2002 foreign investment per capita in Russia was less than 4 percent of the level in the Czech Republic and Slovakia, and about a quarter of the Polish level,[26] but between 2002 and 2006 foreign direct investment in Russia saw an upward trajectory, increasing about

threefold.[27] In 2006, more than 60 percent of foreign investment came from Cyprus (17.9 percent), United Kingdom (12.7), Netherlands (12.0), Luxembourg (10.7), and Germany (9.1); Cyprus and Luxembourg are major destinations of Russia's capital flight—suggesting that some of these investment funds may be repatriated Russian capital or profits.[28] Continued uncertainty and instability regarding government policy, reinforced by the Khodorkovsky case, and a few highly visible murders of prominent business figures, have prevented a stabilization of investor confidence. In addition, in spring 2008, laws delimiting the scope of foreign investment in "strategic sectors," which includes sectors encompassing natural resources but also fields such as telecommunications and fisheries, were approved. While some observers believe that the legislation will inhibit the growth of investment, others argue that explicit regulation such as those provided in the law may provide a more predictable environment.

The geographic focus of Russia's foreign trade activity has shifted significantly since the Soviet period. Whereas in 1994 Ukraine was Russia's most important trading partner, now Germany holds first place, receiving more than 8 percent of Russian exports, and providing 13.6 percent of imports to Russia in 2006. Netherlands received the highest proportion of Russian exports (12.3 percent), with China and Ukraine following Germany in sending goods to Russia. Overall the expanded EU accounts for more than 50 percent of Russia's trade, compared to 14 percent for the countries of the Commonwealth of Independent States (CIS).[29] In 2004, the EU confirmed its support for Russian membership in the World Trade Organization (WTO), as observers speculated a quid pro quo had been reached in exchange for Russian agreement to raise domestic oil prices (since their low level allegedly gives Russian producers an unfair competitive advantage) and to ratify the Kyoto Accord on Climate Change, an important priority of the European Union.

Russia's position in the international political economy remains undetermined. With a highly skilled work force, high levels of educational and scientific achievement, and a rich base of natural resources, Russia has many of the ingredients necessary to become a competitive and powerful force in the global economy. However, if the country's industrial capacity is not restored, reliance on natural resource exports will leave

Russia vulnerable to global economic fluctuations in supply and demand. Furthermore, levels of capital investment and technological innovation have been adequate to fuel increased productivity; even in the lucrative energy sector, experts raise serious concerns about the ability of Russian firms to develop new reserves adequate to meet both domestic needs and contractual obligations to foreign (mainly European) consumers in future years. At the same time, its wealth in natural resources has given Russia advantages compared to its neighbors, since these expensive materials do not need to be imported. In 2006, more than 65 percent of exports were fuels or energy, whereas only about 6 percent were machinery and equipment, with other resources such as metals and timber making up a large part of the balance.[30] Ultimately, Russia's position in the global economy will depend on the ability of the country's leadership to fashion a viable approach to domestic economic challenges and to facilitate differentiation of the country's export base.

Governance and Policy-Making

When Russia became an independent country in December 1991, dramatic changes in state structure and governing processes followed. The new Russian leadership initially endorsed liberal democratic principles as the basis of its new political institutions, and in April 2005 Putin himself declared, "[T]he development of Russia as a free and democratic state [is] the main political and ideological goal."[31] Over time, however, skeptics abound as Putin's measures to strengthen presidential power seem to have undermined many of the Russian Federation's founding democratic principles. Because Putin retains important political power through his post as prime minister in the Medvedev presidency, it seems unlikely that the basic directions of political development will undergo fundamental change in the direction of increasing liberalization unless Medvedev develops his own base of political power and uses it to confront the power of entrenched political forces.

Organization of the State

Ratification of a new Russian constitution in 1993 was a contested political process that followed a violent confrontation between the president and the parliament. The process culminated in a narrowly successful popular referendum on a document reflecting Yeltsin's own preferences. Nonetheless, the new constitution has acquired broad-based popular legitimacy, even if its interpretation is sometimes hotly contested. The document affirms many established principles of liberal democratic governance—competitive elections within a multiparty context, separation of powers, an independent judiciary, federalism, and protection of individual civil liberties. However, another key feature is the strength of the president's executive power. This feature is both a response to the demands for leadership required in a period of radical change and a reflection of Russia's political tradition, which has been characterized by strong central political authority. Despite the constitutional basis for strong executive power, throughout the 1990s the state in practice demonstrated only a weak capacity to govern. Associated declines in economic performance elicited a countertendency after Putin's election in 2000 in the form of a recentralization of political power and a reassertion of control over opposition forces.

The constitution laid the groundwork for institutional conflict between governing structures, which, in the Yeltsin years, often resulted in stalemate. While the executive branch is dominant, new laws must also be passed by the bicameral legislature, the Federal Assembly. Tension between the two branches of government, which are selected in separate electoral processes, was a persistent obstacle to effective governance in the Yeltsin years. Furthermore, the executive itself has two heads (the president and the prime minister), introducing another venue for intrastate tension. Putin's high level of popularity gave him dominance over the government (and prime minister) until his term ended in 2008.

Relations between the executive and judicial branches have at times also been conflictual. They were particularly strained in the Yeltsin years, and the establishment of real judicial independence remains a significant political challenge. Finally, poor salaries and lack of professionalism in the civil service have left the door open to corruption and influence-wielding. Administrative reforms have been ineffective in addressing these problems and corruption remains one of the most important political problems facing Russia. Another area of conflict involves the relationship between the federal government and regional authorities, an issue discussed in depth later in this chapter. Putin's centralizing measures have sought to address all of these areas of contention, but in so doing he may have undermined the very checks and balances that are supposed to offer protection against reestablishment of authoritarian control.

Many of the difficulties facing the new Russian state are, at least in part, legacies of the Soviet period. In the Soviet period, top organs of the Communist Party of the Soviet Union (CPSU) dominated the state. The CPSU was a hierarchical organization. Lower party bodies elected delegates to higher party organs, but these elections were uncontested, and top organs determined candidates for lower party posts. The Politburo, the top party organ, was the real decision-making center. A larger body, the Central Committee, represented the broader political elite, including regional party leaders and representatives of various economic sectors. Alongside the CPSU were Soviet state structures that formally resembled Western parliamentary systems but had little decision-making authority. The state bureaucracy had day-to-day responsibility in both the economic and political spheres but operated in subordination to the party's directives. People holding high state positions were appointed through the *nomenklatura* system, a mechanism that allowed the CPSU to fill key posts with politically reliable individuals. The Soviet constitution provided for legislative, executive, and judicial organs, but separation of powers was considered unnecessary because the CPSU claimed to represent the interests of society as a whole. The Supreme Soviet, the legislative branch of the government, was largely a rubber stamp body. With the power of

appointment firmly under party control, it made little sense to speak of legislative or judicial independence. When the constitution was violated (as it frequently was), the courts had no independent authority to protect its provisions.

Gorbachev tried to reform the system through increased political pluralism, reduced dominance of the CPSU, a revitalized legislature, and constitutional reform. Even before the collapse of the USSR, political institutions began to change in the Russian Republic, a constituent unit of the Soviet Union. A new post of president was created, and on June 12, 1991, Boris Yeltsin was elected by direct popular vote as its first incumbent. In a more radical manner, after the collapse of the USSR, the Yeltsin team tried to wipe the slate clean and start anew. However, some political scientists emphasize the importance of **path dependence**—that is, the manner in which past experience shapes the choices and options available for change.[32] Some observers see in Putin's reforms a reversion to practices and patterns reminiscent of the Soviet period, but many Russian citizens, while cynical about their leaders and institutions, view the current political system as operating quite differently from the Soviet one. The current system is heavily dependent on individual leaders, whereas institutional structures, such as the Communist Party, were stronger in the Soviet period. A crucial turning point was the adoption by referendum of a new Russian constitution in December 1993; this constitution provides the legal foundation for current state institutions (see Figure 11.5). But political practice goes far beyond constitutional provisions and, as this chapter illustrates, sometimes alters their interpretation.

The Executive

The Russian constitution adopted in 1993 establishes a semipresidential system, formally resembling the French system but with stronger executive power. The president is the head of state, and the prime minister, appointed by the president but approved by the lower house of the parliament (the *State Duma*), is the head of government. As a rule of thumb, the president has overseen foreign policy, relations with the regions, and the organs of state security, while the

FIGURE 11.5

Political Institutions of the Russian Federation (R.F.), 2007

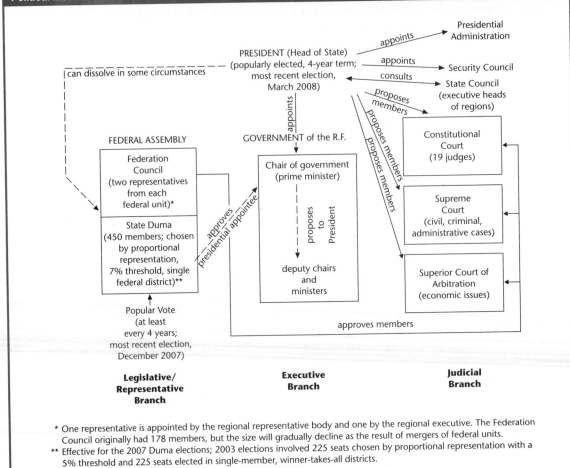

* One representative is appointed by the regional representative body and one by the regional executive. The Federation Council originally had 178 members, but the size will gradually decline as the result of mergers of federal units.

** Effective for the 2007 Duma elections; 2003 elections involved 225 seats chosen by proportional representation with a 5% threshold and 225 seats elected in single-member, winner-takes-all districts.

prime minister has focused his attention on the economy and related issues. However, with Yeltsin's continuing health problems in 1998 and 1999, operative power shifted in the direction of the prime minister. Following the election of Vladimir Putin in March 2000, however, the primary locus of power returned to the presidency.

The president is elected directly by the population every four years, with a limit of two consecutive terms (However, in 2008 a constitutional amendment to extend the presidential term to six years was under consideration.). In 1996, the first presidential

elections returned Yeltsin to power, despite his waning popularity. In December 1999, Yeltsin resigned from office, making the prime minister, Vladimir Putin, acting president until the March 2000 elections, which he won handily. Putin's 2004 electoral victory was even more stunning (winning 71 percent of the vote, with his closest competitor getting under 14 percent), but some international observers alleged that media bias raised questions about its genuine democratic character. The constitution excludes a third consecutive term, and Putin honored this provision. However, to assure stability, Putin "named" his preferred successor, Dmitry Medvedev, following months of speculation; Medvedev was elected with just over 70 percent of the vote with a turnout of nearly 70 percent.

Yeltsin frequently used the power of decree, provided for in the constitution, to address contentious issues. Although presidential decrees may not violate the constitution or specific legislation passed by the bicameral legislature (the Federal Assembly), policy-making by decree can allow the president to ignore an uncooperative or divided parliament. Presidential decrees have the force of law until formal legislation is passed, but because they can be annulled as quickly as they are approved, they do not command the same respect as actual laws. President Putin used the power of decree much less extensively than Yeltsin largely because he had a strong base of support in the parliament. Following the 2004 elections, the party United Russia, closely associated with Putin, held a firm majority in the *Duma*, further reinforced through the outcome of the 2007 *Duma* elections. Thus, the new president, Dmitry Medvedev, is unlikely to face resistance from the *Duma* in putting through his initiatives.

The president has other powers, including the right to call a state of emergency, impose martial law, grant pardons, call referendums, and temporarily suspend actions of other state organs if he deems them to contradict the constitution or federal laws. Some of these actions must be confirmed by other state organs (such as the upper house of the parliament, the Federation Council). The president is commander in chief of the armed forces and conducts affairs of state with other nations. Impeachment of the president is a complicated process involving the *Duma,* the Federation Council, the Supreme Court, and the Constitutional Court. If the president dies in office or becomes incapacitated, the prime minister fills the post until new presidential elections can be held.

The Russian government is headed by the prime minister, flanked by varying numbers of deputy prime ministers. The president's choice of prime minister must be approved by the *Duma*. During Yeltsin's presidency, six prime ministers held office, the longest being Viktor Chernomyrdin, from December 1992 until March 1998, and the final one being Vladimir Putin, appointed in August 1999. Following his move to the presidential post in December 1999, Putin had three prime ministers (and one acting prime minister). The first of these, Mikhail Kasyanov (May 2000 to February 2004), later became an outspoken opposition figure. In May 2008, Putin himself became prime minister, named by Dmitry Medvedev, who was elected to the presidential post in March 2008. Shortly upon taking office, Putin created a new organ, the Presidium of the Russian cabinet, a body that would meet weekly and presumably act as a kind of executive committee of the larger cabinet.

The prime minister can be removed by the *Duma* through two repeat votes of no confidence passed within a three-month period; although the process has been attempted several times in the past decade, usually spearheaded by the Communist Party faction, it has never succeeded. The president has also, on occasion, had difficulty gaining approval of his nominee for prime minister, most notably following the 1998 financial crisis when three prime ministers were in office over a seventeen-month period. Here, too, the *Duma* has ultimately been reluctant to defy the president because rejection of the candidate three times can lead to dissolution of the *Duma* itself. The prime minister has never been a member of the dominant party or coalition in the *Duma*; thus, principles of party accountability that apply in most Western parliamentary systems are not operative in Russia.

The most intriguing question in the current period is how the relationship between the current president, Dmitry Medvedev, and his appointee as prime minister, Vladimr Putin, will unfold. In addition to the inherent difficulties of a shared executive, the interdependence of the two leaders has aroused much speculation about whether Medevdev will emerge as an independent political force or whether he will simply serve as a vehicle of Putin's continued dominance. Shortly after his appointment, Putin made a "cabinet shuffle," which involved shifting some of his former presidential aides to his new post, perhaps a signal that Putin would maintain a strong leadership role. Observers speculated whether the proposal to increase the presidential term to six years anticipated Putin running in the next presidential election.

The National Bureaucracy

The new Russian state inherited a large bureaucratic apparatus. Despite proclaimed intentions, efforts to downsize the executive bureaucratic apparatus have been only partially successful. Alongside the state bureaucracy is the presidential administration, which serves the president directly. With some 2,000 employees, the presidential administration can duplicate or compete with the formal agencies of the state, while some government ministries (such as the Foreign Affairs Ministry, the Federal Security Service, and the Defense Ministry) have traditionally reported directly to the president.[33] The president has various advisory bodies that solicit input from important political and economic actors and also co-opt them into support for government policies. These organs have no constitutional status and thus could be abolished at will. The most important are the Security Council and the State Council. Formed in 1992, the Security Council advises the president in areas related to foreign policy and security (broadly conceived) and includes heads of appropriate government bodies (the so-called power ministries such as Defense and the Federal Security Service), the prime minister, and the heads of seven newly created federal districts. The State Council was formed in September 2000 as part of Putin's attempt to redefine the role of regional leaders in federal decision-making (see below). This body, which includes all of the regional heads, has a consultative role, but without giving the regional executives any real power. A smaller presidium, made up of seven of the regional heads selected by the president, meets monthly.

The bureaucratic agencies that make up the executive branch itself include ministries, agencies, and services. Based on an administrative reform adopted in 2004 (which in part was based on presidential decrees and in part on legislation), ministries are concerned with policy functions or political aspects, whereas services and agencies generally undertake monitoring functions or implementation. The reform is generally considered to have been unsuccessful in achieving its goal of improved bureaucratic efficiency. Other Putin reforms involved reinforcement of central state control vis-à-vis the regional governments. These reforms are discussed below in the section on subnational government.

Ministers other than the prime minister do not require parliamentary approval. The prime minister makes recommendations to the president, who appoints these officials. In the 2008 cabinet shuffle, Putin designated two first deputy prime ministers and five deputy prime ministers, with eighteen ministries and more than fifty other organs.[34] Federal services include bodies such as the Federal Security Service (FSB) and the Tax Inspectorate. Ministers and other agency heads are generally career bureaucrats who have risen through an appropriate government agency, although sometimes more clearly political appointments are made. Many agencies have been reorganized, often more than once. In some cases top leaders also use restructuring to induce political loyalty and place their clients and allies in key positions in the new agencies. Sometimes restructuring signals particular leadership priorities. For example, the State Committee for Environmental Protection was abolished by a May 2000 decree; these responsibilities now lie with the Ministry of Natural Resources and Ecology. The mixing of responsibility for overseeing both use and protection of natural resources in this single agency may be an indicator of the low priority of environmental protection (as compared to resource use). Functions of the State Committee on Northern Affairs were transferred to the Ministry for Economic Development and Trade, viewed by some as a downgrading of northern concerns on the government's agenda. In May 2008, Putin created a new Ministry of Energy, splitting off these functions from those of the Ministry of Industry and Trade. This move reflected the growing importance of this sector to Russia's economy.

Clientelistic networks, which were important in the Soviet period, continue to play a key role in both the presidential administration and other state organs. These linkages are similar to old-boys' networks in the West (and they most often involve men in the Russian case); they underscore the importance of personal career ties between individuals as they rise in bureaucratic or political structures. For example, Putin drew heavily on colleagues with whom he worked earlier in St. Petersburg or in the security establishment (the latter referred to as *siloviki*), in staffing a variety of posts in his administration.

While instituting a merit-based civil service system has been a state goal, it has not yet been achieved in reality. The Russian state bureaucracy continues to suffers low levels of public respect and to be plagued by continuing problems with corruption.

Public and Semipublic Institutions

While privatization policies of the 1990s resulted in the transformation of most state enterprises into joint stock or privatized companies, in limited sectors of the economy, partial or complete state ownership has remained fairly intact or even been restored after earlier privatization was carried out. Public or quasi-public ownership may take the form of direct state or municipal ownership of assets or it may take the form of majority control of shares in a "privatized" firm. Economic sectors more likely to involve public or semipublic ownership include telecommunications (the nonmobile telephone industry in particular), public transport (railways, municipal transport), the electronic media (television), and the energy sector. A prime example from the energy sector is Gazprom, the natural gas monopoly, where the federal government controls just over 50 percent of the shares. The seizure of assets of Yukos, an oil company previously owned by Khodorkovsky (discussed in Section 2), increased government involvement in this part of the energy sector as well. Another oil company, Sibneft, was purchased in the open market by Gazprom, increasing the share of state ownership in the oil sector to more than 30 percent in 2005. Several television stations are publicly owned, either on a national basis (ORT, RTR), by regions, or by municipalities. Many newspapers, including at the regional level, receive financial support from the regional government, and their chief editors may be subject to appointment or approval by local political authorities. Indirect state influence is also realized through the dominant ownership share in many regional TV stations by Gazprom-Media, a subsidiary of the state-controlled natural gas company.

In other areas such as education and health care, while some private facilities and institutions have emerged in recent years, these services are still primarily provided through so-called "budget" (i.e., tax-supported) agencies. Some prestigious new private universities, often with Western economic support, have cropped up in major urban areas, but Russia's large historic universities remain public institutions. Likewise, a state-run medical care system assures basic care to all citizens, even while private clinics and hospitals are taking on growing importance in servicing the more affluent parts of the population. In the public transport sector, smaller private companies that provide shuttle and bus services have grown up alongside publicly owned transport networks. In general, public or semipublic agencies offer services to citizens at a lower price, but often also with lower quality.

Significant parts of the social infrastructure remain under, public or semipublic control. In the Soviet period, many social services were administered to citizens through the workplace. These included daycare, housing, medical, and vacation facilities, as well as food services and some retail outlets. Between 1991 and the end of the 1990s, a process of divestiture resulted in the transfer of most of these assets and responsibilities to other institutions, either to private owners or, often, to municipalities. For example, while many state- or enterprise-owned apartments were turned over to private ownership by their occupants, an important part of the country's housing stock was placed in municipal ownership. Thus local governments play an important role in administering these types of services to the population.

Political authorities, including the president, are responsible for appointing executive officials in many of public and semipublic institutions, so the link between state authorities and these public-sector financial and economic institutions can be quite close. These examples indicate a continuing close relationship between major economic institutions and the state, likely to remain due to the Russian tradition of a strong state and the discrediting of privatization by its association with dismal economic results in the 1990s. Indicative of this trend, the overall share of GDP created in the nonstate sector increased from 5 percent in 1991 to 70 percent in 1997, then fell from 70 percent in 1997 down to 65 percent in 2005–2006.[35]

Other State Institutions

The Military and Security Organs

The Soviet military once ranked as one of the largest and most powerful forces in the world, second only to that of the United States and justifying the country's designation as a superpower. Since the military was represented in the political structures (almost always having at least one representative on the Politburo), political loyalty to the civilian authorities represented a good bargain for the military establishment. The Communist Party controlled military appointments, and, although the military did lobby for particular policies and sometimes played a role in Kremlin intrigues, it never usurped political power. Since the collapse of the communist system, the military has remained loyal to civilian power, even when put to the test. For example, during the August 1991 coup attempt, troops remained loyal to Yeltsin and Gorbachev, even though the minister of defense was among the coup plotters. Again, in October 1993, despite some apparent hesitancy in military circles, military units defended the government's position, this time by firing on civilian protesters, shocking the country.

In the postcommunist period, the political power and prestige of the military have declined radically. Both Gorbachev and Yeltsin oversaw a reduction in military expenditures, which undermined the privileged position of military interests, bringing a decline in facilities for military personnel and a reduction in conventional and nuclear forces. Plans to downsize the military have been a source of tension between the political leadership and the military establishment; during his second term in office, Putin supported an increase in the military budget and Medvedev seems to be continuing that policy. The military's failure to implement a successful strategy in the Chechnya war has led the government to increase the role of the FSB there instead of relying on the army alone.[36] Reports of deteriorating conditions in some Russian nuclear arsenals have raised international concerns about nuclear security. In addition, the situation of military personnel, from the highest officers to rank-and-file soldiers, has deteriorated dramatically, producing a potential source of political unrest.

The Russian Federation still maintains a system of universal male conscription, but noncompliance and draftees rejected for health reasons have been persistent problems; a law to permit alternative military service for conscientious objectors took effect in 2004. Although critics of the military service law welcome the concept, they are critical of the restrictive conditions that the law imposes on alternative service. Government proposals to supplement the conscript army by a smaller professional military corps are on the agenda, but there are no concrete plans to abolish the military draft. However, by 2008, the term of military service had been reduced from two years to one year.

Alongside the military, various security organizations exist in Russia, including government organs such as the FSB and the Ministry of the Internal Affairs (which oversees the police, or militia, including special units). Those officials associated with the security sector in Russia are frequently referred to as the *siloviki*, many of whom have career links to Putin act as a sort of informal interest group.

High crime rates indicate a low capacity of the state to provide legal security to its citizens. Thus, in addition to state security agencies, there is a range of private security agencies that provide protection to businesses and individuals. A network of intrigue and hidden relationships can make it hard to determine the boundaries of state involvement in the security sector, and the government's inability to enforce laws or to apprehend violators may create an impression of state involvement even where they may be none. A prominent example is the case of a former agent of the Russian Federal Security Service, Alexander Litvinenko, who claimed in 1998 that he was threatened after failing to fulfill an FSB order to kill Boris Berezovsky;[37] in 2000 he took political asylum in the United Kingdom and continued his outspoken criticism of the Russian government. In November 2006, Litvinenko was fatally poisoned in London with the rare radioactive isotope Polonium-210; traces of the material were found in public places in London as well as on airlines that had traveled to Moscow, presenting a potential hazard to the general public. On his deathbed, Litvinenko accused the Kremlin of being responsible for his death, an undocumented accusation. In May 2007, the United Kingdom formally requested extradition of Andrei Lugovoi, an ex-KGB agent and Russian politician, to stand trial for the murder, but the Russian government refused, citing a constitutional prohibition. The issue sparked tension between the two countries, including expulsion of diplomats on both sides. These kinds of incidents have generated an atmosphere of insecurity and bizarre linkages reminiscent of cold war-era spy novels.

Because of Vladimir Putin's career background in the Soviet security agency (the KGB), he drew many of his staff from this arena, giving the security establishment increasing importance in the Putin era. This development preceded the events of September 11, 2001. Because many Russians are alarmed by the crime rate and terrorist bombings in the country, restrictions on civil liberties have not elicited the popular concern typical of many Western countries. At the same time, there is widespread public cynicism about the honesty of the ordinary police; many believe that payoffs by the mafia and even by ordinary citizens can buy police cooperation in overlooking crimes or ordinary legal infractions such as traffic tickets. Such suspicions are likely often correct.

The Russian government attributes repeated bombings since 1999 to Chechen terrorists and has claimed that the terrorists have international links to the Al Qaeda network. Since the September 11 attacks, cooperation between Russian and Western security agencies has increased, as Russia has shared security information. However, closer NATO and American ties in neighboring Georgia have been an irritant to Russia, which sees this region as part of its sphere of influence.

The Judiciary

Concepts such as judicial independence and the rule of law were poorly understood in both pre–Revolutionary Russia and the Soviet era. Gorbachev, however, emphasized the importance of constructing a law-based state, judicial independence, and due process. These concepts have been embedded in the new Russian constitution and are accepted by both the public and political elites. However, their implementation has been difficult and not wholly successful, in part because of the continued perception of political interference in the outcomes of high-profile judicial proceedings.

In Russia, a Constitutional Court was formed in 1991. Its decisions were binding, and in several cases even the president had to bow to its authority. After several controversial decisions that challenged the president's authority, Yeltsin suspended the operations of the court in late 1993. However, the 1993 constitution again provided for a Constitutional Court with the power to adjudicate disputes on the constitutionality of federal and regional laws, as well as jurisdictional disputes between various political institutions. Justices are nominated by the president and approved by the Federation Council, a procedure that produced a stalemate after the new constitution was adopted, so that the court became functional only in 1995. Among the justices are political figures, lawyers, legal scholars, and judges. Since 1995, the court has established itself as a vehicle for resolving conflicts relating to the protection of individual rights and conformity of regional laws with constitutional requirements. The court has been cautious in confronting the executive branch, on which it depends to enforce its decisions.

Alongside the Constitutional Court is an extensive system of lower and appellate courts, with the Supreme Court at the pinnacle. These courts hear ordinary civil and criminal cases. In 1995, a system of commercial courts was also formed to hear cases dealing with issues related to privatization, taxes, and other commercial activities. The Federation Council must approve nominees for Supreme Court judgeships, and the constitution also grants the president power to appoint judges at other levels. Measures to shield judges from political pressures include criminal prosecution for attempting to influence a judge, protections from arbitrary dismissal, and improved salaries for judges. The Russian judicial system operates on a civil code system, similar to most of continental Europe. One innovation in the legal system is the introduction of jury trials for some types of criminal offenses.

Subnational Government

The collapse of the Soviet Union was precipitated by the demands of some union republics for more autonomy and, then, independence. After the Russian Federation became an independent state, the problem of constructing a viable federal structure resurfaced.

The Russian Federation inherited a complex structure of regional subunits from the Soviet period. Between 1991 and 1993, negotiations between the central government and the various regions led to the establishment of a federal structure that included eighty-nine units, with various types of historical origins and designations (twenty-one republics, forty-nine *oblasts,* six *krais,* ten autonomous *okrugs,* one autonomous *oblast,* and two cities with federal status, namely, St. Petersburg and Moscow). Subsequent mergers of regions, requiring approval by popular referendum, reduced the number to eighty-three by March 1, 2008.

One of the first issues to arise in the development of Russia's federal system was whether the regions should all have equal status, a principle finally upheld in the 1993 constitution. The republics have also been the most assertive in putting forth claims for autonomy or even sovereignty. The most extreme example was

Chechnya, whose demand for independence led to a protracted civil war. The Russian government's determination to oppose Chechen secession has been reflective of its fear that separatist sentiments could spread. This has not happened, although other republics have declared sovereignty, an ambiguous claim rejected by the Constitutional Court. The ethnic dimension complicates political relations with some of the republics. For example, in Tatarstan, one of the most populous and most assertive of the republics, the titular nationality (the Tatars) forms about half of the population. In the Republic of Sakha (formerly Yakutia), which has valuable diamond reserves, Yakuts form one-third of the population. The republics tend to be in peripheral areas of the Russian Federation, except for Tatarstan and Bashkortostan, which lie in the center of the country. The titular nationalities (Tatars and Bashkirs) in these two republics, as well as in some of the republics of the Caucasus region, are of Islamic

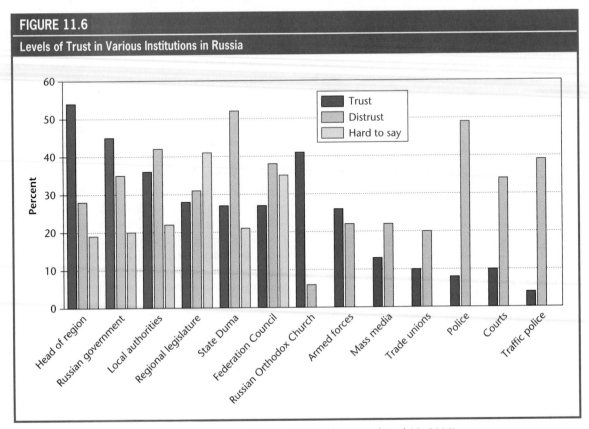

FIGURE 11.6

Levels of Trust in Various Institutions in Russia

Source: Levada Center, http://www.levada.ru/press/2004092702.html (accessed April 28, 2005).

cultural background, but Islamic fundamentalism has not been a significant problem in Russia since decades of Soviet socialization seem to have acculturated most parts of the Muslim population to secular, scientific values.

The republics have been given some special rights, such as declaring a second state language (in addition to Russian) and adopting their own constitutions. From 1994 to 1998, forty-six individual treaties were signed, first between the federal government and several of Russia's republics and then with other units of the federation. These documents were not supposed to contradict the federal constitution, but some provisions actually did. These treaties outlined the jurisdiction of each level of government and granted special privileges, including special rights in relation to natural resource revenues and division of tax revenue—often to the benefit of the ethnic republics. This ad hoc approach produced a system of **asymmetrical federalism**, giving different regions varying privileges. The result was an escalation of regional demands and a drop in the perceived fairness of central policy.

It is no wonder that following the March 2000 election, Putin identified the establishment of a uniform system of federal-regional relations, governed by uniform legal principles, as an important priority. He

Institutional Intricacies: Federalism—Russian Style

Russia is a federal system, according to its constitution. This means that powers are divided between the central government (located in Moscow) and the constituent units. When the Russian constitution was adopted in 1993 there were eighty-nine federal units; due to mergers, there were eighty-three in early 2008.

In comparison to the American federal system, the Russian structure seems complicated.

Some of Russia's federal units are called republics, while others are called *oblasts* (regions), *krais* (another type of region), autonomous *okrugs* (districts), or cities of federal status (Moscow and St. Petersburg). Russia's size and multiethnic population underlie this complexity because diverse ethnic groups in Russia are regionally concentrated, forming the basis for some of the federal units, most notably the fifteen republics and autonomous *okrugs*, which are named after the ethnic groups that reside there. If you think this is complicated, the *okurgs* are located within other federal units, leading to the term "*matrushka* federalism," a name inspired by the Russian wooden dolls that are nested one inside the other. Most of the *okrugs* are, over time, being merged into other federal units.

Russia's federal units are represented in the upper house of the national legislature, the Federation Council. Each region also has two representatives, but their method of selection has been a point of contention. In 1993 they were elected directly by the population. From the mid-1990s, the elected governor (or chief executive) of each region and the head of the regional legislature themselves sat on the Federation Council. Since 2000, the system has again shifted so that these representatives are appointed, one by the region's governor and the other by the region's legislature. All of these changes have occurred in less than fifteen years, making it hard for Russian citizens to keep up.

In the 1990s, Russia's federal government had difficulty controlling what happened in the regions; regional laws sometimes deviated from or even violated federal law. Bilateral treaties between the federal government and some of the republics and regions granted special privileges, producing what some called "asymmetrical federalism." President Putin put measures in place to ensure a greater degree of legal and political uniformity throughout the country. Seven federal districts were created to monitor implementation of federal policy in the regions. Beginning in 1996, regional governors were directly elected, but in 2004 this was replaced by a quasi-appointment procedure, making the governor dependent on the president. Changes to electoral and political party legislation also had a centralizing effect. These measures have led some observers to question whether Russian is really a federal system at all. Although Russia does have a constitutional court to resolve disputes over the jurisdictions of the federal government and the regions, the constitution itself does not provide a strong basis for regional power, since many powers are placed in the hands of the central government while most others are considered "shared" jurisdictions.

immediately took several steps to realize this objective, first by harmonizing regional laws and republic constitutions with federal legislation and constitutional provisions. Another contentious issue was the 2002 deadline for rescinding the special bilateral treaties. While most of these have been annulled, Tatarstan is a hold out. Negotiations to amend the document were finally successful in 2007, resulting in a new treaty that made symbolic concessions to Tatarstan's desire for a special status within the federation.

Other reforms to the federal system strengthened what Putin has called the "**power vertical**." This concept involves an integrated structure of executive power from the top (presidential) level down through to the local level. Critics have questioned whether the idea is actually consistent with federal principles. A first step in this direction was the creation of seven federal districts on top of the existing federal units. Although not designed to replace regional governments, the districts were intended to oversee the work of federal offices operating in the regions and to ensure compliance with federal laws and the constitution. Putin's initial appointees to head these new federal districts included several individuals (all male) with backgrounds in the security services. In practice, the federal districts have been less intrusive in the affairs of the regions than many expected.

A second set of changes to create the power vertical involved a weakening of the independence of regional executives (i.e., the governors and republic presidents). Following the Soviet collapse, they were initially appointed by the president himself, but Yeltsin finally agreed to their popular election, which gave them greater legitimacy and independence from Moscow. Beginning in 1996, the regional executives, along with the heads of each regional legislative body, also sat as members of the upper house of the Russian parliament, the Federation Council. This arrangement gave the regional executives a direct voice in national legislative discussions and a presence in Moscow, but it divided their attention between their executive responsibilities in their home regions and their duties in Moscow. In 2001, Putin gained approval for a revision to the composition of the Federation Council; regional executives were, as of January 2002, no longer members of the Federation Council. Rather, one regional representative is appointed by the regional executive and the other by the regional legislature. Some regional executives resisted this change, seeing it as an assault on their power (they also lost the legal immunity that goes along with being a member of parliament). Putin made concessions to make the change more palatable, for example, giving governors the right to recall their representatives. The State Council was formed to try to assure the regional executives that they would retain some role in the federal policy-making arena, although losing their seats in the Federation Council.

Following the 2000 presidential election, implementation of these changes was accompanied by the exercise of "soft" power mechanisms, namely, the strengthening of clientelistic relations between central authorities, on the one hand, and the governors and presidents of republics, on the other. This use of administrative pressure reinforces a personalistic and clientelistic system of political power.

Following the Beslan massacre, Putin identified corruption and ineffective leadership at the regional level as culprits in allowing terrorists to carry out the devastating school hostage-taking. Accordingly, he proposed an additional reform that created a decisive element of central control over regional politics. Approved by the State *Duma* in December 2004, the change eliminated popular election of regional executives. Now the president nominates regional heads for approval by the regional legislature. Similar to the system for approval of the prime minister, if the regional legislature refuses the nomination three times, the president may disband the body and call for new elections. With governors and republic presidents dependent on the goodwill of the president for appointment and reappointment, a self-perpetuating political process has taken on a formal character, leading some observers to declare the death of Russian federalism and the weakening of Russian democracy. Recent elections of regional legislatures have consolidated the power of the establishment party United Russia in all but exceptional cases, further consolidating the influence of Moscow in the regions.

The distribution of tax revenues among the various levels of government has been another contentious issue. The Soviet state pursued a considerable degree of regional equalization, but regional differences have increased in the Russian Federation. Putin created a more regularized system for determining the distribution of revenues, taking account of both the regional tax base and differences in the needs of various regions (for instance, northern regions have higher expenses to maintain basic services). However, in fact, an increasing proportion of tax revenues are now controlled by Moscow, and regional governments are constantly faced with shortfalls in carrying out their major responsibilities, for example, in social policy. Disparities between rich and poor regions have reached dramatic proportions, with Moscow and resource-rich regions at the top, and areas in Russia's north and southern periphery at the bottom.

The Policy-Making Process

Policy-making occurs through both formal and informal mechanisms. The federal and regional legislatures, the president and his administration, individual deputies, and some judicial bodies may, according to the constitution, propose legislation. Sometimes, the government, deputies, or parliamentary factions have offered competing drafts of laws, leading to protracted and complicated bargaining. Budgetary proposals can be put forth only by the government, and at times have elicited sharp controversy since they can affect key interests and groups, such as regional and local governments, other state agencies, the military, trade unions, enterprise directors, state employees, and pensioners. In the Yeltsin period, conflict between the president and the *Duma* made policy-making a contentious and fractious process; under Putin, the Duma generally went along with proposals made by the president and government, and the proportion of legislation initiated by the executive branch increased significantly. In order for a bill to become law, it must be approved by both houses of the parliament in three readings and signed by the president. If the president

vetoes the bill, it must be passed again in the same wording by a two-thirds majority of both houses of parliament in order to override the veto.

Some policy proclamations are made through presidential or governmental decrees, without formal consultation with the legislative branch. This decision-making process is much less visible and may involve closed-door bargaining rather than an open process of debate and consultation. Often, expert consultants or a special commission are also involved in the policy process, as well as bodies such as the Security Council. Informal groupings also have an important indirect impact on policy-making, very evident in the Yeltsin years. A prominent example is the industrialist lobby, which represents the managerial interests of some of Russia's large privatized industries. Business magnates were able to exert behind-the-scenes influence to gain benefits in the privatization of lucrative firms in sectors such as oil, media, and transport. Putin attempted to reduce the direct political influence of these powerful economic figures and to formalize business input through bodies such as the Entrepreneurship Council. Some observers see this development as an example of corporatism, a system in which the government identifies (or sometimes helps create) organizations that are consulted to represent designated societal interests (in this case, business interests) in the policy-making process. The emerging Russian corporatism seems to be a state corporatist variant, a top-down variety in which the government itself plays an active role in defining these vehicles of societal input.[38] One problem with this approach is that some interests, particularly those that are less powerful or less well organized, may be excluded from the process. In almost all cases, participation in policy-making does not extend to representatives of more broadly based citizens' groups.

SECTION 4   Representation and Participation

Gorbachev's policies in the 1980s brought a dramatic change in the relationship between state and society, as *glasnost* sparked new public and private initiatives. Most restrictions on the formation of social organizations were lifted, and a large number of independent

groups appeared. Hopes rose that these trends might indicate the emergence of **civil society**, an autonomous sphere of social life that could act on the state without being dependent on it. However, just a few years later, only a small stratum of Russian society was actively engaged; the demands of everyday life as well as cynicism about politicians and state institutions have led many people to withdraw into the private domain and to endorse strong political leadership that would ensure stability and continued economic growth. With minor fluctuations, Putin's approval rating stabilized at 65 to 70 percent after his election in 2000, while trust in public institutions remained low and the public's ability to affect policy seemed questionable. To avoid upsetting the delicate social balance that existed, in 2006 and 2007 several laws were passed in an effort to check social forces that could nurture social division without suppressing all forms of constructive civic engagement. These included better oversight of foreign organizations, support for pro-system youth groups, and marginalization of illegal immigrants.

The Legislature

The Russian legislature, the Federal Assembly, came into being after the parliamentary elections of December 12, 1993, when the referendum ratifying the new Russian constitution was also approved. The upper house, the Federation Council, represents Russia's constituent federal units. The lower house, the *Duma,* has 450 members and is currently chosen through a proportional representation (PR) electoral system. This body was named after the short-lived assembly formed by the tsar following the revolution of 1905 and thus emphasizes continuity with the Russian (rather than the Soviet) tradition. The first Federal Assembly served only a two-year term. Subsequent elections to the *Duma* have occurred every four years, in 1995, 1999, 2003, and 2007. As noted in Section 3, in some special circumstances, earlier elections can be called.

Within the *Duma,* factions unite deputies from the same or allied parties. In May 2008 there were four party factions representing the parties elected in the December 2007 vote. The *Duma* has a council (eleven members) and thirty-three committees. Following the 2007 Duma elections twenty-seven of the chairships were held by members of the dominant United Russia faction.[39] The *Duma* elects its own speaker (or chair); since July 2003 this has been Boris Gryzlov, head of the United Russia Party. After the 1995 and 1999 elections, the speaker of the Duma came from the Communist Party, which had the highest electoral showing in those votes.

Compared to the communist period, deputies reflect less fully the demographic characteristics of the population at large. For example, in 1984, 33 percent of the members of the Supreme Soviet were women;[40] in 2005 they constituted less than 10 percent, rising to about 13.5 percent in 2008. In spring 2008, women headed four of the thirty-three committees, two in the traditionally "female" areas (health and women/family/children) and the other two being nature use and ecology, as well as the North/Far East.[41]) In 2000, manual workers made up less than 1 percent of *Duma* deputies, in contrast to 35 percent in the 1985 Supreme Soviet.[42] It is important to remember, however, that the implicit demographic quotas that the CPSU enforced in the Soviet period were primarily symbolic since the Supreme Soviet was largely powerless. On the other hand, the underrepresentation of women and workers in the present *Duma* indicates the extent to which Russian politics is primarily the domain of male elites.

The upper house of the Federal Assembly, the Federation Council, has two members from each of Russia's federal regions and republics, but the method of selection has varied over time. A new procedure, phased in between 2000 and 2002, involves the appointment of one representative by the regional executive and one by the regional legislature; however, from 1995 until that time, the elected governor/president of each region and the regional legislative head had themselves been members. Since 2000, the Federation Council has gradually become quite a compliant organ, although formally it plays a role in the approval of federal laws.[43] Many prominent businessmen are among the appointees, and in some cases the posts may be granted in exchange for political loyalty, raising doubts about the likelihood that the body adequately represents interests of the regions. Party factions do not play a significant role in the Federation Council. Deputies to the Federation Council, as well as to the *Duma,* are granted immunity from criminal prosecution.

The constitution grants parliament powers in the legislative and budgetary areas, but these powers can be exercised effectively only if parliament operates with a high degree of unity. In practice, the president can often override the parliament through mechanisms such as the veto of legislation. To override the veto, two-thirds of the members of the Federal Assembly must support the original wording of the bill. Each house of parliament has the authority to confirm certain presidential appointees, in addition to the prime minister. For example, the *Duma* confirms the chair of the Central Bank of Russia, and the Federation Council confirms judges of higher courts. The Federation Council decides on deployment of troops abroad, and also must approve presidential decrees relating to martial law and state emergency abroad.[44] In some cases, failure to approve the president's nominees has produced a stalemate or prevented certain offices from functioning for a period of time.

Conflict between the president and the legislative branch was frequent in the 1990s. Following electoral rebuffs in the 1993 and 1995 parliamentary elections, Yeltsin confronted a parliament that obstructed many of his proposed policies, but the parliament did not have the power or unity to offer a constructive alternative. Following the 1999 elections, the situation was somewhat less conflictual, and since 2003 the *Duma* has cooperated with the president, since about two-thirds or more (just under 70 percent in 2008) of the deputies have been tied to the United Russia faction, closest to the president; following the 2003 election, the faction was larger than the popular vote received by United Russia (49 percent), but the 2007 vote gave United Russia 64 percent of the vote, closer to its weight in the *Duma*.[45]

Society's ability to affect particular policy decisions through the legislative process is minimal. The blocs and parties in the parliament are isolated from the public at large and suffer low levels of popular respect. Many of the mechanisms that link parties and parliaments to citizens in Western democracies do not exist in Russia: interest associations to lobby the parliament are weak, and the internal decision-making structures of parties are generally elite-dominated.

Political Parties and the Party System

One of the most important political changes following the collapse of communism was the shift from a single-party to a multiparty system. In the USSR, the CPSU not only dominated state organs but also oversaw all social institutions, such as the mass media, trade unions, youth groups, educational institutions, and professional associations. It defined the official ideology for the country, set the parameters for state censorship, and, through the *nomenklatura* system, ensured that loyal supporters occupied all important offices. Approximately 10 percent of adults in the Soviet Union were party members, but there were no effective mechanisms to ensure accountability of the party leadership to its members. Because the CPSU did not have to compete for political office, it was a party of a special kind, whose authority could not be openly questioned.

National competitive elections were held for the first time in the USSR in 1989, but new political parties were not formal participants in Russia until 1993. Since then, a confusing array of political organizations has run candidates in elections (see Table 11.2). A new law on political parties went into effect in July 2001, tightening the conditions for party formation and registration. Parties must have at least 50,000 members, with branches of at least 500 members in at least half of the regions of Russia. Although critics have portrayed these changes as artificially reducing voter choice, defenders argue that they will help to bring order to a chaotic and fragmented party system. In early 2007, thirteen registered parties[46] met these conditions, with eleven appearing on the *Duma* ballot and four winning at least some seats.

In the 1990s, many parties formed around prominent individuals, without a firm social base or stable constituency. Furthermore, other than the Communist Party of the Russian Federation (CPRF), Russian parties are young, so deeply rooted political identifications have not had time to develop. Finally, many citizens do not have a clear conception of their own interests or of how parties might represent them. In this context, image-making is as important as programmatic positions, so that parties appeal to transient voter sentiments. Nonetheless, party membership has grown in recent years.

Russian political parties do not fit neatly on a left–right spectrum. Identity-based issues crosscut economic ideologies, producing the following party tendencies:

- Centrist "parties of power"
- The left
- Nationalist/patriotic forces
- Liberal/reform forces

Table 11.2

Top Parties in the State Duma Elections[a]

Party or Bloc[b]	Percent of 1995 Party List Vote[c]	Percent of 1999 Party List Vote[c]	Percent of 2003 Party List Vote[c]	Percent of Duma Seats 2003[d]	Percent of 2007 Party List Vote[e]	Percent of Duma Seats Based on 2007 Vote	Comments	Party Leader
Centrist/Establishment								
United Russia	—	(23.3)	37.6	49.3	64.3	70.0	Formed as Unity Party in 1999, then merged with Fatherland, All-Russia to form United Russia	Boris Gryzlov, party chair, but Vladimir Putin headed the party list on the ballot (2007)
A Just Russia	—	—	—	—	7.7	8.4	Formed in 2006 from three political parties: Life, Rodina, and the Russian Party of Pensioners	Sergey Mironov
Fatherland, All-Russia	—	13.3	—	—	—	—	Merged into United Russia in 2001	Yuri Lyzhkov, Evgenii Primakov (1999)
Our Home Is Russia	10.1	1.2	—	—	—	—	Chernomyrdin was prime minister, 1992–1998	Viktor Chernomyrdin (1995, 1999)
Liberal/Reform								
Union of Rightist Forces	(3.9)	8.5	4.0	0.7	1.0	0	Russia's Choice (1993), Russia's Democratic Choice/United Russia (1995)	Nikita Belykh
Yabloko	6.9	5.9	4.3	0.9	1.6	0	Opposition liberal/reform party	Grigory Yavlinsky

Communist/Socialist

Party							Leader	Notes
Communist Party of the Russian Federation	22.3	24.3	12.6	11.6	11.6	12.7	Gennady Zyuganov	
Nationalist/Patriotic								
Liberal Democratic Party of Russia	11.2	6.0	11.5	8.0	8.1	8.9	Vladimir Zhirinovsky	In 1999 participated in elections as Bloc Zhirinovsky
Rodina (Motherland Bloc)	—	—	9.0	8.2	—	—	Dmitry Rogozin, Sergey Glaziev (2003)	Left/center nationalist party; merged into A Just Russia

[a] As of 2008, blocs of parties were not permitted to stand in elections.

[b] Figures may not add to 100 percent or to the total number of deputies in the *State Duma* because smaller parties and independents are excluded. Table includes only parties winning at least 4.0 percent of the national party list vote in one of the three elections (but not all such parties).

[c] Percentage of the total popular vote the party or bloc received on the proportional representation portion of the ballot in the year indicated. A dash indicates that the party or bloc was not included on that ballot or did not win a significant portion of the vote. Numbers in parentheses are votes for predecessor parties, similar to the one running in 2003.

[d] The sum of seats won in the proportional representation (party list) vote and the single-member district vote. Number of deputies in the faction changed over time following the elections.

[e] In 2007 all of the seats were allocated according to the party list (proportional representation) ballot for parties receiving at least 7% of that vote; the single-member district vote was discontinued.

Source: Revised and updated from DeBardeleben, Joan, "Russia" in *Introduction to Comparative Politics.* Copyright 2004 by Houghton Mifflin Company. Reprinted with permission. 2007 election results are from the Russian Electoral Commission website, http://www.vybory.izbirkom.ru/region/izbirkom (accessed December 9, 2008).

Nearly all parties express support for the market transition, but those on the left are more muted in their enthusiasm, arguing for a stronger state role in providing social protection for vulnerable parts of the population. The liberal/reform parties, on the other hand, have advocated more rapid market reform, including privatization, free prices, and limited government spending. The now dominant United Russia party charts a middle ground, appealing to voters from a wide ideological spectrum, supporting market reform but in a less radical form. In relation to national identity, nationalist/patriotic parties emphasize the defense of Russian interests over Westernization. Liberal/reform parties, on the other hand, advocate integration of Russia into the global market and the adoption of Western economic and political principles. Again, the United Russia party has articulated an intriguing combination of these viewpoints, identifying Europe as the primary identity point for Russia, but at the same time insisting on Russia's role as a regional power, pursuing its own unique path to democratization and market reform.

Ethnic and regional parties have not had a significant impact on the national scene. Amendments to the party law, noted above, make it even more difficult than previously for regional parties to emerge. Similarly, religion, while an important source of personal meaning for many Russians, has not emerged as a significant basis for political identity among ethnic Russians, who primarily adhere to the Russian Orthodox strain of Christianity. Nonetheless, in recent years, rising expressions of Russian nationalism and ethnic intolerance have erupted, particularly in relation to the primarily Muslim Chechens.

United Russia and A Just Russia: Centrist Parties

Since 2003, one political party, United Russia, has taken on political dominance at both the national and regional levels. A relative newcomer to the political scene, United Russia enjoyed a meteoric rise. Its predecessor, the Unity Party, rose to prominence together with Vladimir Putin in the elections of 1999 and 2000. In 2001, the Unity Party joined with a potential establishment rival, Fatherland/All-Russia, taking the name United Russia in 2004. In its first electoral foray in 1999, the party won 23.3 percent of the party-list vote (and seventy-three seats in the *Duma*); this increased to 37.6 percent in 2003 and 64 percent in 2007.

What explains United Russia's rapid success? Based on its association with Putin, the party has also built an effective political machine that generates persuasive incentives for regional elites to come on board, reinforced by Putin's control of appointments of regional executives (since 2004). The party has a rather poorly defined program, which emphasizes the uniqueness of the Russian approach (as distinct from Western models), an appeal to values of order and law, and a continued commitment to moderate reform. Its official website[47] indicates that the party is more focused on prominent people than on ideas, justifying its designation as a cadre party. The party is, at the same time, truly a "party of power," focused on winning to its side prominent and powerful people who will then use their influence to further bolster the party's position. By 2005, United Russia had, through a combination of carrots and sticks, brought 64 regional executives (governors and heads of republics) into the fold, along with increased influence in regional legislatures.[48]

United Russia has drawn electoral support from every part of the political spectrum, making the party a catchall electoral organization. In the 2007 *Duma* election, there were no real competitors for United Russia's dominance, which was reinforced by slanted media coverage. The second closest rival, the CPRF, won less than 12 percent of the vote. Public opinion polls generally reveal a positive attitude toward United Russia, as a force promoting new ideas and solutions to problems.[49] The question now facing the party is whether it has adequate institutional strength to impose accountability on its leaders and whether it can develop an organizational footing in society.

Another new centrist "establishment" party, A Just Russia, was formed in 2006, based on an amalgam of three small parties (Rodina, Party of Life, and the Party of Pensioners). The party was founded by Putin loyalist Sergey Mironov, chair of Russia's upper legislative body, the Federation Council. Many observers consider that A Just Russia was formed (from above) to demonstrate the competitive nature of Russia's electoral system, while undermining opposition parties that might pose a real threat to United Russia. Mironov espouses support for socialist principles, placing it to the left of United Russia on the political spectrum and offering a political magnet for dissatisfied supporters of the Communist Party.[50] Understandably, Communist Party leaders view such socialist proclamations with a jaundiced eye, suspecting that the party is a Kremlin prop. Mironov's loyalty to Putin was evidenced by his suggestion in March 2007 that the constitution should be amended to allow Putin to run for a third term as president. Many Russians seem confused about the relationship between United Russia and A Just Russia. A February 2007 poll indicated that about a quarter (27 percent) viewe them as "two faces of one 'establishment party,'" just under a half (46 percent) saw them as distinct with separate programs, while another quarter (27 percent) couldn't say.[51] It is expected that A Just Russia will firmly support Putin's initiatives as the Russian prime minister.

The Russian Left: The Communist Party of the Russian Federation (CPRF)

Consistently represented in the *Duma* since 1993, the CPRF, headed by Gennady Zyuganov, was by far the strongest parliamentary party after the 1995 elections, winning more than one-third of the seats in the *Duma*. While maintaining strong electoral performance, the CPRF's relative position was weakened after the 1999 election because the Unity Party gained almost an equal number of votes and seats. In the 2003 elections, CPRF support dropped by about one-half, to 12.6 percent of the party list vote, and in 2007 the party won 11.6 percent. In May 2008, only 13 percent of *Duma* deputies were in the CPRF faction, compared to about 25 percent after the 1999 election and close to 35 percent after the 1995 election.[52] The CPRF, the clearest successor of the old CPSU, is considered by some observers to be the only remaining opposition force represented in the *Duma*. Nonetheless, without the injection of new leadership and ideas, the CPRF may continue to be a party in decline.

In addition to its socialist economic approach, Russian nationalism is also evident in the CPRF program. The party defines its goals as being democracy, justice, equality, patriotism and internationalism, a combination of civic rights and duties, and socialist

renewal. Primary among the party's concerns are the social costs of the reform process. Thus, it has supported state subsidies for industry to ensure timely payment of wages and to prevent enterprise bankruptcies. The party's detractors see its leaders as opportunistic rather than as true democrats, but others point out that in the late 1990s communist governors in some of Russia's regions acted pragmatically rather than ideologically (indeed, many "converted" to the United Russia party in later years). The party has operated within the constitutional framework in pursuing its political goals.

Support for the CPRF is especially strong among older Russians, and economically disadvantaged and rural residents. The party is no longer credible as a vanguard organization representing the working class. Instead, it appears to represent those who have adapted less successfully to the radical and uncertain changes that have occurred since the collapse of the USSR, as well as some individuals who remain committed to socialist ideals. While one might expect Russia to offer fertile ground for social democratic sentiments like those that have been successful in the Scandinavian countries, the CPRF has not capitalized on these sentiments, nor has it made room for a new social democratic party that could be more successful. Its principle failures have been an inability to adapt its public position to attract significant numbers of new adherents, particularly among the young, as well as the absence of a charismatic and attractive political leader. The party also failed to assert its legitimate claim to leadership in the government after its strong showing in the 1995 election, thus sacrificing its reputation as an effective parliamentary opposition force. For this reason, one might lay part of the blame for the weakness of an effective loyal opposition at the door of the CPRF.

The Liberal Democratic (Zhirnovksy) Party: A Nationalist Patriotic Party

To the surprise of many observers, the Liberal Democratic Party of Russia (LDPR), headed by Vladimir Zhirinovsky, received the strongest support on the party ballot in 1993, winning almost 23 percent of the vote; between 1995 and 2007 the party's popular vote has swung between 6 percent (1999) and 11.5 percent (2003). The party finished in third place in 2007 with 8.4 percent. Neither liberal nor particularly democratic in its platform, the party might more properly be characterized as nationalist and populist. Its populism is based on Zhirinovsky's personal charismatic appeal. Some Russians say, "He speaks our language," while others radically oppose Zhirinovsky's provocative style and nationalist rhetoric. In his speeches, Zhirinovsky openly appeals to the anti-Western sentiments that grew in the wake of Russia's decline from superpower status and the government's perceived groveling for Western economic aid. The party has supported revival of an expanded Russian state to include Ukraine, Belarus, and possibly other neighboring areas. Concern with the breakdown of law and order seems to rank high among its priorities. However, despite Zhirinovsky's radical demeanor, he has often supported the government on key issues, including the war in Chechnya. Zhirinovsky's base has been especially strong among working-class men and military personnel. Other parties and leaders have taken up a softer version of the patriotic theme, so the resurgence of support for the LDPR in 2003 suggests that nationalist sentiment in Russia is increasing, not declining. More radical nationalist groups, such as the National Bolsheviks,[53] which combines nationalist and left-wing revolutionary ideology, have also sought influence outside the electoral process, coming under periodic raids or restrictions from the government.

Liberal/Reform Parties: Union of Rightist Forces and Yabloko

More than any other part of the political spectrum, the liberal/reform parties have found it hard to build a stable and unified electoral base. Despite the fact that liberal forces drove Yeltsin's initial reform program in the early 1990s in Russia, by 2007 parties representing this tendency had no seats in the *Duma*. The Union of Rightist Forces (URF) and Yabloko each got less than 2 percent of the vote in the 2007 *Duma* elections.[54]

Leaders of these parties have been outspoken critics of the current government, viewing Russia as on a slide toward authoritarianism. They point to selective enforcement of complex legislation governing elections and political party registration directed against opposition forces. As an example, they refer to the case of regional elections in St. Petersburg *oblast* in March 2007 when the Yabloko party was disqualified due to a contested failure to comply with party registration legislation. Following the 2007 *Duma* election, the party leader, Grigory Yavlinksy, issued a biting criticism of the electoral process: "Today's voting has involved serious violations of all articles of the (election) law without exception," referring, among other things, to "the way [voters'] lists were compiled and absentee vote ballots were issued . . . , mass-scale refusals to release [voting] reports, . . . expulsion of observers from polling stations," and smuggling of fake ballots into ballot boxes. Yavlinksy characterized Russia's political system as "authoritarian, based on oligarchic clans, corrupt, unaccountable to society and pursuing the sole goal of preserving its dominance at any cost."[55] URF party statements echo many of these themes.[56]

While political restrictions on the opposition have likely contributed to the declining electoral success of these parties, more fundamental factors are also at play. First, in the 1990s when liberals enjoyed some popular support, they failed to form a unified political force; Yeltsin's refusal to associate himself with any political party deprived these groups of a strong organizational resource in the early 1990s. Four parties or blocs running on a promarket reform plank won seats in the *Duma* in the 1993 elections; in 1995 several liberal/reform parties split the vote, reducing their representation in the *Duma*. On November 21, 1998, the brutal murder by contract killers of the liberal/reform politician and *Duma* member Galina Starovoitova (one of Russia's most prominent female politicians) resulted in renewed efforts to form a united political bloc in the form of the URF. However this was too late and too little. A second problem has to do with the unpopularity of these parties' programmatic approach, which is associated with the disastrous economic results of Russia's market reform and privatization efforts in the 1990s. Accordingly, support for liberal/reform parties generally is stronger among the young, the more highly educated, urban dwellers, and the well-off. Thus, ironically, those with the best prospects for succeeding in the new market economy have been the least successful in fashioning an effective political party to represent themselves.

Elections

In the postcommunist period, elections seemed to be a constant phenomenon in Russia, partly because presidential, legislative, and regional/local elections are generally held on separate occasions. The initial euphoria with the competitive electoral structure has been replaced by voter fatigue, although turnout in federal elections remains respectable, generally between 60 and 70 percent; it stood at 63 percent in the 2007 *Duma* election and close to 70 percent in the 2008 presidential vote, when the state engaged in assertive voter mobilization. In regional and local contests, participation rates have at times fallen below the required minimum participation rate to make the vote ballot valid (a requirement since eliminated), necessitating repeat balloting. National elections receive extensive media coverage, and campaign activities begin as long as a year in advance. Elections are now big business, involving extensive use of polling firms and public relations experts. Up until 2003, national elections were generally considered to be reasonably fair and free, but international observers have expressed serious concerns about the fairness of both the 2003–2004 and 2007–2008 election cycles, related, for example, to slanted media coverage.[57]

Until 2007, the electoral system for selecting the *Duma* resembled the German system, combining **proportional representation (PR)** with winner-take-all districts; in addition, voters were given the explicit option of voting against all candidates or parties (4.7 percent chose this in 2003). Until 1999, despite the electoral rebuffs in 1993 and 1995, Yeltsin did not install a prime minister reflecting party strength in the *Duma*. In 1999 and 2003, parliamentary elections offered qualified support for the government.

The 2007 election was governed by a new electoral system involving one national proportional representation district, with a minimum threshold for representation of each party raised to 7 percent (from 5 percent). Parties are required to include regional representatives on their lists from across the country. For those parties above the 7 percent threshold, choice of deputies from the list must reflect strength of the vote in the various regions. In addition, according to the 2001 law on political parties, in order to participate in the election, a party must have affiliates in more than half of the regions of Russia, with a certain number of registered members in these regions. Therefore, parties with a strong political base in one or several regions would only be represented in the national parliament if they had organizations of the requisite size in half of the regions in the country *and* if they had gained 7 percent of the national vote. In 2006, national legislation removed the "against all" option from the ballot. Under the new party legislation, the number of successful parties is likely to decline over time, which could help to bring greater clarity about choices to the voter. However, parties will probably be more dependent on national party machines and thus the law is likely to have a strongly centralizing character.

Since 1999, opposition parties have experienced a sharp decline in electoral success, with the rapid ascent of United Russia. One reason is genuine popular support for Putin, as well as the failure of the opposition parties to develop appealing programs or field attractive candidates. However, other factors also play a role. Media coverage has favored the "party of power" and the president. Administrative control measures and selective enforcement have delimited the scope of acceptable political opposition, particularly when this has involved potential elite support for challengers. In addition, the carrot-and-stick method has wooed regional elites, producing a bandwagon effect that has been reinforced by the abolition of elections of regional executives.

Russia has yet to experience a real transfer of power from one political grouping to another, which some scholars consider a first step in consolidating democratic governance. While the CPRF topped the list in the 1995 *Duma* elections, the party leader, Zyuganov, was not able to defeat Yeltsin in the presidential election of 1996. Zyuganov did even more poorly against Putin in the 2000 vote; even in areas of traditional support (the so-called Red Belt in central European Russia), Putin generally outscored him. Zyuganov did not run in 2004, and in 2008 he received 18 percent of the vote (Zhirinovsky came in third with 9 percent). Under the Russian constitution, presidential elections are held every four years (with a proposal to extend this to six years under consideration in 2008). If no candidate receives a majority of the votes in the first round, a runoff election is held between the two top contenders. Although the 1995 election went to a second round (Yeltsin won 35 percent in the first and 54 percent in the second round against Zyuganov), beginning in 2000 no runoff has been required.

Political Culture, Citizenship, and Identity

Political culture can be a source of great continuity in the face of radical upheavals in the social and political spheres. Attitudes toward government that prevailed in the tsarist period seem to have endured with remarkable tenacity. These include acceptance of a tradition of personalistic authority, highly centralized leadership, and a desire for an authoritative source of truth. The Soviet regime embodied these and other traditional Russian values, such as egalitarianism and collectivism; at the same time, the Soviet development model glorified science, technology, industrialization, and urbanization—values superimposed on the traditional way of life of the largely rural population. When communism collapsed, Soviet ideology was discredited, and the government embraced political and economic values from the West. Many citizens and intellectuals are skeptical of this "imported" culture, partly because it conflicts with other traditional civic values such as egalitarianism, collectivism, and a broad scope for state activity. A crisis of identity resulted for both elites and average citizens, and current government priorities collide with some traditional values while appealing to others.

One way to study political culture is to examine evidence from public opinion surveys. Such surveys suggest that there is considerable support in Russia for liberal democratic values such as an independent judiciary, a free press, basic civil liberties, and competitive elections. Colton and McFaul conclude from survey results that "a significant portion of the Russian population acquiesces in the abstract idea of democracy without necessarily looking to the West for guidance."[58] The authors find that Russians are divided on the proper balance between defense of individual rights and the maintenance of order; other experts conclude that Russians' desire for a strong state and strong leaders does not imply support for authoritarian government.[59] On the other hand, democratic values may not be deeply enough entrenched to provide a safeguard against authoritarian rule.

In the Soviet period, the mass media, the educational system, and a variety of other social institutions played key roles in propagating the party's political values. After the collapse of the communist system, students were presented with a wider range of views, print media represent a broad spectrum of political opinion, but the electronic media increasingly reflect the government's position. The electronic media are particularly susceptible to political pressure, given the costs and limited availability of the technology needed to run television stations. Unequal media access, in favor of the propresidential forces, was criticized by international observers in relation to recent elections. Financial interests and mafia attacks on investigative journalists have an inhibiting effect on press freedom. The print media are considerably more diverse than TV, but on occasion political and economic pressure is used by national and regional governments to limit the publication of highly critical viewpoints. Violent attacks on journalists who exposure corruption or who are outspoken in their criticism of established interests present another obstacle to the creation of a responsible and critical press.

Russia is a multiethnic state, and one important aspect of the state's search for identity relates to what it means to be Russian. Thus, the distinction between ethnic identity and civic identity is an important one. The Russian language itself has two distinct words for "Russian": *russkii,* which refers to an ethnicity, and *Rossiiskii,* which has a civic meaning and includes people of various ethnic backgrounds who are Russian citizens. The name of the country, Rossiiskaia Federatsiia, invokes the latter sense. In recent years there have been increasing concerns about the rise of an exclusionary form of Russian nationalism among certain parts of the population. This phenomenon has been manifested in the rise of fringe nationalist parties, extremist nationalist youth movements, and intermittent attacks on visible minorities. Muslim groups from Russia's southern regions have been the target of ethnic stereotyping. In addition, refugee flows from some of the war-torn regions of the Transcaucasus (Georgia, Azerbaijan, and neighboring regions of southern Russia such as Chechnya and Ingushetia) have heightened national tensions. Individuals from these regions play an important role in Russia's trade sector and are viewed by many Russians as speculators and crooks.

Citizen Action

Journalism and Politics

Most Americans wouldn't consider journalism a particularly dangerous profession unless the reporter were posted abroad to a war zone. However, this is different in Russia. A recent high-profile victim, Anna Politkovskaia, was shot on October 7, 2006, at her apartment building in Moscow. Politkovskaia, a reporter for the independent newspaper *Novaia gazeta*, was an outspoken critic of the government, focusing on violations of human rights in Chechnya.[1] Other prominent victims include Dmitriy Kholodov (1994), Larissa Yudina (1998), and Paul Khlebnikov (2004). Kholodov died when a bomb exploded in the editorial office of the popular Russian newspaper *Moskovskii Komsomolets*. Khodolov was known for his publications highlighting corruption in the Russian army. Those put on trial included officers of Russian Special forces, but all were finally acquitted. Yudina, editor of an alternative newspaper in the republic of Kalmykia, was known for her investigative journalism relating to corruption in the republic. Paul Klebnikov, an American of Russian heritage, was editor-in-chief of *Forbes* magazine in Russia; his 2003 book critically profiling a Chechen rebel leader is a presumed motive for his death. All of these cases remain unresolved.

According to the Committee to Protect Journalists, an international NGO devoted to protecting press freedom, these cases are among forty-three journalists murdered in Russia since 1993, making Russia the third most dangerous country for journalists in the world (following Iraq and Algeria).[2] While many of these cases are related to reporting in war-torn Chechnya, others could be classified as contract murders or assassinations.

Why are journalists at risk in Russia? Apart from the war in Chechnya, a fundamental cause may be the incapacity of the state to protect the security of its citizens. Businessman, politicians, and even scholars have also been targets of contract murders. Investigative reporting of criminal activity or organized crime clearly can put journalists at risk.

Apart from the vulnerability of journalists to violent attack, journalists face other obstacles in Russia as well. Article 29 of the Russian constitution states that "freedom of the mass media shall be guaranteed. Censorship shall be prohibited." However, an international organization, *Reporters Without Borders*, placed Russia 147th out of 168 countries surveyed from September 1, 2005–September 1, 2006, based on a press freedom index. In commenting on the rating, the organization noted increasing control of major media outlets by industrial groups close to Putin. While powerful economics interests often own media outlets in Western countries as well, their direct impact on media operations is generally limited by public expectations about journalistic standards and media objectivity.

Russians have access to a wide range of independent newspapers, but readership has declined radically since the Soviet period and news coverage in particular outlets is often openly biased. The lack of a vibrant civil society may partly explain the inadequate public base to generate newspapers in Russia with high professional standards comparable to the *New York Times* or *Washington Post*. Nonetheless, a poll carried out in December 2006 showed that about two-thirds of respondents see journalists as playing a positive role in the life of Russian society.[3]

[1] "Worldwide Press Freedom Index 2006, "North Korean, Turkmenistan, Eritrea: The Worst Violators of Press Freedom," October 23, 2006, http://www.rsf.org/rubrique. php3?id_rubrique=639 (accessed January 1, 2007).

[2] Committee to Protect Journalists, "Journalists Killed: Statistics and Background," http://www.cpj.org/killed/killed_archives/stats.html (accessed Dec. 31, 2006).

[3] Levada Center, http://www.levada.ru/press/2007011504.html.

Recent terrorist attacks have heightened these prejudices. Official state policy, while explicitly opposing these stereotypes, may, in some cases have implicitly fed them. For example, in the context of tensions with neighboring Georgia in 2006, an embargo was placed on imports to Russia, and people of Georgian ethnicity were expelled from public markets and Georgian children from public schools on the grounds that many were in the country illegally. Legislation effective on April 1, 2007, banned noncitizens without proper residence documents and work permits from Russia's numerous outdoor markets, a measure that was more generally threatening to visible minorities and that greatly reduced the number of vendors. A somewhat controversial phenomenon is the youth group, *Nashi* (Ours), that was formed in 2005. While claiming to oppose fascism in Russia, some observers consider the group itself to nurture intolerance and fascist sentiments. The colloquial term "*nashi*" (which means "ours") evokes an "us–them" dichotomy, and members of the group express anti-Western sentiments. Among *Nashi's* goals are to educate youth in Russian history and values, and to form volunteer groups to help maintain law and order. The group has been highly supportive of Putin, seeing him as a defender of Russia's national sovereignty.

Religion has long played a role in shaping Russian identity. Today, the Russian Orthodox Church appeals to many citizens who are looking for a replacement for the discredited values of the communist system. A controversial law passed in 1997 made it harder for new religious groups to organize themselves; the law was directed primarily at Western proselytizers. Human rights advocates and foreign observers protested strongly, again raising questions about the depth of Russia's commitment to liberal democratic values.

Attitudes toward gender relations in Russia reflect traditional family values. It is generally assumed that women will carry the primary responsibility for childcare and a certain standard of "femininity" is expected of women both inside and outside the workplace. The birthrate in Russia fell from 16.6 births per 1,000 people in 1985 to a rate of 10.4 in 2006, while the death rate was 15.2.[60] Although declining birthrates often accompany economic modernization and characterize many West European societies as well, in Russia this phenomenon is less the result of a positive choice than due to daily hardships, future uncertainty, a declining standard of living, and continued housing shortages. In May 2006, Putin announced a doubling of monthly child support payments and a large monetary bonus for women having a second child to boost the birthrate, contributing to its gradual rise. Public opinion surveys indicate that most Russians believe a higher standard of living, including better housing and jobs, would lead to an increase in the birthrate.[61] At the same time, policy-makers are concerned that population decline will hinder economic recovery.

Feminism is not popular in Russia, as many women consider it inconsistent with traditional notions of femininity or with accepted social roles for women. At the same time, a number of civil society organizations have sprung up in Russia to represent the interests of women; some of them advocate traditional policies to provide better social supports for mothers and families, while others challenge traditional gender roles and definitions. Changing cultural norms affect gender relations in other ways as well. A permissive cultural environment, propagated in advertising and through the mass media, represents women more frequently as sex objects. Advertising also reinforces commercialized images of female beauty that may not correspond to cultural expectations or to healthy lifestyles. In the face of unemployment and the breakdown in traditional social linkages, increasing numbers of young women have turned to prostitution to make a living; HIV/AIDS rates are also increasing at a rapid rate, fueled by prostitution, low levels of information, and the rise of drug trafficking related to Russia's more permeable eastern border with countries like Afghanistan.

Social class identity was a major theme in the Soviet period. The Bolshevik revolution was justified in the name of the working class, and the Communist Party of the Soviet Union claimed to be a working-class party that had transformed the Soviet Union into a society free of class conflict, representing the interests of all of the working people. However, many dissidents and average citizens perceived an "us–them" relationship with the political elite in Soviet times, which some dissident intellectuals conceptualized in terms of class conflict between the party leadership and the mass of the Soviet population. Because social class was a major part of the discredited Soviet ideology, in the postcommunist period many Russians were skeptical of claims made by politicians to represent the working class; thus, most postcommunist parties and politicians have not invoked this terminology. Even the Communist Party of the Russian Federation, in its party program, does not explicitly identify itself as a working-class party; characterizing itself as "true to the interests of working people," the CPFR "sees its task as being to join social-class and national-liberatory movements into a unified mass opposition movement and to give it a conscious and purposeful character."[62]

Nonetheless, labor solidarity has played an important role in some sectors of the Russian economy. The official trade unions established under Soviet rule have survived under the title of the Federation of Independent Trade Unions (FITU). However, FITU has lost the confidence of large parts of the work force. In some sectors, such as the coal industry, new independent trade unions have formed, mainly at the local level. Labor actions have become an important form of social protest through spontaneous strikes, transport blockages, and even hunger strikes. In the mid- to late 1990s, the main grievance was late payment of wages, and strikes were most prevalent among coal miners, in the transportation sector, and in the public service. Immediate concessions are often offered in response to such protests, but the underlying problems are rarely addressed. The number of organizations affected by actual labor strikes spiked in 1995, declined, then rose again in 2004–2005, with new waves of strikes and hunger strikes in sectors such as mining. However, according to data from the Federal Statistical Service of the Russian government, the length of time each worker spent on strike was relatively short in 2004–2005, so that apparently these strikes often took the form of one-day protest actions rather than extensive labour disputes that may be more typical of countries with collective bargaining traditions. This suggests that working-class organizations are only weakly oriented toward or able to support sustained collective action. While class conflict as a focus of social organization is momentarily in abeyance, it may well generate more pronounced collective identities, particularly in the context of a global economic recession.

Interests, Social Movements, and Protest

Following the collapse of the USSR, numerous political and social organizations have sprung up in every region of Russia, representing the interests of groups such as children, veterans, women, environmental advocates, pensioners, and the disabled. Other groups include professional unions, sports clubs, trade unions, and cultural organizations. The most successful interest associations have been those formed by better-off elements of society (such as new business entrepreneurs), officials, or, until recently, groups receiving funding from international or foreign agencies. Most locally based interest associations have small staffs and, in addition to foreign support, rely for support on local government, contracts for work carried out, and commercial activities. Dependence on Western aid can divert the agendas of nongovernmental organizations (NGOs) from the concerns of their constituents to the priorities of their foreign sponsors.

Many observers saw such blossoming activism as the foundation for a fledgling civil society that would nurture the new democratic institutions established since 1991. However, there have been many obstacles to realizing this potential. Organizations generally must register with local authorities, and some develop such close relationships with the local administration as to possibly undermine their independence. In January 2006, Putin signed legislation amending laws on public associations and noncommercial organizations. These controversial changes, protested widely by Western governments, provided new grounds for denying registration to such organizations, established new reporting requirements (particularly for organizations receiving funds from foreign sources), and increased government supervisory functions. Particular requirements are placed on foreign noncommercial, nongovernmental organizations operating in Russia; accordingly, several foreign organizations, such as Amnesty International and Human Rights Watch, were forced to temporarily suspend activities while seeking to comply with the new requirements. The new measures were justified as necessary to respond to external terrorist threats, but many commentators see them as an effort to reduce the likelihood that civil society activists with external contacts might foment a colored revolution in Russian similar to what happened in Ukraine in 2004 or in Georgia in 2005.

The government has attempted to channel public activism through official forums, such as the Civic Forum, an unprecedented all-Russian congress of nongovernmental organization activists held in November 2001 in Moscow. Organized with government support, the event elicited both enthusiasm and skepticism in NGO circles. While pleased with the official recognition given to civil society organizations, some activists viewed the event as mainly a public relations effort to indicate the government's openness to social input. A newer initiative is the Public Chamber, created in 2005 by legislation proposed by the president. Based on voluntary participation by presidential appointees and representatives recommended by national and regional societal organizations, the organization is presented as a mechanism for public consultation and input, as well as a vehicle for creating public support for government policy. It appears to reflect a corporatist approach that might serve to co-opt public activists from more disruptive forms of self-expression. A variety of mass-based political organizations protest the current political direction of the government, but in 2007 the authorities tried to restrict use of public demonstrations and protests. An alternative political grouping, The Other Russia, unites a wide range of prominent political critics,[63] while advocating liberal democratic values and human rights. The group held an alternative conference in July 2006 to draw attention to threats to Russian democracy. "Marchs of Dissent" organized periodically since 2006 in Moscow and St. Petersburg have faced bans and obstacles from local authorities; in April 2007 this led to the detention of the group's leaders, including Gary Kasparov, the world chess champion. Other movements, such as the Movement Against Illegal Immigration,[64] lie on the other end of the political spectrum, organizing protests such as a public action called "Moscow—a Russian city" in April 2007. As these examples indicate, public protests span the political spectrum and can come into conflict not only with the authorities but also with one another.

At the time of this writing, one cannot say that civil society has truly formed in Russia. Whatever forms of collective identity have emerged, social forces do not easily find avenues to exert constructive and organized influence on state activity.

SECTION 5   Russian Politics in Transition

In April 2005, in his annual political address to the Federal Assembly, Putin made a dramatic admission: "Above all, we should acknowledge that the collapse of the Soviet Union was a major geopolitical disaster of the century. As for the Russian nation, it became a genuine drama."[65] About the same time, in several cities throughout Russia, local officials decided to erect new monuments to Joseph Stalin to commemorate the sixtieth anniversary of the end of World War II in Europe, a move that Putin neither approved nor obstructed. President George W. Bush, who was visiting Latvia before his arrival in Moscow to celebrate the anniversary, also evoked images of the past, referring to the Soviet Union's unlawful annexation and occupation of the Baltic states.[66] A Kremlin spokesperson vehemently denied this depiction of the postwar events. The verbal sparring was followed by two apparently congenial leaders in Moscow, honoring the veterans who brought the defeat of Naziism. These events show how the Soviet past continues to haunt and obscure not only Russia's path forward, but also relations with neighbors and potential allies.

Political Challenges and Changing Agendas

Russia's future path continues to remain unclear. Will the country move in a "two steps forward, one step backward" progression to a more democratic political system? Or does the free-wheeling atmosphere and political relaxation in the 1990s more likely recall the temporary liberalization that occurred in the 1920s or the short-lived "thaw" of the Khrushchev period? Will Russia be able to reestablish a respected role as a regional and global power? And will the new Russian government be successful in bringing corruption under control, establishing trust in political institutions, and shoring up international confidence? These are some of the key challenges facing the Russian Federation at the dawn of Medvedev's presidency.

When the first edition of this book was published in 1996, five possible scenarios for Russia's future were presented:

- A stable progression toward marketization and democratization

- The gradual introduction of "soft authoritarianism"
- A return to a more extreme authoritarianism of a quasifascist or communist variety
- The disintegration of Russia into regional fiefdoms or de facto individual states
- Economic decline, civil war, and military expansionism[67]

At the time of this writing, a snapshot of Russia would make the "soft authoritarian" scenario seem most likely; however, there are still significant forces that may move Russia back to a more democractic trajectory.

Russia in the World of States

In the international sphere, Russia's flirtation with Westernization in the early 1990s produced ambiguous results, leading to a severe transitional recession and placing Russia in the position of a supplicant state requesting international credits and assistance. Russia's protests against unpalatable international developments, such as NATO expansion, the Desert Fox operation against Iraq in December 1998, and NATO's bombing of Yugoslavia in 1999, revealed Moscow's underlying resentment against Western dominance, as well as the country's relative powerlessness in affecting global developments. The events of September 11, however, provided a new impetus for cooperative ventures, as Russia expressed solidarity with American losses and a commitment to join the battle against international terrorism. Evidence of warmer relations included the formation of a NATO-Russia Council in May 2002, suggesting possibilities for closer cooperation in areas such as control of international terrorism, arms control, nonproliferation, and crisis management.[68] The next month, at the 2002 G-8 summit meeting in Kanaskis, Canada, it was announced that Russia would assume the presidency of the organization in 2006 and host the annual summit meeting.[69] As a further sign of the positive trend in United States–Russia relations, in May 2002 Presidents Bush and Putin agreed to a treaty involving further reductions in the nuclear arsenals of the two countries.

Against this positive background, new tensions emerged in the face of American withdrawal from the Anti-Ballistic Missile Treaty and Russian objections to the American incursion into Iraq in March 2003. In 2004 and 2005, American officials openly criticized Putin's centralizing moves as antidemocratic, and figures in American business circles viewed the attack on Khodorkovsky as interference in business operations, producing inhibitions to investments in the crucial energy sector. A critical element of Russia's relations with both the United States and its West European neighbors rests with Russia's rich endowment of oil and natural gas. The source of about 10 percent of the world's oil production and the country most richly endowed with natural gas (about a third of the world's total reserves), Russia has been dubbed by one expert as a "new energy superpower" (see Figure 11.7). Since 2000, both the EU and the United States have commenced "energy dialogues" to address energy interdependencies. The issue is particularly pressing for the EU, since Russian imports support almost 20 percent of EU gas consumption and 16 percent of oil consumption. In 2004, the EU agreed to support Russia's bid to join the WTO in an implicit quid pro quo involving Russian ratification of the Kyoto climate change protocol, but also Russian agreement to bring a gradual adjustment of its domestic gas prices to bring them closer to world market levels.

Energy issues have also complicated Russia's relations with its "near abroad" (particularly Ukraine and Belarus). As Russia has moved toward applying global market prices to its exports to former Soviet republics, these countries have resisted, resulting in countermeasures on both sides that at times have temporarily cut off some supplies to Western Europe. Russia has resisted opening natural gas transit pipes to European firms, and has sought access to retail markets in Europe. With majority state control of the natural gas monopoly Gazprom, commercial interests, national interest, and state diplomacy can easily become intertwined. At the same time, experts believe that without increased Western investment and technological know-how, Russia will not be able to develop untapped deposits quickly enough to meet both domestic demands and export commitments.

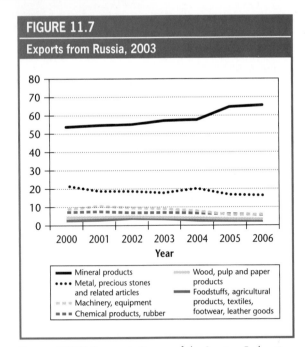

FIGURE 11.7

Exports from Russia, 2003

Year

- ——— Mineral products
- •••• Metal, precious stones and related articles
- ═══ Machinery, equipment
- ▬▬▬ Chemical products, rubber
- ═══ Wood, pulp and paper products
- ——— Foodstuffs, agricultural products, textiles, footwear, leather goods

Source: OECD Economic Survey of the Russian Federation 2004: The Sources of Economic Growth, p. 15, 2004.

Governing the Economy

The upturn in the Russian economy that began in 1999 may have been a watershed in the struggle to overcome the transitional recession that plagued Russia from the late 1980s onward. At the same time, severe disparities in income and wealth remain, meaning that a restoration of economic growth may not bring an improved standard of living for large numbers of Russian citizens, particularly the elderly, children, the disabled, and those living in poorer northern regions. Questions also remain about how much income from oil and gas exports will feed the investment needs of other sectors of the economy and how much is being appropriated by a privileged elite. Making the economy more attractive to foreign investors will require a continued development of the banking sector, legal institutions to ensure enforcement of contracts, and controls on crime and corruption. Although the 1998 devaluation of the ruble brought decreased reliance on Western imports (as they become too expensive), the so-called Dutch disease, in which heavy reliance on export income pushes the value of the currency

Global Connection

Russia and International Organizations

The Russian Federation is now open to global influences, in contrast to the isolation imposed by the Soviet government. The Russian government has sought equal membership in some international organizations from which it was previously excluded, and it has forged partnerships with others. Following are some of the most important international agencies that Russia has become involved with in one way or another over the past fifteen years.

The International Monetary Fund (IMF). The IMF was founded in 1944, and during most of the 1990s it was the most influential international agency in Russia. Its general mandate is to oversee the international monetary system and help maintain stability in exchanges between its 185 member countries, which can draw on the fund's resources. The Soviet Union applied for membership in 1991 but was dissolved before acceptance. Russia was admitted to the IMF in 1992, and

funds were issued to Russia as short- and medium-term credits to help stabilize the ruble and Russia's internal and external monetary balance. The disbursement of these funds was made contingent on the fulfillment of certain conditions by the Russian government, particularly the maintenance of noninflationary fiscal and monetary policies. These policies, in turn, necessitated cutbacks in social services and subsidies to troubled economic sectors. In 1999, a final loan was granted, and since then Russia has forgone further credits, choosing to manage its own macroeconomic fiscal policy. By 2004, Russia had paid off its IMF debt (www.imf.org).

The World Bank. Also founded in 1944, the World Bank has as its purpose to promote and finance economic development in the world's poorer countries. After World War II, this involved assistance in financing reconstruction in war-torn Europe. The agency is an investment bank with 184 member countries. As with the IMF, the Russian Federation was admitted in 1992. Through its International Bank for Reconstruction and Development (IBRD), the World Bank has provided loans to support development programs in Russia in sectors such as agriculture, the environment, energy, and social welfare. From 1991 to 2002, Russia borrowed $12.5 billion from the IBRD, and in January 2005 its outstanding debt stood at $5.7 billion.[1] In 2007, a new three-year Country Partnership Strategy was begun to help Russia achieve sustainable economic growth (www.worldbank.org).

The European Union (EU). The EU initiated the Tacis program in 1991 as a vehicle for providing grants to finance the transfer of knowledge to Russia and other countries in the former Soviet Union. A large source of aid to Russia, annual contributions ran at about 90 million euros in 2002 and 2003. In addition to such assistance efforts, the EU's Partnership and Cooperation Agreement (PCA) with Russia, which entered into force in 1997, set out a strategy for development of "strategic partnership" based on four "Common Spaces": Common Economic Space (to create an integrated market), Common Space for Freedom, Security, and Justice (relating to media, travel, human contact); Common Space for External Security (multilateralism, crisis management, antiterrorism); and Common Space for Research, Education, and Culture (http://europa. eu.int/comm/external_relations/russia/summit_05_ 05/index.htm). Negotiations for renewal of a new partnership agreement, following the expiration of the PCA in 1997, began in 2008.

North Atlantic Treaty Organization (NATO). NATO was formed in 1949 by ten European countries, the United States, and Canada to safeguard the security of its members in response to the perceived Soviet threat. Following the collapse of the communist system in Eastern Europe, NATO has had to rethink its mandate and the nature of potential threats. Among its duties are crisis management, peacekeeping, opposing international terrorism, and prevention of nuclear proliferation. Since 1999 most countries of Central and Eastern Europe were admitted as members of NATO (including Hungary, Czech Republic, and Poland in 1999; Bulgaria, Estonia, Latvia, Lithuania, Romania, Slovakia, and Slovenia in 2004; and Albania, Croatia, and Macedonia (FYROM) are preparing for possible future membership). Russia has objected to the expansion of NATO at each step, and currently the most contentious issue relates to NATO's affirmation of support for future membership for Russia's immediate neighbors, Georgia and Ukraine. Russia has, over time, developed a stronger working relationship with the organization. The Partnership for Peace program was the first important step in the process in 1994, and in 1997, the NATO-Russia Founding Act on Mutual Relations, Cooperation, and Security was concluded. A further step was taken in 2002 with the establishment of the NATO-Russia Council, in which Russia holds an equal seat with the twenty-six NATO member states (http://www.nato. int/issues/nrc/index.html).

The G-8 and Russia. In 1998, Russia was accepted as a full member into the G-8 (Group of Eight), an expanded G-7. The G-8 is an informal international body consisting of the leading industrial nations; G-8 countries hold regular summits dealing with such issues as the international economy, trade relations, and foreign exchange markets. Although Russia is still too weak to exert much influence on G-8 issues, its membership in the organization is valuable, allowing Russia to maintain a presence on the world stage. In July 2006, Russia hosted the G-8 summit.

The World Trade Organization (WTO). The WTO is a powerful international organization, responsible for regulating international trade, settling trade disputes, and designing trade policy through meetings of its 148 member countries. Because of the increasingly global nature of trade, membership in the WTO is an essential prerequisite for increasing economic prosperity and for avoiding international economic isolation. Russia's membership is supported by powerful actors such as the European Union, and an agreement with the United States was reached in November 2006. A series of outstanding issues need to be resolved before Russia is finally admitted. The World Bank estimates that membership will bring Russian annual benefits of $19 billion through increased exports, opening the country to multilateral services and increased foreign direct investment[2] (www.wto.org).

[1] Central Bank of the Russian Federation website, http:// www.cbr.ru/statistics/credit_statistics/print.asp?file=debt.htm (accessed May 10, 2005).

[2] "Russian Economic Report #10: April 2005," The World Bank Group, http://194.84.38.65/mdb/upload/RER10_ eng.pdf (accessed May 10, 2005).

up, now threatens again to undermine prospects for domestic producers and to feed inflationary pressures. The Russian economy is no longer shielded from foreign and international influences; thus, reverberations in international markets and foreign economies have a direct impact on the Russian economy as well, as occurred during the financial crisis of 2008. Perhaps the greatest economic challenge facing the Medvedev administration will be to establish policies to ensure a greater diversity of Russia's economic base, which will require reaching a new social accommodation that will bring a stable environment for economic development. At the same time, the Russian leadership still struggles to find appropriate vehicles for limiting the influence of powerful economic forces on policy-making without undermining legitimate political pluralism.

The Democratic Idea

Russia's initial democratization impulse took a downturn after 2000, and the exercise of public power has been marked by corruption, the power of big money, and limited mechanisms to assure accountability of its leaders. Opinion surveys indicate that Russians consider government performance less than satisfactory across a wide range of policy areas such as crime control, dealing with unemployment, social security, and health care.[70] The continuing disjuncture between high personal support for Putin (and possibly Medvedev) and a continuing lack of confidence in the ability of political institutions to address the country's problems effectively suggests that the legitimacy of the system is still on thin ice. The more positive working relationship between the executive and legislative branches that emerged under Putin's leadership will be tested under the dual-power arrangement between Putin (as prime minster) and Medvedev (as president). Efforts to regularize relations between the center and regions provide prospects for improved institutional performance, but the reduction of vehicles for popular input and heavy-handed efforts to keep regional elites in line and to control political opposition already show signs of producing poor policy choices that may elicit public protests and reinforce public cynicism about the motives of politicians and the trustworthiness of institutions.

The Politics of Collective Identities

Despite changes in social consciousness, the formation of new political identities remains unfinished business. Many people are still preoccupied by challenges of everyday life, with little time or energy to forge new forms of collective action to address underlying problems. Under such circumstances, the appeal to nationalism and other basic sentiments can be powerful. The weakness of Russian intermediary organizations (interest groups, political parties, or associations) means that politicians can more easily appeal directly to emotions because people are not members of groups that help them evaluate the political claims. These conditions reduce safeguards against authoritarian outcomes. Still, the high level of education and increasing exposure to international media may work in the opposite direction. Also, many Russians identify their country as part of Europe and its culture, an attitude echoed by the government (see Table 11.3). Exposure to alternative political systems and cultures may make people become more critical of their own political system and seek opportunities to change it. One might expect that experiences and reforms of the 1990s would have generated effective leaders for this democratic subculture, but so far they have failed to emerge.

Russia remains in what seems to be an extended period of transition. In the early 1990s, Russians frequently hoped for "normal conditions," that is, an

Table 11.3

Attitudes toward Foreign Countries

In general, what is your attitude toward the following foreign countries?

	USA	The European Union	Ukraine
Very positive	6%	6%	7%
Basically positive	57	67	60
Basically negative	22	12	19
Very negative	7	3	4
Hard to say	8	12	10

Note: Based on a survey carried out April 15–18, 2005, among 1,600 residents of Russia (128 sampling points in 46 regions).

Source: Levada Center, http://www.levada.ru/press/2005050401.html.

escape from the shortages, insecurity, and political controls of the past. Now, "normality" has been redefined in less glowing terms than those conceived in the late 1980s. Russians seem to have a capability to adapt to change and uncertainty that North Americans find at once alluring, puzzling, and disturbing.

Russian Politics in Comparative Perspective

The way in which politics, economics, and ideology were intertwined in the Soviet period has profoundly affected the nature of political change in all of the former Soviet republics and generally has made the democratization process more difficult. How has Russia fared compared to some of the other postcommunist systems that faced many of these same challenges, and what can we learn from these comparisons? A rule of thumb, simple as it seems, is that the further east one goes in the postcommunist world, the more difficult and prolonged the transition period has been (with the exception of Belarus, which has liberalized less than one might expect). This is partly because the more westerly countries of Central Europe that were outside the USSR (Poland, Hungary, Czech Republic, Slovakia), as well as the Baltic states, faced the realistic prospect of EU accession and thus had a strong motivation to embark on fundamental reform to meet the EU's conditions. This illustrates the potentially powerful impact of international forces on domestic political developments, given political receptiveness to them. Also, these countries were under communist rule for a shorter period of time. Despite the efforts of the Soviet leadership to establish conformity throughout the region, national differences did remain. The countries of Central Europe had a history of closer ties and greater cultural exposure to Western Europe; ideas of liberalism, private property, and individualism were less foreign to citizens in countries such as Czechoslovakia, East Germany, and Hungary than in regions farther east, including Russia. The Roman Catholic Church in Poland provided a focal point for national identity, and Poland's historical antipathy to Russia produced a stronger resistance to the imposition of the Soviet model than in other Slavic countries of the region. Such cultural, geopolitical, and historical differences affected the shape that communist rule

took, indicating that historical legacies and cultural differences do matter.

In terms of economic performance, postcommunist countries that liberalized the least, such as Uzbekistan and Belarus, suffered less severe recessions in the 1990s because state institutions remained more fully intact. However, these less-reformed economies may face painful adjustments in the future. Russia's experience demonstrates the importance of political institutions if democracy is to be secured; their weakness in the 1990s contributed to high levels of social dislocation, corruption, and personal stress, as well as demographic decline and poor economic adaptation to the market. However, Russia's rich deposits of natural resources have sheltered it from difficulties facing some neighboring countries like Ukraine, but expose other weaknesses, namely difficulties of realizing political accountability in the face of intertwined political and economic power. Environmental protection remains a low priority in Russia, a problem that affects the entire postcommunist region.

Progression along the various dimensions of the quadruple transition are uneven across postcommunist countries, and Russia seems now to be progressing economically, while regressing politically, with nationalism on the rise and aspirations to status of a regional superpower resurfacing. In all of the post–Soviet states (except the Baltic states), the attempt to construct democratic political institutions has been characterized by repeated political crises, weak representation of popular interests, executive–legislative conflict, faltering efforts at constitutional revision, and corruption. Although Russian politics has been highly contentious and the government has operated at very low levels of efficacy and legitimacy for most of the past decade, with the exception of the Chechnya conflict, Russia has escaped major domestic violence and civil war, unlike Yugoslavia, Armenia, Azerbaijan, Georgia, Moldova, and the Central Asian state of Tajikistan.

Russia will undoubtedly continue to be a key regional force in Europe and Asia. Its vast geographic expanse, rich resource base, large and highly skilled population, and the legacy of Soviet rule will ensure this. Yet its former allies in Central Europe, as well as the Baltic states, are gradually drifting into the orbit of Western Europe economically and politically.

Following the 2004 and 2007 enlargements of the EU, Russia's most important Western neighbor, Ukraine, has made clear its aspirations to EU membership, a goal the Russian leadership has not articulated. Although Ukraine is divided internally over its future course, the European dream is an increasingly important reference point. Russian leaders seem to appreciate the isolation this could imply, but seem unwilling to adopt certain crucial aspects of Western political practice. Thus, over the past few years, while Russia has resisted a unipolar world order dominated by the United States and while Russia's leaders have shown a desire and willingness to identify as a European country, Russia has had an ambivalent relationship to accepting crucial norms that would underlie an effective and enduring partnership.

Will Russia be able to find a place for itself in the world of states that meets the expectations of its educated and sophisticated population? Eight years into the new millennium, prospects are still unclear. One thing is certain: Russia will continue to be an important factor by virtue of its size, its energy resources, its historic role, and its nuclear arsenal. If President Medvedev gradually moves Russia on a path closer to liberal democratic development, then this may provide an example to other postcommunist systems further east. On the other hand, if the continuation of existing authoritarian trends is associated with sustained economic growth and stability that benefits the majority of the population, then Russia may settle into a period of soft authoritarianism that reinforces the East–West divide, and that could, if not resisted by the political leadership, feed destructive nationalist tendencies. Finally, if a Russian leadership increasingly insulated from the public generates poor policy outcomes, or if world energy prices trigger an economic downslide, this may stimulate a new process of reflection on Russia's future path and offer an opportunity for democratic forces to reassert themselves and find popular resonance.

Key Terms >>>

patrimonial state
democratic centralism
vanguard party
collectivization
tacit social contract
perestroika
glasnost
demokratizatsiia
market reform
shock therapy
joint-stock companies
privatization voucher
insider privatization

oligarchs
mafia
"state capture"
nomenklatura
path dependence
patron-client networks
siloviki
asymmetrical federalism
"power vertical"
civil society
proportional representation (PR)

Suggested Readings >>>

Aslund, Anders. *Building Capitalism: The Transformation of the Former Soviet Bloc.* Cambridge, UK, and New York: Cambridge University Press, 2002.

Black, J. L. *Vladimir Putin and the New World Order: Looking East, Looking West?* Lanham, Md.: Rowman and Littlefield, 2004.

Colton, Timothy J. *Transitional Citizens: Voters and What Influences Them in the New Russia.* Cambridge: Harvard University Press, 2000.

DeBardeleben, Joan, ed. *The Boundaries of EU Enlargement: Finding a Place for Neighbours.* Houndsmill Basingstoke: Palgrave Macmillan, 2008.

Evans, Jr., Alfred B., Laura A. Henry and Lisa McIntoshe Sundstrom, eds. *Russian Civil Society*. Armonk, N.Y.: M. E. Sharpe, 2006.

Freeland, Chrystia. *Sale of the Century: Russia's Wild Ride from Communism to Capitalism*. New York: Doubleday, 2000.

Getty, J. Arch. *Origins of the Great Purges: The Soviet Communist Party Reconsidered*. Cambridge: Cambridge University Press, 1985.

Hale, Henry E. "Regime Cycles, Democracy, Autocracy and Revolution in Post-Soviet Eurasia," *World Politics* 58 (October 2005): 133–165.

Hoffman, David E. *The Oligarchs: Wealth and Power in the New Russia*. New York: Public Affairs Press, 2002.

Hough, Jerry, and Fainsod, Merle. *How the Soviet Union Is Governed*. Cambridge: Harvard University Press, 1979.

Ledeneva, Alena V. *How Russia Really Works: The Informal Practices That Shaped Post-Soviet Politics and Business*. Ithaca, N.Y.: Cornell University Press, 2006.

Lewin, Moshe. *The Gorbachev Phenomenon: A Historical Interpretation*. Berkeley: University of California Press, 1991.

Motyl, Alexander J., Ruble, Blair A., and Shevtsova, Lilia, eds. *Russia's Engagement with the West: Transformation and Integration in the Twenty-First Century*. Armonk, N.Y.: M. E. Sharpe, 2005.

Pål, Kolsto, and Blakkisrud, Helge, eds. *Nation-Building and Common Values in Russia*. Lanham, Md.: Rowman and Littlefield Publishers, 2004.

Pipes, Richard. *Russia Under the Old Regime*. New York: Scribner, 1974.

Reddaway, Robert, and Orttung, Robert, eds. *The Dynamics of Russian Politics: Putin's Reform of Federal-Regional Relations*. 2 vols. Rowman & Littlefield, 2004 (volume 1); 2005 (volume 2).

Remington, Thomas F. *Politics in Russia,* 3rd ed. Boston: Pearson Education, 2004.

Ross, Cameron, ed. *Local Politics and Democratization in Russia*. London and New York: Routledge, 2008.

Sakwa, Richard. *Putin: Russia's Choice*. London and New York: Routledge, 2008.

Shevstsova, Lilia. *Russia Lost in Transition: The Yeltsin and Putin Legacies*. Washington D.C.: The Carnegie Endowment for International Peace, 2007.

Solomon, Peter H., Jr., and Fogelson, Todd S. *Courts and Transition in Russia: The Challenge of Judicial Reform*. Boulder, Colo.: Westview Press, 2000.

Stoner-Weiss, Kathryn. *Resisting the States: Reform and Retrenchment in Post-Soviet Russia*. Cambridge, UK, and New York: Cambridge University Press, 2006.

Tolz, Vera. *Russia*. London: Arnold; New York: Oxford University Press, 2001.

Tsygankov, Andrei P. *Russia's Foreign Policy: Change and Continuity in National Identity*. Lanham Md.: Rowman and Littlefield Publishers, Inc., 2006.

Weigle, Marcia A. *Russia's Liberal Project: State-Society Relations in the Transition from Communism*. University Park, P.A.: Pennsylvania State University Press, 2000.

Suggested Websites ⟫

The Carnegie Moscow Center
www.carnegie.ru/en/
Center for Russian & East European Studies, University of Pittsburgh
www.ucis.pitt.edu/reesweb
Itar-TASS News Agency
www.itar-tass.com/eng/

Johnson's Russia List
www.cdi.org/russia/johnson/default.cfm
Radio Free Europe/Radio Liberty
www.rferl.org/newsline/
The Moscow News
www.mnweekly.ru

Endnotes ⟫

[1] Richard Pipes, *Russia Under the Old Regime* (London: Widenfelt & Nicolson, 1974).

[2] Ibid., pp. 22–24.

[3] Peter Hauslohner, "Politics Before Gorbachev: De-Stalinization and the Roots of Reform," in Alexander Dallin and Gail W. Lapidus, eds., *The Soviet System in Crisis: A Reader of Western and Soviet Views* (Boulder, Colo.: Westview Press, 1991), pp. 37–63.

[4] Mikhail Gorbachev, *Perestroika: New Thinking for Our Country and the World* (New York: Harper, 1987).

[5] E.g., Michael McFaul, "It's OK to Scold the Backslider," *Los Angeles Times*, May 8, 2005, and the website of the Committee to Protect Journalists, "Special Report 2007: Backsliders" http://www.cpj.org/backsliders/index.html.

[6]See, for example, Joseph Stiglitz, *Globalization and Its Discontents* (New York: W. W. Norton & Co., 2002).

[7]Sergei Peregudov, "The Oligarchic Model of Russian Corporatism," in Archie Brown, ed., *Contemporary Russian Politics: A Reader* (New York: Oxford University Press, 2001), p. 259.

[8]Economist Intelligence Unit (EIU), Country Reports: Russia (London: EIU, March 2005 and October 2007).

[9]Central Intelligence Agency, CIA Factbook, Russia (updated March 15, 2007), https://www.cia.gov/cia/publications/factbook/index.html (accessed March 29, 2007).

[10]E. T. Gurvich, "*Makroekonomicheskaia otsenka roli rossiiskogo neftegazovogo sektora*," [Macroeconomic Evaluation of the Role of the Russian Oil-Gas Sector], *Voprosy ekonomiki*, no. 10 (2004).

[11]Novosti Russian News and Information Agency, June 1, 2007, http://en.rian.ru/russia/20070601/66514271.html (accessed May 31, 2008).

[12]Transparency International, *Annual Report 2006*, p. 21, http://www.transparency.org/publications/annual_report (accessed May 31, 2008).

[13]Joel Hellman and Daniel Kaufmann, "Confronting the Challenge of State Capture in Transition Economies," *Finance and Development* 38, no. 3, September 2001, http://www.imf.org/external/pubs/ft/fandd/2001/09/hellman.htm (accessed May 31, 2008).

[14]Viktor Polterovich and Vladimir Popov, "Democratization, Quality of Institutions and Economic Growth," Social Science Research Network, TIGER Working paper, No. 102, July 1007, p.38,http://papers.ssrn.com/sol3/papers.cfm?abstract_id=1036841 (accessed October 25, 2008).

[15] Economist Intelligence Unit (EIU), *Country Report: Russia* (July 2000, p. 6 and September 2007, p. 12).

[16] EIU, *Country Report: Russia* (March 2002), 13; *Rossiiskii statisticheskii ezhegodnik* [Russian Statistical Yearbook], Moscow: Goskomstat, 2004.

[17]*Rossiiskii statisticheskii ezhegodnik* [Russia Statistics Annual]. Moscow: Federal Service of State Statistics, 2007, http://www.gks.ru/bgd/regl/b07_13/IssWWW.exe/Stg/d02/06-01.htm (accessed May 27, 2008).

[18]Public Opinion Foundation, "National Projects: Preliminary Results and Prospects," January 18, 2007, http://bd.english.fom.ru/cat/societas/society_power/nat_project (accessed October 25, 2008). For the website about the National Projects, see http://www.rost.ru/ (in Russian, accessed October 25, 2008)); also Levada Center, *Obshchestvennoe mnenie* 2007 (Moscow, 2007), pp. 52–53.

[19]Sarah Ashwin and Elaine Bowers, "Do Russian Women Want to Work?" in Mary Buckley, ed., *Post-Soviet Women: From the Baltics to Central Asia* (Cambridge: Cambridge University Press, 1997), p. 23. Also *Rossiiskii statisticheskii ezhegodnik* (2004).

[20]*Rossiiskii statisticheskii ezhegodnik* [Russia Statistics Annual] (Moscow: Federal Service of State Statistics, 2007), http://www.gks.ru/bgd/regl/b07_13/IssWWW.exe/Stg/d01/04-01.htm (accessed May 26, 2008).

[21]*Rossiiskii statisticheskii ezhegodnik* [Russia Statistics Annual] (Moscow: Federal Service of State Statistics, 2007), http://www.gks.ru/bgd/regl/b07_13/IssWWW.exe/Stg/d01/04-01.htm (accessed May 26, 2008).

[22]Victor Zaslavsky, "From Redistribution to Marketization: Social and Attitudinal Change in Post-Soviet Russia," in Gail W. Lapidus, ed., *The New Russia: Troubled Transformation* (Boulder, Colo.: Westview Press, 1994), p. 125.

[23]On attitudes toward corruption see, Rasma Karlkins, *The System Made Me Do It: Corruption in Post-Communist Societies* (Armonk, N.Y.; London, England: M. E. Sharpe, 2005), esp. ch. 4.

[24]Joan DeBardeleben, "Attitudes Toward Privatization in Russia," *Europe-Asia Studies* 51, no. 3 (1999): 447–465, as well as subsequent data from surveys organized in Russia by the author.

[25]Figures adapted from Economist Intelligence Unit, *EIU Quarterly Economic Review of the USSR, Annual Supplement* (London: EIU, 1985): 20.

[26]OECD, "*Obzory investitsionnoi politiki: Rossiiskaia Federaltisiia*" [OECD Investment Policy Review: Russian Federation] (2004), http://www.oecd.org/dataoecd/3/27/34464365.pdf, pp. 20, 24 (accessed October 25, 2008)).

[27]Russian State Statistical Agency, www.gks.ru/free_doc/2006/b06_13/22-15.htm.

[28]Ibid.; www.gks.ru/bgd/regl/b07_13/IssWWW.exe/Stg/d05/23-19.htm (accessed October 25, 2008).

[29]EUI, *Russia: Country Profile 2007*, p. 15.

[30]Ibid, p. 51.

[31]Vladimir Putin, Address to the Federal Assembly, April 25, 2005, http://www.kremlin.ru/appears/2005/04/25/1223_type63372type63374type82634_87049.shtml (accessed October 25, 2008).

[32]For an example of path-dependent analysis, see David Stark and Laszlo Bruszt, *Postsocialist Pathways: Transforming Politics and Property in East Central Europe* (Cambridge and New York: Cambridge University Press, 1998).

[33]Thomas Remington, *Politics in Russia*, 2nd ed. (New York: Longman, 2001), pp. 53–54.

[34]For a chart (in Russian) showing federal executive organs, see the webpage of the Russian government, http://www.government.ru/content/executivepowerservices/(accessed October 25, 2008).

[35]*EBRD Transition Report*, 2006. I am grateful to Vladimir Popov for this reference.

[36]Fred Weir, "Putin's Endgame for Chechen Beartrap," *Christian Science Monitor*, January 25, 2001.

[37]"Russia's Department of Crime," BBC online, November 19, 1998, http://news.bbc.co.uk/1/hi/world/europe/216480.stm (accessed October 25, 2008).

[38]On corporatism, see Philippe C. Schmitter and Gerhard Lehmbruch, *Trends Towards Corporatist Intermediation* (Thousand Oaks, Calif.: Sage, 1979).

[39]Compiled by the author from the website of the *State Duma*, http://www.duma.gov.ru/ (accessed May 20, 2008).

[40]David Lane, *State and Politics in the USSR* (Oxford: Blackwell, 1985), pp. 184–185.

[41]Compiled by the author from the website of the *State Duma*, http://www.duma.gov.ru/ (accessed May 20, 2008).

[42]Remington, p. 102.

[43]See the Constitution of the Russian Federation, Articles 105 and 106, http://www.constitution.ru/en/10003000-06.htm (accessed October 25, 2008).

[44]Ibid., Article 102.

[45]http://www.duma.gov.ru (accessed May 20, 2008).

[46]For a listing of registered parties, see the website of the Federal Electoral Commission of the Russian Federation, http://www.cikrf.ru/cikrf/politparty/(accessed October 25, 2008).

[47]http://www.edinros.ru/index.html (October 25, 2008).

[48]Darrell Slider, "'United Russia' and Russia's Governors: The Path to a One-Party System," paper presented the American Association for the Advancement of Slavic Studies National Convention, Washington, DC, November 17, 2006.

[49]Analytical Center of Yurii Levada (Levada Center), *Obshchestvennoe mnenie 2007* [Russian Public Opinion Annual] (Moscow, 2007), pp. 101–103.

[50]Website of the party at http://www.spravedlivo.ru/. (accessed October 25, 2008).

[51]Levada Center, *Obshchestvennoe mnenie 2007*, p. 102.

[52]These numbers also include seats won in single-member districts that existed until 2007.

[53]See the website at http://nazbol.ru/ (accessed October 25, 2008).

[54]The websites of these parties are also available in English. See www.sps.ru/party/english/ and http://www.eng.yabloko.ru/ (accessed October 25, 2008).

[55]Interfax, Moscow, December 3, 2007, published on the website of the Yabloko party, www.eng.yabloko.ru/Publ/2007/071205_mt2.html (accessed May 20, 2008).

[56]E.g., the statement about the Russian presidential election at www.sps.ru/?id=225741 (accessed May 20, 2008).

[57]Office for Democratic Institutions and Human Rights, "Russian Federation: Election to the *State Duma* 7 December 2003, OSCE/ODHIR Election Observation Mission Report" (Warsaw, January 27, 2004), http://unpan1.un.org/intradoc/groups/public/documents/UNTC/UNPAN016105.pdf (October 25, 2008).

[58]Timothy J. Colton and Michael McFaul, "Are Russians Undemocratic?" *Post-Soviet Affairs* 18 (April–June 2002): 102.

[59]William M. Reisinger, Arthur H. Miller, Vicki L. Hesli, and Kristen Hill Maher, "Political Values in Russia, Ukraine, and Lithuania: Sources and Implications," *British Journal of Political Science* 24 (1994): 183–223.

[60]Goskomstat (Russian Statistical Agency), http://www.gks.ru/bgd/free/b05_00/IswPrx.dll/Stg/d010/i010180r.htm (accessed May 2, 2005); http://www.gks.ru/bgd/free/b07_00/IssWWW.exe/Stg/d01/07-0.htm (accessed October 25, 2008).

[61]Public Opinion Foundation, "The Birthrate in Russia: Views and Forecast," March 22, 2007, http://bd.english.fom.ru/report/whatsnew/ed071222 (accessed October 25, 2008).

[62]Programme of the Communist Party of the Russian Federations, online, http://www.cprf.ru/party/program/ (accessed April 8, 2007), in Russian, translation by the author.

[63]See the website at http://www.theotherrussia.org (accessed October 25, 2008).

[64]See the website at http://www.dpni.org/ (accessed December 9, 2008) .

[65]http://www.kremlin.ru/eng/speeches/2005/04/25/2031_type70029type82912_87086.shtml (accessed October 25, 2008).

[66]Elisabeth Bumille, "Bush, Arriving in Baltics, Steps Into Argument With Russia," *New York Times*, May 7, 2005.

[67]Joan DeBardeleben, "Russia," in Mark Kesselman, Joel Kreiger, and William A. Joseph, eds., *Comparative Politics at the Crossroads* (Lexington, Mass.: Heath, 1996), pp. 355–357.

[68]For the official statement, see the NATO website, "NATO-Russia Relations: A New Quality," Declaration by Heads of State and Government of NATO Member States and the Russian Federation, http://www.nato.int/docu/basictxt/b020528e.htm (October 25, 2008).

[69]For background on the G-8, see the Canadian government site, "About the G8," http://www.g8.gc.ca/menu-en.asp (accessed October 25, 2008).

[70]Based on a survey carried out by the author in conjunction with Russian partners headed by Viktor Khitrov and the Institute of Sociology of the Russian Academy of Sciences. The research was conducted by regional partners in Stavropol *krai*, Nizhnegorodskaia *oblast*, and Orlov *oblast* in 1998 and 2000, and in the same locations in 2004.

Part 4 >> Non-Democracies

Ervand Abrahamian

Chapter 12 ›››**IRAN**

Official Name: **Islamic Republic of Iran (Jomhuri-ye Eslami-ye Iran)**

Location: **Middle East (West Asia)**

Capital City: **Tehran**

Population (2008): **65.8 million**

Size: **approximately 1,648,000 sq. km.; slightly larger than Alaska**

1921
Colonel Reza Khan's military coup

1925
Establishment of the Pahlavi dynasty

1941–1945
Allied occupation of Iran

1951
Nationalization of the oil industry

1953
Coup against Mosaddeq

1963
White Revolution

1975
Establishment of the Resurgence Party

1979
Islamic Revolution

1979–1981
U.S. hostage crisis

December 1979
Referendum on the constitution

January 1980
Bani-Sadr elected president

March 1980
Elections for the First Islamic *Majles*

1980–1988
War with Iraq

June 1981
President Bani-Sadr ousted

October 1981
Khamenei elected president

SECTION 1 · The Making of the Modern Iranian State

Politics in Action

Iran is invariably described as "authoritarian," "dictatorial," and even "totalitarian." Yet its president, who officially heads the executive branch of government, is chosen in relatively democratic elections and often has difficulty persuading the elected parliament to approve his choice of cabinet ministers. What is more, elections both for parliament and the presidency are hotly contested and often produce unpredictable results. In 2005, Mahmud Ahmadinejad, then a little-known ultra-conservative, populist mayor who had come in second in the first round of the presidential elections, managed to win the runoff against a prominent figure of the conservative establishment. Ahmadinejad won the presidency in part because his opposition was divided between conservatives and reformers, in part because the reformers were themselves divided, in part because a large portion of the electorate abstained, in part because he mobilized fellow veterans of the Iraqi War of 1980–1989, and in part because he ran an effective campaign promising to distribute oil money to the poor, cut to size the ruling power elite, and stand up to the demands of the United States—especially on the highly charged issue of Iran's development of nuclear power.

Two presidential elections earlier, in 1997, Muhammad Khatami, a relatively unknown middle-ranking cleric, had won an even more surprising victory against a prominent high-ranking cleric endorsed by much of the establishment. Khatami had run on a liberal ticket promising to reform the "sick economy," initiate a "dialogue" with the West, and nourish **civil society** in Iran by protecting individual liberties, freedom of expression, women's rights, rule of law, and political pluralism. Khatami won nearly 70 percent of the vote in an election where some 80 percent of the electorate participated. He expanded his support in his second run for the presidency in 2001. Much of his support came from women, wage earners, and youth—especially high school graduates and college students. He was unable to run again in 2005 because of term limits laid down by the constitution.

These electoral outcomes, as well as the contrast between the conventional imagery and complex reality of the country, go to the very heart of the paradox that is modern Iran, which, to borrow Winston Churchill's famous quote about the Soviet Union, is a "a riddle wrapped in a mystery inside an enigma." At the core of this enigma lies a written constitution that tries to synthesize **theocracy** (rule by the religious clergy) with democracy, religion with politics, spiritual authority with popular sovereignty, divine rights with human rights, the *shari'a* (Islamic law) with the modern judicial processes, the **mosque** (house of prayer) with the state, and, most important of all, concepts grounded in early Islam with modern principles derived from the West—especially from the Enlightenment. Iran

1984	1989	1996	2001	2005
Elections for the Second Islamic *Majles*	Khomeini dies; Khamenei appointed Leader; Rafsanjani elected president	Elections for the Fifth Islamic *Majles*	Khatami reelected president	Ahamadinejad elected president
1988	**1992**	**1997**	**2004**	**2008**
Elections for the Third Islamic *Majles*	Elections for the Fourth Islamic *Majles*	Khatami elected president	Elections for the Seventh Islamic *Majles*	Elections for the Eighth Islamic *Majles*
		2000		
		Elections for the Sixth Islamic *Majles*		

has regular nationwide elections for local officials, for the presidency, and for the ***Majles*** (parliament). But ultimate power resides in the **Leader** (*Rahbar*) known in the West as the **Supreme Leader**. This Leader, who has to be a cleric elected by an assembly of clerics, has the authority not only to "guide" the nation and "supervise" the state, but also make major appointments—especially to the powerful **Guardian Council,** which vets candidates running for high office and vetoes bills passed by parliament. Thus the *Majles*, as the main legislative body, has the authority to draft laws. But the clerically dominated Guardian Council has the power to determine whether such laws conform to its own understanding of Islamic law and the Islamic Constitution. The constitution itself opens with the grand assurance that the document will remain intact until Judgment Day and the Return of the Messiah. But, tucked away in its many clauses, it mentions that parliament, with a two-thirds majority, can call for a nationwide referendum to change any part of the constitution.

Many argue that the Islamic Republic of Iran is bound to collapse because it is founded on these two contradictory foundations—theocracy and democracy. Before we accept such dire predictions, we should remember that the Islamic Republic has managed to survive now for more than thirty years. We should also contemplate the fact that modern democracy itself is

FIGURE 12.1

The Iranian Nation at a Glance

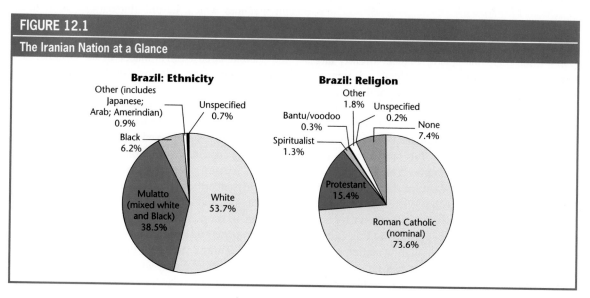

Brazil: Ethnicity

Other (includes Japanese; Arab; Amerindian) 0.9%
Unspecified 0.7%
Black 6.2%
Mulatto (mixed white and Black) 38.5%
White 53.7%

Brazil: Religion

Other 1.8%
Unspecified 0.2%
Bantu/voodoo 0.3%
None 7.4%
Spiritualist 1.3%
Protestant 15.4%
Roman Catholic (nominal) 73.6%

Table 12.1	
Political Organization	
Political System	A mixture of democracy and theocracy (rule of the clergy) headed by a cleric with the title of the Leader
Regime History	Islamic Republic since the 1979 Islamic Revolution
Administrative Structure	Centralized administration with thirty provinces. The interior minister appoints the provincial governor-generals.
Executive	President and his cabinet. The president is elected by the general electorate every four years. The president chooses his cabinet ministers, but they need to obtain the approval of the *Majles* (parliament).
Legislature	Unicameral. The *Majles*, formed of 290 seats, is elected every four years. It has multiple-member districts with the top runners in the elections taking the seats. Bills passed by the *Majles* do not become law unless they have the approval of the clerically dominated Council of Guardians.
Judiciary	A Chief Judge and a Supreme Court independent of the executive and legislature but appointed by the Leader
Party System	The ruling clergy restricts most party and organizational activities.

based on two contradictory principles—that of liberty and equality. To have real equality, we would need to drastically restrict individual liberty. And to give individual liberty unlimited reign would result in a high degree of inequality. Democracies have survived and thrived by balancing these two contradictory ideals. The Islamic Republic might do likewise by balancing *vox Dei* (voice of God) with *vox populi* (voice of the people).

Geographic Setting

Iran—three times the size of France, slightly larger than Alaska, and much larger than its immediate neighbors—is notable for two geographic features. The first is that most of its territory is inhospitable to agriculture. A vast arid zone known as the Great Salt Desert covers much of the central plateau from the capital city, Tehran, to the borders with Afghanistan and Pakistan. The Zagros mountain range takes up the western third of the country. Another range, the Elborz, stretches across the north. Rain-fed agriculture is confined mostly to the northwest and the provinces along the Caspian Sea. In the rest of the country, population settlements are located mostly on oases, on the few rare rivers, and on constructed irrigation networks. Only pastoral

nomads can survive in the semiarid zones and in the high mountain valleys. Thus, 67 percent of the total population of 68 million is concentrated on 27 percent of the land—mostly in the Caspian region, in the northwest provinces, and in the cities of Tehran, Qom, Isfahan, Shiraz, and Ahwaz.

In the past, Iran's inhospitable environment was a major obstacle to economic development. In recent decades, this has been overcome by the inflow of oil revenues which, despite fluctuations, brought on average $15 billion a year through the 1980–1990s, and totaled as much as $30 billion in 2008. Iran is the second largest oil producer in the Middle East and the fourth largest in the world, and oil revenues account for the fact that Iran is now an urbanized and partly industrialized country. More than 67 percent of the population lives in urban centers; 70 percent of the labor force is employed in industry and services; 80 percent of adults are literate; life expectancy has reached seventy years; and the majority of Iranians enjoy a standard of living well above that found in most of Asia and Africa.

Iran's second notable geographic feature is that it lies on the strategic crossroads between Central Asia and Turkey, between the Indian subcontinent and the Middle East, and between the Arabian Peninsula and the Caucasus Mountains, which are

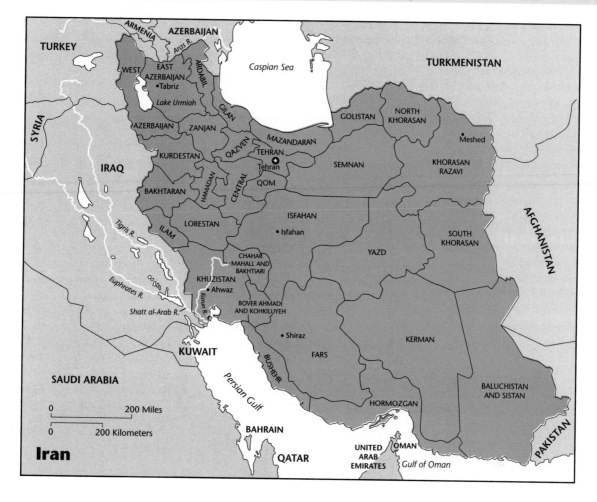

Iran

often considered a boundary between Europe and Asia. This has made the region vulnerable to invaders: Indo-Europeans in the distant past giving the country the name Iran—"Land of the Aryans"; Arab tribes in the seventh century bringing with them the religion of Islam; and series of Turkic incursions in the Middle Ages introducing Turkish-speaking populations in the region.

The population today reflects these historic invasions. Some 51 percent of the country speaks Persian **(Farsi),** an Indo-European language, as their first language; 26 percent speak various dialects of Turkic, mainly Azeri and Turkman; 8 percent speak Gilaki or Mazandarani, distant Persian dialects; 7 percent speak Kurdish, another Indo-European language; and 3 percent speak Arabic. Europeans long referred to

the country as Persia, but since the third century Iranians have called their country Iran and their main language Farsi, after the central province (Fars), the original home of the language. In 1935, Iran formally asked the international community to cease calling the country Persia. Although Persian is the native language of only 51 percent of the population, the dramatic expansion of the educational system after the 1979 revolution has spread its use throughout the country. By 2008, more than 90 percent of the population could speak and understand Persian. The non-Persian speakers were confined to the periphery—some Kurds in the northwest, Turkmans in the northeast, and Baluchis in the far southeast. Iran is now a monolingual state despite continuing to be a multiethnic society.

Critical Junctures

Although modern Iran traces its roots to an ancient empire of the sixth century B.C. and its Islamic religion to the Arab invasions of the seventh century, its current national identity, geographic boundaries, particular interpretation of Islam—**Shi'ism**—and political system were formed by four more recent critical junctures: the Safavid (1501–1722), Qajar (1794–1925), and Pahlavi (1925–1979) dynasties, and the Revolution of 1979, which led to establishment of the current Islamic Republic.

The Safavids (1501–1722)

Modern Iran, with its Shi'i Islamic identity and its present-day boundaries, can be traced to the sixteenth century, when the Safavid family conquered the territory with the help of fellow Turkic-speaking tribes. They revived the ancient Iranian titles of Shah-in-Shah (King of Kings) and Shadow of God on Earth, and proceeded to forcibly convert their subjects to Shi'ism. Although small Shi'i communities had existed in this area since the beginning of Islam, the vast majority had adhered to the majority Sunni branch (see "Background: Islam and Shi'ism"). The Safavid motivation for this drastic conversion was to give their kingdom and population a distinct identity separate from the surrounding Sunni powers: the Ottomans in the west, the Uzbeks in the north, and the Afghans in the east.

By the mid-seventeenth century, the Safavid dynasty had succeeded in converting nearly 90 percent of their subjects to Shi'ism. Sunnism survived only among tribal groups at the periphery: Kurds in the northwest, Turkmans in the northeast, and Baluchis in the southeast. It should be noted that the Safavids failed to capture from the Ottomans the two most holy Shi'i sights: Karbala in Iraq where Imam Husayn had been martyred in 680 A.D.; and nearby Najaf, where Imam Ali had been martyred. Najaf, with its collections of seminaries, became the major theological center for the Shi'i world. This had profound ramifications for Iran. It meant that the rulers of Iran could not control the main Shi'i scholars.

In addition to the Sunni minority, Safavid Iran contained small communities of Jews, Zoroastrians, and Christians (Armenians and Assyrians). These small minorities lived mostly in Isfahan, Shiraz, Kerman, Yazd, and Azerbaijan. Jews had lived in Iran since ancient times, predating the great diaspora prompted by the Roman destruction of Jerusalem. Zoroastrians were descendants of Iranians who retained their old religion after the Arab invasions. The Christians had lived in the northwest long before the advent of Islam in Iran. To strengthen their foothold in central Iran, the Safavids transported there some 100,000 Armenians, encouraging them to become craftsmen and merchants, especially in the lucrative silk trade. The Safavids, like most other Muslim rulers, but unlike medieval Christian kings, tolerated religious minorities as long as they paid special taxes and accepted royal authority. According to Islam, Christians, Jews, and Zoroastrians were to be tolerated as legitimate **People of the Book.** They were respected both because they were mentioned in the Holy **Qur'an** and because they had their own sacred texts: the Bible, the Torah, and the Avesta.

The Safavids established their capital in Isfahan, a Persian-speaking city, and recruited Persian scribes into their court administration. Such families had helped administer the ancient Iranian empires. They proceeded to govern not only through these Persian scribes and Shi'i clerics but also through local notables, especially tribal chiefs and large landowners, as well as through religious leaders, city merchants, guild elders, and ward elders.

The Safavid army was formed mostly of cavalry led by tribal chieftains. Financial constraints prevented the Safavids from creating a large bureaucracy or an extensive standing army. Their revenues came mostly from land taxes levied on the peasantry. In theory, the Safavids claimed absolute power; in reality, their power was limited since they lacked a central state and had no choice but to work along with many semi-independent local leaders. The central government was linked to the general population not so much through coercive institutions as through provincial and hereditary notables. It survived for the most part because the society below was sharply fragmented by geographic barriers (especially mountains) as well as by tribal, communal, and ethnic differences. Moreover, many senior Shi'i clerics who might have opposed the dynasty resided in Najaf, Iraq, at a safe distance from

Background: Islam and Shi'ism

Islam, with some 1 billion adherents, is the second largest religion in the world. Islam means literally "submission to God," and a Muslim is someone who has submitted to God—the same God that Jews and Christians worship. Islam has one central tenet: "There is only one God, and Muhammad is His Prophet." Muslims, in order to consider themselves faithful, need to perform the following four duties to the best of their ability: give to charity; pray every day facing Mecca, where Abraham is believed to have built the first place of worship; make a pilgrimage at least once in a lifetime to Mecca, which is located in modern Saudi Arabia; and fast during the daytime hours in the month of Ramadan to commemorate God's revelation of the Qur'an (Koran, or Holy Book) to the Prophet Muhammad. These four duties, together with the central tenet, are known as the Five Pillars of Islam.

From its earliest days, Islam has been divided into two major branches: Sunni, meaning literally "followers of tradition," and Shi'i, literally "partisans of Ali." Sunnis are by far in the majority. Shi'is total less than 10 percent of Muslims worldwide. They are concentrated in Iran, Azerbaijan, eastern Turkey, southern Lebanon, and around the Persian Gulf—in southern Iraq, Bahrain, and northeastern Saudi Arabia.

Although both branches accept the Five Pillars, they differ mostly over who should have succeeded the Prophet Muhammad (d. 632). The Sunnis recognized the early dynasties that ruled the Islamic empire with the exalted title of caliph ("Prophet's Deputy"). The Shi'is, however, argued that as soon as the Prophet died, his authority should have been passed on to Imam Ali, the Prophet's close companion, disciple, and son-in-law. They further argue that Imam Ali passed his authority to his direct male heirs, the third of whom, Imam Husayn, had been martyred fighting the Sunnis in 680, and the twelfth of whom had supposedly gone into hiding in 941.

The Shi'is are also known as Twelvers, since they follow the Twelve Imams. They refer to the Twelfth Imam as the *Mahdi*, the Hidden Imam, and believe him to be the Messiah whose reappearance will herald the end of the world. Furthermore, they argue that in his absence, the authority to interpret the *shari'a* (religious law) should be in the hands of senior clerical scholars—the **ayatollahs** ("signs of God"). Thus, from the beginning, the Shi'is harbored ambivalent attitudes toward the secular state, especially if the rulers were Sunnis or lacked genealogical links to the Twelve Imams. For Sunnis, the *shari'a* is based mostly on the Qur'an and the teachings of the Prophet. For Shi'is, it is based also on the teachings of the Twelve Imams as interpreted by the ayatollahs.

the seat of power of Iran. The Safavid shah did not control Iranian society. Rather, he hovered over it, systematically orchestrating its many existing rivalries.

The Qajars (1794–1925)

The Safavid dynasty collapsed in 1722 when Afghan tribesmen invaded the capital. The invasion was followed by a half-century of civil war until the Qajars, another Turkic tribe, reconquered much of Iran. The Qajars moved the capital to Tehran and recreated the Safavid system of central manipulation and court administration, including the Persian scribes. They also declared Shi'ism to be the state religion even though they, unlike the Safavids, did not boast of genealogical links to the Twelve Imams. This was to have far-reaching repercussions. Since these new shahs did

not pretend to wear the imam's mantle, the Shi'i clerical leaders could claim to be the main interpreters of Islam. In addition, many of them safeguarded their independence from the state by continuing to reside in Iraq and collecting religious contributions directly from the faithful in Iran. These contributions came mainly from wealthy merchants.

Qajar rule coincided with the peak of nineteenth-century European imperialism. After a series of invasions, the Russians seized parts of Central Asia and the Caucasus, thereby giving Iran borders that have continued more or less intact into the present age. Thus national identity in Iran is strengthened not only by a long history and a common religion but also by fairly consistent borders. It should also be noted that in the last two centuries Iran has never invaded its neighbors but has itself been invaded at least twelve times—four times by the British and six by the Russians, and, most recently, by Saddam Hussein's Iraq in 1980. In addition to territories, the Russians extracted a series of major economic concessions, including a monopoly to fish for sturgeon (the source of the delicacy caviar) in the Caspian Sea and exemption from import duties, internal tariffs, and the jurisdiction of local courts. The British Imperial Bank won the monopoly to issue paper money. The Indo-European Telegraph Company got a contract to extend communication lines through the country. Exclusive rights to drill for oil in the southwest were sold to a British citizen. The later Qajars also borrowed heavily from European banks to meet lavish court expenses. By the end of the nineteenth century, these loans had become so heavy that the Qajars were obliged to guarantee repayments by placing the country's entire customs service under European supervision. Iranians felt that the shah was auctioning off the country with these concessions. These concessions became notorious as "capitulations."

These resentments culminated in the constitutional revolution of 1905–1909. The revolution began with shopkeepers and moneylenders protesting the hand-over of customs collections to Europeans. They suspected that the shah would renege on local debts in favor of repaying his foreign loans. They also protested that the government was not doing enough to protect native merchants and industries. The protests intensified when the government, faced with soaring sugar prices due to political turmoil in Russia (Iran's major source of the commodity), tried to stem inflation by publicly whipping two major importers.

The revolutionary movement peaked in 1906, when some 14,000 protesters took sanctuary inside the gardens of the British legation in Tehran and demanded a written constitution. After weeks of haggling, the shah conceded, in part because British diplomats advised compromise and in part because the ruler's praetorian guards, the Cossack Brigade, threatened to join the protesters. A British diplomat commented, "The shah with his unarmed, unpaid, ragged, starving soldiers, what can he do in face of the menace of a general strike and riots?"[1]

The 1906 constitution introduced essential features of modern government into Iran: elections, separation of powers, laws made by a legislative assembly, and the concepts of popular sovereignty and the nation

(*mellat*). It also generated a heated debate, with some arguing that democracy was inherently incompatible with Islam and others countering that true Islam could not be practiced unless the government was based on popular support. Some even argued in favor of secularism—complete separation of religion from politics, church from state, and clergy from government authority. The new constitution retained the monarchy, but centered political power in a national assembly called the *Majles*. It hailed this assembly as "representing the whole people" and guaranteed seats to the recognized religious minorities: Jews, Zoroastrians, and Christians. But, significantly, no seats were given to the Baha'is, a nineteenth-century offshoot of Shi'ism. The clerical leaders deemed the Baha'is to be not only apostates from Islam but also "sinister heretics linked to the imperial powers."

The constitution endowed the *Majles* with extensive authority over all laws, budgets, treaties, loans, concessions, and the composition of the cabinet. The ministers were accountable to the *Majles,* not to the shah. "Sovereignty," declared the constitution, "is a trust confided (as a divine gift) by the people to the person of the shah." The constitution also included a bill of rights guaranteeing equality before the law, protection of life and property, safeguards from arbitrary arrest, and freedom of expression and association.

Although the constitution was modeled on the European liberal secular system of government, it made some concessions to Shi'ism. Shi'ism was declared Iran's official religion. Only Shi'is could hold cabinet posts. Clerical courts retained the right to implement the *shari'a,* especially in family matters. A Guardian Council formed of senior clerics elected by the *Majles* was given veto power over parliamentary bills deemed un-Islamic. In short, popular sovereignty was to be restricted by clerical veto power. In actual fact, this Guardian Council was not convened until the Islamic Revolution of 1979. It was not convened in part because of opposition within parliament and in part because of divisions within the clerical establishment itself.

The initial euphoria that greeted the 1905 constitutional revolution gave way to deep disillusionment in the subsequent decade. Pressures from the European powers continued, and a devastating famine after World War I took some 1 million lives, almost 10 percent of the total population. Internal conflicts polarized the *Majles* into warring liberal and conservative factions. The former, mostly members of the intelligentsia, championed social reforms, especially the replacement of the *shari'a* with a modern legal code. The latter, led by landlords, tribal chiefs, and senior clerics, vehemently opposed such reforms, particularly land reform, women's rights, and the granting of full equality to religious minorities.

Meanwhile, the central government, lacking any real army, bureaucracy, or tax-collecting machinery, was unable to administer the provinces, especially the regions inhabited by the Kurds, Turkmans, and Baluchis. Some tribes, equipped with modern European rifles, had more firepower than the central government. Moreover, during World War I, Russia and Britain formally carved up Iran into three zones. Russia occupied the north and Britain the south. Meanwhile, the Ottomans invaded from the west. Iran was left with a small "neutral zone" in the middle.

By 1921, Iran was in complete disarray. The shah was gathering the crown jewels to flee south. The British, in their own words, were hoping to "salvage" some "healthy limbs" of the fractured country in their southern zone. Left-wing rebels, helped by the new communist regime in Russia, had taken over Gilan province and were threatening nearby Azerbaijan, Mazandaran, and Khorasan. According to a British diplomat, the propertied classes, fearful of communism, were anxiously seeking "a savior on horseback."[2]

The Pahlavis (1925–1979)

That savior appeared in February 1921 in the person of General Reza Khan, the recently appointed commander of the elite 3,000-strong Cossack Brigade. Carrying out a typical military **coup d'état**, he replaced the cabinet and, while paying lip service to the monarch, consolidated power in his own hands, especially the post of commander in chief of the armed forces. Four years later, he emerged from behind the throne; deposed the Qajars; crowned himself shah-in-shah in the style of his hero, the French emperor Napoleon; and established the Pahlavi dynasty, adopting a name associated with the glories of ancient Iran. This was the first nontribal dynasty to rule the whole of Iran. To forestall opposition from Britain and the Soviet Union, he assured both countries that Iran would remain strictly nonaligned. A compliant *Majles* endorsed this transfer of power from the Qajars to the Pahlavis.

Reza Shah ruled with an iron fist until 1941, when the British and the Soviets invaded Iran to stop Nazi Germany from establishing a foothold there. Reza Shah promptly abdicated in favor of his son, Muhammad Reza Shah, and went into exile, where he soon died. In the first twelve years of his reign, the young shah retained control over the armed forces but had to live with a free press, an independent judiciary, competitive elections, assertive cabinet ministers, and boisterous parliaments. He also had to confront two vigorous political movements: the communist Tudeh (Masses) Party; and the nationalist movement led by the charismatic Dr. Muhammad Mosaddeq (1882–1967).

The Tudeh drew its support mostly from working-class trade unions. The nationalist movement, organized by Mosaddeq's National Front, drew its support mainly from the salaried middle classes. It called for the nationalization of the British company that controlled the petroleum industry in Iran. Mosaddeq also wanted to sever the shah's links with the armed forces. He argued that according to the constitution, the monarch should reign, not rule, and that the armed forces should be supervised by cabinet ministers responsible to parliament. In 1951, Mosaddeq was elected prime minister and promptly nationalized the oil industry. The period of relative freedom, however, ended abruptly in 1953, when royalist army officers overthrew Mosaddeq and installed the shah with absolute power. The coup was financed by the U.S. Central Intelligence Agency (CIA) and the British. The coup not only intensified anti-British sentiment in Iran and created a deep well of distrust for the United States, it also made the shah appear to be a puppet of the imperial powers. Muhammad Reza Shah ruled much in the style of his autocratic father until he was overthrown by the 1979 Islamic Revolution.

During its fifty-four-year rule, the Pahlavi dynasty built the first highly centralized state in Iran's history. This state rested on three pillars: the armed forces, the bureaucracy, and the royal patronage system. The armed forces grew from fewer than 40,000 in 1925 to

124,000 in 1941, and to more than 410,000 in 1979, by which time Iran had the fifth largest army in the world, the largest navy in the Persian Gulf, and the largest air force in western Asia. These regular forces were supplemented by a pervasive secret police notorious as SAVAK—the Persian acronym for the Organization to Protect and Gather Information for the State.

The bureaucracy expanded from a haphazard collection of hereditary scribes, some without fixed offices, to twenty-one ministries in 1979 employing more than 300,000 civil servants. The Ministry of Education grew twentyfold, administering to 4 million children in 26,000 primary schools and 740,000 in 1,850 secondary schools. Meanwhile, the Ministry of Higher Education supervised 227,000 students in 750 vocational schools and 154,000 in thirteen universities. The Interior Ministry appointed provincial governors, town mayors, district superintendents, and village headmen. Since it also appointed electoral supervisors, it could rig *Majles* elections and provide the shah with rubberstamp parliaments.

The Justice Ministry supplanted the *shari'a* with a European-style civil code and the clerical courts with a modern judicial system culminating in a Supreme Court. Lawyers and judges had to pass government-administered exams based on European jurisprudence. The legal system was further secularized in the 1960s, when the shah decreed a controversial Family Protection Law that contradicted the traditional interpretation of the *shari'a* on a number of points. It raised the marriage age for men to twenty and to eighteen for women. It allowed women to override spousal objections and work outside the home if they got court permission. It also restricted polygamy by stipulating that husbands could have more wives only if they first obtained permission from the current wife (or wives) and the courts.

Other ministries experienced similar expansion. For example, the Transport Ministry built an impressive array of bridges, ports, highways, and railroads known as the Trans-Iranian Railway. The Ministry of Industries financed the construction of numerous factories specializing in consumer goods. The Agricultural Ministry attained prominence in 1963 when the shah made land reform the centerpiece of his much-heralded "White Revolution," which was designed partly to forestall the possibility of a communist-led "red revolution." The government bought land from large absentee owners and sold it to small farmers through low-interest, long-term mortgages. It also undertook the task of transforming small farmers into modern commercial entrepreneurs by providing them with fertilizers, cooperatives, distribution centers, irrigation canals, dams, and tractor repair shops. The White Revolution included the extension of the vote to women and a Literacy Corps to eradicate illiteracy in the countryside. Thus, by the late 1970s, the state had set up a modern system of communications, initiated a minor industrial revolution, and extended its reach into even the most outlying villages.

The state also controlled a number of major institutions: the National and the Central Banks; the Industrial and Mining Development Bank, which channeled money to private entrepreneurs; the Plan Organization, which drew up Five Year Plans; the National Iranian Radio and Television, which monopolized the airwaves; and most important, the National Iranian Oil Company, which, while not actually controlling the industry, became the main recipient of the petroleum revenues. On paper, it became one of the world's largest oil companies.

The Pahlavi state was further bolstered by court patronage. The dynasty's founder, Reza Shah, the son of a small landowner, used coercion, confiscations, and diversion of irrigation water to make himself one of the largest landowners in the Middle East. As a British diplomat put it, Reza Shah had an "unholy interest in property," especially other people's property.[3] This wealth transformed the royal court into a large military-landed complex, providing work for thousands in its palaces, hotels, casinos, charities, and beach resorts. This patronage system expanded dramatically under his son, particularly after the establishment of the state-subsidized and tax-exempt Pahlavi Foundation in 1958. By 1979, the Pahlavi Foundation controlled more than $3 billion and administered 207 large companies active in banking, insurance, tourism, agribusiness, real estate, mining, construction, and manufacturing.

The Pahlavi drive for secularization, centralization, industrialization, and social development won some favor from the urban propertied classes. But the 1953 coup, the disregard for constitutional liberties, and the stifling of independent newspapers, political parties, and professional associations produced widespread resentment, particularly among the clergy, the intelligentsia, and the urban working class. In short, this state appeared strong in that it controlled the modern instruments of coercion and administration. But its roots were very shallow in that it failed to link the new state institutions into the country's social structure. The Pahlavis, like the Safavids and the Qajars, hovered over, rather than embedding themselves into, society at large. Furthermore, the creation of the modern state tended to suffocate the conventional liberties enjoyed by civil society in traditional Iran.

This tendency was exacerbated in 1975 when the shah, without warning, announced the formation of the Resurgence Party. He declared the country to be a one-party state and threatened imprisonment and exile to those refusing to join the party. In heralding the new order, he replaced the traditional Islamic calendar with a new royalist one, jumping from the Muslim year 1355 to the royalist year 2535; 2,500 years were allocated to the monarchy in general and 35 years for the shah's own reign. He also gave himself two new titles: *Rahbar* (Leader) of the New Great Civilization; and *Arya Mehr* (Light of the Aryan Race).

The Resurgence Party was designed to create yet another organizational link with the population, especially with the **bazaars** (traditional marketplaces), which, unlike the rest of society, had managed to retain their guilds and thus escape direct government control. The Resurgence Party promptly established its own bazaar guilds as well as newspapers, women's organizations, professional associations, and labor unions. It also prepared to create a Religious Corps, modeled on the Literacy Corps, to go into the countryside to teach the peasants "true Islam." The Resurgence Party promised to establish an "organic relationship between rulers and ruled," "synthesize the best of capitalism and socialism," and chart the way toward the New Great Civilization. It also praised the shah for curbing the "medieval clergy," eradicating "class warfare," and becoming a "spiritual guide" as well as a world-renowned statesman. For his part, the shah told an English-language newspaper that the party's philosophy was "based on the dialectical principles of the White Revolution" and that nowhere else in the world was there such a close relationship between a ruler and his people. "No other nation has given its commander such a *carte-blanche* [blank check]."[4] The terminology, as well as the boast, revealed much about the shah—or, as some suspected, his megalomania at the height of his power.

The Islamic Revolution (1977–1979)

On the eve of the Islamic Revolution, a newspaper published by Iranian exiles denounced the Pahlavis in an issue entitled "Fifty Indictments of Treason during Fifty Years of Treason."[5] It charged the shah and his family with establishing a military dictatorship, collaborating with the CIA, trampling on the constitution, creating SAVAK and a fascistic one-party state, rigging parliamentary elections, taking over the religious establishment, and undermining national identity by disseminating Western culture. It also accused the regime of inducing millions of landless peasants to migrate into urban shantytowns, widening the gap between rich and poor, funneling money away from the small business owners into the pockets of the wealthy the entrepreneurs linked to foreign companies and multinational corporations, wasting resources on bloated military budgets, and reverting to nineteenth-century imperialism by granting "capitulations" to America.

These grievances were given greater articulation when a leading anti-shah cleric, Ayatollah Ruhollah Khomeini, began to formulate a new version of Shi'ism (see "Leaders: Ayatollah Ruhollah Khomeini"). His version has often been labeled Islamic **fundamentalism;** it would better be described as Shi'i populism or political Islam. The term *fundamentalism,* derived from American Protestantism, implies religious dogmatism, theological purity, intellectual inflexibility, political traditionalism, social conservatism, rejection of the modern world, and literal interpretations of scriptural texts. Khomeini, however, was concerned less about literal interpretations than about sociopolitical grievances against the ruling elite and the United States. He was more of a political revolutionary than a social conservative or a dogmatic theologian.

Khomeini denounced monarchies in general and the Pahlavis in particular as part and parcel of the corrupt elite exploiting the oppressed masses. For him, the oppressors consisted of courtiers, large landowners,

Leaders

Ayatollah Ruhollah Khomeini

Ruhollah Khomeini was born in 1902 into a landed clerical family in central Iran. During the 1920s, he studied in Fayzieh Seminary in Qom with the leading theologians of the day, most of whom were scrupulously apolitical. He taught at the seminary from the 1930s through the 1950s, avoiding politics even during the mass campaign to nationalize the British-owned oil company. His entry into politics did not come until 1962–1963, when he, along with many other clerical leaders, denounced Muhammad Reza Shah both because of the White Revolution and because he had granted American military advisers immunity from Iranian laws. He denounced these as "capitulations" reminiscent of nineteenth-century imperialism. Forced into exile, Khomeini taught at the Shi'i center of Najaf in Iraq from 1964 until 1978.

During these years, Khomeini developed his own version of Shi'i populism by incorporating socioeconomic grievances into his sermons and denouncing not just the shah but the whole ruling class. Returning home triumphant in the midst of the Iranian Revolution after the shah was forced from power in 1979, he was declared the Imam and Leader of the new Islamic Republic. In the past, Iranian Shi'is, unlike the Arab Sunnis, had reserved the special term *Imam* only for Imam Ali and his twelve direct heirs, whom they deemed to be semidivine and thereby infallible. For many Iranians in 1979, Khomeini was charismatic in the true sense of the word: a man with a special gift from God. Khomeini ruled as Imam and Leader of the Islamic Republic until his death in 1989.

senior military officers, foreign-connected capitalists, and palace dwellers. The oppressed consisted of the masses, especially landless peasants, wage earners, bazaar shopkeepers, and shantytown dwellers. His proclamations often cited the Qur'anic term *mostazafin* (dispossessed) and the biblical promise that "the poor (meek) shall inherit the earth."

In calling for the overthrow of the Pahlavi monarchy, Khomeini injected a radically new meaning into the old Shi'i term *velayat-e faqih* (**jurist's guardianship).** He argued that jurist's guardianship gave the senior clergy—namely, the grand ayatollahs such as himself—all-encompassing authority over the whole community, not just over widows, minors, and the mentally disabled, as had been the prevailing interpretation. He insisted that only the senior clerics had the sole competence to understand the *shari'a;* that the divine authority given to the Prophet and the imams had been passed on to their spiritual heirs, the clergy; and that throughout history, the clergy had championed the rights of the people against bad government and foreign powers. He further insisted that the clergy were the people's true representatives since they lived among them, listened to their problems, and shared their everyday joys and pains. He claimed that the shah secretly planned to confiscate all religious funds and replace Islamic values with "cultural imperialism." These pronouncements added fuel to an already explosive situation.

By 1977, Iran needed just a few sparks to ignite the revolution. These sparks came in the form of minor economic difficulties and international pressures to curb human rights violations. In 1977–1978, the shah tried to deal with a 20 percent rise in consumer prices and a 10 percent decline in oil revenues by cutting construction projects and declaring war against "profiteers," "hoarders," and "price gougers." Not surprisingly, shopkeepers felt that the shah was diverting attention from court corruption and planning to replace them with government-run department stores. It was widely suspected that he was intending to destroy the bazaar, which some felt was the real pillar of Iranian society.

The pressure for human rights came from Amnesty International and the Western press, as well as from the recently elected Carter administration in the United States, which was a strong cold war ally of Iran. In 1977, after meeting with the International Commission of Jurists, the shah permitted Red Cross officials to visit prisons and allowed defense attorneys to attend political trials. This international pressure had allowed the opposition to breathe again after decades of suffocation.[6]

This slight loosening of the reins, coming in the midst of the economic recession, sealed the fate of the shah. Political parties, labor organizations, and professional associations—especially lawyers, writers, and university professors—regrouped. Bazaar guilds regained their independence. College, high school, and seminary students, especially in the religious center of Qom, took to the streets to protest the quarter-century of repression. On September 8, 1978, known as Bloody Friday, troops in Tehran fired into a crowded square, killing many unarmed demonstrators. By late 1978, a general strike had brought the whole economy to a halt, paralyzing not only the oil industry, the factories, the banks, and the transport system but also the civil service, the media, the bazaars, and the whole educational establishment. Oil workers vowed that they would not produce any petroleum for export until they had exported the "shah and his forty thieves."[7]

Meanwhile, in the urban centers, local committees attached to the mosques and financed by the bazaars were distributing food to the needy, supplanting the police with militias known as ***pasdaran*** (Revolutionary Guards), and replacing the judicial system with ad hoc courts applying the *shari'a*. Equally significant, anti-regime rallies were now attracting as many as 2 million protesters. The largest rally was held in Tehran in December 1978 on the day commemorating the martyrdom of Imam Husayn. Protesters demanded the abolition of the monarchy, the return of Khomeini from exile, and the establishment of a republic to preserve national independence and provide the masses with social justice in the form of land, decent wages, and an improved standard of living.

Although these rallies were led by pro-Khomeini clerics, they drew support from a broad variety of organizations: the National Front; the Lawyer's, Doctor's, and Women's associations; the Tudeh Party; the Fedayin, a Marxist guerrilla group; and the Mojahedin,

a Muslim guerrilla group formed of nonclerical intellectuals. The rallies also attracted students, from high schools and colleges, as well as shopkeepers and craftsmen from the bazaars. A secret Revolutionary Committee in Tehran coordinated protests throughout the country, kept in telephone contact with Khomeini in Paris, and circulated recordings of his messages within Iran. This was a revolution made in the streets and propelled forward by audiotapes. It was also one of the first revolutions to be televised worldwide. Later on, many felt that these demonstrations inspired the anticommunist revolutions that swept through Eastern Europe in the 1980s.

After a series of such mass rallies in late 1978, the *Washington Post* concluded that "disciplined and well-organized marches lent considerable weight to the opposition's claim of being an alternative government."[8] Similarly, the *Christian Science Monitor* stated that the "giant wave of humanity sweeping through the capital declared louder than any bullet or bomb could the clear message, 'The shah must go.'"[9] Confronted by this opposition and aware that increasing numbers of soldiers were deserting to the opposition, the shah decided to leave Iran. A year later, when he was in exile and dying of cancer, there was much speculation, especially in the United States, that he might have been able to master the upheavals if he had been healthier, possessed a stronger personality, and received full support from the United States. But even a man with an iron will and full foreign backing would not have been able to deal with millions of demonstrators, massive general strikes, and debilitating desertions from his own pampered military.

On February 11, 1979—three weeks after the shah's departure from Iran and ten days after Khomeini's return—armed groups, especially Fedayin and Mojahedin guerrillas, supported by air force cadets, broke into the main army barracks in Tehran, distributed arms, and then assaulted the main police stations, the jails, and eventually the national radio-television station. That same evening, the radio station made the historic announcement: "This is the voice of Iran, the voice of true Iran, the voice of the Islamic Revolution." A few hours of street fighting had completed the destruction of the 54-year-old dynasty that claimed a 2,500-year-old heritage.

The Islamic Republic (1979–2001)

Seven weeks after the February revolution, a nation-wide referendum replaced the monarchy with an Islamic Republic. Of the 21 million eligible voters, more than 20 million—97 percent—endorsed the change. Liberal and lay supporters of Khomeini, including Mehdi Bazargan, his first prime minister, had hoped to offer the electorate a third choice: that of a *democratic* Islamic Republic. But Khomeini overruled them on the grounds that the term democratic was redundant because Islam itself was democratic. The structure of this new republic was to be determined later. Khomeini was now hailed as the Leader of the Revolution, Founder of the Islamic Republic, Guide of the Oppressed Masses, Commander of the Armed Forces, and most potent of all, Imam of the Muslim World.

A new constitution was drawn up in late 1979 by a body named the Assembly of Religious Experts (*Majles-e Khebregan*). Although this seventy-three-man assembly—later increased to eighty-five—was elected by the general public, almost all secular organizations as well as clerics opposed to Khomeini boycotted the elections on the grounds that the state media were controlled, independent papers had been banned, and voters were being intimidated by club-wielding vigilantes known as the **Hezbollahis** ("Partisans of God"). The vast majority of those elected, including fifteen ayatollahs and forty middle-ranking clerics known as **hojjat al-Islams** ("Proofs of Islam"), were pro-Khomeini clergymen. They proceeded to draft a highly theocratic constitution vesting much authority in the hands of Khomeini in particular and the clergy in general—all this over the strong objections of Bazargan, who wanted a French-style presidential republic that would be Islamic in name but democratic in structure.

When Bazargan threatened to submit his own secular constitution to the public, the state television network, controlled by the clerics, showed him shaking hands with U.S. policy-makers. Meanwhile, Khomeini declared that the U.S embassy had been a "den of spies" plotting a repeat performance of the 1953 coup. This led to mass demonstrations, a break-in at the embassy, and the seizure of dozens of American hostages, and the resignation of Bazargan. Some suspect that this hostage crisis—which was to last 444 days—was engineered to undercut Bazargan and ratify the Islamic Constitution.

A month after the embassy break-in, Khomeini submitted the theocratic constitution to the public and declared that all citizens had a divine duty to vote. Although 99 percent of the electorate endorsed it, voter participation was down to 75 percent despite full mobilizations by the mass media, the mosques, and the Revolutionary Guards. Some 5 million voters abstained. The clerics had won their constitution, but at the cost of eroding their broad support.

In the first decade after the revolution, a number of factors helped the clerics consolidate power. First, few people could challenge Khomeini's overwhelming charisma and popularity. Second, the Iraqi invasion of Iran in 1980—prompted by Saddam Hussein's ambition to gain control over vital borders—rallied the Iranian population behind their endangered homeland. Third, international petroleum prices shot up. The price of oil, which had hovered around $30 a barrel in 1979, jumped to more than $50 by 1981. This enabled the new regime, despite war and revolution, to continue to finance not only the existing development projects but also to introduce into the countryside such modern amenities as electricity, indoor plumbing, televisions, telephones, refrigerators, motorcycles, and medical clinics.

The second decade after the revolution, however, brought a number of serious challenges. First, Khomeini's death in June 1989 removed his decisive presence. His successor, Ali Khamenei, lacked not only his charisma but also his scholastic credentials and seminary following. Khamenei had been considered a mere middle-level cleric, a hojjat al-Islam, until the state-controlled press elevated him to the rank of ayatollah and Leader. Few ayatollahs, even grand ayatollahs, deemed him their equal. Second, the 1988 UN-brokered ceasefire in the Iran–Iraq War ended the foreign danger. Third, a drastic fall in world oil prices, plunging to less than $10 a barrel by 1998, placed a temporary brake on economic development. Fourth, by the late 1990s, Khomeini's disciples divided into conservative and liberal wings, with the latter stressing the importance of public participation over clerical hegemony, of political pluralism over social conformity, of populism over fundamentalism, and of civil society

The Shah's statue on the ground, February 1979. *Source:* Abbas/Magnum Photos.

over state authority—in other words, of democracy over theocracy. It was the emergence of this liberal reform wing that brought about the unexpected victory of Khatami in the 1997 presidential elections mentioned at the beginning of this chapter. Khatami, a middle-ranking cleric, was a mild-mannered head of the National Library and former minister of culture who sprinkled his campaign speeches with references to Locke, Hume, Voltaire, Rousseau, Kant, and Tocqueville.

Iran after September 11 (2001 to the Present)

The terrorist attacks of September 11, 2001, and the subsequent American invasions of Afghanistan in October 2001 and Iraq in March 2002, had a profound impact on Iran—probably more profound than on any other country (with the exception of the three countries directly involved in the "war on terror"). At first, these events brought Iran and the United States closer together, since Iran for years had seen both the Taliban and Saddam Hussein as its own mortal enemies. Saddam Hussein was hated for the obvious reason that he had invaded Iran in 1980. The Sunni Taliban was hated in part because it had been created by Pakistan—Iran's main rival to the east; in

part because it had massacred Shi'i Afghans; and in part because it was associated with Saudi Arabia, a state dominated by the ultraconservative Sunni fundamentalist sect known as Wahhabis that considers Shi'is to be worse than infidels. Not surprisingly, Iran helped the United States displace the Taliban in Afghanistan. It also used its considerable influence among Iraqi Shi'is to install a pro-American government in Baghdad after the American invasion. To further improve these ties, Iran in 2003 proposed to the U.S. a "grand bargain," an offer to negotiate all major issues of difference, including its nuclear program, its refusal to recognize Israel, its role in the Persian Gulf, and its open support for Hamas in Palestine and Hezbollah in Lebanon—the U.S. deemed both organizations to be "terrorists." There was some hope that diplomatic relations between the two countries, broken ever since the 1979 hostage crisis, might soon be restored.

These hopes, however, were dashed in 2003 by President George W. Bush's famous "Axis of Evil" speech, in which he named Iran as part of the "evil enemy," and accused it both of secretly planning to build nuclear weapons and of arming terrorist groups throughout the Middle East. The Bush administration also financed opposition groups, including ethnically based dissidents, called for U.S.-promoted "regime change" as in Iraq, and talked of the possibility of using force to destroy Iran's nuclear plants. Such inflammatory language played a major role in undermining the relatively moderate president Khatami and paving the way for the electoral victory of the bellicose Ahmadinejad. Reformers in Iran could not afford to be associated with an American administration that seemed intent on pulling off another 1953-type of coup. Conservatives, on the other hand, argued that the only way for the Islamic Republic to survive was to stand up firmly against the U.S.

These events brought the Iran and the United States into a dangerous confrontation—some describe it as a new cold war that could easily escalate into a hot war. In this standoff, both nations have major advantages as well as disadvantages. On one hand, the United States can continue to put economic pressures on Iran through its own embargoes, and through the UN Security Council and its European allies. The United States government has managed to persuade Europe not to invest large sums in Iran's hydrocarbon enterprises—ventures important to Tehran's budget. What is more, the U.S. certainly has the military upper hand, and not only in terms of its overwhelming firepower. It now has bases surrounding Iran—in Iraq, Afghanistan, Central Asia, the Caucasus, and the Persian Gulf. And its main regional allies far outspend Iran in buying modern weapons. Whereas the annual military budget of Iran on average is less than $4.5 billion, that of Turkey is more than $10 billion, that of Israel near $10 billion, and that of Saudi Arabia more than $21 billion. The tiny Sheikhdom of Kuwait spends more on arms than Iran. This questions the image often given of Iran as an "aggressive," "expansionist," "hegemonic," and even "imperialistic" power intent on creating a new "Shi'i Crescent," if not recreating the ancient Persian Empire to threaten Israel, the United States, and the whole Sunni Arab World.

On the other hand, Iran does hold some important advantages. It is far too big to be occupied by the United States—especially now that the latter is bogged down in the quagmires of Iraq and Afghanistan. It continues to be a major exporter of petroleum, and any military confrontation would raise oil prices to an all-time high of $200 per gallon. It could prompt the Lebanese Hezbollah to attack Israel. What is more, Iran could easily further undermine America's already fragile

positions both in Baghdad and Kabul. Tehran helped set up both governments. Tehran could not only undo both but could also give a green light to groups in both countries eager to take on the Americans. In such an eventuality, the U.S. would be forced either to withdraw from a region considered "vital for its interests" or to bring in an army of two million to retain control. This, of course, would necessitate the reintroduction of the draft.

Themes and Implications

Historical Junctures and Political Themes

The critical historical junctures discussed above shape contemporary Iran—the way it behaves in the world of states, governs the economy, handles the democratic idea, and deals with the politics of collective identity.

The main driving force behind Iran's foreign relations has been nationalism—this is as true under the Islamic Republic as under the Pahlavi monarchy. This force has also been fueled by the long experience of imperial intrigues, interventions, invasions, and occupations. Iranian nationalism, however, has often taken diverse directions. Under the shah, Iran tried to become a major force in the Persian Gulf by allying with the West, buying vast sums of ultramodern weaponry from America, and appointing itself the latter's policeman in the region.

In the decade after 1979, the Islamic Republic, in a fit of revolutionary enthusiasm, tried to lead the Muslim World against the West and its local allies—including the monarchies and sheikhdoms in the Arab world as well as the state of Israel. Its slogan was "Muslims of the World Unite against Imperialism and Zionism." This enthusiasm faded with the death of Khomeini and the failure to export the revolution. In the following decade, nationalism took a more pragmatic form. Iran mended ties with the Gulf states; initiated détente with Europe; signed important agreements with the World Bank and the International Monetary Fund; tacitly supported Russia in its war in Chechnya; and openly sided with Christian Armenia against Muslim Azerbaijan—the latter had territorial claims on northern Iran. President Khatami even came close to recognizing Israel. He openly stated if Palestinians were willing to accept a two-state solution, Iran would also do so. In pursuing these pragmatic policies, Iran hoped to obtain from the international community, especially the U.S., the following: recognition that it is an important power in the Gulf; assurances that the CIA would not try to overthrow the Islamic Republic; and the lifting of economic sanctions so that it can integrate further into the global economy and obtain the large investments and high technology needed to develop its vast oil and gas reserves.

President Bush's Axis of Evil speech jeopardized many of these pragmatic policies. The new president, Ahmadinejad, wasted no time reverting to some of the early revolutionary rhetoric. He used global forums, including the United Nations, to call for Third World revolutions against international capitalism, imperialism, and Zionism. He first questioned the historical validity of the Holocaust; then argued that even if it had taken place, he did not understand why Palestinians had to pay the price for European atrocities; and finally insisted that the only way to end the problem was by establishing one large state encompassing Jews as well as Arabs. In short, he rejected the two-state solution favored by most Arab moderates in favor of a one-state solution advocated by most Arab radicals. This raised many eyebrows among reformers in Iran but won him immediate acclaim in the Arab streets. He also added more fuel to the fire by proclaiming that the U.S. was too weak to prevent Iran from pursing what was within its legal rights—its nuclear power program, which he insisted was purely for civilian use. This insistence on the nuclear program, coupled with his opposition to Israel, has undermined Iran's attempt to find a place in the world of states.

In internal affairs, the Islamic Republic faces a number of challenges. The Islamic Republic began with the conviction that it could easily develop the economy if it relied less on oil exports and more on agriculture and manufacturing. Although the regime has made impressive strides in increasing food production and expanding social services into the countryside—mainly by trimming the military budget—it continues to be beset by a series of serious economic problems: heavy dependence on fluctuating oil prices; inflation fueled by government expenditures; high concentration of resources in the hands of the central state—the over-bloated state created by the shah becoming even more bloated with the revolutionary takeover of many factories and businesses owned by the previous elite; and high unemployment, especially among educated youth produced by the ever-expanding colleges and high schools—ironically, the regime's educational successes have compounded its economic problems. To tackle the economy, some leaders have advocated conventional state-interventionist policies: price controls, five-year plans, and further redistribution of wealth through taxation and social investments. Others have advocated equally conventional **laissez-faire** policies: open markets, lifting of government controls, more business incentives, privatization of state enterprises, and, most controversial of all, wooing of foreign capital. Some have even argued that the only way to jump-start the economy and thus solve

The American Connection: The Nuclear Power Issue

At the heart of U.S–Iran tensions lies the nuclear issue. For Iran, nuclear technology—always defined as a "civilian program"—is a nonnegotiable right of an independent nation essential not only for its long-term energy needs but also to attain the hallmark of a developed country. It sees nuclear power as a matter of both national sovereignty and economic modernity.

For the United States, nuclear technology in the hands of Iran—even one developed for peaceful uses—is too risky since such technology can easily be expanded into a weapons program. The only way to resolve this impasse is for the United States to accept Iran's civilian program, and Iran, in return, to provide verifiable guarantees that its program would not trespass into the military realm.

the unemployment problem is to attract on a massive scale foreign investments into the oil and gas industry. Of course, this would entail a dramatic improvement of relations with the United States.

The regime also faces the ongoing problem of how to fully reconcile democracy with Islam. Iran has been a Muslim country since the seventh century and Shi'i Muslim since the sixteenth century. It has also aspired to attain democracy, mass participation, and popular sovereignty since the 1905 constitutional revolution. The dual aspirations for Islam and for democracy culminated in the 1979 Islamic Revolution. Khomeini argued that Islam and democracy were compatible since the vast majority supported the clerics, had faith in them, respected them as the true interpreters of the *shari'a,* and wanted them to oversee state officials. Islam and democracy, however, appear less reconcilable now that the public has lost its early enthusiasm for clerical rule. Some Khomeini followers continue to give priority to his concept of theocracy; others emphasize the importance of full democracy. In other words, Khomeinism has divided into two divergent branches: political liberalism and clerical conservatism.

The fate of democracy in Iran is bounded by the very nature of the *shari'a.* Democracy is based partly on the two principles that all individuals are equal, especially before the law, and that all people have inalienable natural rights, including the right to choose their own religion. The *shari'a,* at least in its traditional and conventional interpretations, rejects both of these democratic principles. Formulated in the seventh century, the *shari'a* is based on the principle of inequality, especially between men and women, between Muslims and non-Muslims, between legitimate minorities, known as the People of the Book, and illegitimate ones, known as unbelievers. In addition, the *shari'a,* like all other religious law, not only considers rights to emanate from God rather than nature, but also deems the individual to be subordinate to the larger religious community. This is of special concern for Muslims who lose their faith or join another religion, since the *shari'a* can condemn them to death as apostates. This is no mere technicality; more than 250 Baha'is and more than 400 leftist prisoners who professed atheism have been executed in Iran on just such grounds. But there are many moderate clerics in Iran

who want to reform the *shari'a* to make it compatible with the modern concepts of individual freedom and human rights. They also favor treating those who do not believe in religion in the traditional manner of "don't ask, don't tell."

Finally, the Islamic Republic began with a strong and widely shared collective identity since 99 percent of Iran's population is Muslim. But this major asset has to some extent been eroded. The stress on Shi'ism has naturally alienated the 10 percent of Iranians who are Sunnis. In addition, the regime's insistence on a theocratic constitution antagonized other top clerics as well as lay secular Muslims, who lead most of the political parties. Similarly, the inadvertent association of Shi'ism with the central Persian-speaking regions of Iran carries with it the potential danger of eventually alienating the important Turkic minority in Azerbaijan province. Thus, the Iranian regime, like most other developing states, has to solve the problem of how to allocate scarce resources without exacerbating ethnic, regional, and sectarian differences. This problem threatens to become more serious as the United States, for the first time in its relations with Iran, contemplates playing the ethnic card and inciting Kurds, Arabs, Baluchis, and Azeris against Persian-speakers.

Implications for Comparative Politics

The Iranian Revolution, the emergence of religion as a force in Middle Eastern politics, and the collapse of the Soviet Union convinced many Americans that a new spectre was haunting the West: that of Islamic fundamentalism. Some scholars predicted that a "clash of civilizations" would replace the cold war, arguing that the fault lines in world politics would no longer be over political ideology but over religion and culture. One of the main clashes would be between the West and the Muslim world, headed by the Islamic Republic of Iran.[10] Islam was seen as a major threat not only because of its size but also because it was deemed "inherently bellicose," "militant," and antagonistic to the West.

Such dire predictions have turned out to be gross exaggerations. It is true that the early Islamic Republic began denouncing the United States, arming militants in other parts of the Middle East, and calling for a struggle, sometimes termed a ***jihad*** (crusade), against the West. But these rhetorical denunciations soon became muted. The call for Muslim unity fell on deaf ears, especially in Sunni countries, such as Saudi Arabia. Iranian assistance to Shi'i Muslims remained limited to Iraq, Lebanon, and Afghanistan. What is more, Iranians themselves, including the clerics, have divided sharply into ultraconservative, conservative, liberal, and radical political camps. They even use the Western terms *left, right,* and *center* to describe themselves. Contemporary Iran shows that Muslim politics comes in many forms and, that as a blanket category, it has as little meaning as that of Christian politics.

Iran is an important power in the Middle East—at least, in the Gulf region. It has a large land mass, considerable human resources, a respectable standard of living and gross domestic product (GDP), and vast oil reserves and production. It also has plans, predating the Islamic Revolution, to become a nuclear power. But Iran's power can easily be exaggerated. Its GDP is only about that of New Jersey, and its armed forces are a mere shadow of what they were under the shah. The brutal eight-year conflict with Iraq (1980–1988) made the military war-weary. The officer ranks have been decimated by constant purges. The country's military hardware has been depleted by war, age, and lack of spare parts. In the last years of the shah, military purchases accounted for 17 percent of the GDP; they now account for 3 percent. Plans to build nuclear plants have been delayed, largely because the U.S. has successfully persuaded Europe not to transfer potentially dangerous technology to Iran. Iran is unlikely to obtain nuclear weapons in the immediate future. Moreover, the United States, after 9/11 and the occupation of Iraq in March 2003, has surrounded Iran with a string of military bases.

It is true that Iran has viewed itself as the vanguard of the Islamic world. But that world turns out to be as illusory for its champions as for its detractors. Just as there never was a communist monolith seeking global domination, the Muslim world is formed not of one unitary bloc but of many rival states, each with its own national self-interest. Those who see the future as a clash of civilizations and a replay of the medieval Crusades forget that even during those wars, both Muslims and Christians were often divided and sometimes sided against their own coreligionists. The Muslim world is no more united now than it was then. Iran's rulers may proclaim Islamic solidarity, but like its Muslim neighbors, the Islamic Republic formulates policies based on national interest, not on cultural, religious, and so-called civilizational values.

SECTION 2 Political Economy and Development

State and Economy

In 2002, Iran drafted a new investment law designed to attract foreign capital—especially into the oil industry. It contemplated permitting foreigners to have substantial shares in national companies, to repatriate profits, to be free of state meddling, and to be safe from arbitrary confiscations and high taxation. This was a far cry from the early days of the Islamic Revolution when the new regime had denounced foreign investors as imperialist exploiters, waxed eloquent about economic self-sufficiency, and denounced the shah for trying to attract multinational corporations. Although some leaders have continued to warn against Western consumerism and cultural imperialism, the regime as a whole—perhaps with the exception of Ahmadinejad—is still eager to attract foreign investment and to rejoin the world economy—a process that had started in the nineteenth century.

The Economy in the Nineteenth Century

The integration of Iran into the world system began in a modest way in the latter half of the nineteenth century. Before then, commercial contact with the outside world had been limited to luxury goods and the famous medieval silk route to China. Integration was brought about by the opening up of the Suez Canal; building of the Trans-Caspian and the Batum-Baku railways; laying of telegraph lines across Iran to link India with Britain; outflow of capital from Europe after 1870; granting of economic concessions to Europeans; and, most important, the Industrial Revolution and the subsequent export of European mass-manufactured goods to the rest of the world.

In the course of the nineteenth century, Iran's foreign trade increased tenfold. More than 83 percent of this trade was with Russia and Britain; 10 percent with Germany, France, Italy, and Belgium; and less than 7 percent with countries in the Middle East. Carpets and agricultural products, including silk, raw cotton, opium, dried fruits, rice, and tobacco, constituted much of the exports. Tea, sugar, kerosene, and industrial products such as textiles, glassware, and guns, formed much of the imports. Also some foreign investment flowed into Iran, especially into banking, fishing, carpet weaving, transport, and telegraph communications.

This contact with the West had far-reaching repercussions. It produced economic dependency. Iran, like many other Third World countries, became heavily dependent on the export of raw materials, and thus hostage to the vagaries of the world market and the fluctuations in world commodity prices. This became an especially serious problem in periods when the relative prices of manufactured goods rose while those of raw materials fell. Some economists have argued that this unequal exchange lies at the root of the present-day problems found in much of the Third World. Whether true or not, it did create in Iran, as in other parts of the Third World, the strong desire for tariff protection, self-sufficiency, industry development, and economic diversification.

The influx of mass-manufactured goods from abroad into Iran devastated some traditional handicrafts, especially cotton textiles. The import of cheap, colorful cotton goods undercut not only the local weavers, dyers, and carders, but also the thousands of women who in the past had supplemented their family incomes with cottage industries and home spindles.[11] Other handicrafts, especially carpet and shawl weaving, benefited since they found ready markets in the West. At the same time, the introduction of cash crops for export, especially cotton, tobacco, and opium, reduced the acreage available for wheat and other

edible grains. Many landowners ceased growing food and turned to these commercial crops. This paved the way for a series of disastrous famines in 1860, 1869–1872, 1880, and 1918–1920. Opium cultivation in Iran was particularly encouraged by British merchants eager to meet the rising demands of the Chinese market brought about by the notorious Opium Wars of the mid-nineteenth century.

Furthermore, the foreign competition, together with the introduction of the telegraph and the postal systems, brought many local merchants, shopkeepers, and workshop owners in the bazaars together into a national propertied middle class aware for the first time of their common interests against both the central government and the foreign powers. This new class awareness played an important role in Iran's constitutional revolution of 1905.

The Oil Economy

Greater integration into the world system began in the early twentieth century. Its main engine was oil. British prospectors struck oil in Khuzistan province in 1908; the British government decided in 1912 to fuel its navy—by far the world's largest at the time—with petroleum rather than coal; and to ensure secure supplies it bought controlling shares of the Anglo-Persian Oil Company, which had a monopoly over the petroleum industry in Iran. By 1951, this company was one of the largest in the world and in Abadan ran the world's very largest oil refinery. Not surprisingly, Iran's oil revenues gradually rose from less than $500,000 in the early 1910s to $16 million in 1951. After the nationalization of the industry in 1951 and a new agreement with a consortium of American and European companies in 1955, oil revenues rose further, reaching $34 million in 1956, $5 billion in 1973, and, after the quadrupling of oil prices in 1974, $23 billion in 1976. Between 1953 and 1978, Iran's cumulative oil income totaled near $100 billion.

Oil became Iran's black gold. It financed 90 percent of imports and 80 percent of the annual budget, far surpassing tax revenues. Oil also enabled Iran not to worry about feeding its population, a problem that confronts many developing countries. Instead, it could undertake ambitious development programs that other states implemented only if they could squeeze scarce resources from their populations. In fact, oil revenues created in Iran what is known as a **rentier state,** a country that obtains a lucrative income by exporting raw materials or leasing out natural resources to foreign companies. Iran, as well as Iraq, Algeria, and the Gulf states, received enough money from its oil wells to be able to disregard its internal tax bases. The state thus became relatively independent of society. Society, in turn, had few inputs into the state. Little taxation meant little representation. It also meant that the state was totally reliant on a commodity whose price was dependent on the vagaries of the international market.

Muhammad Reza Shah tried to lessen dependency on oil by encouraging other exports and attracting foreign investment. Neither policy succeeded. Despite modest increases in carpet and pistachio exports, oil continued to dominate: on the eve of the 1979 Islamic Revolution, it still provided as much as 97 percent of the country's foreign exchange. Even after the oil boom, foreign investments, mostly U.S., European, and Japanese, totaled less that $1 billion. And much of this was invested not in industry but in banking, trade, and insurance. In Iran, as in the rest of the Middle East, foreign investors were put off by government corruption, labor costs, small internal markets, potential instability, and fear of confiscations. Apparently they did not share their own government's confidence that Iran was an "island of stability" in the Middle East.

Society and Economy

Muhammad Reza Shah squandered some oil revenue on palaces, bureaucratic waste, outright corruption, ambitious nuclear projects, and ultrasophisticated weapons too expensive even for many NATO countries. But he also channeled much into socioeconomic development. GNP grew at the average rate of 9.6 percent every year from 1960 to 1977, making Iran one of the fastest developing countries in the Third World at that time. Land Reform, the lynchpin of the White Revolution, created more than 644,000 moderately prosperous farms (see Table 12.2). The number of modern factories tripled from fewer than 320 to more than 980 (see Table 12.3). Enrollment

Table 12.2	
Land Ownership in 1977	
Size (hectares)	*Number of Owners*
200+	1,300
51–200	44,000
11–50	600,000
3–10	1,200,000
Landless	700,000

Note: One hectare is equal to approximately 2.47 acres.
Source: E. Abrahamian, "Structural Causes of the Iranian Revolution," *Middle East Research and Information Project,* no. 87 (May 1980).

Table 12.3		
Number of Factories		
Size	*1953*	*1977*
Small (10–49 workers)	Fewer than 1,000	More than 7,000
Medium (50–500 workers)	300	830
Large (over 500 workers)	19	159

Source: E. Abrahamian, "Structural Causes of the Iranian Revolution," *Middle East Research and Information Project,* no. 87 (May 1980).

in primary schools grew from fewer than 750,000 to more than 4 million; in secondary schools, from 121,000 to nearly 740,000; in vocational schools, from 2,500 to nearly 230,000; and in universities, from under 14,000 to more than 154,000. The Trans-Iranian Railway was completed, linking Tehran with Tabriz, Meshed, Isfahan, and the Gulf. At the same time, roads were built connecting most villages with the provincial cities.

Iran's health services also grew. Between 1963 and 1977, the number of hospital beds increased from 24,126 to 48,000; medical clinics, from 700 to 2,800; nurses, from 1,969 to 4,105; and doctors, from 4,500 to 12,750. These improvements, together with the elimination of epidemics and famines, lowered infant mortality and led to a population explosion. In the two decades prior to the 1979 revolution, the population doubled from 18 to nearly 36 million. This explosion gave the country a predominantly youthful age structure. By the mid-1970s, half the population was under sixteen years of age. This was to have far-reaching repercussions in the revolutionary street politics of 1977–1979.

These improvements did not necessarily make the shah popular. On the contrary, his approach to development tended to increase his unpopularity. The Industrial and Mining Development Bank channeled low-interest loans totaling $50 billion to court-connected entrepreneurs. The shah believed that if economic growth benefited those who were already better off, some of the wealth would trickle down to the poor and, in the end, all would benefit. But in Iran, as elsewhere, the wealth failed to trickle down. By the mid-1970s, Iran had one of the very worst income distributions in the entire world.[12] Similarly, land reform, despite high expectations, left the vast majority of peasants landless or nearly landless. More than 1.2 million received less than 10 hectares (approximately 24.7 acres)—not enough to survive as viable farmers (see Table 12.2). Not surprisingly, many flocked to urban shantytowns in search of work. They provided ready fuel for the coming revolution.

The new factories drew criticism on the grounds that they were mere assembly plants and poor substitutes for real industrial development (see Table 12.4). The shah's medical programs left Iran with one of the worst doctor-patient ratios and child mortality rates in the Middle East. Educational expansion created only one place for every five university applicants, failed to provide primary schools for 60 percent of children, and had little impact on the rate of illiteracy, which remained as high as 68 percent. In fact, the population explosion ended up increasing the absolute number of illiterates in the country. The priority given to the development of Tehran increased disparities between the capital and the provinces. By the mid-1970s, Tehran contained half the country's doctors and manufacturing plants. According to one study, the per capita income in the richest provinces was ten times more than in the poorest ones. In fact, Iran's regional income disparity was the second worst in the world (after Brazil).[13] According to another study, the ratio of urban to rural incomes was five to one, one

Table 12.4

Industrial Production

Product	1953	1977
Coal (tons)	200,000	900,000
Iron ore (tons)	5,000	930,000
Steel (tons)	—	275,000
Cement (tons)	53,000	4,300,000
Sugar (tons)	70,000	527,000
Tractors (no.)	—	7,700
Motor vehicles (no.)	—	109,000

Source: E. Abrahamian, "Structural Causes of the Iranian Revolution," *Middle East Research and Information Project,* no. 87 (May 1980), p. 22.

of the biggest gaps between city and countryside in the world.[14] Moreover, some of the crash economic programs brought in their wake environmental degradation: horrendous air pollution in Tehran; lower water levels in the central plateau; and increased salt and sediment deposits around large hydroelectric dams.

These inequalities created a **dual society** in Iran—on one side the modern sector, headed by elites with close ties to the oil state; on the other side the traditional sector, the clergy, the bazaar middle class, and the rural masses. Each sector, in turn, was sharply stratified into unequal classes (see Figure 12.2).

The upper class—the Pahlavi family, the court-connected entrepreneurs, the military officers, and the senior civil servants—constituted less than 0.01 percent of the population. In the modern sector, the middle class—professionals, civil servants, salaried personnel, and college students—formed about 10 percent of the population. The bottom of the modern sector—the urban working class, which included factory workers, construction laborers, peddlers, and unemployed—constituted more than 32 percent. In the traditional sector, the middle class—bazaar merchants, small retailers, shopkeepers, workshop owners, and well-to-do family farmers—made up 13 percent. The rural masses—landless and near-landless peasants, nomads, and village construction workers—made up about 45 percent of the population.

FIGURE 12.2

Iran's Class Structure in the Mid-1970s

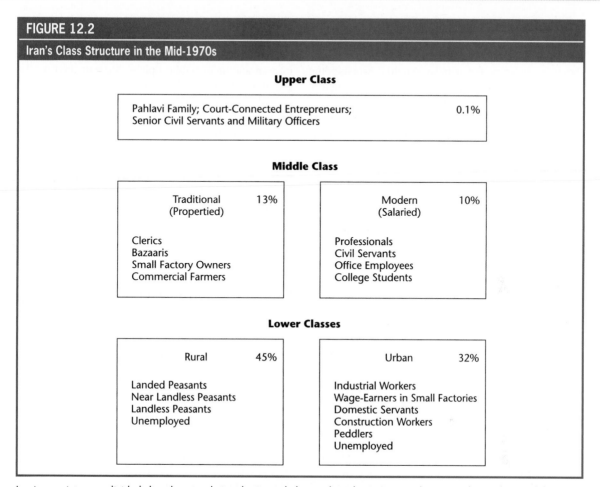

Upper Class

Pahlavi Family; Court-Connected Entrepreneurs; Senior Civil Servants and Military Officers	0.1%

Middle Class

Traditional (Propertied) 13%	Modern (Salaried) 10%
Clerics Bazaaris Small Factory Owners Commercial Farmers	Professionals Civil Servants Office Employees College Students

Lower Classes

Rural 45%	Urban 32%
Landed Peasants Near Landless Peasants Landless Peasants Unemployed	Industrial Workers Wage-Earners in Small Factories Domestic Servants Construction Workers Peddlers Unemployed

Iranian society was divided sharply not only into horizontal classes, but also into vertical sectors—the modern and the transitional, the urban and the rural. This is known as a dual society.

The government's own statistics reveal the widening inequality. In 1972, the richest 20 percent of urban households accounted for 47.1 percent of total urban family expenditures; by 1977, it had risen to 55.5 percent. In 1972, the poorest 40 percent accounted for 16.7 percent of urban family expenditures; by 1977, it had fallen to 11.7 percent (see Table 12.5).

Increasing resentments about this situation were expressed more in cultural and religious terms than in economic and class terms. Among those who articulated them was a gadfly writer named Jalal Al-e-Ahmad (1923–1969). A former communist who had rediscovered his Shi'i roots in the 1960s, Al-e-Ahmad shook his contemporaries by publishing a pamphlet entitled

Table 12.5

Measures of Inequality of Urban Household Consumption Expenditures

	Percentage Share in Total Expenditures		
Year	Poorest 40%	Middle 40%	Richest 20%
1972	16.7	36.2	47.1
1977	11.7	32.8	55.5

Source: V. Nowshirvani and P. Clawson, "The State and Social Equity in Postrevolutionary Iran," in M. Weiner and A. Banuazizi, eds., *The Politics of Social Transformation in Afghanistan, Iran, and Pakistan* (Syracuse, N.Y.: Syracuse University Press, 1994), p. 248.

Gharbzadegi (The Plague from the West). He proclaimed that the ruling class was destroying Iran by mindlessly imitating the West; neglecting the peasantry; showing contempt for popular religion; worshipping mechanization, regimentation, and industrialization; and flooding the country with foreign ideas, tastes, luxury items, and mass-consumption goods. He stressed that developing countries such as Iran could survive this "plague" of Western imperialism only by returning to their cultural roots and developing a self-reliant society, especially a fully independent economy. Al-e-Ahmad's pamphlet initiated the long search for cultural authenticity and economic self-sufficiency that would culminate, a decade after his death, in the Islamic Revolution of 1979.

The themes raised by Jalal Al-e-Ahmad were developed further by another young intellectual, Ali Shariati (1933–1977). Studying in Paris during the turbulent 1960s, Shariati was influenced by Marxist sociology, Catholic liberation theology, the Algerian revolution, and, most important, Frantz Fanon, who, in his famous book *Wretched of the Earth,* had argued that Third World peoples needed to use violence to liberate themselves from the heavy yoke of colonialism. Shariati returned home with a fresh revolutionary interpretation of Shi'ism, echoes of which would later appear in Khomeini's writings.

Shariati argued that history was a continuous struggle between oppressors and oppressed. Each class had its own interests, its own interpretations of religion, and its own sense of right and wrong, justice and injustice, morality and immorality. To help the oppressed, Shariati argued, God periodically sent down prophets, such as Abraham, Moses, Jesus, and Muhammad. The latter had been sent to launch a dynamic community in "permanent revolution" toward the ultimate goal of establishing on earth a classless utopia. Although Muhammad's goal had been betrayed by his illegitimate successors, the caliphs, his radical message had been preserved for posterity by the Shi'i imams, especially by Imam Husayn, who had been martyred to show future generations that human beings had the moral duty to fight oppression in all places at all times. Shariati equated Imam Husayn with Che Guevara, the Latin American guerrilla fighter who helped lead the Cuban Revolution. Shariati considered Iran's contemporary oppressors to be the imperialists, rich capi-

talists, and the "tie-wearers" and "palace dwellers" spreading the "Western plague." He also denounced conservative clerics for having transformed Shi'ism into an apolitical public opiate. Shariati died on the eve of the 1979 revolution, but his prolific works were so widely read and so influential that many felt that he, rather than Khomeini, was the true theorist of the Islamic Revolution.

Iran in the Global Economy

Under the Shah

The oil boom of the 1970s gave the shah the opportunity to play a significant role in regional politics. As the second most important member (after Saudi Arabia) of the **Organization of Petroleum Exporting Countries (OPEC),** Iran could cast decisive votes for raising or lowering oil prices. At times, the shah curried Western favor by moderating prices. At other times, he pushed for higher prices to finance his ambitious projects. These purchases rapidly escalated once President Richard Nixon began to encourage U.S. allies, such as the shah, to take a greater role in policing their regions. Moreover, Nixon's secretary of state, Henry Kissinger, openly argued that the United States should finance ever-increasing oil imports, most of them from the Persian Gulf, by exporting more military hardware to the region. Thus the shah was able to buy from the United States almost any weapon he desired. Arms dealers jested that the shah read their manuals in the same way that some men read *Playboy.* The shah's arms buying from the United States jumped from $135 million in 1970 to $5.7 billion in 1977. Between 1955 and 1978, Iran spent more than $20.7 billion on U.S. arms alone.

This military might gave the shah a reach well beyond his immediate boundaries. He occupied three small but strategically located islands in the Strait of Hormuz, thus controlling the oil lifeline through the Persian Gulf. He talked of establishing a presence well beyond the Gulf on the grounds that Iran's national interests reached into the Indian Ocean. "Iran's military expenditures," according to a 1979 U.S. congressional report, "surpassed those of the most powerful Indian Ocean states, including

Australia, Indonesia, Pakistan, South Africa, and India."[15]

In the mid-1970s, the shah dispatched troops to Oman to help the local sultan fight rebels. He offered Afghanistan $2 billion to break its ties with the Soviet Union, a move that probably prompted the Soviets to intervene militarily in that country, which, in turn, created the conditions for the rise to power of the Taliban. The shah, after supporting Kurdish rebels in Iraq, forced Saddam Hussein to give Iran concessions on the Shatt al Arab estuary. This had been a bone of contention between the two countries ever since Iraq had come into existence as a distinct nation-state after World War I. A U.S. congressional report summed up Iran's overall strategic position: "Iran in the 1970s was widely regarded as a significant regional, if not global, power. The United States relied on it, implicitly if not explicitly, to ensure the security and stability of the Persian Gulf sector and the flow of oil from the region to the industrialized Western world of Japan, Europe, and the United States, as well as to lesser powers elsewhere."[16]

These vast military expenditures, as well as the oil exports, tied Iran closely to the industrial countries of the West and to Japan. Iran now imported millions of dollars' worth of rice, wheat, industrial tools, construction equipment, pharmaceuticals, tractors, pumps, and spare parts, the bulk of which came from the United States. Trade with developing countries was insignificant. "Iran's rapid economic development," admitted the U.S. Department of Commerce, "provides America with excellent business opportunities."[17]

The oil revenues thus had major consequences for Iran's political economy, all of which paved the way for the Islamic Revolution. They allowed the shah to pursue ambitious programs that inadvertently widened class and regional divisions within the dual society. They drastically raised public expectations without necessarily meeting them. They made the rentier state independent of society. They also made Iran an oil-addicted rentier state highly dependent on oil prices and imported products and vulnerable to the world market. Economic slowdowns in the industrial countries could lead to a decline in their oil demands, which could diminish Iran's ability to buy such essential goods as food, medicine, and industrial spare

parts. One of the major promises made by the Islamic Revolution was to end this economic dependency on oil and the West.

Under the Islamic Republic (1979 to the Present)

The Islamic Republic began with high hopes of rapidly developing the economy and becoming fully independent of oil and the West. The results have been mixed.

The main economic problem plaguing the Islamic Republic has been instability in the world oil market despite OPEC's attempts to preserve prices by limiting production and setting quotas for its members. The price of a barrel of oil, which had quadrupled from $5 to $20 in 1974, reached $52 in late 1980 but plunged sharply thereafter, reaching $18 in 1985, hovering around $12 to $14 in the late 1980s and 1990s, and descending to a new low of $10 in 1999. This meant that Iran's oil revenues, which continued to provide the state with 80 percent of its hard currency and 75 percent of its total revenues, fell from $20 billion in 1978 to less than $10 billion in 1998. They did not rise significantly until the early 2000s, when oil prices began to edge upward first slowly and then dramatically after the U.S. invasion of Iraq, hitting the new peak of $138 a barrel in mid-2008 and then falling to $60 in late 2008. Still a rentier state, Iran remains vulnerable to the vagaries of the international petroleum market.

These economic problems were compounded by a population explosion, the Iran–Iraq war, and the emigration of some 3 million Iranians, mostly to Europe and the U.S. The annual population growth rate, which had hit 2.5 percent in the late 1970s, jumped to nearly 4 percent by the late 1980s, mainly because the new regime encouraged large families. This was the highest rate in the world, causing a major strain on government resources, especially social services and food imports. The Iraqi war not only wrecked the oil refinery and the border regions—causing as much as $600 billion in damages—but also killed and injured as many as a quarter-million Iranians. The media hyped this into 1 million in order to fan Iranian nationalism in support of the regime. The Islamic Revolution itself frightened many professionals and highly skilled technicians, as well as wealthy entrepreneurs and industrialists, into fleeing to the West. Of course, they carried their portable assets with them.

The overall result was a twenty-year economic crisis lasting well into the late 1990s. GDP fell 50 percent, per capita income declined 45 percent, and inflation hovered around 20 to 30 percent every year. Real (after inflation) incomes dropped by as much as 60 percent. Unemployment hit 20 percent; more than two-thirds of entrants into the labor force could not find jobs. The absolute number of illiterates actually increased. Peasants continued to flock to urban shantytowns. Tehran grew from 4.5 million to 12 million people. The total number of families living below the poverty level also increased.[18] Shortages in foreign exchange curtailed vital imports, even of essential manufactured goods. The value of Iran's currency on the international market plummeted. Before the revolution, the U.S. dollar had been worth 70 Iranian rials; by 1998, it was worth as much as 1,750 rials on the official exchange rate, and more than 9,000 rials on the black market. What is more, the regime that came to power advocating self-sufficiency now owed foreign banks and governments more than $30 billion, forcing it to renegotiate foreign loans constantly.

Despite these economic failures, the Islamic Republic did manage to score some successes. The Reconstruction Ministry, established mainly to serve the rural population, paved 30,000 miles of roads, and built more than 40,000 schools and 7,000 libraries. It brought electricity and running water to most villages. It also replaced shantytowns with housing complexes. The number of registered vehicles on the roads increased from 27,000 in 1990 to more than 2.9 million in 1996. The Agricultural Ministry not only built more dams and irrigation canals but also distributed some 630,000 hectares of confiscated arable land to poor peasants. It also gave farmers more favorable prices, especially for wheat. By the late 1990s, most independent farmers had such consumer goods as radios, televisions, refrigerators, and pickup trucks. The extension of social services narrowed the gap between town and country, urban poor and middle class. The adult literacy rate grew from 50 to 76 percent; by 2008 illiteracy

among school-age children had been wiped out. The infant mortality rate fell from 104 to 30 per 1,000 in the period between 1979 and 2003. Life expectancy climbed from fifty-five years in 1979 to sixty-eight in 1993 and further to seventy-one in 2008—one of the best in the Middle East. The UN estimates that by 2000, 94 percent of the population had access to health services. On the whole, the poor in Iran are better off now than their parents had been before the Islamic Revolution. Moreover, the country, despite initial setbacks, was able to become more self-sufficient in food production. By the mid-1990s, it was importing no more than 5 percent of its wheat, rice, sugar, and meat requirements. The regime has also been able to diversify foreign trade and become less dependent on the West. By 2000, Iran's main trade partners were Japan, South Korea, and Russia.

The regime also made major strides toward population control. At first, it closed down birth control clinics, claiming that Islam approved of large families and that Iran's strength would lie in having a large population. But it drastically reversed direction once the full impact of the population explosion hit the ministries—especially those responsible for social services. In an about-turn, the government in 1989 declared that Islam favored healthy rather than large families and that one literate citizen was better than ten illiterate ones. It reopened birth control clinics, cut subsidies to large families, and announced that the ideal family should consist of no more than two children. By 2003, the regime could boast that it had reduced the annual population growth from 4 to 1.2 percent. This is an impressive accomplishment. It is also a sign that the regime is highly pragmatic when it comes to economic issues.

The rise in oil prices—from $19 per barrel in 1999 to $53 in 2005 and further to $138 in 2008—has also helped the situation. Oil revenues jumped from less than $10 billion in 1998 to more than $30 billion in 2004. Foreign reserves increased to $4.8 billion, wiping out Iran's foreign debt, stabilizing the currency, and improving the country's creditworthiness. Iran became one of the few developing countries to be free of foreign debt. It is even able set aside some revenues as a hedge against leaner times. Annual GDP growth reached a recent peak in 2002–2003, when it was more than 7 percent per year; it slowed down to around 5 percent through 2007, but will certainly get a boost by the rapid increase in oil prices that started in 2008. Both the official unemployment and inflation rates, while still high, have fallen, and the currency has stabilized. These successes help explain why the Islamic Republic—despite all contrary predictions—has managed to survive and remain relatively strong for more than thirty years.

SECTION 3 Governance and Policy-Making

Iran's political system, with its strange mixture of theocracy and democracy, is unique in the contemporary world—also in world history. It can be described as a theocracy (from the Greek, "god rules") in that religious clergy fill the most powerful political positions. It can also be described as at least partly democratic in that some high officials, including the president, are elected by the people.

Organization of the State

The Iranian state rests on the Islamic Constitution drawn up by the Assembly of Religious Experts immediately after the 1979 revolution. It was amended in 1989 during the last months of Khomeini's life by the Council for the Revision of the Constitution. The final document, with 175 clauses and some 40 amendments (ratified by a nationwide referendum in July 1989) is a highly complex mixture of theocracy and democracy.

Its preamble affirms full belief in God, Divine Justice, the Qur'an, Day of Judgment, the Prophet Muhammad, the Twelve Imams, and the eventual return of the Hidden Imam (the *Mahdi*). It also declares full faith in Khomeini's doctrine of *velayat-e faqeh* ("Guardianship of the Islamic Jurists") that endows the senior religious clerics with ultimate authority in guiding the whole nation. It declares categorically that all laws, institutions, and state organizations have to conform to these "divine principles."

The Leader

The constitution named Khomeini to be the Leader for life on the grounds that the public overwhelmingly recognized him as the "most just, pious, informed, brave, and enterprising" of the senior jurists—the grand ayatollahs. It further described him as the Leader of the Revolution, the Founder of the Islamic

Leaders

Ayatollah Ali Khamenei

Ali Khamenei succeeded Khomeini as Leader in 1989. He was born in 1939 in Meshed into a minor clerical family originally from Azerbaijan. He studied theology under Khomeini in Qom and was briefly imprisoned by the shah's regime in 1962. Active in the anti-shah opposition movement in 1978, he was given a series of influential positions immediately after the revolution, even though he was only a hojjat al-Islam. He became Friday prayer leader of Tehran, head of the Revolutionary Guards, and, in the last years of Khomeini's life, president of the republic. After Khomeini's death, he was elevated to the rank of

Leader even though he was neither a grand ayatollah nor a recognized senior expert on Islamic law. He had not even published a theological treatise. The government-controlled media, however, began to refer to him as an ayatollah. Some ardent followers even referred to him as a grand ayatollah qualified to guide the world's whole Shi'i community. After his elevation, he built a constituency among the Islamic Republic's more diehard elements: traditionalist judges, conservative war veterans, and anti-liberal ideologues. In his earlier career, he had often sported a pipe—mark of a cultured intellectual.

Republic, and, most important, the Imam of the whole community. It stipulated that if no single Leader emerged after his death, then all his authority would be passed on to a leadership council of senior clerics. After Khomeini's death, however, his followers so distrusted the other senior clerics—most of whom rejected the notion of *velayat-e faqeh*—that they did not set up such a council. Instead, they elected one of their own, Ali Khamenei, a middle-ranking cleric, to be the new Leader. Most of Khomeini's titles, with the exception of Imam, were bestowed on Khamenei. The Islamic Republic has often been described as a regime of the ayatollahs. It could be more aptly called a regime of middle-ranking hojjat al-Islams.

The constitution gives wide-ranging powers to the Leader. Enshrined as the vital link between the three branches of government, he can mediate between the legislature, the executive, and the judiciary. He can "determine the interests of Islam," "supervise implementation of general policy," and "set political guidelines for the Islamic Republic." He can grant amnesty. As commander in chief, he can mobilize the armed forces, declare war and peace, and convene the Supreme Military Council. He can also appoint and dismiss the commanders of the regular army, navy, and air force as well as those of the Revolutionary Guards.

The Leader has extensive power over the judicial branch. He can nominate and remove the chief judge, the chief prosecutor, and the revolutionary tribunals (the lowest levels of the judicial system). He can dismiss lower court judges. He can nominate six clerics to the powerful twelve-man Guardian Council, which has the authority to veto parliamentary bills and approve all candidates for the presidency and the *Majles*. The other six members of the Guardian Council are lawyers trained in Islamic law and nominated by the chief judge and approved by the *Majles*. Furthermore, the Leader appoints an **Expediency Council,** which has the authority to resolve differences between the Guardian Council and the *Majles* (the legislature). It also has the power to initiate laws.

The Leader is also authorized to fill important posts outside the official state structure: the **Imam Jum'ehs** (Friday Mosque Preachers) in the main cities; the director of the national radio-television network; and the heads of the main religious endowments, especially the **Foundation of the Oppressed** (see below). By 2001,

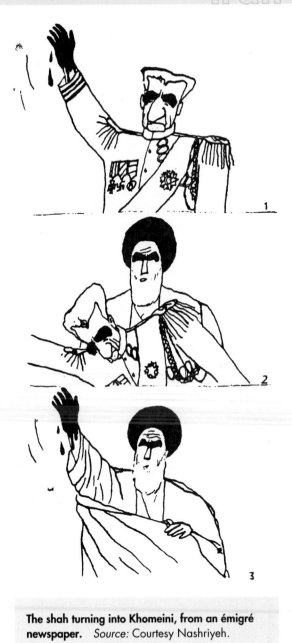

The shah turning into Khomeini, from an émigré newspaper. *Source:* Courtesy Nashriyeh.

the Office of the Leader employed more than six hundred in Tehran alone and had representatives in most sensitive institutions throughout the country. Thus the Leader has obtained more constitutional authority than ever dreamed of by the power-hungry shah.

FIGURE 12.3

The Islamic Constitution

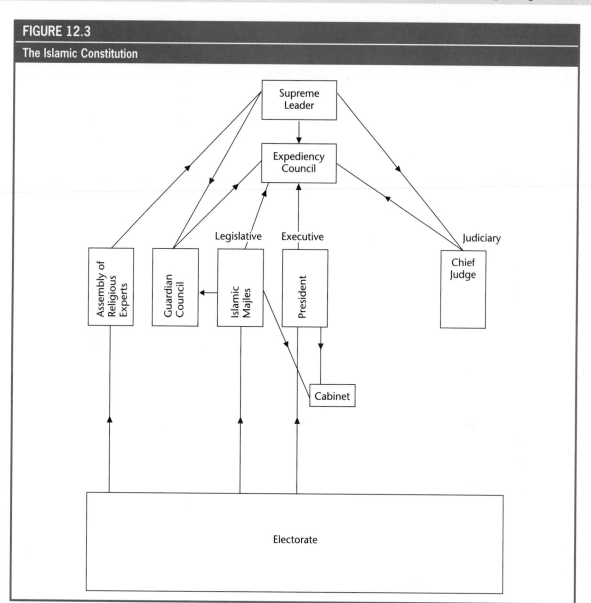

The general public elects the *Majles*, the president, and the Assembly of Religious Experts. But the Supreme Leader and the cleric-dominated Guardian Council decide who can compete in these elections.

The 1989 amendments elevated the Assembly of Religious Experts into what in effect has become a senate—an upper house—of the legislature comprised only of clerics. These amendments expanded Assembly membership to eighty-six; instituted ten-year terms; and stipulated that its members—elected through universal adult suffrage—had to have seminary degrees and pass special theology exams drafted by the Guardian Council. The amendments also gave the Assembly of Religious Experts the power to dismiss the Leader if they found him "mentally and physically incapable of fulfilling his arduous duties."

The Executive

The President and the Cabinet

The constitution reserves some power for the president. He is described as the chief executive and the highest official after the Leader. He is chosen every four years through national elections. If a candidate does not win a majority in the first round, a runoff chooses between the two top vote-getters. The president cannot serve more than two consecutive terms. The constitution says the president must be a pious Shi'i faithful to the Islamic Republic, of Iranian origin, and between the ages of fifteen and seventy-five. He must also demonstrate "administrative capability and resourcefulness." There is some dispute whether the language used restricts the position to males.

The president has the power to conduct the country's internal and external policies, including signing international treaties, laws, and agreements; chair the National Security Council, which is responsible for defense matters; draw up the annual budget, supervise economic matters, and chair the plan and budget organization; propose legislation to the *Majles*; appoint cabinet ministers; appoint most other senior officials, including provincial governors, ambassadors, and the directors of the National Oil Company, the National Bank, and the National Electricity Board.

The president has no vice-president but can appoint as many "deputies" as he wishes. There are currently ten deputy presidents specializing in such fields as atomic energy and veteran's affairs. One is a woman. She has a Ph.D. in geology and is in charge of environmental issues.

Before the revolution, Khomeini had often promised that technocrats—not clerics—would run the executive branch. But, in fact, clerics had filled the presidency for

Leaders

Mahmoud Ahmadinejad

Mahmoud Ahmadinejad was elected president of Iran in 2005. Born in 1956 into a working-class family in a small town in central Iran, he grew up mostly in Tehran, where his father worked as a blacksmith. At the outbreak of the Islamic Revolution, he was studying engineering in Tehran and was active in the student movement. He volunteered to participate in the Iraqi war, and, after the cease-fire, returned to Tehran to complete a Ph.D. in urban planning.

Mentored by conservative clerics, Ahmadinejad was appointed first governor of Ardabil province and then mayor of Tehran (2003–2005). As mayor of Iran's capital city, he rolled back some of the reforms that had been implemented before he took office. For example, he ordered that men and women use separate elevators in city office buildings. This earned him a reputation as a hard-line conservative and a political following among those who believed that president Khatami was too liberal. His presidential campaign was based on a combination of a pledge to restore the values of the Islamic Revolution and to attend to the needs of the poor.

Since becoming president, Ahmadinejad has continued to promote conservative policies and reversed steps taken by the previous government to improve relations with the United States. He insists on Iran's right to develop nuclear power, including weapons, although he asserts that the country has only peaceful intentions. He has been very critical of both the U.S. and Israel.

There are signs that Ahmadinejad's popularity is weakening—especially since his economic promises to the poor have failed to bear fruit. On the contrary, some of his policies have further inflamed inflation and unemployment. In December 2006, there was a fairly large demonstration by Iranian students denouncing the "International Conference to Review the Global Vision of the Holocaust" convened by Ahmadinejad as bringing shame to Iran because of the prominence given to Holocaust deniers on the program. In the same month, conservative candidates allied with the president did not do well in elections for the Assembly of Experts and local councils. This election, for which there was a 60 percent turnout, indicates that the public mood may be shifting against Ahmadinejad. The next presidential election, scheduled for, 2009 will be an important indicator of the balance of power in Iran.

half of the time. Of the six men who have filled the office since the revolution, three—Khamenei, Rafsanjani, and Khatami—have been clerics. The first president of the Islamic Republic, Abol-Hassan Bani-Sadr, was a noncleric, but he was ousted in 1981 precisely because he denounced the regime as "a dictatorship of the mullahtariat," comparing it to a communist-led "dictatorship of the proletariat" (*mullah* is a derogatory term for cleric). Another noncleric president was assassinated a few days after taking office. The current president, Ahmadinejad, is a noncleric, but he is considered by many reformers to be even more clerical-minded that most conservative clerics.

The Bureaucracy

The president, as the chief of the executive branch, heads a huge bureaucracy. Even though Khomeini had often taken the shah to task for having a bloated government, the bureaucracy continued to proliferate after the revolution. It expanded, for the most part, to provide jobs for the many college and high school graduates. On the eve of the revolution, the ministries had 300,000 civil servants and 1 million employees. By the early 1990s, they had more than 600,000 civil servants and 1.5 million employees. The Iranian Revolution, like many others, ended up creating a bigger bureaucracy than that of the government it overthrew.

The largest bureaucracies in the Iranian government include the Ministries of Culture and Islamic Guidance, which controls the media and enforces "proper public conduct"; Intelligence, which has replaced the dreaded SAVAK; Heavy Industries, which manages the nationalized factories; and Rural Reconstruction, which has the task of not only expanding social services and building rural roads, bridges, and houses, but also schools, libraries, and mosques so that peasants will be "exposed for the first time to the true teachings of Islam."[19]

The clergy dominate the bureaucracy as they do the presidency. They monopolize the most sensitive ministries—Intelligence, Interior, Justice, and Culture and Islamic Guidance. They also allocate other ministries to their relatives and protégés. These ministers appear to be highly trained technocrats, sometimes with advanced degrees from the West, but in fact are powerless individuals chosen by, trusted by, and related to the ruling clergy.

Semipublic Institutions

The Islamic Republic has set up a number of semipublic institutions called "Foundations" that play an important role in the state. They include the Foundation of the Oppressed, the Alavi Foundation (named after Imam Ali), the Martyrs Foundation, the Pilgrimage Foundation, the Housing Foundation, and the Foundation for the Publication of Imam Khomeini's Works. Although supposedly autonomous of the government, these foundations are directed by clerics appointed personally by the Leader. According to some estimates, their annual income may be as much as half that of the government.[20] They are exempt from paying state taxes and are allocated foreign currencies, especially U.S. dollars, at highly favorable exchange rates. Most of their assets are property confiscated from the old elite.

The largest of them, the Foundation for the Oppressed, is the direct heir of the Pahlavi Foundation established by the last shah. It administers as many as 140 factories, 120 mines, 470 agribusinesses, and 100 construction companies. It also owns the country's two leading newspapers, *Ettela'at* and *Kayhan*. The Martyrs Foundation, in charge of helping war veterans, controls confiscated property that was not handed over to the Foundation for the Oppressed. Together these foundations employ more than 400,000 and control as much as \$12 billion. They are states within the state—or rather, clerical fiefdoms. The senior clergy administer the endowment funds linked to the major seminaries. Much of the real estate around the cities of Qom and Mashed belongs to these religious endowments.

Other State Institutions

The Military

The clergy have taken special measures to control Iran's armed forces, which consist of both the regular army of 370,000, including 220,000 conscripts, and the paramilitary forces, the 120,000 Revolutionary Guards established during the revolution, and the 200,000 volunteers of the *Basej-e Mostazafin* (Mobilization for the Oppressed) created during the Iraqi war. The Leader, as commander in chief, makes all the key military appointments. He also picks the minister of intelligence, who reports directly to him, bypassing the president and the cabinet.

Immediately after the revolution, the new regime purged the top ranks of the military, promoted young officers, and built up the Revolutionary Guards to be a parallel force to the regular armed forces. They were given their own uniforms, budgets, munitions factories, recruitment centers, and even a navy and air force. The constitution spells out a division of labor between the Revolutionary Guards and the regular army—the former protects the republic from internal enemies, the latter defends the borders from external ones. To ensure the loyalty of the regular armed forces, the new regime introduced its own form of the communist commissar system under which a political officer was placed with most military units. The Islamic Republic has placed Muslim chaplains—handpicked by the Leader's Office—in many of the regular divisions. Their main function is to keep a keen theological and political eye on the professional officers.

The Judiciary

The Islamic Republic regime Islamized the judiciary by enacting a penal code, the Retribution Law, based on a reading of the *shari'a* that was so narrow that it prompted many modern-educated lawyers to resign in disgust, charging that it contradicted the United Nations Charter on Human Rights. It permitted injured families to demand blood money on the biblical and Qur'anic principle of "an eye for an eye, a tooth for a tooth, a life for a life." It mandated the death penalty for a long list of "moral transgressions," including adultery, homosexuality, apostasy, drug trafficking, and habitual drinking. It sanctioned stoning, live burials, and finger amputations. It divided the population into male and female and Muslims and non-Muslims, and treated them unequally. For example, in court, the evidence of one male Muslim is equal to that of two female Muslims. The regime also passed a "law on banking without usury" to implement the *shari'a* ban on all forms of interest taking. Many of these conservative laws were soon challenged by the reform movement.

Although the law was Islamized, the modern centralized judicial system was not dismantled. For years, Khomeini argued that in a truly Islamic society, the local *shari'a* judges would pronounce final verdicts without the intervention of the central authorities. Their verdicts would be swift and decisive. This, he insisted, was the true spirit of the *shari'a*. After the revolution, however, he discovered that the central state needed to retain ultimate control over the justice system, especially over life and death issues. Thus, the revolutionary regime retained the appeals system, the hierarchy of state courts, and the power to appoint and dismiss all judges. State interests took priority over the spirit of the *shari'a*.

Practical experience also led the regime to gradually broaden the narrow interpretation of the *shari'a*. To permit the giving and taking of interest, without which modern economies would not function, the regime allowed banks to offer attractive rates as long as they avoided the taboo term *usury*. To meet public sensitivities as well as international objections, the courts rarely implemented the harsh penalties stipulated by the *shari'a*. They adopted the modern method of punishment, imprisonment, rather than the traditional one of corporal public punishment. By the early 1990s, those found guilty of breaking the law were treated much as they would be in the West: fined or imprisoned rather than flogged in the public square.

Subnational Government

Although Iran is a highly centralized state, it is divided administratively into provinces, districts, subdistricts, townships, and villages. Provinces are headed by governors-general, districts by governors, subdistricts by lieutenant governors, towns by mayors, and villages by headmen. The constitution declares that the management of local affairs in every village, town, subdistrict, district, and province will be under the supervision of councils elected directly by the local population. It also declares that governors-general, governors, mayors, and other regional officials have to consult local councils. These clauses creating local councils had been incorporated into the constitution mainly because of mass demonstrations organized in 1980 by the Left—notably the Mojahedin and the Fedayin. The **Assembly of Religious Experts** had not contemplated such forms of grassroots democracy.

Because of conservative opposition, no steps were taken to hold council elections until 1999, when Khatami, the newly elected president, insisted on having such elections. More than 300,000 candidates, including 5,000 women, competed for 11,000 council seats—3,900 in towns and 34,000 in villages. Khatami's supporters won a landslide victory, taking 75 percent of the seats, including twelve of the fifteen in Tehran. The top vote-getter in Tehran was Khatami's former interior minister, who had been impeached by the conservative *Majles* for issuing too many publishing licenses to reform-minded newspapers. These results again proved the vitality of electoral politics in Iran. But in February 2003, conservatives won fourteen of the fifteen council seats in Tehran. This swing was due largely to many reformers boycotting the elections to show their disgust at the Guardian Council for disqualifying many liberal candidates. Only 10 percent of the Tehran electorate voted.

The Policy-Making Process

Policy-making in Iran is highly complex in part because of the cumbersome constitution and in part because factionalism within the ruling clergy has resulted in more amendments, which have made the original constitution even more complicated. Laws can originate in diverse places, and they can be modified by pressures coming from numerous directions. They can also be blocked by a wide variety of state institutions. In short, the policy-making process is highly fluid and diffuse, often reflecting the regime's factional divisions.

The clerics who destroyed Iran's old order remained united while building the new one. They formed a distinct social stratum as well as a cohesive political group. They were convinced that they alone had the divine mandate to govern. They followed the same leader, admired the same texts, cited the same potent symbols, remembered the same real and imaginary indignations under the shah, and, most important, shared the same vested interest in preserving the Islamic Republic. Moreover, most had studied at the same seminaries and came from similar lower-middle-class backgrounds. Some were even related to each other through marriage and blood ties.

But once the constitution was in place, the same clerics drifted into two loose but identifiable blocs: the Society (*Majmu'eh*) of the Militant Clergy, and the Association (*Jam'eh*) of the Militant Clergy. The former can be described as statist reformers or populists, and the latter as laissez-faire (free-market) conservatives. The reformers hoped to consolidate lower-class support by using state power for redistributing wealth,

eradicating unemployment, nationalizing enterprises, confiscating large estates, financing social programs, rationing and subsidizing essential goods, and placing price ceilings on essential consumer goods. In short, they espoused the creation of a comprehensive welfare state. The conservatives hoped to retain middle-class support, especially in the bazaars, by removing price controls, lowering business taxes, cutting red tape, encouraging private entrepreneurs, and balancing the budget, even at the cost of sacrificing subsidies and social programs. In recent years, the statist reformers have begun to emphasize the democratic over the theocratic features of the constitution, stressing the importance of individual rights, the rule of law, and government accountability to the electorate. In many ways, they have become like **social democrats** the world over (such as the British Labour Party) who want to reform the capitalist system through state regulation, particularly to reduce inequalities in wealth and access to public services.

The conservatives were originally labeled middle-of-the-roaders and traditionalists. The statists were labeled progressives, seekers of new ideas, and followers of the imam's line. The former liked to denounce the latter as extremists, leftists, and pro-Soviet Muslims. The latter returned the insult by denouncing the free-marketers as medievalists, rightists, greedy capitalists, mafia bazaaris, and pro-American Muslims. Both could bolster their arguments with apt quotes from Khomeini.

This polarization created a major constitutional gridlock, since the early Islamic *Majles* was dominated by the reformers, whereas the Guardian Council was controlled by the conservatives who had been appointed by Khomeini. Between 1981 and 1987, more than one hundred bills passed by the reformer-dominated *Majles* were vetoed by the Guardian Council on the grounds that they violated the *shari'a,* especially the sanctity of private property. The vetoed legislation included a labor law, land reform, nationalization of foreign trade, a progressive income tax, control over urban real estate transactions, and confiscation of the property of émigrés whom the courts had not yet found guilty of counterrevolutionary activities. These bills were introduced by individual deputies or cabinet ministers and received quick passage because the radical statists controlled the crucial *Majles* committees and held a comfortable majority on the *Majles* floor. Some ultraconservatives had countered by encouraging

The clerical regime and its two stilts: the sword and the oil wells.   *Source:* Courtesy Mojahed (in exile).

the faithful not to pay taxes and instead to contribute to the grand ayatollahs of their choice. After all, they argued, one could find no mention of income tax anywhere in the *shari'a.*

In arguing for their position, the conservative free-marketers referred to the long list of clauses in the Islamic Constitution protecting personal property, promising balanced budgets, and placing agriculture, small industry, and retail trade in the private sector. The reformers referred to an even longer list of constitutional provisions stressing the importance of the public sector and promising all citizens education, medicine, jobs, housing, unemployment benefits, disability pay, pensions, and interest-free loans.

To break the constitutional gridlock, Khomeini surprisingly resorted to the Sunni concept of **maslahat**—that is, "public interest" and "reasons of state." Over the centuries, Shi'i clerics had denounced this term as a Sunni notion designed to bolster the illegitimate power of the secular Caliphs. Khomeini now claimed that a truly Islamic state could safeguard the public interest by suspending important religious rulings, even over prayer, fasting, and the pilgrimage to Mecca. He declared public interest to be a primary ruling and the others mere secondary rulings. In other words, the state could overrule the views of the highest-ranking clerics. In the name of public interest, it could destroy mosques, confiscate private property, and cancel religious obligations. Khomeini added that the Islamic state had absolute authority, since the Prophet Muhammad had exercised absolute (*motalaq*) power, which he had passed on to the Imams and thus eventually to the Islamic Republic. Never before had a Shi'i religious leader claimed such powers for the state, especially at the expense of fellow clerics.

Khomeini proceeded to establish the Expediency Council for Determining the Public Interest of the Islamic Order. He entrusted the Expediency Council with the task of resolving conflicts between the Islamic *Majles* and the Guardian Council. He packed it with thirteen clerics, including the president, the chief judge, the speaker of the *Majles,* and six jurists from the Guardian Council. The Expediency Council eventually passed some of the more moderate bills favored by the reformers. These included a new income tax, banking legislation, and a much-disputed labor law providing workers in large factories with a minimum wage and some semblance of job security.

Constitutional amendments introduced after Khomeini's death institutionalized the Expediency Council. The Leader could now not only name its members but also determine its tenure and jurisdiction. Not surprisingly, the new Leader, Khamenei, packed it with his supporters—none of them prominent grand ayatollahs. He also made its meetings secret and allowed it to promulgate new laws rather than restrict itself to resolving legislative differences between the Guardian Council and the *Majles.* In effect, the Expediency Council is now a secretive supraconstitutional body accountable only to the Leader. In this sense, it has become a very powerful body rivaling the Islamic *Majles* even though it did not exist in the original constitution. In 2008 the Expediency Council contained thirty-two members. They included the president; chief judge; speaker of the *Majles;* ministers of intelligence, oil, culture, and foreign affairs; chief of the armed forces; jurists from the Guardian Council; directors of radio and television as well as of the Central Bank, Atomic Energy Organization, and National Oil Company; heads of the main religious foundations; chairman of the Chamber of Commerce; and editors of the main conservative newspapers. Seventeen were clerics. These thirty-two members can be considered the inner circle within Iran's policy-making elite.

SECTION 4 Representation and Participation

Although the Islamic Republic is predominantly a theocracy, it incorporates some aspects of the democratic idea. According to the constitution, the general electorate chooses the president as well as the Assembly of Religious Experts, which in turn chooses the Leader. What is more, the elected legislature, the *Majles,* exercises considerable power. According to one of the republic's founding fathers, the *Majles* is the centerpiece of the Islamic Constitution.[21] Another founding father argued that the people, by carrying out the Islamic Revolution, implicitly favored a type of democracy confined within the boundaries of Islam and the guardianship of the jurist.[22] Yet another declared that if he had to choose between the democracy and power of the clergy as specified in the concept of jurist's guardianship, he would not hesitate to choose the latter since it came directly from God.[23] On the eve of the initial referendum on the constitution, Khomeini himself declared: "This constitution, which the people will ratify, in no way contradicts democracy. Since the people love the clergy, have faith in the clergy, want to be guided by the clergy, it is only right that the supreme religious authority oversee the work of the [government] ministers to ensure that they don't make mistakes or go against the Qur'an."[24]

The Legislature

According to the constitution, the *Majles* "represents the nation." As such it is endowed with wide-ranging power, including the authority to enact or change laws (with the approval of the Guardian Council), investigate and supervise all affairs of state, and approve or oust the cabinet ministers. In describing the legislature, the constitution uses the term *qanun* (statutes) rather than *shari'a* (divine law) so as to gloss over the fundamental question of whether laws come from God or the people. It accepts the rationale that God formulates divine law (*shari'a*) but elected representatives can draw up statutes (*qanuns*).

The *Majles* has 290 members and is elected by citizens—both male and female—over the age of eighteen. It can pass *qanun* as long as the Guardian Council deems them compatible with the *shari'a* and the constitution. It can choose, from a list drawn up by the chief judge, six of the twelve-man Guardian Council. It can investigate at will cabinet ministers, affairs of state, and public complaints against the executive and the judiciary. It can remove cabinet members—with the exception of the president—through a parliamentary vote of no confidence. It can withhold approval for government budgets, foreign loans, international treaties, and cabinet appointments. It can hold closed debates, provide members with immunity from arrest, and regulate its own internal workings, especially the committee system.

The *Majles* plays an important role in Iran's national politics. On occasion, it has changed government budgets, criticized cabinet policies, modified development plans, and forced the president to replace his ministers. In 1992, 217 deputies circulated an open letter that explicitly emphasized the prerogatives of the *Majles* and thereby implicitly downplayed those of the Leader. Likewise, the speaker of the House in 2002 threatened to close down the whole *Majles* if the judiciary violated parliamentary immunity by arresting one of the reformist deputies.

Political Parties and the Party System

Iran's constitution guarantees citizens the right to organize, and a law passed in 1980 permits the Interior Ministry to issue licenses to political parties. But political parties were not encouraged until the coming of the Khatami administration in 1997. Since then, three important parties have emerged: the Islamic Iran Participation Front formed of Khatami's supporters; the Servants of Reconstruction created by Hojjat al-Islam Ali-Akbar Hashemi Rafsanjani, the former president and now chairman of the Expediency Council; and the *Osulgarayan* (Principalists) headed by Ahmadinejad. In addition, the two main clerical clusters—the conservative Association of Militant Clergy and the more liberal Society of Militant Clergy—continued to function, especially during elections. According to the Interior Ministry, some seven hundred organizations have received licenses to function. But most are nonpolitical professional associations trusted by members of the ruling elite, such as the Islamic Engineers Association and the Islamic Doctors Association.

Elections

The constitution of the Islamic Republic promises free elections. And in the thirty years since the revolution, the country has had seven presidential elections, two local council elections, and as many as eight separate parliamentary elections. In practice, however, elections have varied from relatively free but disorderly in the early days of the Islamic Republic, to controlled in the middle years, and back again to relatively free, but orderly in the late 1990s. At present the actual voting is generally free of intimidation, but the electoral choice is highly constrained. In some ways, elections are really selections.

In the 1980s, ballot boxes were placed in mosques supervised by the Revolutionary Guards. Neighborhood clerics were on hand to help illiterates complete their ballots. Club-wielding gangs assaulted regime opponents. Now electoral freedom is restricted less heavy-handedly by the government-controlled radio-television network, the main source of information for the vast majority of citizens. The Interior Ministry can ban organizations and their newspapers on grounds they don't fully subscribe to the concept of *velayat-e faqeh*.

But the main obstacle to fair elections has been the Guardian Council with its power to approve candidates. For example, the Council in 2004 excluded some 3,500 candidates (nearly half of the total and many of them reformers) from running for the Seventh *Majles*. This purge was facilitated also by President Bush's labeling of Iran as a member of the global "Axis of Evil." Reluctant to rock the boat at a time of apparent "national danger," most reformers restrained themselves and withdrew from active politics. Not surprisingly, the

📢 Leaders

Hojjat al-Islam Ali-Akbar Hashemi Rafsanjani

Rafsanjani was born in 1934 into a fairly prosperous business and farming family in the heartland of the Shi'i and Persian-speaking provinces. He studied in Qom under Khomeini; found himself in prison four times during the 1960s; set up a number of commercial companies, including one that exported pistachios; and wrote a book praising a nineteenth-century prime minister who had made an abortive attempt to industrialize the country. Nevertheless, Rafsanjani remained active enough in clerical circles to be considered a hojjat al-Islam. After the revolution, he became a close confidant of Khomeini and attained a number of cabinet posts, culminating with the presidency in 1989. After serving two consecutive four-year terms, the maximum allowed by the constitution, he was given the chairmanship of the Expediency Council. He also obtained the chairmanship of the Assembly of Religious Experts in 2005 after losing the presidential election to Ahmadinejad. Thus Rafsanjani remains one of the most powerful clerics in the Islamic Republic.

Electoral campaigners.
Source: © Lynsey Addario/Corbis.

conservatives won a hollow victory. They received a clear majority of the seats, but voter turnout was less than 51 percent. In Tehran, it was as low as only 28 percent. This was the worst showing since 1979. For a regime that liked to boast about mass participation, this was seen as a major setback—even as a crisis of legitimacy. Khatami's reformers had carried the previous *Majles* with a voter participation of more than 70 percent.

The 2008 elections for the Eighth *Majles* was a repeat performance of 2004. The Guardian Council, this time helped by the Interior Ministry, disqualified more than 3,000 potential candidates, including some of the leading reformers who had sat in the Seventh *Majles.* Despite this, forty reformers managed to get elected—many from provincial constituencies. These reformers were supported by Khatami's Islamic Iran Participation Front and Rafsanjani's Servants of Reconstruction. The conservatives, led by Ahmadinejad's Principalists, took 190 seats. But many of them were openly critical of Ahmadinejad's highly populist rhetoric. Rafsanjani claimed that more than 160 of them were really pragmatic conservatives. It is not certain the conservative bloc will manage to preserve any semblance of unity in future elections.

The other sixty seats went to independents, some of whom were reformers in sympathy if not in name. The government claimed that more than 50 percent of the electorate participated. But the real number was probably as low as in the previous *Majles* elections. Staying home was one way of showing disgust at the Guardian Council for barring so many reformers.

The reformers hope to revive some time in the future many of the 100 reform bills passed in Sixth *Majles* but vetoed by the Guardian Council. Some of these vetoed bills implicitly contradicted conventional readings of the *shari'a*. They eliminated legal distinctions between Muslims and non-Muslims, between men and women; raised the marriage age for girls; granted women scholarships to study abroad; stipulated that divorce courts should divide property equally; allowed women deputies to wear the *hejab* (headscarf) instead of the *chadour* (full covering); permitted schoolgirls to dress in colorful clothing; and ratified the UN Convention on the Elimination of Discrimination against Women—a declaration too radical even for the U.S. Congress. The reformers used their parliamentary power to purge the Intelligence Ministry of "rogue elements" who had carried political assassinations; set up committees to investigate prison conditions; and hosted visits from the European Human Rights Commission. They tried to separate the function of prosecutors from judges and introduce trial by juries as well as mandatory defense counsels. They required judges in serious court trials to have at least ten years' experience. They reiterated the constitutional ban on torture, decreeing that prisoners under no circumstances were to be blindfolded, hooded, deprived of sleep, or placed in solitary confinement. They tried to protect the press from the conservative judiciary by instituting a special court to handle all libel and censorship cases. Even more contentious, they passed a bill stripping the Guardian Council of the authority to vet parliamentary and presidential candidates. Although most of these bills were overruled by the Guardian Council, the reform movement hopes that some time in the future a more flexible Leader or Guardian Council will accept them. It also knows that the constitution contains clauses permitting amendments—amendments that could in theory shift the balance of power away from theocracy toward democracy.

Political Culture, Citizenship, and Identity

In theory, the Islamic Republic of Iran should be a highly viable state. After all, Shi'ism is the religion of both the state and the vast majority of the population. Shi'ism can also be described as the central component of Iranian popular culture. Moreover, the constitution guarantees basic rights to religious minorities as well as to individual citizens. All citizens, regardless of race, color, language, or religion, are promised the rights of free expression, worship, and organization. They are guaranteed freedom from arbitrary arrest, torture, and police surveillance.

The constitution extends additional rights to the recognized religious minorities: Christians, Jews, and Zoroastrians. Although Christians (Armenians and Assyrians), Jews, and Zoroastrians form just 1 percent of the total population, they are allocated five *Majles* seats. They are permitted their own community organizations, including schools, their own places of worship, and their family laws. The constitution, however, is ominously silent about Baha'is and Sunnis. The former are deemed heretics; the latter are treated

in theory as full citizens but their actual status is not spelled out.

The constitution also gives guarantees to non-Persian speakers. Although now more than 83 percent of the population understands Persian, thanks to the educational system, more than 50 percent continue to speak non-Persian languages at home—Azeri, Kurdish, Gilaki, Mazandarani, Arabic, and Baluchi. The constitution promises them rights unprecedented in Iranian history. It states that "local and native languages can be used in the press, media, and schools." It also states that local populations have the right to elect provincial, town, and village councils. These councils can watch over the governors-general and the town mayors, as well as their educational, cultural, and social programs.

These generous promises have often been honored more in theory than in reality. The local councils—the chief institutional safeguard for the provincial minorities—were not convened until twenty years after the revolution. Subsidies to non-Persian publications and radio stations remain meager. Jews have been so harassed as "pro-Israeli Zionists" that more than half—40,000 out of 80,000—have left the country in the Islamic Revolution. Armenian Christians have had to end coeducational classes, adopt the government curriculum, and abide by Muslim dress codes, including the veil. The Christian population has declined from more than 300,000 to fewer than 200,000.

The Baha'is, however, have borne the brunt of religious persecution. Their leaders have been executed as "apostates" and "imperialist spies." Adherents have been fired from their jobs, had their property confiscated, and been imprisoned and tortured to pressure them to convert to Islam. Their schools have been closed, their community property expropriated, and their shrines and cemeteries bulldozed. It is estimated that since the revolution, one-third of the 300,000 Baha'is have left Iran. The Baha'is, like the Jews and Armenians, have migrated mostly to Canada and the United States. This persecution did not ease until the election of President Khatami in 1997.

The Sunni population, which forms 9 percent of the country, has other reasons for being alienated. The state religion is Shi'ism, and high officials have to be Shi'i. Citizens must abide by Khomeini's concept of jurists' guardianship, a notion derived from

Executions in Kurdestan, 1979. *Source:* © Jahangir Razmi, Bettman/Corbis.

Shi'ism. Few institutions cater to Sunni needs. There is not a single Sunni mosque in the whole of Tehran. Iran's Kurds, Turkmans, Arabs, and Baluchis are also Sunnis, and it is no accident that in the immediate aftermath of the 1979 revolution, the newborn regime faced its most serious challenges in precisely the areas of the country where these linguistic minorities lived. It crushed these revolts by rushing in Revolutionary Guards from the Persian Shi'i heartland of Isfahan, Shiraz, and Qom.

The regime's base among the Azeris, who are Shi'i but not Persian speakers, remains to be tested. In the past, the Azeris, who form 24 percent of the population and dwarf the other minorities, have not posed a serious problem to the state. They are part of the Shi'i community and have prominent figures in the Shi'i hierarchy—most notably the current Leader, Khamenei. What is more, many Azeri merchants, professionals, and workers live and work throughout Iran. In short, Azeris can be considered well integrated into Iran. But the creation of the Republic of Azerbaijan on Iran's northern border in 1991 following the disintegration of the Soviet Union has raised new concern since some Azeris on both sides of the border have begun to talk of establishing a larger unified Azerbaijan. It is no accident that in the war between Azerbaijan and Armenia in the early 1990s, Iran favored the latter. So far, the concept of a unified Azerbaijan has little appeal among Iranian Azeris.

Interests, Social Movements, and Protest

In the first two decades after its founding, the government of the Islamic Republic was extremely repressive. It closed down newspapers, professional associations, labor unions, and political parties. It banned demonstrations and public meetings. It incarcerated tens of thousands and executed some 25,000 political prisoners, all without due process of law. It systematically tortured prisoners to extract false confessions and public recantations. Many victims were Kurds, military officers from the old regime, leftists, especially members of the Mojahedin and Fedayin guerrilla organizations. The middle class was also targeted. The United Nations, Amnesty International, and Human Rights Watch all took Iran to task for violating the UN Human Rights Charter as well its own Islamic Constitution.

Although the violation of individual liberties affected the whole population, it aroused special resentment among three social groups: the modern middle class, educated women, and organized labor. The modern middle class, especially the intelligentsia, has been secular and even anticlerical ever since the 1905 revolution. Little love is lost between it and the Islamic Republic. Not surprisingly, the vast majority of those executed in the 1980s, including Kurds, were teachers, engineers, professionals, and college students. College students are a political force to be reckoned with: more than half the current population was born after 1979 and as many as 1.15 million are enrolled in higher education. In 1999, eighteen different campuses, including Tehran University, erupted into mass demonstrations against the chief judge, who had closed down a reformist newspaper. Revolutionary Guards promptly occupied the campuses, killing and seriously injuring an unknown number of students. Again, in late 2002, thousands of students protested the death sentence handed down to a reformist academic accused of insulting Islam. But in 2004, when the Guardian Council barred thousands of reformers from the elections, the campuses remained quiet—partly out of fear, partly out of disenchantment with the reformers for failing to deliver on their promises, and partly because of the concern about the looming danger from the American military presence in Iraq.

Educated women in Iran also harbor numerous grievances against the conservative clerics in the regime, especially in the judiciary. Although the Western press often dwells on the veil, Iranian women consider the veil one of their less important problems. Given a choice, most would probably continue to wear it out of personal habit and national tradition. More important are work-related grievances: job security, pay scales, promotions, maternity leave, and access to prestigious professions. Despite patriarchal attitudes held by the conservative clergy, educated women have become a major factor in Iranian society.

They now form 54 percent of college students, 45 percent of doctors, 25 percent of government employees, and 13 percent of the general labor force, up from 8 percent in the 1980s. They have established their own organizations and journals and have reinterpreted Islam to conform to modern notions of gender equality. Women do serve in the *Majles* and on local councils, and one grand ayatollah has even argued that they should be able to hold any job, including president, Leader, and court judge, positions from which women have been barred since 1979. The women's movement scored a major victory in 2003 when a woman, Shiren Ebadi, a life-long human rights lawyer, won the Nobel Peace Prize. With such international prominence, the conservatives dare not silence her or close down her office.

Factory workers in Iran are another significant social group with serious grievances. Their concerns deal mostly with high unemployment, low wages, declining incomes, lack of decent housing, and an unsatisfactory labor law, which, while giving them mandatory holidays and some semblance of job security, denies them the right to call strikes and organize independent unions. Since 1979, wage earners have had a Workers' House— a government-influenced organization—and its affiliated newspaper, *Kar va Kargar* (*Work and Worker*), and, since 1999, the Islamic Labor Party to represent their interests. In most years, the Workers' House flexes its political muscle by holding a May Day rally. In 1999, the rally began peacefully with a greeting from a female member of the city council who had received the second-most votes in the 1996 Tehran municipal elections. But the rally turned into a protest when workers began to march to parliament denouncing conservatives who had spoken in favor of further watering down of the Labor Law. Bus drivers spontaneously joined the protest, shutting down most of central Tehran.

President Khatami's reform movement drew much of its core support precisely from these three social groups: college youth, women, and workers. In the 1997 and 2001 presidential campaigns, as well as in the elections for municipal councils and the Sixth *Majles,* crucial roles were played by the Islamic Student Associations, the Office of Student Solidarity, the Islamic Women's Association, and the Workers' House. The reformers were also supported by a number of newspapers, which have quickly gained a mass circulation, even though they initially catered mainly to the intelligentsia. For example, the reformist *Hayat-e* *No,* launched in late 2000, had a circulation of more than 235,000 by April 2001, almost double that of the long-established conservative newspaper *Ettela'at.*

SECTION 5 **Iranian Politics in Transition**

Political Challenges and Changing Agendas

Contemporary Iran faces two major challenges—one internal, the other external. Internally, the Islamic Republic continues to grapple with the vexing question of how to synthesize theocracy with democracy, and clerical authority with mass participation. The conservative clerics, who already controlled the judiciary, took over the *Majles* in 2004 and the presidency in June 2005. Even though the conservatives appear to control the political heights, they have lost much of their support in the general public. The ruling conservatives thus face the challenge of how to maintain some semblance of mass participation while not actually sharing power with the reformers.

This challenge is particularly vexing since the country has in recent decades gone through a profound cultural revolution, embracing such key concepts as political pluralism, mass participation, civil society, human rights, and individual liberties. Even conservatives have started to incorporate such terms into their own language, openly describing themselves as "neoconservatives" and "pragmatic." Meanwhile, those in the general public who feel excluded from national politics continue to be active in nongovernmental organizations. If they are completely excluded from the political arena, they may well conclude that reform is not possible. So far, however, reformers such as Nobel Peace Prize winner Shiren Ebadi have preferred not to actually challenge the whole system.

The major external challenge to the Islamic Republic comes from the United States. The Bush administration, by naming Iran as a member of the Axis of Evil and openly calling for "regime change," dramatically increased pressures on Iran—pressures that already existed because of economic sanctions, lack of diplomatic relations, and successful barring of

Iran from the World Trade Organization. In the past, the United States has accused Iran of sabotaging the Arab–Israeli peace process; helping terrorist organizations, especially Hamas in Palestine and Hezbollah in Lebanon; and "grossly violating" democratic and human rights of its own citizens. More recently, it has highlighted the danger of weapons of mass destruction in Iran and accused the country of intending to transform its nuclear energy program into a nuclear weapons program. Of course, the external challenge to Iran drastically increased once the United States occupied Iran's neighbors, Afghanistan and Iraq. It was further increased in 2008 when the U.S. administration began to accuse Iran of arming, training, and financing unspecified anti-American Shi'i groups in Iraq. Some administration officials talked as if the U.S. were on the verge of going to war with Iran. U.S.–Iran relations will be an important item on the agenda of the next American president, Barack Obama.

The conservatives in Iran have been able to inadvertently transform this external threat from the U.S. into an asset. They intimidated many reformers into toning down their demands, even silencing them, by declaring that the country was in danger, that the enemy was at the gates, and that any opposition to the government in such times would play into the hands of foreigners. Few reformers were willing to appear unpatriotic at a time when the nation was perceived as facing imminent invasion.

Iranian Politics in Comparative Perspective

Iran is unlike most developing countries in that it is an old state with institutions that go back to ancient times. It is also not a country that only relatively recently achieved independence, since it was never formally colonized by the European imperial powers.

Unlike many other Third World states that have a weak connection with their societies, Iran has a religion that links the elite with the masses, the cities with the villages, the government with the citizenry. Shi'ism, as well as Iranian identity, serves as social and cultural cement, giving the population a strong national identity. Iran also has the advantage of rich oil resources that give it the potential for rapid economic growth that would be the envy of most developing countries. Finally, Iran produced two popular upheavals in the twentieth century: the constitutional (1905) and the Islamic (1979) revolutions, in which the citizenry actively intervened in politics, overthrew the old regime, and shaped the new. Both of these revolutions were the result of authentic homegrown political movements, not foreign imports.

Yet Iran also shares some problems with other Third World countries. Its economy remains underdeveloped, highly dependent on one commodity, and unable to meet the rising expectations of its population. Iran's collective identity, although strong in religious terms, is strained by other internal fault lines, especially those of class, ethnicity, gender, and interclerical political conflicts. And its ambition to enter the world of states as an important regional player has been thwarted by international as well as domestic and regional realities. These have combined to keep the country pretty much on the global sidelines.

The democratic idea in Iran has been constricted by theocracy. Some argue that Islam has made this inevitable. But Islam, like Christianity and other major religions, can be interpreted in ways that either support or oppose the democratic idea. Some interpretations of Islam stress the importance of justice, equality, and consultation as political principles. Islam also has a tradition of tolerating other religions, and the *shari'a* explicitly protects life, property, and honor. In practice, Islam has often separated politics from religion, government legal statutes from holy laws, spiritual affairs from worldly matters, and the state from the clerical establishment.

Moreover, theocracy in Iran originates not in Islam itself but in Khomeini's concept of the jurist's guardianship. On the whole, Sunni Islam considers clerics to be theological scholars, not a special political stratum, which helps explain why the Iranian regime has found it difficult to export the revolution to other parts of the Muslim world. The failure of democracy in Iran should be attributed less to anything intrinsic in Islam than to the confluence of crises between 1979 and 1981 that allowed a particular group of clerics to seize power. Whether they remain in power depends not so much on Islam but on how they handle economic problems and the demands for public participation—in other words, how they deal with the challenges of governing the economy and synthesizing theocracy with the democratic idea.

Politics in the Islamic Republic of Iran remains sharply divided over the question of how to govern an economy beset by rising demands, fluctuating petroleum revenues, and the nightmarish prospect that in the next two generations the oil wells will run dry. Most clerics favor a rather conventional capitalist road to development, hoping to liberalize the market, privatize industry, attract foreign capital, and encourage the propertied classes to invest. Others envisage an equally conventional statist road to development, favoring central planning, government industries, price controls, high taxes, state subsidies, national self-reliance, and ambitious programs to eliminate poverty, illiteracy, slums, and unemployment. President Khatami charted a third way, combining elements of state intervention with free enterprise that is strikingly similar to the social democracy favored in some other parts of the world such as the Labour Party in Britain. Ahmadinejad, on the other hand, favors a state-controlled economy that would implement radical populist programs. Both claim to find their inspiration in Islam, Shi'ism, and Iranian history.

As the clock of history ticks, Iran's population grows, oil revenues fluctuate, and the per capita national income could stagnate or fall again. Economic problems like those that undermined the monarchy could well undermine the Islamic Republic. The country's collective identity has also come under great strain in recent years. The emphasis on Shi'ism has antagonized Iran's Sunnis as well as its non-Muslim citizens. The emphasis on clerical Shi'ism has further alienated all secularists, including lay liberals, radical leftists, and moderate nationalists. Furthermore, the official emphasis on Khomeini's brand of Shi'ism has alienated those Shi'is who reject the whole notion of jurist's guardianship. The elevation of Khamenei as the Leader has also antagonized many early proponents of jurist's guardianship on the grounds that he lacks the scholarly qualifications to hold the position that embodies the sacred and secular power of the Islamic Republic.

In sum, Iran's ruling regime has gradually reduced the social base that brought it to power. Only time will tell whether growing discontent will be expressed through apolitical channels, such as drug addiction, emigration, and quietist religion, or whether those seeking change will look to reformist movements that work within the system or turn to more radical insurrectionary organizations or ethnic-based movements.

Finally, the Islamic Republic's initial attempt to enter the world of states as a militant force for the spread of its theocratic version of Islam proved counterproductive.

This effort diverted scarce resources to the military. It frightened Saudi Arabia and the Gulf sheikdoms into the arms of the United States. It prompted the United States to isolate Iran, discouraging investment and preventing international organizations from extending economic assistance. Militancy also alarmed nearby secular states such as Turkey, Tadzhikistan, and Azerbaijan. In recent years, the regime has managed to overcome many of these problems. It has won over the Arab states and has established cordial relations with its neighbors. Most important, it has managed to repair bridges to the European Community. Only time will show how its tortuous relations with the United States will work out and how this will affect the future of politics in Iran.

Key Terms >>>

civil society
theocracy
shari'a
mosque
Majles
Leader
Supreme Leader
Guardian Council
Farsi
Shi'ism
ayatollah
People of the Book
Qur'an
coup d'état
bazaars
fundamentalism

jurist's guardianship
pasdaran
Hezbollahis
hojjat al-Islam
laissez-faire
jihad
rentier state
dual society
Organization of Petroleum Exporting Countries (OPEC)
Expediency Council
Imam Jum'ehs
Foundation of the Oppressed
Assembly of Religious Experts
social democrats
maslahat

Suggested Readings >>>

Abrahamian, E. *Iran A History of Modern Iran*. Cambridge: Cambridge University Press, 2008.

———. *Khomeinism*. Berkeley: University of California Press, 1993.

Ansari, A. *Modern Iran Since 1921*. New York: Longman, 2003.

Azimi, F. *The Quest for Democracy in Iran*. Cambridge: Harvard University Press, 2008.

Bakhash, S. *Reign of the Ayatollahs*. New York: Basic Books, 1984.

Beeman, W. *The "Great Satan" vs the "Mad Mullahs."* Chicago: University of Chicago Press, 2005.

Bill, J. *The Eagle and the Lion.* New Haven, Conn.: Yale University Press, 1988.

Brumberg, D. *Reinventing Khomeini: The Struggle for Reform in Iran.* Chicago: University of Chicago Press, 2001.

Buchta, W. *Who Rules Iran?* Washington, D.C.: Washington Institute for Near East Policy, 2000.

Chehabi, H. *Iranian Politics and Religious Modernism.* Ithaca, N.Y.: Cornell University Press, 1990.

Dabashi, H. *Theology of Discontent: The Ideological Foundation of the Islamic Revolution in Iran.* New York: New York University Press, 1993.

Ebadi, S. *Iran Awakening: A Memoir of Revolution and Hope.* New York: Random House, 2006.

Garthwaite, F. *The Persians.* Oxford: Blackwell, 2005.

Gheissari, A. & Nasr, V. *Democracy in Iran: History and the Quest for Liberty.* New York: Oxford University Press, 2007.

Hooglund, E. *Twenty Years of Islamic Revolution.* Syracuse, N.Y.: Syracuse University Press, 2002.

Kazemi, F. "Civil Society and Iranian Politics." In A. Norton, ed. *Civil Society in the Middle East.* Leiden: Brill, 1996.

Keddie, N. *Modern Iran: Roots and Results of Revolution.* New Haven, Conn.: Yale University Press, 2004.

Kurzman, C. *The Unthinkable Revolution in Iran.* Cambridge: Harvard University Press, 2004.

Milani, M. *The Making of Iran's Islamic Revolution.* Boulder, Colo.: Westview Press, 1994.

Mir-Hosseini, Z. *Islam and Gender.* Princeton, N.J.: Princeton University Press, 1999.

Moin, B. *Khomeini: Life of the Ayatollah.* London: Tauris, 1999.

Mottahedeh, R. *The Mantle of the Prophet.* New York: Simon & Schuster, 1985.

Pollack, K. *The Persian Puzzle: The Conflict between Iran and America.* New York, Random House, 2003.

Satrapi, M. *Persepolis.* New York: Pantheon, 2003.

Schirazi, A. *The Constitution of Iran.* London: Tauris, 1997.

Takeyh, R. *Hidden Iran: Paradox and Power in the Islamic Republic.* New York: Times Books, 2006.

Suggested Websites ≫

University of Texas—Iran Maps
www.lib.utexas.edu/maps/iran.html
Columbia University—The Gulf/2000 Project's Map Collection
gulf2000.columbia.edu/maps.shtml
The Story of the Revolution, British Broadcasting Corporation
www.bbc.co.uk/persian/revolution

Iranian Mission to the United Nations
www.un.int/iran
Iran Report, Radio Free Europe
www.rferl.org/reports/iran-report
News Related to Iran
www.farsinews.net

Endnotes ≫

[1] Quoted in E. Browne, *The Persian Revolution* (New York: Barnes and Noble, 1966), p. 137.

[2] British Financial Adviser to the Foreign Office in Tehran, *Documents on British Foreign Policy, 1919–39* (London: Her Majesty's Stationery Office, 1963), First Series, XIII, pp. 720, 735.

[3] British Minister to the Foreign Office, *Report on the Seizure of Lands,* Foreign Office 371/Persia 1932/File 34–16007.

[4] *Kayhan International,* November 10, 1976.

[5] "Fifty Indictments of Treason During Fifty Years of Treason," *Khabarnameh,* no. 46 (April 1976).

[6] M. Bazargan, "Letter to the Editor," *Ettela'at,* February 7, 1980.

[7] *Iran Times,* January 12, 1979.

[8] *Washington Post,* December 12, 1978.

[9] *Christian Science Monitor,* December 12, 1978.

[10] Samuel P. Huntington, *The Clash of Civilizations and the Remaking of World Order* (New York: Simon & Schuster, 1996).

[11] Mirza Hosayn Khan Tahvildar-e Isfahan, *Jukhrafiha-ye Isfahan* [The Geography of Isfahan] (Tehran: Tehran University Press, 1963), pp. 100–101.

[12] International Labor Organization, "Employment and Income Policies for Iran" (Unpublished report, Geneva, 1972), Appendix C, p. 6.

[13] A. Sharbatoghilie, *Urbanization and Regional Disparity in Post-Revolutionary Iran* (Boulder, Colo.: Westview Press, 1991), p. 4.

[14] *Wall Street Journal,* November 4, 1977.

[15] U.S. Congress, *Economic Consequences of the Revolution in Iran* (Washington, D.C.: U.S. Government Printing Office, 1979), p. 184.

[16]U.S. Congress, *Economic Consequences of the Revolution in Iran,* p. 5.

[17]U.S. Department of Commerce, *Iran: A Survey of U.S. Business Opportunities* (Washington, D.C.: U.S. Government Printing Office, 1977), pp. 1–2.

[18]Cited in H. Amirahmadi, *Revolution and Economic Transition* (Albany: State University of New York Press, 1960), p. 201.

[19]Cited in *Iran Times,* July 9, 1993.

[20]J. Amuzegar, *Iran's Economy Under the Islamic Republic* (London: Taurus Press, 1994), p. 100.

[21]A. Rafsanjani, "The Islamic Consultative Assembly," *Kayhan,* May 23, 1987.

[22]S. Saffari, "The Legitimation of the Clergy's Right to Rule in the Iranian Constitution of 1979," *British Journal of Middle Eastern Studies* 20, no. 1 (1993): 64–81.

[23]Ayatollah Montazeri, *Ettela'at,* October 8, 1979.

[24]O. Fallaci, "Interview with Khomeini," *New York Times Magazine,* October 7, 1979.

William A. Joseph

Chapter 13 »**CHINA**

Official Name: **People's Republic of China (Zhonghua Remin Gongheguo)**

Location: **East Asia**

Capital City: **Beijing**

Population (2008): **1.3 billion**

Size: **9,596,960 sq. km.; slightly smaller than the United States**

1911
Revolution led by Sun Yat-sen overthrows 2,000-year-old imperial system and establishes the Republic of China

1912
Sun Yat-sen founds the Nationalist Party (*Guomindang*) to oppose warlords who have seized power in the new republic

1921
Chinese Communist Party (CCP) is founded

1927
Civil war between Nationalists (now led by Chiang Kai-shek) and Communists begins

1934
Mao Zedong becomes leader of the CCP.

1937
Japan invades China, marking the start of World War II in Asia.

1949
Chinese Communists win the civil war and establish the People's Republic of China.

SECTION 1 · The Making of the Modern Chinese State

Politics in Action

The 2008 Beijing Olympics were widely touted as China's "coming-out party." They were seen as signifying global recognition of China's emergence as a rising power in world affairs. In terms of sports and spectacle, it was quite a party! The opening ceremonies provided a breathtaking visual and musical tour of China's cultural history from ancient to modern times via high technology, flawless choreography of a cast of thousands, and a fireworks display that used 29,000 rockets to light the sky. The host country proudly won the most gold medals and numerous world records were set in state-of-the art architectural wonders such as the Birds Nest stadium and the Water Cube swimming venue. With a price tag of more than $43 billion, the Beijing games were by far the most expensive Olympics ever—they were three times the cost of the 2004 Athens games.

Faced with worries that Beijing's notorious smog would impair the performance of athletes—or even endanger their health—the Chinese government seemed to work a bit of a miracle by getting the air quality to levels that ranged from acceptable to very good during the games. This was partly achieved through what's been called "the most furious anti-pollution effort of all time,"[1] which involved pulling more than 2 million automobiles off the road, closing hundreds of factories, and halting all construction near the capital.

But the glitter of the gold medals and the blue skies could not completely conceal the fact that China is ruled by a Communist Party that maintains a tight and often repressive grip on power. Several incidents before and during the Olympics reflected the political tensions that have persisted alongside the country's remarkable economic transformation over the last three decades.

Numerous known dissidents were harassed or detained in the run-up to the Games to insure that they wouldn't make trouble while the world's attention was focused on Beijing. The Chinese authorities promised the International Olympics Committee that peaceful protests would be allowed—although limited to three public parks, and requiring the organizers to obtain a police permit—but no such protests took place. Two elderly women applied four times for a permit to protest against the forced evictions from their homes to make way for an Olympics construction project; they not only were not given a permit, but were interrogated by the police for hours and threatened with a year in a "re-education through labor" camp if they persisted.

There was also political unrest far from Beijing. In March 2008, large-scale protests against Chinese rule in Tibet were crushed by military force. In Xinjiang, an area in western China with a large Muslim population, a suicide attack attributed to Islamic terrorists killed sixteen Chinese police officers just a few days before the start of the Olympics.

1958–1960	1976	1978	1989	1997	2002–2003	2008
Great Leap Forward	Mao Zedong dies.	Deng Xiaoping becomes China's most powerful leader and launches the nation on the path toward rapid economic growth.	Tiananmen massacre	Deng Xiaoping dies; Jiang Zemin becomes China's top leader.	Hu Jintao succeeds Jiang as head of the CCP and president of the People's Republic of China; re-elected to those positions in 2007–2008.	Hosted the Olympic Games in Beijing
1966–1976						
Great Proletarian Cultural Revolution						

In the mid-1970s, the People's Republic of China (PRC) was not only among the world's poorest nations, but it also had one of the most tyrannical political systems. The Beijing games were a grand showcase for the country's stunning economic progress. And there has been significant political change, too. The Chinese people, on the whole, enjoy a level of both prosperity and freedom that was unimaginable just a generation ago. But the PRC is one of only a handful of countries that is still a **communist-party state** in which the ruling party claims and enforces an exclusive monopoly on political power and proclaims allegiance (at least officially) to the ideology of **Marxism-Leninism**. The rift between China's authoritarian political system and its increasingly modern and globalized society remains deep and ominous.

Geographic Setting

China is located in the eastern part of mainland Asia. It is at the heart of one of the world's most strategically important regions. It shares land borders with

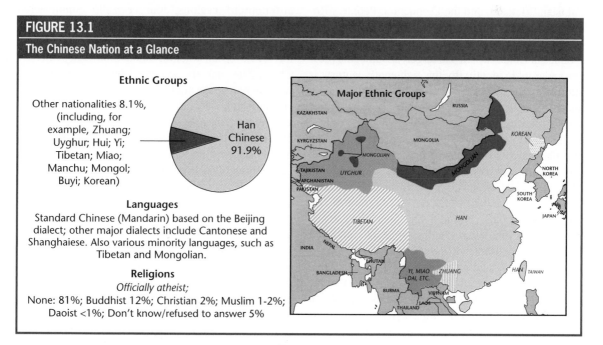

FIGURE 13.1

The Chinese Nation at a Glance

Ethnic Groups

Other nationalities 8.1%, (including, for example, Zhuang; Uyghur; Hui; Yi; Tibetan; Miao; Manchu; Mongol; Buyi; Korean)

Han Chinese 91.9%

Languages

Standard Chinese (Mandarin) based on the Beijing dialect; other major dialects include Cantonese and Shanghaiese. Also various minority languages, such as Tibetan and Mongolian.

Religions

Officially atheist;

None: 81%; Buddhist 12%; Christian 2%; Muslim 1–2%; Daoist <1%; Don't know/refused to answer 5%

Major Ethnic Groups (map)

Table 13.1

Political Organization

Political System	Communist party-state; officially, a socialist state under the people's democratic dictatorship
Regime History	Established in 1949 after the victory of the Chinese Communist Party (CCP) in the Chinese civil war
Administrative Structure	Unitary system with twenty-two provinces, five autonomous regions, four centrally administrated municipalities, and two Special Administrative Regions (Hong Kong and Macao)
Executive	Premier (head of government) and president (head of state) formally elected by legislature, but only with approval of CCP leadership; the head of the CCP, the general secretary, is in effect the country's chief executive, and usually serves concurrently as president of the PRC.
Legislature	Unicameral National People's Congress; about 3,000 delegates elected indirectly from lower-level people's congresses for five-year terms. Largely a rubber-stamp body for Communist Party policies, although in recent years has become somewhat more assertive.
Judiciary	A nationwide system of people's courts, which is constitutionally independent but, in fact, largely under the control of the CCP; a Supreme People's Court supervises the country's judicial system and is formally responsible to the National People's Congress, which also elects the court's president.
Party System	A one-party system, although in addition to the ruling Chinese Communist Party, there are eight politically insignificant "democratic" parties.

more than a dozen countries, including Russia, India, Pakistan, Vietnam, and the Democratic People's Republic of Korea (North Korea), and is a relatively short distance by sea from Japan, the Philippines, and Indonesia. China, which had largely assumed its present geographic identity by the eighteenth century, is slightly smaller than the United States in land area, and is the fourth largest country in the world, after Russia, Canada, and the United States.

The PRC is bounded on all sides by imposing physical barriers: the sea to the east; mountains to the north, south, and west (including the world's highest, Mount Everest); deserts, vast grasslands, and dense forests in various parts of the north; and tropical rain forests to the south. In traditional times, these barriers isolated China from extensive contact with other peoples and contributed to the country's sense of itself as the "Middle Kingdom" (which is the literal translation of the Chinese term for China, *zhongguo*) that lay not only at the physical, but also at the political and cultural center of the world.

The PRC is made up of twenty-two provinces, five **autonomous regions**, four centrally administered cities (including the capital, Beijing), and two Special Administrative Regions, Hong Kong and Macao, former European colonies that are indirectly ruled by China. The sparsely populated but territorially vast western part of the country is mostly mountains, deserts, and high plateaus. The northeast is much like the U.S. plains states in terms of weather and topography. It is a wheat-growing area and China's industrial heartland. Southern China has a much warmer climate. In places it is even semitropical, which allows year-round agriculture and intensive rice cultivation. The country is very rich in natural resources, particularly coal and petroleum (including significant but untapped onshore and offshore reserves). It has the world's greatest potential for hydroelectric power. Still, China's astounding economic growth in recent decades has created an almost insatiable demand for energy resources. This, in turn, has led the PRC to look abroad for critical raw materials.

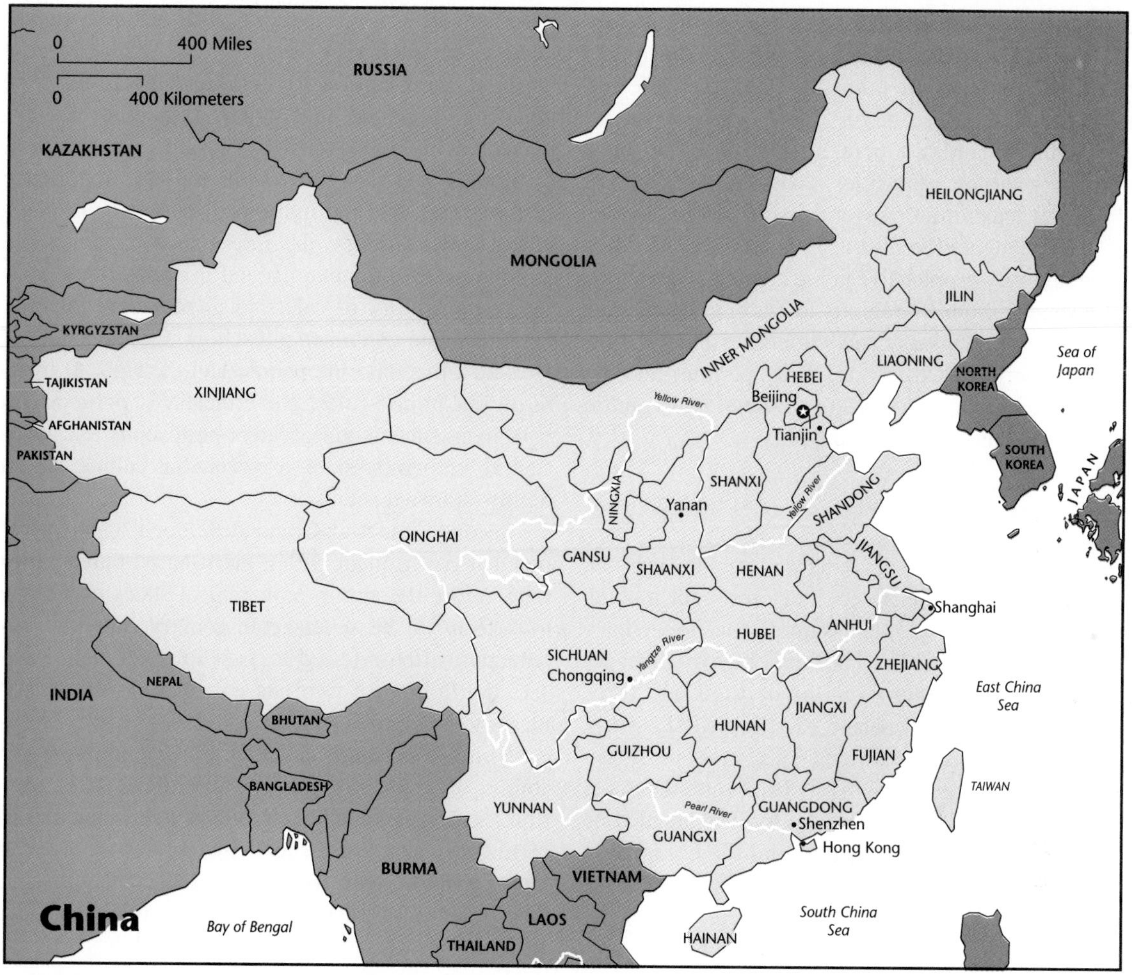
0 400 Miles
0 400 Kilometers
RUSSIA
KAZAKHSTAN
MONGOLIA
HEILONGJIANG
JILIN
KYRGYZSTAN
INNER MONGOLIA
LIAONING
Sea of Japan
TAJIKISTAN
XINJIANG
HEBEI
NORTH KOREA
AFGHANISTAN
Beijing
Yellow River
Tianjin
PAKISTAN
SOUTH KOREA
JAPAN
SHANXI
NINGXIA
Yellow River
SHANDONG
Yanan
QINGHAI
GANSU
JIANGSU
SHAANXI
HENAN
TIBET
Shanghai
ANHUI
HUBEI
Yangtze River
SICHUAN
ZHEJIANG
Chongqing
East China Sea
INDIA
NEPAL
JIANGXI
BHUTAN
HUNAN
GUIZHOU
FUJIAN
BANGLADESH
TAIWAN
YUNNAN
Pearl River
GUANGDONG
Shenzhen
GUANGXI
Hong Kong
BURMA
VIETNAM
China
LAOS
South China Sea
Bay of Bengal
HAINAN
THAILAND

Although China and the United States are roughly equal in geographic size, China's population (1.3 billion, the world's largest) is more than four times greater. Less than 15 percent of its land is usable for agriculture. China has a little more than 20 percent of the world's population but only 10 percent of the world's arable land and 6 percent of water resources. The precarious balance between people and the land needed to feed them has been a dilemma for China for centuries. It remains one of the government's major concerns.

China has more than 140 cities with a population of a million or more (compared with 35 in Europe). The three largest are Shanghai (18.5 million), Beijing (17.4 million), and Tianjin (10.4 million). In 1997, the former British colony of Hong Kong became part of the PRC. It is one of the world's great commercial centers (population 6.9 million). Nevertheless, about 55 percent of China's people still live in rural areas. The countryside has played—and continues to play—a very important role in China's political development.

China's population is highly concentrated along the eastern seaboard and in the most agriculturally fertile areas around three great rivers: the Yellow River in north China, the Yangtze (Yangzi) in the central part of the country, and the Pearl River in the south. The overwhelming majority (92 percent) of China's citizens are ethnically Chinese (referred to as the *Han*, after one of China's earliest dynasties). The remaining 8 percent is made up of more than fifty ethnic minorities, who differ from the Han in at least one of several major ways, including race, language, culture, and religion. Most of these minority peoples live in the country's geopolitically sensitive border regions, including Tibet. This makes the often uneasy and sometimes hostile relationship between China's minority peoples and the central government in Beijing a crucial and volatile issue in Chinese politics today.

Critical Junctures

The People's Republic of China was founded in 1949. But understanding the critical junctures in the making of the modern Chinese state requires that we go back much further into China's political history. Broadly considered, that history can be divided into three periods: the imperial period (221 B.C.–1911 A.D.), during which China was ruled by a series of dynasties and emperors; the relatively brief republican period (1912–1949), when the country was plagued by civil war and foreign invasion; and the communist period, from the founding of the PRC in 1949 to the present.

From Empire to Republic (221 B.C.–1911 A.D.)

Modern China is heir to one of the world's oldest cultural and political traditions. The roots of Chinese culture date back more than 4,000 years, and the Chinese empire first took political shape in 221 B.C., when a number of small kingdoms were unified under China's first emperor, who laid the foundation of an imperial system that lasted for more than twenty centuries until its overthrow in 1911–12. During those many centuries, China was ruled by more than a dozen different family-based dynasties and experienced extensive geographic expansion and far-reaching political, economic, social, and cultural changes. Nevertheless, many of the core features of the imperial system remained remarkably consistent over time.

There are several reasons that the Chinese empire survived for such a long time.

First, the traditional order was supported by the enduring influence in Chinese society of Confucianism. This philosophy, based on the teachings of Confucius (c. 551–479 B.C.), stresses the importance of the group over the individual, deference to one's elders and superiors, the importance of education, and the need to maintain social harmony, as well as the responsibility of rulers to govern benevolently. Confucianism contained a teaching, the "Mandate of Heaven," that said the people had the right to overthrow an unjust ruler. Nevertheless, Confucianism was, in essence, a conservative philosophy that justified an autocratic state, a patriarchal culture, and a highly stratified society.

Second, imperial China developed an effective national government with a merit-based bureaucracy long before the strong monarchical states of Europe took form in the seventeenth century. Imperial bureaucrats, often referred to as scholar-officials, were selected through a rigorous examination that tested mastery of Confucian classics.

Third, the traditional Chinese economy was a source of great strength to the empire. Urbanization expanded in China much sooner than it did in Europe, and Westerners, like Marco Polo, who journeyed to China as early as the thirteenth century, were amazed by the grandeur of the Middle Kingdom's cities.

Fourth, the structure of traditional Chinese society, especially in the million or more small villages that were its foundation, gave imperial China great staying power. The vast majority of the village population was made up of poor and relatively poor peasants. But life was dominated by landlords and other local elites who worked with the national government to maintain and sustain the system.

Finally, the Chinese imperial system endured because, throughout most of its history, China was by far the dominant political, military, and cultural force in its known world. Even when the Middle Kingdom was conquered from the outside, as it was in 1214 A.D. by the Mongols and in 1644 A.D. by the Manchus, the invaders wound up establishing a new dynasty much on the pattern of the old and adapting many aspects of Chinese civilization.

Imperial China experienced many internal rebellions, often quite in large scale, during its lengthy history. Some even led to the overthrow of the ruling dynasty. But new dynasties were always built on traditional foundations. However, in the late eighteenth and nineteenth centuries, the Chinese empire faced an unprecedented combination of internal crises and external challenges. A population explosion (the result of a long spell of peace and prosperity) led to economic stagnation. Official corruption in the bureaucracy and exploitation of the peasants by both landlords and the government increased and caused widespread social unrest. One massive revolt, the Taiping Rebellion (1850–1864), took 20 million lives and nearly overthrew the imperial government.

By the early nineteenth century, the European powers had surged far ahead of China in industrial and military development. They were pressing the country to open its markets to foreign trade. China showed little interest in such overtures and tried to limit the activities of Westerners. But Europe, most notably Britain, was in the midst of its era of great commercial and colonial expansion and used its military supremacy to compel China to engage in "free" trade with the West. Britain made huge profits from selling opium in China, which it used to more than offset the vast quantities of tea that it was importing. Chinese efforts to stop the opium trade led to military conflict. After suffering a humiliating defeat by the British in the Opium War (1839–1842), China was literally forced to sign a series of unequal treaties that opened its borders to foreign merchants, missionaries, and diplomats on terms dictated by Britain and other Western powers. China also lost control of significant pieces of its territory to other countries (including Hong Kong), and important sectors of the Chinese economy fell into foreign hands.

There were many efforts to revive or reform the imperial government in the late nineteenth and early twentieth centuries. But political power in China remained largely in the hands of staunch conservatives who resisted change. When change came in 1911–12, it came in the form of a revolution that not only toppled the ruling dynasty, but also brought an end to the 2,000-year-old dynastic system.

Warlords, Nationalists, and Communists (1912–1949)

The Republic of China was established on January 1, 1912. Dr. Sun Yat-sen*, then China's best-known revolutionary, became president. However, the Western-educated Sun could not hold on to power. China soon fell into a lengthy period of conflict and disintegration with parts of the country run by rival military leaders known as warlords. Sun set about making plans to launch another revolution to reunify the country under his Nationalist Party (the *Guomindang*).

In 1921, a few intellectuals, inspired by the Russian revolution in 1917 and supported by the Soviet Union, organized the Chinese Communist Party (CCP). They were looking for more radical solutions to China's problems. In 1924, the small CCP joined with Sun Yat-sen's much larger Nationalist party to fight the warlords. After some initial successes, this alliance came to a tragic end in 1927. Chiang Kai-shek, a military leader who had become the head of the Nationalist Party after Sun's death in 1925, turned against his communist partners. He ordered a bloody suppression that nearly wiped out the CCP. Chiang proceeded to unify the Republic of China under his personal rule. He did this largely by striking deals with some of the country's most powerful remaining warlords, who supported him in suppressing the Communists.

In order to survive, the Communist Party had to relocate its headquarters deep into the Chinese countryside. Ironically, this retreat created the conditions for the eventual rise to power of the man who would lead the CCP to nationwide victory, Mao Zedong. Mao had been one of the junior founders of the Communist Party. He had strongly advocated paying more attention to China's suffering peasants as a potential source of support for the revolution. "In a very short time," he wrote in 1927, "several hundred million peasants will rise like a mighty storm, like a hurricane, a force

---

*In Chinese, the *family* name comes before the *personal* name. Thus, Sun Yat-sen's family name is Sun, and he is known as Dr. Sun. Family names are almost always made up of one syllable, while personal names usually have two syllables.

so swift and violent that no power, however great, will be able to hold it back."[2] While the CCP was based in the rural areas, Mao began his climb to the top of the party leadership.

In late 1934, the CCP was surrounded by Chiang Kai-shek's army and forced to begin a yearlong, 6,000-mile journey called the Long March, that took them across some of the most remote parts of China. In October 1935, the Communists established a base in a remote and impoverished area of northwestern China called Yan'an, where they would remain for nearly a decade. Although less than 10 percent of the 80,000 or so original Long Marchers made it to Yan'an, the CCP found itself in relative isolation that protected it from sustained assault from Chiang's forces. It was in Yan'an that Mao consolidated his political and ideological control of the CCP, sometimes through ruthless means. He was elected party chairman in 1943, a position that he held until his death in 1976. The CCP also implemented land reform and other policies that benefited the peasants in the areas under its control.

In 1937 Japan invaded China, starting World War II in Asia. The Japanese army pushed Chiang Kai-shek's Nationalist government to the far southwestern part of the country. This effectively eliminated the Nationalists as an active combatant against Japanese aggression. In contrast, the CCP base in Yan'an was on the front line against Japan's troops. Mao and the Communists successfully mobilized the peasants to use **guerrilla warfare** to fight the invaders.

By the end of World War II in 1945, the CCP had vastly expanded its membership and had developed a solid military force of its own. It controlled much of the countryside in north China and had widespread support among the population. In contrast, the Nationalists were cut off from most of China and unpopular with many Chinese because of corruption, political repression, economic mismanagement, and what was seen as a failure to effectively resist the Japanese.

After Japan's surrender, the Chinese civil war quickly resumed. The Communists won a decisive victory over the U.S.-backed Nationalists. Chiang Kai-shek and his supporters had to flee to the island of Taiwan, 90 miles off the Chinese coast. (See "Global Connection: The Republic of China on Taiwan.") On October 1, 1949, Mao Zedong declared the founding of the People's Republic of China.

Mao in Power (1949–1976)

The CCP came to power on a wave of popular support because of its reputation as a party of social reformers and patriotic fighters. Chairman Mao and the CCP quickly turned their attention to some of the country's most glaring problems. A nationwide land reform campaign redistributed property from the rich to the poor and increased agricultural production in the countryside. Highly successful drives eliminated opium addiction and prostitution from the cities. A national law greatly enhanced the legal status of women in the family. It allowed many women to free themselves from unhappy arranged marriages. The CCP did not hesitate to use force to achieve its objectives and silence opponents. Nevertheless, the party gained considerable legitimacy among many parts of the population because of its successful policies during the first period of its rule.

Between 1953 and 1957, the PRC began building a centrally planned economy like that in the Soviet Union. The complete nationalization of industry and **collectivization** of agriculture carried out as part of this plan were decisive steps away from the mixed state-private economy of the early 1950s and toward **socialism**. Although the plan achieved good economic results for the country, Mao was troubled by the growth of the government bureaucracy and the persistence of inequalities, especially those caused by the emphasis on industrial and urban development and the relative neglect of the countryside.

In 1956, Mao used the media to issue a call to the Chinese people to "let a hundred flowers bloom, let a hundred schools of thought contend"; that is, they should come forward to offer their frank opinions about how the Communist Party was governing China. His goals for this **Hundred Flowers Movement** were to shake up the bureaucrats and encourage broader participation in making public policy, especially among the country's intellectuals. But the outpouring of public criticism and a wave of large-scale industrial strikes revealed the fact that many people were harboring deep resentments about communist policies and about the growing political dictatorship.

Mao's reaction to the unexpectedly severe Hundred Flowers criticism was to order a vicious crackdown—the **Anti-Rightist Campaign** of 1957—in which hundreds of thousands of people were accused of being enemies of the revolution ("Rightists") and punished by being demoted, fired, or sent to labor camps. This campaign completely stifled political debate in China and "destroyed the hope that China's 'transition to socialism' might proceed on the basis of some form of popular democracy and with some

Global Connection

The Republic of China on Taiwan

Despite being defeated by Mao Zedong and the Communists on the mainland in October 1949, Chiang Kai-shek's Nationalist Party and the Republic of China (ROC) continued to function on the island of Taiwan, just 90 miles off the coast. The Chinese Communists would likely have taken over Taiwan if the United States had not intervened to prevent an invasion. Taiwan remains politically separate from the People's Republic of China and still formally calls itself the Republic of China.

The Nationalist Party imposed a harsh dictatorship on Taiwan after its forced exile from the mainland in 1949. This deepened the sharp divide between the "mainlanders," who had arrived in large numbers in 1949, and the native Taiwanese majority, whose ancestors had settled there centuries before and who spoke a distinctive Chinese dialect.

But with large amounts of U.S. aid and advice, the Nationalist government under Chiang Kai-shek sponsored a successful and peaceful program of land reform and rural development. It attracted extensive foreign investment and promoted economic growth by producing very competitive exports. The government also modernized Taiwan's roads and ports. It implemented policies that have given the island health and education levels that are among the best in the world. Its standard of living is one of the highest in Asia. By the early 1970s, Taiwan had become a model **newly industrializing country (NIC)**.

After Chiang Kai-shek died in 1975, his son, Chiang Ching-kuo, became president of the Republic of China and head of the Nationalist Party. Most people expected him to continue **authoritarian** rule. Instead, he permitted some opposition and dissent. He gave important government and party positions, previously dominated by mainlanders, to the Taiwanese. When he died in 1988, the Taiwanese vice president, Lee Teng-hui, became president and party leader.

Under President Lee, Taiwan made big strides toward democratization. Laws used to imprison dissidents were revoked, the media were freed of all censorship, and open multiparty elections were held for all local and island-wide positions. In the 1996 presidential elections, Lee won 54 percent of the vote in a hotly contested four-way race. Lee's relatively small margin of victory reflected the new openness of the political system, but his victory reflected the credit that voters gave the Nationalist Party for the island's progress.

In 2000, an opposition party candidate, Chen Shui-bian of the Democratic Progressive Party (DPP), won the presidency. Chen's victory was due in part to a combination of the desire for change, especially in light of a serious downturn in the island's economic growth, and a split within the Nationalist Party. It was also evidence of the further maturing of Taiwan's democracy.

The most contentious political issue in Taiwan is whether the island should continue to work, however slowly, toward reunification with the mainland. This was the Nationalists' policy under Lee Teng-hui. Or should it declare formal independence from China? A big factor in Chen's election was the growing appeal of the DPP's position that Taiwan should seriously consider independence.

Chen was reelected in 2004, but his popularity declined sharply during his second term due largely to corruption in his administration and the feeling that the DPP had gone too far in antagonizing the PRC on the question of Taiwan–mainland relations. The Nationalist Party won both control of the legislature and the presidency in the 2008 elections. Most people now seem to support closer relations with the PRC. But they also prefer the status quo in which Taiwan is, for all intents and purposes (including its own strong military), a separate political entity from China, but does not seek international recognition as an independent country.

(continued)

Global Connection

The Republic of China on Taiwan (*continued*)

The U.S. is committed to a "peaceful solution" of the Taiwan issue. It continues to sell military technology to Taiwan so it can defend itself. China regards Taiwan as a part of China, and Beijing has refused to renounce the use of force if the island moves toward formal separation. The PRC government often criticizes American policy toward Taiwan as interference in China's internal affairs, even though the United States, like most other nations, only has informal diplomatic relations with Taiwan.

Taiwan and China have developed extensive economic relations with trade at more than $100 billion per year. Millions of people from Taiwan have gone to the mainland to do business, visit relatives, or just sightsee. The governments of the PRC and Taiwan have engaged in direct negotiations about further reconciliation and possible reunification—but both acknowledge that any real possibility of that is a long way off.

	Taiwan
Land area	13,895 sq mi/35,980 sq km (slightly smaller than Maryland and Delaware combined)
Population	22.9 million
Ethnic composition	Taiwanese 84 percent, mainland Chinese 14 percent, aborigine 2 percent
Annual GDP at purchasing power parity	US$698.8 billion—which would give it a rank of 21 in the world, behind Iran and ahead of the Netherlands
Annual GDP per capita at purchasing power parity	US$30,100—about the same as Greece or Italy
Annual GDP growth rate (2007)	5.7 percent

real measure of intellectual freedom. It reinforced . . . that the exercise of state power was a monopoly of the Communist Party."[3]

Mao's discontent with the direction in which he perceived the PRC to be heading continued to build, even after his critics had been silenced. In response, he launched the **Great Leap Forward** (1958–1960), a utopian effort to accelerate the country's economic development by relying on the labor power and revolutionary enthusiasm of the masses while also propelling China into the era of true **communism**, in which there would be almost complete economic and social equality.

The Great Leap Forward turned into "one of the most extreme, bizarre, and eventually catastrophic episodes in twentieth-century political history."[4] In the rural areas, irrational policies, wasted resources, poor management, and the suppression of any criticism

and dissent combined with bad weather to produce a famine that claimed at least 30 million lives. An industrial depression soon followed the collapse of agriculture. China suffered a terrible setback in economic development.

In the early 1960s, Mao took a less active role in day-to-day decision-making. Two of China's other top leaders and long-time comrades of Chairman Mao, Liu Shaoqi and Deng Xiaoping, took charge of efforts to revive the economy. They completely abandoned the radical strategy of the Great Leap and used a combination of careful government planning and market-oriented policies to stimulate production, particularly in agriculture.

This approach did revive the Chinese economy. Once again, however, Mao became profoundly unhappy with the political and social consequences of China's development. By the mid-1960s, the Chairman had concluded that the policies of Liu and Deng had led to a resurgence of elitism and inequality in the country. He worried that his revolutionary goals were being undermined and that rather than moving toward socialism and communism, China was, in fact, headed down the road to capitalism.

Mao's disquiet about trends in China was compounded by a sharp deterioration in Sino-Soviet relations. Moscow had provided the PRC with substantial aid and advice for most of the 1950s. But differences between the two communist powers over, among other matters, how to handle relations with the United States (the Soviets advocated peaceful coexistence, whereas the Chinese wanted to keep up the global struggle against American imperialism) mounted, particularly after Nikita Khrushchev replaced Stalin as head of the Soviet Communist Party. By the early 1960s, Mao had reached the conclusion that the Soviet Union was no longer a revolutionary country and had, in fact, experienced a "restoration of capitalism" under Khrushchev.

The result of Mao's uneasiness was the **Great Proletarian Cultural Revolution** (1966–1976), an ideological crusade designed to jolt China back toward Mao's vision of socialism and communism and prevent the PRC from falling prey to the kind of ideological degeneration that had infected the Soviet Union. Like the Great Leap Forward, the Cultural Revolution was a campaign of mass mobilization and utopian idealism. Its methods, though, were much more violent, and its main objective was not accelerated economic development, but the political purification of the party and the nation through struggle against alleged class enemies who had wormed their way into every organization, even the Chinese Communist Party.

Using his unmatched political clout and charisma, Mao put together a potent coalition of radical party leaders, loyal military officers, and student rebels, called Red Guards, to support him and attack anyone thought to be guilty of betraying his version of communist ideology, known as Mao Zedong Thought.

In the Cultural Revolution's first phase (1966–1969), 20 million or so Red Guards went on a rampage across the country. They harassed, tortured, and killed people accused of being class enemies, particularly intellectuals and discredited party leaders, and destroyed many invaluable cultural artifacts that were seen as remnants from the imperial past. Among the top leaders targeted by the Red Guards were Liu Shaoqi and Deng Xiaoping. Liu was subjected to vicious public denunciation and left to die in prison; Deng, though criticized and purged, was "only" sent to live and work on a farm in southern China.

During the next phase of the Cultural Revolution (1969–1971), Mao called on the People's Liberation Army (PLA) to restore political order. Many Red Guards were sent to live and work in the countryside. The final phase of the movement (1972–1976) involved intense factional conflict over who would succeed the old and frail Mao as the leader of the Chinese Communist Party. At stake was not just political power, but also whether China would continue the radical policies of the Cultural Revolution or turn in a more moderate direction.

Mao died in September 1976 at age eighty-two. A month later, a group of relatively moderate leaders, who had survived the Cultural Revolution, but thought it had gone on long enough, staged a **coup d'etat** and arrested their radical rivals, the so-called Gang of Four, led by Mao's wife, Jiang Qing. The arrest of the Gang (who were sentenced to long prison terms) marked the end of the Cultural Revolution, which had claimed at least a million lives and brought the nation to the brink of civil war.

Deng Xiaoping and the Transformation of Chinese Communism (1977–1997)

To repair the damage caused by the Cultural Revolution, China's new leaders restored to power many veteran officials who had been purged by Mao and the radicals. These included Deng Xiaoping. By 1978, Deng, through very skillful political maneuvering, had clearly become the country's most powerful leader, although he never took for himself the formal positions of head of the party or government. Instead he appointed younger, loyal men to those positions.

Deng lost little time in using his power to put China on a path of reform that dramatically transformed the nation. His policies were a profound break with the Maoist past. State control of the economy was significantly reduced. Market forces were allowed to play an increasingly important role. Private enterprise was encouraged. The government allowed unprecedented levels of foreign investment. Chinese artists and writers saw the shackles of party control that had bound them for decades greatly loosened. Deng took major steps to revitalize China's government by bringing in younger, better-educated officials. After decades of stagnation, the Chinese economy experienced spectacular growth throughout the 1980s (see Section 2).

Deng Xiaoping gathered global praise for his leadership of the world's most populous nation. He was twice named *Time* magazine's Man of the Year, first for 1978, then again for 1985. But, in spring of 1989, he and the CCP were faced with a serious challenge when discontent over inflation and corruption, as well as a desire—especially among students and intellectuals—for more political freedom inspired large-scale demonstrations in Beijing and several other Chinese cities. At one point, more than a million people from all walks of life gathered in and around Tiananmen Square in the center of Beijing to voice their concerns. A very large contingent of students set up a camp in the Square, which they occupied for about two months. For quite awhile, the CCP leadership, constrained by internal divisions about how to handle the protests and intensive international media coverage, did little other than engage in some threatening rhetoric to dissuade the demonstrators. But China's leaders ran out of patience, and the army was ordered to use force to clear the square during the very early morning hours of June 4. By the time dawn broke in Beijing, Tiananmen Square had indeed been cleared, but with a death toll that still has not been revealed. Indeed, the Chinese government still insists that it did the right thing in the interests of national stability.

Following the Tiananmen crisis, China went through a few years of intense political repression and a slowdown in the pace of economic change. Then, in early 1992, Deng Xiaoping took some bold steps to accelerate reform of the economy. He did so in large part hoping that economic progress would help the PRC avoid a collapse of China's communist

system such as had occurred just the year before in the Soviet Union.

From Revolutionaries to Technocrats (1997 to the Present)

Another important consequence of the 1989 Tiananmen crisis was the replacement as formal head of the CCP of one Deng protégé, Zhao Ziyang, by another, Jiang Zemin. Zhao had been ousted by Deng because he was considered too sympathetic to the student demonstrators, and Jiang was promoted from his previous posts as mayor and CCP chief of Shanghai because of his firm but relatively bloodless handling of similar protests in that city. Although Deng remained the power behind the throne for several years, he gradually turned over greater authority to Jiang, who, in addition to his positions as head (general secretary) of the CCP and chair of the powerful Central Military Commission, became president of the PRC in 1993. When Deng Xiaoping died in February 1997, Jiang was secure in his position as China's top leader.

Under Jiang's leadership, China continued its economic reforms and remarkable economic growth. The PRC became an even more integral part of the global economy and enhanced its regional and international stature as a rising power. Overall, China was politically stable during the Jiang era. But the country also faced serious problems, including mounting unemployment, pervasive corruption, and widening gaps between the rich and the poor. And the CCP still repressed any individual or group it perceived as challenging its authority.

Upon Jiang's retirement, Hu Jintao, China's vice president, became CCP general secretary in November 2002 and PRC president in March 2003. Hu was sixty years old when he took over the highest party and government offices, which was considerably younger than most of China's recent leaders. Both Jiang and Hu represented a new kind of leader for the PRC. Mao Zedong and Deng Xiaoping were career revolutionaries who had participated in the CCP's long struggle for power and were among the founders of the communist regime when it was established in 1949. In contrast, Jiang and Hu were **technocrats**, officials with academic training (in their cases, as engineers) who had worked their way up the party ladder of power by a combination of professional competence and political loyalty.

The transfer of power from Jiang to Hu was remarkably predictable and orderly. Jiang had retired after two terms in office, as required by both party rules and the state constitution, and Hu had, for several years, been expected to succeed Jiang. This leadership change was the first relatively tranquil top-level political succession in China in more than 200 years.

Hu Jintao was reelected to second five-year terms as both CCP general secretary (in October 2007) and PRC president (in March 2008). He has tried to project himself as a populist leader by placing greater emphasis on dealing with the country's most serious socioeconomic problems, such as the enormous inequalities between regions and the terribly inadequate public health system. But Hu has taken a hard line on political dissent. There is little reason to expect that Chinese politics at the top will change much under Hu Jintao. Nor is he likely to deviate significantly from the combination of economic reform and political repression that has been the CCP's formula for maintaining power since the days of Deng Xiaoping.

Themes and Implications

Historical Junctures and Political Themes

The World of States.   At the time the People's Republic was established in 1949, China occupied a weak position in the international system. For more than a century, its destiny had been shaped by incursions and influences from abroad that it could do little to control. Mao made many tragic and terrible blunders during his years in power. But one of his great achievements was to build a strong state able to affirm and defend its sovereignty. China's international stature has increased as its economic and military strength have grown. Although still a relatively poor country by many per capita measures, the sheer size of its economy makes the PRC an economic powerhouse. Its import and export policies have an important impact on many other countries and on the global economy. China is a nuclear power with the world's largest conventional military force. It is an active and influential member of nearly all international organizations, including the United Nations, where it sits as one of the five permanent members of the Security Council. China has become a major player in the world of states.

Governing the Economy.   Throughout its history the PRC has experimented with a series of very different economic systems: a Soviet-style planning system in the early 1950s, the radical egalitarianism of the Maoist model, and market-oriented policies implemented by Deng Xiaoping and his successors. Ideological disputes over these development strategies were the main cause of ferocious political struggles within the CCP. Deng began his bold reforms in the hope that improved living standards would restore the legitimacy of the CCP, which had been badly tarnished by the economic failings and political chaos of the Maoist era. The remarkable successes of China's leaders in governing the economy have helped to sustain the CCP at a time when most of the world's other communist regimes have disappeared.

The Democratic Idea.   Any hope that the democratic idea might take root in the early years of communist rule in China quickly vanished by the mid-1950s with the building of a one-party communist state and Mao's unrelenting campaigns against alleged enemies of his revolution. The

Deng Xiaoping era brought much greater economic, social, and cultural freedom. But time and again the CCP has strangled the stirrings of the democratic idea, most brutally in Tiananmen Square in 1989. Jiang Zemin and Hu Jintao have been faithful disciples of Deng. They have vigorously championed economic reform in China. They have also made sure that the CCP retains its firm grip on power.

The Politics of Collective Identity.   Because of its long history and ancient culture, China has a very strong sense of collective national identity. Memories of past humiliations and suffering at the hands of foreigners still influence the international relations of the PRC. And as faith in communist ideology has weakened as the country embraces capitalist economic policies, CCP leaders have increasingly turned to

In an act of outrage and protest, an unarmed civilian stood in front of a column of tanks leaving Tiananmen Square the day after the Chinese army had crushed the prodemocracy demonstration in June 1989. This "unknown hero" disappeared into the watching crowd. Neither his identity nor his fate are known.   *Source:* Jeff Widener/AP Images.

nationalism as a means to rally the Chinese people behind their government. China's cultural and ethnic homogeneity has also spared it the kind of widespread communal violence that has plagued so many other countries in the modern world. The exception has been in the border regions of the country where there is a large concentration of minority peoples, including Tibet and the Muslim areas of China's northwest (see Section 4).

Implications for Comparative Politics

First, the People's Republic of China can be compared with other communist party-states with which it shares or has shared many political and ideological features. From this perspective, China raises intriguing questions: Why has China's communist party-state so far proved more durable than that of the Soviet Union and nearly all other similar regimes? By what combination of reform and repression has the CCP held on to power? What signs are there that it is likely to continue to be able to do so for the foreseeable future? What signs suggest that communist rule in China may be weakening? What kind of political system might replace China's communist party-state if the CCP were to lose or relinquish power?

China can also be compared with other developing nations that face similar economic and political challenges. Although the PRC is part of the Third World as measured by the average standard of living of its population, its record of growth in the past several decades has far exceeded almost all other developing countries. Furthermore, the educational and health levels of the Chinese people are quite good when compared with many other countries at a similar level of development, for example, India and Nigeria. How has China achieved such relative success in its quest for economic and social development? By contrast, much of the Third World has become more democratic in recent decades. How and why has China resisted this wave of democracy? What does the experience of other developing countries say about how economic modernization might influence the prospects for democracy in China?

Napoleon Bonaparte, emperor of France in the early nineteenth century, is said to have remarked, "Let China sleep. For when China wakes, it will shake the world."[5] It has taken awhile, but China certainly has awakened. Given the country's geographic size, vast resources, huge population, surging economy, and formidable military might, the PRC is certain to be among the world's great powers in the near future. Will it shake the world?

SECTION 2   Political Economy and Development

The growth of China's economy since the late 1970s has been called "one of the century's greatest economic miracles," which has led to "one of the biggest improvements in human welfare anywhere at any time."[6] Such superlatives seem justified in describing overall economic growth rates that have averaged close to 10 percent per year for nearly three decades, while most of the world's other major economies have been growing much more slowly. Measured in terms of **purchasing power parity (PPP)** (which adjusts for price differences between countries), China now has the second largest economy in the world after the

United States, and per capita incomes in the cities have increased fortyfold since 1978, while in the rural areas (where the majority of people still live), they are up by more than thirty-five times. Although there are still many very poor people in China, more than 400 million have been lifted from absolute poverty to a level where they have a minimally adequate supply of food, clothing, and shelter. China's economic miracle has involved much more than growth in GDP and personal income. There has also been a profound transformation of the basic nature of economic life in the PRC from what it had been during the Maoist era.

State and Economy

The Maoist Economy

When the Chinese Communist Party came to power in 1949, China's economy was suffering from more than a hundred years of rebellion, invasion, civil war, and bad government. The first urgent task of China's new communist rulers was the stabilization and revival of the economy. Although a lot of property was seized from wealthy landowners, rich industrialists, and foreign companies, much private ownership and many aspects of capitalism were allowed to continue in order to gain support for the government and get the economy going again.

Once production had been restored, the party turned its attention to economic development by following the Soviet model of **state socialism**. The essence of this model was a **command economy**, in which the state owns or controls most economic resources, and economic activity is driven by government planning and commands rather than by market forces. The command economy in China was at its height during the so-called First Five-Year Plan of 1953–1957, when the government took control of the production and distribution of nearly all goods and services and, for all intents and purposes, the market economy ceased to exist.

The Plan yielded impressive economic results. But it also created huge bureaucracies and new inequalities, especially between the heavily favored industrial cities and the investment-starved rural areas. Both the Great Leap Forward (1958–1961) and the Cultural Revolution (1966–1976) embodied the unique and radical Maoist approach to economic development that was intended to be less bureaucratic and more egalitarian than the Soviet model.

For example, in the Great Leap, more than a million backyard blast furnaces were set up throughout the country to prove that steel could be produced by peasants in every village, not just in a few gigantic modern factories in the cities. In the Cultural Revolution, revolutionary committees, controlled by workers and communist activists, replaced the Soviet-style system of letting managers run industrial enterprises. Both of these Maoist experiments were less than successful. The backyard furnaces yielded great quantities of useless steel and squandered precious resources, while the revolutionary committees led many factories to pay more attention to politics than production.

The economic legacy of Maoism was mixed. Under Mao, the PRC "did accomplish, in however flawed a fashion, the initial phase of industrialization of the Chinese economy, creating a substantial industrial and technological base that simply had not existed before."[7] In addition, by the end of the Maoist era, the people of China were much healthier and more literate than they had been in the early 1950s.

But for all of its radical rhetoric, the Maoist strategy of development never broke decisively with the basic precepts of the command system. Political interference, poor management, and ill-conceived projects led to wasted resources of truly staggering proportions. Overall, China's economic growth rates, especially in agriculture, barely kept pace with population increases, and the average standard of living changed little between the 1950s and Mao's death in 1976.

China Goes to Market

After Deng Xiaoping consolidated power in 1978, he took China in an economic direction far different from Mao's or that of any other communist party-state. Politics and ideology took a back seat to economic goals, capitalist-style free-market policies were introduced, and the scope of the command economy was cut back in order to stimulate production. Deng's pragmatic views on how to promote development were captured in his famous 1962 statement, "It doesn't matter whether a cat is white or black, as long as it catches mice."[8] Deng meant that the CCP should not be overly concerned about whether a particular policy was socialist or capitalist if it in fact helped the economy. Deng made these remarks when he was in charge of helping China recover from the terrible famine of the Great Leap Forward. But it was just such sentiment that also got him in political trouble with Mao and made Deng one of the principal victims of the Cultural Revolution.

Deng's reforms redefined the role of the Communist Party in governing the economy and the meaning of socialism in China. Authority for making economic decisions passed from government bureaucrats to families, factory managers, and even the owners of private businesses. Individuals were encouraged to work harder and more efficiently to make money for themselves rather than to "serve the people" as had been the slogan during the Maoist era.

In most sectors of the economy the state no longer dictates what to produce and how to produce it. At the start of the reform period in 1978, all prices were set by the government. Now more than 80 percent are determined according to market forces such as supply and demand. Many government monopolies have given way to fierce competition between state-owned and non-state-owned firms. In the late 1980s, there were still more than 200,000 state-owned enterprises (SOEs) in China controlled by various levels of government, many of which were considered to be economic dinosaurs. Now there is about a half that number, and only 150 or so very large ones that are operated by the central government. In 1978, SOEs generated about 80 percent of China's gross domestic product; by 2008, the number had dropped to about 30 percent. Tens of millions of workers were laid off, but the remaining SOEs still employ more than 60 million workers. They also dominate critical parts of the economy such as steel, petroleum, banking, and telecommunications.

However, even SOEs must now respond to market forces. If they cannot turn a profit, they have to restructure or perhaps go into bankruptcy. Some have been semi-privatized and become open to foreign investment and even become "dynamic dynamos"[9] in China's modernizing economy. But many are vastly overstaffed, with outdated facilities and machinery that make them unattractive to potential investors. The state-owned sector remains an enormous drag on the country's government-owned banks, which are still required to bail out many failing SOEs. These large loans are rarely, if ever, paid back. Many economists think that even more drastic SOE reform is needed. The country's leaders understandably fear the political and social consequences that would result from an even more massive layoff of industrial workers.

Although it is somewhat ironic, the Chinese Communist Party now strongly encourages and supports private businesses. The private sector is the fastest-growing part of China's economy. There are tens of millions private businesses in China, ranging from individual street vendors to giant multinational corporations. The private sector currently accounts for more than two-thirds of the PRC's total GDP and employs more than 100 million workers. In 2004, the Chinese constitution was amended to guarantee private-property rights, and in October 2007, a detailed property law went into effect that was especially important in reassuring both domestic and foreign investors that their assets were safe from seizure by the government and that their rights were enforceable in the courts.

The economic results of China's move from a command toward a market economy have been phenomenal (see Figure 13.2). The PRC has been the fastest-growing major economy in the world for nearly three decades. China's GDP per capita (that is, the total output of the economy divided by the total population) grew at an average rate of nearly 9 percent per year from 1978 to 2007. The per capita GDP of the United States and Japan grew at about 2 percent per year during the same period, and India's at a little less than 4 percent.

There has also been a consumer revolution in China. In the late 1970s, people in the cities could only shop for most consumer goods at state-run stores. These carried a very limited range of products, many of which were of shoddy quality. Today most of China's urban areas are becoming shopping paradises. They have domestic and foreign stores of every kind, huge, ultra-modern malls, fast food outlets, and a great variety of entertainment options. A few decades ago, hardly anyone owned a television. Now nearly every urban household and 75 percent of rural households have a color TV. Cell phones are everywhere. In the cities, the new middle class—the 10 percent of the population that are able to live comfortably and even with some degree of luxury—is starting to buy houses, condominiums, and cars, travel abroad, and play golf. China is even developing a class of "super-rich" millionaires and billionaires.

The PRC says that it currently has a **socialist market economy**. Although this terminology may seem to be mere ideological window dressing to allow the introduction of capitalism into a country still ruled by a communist party, the phrase conveys the fact that China's economy now combines elements of both socialism and capitalism. In theory, the market

FIGURE 13.2

The Economic Transformation of China

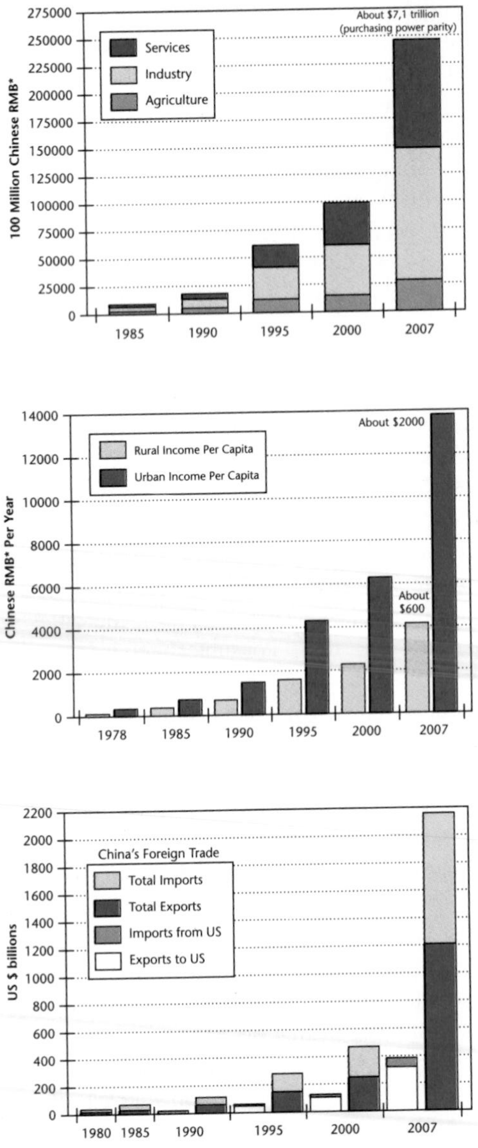

*RMB = Renminbi (people's currency)

These charts show how dramatically the Chinese economy has been transformed since market reforms were introduced by Deng Xiaoping in the late 1970s.

Sources: China Statistical Yearbooks, United States-China Business Council. Chinability.com.

remains subordinate to government planning and CCP leadership, which is supposed to prevent too much capitalist-like exploitation and inequality.

China is, by no means, a fully free-market capitalist economy. Although government commands and central planning have been greatly refined and reduced in scope, they have not disappeared altogether. National and local bureaucrats continue to exercise a great deal of control over the production and distribution of goods, resources, and services, and the state still controls critical nodes in the economy. Market reforms have gained substantial momentum that would be nearly impossible to reverse. But the CCP leadership still wields the power to make the policies that decide the direction of China's economy.

Remaking the Chinese Countryside

One of the first revolutionary programs launched by the Chinese Communist Party when it came to power in 1949 was land reform that confiscated the property of landlords and redistributed it as private holdings to the poorer peasants. But in the mid- to late1950s, peasants were reorganized by the state into collective farms and communes in which the village, not individuals, owned the land and government officials directed all production and labor. Individuals were paid according to how much they worked on the collective land. Most crops and other farm products had to be sold to the state at low fixed prices. The system of collectivized agriculture was one of the weakest links in China's command economy. Per capita agricultural production and rural living standards were stagnant from 1957 to 1977.

Deng Xiaoping made the revival of the rural economy one of his top priorities. He abolished collective farming and established a **household responsibility system**, which remains in effect today. Farmland is now contracted out for thirty years or more by the villages (which still technically own the land) to individual families, who take full charge of the production and marketing of crops. The freeing of the rural economy from the constraints of the communal system has led to a sharp increase in agricultural productivity and income for most farm families.

In response to these reforms, agricultural production grew at an average annual rate of a little more than 6 percent during the 1980s to a high of 12.9 percent in 1984. The biggest factor in generating the growth of agriculture was the change from the collective to the household responsibility system and the impact this had on labor incentives and productivity. At a certain point, the boom effect of this organizational change wore off, and agriculture grew at an average annual rate of only 3.6 percent from 1991 to 2003. In recent years it has crept up to 5 to 6 percent in response to government efforts to stimulate the rural economy through increased investment, and improvement of rural living standards is one of the current leadership's highest priorities.

In late 2008, the CCP leadership proposed a new land reform law, which, it hoped, would stimulate agricultural production, raise rural incomes, and stem the tide of corruption in the countryside. The transfer, subletting, or sale of land use contracts would both be made easier and better regulated. Entrepreneurial farmers would be able to acquire the contracts for adjacent plots of land. This would facilitate economies of scale by overcoming the pattern of small-scale, inefficient "noodle strip" farming that has characterized the system in which each village household is given a relatively equal share of the land. Those rural people who chose to get out of farming would be assured a fair price for their contracts. The stated goal of this reform is to double rural incomes by the year 2020. There has been no move to privatize land ownership, which most CCP leaders still regard as ideologically unacceptable.

But nothing has contributed more to the remaking of the Chinese countryside than the spread of a rural industrial and commercial revolution that, in speed and scope, was unprecedented in the history of the modern world. The foundations of rural industrialization were laid during the Maoist period when communes were expected to run factories to meet their own needs for products like agricultural tools and building supplies. When agriculture was decollectivized in the early 1980s, so-called **township and village enterprises (TVEs)** sprang up everywhere in the countryside. These rural factories and businesses varied greatly in size, from a handful of employees to thousands. They were initially owned and run by local governments but operated outside the state plan (often in competition with state-owned enterprises), made their own decisions about all aspects of the business process, and were responsible for their profits and losses.

For much of the 1980s and 1990s, TVEs were the fastest-growing sector of the Chinese economy. They came to dominate the production of light industrial and consumer goods, including textiles, toys, and furniture. Because of their very low labor costs, TVEs attracted considerable foreign investment and became a vital part of China's emergence as export giant.

But the economic Darwinism of the market caught up with the rapid expansion of TVEs by the turn of the century, and many were forced out of business. Many of those that survived have been privatized. Their rate of growth has slowed considerably, but they still contribute about a third of China's total GDP. They also employ more than 190 million people and have played a critical role in absorbing the vast pool of rural surplus labor.

Society and Economy

Market reform and globalization of the economy have made Chinese society much more diverse and open. People are vastly freer to choose jobs, travel about the country and internationally, practice their religious beliefs, buy private homes, join nonpolitical associations, and engage in a wide range of other activities that were prohibited or severely restricted during the Maoist era. But economic change has also caused serious social problems. Crime, prostitution, and drug use have sharply increased. Although such problems are still far less prevalent in China than in many other countries, they are severe enough to worry national and local authorities.

Economic reform has also brought significant changes in China's basic system of social welfare. The Maoist economy was characterized by what was called the **iron rice bowl**. As in other state socialist economies such as the Soviet Union, the government guaranteed employment, a certain standard of living (although a low one), and basic cradle-to-grave benefits to most of the urban and rural labor force. In the cities, the workplace was more than just a place

A view of Shanghai's ultramodern skyline. The city is China's financial and commercial center and one of the world's busiest ports. *Source:* © Xiaoyang Liu/Corbis.

to work and earn a salary. It also provided housing, health care, day care, and other services.

China's economic reformers believed that such guarantees led to poor work motivation and excessive costs for the government and businesses. They implemented policies designed to break the iron rice bowl. Income and employment are no longer guaranteed. They are now directly tied to individual effort. Workers in the remaining state-owned enterprises still have rather generous health and pension plans, but employees in the rapidly expanding private sector usually have few benefits. The social services safety net provided for China's rural dwellers by the communes has all but disappeared with the return to household-based farming and the market economy. Many rural clinics and schools closed once government financial support was eliminated. The availability of health care, educational opportunities, disability pay, and retirement funds now depends on the relative wealth of families and villages.

China's public health system—once touted as a model for the Third World because of its success in delivering at least essential primary care to almost the entire population—is in shambles. Less than a quarter of the urban population, and only 10 percent of those who live in the rural areas, have health insurance. The World Health Organization ranks China among the worst countries in terms of the allocation of medical resources.

The breaking of the iron rice bowl has motivated people to work harder in order to earn more money. But it has also led to a sharp increase in urban unemployment. An estimated 45 to 60 million workers have been laid off in recent years. Many are too old or too unskilled to find good jobs in the modernized and marketized economy, and China has very little in the way of unemployment insurance or social security for its displaced workers. The official unemployment rate is about 4 percent of the urban labor force, but it is generally believed to be at least twice that and as high as 40 or 50 percent in some parts of the country.

Work slowdowns, strikes, and large-scale demonstrations are becoming more frequent, particularly in China's northeastern rust belt, where state-owned heavy industries like steel were the largest employer. If unemployment continues to surge, labor unrest could be a political time bomb for China's communist party-state.

Market reforms have also opened China's cities to a flood of rural migrants. After the agricultural communes were disbanded in the early 1980s, many of the peasants who were not needed in the fields found work in the rapidly expanding township and village enterprises. But many others, no longer constrained by the strict limits on internal population movement enforced in the Mao era, headed to the urban areas to look for jobs. The 150–200 million people who make up this so-called "floating population" are mostly employed in low-paying temporary jobs such as unskilled construction work.

These migrants are filling an important niche in China's changing labor market, but they are also putting increased pressure on urban housing and social services. In Shanghai, China's largest city, nearly half the population of 18.5 million is made up of migrant workers. Their presence in Chinese cities could become politically destabilizing if they find their economic aspirations thwarted by a stalled economy or if they are treated too roughly or unfairly by local governments, which often see them as intruders. With another 150 million un- or underemployed rural dwellers, the floating population is expected to keep growing for years to come.

China's economic boom has also created enormous opportunities for corruption. In a country in transition from a command to a market economy, officials still control numerous resources and retain power over many economic transactions from which large profits can be made. Bribes are common in this heavily bureaucratized and highly personalized system. Because the rule of law is often weaker than personal connections (called *guanxi* in Chinese), nepotism and cronyism are rampant. Recognizing the threat that corruption poses to its legitimacy, the government has repeatedly launched well-publicized campaigns against official graft, with severe punishment for some serious offenders. Targets have included some very high-ranking officials. In May 2007, the one-time head of the State Food and Drug Administration was found guilty of taking $850,000 in bribes; he was sentenced to death by the court and executed two months later. But, all in all, these campaigns have had little effect in curbing such nefarious practices. A report in October 2007 by the Carnegie Endowment for International Peace in Washington, D.C., concluded that corruption cost China about $86 billion per year (3 percent of GDP) and that the "odds of an average corrupt official going to jail in China was less than 3 in 100—making corruption a high-return, low-risk opportunity."[10]

The benefits of economic growth have reached most of China. But the market reforms and economic boom that created sharp class differences and inequalities between people and parts of the country have risen significantly. A very large gap separates the average incomes of urban residents and those in the countryside (see Figure 13.2). Farmers in China's poorer areas have faced years of stagnating or even declining incomes. The gap is also widening between the prosperous coastal regions and the inland areas of the country.

Such inequalities present a contradiction for a party that still claims to believe in communist ideals. The current administration of Hu Jintao has begun to promote the development of what it calls a "harmonious socialist society." This emphasizes not only achieving a higher average standard of living for everyone, but a more equitable distribution of income and basic social welfare, including health and education. In particular, there is more attention being paid to the rural economy, and new poverty alleviation programs and increased investment have brought some progress to the less developed western regions. At the start of 2007, the government abolished all taxes on agriculture.

Gender inequalities have also increased in some ways since the introduction of the market reforms. There is no doubt that the overall situation of women in China has improved enormously since 1949 in terms of social status, legal rights, employment, and education. Women have also benefited from rising

living standards and expanded economic opportunities that the reforms have brought. But the trend toward marketization has not benefited men and women equally. In the countryside, it is almost always the case that only male heads of households sign contracts for land and other production resources, and therefore men dominate rural economic life. This is true despite the fact that farm labor has become increasingly feminized as many men move to jobs in rural industry or migrate to the cities. Only 1 percent of the leaders in China's 700,000 villages are women. More than 70 percent (about 120 million) of illiterate

Current Challenges

China's One-Child Policy

By the 1970s, China's population exceeded 800 million. Greatly improved health conditions had allowed it to grow at about 2.8 percent per year, which is a very high rate of population increase. The Chinese population was on pace to double in just twenty-five years, and cutting the birthrate came to be seen as a major requirement for economic development. Beginning in the 1980s, the Chinese government has enforced a strict population control policy that has, over time, used various means to encourage or even force couples to have only a single child. This is called the "One-Child Policy."

Intensive media campaigns laud the patriotic virtues and economic benefits of small families. Positive incentives such as more farmland or preferred housing have been offered to couples with only one child. Fines or demotions have punished violators. In some places, workplace medics or local doctors monitor contraceptive use and women's fertility cycles, and a couple must have official permission to have a child. Defiance has sometimes led to forced abortion or sterilization.

The combination of the one-child campaign, the modernizing economy, and a comparatively strong record in improving educational and employment opportunities for women have brought China's population growth rate to about 0.6 percent per year. This is even lower than the population growth rate of the United States, which is 0.9 percent per year. China's rate of population increase is *very* low for a country at its level of economic development. India, for example, has also had some success in promoting family planning. But its annual population growth rate is 1.4 percent. Nigeria's is 2.4 percent. These may not seem like big differences, but consider

this: at these respective growth rates, it will take 116 years for China's population to double, whereas India's population will double in fifty years and Nigeria's in just twenty-nine years!

However, the compulsory, intrusive nature of China's family planning program and the extensive use of abortion as one of the major means of birth control have led to a lot of international criticism. Many farmers have also evaded the one-child policy because their family income now depends on having more people to work. Furthermore, the still widespread belief that male children will make greater economic contributions to the family and that a male heir is necessary to carry on the family line causes some rural families to take drastic steps to make sure that they have a son. Female infanticide and the abandonment of female babies have increased dramatically. Ultrasound technology has led to large number of sex-selective abortions of female fetuses. As a result, China has an unusual gender balance among its young population. One estimate suggests that there are 70 million more males in China than females.

Partly in response to rural resistance and international pressure, the Chinese government has relaxed its population policies. Forced abortion and infanticide are now infrequent. Rural couples are often allowed to have two children. The government is also offering special pensions to those who have only one son or two daughters so they will be less dependent on their children for support in their old age. In the cities, where there has been more voluntary compliance with the policy because of higher incomes and limited living space, the one-child policy is still basically in effect.

adults in China are female. Although China has one of the world's highest rates of female urban labor participation, the market reforms have "strengthened and in some cases reconstructed the sexual division of labor, keeping urban women in a transient, lower-paid, and subordinate position in the workforce."[11] Women workers are the first to be laid off or are forced to retire early when a collective or state-owned enterprise downsizes. Economic and cultural pressures have also led to an alarming suicide rate (the world's highest) among rural women. China's unique and stringent population policy has had a particularly significant impact on women, and certainly one that has not always been to their benefit. (See "Current Challenges: China's One-Child Policy.")

Finally, the momentous economic changes in China have had severe environmental consequences. Industrial expansion has been fueled primarily by highly polluting coal. This has made the air in China's cities and even many rural areas among the dirtiest in the world. Soil erosion, the loss of arable land, and deforestation are serious problems. The dumping of garbage and toxic wastes goes virtually unregulated. It is estimated that 80 percent of China's rivers are badly polluted. One of the most serious problems is a critical water shortage in north China due to urbanization and industrialization. Private automobile use is just starting to take off. This will greatly add to the country's pollution concerns (and demand for more oil) in the very near future. **Sustainable development**, which balances economic growth and environmental concerns, is a key part of the party-state's current emphasis on building a "harmonious socialist society." However, as one journalist with long experience in China observed, "It still seems that every environmentally friendly measure is offset by a greater number of abuses" in the quest for rapid economic development.[12]

Dealing with some of the negative consequences of fast growth and market reforms is one of the main challenges facing China's government. The ability of citizen associations—including labor, women's, and environmental organizations—to place their concerns about these problems on the nation's political agenda remains limited by the party's tight control of political life and by restrictions on the formation of autonomous interest groups (see Section 4).

China in the Global Economy

China was not a major trading nation when Deng Xiaoping took power in 1978. Total foreign trade was around $20 billion (approximately 10 percent of GDP). Foreign investment in China was minuscule. The stagnant economy, political instability, and heavy-handed bureaucracy did not attract potential investors from abroad.

Opening China's economy to the outside world was one of the main goals of Deng's reform program. In the early 1980s, China embarked on a strategy of using trade as a central component of its drive for economic development. In some ways it followed the model of export-led growth pioneered by Japan and **newly industrializing countries (NICs)** such as the Republic of Korea (South Korea). This model takes advantage of low-wage domestic labor to produce goods that are in demand internationally. It then uses the earnings from the export of those goods to modernize the economy.

China is now the world's second largest trading nation behind the United States, and its imports and exports continue to grow at more than 20 percent per year. It is projected to surpass the U.S. in total trade volume sometime between 2015 and 2020. China's main exports are office machines, consumer electronics, data-processing and telecommunications equipment, clothing and footwear, toys, and sporting goods. In 2007–08, a large number of Chinese goods, including pet food, seafood, toys, and tires were recalled from the American market because of health and safety concerns. This reflected both the enormous growth of China as a key part of the "global factory" of the twenty-first century and the lack of effective regulation in many sectors of China's part-command, part-market economy.

China mostly imports industrial machinery, technology and scientific equipment, iron and steel, raw materials (including oil) needed to support economic development, and increasingly, agricultural products. Despite having large domestic sources of petroleum and significant untapped reserves, China is now a net importer of oil because of the massive energy demands of its economic boom. And in 2002, in order to meet the voracious appetite for steel generated by a construction boom and a surge in automobile production, China surpassed the United States as the world's largest importer of that commodity, even though it already produces more steel than the United States and Japan combined.

Much of China's trade is in East Asia, particularly with Japan, South Korea, Taiwan, and Hong Kong, which is now administratively part of the PRC, but is a highly developed, capitalist economy. The United States is also one of the PRC's major trading partners and is now the biggest market for Chinese exports. For quite a few years, the United States has had an enormous trade deficit (that is, imports exceed exports), which topped $250 billion in 2007.

This huge imbalance has become a source of tension in U.S.–China relations, particularly because quite a few Americans think that the PRC is engaging in trade practices (such as undervaluing its currency and restricting market access) that give its products an unfair advantage in global commerce. Some politicians, business leaders, and labor union officials, who also believe that Americans are losing jobs because U.S. companies are "outsourcing" production to China to take advantage of its very low labor costs, are calling for the government to impose restrictions on Chinese imports. But others point out how trade with the PRC benefits the U.S. economy—for example, by bringing inexpensive goods into stores that have saved American consumers hundreds of billions of dollars over the last decade or so. They also note that China uses some of its export earnings to buy U.S. government bonds. These bonds provide the U.S. government with revenue to finance America's large budget deficit, the result of spending on the war in Iraq and tax cuts enacted by the Bush administration. If China (and other nations) had not purchased these government bonds, the U.S. mortgage crisis would probably have hit earlier and been even worse.

Foreign investment in the PRC has also skyrocketed. China is now the one of the world's largest targets of foreign direct investment. Each year tens of billions of dollars are invested in tens of thousands of businesses and projects. More than 400 of the world's 500 top corporations have operations in the PRC. Foreign firms operating in China generally pay their workers considerably more than the average wage of about 60 cents per hour in Chinese-owned factories. But the low cost of labor in China is still a major attraction to investors from abroad, although labor costs in the PRC are increasing and face competition from other countries such as Vietnam and India. The real challenge to the Chinese export industry is whether it can make the transition to producing more sophisticated products, as did Japan and Korea when they were making their way up in the global economy.

Another lure to foreign investment is the gigantic Chinese domestic market. As incomes rise, corporations like Coca-Cola, General Motors, Starbucks, and Wal-Mart have poured vast amounts of money into China. American tobacco companies are hoping that China's 350 million smokers can make up for sharply declining cigarette sales in the United States. In 2005, Philip Morris signed an agreement with a Chinese company to jointly produce Marlboros to be sold in China, expecting that sales would amount to billions of cigarettes per year.

China is itself becoming a major foreign investor. In a sign of how far the PRC has come as a world economic power, a Chinese company, the Lenovo Group, bought IBM's personal computer business in late 2004 and is now aggressively marketing its machines in the United States and other countries.

The global economic meltdown that infected most of the world beginning in 2008 didn't spare China, although its economy has been growing so rapidly that the impact was less severe. Nevertheless, the rate of growth was expected to dip below 10 percent for the first time in decades and exports were down sharply as China's major trading partners—including the United States—cut back orders. Business closings—small firms, not financial giants—were causing a rise in unemployment. In November 2008, the government of the PRC announced a $600 billion economic stimulus package aimed mostly at new construction in areas such as low-income urban housing, transportation projects, educational facilities, and environmental improvement. Clearly, if China's economy slumps badly, the consequences would be felt throughout the world.

China now occupies an extremely important, but somewhat contradictory, position in the international economy. On the one hand, the PRC's relatively low level of economic and technological development makes it very much a part of the Third World. On the other hand, the total output and rapid growth of its economy, expanding trade, and vast resource base (including its population) make it a rising economic superpower among nations.

Governance and Policy-Making

Organization of the State

The People's Republic of China, Cuba, Vietnam, North Korea, and Laos are the only remaining communist party-states in the world. Like the Soviet Union before its collapse in 1991, the political systems of these countries are characterized by Communist Party domination of all government and social institutions, the existence of an official state ideology based on Marxism-Leninism, and, to varying and changing degrees, state control of key aspects of the economy.

The Chinese Communist Party claims that only it can govern in the best interests of the entire nation and therefore has the right to exercise the "leading role" throughout Chinese society. Although China has moved sharply toward a market economy in recent decades, the CCP still asserts that it is building socialism with the ultimate objective of creating an egalitarian and classless communist society.

The underlying principles of China's party-state appear in the country's constitution. The preamble of the constitution repeatedly states that the country is under "the leadership of the Communist Party of China." Article 1 defines the PRC as "a socialist state under the people's democratic dictatorship." It also declares that "disruption of the socialist system by any organization or individual is prohibited." Such provisions imply that the Chinese "people" (implicitly, supporters of socialism and the leadership of the party) enjoy democratic rights and privileges under party guidance. But the constitution also gives the CCP authority to exercise dictatorship over any person or organization that, it believes, opposes socialism and the party.

Marxism-Leninism, the foundation of communist ideology, remains an important part, at least officially, of the Chinese party-state. Marxism refers to the part of communist ideology based on the writing of Karl Marx (1818–1883) that presents a theory of human history emphasizing economic development and the struggle between rich property-owning and poor working classes that inevitably leads to revolution. Leninism refers to the theories developed by the Russian revolutionary, Vladimir Lenin (1870–1924),

who founded the Soviet Union. It focuses on how the workers should be organized and led by a communist party to seize political power.

The CCP says that Mao Zedong made a fundamental contribution to communist ideology. He adapted Marxism-Leninism, which evolved in Europe and Russia, to China's special circumstances. In particular, he emphasized the crucial role of peasants in the revolution that brought the Communist Party to power in China. Although the current CCP leadership acknowledges that Mao made serious mistakes such as the Great Leap Forward and the Cultural Revolution, the party continues to praise Mao and his ideology, which they call "Mao Zedong Thought." The constitution of the PRC is less a governing document that embodies enduring principles than a political statement. Constitutional change (from minor amendments to total replacement) during the last fifty years has reflected the shifting political winds in China. The character and content of the constitution in force at any given time bear the ideological stamp of the prevailing party leadership. The constitutions of the Mao era stressed the importance of class struggle and continuing the revolution, while the current one (adopted in 1982) emphasizes national unity in the pursuit of economic development and modernization.

Nevertheless, China's constitution does specify the structures and powers of the national and subnational levels of government in the PRC. China is not a federal system (like Brazil, Germany, India, Nigeria, and the United States) that gives subnational governments considerable policy-making autonomy. Provincial and local authorities in the PRC operate "under the unified leadership of the central authorities" (Article 3). This makes China a unitary state like France and Japan in which the national government exercises a high degree of control over other levels of government.

The Executive

The government of the People's Republic of China is organizationally and functionally distinct from the Chinese Communist Party. For example, the PRC executive consists of both a premier (prime minister) and a president, whereas the CCP is headed by a general secretary. But there is no alternation of parties in power in China, and the Communist Party exercises direct or indirect control over all government organizations and personnel. All high-ranking government officials with any substantive authority are also members of the important CCP leaders. Therefore, real executive power in the Chinese political system lies with the top leaders and organizations of the CCP.

The government of the PRC essentially acts as the administrative agency for carrying out and enforcing policies made by the party. Nevertheless, to fully understand governance and policy-making in China, it is necessary to look at the structure of both the Chinese Communist Party and the government of the People's Republic of China (the "state") and the relationship between the two.

The Party Executive

According to the CCP constitution (a wholly different document than the constitution of the PRC), the "highest leading bodies" of the party are the National Party Congress and the Central Committee (see Figure 13.3). But the National Party Congress meets for only one week every five years, and it has more than 2,100 delegates. This means that the role of the Congress is more symbolic than substantive. The essential function of the National Party Congress is to approve decisions already made by the top leaders and to provide a showcase for the party's current policies. There is little debate about policy and no contested voting of any consequence. The party congress does not function as a legislative check or balance on the power of the party's executive leadership.

The Central Committee (with 204 full and 167 alternate members) is the next level up in the pyramid of party power. It consists of CCP leaders from around the country who meet annually for about a week. Members are elected for a five-year term by the National Party Congress by secret ballot, with a limited choice of candidates. Contending party factions may jockey to win seats, but the overall composition of the Central Committee is closely controlled by the top leaders to ensure compliance with their policies.

In theory, the Central Committee directs party affairs when the National Party Congress is not in session. But its size and short, infrequent meetings (called plenums) also greatly limit its effectiveness. However, Central Committee plenums and occasional informal work conferences do represent significant gatherings of the party elite. They can be a very important arena of political maneuvering and decision-making.

The most powerful political organizations in China's communist party-state are the two small executive bodies at the very top of the CCP's structure: the Politburo (or Political Bureau) and its even more exclusive Standing Committee. These bodies are elected by the Central Committee from among its own members under carefully controlled and secretive conditions. The current Politburo has twenty-five members. Nine of them also belong to the Standing Committee, the formal apex of power in the CCP.

China's top leaders are, as a whole, very well educated. Eight of the nine members of the Standing Committee were trained as engineers before beginning political careers, while the other has a Ph.D. in economics. All but one of the remaining sixteen members of the Politburo have undergraduate or advanced degrees in subjects ranging from engineering (five) to history, political science, and law. This is dramatic evidence of the shift in China's ruling circles from the revolutionary leaders of Mao's and Deng's generations to technocrats who place highest priority on science, technology, and higher education as the keys to the country's development. No wonder China's government is sometimes called a "technocracy." Given how intellectuals were persecuted during the Maoist era, Time.com referred to the rise to power of engineers and other well-educated technocrats in China as "The Revenge of the Nerds"![13]

The Politburo and Standing Committee are not accountable to the Central Committee or any other institution in any meaningful sense. The operations of these organizations are generally shrouded in secrecy. Top leaders work and often live in a huge walled compound called Zhongnanhai ("Middle Southern Sea") on a lake in the center of Beijing. Zhongnanhai is not only heavily guarded, as any government executive headquarters would be, but it also has no identifying signs on its exterior other than some party slogans, nor is it identified on any public maps. Still, there is now

FIGURE 13.3

Organization of the Chinese Communist Party (73 million members)

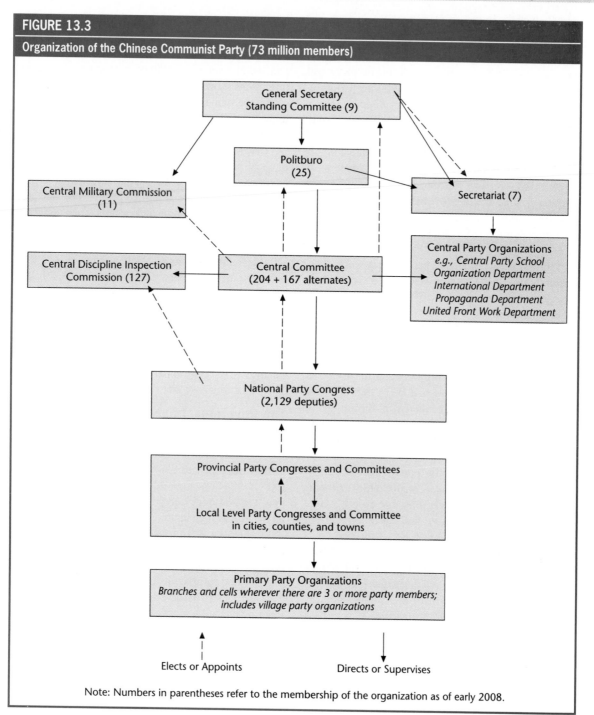

Note: Numbers in parentheses refer to the membership of the organization as of early 2008.

a little more openness about the timing and subjects covered at Politburo and Standing Committee meetings.

Prior to 1982, the top position in the party was the chairman of the Politburo's Standing Committee, which was occupied by Mao Zedong (hence *Chairman* Mao) for more than three decades until his death in 1976. The title of chairman was abolished in 1982 to symbolize a break with Mao's highly personal and often arbitrary style of leadership. Since then, the party's leader has been the general secretary, who presides over the Politburo and the Standing Committee, a position most recently held by Jiang Zemin (1989–2002) and Hu Jintao (2002 to the present).

Neither Jiang nor Hu has had the personal clout or charisma of either Deng or Mao, and therefore both have governed as part of a collective leadership that included their fellow members on the Standing Committee and Politburo. Nevertheless, both have tried to put their own stamp on the party's major policy direction, Jiang by embracing the private sector and forging sort of a partnership between the CCP and the country's entrepreneurs, and Hu by calling for attention to problems like inequality, pollution, health care, and social security as part of the development of a "harmonious socialist society" (see "Leaders: Hu Jintao").

Retired members of the party's top leadership often continue to exercise considerable influence on decision-making after they have left office, sometimes well into their eighties or nineties. Deng Xiaoping remained the most powerful person in China for several years after he had retired from all party and government positions in 1989. Today, none of the party elders have that kind of power, but there are about twenty-five of them, most notably, Jiang Zemin, to whom current leaders show considerable deference.

Two other executive organizations of the party deserve brief mention. The Secretariat manages the day-to-day work of the Politburo and Standing Committee and coordinates the party's complex and far-flung structure with considerable authority in organizational and personnel matters. The Central Commission for Discipline Inspection (CCDI) is responsible for monitoring the compliance of party members with the CCP constitution and other rules. Recently, the commission has been used as a vehicle against corruption. Between December 2002 and June 2007, the CCDI reportedly punished a total of 518,484 party members for various infractions. Minor offenses may lead to a reprimand or probation, while the most serious cases are turned over to the courts for prosecution and may result in jail time or even execution.

Below the national level, the CCP has a hierarchy of local party organizations in provinces, cities, and counties, each headed by a party secretary and party committee. There are about 3.6 million primary party organizations, called branches or cells. These are found throughout the country in workplaces, government offices, schools, urban neighborhoods, rural towns, villages, and army units—wherever there are three or more party members: There is even a CCP branch organization at Wal-Mart's China headquarters in the southern city of Shenzhen. Local and primary organizations extend the CCP's reach throughout Chinese society. They are also designed to ensure coordination within the vast and complex party structure and subordination to the central party authorities in Beijing.

The Government Executive

Government (or state) authority in China is formally vested in a system of people's congresses that begins at the top with the National People's Congress (NPC), which is a completely different organization than the National *Party* Congress. The NPC is China's national legislature and is discussed in more detail in Section 4. There are also people's congresses at the subnational levels of government, including provincial people's congresses, city people's congresses, and rural township people's congresses, (see Figure 13.4). In theory, these congresses (the legislative branch) are empowered to supervise the work of the "people's governments" (the executive branch) at the various levels of the system. But in reality, government executives (such as cabinet ministers, provincial governors, and mayors) are more accountable to party authority than to the people's congresses. For example, the city of Shanghai has both a mayor and a party secretary, each with distinct and important powers. But the party secretary's power is more consequential.

Leaders

Hu Jintao

China's current president and Communist Party leader, Hu Jintao, is, in many ways, typical of the kind of people who now lead the country. For a Chinese leader, he was relatively young (60) when he assumed power in 2002–2003. He is also well educated and had a more-or-less smooth rise to the top up the party career ladder. He fits the definition of a "technocrat," a term often used to describe China's current generation of leaders who have backgrounds in technical fields and spent most of their working lives as bureaucrats within the Chinese Communist Party.

Hu was born into a family of tea merchants in 1942, and grew up in a small city in the central coastal province of Jiangsu, not far from Shanghai. He was just six years old when the Chinese Communist Party came to power. Hu did very well in school and attended Qinghua University, China's best school of science and technology. He joined the Communist Party while at Qinghua. He graduated in 1965. This was right before the start of Chairman Mao's Great Proletarian Cultural Revolution, a period of political and social chaos when China's universities were shut down as part of the campaign to destroy those who were seen as enemies of Chinese Communist Party.

Hu Jintao did not participate as a Red Guard in the Cultural Revolution. However, he did witness a lot of violence, and his father was persecuted for being a "capitalist" and imprisoned. This experience is one influence that made Hu turn against the kind of radical communism preached by Chairman Mao.

In the late 1960s, Hu was among the millions of young people sent to rural areas and the frontier as part of their revolutionary education. He spent about a decade living and working in the poor, remote desert province of Gansu in China's far west. At first he did manual labor in housing construction, but he was transferred to work in the provincial ministry of water resources and electric power because of his high level of specialized training. It was then that he also became actively involved in Communist Party politics.

In Gansu, Hu formed a close relationship with the top party official in the province—also a Qinghua University graduate—who became a member of the CCP's powerful Standing Committee after Deng Xiaoping had consolidated his power as China's dominant leader in the early 1980s. Hu's political career rose with that of his mentor—a good example of the importance of *guanxi* ("connections") in Chinese politics. He was given the critical opportunity to study at the Central Party School in Beijing, which is a training ground for the CCP's future elite. He became a specialist in youth affairs and rose to the position of head of the Communist Youth League.

Hu was then appointed to be Communist Party leader in Guizhou province and Tibet. These appointments gave him an unusual amount of experience in areas of the country inhabited by large numbers of China's minorities (see Section 4). When he was the party leader in Tibet, he imposed **martial law** to suppress demonstrations in favor of Tibetan independence. In 1992, he joined the CCP Secretariat, a key group that manages the party leadership's day-to-day work. In the late 1990s, he became a member of the powerful Standing Committee and China's vice president. He also emerged as Deng Xiaoping's choice to succeed Jiang Zemin as head of the Communist Party and the country. The fact that Deng could anoint not only his successor but also his successor's successor reflected both the extent of Deng's personal power and the informal means by which such important decisions are made in China.

Hu Jintao became general secretary of the Chinese Communist Party in 2002 (reelected in 2007) and president of the People's Republic of China in 2003 (reelected in 2008). Like Deng and Jiang, he has been committed both to promoting rapid economic growth and free-market reforms and to maintaining the rule of the Communist Party. He has also proclaimed that his goal for China is to create a "harmonious socialist society" that pays more attention to problems like the growing inequality, rural poverty, and pollution that have accompanied the PRC's rapid development. In late 2007, the meeting of the National Congress of the Chinese Communist Party (held every five years) was a showcase for Hu's power and policies, and his "Scientific Outlook on Development" was added to the party's constitution as a key part of the CCP's current guiding version of Marxism-Leninism.

FIGURE 13.4

Organization of the Government of the People's Republic of China (PRC)

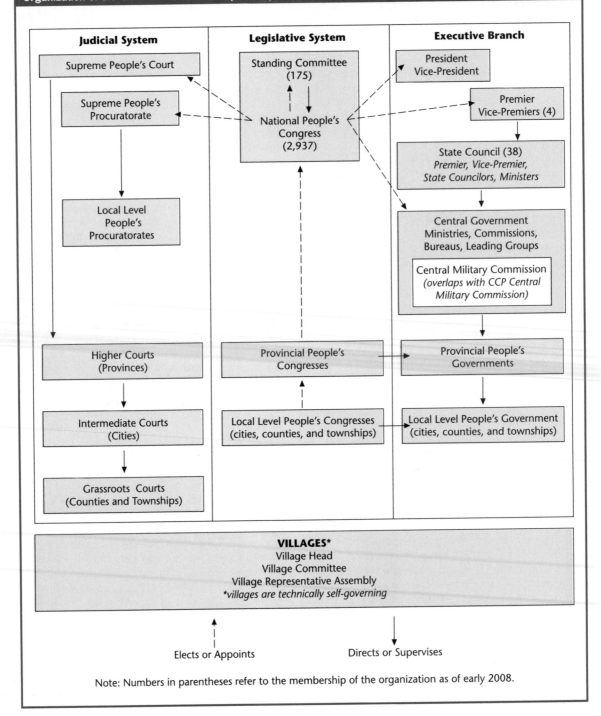

Judicial System	**Legislative System**	**Executive Branch**

Supreme People's Court

Supreme People's Procuratorate

Local Level People's Procuratorates

Standing Committee (175)

National People's Congress (2,937)

President Vice-President

Premier Vice-Premiers (4)

State Council (38)
Premier, Vice-Premier, State Councilors, Ministers

Central Government Ministries, Commissions, Bureaus, Leading Groups

Central Military Commission
(overlaps with CCP Central Military Commission)

Higher Courts (Provinces)

Provincial People's Congresses

Provincial People's Governments

Intermediate Courts (Cities)

Local Level People's Congresses (cities, counties, and townships)

Local Level People's Government (cities, counties, and townships)

Grassroots Courts (Counties and Townships)

VILLAGES*
Village Head
Village Committee
Village Representative Assembly
*villages are technically self-governing

Elects or Appoints

Directs or Supervises

Note: Numbers in parentheses refer to the membership of the organization as of early 2008.

The National People's Congress formally elects the president and vice president of China. But there is only one candidate, chosen by the Communist Party, for each office. The president's term is concurrent with that of the congress (five years). There is a two-term limit. The position is largely ceremonial, although a senior Communist Party leader has always held it. As China's head of state, the president meets and negotiates with other world leaders. Both Jiang Zemin and Hu Jintao served concurrently as both CCP general secretary and PRC president.

The premier (prime minister) has authority over the government bureaucracy and policy implementation. The premier is formally appointed by the president with the approval of the National People's Congress. But in reality, the Communist Party decides who will serve as premier. A very high-ranking member of the CCP Standing Committee has always held that post. Like the president, the premier may serve only two five-year terms.

The current premier, Wen Jiabao, is a geological engineer by training, and has gained something

of a reputation as the "people's premier" for his relatively direct and accessible approach to governing. For example, he flew to the site of the massive killer earthquake in western China's Sichuan province in the spring of 2008 within hours after it struck to investigate the scene, take charge of the rescue effort, and provide a gesture of comfort and support for the people of the area. Such a hands-on and face-to-face style of leadership is not common among China's top officials.

The premier directs the State Council, which constitutionally is "the highest organ of state administration" (Article 85) in the PRC. The National People's Congress appoints the State Council, although its membership is determined by the party leadership. It functions much like the cabinet in a parliamentary system. It includes the premier, a few vice premiers, the heads of government ministries and commissions, and several other senior officials.

The size of the State Council varies as ministries and commissions are created, merged, or disbanded to meet changing policy needs. At the height of the

The Chinese Communist Party Standing Committee.   *Source:* Ng Han Guan/AP Images.

state socialist-planned economy, there were more than one hundred ministerial-level officials. In the 1990s, there were forty ministries and commissions, and in 2003 the number was cut to twenty-eight, reflecting the decreased role of central planning and the administrative streamlining undertaken to make the government more efficient. State Council ministers run either functionally specific departments, such as the Ministry of Education, or organizations with more comprehensive responsibilities, such as the Commission of Science, Technology and Industry for National Defense. Beneath the State Council is an array of support staffs, research offices, and bureaucratic agencies charged with policy implementation. The government announced plans in early 2008 to create five "super ministries"—the Ministry of Industry and Information, the Ministry of Human Resources and Social Security, the Ministry of Environmental Protection, the Ministry of Housing and Urban-Rural Construction, and the Ministry of Transport—that will combine areas of responsibility that have been scattered among numerous organization.

One of the major challenges of governance that China faces is the creation of truly independent regulatory agencies that set and enforce standards in specific policy areas. Such agencies are part of the government, yet function with enough autonomy to be free of political pressure in their operations. Effective regulatory bodies are crucial in any modern economy. In recent years, China has established, among others, the Securities Regulatory Commission (to oversee the stock market), the Banking Regulatory Commission, the General Administration of Civil Aviation, and the State Environmental Protection Agency. There is substantial debate about how effective these watchdogs have been, but getting them to function as they should is particularly difficult in China's mixed-economy. The persisting presence of large numbers of full and partly state-owned enterprises in crucial areas of regulation essentially means the government is watching the government, a situation in which the integrity of regulatory procedures is easily compromised. Furthermore, many of the individual regulators previously worked for the one-time state-owned, but now privatized, firms they are supposed to regulate.

China's bureaucracy is immense in size and in the scope of its reach throughout the country. The total number of **cadres**—people in positions of authority paid by the government or party—in the PRC is around 40 million. Not all cadres are party members and not all party members are cadres. The vast majority of cadres work at the county level or below, and a minority work directly for the government or the CCP. The remainder occupy key posts in economic enterprises (such as factory directors); schools (such as principals); and scientific, cultural, and other state-run institutions. There have been important moves toward professionalizing the bureaucracy, particularly at the city level of government. More official positions are now subject to competition through civil service exams rather than by appointment from above, and the educational level of cadres has increased significantly since the 1980s.

One of the most significant administrative reforms of the post–Mao era—quite unprecedented in a communist party-state—has been to take measures to limit how long officials can stay in their jobs. Depending on their position, both government and party cadres must now retire between the ages of sixty and seventy. A two-term limit has been set for all top cadres, including party and state leaders.

Other State Institutions

The Military and the Police

China's People's Liberation Army (PLA) encompasses all of the country's ground, air, and naval armed services. It is the world's largest military force, with about 2.3 million active personnel (down from nearly 4 million in 1989). On a per capita basis, the PRC had 2.15 active military personnel per 1,000 of its population in the early 2000s, considerably smaller than the U.S. ratio of 4.60 per 1,000. The PLA also has a formal reserve of another 500,000 to 800,000 and a people's militia of 10 to 12 million, which can be mobilized in the event of war or for relief work after a natural disaster. The level of training and weaponry available to the militia are generally minimal.

The PRC has a Military Service Law that applies to all citizens between the ages of eighteen and twenty-two and gives the government the power to conscript both men and women as necessary to meet the country's security needs (although only males must register when they turn 18). But the military does not have to rely on conscription to fill its ranks since serving in the PLA is considered a prestigious option for many young people, particularly for rural youth who might not have many other opportunities for upward mobility.

China has increased military spending by double-digit percentages nearly every year for more than a decade in order to modernize its armed forces and raise the pay of military personnel. It was projected to spend $58.8 billion on defense in 2008, a 17.6 percent increase over the year before. Many analysts think that the PRC vastly understates its defense budget. They estimate that it is at least two times the official figures. Still, China spends much less in total and vastly less per capita on military expenditures than does the United States, which spent about $650 billion on defense in 2007.

The key organizations in charge of the Chinese armed forces are the Military Commissions (CMC) of the CCP and PRC. On paper, these are two distinct organizations. In fact, they overlap entirely in membership and function, with membership determined by the CCP Standing Committee. The chair of the CMC is, in effect, the commander in chief of China's armed forces. This position has almost always been held by the head of the party, currently Hu Jintao. The major exception was Deng Xiaoping: Although he never took the top positions in the party (chairman/general secretary) or state (president/premier), he was chair of the CMC from 1981–1989, which reflected the fact that he wanted to be sure that the PLA was under his authority.

China's internal security apparatus consists of several different organizations. A 1.5 million strong People's Armed Police (PAP) guards public officials and buildings and carries out some border patrol and protection. It also quells serious public disturbances, including worker or peasant unrest. The Ministry of State Security, with a force of about 1.7 million, is responsible for combating espionage and gathering intelligence at home and abroad. The Ministry of Public Security is the main policing organization in the PRC and is responsible for the prevention and investigation of crimes and surveillance of Chinese citizens and foreigners in China suspected of being a threat to the state. Local public security bureaus, which carry out day-to-day police work, are under the command of the central ministry in Beijing. In effect, this gives China a national police force stationed throughout the country.

In addition to a regular prison system, the Ministry of Public Security maintains an extensive system of labor reform camps for people convicted of particularly serious crimes, including political ones. These camps, noted for their harsh conditions and remote locations, are estimated to have millions of prisoners. Public Security Bureaus have the authority to detain indefinitely people suspected of committing a crime without making a formal charge and can use administrative sanctions, that is, penalties imposed outside the court system, to levy fines or sentence detainees for up to four years of "re-education through labor." There is a special system of more than 300 labor camps for such detainees (estimated at 300,000), who include prostitutes, drug users, petty criminals, as well as some who might be considered political prisoners. In a sign of the somewhat freer political environment, a few lawyers and scholars in China have begun openly arguing that administrative sanctions are contrary to the country's efforts to establish a fairer legal system.

The Judiciary

China has a four-tiered "people's court" system reaching from a Supreme People's Court down through higher (provincial-level), intermediate (city-level), and grassroots (county- and township-level) people's courts. The Supreme People's Court supervises the work of lower courts and the application of the country's laws, but it hears few cases and does not exercise judicial review over government policies. A nationwide organization called the "People's Procuratorate" serves in the courts as public prosecutor and also has investigatory functions in criminal cases.

China's judicial system came under attack as a bastion of elitism and revisionism during the Cultural Revolution. The formal legal system pretty much ceased to operate during that period, and many of its functions were taken over by political or police organizations, which often acted arbitrarily in making arrests or administering punishments.

In recent decades, the legal system of the PRC has been revitalized. There are now more than 100,000 lawyers in China (by way of comparison, there are about a million in the United States), and legal advisory offices have been established throughout the country to provide citizens and organizations with legal assistance. Many laws and regulations have been enacted, including new criminal and civil codes, in the effort to regularize the legal system.

There has been an enormous surge in the number of lawsuits filed (and often won) by people against businesses, local officials, and government agencies. Chinese courts can provide a real avenue of redress to the public for a wide range of nonpolitical grievances, including loss of property, consumer fraud, and even unjust detention by the police. Citizen mediation committees based in urban neighborhoods and rural villages play an important role in the judicial process by settling a majority of civil cases out of court.

China's criminal justice system works swiftly and harshly. Great faith is placed in the ability of an official investigation to find the facts of a case. The outcome of cases that actually do come to trial is pretty much predetermined. The conviction rate is 98–99 percent for all criminal cases. Prison terms are long and subject to only cursory appeal. A variety of offenses in addition to murder—including, in some cases, rape and especially major cases of embezzlement and other "economic crimes"—are subject to capital punishment.

All death penalty sentences must be approved by the country's Supreme People's Court. The court has recently started to be more rigorous in this review process, and quite a few death sentences have been reduced to prison terms. But appeals are handled quickly. Capital punishment cases do not linger in the courts for years, or even months. Execution is usually by a single bullet in the back of the convicted person's head, although the country is moving toward lethal injection. Amnesty International said that China led the world in the application of the death penalty in 2007, with about 470 executions that it could verify, followed by Iran (317), Saudi Arabia (143), Pakistan (135) and the United States (42). However, death penalty statistics are officially a state secret in the PRC, and some estimates suggest that the actual number of executions in China was in the 6,000 range.

Although the PRC constitution guarantees judicial independence, China's courts and other legal bodies remain under party control. The appointment of judicial personnel is subject to party approval, and the CCP can and does bend the law to serve its interests. Legal reform in China has been undertaken because China's leaders are well aware that economic development requires detailed laws, professional lawyers and judicial personnel, predictable legal processes, and binding documents such as contracts. China has, by and large, become a country where there is rule *by* law, which means that the party-state uses the law to carry out its policies and enforce its rule. But it is still far from having established the rule *of* law, in which everyone and every organization, including the Communist Party, is accountable and subject to the law.

Subnational Government

There are four main layers of state structure beneath the central government in China: provinces, cities, counties, and rural towns. There are also four very large centrally administered cities (Beijing, Shanghai, Tianjin, and Chongqing) and five autonomous regions, areas of the country with large minority populations (such as Tibet and Mongolia). Each of these levels has a representative people's congress that meets infrequently, and plays a limited, but increasingly active, role in managing affairs in its area. Executive officials, such as governors and mayors, have much greater authority than they did in the recent past, but they, too, are always subject to supervision by the central government and the Communist Party organization at their level.

Government administration in China has become increasingly decentralized over the last two decades as the role of central planning has been reduced and more power has been given to provincial and local authorities, particularly in economic matters. Efforts have also been made to reduce party interference in administrative work.

Nevertheless, the central government retains considerable power to intervene in local affairs when and where it wants. This power of the central authorities derives not only from their ability to set binding national priorities but also from their control over the military and the police, critical energy sources, resource allocation, and the construction of major infrastructure projects. A number of political scientists in

China and abroad have suggested that the PRC, given its continental size and great regional diversity, would be better served by a federal system with a more balanced distribution of power between the national, provincial, and local levels of government. However, such a move would be inconsistent with the highly centralized structure of a communist party-state.

Beneath the formal layers of state administration are China's 700,000 or so rural villages, which are home to the majority of the country's population. These villages, with an average population of roughly 500–1,000 each, are technically self-governing and are not formally responsible to a higher level of state authority. In recent years, village leaders have been directly and competitively elected by local residents, while village representative assemblies have become more vocal. These trends have brought an important degree of grassroots democracy to village government (see Section 4). However, the most powerful organization in the village is the Communist Party branch, and the single most powerful person is the local Communist Party leader (the party secretary).

The Policy-Making Process

At the height of Mao Zedong's power, many scholars described policy-making in China as a simple top-down "Mao-in-command" system. Then the Cultural Revolution led analysts to conclude that policy outcomes in the PRC were best understood as a result of factional and ideological struggles within the Chinese political elite. Now, a much more nuanced model, "fragmented authoritarianism," is often used to explain Chinese policy-making. This model recognizes that China is still fundamentally an authoritarian state and is far from being a democracy in which public opinion, party competition, media scrutiny, and independent interest groups have an impact on policy decisions. But it also takes into account that power in China has become much more dispersed, or fragmented, than it was during the Maoist era. It sees policy as evolving not only from commands from above, but also as a complex process of cooperation, conflict, and bargaining among political actors at various levels of the system.[14] The decentralization of power that has accompanied economic reform has given provincial and local governments a lot more

clout in the policy process, and the national focus on economic development has also led to the growing influence of nonparty experts and organizations in the policy loop.

The fragmented authoritarian model acknowledges that policy-making in China is still ultimately under the control of the Chinese Communist Party and that the top two dozen or so party leaders who sit on the party's Politburo wield nearly unchecked power. The CCP uses a weblike system of organizational controls to make sure that the government bureaucracy complies with the party's will in policy implementation. In the first place, almost all key government officials are also party members. Furthermore, the CCP exercises control over the policy process through party organizations that parallel government agencies at all levels of the system. For example, each provincial government works under the watchful eye of a provincial party committee. In addition, the Communist Party maintains an effective presence inside every government organization through a "leading party group" that is made up of key officials who are also CCP members.

The CCP also influences the policy process by means of the "cadre list," or as it was known in the Soviet Union where the practice was developed, the *nomenklatura* system. The cadre list covers millions of positions in the government and elsewhere (including institutions such as universities, banks, trade unions, and newspapers). Any personnel decision involving an appointment, promotion, transfer, or dismissal that affects a position on this list must be approved by a party organization department, whether or not the person involved is a party member. In recent years, the growth of nonstate sectors of the economy and administrative streamlining have led to a reduction in the number of positions directly subject to party approval. Nevertheless, the *nomenklatura* system remains one of the major instruments by which the CCP tries to "ensure that leading institutions throughout the country will exercise only the autonomy granted to them by the party."[15]

The work of the State Council (and the CCP Politburo) is supported by flexible issue-specific task forces called "leadership small groups." These informal groups bring together top officials from various ministries, commissions, and committees in order to coordinate policy-making and implementation on matters that cross the jurisdiction of any single organization Some groups, such the Central Leading Group on Foreign Affairs, are more or less permanent fixtures in the party-state structure, while others may be convened on an ad hoc basis to deal with short-term matters like a natural disaster or an epidemic. Since most of the members are high-ranking CCP officials, they are also meant to insure party supervision of policy in that particular area.

No account of the policy process in China is complete without noting again the importance of *guanxi* ("connections"), the personal relationships and mutual obligations based on family, friendship, school, military, professional, or other ties. The notion of *guanxi* has its roots in Confucian culture and has long been an important part of political, social, and economic life in China. These connections are still a basic fact of life within the Chinese bureaucracy, where personal ties are often the key to getting things done. Depending on how they are used, *guanxi* can either help cut red tape and increase efficiency or bolster organizational rigidity and feed corruption.

In sum, the power of the Communist Party is the most basic fact of political life in the People's Republic of China. Party dominance, however, does not mean that the system "operates in a monolithic way"; in fact, it "wriggles with politics" of many kinds, formal and informal.[16] In order to get a more complete picture of governance and policy-making in China, it is important to look at how various influences, including ideology, factional maneuverings, bureaucratic interests, citizen input (discussed in Section 4), and *guanxi,* shape the decisions ultimately made by Communist Party leaders and organizations.

SECTION 4 Representation and Participation

The Chinese Communist Party claims to represent the interests of all the people of China and describes the People's Republic as a **socialist democracy**. In the CCP's view this is superior to democracy in capitalist countries where wealthy individuals and corporations dominate politics and policy-making despite multiparty politics. China's *socialist* democracy is based on the unchallengeable role of the CCP as the country's only ruling party and should not be confused with the *social* **democracy** of Western European center-left political parties, which is rooted in a commitment to competitive politics.

Representation and participation play important roles as instruments of socialist democracy in the PRC political system. Legislatures, elections, and organizations like labor unions provide citizens with ways of influencing public policy-making and the selection of some government leaders. But the Chinese Communist Party limits and controls such democratic elements of China's socialist democracy.

The Legislature

China's constitution grants the National People's Congress (NPC) the power to enact and amend the country's laws, approve and monitor the state budget, and declare and end war. The NPC is also empowered to elect (and recall) the president and vice president, the chair of the state Central Military Commission, the head of China's Supreme Court, and the procurator-general (something like the U.S. attorney general). The NPC has final approval over the selection of the premier and members of the State Council. On paper, China's legislature certainly looks to be the most powerful branch of government. In fact, these powers, which are not insignificant, are exercised only as allowed by the Communist Party.

The National People's Congress is a unicameral legislature. Members (called deputies) are elected for a five-year term and meet for only about two weeks every March. Deputies are not full-time legislators and remain in their regular jobs and home areas except for the brief time when the congress is in session.

The size of the NPC is set by law prior to each five-year electoral cycle. The NPC elected in 2008 consisted of nearly 3,000 deputies. All delegates, except those from the People's Liberation Army, are chosen on a geographic basis from China's provinces, autonomous regions, and major municipalities.

Global Connection

Hong Kong: From China to Britain—and Back Again

Hong Kong became a British colony in three stages during the nineteenth century as a result of what China calls the "unequal treaties" imposed under military and diplomatic pressure from the West. Two parts of Hong Kong were given *permanently* to Britain in 1842 and 1860. But the largest part of the tiny territory was given to Britain in 1898 with a ninety-nine-year lease. The anticipated expiration of that lease led to negotiations between London and Beijing in the 1980s. In December 1984, Britain agreed to return all of Hong Kong to Chinese sovereignty on July 1, 1997. On that date, Hong Kong became a Special Administrative Region (SAR) of the People's Republic of China.

Britain ruled Hong Kong for more than 100 years in a traditional, if generally benevolent, colonial fashion. A governor from London presided over an administration in which British rather than local people exercised most of the power. There was a free press, a fair and effective legal system, and other important features of a democratic system. In the last years of their rule, the British appointed more Hong Kong Chinese to higher administrative positions. They also expanded the scope of elections for choosing some members of the colony's executive and representative bodies. The British were criticized for taking steps toward democratization only on the eve of their departure from the colony. They allowed only a small number of Hong Kong residents to emigrate to the United Kingdom before the start of Chinese rule.

Hong Kong flourished economically under the free-market policies of the British. It became one of the world's great centers of international trade and finance. It now has the highest standard of living in Asia outside of Japan and Singapore. Hong Kong is also characterized by extremes of wealth and poverty. When China took over Hong Kong in 1997, it pledged not to impose its political or economic system on the HKSAR for fifty years. The PRC has a strong motivation not to do anything that might destroy Hong Kong's economic dynamism.

Although the PRC took over full control of Hong Kong's foreign policy and has stationed troops of the People's Liberation Army in Hong Kong, Beijing has generally fulfilled its promise that the SAR will have a high degree of political as well as economic autonomy. Civil liberties, the independence of the judiciary, and freedom of the press have largely been maintained.

Nevertheless, China has made sure that it keeps a grip on power in Hong Kong. The SAR is headed by a chief executive, who, along with other top civil servants, must be approved by the PRC. Politicians favoring democracy in Hong Kong have a strong presence in the SAR's elected legislature, but the legislature itself is relatively powerless to make policy. In a telling example of the tug-of-war over the direction of Hong Kong's political future, the PRC's plan to implement a law prohibiting "any act of treason, secession, sedition, subversion against the Central People's Government, or theft of state secrets" was withdrawn in 2004 after large-scale protests by those who worry that British colonialism in Hong Kong might be replaced by Chinese authoritarianism.

	Hong Kong
Land area	401.5 sq mi/1,092 sq km (about six times the size of Washington, D.C.)
Population	7.0 million
Ethnic composition	Chinese, 95 percent; other, 5 percent
Annual GDP at purchasing power parity	US$293.3 billion—making it the 41st largest economy in the world, just behind Nigeria and ahead of the Czech Republic
Annual GDP per capita at purchasing power parity	US$42,000—very close to that of the United States
Annual GDP growth rate (2007)	6.4 percent

There are representatives from China's two indirectly ruled Special Administrative Regions, the tiny former Portuguese colony and now gambling haven of Macao, and the former British colony and now bustling commercial city of Hong Kong (see "Global Connection: Hong Kong: From China to Britain—and Back Again"). To symbolize China's claim to Taiwan, delegates representing the island are chosen from among PRC residents with Taiwanese ancestry or other ties.

When the NPC is not in session, state power is exercised by its Standing Committee, which normally meets every other month. The NPC Standing Committee has about 150 members, and its chair also presides over the regular annual sessions of the congress. The NPC chair is always also a member of the CCP Standing Committee. The Chair's Council of about fifteen members conducts the day-to-day business of the NPC.

A large majority of the deputies to the NPC are members of the CCP, but many belong to one of China's eight noncommunist (and powerless) political parties (see below) or have no party affiliation. In the NPC that served from 2003–2008, workers and farmers made up 18.5 percent of deputies, while intellectuals and professionals made up a little more than 20 percent. Government and party cadres accounted for a third of the deputies; 9 percent were from the military. The remainder represented other occupational categories, such as business people. Women make up around 20 percent of NPC deputies and ethnic minorities 15 percent. Most NPC deputies are now chosen because of their ability to contribute to China's modernization or to represent important constituencies rather than simply on the basis of political loyalty. The educational level of deputies has increased significantly in recent years, with more than ninety percent having junior college degrees or above, and more than half have advanced degrees. There has been an effort to increase the number of "grassroots" deputies, principally farmers and workers. In a new category of representation, three migrant workers (out of a national total of 150-200 million) were elected in 2008. In all cases, however, the CCP monitors the election process to make sure that no outright dissidents are elected as deputies.

Despite great fanfare in the press as examples of socialist democracy at work, legislation is passed and state leaders are elected by the National People's Congress with overwhelming majorities. The NPC never deals with sensitive political issues. The annual sessions are largely taken up by the presentation of *very* long reports on the work in the previous year by the premier and other state leaders. Legislation may be introduced by groups of at least thirty deputies; in fact, most legislation comes from the State Council or the NPC Standing Committee.

Some deputies have become a bit more assertive on issues like corruption and environmental problems, and some dissent and debate does occur. In 1992, about a third of NPC deputies either voted against or abstained from voting on the hugely expensive (officially, $22 billion) and ecologically controversial Three Gorges dam project on the Yangtze River. Government legislative initiatives have occasionally been defeated or tabled. The property rights law—which included the protection of private property—that was finally passed in March 2007 had first been put on the NPC agenda in 2002. It generated enough controversy among deputies, party-state leaders, and academics that it had to be revised several times before it was affirmed by 96.9 percent (fifty-three against, and thirty-seven abstentions) of the vote. Some objected to the law because they thought providing such guarantees to private property owners was contrary to communist principles; others feared that corrupt officials would use the law to enrich themselves through the "asset-stripping" of privatized state-owned enterprises as happened on a grand scale when Russia went from a command to a planned economy. But, in a reflection of the limits on the discussion of controversial issues, the Chinese press was not allowed to cover the property law debate or print editorial opinions on the issue.

Legislatures in communist party-states are often called "rubber stamps," meaning they automatically and without question approve party policies. But as economics has replaced ideology as the main motivation of China's leaders, the NPC has become a much more significant and lively part of the Chinese political system. The NPC is still not part of an independent branch of government in a system of checks and balances; but it also is no longer merely a "rubber stamp" of the Chinese Communist Party.

Political Parties and the Party System

China is usually called a one-party system because the country's politics are so thoroughly dominated by the Chinese Communist Party. In fact, China has eight political parties in addition to the CCP. These parties neither challenge the basic policies of the CCP nor play a significant part in running the government, although they increasingly provide advice in the policy-making process.

The Chinese Communist Party

The Chinese Communist Party has grown steadily since it came to power in 1949, when it had just under 4.5 million members. Only during the Cultural Revolution was there a sharp drop in membership due to the purge of "capitalist roaders" from party ranks, and many of those purged were welcomed back into the CCP after the death of Mao.

With about 73 million members, the CCP is by far the largest political party in the world. But its membership makes up a very small minority of the population (about 8 percent of those over eighteen, the minimum age for joining the party). This is consistent with the party's view that it is a "vanguard" party that admits only those who are truly dedicated to the communist cause.

The social composition of the CCP's membership has changed dramatically since the party came to power in 1949. In the mid-1950s, peasants made up nearly 70 percent of the party, reflecting the revolution's rural roots; in mid-2007, peasants, now called farmers, are just 31.4 percent of the party. The rest of the organization consists of managerial and technical personnel (22.4 percent); retirees (18.9 percent); industrial workers (10.1 percent); party and state cadres (7.5 percent); private entrepreneurs (5.1 percent); students (2.5 percent); and military and armed police personnel (2.1 percent). Women make up only about 20 percent of the CCP as a whole, and 6.3 percent of the 204 full members of the Central Committee (and 14.4 percent of the 167 alternates) elected in 2007. The twenty-five-member Politburo has one female, Liu Yandong, who concurrently serves on the government's cabinet, the State Council. Like many of China's top technocratic leaders, she was educated as an engineer and worked in industry before beginning her climb of the party political ladder. She later received an advanced degree in political science. Her main responsibility within the party leadership is to work with noncommunist organizations and parties (see below).

The CCP claims to represent the interests of the overwhelming majority of people in China. It says that all those over the age of eighteen who accept the party's goals, are willing to be active in a party organization and carry out party decisions, and pay their dues may apply for membership. Even though many Chinese believe that communist ideology is irrelevant to their lives and the nation's future, being a party member still provides unparalleled access to influence and resources. It remains a prerequisite for advancement in many careers, particularly in government. More than 2 million people join the CCP each year, most of them under the age of thirty-five.

The party has been particularly active in the last few years in recruiting members from what is referred to as the "new social stratum," which includes owners of private businesses ("entrepreneurs"), employees of private or foreign-funded companies, and the self-employed. Approximately 35–40 percent of private entrepreneurs are party members, the so-called "Red Capitalists,"[17] and, as noted above, about 5 percent of party members work in private enterprises. Many of these belonged to the CCP *before* they went into business. In fact, that's one of the CCP's motives in opening its doors to the new social stratum; another is that the party wants to broaden its social base to incorporate (or co-opt) the group that is the cutting edge of China's economic development. This is quite a change from the Maoist era, when any hint of capitalism was crushed. Such political and ideological (discussed below) adaptability to the realities of a rapidly changing China is a major reason why the CCP has been able to stay in power.

China's Noncommunist "Democratic Parties"

China describes its political system as one of multiparty cooperation and consultation under the leadership of the Chinese Communist Party. There are eight officially recognized political parties in addition to the CCP. They are referred to as the "democratic parties," which is meant to signify the role they play in representing different interests in the political process. Each noncommunist party draws its membership from a particular group in Chinese society. For example, the China Democratic League consists mostly of intellectuals, whereas the Chinese Party for the Public Interest draws on returned overseas Chinese and experts with overseas connections.

All of these parties, which have a total membership of about 800,000, were founded before the CCP came to power in 1949. They do not contest for power or challenge CCP policy. Their function is to provide advice to the CCP and generate support within their particular constituencies for CCP policies. Individual members of the parties hold many important government positions, including the heads or deputy heads of several state ministries. But organizationally these parties are relatively insignificant and function as little more than "a loyal nonopposition."[18]

The main forum through which the noncommunist parties express their views on national policy is the Chinese People's Political Consultative Conference (CPPCC). The CPPCC is an advisory, not a legislative, body which, according to its charter, operates under the guidance of the Communist Party. It meets in full session once a year for about two weeks at the same time as the National People's Congress (NPC), which CPPCC members attend as nonvoting deputies. The large majority of the more than 2,000 delegates to the CPPCC are noncommunists, representing the "democratic parties" or various constituencies such as education, the arts, and medicine, but all delegates are chosen through a process supervised by the CCP, and a high-ranking party leader heads the CPPCC itself. CPPCC delegates are increasingly speaking out about national problems, but they do not express serious dissent from the party line on any matter.

New political parties are not allowed to form. A group of activists who had been part of the 1989 Tiananmen protests established a China Democracy Party in 1998 to promote multiparty politics. They tried to register the party with the local authorities, as all new organizations are required to do. But their registration was not accepted, and the party's founders were soon arrested, given stiff prison terms, and the party was banned.

Elections

Elections in the PRC are basically mechanisms to give the communist party-state greater legitimacy by allowing large numbers of citizens to participate in the political process under very controlled circumstances. But elections have become somewhat more democratic and more important in providing a way for citizens to express their views and to hold some officials accountable.

Most elections in China are "indirect." In other words, it is the members of an already existing body that elect, mostly from among themselves, those who will serve at the next highest level in the power structure. For example, deputies to a provincial people's congress, not all the eligible citizens of the province, elect delegates who will represent the province to the National People's Congress. A parallel would be a situation in which state legislatures in the United States elected from among their own members those who would serve in the House of Representatives rather than being elected directly and separately through the state's congressional districts. In fact, until 1913, U.S. senators were elected by state legislatures!

Direct elections are elections in which all the voters in the relevant area get to cast ballots for candidates for a particular position. Direct elections are most common in China at the village level, although there have been a few experiments with letting all voters choose officials and representatives at the next rung up the administrative ladder (the township). The authorities have been very cautious in expanding the scope of direct elections. The CCP wants to prevent them from becoming a forum for open campaigning or dissent. The most powerful positions in the government, such a city mayors and provincial governors, are not elected, but are appointed by the Communist Party.

Many direct and indirect elections in China now have multiple candidates, with the winner chosen by secret ballot. A significant number of independently nominated candidates have defeated official nominees, although even independent candidates have to be approved by the CCP.

The most significant progress toward real democratic representation and participation in China has occurred in the rural villages. Laws implemented since the late 1980s have provided for direct election of the village head and other members of the village's governing committee. Local leaders had previously been appointed by and responsible to higher-level authorities. In most villages, any voter can nominate candidates (in others, it requires a group). Village elections are now generally multicandidate, with limited active campaigning and voting by secret ballot, while primaries and runoffs are becoming more commonplace.

These elections have certainly given villagers more power in local affairs. Studies have shown that they produce more responsive and responsible leaders. They have also been used to remove incompetent or corrupt leaders from office. Most villages also have a representative assembly whose members are chosen from each household or group of households. These assemblies, which meet only once or twice a year, have taken a more active role in supervising the work of local officials and in the decision-making in matters affecting community finances and welfare.

As noted in the previous section, real power in a Chinese village resides in the local CCP branch and party leader (the secretary). Villagers who are members of the CCP—usually a small minority of the residents—are the only ones who have a say in who becomes party secretary. This certainly can be a constraint on the authority of the elected village leaders. However, there are many cases in which the local Communist Party leader has been chosen to serve simultaneously as the village head in a competitive election. This may sometimes simply be the result of arm-twisting or worse by the party, but it also often happens because the Communist Party leader is a well-respected person who has the confidence and support of the villagers.

Some observers see direct grassroots elections and the representative assemblies in the Chinese countryside as seeds of real democracy that may take root and spread to higher levels of the political system. Others argue that such elections are merely

Rural residents vote in a village election in China. In recent years, such grassroots democracy has become widespread in the countryside, although it is always closely monitored by the Chinese Communist Party.   *Source:* China Photos/Getty Images.

a facade to appease international critics and give the rural population a way to express discontent with some officials without challenging the country's fundamental political organization. In any case, they do have an impact on the lives of the more than 700 million Chinese who live in the countryside and are certainly worth watching for anyone interested in China's political development.

Recent electoral reform has certainly increased popular representation and participation in China's government. But elections in the PRC still do not give citizens a means by which they can exercise effective control over the party officials and organizations that have the real power in China's political system.

Political Culture, Citizenship, and Identity

From Communism to Consumerism

Since its founding in 1949, the PRC's official political culture has been based on communist ideology. The party-state has made extensive efforts to influence people's political attitudes and behavior to conform to whatever was the prevailing version of Marxism-Leninism in the CCP leadership.

At the height of the Maoist era, Mao Zedong Thought was hailed as "an inexhaustible source of strength and a spiritual atom bomb of infinite power" that held the answer to all of China's problems in domestic and foreign policy.[19] By the mid-1970s, however, the debacles of the Mao years had greatly tarnished the appeal, to most people in China, not only of Maoism, but of communist ideology in general.

After Deng Xiaoping came to power in 1978, he set about trying to restore the legitimacy of the Communist Party through economic reforms and to revive communist ideology by linking it directly to China's development aspirations. After Deng's death in 1997, the CCP amended the party constitution to add "Deng Xiaoping Theory" to its official ideology. One key part of Deng's theory, often referred to under the rubric of "Building Socialism with Chinese Characteristics," was a major departure from Maoism in its central claim that, given China's relative poverty, the main task of the CCP was to promote economic development by any means necessary, even capitalist ones.

The other core component of Deng's ideology, which is fully consistent with Maoist theory and practice, consists of the "**Four Cardinal Principles**" that he spelled out in 1979. These principles—upholding the socialist road, the people's democratic dictatorship, the leadership of the Communist Party, and Marxism-Leninism—were to be the foundation on which economic reform was to take place; as he said at the time, "To undermine any of the four cardinal principles is to undermine the whole cause of socialism in China, the whole cause of modernization."[20] In essence, then, Deng Xiaoping Theory is an ideological rationale for the combination of economic liberalization and party dictatorship that characterizes contemporary China. Both of Deng's successors, Jiang Zemin and Hu Jintao, have time and again reaffirmed the Four Cardinal Principles. For example, in his major address to the CCP's national congress in October 2007, general secretary Hu Jintao reaffirmed that, "The Four Cardinal Principles are the very foundation for building our country and the political cornerstone for the survival and development of the Party and the nation."[21]

In an effort to have himself placed on the CCP's ideological pedestal along Deng and Mao, Jiang Zemin offered his own variation on Chinese communism as he neared retirement in the early 2000s. Jiang's particular contribution was dubbed the "Three Represents," which according to the yet again amended party constitution depicted the CCP as the faithful representative of the "development trend of China's advanced productive forces, the orientation of China's advanced culture, and the fundamental interests of the overwhelming majority of the Chinese people." This is a reaffirmation of Deng's emphasis on economic development, but it is also an ideological rationale for recruiting private entrepreneurs into the Communist Party and accommodating the many existing party members who had gone into private business.

Hu Jintao has also made a move to carve out his own ideological niche relatively early in his tenure as party leader. Even before the end of his first five-year term as general secretary, he laid out his program to achieve a "harmonious socialist society," which meant economic development should be seen as involving more than sheer GDP growth and rising living standards (as Jiang had emphasized), but must also pay attention to poverty, inequality, health care, and the environment. This was codified as the "Scientific Outlook on Development" and inserted in the party constitution in late 2006 as being an approach that "puts people first" and is "in the same line as Marxism-Leninism, Mao Zedong Thought, Deng Xiaoping Theory, the important thought of Three Represents, and keeps up with the times."

This may seem like a lot of theoretical and rhetorical contortion simply to give Marxist-Leninist legitimacy to the policies of the current party leadership, and ideology might be much less important in China now given the almost single-minded focus on economic growth. But the Chinese communist variant of Marxism-Leninism still provides the language of formal politics in China, sets the framework for governance and policy-making, and marks the boundaries for what is permissible in politics in general. Different iterations of that ideology also reflect significant shifts of priority in the CCP, which, in turn, says a lot about the distribution of power in China's political elite.

The CCP tries to keep communist ideology visible and viable by continuing efforts to influence public opinion and socialization—for instance, by controlling the media and overseeing the educational system. Although China's media are much livelier and more open than during the Maoist period, there is no true freedom of the press. Reduced political control of the media has, to a large extent, meant only the freedom to publish more entertainment news, human interest stories, local coverage, and some nonpolitical investigative journalism. For example, in the summer of 2007, the news media helped expose the use of slave labor (including many children) in thousands of brick kilns and coal mines in two provinces in central China. There was also relative openness to press reporting on the Sichuan earthquake in the spring of 2008, but most of the emphasis was on the heroic rescue efforts of local people, the army, and government agencies.

The arts, in general, are the area of life in which there has been the greatest political change in China in recent years, in the sense that there is much less direct (but not totally absent) censorship. The Chinese film industry, for example, has emerged as one of the best in the world, with many of its directors, stars, and productions winning global acclaim, and the modern art scene in China is vibrant, with the work of some young artists commanding both international attention and astronomical prices. Nevertheless, both party and state censorship organizations, under the authority of the CCP's Central Propaganda Department, remain powerful and vigilant. Films, art, and publications of all kinds are censored or banned if they are judged to violate political or moral standards, some of which are set out in documents such as the "Regulations Regarding Strengthening the Administration of Publications Describing Major Party and National Leaders."

The rapid expansion of Internet access in China has provided the censors with a challenge. There were more than 230 million Internet users in the PRC in mid-2008. Private ownership of personal computers is growing, Internet cafés abound in most cities and can even be found in some quite remote towns, and better-off rural villages are getting wired for the Web. The government worries about the influence of e-mail and other electronic information it cannot control. It frequently blocks access to certain foreign Web sites, shuts down unlicensed cybercafés, which it has likened to opium dens, and has arrested people it has accused of disseminating subversive material over the Internet.

Web access in China is tightly controlled by the licensing of just a few Internet service providers, who are themselves responsible for who uses their systems and how. A special state organization under the Ministry of Public Security, with an estimated 50,000 employees, has been established to police the Internet; it states its mission quite clearly in the designation of its official URL: http://www.cyberpolice.cn/! The government is investing huge sums to develop the "Golden Shield Project" (referred to outside the country as the "Great Firewall of China") to strengthen its ability to monitor and control websites, e-mail, chat rooms, and blogs. This project has received technical assistance from Western companies, and Microsoft, Yahoo, and Google along with several other American firms have been criticized by human rights organizations for agreeing to political restrictions on their portals in China exchange for the right to do business there. The Chinese party-state knows that cutting-edge technology is critical to its modernization plans and wants its citizens to become computer literate; but, as with so much else in China, the party-state wants to define the way this happens and to dictate the rules.

Schools are one of the main institutions through which all states instill political values in their young citizens. The expansion of educational opportunities throughout the country and at all levels has been one of the great successes of the government of the PRC. Primary school enrollment is close to 100 percent of the age-eligible population (ages six to eleven), but drops sharply at the secondary (75 percent) and college (21 percent) levels. In Maoist China, students at all levels spent a considerable amount of time studying politics and working in fields or factories, and teaching materials were often overlaid with a heavy dose of political propaganda. Today, political study is a required but minor part of the curriculum throughout the education system. Much greater attention is paid to urging students to gain the skills and knowledge they need to further their own careers and help China modernize.

Academic freedom in China has expanded considerably, and college campuses, in particular, are the sites of unconstrained discussions and exchange of views. Yet Chinese schools are by no means centers of seriously critical or independent thinking, and teachers and students are still monitored for political reliability. In March 2005, a journalism professor at Beijing University (China's most prestigious university) was fired for his public criticism of party censors, whom he compared to those in Nazi Germany. More than 80 percent of China's students between the ages of seven and fourteen belong to the Young Pioneers, an organization designed to promote good social behavior, patriotism, and loyalty to the party. Most Young Pioneers go on to join the Communist Youth League (ages 14 to 28), which has more than 70 million members, and serves as the main source of recruitment of new party members.

Alternative sources of socialization and beliefs are growing in importance in China. These do not often take expressly political forms, however, because of the threat of repression. In the countryside, peasants have replaced portraits of Mao and other communist heroes with statues of folk gods and ancestor worship tablets. The influence of extended kinship groups such as clans often outweighs the formal authority of the party branch or village committee in the rural areas. In the cities, popular culture, including gigantic rock concerts, shapes youth attitudes much more profoundly than party propaganda. Consumerism ("buying things") is probably the most widely shared value in China today. Many observers have spoken of a moral vacuum in the country, which is not uncommon for societies undergoing such rapid, multifaceted change.

Organized religion, which was ferociously repressed during the Mao era, is attracting an increasing number of adherents. Buddhist temples, Christian churches, Islamic mosques, and other places of worship operate more freely than they have in decades, and the government says there are more than 100 million believers in the country, though the actual number is estimated to be several times that. Freedom of religion is guaranteed by the PRC constitution (as is the freedom not to believe in any religion). The CCP is officially an atheist organization, but the party constitution was amended in late 2007 to include its first ever mention of religion with the statement that "The Party strives to fully implement its basic principle for its work related to religious affairs, and rallies religious believers in making contributions to economic and social development."

But religious life is still closely controlled and limited to officially approved organizations and venues. Clergy of any religion who defy the authority of the party-state are often imprisoned. Clandestine Christian communities, called house churches, have sprung up in many areas among people who reject the government's control of religious life and are unable to worship in public. Though local officials sometimes tolerate or even belong to these churches, in numerous cases, house church leaders and lay people have been arrested and the private homes where services are held have been bulldozed. The Chinese Catholic Church is prohibited from recognizing the authority of the pope, although there have been recent signs of a thaw between Beijing and the Vatican.

Citizenship and National Identity

The Chinese people have a very strong sense of their cultural identity. But the views of China's citizens about what ties them to the state—their sense of national identity—are going through a profound and uncertain transformation. Party leaders realize that most citizens are skeptical or dismissive of communist ideology, and that appeals to socialist goals and revolutionary virtues no longer inspire loyalty. The CCP has turned increasingly to patriotic themes to rally the country behind its leadership. The official media put considerable emphasis on the greatness and antiquity of Chinese culture to stoke national pride. They send the not-so-subtle message that it is time for China to reclaim its rightful place in the world order—and that only the CCP can lead the nation in achieving this goal.

The party-state also does all it can to get political capital by touting its role in managing China's impressive economic achievements, winning the 2008 Summer Olympics for Beijing, and securing the return to China of territories like Hong Kong and Macao (a former Portuguese colony) that were lost long ago to Western imperialist powers. In the view of some, such officially promoted nationalist sentiments could lead to a more aggressive foreign and military policy, particularly—given the country's growing need for energy resources—toward areas such as the potentially oil-rich South China Sea, where the PRC's historical territorial claims conflict with those of other countries including Vietnam and the Philippines.

The government of the PRC and the Chinese people can be very sensitive about what they consider slights to their national dignity. For example, many Chinese feel that Japan has not done enough to acknowledge or apologize for the atrocities its army committed in China during World War II. This has been a strain in relations between the two countries and has sometimes led to spontaneous (with some official encouragement to continue) anti-Japanese demonstrations by Chinese students.

China's Non-Chinese Citizens

The PRC calls itself a multinational state with fifty-six officially recognized ethnic groups, one of which is the majority Han people (named after an early dynasty). The Han make up 91.5 percent of the total population. The defining elements of a minority group involve some combination of language, culture (including religion), and race that distinguish them from the Han. The fifty-five minorities number a little more than 100 million, or about 8.5 percent of the total population. These groups range in size

from 16 million (the Zhuang of southwest China) to about 2,000 (the Lhoba in the far west). Most of these minorities have come under Chinese rule over many centuries through the expansion of the Chinese state rather than through migration into China.

China's minorities are highly concentrated in the five autonomous regions of Guangxi, Inner Mongolia, Ningxia, Tibet, and Xinjiang. Only in the last two, however, do minority people outnumber Han Chinese, who have been encouraged to migrate to these regions. The five autonomous regions are sparsely populated, yet they occupy about 60 percent of the total land area of the PRC. Some of these areas are resource rich. All are located on strategically important borders of the country, including those with Vietnam, India, and Russia. In addition to the autonomous regions, which are the equivalent of provinces in the state structure, there are also numerous autonomous counties and other administrative units in many parts of the country where the majority or a large percentage of the population consists of ethnic minorities.

The Chinese constitution grants these autonomous areas the right of self-government in certain matters, such as cultural affairs. But minority regions remain firmly under the control of the central authorities. Minority peoples enjoy some latitude to develop their local economies as they see fit. Religious freedom is generally respected, and the use of minority languages in the media and literature is encouraged, as is, to a certain extent, bilingual education. In order to keep the already small minority populations from dwindling further, China's stringent family planning policy is applied much more loosely among minorities, who are often allowed to have two or more children per couple rather than the one-child limit prescribed for most Chinese.

There has been a concerted effort to recruit and promote minority cadres to run local governments in autonomous areas. The chairman (governor) of all five autonomous regions comes from the major ethnic group of the region. But, as is the case at all important points in China's political system, the most powerful individual in the autonomous regions is the head of the Communist Party, and all those positions are held by Han Chinese. Also, despite significant progress in modernizing the economies of the minority regions, these areas remain among the poorest in China.

The most extensive ethnic conflict in China has occurred in Tibet, which has been under Chinese military occupation since the early 1950s. Hu Jintao, the current president of the PRC and general secretary of the CCP, served as the party chief in Tibet from 1988 to 1992. This gives him vastly more personal experience in this troubled part of the country than any previous national leader. Some see this experience as a cause for optimism, while others are critical of Hu's record of enforcing repressive Chinese control of the region (see "Current Challenges: Tibet and China").

Current Challenges

Tibet and China

Tibet is located in the far west of China on the border with India, Burma, Nepal, and Bhutan. It is a large area (about 470,000 square miles, which is nearly 13 percent of China's total area) and is ringed by some of the world's highest mountains, including the Himalayas and Mt. Everest. Ninety-three percent of Tibet's 2.6 million people are Tibetans, who are ethnically, linguistically, and culturally distinct from the Chinese. Another 3 million ethnic Tibetans live elsewhere in China, mostly in provinces adjacent to Tibet.

In the thirteenth century, Tibet became a theocracy in which absolute power was held by a Buddhist priest, called the Dalai Lama, who ruled the country with the help of other clergy and the aristocracy. Traditional Tibetan society was sharply divided between the tiny ruling class and the common people, most of whom were serfs living and working under difficult and often brutal conditions.

Tibet became subordinate to China in the early eighteenth century, although the Dalai Lama and other Tibetan officials continued to govern the country. After the collapse of China's imperial system in 1911, Tibet achieved *de facto* independence. However, Britain, which saw Tibet in the context of its extensive colonial rule in South Asia, exercised considerable influence in Tibetan affairs.

Shortly after coming to power in 1949, the Chinese Communists made known their intention to end foreign intervention in Tibet, which they, like previous Chinese governments, considered to be part of China. In 1951, the Dalai Lama agreed to the peaceful incorporation of Tibet into the People's Republic of China rather than face a full-scale military assault. Although some Chinese troops and officials were sent to Tibet, the Dalai Lama remained in a position of symbolic authority for much of the 1950s. In 1959,

a widespread revolt against Chinese rule led to the invasion of Tibet by the People's Liberation Army. The Dalai Lama and more than 50,000 of his supporters fled to exile in India, and Chinese rule was even more firmly established. In 1965, the Tibetan Autonomous Region was officially formed, but Chinese political and military officials have kept a firm grip on power in Tibet.

During the Maoist era, traditional Tibetan culture was suppressed by the Chinese authorities. Since the late 1970s, Buddhist temples and monasteries have been allowed to reopen, and Tibetans have gained a significant degree of cultural freedom; the Chinese government has also significantly increased investment in Tibet's economic development. However, China still considers talk of Tibetan political independence to be treason, and Chinese troops have violently crushed several anti-China demonstrations in Lhasa, the capital, and elsewhere in Tibet.

The Dalai Lama is very active internationally in promoting greater autonomy for Tibet. In 1989, he won the Nobel Peace Prize. He has met with several U.S. presidents, including President George W. Bush in October 2007, when the U.S. Congress also awarded him its highest civilian honor. In 1999, the U.S. State Department appointed a special coordinator for Tibetan issues. The Chinese government has objected strongly to such American actions, which they regard as proof of tacit U.S. support for Tibetan independence.

In recent years, high-level delegations from the Dalai Lama's government-in-exile have visited Beijing and Lhasa to further explore better relations. The Dalai Lama appears willing to return to Tibet and accept Chinese sovereignty in exchange for guarantees of real autonomy in managing local, particularly religious and cultural, affairs. But the PRC is fearful that his presence would incite greater opposition to Chinese rule and has rejected the Dalai Lama's offer of a compromise as a "disguised" plan to gain independence for Tibet.

In March 2008, serious rioting broke out in Lhasa and several other locations in Tibet. The protests began when 300 Buddhist monks marched in the capital to demand the release of several imprisoned fellow monks. The situation turned violent and spread after the police tried to disperse the monks' demonstration. Tibetan crowds ransacked shops owned by ethnic Chinese and beat Chinese residents. Police and army cars were burned. A large but unknown number of people were injured and some killed on both sides of the protest before order was restored after a few days by the deployment of several thousand troops from the People's Armed Police. Arrests were made of those suspected of engaging in or encouraging violence. At the end of April, thirty of the detained were quickly tried and given sentences ranging from three years to life in prison.

There was an outpouring of international criticism of China's brutal suppression of the protesters, which proved something of an embarrassment for the PRC coming just a few months before the start of the Beijing Olympics. China blamed the Dalai Lama for inciting the riots and justified its actions as necessary for restoring and maintaining order. To defuse the situation, the Chinese government announced that it was willing to resume talks with representatives of the Dalai Lama's government-in-exile. But the two sides are far from any substantive agreement, and tensions between Tibetans and the Chinese in Tibet remain high and potentially explosive.

There are about 20 million Muslims in China. They live in many parts of the country and belong to several different ethnic minority groups. The highest concentration of Muslims is in the far west of China in the Ningxia Hui and Xinjiang Uyghur autonomous regions. The latter borders the Islamic nations of Afghanistan and Pakistan and the Central Asian states of the former Soviet Union.

The more secular Hui are well assimilated into Han Chinese society. But there is growing unrest among Uyghurs in Xinjiang. The Chinese government has clashed with Uyghur militants who want to create a separate Islamic state of "East Turkestan" and have sometimes used violence, including bombings and assassinations, to press their cause. The PRC became an eager ally of the United States in the post–September 11 war on terrorism in part because China could then justify its crackdown on the Xinjiang-based East Turkestan Islamic Movement (ETIM). Washington has included this group on its list of organizations connected to Al Qaeda.

China's minority population is relatively small and geographically isolated. Ethnic unrest has been limited, sporadic, and easily quelled. Therefore, the PRC has not had the kind of intense, identity-based conflict experienced by countries with more pervasive religious and ethnic cleavages, such as India and Nigeria. But it is possible that domestic and global forces will make ethnic identity a more visible and volatile issue in Chinese politics.

Interest Groups, Social Control, and Citizen Protest

The formal structures of the Chinese political system are designed more to extend party-state control of political life than to facilitate citizen participation in politics. Therefore, people make extensive use of their personal connections (*guanxi*) based on kinship, friendship, and other ties to help ease their contacts with the bureaucrats and party officials who wield such enormous power over so many aspects of their lives.

Patron-client politics is pervasive at the local level, particularly in rural China, as it is in many other developing countries where ordinary people have little access to the official channels of power. For example, a village leader (the patron) may help farmers (the clients) avoid paying some taxes by reporting false production statistics in exchange for their support to keep him in office. Such clientelism can be an important way for local communities to resist state policies that they see as harmful to their interests.

A widely used and rather unique way of pursuing interests in China—particularly by individuals or small groups—is through petitioning the authorities. The roots of this practice go back to imperial times when any subject of the realm could make a request or pursue a grievance through a petition to the emperor or his civil servants. Each year in China today, tens of millions of petitions are filed at specially designated state-administered bureaus that cover complaints such as illegal land seizures, police abuse, corruption, and shoddy government facilities. For many poor people, especially from the rural areas, this is the only way they can pursue justice. There are laws and regulations both specifying petition procedures and guaranteeing the rights of petitioners. But abuse of petitioners is fairly common, especially by local officials against whom complaints are being lodged.

Truly independent interest groups and social movements are not permitted to influence the political process in any significant way. The CCP supports several official "mass organizations" as a means to provide a way for interest groups to express their views on policy matters—within strict limits. All such organizations state in their charters that they are under the leadership of the Communist Party.

Total membership of mass organizations in China reaches the hundreds of millions. Two of the most important are the All-China Women's Federation, the only national organization representing the interests of women in general, and the All-China Federation of Trade Unions (ACFTU), to which about 90 million Chinese workers belong. Although neither constitutes an autonomous political voice for the groups it is supposed to represent, the organizations do sometimes act as an effective lobby in promoting the nonpolitical interests of their constituencies. For example, the Women's Federation has become a strong advocate for women on issues ranging from domestic violence to economic rights. The Trade Union Federation has lobbied the government to change the standard workweek from six to five days a week for industrial workers. The ACFTU also represents individual workers with grievances against management, although its first loyalty is to the Chinese communist party-state.

Since the late 1990s, there has been a huge surge in China in the number of **nongovernmental organizations (NGOs)** that are less directly subordinate to the CCP than the official mass organizations. The government has found NGOs to be very useful partners in achieving (and sharing the cost burden of) some of its goals, particularly in the area of social welfare. They are also a useful and nonthreatening way to channel political participation.

There are several hundred thousand national and local NGOs in China—some connected with international organizations, like Save the Children—that are concerned with a wide range of issues. For example, some deal with the environment (China Green Earth Volunteers), health (the China Foundation for the Prevention of STDs and AIDS), charitable work (China Children and Teenagers Fund), and legal issues (the Beijing Center for Women's Law Services). An NGO is supposed to register with the local authorities and have an official government agency as its sponsor, often referred to as its "mother-in-law." NGOs have considerable latitude to operate within their functional areas without direct party interference *if* they steer clear of politics and do not challenge official policies.

Although the various representative bodies and other citizen organizations discussed in this section remain subordinate to the CCP, they should not be dismissed as inconsequential in China's political system. They do "provide important access points between the Party and the organized masses, which allow the voicing of special interests in ways that do not threaten Party hegemony and yet pressure the shaping of policy."[22]

Mechanisms of Social Control

While China has certainly loosened up politically since the days of Mao Zedong, the party-state's control mechanisms still penetrate to the basic levels of society and serve the CCP's aim of preventing the formation of groups or movements that might defy its authority. In the rural areas, the small-scale, closely knit nature of the village facilitates control by the local party and security organizations. The household registration system (or *hukou*), established in the 1950s, was, for many decades, the principal instrument for keeping tabs on and controlling the movement of China's huge rural population. Every family was required to have a residence permit that limited them to living and working in a specific location. Enforcement was carried out—often very vigorously—by local public security bureaus. The *hukou* system certainly restricted freedom of movement, but it was also one reason why China did not have the kind of urban squatter settlements that housed poor rural migrants to many cities in the Third World. The advent of the market reforms in the early 1980s and the resulting wave of still technically illegal rural-to-urban labor migration led to a *de facto* breakdown of the *hukou* system. In 2007, the government of the PRC acknowledged the incompatibility of the household registration system and the market economy and undertook the first steps toward major changes in the nature and function of residency permits.

For most of the history of the People's Republic, the work unit (or ***danwei***) system was the party-state's means of social control in urban china. At the height of the *danwei* system's influence, almost all urban adults belonged to a work unit that was the center of their economic, social, and political lives. Work units were the source not only of a person's salary, but also of housing, health care, and other benefits. The *danwei* would hold mandatory meetings to discuss the official line on important policies or events, and its personnel department kept employment and political dossiers on every person who worked in that unit. The work unit monitored the government's strict population control policy, and a woman had to have her *danwei*'s permission to have a child. If a person changed jobs, which often could be done only with the *danwei*'s approval, the dossier moved too. In these and other ways, the unit acted as a check on political dissent and social deviance. The *danwei* system is still in effect, particularly in economic, educational, and other organizations with official government ties, but its influence in people's daily lives is greatly diminished.

The structure of urban government has also served as an important instrument of social control since the Mao era. Every city in China is made up of districts; Shanghai, for example, has nineteen districts. Each district has under its jurisdiction a number of "street offices," each covering 100 to 1,000 or more households, depending on the size of the city; street offices are, in turn, divided into even smaller residents committees. These organizations effectively extend the unofficial reach of the party-state down to the most basic level of urban society. In many cities, a new form of urban organization, called the "community" (or *shequ*) is being encouraged by local officials to incorporate many of the functions of both the *danwei* and residents committee systems. Residents committees used to be staffed mostly by appointed retired persons (often elderly women), but now, as the basic function of urban grassroots organizations shifts from surveillance to service, such as sanitation or employment agencies, many *shequ* are led by younger and better-educated residents, and in some places committee members are elected by their neighbors.

Government control mechanisms are weakening as Chinese society continues to change under the impact of economic reform and globalization. The growth of private enterprise, increasing labor and residential mobility, and new forms of association (such as discos and coffeehouses) and communication (for example, cell phones, e-mail, fax machines) are just some of the factors that are making it much harder for the party-state to monitor citizens as closely as it has in the past.

Protest and the Party-State

The Tiananmen massacre of 1989 showed the limits of protest in China. The party leadership was particularly alarmed at signs that a number of independent student and grassroots worker organizations were emerging from the demonstrations. The brutal suppression of the democracy movement was meant to send a clear signal that neither open political protest nor the formation of autonomous interest groups would be tolerated.

There have been few large-scale political demonstrations in China since 1989. Prodemocracy groups have been driven deep underground or abroad. Known dissidents are continuously watched, harassed, imprisoned, or expelled from the country, sometimes as a conciliatory diplomatic gesture.

Repression has by no means put an end to all forms of citizen protest in the PRC. Ethnic protests occur sporadically on China's periphery. The biggest and most continuous demonstrations against the party-state in recent years have been carried out by the Falun Gong (literally, "Dharma Wheel Practice"). Falun Gong (FLG) is a spiritual movement that combines philosophical and religious elements drawn from Buddhism and Taoism with traditional Chinese physical exercises (similar to *tai chi*) and meditation. It was founded in the early 1990s by Li Hongzhi, a one-time low-level PRC government employee now living in the United States. The movement claims

70 million members in China and 30 million in more than seventy other countries: these numbers may be exaggerated, but there is no doubt that the FLG has an enormous following. Its promise of inner tranquility and good health has proven very appealing to a wide cross section of people in China as a reaction to some of the side effects of rapid modernization, including crass commercialism, economic insecurity, and the rising crime rate.

The Chinese authorities, reacting to the movement's growing popularity, began a crackdown on Falun Gong in 1999. Ten thousand FLG followers responded that April by holding a peaceful protest outside the gates of Zhongnanhai, the walled compound in the center of Beijing where China's top leaders live and work. The government then outlawed Falun Gong and deemed it an "evil cult" that spread lies, fooled people to the point that they rejected urgently needed medical care, encouraged suicide, and generally threatened social stability. It is not only the movement's size that alarms the Chinese party-state but also its ability to communicate with and mobilize its members and spread its message through both electronic means and by word of mouth.

The intense suppression of Falun Gong has included the destruction of related books and tapes, jamming of websites, and the arrest of thousands of practitioners, many of whom, the movement claims, have been not only jailed but also beaten (sometimes to death) and sent to psychiatric hospitals or labor camps. There have been a few small demonstrations by FLG followers in recent years, including one in Tiananmen Square in January 2001 that involved self-immolation by five believers. But, by and large, the crackdown seems to have been successful, or, at least, Falun Gong has decided not to overtly challenge the party-state for the time being.

Labor unrest is becoming more frequent, with reports of thousands of strikes and other actions in recent years. Workers have carried out big demonstrations at state-owned factories to protest the ending of the iron rice bowl system, layoffs, the nonpayment of pensions or severance packages, and the arrest of grassroots labor leaders. Workers at some foreign-owned enterprises have gone on strike against unsafe working conditions or low wages. Most of these actions have remained limited in scope and duration, so the government has usually not cracked down on the protesters. On occasion, it has actually pressured employers to meet the workers' demands.

In 2007, the Chinese government implemented a new, sweeping labor law, which was largely designed to enhance workers' rights and protection against dangerous working environments and other abuses that are widespread in China's industries. The law requires that employers, even foreign companies, give workers written contracts and regulates the use of temporary laborers. Workers cannot be fired without due process. Some observers see this as an effort to stem the tide of labor unrest. Others see it also as part of Hu Jintao's political platform to create a "harmonious socialist society."

The countryside has also seen a rising tide of protest. In the poorer regions—especially in central China—farmers have attacked local officials and rioted over corruption, exorbitant taxes and extralegal fees, and the government's failure to pay on time for agricultural products it has purchased. Protests in many parts of the country have attacked illegal land seizures by greedy local officials working in cahoots with developers who want to build factories, expensive housing, or even golf courses. The land reform law proposed in 2008 (see Section 2) is designed in part to prevent this kind of corruption by regulating all land transfers, although it remains to be seen how effective its implementation is.

These protests have not spread beyond the locales where they started and have focused on farmers' immediate material concerns, not on grand-scale issues like democracy. They have usually been contained by the authorities through a combination of coercion and concessions to some of the farmers' demands.

Grassroots protests in both the countryside and cities most often target corrupt local officials or unresponsive employers, not the Communist Party. By responding positively to farmer and worker concerns, the party-state can win support and turn what could be regime-threatening activities into regime-sustaining ones.

The overall political situation in China remains rather contradictory. Although people are much freer than they have been in decades and most visitors find Chinese society quite open, repression can still be intense. Public political dissent is almost nonexistent.

But there are many signs that the Chinese Communist Party is losing or giving up some of its ability to control the movements and associations of its citizens and can no longer easily limit access to information and ideas from abroad. Some forms of protest also appear to be increasing and may come to pose a serious challenge to the authority of the party-state.

Political Challenges and Changing Agendas

Scenes from the Chinese Countryside[23]

China has become a lot more modern and urban in recent years. But it is still largely a rural country with a majority of its people living in the countryside. However, depending on where you look in its vast rural areas, you will see a very different China. Take, for example, the following:

Huaxi, Jiangsu Province.   This village, often called China's richest, looks much like an American suburb: spacious roads lined with two-story townhouses, potted plants on doorsteps, green lawns, and luscious shade trees. Homes are air-conditioned with leather living room furniture, studies with computers, and exercise rooms. Every family has at least one car. Things were not always so prosperous in Huaxi. In the early 1980s, most villagers were farmers living in tiny houses and hoping to save enough money to buy a bicycle. Now the residents are entrepreneurs and investors, and have an annual per capita income of nearly $10,000 per year—about 25 times the rural average—plus dividends. This remarkable transformation began about two decades ago when the Maoist communes were dissolved and replaced with household-based farming. Guided by a savvy village leader, enough funds were accumulated to allow the establishment of a few small industries, and over the years these have expanded into an array of fifty-eight different enterprises, many of which are now staffed by migrants from poorer rural areas.

Nanliang, Shaanxi Province.   This village is located in one of the areas known as China's Third World, where persistent poverty rather than growing prosperity is still the common lot in life. The country's economic boom isn't felt here. Per capita income is less than $75 a year. There are no townhouses: Most families live in one-room, mud-brick houses with no running water or electricity; these living quarters are often shared with pigs or other farm animals. One muddy waterhole is used for bathing—by both people and livestock. The village is miles from the nearest paved road. The children, dressed in grimy clothes and ragged cloth shoes, are not starving, but they do not seem to be flourishing either. Education, professional health care, and other social services are minimal or nonexistent. There is no industry, and the poor-quality land barely supports those who work it. Many of the men have made their way to distant cities hoping to find work as migrant laborers. The money they send back is vital to the survival of most families.

Beihe, Shandong Province.   This may be a typical Chinese village, nowhere near as wealthy as Huaxi nor as poor as Nanliang. Per capita income is about $600 per year. Most people work in small, privately owned factories. Many residents have built new, if modest, brick houses, and most have mobile phones and own consumer electronics. There's a local primary school, which all the children attend; quite a few of those go on to attend (at least) the junior high school in a nearby town. Health care is also available in the town, but only at a private clinic; most villagers can't pay the fees and none have insurance. The local enterprises are struggling to survive fierce market competition, and some have gone bankrupt. Many hope to revive village fortunes by leasing out land to expanding businesses in the area.

Zhushan, Hunan Province.   A couple of years ago, an estimated 20,000 villagers descended on the rural town of Zhushan in central China to protest their mounting grievances against the local government.

The protest was sparked by a sharp increase in the price of bus tickets, combined with the demonstrators' perception that corrupt officials were in cahoots with the private entrepreneur who had taken over management of the bus company in order to squeeze more money from the area's residents. Many residents depend on bus transportation almost daily to get to work or, for students, to school. The demonstrators clashed with the more than 1,000 riot police, who were armed with guns and electric cattle prods. The bus station was set on fire, and police cars were burned by the protesters. There were reportedly many injuries and arrests, and at least one death. The disturbance lasted several days and was quelled only when provincial-level officials agreed to rescind the fare increase and look into charges of corruption.

Beiwang, Hebei Province. This was one of the first villages in China to establish a representative assembly and hold democratic elections for local officials. Among the earliest decisions made by the assembly was to reassign the contracts for tending the village's 3,000 pear trees. After the rural communes were disbanded in the 1980s, each of the 500 or so families in the village was given six trees to look after under the new household responsibility system. The assembly, however, decided that it would be better to reassign the trees to a very small number of families who would care for them in a more efficient and productive manner. The village Communist Party branch refused to approve the decision on the grounds that it would enrich just a few people and cause a decline in general public welfare. Nevertheless, assembly representatives were able to generate strong support in the village for their proposal, and the party branch agreed under pressure to recontract the trees to just eleven households. In a short time, pear production zoomed. The new system proved to be economically beneficial not only to the families who looked after the trees but also to the village as a whole because of the local government's share of the increased profits.

These scenes reflect the enormous diversity of the Chinese countryside: prosperity and poverty, mass protests and peaceful politics. It is worth remembering that more than half of China's population—about 700 million people—still live in the rural parts of the country. What happens in the rural towns and villages will have a tremendous impact on China's political and economic future.

The actions of Beiwang's village representative assembly remind us that not all politics rises to national or international significance. The question of who looks after the village pear trees may matter more than what happens in the inner sanctums of the Communist Party or U.S.–China presidential summit meetings. The victory of the Beiwang representatives and elected officials on the pear tree issue shows that even in a one-party state, the people sometimes prevail against those with power, and democracy works on the local level—as long as the basic principle of party leadership is not challenged.

The Huaxi scene shows the astonishing improvement in living standards in much of rural China. But huge pockets of severe poverty, like that in Nanliang, still persist, especially in inland regions far removed from the more prosperous coastal regions. Most of rural China falls between the extremes. And it is in these in-between areas, such as Beihe and Zhushan, where the combination of new hopes brought about by economic progress and the tensions caused by blatant corruption, stagnating incomes, and other frustrations may prove to be politically explosive.

Economic Management, Social Tension, and Political Legitimacy

The situation in the Chinese countryside illustrates a larger challenge facing the leaders of the PRC: how to sustain and effectively manage the economic growth that is the basis of public support for the ruling Communist Party. The CCP is gambling that continued solid economic performance will literally buy it legitimacy and that most citizens will care little about democracy or national politics if their material lives continue to get better. So far this gamble seems to have paid off.

But failure to keep inequality under control, especially between city and countryside, or failure to continue providing opportunities for advancement for the less well-off could lead to social instability and become a liability for a political party that still espouses socialist goals. One of the government's most formidable tasks will be to create enough jobs not only for the millions of workers laid off by the closure or restructuring of state-owned enterprises, but also for the 24 million or so new entrants to the labor force each year.

China's Communist Party leaders will also have to decide how to further nurture the private sector; this is the most dynamic part of the socialist market economy, yet the government bureaucracy still puts daunting obstacles in the way of business owners and investors. The decentralization of economic decision-making has been beneficial to China's development, but it has also fostered a kind of regional protectionism and local bossism that threaten the political control of the central authorities and their ability to govern the economy. Corruption affects the lives of most people more directly than political repression does, and has become so blatant and widespread that it is probably the single most corrosive force eating away at the legitimacy of the Chinese Communist Party.

The public health system is in shambles, with AIDS and other infectious diseases spreading rapidly. China also has a rapidly "graying" population, that is, the percentage of elderly people in the population is growing. The country lacks any kind of adequate pension or social security system to meet the needs of its senior citizens. As mentioned before, these kinds of problems are the target of CCP leader and PRC President Hu Jintao's emphasis on building a "harmonious socialist society." It remains to be seen whether the Chinese government is able to translate this ideal into action.

According to a detailed statistical study by the World Bank, the governance—"the traditions and institutions by which authority in a country is exercised for the common good"—of China actually deteriorated somewhat over the decade between 1996 and 2006.[24] While the PRC fares considerably better in this study than most countries at its level of economic development (lower middle income), there were declines in China's "overall government effectiveness," "regulatory quality," "control of corruption," and "political stability." These categories bear directly on the party-state's ability to manage China's rapidly modernizing economy and radically changing society and portray some of the most important challenges facing the country's leadership.

China and the Democratic Idea

The two other World Bank governance indicators—"voice and accountability" and "rule of law"—reflect an effort to measure issues that are central to the democratic idea in particular countries. In these, too, the World Bank study concludes, China has slipped a bit.

The PRC has evolved in recent decades toward a system of what has been called "Market-Leninism,"[25] a combination of increasing economic openness (a market economy) and continuing political rigidity under the leadership of a Leninist ruling party that adheres to a remodeled version of communist ideology. The major political tests now facing the CCP and the country emerge from the sharpening contradictions and tensions of this hybrid system.

However, as the people of China become more secure economically, better educated, and more aware of the outside world, they will also likely become more politically active. The steadily expanding middle class and private business owners may want political clout to match their wealth. Scholars, scientists, and technology specialists may become more outspoken about the limits on intellectual freedom. The many Chinese who travel or study abroad may find the political gap between their party-state and the world's democracies to be increasingly intolerable.

There are reasons to be both optimistic and pessimistic about the future of the democratic idea in China.[26] On the negative side, China's long history of bureaucratic and authoritarian rule and the hierarchical values of still-influential Confucian culture seem to be heavy counterweights to democracy. And, although some aspects of its social control have broken down, the coercive power of China's communist party-state remains formidable. The PRC's relatively low per capita standard of living, large rural population and vast areas of extreme poverty, and state-dominated media and means of communications also impose some impediments to democratization. Finally, many in China are apathetic about politics or fearful of the violence and chaos that radical political change might unleash. They are quite happy with the status quo of economic growth and overall political stability of the country under the CCP.

On the positive side, the impressive success of democratization in Taiwan in the past decade, including free and fair multiparty elections from the local level up to the presidency, strongly suggests that the values, institutions, and process of democracy are not incompatible with Confucian culture. And though it is still a developing country, China has a higher literacy rate, more extensive industrialization and urbanization, a faster rate of economic growth, and a larger middle class than most countries at its level of economic development—conditions widely seen by social scientists as favorable to democracy.

Despite the CCP's continuing tight hold on power, there have been a number of significant political changes in China that could be harbingers of democracy: the enhanced political and economic power of local governments; the setting of a mandatory retirement age and term limits for all officials; the rise of younger, better educated, and more worldly leaders; the increasingly important role of the National People's Congress in the policy-making process; the introduction of competitive elections in rural villages; the strengthening and partial depoliticization of the legal system; tolerance of a much wider range of artistic, cultural, and religious expression; and the important freedom (unheard of in the Mao era) for individuals to be apolitical.

Furthermore, the astounding spread of the democratic idea around the globe has created a trend that will be increasingly difficult for China's leaders to resist. The PRC has become a major player in the world of states, and its government must be more responsive to international opinion in order to continue the country's deepening integration with the international economy and growing stature as a responsible and mature global power.

One of the most important political trends in China has been the resurgence of **civil society**, a sphere of independent public life and citizen association, which, if allowed to thrive and expand, could provide fertile soil for future democratization. The development of civil society among workers in Poland and intellectuals in Czechoslovakia, for example, played an important role in the collapse of communism in East-Central Europe in the late 1980s by weakening the critical underpinnings of party-state control.

The Tiananmen demonstrations of 1989 reflected the stirrings of civil society in post–Mao China. But the brutal crushing of that movement showed the CCP's determination to thwart its growth before it could seriously contest the party's authority. But as economic modernization and social liberalization have deepened in the PRC, civil society has begun to stir again. Some stirrings, like the Falun Gong movement, have met with vicious repression by the party-state. But others, such as the proliferation and growing influence of nongovernmental organizations, have been encouraged by the authorities. Academic journals and conferences have recently had surprisingly open, if tentative, discussions about future political options for China, including multiparty democracy.

At some point, the leaders of the CCP will face the fundamental dilemma of whether to accommodate or, as they have done so often in the past, suppress organizations, individuals, and ideas that question the principle of party leadership. Accommodation would require the party-state to cede some of its control over society and allow more meaningful citizen representation and participation. But repression would likely derail the country's economic dynamism and could have terrible costs for China.

Chinese Politics in Comparative Perspective

As mentioned at the end of Section 1, students of comparative politics should find it particularly interesting to compare China with other nations from two perspectives. First, the People's Republic of China can be compared with other communist party-states with which it shares or has shared many political characteristics. Second, China can be compared with other developing nations that face similar economic and political situations.

China as a Communist Party-State

Why has the Chinese communist party-state been more durable than other regimes of its type? The PRC's successful economic restructuring and the rapidly rising living standard of most of the people have saved the CCP from the kinds of economic crises that greatly weakened other communist systems, including the Soviet Union. China's leaders believe that one of the biggest mistakes made by the last Soviet party chief, Mikhail Gorbachev, was that he went too far with political reform and not far enough with economic change, and they are convinced that their reverse formula is a key reason that they have not suffered the same fate.

The fact that the Chinese Communists won power through an indigenous revolution with widespread popular backing and did not depend on foreign military support for their victory also sets China apart from the situation of most of the now-deposed East-Central European communist parties. Despite some very serious mistakes over the six decades of its rule in China, the CCP still has a deep reservoir of historical legitimacy among large segments of the population.

But China also has much in common with other communist party-states, including some of the basic features of a totalitarian political system. **Totalitarianism** (a term also applied to fascist regimes such as Nazi Germany) describes a system in which the ruling party prohibits all forms of meaningful political opposition and dissent, insists on obedience to a single state-determined ideology, and enforces its rule through coercion and terror. Such regimes also seek to bring all spheres of public activity (including the economy and culture) and even many parts of its citizens' private lives (including reproduction) under the total control of the party-state in the effort to modernize the country and, indeed, to transform human nature.

China is much less totalitarian than it was during the Maoist era. In fact, the CCP appears to be trying to save communist rule in China by moderating or abandoning many of its totalitarian features. To promote economic development, the CCP has relaxed its grip on many areas of life. Citizens can now pursue their interests without interference by the party-state as long as they avoid sensitive political issues.

The PRC has evolved from totalitarianism toward a less intrusive but still basically dictatorial political system that has been characterized as a "consultative authoritarian regime" that "increasingly recognizes the need to obtain information, advice, and support from key sectors of the population, but insists on suppressing dissent . . . and maintaining ultimate political power in the hands of the Party."[27] China seems, at least for the moment, to be going through a type of post–totalitarian transition characterized by bold economic and social reform that may, in time, nurture

a transition to democracy, but that so far has helped sustain the dictatorial political system.

China as a Third World State

The record of communist rule in China raises many issues about the role of the state in economic development. It also provides an interesting comparative perspective on the complex relationship between economic and political change in the Third World.

When the Chinese Communist Party came to power in 1949, China was a desperately poor country, with an economy devastated by a century of civil strife and world war. It was also in a weak and subordinate position in the post–World War II international order. Measured against this starting point, the PRC has made remarkable progress in improving the wellbeing of its citizens, building a strong state, and enhancing the country's global role.

Why has China been more successful than so many other nations in meeting some of major dilemmas of development? Third World states have often served narrow class or foreign interests more than the national interest. Many political leaders in Africa, Asia, and Latin America have been a drain on development rather than a stimulus. The result is that Third World governments have often become defenders of a status quo built on extensive inequality and poverty rather than agents of needed change; these are often referred to as predatory states. In contrast, the PRC's recent rulers have been quite successful in creating what social scientists call a **developmental state**, in which government power and public policy are used effectively to promote national economic growth.

Whereas much of the Third World seems to be heading toward democracy without development—or at best very slow development—China is following the reverse course of very fast development without democracy. There is a sharp and disturbing contrast between the harsh political rule of the Chinese communist party-state and its remarkable accomplishments in improving the material lives of the Chinese people. This contrast is at the heart of what one journalist has called the "riddle of China" today, where the government "fights leprosy as aggressively as it attacks dissent. It inoculates infants with the same fervor with which it arrests its critics. Partly as a result, a baby born in Shanghai now has a longer life expectancy than a baby born in New York City."[28] This "riddle" makes it difficult to settle on a clear evaluation of the overall record of communist rule in China, particularly in the post–Mao era. It also makes it hard to predict the future of the Chinese Communist Party, since the regime's economic achievements could provide it with the support, or at least compliance, it needs to stay in power despite its serious political shortcomings.

The CCP's tough stance on political reform is in large part based on its desire for self-preservation. But in keeping firm control on political life while allowing the country to open up in other important ways, Chinese Communist Party leaders also believe they are wisely following the model of development pioneered by the newly industrializing countries (NICs) of East Asia such as South Korea, Taiwan, and Singapore.

The lesson that the CCP draws from the NIC experience is that only a strong "neoauthoritarian" government can provide the political stability and social peace required for rapid economic growth. According to this view, democracy—with its open debates about national priorities, political parties contesting for power, and interest groups squabbling over how to divide the economic pie—is a recipe for chaos, particularly in a huge and still relatively poor country.

But another of the lessons from the East Asian NICs—one that most Chinese leaders have been reluctant to acknowledge so far—is that economic development, social modernization, and global integration also create powerful pressures for political change from below and abroad. In both Taiwan and South Korea, authoritarian governments that had presided over economic miracles in the 1960s and 1970s gave way in the 1980s and 1990s to democracy, largely in response to domestic demands. China's leaders look approvingly on the Singapore model of development with its long-lasting combination of "soft authoritarianism" and highly developed modern economy—even if that city-state has a population about 300 times smaller and an area 1/14,000th the size of the PRC.

China's dynamic economic expansion and social transformation over the last thirty years suggest that the PRC is in the early to middle stages of a period of growth and modernization that will lead it to NIC status. However, in terms of the extent of industrialization, per capita income, the strength of the private sector of the economy, and the size of the middle and professional classes, China's development is still far below the level at which democracy succeeded in Taiwan and South Korea. Before concluding that China's communist rulers will soon yield to the forces of modernization, it is important to point out that "authoritarian governments in East Asia pursued market-driven economic growth for decades without relaxing their hold on political power."[29]

Economic reform in China has already created groups and processes, interests and ideas that are likely to evolve as sources of pressure for more and faster political change. And the experiences of many developing countries suggest that such pressures will intensify as the economy and society continue to modernize. Therefore, at some point in the not-too-distant future, the Chinese Communist Party may again face the challenge of the democratic idea. How China's new generation of leaders responds to this challenge is perhaps the most important and uncertain question about Chinese politics in the early decades of the twenty-first century.

Key Terms ≫

communist-party state
Marxism-Leninism
autonomous regions
guerrilla warfare
newly industrializing country (NIC)
authoritarian
collectivization
socialism

Hundred Flowers Movement
Anti-Rightist Campaign
Great Leap Forward
communism
Great Proletarian Cultural Revolution
coup d'etat
technocrats
purchasing power parity

state socialism

command economy

socialist market economy

household responsibility system

township and village enterprises (TVEs)

iron rice bowl

guanxi

sustainable development

martial law

cadres

nomenklatura

socialist democracy

"Four Cardinal Principles"

patron-client politics

nongovernmental organizations (NGOs)

hukou

danwei

civil society

totalitarianism

developmental state

Suggested Readings ≫

Bergsten, Fred, et al., *China The Balance Sheet: What the World Needs to Know Now About the Emerging Superpower.* New York: Public Affairs, 2006.

Blecher, Marc J. *China Against the Tides: Restructuring Through Revolution, Radicalism, and Reform,* 2nd ed., London: Continuum, 2003.

Chang, Jung. *Wild Swans: Three Daughters of China.* New York: Simon & Schuster, 1991.

Cheek, Timothy. *Living with Reform: China Since 1989.* New York: Palgrave McMillan, 2007.

Denoon, David, ed. *China: Contemporary Political, Economic, and International Affairs.* (New York: New York University Press, 2007).

Economy, Elizabeth C. *The River Runs Black: The Environmental Challenge to China's Future.* Ithaca: Cornell University Press, 2004.

Gao Yuan. *Born Red: A Chronicle of the Cultural Revolution.* Stanford, Calif.: Stanford University Press, 1987.

Goldman, Merle. *From Comrade to Citizen: The Struggle for Political Rights in China.* Cambridge, Mass.: Harvard University Press, 2006.

Grasso, June et al., *Modernization and Revolution in China,* 3rd edition. Armonk, N.Y.: M. E. Sharpe, 2004.

Hessler, Peter. *Oracle Bones: A Journey Between China's Past and Present.* New York: Harper Collins, 2006.

Lampton, David M. *Same Bed, Different Dreams: Managing U.S.-China Relations, 1989–2000.* Berkeley: University of California Press, 2001.

McFarquhar, Roderick, and Schoenhals, Michael. *Mao's Last Revolution.* Cambridge, Mass.: Harvard University Press, 2006.

Pomfret, John. *Chinese Lessons: Five Classmates and the Story of the New China.* New York: Henry Holt, 2006.

Spence, Jonathan. *Mao Zedong.* New York: Viking, 1999.

Suggested Websites ≫

China Links, Professor William A. Joseph, Wellesley College
www.wellesley.edu/Polisci/wj/China/chinalinks.html
Embassy of the People's Republic of China in the United States
www.china-embassy.org
Finding News about China
www.chinanews.bfn.org

PRC China Internet Information Center
www.china.org.cn
China Leadership Monitor
http://www.hoover.org/publications/clm

Endnotes ≫

[1] Bryan Walsh, "Beijing Smog Cleanup: Has It Worked?" *Time.com*, August 15, 2008. http://www.time.com/time/health/article/0,8599,1833371,00.html?imw=Y.

[2] Mao Zedong, "Report on an Investigation of the Peasant Movement in Hunan," March 1927, in *Selected Readings from the Works of Mao Tsetung* (Beijing: Foreign Languages Press, 1971), p. 24.

[3] Maurice Meisner, *Mao's China and After: A History of the People's Republic*, 3rd ed. (New York: Free Press, 1999), p. 183.

[4]David Bachman, *Bureaucracy, Economy, and Leadership in China: The Institutional Origins of the Great Leap Forward* (Cambridge: Cambridge University Press, 1991), p. 2.

[5]See, for example, Nicholas D. Kristof and Sheryl WuDunn, *China Wakes: The Struggle for the Soul of a Rising Power* (New York: Time Books, 1994); and James Kynge, *China Shakes the World: A Titan's Rise and Troubled Future—and the Challenge for America* (Boston: Houghton Mifflin, 2006).

[6]"When China Wakes," pp. 3, 15.

[7]Barry Naughton, "The Pattern and Legacy of Economic Growth in the Mao Era," in Kenneth Lieberthal et al., eds., *Perspectives on Modern China: Four Anniversaries* (Armonk, N.Y.: M. E. Sharpe, 1991), p. 250.

[8]Deng Xiaoping first expressed his "cat theory" in 1962 in a speech, "Restore Agricultural Production," in the aftermath of the failure and famine of the Great Leap Forward. In the original speech, he actually quoted an old peasant proverb that refers to a "yellow cat or a black cat," but it is most often rendered "white cat or black cat." See *Selected Works of Deng Xiaoping (1938–1965)* (Beijing: Foreign Languages Press, 1992), p. 293.

[9]D.A. Ralston, et al., "Today's State-Owned Enterprises of China: Are They Dying Dinosaurs or Dynamic Dynamos?" *Strategic Management Journal*, 27 (2006): 825–843.

[10]Minxin Pei, "Corruption Threatens China's Future," *Carnegie Endowment Policy Brief*, No. 55, October 2007.

[11]Emily Honig and Gail Herschatter, *Personal Voices: Chinese Women in the 1980s* (Stanford, Calif.: Stanford University Press, 1988), p. 337.

[12]Jasper Becker, "China's Growing Pains," *National Geographic*, March 2004, p. 81.

[13]Li Cheng, Lynn White, "The Thirteenth Central Committee of the Chinese Communist Party: From Mobilizers to Managers," *Asian Survey*, Vol. 28, No. 4 (Apr., 1988): 371–399; and Kaiser Kuo, "Made in China: The Revenge of the Nerds," *Time.com*, Jun. 27, 2001, http://www.time.com/time/world/article/0,8599,165453,00.html.

[14]Kenneth Lieberthal and David Michael Lampton, eds., *Bureaucracy, Politics, and Decision-Making in Post-Mao China* (Berkeley: University of California Press, 1992).

[15]John P. Burns, *The Chinese Communist Party's Nomenklatura System: A Documentary Study of Party Control of Leadership Selection, 1979–1984* (Armonk, N.Y.: M. E. Sharpe, 1989), pp. ix–x.

[16]Gordon White, *Riding the Tiger: The Politics of Economic Reform in Post-Mao China* (Palo Alto, Calif.: Stanford University Press, 1993), p. 20.

[17] Bruce J. Dickson, *Red Capitalists in China: The Party, Private Entrepreneurs, and Prospects for Political Change* (Cambridge, Cambridge University Press, 2003).

[18]James D. Seymour, *China's Satellite Parties* (Armonk, N.Y.: M. E. Sharpe, 1987), p. 87.

[19]Lin Biao, "Foreword to the Second Edition," *Quotations from Chairman Mao Tse-tung* (Beijing: Foreign Languages Press, 1967), p. iii.

[20]Deng Xiaoping, Uphold The Four Cardinal Principles (excerpts), March 30, 1979.

[21]"Hold high the great banner of socialism with Chinese characteristics and strive for new victories in building a moderately prosperous society in all respects," Report to the Seventeenth National Congress of the Communist Party of China, Oct. 15, 2007; http://www.idcpc.org.cn/english/cpcbrief/17rep.htm.

[22]James R. Townsend and Brantly Womack, *Politics in China*, 3rd ed. (Boston: Little, Brown, 1986), p. 271.

[23]The following scenes are extrapolated from Jonathan Watts, "In China's richest village," *The Guardian*, May 10, 2005; Wang Zhe, "Behind the Dream of a Village," *Beijing Review*, June 14, 2001, 13–16; Lu Xueyi, "The Peasants Are Suffering, the Villages Are Very Poor," *Dushu* (Readings), January 2001, in U.S. Embassy (Beijing, China), PRC Press Clippings; Hannah Beech, "In Rural China, It's a Family Affair" *Time/Asia*, May 27, 2002; "The Silent Majority: A Rare Look inside a Chinese Village," *The Economist*, April 7, 2005; James Reynolds, "Reporting protests in rural China," BBC News, March 16, 2007; Susan V. Lawrence, "Democracy, Chinese-Style: Village Representative Assemblies," *Australian Journal of Chinese Affairs*, no. 32 (July 1994): 61–68.

[24]D. Kaufmann, A. Kraay, and M. Mastruzzi, *Governance Matters 2007: Governance Indicators for 1996–2006* (Washington, D.C.: The World Bank, 2007), http://info.worldbank.org/governance/wgi2007/home.htm.

[25]Nicholas D. Kristof, "China Sees 'Market-Leninism' as Way to Future," *New York Times*, September 6, 1993.

[26]Many of the points in this section are based on Martin King Whyte, "Prospects for Democratization in China," *Problems of Communism* (May–June 1992): 58–69; Michel Oksenberg, "Will China Democratize? Confronting a Classic Dilemma," *Journal of Democracy* 9, no. 1 (January 1998): 27–34; and Minxin Pei, "Is China Democratizing?" *Foreign Affairs* 77, no. 1 (January– February 1998), 68–82.

[27]Harry Harding, *China's Second Revolution: Reform After Mao* (Washington, D.C.: Brookings Institution, 1987), p. 200.

[28]Nicholas D. Kristof, "Riddle of China: Repression as Standard of Living Soars," *New York Times*, September 7, 1993, pp. A1, A10.

[29]Nicholas Lardy, "Is China Different? The Fate of Its Economic Reform," in Daniel Chirot, ed., *The Crisis of Leninism and the Decline of the Left* (Seattle: University of Washington Press, 1991), p. 147.

Glossary »

5 percent rule provision of the German electoral law requiring all parties to win at least 5 percent of the vote to obtain seats for representation.

abertura (Portuguese for "opening"; *apertura* in Spanish) In Brazil, refers to the period of authoritarian liberalization begun in 1974 when the military allowed civilian politicians to compete for political office in the context of a more open political society. See also ***glasnost***.

accommodation an informal agreement or settlement between the government and important interest groups in response to the interest groups' concerns for policy or program benefits.

accountability a government's responsibility to its population, usually by periodic popular elections and by parliament's having the power to dismiss the government by passing a motion of no confidence. In a political system characterized by accountability, the major actions taken by government must be known and understood by the citizenry.

acephalous societies literally "headless" societies. A number of traditional Nigerian societies, such as the Igbo in the precolonial period, lacked executive rulership as we have come to conceive of it. Instead, the villages and clans were governed by committee or consensus.

Administrative Court court that hears cases from private citizens and organizations involving allegations of bureaucratic violations of rules and laws. In Germany, the third branch of the court system, consisting of the Labor Court, the Social Security Court, and the Finance Court. In France, the highest administrative court is the Council of State.

administrative guidance in Japan, informal guidance, usually not based on statute or formal regulation, that is given by a government agency, such as a ministry and its subdivisions, to a private organization, such as a firm, or a lower-level government. The lack of transparency of the practice makes it subject to criticisms as a disguised form of collusion between a government agency and a firm.

---

*Note: Boldface terms *within* a definition can be found as separate entries in the Glossary.

amakudari a Japanese practice, known as "descent from heaven," in which government officials retiring from their administrative positions take jobs in public corporations or private firms with which their own ministry has or recently had close ties.

Amerindians original peoples of North and South America; indigenous people.

ancien régime the monarchical regime that ruled France until the Revolution of 1789, when it was toppled by a popular uprising. The term is used to describe long-established regimes in other countries ruled by undemocratic elites.

anticlericalism opposition to the power of churches or clergy in politics. In some countries, for example, France and Mexico, this opposition has focused on the role of the Catholic Church in politics.

Anti-Rightist Campaign was launched by Chinese Communist Party (CCP) Chairman Mao Zedong in 1957 in the aftermath of the **Hundred Flowers Movement**. The Campaign was aimed at critics of the CCP who were labeled as "rightists," that is, counterrevolutionaries. Millions of people were affected and hundreds of thousands sent to labor reform camps. Many were not released until after Mao's death in 1976.

Articles of Confederation the first governing document of the United States, agreed to in 1777 and ratified in 1781. The Articles concentrated most powers in the states and made the national government largely dependent on voluntary contributions of the states.

Asian Development Bank (ADB) a regional bank established in 1966 to promote economic development in and cooperation among nations in Asia. The bank mediates public and private investments in, and loans for, selected developmental projects. The current members include forty-five nations and areas within the Asian and Pacific region and eighteen outside the region, including the United States.

Asia-Pacific Economic Cooperation (APEC) a regional organization of Asian and Pacific Rim nations established in 1989 to promote cooperation among member states, especially in foreign investment and the standardization and compilation of statistical data. Currently composed of twenty-one members (including the United States and Canada), it advocates "open regionalism," cooperation among nations within the region that neither precludes nor impedes cooperation between them and nations outside the region.

Assembly of Religious Experts (Iran) nominates the **Supreme Leader** and can replace him. The assembly is elected by the general electorate but almost all its members are clerics.

Association of Southeast Asian Nations (ASEAN) an organization formed in 1967 to promote regional economic and political cooperation. As of 2003, ASEAN consisted of ten member states: Brunei, Cambodia, Indonesia, Laos, Malaysia, Myanmar, the Philippines, Singapore, Thailand, and Vietnam.

asymmetrical federalism a system of governance in which political authority is shared between a central government and regional or state governments, but where some subnational units in the federal system have greater or lesser powers than others.

authoritarian see **authoritarianism.**

authoritarianism a system of rule in which power depends not on popular legitimacy but on the coercive force of the political authorities. Hence, there are few personal and group freedoms. It is also characterized by near absolute power in the executive branch and few, if any, legislative and judicial controls. See also **autocracy; partrimonialism.**

autocracy a government in which one or a few rulers has absolute power, thus, a **dictatorship.** Similar to **authoritarianism.**

autonomous region in the People's Republic of China, a territorial unit equivalent to a province that contains a large concentration of ethnic minorities. These regions, for example Tibet, have some autonomy in the cultural sphere but in most policy matters are strictly subordinate to the central government.

ayatollah literally, "sign of God." High-ranking clerics in Iran. The most senior ones—often no more than half a dozen—are known as grand ayatollahs.

balance of payments an indicator of international flow of funds that shows the excess or deficit in total payments of all kinds between or among countries. Included in the calculation are exports and imports, grants, and international debt payments.

Basic Law *(Grundgesetz)* German document establishing the founding of the Federal Republic of Germany (West Germany) in 1949. Similar to a written constitution.

bazaar an urban marketplace where shops, workshops, small businesses, and export–importers are located.

bicameral a legislative body with two houses, such as the U.S. Senate and the U.S. House of Representatives. Just as the U.S. Constitution divides responsibilities between the branches of the federal government and between the federal government and the states, it divides legislative responsibilities between the Senate and the House.

Bill of Rights the first ten amendments to the U.S. Constitution (ratified in 1791), which established limits on the actions of government. Initially, the Bill of Rights limited only the federal government. The Fourteenth Amendment and subsequent judicial rulings extended the provisions of the Bill of Rights to the states.

Brahmin highest caste in the Hindu caste system.

bureaucracy an organization structured hierarchically, in which lower-level officials are charged with administering regulations codified in rules that specify impersonal, objective guidelines for making decisions. In the modern world, many large organizations, especially business firms and political executives, are organized along bureaucratic lines.

bureaucratic authoritarianism (BA) a term developed by Argentine sociologist Guillermo O'Donnell to interpret the common characteristics of military-led authoritarian regimes in Brazil, Argentina, Chile, and Uruguay in the 1960s and 1970s. According to O'Donnell, bureaucratic authoritarian regimes led by the armed forces and key civilian allies emerged in these countries in response to severe economic crises.

bureaucratic rings a term developed by the Brazilian sociologist and president Fernando Henrique Cardoso that refers to the highly permeable and fragmented structure of the state bureaucracy that allows private interests to make alliances with midlevel bureaucratic officers. By shaping public policy to benefit these interests, bureaucrats gain the promise of future employment in the private sector. While in positions of responsibility, bureaucratic rings are ardent defenders of their own interests.

bushi **(samurai)** the warrior class in medieval Japan, also known as samurai. The class emerged around the tenth century A.D., and a dominant band established Japan's first warrior government in the twelfth century. The last warrior government was overthrown in the Meiji Restoration of the mid-nineteenth century.

cabinet government a system of government, as in Britain, in which the cabinet (rather than the prime minister) exercises responsibility for formulating policy and directing both the government and the executive branch. In the UK, cabinet government has been undermined as a check on the power of the prime minister.

cabinet the ministers who direct executive departments. In parliamentary systems, the cabinet and high-ranking sub-cabinet ministers (also known as the government) are considered collectively responsible to parliament.

cadre a person who occupies a position of authority in a **communist party-state;** cadres may or may not be Communist Party members.

caste system India's Hindu society is divided into castes. According to the Hindu religion, membership in a caste is determined at birth. Castes form a rough social and economic hierarchy. See also **Brahmin; untouchables.**

chancellor the German head of government. Functional equivalent of prime minister in other parliamentary systems.

checks and balances a governmental system of divided authority in which coequal branches can restrain each other's actions. For example, the U.S. president must sign legislation passed by Congress for it to become law. If the president vetoes a bill, Congress can override that veto by a two-thirds vote of the Senate and the House of Representatives.

Citizens Action Groups formed in Germany in the 1970s, forerunner of the Green Party.

civil servants state employees who make up the bureaucracy.

civil society refers to the space occupied by voluntary associations outside the state, for example, professional associations (lawyers, doctors, teachers), trade unions, student and women's groups, religious bodies, and other voluntary association groups. The term is similar to *society,* although *civil society* implies a degree of organization absent from the more inclusive term *society.*

clientelism (or patron-client networks) an informal aspect of policy-making in which a powerful patron (for example, a traditional local boss, government agency, or dominant party) offers resources such as land, contracts, protection, or jobs in return for the support and services (such as labor or votes) of lower-status and less powerful clients; corruption, preferential treatment, and inequality are characteristic of clientelist politics. See also **patrimonialism; prebendalism.**

co-determination German legal mechanism that authorizes trade union members in firms with 2,000 or more employees to have nearly 50 percent of the seats on the firm's board of directors.

cohabitation the term used by the French to describe the situation in the Fifth Republic when a president and prime minister belong to opposing political coalitions.

cold war the hostile relations that prevailed between the United States and the USSR from the late 1940s until the demise of the Soviet Union in 1991. Although an actual (hot) war never directly occurred between the two superpowers, they clashed indirectly by supporting rival forces in many wars occurring in the Third World.

collective identities the groups with which people identify, including gender, class, race, region, and religion, and which are the "building blocks" for social and political action. Any given individual has a variety of identities, for example, a Muslim woman who is a member of the Kurdish ethnic group of northern Iraq. There is enormous variation regarding which collective identities are uppermost for particular individuals, which ones are influential within particular countries, and how effectively political systems process conflicts among collective identities. This question is among the most important issues studied in comparative politics.

collectivization a process undertaken in the Soviet Union under Stalin in the late 1920s and early 1930s and in China under Mao in the 1950s, by which agricultural land was removed from private ownership and organized into large state and collective farms.

command economy a form of **socialist** economic organization in which government decisions ("commands") rather than market mechanisms (such as supply and demand) are the major influences in determining the nation's economic direction; also called central planning.

communism a system of social organization based on the common ownership and coordination of production. According to Marxism (the theory of German philosopher Karl Marx, 1818–1883), communism is a culminating stage of history, following capitalism and **socialism.** In historical practice, leaders of China, the Soviet Union, and other states that have proclaimed themselves seeking to achieve communism have ruled through a single party, the Communist Party, which has controlled the state and society in an authoritarian manner, and have applied **Marxism-Leninism** to justify their rule.

communist party-state a type of nation-state in which the communist party attempts to exercise a complete monopoly on political power and controls all important state institutions. See also **communism.**

comparative politics the study of the domestic politics, political institutions, and conflicts of countries. Often involves comparisons among countries and through time within single countries, emphasizing key patterns of similarity and difference.

comparativists   political scientists who study the similarities and differences in the domestic politics of various countries. See also **comparative politics.**

conservative   the belief that existing political, social, and economic arrangements should be preserved. Historically, this has involved a defense of the inequalities (of class, race, gender, and so on) that are part of the existing order; often used to identify the economic and social policies favored by right-of-center parties.

consolidated democracies   political systems that have been solidly and stably democratic for an ample period of time and in which there is relatively consistent adherence to core democratic principles.

constitutional monarchy   a system of government in which the head of state ascends by heredity, but is limited in powers and constrained by the provisions of a constitution.

constructive vote of no confidence   provision in the German political system of requiring any opposition party or group of parties to have an alternative majority government that would replace the current one. This provision was placed into the Basic Law in 1949 to avoid the Weimar practice of voting governments out of office and producing numerous political crises.

corporatism (state corporatism)   a system of interest representation in which the constituent units are organized into a limited number of singular, compulsory, noncompetitive, hierarchically ordered and functionally differentiated categories, recognized or licensed (if not created) by the state and granted a deliberate representational monopoly within their respective categories in exchange for observing certain controls in their selection of leaders and articulation of demands and supports.

corporatist state   a state in which **interest groups** become an institutionalized part of the structure. See also **corporatism; democratic corporatism; state corporatism.**

Corruption Perceptions Index   a measure developed by Transparency International that "ranks countries in terms of the degree to which corruption is perceived to exist among public officials and politicians. It is a composite index, drawing on corruption-related data in expert surveys carried out by a variety of reputable institutions. It reflects the views of businesspeople and analysts from around the world, including experts who are locals in the countries evaluated." Range: 10 (highly clean) to 0 (highly corrupt). See *http://www.transparency.org.*

country   a territorial unit controlled by a single state. Countries vary in the degree to which groups within them have a common culture and ethnic affiliation. See also **nation-state; state.**

coup d'état   a forceful, extra-constitutional action resulting in the removal of an existing government.

critical juncture   an important historical moment when political actors make critical choices, which shape institutions and future outcomes.

danwei   a Chinese term that means "unit" and is the basic level of social organization and a major means of political control in China's **communist party-state.** A person's *danwei* is most often his or her workplace, such as a factory or an office. The *danwei* is has faded in importance as China moves toward a market economy.

decentralization   policies that aim to transfer some decision-making power from higher to lower levels of government, typically from the central government to subnational governments.

Declaration of Independence   the document asserting the independence of the British colonies in what is now the United States from Great Britain. The Declaration of Independence was signed in Philadelphia on July 4, 1776.

democratic centralism   a system of political organization developed by V. I. Lenin and practiced, with modifications, by all communist party-states. Its principles include a hierarchal party structure in which (1) party leaders are elected on a delegate basis from lower to higher party bodies; (2) party leaders can be recalled by those who elected them; and (3) freedom of discussion is permitted until a decision is taken, but strict discipline and unity should prevail in implementing a decision once it is made. In practice, in all Communist parties in China, the Soviet Union, and elsewhere, centralizing elements tended to predominate over the democratic ones.

democratic corporatism   a set of institutions or forums that bring representatives from employers, trade unions, and government together to negotiate issues affecting workplaces, industry structure, and national economic policy.

democratic transition   the process of a state moving from an authoritarian to a democratic political system.

demokratizatsiia   the policy of democratization identified by former Soviet leader Mikhail Gorbachev in 1987 as an essential component of *perestroika*. The policy was part of a gradual shift away from a **vanguard party** approach toward an acceptance of **liberal** democratic norms. Initially, the policy embraced multicandidate elections and a broadening of political competition within the Communist Party itself; after 1989, it involved acceptance of a multi-party system.

deregulation the process of dismantling state regulations that govern social and economic life. Deregulation increases the power of private actors, especially business firms.

developmental state a **nation-state** in which the government carries out policies that effectively promote national economic growth.

developmentalism an ideology and practice in Latin America during the 1950s in which the state played a leading role in seeking to foster economic development through sponsoring vigorous **industrial policy.** See also **import substitution industrialization.**

dictatorship see **authoritarianism; autocracy; totalitarianism.**

dirigisme a French term denoting that the state plays a leading role in supervising the economy. In contrast to **socialism** or communism, firms remain privately owned under a system of *dirigisme.* At the other extreme, *dirigisme* differs from the situation where the state has a relatively small role in economic governance.

distributional politics political conflicts involving the distribution of valued resources among competing groups.

distributive policies policies that allocate state resources into an area that lawmakers perceive needs to be promoted. For example, leaders today believe that students should have access to the Internet. In order to accomplish this goal, telephone users are being taxed to provide money for schools to establish connections to the Internet (which, in large part, uses telephone lines to transfer data).

Domei the Japanese Confederation of Labor founded in 1964 through the merger of several federations of rightwing labor unions opposed to the leftist labor organization *Sohyo.* Dominated by private sector unions and closely allied with the Democratic Socialist Party, *Domei* advocated harmonious management-labor relations and a corporatist relationship with the government. *Domei* was disbanded in 1987 when all its affiliated unions joined *Rengo* at its founding.

dual society a society and economy that are sharply divided into a traditional, usually poorer, and a modern, usually richer, sector.

Economic Community of West African States (ECOWAS) the organization established in 1975 among the sixteen governments in West Africa. Its goals are to strengthen and broaden the economies in the region through the removal of trade barriers among its members (such as import quotas and domestic content laws), freedom of movement for citizens, and monetary cooperation.

economic liberalization the dismantling of government controls on the economy.

ejidatario recipient of an *ejido* land grant in Mexico.

ejido land granted by Mexican government to an organized group of peasants.

Emergency (1975–1977) the period when Indian Prime Minister Indira Gandhi suspended many formal democratic rights and ruled in an **authoritarian** manner.

emir traditional Islamic ruler. The emir presides over an "emirate," or kingdom, in northern Nigeria.

Environmental Performance Index a measure of how close countries come to meeting specific benchmarks for national pollution control and natural resource management. See *http://www.yale.edu/epi.*

ethnic cleansing concerted political violence akin to genocide applied to a minority population in a country or region, usually to force its expulsion or mass destruction.

European Union (EU) an organization of European countries created in 1958 to promote economic integration and political cooperation among European states. At first, the EU's mandate was primarily to reduce tariff barriers among West European states. Since then, more countries throughout Europe have joined the EU, and its powers have vastly expanded to include promoting common policies on immigration, technical standards, and economic and monetary regulation.

executive the agencies of government that implement or execute policy. The highest level of the executive in most countries is a president or prime minister and cabinet. The top executive officeholders supervise the work of administrative departments and bureaus.

Expediency Council a committee set up in Iran to resolve differences between the *Majles* and the Guardian Council.

export-led growth economic growth generated by the export of a country's commodities. Export-led growth can occur at an early stage of economic development, in which case it involves primary products, such as the country's mineral resources, timber, and agricultural products; or at a later stage, when industrial goods and services are exported.

Farsi Persian word for the Persian language. Fars is a province in Central Iran.

favelas in Brazil, huge shantytowns of homes made out of cardboard, wood from dumps, and blocks of mortar and brick. These shantytowns create rings of extreme poverty around cities like Rio de Janeiro and São Paulo. Similar shantytowns can be found in other Latin American cities, although terms to describe them vary by country. In Peru, for example, these shantytowns are called *barriadas*.

Federal Reserve Board   the U.S. central bank established by Congress in 1913 to regulate the banking industry and the money supply. Although the president appoints the chair of the board of governors (with Senate approval), the board operates largely independently. Many criticize its policies as reflecting the needs of banks and international capital over the needs of citizens, particularly workers.

federal system (state)   nation-state with subnational units (states or provinces) that have significant independent political powers. A federal system differs from a unitary state that has few autonomous regional political institutions. See also **federalism.**

federalism   a system of governance in which political authority is shared between the national government and regional or state governments. The powers of each level of government are usually specified in a federal constitution.

foreign direct investment   ownership of or investment in cross-border enterprises in which the investor plays a direct managerial role.

Foundation of the Oppressed   a clerically controlled foundation in Iran set up after the revolution there.

"Four Cardinal Principles"   ideas first enunciated by Chinese leader Deng Xiaoping in 1979 asserting that all policies should be judged by whether they uphold the socialist road, the dictatorship of the proletariat, the leadership of the Communist Party, and Marxism-Leninism–Mao Zedong Thought. The main purpose of the Four Cardinal Principles was to proscribe any challenge to the ultimate authority of the Chinese Communist Party, even during a time of far-reaching economic reform. The Principles have been reaffirmed by Deng's successors and continue to define the boundaries of what is politically permissible in China.

framework regulations   German style of regulation in which the general patterns of public policy are outlined, but specific details of policy are left to policymakers' discretion as long as they remain within the general framework.

free market   a system in which government regulation of the economy is absent or limited. Relative to other advanced democracies, the United States has traditionally had a freer market economically. See **laissez-faire.**

free trade   international commerce that is relatively unregulated or constrained by tariffs (special payments imposed by governments on exports or imports).

Freedom in the World rating   an annual evaluation by the nongovernmental organization (NGO) Freedom House that identifies the level of freedom in countries around the world, measured according to political rights and civil liberties through "a multi-layered process of analysis and evaluation by a team of regional experts and scholars." Countries are ranked in .5 gradations between 1.0 and 7.0, with 1.0–2.5 being "free"; 3.0–5.0, "partly free"; and 5.5–7.0, "not free."

fundamentalism   a term recently popularized to describe radical religious movements throughout the world.

fusion of powers   a constitutional principle that merges the authority of branches of government, in contrast to the principle of **separation of powers.** In Britain, for example, Parliament is the supreme legislative, executive, and judicial authority. The fusion of legislature and executive is also expressed in the function and personnel of the cabinet.

Gastarbeiter **(guest workers)**   a program instituted by the German government in the early 1960s that brought workers from southern Europe into Germany to address a labor shortage.

gender gap   politically significant differences in social attitudes and voting behavior between men and women.

genocide   the intentional and coordinated attempt to destroy a people, defined in national, religious, racial or ethnic terms.

glasnost   Gorbachev's policy of "openness" or "publicity," which involved an easing of controls on the media, arts, and public discussion, leading to an outburst of public debate and criticism covering most aspects of Soviet history, culture, and policy.

Global Gender Gap   a measure of "the extent to which women in 58 countries have achieved equality with men in five critical areas: economic participation, economic opportunity, political empowerment, educational attainment, and health and well-being." See *www.weforum.org.*

globalization   the intensification of worldwide interconnectedness associated with the increased speed and magnitude of cross-border flows of trade, investment, and finance, and processes of migration, cultural diffusion, and communication.

grandes écoles   prestigious and highly selective schools of higher education in France that train top civil servants, engineers, and business executives.

grands corps   elite bureaucratic networks of graduates of selective training schools in France.

grass-roots democracy   term used to describe activist, local political action, and community control. Used frequently by the Green Party in Germany and many social movements elsewhere.

Great Leap Forward a movement launched by Mao Zedong in 1958 to industrialize China very rapidly and thereby propel it toward **communism**. The Leap ended in economic disaster in 1960, causing one of the worst famines in human history.

Great Proletarian Cultural Revolution the political campaign launched in 1966 by Chairman Mao Zedong to stop what he saw as China's drift away from socialism and toward capitalism. The campaign led to massive purges in the Chinese Communist Party, the widespread persecution of China's intellectuals, extensive political violence, and the destruction of invaluable cultural objects. The Cultural Revolution officially ended in 1976 after Mao's death and the arrest of some of his most radical followers.

green revolution a strategy for increasing agricultural (especially food) production, involving improved seeds, irrigation, and abundant use of fertilizers.

gross domestic product (GDP) the total of all goods and services produced within a country; it is used as a broad measure of the size of its economy.

gross national product (GNP) see **gross national income.**

guanxi a Chinese term that means "connections" or "relationships," and describes personal ties between individuals based on such things as common birthplace or mutual acquaintances. *Guanxi* are an important factor in China's political and economic life.

Guardian Council a committee created in the Iranian constitution to oversee the *Majles* (the parliament).

guerrilla warfare a military strategy based on small, highly mobile bands of soldiers (the guerrillas, from the Spanish word for war, *guerra*) who use hit-and-run tactics like ambushes to attack a better-armed enemy.

health insurance funds a semipublic system in Germany that brings all major health interests together to allocate costs and benefits by way of consultation and group participation.

hegemonic power a state that can control the pattern of alliances and terms of the international order, and often shapes domestic political developments in countries throughout the world.

Hezbollahis literally "partisans of God." In Iran, the term is used to describe religious vigilantes. In Lebanon, it is used to describe the Shi'i militia.

hojjat al-Islam literally, "the proof of Islam." In Iran, it means a medium-ranking cleric.

household responsibility system the system put into practice in China beginning in the early 1980s in which the major decisions about agricultural production are made by individual farm families based on the profit motive rather than by a **people's commune** or the government.

Hukou a Chinese term that means "household residency permit" and refers to the system in which all citizens of the People's Republic of China must have an official card that allows them to live, work, and receive benefits only in a specific location. The *hukou* system was used as a means of social control, political surveillance, and internal migration restrictions. The *hukou* system has not been vigorously enforced since China has moved toward a market economy and the need for labor mobility.

Human Development Index a composite number used by the United Nations to measure and compare levels of achievement in health, knowledge, and standard of living. HDI is based on the following indicators: life expectancy, adult literacy rate and school enrollment statistics, and **gross domestic product** per capita at **purchasing power parity.**

Hundred Flowers Movement refers to a period in 1956–1957 when Chinese Communist Party Chairman Mao Zedong encouraged citizens, particularly intellectuals, to speak out ("Let a hundred flowers bloom, let a hundred schools of thought contend!") and give their views on how to improve China's government. Mao was shocked by the depth of the criticism of communist rule and cracked down by silencing and punishing the critics by launching the **Anti-Rightist Campaign** of 1957.

ideology a set of fundamental ideas, values, or beliefs about how a political, economic, or social system should be organized. Examples of ideology include **capitalism, communism,** and **socialism.**

Imam Jum'ehs prayer leaders in Iran's main urban mosques. Appointed by the **Supreme Leader,** they have considerable authority in the provinces.

import substituting industrialization (ISI) strategy for industrialization based on domestic manufacture of previously imported goods to satisfy domestic market demands. See also **developmentalism.**

Indian Administrative Service (IAS) India's civil service, a highly professional and talented group of administrators who run the Indian government on a day-to-day basis.

indicative planning a term used to describe the development of a national economic plan that indicates what the plan specifies as desirable priorities for economic development. Indicative planning can be distinguished from plans developed under **command economies.**

indigenous groups   population of **Amerindian** heritage in Mexico.

indirect rule   a term used to describe the British style of colonialism in Nigeria and India in which local traditional rulers and political structures were used to help support the colonial governing structure.

industrial policy   a generic term to refer to a variety of policies designed to shape leading sectors of the economy and enhance competitiveness, especially for industries that are considered strategic to national interests. Countries differ substantially regarding the degree to which their states consciously pursue industrial policies.

informal sector (economy)   that portion of the economy largely outside government control in which employees work without contracts or benefits. Examples include casual employees in restaurants and hotels, street vendors, and day laborers in construction or agriculture.

insider privatization   a term used in relation to Russia to refer to the transformation of formerly state-owned enterprises into **joint-stock companies** or private enterprises in which majority control of the enterprise is in the hands of employees and/or managers of that enterprise.

institutional design   the institutional arrangements that define the relationships between executive, legislative, and judicial branches of government and between the central government and sub-central units such as states in the United States.

interest groups   organizations that seek to represent the interests—usually economic—of their members in dealings with the government. Important examples are associations representing people with specific occupations, business interests, racial and ethnic groups, or age groups in society.

international financial institutions (IFIs)   generally refers to the International Bank for Reconstruction and Development (the World Bank) and the International Monetary Fund (IMF), but can also include other international lending institutions. See also **structural adjustment program (SAP).**

International Monetary Fund (IMF)   is the "sister organization" of the World Bank and also has more than 180 member states. It describes its mandate as "working to foster global monetary cooperation, secure financial stability, facilitate international trade, promote high employment and sustainable economic growth, and reduce poverty." It has been particularly active in helping countries that are experiencing serious financial problems. In exchange for IMF financial or technical assistance, a country must agree to a certain set of conditions that promote **economic liberalization**. See **Structural Adjustment Program** and **World Bank**.

interventionist   an interventionist state acts vigorously to shape the performance of major sectors of the economy.

interventores   in Brazil, allies of Getúlio Vargas (1930–1945, 1950–1952) picked by the dictator during his first period of rulership to replace opposition governors in all the Brazilian states except Minas Gerais. The *interventores* represented a shift of power from subnational government to the central state. See also **politics of the governors.**

iron rice bowl   a feature of China's socialist economy during the Maoist era (1949–1976) that provided guarantees of lifetime employment, income, and basic cradle-to-grave benefits to most urban and rural workers. Economic reforms beginning in the 1980s that aimed at improving efficiency and work motivation sought to smash the iron rice bowl and link employment and income more directly to individual effort.

iron triangles   a term coined by students of American politics to refer to the relationships of mutual support formed by particular government agencies, members of congressional committees or subcommittees, and interest groups in various policy areas. Synonymous with "cozy triangles," the term has been borrowed by some students of Japanese politics to refer to similar relationships found among Japanese ministry or agency officials, *Diet* (parliament) members, and special interest groups.

jihad   literally "struggle." Although often used to mean armed struggle against unbelievers, it can also mean spiritual struggle for self-improvement.

joint-stock company   a business firm whose capital is divided into shares that can be held by individuals, groups of individuals, or governmental units. In Russia, formation of joint-stock companies has been the primary method for privatizing large state enterprises.

judicial review   the prerogative of a high court (such as the U.S. Supreme Court) to nullify actions by the executive and legislative branches of government that in its judgment violate the constitution.

judiciary   one of the primary political institutions in a country; responsible for the administration of justice and in some countries for determining the constitutionality of state decisions.

Junkers reactionary land-owing elite in nineteenth-century Prussia. Major supporters of Bismarck's unification of Germany in 1871.

jurist's guardianship Khomeini's concept that the Iranian clergy should rule on the grounds that they are the divinely appointed guardians of both the law and the people. He developed this concept in the 1970s.

keiretsu a group of closely allied Japanese firms that have preferential trading relationships and often interlocked directorates and stock-sharing arrangements. The relationships among *keiretsu* member firms have been regarded as collusive and harmful to free trade by some of Japan's principal trading partners.

Keynesianism named after the British economist John Maynard Keynes, an approach to economic policy in which state economic policies are used to regulate the economy in an attempt to achieve stable economic growth. During recession, state budget deficits are used to expand demand in an effort to boost both consumption and investment, and to create employment. During periods of high growth when inflation threatens, cuts in government spending and a tightening of credit are used to reduce demand.

koenkai usually translated as "support association," *koenkai* is a Japanese campaign organization for a particular candidate, consisting mainly of the candidate's relatives, friends, fellow alumni, coworkers, and their acquaintances. For most conservative politicians, especially LDP members of the *Diet* and local legislatures, networks of *koenkai* organizations are far more important and effective than political parties in assisting politicians' election campaigns. Since it costs politicians a great deal of money to maintain these networks, *koenkai*-centered elections encourage corruption.

Kulturkampf "cultural struggle" initiated by Bismarck's Imperial government between Protestant and Catholic forces in late-nineteenth-century Germany.

laissez-faire the term taken from the French, which means, "to let do," in other words, to allow to act freely. In political economy, it refers to the pattern in which state management is limited to such matters as enforcing contracts and protecting property rights, while private market forces are free to operate with only minimal state regulation. See also **free market.**

law-based state a state where the rule of law prevails, so that actions of the government as well of nongovernmental actors are subject to the requirements of the law. The creation of a law-based state in the Soviet Union was one of the explicit goals of Gorbachev's reform process, thus limiting the ability of state agencies or the Communist Party of the Soviet Union arbitrarily to circumvent laws or legal provisions.

"Lay Judge System" (*saibanin-seido*) the quasi-jury system for major criminal cases that will be introduced into Japan's judicial system in May 2009. Guilt or innocence of the accused—and, if convicted, the sentence—will be determined by a judicial panel composed of three professional judges and six laypersons.

Leader Also known in the West as the Supreme Leader. He is the chief cleric who as "guide" heads the Islamic Republic.

legislature one of the primary political institutions in a country, in which elected members are charged with responsibility for making laws and usually providing for the financial resources for the state to carry out its functions.

legitimacy a belief by powerful groups and the broad citizenry that a state exercises rightful authority. In the contemporary world, a state is said to possess legitimacy when it enjoys consent of the governed, which usually involves democratic procedures and the attempt to achieve a satisfactory level of development and equitable distribution of resources.

liberal classically liberal in the nineteenth-century European sense, favoring free-market solutions to economic problems and extensive personal freedoms for individuals.

liberal democracy a political system that combines capitalist organization of the economy with a democratic political system.

lifetime employment the practice common among Japanese government agencies and large business firms to keep newly hired high school and university graduates on payroll until they reach mandatory retirement age. It is in decline in contemporary Japan, where both the general population and work force are rapidly "graying" and the ratios of temporary and part-time employees are rising.

Lok Sabha the lower house of parliament in India where all major legislation must pass before becoming law.

macroeconomic policy government policy intended to shape the overall economic system at the national level by concentrating on policy targets such as inflation or growth.

mafia a term borrowed from Italy and widely used in Russia to describe networks of organized criminal activity that pervade both economic and governmental securities in that country as well as activities such as the demanding of protection money, bribe-taking by government officials, contract killing, and extortion.

Maharajas   India's traditional rulers—monarchs—who retained their positions during the colonial period but were removed from power when the Indian republic was established.

Majles   Arabic term for "assembly"; used in Iran to describe the parliament.

manifest destiny   the public philosophy in the nineteenth century that the United States was not only entitled but also destined to occupy territory from the Atlantic to the Pacific.

maquiladoras   factories that produce goods for export, often located along the U.S.–Mexican border.

Marbury **v.** *Madison*   the 1803 U.S. Supreme Court ruling that the federal courts inherently had the authority to review the constitutionality of laws passed by Congress and signed by the president. The ruling, initially used sparingly, placed the courts centrally in the system of checks and balances.

market reform   a strategy of economic transformation embraced by the Yeltsin government in Russia and the Deng Xiaoping government in China that involves reducing the role of the state in managing the economy and increasing the role of market forces. In Russia, market reform is part of the transition to postcommunism and includes the extensive transfer of the ownership of economic assets from the state to private hands. In China, market reform has been carried out under the leadership of the Chinese Communist Party and involves less extensive privatization.

martial law   a period of time during which the normal procedures of government are suspended and the executive branch enforces the law with military power.

Marxism-Leninism   the theoretical foundation of communism based on the ideas of the German philosopher, Karl Marx (1818–1883), and the leader of the Russian Revolution, V. I. Lenin (1870–1924). Marxism is, in essence, a theory of historical development that emphasizes the struggle between exploiting and exploited classes, particularly the struggle between the bourgeoisie (capitalists) and the proletariat (the industrial working class). Leninism emphasizes the strategy and organization to be used by the communist party to overthrow capitalism and seize power as a first step on the road to communism.

maslahat   Arabic term for "expediency," "prudence," or "advisability." It is now used in Iran to refer to reasons of state or what is best for the Islamic Republic.

mestizo   a person of mixed white, indigenous (Amerindian), and sometimes African descent.

middle-level theory   seeks to explain phenomena in a limited range of cases, in particular, a specific set of countries with particular characteristics, such as parliamentary regimes, or a particular type of political institution (such as political parties) or activity (such as protest).

Minamata disease   organic mercury poisoning caused by eating contaminated river fish and clams, which produces paralysis of limbs and speech impairment. Occurred in Japan in the 1950s and 1960s as a result of industrial firms' discharge of toxic wastes. The disease is regarded as one of the most tragic examples of the widespread industrial pollution that characterized postwar Japanese society at the height of its dramatic economic growth.

Mixed Member Proportional (MMP)   an electoral system that combines (mixes) the proportional features of a party list proportional representation system with the local representation features of a single-member plurality system. Under this mixed system, each voter casts one vote for a party list and another for an individual candidate in a single-member electoral district.

moderating power (*poder moderador*)   a term used in Brazilian politics to refer to the situation following the 1824 constitution in which the monarchy was supposed to act as a moderating power, among the executive, legislative, and judicial branches of government, arbitrating party conflicts, and fulfilling governmental responsibilities when nonroyal agents failed.

monetarism   an approach to economic policy that assumes a natural rate of unemployment determined by the labor market, emphasizes setting targets for the rate of growth of the monetary supply, gives highest priority to controlling inflation, and rejects the instrument of government spending to run budgetary deficits for stimulating the economy.

mosque   Muslim place of worship, equivalent to a church, temple, or synagogue.

most different case analysis   the logic of most different case analysis is that, by comparing cases that differ widely, one seeks to isolate a factor or factors (termed the independent variable or variables) that both cases share—despite their sharp differences in other respects—that might explain an outcome (or dependent variable).

nationalism   an ideology seeking to create a **nation-state** for a particular community; a group identity associated with membership is such a political community. Nationalists often proclaim that their state and nation are superior to others.

nationalization the policy by which the **state** assumes ownership and operation of private companies.

nation-state distinct, politically defined territory in which the state and national identity coincide. See also **country**.

Nazi abbreviation for Adolf Hitler's National Socialist German Worker's Party.

neoliberal see **neoliberalism**.

neoliberalism a term used to describe government policies aiming to reduce state regulation and promote competition among business firms within the market. Neoliberal policies include **monetarism**, **privatization**, reducing trade barriers, balancing government budgets, and reducing social spending.

New State *(Estado Novo)* in Brazil, an authoritarian government led by Getúlio Vargas in 1937 that legitimized its rule through state corporatism, massive public sector investment through **para-statals**, and paternalistic social policies.

newly industrialized countries (NICs) a term used to describe a group of countries that achieved rapid **economic development** beginning in the 1960s, largely stimulated by robust international trade (particularly exports) and guided by government policies. The core NICs are usually considered to be Taiwan, South Korea, Hong Kong, and Singapore, but other countries, including Argentina, Brazil, Malaysia, Mexico, and Thailand, are often included in this category.

nomenklatura a system of personnel selection under which the Communist Party maintained control over the appointment of important officials in all spheres of social, economic, and political life. The term is also used to describe individuals chosen through this system and thus refers more broadly to the privileged circles in the Soviet Union and China.

nongovernmental organization (NGO) a private group that seeks to influence public policy and deal with certain problems that it believes are not being adequately addressed by governments, such as Amnesty International (human rights), Oxfam (famine relief), and Greenpeace (the environment).

nontariff barriers (NTBs) policies—such as quotas, health and safety standards, packaging and labeling rules, and unique or unusual business practices—designed to prevent foreign imports in order to protect domestic industries. A form of protectionism that does not use formal tariffs.

North American Free Trade Agreement (NAFTA) a treaty among the United States, Mexico, and Canada implemented on January 1, 1994, that largely eliminates trade barriers among the three nations and establishes procedures to resolve trade disputes. NAFTA serves as a model for an eventual Free Trade Area of the Americas zone that could include most nations in the Western Hemisphere.

oligarchs a small group of powerful and wealthy individuals who gained ownership and control of important sectors of Russia's economy in the context of the privatization of state assets in the 1990s.

oligarchy narrowly based, undemocratic government, often by traditional elites. See also **autocracy; authoritarianism.**

OPEC Organization of Petroleum Exporting Countries. Founded in 1960 by Iran, Venezuela, and Saudi Arabia, it now includes most oil-exporting states with the notable exceptions of Mexico and former members of the Soviet Union. It tries to regulate prices by regulating production.

other backward classes the middle or intermediary castes in India that have been accorded reserved seats in public education and employment since the early 1990s.

overlapping responsibilities (policy) refers to the unique pattern of German federalism in which federal and state governments share administrative responsibility for implementation of public policies.

panchayats in India, elected bodies at the village, district, and state levels that have development and administrative responsibilities.

para-statals state-owned, or at least state-controlled, corporations, created to undertake a broad range of activities, from control and marketing of agricultural production to provision of banking services, operating airlines, and other transportation facilities and public utilities. See also **interventionist.**

parity law a French law passed in 2000 that directs political parties to nominate an equal number of men and women for most elections.

parliamentary democracy system of government in which the chief executive is answerable to the legislature and may be dismissed by it. Parliamentary democracy stands in contrast to a presidential system, in which the chief executive is elected in a national ballot and is independent of the legislative branch.

parliamentary sovereignty a constitutional principle of government (principally in Britain) by which the legislature reserves the power to make or overturn any law without recourse by the executive, the judiciary, or the monarchy. Only Parliament can nullify or overturn legislation approved by Parliament; and Parliament can force the cabinet or the government to resign by voting a motion of no confidence.

party democracy   a term used to describe the strong role that German political parties are allowed to play in the Federal Republic. Unlike the U.S. Constitution where parties are not mentioned, the Basic Law explicitly enables political parties to play a crucial linking role between citizen and state.

pasdaran   Persian term for guards, used to refer to the army of Revolutionary Guards formed during Iran's Islamic Revolution.

path dependence   a concept used initially by economists and now by political scientists to analyze the manner in which previous institutional structures and conditions constrain and influence opportunities for change; path dependence does not, however, imply determinism, since contingent events and human agency can, within limits, also influence outcomes.

patrimonial state   See **patrimonialism.**

patrimonialism (or **neopatrimonialism**)   a system of governance in which a single ruler treats the state as personal property (patrimony). Appointments to public office are made on the basis of unswerving loyalty to the ruler. In turn, state officials exercise wide authority in other domains, such as the economy, often for their personal benefit and that of the ruler, to the detriment of the general population. See also **authoritarianism; autocracy; prebendalism.**

patron-client networks   See **patron-client relation** and **clientelism.**

patron-client politics   See **clientelism.**

patron-client relation (clientelism)   an informal aspect of policy-making in which a powerful patron (for example, a traditional local boss, government agency, or dominant party) offers resources such as land, contracts, protection, or jobs in return for the support and services (such as labor or votes) of lower-status and less powerful clients; corruption, preferential treatment, and inequality are characteristic of clientelist politics. See also **patrimonialism; prebendalism.**

People of the Book   the Muslim term for recognized religious minorities, such as Christians, Jews, and Zoroastrians.

perestroika   the policy of restructuring embarked on by Gorbachev when he became head of the Communist Party of the Soviet Union in 1985. Initially, the policy emphasized decentralization of economic decision-making, increased enterprise autonomy, expanded public discussion of policy issues, and a reduction in the international isolation of the Soviet economy. Over time, restructuring took on a more

political tone, including a commitment to *glasnost* and *demokratizatsiia*.

personalist politicians   demagogic political leaders who use their personal charisma to mobilize their constituency.

personalized proportional representation   German voters cast two votes on each ballot: the first for an individual candidate and the second for a list of national and regional candidates grouped by party affiliation. This system has the effect of personalizing list voting because voters have their own representative but also can choose among several parties.

police powers   powers that are traditionally held by the states to regulate public safety and welfare. Police powers are the form of interaction with government that citizens most often experience. Even with the growth in federal government powers in the twentieth century, police powers remain the primary responsibility of the states and localities.

political action committee (PAC)   a narrow form of interest group that seeks to influence policy by making contributions to candidates and parties in U.S. politics.

political culture   the attitudes, beliefs, and symbols that influence political behavior; often defined in terms of specific national political-cultural orientations.

political economy   the study of the interaction between the state and the economy, that is, how the state and political processes affect the organization of production and exchange (the economy) and how the organization of the economy affects political processes.

politics of the governors   in Brazil, refers to periods of history in which state governors acquire extraordinary powers over domains of policy that were previously claimed by the federal government. The term refers most commonly to the Old Republic and the current state of Brazilian federalism. See also **federalism.**

populism   gaining the support of popular sectors. When used in Latin American politics, this support is often achieved by manipulation and demagogic appeals.

pork-barrel politics   a term originally used by students of American politics to refer to legislation that benefits particular legislators by funding public works and projects in their districts. More broadly, the term refers to preferential allocation of public benefits or resources to particular districts or regions so as to give electoral advantage to particular politicians or political parties.

power vertical   a term used by Vladimir Putin to describe a unified and hierarchical structure of executive power ranging from the federal level to the local level, which can be reinforced by various mechanisms such as appointment of lower officials by higher-level officials and oversight of activities of lower organs by higher ones.

prebendalism patterns of political behavior that rest on the justification that official state offices should be utilized for the personal benefit of officeholders as well as of their support group or clients. Thus, prebendal politics is sustained by the existence of **patron-client networks.** See also **patrimonialism; clientelism.**

predominant-party regime a multiparty political system in which one party maintains a predominant position in parliament and control of government for a long period of time.

prefects French administrators appointed by the minister of the interior to coordinate state agencies and programs within the one hundred French departments or localities. Prefects had enormous power until decentralization reforms in the 1980s transferred some of their responsibilities to elected local governments.

privatization the sale of state-owned enterprises to private companies or investors. Those who support the policy claim that private ownership is superior to government ownership because for-profit entities promote greater efficiency. Privatization is a common central component of **structural adjustment programs** to curtail the losses associated with these enterprises and generate state revenue when they are sold. For Russia, see **spontaneous privatization.**

privatization voucher a certificate worth 10,000 rubles issued by the government to each Russian citizen in 1992 to be used to purchase shares in state enterprises undergoing the process of privatization. Vouchers could also be sold for cash or disposed of through newly created investment funds.

property taxes taxes levied by local governments on the assessed value of property. Property taxes are the primary way in which local jurisdictions in the United States pay for the costs of primary and secondary education. Because the value of property varies dramatically from neighborhood to neighborhood, the funding available for schools—and the quality of education—also varies from place to place.

proportional representation (PR) a system of political representation in which seats are allocated to parties within multimember constituencies, roughly in proportion to the votes each party receives. PR usually encourages the election to parliament of more political parties than single-member-district winner-take-all systems.

purchasing power parity (PPP) a method of calculating the value of a country's money based on the cost of actually buying certain goods and services in that country in the local currency, rather than calculating how many U.S. dollars they are worth. PPP is widely considered to be a more accurate indicator of comparing standards of living, particularly in countries at very different levels of economic development.

quangos acronym for quasi-nongovernmental organizations, the term used in Britain for nonelected bodies that are outside traditional governmental departments or local authorities. They have considerable influence over public policy in areas such as education, health care, and housing.

Qur'an the Muslim Bible.

rational choice theory an approach to analyzing political decision-making and behavior that assumes that individual actors rationally pursue their aims in an effort to achieve the most positive net result. The theory presupposes equilibrium and unitary actors. Rational choice is often associated with the pursuit of selfish goals, but the theory permits a wide range of motivations, including altruism.

Rayja Sabha India's upper house of parliament; considerably less significant politically than the *Lok Sabha.*

redistributive policies policies that take resources from one person or group in society and allocate them to a different, usually more disadvantaged, group. The United States has traditionally opposed redistributive policies to the disadvantaged.

referendum an election in which citizens are asked to approve (or reject) a policy proposal.

regime a term that is generally synonymous with government or political system.

regulations the rules that explain the implementation of laws. When the legislature passes a law, it sets broad principles for implementation, but how the law is actually implemented is determined by regulations written by executive branch agencies. The regulation-writing process allows interested parties to influence the eventual shape of the law in practice.

Rengo the General Confederation of Japanese Labor founded in 1987 under the leadership of private sector unions. The largest labor organization in Japanese history, *Rengo* consists today of 59 industrial federations of labor unions with the combined membership of about 6.6 million.

rentier state a country that obtains much of its revenue from the export of oil or other natural resources.

rents   above-market returns to a factor of production. Pursuit of economic rents (or "rent-seeking") is profit seeking that takes the form of nonproductive economic activity.

republic   in contemporary usage, a political regime in which leaders are not chosen on the basis of their inherited background (as in a monarchy). A republic may, but need not be, democratic. For Russia, a republic is one of twenty territorial units in the Russian Federation that are defined by the constitution of 1993 to be among the eighty-nine members of the federation with a status equal to that of other federal units such as the *oblasts* and *krai.* A republic generally was originally formed in recognition of the presence of a non-Russian national or ethnic group residing in the territory. In the Soviet period, most of these units were called **autonomous republics.**

reservations   jobs or admissions to colleges reserved by the government of India for specific social groups, particularly underprivileged groups.

revolution   The process by which an established political regime is replaced (usually by force) and a new regime established that introduces radical changes throughout society. Revolutions are different from **coups d'état** in that there is widespread popular participation in revolutions, whereas **coups d'état** are led by small groups of elites.

scheduled castes   the lowest caste groups in India; also known as the **untouchables.**

secularism   a doctrine that mandates maintaining a separation between church and state. Secularism requires state neutrality toward religious faiths, and that public policy should not be dictated by the teaching of any particular religion. A cause of conflict in regimes committed to secularism often involves where to draw the boundary between religion and the public sphere.

Self-Defense Forces (SDF)   inaugurated in Japan as a police reserve force with 75,000 recruits in August 1950, following the outbreak of the Korean War. Known as SDF since 1954, it today consists of approximately 250,000 troops equipped with sophisticated modern weapons and weapons systems. The constitutional status and operational mandates of these forces are controversial.

separation of powers   an organization of political institutions within the state in which the executive, legislature, and judiciary have autonomous powers and no one branch dominates the others. This is the common pattern in presidential systems, as opposed to parliamentary systems, in which there is a fusion of powers.

sexenio   the six-year administration of Mexican presidents.

shari'a   Islamic law derived mostly from the **Qur'an** and the examples set by the Prophet Muhammad.

shock therapy   a variant of **market reform** that involves the state simultaneously imposing a wide range of radical economic changes, with the purpose of "shocking" the economy into a new mode of operation. Shock therapy can be contrasted with a more gradual approach to market reform.

Sikhs   an important religious minority in India.

siloviki   derived from the Russian word *sil,* meaning "force." Russian politicians and government officials drawn from security and intelligence agencies (such as the Soviet KGB or its contemporary counterpart, the FSB), special forces, or the military, many of whom were recruited to important political posts under Vladimir Putin.

Single Non-Transferable Vote (SNTV)   a method of voting used in a multimember election district system. Each voter casts only one ballot for a particular candidate and that vote may not be transferred to another candidate even of the same party. As many candidates with the most votes are elected as the number of posts available in each district.

single-member district (SMD)   an electoral district in which only one representative is elected, most commonly by the first-past-the-post method. In a system that uses this method, the candidate who wins the most votes in each district is elected, whether or not he or she wins an absolute majority of the votes.

single-member plurality (SMP) electoral system   an electoral system in which candidates run for a single seat from a specific geographic district. The winner is the person who receives the most votes, whether or not that is a majority. SMP systems, unlike systems of proportional representation, increase the likelihood that two national coalition parties will form.

social class   common membership in a group whose boundaries are based on a common economic location, notably, income and occupational level. Members of the same social class often share similar political attitudes, although other factors, such as gender and ethnicity, may outweigh the political importance of class.

social democrats   democrats who place as much stress on social rights such as access to education, health services, and housing as on individual rights.

social market economy   term describing the German economy that combines an efficient competitive economy with generous welfare state benefits for large segments of the population.

social movements   grass-roots associations that demand reforms of existing social practices and government policies.

Social movements are less formally organized than interest groups.

social security national systems of contributory and non-contributory benefits to provide assistance for the elderly, sick, disabled, unemployed, and others similarly in need of assistance. The specific coverage of social security, a key component of the welfare state, varies by country.

socialism in a socialist regime, the state plays a leading role in organizing the economy, and most business firms are publicly owned. A socialist regime, unlike a **communist party-state,** may allow the private sector to play an important role in the economy and be committed to political pluralism. In **Marxism-Leninism,** socialism refers to an early stage in development of communism. Socialist regimes can be organized in a democratic manner, in that those who control the state may be chosen according to democratic procedures. They may also be governed in an undemocratic manner when a single party, not chosen in free competitive elections, controls the state and society.

socialist democracy the term used by the Chinese Communist Party to describe the political system of the People's Republic of China. Also called the *people's democratic dictatorship*. The official view is that this type of system, under the leadership of the Communist Party, provides democracy for the overwhelming majority of people and suppresses (or exercises dictatorship over) only the enemies of the people. Socialist democracy is contrasted to bourgeois (or capitalist) democracy, which puts power in the hands of the rich and oppresses the poor.

socialist market economy the term used by the government of China to refer to the country's current economic system. It is meant to convey the mix of state control (socialism) and market forces (capitalism) that China is now following in its quest for economic development. The implication is that socialism will promote equality, while the market (especially the profit motive) will encourage people to work hard and foreign companies to invest.

socialist see **socialism.**

Sohyo the General Council of Trade Unions of Japan founded in 1950 by seventeen left-wing industrial unions drawn mainly from the public sector. Throughout the 1950s and 1960s, *Sohyo* was closely allied with the Japan Socialist Party and played a prominent role in a series of campaigns on controversial issues, such as Japanese rearmament and the United States–Japan Mutual Security Treaty. *Sohyo's* influence began to decline in the mid-1970s, and it was absorbed by *Rengo* in 1989.

sovereignty a state's claim to exercise authority and effective political control of political decisions within a given territory

special relationship a term used to describe the close affinity between the United States and the United Kingdom since World War II, based on common language and close geopolitical ties, and dramatized by Blair's decision to "stand shoulder to shoulder" with the United States when a coalition led by the U.S. invaded Iraq in 2003 to topple the regime of Saddam Hussein.

spring labor offensive an annual event in Japan since 1955, the spring labor offensive refers to a series of negotiations between labor unions in major industries and management that take place each spring. The wage increases and changes in working hours and working conditions negotiated in this manner set the standards for management-union negotiations in other industries in the given year.

state capitalism an economic system that is primarily capitalistic but in which there is some degree of government ownership of the means of production.

state capture the ability of firms to systematically turn state regulations to their advantage through payoffs to officials.

state corporatism a political system in which the state requires all members of a particular economic sector to join an officially designated **interest group.** Such interest groups thus attain public status, and they participate in national policymaking. The result is that the state has great control over the groups, and groups have great control over their members. See also **corporatism; corporatist state.**

state formation the historical development of a state, often marked by major stages, key events, or turning points (**critical junctures**) that influence the contemporary character of the state.

state socialism refers to the type of economic system practiced by a **communist party-state,** including the People's Republic of China and the Soviet Union. Under state socialism, the government (or state) owns or controls most economic resources, including land, businesses, farms, factories, and banks.

state technocrats career-minded bureaucrats who administer public policy according to a technical rather than a political rationale. In Mexico and Brazil, these are known as the *técnicos*. For contrasting concepts, see **clientelism; partrimonial state; prebendalism.**

state the state comprises a country's key political institutions that are responsible for making, implementing, and adjudicating important policies in that country. States have also been defined as those institutions within a country that claim the right to control force within the territory comprising the country and to make binding rules (laws), which citizens of that country must obey. See also **civil society.**

state-led economic development   the process of promoting economic development using governmental machinery.

statism   the doctrine that advocates firm **state** direction of the economy and society.

statist   see **statism.**

structural adjustment program (SAP)   medium-term (generally three to five years) programs (which include both action plans and disbursement of funds) established by the World Bank intended to alter and reform the economic structures of highly indebted Third World countries as a condition for receiving international loans. SAPs often involve the necessity for **privatization,** trade liberalization, and fiscal restraint. See also **international financial institutions (IFIs).**

Supreme Commander for the Allied Powers (SCAP)   the official title of General Douglas MacArthur between 1945 and 1951 when he led the Allied Occupation of Japan.

suspensive veto   if the German *Bundesrat* votes against a bill, the *Bundestag* can override the *Bundesrat* by passing the measure again by a simple majority. If, however, a two-thirds majority of the *Bundesrat* votes against a bill, the *Bundestag* must pass it again by a two-thirds margin.

sustainable development   an approach to promoting economic growth that seeks to minimize environmental degradation and depletion of natural resources. Advocates of sustainable development believe that policies implemented in the present must take into account the impact on the ability of future generations to meet their needs and live healthy lives.

tacit social contract   an idea put forth by some Western analysts that an unwritten informal understanding existed between the population and the party-state in the post–Stalinist Soviet Union, which helped form the basis of social and political stability; the implicit agreement involved citizens granting political support for Soviet rule in exchange for benefits such as guaranteed employment, free social services, a lax work environment, and limited interference in personal life.

Taisho democracy   a reference to Japanese politics in the period roughly coinciding with Emperor Taisho's reign, 1912–1926. The period was characterized by the rise of a popular movement for democratization of government by the introduction of universal manhood suffrage and the reduction of the power and influence of authoritarian institutions of the state.

technocrats   career-minded bureaucrats who administer public policy according to a technical rather than a political rationale. In Mexico and Brazil, these are known as the *técnicos.* For contrasting concepts, see **clientelism; patrimonial state; prebendalism.**

theocracy   a state dominated by the clergy, who rule on the grounds that they are the only interpreters of God's will and law.

Third World   refers to countries with a low or relatively low level of **economic development,** particularly as measured by **gross national income** or **gross domestic product** per capita. Synonymous with developing world.

Tokai Village   a seaside community lying about ninety miles northeast of Tokyo that is Japan's major nuclear research center that hosts reprocessing and enrichment plants. It is also known as the site of the two worst nuclear accidents the nation has experienced. Despite these accidents, Japan continues to rely on nuclear energy for about 12 percent of its total energy needs.

totalitarian   see **totalitarianism.**

totalitarianism   a political system in which the state attempts to exercise total control over all aspects of public and private life, including the economy, culture, education, and social organizations, through an integrated system of ideological, economic, and political control. Totalitarian states rely on extensive coercion, including terror, as a means to exercise power. The term has been applied to both **communist party-states** including Stalinist Russia and Maoist China and fascist regimes such as Nazi Germany.

township and village enterprises (TVEs)   nonagricultural businesses and factories owned and run by local governments and private entrepreneurs in China's rural areas. TVEs operate largely according to market forces and outside the state plan.

transitional democracies   countries that have moved from an **authoritarian** government to a democratic one. Also referred to as newly established democracies. In many transitional democracies, as compared with consolidated democracies, there is less full adherence to core democratic principles.

typology   a method of classifying by using criteria that divide a group of cases into smaller numbers. For example, in this book, we use a typology of countries that distinguishes among **consolidated democracies, transitional democracies,** and **authoritarian** regimes.

unfinished state a **state** characterized by instabilities and uncertainties that may render it susceptible to collapse as a coherent entity.

unitary state by contrast to the federal systems of Germany, India, Canada, or the United States, where power is shared between the central government and **state** or regional governments, in a unitary state (such as Britain), no powers are reserved constitutionally for subnational units of government.

United Nations The association of some 200 countries, headquartered in New York, charged with primary responsibility for maintaining international peace and security and advancing the rule of international law and prospects for economic and social development.

untouchables the lowest caste in India's **caste system,** whose members are among the poorest and most disadvantaged Indians.

USA PATRIOT Act legislation passed by the United States Congress in the wake of the September 11, 2001 attacks on New York and Washington. The legislation dramatically expanded the federal government's ability to conduct surveillance, to enforce laws, to limit civil liberties, and to fight terrorism.

vanguard party a political party that claims to operate in the "true" interests of the group or class it purports to represent, even if this understanding doesn't correspond to the expressed interests of the group itself. The Communist parties of the Soviet Union and China are good examples of vanguard parties.

vertically divided administration also known as "sectionalism," the term refers to the extreme autonomy of each Japanese government agency or its subdivision, a situation that seriously interferes with "horizontal" coordination between two or more agencies or their subdivisions.

warrant chiefs employed by the British colonial regime in Nigeria. A system in which "chiefs" were selected by the British to oversee certain legal matters and assist the colonial enterprise in governance and law enforcement in local areas.

welfare state not a form of **state,** but rather a set of public policies designed to provide for citizens' needs through direct or indirect provisions of pensions, health care, unemployment insurance, and assistance to the poor.

Westminster model a form of democracy based on the supreme authority of Parliament and the **accountability** of

its elected representatives; named after the site of the Parliament building in Westminster, a borough of London.

works councils legally mandated workplace organizations that provide collective representation for workers with their employers. Separate organization from the trade unions.

World Bank (officially the International Bank for Reconstruction and Development). The World Bank provides low-interest loans, no-interest credit, policy advice, and technical assistance to developing countries with the goal of reducing poverty. It is made up of more than 180 nations. All members have voting rights within the Bank, but these are weighted according to the size of each country's financial contribution to the organization. Thus, the United States and other highly developed countries have near veto power over the Bank's operations. See **International Monetary Fund.**

World Trade Organization (WTO) a global international organization that oversees the "rules of trade" among its member states. The main functions of the WTO are to serve as a forum for its members to negotiate new agreements and resolve trade disputes. Its fundamental purpose is to lower or remove barriers to free trade, and the WTO can levy stiff penalties against member states that are found to violate its rules. Most of the world's countries belong to the WTO. To join, a country must agree to certain domestic and international economic policies. WTO membership is voluntary, but nations that don't belong are at a great disadvantage in the contemporary global economy.

zaibatsu giant holding companies in pre–World War II Japan, each owned by and under the control of members of a particular family. The largest were divided into a number of independent firms under the democratization program during the postwar occupation but were later revived as *keiretsu,* although no longer under the control of any of the original founding families.

zamindars landlords who served as tax collectors under the British colonial government. The *zamindari* system was abolished after independence.

zoku members of the Japanese *Diet* (parliament) with recognized experience and expertise in particular policy areas such as agriculture, construction, and transportation, and close personal connections with special interests in those areas.

Zollverein 1834 customs union among various preunification German states. Fostered economic cooperation that led to nineteenth-century German unification.

About the Editors and Contributors »

Ervand Abrahamian is Distinguished Professor of History at Baruch College and the Graduate Center of the City University of New York. His recent publications include *Khomeinism: Essays on the Islamic Republic* (University of California Press, 1993) and *Tortured Confessions: Prisons and Public Recantations in Modern Iran* (University of California Press, 1999).

Christopher S. Allen is the Josiah Meigs Distinguished Teaching Professor of International Affairs at the University of Georgia, where he teaches courses in comparative politics and political economy. He is the editor of *The Transformation of the German Political Party System* (Berghahn, 1999 and 2001), coauthor of *European Politics in Transition, 6th edition* (Houghton Mifflin, 2008), and is doing research on two projects: democratic representation in parliamentary and presidential systems; and ideas, institutions, and organized capitalism.

Amrita Basu is the Dominic Paino Professor of Political Science and Women's and Gender Studies at Amherst College. Her main areas of interest are social movements, religious nationalism, and gender politics in South Asia. She is the author of *Two Faces of Protest: Contrasting Modes of Women's Activism in India* (University of California Press, 1992) and several edited books, including *Localizing Knowledge in a Globalizing World, Community Conflicts and the State in India* (with Atul Kohli) (Syracuse University Press, 2002), and *Appropriating Gender: Women's Activism and Politicized Religion in South Asia* (Routledge, 1998).

Joan DeBardeleben is Professor of Political Science and of European and Russian Studies at Carleton University in Ottawa, Ontario. She has published widely on Russian politics, with a focus on Russian federalism, public opinion, and elections. Recent articles have been published in *Europe-Asia Studies, Sotsiologicheskie issledovaniia* (*Sociological Research*), and *Party Politics.* She is a contributing author to *Microeconomic Change in Central and East Europe* (Carol S. Leonard, ed., Palgrave Macmillan, 2002) and *The Struggle for Russian Environmental Policy* (Ilmo Masso and Veli-Pekka Tynkkynen, eds., Kikimora, 2001). Dr. DeBardeleben is also Director of Carleton University's Centre for European Studies.

Louis DeSipio is Associate Professor in the Departments of Political Science and Chicano/Latino Studies at the University of California, Irvine. He is the author of *Counting on the Latino Vote: Latinos as a New Electorate* (University Press of Virginia, 1996) and the coauthor, with Rodolfo O. de la Garza, of *Making Americans/Remaking America: Immigration and Immigrant Policy* (Westview Press, 1998). He is also the author and editor of an eight-volume series on Latino political values, attitudes, and behaviors. The latest volume in this series, *Beyond the Barrio: Latinos and the 2004 Elections*, was published by the University of Notre Dame Press in 2009.

Shigeko N. Fukai is Professor of Political Science in the Faculty of Policy Studies at Nanzan University and Visiting Professor at Chiba University (Japan). She has written a book on a sustainable world order (in Japanese), and articles/chapters on sustainability, Japan's land problems and policy-making, Japan's role in the emerging regional economic order in East Asia, and Japan's electoral and party politics in English and Japanese.

Haruhiro Fukui is Professor Emeritus at the University of California, Santa Barbara, and former director of the Hiroshima Peace Institute. His recent publications include "East Asian Studies, Politics," in Neil J. Smelser and Paul B. Baltes, eds., *International Encyclopedia of the Social and Behavioral Sciences*, Vol. 6 (Elsevier Science, 2001); "Japan: Recasting the Post-War Security Consensus," in Emil Kirchner and James Sperling, eds., *Global Security Governance: Competing Perceptions of Security in the 21st Century* (Routledge, 2007); and "Japan: Why Parties Fail, Yet Survive," in Kay Lawson and Peter H. Merkl, eds., *When Parties Prosper: The Uses of Electoral Success* (Lynn Rienner, 2007).

Merilee S. Grindle is the Edward S. Mason Professor of International Development at the Harvard Kennedy School of Government and the director of the David Rockefeller Center for Latin American Studies, Harvard University. She is a specialist on the comparative analysis of policy-making, implementation, and public management in developing countries and has written extensively on Mexico. Her most recent book is *Going Local: Decentralization, Democratization, and the Promise of Good Governance* (Princeton University Press, 2007).

William A. Joseph is Professor of Political Science at Wellesley College and an Associate of the Fairbank Center for East Asian Research at Harvard University. His research focuses on contemporary Chinese politics and ideology. He is the editor of *China Briefing: The Contradictions of Change* (M.E. Sharpe, 1997), coeditor of *New Perspectives on the Cultural Revolution* (Harvard University Press, 1991), and contributing editor of *The Oxford Companion to Politics of the World* (Oxford University Press, 2nd ed., 2001).

Mark Kesselman is Professor Emeritus of Political Science at Columbia University. A specialist on the French and European political economy, his publications include contributions to *The Mitterrand Era: Policy Alternatives and Political Mobilization in France* (Macmillan, 1995), *Mitterrand's Legacy, Chirac's Challenge* (St. Martin's Press, 1996), and *Diminishing Welfare: A Cross-National Study of Social Provision* (Greenwood, 2002). He is the coauthor of *A Century of Organized Labor in France* (St. Martin's Press, 1997) and *The Politics of Power: A Critical Introduction to American Politics* (Wadsworth,

2005); editor of *Readings in Comparative Politics, 2nd edition* (Wadsworth/Cengage, 2009); and editor of *Politics of Globalization: A Reader* (Houghton Mifflin, 2007).

Darren Kew is Assistant Professor in the Graduate Program in Dispute Resolution at the University of Massachusetts, Boston. He studies the role of civil society in democratic development and conflict prevention in Africa. Professor Kew has written on elections, civil society, and conflict prevention in Nigeria. He has worked with the Council on Foreign Relations' Center for Preventive Action to provide analysis and blueprints for preventing conflicts in numerous areas around the world, including Nigeria, Central Africa, and Kosovo, and he has also observed elections in Nigeria.

Atul Kohli is the David K.E. Bruce Professor of International Affairs and Professor of Politics and International Affairs at Princeton University. His principal research interests are in the areas of comparative political economy with a focus on the developing countries. He is the author of *The State of Poverty in India* (Cambridge University Press, 1989); *Democracy and Discontent: India's Growing Crisis of Governability* (Cambridge University Press, 1990); and *State-Directed Development: Political Power and Industrialization in the Global Periphery* (Cambridge University Press, 2004). He is the editor of six volumes: *The State and Development in the Third World; India's Democracy; State Power and Social Forces; Community Conflicts and the State in India; The Success of India's Democracy;* and *States, Markets, and Just Growth*. His current research analyzes limits of developing country democracies. He is editor of *World Politics*, associate editor of *Perspectives in Politics*, and has been the recipient of grants and fellowships from the Social Science Research Council, Ford Foundation, and Russell Sage Foundation.

Joel Krieger is the Norma Wilentz Hess Professor of Political Science at Wellesley College. His research focuses on British politics and political economy and analysis of the political effects of globalization. His publications include *Globalization and State Power* (Pearson Longman, 2005); *Blair's War*, coauthored with David Coates (Polity Press, 2004); *British Politics in the Global Age: Can Social Democracy*

Survive? (Polity Press, 1999); and *Reagan, Thatcher, and the Politics of Decline* (Oxford University Press, 1986). He is also coeditor of *Readings in Comparative Politics* (Houghton Mifflin, 2006) and editor-in-chief of *The Oxford Companion to Politics of the World* (Oxford University Press, 1993; 2nd ed., 2001).

Peter Lewis is Associate Professor at the School of International Service, American University. He has written extensively on Nigerian political economy, as well as on broader regional issues of participation, democratic transition, and economic adjustment in Africa. He is currently working on a study of the comparative political economies of Indonesia and Nigeria.

Alfred P. Montero is Associate Professor of Political Science at Carleton College. His research focuses on the political economy of decentralization and comparative federalism in Latin American and European countries. He is the author of *Shifting States in Global Markets: Subnational Industrial Policy in Contemporary Brazil and Spain* (Penn State University Press, 2002) and *Brazilian Politics: Reforming a*

Democratic State in a Changing World (Polity Press, 2006. He is also coeditor of *Decentralization and Democracy in Latin America* (University of Notre Dame Press, 2004). Professor Montero has also published his work in several edited volumes and journals such as *Latin American Politics and Society, Latin American Research Review, Comparative Politics, West European Politics, Studies in Comparative International Development, Publius: The Journal of Federalism,* and the *Journal of Interamerican Studies and World Affairs.*

George Ross is the Morris Hillquit Chair in Labor and Social Thought at Brandeis University and ad personam Jean Monnet Chair at the Université de Montréal. His most recent books include *Euros and Europeans: EMU and the European Model of Society* (with Andrew Martin) (Oxford: Oxford University Press, 2005); *Brave New World of European Labor* (with Andrew Martin, et al.) (New York: Berghahn, 1999); and *Jacques Delors and European Integration* (Cambridge, England, and New York: Polity/Oxford University Press, 1995).

Index >>